# UNIVERSITY CASEBOOK SERIES

CASES AND MATERIALS

# EMPLOYMENT LAW

FOURTH EDITION

*by*

## MARK A. ROTHSTEIN
Hugh Roy and Lillie Cranz Cullen Distinguished Professor of Law
University of Houston

## LANCE LIEBMAN
William S. Beinecke Professor of Law
Columbia University

NEW YORK, NEW YORK
FOUNDATION PRESS
1998

COPYRIGHT © 1987, 1991, 1994 FOUNDATION PRESS
COPYRIGHT © 1998 By FOUNDATION PRESS

11 Penn Plaza, Tenth Floor
New York, NY 10001
Phone (212) 760–8700
Fax (212) 760–8705

**Library of Congress Cataloging-in-Publication Data**
Rothstein, Mark A.
    Cases and materials on employment law  /  Mark A. Rothstein, Lance
Liebman.  — 4th ed.
        p.    cm.  —  (University casebook series)
    Includes index.
    **ISBN** 1–56662–612–9
    1.  Labor laws and legislation—United States—Cases.    I.  Liebman,
Lance.    II.  Title.    III.  Series.
KF3318.R68    1998
344.7301—dc21                                                                98–23388

*To the memory of our fathers*
*Dr. Sidney D. Rothstein*
*Roy Liebman*

\*

# PREFACE TO THE FOURTH EDITION

Developments in employment law continue at a breathtaking pace. New legislation, new regulations, new judicial decisions, new scholarship, and new changes in the social and economic structure of the workplace have made a new edition essential. Although the fourth edition contains many fascinating new issues, there are no new chapters or major structural changes in the book.

Professor Rothstein would like to acknowledge the research support of University of Houston Faculty Services Librarian Harriet Richman and production coordinator Janice Imoisi. Professor Liebman would like to thank Columbia University production coordinators Karen Adardour and Siobhan Kennedy, and research assistants Liza Dabbs, Hagit Elul, Lynna Huang, Dorothy Kim, Michael Lowenstein, Annie Riggle, Shira Rosenblatt, Maryanne Woo, and Bettina Yip.

We are indebted to our colleagues, who gave us many helpful suggestions about how to improve the book, and to our students, whose unique insights continue to challenge us.

We also want to acknowledge the contributions of Andria Knapp, who was our coauthor on the first two editions of the book.

M.R.
L.L.

July 1998

\*

# SUMMARY OF CONTENTS

*

# TABLE OF CONTENTS

**CHAPTER 8 Occupational Safety and Health** ........................ 671

# TABLE OF CASES

Principal cases are in bold type. Non-principal cases are in roman type. References are to Pages.

\*

CASES AND MATERIALS

# EMPLOYMENT LAW

\*

# PART I

# BACKGROUND

# CHAPTER 1

# WORK AND LAW

## A. WORK AND SOCIETY

When asked once to name the most important things in life, Sigmund Freud answered, "Love and work." This text and this course are about the latter, and the law's efforts to regulate the employment relationship. Recognition of the importance of work to human welfare and satisfaction cuts across historical, philosophical, and political lines. "You take my life, When you take the means whereby I live." In referring to work, Shakespeare's words are as timely today as they were nearly 400 years ago. Individual attitudes about work may range from "Am I really getting paid for this?" to "You can take this job and shove it!", but the need to work for sustenance and the desire to work for gratification and self-fulfillment combine to make work one of the most elemental, powerful, complex, and emotionally-charged forces in our daily lives.

In 1995, approximately two-thirds of the U.S. population of working age—124.9 million individuals—was employed; another 7.4 million unemployed would have worked if they could have found jobs. Most of those who work do so for someone else: we are a nation of employees. The amount of time we spend at work generally constitutes the largest single activity of our waking hours, and for many individuals, work provides an identity and extended family that are otherwise missing. But conflict in the employment relationship seems destined to occur. Owners, managers, and administrators of business and government are responsible for the operation of their respective enterprises, which requires them to make decisions that affect the workforce. Looking at the production of goods and services strictly in economic terms, efficiency and profitability of the firm are the hallmarks of a successful operation. Yet what is efficient, expedient, or profitable for a business is not necessarily also beneficial to its employees, and may even be harmful. A textile company's decision to relocate its manufacturing plant overseas because of cheaper production costs may make economic sense for its stockholders but spell economic disaster for the workers. The employee drug test which might enable an employer to reduce the production costs associated with substance abuse in the workforce invades employee privacy.

How should the law handle the inevitable tensions which arise in the employment relationship? Traditionally, the law considered employment to be a matter of private contract between the employer and employee. The law of master and servant developed originally as an offshoot of the law of domestic relations, and master and servant alike were bound by

obligations to each other.   Just as man (in those days) was master of his
home, so too was he master of his business.   He could impose whatever
working conditions he wished on employees.   If he were an unduly harsh
master, however, then he might be unable to hire competent help, but he
was not otherwise subject to sanction.   With the advent of the industrial
revolution in the nineteenth century and the laissez-faire attitude which
pervaded that era, the freedom of contract approach expanded.   In the
United States, the rule was quickly established that the employment
relationship was one which pertained between equals: the employee was
free to quit to seek alternate employment whenever he or she wanted, and
the employer was free to fire the employee at any time.

The law's first serious efforts to regulate the employment relationship
appeared at the end of the nineteenth century.   Growing awareness of the
hazards associated with certain occupations and industries and the inherent inequality of bargaining power between employer and employee led to
the passage of the first protective statutes, many of which were initially
struck down as unconstitutional infringements on the freedom of contract.
Gradually, and in a piecemeal fashion, legislative and judicial activism at
both the state and federal levels began to curtail the employer's freedom of
action.   In 1935, the National Labor Relations Act gave employees the right
to organize into unions and bargain collectively with their employer.
Unionization and collective bargaining are often seen as the way for
employees to obtain better working conditions, but today unionized employees account for less than 15 percent of the workforce.

In 1938, Congress enacted the Fair Labor Standards Act, which provides minimum wage protection and premium pay for overtime.   In 1963,
the Equal Pay Act made it unlawful for employers to discriminate between
men and women with respect to wages.   Title VII of the Civil Rights Act of
1964 prohibited all discrimination in employment on the basis of race,
color, religion, sex, or national origin.   In 1967, the Age Discrimination in
Employment Act prohibited discrimination on the basis of age.   The
Occupational Safety and Health Act of 1970, along with the Mine Safety
and Health Act, established minimum health and safety standards for the
workplace.   Employment rights for individuals with disabilities were enacted with the Rehabilitation Act of 1973.   The Employee Retirement Income
Security Act was enacted in 1974 to protect pension entitlements.   Since
the mid-1980s Congress has enacted, among other employment legislation,
the Worker Adjustment Retraining and Notification Act, the Employee
Polygraph Protection Act, the Americans with Disabilities Act, the Civil
Rights Act of 1991, and the Family and Medical Leave Act.   Many state
legislatures reacted to federal action by passing their own versions of
federal legislation, in some cases providing greater protection than federal
law.

Despite the virtual explosion of legislation, however, significant aspects
of employment, such as a right to be fired only for cause, are not addressed
by virtually any legislation, and large segments of the workforce, such as
managers and executives or agricultural workers, are exempted from many

laws.  The statutory scheme which exists is a patchwork of protection.
Each of the various statutes has its own coverage, its own procedures, and
its own substantive content.  There is no pervasive scheme at the federal
or state level to regulate the employment relationship.  Nor is one likely to
be passed in the foreseeable future.  As a result, recent developments in
the law have included a revival of the common law as a means of regulating
behavior within the employment relationship that is not already subject to
statutory rules and regulations.

This text follows the individual employee through the employment
relationship, starting with applying for a job and ending with separation
from employment, which may occur through quitting, being fired, being
laid off, or retiring.  In between are employer selection procedures, wages
and hours, benefits, working conditions, safety and health, and disabling
injury and illness.  The focus is on individual rights in employment rather
than collective bargaining, which is the topic of a separate course.  The
dominant query is:  How should the law regulate the employment relationship?  A number of secondary themes recur.  How can employee demands
for self-determination in the workplace be reconciled with the employer's
right to control the means and methods of production?  What social or
economic goals can or should be accomplished through the employment
relationship?  How should conflicts between individual rights and collective
rights be resolved?  What is the proper accommodation of parallel or
conflicting state and federal law?

As you study the remaining materials in this chapter, consider the
significance of the attitudes toward work which are presented in the
introductory readings.  What position should the law take toward work,
employer "rights," and employee "rights"?  Can you construct a theory of
employment law?  The *Wagenseller* case provides a context in which to
begin considering possible theories.

## Laborem Exercens:  Encyclical of Pope John Paul II on Human Work

September 14, 1981.

\* \* \*

Through work man must earn his daily bread and contribute to the
continual advance of science and technology and, above all, to elevating
unceasingly the cultural and moral level of the society within which he lives
in community with those who belong to the same family.  And work means
any activity by man, whether manual or intellectual, whatever its nature or
circumstances; it means any human activity that can and must be recognized as work, in the midst of all the many activities of which man is
capable and to which he is predisposed by his very natures, by virtue of
humanity itself.  Man is made to be in the visible universe and image and
likeness of God himself, and he is placed in it in order to subdue the earth.
From the beginning therefore he is called to work.  Work is one of the

characteristics that distinguish man from the rest of creatures, whose activity for sustaining their lives cannot be called work.   Only man is capable of work, and only man works, at the same time by work occupying his existence on earth.   Thus work bears a particular mark of man and of humanity, the mark of a person operating within a community of persons. And this mark decides its interior characteristics, in a sense it constitutes its very nature.

* * *

NOTE

Professor David Gregory, writing about the spiritual role of work, has added the following commentary and grim reminder:

> Work, or at least the aspiration to work, is ubiquitous.   Work permeates, and is often nearly synonymous with, much of both individual and social life.   The individual person is dignified by work; the community is enriched by work.   Society stands condemned by failure to provide meaningful work.   * * *   As *Laborem Exercens* expressly recognizes, "there is no doubt that human work has an ethical value of its own."   Work helps us become more fully human.   * * *

> Unfortunately, most of the world never has known dignified work. Most of the world always has been desperately and inescapably poor.   * * * Without meaningful work, crushing poverty of both material and spiritual life is inevitable.   The majority of the earth's population will never experience any work, let alone have working lives filled with dignity and hope.   Productive work will remain incomprehensible, or, at most, an ineffable and unattainable dream for the majority of the earth's population.   They will die prematurely, in ignorance, and in regimes where lives of unemployment and poverty are the established norm.

David L. Gregory, Catholic Labor Theory and the Transformation of Work, 45 Wash. & Lee L.Rev. 119, 129–30 (1988).

## Work in America, Report of a Special Task Force to the Secretary of Health, Education and Welfare

3–7 (1973).

### The Functions of Work

The economic purposes of work are obvious and require little comment. Work is the means by which we provide the goods and services needed and desired by ourselves and our society.   Through the economic rewards of work, we obtain immediate gratification of transient wants, physical assets for enduring satisfactions, and liquid assets for deferrable gratifications.

For most of the history of mankind, and for a large part of humanity today, the economic meaning of work is paramount.

Work also serves a number of other social purposes. The workplace has always been a place to meet people, converse, and form friendships. In traditional societies, where children are wont to follow in their parents' footsteps, the assumption of responsibility by the children for one task and then another prepares them for their economic and social roles as adults. Finally, the type of work performed has always conferred a social status on the worker and the worker's family. In industrial America, the father's occupation has been the major determinant of status, which in turn has determined the family's class standing, where they lived, where the children went to school, and with whom the family associated—in short, the life style and life chances of all the family members. (The emerging new role of women in our society may cause class standing to be co-determined by the husband's *and* wife's occupations.)

The economic and societal importance of work has dominated thought about its meaning, and justifiably so: a function of work for any *society* is to produce and distribute goods and services, to transform "raw nature" into that which serves our needs and desires. Far less attention has been paid to the *personal* meaning of work, yet it is clear from recent research that work plays a crucial and perhaps unparalleled psychological role in the formation of self-esteem, identity, and a sense of order.

Work contributes to self-esteem in two ways. The first is that, through the inescapable awareness of one's efficacy and competence in dealing with the objects of work, a person acquires a sense of mastery over both himself and his environment. The second derives from the view stated earlier, that an individual is working when he is engaging in activities that produce something valued by other people. That is, the job tells the worker day in and day out that he has something to offer. Not to have a job is not to have something that is valued by one's fellow human beings. Alternatively, to be working is to have evidence that one is needed by others. One of these components of self-esteem (mastery) is, therefore, internally derived through the presence or absence of challenge in work. The other component (how others value one's contributions) is externally derived. The person with high self-esteem may be defined as one who has a high estimate of his value and finds that the social estimate agrees.

The workplace generally, then, is one of the major foci of personal evaluation. It is where one finds out whether he is "making the grade"; it is where one's esteem is constantly on the line, and where every effort will be made to avoid reduction in self-evaluation and its attending sense of failure. If an individual cannot live up to the expectations he has of himself, and if his personal goals are not reasonably obtainable, then his self-esteem, and with it his relations with others, are likely to be impaired.

\* \* \*

Work is a powerful force in shaping a person's sense of identity. We find that most, if not all, working people tend to describe themselves in terms of the work groups or organizations to which they belong.  The question, "Who are you?" often solicits an organizationally related response, such as "I work for IBM," or "I'm a Stanford professor."  Occupational role is usually a part of this response for all classes:  "I'm a steelworker," or "I'm a lawyer."  In short: "People tend to 'become what they do.' "

Several highly significant effects result from work related identification: welfare recipients become "nobodies"; the retired suffer a crucial loss of identity; and people in low-status jobs either cannot find anything in their work from which to derive an identity or they reject the identity forced on them.

* * *

Basic to all work appears to be the human desire to impose order, or structure, on the world.  The opposite of work is not leisure or free time; it is being victimized by some kind of disorder which, at its extreme, is chaos.  It means being unable to plan or to predict.  And it is precisely in the relation between the desire for order and its achievement that work provides the sense of mastery so important to self-esteem.  The closer one's piece of the world conforms with one's structural plans, the greater the satisfaction of work.  And it follows that one of the greatest sources of dissatisfaction in work results from the inability to make one's own sense of order prevail—the assemblyline is the best (or worst) example of an imposed, and, for most workers, unacceptable structure.

## Studs Terkel, Working:  People Talk About What They Do All Day and How They Feel About What They Do*

xlv–xlix, 159–163 (1972).

CARL MURRAY BATES

(Mason)

As far as I know, masonry is older than carpentry, which goes clear back to Bible times.  Stone mason goes back way *before* Bible time: the pyramids of Egypt, things of that sort.  Anybody that starts to build anything, stone, rock, or brick, start on the northeast corner.  Because when they built King Solomon's Temple, they started on the northeast corner.  To this day, you look at your courthouses, your big public buildings, you look at the cornerstone, when it was created, what year, it will be on the northeast corner.  If I was gonna build a septic tank, I would start on the northeast corner.  (Laughs.)  Superstition, I suppose.

With stone we build just about anything.  Stone is the oldest and best building material that ever was.  Stone was being used even by the cavemen that put it together with mud. They built out of stone before they even used logs. He got him a cave, he built stone across the front. And he learned to use dirt, mud, to make the stones lay there without sliding around—which was the beginnings of mortar, which we still call mud. The Romans used mortar that's almost as good as we have today.

Everyone hears these things, they just don't remember 'em. But me being in the profession, when I hear something in that line, I remember it. Stone's my business. I, oh, sometimes talk to architects and engineers that have made a study and I pick up the stuff here and there.

Every piece of stone you pick up is different, the grain's a little different and this and that. It'll split one way and break the other. You pick up your stone and look at it and make an educated guess. It's a pretty good day layin' stone or brick. Not tiring. Anything you like to do isn't tiresome. It's hard work; stone is heavy. At the same time, you get interested in what you're doing and you usually fight the clock the other way. You're not lookin' for quittin'. You're wondering you haven't got enough done and it's almost quittin' time. (Laughs.) I ask the hod carrier what time it is and he says two thirty. I say, "Oh, my Lord, I was gonna get a whole lot more than this."

I pretty well work by myself. On houses, usually just one works. I've got the hod carrier there, but most of the time I talk to myself, "I'll get my hammer and I'll knock the chip off there." (Laughs.) A good hod carrier is half your day. He won't work as hard as a poor one. He knows what to do and make every move count makin' the mortar. It has to be so much water, so much sand. His skill is to see that you don't run out of anything. The hod carrier, he's above the laborer. He has a certain amount of prestige.

I think a laborer feels that he's the low man. Not so much that he works with his hands, it's that he's at the bottom of the scale. He always wants to get up to a skilled trade. Of course he'd make more money. The main thing is the common laborer—even the word *common* laborer—just sounds so common, he's at the bottom. Many that works with his hands takes pride in his work.

* * *

There's not a house in this country that I haven't built that I don't look at every time I go by. (Laughs.) I can set here now and actually in my mind see so many that you wouldn't believe. If there's one stone in there crooked, I know where it's at and I'll never forget it. Maybe thirty years, I'll know a place where I should have took that stone out and redone it but I didn't. I still notice it. The people who live there might not notice it, but I notice it. I never pass that house that I don't think of it. I've got one house in mind right now. (Laughs.) That's the work of my hands.

'Cause you see, stone, you don't prepaint it, you don't camouflage it. It's there, just like I left it forty years ago.

I can't imagine a job where you go home and maybe go by a year later and you don't know what you've done. My work, I can see what I did the first day I started.  All my work is set right out there in the open and I can look at it as I go by.  It's something I can see the rest of my life.  Forty years ago, the first blocks I ever laid in my life, when I was seventeen years old.  I never go through Eureka—a little town down there on the river—that I don't look thataway.  It's always there.

Immortality as far as we're concerned.  Nothin' in this world lasts forever, but did you know that stone—Bedford limestone, they claim—deteriorates one-sixteenth of an inch every hundred years?  And it's around four or five inches for a house.  So that's gettin' awful close. (Laughs.)

## PHIL STALLINGS

(Spot-welder)

I stand in one spot, about two- or three-feet area, all night.  The only time a person stops is when the line stops.  We do about thirty-two jobs per car, per unit.  Forty-eight units an hour, eight hours a day.  Thirty-two times forty-eight times eight.  Figure it out.  That's how many times I push that button.

The noise, oh it's tremendous.  You open your mouth and you're liable to get a mouthful of sparks.  (Shows his arms)  That's a burn, these are burns.  You don't compete against the noise.  You go to yell and at the same time you're straining to maneuver the gun to where you have to weld.

You got some guys that are uptight, and they're not sociable.  It's too rough.  You pretty much stay to yourself.  You get involved with yourself. You dream, you think of things you've done.  I drift back continuously to when I was a kid and what me and my brothers did.  The things you love most are the things you drift back into.

Lots of times I worked from the time I started to the time of the break and I never realized I had even worked.  When you dream, you reduce the chances of friction with the foreman or with the next guy.

It don't stop.  It just goes and goes and goes.  I bet there's men who have lived and died out there, never seen the end of that line.  And they never will—because it's endless.  It's like a serpent.  It's just all body, no tail.  It can do things to you * * * (Laughs.)

Repetition is such that if you were to think about the job itself, you'd slowly go out of your mind.  You'd let your problems build up, you'd get to a point where you'd be at the fellow next to you—his throat.  Every time the foreman came by and looked at you, you'd have something to say.  You just strike out at anything you can.  So if you involve yourself by yourself, you overcome this.

I don't like the pressure, the intimidation.  How would you like to go up to someone and say, "I would like to go to the bathroom?"  If the foreman doesn't like you, he'll make you hold it, just ignore you.  Should I leave this job to go to the bathroom I risk being fired.  The line moves all the time.

* * *

You really begin to wonder.  What price do they put on me?  Look at the price they put on the machine.  If that machine breaks down, there's somebody out there to fix it right away. If I break down, I'm just pushed over to the other side till another man takes my place. The only thing they have on their mind is to keep that line running.

\* \* \*

I know I could find better places to work. But where could I get the money I'm making? Let's face it, $4.32 an hour. That's real good money now. Funny thing is, I don't mind working at body construction. To a great degree, I enjoy it. I love using my hands—more than I do my mind. I love to be able to put things together and see something in the long run. I'll be the first to admit I've got the easiest job on the line. But I'm against this thing where I'm being held back. I'll work like a dog until I get what I want. The job I really want is utility.

\* \* \*

Proud of my work? How can I feel pride in a job where I call a foreman's attention to a mistake, a bad piece of equipment, and he'll ignore it. Pretty soon you get the idea they don't care. You keep doing this and finally you're titled a troublemaker. So you just go about your work. You *have* to have pride. So you throw it off to something else. And that's my stamp collection.

I'd break both my legs to get into social work. I see all over so many kids really gettin' a raw deal. I think I'd go into juvenile. I tell kids on the line, "Man, go out there and get that college." Because it's too late for me now.

When you go into Ford, first thing they try to do is break your spirit. I seen them bring a tall guy where they needed a short guy. I seen them bring a short guy where you have to stand on two guys' backs to do something. Last night, they brought a fifty-eight-year-old man to do the job I was on. That man's my father's age. I know damn well my father couldn't do it. To me, this is humanely wrong. A job should be a job, not a death sentence.

The younger worker, when he gets uptight, he talks back. But you take an old fellow, he's got a year, two years, maybe three years to go. If it was me, I wouldn't say a word, I wouldn't care what they did 'Cause, baby, for another two years I can stick it out. I can't blame this man. I respect him because he had enough will power to stick it out for thirty years.

## B.   LEGAL INTERVENTION

### Wagenseller v. Scottsdale Memorial Hospital

710 P.2d 1025 (Ariz.1985).

■ FELDMAN, JUSTICE.

\* \* \*

FACTUAL BACKGROUND

Catherine Wagenseller began her employment at Scottsdale Memorial Hospital as a staff nurse in March 1975, having been personally recruited by the manager of the emergency department, Kay Smith. Wagenseller was an "at-will" employee—one hired without specific contractual term. Smith was her supervisor. In August 1978, Wagenseller was assigned to the position of ambulance charge nurse, and approximately one year later was promoted to the position of paramedic coordinator, a newly approved management position in the emergency department. Three months later, on November 1, 1979, Wagenseller was terminated.

Most of the events surrounding Wagenseller's work at the Hospital and her subsequent termination are not disputed, although the parties differ in their interpretation of the inferences to be drawn from and the significance of these events. For more than four years, Smith and Wagenseller maintained a friendly, professional, working relationship. In May 1979, they joined a group consisting largely of personnel from other hospitals for an eight-day camping and rafting trip down the Colorado River. According to Wagenseller, "an uncomfortable feeling" developed between her and Smith as the trip progressed—a feeling that Wagenseller ascribed to "the behavior that Kay Smith was displaying." Wagenseller states that this included public urination, defecation and bathing, heavy drinking, and "grouping up" with other rafters. Wagenseller did not participate in any of these activities. She also refused to join in the group's staging of a parody of the song "Moon River," which allegedly concluded with members of the group "mooning" the audience. Smith and others allegedly performed the "Moon River" skit twice at the Hospital following the group's return from the river, but Wagenseller declined to participate there as well.

Wagenseller contends that her refusal to engage in these activities caused her relationship with Smith to deteriorate and was the proximate cause of her termination. She claims that following the river trip Smith began harassing her, using abusive language and embarrassing her in the company of other staff. Other emergency department staff reported a similar marked change in Smith's behavior toward Wagenseller after the trip, although Smith denied it.

Up to the time of the river trip, Wagenseller had received consistently favorable job performance evaluations. Two months before the trip, Smith completed an annual evaluation report in which she rated Wagenseller's performance as "exceed[ing] results expected," the second highest of five possible ratings. In August and October 1979, Wagenseller met first with Smith and then with Smith's successor, Jeannie Steindorff, to discuss some problems regarding her duties as paramedic coordinator and her attitude toward the job. On November 1, 1979, following an exit interview at which Wagenseller was asked to resign and refused, she was terminated.

She appealed her dismissal in letters to her supervisor and to the Hospital administrative and personnel department, answering the Hospital's stated reasons for her termination, claiming violations of the disciplinary procedure contained in the Hospital's personnel policy manual, and requesting reinstatement and other remedies. When this appeal was denied, Wagenseller brought suit against the Hospital, its personnel administrators, and her supervisor, Kay Smith.

\* \* \*

## NOTES AND QUESTIONS

**1.** What rule should the legal system apply to Catherine Wagenseller's lawsuit? At common law, at least since the late nineteenth century, Wagenseller was an employee at will; she could be dismissed for any reason or for no reason. See, e.g., Horace G. Wood, Law of Master and Servant § 134, at 273 (1877):

> With us the rule is inflexible, that a general or indefinite hiring is prima facie a hiring at will, and if the servant seeks to make it out a yearly hiring, the burden is upon him to establish it by proof. \* \* \* [I]t is an indefinite hiring and is determinable at the will of either party.

Should this be the law in the late twentieth century? If not, should there be a right not to be unjustly fired for:

(a) Every worker?

(b) Permanent or long-term workers? Defined how?

(c) Only those workers who exercise their statutory right to form a union and bargain for a contract?

(d) Only those workers who obtain a written contract when they take a job?

If some dismissals should be unlawful, which ones? Wagenseller's? Why? Would the result be that courts sit in judgment about the facts of and the justification for the millions of dismissals that occur every year in the U.S.? Can the courts handle this role?

Can we assume that employers do not fire good and reliable workers? When Smith began harassing Wagenseller after the rafting trip, why did Wagenseller not just quit and go to work for another hospital? If Scottsdale Memorial acquired a reputation for being an oppressive employer it would have to pay its workers more to attract them or would have to promise to refrain from arbitrary action. Would leaving matters such as this to the marketplace be more efficient and permit the parties to bargain for the terms of employment of concern to them?

**2.** Regardless of the specific contributing factors, Wagenseller was discharged because of the deterioration of her relationship with Smith. Should a personal conflict be sufficient to justify a discharge? Should it matter whether the employer is General Motors or a "mom-and-pop" store?

**3.** Suppose that Wagenseller rather than Smith had engaged in mooning and other activities on the rafting trip. Should the hospital be able to discharge her because of this off-work activity?  What type of off-work activity would justify an employee's discipline or discharge?

**4.**  What "rights" do employees have in their jobs?  Are they property rights, contract rights, statutory rights, constitutional rights, or some other rights?  Should these rights depend on whether the employer is private or public, whether the employees are represented by a union, or the basis of the employer's action? If Wagenseller should be given legal protection, what mechanism should be used?  Should establishing employee rights be the province of a court, legislature, administrative agency, or some other entity?  Who should enforce these rights?

**5.**  Should the law also attempt to regulate the hiring of employees?  If so, should the law on hiring be the same as the law on firing?  What system should be used to regulate employment?  The courts?  An administrative agency?  Arbitration?  What are the economic and social costs of legal intervention?  What are the economic and social costs of not intervening?

**6.**  Why is a job so important in our society?  How should this influence the desirability of legal regulation of the employment relationship?

* * *

This book considers all these questions, and many other similar issues about the law of employment relationships in the U.S.  Throughout, you should keep in mind some general questions: What is the proper role of law in establishing and enforcing employer and employee behavior?  Can courts supervise the American workplace?  Is law a good substitute for union representation of workers?  If ideas and norms are changing, how should courts find the values that they express and apply?  Can we use law to establish the kinds of workplaces where we would like to be an employee?  What are the problems and the costs of doing so?

# CHAPTER 2

# THE DEVELOPMENT OF EMPLOYMENT LAW

Chapter 1 explored the social and cultural significance of work. What are the legal consequences of employment? What does it mean to be an employee or an employer? Working for someone (or having someone work for you) establishes a relationship with legal rights and obligations. Historically, employment was governed by the law of master-servant, some of the premises of which were overwhelmed by changes in the nature of employment wrought by the industrial revolution. Currently, legal regulation of the relationship is accomplished in a variety of ways: individual contracts of employment, collective bargaining, and government regulation.

The employer-employee relationship is not monolithic. Indeed, the desire to be characterized as employer and employee may vary according to the legal consequences. In order to avoid the minimum wage standards of the Fair Labor Standards Act, a company may argue that an individual is an independent contractor rather than an employee. But if that same individual is injured in the course of providing services to the business, the company may argue that the individual is an employee, who may not sue in tort and whose only recourse is to file a workers' compensation claim. Should the definition of employer and employee be different for different purposes? What establishes the existence of an employment relationship?

The materials in Chapter 2 trace the development of employment law from master-servant to employment at will to modern workplace regulation. The focus is varied and includes discussions of why the law has developed as it has and whether the law has fostered efficiency and equity. More specifically, how *should* the law regulate employment? Private contract (individual or collective) permits the parties to engage in free bargaining over the terms and conditions of work. Government regulation, by forcing the parties to behave in certain ways, accomplishes social ends that the marketplace does not achieve. Is there an optimal mix of private bargain and government regulation? Is efficient production in conflict with the political and social goals of the various regulatory statutes? Finally, should legal regulation change to take account of the changing demographics, economics, and technology of the workplace? How will the employment policies and relationships of the future affect employment law?

## A.   THE FOUNDATIONS OF EMPLOYMENT LAW

## 1.   MASTER–SERVANT

# Ordinance of Labourers

23 Edw. III (1349).

Edward by the grace of God, &c. to the reverend father in Christ, William, by the same grace archbishop of Canterbury, primate of all England, greeting.  Because a great part of the people, and especially of workmen and servants, late died of the pestilence, many seeing the necessity of masters, and great scarcity of servants, will not serve unless they may receive excessive wages, and some rather willing to beg in idleness, than by labour to get their living;  we, considering the grievous incommodities, which of the lack especially of ploughmen and such labourers may hereafter come, have upon deliberation and treaty with the prelates and the nobles, and learned men assisting us, of their mutual counsel, ordained:

### CAP. 1

Every person able in body under the age of sixty years, not having to live on, being required, shall be bound to serve him that doth require him, or else committed to the gaol, until he find surety to serve.

That every man and woman of our realm of *England,* of what condition he be, free or bond, able in body, and within the age of threescore years, not living in merchandize, nor exercising any craft, nor having of his own whereof he may live, nor proper land, about whole tillage he may himself occupy, and not serving any other, if he in convenient service (his Estate considered) be required to serve, he shall be bounden to serve him which so shall him require.  And take only the wages, livery, meed, or salary, which were accustomed to be given in the places where he oweth to serve, the XX. year of our reign of *England,* or five or six other common years next before.  Provided always, That the lords be preferred before other in their bondmen or their land tenants, so in their service to be retained:  so that nevertheless the said lords shall retain no more than be necessary for them.  And if any such man or woman, being so required to serve, will not the same do, that proved by two true men before the sheriff or the bailiffs of our sovereign lord the King, or the constables of the town where the same shall happen to be done, he shall anon be taken by them of any of them, and committed to the next gaol, there to remain under strait keeping, till he find surety to serve in the form aforesaid.

\* \* \*

NOTE

The Ordinance of Labourers is often considered to be the start of English labor law.  It was enacted in 1349, the year after the ''Black

Death" caused by bubonic plague. The plague greatly reduced the number of available workers and thus wages soared and crops went unharvested. The Ordinance of Labourers (1349) and the Statute of Labourers (1351) fixed wages, regulated other terms of the labor contract, prohibited the enticing away of another's servants, and compelled workers to accept employment. These statutes were later expanded and were the basis of the Elizabethan Statute of Labourers (1562). The importance of these early laws is that they made the employment contract different from other contracts and made illegal any attempt on the part of workers to bargain collectively.

## Sir William Blackstone, Commentaries

410 (1765).

The three great relations in private life are, 1. That of *master and servant,* which is founded in convenience, whereby a man is directed to call in the assistance of others, where his own skill and labour will not be sufficient to answer the cares incumbent upon him. 2. That of *husband and wife;* * * * 3. That of *parent and child,* * * * As for those things which a servant may do on behalf of his master, they seem all to proceed upon this principle, that the master is answerable for the act of his servant, if done by his command, either expressly given, or implied: * * * Therefore, if the servant commit a trespass by the command or encouragement of his master, the master shall be guilty of it, though the servant is not thereby excused, for he is only to obey his master in matters that are honest and lawful. If an innkeeper's servants rob his guests, the master is bound to restitution; for as there is a confidence reposed in him, that he will take care to provide honest servants, his negligence is a kind of implied consent to the robbery; nam, qui non prohibit, cum prohibere possit, jubet. So likewise if the drawer at a tavern sells a man bad wine, whereby his health is injured, he may bring an action against the master: for although the master did not expressly order the servant to sell it to that person in particular, yet his permitting him to draw and sell it at all is impliedly a general command.

NOTES AND QUESTIONS

**1.** Blackstone's view of the master-servant relationship is open to serious criticism:

> This brings us to the second crucial point of difference between Blackstone and his successors. They were to claim that the law was essentially neutral as between persons. Within the state, there was or should be equality of political rights; within private law, there was formal equality of individual legal capacities. By contrast, * * * Blackstone's law of persons contained *only* relations of formal inequality, such as king and subject, noble and commoner, pastor and parishioner, husband and wife, master and servant. His structure suggested that the human universe could

be divided into two parts: a world of hierarchically ordered relations of people to one another, and an egalitarian world in which
people dominated objects. The function of this odd procedure was
to legitimate the status quo. It allowed Blackstone to maintain
that it was *only* in the social world of accepted, hierarchically
arranged roles that the law was the instrument of personal domination. He granted that law involved violence, but by the sharp
segregation of persons and things he was able to maintain that it
was violent only in order to uphold the institutions of royalty, the
established Church, and the extended family consisting of spouses,
children, and servants. Beyond that, it merely ratified man's
control over nature.

Duncan Kennedy, The Structure of Blackstone's Commentaries, 28 Buffalo
L.Rev. 205, 350 (1979).

**2.** The contemporary relevance of master-servant law is almost exclusively in the field of torts. Under tort doctrine, "once it is determined that the
man at work is a servant, the master becomes subject to vicarious liability
for his torts." W. Page Keeton, et al., Prosser and Keeton on Torts § 70,
at 501 (5th ed. 1984). Thus, usually the question of whether someone is a
servant is more important for a third party trying to sue a deep pocket,
than for the employee.

Historically, however, the questions surrounding master-servant law
involved a constellation of social policy issues. A servant owed certain
duties to his master and the master also had certain responsibilities to his
servant. Thus, the question of whether an employee was a servant could
radically change his life and welfare.

## 2.  EMPLOYER-EMPLOYEE

### Marc Linder, *What Is An Employee?  Why it Does, But Should Not, Matter* *
7 Law & Inequality 155 (1989).

Although wage labor in fourteenth and fifteenth-century England
connoted freedom when contrasted to the prior condition of serfdom, it also
signaled a loss of independence. The expropriation of the land or "capital"
which accompanied the change undermined this anti-feudal emancipatory
meaning.

This two-fold sense of "freedom" comprising wage labor still survives.
Wage laborers are both formally free to work when, where and for whom
they please, *and* substantively free from the direct access to the means of
production and subsistence that once undergirded the independence of
small producers. While the wage-earners in capitalist societies have at
times displayed the militancy and autonomy befitting the liberating component of the first meaning, they have also succumbed to their role as the

---

* Reprinted by permission.

dependent creatures of capital contained in the second meaning. Workers promote an ideological view of the state as an agency that can be manipulated to create the modicum of social security and work-related protection that, at least for certain sectors of the working class, cannot be gained directly from their capitalist employers. Fostering this view, workers have come to believe in an image of themselves as passive beneficiaries of forces that operate outside of the employer-employee relationship.

Paradoxically, entitlements to those benefits are almost universally contingent on being an employee, rather than being self-employed. The variety of benefits and protections in the United States conditioned on the existence of an employment relationship is impressive: unemployment compensation, workers compensation, collective bargaining rights, minimum wages and maximum hours, social security, pensions, occupational safety and health, and anti-discrimination protection. What an employee *is*, however, has often been left vague, has varied from benefit program to benefit program and from jurisdiction to jurisdiction, and has changed over time. No sound theoretical or empirical ground justifies this lack of uniformity. Indeed, the very existence of this hodgepodge is largely unknown not only to the affected workers, but also to the legislators, administrators and judges who are responsible for articulating policies, formulating definitions and drawing lines.

* * *

The social policy underlying labor-protective statutes, which forcibly prevent the disparate degrees of bargaining power of the parties from resulting in specific kinds of unacceptable exploitation, is closely related to the policies which support protection of wards (but not of differential birth rights). The crucial difference is that modern ideas of status presuppose and operate through the medium of the employment relationship: the existence and termination of status depend on the parties' volition, while its content is partly determined by norms out of which the parties are not permitted to contract, to the detriment of the weaker party.

Courts conflated a relationship that can (and must) be voluntarily entered into and terminated, with one created without or even against the volition of the affected parties. This result occurred because nineteenth and early twentieth-century Anglo–American jurisprudence persisted in the anachronistic and atavistic tradition, codified by Blackstone, of viewing the master-servant relationship as grounded in semi-feudal and mercantilist statutory compulsion and protection. With the ascendancy of the contractarian mode in the nineteenth century, judges (and lawyers) regarded both residual and nascent statutory protection of the working class as non-market obligatory norms, totally distinct from and operating outside of the context of the employment contract. Unable to integrate these two dimensions of the employment relationship, status and contract, courts tended to identify the mandatory norms as enforceable on the same grounds that applied under the Statutes of Labourers in the fourteenth century—as effluences of status.

## NOTES AND QUESTIONS

**1.** By implication, Professor Linder asserts that the newer employer-employee status relationship is even more important than the master-servant relationship was in Blackstone's time. Why? Do you agree?

**2.** The employer-employee relationship is based on contract. Yet there is an unmistakable influence of property law in the employment setting. The employer's ability to impose a wide range of conditions on employment often is justified because the work is performed on the employer's property, with the employer's materials and equipment, and even utilizing the employer's intangible property such as its good will and trademarks. Does the employee have any such "property" interests in employment? How might greater property rights affect the employment rights of workers?

**3.** Does the categorization of "employee" retain its significance today? Consider the following case.

## Lemmerman v. A. T. Williams Oil Co.

350 S.E.2d 83 (N.C.1986).

■ FRYE, JUSTICE.

The sole issue on this appeal is whether the Court of Appeals correctly affirmed the trial court's conclusion that plaintiff Shane Tucker was an employee of the defendant, A.T. Williams Oil Company. For the reasons set forth in this opinion, we conclude that the Court of Appeals was correct in so affirming.

On 1 December 1982, plaintiff Shane Tucker, then aged eight, slipped on a sidewalk on defendant's property and fell, cutting his hand. He and his mother, plaintiff Sylvia Tucker, filed this action against defendant on 26 June 1984. In their complaint, plaintiffs alleged in essence that Shane Tucker's injuries were proximately caused by defendant's negligence. They sought damages for medical expenses, lost wages, and pain and suffering. R. Douglas Lemmerman was appointed guardian ad litem for the minor plaintiff Shane.

Defendant filed an answer and raised as one of its defenses lack of subject matter jurisdiction. It asserted that the child Shane was its employee as defined by the Workers' Compensation Act and that the Industrial Commission accordingly had exclusive jurisdiction over plaintiffs' claim. Following preliminary discovery, defendant moved to dismiss for lack of subject matter jurisdiction. Upon the parties' stipulation that the trial judge find jurisdictional facts, Judge DeRamus made findings and concluded that Shane was an employee injured within the course and scope of his employment with defendant as defined in the Workers' Compensation Act. The judge therefore dismissed plaintiffs' action for lack of subject matter jurisdiction. Plaintiffs appealed to the Court of Appeals, which affirmed with a dissent by Webb, J., on the question of whether the evidence supported the conclusion that plaintiff Shane was an employee of defendant.

"By statute the Superior Court is divested of original jurisdiction of all actions which come within the provisions of the Workmen's Compensation Act." The Act provides that its remedies shall be an employee's only remedies against his or her employer for claims covered by the Act. N.C.G.S. § 97–10.1 (1985). Remedies available at common law are specifically excluded. Therefore, the question of whether plaintiff Shane Tucker was defendant's employee as defined by the Act is clearly jurisdictional. This issue is not affected by the fact that the minor may have been illegally employed because the Act specifically includes within its provisions illegally employed minors.[1] N.C.G.S. § 97–2(2) (1985).

* * *

Plaintiff Shane testified at his deposition that he routinely accompanied his mother to her job as part-time cashier at defendant's store and service station, a Wilco. According to his description, he ordinarily did his homework, ate a snack, and performed odd jobs about the station. These jobs consisted of picking up trash in the store, taking out the garbage, and stocking cigarettes and drinks. He had been doing these jobs for almost a month at the time of the accident. The child said that the jobs generally took him between half an hour and one hour to complete. In return, the store manager, Ken Schneiderman, would pay him a dollar, occasionally more depending on the amount of work he had done. A fair reading of the child's testimony discloses that he clearly expected to be paid for his efforts.

The child also testified that on the day of the accident he had nearly finished his tasks and was on his way to ask Schneiderman if there was anything else Schneiderman wanted him to do when he slipped and fell. He said at one point that he believed that Schneiderman did later give him his dollar, although he was not clear on this point.

The child's mother, Sylvia Tucker, corroborated Shane's account. She testified that at the time of the accident, she was working from 4 p.m. to 7 p.m. as a part-time cashier at Wilco. Schneiderman had Shane "put up stock, straighten the shelves up and pick up trash inside the building" and occasionally outside as well. Mrs. Tucker testified that her understanding was that the child was going to be paid for what he did. Although she told Schneiderman originally that Shane would work without being paid, he

---

**1.** The argument has been made that since the minor plaintiff may have been illegally employed, see N.C.G.S. § 95–25.5, defendant should not be allowed to prevail upon this defense. However, "[a] universal principle as old as the law is that the proceedings of a court without jurisdiction of the subject matter are a nullity." Burgess v. Gibbs, 262 N.C. 462, 465, 137 S.E.2d 806, 808 (1964). "If a court finds at any stage of the proceedings it is without jurisdiction, it is its duty to take notice of the defect and * * * dismiss the suit." Id. Therefore, if the Industrial Commission has jurisdiction over the claim of an illegally employed minor and the superior court does not, the superior court would have the duty to raise this issue *ex mero motu*.

rejected this offer and told both her and the child that he would pay Shane for his work.   She believed that Schneiderman paid Shane a dollar a day.

\* \* \*

We believe that this evidence amply supports the trial judge's findings that Schneiderman, who had the authority to hire and fire employees, hired the minor plaintiff to do odd jobs as needed in defendant's service station/convenience store business.   Specifically, these tasks included stocking cigarettes and drinks, and picking up trash.   At the time of the accident, Shane was engaged in doing these tasks.

\* \* \*

[P]laintiffs argue that Shane could not have been an employee because Schneiderman did not comply with certain procedural formalities.   He did not take an application from Shane or report him on the list of employees he turned into his supervisor for withholding purposes.   His normal practice was to pay employees from the cash register;   he paid Shane from his pocket.

We do not believe that any of these factors is dispositive.   Our Court of Appeals has held that failure to follow technical procedures such as withholding F.I.C.A. and income taxes is not controlling on the issue of whether an employer-employee relationship exists.   We also do not think that Schneiderman's method of paying Shane was as significant under the facts of this case as it might otherwise be, because all wages came out of Schneiderman's commission.   He therefore paid all of the employees at Wilco out of his own money.

[P]laintiffs contend that Shane was not an employee but instead performed gratuitous services.   In addition to Schneiderman's testimony denying that he hired Shane, rejected by the trial judge, plaintiffs cite Mrs. Tucker's original statement to Schneiderman that he did not have to pay the child.   However, this evidence in fact supports the opposite conclusion, that Shane was an employee.   Schneiderman was offered the chance to avail himself of Shane's gratuitous services, but he specifically rejected it and said that he wanted to pay the child for his work.   The evidence shows, and the judge found, that he did so.

Finally, plaintiffs contend that if Shane was an employee, he was Schneiderman's personal employee.   We disagree.   Schneiderman had the authority to hire employees for defendant, and the evidence shows and the trial judge found that the tasks the child performed were in the course of defendant's business, not Schneiderman's personal affairs.

\* \* \*

For all of the foregoing reasons, the decision of the Court of Appeals is affirmed.

AFFIRMED.

■ MARTIN, JUSTICE, dissenting.

I must respectfully dissent.  First, the majority opinion allows the defendant corporation to profit from its own illegal act.  Here, defendant corporation claims that it hired plaintiff Shane, an eight-year-old child, as an employee.  Defendant's act would be a direct violation of N.C.G.S. § 95–25.5(d), punishable by imposition of civil penalties.  This statute establishes the public policy of this state that it is unlawful for employers to employ children thirteen years of age or less.

The public policy of North Carolina also will not permit a wrongdoer to take advantage of or enrich itself as a result of its own wrong.  "It is a basic principle of law and equity that no man shall be permitted to take advantage of his own wrong.  * * *"  Further citation of authority is not necessary for this basic principle of law.  The principle is especially applicable where, as here, the power of the parties is so disparate—an eight-year-old child versus a large corporation!  The inequity of defendant's plea in bar is thus magnified by the relationship of the parties.

\* \* \*

Even if this Court allows defendant to rely upon an inequitable defense, the evidence fails, in at least one respect, to support a finding that plaintiff child was defendant's employee.  We must not overlook that defendant has the burden of proof to sustain its plea in bar.  As the majority states, the right to demand payment from the *employer,* A.T. Williams Oil Company, is an essential element of the employment status.  Defendant has failed to carry its burden as to this element.

The evidence in many respects is in conflict.  However, defendant has failed to produce a shred of evidence that the eight-year-old child had a right to demand payment for his services from A.T. Williams Oil Company.  Also, there is no evidence that plaintiff child could have made such a demand from Schneiderman, albeit defendant argues that plaintiff was its employee and not Schneiderman's.  All of the testimony showed that the infrequent payment of amounts ranging from twenty-five cents to a dollar came out of Schneiderman's own money, out of his own pocket.  The payments were not made from the cash register, as were payments to defendant's employees.  Thus, the record is simply devoid of any evidence that the child could have demanded payment from the corporate defendant for services he rendered to Schneiderman.

On the other hand, the record is replete with evidence that plaintiff child was *not* an employee of defendant's.  Shane was not a listed employee for workers' compensation purposes;  his name was not reported to the defendant corporation for tax withholding purposes;  Schneiderman testified explicitly that Shane was not an employee.

\* \* \*

Likewise, here defendant desired to employ Sylvia Tucker, plaintiff child's mother, to work in the convenience store.  She could not do so unless defendant agreed to let her eight-year-old son come to the store after school and remain until she completed her work.  Defendant agreed to this plan.  While on the premises the child from time to time performed menial tasks for Schneiderman, who sometimes would give the boy payments ranging from twenty-five cents to a dollar for his work.  This is entirely consistent with the problem of a working mother who needs employment but must also supervise her young child.  Shane was on the premises not as an employee of the corporate defendant, but because it was necessary in order for his mother to work.  Such are the demands of our modern society.

NOTES AND QUESTIONS

**1.**  Was Shane Tucker an "employee" in the ordinary sense of the word?  Before his injury, did Shane, Mrs. Tucker, Mr. Schneiderman, or the A. T. Williams Oil Company consider him an employee?

**2.**  The court suggests that Shane would be entitled to workers' compensation.  Is there something wrong with an eight year-old, who is too young to be a legal employee, receiving workers' compensation?  Does the court's decision further the public policy of prohibiting child labor?

Courts have split over whether illegally employed minors, injured or killed on the job, should be limited to workers' compensation.  See Fanion v. McNeal, 577 A.2d 2 (Me.1990) (minor, even though employed in violation of child labor laws, was limited to remedies provided by workers' compensation act and was precluded from wrongful death action).  Other courts have found this outcome to be unjust and contrary to public policy.  See Blancato v. Feldspar Corp., 522 A.2d 1235 (Conn.1987) (child may void an illegal contract and thus may pursue workers' compensation claim or tort action).

See also S.G. Borello & Sons, Inc. v. Department of Industrial Relations, 769 P.2d 399 (Cal.1989) (agricultural laborers are not independent contractors and therefore are eligible for workers' compensation); Northwest Advancement, Inc. v. State, Bureau of Labor, 772 P.2d 934 (Or.App.), review denied, 779 P.2d 618 (Or.1989), cert. denied, 495 U.S. 932 (1990) (minors, employed as door-to-door salespersons, were employees and not independent contractors for purpose of wage and hour regulations).

**3.**  Because workers' compensation precludes damage awards, injured individuals sometimes argue that they are independent contractors who can sue in tort rather than employees limited to workers' compensation relief.  Eckis v. Sea World, infra p. 830, held that plaintiff, who was bitten by Shamu the killer whale while riding Shamu at Seaworld, was an employee and so could not sue in tort.  The Social Security system focuses upon whether someone is receiving income from labor, with the result that he or she is not "retired" and so does not get full old age benefits, or is getting dividends (a return on capital) and so is "retired" and entitled to full old age payments.  Taubenfeld v. Bowen, infra p. 1247.  For a particularly novel attempt to characterize a personal injury suit as falling under a state workers' compensation act, see Houston v. Quincy Post 5129, 544 N.E.2d 425 (Ill.App.1989) (reversal of trial court's finding that claimant, injured while helping to conduct a bingo game, was employee and not volunteer).

**4.**  The issue of "who is an employee?" arises in many settings.  Could newsboys, whom the Los Angeles newspapers said were independent contractors, make use of the National Labor Relations Act in an attempt to organize and bargain?  In NLRB v. Hearst Publications, Inc., 322 U.S. 111 (1944), the Supreme Court upheld a National Labor Relations Board decision giving the newsboys the status of employee under that statute.

In Nationwide Mutual Insurance Co. v. Darden, 503 U.S. 318 (1992), the Supreme Court said "traditional agency law criteria" should guide the question of who is an employee for the purpose of applying federal pension law.  The pension statute, the Employee Retirement Income Security Act of 1974 (ERISA), is considered at length in Chapter 13.  Justice Souter said, correctly, that the statute's definition of employee ("any individual employed by an employer") is "completely circular and explains nothing." He said the law's reach should be measured by the "general common law of agency rather than * * * the law of any particular State."  Interestingly, similar "circular" definitions of employee and employer are contained in numerous federal and state statutes.  For example, § 3(6) of the Occupational Safety and Health Act (discussed in detail in Chapter 8) defines an employee as "an employee of an employer who is employed in a business of his employer which affects commerce."  It remains to be seen whether the *Nationwide* approach will be applied to these other federal and state statutes.

You will see some of these issues in further detail in the consideration of particular programs later in the book.  There is no single test of "employee"; the relationship is categorized differently for different regulatory purposes.

## 3.   EMPLOYMENT AT WILL

### Jay M. Feinman, *The Development of the Employment at Will Rule*

20 Am.J. Legal Hist. 118 (1976).

American law originally adopted the rules of English law on duration of service contracts.  Toward the end of the nineteenth century, however, English and American law diverged.  While the English used presumptions of long-term hiring and required reasonable notice of termination, American lawyers and courts developed the rule of termination at will.

\* \* \*

English courts at an early point developed a relatively sophisticated approach to the termination of master-servant relationships.  They identified two questions: What is the duration of the relation presumed to be when none is specifically stated?  What length of notice must be given before the relation can be terminated?  The English, unlike the Americans, saw that the questions were not the same and eventually developed a response to the second that mitigated somewhat the strictness of the early response to the first.

The duration of service relationships was a concern in early stages of English law, but the law was best formulated and made prominent only with the statement of a rule and policy by Blackstone:

> If the hiring be general, without any particular time limited, the law construes it to be a hiring for a year; upon a principle of natural equity, that the servant shall serve, and the master maintain him, throughout all the revolutions of the respective seasons, as well when there is work to be done as when there is not.

The rule thus stated expressed a sound principle: injustice would result if, for example, masters could have the benefit of servants' labor during planting and harvest seasons but discharge them to avoid supporting them during the unproductive winter, or if servants who were supported during the hard season could leave their masters' service when their labor was most needed.  But the source of the yearly hiring rule was not solely, as might be supposed from Blackstone's statement, in the judges' concern for fairness between master and servant.  The rule was also shaped by the requirements of the Statutes of Labourers, which prescribed a duty to work and prohibited leaving an employment or discharging a servant before the end of a term, and by the Poor Laws, which used a test of residence and employment to determine which community was responsible for the support of a person.  Thus, despite a concern with the "revolution of the seasons," the rule articulated by Blackstone was not restricted to agricultural and domestic workers.  The presumption that an indefinite hiring was a hiring for a year extended to all classes of servants.  Because the rule was designed for domestic servants broadly construed, however, those who were clearly not in that group were sometimes excluded.  The types of employment now considered usual—where the hours or days of work were limited, or the employment only for a certain job—would sometimes be held not to import a yearly hiring, indicating some sophistication by the law in not extending a concept designed for one purpose beyond its reasonable reach.

* * *

As the law was faced with an increasing variety of employment situations, mostly far removed from the domestic relations which had shaped the earlier law, the importance of the duration of contract question diminished and the second issue, the notice required to terminate the contract, moved to the fore.  Even when they recognized hirings as yearly ones, the courts refused to consider the contracts as entire and instead developed the rule that, unless specified otherwise, service contracts could be terminated on reasonable notice.

What constituted reasonable notice was a question of fact to be decided anew in each case, but certain conventions grew up.  Domestic servants, who presumably no longer needed the benefit of the seasons, could be given a month's notice.  Other types of employees could also be given a month's notice; three months was another common term, although some special cases required six or even twelve months' notice.  Although notice was a separate question in each case, the custom of the trade was often determinative.

\* \* \*

While English law followed a relatively clear path, American law at the same time exhibited a confusion of principles and rules.  Through the middle of the nineteenth century, American courts and lawyers relied heavily on English precedents but often came to different results.

In colonial times some hirings, such as of day laborers, were conventionally terminable at will.  Agricultural and domestic service relations often followed the English rule of yearly hirings.  In the nineteenth century, however, whatever consensus existed about the state of the law dissolved.  For example, Tapping Reeve's pioneering domestic relations treatise at mid-century stated the English presumption of yearly hiring but noted that no such rule existed in Connecticut.  But, in the same year that Reeve's second edition was published, the New York Court of Appeals held that the English rule of yearly hiring was still in effect in New York, even giving Blackstone's "benefit of the seasons" rationale.  Shortly thereafter Charles Manly Smith's treatise on master and servant, the first devoted solely to the subject in the United States, was published in Philadelphia.  Covering English law with reference to American cases, Smith's treatise was noted for its exhaustive discussion of the intricacies of the law and it had significant impact for that reason.  Smith stated a presumption that a general hiring was a yearly hiring for all servants, the presumption was rebuttable by custom or other evidence, and, in spite of a yearly hiring, the relation was terminable on notice where that was customary.

The confusion over the nature of the field of master and servant law contributed to the confusion over the duration of service contracts issue.  Master and servant law was originally classed as a domestic relation.  The master-servant relation was personal, often familial; servants were described as "menial" not derogatorily but because they resided intra moenia, within the walls of the master's house.  As the nineteenth century progressed, however, the true master-servant relation became overshadowed by the number of employees whose relationship to their employers was essentially commercial and therefore did not fit the pattern.  The resulting tension influenced the direction of the law, with the earlier perception acting as a force delaying accommodations to new economic conditions.

\* \* \*

By the 1870's the dissolution of the earlier law was apparent.  Although the presumption of yearly hiring was recognized as anachronistic, the concept of reasonable notice had not caught on.  Attempts were made to provide new, more fitting rules.  \* \* \*

\* \* \*

Thus the time was ripe for a sure resolution of the problem; it was achieved by an Albany lawyer and prolific treatise writer named Horace Gray Wood.  Wood sliced through the confusion and stated the employment at will doctrine in absolutely certain terms:

> With us the rule is inflexible, that a general or indefinite hiring is prima facie a hiring at will, and if the servant seeks to make it out a yearly hiring, the burden is upon him to establish it by proof.  * * * [I]t is an indefinite hiring and is determinable at the will of either party, and in this respect there is no distinction between domestic and other servants.

The puzzling question is what impelled Wood to state the rule that has since become identified with his name.  Wood's master and servant treatise, like his other works, won him acclaim for his painstaking scholarship, but that comprehensiveness and concern for detail were absent in his treatment of the duration of service contracts.  First, the four American cases he cited in direct support of the rule were in fact far off the mark.  Second, his scholarly disingenuity was extraordinary; he stated incorrectly that no American courts in recent years had approved the English rule, that the employment at will rule was inflexibly applied in the United States, and that the English rule was only for a yearly hiring, making no mention of notice.  Third, in the absence of valid legal support, Wood offered no policy grounds for the rule he proclaimed.

Whatever its origin and the inadequacies of its explanation, Wood's rule spread across the nation until it was generally adopted.

———

NOTE

Regardless of Wood's motivation for advancing the employment at will rule, it rapidly became standard doctrine, endorsed even by the Supreme Court.  In Adair v. United States, 208 U.S. 161 (1908), the Court struck down as unconstitutional a federal statute making it a crime for an employer engaged in interstate commerce to discharge an employee solely because of membership in a labor organization.  Such a restriction on the right of contract was perceived by the Court to be an impermissible invasion of personal liberty.  It was inappropriate for government "to compel any person in the course of his business and against his will to accept or retain the personal services of another, or to compel any person, against his will, to perform personal services for another."  The Court viewed the right of the employer to "dispense with the services" of any employee as correlative with the employee's right to quit for whatever reason.  In Coppage v. Kansas, 236 U.S. 1 (1915), the Court applied the same reasoning to state efforts to regulate the employer's right to discharge employees and struck down a Kansas statute which made it unlawful for any firm or individual to require nonmembership in a union as a condition of employment.  The case would be different, the Court reasoned, only if coercion or duress was involved; otherwise, the individual's decision to enter into a contract of employment was seen as one freely entered into, and one which the judiciary would not second-guess. According to the Court, the individual employee had two options: he could be hired (or remain employed) and withdraw from union activities, or if he preferred, he could remain in the union and forego employment. See also Andrew P. Morriss, Exploding Myths: An Empirical and Economic Reassessment of the Rise of Employment At–Will, 59 Mo.L.Rev. 679 (1994).

## Clarke v. Atlantic Stevedoring Co.
163 Fed. 423 (E.D.N.Y.1908).

■ CHATFIELD, DISTRICT JUDGE. The plaintiff in this action is the assignee of 96 colored longshoremen, who went to work at the suggestion and apparently under the direction of the plaintiff, who had received a letter from one Charles M. Tiffany, superintendent of the defendant, which is as follows:

"New York, May 3rd, 1907.

"Mr. William Clarke, New York City—Dear Sir: I have work immediately for 200 colored longshoremen, and can guarantee the above number continuous work, providing they are good men. This Company pays the usual rate of wages, namely, 30¢ per hr. for day and 45¢ per hr. at night. We propose to keep colored men at work as long as they fulfill their part of the program. Attached letter-head will show you the work we do.

"Yours truly,

Chas. M. Tiffany, Supt."

The plaintiff and his 96 assignors went to work for the defendant, and were employed and paid up to the 6th day of July, 1907, when they were discharged and their places filled by white longshoremen. The plaintiff on his behalf, and because of the transactions with each of his assignors, has claimed $1,000 damages each for breach of what he alleges was a contract to furnish continuous employment at a reasonable rate of wages. The complaint alleges that the defendant has failed to give employment to each of the plaintiff's assignors from the time of the breach until the present date.

The defendant has demurred, and claims (1) that the letter was not an offer by the acceptance of which the defendant would be bound to employ any particular person; (2) that, if a contract existed, its duration was indefinite, and in fact amounted to but an employment at will; (3) that the inducement was offered by the superintendent of the defendant, and that the defendant was an undisclosed principal; (4) that the advertisement called for 200 men and that but 96 appear to have gone to work, thus showing a lack of compliance on the part of the libelant. It is unnecessary to discuss these last two grounds. It is impossible upon demurrer to determine whether 96 or 200 men answered the advertisement; the record merely showing that 96 of these men have assigned their claims to the libelant. Nor does the record show the authority of the person who signed the letter. The letter is written upon the paper of the defendant, and the complaint states that the plaintiff went into the service of the defendant, and that the contract signed by the superintendent was made with the defendant.

It can hardly be determined upon the face of this pleading that a prima facie contract with the defendant is not alleged, if the matter was in any sense a contract between the plaintiff's assignors and any person or corporation whatever. We must, therefore, consider the first two grounds of the demurrer, and these would seem to be well founded. The letter recited is at most an advertisement or inducement to enlist the interest and offer of services by the plaintiff. It is manifest that the plaintiff as an individual could not do the work of 200 men, and the letter certainly contemplated the presentation to the defendant either of an offer to furnish longshoremen, or of longshoremen to be put to work, and all arrangements are left in abeyance, and by the terms of the letter would seem to be matters for adjustment at the time of hiring. The statement of a need is not the offer of a position, unless the terms are definite and the offer is so worded as to indicate intent to make a contract by acceptance.

As to the other objection—that, if an arrangement was made, it was terminable at will—the question would seem to be disposed of by the previous discussion. But, in so far as the plaintiff may have shown by his complaint that he and his assignors went to work under a contract of which the letter in question is a written memorandum (assuming for the purpose of this argument that the complaint has been so worded that a contract of this nature might be proven under it, even though on its face it appears to be an allegation of an offer and acceptance), nevertheless the demurrer should be sustained. A contract of hiring, indefinite with respect to the term for which the contract shall run, in the absence of allegations that the term of the contract is fixed by statute or custom, is at most a contract terminable at will. Many cases in the state court supporting this proposition could be cited, and a number of these are referred to, with a quotation from Wood on Master and Servant, p. 272, in the case of The Pokanoket, 156 Fed. 241, 84 C.C.A. 49, which shows the existence of the same rule in the federal courts.

The allegation of the complaint that the colored men were replaced by white, and the date of their discharge showing that the discharges all took place at one time, indicate a complete departure from the intent or mental attitude of the defendant's superintendent, as evidenced by the statement that "we propose to keep colored men at work as long as they fulfill their part of the program." This change of purpose may have caused hardship to a number of innocent workmen, but the matter must be determined according to the parties' legal rights, and not from the standpoint of sympathy or approval of the economic questions involved, and it seems to the court that the plaintiff has shown no agreement with the defendant by which it bound itself to continue the plan of employing colored workmen longer than it might see fit so to do; nor is any contract on the part of the defendant set forth under which the defendant agreed not to change its mind.

The demurrer must be sustained.

NOTES AND QUESTIONS

**1.** The court applied Wood's rule and traditional contract theory. Thus, despite recognizing the "hardship" of the situation, it sustained the defendant's demurrer.

**2.** In Payne v. Western & Atlantic Railroad, 81 Tenn. 507 (1884), the railroad ordered its employees to stop trading at a store owned by the plaintiff. The Supreme Court of Tennessee upheld the railroad's prerogative to discharge its employees, if it so chose, for any reason—for good cause, no cause, or bad cause. Compare Richard A. Epstein, In Defense of the Contract at Will, 51 U.Chi.L.Rev. 947 (1984) (approving result in *Payne*), with Matthew W. Finkin, "In Defense of the Contract at Will"— Some Discussion Comments and Questions, 50 J.Air L. & Comm. 727 (1985) (criticizing *Payne* and Epstein).

**3.** In Henry v. Pittsburgh & L.E.R. Co., 21 A. 157 (Pa.1891), a railroad ticket agent was discharged because there were financial irregularities in his department, even though there was no evidence that the agent was personally responsible. The railroad then told the local newspaper that the agent was terminated for dishonesty. The court held that no action would lie against the railroad. For a contrary modern rule, see Lewis v. Equitable Life Assurance Society, infra at 144.

**4.** Taken together, *Payne, Clarke,* and *Henry* illustrate three aspects of the common law "at will" rule: the employer was free to impose any conditions of employment, to discharge an employee at any time for any reason, and to effect the discharge in virtually any manner.

**5.** Was the common law unable or unwilling to address the issue of race discrimination? For a discussion of the statutory non-discrimination obligation, see part B–4 of this chapter.

**6.** For an analysis of Wood's rule reaching a conclusion contrary to Feinman's, that Wood was correct in his reading of prior cases, see Mayer G. Freed & Daniel D. Polsby, The Doubtful Provenance of "Wood's Rule" Revisited, 22 Ariz.St.L.J. 551 (1990).

## B. SOURCES OF MODERN EMPLOYMENT LAW

This section explores major themes in the development of contemporary employment law. In the late nineteenth century, patronage politics began to give way to a more professional, career-oriented public sector bureaucracy. While state and federal governments have devised detailed procedures for regulating basic elements of hiring, firing, compensation, and conditions of employment, civil service laws still have not resolved the question of the permissible scope of political activities of public employees. A century of litigation, from *McAuliffe* to *Rutan,* has focused on this issue.

The rise of collective bargaining in the late nineteenth and early twentieth centuries culminated in the National Labor Relations Act or Wagner Act of 1935. Although this book addresses individual rather than collective rights, the impact of collective bargaining remains important. The union movement's political agenda often has dictated the legislative regulation of all employment and the recent decline in union density has had consequences for the rights of nonunion employees.

A third theme of this section is the increased governmental role in regulating private sector employment. Originally begun in response to the Great Depression, new waves of regulatory initiatives have centered on occupational safety and health, employee pensions, and fringe benefits. Is workplace regulation effective and efficient? Are we inevitably committed to increased regulation?

Beginning in the 1960s, civil rights laws were enacted at the federal and state levels that prohibit discrimination in employment on the basis of race, color, religion, sex, national origin, age, and disability. This section reviews the historical and conceptual foundations of this legislation. Subsequent chapters (especially Chapter 4) provide detailed analyses of antidiscrimination law.

The 1970s and 1980s saw the courts undertake a major reassessment of the vitality of the at-will doctrine. Recognizing that strict adherence to the doctrine would often cause harsh results, the courts in many jurisdictions carved out a series of tort and contract exceptions. This trend is summarized in this section and explored in depth in Chapter 10.

It is important to remember that, unlike tax law, commercial law, or even labor law, there is no single source of employment law. What has come to be called "employment law" is an amalgam of numerous state and federal constitutional, statutory, regulatory, and common law rights and remedies. Different assumptions and different objectives may underlie each of these attempts to interpose the law into the employment relationship. Because there is no coherent, contemporaneously adopted body of law, there are numerous gaps and overlaps. Thus, preemption and election of remedies are two recurring themes. An important and as yet unresolved issue is illustrated by the *Pryner* case—the relationship between statutes prohibiting discrimination and collective bargaining agreements.

## 1. CIVIL SERVICE/PUBLIC EMPLOYMENT

## McAuliffe v. Mayor & City of New Bedford

29 N.E. 517 (Mass.1892).

■ HOLMES, J. This is a petition for mandamus to restore the petitioner to the office of policeman in New Bedford. He was removed by the mayor upon a written complaint, after a hearing, the mayor finding that he was guilty of violating the thirty-first rule of the police regulations of that city. The part of the rule which the petitioner seems certainly to have violated is as follows: "No member of the department shall be allowed to solicit money or any aid, on any pretense, for any political purpose whatever." There was also evidence that he had been a member of a political committee, which likewise was prohibited. Both parties agree that the city had accepted chapter 319 of the Acts of 1890, by virtue of which the members of the police force held office "during good behavior, and until removed by the mayor * * * for cause deemed by him sufficient, after due hearing." It is argued by the petitioner that the mayor's finding did not warrant the removal; that the part of the rule violated was invalid, as invading the petitioner's right to express his political opinions; and that a breach of it was not a cause sufficient, under the statutes.

One answer to this argument, assuming that the statute does not make the mayor the final judge of what cause is sufficient, and that we have a right to consider it, is that there is nothing in the constitution or the statute to prevent the city from attaching obedience to this rule as a condition to the office of policeman, and making it part of the good conduct required. The petitioner may have a constitutional right to talk politics, but he has no constitutional right to be a policeman. There are few employments for hire in which the servant does not agree to suspend his constitutional rights of free speech as well as of idleness by the implied terms of his contract. The servant cannot complain, as he takes the employment on the terms which are offered him. On the same principle the city may impose any reasonable condition upon holding offices within its control. This condition seems to us reasonable, if that be a question open to revision here.

The petitioner also argues that he has not had due hearing. The first ground for this argument is some testimony reported that the mayor said that he did not care about the evidence; he knew what McAuliffe had been doing; he knew all about it. A sufficient answer to this is that the fact is not found by the judge who tried the case, and, if necessary to support his findings, we should have to assume that he did not believe the evidence. Next, it is said that the charges against the petitioner were not stated specifically, and that when specifications were called for they were refused. The judge was well warranted in finding that the mayor did all that justice required. The complaint was tolerably full, although no doubt, under some circumstances, further specifications properly ought to be demanded. The petitioner attended on notice at the first day appointed for a hearing, and asked for no specifications, and offered no evidence. There was evidence that he said to the mayor, at the hearing, "I admit I am guilty. What's the penalty?" and also said to the mayor at another interview that, if he was going to be removed, he would like to know it, so that he could resign. At an adjourned hearing before the mayor, the petitioner attended with counsel, and his counsel asked for specifications. The mayor refused the request, whereupon the petitioner refused to proceed, and the mayor declared the hearing closed. Under the circumstances, we cannot say that he was wrong.

The next suggestion, that no notice was given to the petitioner that a proceeding to remove him from his office was intended, does not require much answer.  The petitioner had notice of the proceedings, and must be taken to have known their possible consequences.  According to the evidence, he used language to the mayor expressly contemplating those consequences.  Finally, it is said that the case should first have been investigated before the committee on police, as provided by rule 24 of the police regulations.  But since the passage of the act of 1890, if not before, we have no doubt of the power of the mayor to hear all cases on the removal of a police officer in the first instance himself.

Petition dismissed.

QUESTIONS

**1.**  To what extent did Justice Holmes rely on the prevailing theory of employment contracts in the private sector to reach the result in this public sector case?

**2.**  Are there legitimate bases for distinguishing the rights of public sector and private sector employees?  What employees?  What rights?

———

In 1995, about 15 percent of American workers were employed by federal, state, and local governments.  For most of these 19.3 million workers, civil service laws control selection procedures through the use of competitive examinations and merit systems.  Civil service laws also prohibit discrimination based on race, color, sex, religion, national origin, age, disability, and other classifications.  Federal employees are covered by Title VII under § 717;  state and local government employees were brought under the general coverage of Title VII with the 1972 Amendments.

The law of public sector collective bargaining is beyond the scope of this book, as is a study of the myriad regulations and procedures under the various civil service laws.  The following article provides a brief history and current update of civil service in the federal sector.  Issues of political activity, freedom of expression, and related matters are discussed in Chapters 7 and 10.

## Louis Lawrence Boyle, Reforming Civil Service Reform: Should the Federal Government Continue to Regulate State and Local Government Employees? *

7 J.L. & Politics 243, 268–80 (1991).

After President Garfield was assassinated in 1881 by a disgruntled office-seeker, the Pendleton Act was passed in 1883.  The Supreme Court has since stated that the Pendleton Act was passed as a result of the

* Reprinted by permission.

"strong discontent with the corruption and inefficiency of the patronage system of public employment." Not only did the Pendleton Act weaken the spoils system by creating a class of federal employees who had to obtain their offices through a merit system of competitive examinations, but it also prohibited political solicitations of federal employees. This prohibition on political solicitation was continued in 1925 when Congress passed the Federal Corrupt Practices Act in response to such scandals in the Harding Administration as the Teapot Dome Scandal.

Although machine politicians like Plunkitt of Tammany Hall railed against these civil service reforms, the political party in power managed to continue receiving financial support from government employees, despite laws to the contrary. Furthermore, the patronage system, while damaged by the Pendleton Act, was not eliminated. By the turn of the century, the majority of government jobs were not subject to the Civil Service competitive examinations. Even a 1907 executive order issued by President Theodore Roosevelt, a former Civil Service Commissioner, restricting the political activity of civil service employees, did not affect a majority of the federal, state and local government employees.

Although the initial reform of the Pendleton Act was in need of additional reform, a political crisis was necessary for its implementation. Despite the brief surge for reform in response to the scandals in the Harding administration, that significant crisis came in 1939, after the political parties had again shifted in their positions of power. This time with the New Deal Democrats in control, a coalition of Republicans and anti-New Deal Democrats joined forces to pass the Hatch Act, sponsored by Senator Carl Hatch, a New Mexico Democrat. The driving force behind the Hatch Act was a series of charges that President Roosevelt had exploited Works Progress Administration relief workers and its officers, including his failed attempts to purge disloyal Democrats from the ballot in the 1938 primaries.

The 1939 Hatch Act tightened the prohibitions on the political activity of federal employees. Congress acted so quickly in considering the Hatch Act, however, that it had to be amended prior to final passage to exempt the President, the Vice President and members of Congress from its restrictions, which would have prevented these federal employees from seeking re-election.

With Congress acting so fast to enact the Hatch Act, it is not surprising that the very next year Congress was forced to resolve differences of opinion as to exactly what political activities were prohibited by the Hatch Act and whether or not the Civil Service Commission should have authority to issue regulations in this sensitive area. Not satisfied with only restricting federal employees, Senator Hatch, overcoming strong objections, also expanded the 1940 amendments to include state and local government employees whose agency received any federal funds. This provision required further reform in 1942 in order to exempt employees of educational and religious organizations which received federal funds. Thus, within the first three years of the Hatch Act's existence, Congress had to reform the

Act on two separate occasions. Additional reforms proved to be necessary in the 1950s and 1970s, illustrating that reform is a self-perpetuating process.

This brief history of civil service reform demonstrates that political reforms were a reaction to the perceived abuses of the political system as well as to the power of the incumbents who had been elected by that political system. As the Supreme Court has recognized, "[p]atronage thus tips the electoral process in favor of the incumbent party, and where the practice's scope is substantial relative to the size of the electorate, the impact on the process can be significant." Furthermore, the lack of effective means of enforcement of the reforms of the last century along with the lack of application of the reforms to a majority of government employees necessitated further reforms to close these loopholes. An examination of the Hatch Act, its enforcement and the extent of its application to government employees within the last half-century reveals the need for additional reform.

### III.  THE CONTINUING REFORM OF THE HATCH ACT

When Congress passed the Hatch Act in 1939 and then extended its application to state and local government employees in 1940, protests from the states characterized the Hatch Act as "probably the most unpopular legislation ever imposed on our State and local governments." No doubt some of that protest may have been due to the intrusion of the federal government into the regulation of the political activity of state employees. An annoyance for some states is that there is no statute of limitations applicable to Hatch Act cases, so that states may be forced to terminate employment for an individual who long ago may have inadvertently violated the Hatch Act. The most egregious problem which the Hatch Act created for the states appeared in the manner in which Congress chose to have the Hatch Act enforced. Once the federal Civil Service Commission determined that an individual had violated the Hatch Act, the state or local government had two options. The state or local agency could terminate the individual's employment and not rehire that individual for at least eighteen months. Alternatively, the state or local agency where the individual had been employed would lose federal loans or grants equivalent to two years of pay at the rate the employee was receiving when he or she violated the Hatch Act. Due to their opposition to the Hatch Act, however, not all states summarily dismissed their employees for the exercise of their first amendment freedoms. The Supreme Court, in *Oklahoma v. United States Civil Service Commission,* [64] upheld the right of Congress to force state and local governments to choose between federal funds and a potentially valuable employee. To this day, Congress continues to influence state and local government policy by linking compliance with federal funds.

In an effort to appease the opposition of the state governments, Congress in 1950 amended the Hatch Act to allow the Civil Service Commission to determine whether a violation of the Hatch Act warranted

---

64.  330 U.S. 127 (1946).

removal. Although removal had previously been mandatory, it became one of two options in 1950. The second option consisted of a minimum suspension for 90 days without pay, which in 1960 was reduced to 30 days suspension without pay.

\* \* \*

Due to the continuing protests from the states, it is not surprising that, when Congress again became zealous about reform after the Watergate incident in 1972, it turned its attention once again to reforms in the Hatch Act and even included two reforms in the same measure. In 1974, Congress amended the Hatch Act to resolve some of the states' concerns by loosening somewhat the restrictions on the political activity of state and local government employees. When Congress passed the Hatch Act in 1939 and then extended its application to state and local employees in 1940, the state and local government employees were initially subject to the same restrictions as were federal employees. One of the changes Congress made in 1974 was to allow state and local government employees to be candidates in completely nonpartisan elections. Federal courts and administrative agencies have interpreted nonpartisan as allowing participation "only if none of the candidates could be considered partisan." Individuals seeking election as an independent or as a bipartisan candidate do not qualify for this exemption.

Another 1974 amendment was the replacement of the prohibition on taking "an active part in political management or political campaigns" with the prohibition only on being "a candidate for elective office." Federal courts have interpreted this change as allowing state and local employees to participate in political campaigns as long as they do not run for office themselves.

\* \* \*

In 1978, in still another series of reforms, Congress replaced the Civil Service Commission with the Merit Systems Protection Board (MSPB) and potentially brought more federal employees within the coverage of the Hatch Act and the MSPB.

The MSPB now lists five permissible political activities for state and local government employees. Where appropriate, reference is made to cases illustrating these permissible activities. State and local government employees:

— May be a candidate for public office in a nonpartisan election[;]

— May campaign for and hold elective office in political clubs and organizations[;]

— May actively campaign for candidates for public office in partisan and nonpartisan elections[;]

— May contribute money to political organizations or attend political fundraising functions[; and]

— May participate in any activity not specifically prohibited by law or regulation[.]

Likewise, MSPB lists three general prohibitions on the political activity of state and local employees.   Where appropriate, reference is made to cases illustrating these prohibitions.   A state or local government employee may *not*:

— Use his official authority or influence for the purpose of interfering with or affecting the result of an election or a nomination for office; or

— Directly or indirectly coerce, attempt to coerce, command, or advise a [s]tate or local officer or employee to pay, lend, or contribute anything of value to a political party, committee, organization, agency, or person for a political purpose.

— Be a candidate for elective public office in a partisan election.

* * *


## NOTES

**1.**   The Hatch Act Reform Amendments of 1993, Pub.L. 103–94, conferred greater rights on public employees to engage in partisan political activity. In contrast to prior laws, an employee "may take an active part in political management or in political campaigns."   There are exceptions, however, including that an individual may not: (1) solicit campaign contributions from subordinates or persons having business pending before the agency; (2) engage in political activity while on duty;  (3) use government facilities or property for a political purpose;  and (4) run for a partisan political office.

**2.**   Along with the prohibition of political activity, the Hatch Act and its amendments embrace the "merit principle" in the selection and promotion of government employees.   The law also contains a broad range of "prohibited personnel practices."   These include discrimination based on race, color, religion, national origin, age, sex, disability, marital status, or political affiliation.   Nepotism, retaliation, and other treatment violating merit principles also are prohibited.

**3.**   For a further discussion, see William V. Luneburg, The Federal Personnel Complaint, Appeal, and Grievance Systems: A Structural Overview and Proposed Revisions, 78 Ky.L.J. 1 (1989–90).


## Rutan v. Republican Party

497 U.S. 62 (1990).

■ JUSTICE BRENNAN delivered the opinion of the Court:

To the victor belong only those spoils that may be constitutionally obtained.   Elrod v. Burns, 427 U.S. 347 (1976), and Branti v. Finkel, 445

U.S. 507 (1980), decided that the First Amendment forbids government officials to discharge or threaten to discharge public employees solely for not being supporters of the political party in power, unless party affiliation is an appropriate requirement for the position involved. Today we are asked to decide the constitutionality of several related political patronage practices—whether promotion, transfer, recall, and hiring decisions involving low-level public employees may be constitutionally based on party affiliation and support. We hold that they may not.

## I.

The petition and cross-petition before us arise from a lawsuit protesting certain employment policies and practices instituted by Governor James Thompson of Illinois.[1] On November 12, 1980, the Governor issued an executive order proclaiming a hiring freeze for every agency, bureau, board, or commission subject to his control. The order prohibits state officials from hiring any employee, filling any vacancy, creating any new position, or taking any similar action. It affects approximately 60,000 state positions. More than 5,000 of these become available each year as a result of resignations, retirements, deaths, expansion, and reorganizations. The order proclaims that "no exceptions" are permitted without the Governor's "express permission after submission of appropriate requests to [his] office." * * *

Requests for the Governor's "express permission" have allegedly become routine. Permission has been granted or withheld through an agency expressly created for this purpose, the Governor's Office of Personnel (Governor's Office). Agencies have been screening applicants under Illinois' civil service system, making their personnel choices, and submitting them as requests to be approved or disapproved by the Governor's Office. Among the employment decisions for which approvals have been required are new hires, promotions, transfers, and recalls after layoffs.

By means of the freeze, according to petitioners, the Governor has been using the Governor's Office to operate a political patronage system to limit state employment and beneficial employment-related decisions to those who are supported by the Republican Party. In reviewing an agency's request that a particular applicant be approved for a particular position, the Governor's Office has looked at whether the applicant voted in Republican primaries in past election years, whether the applicant has provided financial or other support to the Republican Party and its candidates, whether the applicant has promised to join and work for the Republican Party in the future, and whether the applicant has the support of Republican Party officials at state or local levels. * * *

---

1. The cases come to us in a preliminary posture and the question is limited to whether the allegations of petitioners Rutan et al., state a cognizable First Amendment claim, sufficient to withstand respondents' motion to dismiss under Federal Rule of Civil Procedure 12(b)(6). Therefore, for purposes of our review we must assume that petitioners' well-pleaded allegations are true. * * *

## II.

In *Elrod,* supra, we decided that a newly elected Democratic sheriff could not constitutionally engage in the patronage practice of replacing certain office staff with members of his own party "when the existing employees lack or fail to obtain requisite support from, or fail to affiliate with, that party." The plurality explained that conditioning public employment on the provision of support for the favored political party "unquestionably inhibits protected belief and association." It reasoned that conditioning employment on political activity pressures employees to pledge political allegiance to a party with which they prefer not to associate, to work for the election of political candidates they do not support, and to contribute money to be used to further policies with which they do not agree. The latter, the plurality noted, had been recognized by this Court as "tantamount to coerced belief." At the same time, employees are constrained from joining, working for or contributing to the political party and candidates of their own choice. "[P]olitical belief and association constitute the core of those activities protected by the First Amendment," the plurality emphasized. * * *

The Court then decided that the government interests generally asserted in support of patronage fail to justify this burden on First Amendment rights because patronage dismissals are not the least restrictive means for fostering those interests. The plurality acknowledged that a government has a significant interest in ensuring that it has effective and efficient employees. It expressed doubt, however, that "mere difference of political persuasion motivates poor performance" and concluded that, in any case, the government can ensure employee effectiveness and efficiency through the less drastic means of discharging staff members whose work is inadequate. The plurality also found that a government can meet its need for politically loyal employees to implement its policies by the less intrusive measure of dismissing, on political grounds, only those employees in policymaking positions. Finally, although the plurality recognized that preservation of the democratic process "may in some instances justify limitations on First Amendment freedoms," it concluded that the "process functions as well without the practice, perhaps even better." Patronage, it explained, "can result in the entrenchment of one or a few parties to the exclusion of others" and "is a very effective impediment to the associational and speech freedoms which are essential to a meaningful system of democratic government." * * *

We first address the claims of the four current or former employees. Respondents urge us to view *Elrod* and *Branti* as inapplicable because the patronage dismissals at issue in those cases are different in kind from failure to promote, failure to transfer, and failure to recall after layoff. Respondents initially contend that the employee petitioners' First Amendment rights have not been infringed because they have no entitlement to promotion, transfer, or rehire. We rejected just such an argument in *Elrod* and *Branti,* as both cases involved state workers who were employees at will with no legal entitlement to continued employment. * * *

Likewise, we find the assertion here that the employee petitioners had no legal entitlement to promotion, transfer, or recall beside the point.

Respondents next argue that the employment decisions at issue here do not violate the First Amendment because the decisions are not punitive, do not in any way adversely affect the terms of employment, and therefore do not chill the exercise of protected belief and association by public employees. This is not credible. Employees who find themselves in dead-end positions due to their political backgrounds are adversely affected. They will feel a significant obligation to support political positions held by their superiors, and to refrain from acting on the political views they actually hold, in order to progress up the career ladder. Employees denied transfers to workplaces reasonably close to their homes until they join and work for the Republican Party will feel a daily pressure from their long commutes to do so. And employees who have been laid off may well feel compelled to engage in whatever political activity is necessary to regain regular paychecks and positions corresponding to their skill and experience.

The same First Amendment concerns that underlay our decisions in *Elrod* and *Branti* are implicated here. Employees who do not compromise their beliefs stand to lose the considerable increases in pay and job satisfaction attendant to promotions, the hours and maintenance expenses that are consumed by long daily commutes, and even their jobs if they are not rehired after a "temporary" layoff. These are significant penalties and are imposed for the exercise of rights guaranteed by the First Amendment. Unless these patronage practices are narrowly tailored to further vital government interests, we must conclude that they impermissibly encroach on First Amendment freedoms.

We find, however, that our conclusions in *Elrod* and *Branti* are equally applicable to the patronage practices at issue here. A government's interest in securing effective employees can be met by discharging, demoting or transferring staffmembers whose work is deficient. A government's interest in securing employees who will loyally implement its policies can be adequately served by choosing or dismissing certain high-level employees on the basis of their political views. Likewise, the "preservation of the democratic process" is no more furthered by the patronage promotions, transfers, and rehires at issue here than it is by patronage dismissals.
\* \* \*

Petitioner James W. Moore presents the closely related question whether patronage hiring violates the First Amendment. Patronage hiring places burdens on free speech and association similar to those imposed by the patronage practices discussed above. A state job is valuable. Like most employment, it provides regular paychecks, health insurance, and other benefits. In addition, there may be openings with the State when business in the private sector is slow. There are also occupations for which the government is a major (or the only) source of employment, such as social workers, elementary school teachers, and prison guards. Thus, denial of a state job is a serious privation. \* \* \*

Almost half a century ago, this Court made clear that the government "may not enact a regulation providing that no Republican * * * shall be appointed to federal office." Public Workers v. Mitchell, 330 U.S. 75, 100 (1947). What the First Amendment precludes the government from commanding directly, it also precludes the government from accomplishing indirectly. Under our sustained precedent, conditioning hiring decisions on political belief and association plainly constitutes an unconstitutional condition, unless the government has a vital interest in doing so. We find no such government interest here, for the same reasons that we found the government lacks justification for patronage promotions, transfers or recalls. * * *

If Moore's employment application was set aside because he chose not to support the Republican Party, as he asserts, then Moore's First Amendment rights have been violated. Therefore, we find that Moore's complaint was improperly dismissed.

## III.

We hold that the rule of *Elrod* and *Branti* extends to promotion, transfer, recall, and hiring decisions based on party affiliation and support and that all of the petitioners and cross-respondents have stated claims upon which relief may be granted. We affirm the Seventh Circuit insofar as it remanded Rutan's, Taylor's, Standefer's, and O'Brien's claims. However, we reverse the Circuit Court's decision to uphold the dismissal of Moore's claim. All five claims are remanded for proceedings consistent with this opinion. It is so ordered.

■ JUSTICE STEVENS, concurring:

To avoid the force of * * * authority * * * Justice Scalia would weigh the supposed general state interest in patronage hiring against the aggregated interests of the many employees affected by the practice. This defense of patronage obfuscates the critical distinction between partisan interest and the public interest. It assumes that governmental power and public resources—in this case employment opportunities—may appropriately be used to subsidize partisan activities even when the political affiliation of the employee or the job applicant is entirely unrelated to his or her public service. The premise on which this position rests would justify the use of public funds to compensate party members for their campaign work, or conversely, a legislative enactment denying public employment to nonmembers of the majority party. If such legislation is unconstitutional—as it clearly would be—an equally pernicious rule promulgated by the Executive must also be invalid. * * *

The tradition that is relevant in this case is the American commitment to examine and reexamine past and present practices against the basic principles embodied in the Constitution. The inspirational command by our President in 1961 is entirely consistent with that tradition: "Ask not what your country can do for you—ask what you can do for your country." This case involves a contrary command: "Ask not what job applicants can do for the State—ask what they can do for our party." Whatever traditional support may remain for a command of that ilk, it is plainly an illegitimate excuse for the practices rejected by the Court today.

■ JUSTICE SCALIA, with whom THE CHIEF JUSTICE and JUSTICE KENNEDY join, and with whom JUSTICE O'CONNOR joins as to Parts II and III, dissenting.

Today the Court establishes the constitutional principle that party membership is not a permissible factor in the dispensation of government jobs, except those jobs for the performance of which party affiliation is an "appropriate requirement." It is hard to say precisely (or even generally) what that exception means, but if there is any category of jobs for whose performance party affiliation is not an appropriate requirement, it is the job of being a judge, where partisanship is not only unneeded but positively undesirable. It is, however, rare that a federal administration of one party will appoint a judge from another party. And it has always been rare. See Marbury v. Madison, 1 Cranch 137 (1803). Thus, the new principle that the Court today announces will be enforced by a corps of judges (the Members of this Court included) who overwhelmingly owe their office to its violation. Something must be wrong here, and I suggest it is the Court.

The merit principle for government employment is probably the most favored in modern America, having been widely adopted by civil-service legislation at both the state and federal levels. But there is another point of view, described in characteristically Jacksonian fashion by an eminent practitioner of the patronage system, George Washington Plunkitt of Tammany Hall:

"I ain't up on sillygisms, but I can give you some arguments that nobody can answer.

"First, this great and glorious country was built up by political parties; second, parties can't hold together if their workers don't get offices when they win; third, if the parties go to pieces, the government they built up must go to pieces, too; fourth, then there'll be hell to pay." W. Riordon, Plunkitt of Tammany Hall 13 (1963).

It may well be that the Good Government Leagues of America were right, and that Plunkitt, James Michael Curley and their ilk were wrong; but that is not entirely certain. As the merit principle has been extended and its effects increasingly felt; as the Boss Tweeds, the Tammany Halls, the Pendergast Machines, the Byrd Machines and the Daley Machines have faded into history; we find that political leaders at all levels increasingly complain of the helplessness of elected government, unprotected by "party discipline," before the demands of small and cohesive interest-groups.

The choice between patronage and the merit principle—or, to be more realistic about it, the choice between the desirable mix of merit and patronage principles in widely varying federal, state, and local political contexts—is not so clear that I would be prepared, as an original matter, to chisel a single, inflexible prescription into the Constitution. Fourteen years ago, in Elrod v. Burns, the Court did that. *Elrod* was limited however, as was the later decision of Branti v. Finkel, to patronage firings, leaving it to state and federal legislatures to determine when and where political affiliation could be taken into account in hirings and promotions. Today the Court makes its constitutional civil-service reform absolute, extending to all decisions regarding government employment. Because the First Amendment has never been thought to require this disposition, which may well have disastrous consequences for our political system, I dissent.

## I.

\* \* \*

Once it is acknowledged that the Constitution's prohibition against laws "abridging the freedom of speech" does not apply to laws enacted in the government's capacity as employer the same way it does to laws enacted in the government's capacity as regulator of private conduct, it may sometimes be difficult to assess what employment practices are permissible and what are not. That seems to me not a difficult question, however, in the present context. The provisions of the Bill of Rights were designed to restrain transient majorities from impairing long-recognized personal liberties. They did not create by implication novel individual rights overturning accepted political norms. Thus, when a practice not expressly prohibited by the text of the Bill of Rights bears the endorsement of a long tradition of open, widespread, and unchallenged use that dates back to the beginning of the Republic, we have no proper basis for striking it down. Such a venerable and accepted tradition is not to be laid on the examining table and scrutinized for its conformity to some abstract principle of First–Amendment adjudication devised by this Court. To the contrary, such traditions are themselves the stuff out of which the Court's principles are to be formed. They are, in these uncertain areas, the very points of reference by which the legitimacy or illegitimacy of other practices are to be figured out. When it appears that the latest "rule," or "three-part test," or "balancing test" devised by the Court has placed us on a collision course with such a landmark practice, it is the former that must be recalculated by us, and not the latter that must be abandoned by our citizens. I know of no other way to formulate a constitutional jurisprudence that reflects, as it should, the principles adhered to, over time, by the American people, rather than those favored by the personal (and necessarily shifting) philosophical dispositions of a majority of this Court.   \* \* \*

## II.

Even accepting the Court's own mode of analysis, however, and engaging in "balancing" a tradition that ought to be part of the scales, *Elrod, Branti,* and today's extension of them seem to me wrong.   \* \* \*

The whole point of my dissent is that the desirability of patronage is a policy question to be decided by the people's representatives; I do not mean, therefore, to endorse that system. But in order to demonstrate that a legislature could reasonably determine that its benefits outweigh its "coercive" effects, I must describe those benefits as the proponents of patronage see them: As Justice Powell discussed at length in his *Elrod* dissent, patronage stabilizes political parties and prevents excessive political fragmentation—both of which are results in which States have a strong governmental interest. Party strength requires the efforts of the rank-and-file, especially in "the dull periods between elections," to perform such tasks as organizing precincts, registering new voters, and providing constituent services. Even the most enthusiastic supporter of a party's program will shrink before such drudgery, and it is folly to think that ideological conviction alone will motivate sufficient numbers to keep the party going through the off-years. "For the most part, as every politician knows, the hope of some reward generates a major portion of the local political activity supporting parties." Here is the judgment of one such politician, Jacob Arvey (best known as the promoter of Adlai Stevenson): Patronage is " 'a necessary evil if you want a strong organization, because the patronage system permits of discipline, and without discipline, there's no party organization.' " * * *

Patronage, moreover, has been a powerful means of achieving the social and political integration of excluded groups. By supporting and ultimately dominating a particular party "machine," racial and ethnic minorities have—on the basis of their politics rather than their race of ethnicity—acquired the patronage awards the machine had power to confer. No one disputes the historical accuracy of this observation, and there is no reason to think that patronage can no longer serve that function. The abolition of patronage, however, prevents groups that have only recently obtained political power, especially blacks, from following this path to economic and social advancement. * * *

In emphasizing the advantages and minimizing the disadvantages (or at least minimizing one of the disadvantages) of the patronage system, I do not mean to suggest that that system is best. It may not always be; it may never be. To oppose our *Elrod–Branti* jurisprudence, one need not believe that the patronage system is necessarily desirable; nor even that it is always and everywhere arguably desirable; but merely that it is a political arrangement that may sometimes be a reasonable choice, and should therefore be left to the judgment of the people's elected representatives. The choice in question, I emphasize, is not just between patronage and a merit-based civil service, but rather among various combinations of the two that may suit different political units and different eras: permitting patronage hiring, for example, but prohibiting patronage dismissal; permitting patronage in most municipal agencies but prohibiting it in the police department; or permitting it in the mayor's office but prohibiting it everywhere else. I find it impossible to say that, always and everywhere, all of these choices fail our "balancing" test.

### III.

Even were I not convinced that *Elrod* and *Branti* were wrongly decided, I would hold that they should not be extended beyond their facts, viz., actual discharge of employees for their political affiliation. Those cases invalidated patronage firing in order to prevent the "restraint it places on freedoms of belief and association." The loss of one's current

livelihood is an appreciably greater constraint than such other disappoint-
ments as the failure to obtain a promotion or selection for an uncongenial
transfer.   Even if the "coercive" effect of the former has been held always
to outweigh the benefits of party-based employment decisions, the "coercive" effect of the latter should not be.   We have drawn a line between
firing and other employment decisions in other contexts, see Wygant v.
Jackson Bd. of Education, [infra, Chapter 4], and should do so here as well.

*  *  *

## NOTES AND QUESTIONS

**1.**   Patronage is as old as American government and much older in the
England from which our traditions derived.   Why should the Supreme
Court now declare that this system is unconstitutional?

**2.**   Is Justice Scalia right that this decision will further weaken the
political parties and that the result may be bad for American democracy?

**3.**   Can a Court-mandated civil service system be effective?   How can
judges create the detailed supervisory rules that nonpatronage systems
require?

**4.** Earlier cases had barred political discrimination in discharge.   Should
the Constitution be held to protect the political beliefs of current employees
but to allow politics to govern new hiring?   How would you defend such a
distinction?

**5.**   Besides First Amendment claims involving freedom of expression and
association, two other constitutional arguments are often raised by public
sector employees.   First, the Fourth Amendment has been used to challenge allegedly unconstitutional searches and seizures in the workplace
involving property (e.g., searches of desks, lockers, and cars) and the person
(e.g., urine drug testing).   Second, the Fifth and Fourteenth Amendments
have been the bases of due process and equal protection claims.

## Craig Becker, *With Whose Hands: Privatization, Public Employment, And Democracy* *

6 Yale L. & Pol'y Rev. 88 (1988).

Historians differ in their assessments of the motives and accomplishments of early civil service reforms.   Some agree with Justice Douglas and
root them in a democratic impulse.   Others find they were designed to
ensure government by an elite cadre of experts and thereby to curb urban
ward bosses and their immigrant constituencies.   Notwithstanding the
contradictory purposes in which they originated, however, civil service laws
now extend beyond an elite corps of public officials, providing job security
to secretaries, custodians, and garbage collectors.   Moreover, women and

---

* Reprinted by permission.

minorities have tended to find jobs in the civil service more readily than in the private sector. Thus, the significance of civil service principles in the late twentieth century cannot necessarily be identified with the concerns animating the creation of the administrative state.

Today, civil service laws establish two central requirements: (1) appointment and promotion must be in accord with merit and fitness and (2) discharge may only be for just cause. These restraints not only prohibit the "spoils system," which awards jobs on the basis of political fealty, but also embody a set of positive principles of public administration. These principles are openness, merit, and independence. Privatization of public services is incompatible with each of these ideals.

Civil service laws guarantee that vacancies in government are publicly announced, qualifications are clearly articulated, application is open to all, and selection is according to objective criteria. The commitment to openness in the civil service is designed to ensure that it will be representative of the electorate. Although merit is difficult to define and harder to measure, the system of examinations and qualification standards required by civil service laws provide some assurance that the public business is not delegated simply to workers of a particular color, workers who have given something in return, or workers willing to accept the lowest wage. Private contractors are barred from engaging in certain types of discrimination, but they remain relatively free to hire through a closed and private process. It is not surprising, therefore, that government service opened an avenue to secure and well-paying jobs for women and minorities, while the doors to the corporate boardroom remain closed.

In 1980, 27.1% of black workers were employed by government, as compared with 15.9% of white employees. Black employment in the public sector is even more pronounced at the higher levels of government. Fifty-three percent of all black managers and professionals are in the public service in contrast to only 29% of whites. Similarly, women have found unique opportunities in government service. Only 16% of working men are employed in government, while 21% of working women are employed there. Fifty-five percent of all female professionals are civil servants, compared with only 35% of male professionals. Public employees, then, are more representative of both the racial and gender composition of the workforce than are employees in private business.

## 2.   COLLECTIVE BARGAINING

The Pullman strike of 1894 began an extended period of labor unrest in which workers and capitalists tried to arrive at terms that would make the world of work acceptable to both sides. By 1935, with the enactment of the Wagner Act, the U.S. labor system began to settle into the complex mix of bargaining and regulation that has characterized the past half century. Why did workers press for collective bargaining? Consider the following statement:

**Testimony of John Mitchell, former President of the United Mine Workers, before the U.S. Senate Commission on Industrial Relations, April 6, 1914.**

MR. MITCHELL.  * * * In my judgment there can be no permanent prosperity to the workingmen, there can be no permanent industrial peace, until the principle is firmly and fully established that in industrial life the settlements of wages, hours of labor, and all the important conditions of work, are made between the employers and the workingmen collectively and not between employers and working men individually.  The individual workman theoretically bargains with his employer as to the wages to be paid by his employer; but practically there is no bargaining.  The individual workman must accept the wages and conditions of employment that are offered to him by his employer.  It is a matter of no concern at all to an employer if one workingman refuses employment.  He thinks nothing about it, because there is another workingman ready to take the job.

As a consequence of this system of individual bargaining, which is really nonunionism, the conditions of the best men in the industry are brought down, practically, to a level with those of the weakest men in the industry.  Collective bargaining, of course, means that there shall be a uniform and minimum standard of wages and that there shall be uniform hours of labor.  * * *

I know that in the industry with which I am best acquainted, the coal industry, collective bargaining has not only increased tremendously the earnings of the mine workers, but what is perhaps of more importance it has given the whole mining population a different and a better view of life. That is, instead of being, as they once were, a hopeless, despondent people, whose labor brought them less than that upon which they could live decently, they have become a hopeful people; they have got a different outlook; they regard this as "our country," a country in which they feel an interest, a country that means something to them.

Now, it has given them that feeling of justifiable independence; it has made them better men, better citizens, better fathers, given them better homes; it has meant education for their children, and it has meant, in most cases, a provision for their old age.  * * *

---

From the earliest days of the American trade union movement, business sought help from the judiciary in its struggle against unionization. During the 1880s, equity courts began issuing sweeping injunctions against strike activities by the growing number of labor unions.  Although the English rule initially followed by American courts did not ordinarily permit the issuance of injunctions, many railroads were in receivership and therefore under the control of equity courts, which enjoined strikes by railroad employees.  In In re Debs, 158 U.S. 564 (1895), the Supreme Court upheld the contempt conviction of Eugene V. Debs of the American Railway Union for his part in the Pullman strike of 1894.

After the Pullman strike, President Cleveland appointed the United States Strike Commission to investigate the national labor scene.  The Commission's report recommended that employees be permitted to organize into unions and to bargain collectively.  Congress responded by passing the Erdman Act in 1898.  The law was limited to employees engaged in the operation of interstate trains.  It imposed criminal penalties for the discharge or threatened discharge of employees for union membership and provided for conciliation and mediation of railway labor disputes.  The Act was declared unconstitutional by the Supreme Court in Adair v. United States, 208 U.S. 161 (1908).

In 1914, Congress passed the Clayton Act, §§ 6 and 20 of which provided that the antitrust laws, especially the Sherman Act, did not apply to labor unions.  The Railway Labor Act, passed in 1926, provided that "collective action, without interference, influence, or coercion exercised by either party over the self-organization or designation of representatives by the other" was to be the manner of selection for representatives.  The Act was upheld in Texas & New Orleans Rail Road Co. v. Brotherhood of Railway & Steamship Clerks, 281 U.S. 548 (1930).

The Norris-LaGuardia Act was enacted in 1932.  The Act outlawed "yellow dog" contracts and prohibited the federal courts from issuing injunctions in labor disputes.  The following year Congress passed the National Industrial Recovery Act (NIRA).  Section 7(a) of NIRA granted employees the right to organize and bargain collectively, but it was declared unconstitutional in A.L.A. Schechter Poultry Corp. v. United States, 295 U.S. 495 (1935).

Less than two months later, Congress enacted the National Labor Relations Act (NLRA or Wagner Act).  The NLRA declared it to be the policy of the United States to encourage collective bargaining; established the National Labor Relations Board (NLRB) to regulate union organizing, representation elections, and unfair labor practices; gave employees the rights of self-organization and collective bargaining; and prohibited certain employer unfair labor practices.

The NLRA was held to be constitutional by the Supreme Court by a five-to-four vote, in NLRB v. Jones & Laughlin Steel Corp., 301 U.S. 1 (1937).  According to Chief Justice Hughes, the NLRA "purports to reach only what may be deemed to burden or obstruct * * * commerce, and thus qualified, it must be construed as contemplating the exercise of control within constitutional bounds."

In 1938, Congress passed the Fair Labor Standards Act, which set minimum wage rates, required higher pay for overtime, and prohibited the use of child labor in goods or services involved in interstate commerce.

After World War II unions were much more powerful and largely unchecked by law.  Asserting a need to return a "balance" to labor-management relations, Congress passed the Labor Management Relations Act (LMRA or Taft-Hartley Act) in 1947 over President Truman's veto.  Taft-Hartley amended the NLRA to give employees the right to refrain from (as well as participate in) union activities; expanded the NLRB from three to five members; and added a series of prohibited unfair labor practices by unions.

To control internal union affairs, in 1959 Congress passed the Labor-Management Reporting and Disclosure Act (LMRDA or Landrum-Griffin). This "bill of rights" for union members requires periodic financial and other reports from unions, regulated union elections and union funds, and prohibits Communists and certain ex-felons from holding union office. The LMRDA also makes some minor changes in the NLRA.

The NLRA is based on the commerce clause and covers businesses "affecting commerce." This is determined by the dollar volume of the enterprise. The NLRA specifically excludes federal, state, and local government employees, agricultural employees, supervisory employees, and railway and airline employees (who are covered under the Railway Labor Act).

The vast majority of the NLRB's actions are concerned with: (1) conducting and certifying the results of union representation elections, which if won by the union will require the union and company to bargain in good faith over wages, hours, and terms and conditions of employment; and (2) investigating and prosecuting unfair labor practice charges brought by employees, unions, and employers.

A vast body of substantive law has developed under the NLRA during the last 60 years. It is beyond the scope of this book to explore these developments in any detail. Nevertheless, some brief mention of NLRA law is essential for understanding the framework in which collective bargaining is regulated.

Section 8(a)(1) of the NLRA makes it an unfair labor practice for an employer "to interfere with, restrain, or coerce employees" in the exercise of their rights to self-organization and collective bargaining. An employer may not discharge or otherwise discriminate against employees for discussing unionization (especially during nonwork time and in nonwork areas), wearing union buttons and insignia, or signing union authorization cards. Republic Aviation Corp. v. NLRB, 324 U.S. 793 (1945).

Collective bargaining takes place in bargaining units comprised of employees at a single plant with similar wage scales, hours, job responsibilities, and working conditions. If 30 percent of the employees in a bargaining unit sign cards authorizing a particular union to represent them, the NLRB will order and conduct a representation election. (If more than 50 percent sign cards the employer may voluntarily recognize and bargain with the union although it need not do so. Linden Lumber Division, Summer & Co. v. NLRB, 419 U.S. 301 (1974).) During the election campaign, a period of about two or three weeks, neither side may threaten or coerce voters nor promise benefits based on the outcome of the election. NLRB v. Gissel Packing Co., 395 U.S. 575 (1969). If the union loses (fails to obtain a majority), another election may not be held for at least one year. If the union wins, it is the collective bargaining representative of all the employees in the unit, regardless of whether they supported the union.

Sections 8(a)(5), 8(b)(3), and 8(d) require that the union and employer bargain in good faith over wages, hours, and other terms and conditions of employment. The NLRA does not require that both sides reach an agreement, only that they meet and confer, and bargain in good faith. If an agreement is reached, it will set out the wages, hours, and terms of employment. Most collective bargaining agreements set out disciplinary procedures and prohibit the discharge of employees unless there is "just cause." Grievances and disputes between labor and management are usually subject to arbitration in accordance with the collective bargaining agreement.

Unions sometimes strike to pressure an employer into making concessions in collective bargaining. The primary strike is legal under the NLRA, but secondary strikes (against customers and suppliers) usually are not and may be enjoined by the NLRB. Although the employer may not discharge employees engaged in protected, concerted activity (including the primary strike), the Supreme Court has held that the employer may hire permanent replacements. NLRB v. Mackay Radio & Telegraph Co., 304 U.S. 333 (1938). (In effect, strikers may lose their jobs and need only be placed on a preferential hiring list for the next available opening.) If the employees strike simply to protest employer unfair labor practices the employer may hire only temporary replacements.

Charges of unfair labor practices must be filed with the NLRB within six months of their alleged occurrence. The General Counsel of the NLRB has unreviewable discretion in deciding whether to proceed with an unfair labor practice charge. Initial adjudications are made by an administrative law judge and are then subject to review by the five-member NLRB. Appeals and petitions for enforcement then may be filed in the United States Courts of Appeal. NLRB remedies are usually limited to back pay, reinstatement, orders to bargain, and cease and desist orders.

## NOTE ON UNION SECURITY

An important aspect of an individual's employment relationship concerns whether the individual can be required to or prohibited from joining a union or paying dues or other fees to a union. Section 3 of the Norris-LaGuardia Act, enacted in 1932, proscribed *"yellow dog contracts,"* in which the employee promises not to join a union. In 1935, when the Wagner Act (NLRA) was passed, § 7 declared that employees have the right "to form, join, or assist labor organizations." Thus, although employees could not be prohibited from joining a union, there was no provision that prohibited requiring an employee to join a union as a condition of obtaining or retaining employment.

A union security clause is a provision in a collective bargaining agreement that describes the obligations of employees to support the union. The most demanding provision is one providing for a *closed shop*. A closed shop provision obligates the employer to hire only union members and to discharge employees who drop or lose their membership. Under the Wagner Act the closed shop was legal. Congress was concerned that the closed shop had caused disruptive union activity and had been used to oust dissenters from their jobs by expelling them from union membership. In 1947, the Taft-Hartley Act amended § 7 to add that employees also have the right to refrain from union activity, except "to the extent that such right may be affected by an agreement requiring membership in a labor organization as a condition of employment as authorized in section 8(a)(3)." Section 8(a)(3) outlawed the closed shop by adding a grace period of at least 30 days before an employee can be required to pay union dues or fees. It also banned union fees and dues unless membership is made available to the employee on the same terms as to other members and prohibited an employer from discharging an employee for nonmembership in a union if the employer "has reasonable grounds for believing that membership was denied or terminated for reasons other than the failure of the employee to tender the periodic dues and the initiation fees uniformly required as a condition of acquiring or retaining membership."

Section 8(a)(3) therefore legalizes the *union shop,* whereby an employee may be required to become a union member in order to retain a job, although the employee need not be a member at the time of hiring and has a grace period of at least 30 days to join the union. In NLRB v. General Motors Corp., 373 U.S. 734 (1963), the Supreme Court construed quite narrowly § 8(a)(3)'s use of the word "membership."

> It is permissible to condition employment upon membership, but membership, insofar as it has significance to employment rights, may in turn be conditioned only upon payment of fees and dues. "Membership" as a condition of employment is whittled down to its financial core.

Id. at 742.

While the union shop is legal, in reality, the most demanding provision enforceable is one that mandates an *agency shop,* in which employees need not join the union but are required to pay the union an amount equal to the union's initiation fees and dues. There is one important difference between a union shop and an agency shop. Pursuant to many union constitutions, union discipline (e.g., honoring strikes) may be maintained through the assessment of fines enforceable in state court. Thus, while the agency shop eliminates the problem of "free riders" benefitting from union services without paying, union control is weakened. In 1980, Congress amended § 19 of the NLRA to permit employees with bona fide religious objections to joining or financially supporting labor organizations to contribute an equivalent amount of money to an approved charity. (The permissible reach of union security arrangements for government employees is even narrower. In Abood v. Detroit Board of Education, 431 U.S. 209 (1977), the Supreme Court held that the First Amendment's guarantee of freedom of association prohibits a public sector union from collecting agency fees for political activities to which nonunion members object. According to the Court, agency fees could only be *required* for reasonable costs of contract negotiation and administration.)

Another important change in union security made by the Taft-Hartley amendments is the enactment of § 14(b), which prohibits an agreement requiring membership in a labor organization as a condition of employment in any state or territory with a contrary state law. ("Membership" includes financial contribution under an agency shop. Retail Clerks Local 1625 v. Schermerhorn, 373 U.S. 746 (1963).) Pursuant to § 14(b), at least 21 states, almost all in the south and west, have enacted *right to work laws* proscribing union membership as a condition of employment. For unions, this means that they have both the discipline and free-rider problems. Union density in right to work states is much lower than in states without such laws.

## Paul C. Weiler, Governing the Workplace*

7–13 (1990)

The Rise and Decline of Collective Bargaining

Unquestionably, thirty years ago one would not have dreamed of settling such a contentious issue as drug testing through the use of legal authority in the civil jury process. The favored instrument, instead, would have been direct voluntary negotiation between the employer and a union which the employees had selected for purposes of collective bargaining. Sometimes such problems were explicitly addressed by the parties, which would negotiate detailed programs to deal with them. Alternatively, the matters might first have arisen under the umbrella of the general contract protection against unjust discipline and discharge, and been taken through the grievance arbitration procedure for resolution. Even that process was ultimately subject to the control of the immediate parties, who could select and remove their arbitrators as well as revise arbitration rulings for future cases.

In the eyes of its proponents the institution of collective bargaining had several important virtues. First, while a solitary employee—a Barbara Luck, for example—would probably have little realistic chance of avoiding either invasion of privacy by a drug test or loss of her job if she refused to provide a urine sample, her prospects would be much better if she were to band together with all her fellow employees in pursuit of that goal. At a minimum, such an association would provide a forum in which the employees could discuss and formulate their concerns, then use a skilled representative to voice their position to a management team representing the employer, and in all likelihood exert considerable influence on the design, if not the existence, of any drug testing program.

At the same time, any restraints on management prerogatives would be those that had been mutually accepted by the parties themselves, given their respective needs and priorities. In other employment relationships in which the participants had different views about what was important, they

were free to go their own way on this and other issues.  Indeed, the initial
judgments made in the original setting were equally open to renegotiation
as experience seemed to dictate.  Nor is this just an imaginary scenario
with respect to the drug issue itself.  Inveterate readers of the sports pages
will have observed essentially that scenario unfolding as collective bargaining in the several professional sports has grappled in a variety of ways with
the common problem of drugs and testing throughout the eighties.

In sum, collective bargaining was and is a governance mechanism
which offers employees a blend of *protection* and *participation* through
private, local, and voluntary settlement of workplace problems.  However,
the existence and shape of the institution itself is assumed to be a matter of
public concern and is thus the object of substantial legal support and
influence.  A half century ago the National Labor Relations Act (NLRA)
was enacted to encourage the organization of employees for purposes of
collective bargaining whenever employees in a work unit favored that
option; to protect the employees in question from coercion and restraint in
making their choice; and to require the employer to recognize and deal
with any union that might be selected by a majority of the employees.
Since the mid-thirties, then, our federal labor policy has been to facilitate
the *reconstruction* of the unfettered individualistic labor market so as to
give employees greater group leverage in dealing with what were often
large, powerful corporate employers.  But the actual terms and conditions
of employment which flowed from the bargaining process were, with rare
exceptions, determined by the mutual agreement of the parties.  The
content of their agreement would reflect the parties' respective needs and
resources, shaped both by the state of the labor market and by the external
product and capital markets in which the firm and its employees had to
operate.

For the first twenty years of its life, this New Deal labor policy was
highly successful in its own terms.  The scope of union representation in
collective bargaining, which had been roughly 15 percent of the private
sector labor force just before enactment of the NLRA, soared to nearly 40
percent by the mid-fifties; all indications were that this figure would rise to
45 or even 50 percent some time thereafter.  Indeed, the influence of the
union movement was actually much broader than the direct measures of
"union density" might indicate.  The core of union membership was male,
blue-collar production workers in manufacturing industries, many of whom
were employed by the larger, more successful firms—such as General
Motors, U.S. Steel, and General Electric—which were pacesetters in sophisticated management techniques.  Thus the human resource innovations
developed in collective bargaining between these firms and their unions
soon set a pattern which was imitated by unionized firms for their
nonunion white-collar workers, and by nonunion firms for both their blue-
collar and white-collar labor force.

In the mid-fifties there began a remarkable turnaround in the fortunes
of collective bargaining, and the institution started on a long and inexora-
ble downhill slide.  Associated with the decline was an equally marked

change in the composition of the work force.  The pendulum swung from manufacturing to service industries, from blue-collar to white-collar jobs, from an almost exclusively male work force to a high percentage of female workers, and from the northern to the southern regions of the country. The established unions found that they could not put down substantial roots among the new and growing segments of the labor force (at least in the private if not the public sector); therefore, even if these unions had been able to maintain their existing positions in their traditional constituencies, their proportionate statistical share of the overall labor force would decrease.

But starting in the early seventies, union coverage began to fall even in its traditional bastions.  Union representation typically suffers significant attrition when already organized plants are closed and firms go out of business.  That trend was even more pronounced in the early eighties, when the "rust belt" reeled under the pressures of intensified foreign competition and a deep recession.  Just to stay even, unions annually had to organize their proportionate share of the workers in the new plants and firms which opened to supply new markets.  But the dominant industrial unions such as the United Auto Workers, the Steel Workers, the Electrical Workers, the Teamsters, and the construction building trades were not able to secure bargaining rights in many of the new units, either in the fast-growing "sun belt" or even in the north.  By the mid-eighties, then, private sector union coverage had fallen from its 40 percent share in the mid-fifties to just over 15 percent only three decades later.  Recall that the latter was roughly the same percentage as had obtained a half-century earlier, when the Wagner Act was enacted in order to expand the prospects for collective employee action.  Moreover, there is no reason to suppose that the 15 percent figure is a bottom point in the slide.  Unless the next decade witnesses a change as far-reaching as the one that occurred in the fifties, simple extrapolation of existing trends indicates that union density will be down to less than 10 percent by the turn of the century.

But these empirical trends are not by themselves an index of the failure of the legal policy of the NLRA.  Such a value judgment must ultimately rest on a diagnosis of the reasons fewer and fewer American workers are securing collective bargaining under the auspices of the Act.

For our purposes, the multitude of specific explanations for this phenomenon can be divided into two categories—a decline in the demand for collective bargaining and a decline in the supply of this institution.  On the demand side, on explanation emphasizes that to many of the new breed of white-collar and often female workers, joining a union has had little appeal.  Note that this demographic and attitudinal story could hold true for only private sector employees, because one predominantly female, white-collar occupational category, the school teachers, has actually been the fastest-growing segment of the unionized work force for the last quarter-century.  But in this view, to the extent that this account is generally valid for the private sector covered by the NLRA, the decline in union representation represents only a failure of the unions, not of the labor laws.  After all, the object of the law is simply to give workers the right to collective bargaining if they want it, not to foist it upon worker groups who would rather not have it.

The contrary prescription would follow if the "supply side" diagnosis were valid—that the source of a considerable share of union decline is sustained employer resistance, making collective bargaining less readily available to employees.  From this point of view the problem is that more and more American employers, wanting to remain or to become nonunion, are utilizing a variety of antiunion measures which make it ever more difficult for employees interested in collective bargaining to actually exercise their statutory rights to join a union, at least at a price most workers might reasonably be expected to pay.  If and to the extent this second account is valid, there is clearly much better reason to believe that something in our labor law needs fixing.

Later in this book I present the evidence for the two competing explanations for the downward trend in union membership, and consider the implications for the future design of our national labor policy.  For the moment it is more interesting to speculate on the reasons why a shift might have occurred in either or both the demand for or supply of union representation.

With respect to the apparent decline in employee demand, two factors seem to be operating side by side.  One is that human resource management by many American employers has become more professional, more sophisticated, and more attuned to the needs and interests of the employees.  Increasingly sustained efforts are being made to provide decent wages and benefits, to eliminate unfair treatment of individual employees, and to produce a secure and congenial workplace environment.  Part of the reason for the improvement in personnel practice is the expectation that it will attract and retain a high-quality, well-motivated work force.  Needless to say, another powerful factor is the employer's hope that such measures will head off any felt need among the employees to explore an alternative instrument—unionization—to secure favorable conditions on the job.

At the same time there has been a gradual alteration in the character of unionism itself.  From one perspective, unionization has been and can be viewed as an *activity* of the employees themselves, whereby they participate as a group in the improvement of their own working conditions.  In its current image, though, the union is usually perceived as an *entity* external to the employees: as a large, bureaucratic organization whose full-term officials periodically negotiate a long-term contract behind closed doors with the employer, and then represent a fairly small number of employees who are aggrieved by the way management administers the contract during its lifetime.

Of course, the main reason unionism and collective bargaining have evolved this way is that a large and sophisticated organization and professional staff were needed to deal effectively with even larger and more sophisticated corporations, and to establish the kinds of protection employees want without having to pay an unacceptable price for it.  But whatever the reason for its evolution, the resulting brand of unionism displayed certain negative attributes.

First, even if larger, more highly bureaucratized unions do produce a higher level of employment protection, at least within the standard compass of the labor contract, there is little participation by the employees in the effort. And, until recently at least, little or no attention has been paid to the felt need of workers to have a positive personal influence on the daily character of their jobs and the productive operation of which they are a part.

Even worse, as the union appears increasingly to be an entity separate and apart from the employees—a professional organization analogous in function if not in constituency to the company personnel department—concerns naturally arise about how to protect the employees, individually and collectively, from the union itself and its management. That need will be felt even when the union's leadership ethos is benign, because it is desirable to reduce the incidence of ineffective and inadequate representation. But the unhappy reality is that occasionally the attitude of union officialdom is not benign; union leaders' actions are sometimes motivated by the desire to perpetuate their tenure and to enhance their financial rewards, a situation that may result in an undemocratic and corrupt union organization. Perhaps the ultimate testimony to this human and organizational failing is the recent spate of trusteeships imposed on local unions by courts acting under the auspices of RICO, a piece of criminal legislation which the Congress enacted to fight organized crime.

If the trends I have just described were widespread enough, the combination of a more appealing work situation provided by the employer and a less attractive union alternative could have been sufficient to produce much if not all the decline in union representation observable in the aggregate statistics. But American employers have not been content to allow these forces to play themselves out, with whatever impact they might have on the employees' own sentiments. American business has adopted, instead, a posture of sustained and active resistance to collective bargaining for its employees.

Within the longer-term historical perspective, that posture is not surprising. For the last century management in the United States has been vigorously opposed to union representation, as much if not more so than management in any other industrialized nation. True, in the mid-fifties an *entente cordiale* was seemingly reached with organized labor, but with hindsight that appears to have been merely a temporary lull in the struggle. A number of maverick nonunion employers continued to develop and to demonstrate the effectiveness of a variety of tactics for frustrating union organizing. By the early seventies, more and more supposed business statesmen were beginning to utilize these and other tactics as part of a corporate strategy to achieve as low a level of unionization as possible. The result is that whatever wavering affections American workers might have as between their employer and a union, they now recognize that it will be an arduous, stressful, and risky journey to proceed from an initial interest in collective bargaining, through the representation campaign, and eventually to a first contract with a union representative firmly inside the plant or office.  Unsurprisingly, whatever their personal inclinations, fewer and fewer workers are prepared to undertake that journey.

NOTES AND QUESTIONS

**1.**  In the U.S., widespread opposition to unions among employers has spurred the growth of numerous "management consultants," who advise companies how to thwart union organizing activity, defeat unions in NLRB elections, and frustrate unions in collective bargaining.  Indeed, many corporate personnel policies are designed to preempt unions.  Why are American employers so anti-union?  Why are American employees less willing to commit themselves to the union movement?

**2.**  During the last 25 years, despite problems in organizing workers and at the bargaining table, unions have had a fair degree of success in the political arena.  Due in no small part to union support laws have been enacted on employment discrimination, safety and health, and pensions.  From a union perspective, sweeping national reform may be more efficient and effective than individual collective bargaining.  Also, by establishing minimum standards for all employers, unionized employers (and their employees) are not at a competitive disadvantage with regard to nonunion employers.  Is it also possible, however, that unions are contributing to their own demise?  With the government mandating nondiscrimination, safety and health, and other matters perhaps workers have less need for unions.  Would a statutory prohibition against unjust dismissal be the death knell for unions?  In Western Europe there are both comprehensive social legislation and union density.  Why not here?

**3.**  For a further discussion of these issues, see Richard B. Freeman and James L. Medoff, What Do Unions Do? (1984).

# Pryner v. Tractor Supply Co.

109 F.3d 354 (7th Cir.1997), cert. denied, 118 S.Ct. 294 (1997).

■ POSNER, CHIEF JUDGE.

We have consolidated the appeals in two employment discrimination cases that raise the same two issues: Are arbitration clauses in collective bargaining agreements other than in the maritime, railroad, and other transportation industries subject to the Federal Arbitration Act, 9 U.S.C. §§ 1 et seq.?  And can a collective bargaining agreement compel an employee to arbitrate a claim that he may have under one of the federal statutes, such as Title VII of the Civil Rights Act of 1964, the Age Discrimination in Employment Act, or the Americans with Disabilities Act, that confer litigable rights on employees?  The first issue is critical to our jurisdiction of these appeals; the second is the issue on the merits—which, of course, we can reach only if we satisfy ourselves that we have jurisdiction.

Each of the two plaintiffs is a former employee of one of the defendants, and each was discharged by his employer in alleged violation of federal law.  Pryner is black and complains that he was discharged in violation of Title VII and of 42 U.S.C. § 1981 because of his race and also because he had complained about Tractor Supply's previous racial discrimination against him before he was fired; he also has a claim under the Americans with Disabilities Act.  Tractor Supply has counterclaimed against Pryner, but the counterclaim is not involved in this appeal.  Sobierajski complains of having been discharged because of his age (58 at the time of the discharge), in violation of the Age Discrimination in Employment Act, and because of a disability, in violation of the ADA.

Both plaintiffs were employed under collective bargaining agreements.  The agreement between defendant Thoesen and Sobierajski's union, the automobile mechanics union, provided that "in accordance with applicable Federal and State law, neither the company nor the Union will discriminate against employees covered by this collective bargaining agreement in regard to any terms or conditions of employment on the basis of race, creed, religion, national origin, sex or age."  The agreement between Tractor Supply and Pryner's union, the teamsters, contains a similar provision but does not refer to federal or state law and adds to the prohibition against discrimination in regard to any "terms or conditions of employment" a prohibition against discrimination "with respect to hiring [or] compensation."  Both agreements authorize the employer to impose discipline on an employee, up to and including discharge, for "just cause."  And both contain a clause that creates a grievance procedure, making the union the employee's griever and culminating in arbitration if the matter is not resolved in the earlier stages of the procedure, for disputes involving "interpretation or application" of the agreement.

Both Sobierajski and Pryner invoked the grievance procedure in their respective collective bargaining agreements.  Pryner's union struck out at the earlier stages of the grievance procedure, and has demanded arbitration.  Sobierajski's grievance, however, was abandoned, though whether by his own actions or those of the union is unclear.  Pryner and Sobierajski then filed these discrimination suits, seeking damages (including punitive damages in the case of Pryner), attorneys' fees, and reinstatement.  The defendants moved to stay the suits pending arbitration of the plaintiffs' claims.  The motions were denied and the defendants have appealed from these denials.

* * *

A footnote in United Paperworkers Int'l Union v. Misco, Inc., 484 U.S. 29, 40 n. 9 (1987), says that the arbitration act does not apply to labor arbitration.  But the footnote gives no reason; is inconsistent with the Supreme Court's subsequent decision in Gilmer v. Interstate/Johnson Lane Corp., 500 U.S. 20, 25 n. 2 (1991), which expressly left the question open; and goes on to cite with apparent approval our decision in Pietro Scalzitti Co. v. International Union of Operating Engineers, 351 F.2d 576, 579–80 (7th Cir.1965), which, limiting the exclusion of employment contracts in section 1 to workers engaged in the physical movement of goods in interstate or foreign commerce, holds that the arbitration act applies to labor arbitration in all industries except transportation.

* * *

Even if as we believe the collective bargaining agreements in this case are not excluded from the act's coverage by section 1's reference to employment agreements, they might be excluded, as some courts believe, by section 301 of the Taft–Hartley Act.  Section 301(a), which makes collective bargaining agreements enforceable in the federal courts, was interpreted in Textile Workers Union v. Lincoln Mills, 353 U.S. 448 (1957), to require that principles of federal common law be developed and used to interpret such agreements.  There is no reference in section 301 to arbitration, which becomes an issue in a section 301 case only when a collective bargaining agreement happens to contain (as most such agreements do) an arbitration clause.  The question is then whether, despite its silence about arbitration, section 301 repealed the Federal Arbitration Act with respect to collective bargaining agreements that would otherwise be within the act's scope.  This seems hardly likely, quite apart from the venerable but contested principle that repeals by implication are disfavored and so are to be avoided unless there is no way to reconcile the two statutes.

* * *

Two competing interests have to be considered.  One is the interest in allowing unions and employers to establish a comprehensive regime for the adjustment of employment disputes;  it argues for allowing the collective bargaining agreement to force all such disputes into the grievance and arbitration groove even when the dispute arises out of a claim that a worker's statutory rights have been infringed.  The other is the interest in the effective enforcement of rights designed for the protection of workers whom Congress has classified as belonging to vulnerable groups, generally and in these two cases minority groups—blacks, the disabled, and the aged (though whether persons 40 years old and older, the group protected by the age discrimination law, should be considered a vulnerable segment of the population may certainly be questioned as an original matter).  That interest will be impaired if the right to bring suit in federal district court to enforce these rights is taken away from the workers.

Or will it?  The employers in our two cases, supported by employer groups that have filed amicus curiae briefs, argue that the workers will actually be better off if the employers' position is adopted.  Because the Equal Employment Opportunity Commission has an enormous backlog and limited resources for litigating, the vast majority of workers who have claims under any of the statutes that the Commission enforces have perforce to bring and finance their own lawsuits;  they cannot rely on the Commission to do so for them.  In contrast, a grievance is prosecuted by the worker's collective bargaining representative (the union) at no cost to the worker.  It is true that the plaintiffs in these cases do not wish to abandon their right to invoke the grievance machinery created by the collective bargaining agreements: they just want the option of pursuing judicial remedies on top of or in lieu of their arbitral remedies. But unless the arbitral remedy is exclusive, the company's incentive to agree to negotiate an arbitration clause broad enough to encompass statutory violations will be reduced, as the only effect of such a clause will be to multiply the employee's remedies.

The employers emphasize that these collective bargaining agreements do not take away any of the workers' substantive statutory rights, but merely substitute an arbitral for a judicial proceeding as the means of vindicating the rights. Although the arbitrator's award, whether or not confirmed, can—this is implicit in the notion of binding arbitration—be pleaded as res judicata in the worker's federal district court suit, subject to limitations unnecessary to dwell on here, this is true if the worker wins before the arbitrator as well as if he loses. So there is no curtailment of his substantive rights. The only difference is the forum; the defendants are right. The plaintiffs riposte that it isn't clear that the collective bargaining agreements in our two cases are completely coextensive with the plaintiffs' statutory rights; and it isn't. But a court can properly stay a suit before it if *any* issue in the suit is arbitrable, even if some issues are not. The arbitration act says in fact that the court shall stay the suit, not just a piece of the suit, if the suit is "brought upon" an arbitrable issue, though the cases, perhaps concerned lest the tail wag the dog, treat the question whether to stay the entire case as discretionary in cases involving both arbitrable and nonarbitrable issues. This interpretation was assumed in Dean Witter Reynolds Inc. v. Byrd, 470 U.S. 213, 218–19 and n. 5 (1985), though in the context of issues nonarbitrable as a matter of law, as distinct from those the parties may just not have agreed to arbitrate.

The defendants concede that to the extent that the rights conferred by the collective bargaining agreements, or the sanctions available to the arbitrators, fall short of fully vindicating the plaintiffs' substantive and remedial statutory rights, the plaintiffs will be free to resume their suits after the arbitrators render their awards, having filed the suits within the statute of limitations. But the findings made by the arbitrators might be entitled to collateral estoppel effect in the resumed suits. We say "might" to emphasize the readiness of courts to deny that effect to arbitral awards when the arbitrator has failed to explain his findings adequately or to follow procedures likely to lead to reliable findings—"adequacy" and "reliability" being relative to the importance of the claim that the arbitrator's findings are sought to be used to block.

The honey-tongued assurances of the employers' able counsel and their amici, unusually and perhaps opportunistically aligned with the unions' interest in controlling their members' access to remedies, do not persuade us that there is no genuine conflict between employer and employee interests in these cases. The plaintiffs' rights under the collective bargaining agreements are not as extensive as their statutory rights, so that to obtain complete relief they may have to undergo two trials, one before the arbitrator and the other in the district court.  And by being forced into binding arbitration they would be surrendering their right to trial by jury— a right that civil rights plaintiffs (or their lawyers) fought hard for and finally obtained in the 1991 amendments to Title VII, and that they also have under the age discrimination and disability acts.

Most important, the grievance and arbitration procedure can be invoked only by the union, and not by the worker.  The worker has to persuade the union to prosecute his grievance and if it loses in the early stages of the grievance proceedings to submit the grievance to arbitration. The defendants point out that if the union arbitrarily refuses to prosecute a grievance, let alone refuses on racial or other invidious grounds to do so, the worker can bring a suit against the union for breach of its duty of fair representation of all members of the bargaining unit.  This raises the spectre of three suits to enforce a statutory right—the suit against the union to force it to grieve and if necessary arbitrate the grievance, the arbitration proceeding, and the resumed district court proceeding if the workers' rights under the collective bargaining agreement are more limited than their statutory rights.  In any event, the union has broad discretion as to whether or not to prosecute a grievance.  It may take into account tactical and strategic factors such as its limited resources and consequent need to establish priorities, just as other "prosecutors" must do, as well as its desire to maintain harmonious relations among the workers and between them and the employer.  Corresponding to this expansive and ill-defined discretion, the scope of judicial review of its exercise is deferential. The result is that a worker who asks the union to grieve a statutory violation cannot have great confidence either that it will do so or that if it does not the courts will intervene and force it to do so.  While the grievance machinery could in principle offer the worker a cheaper alternative to suing, it seems unlikely that the union would be any more willing to prosecute a marginal case than a lawyer asked to handle it on a contingent-fee basis.  Indeed, the union might for strategic reasons decline to prosecute a claim that would have enough merit to enable the worker to retain a lawyer on a contingent-fee basis were the worker not bound to the union.

The essential conflict is between majority and minority rights.  The collective bargaining agreement is the symbol and reality of a majoritarian conception of workers' rights.  An agreement negotiated by the union elected by a majority of the workers in the bargaining unit binds all the members of the unit, whether they are part of the majority or for that matter even members of the union entitled to vote for union leaders—they need not be.  The statutory rights at issue in these two cases are rights given to members of minority groups because of concern about the mistreatment (of which there is a long history in the labor movement) of minorities by majorities.  We may assume that the union will not engage in actionable discrimination against minority workers.  But we may not assume that it will be highly sensitive to their special interests, which are the interests protected by Title VII and the other discrimination statutes, and will seek to vindicate those interests with maximum vigor. The employers' position delivers the enforcement of the rights of these minorities into the hands of the majority, and we do not think that this result is consistent with the policy of these statutes or justified by the abstract desirability of allowing unions and employers to cut their own deals. And we are given no reason to believe that the ability of unionized workers to enforce their statutory rights outside of the grievance machinery established by collective bargaining agreements is undermining labor relations.

\* \* \*

We are not holding that workers' statutory rights are never arbitrable. They are arbitrable if the worker consents to have them arbitrated. If the worker brings suit, the employer suggests that their dispute be arbitrated, the worker agrees, and the collective bargaining agreement does not preclude such side agreements, there is nothing to prevent a binding arbitration. All we are holding is that the union cannot consent *for* the employee by signing a collective bargaining agreement that consigns the enforcement of statutory rights to the union-controlled grievance and arbitration machinery created by the agreement.

\* \* \*

Affirmed.

NOTES AND QUESTIONS

**1.** In Alexander v. Gardner–Denver Co., 415 U.S. 36 (1974), the Supreme Court held that prior arbitration of a discrimination claim pursuant to a collective bargaining agreement did not preclude an action under Title VII. In Gilmer v. Interstate/Johnson Lane Corp., 500 U.S. 20 (1991), however, the Court held that a stockbroker, who signed an agreement consenting to arbitrate any dispute arising out of employment, was barred from bringing an action under the Age Discrimination in Employment Act. *Gilmer* distinguished, but did not overrule, *Alexander*. Consequently, it is not clear how much of *Alexander* still remains. The court in *Pryner* was "timid about declaring decisions by the Supreme Court overruled when the Court has not said so."

**2.** *Pryner* illustrates not only the conflicts among the various statutes, but the conflicts of the parties. In this case, the unions are siding with the employers against the employees. Why would a union have an interest in limiting the available relief of one of its members?

**3.** For more on the relationship between collective bargaining agreements and the legal rights of individual workers, see the consideration of Lingle v. Norge in Chapter 10. See also Samuel Estreicher, Predispute Agreements to Arbitrate Statutory Employment Claims, 72 N.Y.U.L.Rev. 1344 (1997).

## 3. GOVERNMENT REGULATION OF EMPLOYMENT

### Sar A. Levitan, Peter E. Carlson, & Isaac Shapiro, Protecting American Workers *

3–6 (1986).

The belief that labor markets should operate unencumbered by federal intervention was widely held by Americans until the Great Depression. Social Darwinism with its strong emphasis on individualism and self-reliance was a widely accepted philosophy—those who made it to the top of the economic ladder deserved to be there; similarly, those who failed received their just reward. The law protected employer interests and employees enjoyed few protections or rights in the workplace.

Although the period before the Great Depression was one of substantial economic growth and immigrants had significantly better opportunities than in their native lands, for every Horatio Alger, there were many workers who remained in destitution. Entire families often worked long hours in sweat shops, but still earned so little that they lived in poverty. Laborers who moved from farms to factories became more vulnerable to economic downturns. The growing interdependence of the economy guaranteed that maladjustments in one sector would cause havoc in other areas. Workers with specialized skills were less adaptable to these economic disruptions and did not raise their own food supply. Because of the growing labor supply created by rural to urban migration and by immigration, workers lacked bargaining power. They had little alternative but to accept difficult working conditions.

The hardships created by industrialization and the unregulated marketplace inevitably resulted in reform movements. The populist movement, with its agrarian roots, was strong in the late 19th century. The socialist movement reached its heyday in the early 20th century. The progressive movement, which flourished at the same time as the socialist movement, accepted capitalism but sought to ameliorate harsh workplace conditions. The union movement was established during this period to advance the interests of labor and to create a more secure and humane work environment.

These reform movements had little success in securing protection for industrial workers. No federal legislation was enacted and even modest state protective legislation was often struck down by the courts. The Supreme Court held the property rights of employers to be paramount and found legislated wage or hourly standards to be an unconstitutional infringement on employers' freedom to contract with their employees. In a 1923 decision striking down a District of Columbia minimum wage law, the Supreme Court held that "The tendency of the times to socialize property rights * * * will prove destructive of our free institutions." The Court ruled that the right of an employee to a living wage was subordinate to the employer's right to determine a "just" wage for services rendered. The Court reasoned that employers would be left without "adequate means of livelihood" if restrained from cutting wages during periods of stress and business downturns. No similar concern was expressed for the economic security of employees.

The Great Depression shook public confidence in the beneficent operations of the free market. Mass joblessness and underemployment, bank and business failures, and the inadequacy of private and state relief efforts convinced the American people of the need for federal regulation. The growing influence of Keynesian economic theory also played a part in the increased role of the federal government. The anticipation of effective federal intervention during sharp economic down-turns provided the public with hope and dispelled the prevailing belief that business cycles must run their course no matter the toll in human suffering.

The initiatives of the New Deal responded to the pressing needs of the time. An income support system was established to mitigate the harsh consequences of widespread unemployment and to ease the burden of caring for the nation's elderly. The only direct intervention into the terms of employment were minimum wage and overtime restrictions, which were intended to guarantee minimal socially acceptable compensation for the working population. Federal law legitimized the role of unions to protect worker interests on the job through collective bargaining as an alternative to coercive, sometimes violent, tactics by employers. An institutional structure was established through which unions could operate and thrive.

These interventions were an explicit recognition that unregulated markets could not adequately protect the welfare of the nation's workers. Although opposition to the New Deal reforms persisted, the Eisenhower administration made no serious effort to alter this expanded federal role. Conservatives accepted the public's support for the New Deal programs, and focused their efforts at the margins—restraining the growth of federal programs and chipping away at labor's legislated advantages.

Three decades of adjustment to the deep social reforms of the New Deal were necessary before a second wave of reform was launched. The doors of economic opportunity had opened for the great majority of Americans during the two decades of postwar prosperity, but prospects for advancement for minorities and women remained bleak. Unemployed and under-employed individuals found their opportunities limited by their lack of education, inadequate job skills, or regional isolation. Gradually, evidence mounted that economic freedom and opportunity for all, even in periods of sustained economic growth, can be realized only if barriers to work and advancement are removed through government action. The initiatives of the Great Society as well as those of the Nixon administration were directed at those who had been left behind. The Johnson and Nixon administrations also responded to the expanding aspirations of mainstream Americans. An affluent and better educated work force demanded workplace protection, leading in the early 1970s to workplace health and safety legislation and provisions for safeguarding private pensions.

## 4.   NONDISCRIMINATION

One great achievement of the civil rights movement of the early 1960s was enactment of the Civil Rights Act of 1964, Title VII of which prohibits discrimination in employment on the basis of race, color, religion, sex, or national origin. The law is notable for numerous reasons, including the theoretical bases and premises underlying its provisions.

In enacting Title VII, the first major piece of federal legislation banning employment discrimination, Congress chose not to prohibit all forms of irrational, invidious employment discrimination. Instead, it prohibited discrimination only on the basis of five proscribed classifications. Why? Why were race, color, religion, sex, and national origin selected?

## Paul Brest, *Foreword: In Defense of the Antidiscrimination Principle* *

90 Harv.L.Rev. 1, 10 (1976).

Racial generalizations usually inflict psychic injury whether or not they are in fact premised on assumptions of differential moral worth. Although all of us recognize that institutional decisions must depend on generalizations based on objective characteristics of persons and things rather than on individualized judgments, we nonetheless tend to feel unfairly treated when disadvantaged by a generalization that is not true as applied to us. Generalizations based on immutable personal traits such as race or sex are especially frustrating because we can do nothing to escape their operation. These generalizations are still more pernicious, for they are often premised on the supposed correlation between the inherited characteristic and the undesirable voluntary behavior of those who possess the characteristic—for example, blacks are less industrious, trustworthy or clean than whites. Because the behavior is voluntary, and hence the proper object of moral condemnation, individuals as to whom the generalization is inaccurate may justifiably feel that the decisionmaker has passed moral judgment on them.

The psychological injury inflicted by generalizations based on race is compounded by the frustrating and cumulative nature of their material injuries. Racial generalizations are pervasive and have traditionally operated in the same direction—to the disadvantage of members of the minority group. A person who is denied one opportunity because he or she is short or overweight will find other opportunities, for in our society height and weight do not often serve as the bases for generalizations determining who will receive benefits. By contrast, at least until very recently, a black was not denied *an* opportunity because of his or her race, but denied virtually *all* desirable opportunities. As door after door is shut in one's face, the

---

* Reprinted by permission.

individual acts of discrimination combine into a systematic and grossly inequitable frustration of opportunity.

The cumulative disadvantage caused by the use of race as a proxy even for legitimate characteristics provides an independent ground for disfavoring nonbenign race-dependent decisions regardless of the integrity of the process by which they were made.  To the unprejudiced employer who would prefer white applicants to blacks solely for reasons of efficiency, the antidiscrimination principle says in effect: "If you were the only one to do this, we would permit you to make efficient generalizations based on race. But so many other firms might employ similar generalizations that black individuals would suffer great cumulative harms.  And, in the absence of an overriding justification, this cannot be permitted."

\* \* \*

Race correlates so weakly with the legitimate characteristics for which it might be used as a proxy that, even if race-dependent decisions are sometimes rational, society loses little if they are presumptively forbidden. By contrast, a presumption prohibiting all decisions that stigmatize or cumulatively disadvantage particular individuals would affect an enormously wide range of practices important to the efficient operation of a complex industrial society.  (Furthermore, a general doctrine disfavoring harmful results could not be administered by the judiciary.)  Therefore, the law has tended to reflect the result-oriented concerns of the antidiscrimination principle, not by operating directly to scrutinize results, but by disfavoring particular classifying traits that tend to be especially harmful and have little social utility.  This approach, as well as suspected defects of process, underlies the expansion of the antidiscrimination principle beyond race to encompass decisions based on ethnic and national origin, alienage, illegitimacy and sex.

## Owen M. Fiss, *A Theory of Fair Employment Laws* \*

38 U.Chi.L.Rev. 235 (1971).

### I.  THE THEORY OF FAIR EMPLOYMENT LAWS AND THE NORM OF COLOR BLINDNESS

Fair employment laws confer benefits upon a class of persons, namely, the actual and likely victims of discrimination.  In the case of the prohibition against racial discrimination, that class consists predominantly of Negroes.  At least on the federal level, enactment was largely a response to patterns of discrimination against Negroes; the resources of public enforcement agencies have been committed primarily to inducing or coercing employers not to discriminate against Negroes; and Negroes were intended to be and, I would venture to guess, have turned out to be the primary and immediate beneficiaries of the prohibition against racial discrimination.

\* Reprinted by permission.

The supporters of fair employment laws are not unrealistic about the race of the class upon whom the law confers its direct benefits. It is black. But the desire to help blacks is qualified. It is qualified, first, by a recognition that discrimination against Negroes violates certain principles that attach no particular importance to which color happens to be the basis of the employment decision. Thus the prohibition is couched in terms of "race" or "color"—without specifying which race or color. Second, the law contemplates conferring only a limited benefit. It does no more than prohibit businessmen from making employment decisions on the basis of race or color—a criterion whose use would in any event impair rather than advance productivity and wealth maximization for the individual business-man and for society as a whole. These two qualifications make the conferral of benefits on blacks particularly palatable, ethically and political-ly, to the political majority. It is from these qualifications that the norm of color blindness emerges.

## A.  *The Aims of the Law:  Securing Equality for Negroes*

Laws prohibiting racial discrimination in employment are inextricably linked to the goal of securing for Negroes a position of "equality." There are, however, two senses to "equality" in this context. One is equal treatment. Individual Negroes should be treated "equally" by employers in the sense that their race should be "ignored," that is, not held against them. This sense of equality focuses on the starting positions in a race: If color is not a criterion for employment, blacks will be on equal footing with whites. The second sense of equality—"equal achievement"—looks to the outcome of the race. It relates to the actual distribution of jobs among racial classes and is concerned with both the quantity and the quality (measured, for example, by pay level and social status) of the jobs. Jobs should be distributed so that the relative economic position of Negroes is approximately equal to that of whites. Disproportionate unemployment and underemployment of blacks should be eliminated or substantially reduced.

These two senses of equality are linked in fair employment laws, but it is not clear which is the goal of the law. Under one interpretation, the aim of a fair employment law is to secure equal treatment, and although equal treatment might alter the actual distribution of jobs and lead to equal achievement, such a result would be only incidental. Under an alternative interpretation, the aim is equal achievement, and the guarantee of equal treatment—the antidiscrimination prohibition—is the chosen method for equalizing the distribution of jobs among racial classes.

The distinction between these two views of the aim of the law is of little moment if it can be assumed that equal treatment will lead to equal achievement. But the assumption may be incorrect. It is conceivable, and indeed likely, that even if color is not given any weight in employment decisions, and in that sense equal treatment obtained, substantial inequalities by race in the distribution of jobs will persist in the immediate and foreseeable future.

* * *

* * * The question that has to be asked is whether the goal of the antidiscrimination prohibition is equal treatment or equal achievement, and a great deal may turn on the answer to that question. For the equal treatment goal will constitute one, though only one, of the pressures to depart from the norm of color blindness. If equal achievement is the goal of the law, and, as may be the case, it is not obtained by color blindness, the desire to improve the relative economic position of blacks will create a greater temptation to construe the legal obligation arising from the command not to base employment decisions on race in a more and more "generous" fashion. There will be considerable pressure to construe the central regulatory device in a manner that would bring the law closer to the attainment of the alleged goal of equalizing the actual distribution of employment opportunities, and such a construction might well entail giving preferential treatment to blacks. On the other hand, the equal treatment goal is more compatible with color blindness; it means that blacks are treated the same as whites and thus would seem to be achieved once all employment decisions are independent of the colors of the prospective employees.

## NOTES AND QUESTIONS

**1.** How would you answer Professor Fiss' question about whether the goal of Title VII is equal treatment or equal achievement? This issue will be important when we consider topics such as affirmative action and "reverse discrimination."

**2.** As you study Chapter 4, consider several questions. First, how has Title VII's original emphasis on race discrimination affected the interpretation of Title VII in cases involving sex, national origin, and religion? Second, how well has Title VII succeeded in accomplishing its goal of eradicating discrimination? Black unemployment is higher today than it was when the statute was passed. Does that mean Title VII is a failure?

**3.** Professor Lea VanderVelde has argued that the Thirteenth Amendment to the U.S. Constitution, which bans both "slavery" and "involuntary servitude," was intended by its congressional sponsors and should be interpreted today as a charter of "fair and just labor relations." In Professor VanderVelde's vision, the Thirteenth Amendment serves not only as a prohibition of chattel slavery and as a constitutional basis for antidiscrimination statutes (see, e.g., Patterson v. McLean Credit Union, 491 U.S. 164 (1989)), but as a judicially-enforceable guarantee to workers of "the opportunities necessary to elevate their condition with the industrious application of labor." Many issues discussed in this book would be constitutionalized by Professor VanderVelde: the right to quit and seek new employment, worker covenants not to compete, employer conspiracies to lower wages, "just and fair" wages, protection of worker privacy against employer interference, and the employment at-will doctrine generally. Lea

VanderVelde, The Labor Vision of the Thirteenth Amendment, 138 U.Pa. L.Rev. 437 (1989).

**4.** For a further discussion, see Larry Alexander, What Makes Wrongful Discrimination Wrongful?  Biases, Preferences, Stereotypes, and Proxies, 141 U.Pa.L.Rev. 149 (1992).

## 5.   JUDICIAL MODIFICATION OF THE AT WILL RULE

### Arthur S. Leonard, *A New Common Law of Employment Termination* *

66 N.C.L.Rev. 631 (1988).

Recent decades have brought significant change and uncertainty to common-law principles governing employment termination.  The employment at will rule that came into general acceptance around the turn of the last century—providing that an employment agreement of unspecified duration is presumed to be terminable without penalty or notice by either the employer or employee for any or no reason—has experienced great erosion, leaving uncertainty and wide variations in law between the states.

Federal and state legislation specifying forbidden motivations for discharge, such as race, sex, religion or national origin, age, union activity, application for workers compensation benefits, or jury service, laid the groundwork for undermining the common-law rule.  These laws sometimes provide an administrative forum to challenge an unlawfully motivated discharge, and reinstatement is a potentially appropriate remedy.  These statutes challenge both the traditional presumption of terminability at will and the traditional restriction against ordering specific performance of employment agreements.  Most of the pertinent legislation was enacted during the New Deal period (in the case of federal labor and employment law) or the years 1960–1975 (in the case of civil rights and related protective labor legislation).  In addition, the organization of substantial numbers of employees into labor unions which negotiated collective bargaining agreements setting a just cause standard for employment termination and establishing a nonjudicial mechanism (neutral binding arbitration) for enforcement, marked a major incursion in the at will regime.

Another important legislative development affecting job security was the move to guarantee accumulated employee rights with respect to benefits entitlements.  The Employee Retirement Income Security Act (ERISA) of 1974, which set minimum vesting periods and required that vested benefits be nonforfeitable, gave employees a property interest in continued employment by strengthening legally enforceable interests which related to benefit entitlements.  ERISA also adopted a nonretaliation principle under which employment terminations would be suspect at various identifiable times during an employee's career.

As legislation and union organization have undermined employment at will, employees have developed new consciousness and expectations about job security. Unionized employees, never a majority of the workforce but still a significant portion, are conscious of their just cause protection, a standard requiring employer justifications based on business reasons. Members of minority groups know they can mount a legal attack against terminations traceable to racial or ethnic animosity or otherwise unrelated to their work performance. Elderly employees no longer need retire solely due to age, and employers must make "reasonable accommodations" to continue employing individuals with physical or mental impairments or who feel compelled by religious belief to perform unconventional practices of dress, diet, or Sabbath observance.

Legislative entitlements to job security have had an effect on the consciousness not only of those directly protected but also of their families, friends, and fellow employees. Supervisory employees are aware of restrictions on their ability to discharge subordinates covered by collective bargaining or statutory protections. Family and friends of public employees become conscious of the job security afforded by civil service laws and caselaw expanding constitutional job protections in the public sector. Simultaneously, other areas of the law have evolved to provide greater protection to the working class in other spheres of their everyday lives. All of these factors undoubtedly have contributed to increased feelings among employees that they have an entitlement to fair treatment in the workplace, particularly regarding job termination.  * * *

The first judicial cracks in the at will citadel involved allegations that a particular discharge decision offended some principle of public policy. A California decision recognizing such a cause of action during the 1950s has been identified as one of the earliest influential cases. During the 1970s and 1980s the highest courts of many states agreed to recognize a "public policy exception" to the at will rule, although they differed in the latitude they would allow in identifying the sources of public policy for determining whether a discharge was actionable. By 1987 a common law public policy exception had become a clear majority rule, with only a few prominent holdouts such as New York. Over sixty percent of the states now recognize an exception grounded in considerations of public policy, sometimes characterized as a basis for a tort action, with punitive damages available as a remedy in some cases.

Another widely accepted exception is an implied contract based either on written statements contained in employee handbooks or oral statements made at the time of hiring or shortly thereafter, which would lead employees reasonably to believe that they had job security. The developing caselaw shows a growing judicial reluctance to let employers enjoy the presumed benefits of such statements without incurring any obligation to abide by them. By 1987 courts in more than half the states had recognized an effective rebuttal of the at will presumption in such cases. The resulting cause of action is a breach of contract, with normal contract damages measured by an expectation interest, reduced by amounts earned in mitigation, as the usual remedy.

A minority of jurisdictions recognize an exception based on an implied covenant of good faith and fair dealing in employment agreements, similar to that implied in commercial contracts covered by the Uniform Commercial Code, and consider a breach of such covenant as the basis for a contract or tort action. Significantly, all the judicially adopted exceptions adhere to the traditional common-law reluctance to order specific performance of employment contracts, favoring damages as the sole remedy, in contrast to legislative exceptions to the at will rule that authorize a reinstatement and back-pay remedy.

Despite the rapid spread of the two principal exception theories— public policy and implied contract—the state courts are reluctant to abandon the underlying concept of a presumption of at will employment. All of the decisions upholding a cause of action do so within the framework of an exception to an underlying at will rule.

NOTES AND QUESTIONS

**1.** At common law an employer could hire or fire any employee at will. Judicial limitations on the at will rule have been concerned exclusively with wrongful discharge. Why have the courts been unwilling to create a cause of action in tort or contract for wrongful refusal to hire? See generally Mark A. Rothstein, Wrongful Refusal to Hire: Attacking the Other Half of the Employment–At–Will Rule, 24 Conn.L.Rev. 97 (1991).

**2.** For a complete discussion of wrongful discharge litigation, see Chapter 10.

## 6.   OTHER SOURCES

The modifications of the at will rule through tort and contract actions are not the only changes in the common law of employment. A variety of other tort doctrines are now being used to redress incursions upon employee privacy, reputation, and other interests. The burgeoning case law of torts in the workplace now encompasses invasion of privacy, intentional infliction of emotional distress, defamation, negligent hiring, and negligent maintenance of records. These developments are explored in subsequent chapters.

A growing number of state and federal laws also have been enacted to address a wide range of employment issues, including the following: polygraphs, drug testing, access to personnel records, migrant labor, employment agencies, other forms of discrimination (e.g., marital status, sexual orientation), and benefits (e.g., parental leave, health insurance).

## C.   THE CHANGING ECONOMIC AND SOCIAL SETTING

## 1.   DEMOGRAPHICS

### Economic Report of the President

145–49, 159–60, 164 (1990).

## THE CHANGING U.S. POPULATION

Chart 5-1

**AGE DISTRIBUTION OF THE U.S. POPULATION.**   The aging of the population means a more experienced work force, a declining share of teenagers, and an increasing share of elderly.

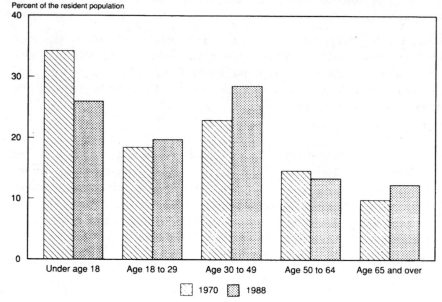

Source:  Department of Commerce.

Several major demographic trends will influence the U.S. economy and its labor markets in the 1990s.  The steady aging of the baby-boom generation will continue to increase the average age of the work force.  As Chart 5–1 shows, the percentage of the population between ages 30 and 49 rose from 23 to 29 percent between 1970 and 1988, and is projected to rise to 31 percent by 2000.  The percentage of the population age 65 and over will also continue to grow, while the percentage age 85 and over will grow even more rapidly.  At the same time, the lower birth rates that followed the baby boom have resulted in a declining number of teenagers and young adults in the population.

In addition, the share of the population composed of racial and ethnic minorities—particularly blacks, Hispanics, and Asians—continues to increase.  Growth in the Hispanic community has been particularly rapid.

Since 1980, as a result of higher birth and immigration rates, the Hispanic population has expanded at a rate five times as fast as the rest of the population.  Inflation-adjusted weekly earnings among full-time minority workers have not risen since 1980.  After several decades of steady growth, relative weekly earnings of black men have also remained flat throughout the 1980s, at about three-fourths of white men's weekly earnings.  Employment has gone up among minority workers, however, increasing labor market income for this group as a whole.

This changing population mix has important implications for the U.S. labor market.  The movement of the baby-boom generation into its thirties and forties means a work force that is, on average, older and therefore somewhat less flexible and mobile.  The declining share of teenagers and young adults has meant labor shortages for those industries that traditionally hire young people for part-time jobs.  At the same time, employment opportunities have increased for those older persons who seek employment.

The growing population of Hispanic and Asian workers, many of whom speak English as a second language, will need to adapt fully to the U.S. labor market.  This population will also create new challenges for schools and employers to offer training and assistance to enable these workers to be fully integrated into the economy.  Historically, this challenge is familiar to the U.S. economy;  current immigration rates, while above those of recent decades, are well below those around the turn of the century.  The labor market successfully absorbed these earlier immigrants, who worked hard for economic security in their adopted country.  The growing share of racial and ethnic minorities in the work force also underscores the importance of ensuring equal economic opportunities for all workers.

Not only is the composition of the U.S. population changing, but so are the ways in which individuals form families and households.  The proportion of individuals who do not live with any relative continues to increase, both because young adults spend more years living on their own and because the number of elderly single individuals has been rising.  The share of female-headed households with children is also increasing, from 5 percent of all households in 1970 to 7 percent in 1988.  Concurrently, the share of married-couple households has declined, from 71 percent of all households in 1970 to 57 percent by 1988.  The nature of these married-couple households has also changed dramatically;  in most of today's marriages, both husband and wife work.  Even among married women with preschool children, 53 percent work at least part-time outside the home.

These trends underscore the increasing importance of women's earnings.  More women are the sole earner in the household, either as single individuals or as single parents.  Moreover, married couples are relying more heavily upon women's earnings.  By 1985, women's earnings provided 28 percent of all income among white households and 46 percent of all income among black households.  Women's wages have risen relative to men's over the past decade, and continued improvements in job opportunities and wages for women will help many low-income households improve their standard of living.

These demographic and household trends set the stage for some of the important labor market challenges of the 1990s:

- Adjusting to an aging labor force and a smaller number of new labor market entrants.

- Absorbing a larger share of workers from varying ethnic and racial backgrounds and ensuring economic opportunities for all workers.

- Continuing the expansion of women's labor market opportunities.

The Department of Labor estimates that more than two-thirds of all new labor market entrants between 1988 and 2000 will be Hispanic, Asian, black, or female.  Strong economic growth depends on finding productive employment opportunities for these workers.

## SKILLS AND EDUCATION:  INVESTING IN HUMAN RESOURCES

A modern growing economy requires an educated and flexible labor force.  The median years of schooling acquired by young adults (aged 25 to 29) rose steadily in this country to an historic high in 1976 of 12.9 years.  But there has been no increase since then, while the need for a more highly skilled labor force continues to grow.  Raising the quality of education in elementary and secondary schools is at least as important as increasing years of schooling.  Higher achievement among students of every age will better prepare tomorrow's workers for productive employment.  The Federal Government can play an important leadership role in stimulating improvement in the education and training of U.S. workers, but it is important to recognize that the primary responsibility for this task resides in State and local governments and in the private sector.

The demand for more highly educated labor has increased steadily for many decades in the United States.  As Chart 5–2 indicates, the share of jobs in occupations requiring greater education has expanded.  In 1970, 21 percent of the work force were in white-collar jobs (professional, administrative, managerial, and technical occupations).  By 1988, 28 percent of workers held these jobs.  Correspondingly, the share of blue-collar jobs (production, craft, operative, labor, and agricultural work) fell from 40 percent to 31 percent.  The share of sales, clerical, and service jobs rose slightly, and there was a shift toward more skilled jobs within these categories.

These occupational changes have been closely related to the declining share of employment in traditional manufacturing industries and the rising share in service-producing industries.  In contrast to the stereotype of service-sector jobs as low-skilled labor, the growing service sector in general contains a higher percentage of jobs requiring more education.  Fully 24

## THE GROWING NEED FOR SKILLED LABOR

Chart 5-2

**TRENDS IN OCCUPATIONS.** Projected growth in white collar and service occupations will demand a more highly skilled labor force in the future.

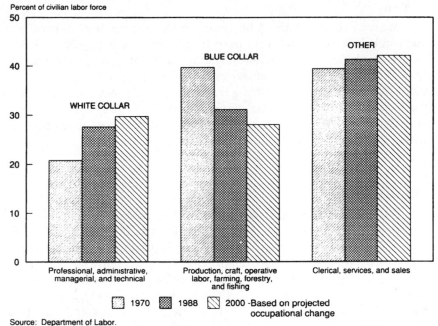

Percent of civilian labor force

1970 ▢  1988 ▨  2000 ◹ -Based on projected occupational change

Source: Department of Labor.

percent of workers in the service-producing sectors of the economy held a college degree in 1980, while only 20 percent had no high school diploma. In contrast, only 11 percent of the workers in the goods-producing sectors held college degrees, while 30 percent had not completed high school.

As the economy continues to shift toward services, the need for skilled labor will continue to rise. The Bureau of Labor Statistics predicts that the fastest employment growth between now and the year 2000 will occur in white-collar occupations, where 57 percent of all workers are college graduates and 97 percent are high school graduates. Blue-collar occupations, where only 5 percent are college graduates and 71 percent are high school graduates, will continue to shrink.

\* \* \*

## LABOR SHORTAGES, WORKER MOBILITY, AND IMMIGRATION

As the U.S. economy enters the 1990s, concerns are growing about the effects of possible labor shortages on production and wages. Employers in some areas of the country report a shortfall of entry-level workers and are paying wages well above the minimum wage to attract new employees. Other firms report difficulties in hiring suitably trained employees for more skilled positions.

In many cases, limited supplies of workers with particular skills or in particular geographic areas have developed from changes in the labor force, forcing employers to intensify their efforts to attract new workers. In other cases, uneven patterns of economic growth and technological change have altered the skill requirements or location of jobs, resulting in labor shortages for employers in growing areas or industries and job losses among workers whose skills have become obsolete or who find themselves in areas with few job opportunities.

Most of the time the labor market has readily and naturally resolved such imbalances.  Employers perceiving a labor shortage have often raised wages to attract workers, encouraging new entry or geographic mobility.  Other firms have relocated to areas with a greater supply of available workers, coupled lower hiring standards with remedial and on-the-job training, or targeted nontraditional sources of labor such as older workers and the handicapped.  Immigration has also been an important source of new workers in particular industries and occupations.

* * *

## IMMIGRATION

When labor market mobility is insufficient to eliminate area- or indus-try-specific labor shortages, employers often turn to immigrants.  Through-out U.S. history, economic growth and job opportunities have drawn millions of foreign-born persons to this country, both legally and illegally.  Of course, factors influencing immigration include family ties and the freedoms offered by the United States.  But whatever their motivation for coming to America, immigrants traditionally have adapted well to the U.S. labor market and have contributed significantly to long-run U.S. economic growth.

Between 1980 and 1988, legal immigration averaged 580,000 persons per year—about one-quarter of 1 percent of the U.S. population.  This rate of immigration was above the pace of the 1970s, but well below the average immigration rate prior to 1921, when numerical restrictions on immigra-tion were first introduced.  Efforts to control illegal immigration, estimated by the U.S. Census Bureau to have added between 100,000 and 300,000 illegal aliens each year in the first half of the 1980s, led to the Immigration Reform and Control Act of 1986.  This act restricted the employment opportunities of illegal aliens by imposing penalties on employers who hired them, but offered legal immigrant status to aliens who were in the United States before 1982.

NOTES AND QUESTIONS

**1.**  Much of this book deals with the legal implications of the demographic developments reported above.  As compared to 1970, the 2000 labor force will include more women, more non-whites, fewer jobs in heavy industry, healthier older persons, and a smaller percentage of union members.  Thus, this book considers in depth issues of race and sex discrimination in hiring, of equal pay and comparable worth, and of mandatory retirement.  With the union movement in retreat, there is more call for legislative and administrative interventions to provide worker protections traditionally obtained through collective bargaining.  Accordingly, the book also addresses issues of legislative protection against arbitrary dismissal, regulatory mechanisms for assuring safety and health, and legislated fringe benefits. A major theme running through the book is the question of whether and how institutions of legal regulation can achieve their purposes fairly and efficiently.

**2.** In 1995, there were 21.3 million workers between 16 and 24. The Bureau of Labor Statistics estimates that in 2005 there will be 23.9 million. New jobs created are expected to exceed people added to the labor force by one million per year. Will workers have increased bargaining power or will the world economy operate to keep down wages? If workers have increased power, what will they do with it? What legal changes will result?

**3.** According to the Bureau of Labor Statistics, between 1990 and 2005, the number of white males in the workforce will increase by only 7%, but white females—19%, black males—29%, black females—33%, Asian males—63%, Hispanic males—72%, Asian females—75%, and Hispanic females—80%. What effects will the new demographic makeup of the workforce have on employment law?

**4.** Other data from the Bureau of Labor Statistics document that between 1979 and 1992, the largest changes in the occupational mix in the economy have been the decline in the percentage of workers in the manufacturing sector (23% to 17%) and the increase in the percentage of workers in the service sector (19% to 27%). What are the economic and employment law consequences of this shift? See generally Robert B. Reich, The Work of Nations (1991).

## 2.   NEW WORK ARRANGEMENTS

Changing demographics, economic conditions, and technology combine to affect the nature of employment in profound ways. What will the workplace look like in the coming decades? Who is the worker of the future? Forecasters have noted various trends arising from the impact of these forces. This note explores some of the ways in which the trends are likely to change the employment relationship.

### 1. *Technology and employment*

Technology is transforming almost every aspect of work. Where computers formerly served to help perform existing job functions more efficiently, they now assist in performing managerial and organizational tasks and in developing financial and marketing strategies. As industries become more sophisticated at applying technological innovation, the adoption of new technology alters the jobs themselves. Some positions are eliminated, while new ones are created.

The introduction of technological innovation may lead to contradictory results. Some analysts contend that technology "deskills" jobs and causes a deterioration in the quality of employment. For instance, insurance companies now use a computer program to perform risk assessment in order to determine the cost of a policy to a particular consumer. This technological application renders obsolete the skill and experience insurance adjusters relied on to provide the same evaluation. On the other hand, other forecasters have observed that technological advances eliminate much routine clerical work, leaving workers with more time to focus on tasks requiring a higher level of expertise and creativity. Whatever the result, it is clear that the rapid technological development presently occurring is creating both problems and new opportunities for workers.

Technological development, along with the rise in foreign competition, also has contributed to the shift in the U.S. from a manufacturing to a service economy. The movement of labor and capital out of the production of goods and into the high-tech and service industries have changed the composition of the workforce. Approximately 30 years ago, almost half of the labor force in the U.S. worked in the goods producing sector; today, seven out of ten workers are employed in either white collar or service occupations.

In relying on computers and telecommunications systems, service industries are no longer constrained by a physical worksite or to a 9–to–5 work schedule. Strong economic incentives exist to introduce a variety of employment options. By offering flexible work schedules or home-based work, industries can reduce the size of their facilities. In addition, they can save on both direct labor costs, by paying only for actual work time, and indirect labor costs such as overhead and benefits. For example, by defining employees as part-time workers or independent contractors, they do not need to provide them with the benefit packages that full-time permanent employees require.

2. *Changing composition of the workforce*

By the end of 1984, white males for the first time no longer comprised the majority of the U.S. workforce. In the coming decades, several population trends will converge to substantially alter the composition of the workforce.

First, women will continue to seek employment in growing numbers. Presently, 50% of women with children under three years old, 60% of women with children aged three to five, and 70% of women with school-age children are working. The dual career couple is now the norm rather than the exception. Also, the "baby boom" generation, which comprises the largest cohort in the workforce, is now faced with the task of caring for its aging parents. The increased family responsibilities and greater tendency for couples to share these demands puts pressure on this large group of workers to seek more flexible employment arrangements.

Second, a much smaller "baby bust" generation is currently entering the workforce, following on the heels of the baby boom generation. Awaiting uncertain pension and Social Security benefits, workers will probably remain in the workforce longer or seek some type of employment after retirement from a conventional career. By the year 2000, 53.2% of the workforce will be between the ages of 35 and 54. As the baby boom generation ages and fewer individuals enter the workforce, employers will need to develop ways to retain an older group of employees in order to meet the demand for skilled workers.

Third, as Hispanics, Asians, and other minorities become a larger part of U.S. society, their presence will be reflected in the workforce. The educational level of prospective minority workers, including their basic math and computer skills, will be extremely important to their employability. Nevertheless, with the current high dropout rate for blacks and other minorities and the continuing loss of unskilled jobs in the manufacturing sector, unless the current trend is reversed our society could face both a labor shortage and severe minority unemployment.

In response to the growth of the service sector and application of technological innovation, employers are likely to pursue skilled workers more aggressively. The typical worker is no longer the sole earner in the household who ventures out each day from 9–to–5, secure in the knowledge that his wife will attend to their children and other domestic responsibilities. Workers are increasingly unwilling or unable to accept a typical work schedule. Older workers prefer to work fewer hours or temporary assignments. The demands of childrearing or caring for elderly relatives prevent many women from entering conventional full-time employment. In dual career households, spouses are sharing childrearing and other household duties. Computerization and telecommunications have liberated preparation of the work product from the worksite, enabling employers to begin to offer alternatives to working in the office. In addition, a growing number of employers are providing alternatives to a 40–hour work schedule in order to make employment more attractive to these potential workers. These alternatives have proven attractive to other groups of potential workers as well, leading more employers and workers to redefine the employment relationship.

### 3.   *The flexible workplace*

Because of technology and the growth of service sector employment, many workers need no longer report to the office in order to perform their job duties. Computers and fax machines facilitate the processing and transfer of information and work products from home to office and elsewhere. New technology has enabled companies to remain competitive in an increasingly global economy by having the opportunity to increase staffing and decrease the expense of maintaining a physical worksite. Moreover, workers are choosing to work at home as a way to resolve the competing demands of family and career. Many entrepreneurs are also taking advantage of developments in telecommunications and other technologies to start businesses in their homes.

Some controversy surrounds the growing availability of home-based work. Its supporters contend that home-based work increases the autonomy of the worker, allowing for flexibility in balancing work and other responsibilities. Its detractors, pointing to historical evidence of exploitation of homeworkers, argue that it forces women back into the home and prevents the development of comprehensive childcare and eldercare programs. Also, critics note that employers can exploit homeworkers more easily than on-site workers, because they are not visible to the public and are isolated from their coworkers.

Despite the potential pitfalls, homework is a growing phenomenon, especially among women with children and older workers. In 1988, 25 million people were doing all or part of their job-related work at home, an increase of 7% over the 1987 figure. It has been estimated that there may be as many as 40 million homeworkers by 2000.

The variety of jobs that can be performed at home extends well beyond unskilled piecework or data processing. In 1988, over half of homeworkers had college degrees and performed managerial or professional jobs. Many larger companies have been slower to integrate a homework option into their employment schedule because they have traditionally relied on direct observation of employees in order to control work production. As employers continue to incorporate technological innovation in more sophisticated ways, however, the organizational structure of businesses will change and homework may become a more widely accepted alternative.

4.  *The flexible work schedule*

Global competition has forced many companies to cut back the size of their permanent workforce. Instead of investing time and capital in training employees for long-term employment with the company, companies are increasingly turning to temporary or part-time professional workers to perform special assignments or to increase the size of their workforce during busy periods. As technology transforms job descriptions, job skills become less industry-specific. Skills are more easily transferable to different industries. The ease of transferability increases the range of opportunities available to workers. As a result, they are more likely to change jobs more frequently, a phenomenon known as "job shifting."

Job security is becoming less important for many people as the available labor pool shrinks and demand for skilled workers increases. Therefore, at the same time employers are less willing to plan for large, long-term employee bases, workers are less likely to be "lifers." Because of the aging of the American workforce, the greater emphasis on personal autonomy, and the decreasing emphasis on job security, workers will increasingly consider temporary employment and a variety of scheduling options as alternatives to a conventional full-time job.

The growing tendency away from a 40-hour work week has led to a dramatic change in the nature and variety of temporary and contract employment available. The number of American workers who earn their primary income in temporary jobs almost doubled to 835,000 workers by 1986 and continues to grow. Business consultants, C.P.A.s, doctors, and lawyers are among the professionals who can opt for temporary assignments. The technical and professional segment of the temporary services industry now accounts for 11% or more of all temporary workers.

Employers are also offering flexible time scheduling to make jobs more attractive to a greater number of skilled workers.  "Flextime" permits workers to adjust their work schedule in order to accommodate other activities by allowing employees to choose starting and quitting times within the limits established by the employer.  Employers find that flextime scheduling significantly reduces employee absenteeism and increases productivity.  Some flextime programs require that an employee be present in the office during a core period in order to permit direct management and staff meetings.  Others allow an employee to work a compressed work week (for example, four 10–hour days), or allow for greater flexibility in determining the work schedule.  U.S. employers may soon follow the example of some of their European counterparts in offering a "flex-year" alternative, where workers are able to schedule the number of hours they intend to work on an annual basis.

Another option more employers are making available is job sharing. In job sharing, duties are shared but each worker is responsible for the whole job.  A wide variety of jobs are conducive to having pairs of workers perform their functions.  Employers have had success in instituting job sharing in high-stress positions such as those of parole officers and teachers, as well as assembly line workers, secretaries, and receptionists.

As technology and economics redefine work functions and society redefines the place and importance of work in life, the character of employment is changing dramatically.  Employers, in their quest for a competitive edge, are becoming more willing to offer alternatives to conventional full-time employment as studies confirm that productivity and worker dedication are enhanced by offering job opportunities with flexible time and place possibilities.  As alternative work schedules become more commonplace in society, workers will be more likely to consider new employment arrangements.

## Donovan v. DialAmerica Marketing, Inc.

757 F.2d 1376 (3d Cir.), cert. denied, 474 U.S. 919 (1985).

■ BECKER, CIRCUIT JUDGE.

This opinion concerns an appeal by the Secretary of Labor (the "Secretary") from the district court's judgment for defendant, DialAmerica Marketing, Inc., in an action brought by the Secretary under the Fair Labor Standards Act, 29 U.S.C. §§ 201–219 (1982) (the "FLSA").  The Secretary alleged that DialAmerica had failed to comply with the minimum-wage and record-keeping provisions of the FLSA.  The district court determined that the two groups of workers in question, persons who research telephone numbers for DialAmerica in their homes and those who also distribute telephone-research work to other home researchers ("distributors"), are independent contractors, not "employees" subject to the provisions of the FLSA.  * * *

Because we believe the district court misapplied the relevant legal test for determining "employee" status under the FLSA, we hold that the court erred in concluding that the home researchers were not employees of DialAmerica.  On the other hand, we hold that the district court did not err in its conclusion that the distributors were independent contractors rather than employees.  * * *

DialAmerica Marketing, Inc., is a telephone marketing firm that operates in twenty states and maintains its principal place of business in Teaneck, New Jersey.  A major aspect of DialAmerica's business is the sale of magazine renewal subscriptions by telephone to persons whose subscriptions have expired or are near expiration.  Under this "expire" program, publishers supply DialAmerica with the names and addresses of subscribers, and DialAmerica locates phone numbers for these subscribers and telephones them in an effort to sell renewal subscriptions.

Initially, DialAmerica located subscribers' phone numbers by employing in-house researchers who would find numbers by consulting telephone books and calling directory-assistance operators.  In 1976, DialAmerica initiated its home-researcher program as a method of increasing its capacity to locate needed telephone numbers.  Under the program, persons would travel to DialAmerica's office in Teaneck and pick up cards, each of which contained the name and address of a subscriber whose telephone number was needed.  They would then take these cards home, use telephone books or operators to locate the telephone numbers of the persons listed, write the numbers on the cards in a specified manner, and then return the completed cards to DialAmerica's office.  The home-research program remained in effect until 1982, when it was discontinued.

In June 1979, DialAmerica began a computerized telephone-number search operation.  During the period from 1979 to 1982, this operation accounted for the locating of about 50% of all telephone numbers searched by DialAmerica.  Another 20% of the numbers were located by the company's in-house researchers.  The home-research program accounted for the discovery of about 4%–5% of all numbers sought;  the remainder apparently were never found.

Upon deciding to begin the home-research program, DialAmerica sought researchers by placing a total of five newspaper advertisements, the last of which ran in May 1979.  After that date, prospective home researchers approached DialAmerica after learning about the program from others.  Those desiring such work met with an officer of the company.  During the meeting, they were instructed how properly to complete the magazine expire cards, and they were asked to sign a document labeled an "Independent Contractor's Agreement."  DialAmerica never rejected anyone who applied for such work, although it did subsequently discharge some home researchers who performed their work inadequately.

Upon signing the agreement to do home-research work, a worker was given an initial box of 500 cards to be researched.  The worker was expected to set up an appointment to return the cards one week later.  Appointments were designed to prevent too many of the home researchers (generally women some of whom brought their small children along) from being present in the office at one time.

Home researchers were free to choose the weeks and hours they wanted to work and the number of cards they wished to research (subject to a 500–card minimum per batch and to the sometimes-limited availability of cards). DialAmerica instructed the researchers not to look for the phone numbers of schools, libraries, government installations, or hospitals. The researchers were instructed to keep all duplicate cards separate. DialAmerica required the use of a black ink or Flair pen and sold such pens to the researchers. The researchers were required to place their initials and the letter "H" (for home researcher) on each card they completed. When DialAmerica installed a machine to read and process the completed cards automatically, DialAmerica required that the home researchers place numbers on the cards by writing them in ink around dots pre-printed on the cards. Finally, the home researchers were instructed not to wear shorts when they came to the office to pick up or deliver cards. DialAmerica did not, however, require the home researchers to keep records of the hours that they worked.

During the course of this program, six or seven of the home researchers acted as distributors for DialAmerica, picking up and delivering the cards of other home researchers. In some cases, the distributors recruited new home researchers and instructed them as to the proper method of completing the cards. Initially, DialAmerica instructed the distributors to require each of their distributees to sign the same independent contractor's agreement that was given to the other home researchers. DialAmerica retained copies of these signed agreements. Later in the program, however, DialAmerica chose not to require distributees to sign the agreements, and it discarded the ones that it had in its possession.

When the program began in 1976, DialAmerica paid its home researchers five cents for every completed telephone-number card. At the same time, DialAmerica was paying its in-house researchers the minimum-wage hourly rate. The piece rate paid to home researchers was eventually raised to seven cents and then to ten cents per card. On special projects, DialAmerica set the piece rate higher to compensate for the lower percentage of correct numbers that were likely to be found. Generally, one week after a home researcher had returned a group of cards, DialAmerica would make payment to that researcher of a check equal to the piece rate times the number of cards completed. DialAmerica made no deductions from these checks. Distributors were paid a lump sum equivalent to one cent more than the going piece rate for every completed card they returned to DialAmerica, regardless of whether the card had been completed by them or their distributees. Initially, DialAmerica instructed the distributors to pay distributees the going piece rate and to keep the remaining one cent per card for themselves. Later, however, DialAmerica gave no instructions as to the amount to be paid to distributees, allowing the distributors to negotiate their own piece rates.

* * *

Congress and the courts have both recognized that, of all the acts of social legislation, the Fair Labor Standards Act has the broadest definition of "employee." In determining whether a worker is an "employee" of another person or organization within the purview of the FLSA, the Supreme Court, in Rutherford Food Corp. v. McComb, 331 U.S. 722 (1947), emphasized that the circumstances of the whole activity should be examined rather than any one particular factor.

In *Rutherford,* the Court held that boners who worked in a slaughterhouse were employees under the FLSA, even though they were paid collectively on a piece-rate basis, owned their own tools, and worked under individual employment contracts. Specific factors examined by the *Rutherford* Court in rendering its decision included: whether the work being done is part of the integrated unit of production: whether the workers shift from one workplace to another as a unit; whether managers from the alleged employer keep in close touch with the workers; and whether the work is more like piecework than an enterprise dependent for success on the workers' initiative, judgment or foresight.

Recently, the Court of Appeals for the Ninth Circuit, in Donovan v. Sureway Cleaners, 656 F.2d 1368 (9th Cir.1981), refined the test for "employee" status originally set forth initially by the Supreme Court in *Rutherford.* This test lists six specific factors for determining whether a worker is an "employee":

(1) the degree of the alleged employer's right to control the manner in which the work is to be performed; 2) the alleged employee's opportunity for profit or loss depending upon his managerial skill; 3) the alleged employee's investment in equipment or materials required for his task, or his employment of helpers; 4) whether the service rendered requires a special skill; 5) the degree of permanence of the working relationship; 6) whether the service rendered is an integral part of the alleged employer's business.

In addition, *Sureway Cleaners* instructs that neither the presence nor absence of any particular factor is dispositive and that courts should examine the "circumstances of the whole activity," and should consider whether, as a matter of economic reality, the individuals "are dependent upon the business to which they render service." The *Sureway Cleaners* test has been previously cited with approval by this court in dicta. We now adopt it as the standard for determining "employee" status under the FLSA, and we will proceed to analyze the district court's decision in relation thereto.

* * *

In its opinion, the district court conceded that three of the six *Sureway Cleaners* factors, when applied to the home researchers, weighed in favor of the conclusion that they were "employees." As the district court stated:

> It cannot be denied that, for the most part, the investment of these workers was not great, the opportunity for profit and loss was small and the skills required were few.

These findings are not only supported in the record, they are clearly correct.

The district court devoted most of its discussion, however, to explaining that defendant had very little control over the manner in which the home researchers did their work. The court emphasized that the home researchers had the freedom to work at any time and for as many hours as they desired, and that they were not directly supervised by defendant. Had the district court been analyzing the status of a group of in-house workers, the court's emphasis on these facts would have been appropriate. But in the context of this case—one involving homeworkers—the court's emphasis was misplaced.

That the home researchers could generally choose the times during which they would work and were subject to little direct supervision inheres in the very nature of home work. Yet, courts have held consistently that the fact that one works at home is not dispositive of the issue of "employee" status under the FLSA. In a seminal decision, Goldberg v. Whitaker House Cooperative, 366 U.S. 28 (1961), the Supreme Court held that members of a cooperative who made knitted goods in their homes and were paid on a piece-rate basis, were "employees" under the FLSA. The Court examined, inter alia, the legislative history of the FLSA and determined that, in general, homeworkers were intended to be encompassed by the Act. The Court then examined the specific homeworkers at issue and, upon analyzing the economic reality of their whole situation, concluded that they were indeed "employees":

> The members are not self-employed; nor are they independent, selling their products on the market for whatever price they can command. They are regimented under one organization, manufacturing what the organization desires and receiving the compensation the organization dictates. Apart from formal differences, they are engaged in the same work they would be doing whatever the outlet for their products. The management fixes the piece rates at which they work; the management can expel them for substandard work or for failure to obey the regulations. The management, in other words, can hire or fire the homeworkers.

Other federal court rulings have been consistent with *Goldberg,* holding that homeworkers in various situations were "employees" under the FLSA. Thus, the facts relied on by the district court in concluding that defendant had only a slight degree of control over the manner in which the home researchers did their work were, to a large extent, insignificant. The district court therefore misapplied and over-emphasized the right-to-control factor in its analysis.

The district court did not apply two other factors specified in the *Sureway Cleaners* test: the degree of permanence of the working relationship and whether the service rendered is an integral part of the alleged employer's business. The working relationship between the home researchers and DialAmerica was, for the most part, not a transitory one. Although there was testimony presented that several researchers performed telephone calling services for other organizations following the termination of their work for the defendant, this was not true generally. Moreover, there was no evidence to show that more than three among dozens of home researchers performed similar services for another organization while he or she was working for the defendant. In short, the home researchers did not transfer their services from place to place, as do independent contractors. Each worked continuously for the defendant, and many did so for long periods of time. As such, the permanence-of-working-relationship factor indicates that the home researchers were "employees" of the defendant.

The district court also did not expressly consider whether the service rendered by the home researchers was an integral part of the defendant's business. Given the evidence in the record, we conclude that it was. Although DialAmerica contends that beginning in June 1979, the home researchers accounted for the location of only 4%–5% of the total number of telephone numbers sought by defendant, this contention bears little relevance to the integral-economic-relationship factor. The factor relates not to the percentage of total work done by the workers at issue but to the nature of the work performed by the workers: does that work constitute an "essential part" of the alleged employer's business? In other words, regardless of the amount of work done, workers are more likely to be "employees" under the FLSA if they perform the primary work of the alleged employer.

In this case, the primary work of the defendant is locating phone numbers of various people and calling them to sell particular products. The home researchers were engaged in the location of phone numbers, and their work was therefore an integral part of defendant's business. Thus, consideration of the integral-economic-relationship factor also weighs in favor of the conclusion that the home researchers were "employees" of the defendant.

The final consideration included within the *Sureway Cleaners* test is whether, as a matter of economic reality, the workers at issue " 'are dependent upon the business to which they render service.' " The district court clearly misinterpreted and misapplied this part of the analysis. The court reasoned that, because many of the home researchers used the money they earned from their work only as a secondary source of income for their households, they were not economically dependent upon DialAmerica. There is no legal basis for this position. The economic-dependence aspect of the *Sureway Cleaners* test does not concern whether the workers at issue depend on the money they earn for obtaining the necessities of life, as the district court suggests. Rather, it examines whether the workers are dependent on a particular business or organization for their continued employment.

The home researchers in this case were not in a position to offer their services to many different businesses and organizations. They worked on a continuous basis with DialAmerica and were able to work only when and if DialAmerica was in need of their services. Consequently, the home researchers were economically dependent on DialAmerica, indicating that they were indeed "employees" of the defendant under the FLSA.

In summary, of the six factors and one general consideration identified by *Sureway Cleaners* as the basis for determining "employee" status, only one factor weighs in favor of the conclusion that the home researchers were not "employees." And that factor, the right-to-control factor, was overemphasized by the district court because homeworkers by their very nature are generally subject to little supervision and control by an alleged employer. Federal courts have consistently held homeworkers of many varieties to be "employees" under the FLSA.

\* \* \*

The district court concluded that the six or seven home researchers who distributed telephone-number research cards to the other home researchers were also not "employees" under the FLSA. In reaching its decision, the court again did not consider all of the factors specified in the *Sureway Cleaners* test for determining "employee" status. Nevertheless, upon application of the entire *Sureway Cleaners* test, we agree that the distributors were not "employees" and were not subject to the minimum-wage protection of the FLSA for their work in delivering cards to and from other home researchers.

With respect to the right-to-control factor, the district court correctly found that the defendant exercised little control over the distributors' delivery of cards. The distributors were permitted to recruit their own distributees, and some of them did so. Although the defendant initially kept records of all distributees, it eventually relied on the distributors to maintain those records.

Moreover, we also defer to the district court's finding that the distributors risked financial loss if they did not manage their distribution network properly. The distributors were responsible for paying all of their expenses, which consisted primarily of transportation expenses. And each distributor had the authority to set the rate at which its distributees would be paid. Thus, theoretically at least, distributors could lose money if their expenses outweighed their revenues.

The distributors also had to make an investment in their business. Again, this investment consisted primarily of transportation expenses. One distributor also used paid advertising in an effort to gain more distributees. Consideration of the investment factor, therefore, supports the conclusion that the distributors were independent contractors.

\* \* \*

Finally, the *Sureway Cleaners* test examines the circumstances of the whole activity and considers whether, in this case, the distributors are economically dependent on the defendant.  It is more likely than not that the distributors were economically dependent.  Although defendant did not prohibit these persons from performing distribution work for other organizations, there was no evidence that any of them did so, either during or following the period in which they worked for the defendant.  Presumably, all of the distributors ceased doing distribution work when defendant ceased providing such work for them.  Thus, for the most part, the distributors were dependent on DialAmerica for continuing their work as distributors.

In summary, all of the factors in the *Sureway Cleaners* test, when applied to the distributors, do not lead to the same conclusion.  Having considered the evidence with appropriate deference to the district court's fact-finding, we note that some factors support the conclusion that the distributors are "employees," while others do not.  Although the question is admittedly close, we hold that the distributors qua distributors were not employees under the FLSA because they operated more like independent contractors than like employees of DialAmerica.  The distributors were subject to minimal oversight or control over their distribution activities.  Moreover, they faced a real opportunity for either a profit or loss in their operations, depending upon the amount of their investment and their skills in management.  Finally, their work as distributors was not an integral part of DialAmerica's business and thus was less likely to be performed by an "employee" of DialAmerica.

* * *

In summary, therefore, we hold that the persons who performed telephone-number research at home were "employees" of DialAmerica under the FLSA.  DialAmerica was obligated to pay them the applicable minimum wage and to comply with the other provisions of the Act.  Those home researchers who also distributed telephone-number research cards to other home researchers were not "employees" while they were engaged in the act of distributing.  Therefore, they were not entitled to the minimum-wage protection of the FLSA for their distribution work.

## NOTES AND QUESTIONS

**1.**  In *DialAmerica,* why are the telephone researchers held to be employees while the telephone research distributors are not?  What are the indicia of independent contractor status?  Under the *Sureway* test, what minimal criteria must be met before an individual is found to be an employee rather than an independent contractor?

**2.**  Why should DialAmerica be held in violation of the FLSA for wage agreements negotiated separately and without its knowledge or consent between the research distributors and the researchers who worked under their direction?

**3.**  The "economic realities" test applied by the court is in extensive use.  An employer-employee relationship has been found even where the parties explicitly agreed in writing to an independent contractor relationship and the employer did not intend to create an employment relationship. See Donovan v. Sandy Retreat Beach Club, 95 Lab.Cas. ¶ 34,239 (S.D.Tex. 1982).

**4.** Some labor market experts think the next decade will see an expansion in work done at home. Technology, computers linked by telephone lines, makes that possible for some work. Work at home may be especially attractive for persons with child care responsibilities. The issue has arisen most prominently in connection with Vermont knitters.

Numerous women in rural Vermont perform piecework for skiwear manufacturers by producing knit outerwear on knitting machines owned and operated by them in their homes. The advantages for the women are flexibility of hours, reduced child care expenses, and no commuting or uniform expenses. The employer, in turn, does not incur the fixed overhead or capital costs associated with building and operating a large factory to house all of its workers. The worker is paid on a piece rate; most women apparently earn at least the minimum wage for their work.

There is one flaw in this arrangement. What the knitters are doing has historically been in violation of the FLSA. Due to concern about sweatshop conditions which then prevailed in metropolitan areas, and to situations in which employees were required to do additional work at home, during the 1940s the Department of Labor prohibited industrial homework in seven industries ranging from knitted outerwear to jewelry and embroideries. In 1984, the Department of Labor rescinded the homework ban in knitted outerwear and replaced it with a certification system, which requires employers wishing to hire homeworkers to obtain a certificate from the department. In 1988, the Department of Labor rescinded the ban on homework for five additional industries: gloves and mittens, handkerchiefs, buttons and buckles, "nonhazardous" jewelry, and embroideries. Despite finding a lack of enforcement under the 1984 certification system, the reviewing court upheld the new regulation. ILGWU v. Dole, 729 F.Supp. 877 (D.D.C.1989).

**5.** How should homework be regulated? The factual situations in *Dial-America* and the Vermont knitters case illustrate the range of possibilities in the performance of work. While some workers—the Vermont knitters—would prefer to work at home, others—telephone researchers and "telecommuters"—may be taken advantage of. Many home-based clerical workers are women with small children who feel they have no choice but to stay home and work from there. A 1986 report by the House Committee on Government Operations found that many homeworkers are not paid the minimum wage and do not receive employee benefits, such as health insurance and workers' compensation. In addition, the study found, home-based workers are not paid for such work-related tasks as setting up equipment and correcting their work, and they often lose opportunities for advancement available to those who work in a traditional setting. While it did not recommend a total ban on homework, the study concluded that additional protections for homeworkers are needed and urged the expansion of child care services in order to ensure that individuals "may make free and unforced choices as to whether, when and under what terms they will work at home." Dissenting members of the committee stated, "Life is full of trade-offs; employment destiny is no exception. * * * That is the beauty of homework."

**6.** A related issue is whether permitting employees with disabilities to work at home is a reasonable accommodation required of employers by the Americans with Disabilities Act or other disability discrimination laws. The few courts to consider the issue have not agreed. Compare *Vande Zande,* infra p. 337 (no duty to allow a paraplegic employee to work at home or to install a computer in her home so that she could avoid using sick leave) with Chirico v. Office of Vocational & Educational Services for Individuals with Disabilities, 627 N.Y.S.2d 815 (App.Div.1995) (reinstating claim where quadriplegic employee sought voice-activated computer at home).

### Jennifer Middleton, Contingent Workers in a Changing Economy: Endure, Adapt, or Organize? *

22 N.Y.U.Rev.L. & Soc. Change 557 (1996).

Current estimates place the number of contingent workers at around thirty-two to thirty-seven million, or about one-quarter of the nation's working population. This figure represents a substantial increase since 1980, when approximately twenty-five to twenty-eight million workers were classified as contingent. The catch-all term "contingent workers" encompasses a wide variety of work arrangements and types of workers. Some forms of contingent work have grown more rapidly than others in the course of the past decade. While data are incomplete for many types of workers, the following sections survey the information available on the growth of each segment of the contingent workforce.

#### A. Part-time Workers

Part-time workers comprise by far the largest segment of contingent workers, almost one-fifth of the entire U.S. workforce. The reasons for the increasing use of part-time workers are many, including some workers' desires to work fewer hours so they may take care of family or other responsibilities or to accommodate needs for nonstandard scheduling arrangements. Disturbingly, however, the number of involuntary part-time workers—those workers who would like full-time employment, but whose employers prefer to hire several part-time employees—is increasing. Many of these workers in fact work full-time hours (thirty-five per week or more), but they do so through holding down two or more part-time jobs, and thus are without the protections of full-time work. The stress of such arrangements is compounded by the need to coordinate shifts and transportation.

Part-time jobs are most common in the clerical, sales, and service industries. They typically offer low pay and few or no benefits, require few

* Reprinted by permission.

skills, and demonstrate high rates of turnover. Part-time jobs are, on average, worse than full-time jobs along nearly every dimension. The median part-time worker earned fifty-eight percent of the hourly wage of the median full-time worker in 1989. Even controlling for disparities in sex, race, education, experience, industry, and occupation, part-timers still earned ten percent less than their full-time counterparts. In 1984, more than one quarter of part-time workers earned the minimum wage, as compared to one in twenty full-time workers. Moreover, only twenty-two percent of part-time workers received health insurance benefits through their jobs in 1988, while seventy-eight percent of full-time workers did. The corresponding numbers for pensions were twenty-six percent for part-timers and sixty percent for full-timers. As discussed below, part-time workers are also frequently exempted from statutory workplace protections. Thus, as a growing proportion of the U.S. workforce works one or more part-time jobs rather than a single full-time job, fewer and fewer workers enjoy the benefits of a living wage, employer-provided insurance, or basic statutory workplace protections.

### B.  Contract Workers

A second segment of the contingent work force is contract workers, those who may be employed by a primary employer but who provide services to a secondary employer on a contract basis. Typical examples include construction, janitorial services, and garment manufacturing, but the trend occurs throughout all segments of the economy. It is impossible to quantify how many workers fall directly into this category. Anecdotal evidence, however, suggests that increasing amounts of work that was once performed in-house by full-fledged employees of the recipient business are now subcontracted to secondary employers. Denominating such contract workers as "business services," Richard Belous of the National Planning Association reports that their numbers have grown from 3.3 million in 1980 to 5.3 million in 1992, a sixty-one percent increase. Kelly Services, one of the nation's leading temporary service agencies, claims that as many as 6.4 million workers labored in the business services sector in 1992, a full 5.5% of the workforce.

Subcontracting relieves employers from responsibilities toward the workers who perform services for them. Jonathan Hiatt, General Counsel to the Service Employees International Union, provides some telling examples of the effects of the trend toward subcontracting:

> One of the larger cleaning contractors in Seattle, ... after successfully positioning himself as the lowest cost bidder on commercial office building accounts in the city, turned around and began "selling" floors of office buildings as "franchises" to individuals—mostly Central American and Asian immigrants. These "franchisees" each pay from $4000 to $7000 for the privilege of "buying" a floor to clean.... [T]he contractor thus disclaims any responsibility for Social Security or unemployment compensation payments, minimum wage or overtime violations, or tax withholdings of any kind.

In the Hartford, Connecticut area, 1,000 school bus drivers lost full-time jobs with good benefits when the school districts privatized their jobs. These workers, who once enjoyed health insurance, pensions, and other fringe benefits, now are employed part-time, and receive virtually no benefits, even though they are performing precisely the same work as before.

The recent corporate ardor for integrated networks of operations, downsizing, and just-in-time production all have contributed to an increase in outsourcing operations to contract workers and a corresponding decline in full-time, steady employment with primary employers.

### C.  Temporary Workers

Temporary workers comprise a third category of contingent workers. The growth in temporary workers over the past decade is the most dramatic among the various types of contingent workers. Temporary agencies supplied two million workers to American companies in 1994, filling one in six new jobs. This compares with only 170,000 temporary workers in 1972. Manpower, Inc., with 560,000 employees in its ranks, is by some definitions the nation's largest private employer. The industry recorded revenues of $18.3 billion in 1992 and includes more than five thousand firms operating at fifteen thousand locations including branches abroad. They placed an average of 1.6 million workers per day in 1993. Increasingly, businesses are establishing exclusive relationships with a single temporary supply agency, effectively cementing their long-term use of temporary workers and subcontracting a chunk of their human relations processes to outside firms.

Temporary workers are still predominantly female and clerical, though temporary agencies increasingly supply a varied and specialized range of workers. About half of temporary workers are clerical, a quarter industrial, and a quarter professional; eighty percent are women. Wages vary widely; the national average is over eight dollars per hour. Participation in the benefit plans that some temporary agencies offer is low, which may be due to the short-term nature of the work as well as high co-payment or minimum hours requirements. Although temporary agencies must pay all employment-related taxes for their personnel and comply with all relevant employment regulations, most have no ability to oversee the work conditions into which they place employees. Because agencies exert little or no control over the employers to whom they send workers, effective monitoring of working conditions by even the most scrupulous of agencies can be difficult. Moreover, the status of temporary workers as nonemployees of the recipient firm may facilitate workplace abuses such as sexual and racial harassment and discrimination, as well as unsafe working conditions.

### D.  Independent Contractors

The self-employed compromise a fourth category of contingent workers. For self-employed professional workers such as consultants or writers, status as a contingent worker may be a misnomer. Rather, the workers in this category who suffer exploitation are those who lose benefits as a result of employers' misclassification.  The legal test for determining employee/independent contractor status is a complex and manipulable multifactor test which invites employers to structure their relationships with employees in whatever manner best evades liability.  Many employers relieve themselves from complying with safety regulations and paying payroll taxes by calling their employees independent contractors, thereby shifting the costs of such workplace protections directly onto the workers.  In addition, misclassified workers have no access to federally-mandated benefits and standards, including unemployment benefits, workers' compensation, pension regulation through ERISA, health and safety standards, antidiscrimination laws, federal disability insurance, and protection under the Fair Labor Standards Act (FLSA).

The definition of an employee as opposed to an independent contractor is unnecessarily complex, involving as many as twenty criteria in an unweighted appraisal of each individual job situation.  The numbers of misclassified independent contractors are impossible to calculate, though attempts at enforcement of tax regulations by the Internal Revenue Service (IRS) demonstrate massive fraud on the part of employers in this area.  Based on a 1984 study, the IRS estimated that, among 5.2 million businesses both small and large, fifteen percent misclassified 3.4 million employees as independent contractors.

\* \* \*

Also included within the independent contractor category are the tens of thousands of day laborers who gather to find work each day in labor pools that have proliferated around the country.  Prospective employers simply drive up to corners where workers gather on a daily basis and take any of the mostly immigrant men to work in construction, landscaping, agriculture, or any number of other trades.  Often, workers are paid by the day, and their wages are sometimes subminimum after employers deduct for provision of tools, transportation, or a meager lunch.  They are given the dirtiest and most hazardous jobs.  Although it is impossible to estimate the number of day laborers, a recent trend toward increased regulation of areas where individuals may solicit work and of labor pool contractors suggests the practice is expanding.

## Vizcaino v. Microsoft Corp.

120 F.3d 1006 (9th Cir.1997) cert. denied, 118 S.Ct. 899 (1998).

■ FERNANDEZ, CIRCUIT JUDGE.

Donna Vizcaino, Jon R. Waite, Mark Stout, Geoffrey Culbert, Lesley Stuart, Thomas Morgan, Elizabeth Spokoiny, and Larry Spokoiny brought this action on behalf of themselves and a court-certified class.  They sued Microsoft Corporation and its various pension and welfare plans, including its Savings Plus Plan, and sought a determination that they were entitled to participate in the plan benefits because those benefits were available to Microsoft's common law employees.  The district court granted summary judgment against the Workers, and they appealed the determinations that they were not entitled to participate in the SPP or in the Employee Stock Purchase Plan. We reversed the district court because we decided that the Workers were common law employees who were not properly excluded from participation in those plans.

However, we then decided to rehear the matter en banc, and we now agree with much of the panel's conclusion and reverse the district court.

At various times before 1990, Microsoft hired the Workers to perform services for it. They did perform those services over a continuous period, often exceeding two years. They were hired to work on specific projects and performed a number of different functions, such as production editing, proofreading, formatting, indexing, and testing. "Microsoft fully integrated [the Workers] into its workforce: they often worked on teams along with regular employees, sharing the same supervisors, performing identical functions, and working the same core hours. Because Microsoft required that they work on site, they received admittance card keys, office equipment and supplies from the company." However, they were not paid for their services through the payroll department, but rather submitted invoices to and were paid through the accounts payable department.

Microsoft did not withhold income or Federal Insurance Contribution Act taxes from the Workers' wages, and did not pay the employer's share of the FICA taxes. Moreover, Microsoft did not allow the Workers to participate in the SPP or the ESPP. The Workers did not complain about those arrangements at that time.

However, in 1989 and 1990 the Internal Revenue Service examined Microsoft's records and decided that it should have been withholding and paying over taxes because, as a matter of law, the Workers were employees rather than independent contractors. It made that determination by applying common law principles. Microsoft agreed with the IRS and made the necessary corrections for the past by issuing W–2 forms to the Workers and by paying the employer's share of FICA taxes to the government.

Microsoft also realized that, because the Workers were employees, at least for tax purposes, it had to change its system. It made no sense to have employees paid through the accounts payable department, so those who remained in essentially the same relationship as before were tendered offers to become acknowledged employees. Others had to discontinue working for Microsoft, but did have the opportunity to go to work for a temporary employment agency, which could then supply temporary Workers to Microsoft on an as-needed basis. Some took advantage of that opportunity, some—like Vizcaino—did not.

The Workers then asserted that they were employees of Microsoft and should have had the opportunity of participating in the SPP and the ESPP because those plans were available to all employees who met certain other participation qualifications, which are not relevant to the issues before us. Microsoft disagreed, and the Workers asked the SPP plan administrator to exercise his authority to declare that they were eligible for the benefits. A panel was convened; it ruled that the Workers were not entitled to any benefits from ERISA plans—for example, the SPP—or, for that matter, from non-ERISA plans—for example, the ESPP. That, the administrative panel seemed to say, was because the Workers had agreed that they were independent contractors and because they had waived the right to participate in benefit plans. This action followed.

. . .

Although the Workers challenge both their exclusion from the SPP and their exclusion from the ESPP, the two plans are subject to rather different legal regimes. The former is a 26 U.S.C. § 401(k) plan, which is governed by ERISA; the latter is a 26 U.S.C. § 423 plan, which is not governed by ERISA. It, instead, is governed, at least in large part, by principles arising out of the law of the State of Washington. Nevertheless, certain issues, perhaps the most critical ones, cut across both regimes, and we will address them first.

It is important to recognize that there is no longer any question that the Workers were employees of Microsoft, and not independent contractors. The IRS clearly determined that they were. In theory one could argue that what the IRS said was fine for withholding and FICA purposes, but that is as far as it goes.

However, the IRS made its determination based upon the list of factors which is generally used to decide whether a person is an independent contractor or an employee. The same essential definition is used for § 401(k) plans and for § 423 plans. That there should be a congruence of approaches is not surprising. As the Supreme Court has pointed out, when Congress uses the word "employee," courts " 'must infer, unless the statute otherwise dictates, that Congress means to incorporate the established meaning' " of that word.... But, again, we recognize that one could still question the IRS's application of those factors in a particular case.

That question is obviated here for, perhaps more to the purpose, both Microsoft and the SPP have conceded for purposes of this appeal that the Workers were common law employees. In fact, they have asserted that the Workers' status is a "nonissue" because they concede that the Workers were common law employees. That is to say, they were employees of Microsoft.

The concession that the Workers were employees would, at first blush, appear to dispose of this case. It means that for legal purposes they, along with the other employees of Microsoft, were subject to Microsoft's control as to both "the manner and means" of accomplishing their job, that they worked for a substantial period, that they were furnished a workplace and equipment, that they were subject to discharge, and the like. If that were all, this would be an exceedingly easy case. Of course, it is not all.

Microsoft also entered into special agreements with the Workers, and it is those which complicate matters to some extent. Each of the Workers and Microsoft signed agreements which stated, among other things not relevant here, that the worker was "an Independent Contractor for [Microsoft]," and nothing in the agreement should be construed as creating an "employer-employee relationship." As a result, the worker agreed "to be responsible for all of [his] federal and state taxes, withholding, social security, insurance, and other benefits." At the same time, Microsoft had the Workers sign an information form, which explained: "[A]s an Independent Contractor to Microsoft, you are self employed and are responsible to pay all your own insurance and benefits.... Microsoft ... will not subject your payments to any withholding.... You are not either an employee of Microsoft, or a temporary employee of Microsoft." We now know beyond peradventure that most of this was not, in fact, true because the Workers actually were employees rather than independent contractors. What are we to make of that?

We now know that as a matter of law Microsoft hired the Workers to perform their services as employees and that the Workers performed those services. Yet we are also obligated to construe the agreements. In doing so, we could take either a negative or a positive view of Microsoft's intent and motives. We could decide that Microsoft knew that the Workers were employees, but chose to paste the independent contractor label upon them after making a rather amazing series of decisions to violate the law. Or we could decide that Microsoft mistakenly thought that the Workers were independent contractors and that all else simply seemed to flow from that status.

Were we to take the former approach, we would have to determine that Microsoft, with the knowledge that the Workers were simply a group of employees, decided to engage in the following maneuvers:

(1) Despite the requirements of federal law that amounts be withheld from employee wages, Microsoft decided it would not withhold.

(2) Despite the fact that the SPP states that "employee" means "any common law employee ... who is on the United States payroll of the employer," Microsoft decided to manipulate the availability of that benefit by routing the wages of these employees through the accounts payable department, so that it could argue that they were not on the United States payroll. Beyond that, it also determined that it would tell the IRS in its "Application for Determination for Defined Contribution Plan," that Microsoft did, indeed, basically include all employees, a category that it knew included the Workers, even though it had contrived to exclude them. Beyond even that, Microsoft excluded these employees when it filed its tax returns for the SPP, even though it knew better.

(3) Despite the fact that the ESPP must, essentially, be made available to all employees, Microsoft excluded these employees and thereby intentionally risked the possibility that the plan would not qualify for favorable tax treatment. It did that, even though the plan itself stated that it covered all regular employees and that it was to be construed to comply with 26 U.S.C. § 423, a law which basically requires that all employees be covered. The officers of Microsoft also decided to eliminate one group of common law employees from the benefits, even though the board of directors and the

shareholders had already made the benefits of the ESPP available to those employees. In doing that, the officers intentionally violated the corporate law of Delaware, to which Microsoft was subject, because the terms of coverage of stock option plans are not in the hands of corporate officers; they are in the hands of the board itself.

On the other hand, in construing the agreements we can view the label as a simple mistake. That is, Microsoft honestly thought that the Workers were independent contractors and took its various actions and inactions based upon that misapprehension. Its actions and the conclusions conveyed to the Workers in the agreements and in the explanation in the information form, which accompanied the agreements, were simply an explication of what the effect of independent contractor status would be and had no separate purpose or effect aside from that explanatory function. That is to say, of course there could neither be withholding from wages nor participation in the benefit plans because those keyed on common law employment status. If the Workers were independent contractors, those would be the inevitable results, even if nothing were said about them in the agreement or the information form. Explaining the meaning of independent contractor status was simply a helpful disclosure.

Absent evidence that the officers of Microsoft used their daedalian talents to follow the first route we have just outlined, we must decide that the second route is a more accurate portrayal of what occurred here. In other words, we should, and we do, consider what the parties did in the best light. In so doing, we do not believe that we are being panglossian; we are merely acting in accordance with the ancient maxim which assumes that "the law has been obeyed."

The evidence does not undercut our approach; it supports it. As soon as Microsoft realized that the IRS, at least, thought that the Workers were employees, it took steps to correct its error. It put some of them on its United States payroll forthwith. It also gave the Workers retroactive pay for overtime hours. If Microsoft had been withholding taxes while failing to provide benefits, that would have suggested that it knew that the Workers were a species of employee. However, its failure to withhold indicates that it did not think that the Workers were a special breed of employee; it simply thought that they were not employees at all. That was underscored when Microsoft told its managers about the status of the Workers. It distinguished the Workers from other employees, both regular full-time and temporary. It did not say that the Workers were employees in some special category; rather, it said that they were not employees at all.

But they were employees, which returns us to the contracts themselves. Viewed in the proper light, it can be seen that the Workers were indeed hired by Microsoft to perform services for it. We know that their services were rendered in their capacities as employees. The contracts indicate, however, that they are independent contractors, which they were not. The other terms of the contracts do not add or subtract from their status or, indeed, impose separate agreements upon them. In effect, the other terms merely warn the Workers about what happens to them if they are independent contractors. Again, those are simply results which hinge on the status determination itself; they are not separate freestanding agreements. Therefore, the Workers were employees, who did not give up or waive their rights to be treated like all other employees under the plans. The Workers performed services for Microsoft under conditions which made them employees. They did sign agreements, which declared that they were independent contractors, but at best that declaration was due to a mutual mistake, and we know that even Microsoft does not now seek to assert that the label made them independent contractors.

. . .

One additional matter must detain us for a moment. It could, perhaps, be argued that the statements about benefits, unlike statements about withholding, stand on their own footing as a waiver of benefits, regardless of the Workers' true status as employees. As we have said, we think that would be an incorrect interpretation of these agreements, and Microsoft assured us at argument that this is not a waiver case. Were it one, we would have to consider whether the waivers based, as they would have been, on the mistaken premise of independent contractor status were knowing and voluntary under ERISA and Washington law. . . .

. . .

However, these issues need not even be mooted once it is recognized that there was no separate waiver at all. Moreover, we need not consider what the result would be if the agreements were of a different form or character. . . .

Therefore, we now determine that the reasons for rejecting the Workers' participation in the SPP and the ESPP were invalid. Any remaining issues regarding the rights of a particular worker in the ESPP and his available remedies must be decided by the district court upon remand. However, any remaining issues regarding the right of any or all of the Workers to participate in the SPP must be decided by the plan administrator upon remand.

REVERSED and REMANDED to the district court as to the ESPP. REVERSED and REMANDED to the district court for further remand to the plan administrator as to the SPP.

■ FLETCHER, CIRCUIT JUDGE, with whom HUG, CHIEF JUDGE, and PREGERSON, HAWKINS and THOMAS, CIRCUIT JUDGES, join, concurring in part and dissenting in part:

We concur in the substance of Judge Fernandez' opinion except that we would not remand the issue of eligibility to participate in the SPP to the Plan Administrator and would hold that the Workers are eligible to participate. Remand is inappropriate and further unnecessary in that we conclude that interpretation of the phrase "on the United States payroll of the employer" is not required.

. . .

■ O'SCANNLAIN, CIRCUIT JUDGE, joined by HALL and T.G. NELSON, CIRCUIT JUDGES, concurring in part and dissenting in part:

I respectfully dissent from ... the court's opinion because Microsoft and the plaintiffs never formed a valid contract under Washington law for the benefits now claimed. . . .

I do not disagree with the court's statement of facts, but it has failed to mention some and may leave a mistaken impression of others.  Thus, I suggest that the following additional facts from the record be taken into account.

The plaintiffs were temporary "freelancers" for Microsoft.  Instead of calling them by this label-which was ubiquitously used within the Microsoft community and by the plaintiffs themselves—the court styles the plaintiffs as "workers."  It then engages in a long discussion of why they were in fact "common law employees" of Microsoft.  Both labels may be true—the plaintiffs did work, and Microsoft has conceded that the plaintiffs satisfy the definition of common law employees for some purposes.  Neither of these labels are relevant to the question before us, however, and both are potentially misleading.  Both labels imply that the plaintiffs were just like any other regular Microsoft employees, and hence should be eligible for the same benefits as regular staff.  The evidence in the record, however, points to the contrary.  I will refer to the plaintiffs by the same term the plaintiffs themselves use "freelancers".

Before going further, it is also important that the statement of facts identify precisely what period of activity is at issue in this case.  All plaintiffs were hired before 1989.  In the fall of that year, the IRS determined, for employment tax purposes, that the freelancers were common law employees.  After that, in late 1989 and during 1990, Microsoft directly hired some of the freelancers as "staff" (with Microsoft benefits) and arranged for the remainder to become employees of unrelated employment agencies (without Microsoft benefits) who had contracts with Microsoft.  For the sake of clarity, I note that all we decide today is whether the freelancers should have been allowed to participate in the ESPP and the SPP during the period leading up to the 1989–90 conversion.  All agree that those freelancers who were converted into employees of outside employment agencies have no valid claim for participation in the ESPP and SPP after the date of their conversion.

When the freelancers were originally retained by contract with Microsoft, they were expressly told that they were not eligible for any Microsoft employee benefits, and that they would have to provide their own benefits.  Indeed, the named plaintiffs admit that they did not think they were entitled to benefits, and did not think benefits were a part of their compensation package.

Moreover, the freelancers each signed contractual documents which expressly stated that they would not receive any benefits, and would have to pay their own taxes and benefits. Specifically, Microsoft required that each plaintiff sign an "Independent Contractor Agreement" ("ICA").

. . .

In the district court, Microsoft's uncontested extrinsic evidence established that the plaintiffs were told, and knew, that benefits were not a part of their compensation. Instead of providing benefits, Microsoft paid the freelancers at a higher hourly rate than Microsoft's regular employees. The freelancers were also treated differently in a host of other ways. They had different color employee badges, different e-mail addresses, and were not invited to company parties and functions. Instead of receiving a regular paycheck from Microsoft's Payroll department (like Microsoft's regular employees), freelancers submitted invoices for their services to the Accounts Payable department.

With these additional relevant facts in mind, we may consider the merits.

As I see it, this is a simple contracts case. The Washington law of contracts governs the freelancers' claim of entitlement to benefits under the Employee Stock Purchase Plan ("ESPP"). No law, state or federal, mandates that Microsoft provide such benefits even to its employees. Plaintiffs are eligible to participate in the ESPP only to the extent that they entered into a valid contract with Microsoft for such participation.

Offer, acceptance, and consideration are requisites to contract formation under Washington law. . . .

Microsoft's board offered the ESPP to employees generally, and then Microsoft told the freelancers: "We aren't offering the ESPP to you; ESPP benefits are not included in your contract." Knowing that they wouldn't get ESPP benefits, the freelancers nevertheless agreed to work for Microsoft. Their contract therefore does not include ESPP benefits because the offer of those benefits was revoked.

Likewise, there was no mutual assent (or "meeting of the minds") as is required for the formation of a unilateral contract. Microsoft did not think it was offering ESPP benefits to the freelancers, and the freelancers did not think they were accepting an offer of ESPP benefits. Had the parties known that a court would force them to include ESPP benefits in their contract, the bargain undoubtedly would have been different.

If this is not enough, the court's alleged contract suffers from another defect: a lack of consideration. There was no detrimental reliance on the ESPP by the freelancers—they did not think they would get ESPP benefits, and they still chose to work for Microsoft on Microsoft's terms. Indeed, it is hard to imagine what consideration the freelancers could have given for the ESPP benefits since they chose to work for Microsoft for several years without benefits. If anything, the freelancers received consideration (a higher hourly rate) for their agreement that they would not get ESPP benefits.

. . .

NOTES AND QUESTIONS

**1.**   The Internal Revenue Service has good reasons for considering these individuals to be employees: collection of taxes and of information about employment from Microsoft is much easier than from thousands of individuals.   But should the IRS definition of an employee control for other employment purposes: for workers' compensation eligibility, for minimum wage, for overtime hours, for vacations, and for pensions?   Should the U.S. system have a single definition of "employee"?   If so, should the federal income tax process dominate the classification for all purposes?

**2.**   Microsoft says: "We will hire you at a high hourly wage; you will escape some of the rules that discipline full-time employees; and you will take care of your own pension, health benefits, and vacations."   Mary Jones says: "I am young and high-tech.   I accept your offer."   Should the legal system interfere with this agreement?   Why?

**3.**   West v. Clarke Murphy, Jr. Self Employed Pension Plan, 99 F.3d 166 (4th Cir.1996), held that employee status under ERISA is determined not by the Internal Revenue Code but by the common law of agency.   Microsoft's concession on this point rendered the issue irrelevant to the decision in *Vizcaino*.

**4.**   For decisions permitting an employer to limit coverage in an ERISA plan to certain employees, see Clark v. E.I. du Pont de Nemours & Co., 105 F.3d 646 (4th Cir.1997);   Abraham v. Exxon Corp., 85 F.3d 1126 (5th Cir.1996);   Stanton v. Gulf Oil Corp., 792 F.2d 432 (4th Cir.1986).   For consideration of ERISA, the Employee Retirement Income Security Act of 1974, see Chapters 6 and 13.

# PART II

# Establishing the Employment Relationship

# CHAPTER 3

# THE HIRING PROCESS

How do people find jobs? There are numerous ways, such as word-of-mouth recruitment, nepotism, walk-in recruitment, employment agencies, newspaper and other advertising, and union hiring halls. Although the process used varies with the job sought, it is often highly unstructured and informal. Until recently, it also has been largely free of legal regulation. This chapter considers the role of law in regulating the job search process. It considers legal regulation of job search, of eligibility, and of certain intrusive methods of employer information gathering.

## A.  INTRODUCTION

### George Ritzer & David Walczak; Working: Conflict and Change *
149–50 (3d ed. 1986).

What is involved in the process of searching for a job? The answer, of course, depends on the nature of the occupation being sought. Looking for jobs as a lawyer, a personnel manager, a laborer, or a pimp clearly involve very different steps. For most occupations, however, a variety of formal steps may be taken. The individual can go to an employment agency, or to the personnel offices of the various organizations that have the kind of work sought. He or she can reply to a public notice or an advertisement in the newspaper. Those who seek an occupation, usually a skilled craft, in which the union does the hiring would probably go to the union hiring hall. These, and many other formal devices, are open to the person in search of work.

However, one of the consistent findings in the study of work is that people in a wide array of occupations are more likely to use informal, rather than formal, means in searching for a job. For some occupations, such as the deviant occupations discussed earlier, there simply are no formal means available. Among the informal means of job search most often used are the reliance on contacts through family, friends, or acquaintances.

A number of studies of blue-collar hirings have shown that informal factors account for between 53 and 80 percent of all hired. Others have shown that such "informal contact networks" are not restricted to low-

* Reprinted by permission of Prentice-Hall, Inc., Englewood Cliffs, N.J.

status blue-collar hirings.  Graves found that in pipeline work, a skilled craft, people rely primarily on kin ties and friends to obtain work.  Similarly, Caplow and McGee have pointed to the importance of personal contacts in obtaining academic jobs.  Granovetter found that a wide range of professional, technical and managerial workers relied on personal contacts to find work.  In short, there is considerable evidence that informal contact networks operate throughout the occupational hierarchy.

One might think that reliance on informal rather than formal means of job search would lead to inefficiency in the process.  But again, various studies have pointed in the opposite direction.  Graves found informal contact networks to be very effective in the pipeline industry, where people are usually needed quickly for short-term jobs.  In such a setting, it would clearly be impossible to rely on more formal and more cumbersome methods of job search.  Similarly, in a wide-ranging study of job-search behavior, Reid concludes that those using informal job-search methods "were no worse off in terms of frictional unemployment, wages or job preference" than those using formal methods.  Granovetter found that professionals, technicians and managers obtain better jobs through personal contacts than through more formal methods.  Among other things, they were more likely to be highly satisfied with their work and to earn high salaries when they found their positions through personal contacts.

Although informal job-search methods seem to work well in various settings, we must not overlook the fact that they are inherently discriminatory.  Those who have the contacts are more likely to find jobs than those who don't, and those who lack contacts are the ones who, in our society, are most often discriminated against because of sex, race, age, or religion.

NOTES AND QUESTIONS

**1.**  As mentioned by Ritzer & Walczak, some of the informal methods of recruitment have led to allegations of discrimination.  See, e.g., Furnco Construction Corp. v. Waters, 438 U.S. 567 (1978) (refusal to consider "walk-in" applicants may be pretext for racial discrimination); Franks v. Bowman Transportation Co., 495 F.2d 398 (5th Cir.1974), rev'd on other grounds, 424 U.S. 747 (1976) (company's reliance on word-of-mouth recruiting not adequate explanation for all-white office workforce).  What must an employer do to prevent discrimination and allegations of discrimination?  See Chapter 4.

**2.**  One of the oldest methods of job placement is nepotism.  This system assured the continuation of skilled crafts and facilitated the training of successive generations of workers.  But do such practices constitute unlawful restrictions of job opportunities?  Consider the following case.

## Kotch v. Board of River Port Pilot Commissioners
330 U.S. 552 (1947).

■ MR. JUSTICE BLACK delivered the opinion of the Court.

Louisiana statutes provide in general that all seagoing vessels moving between New Orleans and foreign ports must be navigated through the

Mississippi River approaches to the port of New Orleans and within it, exclusively by pilots who are State Officers.  New State pilots are appointed by the governor only upon certification of a State Board of River Pilot Commissioners, themselves pilots.  Only those who have served a six month apprenticeship under incumbent pilots and who possess other specific qualifications may be certified to the governor by the board.  Appellants here have had at least fifteen years experience in the river, the port, and elsewhere, as pilots of vessels whose pilotage was not governed by the State law in question.  Although they possess all the statutory qualifications except that they have not served the requisite six months apprenticeship under Louisiana officer pilots, they have been denied appointment as State pilots.  Seeking relief in a Louisiana state court, they alleged that the incumbent pilots, having unfettered discretion under the law in the selection of apprentices, had selected with occasional exception, only the relatives and friends of incumbents; that the selections were made by electing prospective apprentices into the pilots' association, which the pilots have formed by authority of State law; that since "membership * * * is closed to all except those having the favor of the pilots" the result is that only their relatives and friends have and can become State pilots.  The Supreme Court of Louisiana has held that the pilotage law so administered does not violate the equal protection clause of the Fourteenth Amendment, 209 La. 737, 25 So.2d 527.  The case is here on appeal from that decision under 28 U.S.C. § 344(a), 28 U.S.C.A. § 344(a).

\* \* \*

Studies of the long history of pilotage reveal that it is a unique institution and must be judged as such.  In order to avoid invisible hazards, vessels approaching and leaving ports must be conducted from and to open waters by persons intimately familiar with the local waters.  The pilot's job generally requires that he go outside the harbor's entrance in a small boat to meet incoming ships, board them and direct their course from open waters to the port.  The same service is performed for vessels leaving the port.  Pilots are thus indispensable cogs in the transportation system of every maritime economy.  Their work prevents traffic congestion and accidents which would impair navigation in and to the ports.  It affects the safety of lives and cargo, the cost and time expended in port calls, and in some measure, the competitive attractiveness of particular ports.  Thus, for the same reasons that governments of most maritime communities have subsidized, regulated, or have themselves operated docks and other harbor facilities and sought to improve the approaches to their ports, they have closely regulated and often operated their ports' pilotage system.

The history and practice of pilotage demonstrate that, although inextricably geared to a complex commercial economy, it is also a highly personalized calling.  A pilot does not require a formalized technical education so much as a detailed and extremely intimate, almost intuitive, knowledge of the weather, waterways and conformation of the harbor or river which he serves.  This seems to be particularly true of the approaches to New Orleans through the treacherous and shifting channel of the Mississippi River.  Moreover, harbor entrances where pilots can most conveniently make their homes and still be close to places where they board incoming and leave outgoing ships are usually some distance from the port cities they serve.  These "pilot towns" have begun, and generally exist today, as small communities of pilots perhaps near, but usually distinct from the port cities.  In these communities young men have an opportunity to acquire special knowledge of the weather and water hazards of the locality and seem to grow up with ambitions to become pilots in the traditions of their fathers, relatives, and neighbors.  We are asked, in effect, to say that Louisiana is without constitutional authority to conclude that apprenticeship under persons specially interested in a pilot's future is the best way to fit him for duty as a pilot officer in the service of the State.

The States have had full power to regulate pilotage of certain kinds of vessels since 1789 when the first Congress decided that then existing state pilot laws were satisfactory and made federal regulation unnecessary. Louisiana legislation has controlled the activities and appointment of pilots since 1805—even before the Territory was admitted as a State.  The State pilotage system, as it has evolved since 1805, is typical of that which grew up in most seaboard states and in foreign countries.  Since 1805 Louisiana pilots have been State officers whose work has been controlled by the State.

\* \* \*

It is within the framework of this longstanding pilotage regulation system that the practice has apparently existed of permitting pilots, if they choose, to select their relatives and friends as the only ones ultimately eligible for appointment as pilots by the governor.

\* \* \*

The practice of nepotism in appointing public servants has been a subject of controversy in this country throughout our history.  Some states have adopted constitutional amendments or statutes, to prohibit it.  These have reflected state policies to wipe out the practice.  But Louisiana and most other states have adopted no such general policy.  We can only assume that the Louisiana legislature weighed the obvious possibility of evil against whatever useful function a closely knit pilotage system may serve. Thus the advantages of early experience under friendly supervision in the locality of the pilot's training, the benefits to morale and esprit de corps which family and neighborly tradition might contribute, the close association in which pilots must work and live in their pilot communities and on the water, and the discipline and regulation which is imposed to assure the State competent pilot service after appointment, might have prompted the legislature to permit Louisiana pilot officers to select those with whom they would serve.

The number of people, as a practical matter, who can be pilots is very limited.  No matter what system of selection is adopted, all but the few occasionally selected must of necessity be excluded.

\* \* \*

The object of the entire pilotage law, as we have pointed out, is to secure for the State and others interested the safest and most efficiently operated pilotage system practicable.

* * *

[W]e cannot say that the practice appellants attack is the kind of discrimination which violates the equal protection clause of the Fourteenth Amendment.

Affirmed.

■ MR. JUSTICE RUTLEDGE, dissenting.

The unique history and conditions surrounding the activities of river port pilots, shortly recounted in the Court's opinion, justify a high degree of public regulation.  But I do not think they can sustain a system of entailment for the occupation.  If Louisiana were to provide by statute in haec verba that only members of John Smith's family would be eligible for the public calling of pilot, I have no doubt that the statute on its face would infringe the Fourteenth Amendment.  And this would be true, even though John Smith and the members of his family had been pilots for generations. It would be true also if the right were expanded to include a number of designated families.

In final analysis this is, I think, the situation presented on this record. While the statutes applicable do not purport on their face to restrict the right to become a licensed pilot to members of the families of licensed pilots, the charge is that they have been so administered.  And this charge not only is borne out by the record but is accepted by the Court as having been sustained.

The result of the decision therefore is to approve as constitutional state regulation which makes admission to the ranks of pilots turn finally on consanguinity.  Blood is, in effect, made the crux of selection.  That, in my opinion, is forbidden by the Fourteenth Amendment's guaranty against denial of the equal protection of the laws.

* * *

Conceivably the familial system would be the most effective possible scheme for training many kinds of artisans or public servants, sheerly from the viewpoint of securing the highest degree of skill and competence. Indeed, something very worth while largely disappeared from our national life when the once prevalent familial system of conducting manufacturing and mercantile enterprises went out and was replaced by the highly impersonal corporate system for doing business.

But that loss is not one to be repaired under our scheme by legislation framed or administered to perpetuate family monopolies of either private occupations or branches of the public service.  It is precisely because the Amendment forbids enclosing those areas by legislative lines drawn on the basis of race, color, creed, and the like, that, in cases like this, the possibly most efficient method of securing the highest development of skills cannot be established by law. Absent any such bar, the presence of such a tendency or direct relationship would be effective for sustaining the legislation. It cannot be effective to overcome the bar itself. The discrimination here is not shown to be consciously racial in character. But I am unable to differentiate in effects one founded on blood relationship.

* * *

■ MR. JUSTICE REED, MR. JUSTICE DOUGLAS and MR. JUSTICE MURPHY join in this dissent.

## NOTES AND QUESTIONS

**1.** How might some open competitive system for appointment adversely affect the public interest in pilotage?

**2.** To what extent should an individual's ability to work closely with current employees be taken into account? Are there dangers in a widespread application of the concept of coworker preference?

**3.** The Louisiana law at issue in *Kotch* had the effect of excluding the vast majority of citizens, rather than a discrete minority, from working as pilots. Does this fact affect the Court's analysis?

**4.** One of the consequences of the Louisiana pilotage system may have been to institutionalize and perpetuate racial discrimination. If true, does this make the law unconstitutional? Is intent to discriminate required? See Washington v. Davis, 426 U.S. 229 (1976) (intent to discriminate required in constitutionally-based actions). For an update on the issue of harbor pilots, see Michael Totty, Harbor Pilots: Great Job, But Good Luck Getting It, Wall St.J., Nov. 29, 1995.

**5.** Does "family" belong on a list with "race, color, creed and the like," as Justice Rutledge thinks? If Justice Rutledge is right, should a parent be able to turn over to a child the parent's proprietary business? Is there a difference in the "property" involved?

**6.** In Backlund v. Hessen, 104 F.3d 1031 (8th Cir.1997), an applicant for a city firefighter position with the highest test score was passed over in favor of three lower ranking candidates who were related to fire department employees. The plaintiff claimed that the nepotism violated equal protection. In reversing the district court's dismissal of the claim, the Eighth Circuit distinguished *Kotch* and observed that in *Kotch* the state justified its policy in light of "the unique character of river piloting." It held that "*Kotch* makes it abundantly clear that nepotism in governmental hiring requires some measure of justification before it can pass constitutional muster."

**7.** Nepotism, per se, does not violate the nondiscrimination provisions of Title VII of the Civil Rights Act of 1964, but if the effect of nepotism is discrimination on the basis of race, sex, or some other proscribed classification it is illegal. In Asbestos Workers, Local 53 v. Vogler, 407 F.2d 1047 (5th Cir.1969), the union had a policy restricting membership to sons or close relatives of current members. The effect of the policy was to perpetuate the exclusion of minorities from the all-white union.   The court invalidated the policy.

**8.**   Does an employer's antinepotism rule violate a state prohibition on marital status discrimination?   Compare Manhattan Pizza Hut, Inc. v. State Human Rights Appeal Board, 415 N.E.2d 950 (N.Y.1980) (no), with Kraft, Inc. v. State, 284 N.W.2d 386 (Minn.1979) (yes).  Does a city's anti-nepotism policy violate the constitutional right to marry?   See Parks v. City of Warner Robins, 43 F.3d 609 (11th Cir.1995) (held:  no).

**9.**   These issues about prohibited discrimination are considered in depth in Chapter 4.   As you study that chapter, consider whether *Kotch* is good law today.

## EEOC v. Consolidated Service Systems

989 F.2d 233 (7th Cir.1993).

■ POSNER, CIRCUIT JUDGE.

The Equal Employment Opportunity Commission brought this suit in 1985 against a small company which provides janitorial and cleaning services at a number of buildings in the Chicago area.   The owner of the company is a Korean immigrant, as are most of its employees.   The suit charges that the company discriminated in favor of persons of Korean origin, in violation of Title VII of the Civil Rights Act of 1964, 42 U.S.C. § 2000e et seq., by relying mainly on word of mouth to obtain new employees.   After a bench trial, the district judge dismissed the suit on the ground that the Commission had failed to prove discrimination.   * * *

Between 1983, when Mr. Hwang, the company's owner, bought the company from its previous owner, also a Korean, and the first quarter of 1987, 73 percent of the applicants for jobs with Consolidated, and 81 percent of the hires, were Korean.   Less than 1 percent of the work force in Cook County is Korean and at most 3 percent of the janitorial and cleaner work force.   It doesn't take a statistician to tell you that the difference between the percentage of Koreans in Consolidated's work force and the percentage of Koreans in the relevant labor market, however exactly that market is defined, is not due to chance.   But is it due to discrimination? The district judge found it was not, and we do not think his finding was clearly erroneous.

There is no direct evidence of discrimination.   The question is whether the circumstantial evidence compels an inference of discrimination—*intentional* discrimination ("disparate treatment," in the jargon of Title VII cases), for the EEOC has not appealed from the district court's rejection of its disparate-impact theory of liability.

We said that Consolidated is a small company.   The EEOC's lawyer told us at argument that the company's annual sales are only $400,000. We mention this fact not to remind the reader of David and Goliath, or to suggest that Consolidated is exempt from Title VII (it is not), or to express wonderment that a firm of this size could litigate in federal court for seven years (and counting) with a federal agency, but to explain why Mr. Hwang relies on word of mouth to obtain employees rather than reaching out to a broader community less heavily Korean.   It is the cheapest method of recruitment.   Indeed, it is practically costless.   Persons approach Hwang or his employees—most of whom are Korean too—at work or at social events, and once or twice Hwang has asked employees whether they know anyone who wants a job.   At argument the EEOC's lawyer conceded, perhaps improvidently but if so only slightly so, that Hwang's recruitment posture could be described as totally passive.   Hwang did buy newspaper advertisements on three occasions—once in a Korean-language newspaper and twice in the *Chicago Tribune*—but as these ads resulted in zero hires, the experience doubtless only confirmed him in the passive posture.   The EEOC argues that the single Korean newspaper ad, which ran for only three days and yielded not a single hire, is evidence of discrimination.   If so, it is very weak evidence.   The Commission points to the fact that Hwang could have obtained job applicants at no expense from the Illinois Job Service as further evidence of discrimination.   But he testified that he had never heard of the Illinois Job Service and the district judge believed him.

If an employer can obtain all the competent workers he wants, at wages no higher than the minimum that he expects to have to pay, without beating the bushes for workers—without in fact spending a cent on recruitment—he can reduce his costs of doing business by adopting just the stance of Mr. Hwang.   And this is no mean consideration to a firm whose annual revenues in a highly competitive business are those of a mom and pop grocery store.   Of course if the employer is a member of an ethnic community, especially an immigrant one, this stance is likely to result in the perpetuation of an ethnically imbalanced work force.   Members of these communities tend to work and to socialize with each other rather than with people in the larger community.   The social and business network of an immigrant community racially and culturally distinct from the majority of Americans is bound to be largely confined to that community, making it inevitable that when the network is used for job recruitment the recruits will be drawn disproportionately from the community.

No inference of intentional discrimination can be drawn from the pattern we have described, even if the employer would prefer to employ people drawn predominantly or even entirely from his own ethnic or, here, national-origin community.   Discrimination is not preference or aversion; it is acting on the preference or aversion.   If the most efficient method of hiring, adopted because it is the most efficient (not defended because it is efficient—the statute does not reference to efficiency, 42 U.S.C. § 2000e–2(k)(2)), just happens to produce a work force whose racial or religious or ethnic or national-origin or gender composition pleases the employer, this is not intentional discrimination.   EEOC v. Chicago Miniature Lamp Works, 947 F.2d 292, 299 (7th Cir.1991).   The motive is not a discriminatory one.   "Knowledge of a disparity is not the same thing as an intent to cause or maintain it."   Or if, though the motives behind adoption of the method were a mixture of discrimination and efficiency, Mr. Hwang would have adopted the identical method of recruitment even if he had no interest in the national origin of his employees, the fact that he had such an interest would not be a "but for" cause of the discriminatory outcome and again there would be no liability.   There is no evidence that Hwang is biased in favor of Koreans or prejudiced against any group underrepresented in his work force, except what the Commission asks us to infer from the imbalance in that force and Hwang's passive stance.

We said the passive stance is the cheapest method of recruitment.   It may also be highly effective in producing a good work force.   There are two reasons.   The first is that an applicant referred by an existing employee is likely to get a franker, more accurate, more relevant picture of working conditions than if he learns about the job from an employment agency, a newspaper ad, or a hiring supervisor.   The employee can give him the real low-down about the job.   The result is a higher probability of a good match, and a lower probability that the new hire will be disappointed or disgruntled, perform badly, and quit.   Second, an employee who refers someone for employment may get in trouble with his employer if the person he refers is a dud;   so word of mouth recruitment in effect enlists existing employees to help screen new applicants conscientiously.

If this were a disparate-impact case (as it was once, but the Commission has abandoned its claim of disparate impact), and, if, contrary to EEOC v. Chicago Miniature Lamp Works, word of mouth recruitment were deemed an employment practice and hence was subject to review for disparate impact, as assumed in Clark v. Chrysler Corp., 673 F.2d 921, 927 (7th Cir.1982), and held in Thomas v. Washington County School Board, 915 F.2d 922, 924–26 (4th Cir.1990), then the advantages of word of mouth recruitment would have to be balanced against its possibly discriminatory effect when the employer's current work force is already skewed along racial or other disfavored lines.   But in a case of disparate treatment, the question is different.   It is whether word of mouth recruitment gives rise to an inference of intentional discrimination.   Unlike an explicit racial or ethnic criterion or, what we may assume without deciding amounts to the same thing, a rule confining hiring to relatives of existing employees in a racially or ethnically skewed work force, as in *Thomas,* word of mouth recruiting does not compel an inference of intentional discrimination.   At least it does not do so where, as in the case of Consolidated Services Systems, it is clearly, as we have been at pains to emphasize, the cheapest and most efficient method of recruitment, notwithstanding its discriminatory impact.   Of course, Consolidated had some non-Korean applicants for employment, and if it had never hired any this would support, perhaps decisively, an inference of discrimination.   Although the respective percentages of Korean and of non-Korean applicants hired were clearly favorable to Koreans (33 percent to 20 percent), the EEOC was unable, as explained more fully below, to find a single person out of the 99 rejected non-Koreans who could show that he or she was interested in a job that Mr. Hwang ever hired for.   Many, perhaps most, of these were persons who responded to the ad he placed in the *Chicago Tribune* for a contract that he never got, hence never hired for.

The Commission cites the statement of Consolidated's lawyer that his client took advantage of the fact that the Korean immigrant community offered a ready market of cheap labor as an admission of "active" discrimination on the basis of national origin. It is not discrimination, and it is certainly not active discrimination, for an employer to sit back and wait for people willing to work for low wages to apply to him. The fact that they are ethnically or racially uniform does not impose upon him a duty to spend money advertising in the help-wanted columns of the *Chicago Tribune*. The Commission deemed Consolidated's "admission" corroborated by the testimony of the sociologist William Liu, Consolidated's own expert witness, who explained that it was natural for a recent Korean immigrant such as Hwang to hire other recent Korean immigrants, with whom he shared a common culture, and that the consequence would be a work force disproportionately Korean. Well, of course. People who share a common culture tend to work together as well as marry together and socialize together. That is not evidence of illegal discrimination.

Although the Commission's witness list contained the names of 99 persons whom Hwang had refused to hire allegedly because they were not Korean, at trial it presented only four of these persons as witnesses. One was a woman whose national origin the record does not disclose, but we shall assume that she is not Korean. She applied for a job with Consolidated in response to one of the ads he had placed in the *Tribune*. She was not hired. Hwang testified that he hired no one who responded to the ad because he failed to receive the contract which he had placed the ad in expectation of receiving. The district judge believed him. The judge also thought it odd that this witness had been a receptionist both before she applied for the job with Consolidated and after she failed to get it. He doubted that she had really wanted a job cleaning buildings.

The next witness had responded to the same ad. His national origin, too, is not of record but we may assume from his name and from the fact that the EEOC offered him as a witness that he is not Korean. Apart from believing Hwang's testimony that the ad had been placed to obtain workers for a job that never materialized, the judge found this witness's testimony "incredible," in part because he gave contradictory evidence. The judge disbelieved the third witness as well, sensing that he had not really wanted a job with Consolidated because he had just quit a higher-paying job. The last witness was adamant that he had learned about the job opening at Consolidated from the *Chicago Sun–Times,* in which Consolidated had never advertised. In addition, he had been fired from his previous job because he had been caught stealing from his employer. He also testified that he was seeking a job that paid almost twice what Consolidated was offering.

This was a sorry parade of witnesses, especially when we recall that the Commission culled it from a list of 99. We can hardly fault the district judge for concluding from all the evidence that the Commission had failed to prove that Consolidated was deliberately discriminating in favor of Koreans.

In a nation of immigrants, this must be reckoned an ominous case despite its outcome. The United States has many recent immigrants, and today as historically they tend to cluster in their own communities, united by ties of language, culture, and background. Often they form small businesses composed largely of relatives, friends, and other members of their community, and they obtain new employees by word of mouth. These small businesses—grocery stores, furniture stores, clothing stores, cleaning services, restaurants, gas stations—have been for many immigrant groups, and continue to be, the first rung on the ladder of American success. Derided as clannish, resented for their ambition and hard work, hated or despised for their otherness, recent immigrants are frequent targets of discrimination, some of it violent. It would be a bitter irony if the federal agency dedicated to enforcing the antidiscrimination laws succeeded in using those laws to kick these people off the ladder by compelling them to institute costly systems of hiring. There is equal danger to small black-run businesses in our central cities. Must such businesses undertake in the name of nondiscrimination costly measures to recruit non-black employees?

\* \* \*

AFFIRMED.

NOTES AND QUESTIONS

✓**1.** To what extent is the court concerned about a small, minority-owned business? Suppose the business were neither small nor minority-owned. Would word-of-mouth recruitment be more objectionable? Suppose the result of word-of-mouth recruitment were the *exclusion* of minorities. Would the court be as willing to sanction the use of this technique?

**2.** Judge Posner focuses on the asserted efficiency of word-of-mouth recruitment for this small employer. Is this the proper province of the court, or are matters of weighing efficiency against nondiscrimination and other societal values the proper role of the legislature?

**3.** Should Title VII be concerned about fairness in process or fairness in outcomes? What costs are reasonable to impose on employers to engage in "unnecessary" efforts to recruit a more diverse work force?

**4.** Between 1979 and 1987, a Chicago wire press shop hired 87 people for low-skilled press jobs, none of whom were black. There was no other specific evidence of discrimination. The employer's defense was that blacks were unwilling to work in the jobs because they were held mostly by Polish- and Spanish-speaking workers. Has the employer violated Title VII? See EEOC v. O & G Spring & Wire Forms Specialty Co., 38 F.3d 872 (7th Cir.1994), cert. denied, 513 U.S. 1198 (1995) (held: yes).

**5.** For a general discussion of the issue raised in *Consolidated Service,* see Jonathan Kaufman, Help Unwanted: Immigrants' Businesses Often Refuse to Hire Blacks in Inner City, Wall St.J., June 6, 1995, at A1, col. 1.

## A NOTE ON INFORMATION AND REFERRAL SOURCES

### A. *Want Ads*

Discriminatory want ads are expressly prohibited by Title VII of the Civil Rights Act of 1964 and the Age Discrimination in Employment Act (ADEA). Section 704(b) of Title VII provides:

It shall be an unlawful employment practice for an employer, labor organization, [or] employment agency * * * to print or publish or cause to be printed or published any notice or advertisement relating to employment by such an employer or membership in or any classification or referral for employment by such labor organization, or relating to any classification or referral for employment by such an employment agency, * * * indicating any preference, limitation, specification, or discrimination, based on race, color, religion, sex, or national origin, except that such a notice or advertisement may indicate a preference, limitation, specification, or discrimination based on religion, sex, or national origin when religion, sex, or national origin is a bona fide occupational qualification for employment.

Most of the litigation under § 704(b) has involved alleged sex discrimination, where ads for "boys," "girls," "men," and "women" have been struck down. What about an ad for a salesman, bus boy, waitress, or longshoreman? In Hailes v. United Air Lines, 464 F.2d 1006 (5th Cir.1972), it was held to violate Title VII for United to advertise for "stewardesses."

Although the content of want ads has been regulated, the ads themselves may be run in publications with a limited readership. For example, a want ad run in a general circulation newspaper could not indicate that the Chung Fu Restaurant had openings for Chinese waiters. But, it would not be unlawful for Chung Fu to place a want ad only in a Chinese newspaper. Similarly, Way Out Fashions could not run a want ad seeking college age students to work as sales clerks. But, Way Out could announce sales openings in a want ad run only in a campus newspaper. Is the current state of the law realistic? Is more or less regulation appropriate? Is *Consolidated Service Systems* the appropriate judicial response?

### B. *Employment Agencies*

Most states began licensing and regulating employment agencies during the Great Depression, when high unemployment led to some unscrupulous and exploitative agency practices. These laws typically required employment agency licensing and bonding, prohibited advance charging, and set maximum fees. The laws were challenged as being unconstitutional, but they were upheld as being necessary and reasonable regulations. See, e.g., National Employment Exchange v. Geraghty, 60 F.2d 918 (2d Cir.1932); Abbye Employment Agency, Inc. v. Robinson, 2 N.Y.S.2d 947 (App.Div.1938).

Today, in addition to the regulation of fees, discrimination in referrals is prohibited. Section 703(b) of Title VII provides: "It shall be an unlawful employment practice for an employment agency to fail or refuse to refer for employment, or otherwise to discriminate against, any individual because of his race, color, religion, sex, or national origin, or to classify or refer for employment on the basis of his race, color, religion, sex, or national origin." Section 701(c) of Title VII provides: "The term 'employment agency' means any person regularly undertaking with or without compensation to procure for employees opportunities to work for an employer and includes an agent of such person."

In Kaplowitz v. University of Chicago, 387 F.Supp. 42 (N.D.Ill.1974), the court held that a law school placement office was an employment agency for purposes of Title VII. But see Bonomo v. National Duckpin Bowling Congress, Inc., 469 F.Supp. 467 (D.Md.1979) (criticizing *Kaplowitz*). In United States v. Philadelphia, 798 F.2d 81 (3d Cir.1986), the Third Circuit held that the supremacy clause bars Philadelphia from applying its human rights law to stop the Temple Law School placement office from allowing the Army, Navy, and Marines to recruit students, even though these armed services (but not the Air Force) refuse to hire gay or lesbian persons.

The federal government does not regulate private employment agencies. Two laws, however, regulate farm labor contractors. The Migrant and Seasonal Agricultural Worker Protection Act, 29 U.S.C. § 1801 et seq., and the Wagner–Peyser Act, 29 U.S.C. § 49 et seq., provide, among other things, that labor contractors must disclose to potential employees, "in writing in a language in which the worker is fluent," all of the terms and conditions of employment. For a discussion of the two statutes, see Espinoza v. Stokely–Van Camp, Inc., 641 F.2d 535 (7th Cir.1981), cert. dismissed, 453 U.S. 950 (1981).

Every state has its own state employment service, which attempts to find appropriate jobs for the unemployed. These state agencies, mandated by a provision of the Federal Unemployment Tax Act, 26 U.S.C. § 3301, also are responsible for the distribution of insurance benefits. For further discussion of unemployment insurance, see Chapter 12.

In addition to statutory duties, employment agencies owe a common law duty of reasonable care to their clients. For example, in one case an employment agency received a phone call from a man who asked them to send over someone to do routine office work at a motorcycle repair shop. The agency dispatched a woman to the caller's "office," which was an empty room. The man then repeatedly sexually assaulted her and kidnapped her. Another employment agency had refused to refer anyone to the purported employer because he sounded "fishy." The employment agency's failure to make further inquiries of the caller made it liable for negligence. Keck v. American Employment Agency, 652 S.W.2d 2 (Ark. 1983).

## C. *Hiring Halls*

In some industries, such as construction and longshoring, unions serve as a job referral service. An employer needing workers would merely contact the union. In theory, the use of a hiring hall benefits both employers and workers. For employers, it facilitates recruitment and allows flexibility in hiring a workforce only as needed. For workers, it simplifies the job search process.

The problem with hiring halls has centered around the union's role in administering them. Section 8(b)(2) of the National Labor Relations Act (NLRA) makes it an unfair labor practice for a union "to cause or attempt to cause an employer to discriminate against an employee" in violation of § 8(a)(3). Section 8(a)(3) makes it an unfair labor practice for an employer "by discrimination in regard to hire or tenure of employment or any term or condition of employment to encourage or discourage membership in any labor organization."

In International Brotherhood of Teamsters, Local 357 v. NLRB, 365 U.S. 667 (1961), the Supreme Court held that union hiring halls are not illegal per se. According to the Court, § 8(a)(3) only prohibits encouragement or discouragement of union membership accomplished by discrimination. Therefore, even if a hiring hall encourages union membership, it is not illegal if the hiring hall is run in a nondiscriminatory manner. In another words, union members may not be given preference over nonunion workers in job referrals. Discrimination by a union in hiring hall referrals is actionable under § 301 of the Labor Management Relations Act, in addition to being an unfair labor practice under the NLRA. Breininger v. Sheet Metal Workers Local Union No. 6, 493 U.S. 67 (1989). Hiring halls also have been held not to violate a state right to work law. Stricker v. Swift Brothers Construction Co., 260 N.W.2d 500 (S.D.1977).

A union hiring hall is permitted to use other reasonable criteria in making referrals. Thus, referrals may be made on the basis of seniority in the industry, *Teamsters;* residence in a particular area, Local Union 8, Electrical Workers (IBEW), 221 N.L.R.B. 1131 (1975); or passing a union-administered examination, Electrical Workers (IBEW) Local 592 (United Engineering & Construction Co.), 223 N.L.R.B. 899 (1976).

Another area in which unions control job opportunities is through apprenticeships and training programs. Race or gender discrimination in admission to such programs may violate Title VII. Some of the practices found to be discriminatory include the use of tests and admissions criteria which are not job related, Hameed v. International Association of Bridge, Structural, & Ornamental Iron Workers, 637 F.2d 506 (8th Cir.1980); recruitment efforts aimed only at whites, United States v. Sheet Metal Workers, Local Union 36, 416 F.2d 123 (8th Cir.1969); and discriminatory application of admissions requirements, Sims v. Sheet Metal Workers, Local Union 65, 489 F.2d 1023 (6th Cir.1973).

The Job Training Partnership Act (JTPA), 29 U.S.C. §§ 1501–1781, enacted in 1982, authorizes programs to train youth and unskilled adults for entry into the labor force. It also provides job training to the economically disadvantaged and to individuals facing language, education, handicap, and other barriers. The JTPA is a cooperative program of the federal and state governments and private employers. It attempts to train workers for occupations where there is a demonstrated local need. See Royal S. Dellinger, Implementing the Job Training Partnership Act, 35 Lab.L.J. 195 (1984).

## B. LEGAL RESTRICTIONS ON ACCESS TO JOBS

### 1. RESIDENCY REQUIREMENTS

## Wardwell v. Board of Education

529 F.2d 625 (6th Cir.1976).

■ WILLIAM E. MILLER, CIRCUIT JUDGE.

This appeal requires us to consider the constitutionality of a rule adopted by the Board of Education of the City of Cincinnati requiring all teachers in the Cincinnati schools hired after November 13, 1972, to establish within 90 days of employment residency within the city school district.

In December, 1972, plaintiff, Terry Wardwell, was hired to teach in the Cincinnati schools. As a condition of employment he agreed to move into the city school district pursuant to a rule announced by the school superintendent in November, 1972, that all newly-employed teachers must establish residence within the district within 30 days after employment. In January, 1973, the Board adopted the following resolution, essentially ratifying the superintendent's rule:

"RESOLVED, That any employee hired by the Cincinnati Schools after November 13, 1972 must either reside within the Cincinnati School District, or agree, as a condition of employment, to establish residency within the district within ninety days of employment. Employees who live in the district must continue to reside therein as long as they are so employed. This policy does not affect in any way personnel hired before the above date."

Plaintiff Wardwell lived outside the district but within the State of Ohio. Despite the requirement he failed to change his residence. He filed the present action in July, 1973, under 28 U.S.C. § 1343 and 42 U.S.C. § 1983, challenging the residency requirement on equal protection grounds and seeking injunctive relief and attorney's fees. No preliminary injunction was requested because enforcement of the rule had been stayed by a preliminary injunction issued by a state court. Since being hired, plaintiff Wardwell has taught at one time in a predominantly white school located within a ten minute drive from his home and later at a predominantly black school about twenty minutes from his home outside the district.

The district court denied the request for an injunction and upheld the validity of the rule, relying heavily on the Fifth Circuit's reasoning in Wright v. City of Jackson, 506 F.2d 900 (5th Cir.1975).

Plaintiff argues that the Board's residency requirement infringes his constitutionally protected right to travel as defined in Shapiro v. Thompson, 394 U.S. 618 (1969), and in Dunn v. Blumstein, 405 U.S. 330 (1972), extending the protection, as he contends, to both intrastate and interstate travel and embracing as a necessary corollary the right to remain in one place.

We find no support for plaintiff's theory that the right to intrastate travel has been afforded federal constitutional protection. An examination of [prior cases] convinces us that the aspect of the right to travel with which the Court was concerned in those cases is not involved here. It is clear that the Court was dealing with the validity of durational residency requirements which penalized recent interstate travel. Such *durational* residency requirements or restrictions affecting the interstate aspect of travel will not pass constitutional muster "absent a compelling state interest."

\* \* \*

We conclude that the "compelling state interest" test is the applicable test in cases involving infringement of the right to interstate travel by *durational* residency requirements. On the other hand, where, as in the present case, a *continuing* employee residency requirement affecting at most the right of intrastate travel is involved, the "rational basis" test is the touchstone to determine its validity.

We find a number of rational bases for the residency requirement of the Cincinnati School Board. The Cincinnati school superintendent testified that promulgation of the rule was based on the following conclusions: (1) such a requirement aids in hiring teachers who are highly motivated and deeply committed to an urban educational system, (2) teachers who live in the district are more likely to vote for district taxes, less likely to engage in illegal strikes, and more likely to help obtain passage of school tax levies, (3) teachers living in the district are more likely to be involved in school and community activities bringing them in contact with parents and community leaders and are more likely to be committed to the future of the district and its schools, (4) teachers who live in the district are more likely to gain sympathy and understanding for the racial, social, economic, and urban problems of the children they teach and are thus less likely to be considered isolated from the communities in which they teach, (5) the requirement is in keeping with the goal of encouraging integration in society and in the schools. These conclusions appear to us clearly to establish rational bases for the residency requirement imposed by the Cincinnati Board.

Appellant insists that the basic purpose of the residency rule is to advance "quality integrated" education and to help in eliminating racial segregation in the community and school system. The rule is not rationally related to this objective, appellant claims, because school and community integration would only be promoted by requiring teachers to live in the attendance districts of the schools at which they teach. Integration is not encouraged, it is argued, by a regulation such as the present which requires teachers to live somewhere in the district at large when the district itself contains many segregated areas. This argument overlooks the various other convincing and rational bases for adoption of the rule. Although it is possible that the rule will not materially contribute to racial integration, we consider that the numerous other legitimate objectives of the rule are wholly adequate to demonstrate that the residency classification fully comports with the rational basis test. Many other courts have recognized the importance of employees being highly committed to the area in which they work and motivated to find solutions for its problems. Such commitment and motivation, it is not unreasonable to suppose, may best be fostered by requiring teachers to live and pay taxes in the place in which they are employed to work.

Other arguments against the validity of this residency requirement are advanced. First, it is said that the right to teach, which in Ohio is controlled by state law through the issuance of a teaching certificate, entitles a teacher to be considered for employment only on his merits as prescribed by statute. This right may not be withheld on constitutionally impermissible grounds. The state certification of teachers distinguishes teachers as a group from municipal employees performing other functions. We agree with appellee, however, that the possession of an Ohio certificate establishes only that a teacher has met certain minimum standards. It does not entitle him to a teaching position with any particular local school board. Local boards are free to impose additional qualifications and conditions of employment or to adopt higher standards.

Finally, appellant argues that the residency requirement is invalid because it requires newly-hired teachers to move into and remain in the district and permits those already hired to remain or move outside the district. Appellee replies that distinguishing between new teachers and teachers with experience who may have tenure and who did not know of the requirement when they accepted employment, is a reasonable distinction which the state is free to make. While we recognize that the limited applicability of the rule may be its most questionable feature, we do not believe that the residency requirement must fail because it does not apply to all teachers employed by the Cincinnati schools. The Supreme Court has pointed out that there is no constitutional requirement that regulations must cover every class to which they might be applied. It has further stated that "if the classification has some reasonable basis, it does not offend the constitution simply because the classification 'is not made with mathematical nicety or because in practice it results in some inequality.'" Dandridge v. Williams, 397 U.S. 471, 485 (1970).

Affirmed.

NOTES AND QUESTIONS

**1.** Do the reasons for the residency requirement asserted by the Board of Education provide a "rational basis" for the rule? Are they "compelling"?

**2.** Many of the reasons supporting the residency requirement, such as the need for teachers committed to an urban educational system and sympathetic to urban children, apply primarily to teachers. Would these justifications support a residency requirement for school janitors? What about other public employees?

In Salem Blue Collar Workers Association v. City of Salem, 33 F.3d 265 (3d Cir.1994), cert. denied, 513 U.S. 1152 (1995), a laborer was discharged for violating the city's residency ordinance. The reasons for the ordinance were to reduce unemployment in the city, improve relations among city employees, enhance the quality of employee performance by greater personal knowledge of conditions and problems in the city, promote a feeling of personal interest in the city's progress, reduce possible tardiness and absenteeism, provide ready personnel for emergency situations, and provide economic benefits to the city. Which of these reasons most persuaded the city to adopt the ordinance? Do these reasons establish a rational basis? The Third Circuit upheld the ordinance.

**3.** The Supreme Court has upheld municipal employee residency requirements against a variety of constitutional challenges. In McCarthy v. Philadelphia Civil Service Commission, 424 U.S. 645 (1976), the Court upheld a residency requirement for Philadelphia firefighters against a challenge based on equal protection. In White v. Massachusetts Council of Construction Employers Inc., 460 U.S. 204 (1983), the Court held that the commerce clause was not violated by an executive order of the Mayor of Boston requiring that on all construction projects funded in whole or in part by the city, at least half of the employees had to be residents of Boston. And in United Building & Construction Trades Council v. Mayor of Camden, 465 U.S. 208 (1984), the Court held that a similar Camden, New Jersey, ordinance requiring at least 40 percent of construction workers on city funded projects to be Camden residents did not violate the privileges and immunities clause of article IV because a "substantial reason" for the ordinance was shown. Cf. New Hampshire v. Piper, 470 U.S. 274 (1985) (New Hampshire failed to prove substantial reason for refusing to permit nonresidents to be members of the state bar); Hicklin v. Orbeck, 437 U.S. 518 (1978) (invalidating preference for Alaska residents in pipeline contracts).

**4.** Since the Civil War, many federal and state civil service laws have contained provisions giving honorably discharged veterans a preference in appointment, promotion, and retention. In Personnel Administrator v. Feeney, 442 U.S. 256 (1979), the Supreme Court held that veterans preference statutes which accord an absolute employment preference to veterans are legitimate rewards for military service and do not violate the equal protection clause even though the preference operates to exclude women.

Section 712 of Title VII provides: "Nothing contained in this title shall be construed to repeal or modify any Federal, State, territorial, or local law creating special rights or preference for veterans." Would an employer violate Title VII by *voluntarily* giving a preference to veterans? See Woody v. West Miami, 477 F.Supp. 1073 (S.D.Fla.1979) (violation of Title VII to reject female applicant for police officer position because of preference for veterans).

The New York Constitution and Civil Service Law grant a civil service employment preference, in the form of points added to examination scores, to New York residents who are honorably discharged veterans, served during time of war, and were New York residents when they entered military service.  Is this type of veterans preference constitutional?  See Attorney General of New York v. Soto-Lopez, 476 U.S. 898 (1986) (violation of right to travel and equal protection).

**5.**  For a discussion of constitutional protections in politically-motivated hirings, see Rutan v. Republican Party, supra p. 37; for a discussion of politically-motivated discharges, see Chapters 7 and 10.

## 2.  UNDOCUMENTED ALIENS

According to the Bureau of the Census, in 1986 there were between three million and five million undocumented aliens living in the United States.  The number grows by between 100,000 and 300,000 each year.  To reduce the flow of illegal aliens and to remove the cloud over longtime resident undocumented aliens, Congress enacted the Immigration Reform and Control Act of 1986.

Prior to passage of this law, there were few restrictions on the hiring of undocumented workers.  Some states, such as California, provided for employer fines for hiring undocumented workers.  See De Canas v. Bica, 424 U.S. 351 (1976) (upholding constitutionality of California law).  In addition, the Federal Migrant and Seasonal Agricultural Worker Protection Act, 29 U.S.C. § 1816, provides that "No farm labor contractor shall recruit, hire, employ, or use, with knowledge, the services of any individual who is an alien not lawfully admitted for permanent residence or who has not been authorized by the Attorney General to accept employment."  A bona fide inquiry into each worker's status is required.  A contractor's reliance upon "instinct" is insufficient.  Counterman v. United States Department of Labor, 607 F.Supp. 286 (W.D.Tex.1985), affirmed, 776 F.2d 1247 (5th Cir.1985).  Farm labor contractors are required to have a certificate of registration from the Secretary of Labor, 29 U.S.C. § 1811, and the certificate will be revoked if, among other things, the contractor uses undocumented workers, 29 U.S.C. § 1813(a).  Farm labor contractors who operate without proper certification are subject to a fine of up to $10,000, three years in prison, or both, 29 U.S.C. § 1851(b).

The 1986 immigration law applies to all employers, regardless of size or industry.  It prohibits employers from hiring undocumented workers and provides civil penalties of $250 to $2,000 for each undocumented worker hired.  For subsequent offenses, penalties of up to $10,000 may be assessed and for a "pattern or practice" of violations, the employer is subject to a $3,000 criminal fine and six months imprisonment.

Employers are required to ask all job applicants for documents, such as a passport, a birth certificate, or a driver's license, to confirm that they are either citizens or aliens authorized to work in the United States.  The employer is not required to check the authenticity of documents.

The Act also offers legal status to aliens who entered the United States illegally before January 1, 1982, and have resided continuously since then.

An alien who makes false statements in an application for legal status is subject to a $2,000 fine and up to five years imprisonment.

Most undocumented aliens come to the United States specifically to find work. Congress enacted the 1986 immigration law after extensive debate over whether the effort to combat illegal immigration should focus on employers. Critics of employer sanctions contend, among other things, that it will lead to employment discrimination against persons legally entitled to work.

The employment rights of lawful resident aliens are discussed in Chapter 4.

## Collins Foods International, Inc. v. Immigration & Naturalization Service

948 F.2d 549 (9th Cir.1991).

■ Canby, Circuit Judge:

Collins Foods International appeals from the decision of an Administrative Law Judge (ALJ) holding Collins Foods subject to a civil penalty for hiring an alien, knowing him to be unauthorized to work in the United States, in violation of 8 U.S.C. § 1324a(a)(1)(A). The ALJ found that Collins Foods had constructive knowledge of the alien's status, and that this constructive knowledge was sufficient to establish the knowledge element of section 1324a(a)(1).

We reverse.

### FACTS

Ricardo Soto Gomez (Soto), an employee at a Phoenix Sizzler Restaurant, is authorized to hire other Sizzler employees for that location. Soto extended a job offer to Armando Rodriguez in a long-distance telephone conversation; Soto was in Phoenix and Rodriguez was in California. Rodriguez said nothing in the telephone conversation to indicate that he was not authorized to work in the United States. Rodriguez was working for Sizzler in California at the time Soto extended the offer of employment in Phoenix.

When Rodriguez came to Phoenix, he reported to Sizzler for work. Before allowing Rodriguez to begin work, Soto asked Rodriguez for evidence of his authorization to work in the United States. Rodriguez informed Soto that he did not have the necessary identification with him. At that point, Soto did not let Rodriguez begin work, but sent him away with the understanding that he would return with his qualifying documents.

Rodriguez returned with a driver's license and what appeared to be a Social Security card. Soto looked at the face of the documents and copied information from them onto a Form I–9. Soto did not look at the back of the Social Security card, nor did he compare it with the example in the INS handbook. After Soto completed the necessary paperwork, Rodriguez began work at the Sizzler in Phoenix. Rodriguez, it turned out, was an alien not authorized to work in the United States, and his "Social Security card" was a forgery.

## DISCUSSION

The INS charged Collins Foods with one count of hiring an alien, knowing him to be unauthorized to work in the United States, in violation of 8 U.S.C. § 1324a(a)(1)(A). Upon receiving INS' Notice of Intent to Fine, Collins Foods requested a hearing. Inasmuch as it was uncontroverted that Rodriguez was unauthorized to work in the United States, the only issue to be decided at the hearing was whether Collins Foods knew that Rodriguez was unauthorized at the time of hire. The ALJ declined to decide that Collins Foods had actual knowledge of the fact that Rodriguez was an illegal alien, but decided instead that it had "constructive knowledge." The ALJ based his "constructive knowledge" conclusion on two facts: first, that Soto offered the job to Rodriguez over the telephone without having seen Rodriguez' documentation; and, second, that Soto failed to compare the back of the Social Security card with the example in the INS manual. While we do not disturb the factual determinations made by the ALJ, we hold that these two facts cannot, as a matter of law, establish constructive knowledge under 8 U.S.C. § 1324a(a)(1)(A).

## I. *Job Offer Prior to Verification of Documents*

The first of these facts, as a matter of law, cannot support a finding of constructive knowledge. Nothing in the statute prohibits the offering of a job prior to checking the documents; indeed, the regulations contemplate just such a course of action.

The statute that Collins Foods is charged with violating prohibits "a person or other entity [from] hir[ing] for employment" an alien not authorized to work. The Regulations define "hiring" as "the actual commencement of employment of an employee for wages or other remuneration." As Rodriguez had not commenced employment for wages at the time Soto extended a job offer to him over the telephone, Rodriguez was not yet "hired" for purposes of section 1324a. Soto was therefore not required to verify Rodriguez' documentation at that time.

Another regulation addresses the issue of the timeliness of verification, and it suggests the same result. Under 8 C.F.R. § 274a.2(b)(ii), employers are required to examine an employee's documentation and complete Form I–9 "within three business days of the hire." Because Soto had examined Rodriguez' documents and completed the necessary paperwork by the time Rodriguez began work for wages, Soto was not delinquent in verifying Rodriguez' documentation.

There are additional, highly cogent reasons for rejecting the ALJ's reliance on the fact that Soto "told Rodriguez he would be hired long before Soto ever saw, or had any opportunity to verify, *any* evidence of Rodriguez' work authorization." To hold such a failure of early verification against the employer, as the ALJ did, places the employer in an impossible position. Pre-employment questioning concerning the applicant's national origin, race or citizenship exposes the employer to charges of discrimination if he does not hire that applicant. The Equal Employment Opportunity Commission has held that pre-employment inquiries concerning a job applicant's race, color, religion, national origin, or citizenship status "may constitute evidence of discrimination prohibited by Title VII." EEOC, *Pre-Employment Inquiries* (1981), *reprinted in* 2 Employment Practices Guide ¶ 4120, 4163 (CCH 1985). An employer who makes such inquiries will have the burden of proving that the answers to such inquiries "are not used in making hiring and placement decisions in a discriminatory manner prohibited by law." For that reason, employers attempting to comply with the Immigration Reform and Control Act of 1986 ("IRCA"), are well advised not to examine documents until after an offer of employment is made:

WARNING

Although the law does not prevent an employer from reviewing the documents and completing the Form I–9 prior to the first day of work, prudent employers will delay the process until at least after extending an offer of employment. This will prevent a job applicant who is rejected for employment after having shown his or her documentation which may contain age, and in some cases, national origin information, from using the verification process to claim discrimination under Title VII of the Civil Rights Act of 1964 or under the unfair immigration-related employment practice provisions contained in [IRCA].

Hope M. Frye and H. Ronald Klasko, 1 *Employers' Immigration Compliance Guide* § 3.03(3) at 3–24 (1991).

The ultimate danger, of course, is that many employers, faced with conflicting commands from the EEOC and the INS, would simply avoid interviewing any applicant whose appearance suggests alienage. The resulting discrimination against citizens and authorized aliens would frustrate the intent of Congress embodied in both Title VII of the Civil Rights Act of 1964, 42 U.S.C. § 2000e et seq., and the 1986 Immigration Reform Act itself. We discuss below some of the legislative history of the latter Act. The legislative history cannot be squared with the ruling of the ALJ regarding Soto's telephone offer of employment to Rodriguez.

Soto complied with the statute and regulations, and followed the course of action recommended by the EEOC, in waiting until the day Rodriguez began work to verify Rodriguez' authorization to work and to complete the Form I–9. Soto's offer of employment prior to that verification cannot serve to establish that Collins Foods had constructive knowledge of Rodriguez' unauthorized work status.

II.  *Verification of Documents*

The portion of the statute that Collins Foods allegedly violated prohibits the hiring of an alien while "knowing" the alien is not authorized to work.   The statute also prohibits the hiring of an individual without complying with the verification requirements outlined in the statute at section 1324a(b)(1)(A).   These two actions, failing properly to verify an employee's work-authorization documents, and hiring an alien knowing him to be unauthorized to work, constitute separate offenses under the IRCA.   Nevertheless, the INS argues, and the ALJ held, that Collins Foods' failure to comply with the verification provisions of the statute establishes the knowledge element of subsection (a)(1)(A), hiring an alien knowing him to be unauthorized.   We need not decide, however, whether a violation of the verification requirement establishes the knowledge element of section (a)(1)(A);  Collins Foods complied with the verification requirement.

The statute, at 8 U.S.C. § 1324a(b)(1)(A), provides that an employer will have satisfied its verification obligation by examining a document which "reasonably appears on its face to be genuine."   Soto examined the face of both Rodriguez' false Social Security card and his genuine driver's license, but failed to detect that the Social Security card was invalid.   But as the ALJ acknowledged, even though Rodriguez was spelled "Rodriquez" on the front of the social security card, at a glance the card on its face did not appear to be false.

Although the verification requirement of the statute requires only that the document "reasonably appear[ ] on its face to be genuine," *id.*, the ALJ held that Collins Foods did not satisfy its verification obligation because Soto did not compare the back of Rodriguez' social security card with the example in the INS handbook.   We can find nothing in the statute that requires such a comparison.   Moreover, even if Soto had compared the card with the example, he still may not have been able to discern that the card was not genuine.   The handbook contains but one example of a Social Security card, when numerous versions exist.   The card Rodriguez presented was not so different from the example that it necessarily would have alerted a reasonable person to its falsity.   Collins Foods, through its employee Soto, did all that it was required to do by statute to satisfy its verification obligation.

Moreover, the legislative history of section 1324a indicates that Congress intended to minimize the burden and the risk placed on the employer in the verification process.   The Judiciary Committee Report on the statute shows that Congress did not intend the statute to cause employers to become experts in identifying and examining a prospective employee's employment authorization documents.   The Judiciary Committee Report states that "[i]t is not expected that employers ascertain the legitimacy of documents presented during the verification process."   H.R.Rep. No. 99–682 (Part 1), 99 Cong.2d Sess. 61 (1986).   The Report goes on to say that "[t]he 'reasonable man' standard is to be used in implementing this provision and the Committee wishes to emphasize that documents that reasonably appear to be genuine should be accepted by employers without requiring further investigation of those documents."   The primary enforcement threat in the legislation is directed at the unauthorized alien presenting the false documentation; the statute provides criminal penalties against that party.

Congress carefully crafted section 1324a to limit the burden and the risk placed on employers. The ALJ's holding in this case places on employers a verification obligation greater than that intended by Congress and beyond that outlined in the narrowly-drawn statute.

In addition, the ALJ's holding extends the constructive knowledge doctrine far beyond its permissible application in IRCA employer sanction cases. IRCA, as we have pointed out, is delicately balanced to serve the goal of preventing unauthorized alien employment while avoiding discrimination against citizens and authorized aliens. The doctrine of constructive knowledge has great potential to upset that balance, and it should not be expansively applied. The statute prohibits the hiring of an alien "*knowing* the alien is an unauthorized alien ... with respect to such employment." Insofar as that prohibition refers to actual knowledge, as it appears to on its face, any employer can avoid the prohibited conduct with reasonable ease. When the scope of liability is expanded by the doctrine of constructive knowledge, the employer is subject to penalties for a range of undefined acts that may result in knowledge being imputed to him. To guard against unknowing violations, the employer may, again, avoid hiring anyone with an appearance of alienage. To preserve Congress' intent in passing the employer sanctions provisions of IRCA, then, the doctrine of constructive knowledge must be sparingly applied.

Indeed, the only federal cases we have found that have allowed constructive knowledge to satisfy the knowledge element of section 1324a(a)(1)(A) are two recent decisions of this court. A comparison of those cases with the one before us illustrates why constructive knowledge cannot be found here.

In Mester Mfg. Co. v. INS, 879 F.2d 561 (9th Cir.1989), the INS had visited the employer's plant and obtained a list of employees. It then notified the employer that certain employees were suspected unlawful aliens, and if their green cards matched the numbers listed in the INS' letter to the employer, then they were using false cards or cards belonging to someone else. The employer did not take any corrective action, and continued to employ the unlawful aliens. We found constructive knowledge.

New El Rey Sausage Co. v. INS, 925 F.2d 1153 (9th Cir.1991), is essentially the same case. The INS visited the employer to inspect paperwork. After running checks on the alien registration numbers of the workers, the INS found several using improper or borrowed numbers. The INS then hand-delivered a letter to the employer reciting the results of its investigation and saying: "Unless these individuals can provide valid employment authorization from the United States Immigration and Naturalization Service, they are to be considered unauthorized aliens, and are therefore not authorized to be employed in the United States. Their continued employment could result in fine proceedings...." Id. at 1155.

The employer simply accepted the word of the aliens as to their legal status, and continued to employ them. We found constructive knowledge.

These cases lead us to conclude that a finding of constructive knowledge under the hiring violation statute requires more than the ALJ found to exist here. Failure to compare the back of a Social Security card with the example in the INS handbook, when neither statute nor regulation requires the employer to do so, falls far short of the "willful blindness" found in *Mester* and *New El Rey Sausage.* To expand the concept of constructive knowledge to encompass this case would not serve the intent of Congress, and is certainly not required by the terms of ICRA.

## CONCLUSION

Collins Foods did not have the kind of positive information that the INS had provided in *Mester* and *New El Rey Sausage* to support a finding of constructive knowledge. Neither the failure to verify documentation before offering employment, nor the failure to compare the back of the applicant's Social Security card with the example in the INS manual, justifies such a finding. There is no support in the employer sanctions provisions of IRCA or in their legislative history to charge Collins Foods, on the basis of the facts relied on by the ALJ here, with constructive knowledge of Rodriguez' unauthorized status. Accordingly, we reverse.

REVERSED.

## NOTES AND QUESTIONS

**1.** For every individual hired after November 6, 1986, an employer must execute and maintain an Employment Eligibility Verification Form, known as Form I–9. Employers are required to ask all job applicants for a passport, birth certificate, or driver's license, to confirm that they are either citizens or aliens authorized to work in the United States. The employer is not required to check the authenticity of the documents.

The INS has implemented a telephone verification service to permit employers to check an alien's registration number against an INS data bank. Do you think this service affects the employer's responsibility to make a good faith effort at compliance?

**2.** Do you think the court in *Collins* strikes the correct balance in imposing obligations on the employer?

**3.** Suppose the employer received an anonymous phone tip that one of its employees was using a false "green card"? Could the INS charge that the employer was put on notice of the employee's unauthorized status? Do you think the INS should consider this factor?

**4.** Under IRCA, the INS can levy either civil or criminal penalties against employers found guilty of paperwork or illegal hiring violations. Civil penalties of $250 to $10,000 may be assessed against an employer who knowingly hires or continues to hire an unauthorized worker. An employer who engages in a "pattern or practice" of hiring undocumented workers is subject to criminal fines of up to $3,000 for each undocumented employee and up to six months in jail.

**5.** Under IRCA, fines for repeated violations of the illegal hiring provisions of the Act are more severe than "first level" fines. In Furr's/Bishop's Cafeterias, L.P. v. Immigration & Naturalization Service, 976 F.2d 1366 (10th Cir.1992), the Attorney General asserted that enhanced fines against a company for a subsequent IRCA violation at a different establishment of the company were appropriate because the company retained the power to terminate unauthorized employees, discipline managers, and conduct company wide education programs. The company argued that each establishment should be considered separately. The Tenth Circuit upheld the increased fines.

**6.** Employer sanctions present a special problem for employers who cannot find qualified U.S. workers to fill certain skilled or professional positions. U.S. law permits employers to "sponsor" aliens for permanent residence by proving through a Department of Labor procedure known as "labor certification" that no U.S. workers are qualified or available for the job offered. Even after approval, however, aliens often face a long wait under the visa quota system before they can actually apply for permanent resident status. The INS has declared that an employer is subject to sanctions upon learning through the labor certification process that an alien is not authorized to work in the United States. This policy will certainly deter employers from assisting aliens with the labor certification process and may have a negative impact on sectors where U.S. workers are typically in short supply.

**7.** In American Friends Service Committee Corp. v. Thornburgh, 718 F.Supp. 820 (C.D.Cal.1989), the court rejected a First Amendment challenge to the employer sanctions provisions of IRCA. According to the court, even if the provision had a substantial impact on the free exercise of rights of a religious organization, those interests did not outweigh the government's interest in immigration control.

**8.** Do employer sanctions under IRCA increase employment discrimination based on national origin? See Steven M. Kaplan, Note, The Employer Sanctions Provisions of IRCA: Deterrence or Discrimination?, 6 Geo. Immigration L.J. 545 (1992). See also Maria L. Ontiveros, To Help Those Most in Need: Undocumented Workers' Rights and Remedies under Title VII: 20 N.Y.U.Rev.L. & Soc. Change 607 (1993–94).

## C. THE EMPLOYER'S INFORMATION-GATHERING PROCESS

## 1. APPLICATIONS

# Sullivan v. United States Postal Service

944 F.Supp. 191 (W.D.N.Y.1996).

■ LARIMER, CHIEF JUDGE.

### *BACKGROUND*

Plaintiff, Rodger R. Sullivan ("Sullivan"), filed a complaint on April 2, 1994, against the United States Postal Service ("Postal Service") and Rodney Brown ("Brown"), a Postal Service employee. Plaintiff claims that the Postal Service violated his rights under the Privacy Act (5 U.S.C. § 552a(b)). Plaintiff also brings a *Bivens* [1] claim against Brown alleging that Brown violated Sullivan's constitutional rights by infringing on his right to privacy. Defendants move for summary judgment on both claims. Defendants' summary judgment motion is granted in part and denied in part. The constitutional violation is dismissed but the claim under the Privacy Act may proceed.

### *FACTS*

The facts as alleged by Sullivan are the following.

Sometime in 1988 Sullivan took a civil service test for employment with the Postal Service. In September, 1993, Sullivan was hired by Lewis General Tires as a management trainee. In late December, 1993, Sullivan received a notice in the mail informing him of an opening at the Postal Service. On or about January 2, 1994, Sullivan completed an employment application with the Postal Service. One part of the application requested the applicant to name his current employer. Sullivan identified Lewis General Tires as his current employer but checked "No" next to that part of the application that asked if the Postal Service could contact his current employer.

Sullivan, along with three other applicants, was interviewed for the position by defendant Brown on January 4, 1994. According to Sullivan, Brown failed to inform the applicants of their rights under the Privacy Act. During the interview, Brown did inform the applicants that he would make his selection for the available position based on test scores, orientation, background and information from employers. After the interview, in spite of Sullivan's instructions to the contrary, Brown contacted Sullivan's employer, Lewis General Tires, and informed them that Sullivan had applied for employment with the Postal Service. According to Sullivan, as a result of the disclosure, he was terminated from his employment at Lewis

1. Bivens v. Six Unknown Agents, 403 U.S. 388 (1971).

General Tires on February 17, 1994.  He was not hired by the Postal Service.

*  *  *

### III.  Privacy Act

Sullivan alleges that the Postal Service violated his rights under the Privacy Act, 5 U.S.C. § 552a, which provides in part that "[n]o agency shall disclose any record which is contained in a system of records .. to any person, or to another agency, except pursuant to a written request by, or with the prior written consent of, the individual to whom the record pertains, ...".

The Postal Service contends that Sullivan's claim must fail because: (1) Brown did not "disclose" a Privacy Act record; (2) Brown's telephone call to Sullivan's employer was not the proximate cause of Sullivan's termination; and (3) Brown's action was not intentional and willful.

Although the Postal Service appears to concede that Sullivan's application for employment with the Postal Service was a "record" for purposes of the Privacy Act, it contends, nevertheless, that there was no violation of the Act because Brown did not disclose any information from the application to a third party.  The Postal Service attempts to distinguish between disclosing the fact that a record existed and disclosing information contained in the record.  I am not persuaded by this argument.

The Privacy Act defines "record" as "... any item, collection, or grouping of information about an individual that is maintained by an agency, including, but not limited to, his education, financial transactions, medical history, and criminal or employment history and that contains his name ..."  5 U.S.C. § 552a(a)(4).

As stated above, the Postal Service concedes as it must that the employment application Sullivan completed was a "record" for Privacy Act purposes.  Sullivan's name was part of the information contained on the record.  Brown disclosed information that a current employee named Sullivan had applied for employment by telephoning the employer and apprising him of that information.  It is true that Brown did not disclose any other information from the application but defendants' claim that Brown did not disclose any information is simply incorrect.

"While the [Privacy] Act does not specifically define "disclosure," common sense requires that this term be taken to denote the imparting of information which in itself has meaning and which was previously unknown to the person to whom it was imparted."

Brown's telephone call to Sullivan's employer during which Brown informed the employer that Sullivan had filed an employment application with the Postal Service had meaning in itself and disclosed to the employer information about Sullivan that he had not previously known.  Thus, I find that Brown's action constituted a "disclosure" of a record for the purpose of the Privacy Act.  On this summary judgment motion, I am unable to rule as defendants request that Brown's acts did not constitute disclosure of protected information.

Defendants further contend that even if Brown's call constituted an improper disclosure, Sullivan's claim should be dismissed because the disclosure was not the proximate cause of Sullivan's termination from his employment. However, the question of proximate cause is a disputed question of material fact. The record indicates that: Sullivan's employer rated his work "satisfactory" several weeks prior to the decision to terminate him; the employer had no intention of terminating Sullivan's employment prior to receiving the telephone call from Brown; and the telephone call from Brown was the "ultimate" reason for the employer's decision to terminate Sullivan's employment. While it is true that there is also evidence in the record indicating that Sullivan's employer was concerned about Sullivan's work performance prior to Brown's telephone call, given the record before me it is inappropriate on this motion to resolve issues concerning proximate cause.

Lastly, defendants claim that Brown's action was not "intentional or willful." To prevail in an action brought pursuant to the Privacy Act, a plaintiff must prove that "the agency acted in a manner which was intentional or willful." "The legislative history describes this standard as 'somewhat greater than gross negligence.'" In the present case, the Postal Service contends that Brown's disclosure was not intentional but rather the result of a mistake. This also is a disputed fact issue. The Postal Service contends that Brown did not have much experience in hiring personnel and was unaware of the rule against contacting the current employer of an applicant without the applicant's consent. Sullivan, on the other hand, contends that Brown's action was intentional and willful as evidenced by the fact that Brown admitted that he knew that the employment application was covered by the Privacy Act; admitted that he had received training concerning the Privacy Act; and admitted that "waiver" forms existed but that he took no steps to obtain a waiver permitting him to contact Sullivan's employer. Brown also acknowledged that the employer's name and telephone number was on the application directly below the box where Sullivan had checked "no" when asked if he was willing to have his current employer contacted.

Whether Brown's disclosure was intentional or willful is a question of fact which cannot be disposed of summarily on the record before me.

I have considered defendants' other arguments in support of their summary judgment motion and find them to be without merit.

### *CONCLUSION*

The Postal Service's motion for summary judgment on Sullivan's first cause of action alleging a Privacy Act violation is DENIED.

IT IS SO ORDERED.

NOTES AND QUESTIONS

**1.** If Sullivan had applied for a private sector job, would he have a remedy? What theory? Should the action be against his prospective employer or his former employer?

**2.** Title VII of the Civil Rights Act of 1964 does not specifically prohibit employers from asking any questions about an applicant's race, color, religion, sex, or national origin. Nevertheless, "inquiries which either directly or indirectly disclose such information, unless otherwise explained, may constitute evidence of discrimination prohibited by Title VII." EEOC, Pre-Employment Inquiries (Office of Pub. Affairs 1981). Thus, by declining to ask such questions the employer is seeking to give assurances of its practice of nondiscrimination, which it notes at the bottom of the form.

3. The equal employment laws of many states go beyond the Title VII prohibitions, especially in the area of preemployment inquiries. The following preemployment inquiry guide was issued by the West Virginia Human Rights Commission under the West Virginia Human Rights Act.

| Subject | Lawful Preemployment Inquiries | Unlawful Preemployment Inquiries |
|---|---|---|
| Name | First, Middle, Last. Name used if previously employed under different name. | To require prefix to applicant's name, (Mr., Mrs., Miss, Ms). Inquiry into marital status. Inquiry into previous name where it has been changed by court order. |
| Sex | | Inquiry into sex of applicant. |
| Height & Weight | | It is unlawful for an employer to set minimum height or weight requirements for hiring unless based on a legitimate job need. |
| Address | Applicant's place of residence and length of residence. | Inquiry into foreign addresses which would indicate national origin. |
| Age | Are you under 18 or over 70? If there is question as to applicant being of legal working age, proof may be requested in form of work permit. | Requesting an individual's date of birth **prior** to employment is prohibited. |
| Number of Dependents | This information may be requested only **after** hiring for legitimate purposes. | Asking an applicant's number of dependents **prior** to employment is prohibited. |
| Race or Color | | Any inquiry which would indicate race or color is prohibited. |
| Color of Hair or Eyes | | Inquiry into color of hair or eyes is prohibited. |
| Photographs | Photograph may be requested only **after** hiring and then only for legitimate business purpose. | Any request for photograph **prior** to hiring is prohibited. |
| Religion, Creed | May be asked only **after** hiring if employer informs applicant it is to be used for emer- | Inquiry into applicant's religious denomination, religious affiliations, church, |

| Subject | Lawful Preemployment Inquiries | Unlawful Preemployment Inquiries |
|---|---|---|
| | gency purpose only. | parish, pastor or religious holidays observed **prior** to hiring is prohibited. |
| Citizenship | Are you a citizen of the United States? If applicant is not a citizen, employer may require a work permit or evidence of alien status. | To ask if applicant is naturalized or a native-born citizen; or to ask the date applicant acquired citizenship. To require **prior** to hiring that applicant produce naturalization papers or first papers. To ask if applicant's spouse or parents are citizens of the United States. |
| Birthplace | Proof of citizenship may be requested after hiring. | Inquiry into birthplace of applicant, or birthplace of applicant's parents, spouse or relatives. Require **prior** to hiring, birth certificate, naturalization or baptismal record. |
| National Origin | To inquire what languages applicant reads, speaks and writes fluently. | Inquiry into an applicant's lineage, ancestry, national origin, descent, parentage, or nationality. Nationality of parents or spouse. Inquiry into how applicant acquired ability to read, write, or speak a foreign language. |
| Education | Inquiry into what academic, professional or vocational schools attended. | It is unlawful to ask specifically the nationality, racial or religious affiliation of a school attended by the applicant. |
| Prior Arrest Record | | The requiring of arrest information has been shown to have a disparate effect on minorities. |
| Criminal Record | | Inquiry advisable only if job related. |
| Relatives | Inquiry into name and address and relationship of persons to be notified in case of emergency. This information may be solicited only **after** hiring. | Inquiry into the location of relatives' places of business. Inquiry to determine if relatives of applicant are or have previously been employed by the employer. |
| Military Service | Inquiry into applicant's experience or duties in United States Armed Forces. | To require copy of military discharge paper or military discharge number. |
| Organizations | Inquiry into organization memberships, excluding those | Unlawful to inquire into organizations which may indi- |

| Subject | Lawful Preemployment Inquiries | Unlawful Preemployment Inquiries |
|---|---|---|
|  | organizations which may indicate race, religion, color, sex, national origin, ancestry, or handicap of their members. | cate race, religion, color, sex, national origin, ancestry, or handicap of their members. |
| Character | Permissible to ask applicant for character references. | It is unlawful to inquire from references any information that is directly prohibited by West Virginia Human Rights Act. |
| Handicaps–Physical or Mental | Have you any disability which would prevent you from performing the duties of the job for which you are applying?  If yes, explain: | It is unlawful to discriminate against an individual who is handicapped, if the individual is able and competent with reasonable accommodation to perform the services required. |
| Economic Status |  | It is inadvisable to inquire as to bankruptcy, car ownership, rental or ownership of a house, length of residence at an address, or past garnishment of wages as poor credit ratings have a disparate impact on women and minorities. |

**4.**   The West Virginia guidelines are based on a specific statutory provision prohibiting preemployment inquiry about race, religion, color, national origin, ancestry, sex, or age.   W.Va.Code § 5–11–9(2)(A).   Other states follow Title VII and do not specifically prohibit soliciting the information, although a discriminatory inference may be drawn if the employer solicits such information.   See, e.g., Neb.Rev.Stat. § 48–1104.   In other states, there are additional statutory prohibitions.   For example, California prohibits asking applicants about arrests not leading to conviction, Cal.Lab. Code § 432.7, and about marijuana convictions more than two years old, Cal.Lab.Code § 432.8.   New Jersey prohibits an employer from asking about draft status and marital status.   N.J.Stat.Ann. § 10:5–12.

**5.**   Preemployment inquiries may run afoul of other laws.   For example, § 8(a)(3) of the National Labor Relations Act makes it an unfair labor practice for an employer to discriminate "in regard to hire or tenure of employment or any term or condition of employment to encourage or discourage membership in any labor organization * * *."   Thus, an employer may not refuse to hire an applicant because the applicant belongs to a union.

**6.**   Applicants who misstate their background, qualifications, work history, or other matters need not be hired when the misstatements are discovered. If the misstatements are not discovered until after the individual begins work, the misstatements will establish cause for discharge.   If the misstatement is not discovered until after an allegedly unlawful discharge, the courts will determine the applicability of the "after-acquired evidence," which will decide what effect, if any, the post-discharge evidence of wrong-doing (which may include preemployment and employment related matters) should have.  For a further discussion, see McKennon v. Nashville Banner Publishing Co., infra pp. 991–992.

## 2.   INTERVIEWS

# Lysak v. Seiler Corp.

614 N.E.2d 991 (Mass.1993).

■ O'CONNOR, JUSTICE.

The plaintiff, Patricia Lysak, states in her complaint that her employer, the defendant, The Seiler Corporation, terminated her employment because she was pregnant, and that therefore the termination violated the prohibition found in G.L. c. 151B, § 3, against discrimination in employment because of sex.  [T]his court [has] held that pregnancy is a sex-linked classification.  After a jury trial, the jury found for the defendant and a judgment was entered accordingly.  The plaintiff appealed and we transferred the case here on our own initiative.  On appeal, the plaintiff argues that the trial judge erred by not directing a verdict in her favor pursuant to her request.  She also argues that the judge erred by not giving a jury instruction that she had requested and by excluding testimony concerning her emotional distress.  We affirm the judgment.

We summarize the evidence relevant to the first two issues, beginning with the plaintiff's testimony.  The plaintiff testified that, after being interviewed on February 20, 1987, by William Zammer, the defendant's president, she was employed by the defendant as its marketing director beginning March 23, 1987.  On April 24, 1987, she told Zammer that she was pregnant.  Zammer was extremely upset by that revelation.  He told her that the situation was "untenable" and that she could not continue in the position for which she had been employed.  He said that he felt "personally betrayed."  Zammer told her that she had lied to him about being career oriented.  She denied that she had lied.  On the Monday following April 24, the plaintiff proposed to Zammer that her employee status be terminated and that, instead, she be considered an independent contractor.  The plaintiff and defendant then entered into such a relationship which lasted until the middle of July, 1987.

According to the plaintiff's testimony, when Zammer interviewed her for employment on February 20, 1987, Zammer and she did not discuss any plans she might have had with regard to either having or not having more children.  The plaintiff was pregnant at the time of her interview with Zammer and, because of positive laboratory tests and her doctor's confirmation, she knew at that time that she was pregnant.

Zammer's testimony in substance was that, when he and the plaintiff first met on February 20, 1987, she told him, without any solicitation by him, that her husband stayed home and took care of their two children with the help of an au pair and that "she was not planning on having any more kids." Zammer's testimony was that he would have hired the plaintiff if he had known she was pregnant, but, because she told him, without being asked, that she had no intention of having more children and that was a lie, he felt betrayed. Zammer testified that on the Monday following the April 24 disclosure of her pregnancy, the plaintiff told him that she had made a mistake, that she had lied to him and wanted to make it up to him. According to his testimony, Zammer told the plaintiff that she had lied to him and he would not be able to trust her anymore. Nevertheless, he accepted her proposal that she and the defendant would enter into an independent contractor relationship because the defendant had some unfinished projects that needed prompt completion and she could complete them.

On appeal, the plaintiff's first contention is that she was denied a directed verdict to which she was entitled. It is very seldom that a verdict dependent on oral evidence can be directed in favor of the party with the burden of proof. Nevertheless, the plaintiff says she was entitled to a directed verdict in this case because of the principle articulated in Kraft v. Police Comm'r of Boston, 410 Mass. 155, 571 N.E.2d 380 (1991). In that case, the plaintiff was required to complete two forms under oath in connection with his application for appointment as a police officer. The forms unlawfully required him to give information about his mental health history. He gave false information and several years later the defendant commissioner terminated his employment because he "had failed to disclose his Veteran[s'] Administration Hospital admissions on his answers to application questions." The defendant commissioner argued to this court that the relevant statute, G.L. c. 151B, § 4(9A) (1988 ed.), did not bar him from inquiring into the mental health hospitalization history of an applicant for a position that would require the carrying of a gun. We held that the inquiries were prohibited by the statute, and that "[t]he commissioner had no authority to discharge [the plaintiff] for giving false answers to questions that the commissioner under law had no right to ask." Based on *Kraft,* the plaintiff argues that, "accepting the defendant's version of the facts," that is, that Zammer discharged the plaintiff for giving unsolicited false information about whether she was pregnant, Zammer, and therefore the defendant, violated the law by discharging the plaintiff, at least constructively, on April 24, 1987. Therefore, the plaintiff argues, the discharge cannot stand.

*Kraft* does not help the plaintiff. A rule that bars an employer from discharging an employee because of the employee's false responses to the employer's unlawful inquiries, does not bar a discharge due to unsolicited, volunteered, false statements made by the employee. Any result other than the one reached in *Kraft* at best would have ignored the employer's unlawful inquiries, and at worst would have rewarded the employer for them. In either event, employers in the future would have been encouraged to violate the law. Here, however, there was no evidence, binding on the defendant, that unlawful inquiries had been made. Therefore, the evidence warranted the jury's verdict that the defendant's discharge of the plaintiff was lawful, and the plaintiff was not entitled to a directed verdict.

Next, the plaintiff contends that it was error for the trial judge not to give proposed jury instruction number 17.  The first of that proposed instruction's two sentences states:  "Because the Defendants [could] not legally make any employment decisions based solely on the fact that Mrs. Lysak was pregnant, and because they also could not legally inquire whether she was pregnant, you are instructed that, as a matter of law, they could not base any employment decision on any alleged misrepresentation by Mrs. Lysak concerning her pregnancy."  That instruction could not properly have been given for the same reason, stated above, that the plaintiff was not entitled to a directed verdict.  Contrary to the requested instruction, the defendant could properly have based an employment decision on an unsolicited misrepresentation by the plaintiff concerning pregnancy if the jury found those to be the facts.

The second and final sentence of the proposed instruction at issue on appeal states:  "Therefore, if you find that the Defendants did in fact base an employment decision in whole or in part on the alleged misrepresentation by Mrs. Lysak about the pregnancy, the Defendants must prove that the same decision would have been made absent a consideration of any information about the pregnancy."  The second sentence would have been an incorrect instruction, too, because, although it is less than clear, it appears to be based on the same incorrect legal premise that underlies the first sentence.  Furthermore, the plaintiff did not preserve for review the judge's failure to give the requested second sentence as required by Mass.R.Civ.P. 51(b), 365 Mass. 816 (1974).  At the conclusion of the jury instructions, plaintiff's counsel protested to the judge his failure to give the requested "instruction that a lie about a protected category of information is not a defense towards sex discrimination."  The proposed second sentence of requested instruction number 17 focused on a different issue regarding shifting of the burden of proof as to causation once unlawful discrimination has been shown to be a factor motivating discharge.  Plaintiff's counsel did not discuss that issue with the judge.

* * *

*Judgment affirmed.*

NOTES AND QUESTIONS

**1.**  Does the holding in *Kraft,* that an employee may not be discharged for giving a false response to a question that the employer had no lawful right to ask, constitute adequate protection for employees who are asked unlawful questions?  Is there a better solution?

**2.**  A county veterans service agency was interviewing candidates for the position of director of the agency.  When Maureen Barbano interviewed for the position, one of the members of the interviewing committee told her that he would not consider "some woman" for the position;  he also asked what her plans were for having a family and whether her husband would object to her transporting male veterans.  The Second Circuit held that the county violated Title VII by rejecting her application.  Barbano v. Madison County, 922 F.2d 139 (2d Cir.1990).  Suppose that, despite the discriminatory interview, the applicant is found to be unqualified for the position. Has the employer violated Title VII?  See Mitchell v. Jones Truck Lines, Inc., 754 F.Supp. 584 (W.D.Tenn.1990) (held: no).

**3.**  A frequent criticism of the interview technique is that interviewers tend to prefer individuals who are most like themselves.  If valid, what legal problems might follow from this observation? As counsel for an employer, what would you advise the employer to do to make the interview process fairer in both appearance and reality?

**4.**  Although the purpose of most interviews is to evaluate the applicant, it also may be used as a recruitment device, giving the interviewer an opportunity to extoll the virtues of the company.  During this process, however, the interviewer may make representations which will bind the employer.  For example, in Weiner v. McGraw-Hill, Inc., 443 N.E.2d 441 (N.Y.1982), Mr. Weiner was assured in the initial employment interview that McGraw-Hill terminated employees only for just cause.  His employment application specified that employment would be subject to the provisions of McGraw-Hill's "Handbook on Personnel Policies and Procedures," which stated that "the company will resort to dismissal for just and sufficient cause only * * *."  The New York Court of Appeals held that an action for breach of contract would lie based on Mr. Weiner's dismissal.

**5.**  Another potential problem for employers associated with interviews is that the interviewers may make discriminatory statements to the interviewees, which later will be used as evidence in an action for employment discrimination.  See King v. New Hampshire Department of Resources & Economic Development, 562 F.2d 80 (1st Cir.1977).

## 3.  REFERENCES

## Chambers v. American Trans Air, Inc.

577 N.E.2d 612 (Ind.App.1991).

■ RUCKER, JUDGE.

Becky Chambers filed suit for defamation against her former employer, American Trans Air, Inc., and two former supervisors, Laura Knowles and John Piburn.  The trial court entered summary judgment against Chambers and she appeals.  The sole issue presented for our review is whether the trial court erred in granting summary judgment in favor of American Trans Air, Inc., Laura Knowles and John Piburn.  Finding no error, we affirm.

Chambers was employed by American Trans Air, Inc. (ATA) from October 1982 to July 1987.  During part of that time Knowles was Chambers' supervisor and Piburn was Knowles' supervisor.

Chambers resigned from ATA after a dispute over working conditions.  She then sought new employment.  When asked by prospective employers the names of her supervisors at ATA, Chambers named Knowles and Piburn as references.  Chambers began experiencing difficulty in finding new employment and the pattern of responses Chambers was receiving from prospective employers led her to become suspicious of the ATA references.

In an effort to determine the nature of the references ATA was providing prospective employers, Chambers instructed her mother to call ATA, represent herself as a prospective employer and ask to speak with Chambers' supervisors. Chambers was aware of ATA policy that inquiries concerning former employees should be directed to the company's personnel department. However, Chambers' instructions to her mother were tailored to avoid having the inquiries forwarded to personnel.

Chambers' mother was able to speak with Knowles and to ask specific questions concerning Chambers. In response Knowles made the following statements: "could work without supervision on occasion," "did not get along well with other employees," and "was somewhat dependable."

At Chambers' request, Chambers' boyfriend also called ATA, represented himself as a prospective employer and spoke to Piburn. In response to specific questions posed to him Piburn replied that Chambers: "does not work good with other people," "is a trouble maker," "was not an accomplished planner," and "would not be a good person to rehire."

Chambers brought this action against ATA, Knowles and Piburn, alleging that the foregoing statements were defamatory. Chambers contends the defendants have similarly defamed her with prospective employers. However, there is no evidence indicating any prospective employers of Chambers spoke to Knowles or Piburn or contacted ATA for a reference.

ATA, Knowles, and Piburn moved for summary judgment advancing various theories including lack of publication, consent, and qualified privilege. The trial court determined that as a matter of law there was no publication of the statements of Knowles and Piburn and entered summary judgment against Chambers.

* * *

The basic elements of an action in defamation are a defamatory imputation, malice, publication, and damages. In granting summary judgment the trial court determined there was no publication of the alleged defamatory statements because Chambers' mother and boyfriend were acting as her agents.  * * *

We have no need to address [this issue] here because the trial court's judgment can be readily sustained on the ground of qualified privilege.

Qualified privilege is a defense to a defamation action and it applies to "communication made in good faith on any subject matter in which the party making the communication has an interest or in reference to which he has a duty, either public or private, either legal, moral, or social, if made to a person having a corresponding interest or duty." The privilege arises out of the necessity for full and unrestricted communication on matters in which the parties have a common interest or duty.

Whether a statement is protected by a qualified privilege is a matter of law, unless facts giving rise to the privilege are in dispute. This court has held that various communications are protected as privileged, including those between employers and employees, business partners, members of fraternal organizations, creditors and credit agencies. We have not, however, had occasion to determine whether a qualified privilege exists regarding a former employer's statements given to a prospective employer concerning a former employee. We now hold that it does.

As a general rule an employee reference given by a former employer to a prospective employer is clothed with the mantle of a qualified privilege. A former employer has an interest in open communications with a prospective employer regarding a former employee's work characteristics. Without the protection of the privilege, employers might be reluctant to give sincere yet critical responses to requests for an appraisal of a prospective employee's qualifications.

We agree with the viewpoint of the foregoing authorities and find them consistent with our existing case law. There is a self-evident social utility in free and open communications between former and prospective employers concerning an employee reference. Accordingly, we hold that such communications are protected by a qualified privilege.

In the case before us, both Knowles and Piburn were under the impression they were communicating with a prospective employer of Chambers. Their responses to specific questions represented appraisals of Chambers' employment qualifications. The communications under these circumstances are entitled to the protection of a qualified privilege.

However, a statement otherwise protected by the doctrine of qualified privilege may lose its privileged character upon a showing of abuse, namely: (1) The communicator was primarily motivated by ill will in making the statement; (2) there was excessive publication of the defamatory statement; or (3) the statement is made without belief or grounds for belief in its truth.

Here, ATA met its initial burden as movant for summary judgment by showing that the statements of Knowles and Piburn were protected by a qualified privilege based on their belief that they were speaking to a prospective employer. Summary judgment was properly entered against Chambers unless she came forward with specific facts demonstrating that the protection of the qualified privilege was lost. Chambers has the burden of showing that Knowles and Piburn were either primarily motivated by a feeling of ill will toward her, or that there was excessive publication of the alleged defamatory statements, or that Knowles and Piburn made the statements without belief or grounds for belief in its truth.

Chambers does not argue the alleged defamatory statements were excessively published. Rather, she contends that Knowles' statements were primarily motivated by ill will. In support of her contention Chambers directs our attention to deposition testimony which indicates there was an ATA policy which provided that all calls from prospective employers were to be directed to the ATA personnel department; that Knowles was aware of the policy; Knowles did not direct the inquiry from Chambers' mother to personnel and therefore, according to Chambers, Knowles lost any qualified privilege by "stepping outside the scope of the privilege". We are not persuaded.

Chambers was also aware of the ATA policy that inquiries concerning former employees should be directed to the personnel department. Consequently Chambers' instructions to her mother were specifically designed to circumvent the policy and to insure that her inquiries were made directly to Knowles. Moreover Chambers testified it was her belief that any prospective employer would attempt to bypass personnel, if possible, in favor of speaking to the supervisor who actually had first hand knowledge of a former employee.

We cannot agree Knowles abused the protection afforded by a qualified privilege in responding to inquiries from Chambers' mother rather than directing those inquiries to personnel.

In further support of her claim that Knowles' statements were primarily motivated by ill will Chambers asserts Knowles did not like her and was jealous of her because Chambers was unmarried; that Knowles was rude and "nasty" to her, as evidenced by incidents in which Knowles jerked paperwork out of her hand and snapped her fingers at Chambers in a peremptory fashion; and that Knowles generally talked about people behind their backs and that Knowles talked "down" to Chambers in a tone that she did not use with other workers at ATA.

To the extent the foregoing constitutes admissible evidence at all, at most Chambers has merely shown that while she was employed at ATA animosity existed between her and Knowles. That is not enough to overcome the defense of qualified privilege. The animosity must provide the underlying basis for the otherwise privileged statement.

Chambers presented no material facts to the trial court showing Knowles' alleged defamatory statements were primarily motivated by feelings of ill will.

Next, Chambers argues the statements of Knowles and Piburn were made without belief or grounds for belief in their truthfulness. "Lack of grounds for belief" has been equated to reckless disregard for the truth. In support of her claim Chambers points to her deposition and the deposition of Knowles which in summary indicate: Chambers' work habits while employed at ATA were satisfactory; there were employees whose overall performance was superior to Chambers, but Knowles did not observe that Chambers was slower or made more mistakes than the others; the group in which Chambers worked had a problem with deadlines, but Knowles could not specify the precise nature of the problem; Chambers had difficulty in getting along with co-workers, but Knowles got along as well with Chambers as she did with other employees; Knowles did not perceive that Chambers had any more difficulty getting along with her than did any other employee.

The thrust of Chambers' argument is that the allegedly defamatory statements of Knowles and Piburn did not reflect an honest evaluation of Chambers' work performance.  However the relevant inquiry here is whether the statements of Knowles and Piburn lost the protection of a qualified privilege.  Chambers has not presented sufficient evidence to demonstrate that either Knowles or Piburn uttered the alleged defamatory statements with reckless disregard for the truth.

ATA, Knowles and Piburn have met their burden of showing the lack of material fact as to the existence of a qualified privilege, and Chambers has made no showing of abuse of that privilege.  The trial court properly granted summary judgment.

Judgment affirmed.

NOTES AND QUESTIONS

**1.**  In general, communications to prospective employers, to the state employment security department and other public officials, as well as internal communications, are all subject to a qualified or conditional privilege.  In Circus Circus Hotels, Inc. v. Witherspoon, 657 P.2d 101 (Nev.1983), Witherspoon was discharged because an agent of the Nevada Gaming Control Board allegedly saw him "past posting" a toke bet, which constitutes the crime of swindling in Nevada.  Witherspoon sued the casino over a letter it sent to the Nevada Employment Security Department about his eligibility for unemployment compensation and a statement it made to a prospective employer that Witherspoon "was a good kid, and he went sour."  Citing precedent from Kansas, Scarpelli v. Jones, 626 P.2d 785 (Kan.1981), and Hawaii, Hamm v. Merrick, 605 P.2d 499 (Hawaii 1980), the Nevada Supreme Court held that statements to the state Employment Security Department were "absolutely privileged" as long as the communication has "some bearing on the subject matter of the proceeding."  Regarding the casino's statement to a prospective employer, the court stated, "A qualified or conditional privilege exists where a defamatory statement is made in good faith on any subject matter in which the person communicating has an interest, or in reference to which he has a right or a duty, if it is made to a person with a corresponding interest or duty."  Specifically, the court held, "A former employer has a qualified or conditional privilege to make otherwise defamatory communications about the character or conduct of former employees to present or prospective employers, as they have a common interest in the subject matter of the statements."

**2.**  Is it libelous for a former employer to write to a prospective employer: "I do not recommend these people"?  See Davis v. Ross, 754 F.2d 80 (2d Cir.1985) (held:  letter written by singer Diana Ross about her former executive assistant *was* libelous).

**3.**  From a personnel standpoint, reference checks have questionable value.  There has been little research on whether negative or positive reference data correlates with job performance.  "The employee discharged for dishonesty may have learned his or her lesson.  Hiring someone with a spotless record is no guarantee of honesty in the future."  Mitchell S.

Novit, Essentials of Personnel Management 83 (2d ed. 1986). Moreover, companies are often reluctant to put negative information in writing. The main value of reference checks may well be the opportunity they provide to confirm facts and to check the applicant's candor and accuracy. Nevertheless, refusals to hire based on unfavorable references have been upheld, even where there is evidence of discrimination by the employer generally. See Parham v. Southwestern Bell Telephone Co., 433 F.2d 421 (8th Cir.1970); Piascik v. Cleveland Museum of Art, 426 F.Supp. 779 (N.D.Ohio 1976).

**4.** In addition to information from prior employers, there is evidence that employers have been able to obtain vast amounts of personal information via inter-corporate computer banks, insurance companies, banks, and other public and private institutions. Staff of Subcommittee on Labor-Management Relations, House Comm. on Education & Labor, 96th Cong., 2d Sess. 7–11 (Comm.Print 1980).

The Fair Credit Reporting Act, 15 U.S.C. §§ 1681–1681u, enacted in 1980, is the most sweeping congressional attempt to limit private sector information abuse. The Act requires consumers to be informed if they are the subject of a consumer credit report and, if an adverse decision is reached, they may obtain disclosure of information in their file. Consumers may request deletion of erroneous material in their file and may submit their own statement disputing file contents. The Act also prohibits dissemination of information more than seven years old and requires reasonable recordkeeping and reporting procedures. Violators of the Act are subject to criminal penalties and civil liability. See generally Virginia G. Maurer, Common Law Defamation and the Fair Credit Reporting Act, 72 Geo.L.J. 95 (1983); Comment, The New Commercial Speech and the Fair Credit Reporting Act, 130 U.Pa.L.Rev. 131 (1981).

**5.** A related issue involves background and security checks by employers. In one case an employee of a telephone equipment installer refused to sign a form consenting to an investigation designed to screen out security risks. He then brought an action alleging, among other things, that the employer committed the tort of invasion of privacy. Spencer v. General Telephone Co., 551 F.Supp. 896 (M.D.Pa.1982) (held: no invasion of privacy). Under what circumstances could a security investigation constitute an invasion of privacy?

**6.** Many states require the fingerprinting of workers in a variety of job classifications, such as alcoholic beverage workers, farm labor contractors, jockeys, pawnbrokers, private detectives, professional boxers, school bus drivers, stock brokers, and taxi drivers. Do such requirements constitute an unlawful invasion of privacy? Is it legal for a city to require employees of establishments serving liquor by the drink to register with the police department, be fingerprinted and photographed, and procure an identification card? See Iacobucci v. City of Newport, 785 F.2d 1354 (6th Cir.1986), reversed on other grounds, 479 U.S. 92 (1986) (held: yes). New York, N.Y.Labor Code § 201–a, and California, Cal.Labor Code § 1051, limit employer use of fingerprints. What employee interests are furthered by these laws?  New York's law was passed to prevent private employers from using fingerprinting as a way of blacklisting union leaders and members. Friedman v. Valentine, 30 N.Y.S.2d 891 (Sup.Ct.1941), affirmed, 42 N.Y.S.2d 593 (App.Div.1943).

**7.**  Should a rejected applicant have the right to learn the reason for not being hired?  Statutes give this right to rejected credit applicants; why not to applicants for employment?

## Lewis v. Equitable Life Assurance Society

389 N.W.2d 876 (Minn.1986).

■ AMDAHL, CHIEF JUSTICE:—Plaintiffs, Carole Lewis, Mary Smith, Michelle Rafferty, and Suzanne Loizeaux, former employees of defendant, the Equitable Life Assurance Society of the United States (company), all hired for indefinite, at-will terms, were discharged for the stated reason of "gross insubordination."  They claim that they were discharged in breach of their employment contracts, as determined by an employee handbook, and that they were defamed because the company knew that they would have to repeat the reason for their discharges to prospective employers.  A Ramsey County jury awarded plaintiffs compensatory and punitive damages.  The Minnesota Court of Appeals affirmed the award but remanded on the issue of contract damages for future harm.  We affirm in full the award of compensatory damages but reverse the award of punitive damages.

In spring 1980, the company hired plaintiffs as dental claim approvers in its St. Paul office.  During the application process, a manager or supervisor of the company interviewed plaintiffs and assured them that if hired, their employment would continue as long as their production remained at a satisfactory level.  Plaintiffs did not execute written contracts of employment.  They were employed for an indefinite time pursuant to oral agreements, and each received a copy of the company's employee handbook.  Among other topics, the handbook discussed policies regarding job security, dismissals, and severance pay.[1]

In fall 1980, the company's Pittsburgh office requested assistance from its St. Paul office.  Claim approvers from St. Paul were sent to Pittsburgh beginning in September.  In October, plaintiffs, who had never traveled on company business before, were among two groups of employees sent to assist the Pittsburgh office for 2-week periods.

---

**1.**  With respect to dismissals, the handbook provided:

Dismissals usually come about because of an individual's indifference to work quality or attendance standards.  Except for misconduct serious enough to warrant immediate dismissal, no employee will be discharged without previous warning and a period in which to bring performance up to a satisfactory level.  When a dismissal is necessary and the employee has been with [the company] for six months or longer, severance pay may be granted, depending on the reason for the dismissal.

At the time plaintiffs departed for Pittsburgh, the company had written policies concerning travel expenses.  Guidelines were set forth on the back of company expense report forms and in management manuals, and the company's St. Paul office manager was responsible for instructing prospective travelers regarding the company's policies.  Because he was out of the office at the time the first group departed, the office manager delegated the responsibility to his secretary.  A supervisor in the St. Paul office was given responsibility for advising the second group.  Neither the secretary nor the supervisor had performed such duties prior to instructing plaintiffs.  As a result, they did not review available written guidelines, they did not give plaintiffs any written instructions, and they did not tell plaintiffs that expense reports would have to be filed.  Plaintiffs were only orally given information on the company's daily allowances for meals and maid tips and they were told to keep receipts for hotel bills and airfare.  In addition, each received a $1,400 travel advance which, having no instruction to the contrary, they spent in full.

When plaintiffs returned to St. Paul, each received a personal letter from management commending them on their job performance while in Pittsburgh.  Upon their return, and after they had spent their travel advances, they were also informed for the first time that they would have to submit expense reports detailing their daily expenditures while in Pittsburgh.  Plaintiffs complied with the company's request and prepared expense reports in which they attempted to reconstruct their expenses.  Upon submission, however, they were asked to change the reports with respect to maid tips because the initial instructions had been erroneous.  Plaintiffs complied with this second request.  However, plaintiffs were yet again told to change their reports to reflect lower overall totals.  Apparently, the company sought to recoup from each plaintiff approximately $200.[2]

Not until late November 1980 did plaintiffs receive written guidelines for completing the expense reports.  The guidelines differed from the instructions given prior to their departures.  At this point, the company asked plaintiffs to make additional changes in their expense reports. Plaintiffs this time refused to make further changes, maintaining that the expenses shown on their original reports had been honestly and reasonably incurred and were submitted based upon the instructions they had received prior to leaving for Pittsburgh.  The company did not dispute the claims that these expenses were honestly incurred.

Nevertheless, in January 1981, plaintiffs each received a letter from the office manager requesting again that they revise their expense reports. The letter set out still another, different set of guidelines to be followed. Additionally, three plaintiffs met individually with a manager from the company's Chicago office.  At the meetings they were once again asked to conform to company policies.  They refused and were told that they were

---

**2.**  Just prior to the expense report controversy it was discovered that another employee in the office had embezzled $10,000 from the company.  Although that incident was a criminal act involving more than ten times as much money as was at stake in all plaintiffs' expense reports combined, the company chose not to prosecute the case.

being put on probation.  They were also warned, for the first time, that termination might be considered.  At trial, company managers testified that the "probation" imposed on the three plaintiffs was not given in reference to the company's dismissal policies, but was primarily for the benefit of company management, to provide time to decide whether to terminate plaintiffs.

A week later, the office manager received orders from Chicago to obtain from two of the plaintiffs monies they had agreed to refund to the company and then to fire all four.  The office manager called the two to his office and had them refund the money, saying nothing of the fact that they were to be terminated later that day.  Late in the afternoon, he called each plaintiff to his office individually and again asked them to change their reports.  When they stated that they were standing by their reports, he terminated them for "gross insubordination."[3]  Another employee involved in the expense-account dispute was not terminated because she agreed to change her report and to refund $200 to the company.

Because they were fired for "gross insubordination," plaintiffs received no severance pay.  Had they been fired for other reasons they would have been entitled to as much as one month's severance pay.

The company admitted that the production and performance of plaintiffs was at all times satisfactory and even commendable.  Company managers acknowledged that plaintiffs should have been given more thorough instructions and that the company's written guidelines should have been reviewed prior to their departures for Pittsburgh.  Management also admitted that the problems could have been avoided had plaintiffs been given proper guidelines prior to their departures.

In seeking new employment, plaintiffs were requested by prospective employers to disclose their reasons for leaving the company, and each indicated that she had been "terminated."  When plaintiffs received interviews, they were asked to explain their terminations.  Each stated that she had been terminated for "gross insubordination" and attempted to explain the situation.  The company neither published nor stated to any prospective employer that plaintiffs had been terminated for gross insubordination.  Its policy was to give only the dates of employment and the final job title of a former employee unless specifically authorized in writing to release additional information.

Only one plaintiff found employment while being completely forthright with a prospective employer about her termination by the company.  A second plaintiff obtained employment after she misrepresented on the application form her reason for leaving the company.  She did, however,

---

**3.**  Plaintiffs were terminated pursuant to the company's human resources manual, which provides in relevant part:

> Gross misconduct is a serious violation of accepted standards of behavior.  Examples are: assaulting another employee, involvement in drug traffic, theft or destruction of Equitable's or another employee's property, or misusing an I.D. card.  Gross misconduct also includes gross insubordination and falsification of any Equitable records including employment papers.

explain the true reason in her interview.  A third plaintiff obtained employment only when she left blank the question on the application form requesting her reason for leaving her last employment;  the issue never arose in her interview.  The fourth plaintiff has been unable to find full-time employment.  All plaintiffs testified to suffering emotional and financial hardship as a result of being discharged by the company.

* * *

In order for a statement to be considered defamatory, it must be communicated to someone other than the plaintiff, it must be false, and it must tend to harm the plaintiff's reputation and to lower him or her in the estimation of the community.  Generally, there is no publication where a defendant communicates a statement directly to a plaintiff, who then communicates it to a third person.  Company management told plaintiffs that they had engaged in gross insubordination, for which they were being discharged.  This allegedly defamatory statement was communicated to prospective employers of each plaintiff.  The company, however, never communicated the statement.  Plaintiffs themselves informed prospective employers that they had been terminated for gross insubordination.  They did so because prospective employers inquired why they had left their previous employment.  The question raised is whether a defendant can ever be held liable for defamation when the statement in question was published to a third person only by the plaintiff.

We have not previously been presented with the question of defamation by means of "self-publication."  Courts that have considered the question, however, have recognized a narrow exception to the general rule that communication of a defamatory statement to a third person by the person defamed is not actionable.  These courts have recognized that if a defamed person was in some way compelled to communicate the defamatory statement to a third person, and if it was foreseeable to the defendant that the defamed person would be so compelled, then the defendant could be held liable for the defamation.

* * *

The trend of modern authority persuades us that Minnesota law should recognize the doctrine of compelled self-publication.  We acknowledge that recognition of this doctrine provides a significant new basis for maintaining a cause of action for defamation and, as such, it should be cautiously applied.  However, when properly applied, it need not substantially broaden the scope of liability for defamation.  The concept of compelled self-publication does no more than hold the originator of the defamatory statement liable for damages caused by the statement where the originator knows, or should know, of circumstances whereby the defamed person has no reasonable means of avoiding publication of the statement or avoiding the resulting damages; in other words, in cases where the defamed person was compelled to publish the statement.  In such circumstances, the damages are fairly viewed as the direct result of the originator's actions.

Properly applied, the doctrine of compelled self-publication does not unduly burden the free communication of views or unreasonably broaden the scope of defamation liability. Accordingly, we hold that in an action for defamation, the publication requirement may be satisfied where the plaintiff was compelled to publish a defamatory statement to a third person if it was foreseeable to the defendant that the plaintiff would be so compelled.

In the present action, the record indicates that plaintiffs were compelled to repeat the allegedly defamatory statement to prospective employers and that the company knew plaintiffs would be so compelled. The St. Paul office manager admitted that it was foreseeable that plaintiffs would be asked by prospective employers to identify the reason that they were discharged. Their only choice would be to tell them "gross insubordination" or to lie. Fabrication, however, is an unacceptable alternative.

Finding that there was a publication, we next turn to the issue of truth. True statements, however disparaging, are not actionable. Since it is true that plaintiffs were fired for gross insubordination, the company argues, they cannot maintain an action for defamation. The company contends the relevant statement to consider when analyzing the defense of truth is the one that plaintiffs made to their prospective employers, that is, that they had been fired for gross insubordination. Plaintiffs counter that it is the truth or falsity of the underlying statement—that plaintiffs engaged in gross insubordination—that is relevant.

The company relies for its authority solely upon language of this court in Johnson v. Dirkswager, 315 N.W.2d 215, 218–19 (Minn. 1982), where we raised the question whether truth as a defense goes to the verbal accuracy of the statement or to the underlying implication of the statement. In *Dirkswager*, however, it was unnecessary to resolve the question. Moreover, that case is distinguishable from the present case because there the underlying statements were presented merely as "allegation of misconduct." Here, the company's charges against plaintiffs went beyond accusations and were conclusory statements that plaintiffs had engaged in gross insubordination.

Requiring that truth as a defense go to the underlying implication of the statement, at least where the statement involves more than a simple allegation, appears to be the better view. Moreover, the truth or falsity of a statement is inherently within the province of the jury. This court will not overturn a jury finding on the issue of falsity unless the finding is manifestly palpably contrary to the evidence. Thus, we find no error on this point because the record amply supports the jury verdict that the charge of gross insubordination was false.

Even though an untrue defamatory statement has been published, the originator of the statement will not be held liable if the statement is published under circumstances that make it conditionally privileged and if privilege is not abused.

* * *

Plaintiffs argue that a self-publication case does not properly fit within the qualified privilege doctrine. Two of the cases which plaintiffs cite in support of the self-publication doctrine, however, appear to agree that the employer's qualified privilege does apply. Also, the logic of imposing liability upon a former employer in a self-publication case appears to compel recognition of a qualified privilege. A former employer in a compelled self-publication case may be held liable as if it had actually published the defamatory statement directly to prospective employers. Where an employer would be entitled to a privilege if it had actually published the statement, it makes little sense to deny the privilege where the identical communication is made to identical third parties with the only difference being the mode of publication. Finally, recognition of a qualified privilege seems to be the only effective means of addressing the concern that every time an employer states the reason for discharging an employee it will subject itself to potential liability for defamation. It is in the public interest that information regarding an employee's discharge be readily available to the discharged employee and to prospective employers, and we are concerned that, unless a significant privilege is recognized by the courts, employers will decline to inform employees of reasons for discharges. We conclude that an employer's communication to an employee of the reason for discharge may present a proper occasion upon which to recognize a qualified privilege.

This conclusion does not necessarily determine that the company's statements were privileged. A qualified privilege may be lost if it is abused. The burden is on the plaintiff to show that the privilege has been abused. While the initial determination of whether a communication is privileged is a question of law for the court to decide, the question of whether the privilege was abused is a jury question. * * * The court should not have submitted the issue of the company's entitlement to the qualified privilege to the jury. Absent abuse, the company was entitled to the privilege.

This error, however, was not prejudicial because the jury found that the company's statements were "actuated by actual malice." A qualified privilege is abused and therefore lost if the plaintiff demonstrates that the defendant acted with actual malice. The jury instructions correctly placed the burden of demonstrating malice on the plaintiff. Most importantly, the jury's special verdict finding on actual malice did not depend upon a finding that there was a qualified privilege. Even though the jury was not properly instructed on the qualified privilege, it nevertheless found the actual malice which negates the company's entitlement to the privilege. Thus, the company was not prejudiced.

NOTES AND QUESTIONS

**1.** In *Lewis* the employer was found liable for disclosing only to its employees the reason for their discharge. In effect, the court treated the plaintiffs' republishing the alleged defamation as if Equitable had published the defamation. Is this valid?

**2.** Equitable had a policy of refusing to discuss its former employees with other companies. Perhaps this was to avoid actions for defamation. Yet, this policy may have contributed to the foreseeability of the self-publication by the plaintiffs and therefore the liability of the company. Does the decision in *Lewis* encourage employers not to give employees any reason for discharge? Is this desirable? Should employees have the right to know the reason for their discharge?

**3.** The plaintiffs were, *in fact*, fired for "gross insubordination." According to the court, the issue was not whether the firing was proper, but whether the characterization of the discharge—knowing of the likely self-republication—was done with malice, so as to destroy the conditional privilege. Is this a plausible distinction or one jurors are likely to be able to draw? Did the case ultimately turn on whether the discharge was justified?

**4.** The court affirmed damages of $75,000 for each plaintiff based on defamation (as well as damages for breach of contract). The court reversed awards of $150,000 in punitive damages for each plaintiff on the ground that such an award would tend to encourage self-publication of defamatory statements and may deter employers from communicating reasons for discharge.

**5.** In 1987, the Minnesota legislature responded to *Lewis* by enacting a statute providing that an employee who has been discharged may, within five working days following the discharge, request in writing that the employer inform the employee of the reason for the discharge. The employer then has five working days to inform the employee in writing of the "truthful reason" for the discharge. The statement furnished to the employee may not be used as the basis of an action for defamation. Minn.Stat.Ann. § 181.933. What effect, if any, do you think this statute will have on claims for defamation? By contrast, the Colorado legislature has prohibited all defamation claims based on compelled self-publication. Colo.Rev.Stat.Ann. § 13–25–125.5. See generally Markita D. Cooper, Between a Rock and a Hard Case: Time for a New Doctrine of Compelled Self–Publication, 72 Notre Dame L.Rev. 373 (1997).

**6.** When Larry Buck was fired without reason by Frank B. Hall & Co., Buck hired a private investigator, Lloyd Barber, to discover Hall's true reasons for firing him. Barber contacted three managers of the Hall company. He told them he was an investigator, but claimed that he was seeking information about Buck because Buck was under consideration for a position of trust and responsibility with another company. Barber taped the interviews in which Buck was described as untrustworthy, untruthful, disruptive, paranoid, hostile, guilty of padding his expense account, irrational, ruthless, disliked by office personnel, a "classical sociopath," "a zero," and a Jekyll and Hyde personality who lacked scruples. Otherwise, they said he was a nice guy. Do these statements constitute actionable defamation? See Frank B. Hall & Co. v. Buck, 678 S.W.2d 612 (Tex.App. 1984), cert. denied, 472 U.S. 1009 (1985) (held: statements were published even though publishers were mistaken as to the identity of the person to whom the publication was made).

**7.**  At the turn of the century, one of the ways in which employers sought to dispel unionization was to circulate lists of former employees who were union organizers or members.  "Blacklisting" laws, which prohibit an employer from preventing or attempting to prevent a former employee from obtaining other employment, were enacted in 24 states.  See, e.g., N.M.Stat.Ann. § 30–13–3.  Eleven states have "service letter" laws, which require that employers state a specific cause for discharge.  See, e.g., Mo.Rev.Stat. § 290.140;  Stark v. American Bakeries Co., 647 S.W.2d 119 (Mo.1983).

## 4.  NEGLIGENT HIRING

The preceding sections of this chapter explored the ineffectiveness, inaccuracy, intrusiveness, and undesirability of many of the commonly used employee selection criteria.  What are the alternatives?  Is the appropriate reaction to the "perfect worker" syndrome for employers to use only minimal hiring criteria, with little or no inquiry into an employee's prior employment record?  Consider the following case.

## Malorney v. B & L Motor Freight, Inc.

496 N.E.2d 1086 (Ill.App.1986).

■ JUSTICE MURRAY delivered the opinion of the court:

This is an interlocutory appeal pursuant to Supreme Court Rule 308 by defendant B & L Motor Freight, Inc. (B & L) from a trial court order denying its motion for summary judgment.  This court granted defendant's motion for leave to appeal upon certification of the issue by the trial court. The issue certified is whether defendant had a duty under the circumstances of this case to investigate Edward Harbour's non-vehicular criminal record and to verify his negative response regarding criminal offenses which he furnished on his employment application prior to employing him and furnishing him an over-the-road truck with sleeping facilities.

The circumstances of this case are as follows.  Edward Harbour applied for a position of over-the-road driver with defendant B & L.  On the employment application, Harbour was questioned as to whether he had any vehicular offenses or other criminal convictions.  His response to the vehicular question was verified by B & L; however, his negative answer regarding criminal convictions was not verified by B & L.  In fact, Harbour had a history of convictions for violent sex-related crimes and had been arrested the year prior to his employment with B & L for aggravated sodomy of two teenage hitchhikers while driving an over-the-road truck for another employer.  Upon being hired by B & L, Harbour was given written instructions and regulations, including a prohibition against picking up hitchhikers in a B & L truck.

Subsequently, on January 24, 1978, at an Indiana toll road plaza, Harbour picked up plaintiff Karen Malorney, a 17-year-old hitchhiker. In the sleeping compartment of his truck, he repeatedly raped and sexually assaulted plaintiff, threatened to kill her, and viciously beat her. After being released, plaintiff notified police. Harbour was arrested, convicted, and sentenced to 50 years with no parole. Plaintiff's complaint charges defendant B & L with recklessness and wilful and wanton misconduct in negligently hiring Harbour as an over-the-road driver without adequately checking his background and providing him a vehicle with a sleeping compartment. Plaintiff seeks compensatory and punitive damages from B & L.

Defendant B & L filed a motion for summary judgment contending that it had no duty to verify Harbour's negative response to the question regarding criminal convictions. In denying defendant's motion, the trial court found that (1) Harbour was hired as an over-the-road driver and furnished with a truck equipped with sleeping quarters; (2) B & L instructed Harbour not to pick up hitchhikers; and (3) it is common knowledge that hitchhikers frequent toll plazas which would show that B & L knew drivers are prone to give rides to hitchhikers. The court concluded that these facts show that B & L had a duty to check Harbour's criminal background and certified the issue for interlocutory appeal.

Defendant argues that it had no duty to investigate Harbour's non-vehicular criminal background nor to verify his denial thereof because of a lack of foreseeability that he would use the truck to pick up and sexually assault a hitchhiker. To impose such a duty would be against public policy by placing too great a burden on employers. On the other hand, plaintiff posits the argument that factual issues exist which preclude summary judgment and require a jury determination. We agree and must affirm the trial court for the following reasons.

Defendant correctly argues that the existence of a duty is a question of law to be determined by the court, rather than by the factfinder. However, once a duty has been found, the question of whether the duty was properly performed is a fact question to be decided by the trier of fact, whether court or jury.

The existence of a legal duty is not dependent on foreseeability alone, but includes considerations of public policy and social requirements. In Illinois, two duties, among others not pertinent here, are imposed by law on owners of vehicles who permit or hire other persons to drive on our highways. The first duty requires that the degree of care which an owner should exercise in selecting a driver is that which a reasonable person would exercise under the circumstances. An owner or employer also owes a duty in connection with the entrustment of vehicles to others. In other words, a vehicle owner has a duty to deny the entrustment of a vehicle to a driver it knows, or by the exercise of reasonable diligence could have known, is incompetent. In addition to these duties, it is well settled in Illinois that a cause of action exists against an employer for negligently hiring a person the employer knew, or should have known, was unfit for the job.

B & L contends that a reasonable and prudent motor carrier could not foresee that one of its drivers would rape and assault a hitchhiker.   The court in Neering v. Illinois Central R.R. Co. (1943), 383 Ill. 366, 50 N.E.2d 497, in discussing foreseeability stated that the ultimate injury must be the natural and probable result of the negligent act or omission such that an ordinary and prudent person ought to have foreseen as likely its occurrence as a result of the negligence.   It is not essential that one should have foreseen the precise injury which resulted from the act or omission.   This interpretation thus requires an employer to exercise that degree of care reasonably commensurate with the perils and hazards likely to be encountered in the performance of an employee's duty, i.e., such care as a reasonably prudent person would exercise in view of the consequences that might reasonably be expected to result if an incompetent, careless, or reckless agent was employed for a particular duty.

Applying these principles to the present case, it is clear that B & L had a duty to entrust its truck to a competent employee fit to drive an over-the-road truck equipped with a sleeping compartment.   Lack of forethought may exist where one remains in voluntary ignorance of facts concerning the danger in a particular act or instrumentality, where a reasonably prudent person would become advised, on the theory that such ignorance is the equivalent of negligence.   Bearing in mind the facts that B & L gave Harbour an over-the-road vehicle with a sleeping compartment and that B & L probably knew, or should have known, that truckers are prone to give rides to hitchhikers despite rules against such actions, the question now becomes one of fact—whether B & L breached its duty to hire a competent driver who was to be entrusted with a B & L over-the-road truck.

Regarding defendant's public policy argument, there is no evidence in the record to justify the contention that the cost of checking on the criminal history of all truck driver applicants is too expensive and burdensome when measured against the potential utility of doing so.

Finally, we note that a question of foreseeability is at times a question for the court and at times, if varying inferences are possible, a question for the jury.   In the present case, B & L did have a duty to check into Harbour's background so as to ascertain whether he would be a fit employee.   Based on the circumstances of this case, it is apparent that reasonable persons could arrive at different conclusions as to whether B & L used due care in the performance of this duty when it employed Harbour. Questions which are composed of such qualities sufficient to cause reasonable persons to arrive at different results should never be determined as matters of law.   Questions of negligence, due care, and proximate cause are questions of fact to be determined by the factfinder.

In affirming the trial court's denial of summary judgment, we are not expressing any opinion as to the resolution of the facts in this case. Plaintiff has the heavy burden of proving that defendant B & L negligently performed a duty it owed her in entrusting Harbour with an over-the-road truck, and if negligence is found, that it proximately caused her injury. These questions, including the issue of whether defendant negligently hired Harbour by not checking his criminal background, are questions for the trier of fact and become a question of law only when the ultimate facts have been determined by the factfinder.

For these reasons, the order denying summary judgment for defendant is affirmed and the cause is remanded for further proceedings.

Affirmed and remanded.

■ LORENZ and PINCHAM, JJ., concur.

## NOTES AND QUESTIONS

**1.** If B & L had checked with Harbour's prior employer, do you think the prior employer would have been forthcoming with the information of his arrest for aggravated sodomy? Is there a reluctance to divulge this type of information for fear of liability for defamation? For a decision contrary to *Malorney* based on similar facts, see C.C. v. Roadrunner Trucking, Inc., 823 F.Supp. 913 (D.Utah 1993). Would B & L be liable if Harbour sexually assaulted a hotel clerk rather than a hitchhiker? See Connes v. Molalla Transport Systems, Inc., 831 P.2d 1316 (Colo.1992) (held: no liability under theory of negligent entrustment).

**2.** Suppose B & L hired Harbour based on reliance on a non-negative recommendation. Could Malorney sue Harbour's prior employer? See Moore v. St. Joseph Nursing Home, Inc., 459 N.W.2d 100 (Mich.App.1990) (former employer had no duty to disclose former employee's dangerous proclivities to inquiring prospective employer).

**3.** If the former employer knows of the former employee's dangerous proclivities, should there be a difference between giving no recommendation, giving a non-negative recommendation, and giving a positive recommendation? When Robert Gadams applied for the position of vice principal in the Livingston Union School District, his former employers wrote letters of recommendation for him in which they described him as dependable and reliable, as having a pleasant personality, as setting high standards, and as an "administrator who relates well to his students." They neglected to disclose that he had resigned under pressure due to charges of sexual misconduct involving several incidents of touching or molesting female students. Are these former employers liable when the individual is hired and then engages in additional acts of sexual misconduct? See Randi W. v. Muroc Joint Unified School District, 929 P.2d 582 (Cal.1997) (former employer writing a letter of recommendation owed to prospective employer and third persons a duty not to misrepresent the facts surrounding the qualifications and character of former employee).

Many employers believe they have been placed in a dilemma. If they fail to check out their employees, they may be liable for negligent hiring or some other tort. If they check out their employees too aggressively, they may be liable for invasion of privacy, discrimination, or some other cause of action. Is there a way to reconcile the employers' conflicting obligations?

See generally Stephen F. Befort, Pre-Employment Screening and Investigation: Navigating Between a Rock and a Hard Place, 14 Hofstra Lab.L.J. 365 (1997).

**4.**  In many states information about criminal convictions (or other contacts with the criminal justice system) is restricted, and not easily available to prospective or current employers.  See, e.g., Massachusetts Criminal Offender Record Information System Act, Mass.Gen.Laws Ch. 6 §§ 167–178; Massachusetts Fair Information Practices Act, Mass.Gen.Laws Ch. 66A §§ 1–3.  Some state laws allow persons to apply for jobs without revealing their criminal records.  See, e.g., Mass.Gen.Laws Ch. 276 § 100C.

**5.**  Suppose B & L refused to hire any person who had an arrest record. Would this be permissible?  Suppose blacks were shown to be arrested at a rate much greater than whites (especially arrests for "suspicion").  Would this policy violate Title VII?  See Gregory v. Litton Systems, Inc., 316 F.Supp. 401 (C.D.Cal.1970), modified on other grounds, 472 F.2d 631 (9th Cir.1972) (held: yes).  Suppose the policy were limited to convictions?  See Green v. Missouri Pacific Railroad, 549 F.2d 1158 (8th Cir.1977) (held: to be lawful, policy must consider the nature and gravity of the offense, the time elapsed since conviction, and the nature of the job involved).

**6.**  There are two types of negligent hiring cases.  First, the employee injures some third party.  E.g., *Malorney*; Cramer v. Housing Opportunities Commission, 501 A.2d 35 (Md.1985).  Second, the employee injures a co-employee.  In the second type of case the issue is often raised whether the injured worker's exclusive remedy is workers' compensation.  See Sheerin v. Holin Co., 380 N.W.2d 415 (Iowa 1986) (injured workers permitted to sue employer in tort).  For a further discussion of actions brought against employers for workplace injuries and illnesses, see Chapter 9.

**7.**  A preemployment psychological test reveals that an applicant for a job as a pharmaceutical sales representative was a person of "high aggression." The man was hired and, while on a sales trip, got into a fight with another motorist.  Is the employer liable for negligent hiring?  See Thatcher v. Brennan, 657 F.Supp. 6 (S.D.Miss.1986) (held: no; "high aggression" is not synonymous with "violent"), affirmed mem., 816 F.2d 675 (5th Cir. 1987).

**8.**  Does the tort of negligent hiring require proof that the misconduct was within the wrongdoer's scope of employment?  See J. v. Victory Tabernacle Baptist Church, 372 S.E.2d 391 (Va.1988) (held: no; negligent hiring is independent tort and is not dependent on respondeat superior).

**9.**  In Haybeck v. Prodigy Services Co., 944 F.Supp. 326 (S.D.N.Y.1996), the plaintiff met a Prodigy employee in an on-line sex chat room that he ran for Prodigy.  She later became HIV positive after having unprotected sex with him and sued Prodigy.  In dismissing the action the court held that there was no respondent superior liability because the employee's alleged concealing of his HIV status was not within the scope of employment.  In addition, under New York law, an employer's duty in negligent hiring and retention cases is limited.  "Here, the conduct complained of, whether it is the act of sex or [the employee's] failure to disclose his HIV status, unquestionably took place outside the employer's premises and without the employer's chattels."

**10.**   In Board of County Commissioners of Bryan County v. Brown, 117 S.Ct. 1382 (1997), the Supreme Court held that a municipality was not liable under 42 U.S.C. § 1983 where one of its police officers allegedly used excessive force in making an arrest.  "Deliberate action" rather than mere negligent hiring is required to establish a constitutional violation.  "A failure to apply stringent culpability and causation requirements raises serious federalism concerns, in that it risks constitutionalizing particular hiring requirements that States have themselves not elected to impose."

**11.**   The National Child Protection Act of 1993, 42 U.S.C. § 5119, establishes procedures for national criminal background checks for child care workers.  In each state, an authorized criminal justice agency reports child abuse crime information to the national criminal history background check system.  The states may then require certain "entities"—public, private, for-profit, not-for-profit, or voluntary providers of child care or child care placement services—to contact the authorized state agency to request a national background check on the individual to determine if the individual "has been convicted of a crime that bears upon an individual's fitness to have responsibility for the safety and well-being of children."

**12.**   Should there be any limits placed on an employer's ability to refuse to hire an individual for any job because of the individual's prior criminal record?  If, upon completing their sentences for any crime, all ex-convicts were unemployable, then they would be much more likely to engage in future criminal conduct.  Is there a way for public policy to balance both the public interests at stake?  Cf. Selix v. Boeing Co., 919 P.2d 620 (Wash.Ct.App.1996), review denied, 930 P.2d 1230 (Wash.1997) (discharge of employee based on prior assault conviction did not violate public policy of rehabilitation of felons).

---

## D.   TRUTH-DETECTING DEVICES AND PSYCHOLOGICAL AND PERSONALITY TESTING

### 1.   THE POLYGRAPH

### Office of Technology Assessment, U.S. Congress, Scientific Validity of Polygraph Testing
11 (1983).

**Polygraph Instrument**

Although there are numerous variations in testing procedures, the polygraph instrument itself is fairly standard.  The polygraph measures several, usually three, physiological indicators of arousal.  Changes in physiological arousal exhibited in response to a set of questions are taken to indicate deception or truthfulness.  The polygraph instrument, it should be noted, is not a "lie detector" per se; i.e., it does not indicate directly whether a subject is being deceptive or truthful.  There is no known physiological response that is unique to deception.  Instead, a polygraph examiner obtains a subject's responses to a carefully structured set of questions, and based on the pattern of arousal responses, infers the subject's veracity.  This assessment has been called the "diagnosis" of truthfulness or deception.

In actual field testing, subjects' physiological responses are measured by a three- or four-channel polygraph machine that records responses on a moving chart.  Usually, three different types of physiological responses are measured.  The rate and depth of respiration is measured by pneumographs strapped around the chest and the abdomen.  A blood pressure cuff (sphygmomanometer) placed around the bicep is used to measure cardiovascular activity.  In modern polygraph instruments, sphygmomanometer readings are electronically enhanced so as to permit lower pressure in the cuff.  The electrodermal response (EDR), a measure of perspiration, requires electrodes attached to the fingertips.  This has also been referred to as galvanic skin response (GSR) or skin conductance response (SCR).  Each of these physiological assessments has been shown to be related to physiological arousal.  There is some literature to suggest that one or more of the physiological channels (EDR, in particular) is most sensitive.  Actual field testing, however, almost always involves measurement of all three types of responses.

NOTE

The 1983 study by the Congressional Office of Technology Assessment (OTA) is the most detailed review of the literature on the accuracy of polygraphs in various settings.

Although there have been a number of studies of polygraphs, only two have been done on the use of polygraphs in the preemployment setting.  OTA considered one of the studies to have "a number of problems" with its methodology and the other study to "raise serious questions about the usefulness * * * of polygraph testing for preemployment and counterintelligence purposes, especially if done alone."  A review of the nonemployment literature suggested accuracy rates varying from 50 percent to 90 percent.

"OTA concluded that, while there is some evidence for the validity of polygraph testing as an adjunct to criminal investigations, there is very little research or scientific evidence to establish polygraph test validity in screening situations, whether they be preemployment, preclearance, periodic or aperiodic, random, or 'dragnet.' "

A recent survey of psychologists and psychophysiologists indicated that most respondents believed that polygraphic lie detection is not theoretically sound, claims of high validity for these tests cannot be sustained, the tests can be beaten by easily learned countermeasures, and polygraph results should not be admitted into evidence in courts of law.  W.G. Iacono & D.T.

Lykken, The Validity of the Lie Detector: Two Surveys of Scientific Opinion, 82 J. Applied Psychology 426 (1997).

The polygraph actually is most accurate in the law enforcement setting because, through traditional detective work, the pool of suspects given examinations is likely to have a relatively high percentage of guilty persons. By contrast, when polygraphs are used where there is a lower percentage of guilty persons, such as in mass preemployment screening, the accuracy of the test goes down sharply. Yet, polygraph results are inadmissible in criminal cases but are responsible for thousands of employment decisions.

Despite scientific evidence of the inaccuracy of polygraphs, numerous employers assert that they are highly effective in screening out workers who steal and engage in other forms of misconduct. In fact, often the reason for the "effectiveness" of the polygraph is that many people who take polygraphs think the test is accurate and that it will detect lies. Therefore, they admit to various kinds of wrongdoing and are not hired or are fired as a result. The polygraph is credited with ferreting out these people. Is influencing people to divulge wrongdoing a justification for using polygraphs?

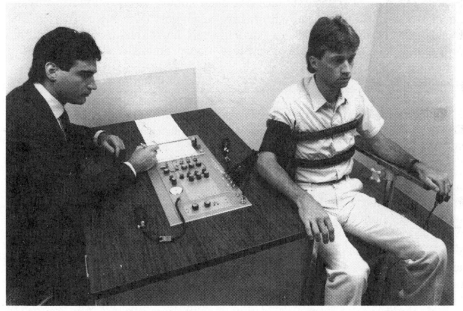

Photo courtesy of John E. Reid and Associates, Inc. The examiner is Michael Adamec and the subject is portrayed by Michael Masokas, both of John E. Reid and Associates, Inc. Note: Pneumograph tubes are placed around the subject's chest and abdomen to measure abdominal and thoracic respiration; the blood pressure cuff around the right arm measures blood pressure and pulse; electrodes attached to two fingers of the left hand measure galvanic skin response; the back of the chair and the chair seat have inflatable rubber bladders to record muscular contractions and pressures. The subject is placed in a position so that he or she looks straight ahead, with the instrument and examiner to the right side and rear.

## EMPLOYEE POLYGRAPH PROTECTION ACT

The federal Employee Polygraph Protection Act, 29 U.S.C. §§ 2001–2009, went into effect in 1988.  The Act, applicable to most private employers, prohibits most uses of polygraphs in employment.  The Act does not prohibit the use of paper and pencil honesty questionnaires or tests.  Employers who violate the Act are subject to a civil penalty of $10,000, injunctive actions by the Secretary of Labor, and private civil actions.

The Act contains the following exemptions:  (1) it does not apply to federal, state, or local government employers;  (2) it does not prohibit the testing by the federal government of experts, consultants, or employees of federal contractors engaged in national security intelligence or counterintelligence;  (3) it permits the testing of employees who are reasonably suspected of involvement in a workplace incident that results in economic loss or injury to the employer's business;  (4) it permits the testing of some prospective employees of private armored car, security alarm, and security guard firms;  and (5) it permits the testing of some current and prospective employees in firms authorized to manufacture, distribute, or dispense controlled substances.

In polygraph examinations under the last three exemptions, some specific additional provisions apply.  Among other things, the examinee may not be asked any questions about religious beliefs, racial beliefs, political beliefs, sexual behavior, or union affiliation. See Mennen v. Easter Stores, 951 F.Supp. 838 (N.D.Iowa 1997) (employer violated Employee Polygraph Protection Act where it failed to comply with procedural guidelines for use of polygraph to investigate theft).

The Act is enforced by the Secretary of Labor, who has promulgated implementing regulations at 29 C.F.R. Part 801.

## NOTES AND QUESTIONS

**1.**  As many as two million polygraphs were performed each year in the private sector prior to the passage of the Employee Polygraph Protection Act.  Roughly 85 percent of these polygraphs are now prohibited.

**2.**  Before enactment of the federal law in 1988, 18 states and the District of Columbia had laws regulating or prohibiting the use of polygraphs, 25 states had licensing requirements for polygraph examiners, and only 14 states neither prohibited polygraphs nor licensed examiners.

**3.**  The Employee Polygraph Protection Act prohibits the use of polygraphs by "employers."  Is a company that performs polygraphs under contract for the employer amenable to suit by an employee as a statutory "employer"?  See Rubin v. Tourneau, Inc., 797 F.Supp. 247 (S.D.N.Y.1992) (held:  defendant's motion to dismiss denied).

**4.**  Is it possible for the victim of an alleged erroneous polygraph examination to bring a negligence action against the polygraph examiner?  See Zampatori v. United Parcel Service, 479 N.Y.S.2d 470 (Sup.Ct.1984) (held: yes).

## PROBLEM FOR DISCUSSION: SHOULD POLYGRAPHS BE USED IN THE PREEMPLOYMENT SETTING?

Joe Smith applies for the job of security guard with Ace Security Company. Ace has the contract to supply security guards at a day care center. At a preemployment polygraph examination he is asked the following question: "Have you ever molested a child?" Joe says "no." The polygraph examiner claims he is lying.

Assume that 1% of applicants *have* molested children (a high estimate). Further assume that the polygraph is 80% "accurate" (a high estimate). Note: 80% accurate means that the polygraph can correctly identify as positive 80% of all individuals tested who have the tested-for trait (sensitivity) and can correctly identify as negative 80% of all individuals who do not have the tested-for trait (specificity).

If 1,000 applicants were given a polygraph the results would be as follows:

| Subjects | No. with Positive Test | No. with Negative Test |
|---|---|---|
| 10 child molesters | 8 (true positives) | 2 (false negatives) |
| 990 Not child molesters | 198 (false positives) | 792 (true negatives) |

Of the 206 individuals with a positive test result only 8 would actually be child molesters. The predictive value of any positive result is $\frac{8}{206}$, or 3.88%. Therefore, even if Joe has a "positive" test result the odds of him actually being a child molester are only 1 in 25.

1. You are an attorney who has been called by Joe. He really needs the job and feels terribly that people think that he might be a child molester. He knows that the administrator of the day care center (who approves all security guards) is considering whether to accept the polygraph findings. You schedule a meeting with the administrator to argue that the polygraph is unreliable. What arguments would you make?

2. Suppose you were counsel to Ace or the day care center. Using the polygraph is 4 times more accurate than not using anything. In addition, if you find another applicant who "passes" the polygraph, the predictive value (negative) is $\frac{792}{794}$ or 99.7%. Thus, you would be 99.7% sure that the person you hired would not be a child molester. What responsibility does the day care center owe to the children and their parents? What do you recommend?

## 2.   OTHER TRUTH–DETECTING DEVICES AND PSYCHOLOGICAL AND PERSONALITY TESTS

### David T. Lykken, A Tremor in the Blood *
195–96, 199–201 (1981).

In the fall of 1976, the Minnesota Legislature was considering a bill to ban polygraph testing of employees.  An unexpected witness at the first committee hearing was Sister Terressa, a member of a teaching order, whose forthright and determined manner carried no suggestion of the cloister.  She told the committee that some months earlier she had applied for a part-time job with B. Dalton Bookstores in Minneapolis.  The application procedure included a disconcerting questionnaire called the Reid Report.  Inquiry revealed that B. Dalton used the results on this test, scored by John E. Reid Associates in Chicago, as their basis for assessing the trustworthiness of potential employees.  After weeks had passed without further word, Sister Terressa called the bookstore to learn the fate of her application.  She was told that she had been rejected because of her performance on the Reid Report.  "They said I had the lowest score on the 'honesty test' that they had ever seen!"  Partly because of Sister Terressa's indignant and effective testimony, the present Minnesota statute forbids the use in employment applications of polygraph tests, voice stress analysis, or "any test purporting to test the honesty of any employee or prospective employee."

The misclassification of one outraged nun is not a sufficient reason for the statutory prohibition of a test.  B. Dalton, like every other retailer, suffers losses from employee theft.  If the Reid Report is generally accurate as a predictor of trustworthiness, then its use will diminish these losses.  No test, no predictor, is perfect;  if an employer uses any selection criterion whatsoever, then there will be a few persons rejected, like Sister Terressa, who would have been entirely satisfactory employees.

\* \* \*

The new honesty questionnaires like the Reid Report, the Stanton Survey, the Personnel Security Inventory, were constructed by polygraphers for use by business clients unwilling or unable to pay the higher cost of polygraph screening.  The provenance of these questionnaires is readily apparent when one studies the test items.  One group of questions invites the respondent to admit to various crimes misdemeanors ranging from homicide, to forgery, to stealing from the company, to lying to the boss.  These yes-no items are supplemented by rating scales such as:

What total value in merchandise and property have you taken without permission from employers?  (Circle nearest value.)

$5,000   $2,500   $1,000   $750   $500   $250   $100   $50   $0

Or:

* Reprinted by permission of McGraw-Hill Book Company, New York, N.Y.

How honest are you?  Be objective and do not exaggerate.

| High Above Average | Above Average | About Average | Slightly Below Average | Below Average |
|---|---|---|---|---|

Dr. Philip Ash, research director for the Reid organization, explains: "Incredible as it may seem, applicants in significant numbers do admit to practically every crime in the books."

Supplementing these "admissions" items are sets of questions intended to measure the respondent's "punitiveness" and his "attitudes toward theft."  Typical "punitiveness" items are:

An employer discovers that a long-service, trusted employee has been taking a few dollars out of the cash register every week. Should the employer have him arrested?

Or:

What should be done if an employee occasionally smokes marijuana on the job?  (Circle one)

| Ignore | Warn | Suspend | Fire | Arrest |
|---|---|---|---|---|

Some "theft attitude" items:

How many people that you know are really honest?

| 95% | 80% | 60% | 40% | 20% | 5% |
|---|---|---|---|---|---|

How many employees take small things from their employers from time to time?

| 95% | 80% | 60% | 40% | 20% | 5% |
|---|---|---|---|---|---|

How many people cheat on their income tax?

| 95% | 80% | 60% | 40% | 20% | 5% |
|---|---|---|---|---|---|

If you would like to see how you might fare on an honesty test, decide how you would answer these sample questions.  Did you recommend jailing that old, trusted employee who's been taking a few dollars from the till each week?  And also the young man caught smoking marijuana?  Then you are doing well so far.  Did you say that nearly all the people you know are really honest?  And did you think that almost no one steals from his employer or cheats on his income taxes?  Then, unless you have confessed to something serious on the "admissions" questions, you will probably get the job.

The rationale for such scoring is that a thief will be unlikely to recommend harsh punishment for acts he might himself commit and he will probably contend that most people are as dishonest as he.  The trouble with this rationale is that the logic does not work in both directions.  It is not likely that most people who recommend leniency are thieves.  It is not true that all those who see the world as a sinful place are great sinners themselves.  Ironically, polygraphers insist that most employees are occasionally dishonest and they are so sure that most people cheat on their income taxes that this situation is often used as a "known lie" control question in polygraph tests. Yet, when a job applicant reveals a similar degree of cynicism on the honesty questionnaire, the report to the employer will be "Not recommended for employment."

We can now begin to understand why it was that Sister Terressa got such a bad score on the Reid Report. We may doubt that she had anything sinister to reveal on the "admissions" questions (although no doubt she honestly confessed whatever youthful misdeeds she could remember). But Sister Terressa was handicapped by Christian charity, which ensured that she would do badly on the "punitiveness" items. And she was an intelligent, educated woman, with some experience of the world, and these qualities prevented her from expressing the naive assessment of humankind required to do well on the "attitude toward theft" items. A clever thief might achieve a good score on the honesty questionnaire—by answering deceptively. But, if the questions are to be answered honestly, then what is required is a punitive, authoritarian personality combined with a worldview like that of the three monkeys who hear-no-evil, see-no-evil, speak-no-evil. Oh, brave new world of work, that has such creatures in it!

## NOTES AND QUESTIONS

**1.** In 1988, an estimated 3.5 million honesty tests were given to applicants and employees. These tests are only prohibited in Massachusetts, Mass. Gen.Laws Ann. ch. 149, § 19(B)(1). In Rhode Island they may be used so long as they are not the "primary basis for an employment decision." R.I.Gen.Laws §§ 28–6.1–1 to 28–6.1–4. In all other states they may be used without qualification.

**2.** States without legislation specifically prohibiting written honesty tests have been unsuccessful in using their anti-polygraph laws against these tests. For example, in State v. Century Camera, Inc., 309 N.W.2d 735 (Minn.1981), the Supreme Court of Minnesota construed the state anti-polygraph law's language prohibiting the use of "any test purporting to test honesty." It held that the prohibition is limited to tests which "purport to measure physiological changes in the subject tested * * *." Therefore, the prohibition does not apply to written honesty questionnaires. The court was concerned that without such a construction the statute would be unconstitutionally vague. See also Pluskota v. Roadrunner Freight Systems, Inc., 524 N.W.2d 904 (Wis.App.1994) review denied, 531 N.W.2d 325 (Wis.1995) (Wisconsin law barring employer's use of polygraphs, voice stress analysis, or psychological stress evaluators does not extend to paper and pencil honesty tests). See generally David C. Yamada, The Regulation of Pre–Employment Honesty Testing: Striking a Temporary(?) Balance Between Self–Regulation and Prohibition, 39 Wayne L.Rev. 1549 (1993); Katrin U. Byford, Comment, The Quest for the Honest Worker: A Proposal for Regulation of Integrity Testing, 49 S.M.U.L.Rev. 329 (1996).

**3.** One part of the Reid Report includes 100 questions about theft and honesty. A second part includes 93 questions about gambling, drinking, drug habits, outstanding loans, alimony, spouse's salary, and other matters. The honesty section is scored by Reid Associates, which reports to the employer that the applicant is recommended for employment, qualifiedly recommended, not recommended, or gives no opinion. The 93-item factual questionnaire with the personal data is returned to the employer to be placed in the employee's personnel file.

**4.** The Reid Report is most commonly used in banks, discount stores, insurance companies, drug stores, brokerage houses, trucking firms, and fast food restaurants.

**5.** Would a claim for wrongful discharge lie based on the refusal to take the Reid Report or based on its results?

**6.** What legal actions could have been brought by Sister Terressa?

**7.** Another test used by employers is the Psychological Stress Evaluator (PSE). This and other voice analyzers seek to detect the tension in the voice of someone who is lying. Some employers use the PSE to analyze tape recordings of telephone conversations with applicants, who are asked questions on the phone. Presumably, this is less expensive than a personal interview.

## PROBLEM FOR DISCUSSION: PREVENTING EMPLOYEE THEFT

Estimates of the amount of employee theft in the United States each year range from $10 to $50 billion. If polygraphs and honesty questionnaires cannot be used, what is an employer to do? Would shifting the focus from the hiring stage to the working stage be better or would employers be encouraged to use surveillance cameras, locker searches, frisking of workers, and other techniques that are actually more invasive than an honesty questionnaire or polygraph?

Dr. Lykken, an outspoken critic of polygraphs, recommends checking references more closely, instituting better security procedures, boosting employee morale such as through profit-sharing plans, and nonintrusive surveillance and sanctions. Are these measures likely to be effective? Do they raise other legal or economic concerns?

If you represented a retailer, what would you recommend?

## William D. Hooker, *Psychological Testing in the Workplace* *

11 Occup.Med.: State of the Art Revs. 699 (1996).

Psychological testing has played a significant role in the workplace for more than 50 years. This involvement continues to grow as the number of disability and accommodation claims increase and as ongoing psychology research in personnel selection and productivity assists employers to pick the right person for the job. At least 3,000 different tests are sold commercially by at least 450 vendors targeted at the workplace. In the

* Reprinted by permission.

testing situation, the behavior or test response is measured in correctness, speed, accuracy, or quality.

Psychological tests are used extensively in preemployment screening and personnel selection. Selecting the right person for the job is the goal of using achievement, aptitude, and personality tests at the preemployment stage. Achievement tests measure proficiency in a specific area. Achievement tests are used in personnel selection if the specific knowledge, skill, or ability (KSAs) relevant to that job can be identified. It is assumed that the knowledge, skill, or ability being measured on the test is transferable to the task demands of the job itself. Achievement tests can take the form of paper-and-pencil tests, hands-on demonstrations, or work samples. Examples of achievement tests are a multiple-choice test of drug knowledge for a pharmacy technician applicant, a hand-on demonstration of a word processing program by a transcriptionist applicant, or a medical board examination for a physician.

Aptitude testing is commonly used instead of achievement testing because most jobs are too multifaceted for achievement testing to be practical. Aptitude tests are used as a general measure of a person's potential to learn a specific body of knowledge. Aptitude tests are extensively used in the military and civilian workplace as personnel selection tools because they generally do a good job of predicting overall job performance. Types of aptitude tests include measures of manual dexterity, psychomotor speed, verbal reasoning, numerical ability, spatial perception and reasoning, ability to learn and remember, and other cognitive abilities. They are sometimes referred to as cognitive ability tests. Cognitive ability tests that have predictive validity for subsequent job performance are used for personnel selection. Other specialized tests of cognitive ability, such as intelligence and neuropsychological measures, are used in evaluations of disability, fitness for duty, and vocational rehabilitation.

The last type of psychological testing is personality and psychological functioning assessment. These tests measure personality traits, temperament, personal preferences, interests and attitudes, ways of thinking about oneself, styles of relating to others, and psychological symptoms and problems. In the personnel selection phase, these types of tests have special applications as well as limitations. A limited version of personality testing termed "honesty" or "integrity" tests are increasingly used to select employees who will more likely display productive workplace behavior. More extensive personality testing is frequently used in personnel selection for high-risk jobs in which public safety is at stake. Personality and psychological functioning tests are extensively used in disability, fitness for duty, and vocational rehabilitation evaluations.

The development and use of psychological tests in a scientifically valid manner is one of the major attributes that defines the field of psychology and distinguishes it from psychiatry or social work. Psychological tests are different from the pop questionnaires found in self-help magazines. They must meet technical standards for construction and validation based on research, and users would possess the test knowledge and professional training to use them correctly.  Not all psychological tests that are market-ed to the employer meet scientific standards.  Information about the reliability and validity of tests targeted for the workplace is not uniformly made available by the publishers.  The employer using these tests for personnel selection is legally bound to demonstrate that the test is valid and necessary to fill a specific job.  Employers must rely on publishers' claims that these tests are valid for their intended use.  However, the literature from some of the smaller or single-test publishers are often full of exaggerated claims and the potential for misuse is high.  Not all test users will understand the test and recognize its applications and its limitations.

## Soroka v. Dayton Hudson Corp.

1 Cal.Rptr.2d 77 (Cal.App.1991), review dismissed, 862 P.2d 148 (Cal.1993).

■ REARDON, ASSOCIATE JUSTICE.

Appellants Sibi Soroka, Sue Urry and William d'Arcangelo filed a class action challenging respondent Dayton Hudson Corporation's practice of requiring Target Store security officer applicants to pass a psychological screening.  The trial court denied Soroka's motion for a preliminary injunction to prohibit the use of this screening pending the outcome of this litigation.  It also denied Soroka's motion for class certification and grant-ed Dayton Hudson Corporation's motion to deny class certification.  Soroka appeals from these orders, contending that a preliminary injunction should issue because he is likely to prevail on the merits of his constitutional and statutory claims.  He also urges us to find that the trial court should have certified the class.  The American Civil Liberties Union (ACLU) filed an amicus brief in support of Soroka's constitutional right to privacy claims. We reverse the trial court's order denying a preliminary injunction and remand the matter to the trial court for further proceedings on class certification.

### FACTS

Respondent Dayton Hudson Corporation owns and operates Target Stores throughout California and the United States.  Job applicants for store security officer (SSO) positions must, as a condition of employment, take a psychological test that Target calls the "Psychscreen."  An SSO's main function is to observe, apprehend and arrest suspected shoplifters. An SSO is not armed, but carries handcuffs and may use force against a suspect in self-defense.  Target views good judgment and emotional stabili-ty as important SSO job skills.  It intends the Psychscreen to screen out SSO applicants who are emotionally unstable, who may put customers or employees in jeopardy, or who will not take direction and follow Target procedures.

The Psychscreen is a combination of the Minnesota Multiphasic Per-sonality Inventory and the California Psychological Inventory.  Both of these tests have been used to screen out emotionally unfit applicants for public safety positions such as police officers, correctional officers, pilots, air traffic controllers and nuclear power plant operators. The test is composed of 704 true-false questions. At Target, the test administrator is told to instruct applicants to answer every question.

The test includes questions about an applicant's religious attitudes, such as: "[¶] 67. I feel sure that there is only one true religion.... [¶] 201. I have no patience with people who believe there is only one true religion.... [¶] 477. My soul sometimes leaves my body.... [¶] 483. A minister can cure disease by praying and putting his hand on your head.... [¶] 486. Everything is turning out just like the prophets of the Bible said it would.... [¶] 505. I go to church almost every week. [¶] 506. I believe in the second coming of Christ.... [¶] 516. I believe in a life hereafter.... [¶] 578. I am very religious (more than most people).... [¶] 580. I believe my sins are unpardonable.... [¶] 606. I believe there is a God.... [¶] 688. I believe there is a Devil and a Hell in afterlife."

The test includes questions that might reveal an applicant's sexual orientation, such as: "[¶] 137. I wish I were not bothered by thoughts about sex.... [¶] 290. I have never been in trouble because of my sex behavior.... [¶] 339. I have been in trouble one or more times because of my sex behavior.... [¶] 466. My sex life is satisfactory.... [¶] 492. I am very strongly attracted by members of my own sex.... [¶] 496. I have often wished I were a girl. (Or if you are a girl) I have never been sorry that I am a girl.... [¶] 525. I have never indulged in any unusual sex practices.... [¶] 558. I am worried about sex matters.... [¶] 592. I like to talk about sex.... [¶] 640. Many of my dreams are about sex matters." [5]

An SSO's completed test is scored by the consulting psychologist firm of Martin–McAllister. The firm interprets test responses and rates the applicant on five traits: emotional stability, interpersonal style, addiction potential, dependability and reliability, and socialization—i.e., a tendency to follow established rules. Martin–McAllister sends a form to Target rating the applicant on these five traits and recommending whether to hire the applicant. Hiring decisions are made on the basis of these recommendations, although the recommendations may be overridden. Target does not receive any responses to specific questions. It has never conducted a formal validation study of the Psychscreen, but before it implemented the test, Target tested 17 or 18 of its more successful SSO's.

Appellants Sibi Soroka, Susan Urry and William d'Arcangelo were applicants for SSO positions when they took the Psychscreen. All three were upset by the nature of the Psychscreen questions. Soroka was hired by Target. Urry—a Mormon—and d'Arcangelo were not hired. In August 1989, Soroka filed a charge that use of the Psychscreen discriminated on

**5.** Soroka challenges many different types of questions on appeal. However, we do not find it necessary to consider questions other than those relating to religious beliefs and sexual orientation.

the basis of race, sex, religion and physical handicap with the Department of Fair Employment and Housing.

Having exhausted their administrative remedies, Soroka, Urry and d'Arcangelo filed a class action against Target in September 1989 to challenge its use of the Psychscreen. The complaint was amended twice. The second amended complaint alleged that the test asked invasive questions that were not job-related. Soroka alleged causes of action for violation of the constitutional right to privacy, invasion of privacy, disclosure of confidential medical information, fraud, negligent misrepresentation, intentional and negligent infliction of emotional distress, violation of the Fair Employment and Housing Act, violation of sections 1101 and 1102 of the Labor Code, and unfair business practices. This complaint prayed for both damages and injunctive relief.

In June 1990, Soroka moved for a preliminary injunction to prohibit Target from using the Psychscreen during the pendency of the action. A professional psychologist submitted a declaration opinion that use of the test was unjustified and improper, resulting in faulty assessments to the detriment of job applicants. He concluded that its use violated basic professional standards and that it had not been demonstrated to be reliable or valid as an employment evaluation. For example, one of the two tests on which the Psychscreen was based was designed for use only in hospital or clinical settings. Soroka noted that two of Target's experts had previously opined that the Minnesota Multiphasic Personality Inventory was virtually useless as a preemployment screening device. It was also suggested that the Psychscreen resulted in a 61 percent rate of false positives—that is, that more than 6 in 10 qualified applicants for SSO positions were not hired.

Target's experts submitted declarations contesting these conclusions and favoring the use of the Psychscreen as an employment screening device. Some Target officials believed that use of this test has increased the quality and performance of its SSO's. However, others testified that they did not believe that there had been a problem with the reliability of SSO applicants before the Psychscreen was implemented. Target's vice president of loss prevention was unable to link changes in asset protection specifically to use of the Psychscreen. In rebuttal, Soroka's experts were critical of the conclusions of Target's experts. One rebuttal expert noted that some of the intrusive, non-job-related questions had been deleted from a revised form of the test because they were offensive, invasive and added little to the test's validity.

The trial court denied Soroka's motion to certify the class and granted Target's motion to deny class certification. The court concluded that the case was not an appropriate one for certification because of the predominantly individual nature of the claims. It found no well-defined community of interest among class members. The court also denied the motion because it could not conclude that the class would be fairly and adequately represented by Soroka, Urry, d'Arcangelo and their counsel, although it noted that counsel was extremely qualified in employment litigation. The court stated that because Soroka's answers to the Psychscreen test that he took had twice been made public, that disclosure would likely be an issue of substantial import to the invasion of privacy claims at trial.

The trial court also denied Soroka's motion for preliminary injunction. It ruled that he had not demonstrated a reasonable probability of prevailing on the merits of the constitutional or statutory claims at a trial.  The court found that Target demonstrated a legitimate interest in psychologically screening applicants for security positions to minimize the potential danger to its customers and others.  It also found that Target's practice of administering this test to SSO applicants was not unreasonable.  Finally, the trial court denied both parties' motions for summary adjudication. This appeal followed.

* * *

## A.   *Constitutional Claim*

First, Soroka argues that he is likely to prevail at trial on his constitutional right to privacy claim.  The parties dispute the standard to be applied to determine whether Target's violation of Soroka's privacy was justified.  In order to understand the various legal issues underlying this contention, a review of the basic legal concepts that guide us is in order.

### 1.   *The Right to Privacy*

The California Constitution explicitly protects our right to privacy. Article I, section 1 provides: "All people are by nature free and independent and have inalienable rights.  Among these are enjoying and defending life and liberty, acquiring, possessing, and protecting property, and pursuing and obtaining safety, happiness, and privacy." "By this provision, California accords privacy the constitutional status of an inalienable right, on a par with defending life and possessing property."  Before this constitutional amendment was enacted, California courts had found a state and federal constitutional right to privacy even though such a right was not enumerated in either constitution, and had consistently given a broad reading to the right to privacy.  Thus, the elevation of the right to privacy to constitutional stature was intended to expand, not contract, privacy rights.

Target concedes that the Psychscreen constitutes an intrusion on the privacy rights of the applicants, although it characterizes this intrusion as a limited one.  However, even the constitutional right to privacy does not prohibit *all* incursion into individual privacy.  The parties agree that a violation of the right to privacy may be justified, but disagree about the standard to be used to make this determination.  At trial, Target persuaded the court to apply a reasonableness standard because Soroka was an applicant, rather than a Target employee.  On appeal, Soroka and the ACLU contend that Target must show more than reasonableness—that it must demonstrate a compelling interest—to justify its use of the Psychscreen.

2. *Applicants vs. Employees*

Soroka and the ACLU contend that job applicants are entitled to the protection of the compelling interest test, just as employees are. The trial court disagreed, employing a reasonableness standard enunciated in a decision of Division Three of this District which distinguished between applicants and employees.

In Wilkinson v. Times Mirror Corp., 215 Cal.App.3d 1034, 264 Cal. Rptr. 194 (1989), a book publisher required job applicants to submit to drug urinalysis as part of its preemployment physical examination. The appellate court rejected the applicants' contention that the compelling interest test should apply to determine whether the publisher's invasion of their privacy interests was justified under article I, section 1. Instead, the court fashioned and applied a lesser standard based on whether the challenged conduct was reasonable. When setting this standard, the most persuasive factor for the *Wilkinson* court appears to have been that the plaintiffs were applicants for employment rather than employees. "Any individual who chooses to seek employment necessarily also chooses to disclose certain personal information to prospective employers, such as employment and educational history, and to allow the prospective employer to verify that information." This applicant-employee distinction was pivotal for the *Wilkinson* court. "Simply put, applicants for jobs * * * have a choice; they may consent to the limited invasion of their privacy resulting from the testing, or may decline both the test and the conditional offer of employment."

Our review of the ballot argument satisfies us that the voters did not intend to grant less privacy protection to job applicants than to employees. The ballot argument specifically refers to job applicants when it states that Californians "are required to report some information, regardless of our wishes for privacy or our belief that there is no public need for the information. Each time we * * * *interview for a job,* * * * a dossier is opened and an informational profile is sketched." (Ballot Pamp., Proposed Amends. to Cal. Const. with arguments to voters, Gen. Elec. (Nov. 7, 1972) p. 27, emphasis added.) Thus, the major underpinning of *Wilkinson* is suspect.

Appellate court decisions predating *Wilkinson* have also applied the compelling interest standard in cases involving job applicants. Target attempts to distinguish these cases as ones involving public, not private, employers, but that is a distinction without a difference in the context of the state constitutional right to privacy. Private and public employers alike are bound by the terms of the privacy provisions of article I, section 1.

The legislative history and the prior California law are sufficient to convince us that no distinction should be made between the privacy rights of job applicants and employees.

* * *

In conclusion, we are satisfied that any violation of the right to privacy of job applicants must be justified by a compelling interest. This conclusion is consistent with the voter's expression of intent when they amended article I, section 1 to make privacy an inalienable right and with subsequent decisions of the California Supreme Court.

### 3.   *Nexus Requirement*

Soroka and the ACLU also argue that Target has not demonstrated that its Psychscreen questions are job-related—i.e., that they provide information relevant to the emotional stability of its SSO applicants. Having considered the religious belief and sexual orientation questions carefully, we find this contention equally persuasive.

Although the state right of privacy is broader than the federal right, California courts construing article I, section 1 have looked to federal precedents for guidance.  Under the lower federal standard, employees may not be compelled to submit to a violation of their right to privacy unless a clear, direct nexus exists between the nature of the employee's duty and the nature of the violation.  We are satisfied that this nexus requirement applies with even greater force under article I, section 1.

* * *

*Wilkinson* attempted to address this nexus requirement but its conclusion is inconsistent with federal law, which affords less protection than that provided by the state constitutional privacy amendment.  *Wilkinson* held that an employer has a legitimate interest in not hiring individuals whose drug abuse may render them unable to perform their job responsibilities in a satisfactory manner.  Federal courts have held that this sort of generalized justification is not sufficient to justify an infringement of an employee's Fourth Amendment rights.  If this justification is insufficient to satisfy a lesser Fourth Amendment test, then it cannot pass muster under the more stringent compelling interest test.

### 4.   *Application of Law*

Target concedes that the Psychscreen intrudes on the privacy interests of its job applicants.  Having carefully considered *Wilkinson*, we find its reasoning unpersuasive.  As it is inconsistent with both the legislative history of article I, section 1 and the case law interpreting that provision, we decline to follow it.  Under the legislative history and case law, Target's intrusion into the privacy rights of its SSO applicants must be justified by a compelling interest to withstand constitutional scrutiny.  Thus, the trial court abused its discretion by committing an error of law—applying the reasonableness test, rather than the compelling interest test.

While Target unquestionably has an interest in employing emotionally stable persons to be SSO's, testing applicants about their religious beliefs and sexual orientation does not further this interest.  To justify the invasion of privacy resulting from use of the Psychscreen, Target must demonstrate a compelling interest and must establish that the test serves a job-related purpose.  In its opposition to Soroka's motion for preliminary injunction, Target made no showing that a person's religious beliefs or sexual orientation have any bearing on the emotional stability or on the ability to perform an SSO's job responsibilities. It did no more than to make generalized claims about the Psychscreen's relationship to emotional fitness and to assert that it has seen an overall improvement in SSO quality and performance since it implemented the Psychscreen. This is not sufficient to constitute a compelling interest, nor does it satisfy the nexus requirement. Therefore, Target's inquiry into the religious beliefs and sexual orientation of SSO applicants unjustifiably violates the state constitutional right to privacy. Soroka has established that he is likely to prevail on the merits of his constitutional claims.

B. *Statutory Claims*

Soroka also contends that he is likely to prevail on the merits of his statutory claims. He makes two statutory claims—one based on the Fair Employment and Housing Act (FEHA) and another based on the Labor Code. As we have already found that portions of the Psychscreen as administered to Target's SSO applicants violate the constitutional right to privacy, it is not necessary for us to address the statutory issues to resolve the question of whether the preliminary injunction should issue. However, for the benefit of the trial court at the later trial, we will address these statutory claims.

1. *Fair Employment and Housing Act*

Soroka contends that the trial court abused its discretion by concluding that he was unlikely to prevail on his FEHA claims. These claims are based on allegations that the questions require applicants to divulge information about their religious beliefs. In its ruling on Soroka's motion for summary adjudication, the trial court found that he did not establish that Target's hiring decisions were based on religious beliefs, nor that the questions asked in the Psychscreen were designed to reveal such beliefs.

In California, an employer may not refuse to hire a person on the basis of his or her religious beliefs. Likewise, an employer is prohibited from making any non-job-related inquiry that expresses "directly or indirectly, any limitation, specification, or discrimination as to * * * religious creed * * *." FEHA guidelines provide that an employer may make any preemployment inquiry that does not discriminate on a basis enumerated in FEHA. However, inquiries that identify an individual on the basis of religious creed are unlawful unless pursuant to a permissible defense. Job-relatedness is an affirmative defense. A means of selection that is facially neutral but that has an adverse impact on persons on the basis of religious creed is permissible only on a showing that the selection process is sufficiently related to an essential function of the job in question to warrant its use.

The trial court committed an error of law when it found that questions such as "I feel sure that there is only one true religion," "Everything is turning out just like the prophets of the Bible said it would," and "I believe in the second coming of Christ" were not intended to reveal religious beliefs.  Clearly, these questions were intended to—and did—inquire about the religious beliefs of Target's SSO applicants.  As a matter of law, these questions constitute an inquiry that expresses a "specification [of a] religious creed."

Once Soroka established a prima facie case of an impermissible inquiry, the burden of proof shifted to Target to demonstrate that the religious beliefs questions were job-related.  As we have already determined, Target has not established that the Psychscreen's questions about religious beliefs have any bearing on that applicant's ability to perform an SSO's job responsibilities.  Therefore, Soroka has established the likelihood that he will prevail at trial on this statutory claim.[10]

2.  *Labor Code Sections 1101 and 1102*

\* \* \*

Under California law, employers are precluded from making, adopting or enforcing any policy that tends to control or direct the political activities or affiliations of employees.  Employers are also prohibited from coercing, influencing, or attempting to coerce or influence employees to adopt or follow or refrain from adopting or following any particular line of political activity by threatening a loss of employment.  These statutes have been held to protect applicants as well as employees.

\* \* \*

The trial court committed an error of law when it determined that Psychscreen questions such as "I am very strongly attracted by members of my own sex" were not intended to reveal an applicant's sexual orientation.  On its face, this question directly asks an applicant to reveal his or her sexual orientation.  One of the five traits that Target uses the Psychscreen to determine is "socialization," which it defines as "the extent to which an individual subscribes to traditional values and mores and feels an obligation to act in accordance with them."  Persons who identify themselves as homosexuals may be stigmatized as "willing to defy or violate" these norms, which may in turn result in an invalid test.

As a matter of law, this practice tends to discriminate against those who express a homosexual orientation.  It also constitutes an attempt to coerce an applicant to refrain from expressing a homosexual orientation by threat of loss of employment.  Therefore, Soroka has established that he is likely to prevail at trial on this statutory basis, as well.

\* \* \*

## CONCLUSION

Target's preemployment requirement of psychological screening violates both the constitutional right to privacy and statutory prohibitions

---

**10.**  Soroka also challenges questions relating to physical handicaps or conditions.  As we find that use of the Psychscreen violates FEHA regulations against questioning about an applicant's religious beliefs, we need not address these additional claims of error.

against improper preemployment inquiries and discriminatory conduct by inquiring into its applicants' religious beliefs and sexual orientation. At trial, Soroka is likely to prevail on the merits of his complaint. The interim harm to Soroka and others if the preliminary injunction does not issue outweighs the harm to Target from being precluded from giving the Psychscreen in its present form during the pendency of this litigation.

The order denying the preliminary injunction is reversed. The order denying Soroka's motion for class certification and granting Target's motion to deny class certification is remanded to the trial court for further proceedings in accordance with this opinion. Target shall bear all costs on appeal, the amount of which shall be fixed by the trial court.

## NOTES AND QUESTIONS

**1.** On July 9, 1993, while the case was pending before the California Supreme Court, Target Stores agreed to pay more than $2 million to settle the class action in *Soroka*. The company set up a $1.3 million fund to be divided among the 2,500 applicants who took the Psychscreen for security job positions at Target's 113 California stores. An additional $60,000 was divided among the named plaintiffs, plus the company paid the plaintiffs' attorney fees and costs. Target stopped using the test in 1991 because of concerns that it might violate the Americans with Disabilities Act.

**2.** Assuming that the use of the Psychscreen does not have a disparate impact along the lines of religion or sexual orientation, should the entire test be banned because of certain of the numerous questions? Cf. Connecticut v. Teal, 457 U.S. 440 (1982) (5–4 decision rejecting "bottom line" defense). Should only those questions be banned?

**3.** Would it be lawful under Title VII for the employer to ask applicants what their religion and sexual orientation was on an application form if it did not use the information in making employment decisions?

**4.** Why should the employer have to demonstrate a compelling interest in the use of the test?

**5.** The MMPI remains one of the most widely used psychological tests. This test was originally devised to identify and classify individuals who were mentally ill and there is no evidence of its utility as a preemployment test. Moreover, its 567 questions touch on a variety of sensitive and personal matters; the answers presumably would become a part of the employee's personnel file. The following is a sample of questions from the revised, 1989 version of the MMPI:

True or False

12. My sex life is satisfactory.
20. I am very seldom troubled by constipation.
121. I have never indulged in any unusual sex practices.
142. I have never had a fit or convulsion.
189. I like to flirt.
209. I like to talk about sex.

246. I believe my sins are unpardonable.
270. It does not bother me particularly to see animals suffer.
287. Many of my dreams are about sex.
336. Someone has control over my mind.
371. I have often wished I were a member of the opposite sex.
379. I got many beatings when I was a child.
416. I have strong political opinions.
429. Except by doctor's orders I never take drugs or sleeping pills.
489. I have a drug or alcohol problem.
556. I worry a great deal over money.

**6.** Another surprisingly popular personality assessment technique is handwriting analysis ("graphology" or "graphoanalysis"). An estimated 2,000 to 2,500 U.S. employers use handwriting analysis to predict the personalities of individuals. It is cheaper ($25 to $350) and simpler (12 to 14 lines of handwriting on unlined paper) than traditional psychological tests, but its scientific validity is far from established. Many of the "handwriting consultants" to industry have no formal training or learned handwriting analysis through a correspondence course. The following figure gives some samples of handwriting analysis.

### Handwriting Analysis Techniques

Source: *Handwriting Analysis*, 37 BNA Bull. to Management No. 19 (May 8, 1986), p. 152.

**7.** Are there legal and policy questions surrounding the use of personality and psychological tests? If you question the use of these tests is it because (a) they have not been proven to be accurate as a preemployment test; (b) they are irrelevant to legitimate job-related concerns; (c) they are overly intrusive and ask personal and sensitive questions; (d) they generate personnel files with information of an extremely personal nature; (e) they result in hiring a homogeneous and passive work force; or (f) they incorrectly seek a "hi-tech" shortcut to eliminate interviews, references, and traditional employee selection measures?

PROBLEM FOR DISCUSSION: LIMITING PSYCHOLOGICAL AND PERSONALITY TESTING IN EMPLOYMENT

There are many occupations, such as police officer, airline pilot, and physician, in which an individual's mental state is extremely relevant to ability to perform the job. Similarly, in numerous job placement situations an individual's personality is an extremely important factor. For example, it may be very important to know whether an individual likes working alone, traveling, or large crowds or whether the individual is outgoing or reserved or patient or short-tempered. Should an employer be permitted to inquire into these matters? If so, how?

If you were to draft a state statute seeking to prohibit some of the abuses of psychological and personality testing yet permit limited employer inquiries, what would you include in your law?

## E. MEDICAL SCREENING

## 1. PURPOSE

## Mark A. Rothstein, Medical Screening and the Employee Health Cost Crisis *

1–6 (1989).

Medical screening of workers has become an established practice in many industries. It involves the use of medical criteria in the selection and maintenance of a work force and is sometimes referred to as "selection screening." Medical screening, of course, is not new. Since the turn of the century large industrial companies have employed "factory surgeons" to determine whether applicants and employees were free of disease and had the necessary strength, stamina, vision, hearing, and other physical attributes to perform the job. For example, in 1909 Dr. Harry E. Mock began a program of physical examinations at Sears, Roebuck and Company to discover and isolate individuals with tuberculosis.

In recent years, medical screening has changed both qualitatively and quantitatively. The purpose of screening no longer is simply "diagnostic," that is, to decide whether an individual is free of contagious diseases and capable of performing the job. Increasingly, "predictive screening" attempts to identify whether currently capable individuals are at risk of developing a medical impairment at some future time. This new form of medical screening is greatly affected by technological advancements and is likely to become an increasingly important part of the employee selection process.

Each year American companies require their employees to submit to millions of blood tests, urine tests, x-rays, pulmonary function tests, and other medical and laboratory procedures. In fact, with the exception of

---

* Reprinted by permission of the Bureau of National Affairs, Inc., Washington, D.C.

typing and similar skills tests for office and clerical employees, medical screening is the most widely used preemployment test in all major employment categories.  Merely looking at the increasing number of tests performed each year, however, does not convey the sense of change in medical screening—changes that already have occurred and that are likely to occur in the future.  * * *

The increase in the various types of medical screening may be attributable to a number of factors.  First, for employees exposed to toxic substances such as asbestos, lead, and ethylene oxide, Occupational Safety and Health Administration (OSHA) standards require preplacement and periodic medical examinations.  This would account for increases in periodic pulmonary function tests, for example.  Second, some employees working under a collective bargaining agreement may be subject to periodic medical examinations pursuant to a safety and health provision in the agreement.  Approximately one-third of all union contracts contain a provision relating to medical examinations.

These two factors may explain the increased medical screening by large employers (which are more likely to be unionized), in certain industries (e.g., where there is exposure to toxic substances), and in the use of certain procedures (e.g., chest x-rays, pulmonary function tests).  Other medical screening procedures may be required of federal government contractors.  Nevertheless, * * * the largest percentage increases [have] occurred in categories less likely to be affected by OSHA requirements, collective bargaining, or government contracts:  preplacement examinations in small plants, blood and urine tests, and testing in the service sector.  In other categories there * * * actually [has been] a decline.  The reasons behind the increases offer the best evidence of the future direction of medical screening.

It has become increasingly clear that the newer forms of medical screening are not concerned with employee susceptibility to workplace hazards so much as with employee health in general.  Simply stated, some medical procedures have been instituted as a cost-containment measure.  A healthy work force means lower workers' compensation costs, reduced absenteeism, less turnover, lower disability and health insurance costs, reduced tort liability (such as asbestos products liability suits), and higher productivity.  Of course, some medical screening is performed because of altruistic concerns with having a safe and healthy work force.

Of all the costs associated with employee illness, the largest and most rapidly increasing cost is health insurance.  According to a recent study, 97 percent of medium and large companies offer health insurance as an employee benefit.  Employee health benefits costs increased from 8.9 percent in 1986 to 9.7 percent in 1987 of total payroll costs—about $1,985 per employee.  Both self-insured companies and experience-rated, privately insured companies had substantial increases in health benefits costs.  Despite celebrated efforts at corporate cost containment, in 1988 health costs soared 18.6 percent to $2,354 per employee.  The largest employers (40,000 or more employees) had costs of $2,605, and self-funded plans had increases of 24.8 percent.

Increased health care costs also have led to more medical screening by small employers. According to Dr. Dominick S. Zito, medical director of Preventive Plus, a company that performs medical examinations for industry: "Small companies find their liability insurance and benefits packages are getting so expensive that they are looking for any way to cut costs." If the per incident cost of employee and retiree health care cannot be controlled, there will be increasing pressure on companies of all sizes to use medical screening to avoid hiring people who are likely to be extensive users of health care resources.

## NOTES

**1.** See generally Lance Liebman, Too Much Information: Predictions of Employee Disease and the Fringe Benefit System, 1988 U.Chi.Legal F. 57; Mark A. Rothstein, Medical Screening and Employment Law: A Note of Caution and Some Observations, 1988 U.Chi.Legal F.1.

**2.** For a further discussion of health benefits, see Chapter 6.

## 2. Medical Questionnaires

### Griffin v. Steeltek, Inc.

964 F.Supp. 317 (N.D.Okl.1997).

■ Kern, Chief Judge.

This case involves a claim of employment discrimination under the Americans With Disabilities Act of 1990, 42 U.S.C. § 12101 et seq. ("ADA").

On April 26, 1996, Plaintiff filled out an application for employment as a grinder with Defendant pursuant to a newspaper advertisement for the position. The application form asked various questions regarding the Plaintiff's education and work experience, and also included the following questions: "Have you received Workers' Compensation or Disability Income payments?" "Have you any physical defects which preclude you from performing certain jobs?" "If yes, describe." On the application form, Plaintiff described his Worker's Compensation/Disability Income payment as "3 degree burn to hand and foot, surgery to elbow, spain [sic] in shoulder". Plaintiff did not describe any physical defects which would preclude him from performing certain jobs. Plaintiff claims that he was told at the time that he was the most qualified applicant at that time, which he understood to indicate that he would be hired. Several days later, the Plaintiff called the Defendant to check the status of his application, and was informed that no decision had been made. Later, the Plaintiff was informed that someone else was hired for the position.

The Defendant has submitted affidavits indicating that the position in question had an unwavering requirement of two years of prior experience as a grinder, and that the Plaintiff was not hired solely because he did not possess the requisite experience level.  However, the parties dispute whether this requirement was ever revealed to the Plaintiff, or whether the requirement actually existed.

\* \* \*

Defendant argues that summary judgment should be granted in this case because the Plaintiff has failed to establish a prima facie case of disability discrimination under the ADA.  Specifically, Defendant asserts that the Plaintiff was neither disabled as defined under the ADA, nor qualified for an employment position as a grinder.  Plaintiff asserts that summary judgment is inappropriate, because the Defendant violated the ADA by asking improper questions regarding Plaintiff's disabilities before an offer of conditional employment was made.  Defendant responds by insisting that the Plaintiff has no standing to bring a claim under the ADA as he is not a person with a disability under the Act.  The Plaintiff admitted in his response brief that he is not claiming to be either disabled or perceived as disabled, but that his claim is based solely on the fact that the Defendant violated the ADA by asking prohibited questions.  Thus, it appears that the issue presented is whether the provisions of the ADA prohibiting pre-employment, non-business related medical inquiries provide a cause of action for an individual who is not disabled as defined under the ADA.

The ADA prohibits discrimination against qualified individuals with a disability because of the disability of such individual in regard to job application procedures, hiring, discharge, and other terms, conditions, and privileges of employment.  Additionally, the ADA prohibits employers from conducting a medical examination or making inquiries of a job applicant as to whether such applicant is an individual with a disability or as to the nature or severity of such disability.  The Equal Employment Opportunities Commission ("EEOC") has promulgated interpretive guidelines pertaining to these provisions which make it clear that employers are not to inquire about an applicant's workers' compensation history.

There is no explicit language in Title I of the ADA providing a cause of action for nondisabled job applicants pursuant to 42 U.S.C. § 12112(d)(2)(A).  Although that subsection does define such inquiries as discrimination, it also makes a direct reference to subsection (a), which is the general rule prohibiting discrimination against a *qualified individual with a disability*.  Additionally, the EEOC regulations specify only defenses to disparate treatment charges brought under §§ 1630.4 through 1630.8, and 1630.11 through 1630.12.  There is no mention in the regulations of a defense to a disparate treatment charge arising solely out of a 42 U.S.C. § 12112(d)(2)(A) violation.  Similarly, the purpose statement of the ADA clearly indicates that the ADA was intended to prevent discrimination against individuals who are disabled, or who suffer discrimination because they are perceived as disabled.  The Court has found only one case addressing this issue.

In Armstrong v. Turner Indus., Ltd., 950 F.Supp. 162 (M.D.La.1996), the plaintiff alleged that he was denied a job as a pipefitter because he was regarded as having a disability. Additionally, the plaintiff alleged that, whether he was perceived as disabled or not, he was subjected to prohibited medical inquiries before a conditional offer of employment was extended, and thus was entitled to bring a cause of action against the defendant. The defendant in *Armstrong* contended that it was entitled to summary judgment on the ground that the plaintiff was not perceived as disabled. The defendant further argued that even if the plaintiff were perceived as disabled, he was fired because he falsified job application forms rather than because of any disability. The defendant also maintained that, because the plaintiff was not disabled as defined in the ADA, he could not assert a violation of 42 U.S.C. 12112(d)(2)(A).

After determining that the plaintiff was not disabled as defined in the ADA, the *Armstrong* court held that the plaintiff could not maintain a separate cause of action based upon the defendant's alleged misconduct in making inquiries regarding the plaintiff's medical condition. This Court agrees with the *Armstrong* decision, and holds that a prima facie case of employment discrimination under § 102 of the ADA necessarily requires a finding of disability as defined under the ADA.

Because Plaintiff has failed to allege either that he was disabled or perceived as disabled as defined under the ADA, he was not established a prima facie case of disability discrimination. For this reason, the Defendant is entitled to judgment as a matter of law. Defendant's Motion for Summary Judgment (docket # 4) is Granted.

### NOTES AND QUESTIONS

**1.** Is there any way that the court could have interpreted the ADA to produce the opposite result, that all unlawful preemployment medical inquiries are actionable?

**2.** When Julius Caldwell applied for a job he was required to complete an employment application form which asked numerous questions about his health, all of which violated the ADA's prohibition of preemployment medical inquiries. One of the questions asked whether he had ever been treated for back problems. Despite injuring his back while working for a prior employer, he wrote "no" to the back injury question. He was hired as a lathe operator. Within two weeks of his hiring, he reinjured his back. His employer contested any workers' compensation payments on the ground that Caldwell misrepresented his health status. Should his untruthful answer to the illegal question bar his workers' compensation recovery? See Caldwell v. Aarlin/Holcombe Armature Co., 481 S.E.2d 196 (Ga.1997) (held: yes). For a contrary result, see Huisenga v. Opus Corp., 494 N.W.2d 469 (Minn.1992) (based on specific state statute, false answers to illegal medical questions cannot be used to deny workers' compensation benefits).

PROBLEM FOR DISCUSSION: REFUSING TO HIRE SMOKERS

According to the Surgeon General, cigarette smoking causes over 400,000 deaths a year in the United States. A substantial portion of the economic consequences of these deaths (and illnesses) is borne by employers in lost productivity, health care costs, and increased insurance.

Traditionally, employers attempting to dissuade employees from smoking have prohibited smoking on the job and have instituted or supported smoking cessation programs. A relatively new approach is to refuse to hire individuals who smoke. These policies stem from three separate premises. First, cigarette smoke has a synergistic relationship with some workplace exposures (such as asbestos) that greatly magnifies the toxic effect of the substance. These policies aim to decrease occupational illness and related claims. Second, in some states "heart and lung" laws establish a legal presumption that any heart or lung illness suffered by a police officer or firefighter is work related. Hiring only nonsmokers saves money by eliminating compensable cigarette-related illnesses. Third, because morbidity and mortality rates for smokers greatly exceed those for nonsmokers, hiring only nonsmokers saves money.

Those who support policies of refusing to hire smokers argue that it is a controllable behavioral problem, that employers have a legitimate right to limit health care expenditures, and that these policies will reduce smoking and save lives. Those who oppose these policies argue that many smokers are unable to quit, that if all employers adopted such policies there would be a large class of unemployable individuals, and that smoking should be discouraged by other means. They also assert that to verify whether employees were not smoking at home, employers would be tempted to use surveillance, polygraphs, urine screens, and other intrusive measures.

What are your views? If you believe that employers should not be able to refuse to hire smokers, what legal approaches would you recommend to protect these individuals?

About half the states have enacted laws prohibiting employers from conditioning employment on an employee's refraining from using "lawful tobacco products" or engaging in "lawful activities" during nonworking hours.

In Grusendorf v. City of Oklahoma City, 816 F.2d 539 (10th Cir.1987), the court upheld the dismissal of a fire fighter trainee who violated a no smoking rule of the fire department by taking three puffs of a cigarette during a lunch break. Similarly, in City of North Miami v. Kurtz, 653 So.2d 1025 (Fla.1995), cert. denied, 516 U.S. 1043 (1996), the Florida Supreme Court upheld a city policy requiring all applicants to sign an affidavit stating that they have not smoked within the last year. Rejecting the argument that this violated state or federal constitutional privacy, the court held that the regulation was justified by the city's interest in reducing the costs from smoking-related illnesses. For a further discussion, see Mark A. Rothstein, Refusing to Employ Smokers: Good Public Health or Bad Public Policy?, 62 Notre Dame L.Rev. 940 (1987).

## 3.   MEDICAL EXAMINATIONS

## Green v. Walker

910 F.2d 291 (5th Cir.1990).

■ POLITZ, CIRCUIT JUDGE:

Joni Green, individually and on behalf of her minor child, appeals an adverse summary judgment which dismissed her claims against Leslie Walker, M.D., on the grounds that Dr. Walker owed Sidney Green, her now deceased husband, no duty of care in the conduct of an annual employment physical. Holding that the examining physician-examinee relationship which existed gave rise to an obligation to perform the examination with due care and to appropriately report thereon, we reverse and remand for further proceedings.

*Background*

Sidney Green was employed as an offshore cook by ARA/GSI International. As a condition of continued employment ARA/GSI required that its employees undergo an annual physical examination that included a thorough examination of the physical systems, a urine test, and x-rays of the chest and spine. ARA/GSI contracted with Dr. Walker to conduct these examinations in accordance with an outlined protocol. Green submitted to his annual employment physical with Dr. Walker on May 6, 1985. According to the report submitted to ARA/GSI, Dr. Walker found all test results normal and classified Green as "employable without restriction," the best possible rating on the report. Approximately one year later Green was diagnosed with lung cancer, necessitating extensive diagnostic and surgical procedures.

Sidney and Joni Green, individually and on behalf of their minor daughter, filed suit against Dr. Walker, claiming that he had negligently failed to diagnose the beginnings of the cancer at the time of the May 1985 physical examination, and had failed to disclose these findings timely, thus lessening Sidney Green's chances of survival and reducing his life expectancy. Sidney Green has since died. Dr. Walker moved for summary judgment contending that his examination of Green had been conducted pursuant to a contract with Green's employer and that therefore no physician-patient relationship, on which a malpractice claim could be based, existed between him and Green. The district court granted summary judgment and Joni Green timely appealed. The sole question posed on appeal may be stated thusly: Did Dr. Walker have a duty to Sidney Green to perform the prescribed examination with due care, consistent with the medical skills he held out to the public, and to report his findings, particularly any finding which appeared to pose a threat to the physical or mental health of Sidney Green? The district court answered this question in the negative. We now answer it affirmatively.

*Analysis*

The traditional malpractice paradigm.

It is a long-established principle of law that liability for malpractice is dependent on the existence of a physician-patient relationship. Whereas malpractice liability lies primarily in tort, the existence of the traditional physician-patient relationship on which such liability hinges uniformly has been held to depend upon the existence of a contract, express or implied, that the doctor will undertake to treat the patient or at least engage in diagnosis as a prelude to treatment.

Emphasizing a distinction between treatment and a consultative physical examination conducted at the request and for the benefit of a third party, state courts addressing the issue generally have held that no physician-patient relationship exists between "(a) a prospective or actual insured and the physician who examines him for the insurance company; or (b) a prospective or actual employee and the doctor who examines him for the employer." Hoover v. Williamson, 236 Md. 250, 203 A.2d 861 (1964); *see* Thomas v. Kenton, 425 So.2d 396 (La.App.1982); Lotspeich v. Chance Vought Aircraft, 369 S.W.2d 705 (Tex.Civ.App.1963).

*Erie* obligations.

Focusing on our obligations as a federal court sitting in diversity, Erie R. Co. v. Tompkins, 304 U.S. 64 (1938), both sides to this dispute earnestly contend that Louisiana caselaw mandates our resolution of this appeal in their favor. Mrs. Green contends that we must reverse the district court, citing the decision of the Louisiana Supreme Court in Ducote v. Albert, 521 So.2d 399 (La.1988). Dr. Walker counters that we are bound to follow the lead of an intermediate appellate court in Thomas v. Kenton, 425 So.2d 396 (La.App.1982), and affirm the district court.

Albeit persuasive, and of some guidance as we walk a dimly blazed trail, neither case is truly dispositive. In *Ducote* the Louisiana Supreme Court adopted the "dual capacity" doctrine, holding that the Louisiana Worker's Compensation Law does not provide a company doctor with immunity from civil liability for medical malpractice. As Dr. Walker points out, however, *Ducote* involved a situation in which the plaintiff-employee had seen the company physician for treatment of his injured hand; whether the physician had rendered "treatment," thereby creating a physician-patient relationship in the traditional sense, was not in dispute. *Ducote,* therefore, arguably may stand merely for the proposition that a company physician committing malpractice may not raise his co-employee status as a defense to a malpractice claim.

Alternatively, *Thomas v. Kenton* arguably is on all fours with the case at bar. Thomas's employer had retained a physician to conduct annual or biennial physical examinations of its employees to assess their continued employability; the examinations were neither initiated by Thomas nor conducted to diagnose and treat a particular ailment. Thomas sued the examining physician, claiming that he had failed in the course of the examination to diagnose and disclose a condition from which Thomas suffered, thus allowing the condition to progress without Thomas's knowledge.

Adopting the reasoning of other jurisdictions that had considered "strikingly similar" situations, such as *Hoover* and *Lotspeich,* the *Thomas* court held that there was no physician-patient relationship between a prospective or actual employee and the doctor conducting an examination at the employer's request.   In the absence of such a relationship, the *Thomas* court concluded, there could be no liability for malpractice.   Above all, the *Thomas* court was impressed that it was the employer, not the employee, who was the intended beneficiary of the doctor's contractual obligations:

> The doctor was hired by the company for their benefit and any benefit that their employees receive from having a doctor there to conduct these examinations was only secondary in nature.

The directive of *Erie* in a diversity case limits but does not eliminate the federal decision-making process for *Erie* "does not command blind allegiance to [any] case on all fours with the case before the court."   The decision of an intermediate appellate state court guides, but does not necessarily control a federal court's determination of the applicable state law.

If anything, this flexibility is even greater when a federal court sits as an *Erie* court applying the Louisiana civil law.   In such cases, "the *Erie* obligation is to the [Civil] Code, the 'solemn expression of legislative will.'"   The Louisiana Supreme Court has taken great pains to "plainly state that, particularly in the changing field of delictual responsibility, the notion of *stare decisis,* derived as it is from the common law, should not be thought controlling in this state."   While caselaw in the State of Louisiana is acknowledged as "invaluable as previous interpretation of the broad standard of Article 2315" [the general standard of conduct in torts referred to as "the keystone of responsibility,"] it is nonetheless properly regarded as "secondary information."   As our constant focus, "we must never forget that it is a Code we are expounding."

Duty of care—general obligation.

Unlike the fact-oriented questions of breach and causation, which we do not address today, determining the existence of an obligation or duty in particular situations is a question of law.   See Pitre v. Opelousas General Hosp., 530 So.2d 1151 (La.1988).   The Louisiana Civil Code establishes the standard of conduct required of all persons in Louisiana in all of their relationships in broad, simple terms: "Every act whatever of man that causes damage to another obliges him by whose fault it happened to repair it."   La.Civ.Code art. 2315.   The drafters of the Civil Code made no effort to define the concept of "fault."   Instead,

> [they] conceived of fault as a breach of a preexisting obligation, for which the law orders reparation, when it causes damage to another, and they left it to the court to determine in each case the existence of an anterior obligation which would make an act constitute fault.

In determining whether article 2315 contemplates the existence of a previously undefined duty, the Louisiana Supreme Court has looked to the foreseeability of the risks involved as well as "policy considerations, including social, moral and economic elements."

Duty of care—physicians.

Like any person, a physician "is responsible for the damage he occasions not merely by his act, but by his negligence, his imprudence, or his want of skill." La.Civ.Code art. 2316. As the Louisiana Supreme Court acknowledged in *Pitre,* however, the Louisiana Legislature has expressly provided that a physician's professional status carries with it additional legal obligations. A physician practicing as a general practitioner must possess the degree of knowledge or skill possessed and exercise the degree of care ordinarily exercised by physicians in active practice in a similar community under similar circumstances.

The issue presented by the instant case is whether Louisiana jurisprudence supports an extension of the traditional physician-patient relationship to admit of a legal relationship between examining physician and examinee, thus imposing the physician's duty of due care in that situation. The Louisiana Supreme Court's recent enunciation of the principles underlying article 2315, as applied to physicians in *Pitre,* convinces us that the Civil Code permits the articulation of a duty of care that would protect physical examinees, if they are to be deemed other than "patients," a position we do not here concede:

> The persons at whose disposal society has placed the potent implements of technology owe a heavy moral obligation to use them carefully and to avoid foreseeable harm to present or future generations. In the field of medicine, as in that of manufacturing, the need for compensation of innocent victims of defective products and negligently delivered services is a powerful factor influencing tort law. Typically in these areas also the defendants' capacity to bear and distribute the losses is far superior to that of consumers. Additionally these defendants are in a much better position than the victims to analyze the risks involved in the defendants' activities and to either take precautions to avoid them or to insure against them. Consequently, a much stronger and more effective incentive to prevent the occurrence of future harm will be created by placing the burden of foreseeable losses on the defendants than upon the disorganized, uninformed victims.

From this linchpin the *Pitre* court held that when a physician knows or should know that there is an unreasonable risk that a child will be born with a foreseeable birth defect, he owes a duty, not only to that child's parents, *but to the not as yet conceived child,* to exercise reasonable care to warn the potential parents and assist them to avoid conception of the foreseeably deformed child. If article 2315 supports such a duty we cannot but conclude that it also supports a duty between an examining physician and the person present and consenting to the examination, notwithstanding the claim that the examination is being conducted ostensibly for the benefit of another.

We live in an age in which the drive for an increasingly productive workforce has led employers increasingly to require that employees subject their bodies (and minds) to inspection in order to obtain or maintain employment. In placing oneself in the hands of a person held out to the world as skilled in a medical profession, albeit at the request of one's employer, one justifiably has the reasonable expectation that the expert will warn of "any incidental dangers of which he is cognizant due to his peculiar knowledge of his specialization."

We therefore now hold that when an individual is required, as a condition of future or continued employment, to submit to a medical examination, that examination creates a relationship between the examining physician and the examinee, at least to the extent of the tests conducted. This relationship imposes upon the examining physician a duty to conduct the requested tests and diagnose the results thereof, exercising the level of care consistent with the doctor's professional training and expertise, and to take reasonable steps to make information available timely to the examinee of any findings that pose an imminent danger to the examinee's physical or mental well-being. To impose a duty upon the doctor who performs such tests to do so in accordance with the degree of care expected of his/her profession for the benefit of the employee-examinee, as well as the employer, is fully consistent with the very essence of Civil Code article 2315.

The decision of the district court is REVERSED and the matter is REMANDED for further proceedings consistent herewith.

NOTES AND QUESTIONS

**1.** The traditional view is that there is no physician-patient relationship between an applicant or employee and a physician retained by an employer to assess the health of the applicant or employee. See, e.g., Lotspeich v. Chance Vought Aircraft, 369 S.W.2d 705 (Tex.Civ.App.1963). This is because the examination is not performed for the benefit of the examinee nor is there any contemplation of treatment. As a result, there may be no duty on the part of the physician to notify the individual of test results or diagnoses or to refer the individual for treatment. Do you think the court in Green v. Walker struck the right balance? For a similar case involving preemployment medical examinations, see Daly v. United States, 946 F.2d 1467 (9th Cir. 1991).

Many individuals who undergo preplacement medical examinations are unaware of the legal relationships that exist or do not exist. What disclosures should be made at the outset by the physician and company about who has retained the physician, the scope of the examination, the use of medical findings, the availability of medical reports, and other matters? See Mark A. Rothstein, Legal Issues in the Medical Assessment of Physical Impairment by Third-Party Physicians, 5 J. Legal Med. 503 (1984).

**2.** In what form should occupational physicians provide management with medical assessments? Should they provide the actual work-up sheets and laboratory reports, summaries of findings, or simply conclusions of employability? The American College of Occupational and Environmental Medicine Code of Ethical Conduct (1993), provides in pertinent part:

> 6. Physicians should recognize that employers may be entitled to counsel about an individual's medical work fitness, but not to diagnoses or specific details, except in compliance with laws and regulations.

This provision, however, merely states that it is ethical so long as it is legal, such as where it is in accordance with the Americans with Disabilities Act, discussed infra. For a criticism of this code provision, see Mark A. Rothstein, A Proposed Revision of the ACOEM Code of Ethics, 39 J.Occup. & Envt'l Med. 616 (1997).

**3.** Employee medical records often contain sensitive personal information on topics such as psychiatric problems, drug and alcohol abuse, and reproductive matters. They also contain the medical data upon which personnel decisions frequently are made. Despite the crucial nature of these records, employees usually have no legal right to see them; and despite their often sensitive nature, there are few restrictions on the intra-company and extra-company disclosure of such records.

In Bratt v. IBM Corp., 467 N.E.2d 126 (Mass.1984), the court applied a balancing test to decide whether an employer's legitimate interests in disseminating medical information outweigh the employee's privacy interests. "A physician retained by the employer may disclose to the employer medical information concerning an employee if receipt of the information is reasonably necessary to serve a substantial and valid business interest of the employer."

Some states have laws giving all employees a right to see their personnel files or medical records. See, e.g., Conn.Gen.Stat.Ann. § 31–128c; Wis.Stat.Ann. § 103.13. In addition, OSHA's Access to Employee Exposure and Medical Records Standard, 29 C.F.R. § 1910.20, requires that the employer provide access to both exposure records and medical records. The standard, however, does not apply to applicants and only covers employees who are exposed to toxic substances.

Regarding disclosure of information, California's Confidentiality of Medical Information Act, Cal.Civ.Code Ann. §§ 56 to 56.37, is the most extensive state law. It provides in part:

> Each employer who receives medical information shall establish appropriate procedures to ensure the confidentiality and protection from unauthorized use and disclosure of that information. These procedures may include, but are not limited to, instruction regarding confidentiality of employees and agents handling files containing medical information, and security systems restricting access to files containing medical information.

\* \* \* No employer shall use, disclose, or knowingly permit its employees or agents to use or disclose medical information which the employer possesses pertaining to its employees without the patient having first signed an authorization \* \* \* permitting such use or disclosure [except if the disclosure of the records is compelled by legal process, the records are an issue in a pending legal action, the information is used in administering an employee benefits plan, or the information is used in diagnosis or treatment].

Under the law, an individual whose records have been disclosed may recover compensatory damages, punitive damages up to $3,000, attorney fees up to $1,000, and costs of litigation. Violations are also punishable as misdemeanors. This statute is, by far, the most sweeping protection for employee privacy.

**4.** A truck driven by an employee of Wharton Transport Corporation struck the rear of a car parked on the side of a road and occupied by a family. The collision resulted in the death of one child, severe injuries to three other children, and minor injuries to the father. The truck driver was not hurt. Wharton paid $426,314.25 to settle the case brought by the occupants of the car and then brought an indemnity action against Dr. Bridges, the physician it had retained to determine whether the truck driver was physically fit to drive a truck in interstate commerce (as required by ICC regulations). Wharton alleged that Dr. Bridges was negligent in certifying the driver as physically fit when a subsequent examination indicated that the driver had a variety of severe impairments, as follows: (1) only 5 percent vision in his left eye and blurred vision in his right eye caused by chorioretinitis; (2) severe osteoarthritis in both legs causing a loss of flexion and range of motion; (3) chronic degenerative disc disease in his neck and lower back which impaired his ability to move his neck and head; and (4) chronic fatigue, depression, and emotional exhaustion. Can Wharton recover from Dr. Bridges? See Wharton Transport Corp. v. Bridges, 606 S.W.2d 521 (Tenn.1980) (held: yes). Could the injured family members recover from Dr. Bridges?

**5.** Donald Armstrong applied for the position of Vice President of Credit of the Zale Corporation. He was required to have a physical examination performed by Dr. Melvin Morgan to determine his health status. Dr. Morgan was negligent in his diagnosis and erroneously reported to Zale that Armstrong was in very poor health. Can Armstrong recover from Dr. Morgan? If so, what damages and under what theory? Would it matter whether Dr. Morgan was an employee of Zale or an independent physician hired by Zale? See Armstrong v. Morgan, 545 S.W.2d 45 (Tex.Civ.App. 1976) (held: Armstrong could recover under negligence theory).

## MEDICAL EVALUATIONS UNDER THE AMERICANS WITH DISABILITIES ACT

The Americans with Disabilities Act of 1990 (ADA) mandates major changes in the way companies conduct medical examinations and inquiries of applicants and employees.  The employment provisions of the ADA take effect in 1992 for employers with 25 or more employees and take effect in 1994 for employers with 15 or more employees.

Section 102(d)(2) of the ADA prohibits "traditional" preemployment medical examinations and questionnaires.  An employer may not "conduct a medical examination or make inquiries of a job applicant as to whether such applicant is an individual with a disability or as to the nature or severity of such disability."  The only permissible inquiries are about the ability of the applicant to perform job-related functions.

After a conditional offer of employment an employer may require an "employment entrance examination" (preplacement examination) pursuant to § 102(d)(3).  These examinations, need not be job-related, but they must be given to all employees in a job category regardless of disability.  The information obtained must be stored in separate files and treated as confidential.  Supervisors and managers may be told only about an employee's work restrictions and necessary accommodations.

Similar provisions apply to periodic medical examinations of employees.  Under § 102(d)(4), all medical examinations and inquiries must be "job-related and consistent with business necessity."  Employers may offer medical examinations of a non-job-related nature, such as comprehensive medical examinations and wellness programs, but employee participation must be voluntary.

## F.  DRUG TESTING AND OTHER LABORATORY PROCEDURES

## 1.  DRUG TESTING

### Mark A. Rothstein, *Drug Testing in the Workplace: The Challenge to Employment Relations and Employment Law*

63 Chi.–Kent L.Rev. 683 (1987).

### III.  DRUG TESTING—HOW IT WORKS AND WHAT IT MEASURES

#### A.  *Drug Testing Technology*

In the last decade, technological advances in drug testing and the commercial exploitation of these advances have made workplace drug testing commonplace.  Despite the frequency of drug testing, however, there remains widespread misunderstanding about how the tests work, what they measure, and how their accuracy is determined.

Drug tests analyze a body specimen for the presence of drugs or their by-products, metabolites.  The most commonly used specimen for workplace testing is urine, although blood, breath, saliva, hair, and other specimens have been used in settings other than the workplace.  Blood testing by employers is mostly limited to retrospective testing after the occurrence of an accident.

Scientifically valid drug testing is a two-step process. In the initial step, a "screening" test eliminates from further testing those specimens with negative results, indicating either the absence of targeted substances or the presence of levels below a designated threshold or "cut-off" point. A result which reveals substance levels at or above the cut-off is considered positive. All positive specimens are then retested using a "confirmatory" test. According to the Toxicology Section of the American Academy of Forensic Sciences, the confirmatory test must be "based upon different chemical or physical principles than the initial analysis method(s)." Confirmatory testing is essential to establish both the identity and quantity of the substances in the specimen.

There are three main types of initial screening tests: color or spot tests, thin layer chromatography and immunoassays. The most widely used are the immunoassays, which are of three types, enzyme, radio, and fluorescence. All of these latter tests are based on immunological principles. A known quantity of the tested-for drug is bound to an enzyme or radioactive iodine and is added to the urine. If the urine contains the drug, the added, "labeled" drug competes with the drug in the specimen and cannot bind to the antibodies. As a result, the enzyme or radioactive iodine remains active. By measuring enzyme activity or radioactivity, the presence and amount of the drug can be determined.

The most commonly used immunoassay is the enzyme multiplied immunoassay technique or EMIT. An advantage of EMIT is that it tests for a broad spectrum of drugs and their metabolites, including opiates, barbiturates, amphetamines, cocaine and its metabolite, benzodiazepines, methaqualone, methadone, phencyclidine, and cannabinoids. It is also fast and cheap. A single test may cost about five dollars. In addition, portable kits starting at $300 are sold for on-site use by individuals with minimal training.

The radioimmunoassay (RIA) can measure only one drug at a time, but has broad-spectrum detection capabilities similar to EMIT. RIA is more expensive than EMIT, however, and requires a more highly trained technician. The fluorescence polarization immunoassay (FPIA) is a relatively new technique and, as yet, not widely used.

The most widely used confirmatory test is gas chromatography/mass spectrometry (GC/MS). In GC the sample is pretreated to extract drugs from the urine. The drugs are converted to a gaseous form and transported through a long glass column of helium gas. By application of varying temperatures to the column the compounds are separated according to their unique properties, such as molecular weight and rate of reaction. These particular properties are used to identify the compound. Although GC can be used alone, the superior method combines it with a mass spectrometer (MS), which breaks down the compound molecules into electrically charged ion fragments. Each drug or metabolite produces a unique fragment pattern, which can be detected by comparison with known fragment patterns. GC/MS requires expensive equipment and highly trained technicians to prepare the sample and interpret test results. The process is also time-consuming because only one sample and one drug per sample may be tested at a time.  High performance liquid chromatography (HPLC) is also used as a confirmatory test, but GC/MS has become the standard confirmatory test.

The pricing structures for drug tests vary widely.  Some laboratories charge customers a flat fee per specimen tested; others divide the fee so that those samples requiring a confirmatory test incur an additional charge.  Other factors affecting price are the type of analysis used, the number of specimens tested, and the types of drugs tested for.  In general, laboratory charges for single-procedure methods range from $5 to $20; GC/MS confirmation costs from $30 to $100.

### B.  What the Tests Measure

It is essential to understand that a positive result on a drug test does not indicate impairment of the subject.  Drug metabolites detected in urine are the inert, inactive by-products of drugs and cannot be used to determine impairment.  Although a blood test can reveal the presence of drugs in the blood in their active state, with the exception of ethanol, there is no known correlation between the detection of metabolites in urine and blood concentrations.  Moreover, there is no agreement among experts on what level of drug indicates impairment.

Many variables influence how a drug will affect an individual user, including the type of drug, dose, time lapse from administration, duration of effect and use, and interactions with other drugs.  The individual's age, weight, sex, general health state, emotional state, and drug tolerance also are important factors.  Consequently, the wide individual variations make generalizing extremely speculative.  According to one expert:

> Testing does only one thing.  It detects what is being tested.  It does not tell us anything about the recency of use.  It does not tell us anything about how the person was exposed to the drug.  It doesn't even tell us whether it affected performance.

A final factor that complicates interpretation of a positive result is the often-considerable duration of detectability of drugs in urine.  As indicated in the following table, drug metabolites can be detected in urine from one day to several weeks following exposure.

Table 2

Approximate Duration of Detectability of
Selected Drugs in Urine

| Drugs | Approximate Duration of Detectability |
|---|---|
| Amphetamines | 2 days |
| Barbiturates | 1–7 days |
| Benzodiazepines | 3 days |
| Cocaine metabolites | 2–3 days |
| Methadone | 3 days |
| Codeine | 2 days |

| *Drugs* | *Approximate Duration of Detectability* |
|---|---|
| PCP | 8 days |
| Cannabinoids, single use | 3 days |
| moderate smoker (4 times/week) | 5 days |
| heavy smoker (daily) | 10 days |
| chronic heavy smoker | 21 days |

The usual *effects* of most drugs persist for only a few hours after use. Therefore, drugs are detectable long after their effects have subsided and any correlations between a positive test and impairment are impossible.

### C.  How Accurate are the Tests?

Before discussing the accuracy of drug tests, it is important to review how accuracy in medical tests is measured.  The key concepts are "sensitivity" and "specificity."  The sensitivity of a test is a measure of its ability to identify persons with the tested-for condition.  It is the percentage of persons with the condition who register a positive test result:

$$\frac{\text{true positive test results}}{\text{persons with condition (true positives + false negatives)}} \times 100 \text{ percent}$$

Therefore, if 100 persons have a condition and the test is able to identify 90 of them, the test would be 90% sensitive.

The specificity of a test is a measure of its ability to identify persons who do not have a condition.  It is the percentage of persons free of the condition who register a negative test result:

$$\frac{\text{true negative test results}}{\text{persons free of condition (true negatives + false positives)}} \times 100 \text{ percent}$$

Therefore, if 100 persons are free of a condition and the test is able to identify 90 of them, the test would be 90% specific.

The "positive predictive value" of a test refers to the value of a positive test result in identifying the presence of a condition.  It is the percentage of persons whose test results are positive who actually have the condition:

$$\frac{\text{persons with condition (true positives)}}{\text{positive test results (true positives + false positives)}} \times 100 \text{ percent}$$

According to independent studies, the EMIT test has a sensitivity of about 99% and a specificity of about 90%.  The positive predictive value of the test, however, varies greatly depending on the prevalence of drug usage in the tested population.  The following tables illustrate how important prevalence is to the predictive value of a test.

Table 3

Predictive Value of EMIT Test with 99% Sensitivity, 90% Specificity, 50% Prevalence, and 10,000 Subjects

| *Subjects* | *True Positives* | *False Negatives* |
|---|---|---|
| 5000 + | 4950 | 50 |
| | *False Positives* | *True Negatives* |
| 5000 − | 500 | 4500 |

Table 3 assumes a 50% prevalence—perhaps individuals in a drug treatment program or, in a workplace setting, individuals selected for testing based upon reasonable suspicion. The test correctly identifies 4950 of the 5000 true positives, with 50 false negatives. It correctly identifies 4500 of the 5000 true negatives, with 500 false positives. Therefore, of the 5450 positives, 4950 are true positives. The positive predictive value of the test is $^{4950}\!/_{5450}$ or 90.8%.

### Table 4
#### Predictive Value of EMIT Test with 99% Sensitivity, 90% Specificity, 5% Prevalence, and 10,000 Subjects

| Subjects | True Positives | False Negatives |
|---|---|---|
| 500 + | 495 | 5 |
| | False Positives | True Negatives |
| 9500 − | 950 | 8550 |

Table 4 assumes a 5% prevalence—a reasonable estimate of the prevalence of recent drug users among job applicants. The test correctly identifies 495 of the 500 true positives, with 5 false negatives. It correctly identifies 8550 of the 9500 true negatives, with 950 false positives. Therefore, of the 1445 positives, 495 are true positives. The positive predictive value of the test is $^{495}\!/_{1445}$ or 34.3%.

Table 4 demonstrates why it is essential to use confirmatory tests. Two out of three positives identified by the test will be false positives. Unfortunately, pre-employment drug tests, where the prevalence and predictive values are low, are also the tests least likely to be confirmed due to cost considerations.

### Table 5
#### Some Commonly Available Substances That Cross–React with Widely Tested–For Drugs

| Type of Drug | Cross–Reactants |
|---|---|
| amphetamines | 1. over-the-counter cold medications (decongestants) |
| | 2. over-the-counter and prescription dietary aids |
| | 3. asthma medications |
| | 4. anti-inflammatory agents |
| barbiturates | 1. anti-inflammatory agents |
| | 2. phenobarbital (used to treat epilepsy) |
| cocaine | 1. herbal teas (made from coca leaves) |
| marijuana (cannabinoids) | 1. nonsteroidal anti-inflammatory agents |
| | 2. Ibuprofen (Advil, Motrin, Nuprin) |
| morphine, opiates | 1. codeine |
| | 2. prescription analgesics and antitussives |
| | 3. poppy seeds |
| | 4. over-the-counter cough remedies |
| Phencyclidine (PCP) | 1. prescription cough medicines |
| | 2. Valium |

Because drug tests detect metabolites of drugs rather than the drugs themselves, commonly used screening tests (and to a lesser extent confirmatory tests as well) sometimes incorrectly identify as metabolites of illicit drugs the metabolites of other substances or normal human enzymes such as lysozyme and malate dehydrogenase.  Table 5 indicates some of the substances for which this effect, cross-reactivity, has been documented.

The problem of cross-reactivity is one important reason why it is important to use pretest questionnaires inquiring about medications and other cross-reactants and to give individuals an opportunity to explain a positive result.  A related concern is that a drug test will be positive because of "passive inhalation."  There is disputed evidence about whether a marijuana test using a cutoff of 20 nanograms per milliliter of urine will test positive if the subject was exposed to the marijuana smoke of other people.  Using a higher cutoff, however, such as 100 nanograms per milliliter of urine, will eliminate this problem.

The accuracy of drug tests also may be affected by several other factors.  Alteration of the specimen, such as by substitution or dilution, improper calibration of equipment or cleaning of equipment (the so-called "carry-over effect"), mislabeling, contamination, or technician error all may undermine test accuracy.  Indeed, even the best methodologies will yield valid results only to the extent that the testing laboratory adheres to rigid standards of quality control.  Laboratory proficiency criteria, however, have been extremely inadequate.

### IV.  Drug Testing—Who Is Doing It and Why

#### A.  Public Employers

A limited amount of drug testing long has been used in the private sector, but the major impetus for widespread testing has come from the federal government.  Drug testing was begun in the military in 1981 and by 1985 over three million drug tests were performed annually at a cost of over one-half billion dollars.  The Department of Defense credits the drug testing program for a decline in drug usage.

In July 1983, President Reagan established the President's Commission on Organized Crime.  In its March 1986 report on drug abuse the Commission recommended drug testing for public and private sector employers.

> The President should direct the heads of all Federal agencies to formulate immediately clear policy statements, with implementing guidelines, including suitable drug testing programs, expressing the utter unacceptability of drug abuse by Federal employees. State and local governments and leaders in the private sector should support unequivocally a similar policy that any and all use of drugs is unacceptable.  Government contracts should not be awarded to companies that fail to implement drug programs, including suitable drug testing.

In July 1986 the Office of Personnel Management proposed that drug tests be required of all federal employees, that dismissal occur after a second positive drug test, and that the law allowing dismissal only upon a finding of drug-related impairment be repealed. The White House rejected this proposal. The following month the White House Domestic Policy Council recommended that drug testing be conducted on federal employees in sensitive positions, those creating reasonable suspicion of drug use, and all job applicants. The Council also proposed random testing of workers in critical positions. On September 15, 1986, President Reagan issued Executive Order 12,564. Based largely on the Council's recommendations, the Order requires the head of each Executive agency to establish a program to test for illegal drug use by employees in sensitive positions. "Sensitive positions" is defined as: those handling classified information, those serving as Presidential appointees, those in positions related to national security, law enforcement officers, those charged with the protection of life, property, and public health and safety, and those in jobs requiring a high degree of trust and confidence. This extremely broad definition authorizes the testing of 1.1 million of the nation's 2.1 million federal employees.

The Executive Order specifically authorizes testing under four circumstances: (1) where there is reasonable suspicion of illegal drug use; (2) in conjunction with the investigation of an accident; (3) as a part of an employee's counseling or rehabilitation for drug use through an employee assistance program (EAP); and (4) to screen any job applicant for illegal drug use. The Order mandates confirmatory testing and allows the employee to provide a urine specimen in private unless there is reason to believe adulteration will occur.

\* \* \*

The Department of Health and Human Services (HHS) is charged with promulgating scientific and technical guidelines for the federal drug testing program. The Guidelines, issued in August 1987, detail the scientific and technical requirements, including collection of specimens, laboratory analysis, and transmittal and interpretation of test results. The Guidelines require testing for marijuana and cocaine and permit testing for any drug listed in Schedule I or II of the Controlled Substances Act. The Guidelines also include specific information on other drugs "most likely to be included in agency drug testing programs"—opiates, amphetamines, and PCP. Significantly, the Guidelines contain no specific mention of testing for alcohol or other legal drugs of abuse. This fact tends to refute official claims that the testing program is an attempt to assure safety and productivity rather than a law enforcement measure.

The specimen collection procedures detailed in the Guidelines have generated considerable controversy. The employee may urinate in privacy "unless there is reason to believe that a particular individual may alter or substitute the specimen to be provided." "To ensure that unadulterated specimens are obtained," the Guidelines also detail the "minimum precautions" to be taken in the collection of urine specimens: (1) toilet bluing agents must be placed in the toilet bowl (presumably to prevent dilution of the sample); (2) there is to be no other source of water available in the area where the sample is given; (3) the person must present photo identification upon arrival; (4) the person must remove any unnecessary outer garments that could conceal items used to adulterate the sample; (5) the person must wash his or her hands upon arrival but may not wash again until after the sample collection has been completed; (6) immediately after collection the sample must be inspected for color and signs of contaminants and, within four minutes of urination, its temperature must be measured; and (7) if the temperature of the specimen gives rise to reasonable suspicion of adulteration or if other cause for suspicion is established, a second specimen must be obtained under direct observation.

The Guidelines provide procedures to verify the chain of custody and also detail the required analytical procedures. The initial screen must be an immunoassay with confirmation using GC/MS. The Guidelines also set forth the necessary quality assurance measures, including laboratory proficiency testing.

## B.  Private Employers

Although drug testing began in the private sector, it was not until public employers began testing that private sector drug testing became so widespread. For the most part, it is the large companies that have embraced drug testing. Among Fortune 500 corporations, only ten percent performed urinalysis in 1982; by 1985 the figure had reached twenty-five percent; and by 1987 nearly fifty percent of the largest corporations performed drug testing.

As the size of the company declines, so too does the prevalence of drug testing. In a 1987 survey of companies with more than 500 employees, seventeen percent of the companies tested current workers for drugs and twenty-three percent tested applicants. Smaller companies reported less testing. Transportation and manufacturing companies were most likely to test, electronics/communications and insurance/finance companies were least likely to test. The specifics of drug testing also vary by size of the company, geography, industry, and other factors. Larger companies are more likely to use confirmatory testing and refer those testing positive to an employee assistance program; smaller companies are more likely to use only screening tests and to respond to a positive test with summary dismissal.

According to one study, almost all of the companies (94.5%) that perform urinalysis test job applicants and nearly three-fourths of the companies (73%) test current employees on a "for cause" basis. Only fourteen percent conducted random tests and those companies tended to be smaller, with a significant number of them testing people in jobs of a "sensitive or high risk nature." The most widely cited reason for testing (37%) was health and safety. Other reasons for testing were the identification of a workplace substance abuse problem (21%), the awareness of drugs as a national problem (11%), and the high-risk nature of the job (9%).

It is also valuable to consider why the companies without drug testing programs have declined to engage in testing.  According to the American Management Association, the most common reasons for not performing drug testing are as follows:  moral issues or privacy (68%); inaccuracy of tests (63%); negative impact on morale (53%); tests show use, not abuse (43%); employee opposition (16%); and union opposition (7%).  Interestingly, fear of litigation was not mentioned, but it certainly may be an increasingly significant consideration.

## National Treasury Employees Union v. Von Raab

489 U.S. 656 (1989).

■ JUSTICE KENNEDY delivered the opinion of the Court.

We granted certiorari to decide whether it violates the Fourth Amendment for the United States Customs Service to require a urinalysis test from employees who seek transfer or promotion to certain positions.

The United States Customs Service, a bureau of the Department of the Treasury, is the federal agency responsible for processing persons, carriers, cargo, and mail into the United States, collecting revenue from imports, and enforcing customs and related laws.  An important responsibility of the Service is the interdiction and seizure of contraband, including illegal drugs.  In 1987 alone, Customs agents seized drugs with a retail value of nearly 9 billion dollars.  In the routine discharge of their duties, many Customs employees have direct contact with those who traffic in drugs for profit.  Drug import operations, often directed by sophisticated criminal syndicates, may be effected by violence or its threat.  As a necessary response, many Customs operatives carry and use firearms in connection with their official duties.

In December 1985, respondent, the Commissioner of Customs, established a Drug Screening Task Force to explore the possibility of implementing a drug screening program within the Service.  After extensive research and consultation with experts in the field, the Task Force concluded "that drug screening through urinalysis is technologically reliable, valid and accurate."  Citing this conclusion, the Commissioner announced his intention to require drug tests of employees who applied for, or occupied, certain positions within the Service.  The Commissioner stated his belief that "Customs is largely drug-free," but noted also that "unfortunately no segment of society is immune from the threat of illegal drug use."  Drug interdiction has become the agency's primary enforcement mission, and the Commissioner stressed that "there is no room in the Customs Service for those who break the laws prohibiting the possession and use of illegal drugs."

In May 1986, the Commissioner announced implementation of the drug-testing program.  Drug tests were made a condition of placement or employment for positions that meet one or more of three criteria.  The first is direct involvement in drug interdiction or enforcement of related laws, an activity the Commissioner deemed fraught with obvious dangers to the mission of the agency and the lives of customs agents. The second criterion is a requirement that the incumbent carry firearms, as the Commissioner concluded that "[p]ublic safety demands that employees who carry deadly arms and are prepared to make instant life or death decisions be drug free." The third criterion is a requirement for the incumbent to handle "classified" material, which the Commissioner determined might fall into the hands of smugglers if accessible to employees who, by reason of their own illegal drug use, are susceptible to bribery or blackmail.

After an employee qualifies for a position covered by the Customs testing program, the Service advises him by letter that his final selection is contingent upon successful completion of drug screening. An independent contractor contacts the employee to fix the time and place for collecting the sample. On reporting for the test, the employee must produce photographic identification and remove any outer garments, such as a coat or a jacket, and personal belongings. The employee may produce the sample behind a partition, or in the privacy of a bathroom stall if he so chooses. To ensure against adulteration of the specimen, or substitution of a sample from another person, a monitor of the same sex as the employee remains close at hand to listen for the normal sounds of urination. Dye is added to the toilet water to prevent the employee from using the water to adulterate the sample.

Upon receiving the specimen, the monitor inspects it to ensure its proper temperature and color, places a tamper-proof custody seal over the container, and affixes an identification label indicating the date and the individual's specimen number. The employee signs a chain-of-custody form, which is initialed by the monitor, and the urine sample is placed in a plastic bag, sealed, and submitted to a laboratory.

The laboratory tests the sample for the presence of marijuana, cocaine, opiates, amphetamines, and phencyclidine. Two tests are used. An initial screening test uses the enzyme-multiplied-immunoassay technique (EMIT). Any specimen that is identified as positive on this initial test must then be confirmed using gas chromatography/mass spectrometry (GC/MS). Confirmed positive results are reported to a "Medical Review Officer," "[a] licensed physician * * * who has knowledge of substance abused disorders and has appropriate medical training to interpret and evaluate the individual's positive test result together with his or her medical history and any other relevant biomedical information." After verifying the positive result, the Medical Review Officer transmits it to the agency.

Customs employees who test positive for drugs and who can offer no satisfactory explanation are subject to dismissal from the Service. Test results may not, however, be turned over to any other agency, including criminal prosecutors, without the employee's written consent.

Petitioners, a union of federal employees and a union official, commenced this suit in the United States District Court for the Eastern District of Louisiana on behalf of current Customs Service employees who seek covered positions. Petitioners alleged that the Custom Service drug-testing program violated, inter alia, the Fourth Amendment. The District Court agreed. The court acknowledged "the legitimate governmental interest in a drug-free work place and work force," but concluded that "the drug testing plan constitutes an overly intrusive policy of searches and seizures without probable cause or reasonable suspicion, in violation of legitimate expectations of privacy." The court enjoined the drug testing program, and ordered the Customs Service not to require drug tests of any applicants for covered positions.

A divided panel of the United States Court of Appeals for the Fifth Circuit vacated the injunction.

We granted certiorari. We now affirm so much of the judgment of the court of appeals as upheld the testing of employees directly involved in drug interdiction or required to carry firearms. We vacate the judgment to the extent it upheld the testing of applicants for positions requiring the incumbent to handle classified materials, and remand for further proceedings.

In Skinner v. Railway Labor Executives Assn., [109 S.Ct. 1402 (1989)] decided today, we hold that federal regulations requiring employees of private railroads to produce urine samples for chemical testing implicate the Fourth Amendment, as those tests invade reasonable expectations of privacy. Our earlier cases have settled that the Fourth Amendment protects individuals from unreasonable searches conducted by the Government, even when the Government acts as an employer, and, in view of our holding in *Railway Labor Executives* that urine tests are searches, it follows that the Customs Service's drug testing program must meet the reasonableness requirement of the Fourth Amendment.

While we have often emphasized, and reiterate today, that a search must be supported, as a general matter, by a warrant issued upon probable cause, our decision in *Railway Labor Executives* reaffirms the longstanding principle that neither a warrant nor probable cause, nor, indeed, any measure of individualized suspicion, is an indispensable component of reasonableness in every circumstance. As we note in *Railway Labor Executives,* our cases establish that where a Fourth Amendment intrusion serves special governmental needs, beyond the normal need for law enforcement, it is necessary to balance the individual's privacy expectations against the Government's interests to determine whether it is impractical to require a warrant or some level of individualized suspicion in the particular context.

It is clear that the Customs Service's drug testing program is not designed to serve the ordinary needs of law enforcement. Test results may not be used in a criminal prosecution of the employee without the employee's consent. The purposes of the program are to deter drug use among those eligible for promotion to sensitive positions within the Service and to prevent the promotion of drug users to those positions. These substantial interests, no less than the Government's concern for safe rail transportation at issue in *Railway Labor Executives,* present a special need that may justify departure from the ordinary warrant and probable cause requirements.

Petitioners do not contend that a warrant is required by the balance of privacy and governmental interests in this context, nor could any such contention withstand scrutiny. We have recognized before that requiring the Government to procure a warrant for every work-related intrusion "would conflict with 'the common-sense realization that government offices could not function if every employment decision became a constitutional matter.'" Even if Customs Service employees are more likely to be familiar with the procedures required to obtain a warrant than most other Government workers, requiring a warrant in this context would serve only to divert valuable agency resources from the Service's primary mission. The Customs Service has been entrusted with pressing responsibilities, and its mission would be compromised if it were required to seek search warrants in connection with routine, yet sensitive, employment decisions.

Furthermore, a warrant would provide little or nothing in the way of additional protection of personal privacy. A warrant serves primarily to advise the citizen that an intrusion is authorized by law and limited in its permissible scope and to interpose a neutral magistrate between the citizen and the law enforcement officer "engaged in the often competitive enterprise of ferreting out crime." But in the present context, "the circumstances justifying toxicological testing and the permissible limits of such intrusions are defined narrowly and specifically * * *, and doubtless are well known to covered employees." Under the Customs program, every employee who seeks a transfer to a covered position knows that he must take a drug test, and is likewise aware of the procedures the Service must follow in administering the test. A covered employee is simply not subject "to the discretion of the official in the field." The process becomes automatic when the employee elects to apply for, and thereafter pursue, a covered position. Because the Service does not make a discretionary determination to search based on a judgment that certain conditions are present, there are simply "no special facts for a neutral magistrate to evaluate."

Even where it is reasonable to dispense with the warrant requirement in the particular circumstances, a search ordinarily must be based on probable cause. Our cases teach, however, that the probable-cause standard "is peculiarly related to criminal investigations." In particular, the traditional probable-cause standard may be unhelpful in analyzing the reasonableness of routine administrative functions, especially where the Government seeks to *prevent* the development of hazardous conditions or to detect violations that rarely generate articulable grounds for searching any particular place or person. Our precedents have settled that, in certain limited circumstances, the Government's need to discover such latent or hidden conditions, or to prevent their development, is sufficiently compelling to justify the intrusion on privacy entailed by conducting such searches without any measure of individualized suspicion. We think the Government's need to conduct the suspicionless searches required by the Customs program outweighs the privacy interests of employees engaged directly in drug interdiction, and of those who otherwise are required to carry firearms.

The Customs Service is our Nation's first line of defense against one of the greatest problems affecting the health and welfare of our population. We have adverted before to "the veritable national crisis in law enforcement caused by smuggling of illicit narcotics." Our cases also reflect the traffickers' seemingly inexhaustible repertoire of deceptive practices and elaborate schemes for importing narcotics. The record in this case confirms that, through the adroit selection of source locations, smuggling routes, and increasingly elaborate methods of concealment, drug traffickers have managed to bring into this country increasingly large quantities of illegal drugs. The record also indicates, and it is well known, that drug smugglers do not hesitate to use violence to protect their lucrative trade and avoid apprehension.

Many of the Service's employees are often exposed to this criminal element and to the controlled substances they seek to smuggle into the country. The physical safety of these employees may be threatened, and many may be tempted not only by bribes from the traffickers with whom they deal, but also by their own access to vast sources of valuable contraband seized and controlled by the Service. The Commissioner indicated below that "Customs [o]fficers have been shot, stabbed, run over, dragged by automobiles, and assaulted with blunt objects while performing their duties." At least nine officers have died in the line of duty since 1974. He also noted that Customs officers have been the targets of bribery by drug smugglers on numerous occasions, and several have been removed from the Service for accepting bribes and other integrity violations.

It is readily apparent that the Government has a compelling interest in ensuring that front-line interdiction personnel are physically fit, and have unimpeachable integrity and judgment. * * * This national interest in self protection could be irreparably damaged if those charged with safeguarding it were, because of their own drug use, unsympathetic to their mission of interdicting narcotics. A drug user's indifference to the Service's basic mission or, even worse, his active complicity with the malefactors, can facilitate importation of sizable drug shipments or block apprehension of dangerous criminals. The public interest demands effective measures to bar drug users from positions directly involving the interdiction of illegal drugs.

The public interest likewise demands effective measures to prevent the promotion of drug users to positions that require the incumbent to carry a firearm, even if the incumbent is not engaged directly in the interdiction of drugs. Customs employees who may use deadly force plainly "discharge duties fraught with such risks of injury to others that even a momentary lapse of attention can have disastrous consequences." We agree with the Government that the public should not bear the risk that employees who may suffer from impaired perception and judgment will be promoted to positions where they may need to employ deadly force. Indeed, ensuring against the creation of this dangerous risk will itself further Fourth Amendment values, as the use of deadly force may violate the Fourth Amendment in certain circumstances.

Against these valid public interests we must weigh the interference with individual liberty that results from requiring these classes of employees to undergo a urine test. The interference with individual privacy that results from the collection of a urine sample for subsequent chemical analysis could be substantial in some circumstances. We have recognized, however, that the "operational realities of the workplace" may render entirely reasonable certain work-related intrusions by supervisors and co-workers that might be viewed as unreasonable in other contexts. While these operational realities will rarely affect an employee's expectations of privacy with respect to searches of his person, or of personal effects that the employee may bring to the workplace, it is plain that certain forms of public employment may diminish privacy expectations even with respect to such personal searches. Employees of the United States Mint, for example, should expect to be subject to certain routine personal searches when they leave the workplace every day. Similarly, those who join our military or intelligence services may not only be required to give what in other contexts might be viewed as extraordinary assurances of trustworthiness and probity, but also may expect intrusive inquiries into their physical fitness for those special positions.

We think Customs employees who are directly involved in the interdiction of illegal drugs or who are required to carry firearms in the line of duty likewise have a diminished expectation of privacy in respect to the intrusions occasioned by a urine test. Unlike most private citizens or government employees in general, employees involved in drug interdiction reasonably should expect effective inquiry into their fitness and probity. Much the same is true of employees who are required to carry firearms. Because successful performance of their duties depends uniquely on their judgment and dexterity, these employees cannot reasonably expect to keep from the Service personal information that bears directly on their fitness. While reasonable tests designed to elicit this information doubtless infringe some privacy expectations, we do not believe these expectations outweigh the Government's compelling interests in safety and in the integrity of our borders.

Without disparaging the importance of the governmental interests that support the suspicionless searches of these employees, petitioners nevertheless contend that the Service's drug testing program is unreasonable in two particulars. First, petitioners argue that the program is unjustified because it is not based on a belief that testing will reveal any drug use by covered employees. In pressing this argument, petitioners point out that the Service's testing scheme was not implemented in response to any perceived drug problem among Customs employees, and that the program actually has not led to the discovery of a significant number of drug users. Counsel for petitioners informed us at oral argument that no more than 5 employees out of 3,600 have tested positive for drugs. Second, petitioners contend that the Service's scheme is not a "sufficiently productive mechanism to justify [its] intrusion upon Fourth Amendment interests," because illegal drug users can avoid detection with ease by temporary abstinence or by surreptitious adulteration of their urine specimens. These contentions are unpersuasive.

Petitioners' first contention evinces an unduly narrow view of the context in which the Service's testing program was implemented. Petitioners do not dispute, nor can there be doubt, that drug abuse is one of the most serious problems confronting our society today. There is little reason to believe that American workplaces are immune from this pervasive social problem, as is amply illustrated by our decision in *Railway Labor Executives.* * * *

The mere circumstance that all but a few of the employees tested are entirely innocent of wrongdoing does not impugn the program's validity. * * * The Service's program is designed to prevent the promotion of drug users to sensitive positions as much as it is designed to detect those employees who use drugs. Where, as here, the possible harm against which the Government seeks to guard is substantial, the need to prevent its occurrence furnishes an ample justification for reasonable searches calculated to advance the Government's goal.

We think petitioners' second argument—that the Service's testing program is ineffective because employees may attempt to deceive the test by a brief abstention before the test date, or by adulterating their urine specimens—overstates the case. As the Court of Appeals noted, addicts may be unable to abstain even for a limited period of time, or may be unaware of the "fade-away effect" of certain drugs. More importantly, the avoidance techniques suggested by petitioners are fraught with uncertainty and risks for those employees who venture to attempt them. A particular employee's pattern of elimination for a given drug cannot be predicted with perfect accuracy, and, in any event, this information is not likely to be known or available to the employee. * * * Thus, contrary to petitioners' suggestion, no employee reasonably can expect to deceive the test by the simple expedient of abstaining after the test date is assigned. Nor can he expect attempts at adulteration to succeed, in view of the precautions taken by the sample collector to ensure the integrity of the sample. In all the circumstances, we are persuaded that the program bears a close and substantial relation to the Service's goal of deterring drug users from seeking promotion to sensitive positions.

In sum, we believe the Government has demonstrated that its compelling interests in safeguarding our borders and the public safety outweigh the privacy expectations of employees who seek to be promoted to positions that directly involve the interdiction of illegal drugs or that require the incumbent to carry a firearm. We hold that the testing of these employees is reasonable under the Fourth Amendment.

We are unable, on the present record, to assess the reasonableness of the Government's testing program insofar as it covers employees who are required "to handle classified material." We readily agree that the Government has a compelling interest in protecting truly sensitive information from those who, "under compulsion of circumstances or for other reasons, * * * might compromise [such] information." We also agree that employees who seek promotions to positions where they would handle sensitive information can be required to submit to a urine test under the Service's screening program, especially if the positions covered under this category require background investigations, medical examinations, or other intrusions that may be expected to diminish their expectations of privacy in respect of a urinalysis test.

It is not clear, however, whether the category defined by the Service's testing directive encompasses only those Customs employees likely to gain access to sensitive information. Employees who are tested under the Service's scheme include those holding such diverse positions as "Accountant," "Accounting Technician," "Animal Caretaker," "Attorney (All)," "Baggage Clerk," "Co-op Student (All)," "Electric Equipment Repairer," "Mail Clerk/Assistant," and "Messenger." We assume these positions were selected for coverage under the Service's testing program by reason of the incumbent's access to "classified" information, as it is not clear that they would fall under either of the two categories we have already considered. Yet it is not evident that those occupying these positions are likely to gain access to sensitive information, and this apparent discrepancy raises in our minds the question whether the Service has defined this category of employees more broadly than necessary to meet the purposes of the Commissioner's directive.

We cannot resolve this ambiguity on the basis of the record before us, and we think it is appropriate to remand the case to the court of appeals for such proceedings as may be necessary to clarify the scope of this category of employees subject to testing. Upon remand the court of appeals should examine the criteria used by the Service in determining what materials are classified and in deciding whom to test under this rubric. In assessing the reasonableness of requiring tests of these employees, the court should also consider pertinent information bearing upon the employees' privacy expectations, as well as the supervision to which these employees are already subject.

\* \* \*

The judgment of the Court of Appeals for the Fifth Circuit is affirmed in part and vacated in part, and the case is remanded for further proceedings consistent with this opinion.

*It is so ordered.*

■ JUSTICE MARSHALL, with whom JUSTICE BRENNAN joins, dissenting.

For the reasons stated in my dissenting opinion in Skinner v. Railway Labor Executives' Association, I also dissent from the Court's decision in this case. Here, as in *Skinner,* the Court's abandonment of the Fourth Amendment's express requirement that searches of the person rest on probable cause is unprincipled and unjustifiable. But even if I believed that balancing analysis was appropriate under the Fourth Amendment, I would still dissent from today's judgment, for the reasons stated by Justice Scalia in his dissenting opinion and for the reasons noted by the dissenting judge below relating to the inadequate tailoring of the Customs Service's drug-testing plan.

■ JUSTICE SCALIA, with whom JUSTICE STEVENS joins, dissenting.

The issue in this case is not whether Customs Service employees can constitutionally be denied promotion, or even dismissed, for a single instance of unlawful drug use, at home or at work. They assuredly can. The issue here is what steps can constitutionally be taken to *detect* such drug use. The Government asserts it can demand that employees perform "an excretory function traditionally shielded by great privacy," Skinner v. Railway Labor Executives' Assn., while "a monitor of the same sex * * * remains close at hand to listen for the normal sounds," and that the excretion thus produced be turned over to the Government for chemical analysis. The Court agrees that this constitutes a search for purposes of the Fourth Amendment—and I think it obvious that it is a type of search particularly destructive of privacy and offensive to personal dignity.

Until today this Court had upheld a bodily search separate from arrest and without individualized suspicion of wrongdoing only with respect to prison inmates, relying upon the uniquely dangerous nature of that environment. Today, in *Skinner,* we allow a less intrusive bodily search of railroad employees involved in train accidents. I joined the Court's opinion there because the demonstrated frequency of drug and alcohol use by the targeted class of employees, and the demonstrated connection between such use and grave harm, rendered the search a reasonable means of protecting society. I decline to join the Court's opinion in the present case because neither frequency of use nor connection to harm is demonstrated or even likely. In my view the Customs Service rules are a kind of immolation of privacy and human dignity in symbolic opposition to drug use. * * *

What is absent in the Government's justifications—notably absent, revealingly absent, and as far as I am concerned dispositively absent—is the recitation of *even a single instance* in which any of the speculated horribles actually occurred: an instance, that is, in which the cause of bribe-taking, or of poor aim, or of unsympathetic law enforcement, or of compromise of classified information, was drug use. Although the Court points out that several employees have in the past been removed from the Service for accepting bribes and other integrity violations, and that at least nine officers have died in the line of duty since 1974, there is no indication whatever that these incidents were related to drug use by Service employees. Perhaps concrete evidence of the severity of a problem is unnecessary when it is so well known that courts can almost take judicial notice of it; but that is surely not the case here. The Commissioner of Customs himself has stated that he "believe[s] that Customs is largely drug-free," that "[t]he extent of illegal drug use by Customs employees was not the reason for establishing this program," and that he "hope[s] and expect[s] to receive reports of very few positive findings through drug screening." The test results have fulfilled those hopes and expectations. According to the

Service's counsel, out of 3,600 employees tested, no more than 5 tested positive for drugs.

The Court's response to this lack of evidence is that "[t]here is little reason to believe that American workplaces are immune from [the] pervasive social problem" of drug abuse. Perhaps such a generalization would suffice if the workplace at issue could produce such catastrophic social harm that no risk whatever is tolerable—the secured areas of a nuclear power plant, for example. But if such a generalization suffices to justify demeaning bodily searches, without particularized suspicion, to guard against the bribing or blackmailing of a law enforcement agent, or the careless use of a firearm, then the Fourth Amendment has become frail protection indeed. * * * In *Skinner,* for example, we pointed to a long history of alcohol abuse in the railroad industry, and noted that in an 8–year period 45 train accidents and incidents had occurred because of alcohol- and drug-impaired railroad employees, killing 34 people, injuring 66, and causing more than $28 million in property damage. In the present case, by contrast, not only is the Customs Service thought to be "largely drug-free," but the connection between whatever drug use may exist and serious social harm is entirely speculative. * * *

Today's decision would be wrong, but at least of more limited effect, if its approval of drug testing were confined to that category of employees assigned specifically to drug interdiction duties. Relatively few public employees fit that description. But in extending approval of drug testing to that category consisting of employees who carry firearms, the Court exposes vast numbers of public employees to this needless indignity. Logically, of course, if those who carry guns can be treated in this fashion, so can all others whose work, if performed under the influence of drugs, may endanger others—automobile drivers, operators of other potentially dangerous equipment, construction workers, school crossing guards. A similarly broad scope attaches to the Court's approval of drug testing for those with access to "sensitive information." Since this category is not limited to Service employees with drug interdiction duties, nor to "sensitive information" specifically relating to drug traffic, today's holding apparently approves drug testing for all federal employees with security clearances— or, indeed, for all federal employees with valuable confidential information to impart. Since drug use is not a particular problem in the Customs Service, employees throughout the government are no less likely to violate the public trust by taking bribes to feed their drug habit, or by yielding to blackmail. Moreover, there is no reason why this super-protection against harms arising from drug use must be limited to public employees; a law requiring similar testing of private citizens who use dangerous instruments such as guns or cars, or who have access to classified information would also be constitutional.

There is only one apparent basis that sets the testing at issue here apart from all these other situations—but it is not a basis upon which the Court is willing to rely. I do not believe for a minute that the driving force behind these drug-testing rules was any of the feeble justifications put forward by counsel here and accepted by the Court.  The only plausible explanation, in my view, is what the Commissioner himself offered in the concluding sentence of his memorandum to Customs Service employees announcing the program:  "Implementation of the drug screening program would set an important example in our country's struggle with this most serious threat to our national health and security."  Or as respondent's brief to this Court asserted:  "if a law enforcement agency and its employees do not take the law seriously, neither will the public on which the agency's effectiveness depends."  What better way to show that the Government is serious about its "war on drugs" than to subject its employees on the front line of that war to this invasion of their privacy and affront to their dignity?  To be sure, there is only a slight chance that it will prevent some serious public harm resulting from Service employee drug use, but it will show to the world that the Service is "clean," and—most important of all—will demonstrate the determination of the Government to eliminate this scourge of our society!  I think it obvious that this justification is unacceptable;  that the impairment of individual liberties cannot be the means of making a point;  that symbolism, even symbolism for so worthy a cause as the abolition of unlawful drugs, cannot validate an otherwise unreasonable search.

There is irony in the Government's citation, in support of its position, of Justice Brandeis's statement in Olmstead v. United States, 277 U.S. 438, 485 (1928) that "[f]or good or for ill, [our Government] teaches the whole people by its example."  Brandeis was there *dissenting* from the Court's admission of evidence obtained through an unlawful Government wiretap. He was not praising the Government's example of vigor and enthusiasm in combatting crime, but condemning its example that "the end justifies the means."  An even more apt quotation from that famous Brandeis dissent would have been the following:

> "[I]t is * * * immaterial that the intrusion was in aid of law
> enforcement.  Experience should teach us to be most on our guard
> to protect liberty when the Government's purposes are beneficent.
> Men born to freedom are naturally alert to repel invasion of their
> liberty by evil-minded rulers.  The greatest dangers to liberty lurk
> in insidious encroachment by men of zeal, well-meaning but with-
> out understanding."

Those who lose because of the lack of understanding that begot the present exercise in symbolism are not just the Customs Service employees, whose dignity is thus offended, but all of us—who suffer a coarsening of our national manners that ultimately give the Fourth Amendment its content, and who become subject to the administration of federal officials whose respect for our privacy can hardly be greater than the small respect they have been taught to have for their own.

NOTES AND QUESTIONS

1.  In Skinner v. Railway Labor Executives' Association, 489 U.S. 602 (1989), the Supreme Court by a seven-to-two vote upheld Federal Railroad

Administration regulations requiring railroads to conduct post-accident drug tests of railroad crews. Justices Marshall and Brennan dissented. Part of the dissent is as follows:

> The issue in this case is not whether declaring a war on illegal drugs is good public policy. The importance of ridding our society of such drugs is, by now, apparent to all. Rather, the issue here is whether the Government's deployment in that war of a particularly draconian weapon—the compulsory collection and chemical testing of railroad workers' blood and urine—comports with the Fourth Amendment. Precisely because the need for action against the drug scourge is manifest, the need for vigilance against unconstitutional excess is great. History teaches that grave threats to liberty often come in times of urgency, when constitutional rights seem too extravagant to endure. The World War II relocation-camp cases, Hirabayashi v. United States, 320 U.S. 81 (1943); Korematsu v. United States, 323 U.S. 214 (1944), and the Red Scare and McCarthy–Era internal subversion cases, Schenck v. United States, 249 U.S. 47 (1919); Dennis v. United States, 341 U.S. 494 (1951), are only the most extreme reminders that when we allow fundamental freedoms to be sacrificed in the name of real or perceived exigency, we invariably come to regret it.

\* \* \*

In his first dissenting opinion as a Member of this Court, Oliver Wendell Holmes observed:

> "Great cases, like hard cases, make bad law. For great cases are called great, not by reason of their real importance in shaping the law of the future, but because of some accident of immediate overwhelming interest which appeals to the feelings and distorts the judgment. These immediate interests exercise a kind of hydraulic pressure which makes what previously was clear seem doubtful, and before which even well settled principles of law will bend." Northern Securities Co. v. United States, 193 U.S. 197, 400–401 (1904).

A majority of this Court, swept away by society's obsession with stopping the scourge of illegal drugs, today succumbs to the popular pressures described by Justice Holmes. In upholding the FRA's plan for blood and urine testing, the majority bends time-honored and textually-based principles of the Fourth Amendment—principles the Framers of the Bill of Rights designed to ensure that the Government has a strong and individualized justification when it seeks to invade an individual's privacy. I believe the Framers would be appalled by the vision of mass governmental intrusions upon the integrity of the human body that the majority allows to become reality. The immediate victims of the majority's constitutional timorousness will be those railroad workers whose bodily fluids the Government may now forcibly collect and analyze.  But ultimately, today's decision will reduce the privacy all citizens may enjoy, for, as Justice Holmes understood, principles of law, once bent, do not snap back easily.  I dissent.

**2.**  As with Justice Scalia's dissent in *Von Raab*, Justice Marshall's dissent in *Skinner* suggests that the facts of the case led the majority to reach an unsound legal conclusion.  Do you agree?  What facts are most compelling for each side?

**3.**  Justice Scalia charged that the drug testing program was "symbolic," i.e., politically motivated.  Does Justice Kennedy reject this argument or does he say, in effect, that regardless of the motivation the drug testing program is reasonable?

**4.**  Constitutional challenges to government-mandated drug testing after *Von Raab* have focused on the government's need to test.  This determination often is based on the nature of the employees' duties.  See, e.g., American Federation of Government Employees v. Martin, 969 F.2d 788 (9th Cir.1992) (upholding testing of Labor Department employees in safety-sensitive or security-sensitive positions); American Federation of Government Employees Local 1533 v. Cheney, 944 F.2d 503 (9th Cir.1991) (upholding Navy's testing of civilian employees required to hold top secret security clearances); American Postal Workers Union v. Frank, 725 F.Supp. 87 (D.Mass.1989) (striking down testing of all postal workers without individualized suspicion).  What factors should the courts consider in deciding whether government-mandated drug testing is constitutional?

**5.**  The Drug–Free Workplace Act of 1988, 41 U.S.C. §§ 701 et seq., applies to employers with federal contracts in excess of $25,000.  Under the Act, each covered employer must publish and distribute a policy prohibiting the unlawful manufacture, distribution, dispensing, possession, or use of controlled substances in the workplace;  provide for penalties for employees convicted of drug related violations on the job;  and establish an employee awareness program on the dangers and penalties of workplace drug abuse, and the availability of resources for drug rehabilitation and counseling.  Employers failing to meet these requirements may have their federal contracts terminated and may be debarred from future contracts for up to five years.

**6.**  The Omnibus Transportation Employee Testing Act, 49 U.S.C. §§ 45101–45106, codified earlier Department of Transportation regulations requiring the drug testing of employees in the transportation industry.  It also adds the requirement of random alcohol testing for six million employees.  See 49 C.F.R. Part 40.

**7.**  Nine states have enacted laws limiting drug testing.  The laws in seven states, Connecticut, Iowa, Maine, Minnesota, Montana, Rhode Island, and Vermont, are similar in the following respects:  (1) all of the laws seek to limit drug testing, but do not prohibit testing completely;  (2) all of the laws permit the preemployment testing of applicants and some permit the periodic testing of employees if advance notice is given;  (3) exceptions are often made for public safety officers and employees in safety-sensitive jobs; (4) "for cause" testing is generally allowed if there is "probable cause," "reasonable cause," or "reasonable suspicion" that an employee is impaired; (5) most of the laws require that the sample collection be performed in private; (6) all of the laws require confirmatory testing; and (7) most of the laws specifically require that drug testing records be kept confidential.

Nine other states, Florida, Hawaii, Illinois, Louisiana, Mississippi, Nebraska, Nevada, North Carolina, and Oregon, regulate various procedures used in private or public sector drug testing. For example, they specify that notices must be posted to advise employees of the testing, require the use of certified laboratories, or grant employees the right to have the sample retested.

Utah's Drug and Alcohol Testing Act, Utah Code Ann. §§ 34–38–1 to 34–38–15, differs significantly from the other laws. The Utah law permits drug testing as a condition of hiring or continued employment so long as employers and managers also submit to testing periodically. In encouraging drug testing, the statute requires that employers performing drug testing have a written testing policy and that confirmatory tests be used. If an employer satisfies these requirements, the law immunizes the employer from liability for defamation or other torts based on the drug testing. It also prohibits any action based on the failure to conduct a drug test.

In Chandler v. Miller, 117 S.Ct. 1295 (1997), the Supreme Court struck down a Georgia statute that required candidates for designated state offices to present a certificate from a state-approved laboratory that they have taken and have had a negative result on a urinalysis drug test within 30 days prior to qualifying for nomination or election. The Court held that the purely "symbolic" function of the law was insufficient to pass scrutiny under the Fourth Amendment.

**8.** Challenges to private sector drug testing have relied on various theories, including the claim that the testing violates a state constitution's right to privacy. These challenges generally have been unsuccessful. Compare Luedtke v. Nabors Alaska Drilling, Inc., 768 P.2d 1123 (Alaska 1989) (rejecting theory) with Semore v. Pool, 266 Cal.Rptr. 280 (Cal.App.1990) (adopting theory). See also Alverado v. Washington Public Power Supply System, 759 P.2d 427 (Wash.1988), cert. denied, 490 U.S. 1004 (1989) (state law claim preempted by federal regulation of nuclear power plant).

**9.** Section 104(d) of the Americans with Disabilities Act (ADA) provides that "a test to determine the illegal use of drugs shall not be considered a medical examination." Consequently, they may be given at any time, including at the preemployment stage. At the preemployment stage, however, the ADA prohibits employers from asking applicants about the prescription medications they are taking. Because knowledge of prescription medications is important in drug testing in ruling out "cross-reactivity," is it lawful for employers to ask about prescription drug use as part of an otherwise lawful, preemployment drug test? EEOC, in its Guidance on Pre-employment Inquiries (1994), said that after an initial positive screening test an employer may ask about prescription medications. Why do you think most employers prefer to perform drug testing at the preemployment rather than the preplacement stage?

## Mark A. Rothstein, *Does Employee Drug Testing Work?*
4 Employment Testing 716 (1991).

Each year millions of workers, in jobs ranging from accountant to zookeeper, submit to drug testing. There has been much discussion about whether the tests are accurate or legal. There has been little discussion, however, about whether drug testing actually works. In other words, does drug testing reduce the use of illicit substances by employees and improve productivity and safety?

Because of the expense and intrusiveness of urine drug testing, it would seem appropriate that the proponents of drug testing have the burden of proving that drug testing is, among other things, necessary and effective. Drug testing advocates often cite three sets of data to buttress their claim that drug testing works: (1) declining drug use by employees, (2) improvements in productivity and safety, and (3) employee surveys endorsing drug testing. Each of these reasons deserves further review.

### Declining Rates of Drug Use

Some companies that have been performing drug tests on applicants for a few years report that the percentage of applicants testing positive has declined. Two reasons are often cited for this drop. First, it has been asserted that widespread drug testing by employers has reduced overall drug consumption because drug users know they will not be able to get a job. Second, it also has been argued that when drug testing of applicants by a particular company becomes well known in a community, drug-using individuals do not even bother to apply for a job with that company.

There are no studies addressing why illicit drug users seek employment with one company instead of another. It may be that drug testing helps companies avoid hiring some problem employees. On the other hand, those companies probably lose some potentially valuable employees whose occasional drug use would not affect their performance, as well as other individuals who do not use drugs but who are offended at having to take a drug test.

The other assertion—that widespread employee drug testing has caused or contributed to a nationwide decline in drug use—is almost certainly incorrect. According to the National Institute on Drug Abuse (NIDA), the number of adult cocaine users declined from 5.8 million in 1985 to 1.6 million in 1990, and the number of adults who used any illicit drug declined from 23.0 million in 1985 to 12.9 million in 1990. This decline in the number of drug users began before the widespread institution of employee drug testing.

Despite a contrary impression from the media, the rate of illicit substance abuse in the United States has declined sharply. Unfortunately, the number of drug addicts has declined only slightly, and the percentage of drug users who are addicted has increased.  Thus, there are relatively more addicts but many fewer "casual" users.  The decline in casual drug use suggests a general lessening of the need for employers to perform drug testing.  Casual drug users actually pose the greater threat to employers. Hard core drug addicts are much less likely to seek and maintain traditional employment and are much more easily detected without drug testing at a preemployment medical examination and, if hired, by supervisory personnel.

The most convincing reason why workplace drug testing is not responsible for the decline in drug use by workers is that a similar decline has been measured in a group that has not been subject to drug testing—high school students.  The University of Michigan's annual survey of high school seniors nationwide showed a drop in cocaine use from 6.7 percent in 1985 to 1.9 percent in 1990.  This is similar to the decline in cocaine use by adults reported by NIDA.  Moreover, marijuana use has declined steadily from 37.1 percent in 1978 to 14.0 percent in 1990.  Thus, rates of illicit drug use have declined irrespective of drug testing.

### Productivity and Safety

Some drug testing advocates point to anecdotal reports of improved productivity and safety (e.g., fewer drug-related absences and accidents) as being directly attributable to drug testing.  Because of reduced drug usage, however, these improvements probably would have occurred in any event. Moreover, the use of illegal drugs actually has relatively little effect on overall safety rates when compared with alcohol and prescription drugs.  In a study, for example, of work-related fatalities in Harris County, Texas, drug and alcohol testing was performed at 173 of 196 autopsies.  The results showed that 23 workers had a detectable blood alcohol content, 11 workers had detectable traces of prescription drugs with the potential to alter physical functions needed to avoid injury, and only 1 worker tested positive for marijuana.

Even assuming that improvements in safety have resulted from employer action related to drugs, it is clear that improvements would have taken place without drug *testing*.  For some companies, employee drug testing was the first and only effort to do something about substance abuse. Therefore, for some companies, drug testing is being compared with doing nothing.  In scientific terms, it is an experiment without a control.  Employers who institute drug education programs, supervisory training programs, and employee assistance programs may well achieve the same safety and productivity improvements without resorting to drug testing.

There are no studies comparing the effectiveness of drug testing with these other methods of dealing with workplace drug abuse.  Few scientific studies exist that document the hardly surprising conclusion that individuals testing positive for marijuana or cocaine at a pre-employment drug test are more likely to be fired, injured, or disciplined.  A November 1990 study of postal workers published in the *Journal of the American Medical Association* found a much smaller correlation between a positive drug test and reduced productivity than those claimed by drug testing advocates. According to the authors of the study, "the findings * * * suggest that many of the claims cited to justify preemployment drug screening have been exaggerated." Nevertheless, a headline published the same day in the *Wall Street Journal* read: "Study May Spur Job–Applicant Drug Screening."

### Employee Support

Some companies justify drug testing by citing surveys in which their employees appear to favor drug testing. These surveys need to be put in perspective. Employees may not be knowledgeable about drug usage rates, alternatives to drug testing, or the limitations of drug testing. As with management, many employees may not realize that drug testing does not indicate when the drug was taken, how much was taken, whether the individual was impaired at the time of ingestion, whether the individual is currently impaired, or what effects the drug has on job performance. They also may not realize that the more widespread use of alcohol, prescription drugs, and over-the-counter medications (not usually part of a drug test) makes these substances more of a safety risk than illicit drugs. Finally, they may not realize that, at least in the private sector, employees usually have no right to challenge an erroneous result and that a "drug-related" discharge could damage their employment prospects long into the future.

### Conclusion

Drug testing is expensive, intrusive, and, unless done carefully by a qualified laboratory, may be inaccurate. It may undermine labor-management relations, and it is also increasingly subject to legal challenge. On the other hand, drug testing is an important part of aftercare for individuals in drug rehabilitation programs; drug testing may provide an added margin of safety for employees in certain unsupervised, ultrahazardous jobs; and it may reassure members of the public that workers on whom they depend are drug free.

The decision to implement workplace drug testing should not be made without the careful consideration of a number of factors. It also should not be made on the assumption that employee drug testing is effective. There is simply far too little evidence at present to support such a claim.

NOTE

For a further discussion, see National Research Council/Institute of Medicine, Under the Influence? Drugs and the American Work Force (1994); Mark A. Rothstein, Workplace Drug Testing: A Case Study in the Misapplication of Technology, 5 Harv. J.L. & Tech. 65 (1991).

## 2.  GENETIC TESTING

## Mark A. Rothstein, *Genetic Discrimination in Employment and the Americans With Disabilities Act*
29 Hous.L.Rev. 23, 24–33 (1992).

Genes provide the blueprint for the biological component of human individuality. Biologically speaking, genes determine the unique characteristics of every human being and make *Homo sapiens* a heterogeneous and variegated species. The Human Genome Project promises to expand our knowledge of genetics in ways and to an extent that are unprecedented. With the potential to predict the future health of individuals, however, the Human Genome Project also raises profound ethical, legal, moral, and social issues.

The Human Genome Project is not a single "project," but a collection of conceptually related, independent, worldwide research efforts with the common goal of analyzing the structure of human DNA and mapping and sequencing the estimated 100,000 human genes. This vast undertaking, which will cost an estimated $3 billion over fifteen years, began in 1990. It is widely thought to be one of the most important scientific research projects ever undertaken. Among the many ways in which the Human Genome Project will influence medicine are reproductive planning, prenatal diagnosis and treatment, preventive health, and eventually therapies to cure a wide range of illnesses with a genetic component.

The Human Genome Project will not only reconfirm the fundamental genetic similarity of all humans, but will also lead to the discovery of subtle and profound variations among individuals at the molecular level. With the increased understanding of what makes individuals distinct and polymorphic, the opportunity to classify or categorize individuals based upon genetic criteria will exist. Recognizing distinctions among individuals may lead to differentiation in their treatment and, consequently, genetic discrimination.

In the employment setting, discrimination among individuals has long been legally, ethically, and socially acceptable. For example, employers "discriminate" among job applicants based on qualifications such as education and experience. Only invidious discrimination is ethically unacceptable and only some specific forms of invidious discrimination, such as discrimination based on race, color, religion, sex, national origin, age, or disability, are illegal.

Employers already discriminate on the basis of genetics, either in absolute terms (e.g., refusing to employ someone lacking relevant physical qualifications) or in relative terms (e.g., preferring one person over another because of their superior physical qualifications). This discrimination, however, is based largely on the *effects* of genes. The Human Genome Project will greatly expand the ability to predict which unexpressed genes may, at some time in the future, lead to gene expression. The most frequent concerns voiced about future gene expression are about genes with deleterious health consequences.

There has been much discussion about the possibility that new genetic technologies could bring about horrendous social consequences, including the creation of a biological underclass of unemployable and uninsurable people. Is this concern well founded? In answering this question, it would be very helpful to know the extent of genetic screening in employment today and the extent to which screening will be used in the future. The most authoritative study, a 1990 report, *Genetic Monitoring and Screening in the Workplace,* by the Congressional Office of Technology Assessment (OTA), reported the results of its 1989 survey of the *Fortune* 500 companies, the fifty largest utilities, and thirty-three major unions. Of the 330 responding companies, only twelve reported using biochemical genetic screening and none indicated that they anticipated using direct DNA screening in the next five years.

It is tempting to read the OTA survey in a reassuring way—as suggesting that there is no problem with genetic screening today, that there is not likely to be a problem in the future, and that concerns about future genetic screening are unfounded and alarmist. Such a reading, however, is misguided. The OTA's survey design was constrained by the need to follow up a similar survey done in 1982 and by a desire to avoid speculation. Nevertheless, one must wonder whether similar disinterest in genetic screening would continue if the following three questions were asked to employers:

1. If a simple, cheap, and accurate test were available that would indicate whether an applicant or employee was likely to get a future illness costing many thousands of dollars to treat, would you have any interest in using such a test?

2. If you had access to the results of a medical test taken by one of your applicants or employees, and the test indicated that he or she was likely to get a future illness costing many thousands of dollars, would you have an interest in seeing such test results?

3. If you knew, from a medical test or record, that an applicant or employee had or was likely to get an illness costing many thousands of dollars to treat, as a self-insured company, would you consider preexisting condition exclusions, waivers of specific disease coverage, caps on pay-outs, or other measures to limit the company's health care exposure?

A wealth of information is available to suggest that many employers would indeed answer one or more of these questions in the affirmative. First, considerable anecdotal evidence of genetic discrimination in employment has been compiled. Second, the OTA's survey data, published separately in 1991, indicated that forty-two percent of the companies considered a job applicant's health insurance risks a factor in determining employability. In addition, thirty-six percent of the companies actively engaged in health insurance risk assessments of job applicants. Thus, the OTA concluded that health insurance cost containment could lead to the genetic testing of job applicants.

\* \* \*

Third, genetic discrimination may be viewed merely as a subset of health-based discrimination, which is already a significant problem and likely to get much worse because of the economic pressures placed on employers to reduce health care expenditures. From 1985 to 1991, employer health insurance costs per employee increased from $1,724 to $3,605 per year. Insurance costs continue to increase at least ten to twenty percent a year.  In some industries, depending on the type of coverage provided, health costs are already much higher.  For example, in the automobile industry, annual health care costs in 1988 were $5,800 per employee, representing approximately $700 per car.  In 1989 health care costs in all industries were fifty-six percent of pretax company profit, compared with eight percent in 1965.

Employers' responses to these increasing costs have been well documented.  Employer efforts at cost containment and cost shifting are the main reasons that the leading cause of labor strikes is now health benefits.  Employers also have attempted to restrict the employment of high-cost users of health care, such as cigarette smokers, people infected with HIV, and even people with high cholesterol levels.  Both large, self-insured companies and small-to-medium sized, experience-rated companies are acting much like commercial health insurers who have financial incentives to screen out health risks.  Commercial health insurers engage in detailed medical screening for individually underwritten policies.  From a purely economic standpoint, many employers probably will want to do the same.

If genetic discrimination in employment becomes widespread, what legal remedies will be available?  The legal response to genetic discrimination in employment dates back only twenty years.  During the early 1970s, sickle cell testing became a national health priority.  Sickle cell testing in black communities became common, but these federally-funded screening programs "evolved in a rapid, haphazard, often poorly planned fashion, generated in large measure by public clamor and political pressure."  Inadequate counseling and public education meant that many people were unable to distinguish sickle cell anemia from sickle cell trait.  Consequently, many unaffected heterozygotes were subject to discrimination in employment in a wide range of jobs.  To combat this irrational discrimination, Florida, Louisiana, and North Carolina enacted laws prohibiting employment discrimination based on sickle cell trait.  These statutes were the first employment laws specifically directed at genetic discrimination.

As the prospects have increased for more broadly based genetic discrimination, other state laws have been enacted.  In 1981 New Jersey enacted a law prohibiting employment discrimination based on an individual's "atypical hereditary cellular or blood trait," defined to include sickle cell trait, hemoglobin C trait, thalassemia trait, Tay–Sachs trait, and cystic fibrosis trait.  In 1989 Oregon amended its unlawful employment practices act to prohibit employers from requiring applicants or employees to undergo "genetic screening," although the term itself is not further defined.  In 1990 New York enacted a law prohibiting genetic discrimination based on sickle cell trait, Tay–Sachs trait, or Cooley's anemia (beta thalassemia) trait.  Finally, in 1992 Wisconsin enacted a law barring employers from requiring applicants or employees to undergo genetic testing or from using information from such tests in employment decisions.  Additional state legislation looms on the horizon.

* * *

The newest and most important law prohibiting discrimination in employment on the basis of disability is the Americans with Disabilities Act of 1990 (ADA). This comprehensive federal law is the first to prohibit discrimination in public and private employment on the basis of disability. It is a complex and far-reaching law, but one that was not specifically drafted with the problems of genetic discrimination in mind. Nevertheless, the broad policy of the ADA to prohibit discrimination based on health status encompasses most genetic conditions.

Fueled by the growing crisis in employer-provided health benefits, the economic interests of employers and the principle of nondiscrimination in employment are on a collision course. By greatly expanding the ability to engage in predictive screening, the Human Genome Project will accelerate this collision. How will law and public policy resolve this dilemma? Are current laws, including the ADA, adequate to regulate this complex issue?

NOTES AND QUESTIONS

**1.** To what extent do you think health care reform (discussed in Chapter 6, infra), giving access to health insurance to all Americans regardless of their medical condition, will eliminate the incentive for employers to engage in genetic discrimination?

**2.** Is genetic discrimination any different from other forms of medical discrimination? If so, how?

**3.** In March 1995, the EEOC issued its first official interpretation of the coverage of genetic predisposition under the ADA.

> This part of the definition of "disability" applies to individuals who are subjected to discrimination on the basis of genetic information related to illness, disease, or other disorders. Covered entities that discriminate against individuals on the basis of such genetic information are regarding the individuals as having impairments that substantially limit a major life activity. Those individuals, therefore, are covered by the third part of the definition of "disability."

EEOC Compliance Manual, Volume 2, EEOC Order 915.002, Definition of the Term "Disability," at 902–45, reprinted in Daily Lab.Rep., Mar. 16, 1995, at E–1, E–23.

**4.** Laws enacted in over a dozen states prohibit discrimination based on genetic tests or genetic information. There are two main problems. First, while "genetic test" is underinclusive (not covering genetic information based on family health histories), "genetic information" may be overinclusive (including medical information about common multi-factorial disorders such as heart disease, cancer, diabetes, and asthma). Second, while prohibiting discrimination, the laws do not prohibit employers from requiring individuals from signing a release of their individual medical records, which may contain genetic information.

**5.** In Norman–Bloodsaw v. Lawrence Berkeley Laboratory, 135 F.3d 1260 (9th Cir.1998), the Ninth Circuit reversed the district court and held that employees who alleged that their blood was tested for, among other things, sickle cell trait, without their consent had stated a valid claim under the federal and state constitutions and Title VII.

## 3. THE EFFECTS OF WORKPLACE SCREENING

### Mark A. Rothstein, *The Perfect Worker*
Chicago Tribune, Dec. 30, 1985.

In the last ten years, a growing number of companies have begun performing increasingly detailed medical screening tests on applicants and employees. The companies engaged in this practice attempt to determine not only which individuals are currently unable to perform the job, but which ones have an increased risk of medical problems in the future. Identifying these individuals in advance could, theoretically, save the companies considerable amounts of money in workers' compensation and health insurance costs, as well as reducing sick leave, absenteeism, turnover, and the like.

After reflecting on this phenomenon, it occurred to me that maybe these companies were going about it all wrong. Instead of focusing on the traits that make workers unacceptable, perhaps they should be focusing on the traits that make workers particularly desirable from a medical and personnel standpoint. To confirm this hypothesis, I needed to locate a single individual who embodied all of the most desirable medical and personal characteristics. In short, I had to find the perfect worker.

I secured a grant from the well-known Boondoggle Philanthropic Foundation and began my research by developing a computer program to identify essential genetic, biochemical, physiological, and psychological attributes. Then I attempted to match this profile with known medical criteria of numerous companies. Finally, my team of researchers, epidemiologists, and physicians and I scoured the country in search of this elusive, single individual.

After an entire year of searching, it seemed that the project had to be abandoned. We had reviewed thousands of medical records and had interviewed thousands of workers. Whenever an individual looked particularly promising, further questioning or testing invariably indicated an atypical genetic trait, allergy, prior occupational exposure, or medical finding that made the individual statistically more likely to contract a certain rare disease under a remote circumstance. I was beginning to question my own hypothesis: maybe there was no perfect worker.

Then, one morning I was passing through a small town in rural Tennessee. I met an unusual young man and the more I questioned him the more intrigued I became. He not only checked out positively in all of my listed categories, but in other ways that I had not even thought about in advance. Could he be the perfect worker?

His name was Fritz Gonzalez and I soon learned that his mother is German-American and his father is Mexican-American. (Immediately, I recognized that this lineage would provide a good cross-breeding of ethnic backgrounds with relatively low cancer rates.)  Fritz is an only child, is single, and lives alone.  After contemplating a career in the clergy, Fritz decided to remain celibate.  (This fact eliminates a multitude of problems. Living alone minimizes viral contact and the risk of infectious disease.  His celibacy precludes AIDS, herpes, and various sexually transmitted illnesses. Without a wife and children an employer eliminates medical insurance or other costs for childbirth, "parenting" leave, child care, and health insurance coverage for any chronically ill children.  An employer also need not fear about exposures to gametotoxins or mutagens.)

It was time to call in the medical team for a complete evaluation. Fritz was 24 years old, stood six feet tall and weighed 180 pounds.  From his mother Fritz inherited broad shoulders, a strong build, and a musculoskeletal system that makes him ideal for strenuous work.  From his father, Fritz inherited dark hair, eyes, and skin, which makes him less sensitive to ultraviolet sun rays and therefore less likely to contract skin cancer from working outdoors.

Fritz's biochemical genetic makeup was unremarkable, with no inborn errors of metabolism.  He showed no genetic predisposition to illness. There is no history in Fritz's family of cancer, diabetes, cardiovascular disease, or respiratory problems.  He has no known allergies and has been in perfect health except for the common childhood illnesses that serve to establish immunity in adults.  Fritz has no hearing or vision problems. (This would save money on company-furnished hearing aids and glasses.) Fritz has perfect teeth.  (No need to worry about dental bills, either.) Fritz has never received an X-ray, but he has had annual medical checkups.

Fritz was sounding too good to be true.  We decided to do a behavioral history.  We learned that Fritz lived his entire life in rural Tennessee, a state with one of the lowest cancer rates.  He has never lived in a city and has never even visited New Jersey.  (Air and water pollution are thought to be responsible for high cancer rates in certain areas.)  Fritz's diet consists mostly of tofu, yogurt, and home-grown fruits and vegetables.  It is high in fiber, low in animal fats, and without artificial additives, sugar, or salt.  We were delighted to learn that Fritz does not smoke (each smoker costs an employer an estimated $400–$700 per year in health insurance, fire losses, workers' compensation, absenteeism, productivity losses, and involuntary exposure to tobacco smoke), or use alcohol or other drugs (no need to worry about expensive drug screening, rehabilitation programs, or productivity losses).  Fritz was clean-shaven.  (A beard makes it difficult to wear a respirator.)  Fritz's hobbies were safe and healthful: growing food in his garden, vigorous calisthenics, yoga, and reading.

During a break in our interview, and waiting for some results from our mobile lab, I inquired into Fritz's work history.  Although a college graduate, Fritz enjoys working with his hands.  He has worked for a manufacturing company in Tennessee for three years and has an excellent work record.  At work he has not been exposed to any toxic substances. (Some employers refuse to hire otherwise healthy workers with prior exposure to toxic substances.)  He is a safe worker, but believes his employer—not some government agency such as OSHA—should be responsible for safety.  Fritz is extremely loyal and believes in working overtime to help out the company.  He also thinks that discipline, obedience, and following orders are especially positive traits.  He gets along well with his coworkers, but volunteered that he hates unions because they interfere with an employer's salary structure and other management prerogatives.  It was obvious to me that Fritz would be an ideal worker in the short run, but what about the future?  Fritz told us that all of his ancestors had been productive and in excellent health until their retirement at age 70.  Then, within a few months of retirement they would die in their sleep of natural causes.  (A worker who dies shortly after retirement with no dependents could save a company thousands of dollars on a self-insured pension, annuity, or retirement benefits.)

I was almost convinced about Fritz, but talking about his retirement led me to ask Fritz one final question.  "Fritz," I asked, "if you died with no family whatsoever, what would you do with all of the money you saved?"  He replied without any hesitation:  "Sir, I plan to leave it all to my work family—my employer—for renovation of the executive lounge."  Now I was sure I had found the perfect worker.

## NOTES AND QUESTIONS

**1.**  Is the prospect of companies searching for "perfect" or "near-perfect" workers one that is a realistic concern?  What is wrong with employers meticulously screening their workers?  Are such efforts cost-effective for the companies and for society?

**2.**  Because of the demographic changes in the workforce discussed in Chapter 2, pp. 72–81 supra, employers may not be able to engage in such detailed screening even if they want to.  Are these demographic changes and market forces sufficient counter-balances to offset the possible negative effects of excessive screening?

**3.**  For a further discussion on the "perfect worker" theme, see Elinor P. Schroeder, On Beyond Drug Testing:  Employer Monitoring and the Quest for the Perfect Worker, 36 Kan.L.Rev. 869 (1988).  See also Clifton K. Meador, The Last Well Person, 330 New Eng.J.Med. 440 (1994).

**4.**  The cases and readings in this chapter have focused on the practical, legal, and policy problems raised by commonly used hiring tools such as interviews, references, polygraphs, psychological tests, medical examinations, and drug testing.  If these and similar selection methods are "more trouble than they are worth," then what measures should be used in the hiring process?  What is the proper role of the law in regulating this process?

# CHAPTER 4

# DISCRIMINATION

After gathering information about interested applicants, an employer must select one individual to fill a particular job opening. Generally, employers and personnel directors speak in terms of "hiring the best person for the job" from the available applicant pool. But how does an employer determine who is the "best" from a number of candidates? Whether the position available is skilled or unskilled, that task is not easy, nor would different employers necessarily reach the same conclusion about a single applicant.

Traditionally, employers have had the right to hire whomever they pleased, and selection methods still reflect considerable diversity. Employers with large numbers of relatively unskilled jobs to fill can hire applicants on a "first come, first served" basis once a minimal threshold of competence is established. Frequently, however, the employer needs to be more critical in its selection procedures. When the employer has too many applicants to consider each one individually, the typical response is to narrow the original applicant pool by imposing initial qualifications which the employer believes will improve the overall quality of the workforce and which an applicant must meet before his or her application will be considered. Examples of this are requirements that employees have a high school diploma or achieve a certain score on a standardized test.

Once the applicant pool is narrowed in size, the employer will consider individual qualifications, education, experience, references, test and interview results, and other characteristics—the information garnered through procedures discussed in Chapter 3—in an effort to determine the best qualified candidate. Some skills are objectively quantifiable, such as the ability to type or to operate a drill press. Intangible traits or characteristics—reliability, interpersonal skills, analytical ability, leadership, or creativity—may be equally important to successful job performance, however. As a result, an employer usually seeks a mix of qualities rather than a single measurable trait or skill. Because many desirable traits are not quantifiable, much of the employer's final decisionmaking is ultimately subjective. Different applicants have different mixes of characteristics, and it is often difficult to single out one who stands head and shoulders above the others. Faced with several candidates who have relatively equal qualifications, the employer will nonetheless find some criterion on which to base the final selection: more education, higher test scores, more years of experience, family connections, an amorphous "gut feeling" arising from

the interview process. Nepotism and the "old boy" network of personal
and professional contacts are classic ways for small employers especially to
fill infrequent job openings, or for larger employers to fill top-level managerial and executive positions.

Historically, these selection methods, left unregulated, have resulted in
identifiable groups, such as women, blacks, and other minorities, being
underrepresented in the more desirable sectors of the workforce relative to
their availability and ability to work. Title VII of the Civil Rights Act of
1964, 42 U.S.C. § 2000e et seq., was enacted to eliminate discrimination in
employment on the basis of "race, color, religion, sex, or national origin."
Later, the non-discrimination principle was extended to other classifications. See, e.g., the Age Discrimination in Employment Act of 1967 and
the Americans with Disabilities Act of 1990, both discussed in this chapter.
State laws provide parallel or extended coverage. This chapter shows the
continuing struggle to alter employment practices through legal regulation
and the continuing controversy over the dividing line between appropriate
bases for employer decision making and illegal use of prejudicial criteria.

The concept of non-discrimination is not easy to define and apply.
Employers seek the authority to choose the best individual for a job, and
legislators and judges are reluctant to infringe on the employer's managerial prerogatives. Reasonable persons differ over interpretation of both the
employer's obligations under the law and the consequences of the employer's actions; these differences of opinion have required the courts to
develop a jurisprudence which balances the employer's right to manage its
business free from unnecessary governmental intrusion and the statutory
rights of different individuals competing for the same position. Essentially,
the law plays a negative role in employee selection. While it proscribes
certain practices, the law does not prohibit irrationality per se (such as
hiring only individuals whose Social Security numbers end with an even
digit); it only prohibits employer action—rational or irrational in terms of
economic efficiency—that is improperly motivated or has unacceptable
consequences.

As you read the materials in this chapter, consider the following
questions: Should the law prohibit discrimination only when it involves
certain impermissible criteria? Why have we chosen the current list of
proscribed criteria? Is the law interfering unduly with employer prerogatives? What are the societal consequences of legal intervention or nonin-
tervention?

Although this chapter includes the major treatment of discrimination,
the topic is covered elsewhere in the book, including Chapter 5 (equal pay
and comparable worth), Chapter 6 (discrimination in benefits), Chapter 7
(sexual harassment and discrimination in promotions), Chapter 10 (discharge), and Chapter 13 (mandatory retirement).

## A. DISCRIMINATION ON THE BASIS OF RACE OR SEX

## 1. SOURCES OF PROTECTION

### a. TITLE VII OF THE CIVIL RIGHTS ACT OF 1964

The Civil Rights Act of 1964, 42 U.S.C. § 2000, is the most sweeping and important civil rights legislation ever enacted. The law contains 11 titles barring discrimination in voting rights, public accommodations, education, employment, and use of federal funds. In Heart of Atlanta Motel, Inc. v. United States, 379 U.S. 241 (1964), and Katzenbach v. McClung, 379 U.S. 294 (1964), the Supreme Court upheld the constitutionality of the Act under the commerce clause and the fourteenth amendment.

Title VII, dealing with employment, prohibits discrimination based on race, color, religion, sex, and national origin. The legislative history of Title VII shows that the primary focus of the law was racial discrimination. It also shows that Congress was concerned with eliminating not only specific instances of employment discrimination, but its broader economic and social effects as well.

President Lyndon Johnson signing the Civil Rights Act of 1964. Seated in the front row were, from the left, Senators Everett M. Dirksen and Hubert H. Humphrey and Representatives Charles A. Halleck and Emanuel Celler. Other notables include, in the second row, George Meany of the AFL–CIO, and Dr. Martin Luther King, Jr.
**Source:** The New York Times/George Tames

*(i) Legislative History of the Civil Rights Act of 1964*

## U.S. Code Cong. & Admin.News

88th Cong., 2d Sess. (1964), at 2513–2517.

### TITLE VII—EQUAL EMPLOYMENT OPPORTUNITY

In other titles of this bill we have endeavored to protect the Negro's right to first-class citizenship. Through voting, education, equal protection of the laws, and free access to places of public accommodations, means have been fashioned to eliminate racial discrimination.

The right to vote, however, does not have much meaning on an empty stomach. The impetus to achieve excellence in education is lacking if gainful employment is closed to the graduate. The opportunity to enter a restaurant or hotel is a shallow victory where one's pockets are empty. The principle of equal treatment under law can have little meaning if in practice its benefits are denied the citizen.

Testimony supporting the fact of discrimination in employment is overwhelming. * * *

In 1962, nonwhites made up 11 percent of the civilian labor force but 22 percent of the unemployed. Approximately 900,000 nonwhites were without jobs during the year—thereby constituting an unemployment rate of 11 percent. This was more than twice the rate of white unemployed workers. The breakdown among age, sex, and occupational categories is even more striking as the above table reveals. Moreover, among Negroes who are employed, their jobs are largely concentrated among the semi-skilled and unskilled occupations. This has the effect of severely retarding the economic standards of the Negro population. Likewise, concentration at the lower levels of employment heightens the chances of early and long duration layoffs. This is particularly evident today with the rapid upgrading of job skills which is closely associated with automation.

Similarly, a comparison of median annual incomes of whites and nonwhites from 1939 to 1960 as published by the Department of Labor, reveals the economic straitjacket in which the Negro has been confined.

| Table 3 Median annual wage and salary incomes of white and nonwhite persons, 1939, 1947, 1957, 1960 | | | | |
|---|---|---|---|---|
| | 1939 | 1947 | 1957 | 1960 |
| Males: | | | | |
| White | $1,112 | $2,357 | $4,396 | $5,137 |
| Nonwhite | $460 | $1,279 | $2,436 | $3,075 |
| Nonwhite as a percent of white | 41.4 | 54.3 | 55.4 | 59.9 |
| Females: | | | | |
| White | $676 | $1,269 | $2,240 | $2,537 |
| Nonwhite | $246 | $432 | $1,019 | $1,276 |
| Nonwhite as a percent of white | 36.4 | 34.0 | 45.5 | 50.3 |

The failure of our society to extend job opportunities to the Negro is an economic waste. The purchasing power of the country is not being fully developed. This, in turn, acts as a brake upon potential increases in gross national product. In addition, the country is burdened with added costs for the payment of unemployment compensation, relief, disease, and crime.

National prosperity will be increased through the proper training of Negroes for more skilled employment together with the removal of barriers for obtaining such employment. Through toleration of discriminatory practices, American industry is not obtaining the quantity of skilled workers it needs. With 10 percent of the work force under the bonds of racial inequality, this stands to reason. Similarly, an examination of job openings that are regularly advertised discloses that the country is not making satisfactory use of its manpower. Consider how our shortage of engineers, scientists, doctors, plumbers, carpenters, technicians, and the myriad of other skilled occupations could be overcome in due time if we eliminate job discrimination.

A nation need not and should not be converted into a welfare state to reduce poverty, lessen crime, cut down unemployment, or overcome shortages in skilled occupational categories. All that is needed is the institution of proper training programs and the elimination of discrimination in employment practices.

### (ii) How Title VII Works

While this chapter focuses on discrimination in hiring, Title VII's proscription against discrimination applies broadly to all aspects of employment. The most important section of Title VII is § 703:

Sec. 703(a) It shall be an unlawful employment practice for an employer—(1) to fail or refuse to hire or to discharge any individual, or otherwise to discriminate against any individual with respect to his compensation, terms, conditions, or privileges of employment, because of such individual's race, color, religion, sex, or national origin; or

(2) to limit, segregate, or classify his employees or applicants for employment in any way which would deprive or tend to deprive any individual of employment opportunities or otherwise adversely affect his status as an employee, because of such individual's race, color, religion, sex, or national origin.

Section 703(b) prohibits discrimination by employment agencies on similar grounds (see Chapter 3, supra), and § 703(c) prohibits such discrimination by labor unions.

When Title VII was first proposed, it did not include protection against gender-based discrimination. Representative Howard W. Smith (D.Va.) was seeking to kill Title VII, and thought that including the ban on sex discrimination would encourage other representatives to oppose the legislation. Recent scholarship has emphasized the efforts of such groups as the National Woman's Party to lay the groundwork for laws prohibiting employment discrimination on the basis of gender. See, e.g., Jo Freeman,

How "Sex" Got into Title VII: Persistent Opportunism as a Maker of Public Policy, 9 J.L. & Equality 163 (1991).

The Act applies to all private employers with 15 or more employees. It also applies to federal, state, and local government employers. All employees of a covered employer are protected, regardless of their status (i.e., management personnel, professionals). Exclusions from the Act's coverage include: educational institutions owned or supported by a religion and employing members of that religion; businesses operating on or near an Indian reservation and giving preferential treatment to Indians; and members of the Communist party.

In Walters v. Metropolitan Educational Enterprises, Inc., 117 S.Ct. 660 (1997), the Supreme Court agreed with the EEOC's "payroll" approach, under which all employees on the payroll are counted toward meeting the jurisdictional minimum, regardless of whether every employee worked or was compensated on any given day.

Section 703 also contains important exceptions to the nondiscrimination obligation. Under certain circumstances, discrimination may be permitted where:

(1) religion, sex, or national origin (but not race) is a bona fide occupational qualification (BFOQ) reasonably necessary to the normal operation of the business;

(2) the employer acts pursuant to a bona fide seniority or merit system, or measures earnings by quantity or quality of production;

(3) the employer acts on the results of a professionally developed ability test that "is not designed, intended, or used to discriminate because of race, color, religion, sex, or national origin";

(4) differences in pay based upon sex are authorized by the Equal Pay Act of 1963 (discussed in Chapter 5).

Title VII has been amended three times. The Equal Employment Opportunity Act of 1972 substantially expanded the Act's coverage and increased the EEOC's enforcement power. The Pregnancy Discrimination Act of 1978 added § 701(k), which expanded the definition of sex discrimination to include discrimination on the basis of "pregnancy, childbirth, and related medical conditions." (The issue of pregnancy-based discrimination in benefits is discussed in Chapter 6.) The Civil Rights Act of 1991 overruled Supreme Court cases related to the burden of proof and other issues, provided for the right to a jury trial, added compensatory and punitive damages to the available relief, and made other changes discussed below.

The District of Columbia Circuit upheld an award of punitive damages, in addition to back pay and compensatory damages, to an African–American hospital administrator who was not hired by a medical management company because of his race because the plaintiff was able to show an "evil motive or intent" to violate his protected civil rights. Barbour v. Merrill, 48 F.3d 1270 (D.C.Cir.1995), cert. dismissed, 116 S.Ct. 1037 (1996).

Section 706 describes the procedures for enforcing Title VII. The statute is administered by the Equal Employment Opportunity Commission

(EEOC), an independent executive agency consisting of five presidentially-appointed members who serve five-year terms. Violations of the statute are brought to the EEOC's attention by agency investigation, recordkeeping, and compliance activity as well as by individual complaints.

A complaint or "charge" must be filed with the EEOC within 180 days after the occurrence of the alleged unlawful employment practice, unless there is a state or local antidiscrimination law similar to Title VII (and virtually every state has one), with its own procedure for investigating and resolving complaints. In those cases, the procedure is modified, to encourage resolution of claims at the local level. Charges may be filed with either the EEOC or the state or local agency. If the charge is initially filed with the state or local agency, an EEOC charge may be filed up to 300 days after the occurrence of the alleged discrimination or 30 days after notice of termination of local proceedings, whichever comes first. If the charge is filed first with EEOC, it must defer to local proceedings for 60 days before undertaking its own investigation.

After a Title VII charge has been filed, the EEOC must serve notice of the charge on the respondent within ten days. EEOC then investigates and determines if there is reasonable cause to believe discrimination has occurred. If cause is found, EEOC attempts conciliation. If no conciliation can be reached, the EEOC may bring a civil action in United States district court. If no cause is found, or if within 180 days of the filing of the charge there has been no conciliation or civil action filed by the EEOC, the EEOC notifies the complainant in a "right to sue" letter. The charging party has 90 days after receipt of the right to sue letter to bring a civil action in federal district court.

All district court proceedings under Title VII are de novo. If the court finds an unlawful employment practice, it may enjoin the practice and grant affirmative relief including reinstatement, retroactive seniority, and back pay. Compensatory and punitive damages also may be awarded, up to $300,000 for companies with more than 500 employees. Section 706(g) limits back pay to two years before the filing of the charge with the EEOC. The court may also award attorneys' fees to prevailing parties.

For a detailed discussion of Title VII procedures, see Barbara Lindemann & Paul Grossman, Employment Discrimination Law, chs. 29–37 (3d ed. 1996).

## NOTES AND QUESTIONS

**1.** Does Title VII protect former employees from retaliation by their employers after they have filed a discrimination suit? In Robinson v. Shell Oil Co., 117 S.Ct. 843 (1997), an African–American sales representative was fired and sued unsuccessfully under Title VII. When he applied for another job, the prospective employer received an unfavorable reference. Robinson then sued Shell for retaliation. The Supreme Court read § 704(a) as prohibiting retaliation against former employees as well as current ones.

**2.** Whether plaintiffs in Title VII actions may bring suit against agents of their employers in their individual capacities has also been the subject of a split among the circuits.   The Second Circuit has recently decided that such suits are not permitted and thus that plaintiffs will only be able to obtain relief from their employers.   Tomka v. Seiler Corp., 66 F.3d 1295 (2d Cir.1995).   The court said that since Title VII covers only employers with 15 or more employees, Congress did not intend to hold individuals liable, and therefore an employee who was sexually assaulted by two co-workers and her supervisor after a social dinner could not recover from them in their individual capacities.   The Supreme Court has so far declined to resolve this issue.

### b.   STATE FAIR EMPLOYMENT PRACTICE LAWS

Section 708 of Title VII specifically permits parallel state regulation of employment discrimination as long as the state law does not conflict with Title VII.   Every state has a law which prohibits discrimination in employment.   Although most of the laws are patterned after Title VII, there are two important distinctions.   First, state fair employment practice (FEP) laws usually do not exempt small employers as Title VII does, so that state law may be the only source of protection against discrimination for some applicants and employees.   Second, some state legislatures have gone beyond the federal proscriptions against discrimination on the basis of race, color, religion, sex, and national origin (Title VII), age (ADEA), and disability (Americans with Disabilities Act) to ban discrimination based on other criteria. Marital status and sexual orientation are some common bases of state anti-discrimination law, but there are others.   For example, Minnesota prohibits discrimination against recipients of public assistance, Minn.Stat.Ann. § 363.03.

### c.   THE FOURTEENTH AMENDMENT AND RECONSTRUCTION ERA CIVIL RIGHTS STATUTES

During Reconstruction, Congress enacted the Civil Rights Act of 1866 over the veto of President Andrew Johnson.   The Act was a response to "black codes," which had been enacted in several southern states, and which imposed severe legal restrictions on blacks.   There were some doubts at the time of passage about the constitutionality of this law.   In 1868, however, the fourteenth amendment was ratified—at least in part to validate the Civil Rights Act of 1866.

### AMENDMENT XIV (1868)

§ 1.   All persons born or naturalized in the United States, and subject to jurisdiction thereof, are citizens of the United States and of the State wherein they reside.   No State shall make or enforce any law which shall abridge the privileges or immunities of citizens of the United States; nor shall any State deprive any person of life, liberty, or property, without due process of law; nor deny to any person within its jurisdiction the equal protection of the laws.

* * *

§ 5.   The Congress shall have power to enforce, by appropriate legislation, the provisions of this article.

In 1870 the Civil Rights Act of 1866 was reenacted under the Enforcement Act of 1870, in order to remove any doubt about the act's constitutionality.

The main provision of the Civil Rights Act of 1866, reenacted in 1870, is currently codified at 42 U.S.C. § 1981.

§ 1981.   Equal rights under the law

(a) All persons within the jurisdiction of the United States shall have the same right in every State and Territory to make and enforce contracts, to sue, be parties, give evidence, and to the full and equal benefit of all laws and proceedings for the security of persons and property as is enjoyed by white citizens, and shall be subject to like punishment, pains, penalties, taxes, licenses, and exactions of every kind, and to no other.

(b) For purposes of this section, the term "make and enforce contracts" includes the making, performance, modification, and termination of contracts, and the enjoyment of all benefits, privileges, terms, and conditions of the contractual relationship.

(c) The rights protected by this section are protected against impairment by nongovernmental discrimination and impairment under color of State law.

In 1975, in Johnson v. Railway Express Agency, Inc., 421 U.S. 454 (1975), the Supreme Court held that § 1981 prohibits purely private discrimination in contracts, including employment.  By its clear language, § 1981 permits blacks to sue for racial discrimination.  Until 1976, however, it was not clear whether the "as is enjoyed by white citizens" language would permit whites to sue for discrimination under § 1981.  In McDonald v. Santa Fe Trail Transportation Co., 427 U.S. 273 (1976), the Supreme Court held that § 1981 was intended "to proscribe discrimination in the making or enforcement of contracts against, or in favor of, any race."  Id. at 295.

In Saint Francis College v. Al-Khazraji, 481 U.S. 604 (1987), the Supreme Court permitted a § 1981 action by a U.S. citizen born in Iraq who alleged that as an Arab he had been discriminated against when denied tenure.  Justice White wrote: "Plainly all those who might be deemed Caucasian today were not thought to be of the same race at the time § 1981 became law."  He showed references in the 1866 congressional debate to the Chinese, Spanish, Anglo–Saxon, Jewish, Mexican, Mongolian, German, and gypsy races.  The law thus applied to "identifiable classes of persons who are subjected to intentional discrimination solely because of their ancestry or ethnic characteristics."  For the plaintiff to prevail under § 1981, he must prove that he was discriminated against because he is an Arab, and not solely because of his place of origin or his religion.

Procedurally, § 1981 actions may be brought in state or federal court.  There is no minimum number of employees before an employer is covered.

State statutes of limitations apply and there is no administrative exhaustion requirement.   Compensatory and punitive damages are available.

The other relevant Reconstruction Era Civil Rights Act is the Civil Rights Act of 1871, also known as the Ku Klux Klan Act.   The Act contains both civil and criminal sections.   The two most important civil sections are now codified at 42 U.S.C. §§ 1983 and 1985.

### § 1983.   Civil action for deprivation of rights

Every person who, under color of any statute, ordinance, regulation, custom, or usage, of any State or Territory or the District of Columbia, subjects, or causes to be subjected, any citizen of the United States or other person within the jurisdiction thereof to the deprivation of any rights, privileges, or immunities secured by the Constitution and laws, shall be liable to the party injured in an action at law, suit in equity, or other proper proceeding for redress.

### § 1985.   Conspiracy to interfere with civil rights—Preventing officer from performing duties

#### Depriving persons of rights or privileges

(3) If two or more persons in any State or Territory conspire or go in disguise on the highway or on the premises of another, for the purpose of depriving, either directly or indirectly, any person or class of persons of the equal protection of the laws, or of equal privileges and immunities under the laws;  in any case of conspiracy set forth in this section, if one or more persons engaged therein do, or cause to be done, any act in furtherance of the object of such conspiracy, whereby another is injured in his person or property, or deprived of having and exercising any right or privilege of a citizen of the United States, the party so injured or deprived may have an action for the recovery of damages, occasioned by such injury or deprivation, against any one or more of the conspirators.

Under § 1983 the plaintiff may be any citizen whose civil rights have been violated.   Protected civil rights include due process, equal protection, privileges and immunities of citizenship, and statutory rights.   Employment discrimination based on race, color, religion, sex, national origin, and other classifications not rationally related to a legitimate state interest may be redressed under § 1983.

Under the Fourteenth Amendment and the "under color of" language in § 1983 itself, "state action" is required before a violation of § 1983 can be found.   Therefore, § 1983 may not be used in actions against federal officials or in cases of private discrimination.   In Monell v. Department of Social Services, 436 U.S. 658 (1978), the Supreme Court held that municipalities may be sued under § 1983 for both damages and injunctive relief.   In Alabama v. Pugh, 438 U.S. 781 (1978), however, the court held that the eleventh amendment precludes § 1983 actions against states per se, although state officials may be sued in their individual and official capacities. Actions under § 1983 may be brought in state or federal court.

In Great American Federal Savings & Loan Association v. Novotny, 442 U.S. 366 (1979), the Supreme Court held that conspiracies to deprive an individual of fourteenth amendment rights under § 1985 require state action, severely limiting the utility of § 1985 as a cause of action separate from §§ 1981 and 1983.

When Title VII was originally enacted in 1964, government employers were not covered by the statute, and the Fourteenth Amendment and the civil rights acts were the only means by which government employees could redress discrimination in employment. The 1972 amendments to Title VII brought government employers under its coverage. While §§ 1981, 1983, and 1985 offer possible alternatives to Title VII, Title VII remains the workhorse of employment discrimination law, because of its extensive coverage and the availability of the EEOC to assist individuals in pressing and resolving charges of discrimination. The civil rights acts are most useful for individuals not covered by Title VII and for those who have missed the relatively short statute of limitations for filing a Title VII charge. Over half the state laws have broader coverage than Title VII, and 10 jurisdictions extend protection to individuals working for employers with one or more employees.

## d.  EXECUTIVE ORDER 11246

On September 24, 1965, President Johnson issued Executive Order 11246. The key provision of the Executive Order is § 202, which prohibits employment discrimination by government contractors.

> The Contractor will not discriminate against any employee or applicant for employment because of race, creed, color, or national origin. The Contractor will take affirmative action to ensure that applicants are employed, and that employees are treated during employment, without regard to their race, creed, color, or national origin. Such action shall include, but not be limited to, the following: employment, upgrading, demotion, or transfer; recruitment or recruitment advertising; layoff or termination; rates of pay or other forms of compensation; and selection for training, including apprenticeship.

On October 13, 1967, the President issued Executive Order 11375, adding sex to the categories for which nondiscrimination and affirmative action are mandated by government contractors. The Executive Orders, which cover about one-third of all workers, are important because they force many employers to go beyond Title VII nondiscrimination to implement affirmative action programs.

The contractor's nondiscrimination and affirmative action obligations also apply to subcontractors and vendors with which it trades. Failure to comply with the Order may subject the contractor to cancellation, termination, or suspension of the contract, and, in the most egregious cases, debarment from further government contracts.

The Executive Order's dual requirements of nondiscrimination and affirmative action are enforced by the Office of Federal Contract Compliance Programs (OFCCP) within the Department of Labor and monitored through reporting requirements contained in the Executive Order. The Secretary of Labor has issued detailed regulations implementing the Executive Order, 41 C.F.R. Chapter 60. All government contracts in excess of $10,000 are subject to the Order. Contractors with 50 or more employees and contracts for more than $50,000 are required to have a written affirmative action plan. If a contract is in excess of $1,000,000, the contract cannot be awarded until a pre-award compliance review of the affirmative action program has been completed and approved. Contractors in violation of the Order are subject to administrative enforcement proceedings by the OFCCP. These administrative remedies are exclusive and individuals may not sue the contractor directly. Individuals, however, may file complaints with OFCCP and may sue the Secretary of Labor to compel performance of obligations under the Executive Order.

## 2.   What Is Unlawful Discrimination?

### Griggs v. Duke Power Co.
401 U.S. 424 (1971).

■ Mr. Chief Justice Burger delivered the opinion of the Court.

We granted the writ in this case to resolve the question whether an employer is prohibited by the Civil Rights Act of 1964, Title VII, from requiring a high school education or passing of a standardized general intelligence test as a condition of employment in or transfer to jobs when (a) neither standard is shown to be significantly related to successful job performance, (b) both requirements operate to disqualify Negroes at a substantially higher rate than white applicants, and (c) the jobs in question formerly had been filled only by white employees as part of a longstanding practice of giving preference to whites.

Congress provided, in Title VII of the Civil Rights Act of 1964, for class actions for enforcement of provisions of the Act and this proceeding was brought by a group of incumbent Negro employees against Duke Power Company. All the petitioners are employed at the Company's Dan River Steam Station, a power generating facility located at Draper, North Carolina. At the time this action was instituted, the Company had 95 employees at the Dan River Station, 14 of whom were Negroes; 13 of these are petitioners here.

The District Court found that prior to July 2, 1965, the effective date of the Civil Rights Act of 1964, the Company openly discriminated on the basis of race in the hiring and assigning of employees at its Dan River plant. The plant was organized into five operating departments: (1) Labor, (2) Coal Handling, (3) Operations, (4) Maintenance, and (5) Laboratory and Test. Negroes were employed only in the Labor Department where the highest paying jobs paid less than the lowest paying jobs in the other four "operating" departments in which only whites were employed.[2] Promotions were normally made within each department on the basis of job seniority. Transferees into a department usually began in the lowest position.

In 1955 the Company instituted a policy of requiring a high school education for initial assignment to any department except Labor, and for transfer from the Coal Handling to any "inside" department (Operations, Maintenance, or Laboratory). When the Company abandoned its policy of restricting Negroes to the Labor Department in 1965, completion of high school also was made a prerequisite to transfer from Labor to any other department. From the time the high school requirement was instituted to the time of trial, however, white employees hired before the time of the high school education requirement continued to perform satisfactorily and achieve promotions in the "operating" departments. Findings on this score are not challenged.

The Company added a further requirement for new employees on July 2, 1965, the date on which Title VII became effective. To qualify for placement in any but the Labor Department it became necessary to register satisfactory scores on two professionally prepared aptitude tests, as well as to have a high school education. Completion of high school alone continued to render employees eligible for transfer to the four desirable departments from which Negroes had been excluded if the incumbent had been employed prior to the time of the new requirement. In September 1965 the Company began to permit incumbent employees who lacked a high school education to qualify for transfer from Labor or Coal Handling to an "inside" job by passing two tests—the Wonderlic Personnel Test, which purports to measure general intelligence, and the Bennett Mechanical Comprehension Test. Neither was directed or intended to measure the ability to learn to perform a particular job or category of jobs. The requisite scores used for both initial hiring and transfer approximated the national median for high school graduates.[3]

\* \* \*

The Court of Appeals was confronted with a question of first impression, as are we, concerning the meaning of Title VII. After careful analysis a majority of that court concluded that a subjective test of the employer's intent should govern, particularly in a close case, and that in this case there was no showing of a discriminatory purpose in the adoption of the diploma

---

**2.** A Negro was first assigned to a job in an operating department in August 1966, five months after charges had been filed with the Equal Employment Opportunity Commission. The employee, a high school graduate who had begun in the Labor Department in 1953, was promoted to a job in the Coal Handling Department.

**3.** The test standards are thus more stringent than the high school requirement, since they would screen out approximately half of all high school graduates.

and test requirements. On this basis, the Court of Appeals concluded there was no violation of the Act.

The Court of Appeals reversed the District Court in part, rejecting the holding that residual discrimination arising from prior employment practices was insulated from remedial action. The Court of Appeals noted, however, that the District Court was correct in its conclusion that there was no showing of a racial purpose or invidious intent in the adoption of the high school diploma requirement or general intelligence test and that these standards had been applied fairly to whites and Negroes alike. It held that, in the absence of a discriminatory purpose, use of such requirements was permitted by the Act. In so doing, the Court of Appeals rejected the claim that because these two requirements operated to render ineligible a markedly disproportionate number of Negroes, they were unlawful under Title VII unless shown to be job related. We granted the writ on these claims.

The objective of Congress in the enactment of Title VII is plain from the language of the statute. It was to achieve equality of employment opportunities and remove barriers that have operated in the past to favor an identifiable group of white employees over other employees. Under the Act, practices, procedures, or tests neutral on their face, and even neutral in terms of intent, cannot be maintained if they operate to "freeze" the status quo of prior discriminatory employment practices.

The Court of Appeals' opinion, and the partial dissent, agreed that, on the record in the present case, "whites register far better on the Company's alternative requirements" than Negroes.[6] This consequence would appear to be directly traceable to race. Basic intelligence must have the means of articulation to manifest itself fairly in a testing process. Because they are Negroes, petitioners have long received inferior education in segregated schools and this Court expressly recognized these differences in Gaston County v. United States, 395 U.S. 285 (1969). There, because of the inferior education received by Negroes in North Carolina, this Court barred the institution of a literacy test for voter registration on the ground that the test would abridge the right to vote indirectly on account of race. Congress did not intend by Title VII, however, to guarantee a job to every person regardless of qualifications. In short, the Act does not command that any person be hired simply because he was formerly the subject of discrimination, or because he is a member of a minority group. Discriminatory preference for any group, minority or majority, is precisely and only what Congress has proscribed. What is required by Congress is the removal of artificial, arbitrary, and unnecessary barriers to employment

---

**6.** In North Carolina, 1960 census statistics show that, while 34% of white males had completed high school, only 12% of Negro males had done so. U.S. Bureau of the Census, U.S. Census of Population: 1960, Vol. 1, Characteristics of the Population, pt. 35, Table 47.

Similarly, with respect to standardized tests, the EEOC in one case found that use of a battery of tests, including the Wonderlic and Bennett tests used by the Company in the instant case, resulted in 58% of whites passing the tests, as compared with only 6% of the blacks.

when the barriers operate invidiously to discriminate on the basis of racial or other impermissible classification.

Congress has now provided that tests or criteria for employment or promotion may not provide equality of opportunity merely in the sense of the fabled offer of milk to the stork and the fox.  On the contrary, Congress has now required that the posture and condition of the job-seeker be taken into account.  It has—to resort again to the fable—provided that the vessel in which the milk is proffered be one all seekers can use.  The Act proscribes not only overt discrimination but also practices that are fair in form, but discriminatory in operation.  The touchstone is business necessity.  If an employment practice which operates to exclude Negroes cannot be shown to be related to job performance, the practice is prohibited.

On the record before us, neither the high school completion requirement nor the general intelligence test is shown to bear a demonstrable relationship to successful performance of the jobs for which it was used.  Both were adopted, as the Court of Appeals noted, without meaningful study of their relationship to job-performance ability.  Rather, a vice president of the Company testified, the requirements were instituted on the Company's judgment that they generally would improve the overall quality of the work force.

The evidence, however, shows that employees who have not completed high school or taken the tests have continued to perform satisfactorily and make progress in departments for which the high school and test criteria are now used.  The promotion record of present employees who would not be able to meet the new criteria thus suggests the possibility that the requirements may not be needed even for the limited purpose of preserving the avowed policy of advancement within the Company.  In the context of this case, it is unnecessary to reach the question whether testing requirements that take into account capability for the next succeeding position or related future promotion might be utilized upon a showing that such long-range requirements fulfill a genuine business need.  In the present case the Company has made no such showing.

The Court of Appeals held that the Company had adopted the diploma and test requirements without any "intention to discriminate against Negro employees."  We do not suggest that either the District Court or the Court of Appeals erred in examining the employer's intent; but good intent or absence of discriminatory intent does not redeem employment procedures or testing mechanisms that operate as "built-in headwinds" for minority groups and are unrelated to measuring job capability.

The Company's lack of discriminatory intent is suggested by special efforts to help the undereducated employees through Company financing of two-thirds the cost of tuition for high school training.  But Congress directed the thrust of the Act to the *consequences* of employment practices, not simply the motivation.  More than that, Congress has placed on the employer the burden of showing that any given requirement must have a manifest relationship to the employment in question.

The facts of this case demonstrate the inadequacy of broad and general testing devices as well as the infirmity of using diplomas or degrees as fixed measures of capability. History is filled with examples of men and women who rendered highly effective performance without the conventional badges of accomplishment in terms of certificates, diplomas, or degrees. Diplomas and tests are useful servants, but Congress has mandated the common-sense proposition that they are not to become masters of reality.

\* \* \*

Nothing in the Act precludes the use of testing or measuring procedures; obviously they are useful. What Congress has forbidden is giving these devices and mechanisms controlling force unless they are demonstrably a reasonable measure of job performance. Congress has not commanded that the less qualified be preferred over the better qualified simply because of minority origins. Far from disparaging job qualifications as such, Congress has made such qualifications the controlling factor, so that race, religion, nationality, and sex become irrelevant. What Congress has commanded is that any tests used must measure the person for the job and not the person in the abstract.

The judgment of the Court of Appeals is, as to that portion of the judgment appealed from, reversed.

NOTES AND QUESTIONS

**1.** Do you believe the company intentionally discriminated against blacks? The Supreme Court regards itself as bound by the trial judge's conclusion that no intentional discrimination occurred. Why, then, is the company held to have violated the law?

**2.** What standard does the Court establish for employers to meet in order to avoid liability for facially neutral selection practices which have an adverse impact on categories of individuals protected by Title VII? What was wrong with the employer's efforts to meet that standard in *Griggs?*

**3.** What is wrong with an employer's wanting to upgrade its workforce? Why should the law constrain the employer's determination of the qualifications it seeks in its employees? Does Title VII prohibit an employer from hiring an "overqualified" workforce?

**4.** Assuming that Duke Power had acted in good faith in implementing the testing and diploma requirements, should this be a defense?

Duke Power Company would finance two-thirds of the cost of tuition for high school training for any of its employees who wanted to complete their education on their own time. What effect should that program have on the Court's evaluation of Duke Power's liability under the law?

**5.** The Court takes judicial notice of the inferior education received by blacks in North Carolina in the early 1960's to establish the adverse impact of the high school diploma requirement for plaintiffs, in a context where the Court concluded that a diploma requirement was not job related. In other circumstances, courts have been willing to take judicial notice of the job relatedness of an education requirement.  See, e.g., Aguilera v. Cook County Police & Corrections Merit Board, 760 F.2d 844 (7th Cir.), cert. denied, 474 U.S. 907 (1985):

> Sometimes the appropriateness of an educational requirement is sufficiently obvious to allow dispensing with empirical validation. No one would insist that a law school validate statistically the "business need" behind requiring that its faculty members have law degrees (which might, indeed, be quite difficult to do), or that a hospital validate a requirement that its doctors have medical degrees.  * * * [T]here has now been enough judicial and professional experience with educational requirements in law enforcement to establish a presumption in civil rights cases that a high school education is an appropriate requirement for anyone who is going to be a policeman, * * * and therefore to excuse civil rights defendants from having to prove, over and over again, that such requirements really are necessary for such jobs.

Is this holding wrong?  That is, should all diploma and test requirements be subjected to a strict test of business necessity?  For the argument that *Griggs* should be applied even to airline pilots and law school applicants, see Elizabeth Bartholet, Application of Title VII to Jobs in High Places, 95 Harv.L.Rev. 945 (1982).

**6.**   The I.Q. Taxi Company had a policy of hiring only unemployed Ph.D.s. In its advertising, I.Q. urged customers to ride in I.Q. cabs and "have an intellectual discussion with our drivers on the way to the airport or wherever you may be going."  In a Title VII challenge to I.Q.'s hiring (based on alleged disparate impact race discrimination), can the hiring policy be sustained?  Should it matter whether I.Q. charged more than other taxis, advertised the education of its drivers, or required a high school diploma instead of a Ph.D.?  Cf. Wileman v. Frank, 979 F.2d 30, 37 (4th Cir.1992) (in reversing the district court's holding that any consideration of educational differences beyond minimum requirements was per se pretextual, the Fourth Circuit held that "[w]hen two applicants meet the minimum educational qualifications of a position, Title VII does not prevent an employer from preferring the applicant who has educational qualifications which surpass the minimum requirements of the position."). Does this mean that Duke Power Co. could not *require* a high school diploma, but could *prefer* applicants who had one?

**7.**   What of a discriminatory impact that results from the policy of a religious group whose activities are constitutionally protected?  See Murphy v. Derwinski, 776 F.Supp. 1466 (D.Colo.1991), affirmed, 990 F.2d 540 (10th Cir.1993), holding that a Veteran's Administration requirement that chaplains be ordained discriminated against women who cannot be ordained by the Catholic Church but who can, instead, be "endorsed" by an ecclesiastical agency.

In INTERNATIONAL BROTHERHOOD OF TEAMSTERS v. UNITED STATES, 431 U.S. 324 (1977), the Supreme Court approved the use of statistics to prove discrimination. The government had sued T.I.M.E.–D.C., Inc., a motor freight carrier, and the Teamsters for discriminating against minorities in hiring, job assignment, and promotions and transfers. As to whether the government had made a prima facie case that the company had discriminated, the Court stated:

> We agree with the District Court and the Court of Appeals that the Government carried its burden of proof. As of March 31, 1971, shortly after the Government filed its complaint alleging systemwide discrimination, the company had 6,472 employees. Of these, 314 (5%) were Negroes and 257 (4%) were Spanish-surnamed Americans. Of the 1,828 line drivers, however, there were only 8 (0.4%) Negroes and 5 (0.3%) Spanish-surnamed persons, and all of the Negroes had been hired after the litigation had commenced. With one exception—a man who worked as a line driver at the Chicago terminal from 1950 to 1959—the company and its predecessors *did not employ a Negro on a regular basis as a line driver until 1969.* And, as the Government showed, even in 1971 there were terminals in areas of substantial Negro population where all of the company's line drivers were white.[17] A great majority of the Negroes (83%) and Spanish-surnamed Americans (78%) who did work for the company held the lower-paying city operations and serviceman jobs, whereas only 39% of the nonminority employees held jobs in those categories.

> The Government bolstered its statistical evidence with the testimony of individuals who recounted over 40 specific instances of discrimination. * * *

> The company's principal response to this evidence is that statistics can never in and of themselves prove the existence of a pattern or practice of discrimination, or even establish a prima facie case shifting to the employer the burden of rebutting the inference raised by the figures. But, as even our brief summary of the evidence shows, this was not a case in which the Government relied on "statistics alone." The individuals who testified about their personal experiences with the company brought the cold numbers convincingly to life.

> In any event, our cases make it unmistakably clear that "[s]tatistical analyses have served and will continue to serve an important role" in cases in which the existence of discrimination is

---

**17.** In Atlanta, for instance, Negroes composed 22.35% of the population in the surrounding metropolitan area and 51.31% of the population in the city proper. The company's Atlanta terminal employed 57 line drivers. All were white. In Los Angeles, 10.84% of the greater metropolitan population and 17.88% of the city population were Negro. But at the company's two Los Angeles terminals there was not a single Negro among the 374 line drivers. The proof showed similar disparities in San Francisco, Denver, Nashville, Chicago, Dallas, and at several other terminals.

a disputed issue.  We have repeatedly approved the use of statistical proof, where it reached proportions comparable to those in this case, to establish a prima facie case of racial discrimination in jury selection cases.  Statistics are equally competent in proving employment discrimination.[20]  We caution only that statistics are not irrefutable;  they come in infinite variety and, like any other kind of evidence, they may be rebutted.  In short, their usefulness depends on all of the surrounding facts and circumstances.

431 U.S. at 337–40.  The Court further delineated the appropriate role of statistics in establishing adverse impact in Hazelwood School District v. United States, 433 U.S. 299 (1977), when it narrowed the application of statistical data to the "relevant labor market."  In *Teamsters,* the government had compared the employer's hiring record to the percentage of blacks in the population in the surrounding area.  In *Hazelwood,* the Court distinguished the job requirement in *Teamsters*—the ability to drive, which is widely held in the adult population—from the more specialized job requirement in *Hazelwood* of having a teaching certificate.  In *Hazelwood,* the "relevant labor market" was not the general population in the greater St. Louis area, but the population of individuals having teaching certificates.

## NOTES AND QUESTIONS

**1.**  In addition to the statistical evidence about the company's hiring and selection practices, the Court in *Teamsters* also had before it testimony from a number of individual blacks who had been discriminated against.  Would statistical evidence alone be sufficient to establish a prima facie case against the employer even if there were no individual testimony to support the statistics?  On what basis?

**2.**  The employer's workforce data in *Teamsters* was compared to the percentage of blacks in the general population, while *Hazelwood* focused on comparisons between the School District's hiring data and the "relevant labor market."  Under what circumstances are general population comparisons still useful?  What factors determine the "relevant labor market"?

**3.**  Another possible data base to use is "applicant flow data."  What advantages and disadvantages does such information present for a court charged with the task of determining whether the employer's hiring practices have had an adverse impact on a protected group?

---

**20.**  Petitioners argue that statistics, at least those comparing the racial composition of an employer's work force to the composition of the population at large, should never be given decisive weight in a Title VII case. * * *

* * *  Statistics showing racial or ethnic imbalance are probative in a case such as this one only because such imbalance is often a telltale sign of purposeful discrimination; absent explanation, it is ordinarily to be expected that nondiscriminatory hiring practices will in time result in a work force more or less representative of the racial and ethnic composition of the population in the community from which employees are hired.  Evidence of longlasting and gross disparity between the composition of a work force and that of the general population thus may be significant even though § 703(j) makes clear that Title VII imposes no requirement that a work force mirror the general population.

**4.** Once the proper quantitative data comparison has been established, some measure of the qualitative usefulness of the data is necessary before a court can conclude that a particular hiring pattern has an "adverse impact" within the meaning of the law. In *Hazelwood,* the Supreme Court endorsed the use of standard deviations, a mathematical measure of statistical significance, to determine whether data has legal significance as well. Standard deviations measure the likelihood that a particular set of numbers is the result of chance rather than what one would expect to occur naturally as a result of the employer's selection processes. What the Supreme Court has not done, however, is indicate precisely what level of statistical significance is legally determinative. As a result, many complex adverse impact cases have involved sophisticated statistical battles between mathematical experts debating the relative merits of various measures of significance, particularly multiple regression analysis.

**5.** Sample size is an important component of statistical probability analysis. The fewer employment decisions an employer makes, the more difficult it is to conclude that differences in selection rates are meaningful. How does one prove discrimination in such cases? The First Circuit has offered guidance on this problem:

> Widely accepted statistical techniques have been developed to determine the likelihood an observed disparity resulted from mere chance. Where a plaintiff relies exclusively on a narrow base of data, * * * it is crucial for the court to consider the possibility that chance could account for the observed disparity.

> We think that in cases involving a narrow data base, the better approach is for the courts to require a showing that the disparity is statistically significant, or unlikely to have occurred by chance, applying basic statistical tests as the method of proof. When statistical tests sufficiently diminish chance as a likely explanation, it can then be presumed that an apparently substantial difference in pass rates is attributable to discriminatory bias, thus shifting the burden to defendants to show job relatedness. If the probability is sufficiently high that the disparity resulted from chance, the plaintiff must present additional evidence of disproportionate impact in order to establish a prima facie case.

Fudge v. Providence Fire Department, 766 F.2d 650 (1st Cir.1985). An additional problem surfaces when an employer changes its testing procedures, making it impossible to compare test results from one time period to another.

**6.** The EEOC Guidelines establish a "four-fifths rule of thumb" for determining when an adverse impact exists in an employer's selection processes. If the *selection rate* for a protected group of employees is less than four-fifths, or 80 percent, of the selection rate for the rest of the workforce or applicant pool, the selection process will be presumed to have an adverse impact. While some courts use the rule as a guideline, it has not been universally adopted. What problems exist in applying such a rule? See Elaine W. Shoben, Differential Pass-Fail Rates in Employment

Testing: Statistical Proof Under Title VII, 91 Harv.L.Rev. 793 (1978). See also Kingsley R. Browne, Statistical Proof of Discrimination: Beyond "Damn Lies," 68 Wash.L.Rev. 477 (1993).

*Griggs* focused attention on employer attempts to show that selection methods satisfy the standard of "job relatedness" or "business necessity" (phrases *Griggs* seemed to use interchangeably). The leading case was ALBEMARLE PAPER CO. v. MOODY, 422 U.S. 405 (1975), which rejected the company's attempt to show the validity of its high school diploma and standardized test requirements:

The [Albemarle] plant, which now employ[s] about 650 persons converts raw wood into paper products. It is organized into a number of functional departments, each with one or more distinct lines of progression, the theory being that workers can move up the line as they acquire the necessary skills; .... [U]ntil 1964 ... skilled lines were expressly reserved for white workers.... After 1964, when it discontinued overt segregation in the lines of progression, the Company allowed Negro workers to transfer to the skilled lines if they could pass the Beta and Wonderlic Tests, but few succeeded in doing so....

Measured against the Guidelines, Albemarle's validation study is materially defective in several respects:

(1) Even if it had been otherwise adequate, the study would not have "validated" the Beta and Wonderlic test battery for all of the skilled lines of progression for which the two tests are, apparently, now required. The study showed significant correlations for the Beta Exam in only three of the eight lines. Though the Wonderlic Test's Form A and Form B are in theory identical and interchangeable measures of verbal facility, significant correlations for one form but not for the other were obtained in four job groupings. In two job groupings neither form showed a significant correlation. Within some of the lines of progression, one form was found acceptable for some job groupings but not for others. Even if the study were otherwise reliable, this odd patchwork of results would not entitle Albemarle to impose its testing program under the Guidelines. A test may be used in jobs other than those for which it has been professionally validated only if there are "no significant differences" between the studied and unstudied jobs. 29 CFR § 1607.4(c)(2). The study in this case involved no analysis of the attributes of, or the particular skills needed in, the studied job groups. There is accordingly no basis for concluding that "no significant differences" exist among the lines of progression, or among distinct job groupings within the studied lines of progression. Indeed, the study's checkered results appear to compel the opposite conclusion.

(2) The study compared test scores with subjective supervisorial rankings. While they allow the use of supervisorial rankings in test validation, the Guidelines quite plainly contemplate that the rankings will be elicited with far more care than was demon-

strated here.  Albemarle's supervisors were asked to rank employees by a "standard" that was extremely vague and fatally open to divergent interpretations.  As previously noted, each "job grouping" contained a number of different jobs, and the supervisors were asked, in each grouping, to

> "determine which ones [employees] they felt irrespective of the job that they were actually doing, but in their respective jobs, did a better job than the person they were rating against. * * *"

There is no way of knowing precisely what criteria of job performance the supervisors were considering, whether each of the supervisors was considering the same criteria or whether, indeed, any of the supervisors actually applied a focused and stable body of criteria of any kind.  There is, in short, simply no way to determine whether the criteria *actually* considered were sufficiently related to the Company's legitimate interest in job-specific ability to justify a testing system with a racially discriminatory impact.

(3) The Company's study focused, in most cases, on job groups near the top of the various lines of progression.  * * *  The fact that the best of those employees working near the top of a line of progression score well on a test does not necessarily mean that that test, or some particular cutoff score on the test, is a permissible measure of the minimal qualifications of new workers entering lower level jobs.  In drawing any such conclusion, detailed consideration must be given to the normal speed of promotion, to the efficacy of on-the-job training in the scheme of promotion, and to the possible use of testing as a promotion device, rather than as a screen for entry into low-level jobs.  * * *

(4) Albemarle's validation study dealt only with job-experienced, white workers; but the tests themselves are given to new job applicants, who are younger, largely inexperienced, and in many instances nonwhite.  The APA Standards state that it is "essential" that

> "[t]he validity of a test should be determined on subjects who are at the age or in the same educational or vocational situation as the persons for whom the test is recommended in practice."

The EEOC Guidelines likewise provide that "[d]ata must be generated and results separately reported for minority and nonminority groups wherever technically feasible."  29 CFR § 1607.5(b)(5).  In the present case, such "differential validation" as to racial groups was very likely not "feasible," because years of discrimination at the plant have insured that nearly all of the upper level employees are white.  But there has been no clear showing that differential validation was not feasible for lower level jobs.

422 U.S. at 431–35.

## NOTES AND QUESTIONS

**1.** *Albemarle* is best known for illustrating to employers how *not* to validate a selection procedure; the Court is explicit on what the weaknesses of the employer's validation efforts were. Footnote 25 from the majority opinion illustrates in part how the company had gone about validating its test requirements:

> In the course of a 1971 validation effort * * *, test scores were accumulated for 105 incumbent employees (101 of whom were white) working in relatively high-ranking jobs. Some of these employees apparently took the tests for the first time as part of this study. The Company's expert testified that the test cutoff scores originally used to screen these incumbents for employment or promotion "couldn't have been * * * very high scores because some of these guys tested very low, as low as 8 in the Wonderlic test, and as low as 95 in the Beta. They couldn't have been using very high cut-off scores or they wouldn't have these low testing employees."

**2.** If you were counsel to the paper company, how would you advise it to modify its employee selection procedures in order to comply with the Court's opinion? Keep in mind that an employer has two options when faced with a selection process that has an adverse impact: validate the selection procedure or eliminate the adverse impact. There is no validation requirement when a selection process has no adverse impact.

**3.** The degree to which a strict job relatedness requirement is applied to all hiring criteria depends on the nature of the job involved. This is particularly true with regard to jobs in which public safety is an issue. For example, United Airlines required that its flight officers have a college degree (in addition to a commercial pilot's license and instrument rating). This requirement had a disparate impact upon blacks and, in fact, only nine of United's 5900 flight officers were black. Nevertheless, the college degree requirement was upheld:

> When a job requires a small amount of skill and training and the consequences of hiring an unqualified applicant are insignificant, the courts should examine closely any pre-employment standard or criteria which discriminate against minorities. In such a case, the employer should have a heavy burden to demonstrate to the court's satisfaction that his employment criteria are job-related. On the other hand, when the job clearly requires a high degree of skill and the economic and human risks involved in hiring an unqualified applicant are great, the employer bears a correspondingly lighter burden to show that his employment criteria are job-related.

Spurlock v. United Airlines, Inc., 475 F.2d 216, 219 (10th Cir.1972). A similar approach has been taken in cases decided under age and handicap discrimination laws, discussed later in this chapter.

Griggs v. Duke Power Co. was the first major decision from the Supreme Court interpreting the reach of Title VII with respect to hiring practices. In *Griggs,* the Supreme Court distinguished between two types of discriminatory treatment by employers: practices which constitute deliberate differential, or disparate, treatment, and practices such as the high school diploma requirement which, while neutral on their face, nonetheless have the consequence of discriminating on the basis of a classification proscribed by Title VII. Cases in this second category are labelled adverse impact or disparate impact cases. Adverse impact cases assert that the discriminatory impact of an employer's facially neutral practice sweeps broadly to cause unlawful discrimination. Disparate treatment, however, focuses on intent rather than effects, such as when an employer refuses to let women apply for certain jobs.

## a. DISPARATE TREATMENT

In McDONNELL DOUGLAS CORP. v. GREEN, 411 U.S. 792 (1973), the Supreme Court set out the elements of proof which must be met in a Title VII disparate treatment case based on discrimination in selection:

> The complainant in a Title VII trial must carry the initial burden under the statute of establishing a prima facie case of racial discrimination. This may be done by showing (i) that he belongs to a racial minority; (ii) that he applied and was qualified for a job for which the employer was seeking applicants; (iii) that, despite his qualifications, he was rejected; and (iv) that, after his rejection, the position remained open and the employer continued to seek applicants from persons of complainant's qualifications. In the instant case, we agree with the Court of Appeals that respondent proved a prima facie case. Petitioner sought mechanics, respondent's trade, and continued to do so after respondent's rejection. Petitioner, moreover, does not dispute respondent's qualifications and acknowledges that his past work performance in petitioner's employ was "satisfactory."

> The burden then must shift to the employer to articulate some legitimate, nondiscriminatory reason for the employee's rejection. We need not attempt in the instant case to detail every matter which fairly could be recognized as a reasonable basis for a refusal to hire. Here petitioner has assigned respondent's participation in unlawful conduct against it as the cause for his rejection.

> \* \* \*

> Petitioner's reason for rejection thus suffices to meet the prima facie case, but the inquiry must not end here. While Title VII does not, without more, compel rehiring of respondent, neither does it permit petitioner to use respondent's conduct as a pretext for the sort of discrimination prohibited by § 703(a)(1). On remand, respondent must, as the Court of Appeals recognized, be afforded a fair opportunity to show that petitioner's stated reason

for respondent's rejection was in fact pretext. Especially relevant
to such a showing would be evidence that white employees involved in acts against petitioner of comparable seriousness to the
"stall-in" were nevertheless retained or rehired. Petitioner may
justifiably refuse to rehire one who was engaged in unlawful,
disruptive acts against it, but only if this criterion is applied alike
to members of all races.

Other evidence that may be relevant to any showing of pretext
includes facts as to the petitioner's treatment of respondent during
his prior term of employment; petitioner's reaction, if any, to
respondent's legitimate civil rights activities; and petitioner's general policy and practice with respect to minority employment. On
the latter point, statistics as to petitioner's employment policy and
practice may be helpful to a determination of whether petitioner's
refusal to rehire respondent in this case conformed to a general
pattern of discrimination against blacks. * * * In short, on the
retrial respondent must be given a full and fair opportunity to
demonstrate by competent evidence that the presumptively valid
reasons for his rejection were in fact a coverup for a racially
discriminatory decision.

411 U.S. at 802–05.

———————

*McDonnell Douglas'* three-part structure for proving discrimination
has been universally followed. In subsequent cases, however, it became
clear that the exact allocation of the burdens of proof between plaintiff and
defendant was ambiguous under the *McDonnell Douglas* standards, particularly with respect to how a defendant employer could rebut the plaintiff's
prima facie case of discrimination. In TEXAS DEPARTMENT OF COM-
MUNITY AFFAIRS v. BURDINE, 450 U.S. 248 (1981), the Supreme Court
clarified the respective burdens of plaintiff and defendant:

The nature of the burden that shifts to the defendant should
be understood in light of the plaintiff's ultimate and intermediate
burdens. The ultimate burden of persuading the trier of fact that
the defendant intentionally discriminated against the plaintiff
remains at all times with the plaintiff. * * *

The burden of establishing a prima facie case of disparate
treatment is not onerous. The plaintiff must prove by a preponderance of the evidence that she applied for an available position
for which she was qualified, but was rejected under circumstances
which give rise to an inference of unlawful discrimination. The
prima facie case serves an important function in the litigation: it
eliminates the most common nondiscriminatory reasons for the
plaintiff's rejection. As the Court explained in Furnco Construction Corp. v. Waters, 438 U.S. 567, 577 (1978), the prima facie case
"raises an inference of discrimination only because we presume

these acts, if otherwise unexplained, are more likely than not based on the consideration of impermissible factors." Establishment of the prima facie case in effect creates a presumption that the employer unlawfully discriminated against the employee. If the trier of fact believes the plaintiff's evidence, and if the employer is silent in the face of the presumption, the court must enter judgment for the plaintiff because no issue of fact remains in the case.

The burden that shifts to the defendant, therefore, is to rebut the presumption of discrimination by producing evidence that the plaintiff was rejected, or someone else was preferred, for a legitimate, nondiscriminatory reason. The defendant need not persuade the court that it was actually motivated by the proffered reasons. It is sufficient if the defendant's evidence raises a genuine issue of fact as to whether it discriminated against the plaintiff. To accomplish this, the defendant must clearly set forth, through the introduction of admissible evidence, the reasons for the plaintiff's rejection. The explanation provided must be legally sufficient to justify a judgment for the defendant. If the defendant carries this burden of production, the presumption raised by the prima facie case is rebutted, and the factual inquiry proceeds to a new level of specificity. Placing this burden of production on the defendant thus serves simultaneously to meet the plaintiff's prima facie case by presenting a legitimate reason for the action and to frame the factual issue with sufficient clarity so that the plaintiff will have a full and fair opportunity to demonstrate pretext. The sufficiency of the defendant's evidence should be evaluated by the extent to which it fulfills these functions.

The plaintiff retains the burden of persuasion. She now must have the opportunity to demonstrate that the proffered reason was not the true reason for the employment decision. This burden now merges with the ultimate burden of persuading the court that she has been the victim of intentional discrimination. She may succeed in this either directly by persuading the court that a discriminatory reason more likely motivated the employer or indirectly by showing that the employer's proffered explanation is unworthy of credence.

450 U.S. at 253–56.

The Supreme Court revisited the issue of the *McDonnell Douglas– Burdine* three-part structure in ST. MARY'S HONOR CENTER v. HICKS, 509 U.S. 502 (1993). For the first time the Court addressed a situation where the fact-finder rejected the defendant's proffered nondiscriminatory explanation for its adverse employment decision:

[Defendants] sustained their burden of production by introducing evidence of two legitimate, nondiscriminatory reasons for their actions.... Our cases make clear that at that point the shifted burden of production became irrelevant. "If the defendant carries this burden of production, the presumption raised by the prima facie case is rebutted." *Burdine.*

* * *

The presumption, having fulfilled its role of forcing the defendant to come forward with some response, simply drops out of the picture. *Burdine.* The defendant's "production" (whatever its persuasive effect) having been made, the trier of fact proceeds to decide the ultimate question: whether plaintiff has proven "that the defendant intentionally discriminated against [him]" because of his race, *Id.* The factfinder's disbelief of the reasons put forward by the defendant (particularly if disbelief is accompanied by a suspicion of mendacity) may, together with the elements of the prima facie case, suffice to show intentional discrimination. Thus, rejection of the defendant's proffered reasons will permit the trier of fact to infer the ultimate fact of intentional discrimination.

See generally Mark S. Brodin, The Demise of Circumstantial Proof in Employment Discrimination Litigation: St. Mary's Honor Center v. Hicks, Pretext, and the "Personality" Excuse, 18 Berkeley J. Employment & Lab.L. 183 (1997).

For an interesting debate on the relevance of *St. Mary's* when a plaintiff proves that defendant's proffered justifications are false, see the Second Circuit's en banc opinion in Fisher v. Vassar College, 114 F.3d 1332 (1997). Six circuit judges in *Fisher,* in a majority opinion written by Judges Jacobs and Leval, held that "once an employer has proffered a non-discriminatory reason for an adverse employment action, a plaintiff in a discrimination case must show by a 'preponderance of the evidence' that the reason for the adverse employment action was illegal discrimination . . . . 'that the proffered reason was not the true reason for the employment decision, and that race was.' " *St. Mary's.* The majority thus held that once a defendant proffered evidence of a non-discriminatory reason for its action, the plaintiff was required to prove both that the defendant's proffered reasons were pretextual *and* that discrimination was the real reason for the defendant's action.

Three judges joined a dissenting opinion written by Judge Winter: "My colleagues in the majority . . . hold the following: (1) a Title VII/ ADEA plaintiff's presentation of a *McDonnell Douglas* prima facie case will, if the defendant stands mute as to the reasons for the adverse employment decision, result in liability; but (2) the very same plaintiff's case can, if the defendant responds with a lie, be dismissed on insufficiency grounds. . . . This view leads to peculiar results. For example, under the majority's reasoning, a prima facie case plus the proffer of pretextual defense is weaker (from the plaintiff's standpoint) than an unanswered prima facie case."

Ann Hopkins in front of the Supreme Court.
**Source:** Bruce Young/New York Times

# Price Waterhouse v. Hopkins

490 U.S. 228 (1989).

■ JUSTICE BRENNAN announced the judgment of the Court and delivered an opinion, in which JUSTICE MARSHALL, JUSTICE BLACKMUN and JUSTICE STEVENS join.

Ann Hopkins was a senior manager in an office of Price Waterhouse when she was proposed for partnership in 1982. She was neither offered nor denied admission to the partnership; instead, her candidacy was held for reconsideration the following year. When the partners in her office later refused to repropose her for partnership, she sued Price Waterhouse under Title VII of the Civil Rights Act of 1964, charging that the firm had discriminated against her on the basis of sex in its decisions regarding partnership. * * *

At Price Waterhouse, a nationwide professional accounting partnership, a senior manager becomes a candidate for partnership when the partners in her local office submit her name as a candidate. All of the other partners in the firm are then invited to submit written comments on each candidate—either on a "long" or a "short" form, depending on the partner's degree of exposure to the candidate. Not every partner in the firm submits comments on every candidate. After reviewing the comments and interviewing the partners who submitted them, the firm's Admissions Committee makes a recommendation to the Policy Board. This recommendation will be either that the firm accept the candidate for partnership, put her application on "hold," or deny her the promotion outright. The Policy Board then decides whether to submit the candidate's name to the entire partnership for a vote, to "hold" her candidacy, or to reject her. The recommendation of the Admissions Committee, and the decision of the Policy Board, are not controlled by fixed guidelines: a certain number of positive comments from partners will not guarantee a candidate's admission to the partnership, nor will a specific quantity of negative comments necessarily defeat her application. Price Waterhouse places no limit on the number of persons whom it will admit to the partnership in any given year.

Ann Hopkins had worked at Price Waterhouse's Office of Government Services in Washington, D.C., for five years when the partners in that office proposed her as a candidate for partnership. Of the 662 partners at the firm at that time, 7 were women. Of the 88 persons proposed for partnership that year, only 1—Hopkins—was a woman. Forty-seven of these candidates were admitted to the partnership, 21 were rejected, and 20—including Hopkins—were "held" for reconsideration the following year.[1] Thirteen of the 32 partners who had submitted comments on Hopkins supported her bid for partnership. Three partners recommended that her candidacy be placed on hold, eight stated that they did not have an informed opinion about her, and eight recommended that she be denied partnership.

In a jointly prepared statement supporting her candidacy, the partners in Hopkins' office showcased her successful 2–year effort to secure a $25 million contract with the Department of State, labeling it "an outstanding performance" and one that Hopkins carried out "virtually at the partner level." Despite Price Waterhouse's attempt at trial to minimize her contribution to this project, Judge Gesell specifically found that Hopkins had "played a key role in Price Waterhouse's successful effort to win a multi-million dollar contract with the Department of State." Indeed, he went on, "[n]one of the other partnership candidates at Price Waterhouse that year had a comparable record in terms of successfully securing major contracts for the partnership."

The partners in Hopkins' office praised her character as well as her accomplishments, describing her in their joint statement as "an outstanding professional" who had a "deft touch," a "strong character, independence and integrity." Clients appear to have agreed with these assessments. At trial, one official from the State Department described her as "extremely competent, intelligent," "strong and forthright, very productive, energetic and creative." Another high-ranking official praised Hopkins' decisiveness, broadmindedness, and "intellectual clarity"; she was, in his words, "a stimulating conversationalist." Evaluations such as these led

---

**1.** Before the time for reconsideration came, two of the partners in Hopkins' office withdrew their support for her, and the office informed her that she would not be reconsidered for partnership. Hopkins then resigned. Price Waterhouse does not challenge the Court of Appeals' conclusion that the refusal to repropose her for partnership amounted to a constructive discharge. That court remanded the case to the District Court for further proceedings to determine appropriate relief, and those proceedings have been stayed pending our decision. We are concerned today only with Price Waterhouse's decision to place Hopkins' candidacy on hold. Decisions pertaining to advancement to partnership are, of course, subject to challenge under Title VII. Hishon v. King & Spalding, 467 U.S. 69 (1984).

Judge Gesell to conclude that Hopkins "had no difficulty dealing with clients and her clients appear to have been very pleased with her work" and that she "was generally viewed as a highly competent project leader who worked long hours, pushed vigorously to meet deadlines and demanded much from the multidisciplinary staffs with which she worked."

On too many occasions, however, Hopkins' aggressiveness apparently spilled over into abrasiveness. Staff members seem to have borne the brunt of Hopkins' brusqueness. Long before her bid for partnership, partners evaluating her work had counseled her to improve her relations with staff members. Although later evaluations indicate an improvement, Hopkins' perceived shortcomings in this important area eventually doomed her bid for partnership. Virtually all of the partners' negative remarks about Hopkins—even those of partners supporting her—had to do with her "interpersonal skills." Both "[s]upporters and opponents of her candidacy," stressed Judge Gesell, "indicated that she was sometimes overly aggressive, unduly harsh, difficult to work with and impatient with staff."

There were clear signs, though, that some of the partners reacted negatively to Hopkins' personality because she was a woman. One partner described her as "macho"; another suggested that she "overcompensated for being a woman"; a third advised her to take "a course at charm school." Several partners criticized her use of profanity; in response, one partner suggested that those partners objected to her swearing only "because it[']s a lady using foul language." Another supporter explained that Hopkins "ha[d] matured from a tough-talking somewhat masculine hard-nosed mgr to an authoritative, formidable, but much more appealing lady ptr candidate." But it was the man who, as Judge Gesell found, bore responsibility for explaining to Hopkins the reasons for the Policy Board's decision to place her candidacy on hold who delivered the *coup de grace:* in order to improve her chances for partnership, Thomas Beyer advised, Hopkins should "walk more femininely, talk more femininely, dress more femininely, wear make-up, have her hair styled, and wear jewelry."

Dr. Susan Fiske, a social psychologist and Associate Professor of Psychology at Carnegie–Mellon University, testified at trial that the partnership selection process at Price Waterhouse was likely influenced by sex stereotyping. * * *

In previous years, other female candidates for partnership also had been evaluated in sex-based terms. * * *

Judge Gesell found that Price Waterhouse legitimately emphasized interpersonal skills in its partnership decisions, and also found that the firm had not fabricated its complaints about Hopkins' interpersonal skills as a pretext for discrimination. Moreover, he concluded, the firm did not give decisive emphasis to such traits only because Hopkins was a woman; although there were male candidates who lacked these skills but who were admitted to partnership, the judge found that these candidates possessed other, positive traits that Hopkins lacked.

The judge went on to decide, however, that some of the partners' remarks about Hopkins stemmed from an impermissibly cabined view of the proper behavior of women, and that Price Waterhouse had done nothing to disavow reliance on such comments. He held that Price Waterhouse had unlawfully discriminated against Hopkins on the basis of sex by consciously giving credence and effect to partners' comments that resulted from sex stereotyping. Noting that Price Waterhouse could avoid equitable relief by proving by clear and convincing evidence that it would have placed Hopkins' candidacy on hold even absent this discrimination, the judge decided that the firm had not carried this heavy burden. * * *

In passing Title VII, Congress made the simple but momentous announcement that sex, race, religion, and national origin are not relevant to the selection, evaluation, or compensation of employees. Yet, the statute does not purport to limit the other qualities and characteristics that employers *may* take into account in making employment decisions. The converse, therefore, of "for cause" legislation, Title VII eliminates certain bases for distinguishing among employees while otherwise preserving employers' freedom of choice. This balance between employee rights and employer prerogatives turns out to be decisive in the case before us.

Congress' intent to forbid employers to take gender into account in making employment decisions appears on the face of the statute. In now-familiar language, the statute forbids an employer to "fail or refuse to hire or to discharge any individual, or otherwise to discriminate with respect to his compensation, terms, conditions, or privileges of employment," or to "limit, segregate, or classify his employees or applicants for employment in any way which would deprive or tend to deprive any individual of employment opportunities or otherwise adversely affect his status as an employee, *because of* such individual's * * * sex." We take these words to mean that gender must be irrelevant to employment decisions. To construe the words "because of" as colloquial shorthand for "but-for causation," as does Price Waterhouse, is to misunderstand them.

But-for causation is a hypothetical construct. In determining whether a particular factor was a but-for cause of a given event, we begin by assuming that that factor was present at the time of the event, and then ask whether, even if that factor had been absent, the event nevertheless would have transpired in the same way. The present, active tense of the operative verbs of § 703(a)(1) ("to fail or refuse"), in contrast, turns our attention to the actual moment of the event in question, the adverse employment decision. The critical inquiry, the one commanded by the words of § 703(a)(1), is whether gender was a factor in the employment decision *at the moment it was made*. Moreover, since we know that the words "because of" do not mean "*solely* because of," we also know that Title VII meant to condemn even those decisions based on a mixture of legitimate and illegitimate considerations. When, therefore, an employer considers both gender and legitimate factors at the time of making a decision, that decision was "because of" sex and the other, legitimate considerations—even if we may say later, in the context of litigation, that the decision would have been the same if gender had not been taken into the account.

To attribute this meaning to the words "because of" does not, as the dissent asserts, divest them of causal significance. A simple example illustrates the point. Suppose two physical forces act upon and move an object, and suppose that either force acting alone would have moved the object. As the dissent would have it, *neither* physical force was a "cause" of the motion unless we can show that but for one or both of them, the object would not have moved; to use the dissent's terminology, both forces were simply "in the air" unless we can identify at least one of them as a but-for cause of the object's movement. Events that are causally overdetermined, in other words, may not have any "cause" at all. This cannot be so.

We need not leave our common-sense at the doorstep when we interpret a statute. It is difficult for us to imagine that, in the simple words "because of," Congress meant to obligate a plaintiff to identify the precise causal role played by legitimate and illegitimate motivations in the employment decision she challenges. We conclude, instead, that Congress meant to obligate her to prove that the employer relied upon sex-based considerations in coming to its decision.

\* \* \*

To say that an employer may not take gender into account is not, however, the end of the matter, for that describes only one aspect of Title VII. The other important aspect of the statute is its preservation of an employer's remaining freedom of choice. We conclude that the preservation of this freedom means that an employer shall not be liable if it can prove that, even if it had not taken gender into account, it would have come to the same decision regarding a particular person. \* \* \*

\* \* \* The central point is this: while an employer may not take gender into account in making an employment decision (except in those very narrow circumstances in which gender is a BFOQ), it is free to decide against a woman for other reasons. We think these principles require that, once a plaintiff in a Title VII case shows that gender played a motivating part in an employment decision, the defendant may avoid a finding of liability only by proving that it would have made the same decision even if it had not allowed gender to play such a role. This balance of burdens is the direct result of Title VII's balance of rights.

\* \* \*

In saying that gender played a motivating part in an employment decision, we mean that, if we asked the employer at the moment of the decision what its reasons were and if we received a truthful response, one of those reasons would be that the applicant or employee was a woman. In the specific context of sex stereotyping, an employer who acts on the basis of a belief that a woman cannot be aggressive, or that she must not be, has acted on the basis of gender.

Although the parties do not overtly dispute this last proposition, the placement by Price Waterhouse of "sex stereotyping" in quotation marks throughout its brief seems to us an insinuation either that such stereotyping was not present in this case or that it lacks legal relevance. We reject both possibilities. As to the existence of sex stereotyping in this case, we are not inclined to quarrel with the District Court's conclusion that a number of the partners' comments showed sex stereotyping at work. As for the legal relevance of sex stereotyping, we are beyond the day when an employer could evaluate employees by assuming or insisting that they matched the stereotype associated with their group, for " '[i]n forbidding employers to discriminate against individuals because of their sex, Congress intended to strike at the entire spectrum of disparate treatment of men and women resulting from sex stereotypes.' " An employer who objects to aggressiveness in women but whose positions require this trait places women in an intolerable and impermissible Catch–22: out of a job if they behave aggressively and out of a job if they don't. Title VII lifts women out of this bind.

Remarks at work that are based on sex stereotypes do not inevitably prove that gender played a part in a particular employment decision. The plaintiff must show that the employer actually relied on her gender in making its decision. In making this showing, stereotyped remarks can certainly be *evidence* that gender played a part.

The courts below held that an employer who has allowed a discriminatory impulse to play a motivating part in an employment decision must prove by clear and convincing evidence that it would have made the same decision in the absence of discrimination. We are persuaded that the better rule is that the employer must make this showing by a preponderance of the evidence.

* * *

Price Waterhouse appears to think that we cannot affirm the factual findings of the trial court without deciding that, instead of being overbearing and aggressive and curt, Hopkins is in fact kind and considerate and patient. If this is indeed its impression, petitioner misunderstands the theory on which Hopkins prevailed. The District Judge acknowledged that Hopkins' conduct justified complaints about her behavior as a senior manager. But he also concluded that the reactions of at least some of the partners were reactions to her as a *woman* manager. Where an evaluation is based on a subjective assessment of a person's strengths and weaknesses, it is simply not true that each evaluator will focus on, or even mention, the same weaknesses. Thus, even if we knew that Hopkins had "personality problems," this would not tell us that the partners who cast their evaluations of Hopkins in sex-based terms would have criticized her as sharply (or criticized her at all) if she had been a man. It is not our job to review the evidence and decide that the negative reactions to Hopkins were based on reality; our perception of Hopkins' character is irrelevant. We sit not to determine whether Ms. Hopkins is nice, but to decide whether the partners reacted negatively to her personality because she is a woman.

We hold that when a plaintiff in a Title VII case proves that her gender played a motivating part in an employment decision, the defendant may avoid a finding of liability only by proving by a preponderance of the evidence that it would have made the same decision even if it had not taken the plaintiff's gender into account. Because the courts below erred by deciding that the defendant must make this proof by clear and convincing evidence, we reverse the Court of Appeals' judgment against Price Waterhouse on liability and remand the case to that court for further proceedings.

It is so ordered.

■ JUSTICE O'CONNOR, concurring in the judgment.

* * *

Where an individual disparate treatment plaintiff has shown by a preponderance of the evidence that an illegitimate criterion was a *substantial* factor in an adverse employment decision, the deterrent purpose of the statute has clearly been triggered. More importantly, as an evidentiary matter, a reasonable factfinder could conclude that absent further explanation, the employer's discriminatory motivation "caused" the employment decision. The employer has not yet been shown to be a violator, but neither is it entitled to the same presumption of good faith concerning its employment decisions which is accorded employers facing only circumstantial evidence of discrimination. Both the policies behind the statute, and the evidentiary principles developed in the analogous area of causation in the law of torts, suggest that at this point the employer may be required to convince the factfinder that, despite the smoke, there is no fire.

* * *

* * * In this case, the District Court found that a number of the evaluations of Ann Hopkins submitted by partners in the firm overtly referred to her failure to conform to certain gender stereotypes as a factor militating against her election to the partnership. The District Court further found that these evaluations were given "great weight" by the decisionmakers at Price Waterhouse. In addition, the District Court found that the partner responsible for informing Hopkins of the factors which caused her candidacy to be placed on hold, indicated that her "professional" problems would be solved if she would "walk more femininely, talk more femininely, wear make-up, have her hair styled, and wear jewelry." As the Court of Appeals characterized it, Ann Hopkins proved that Price Waterhouse "permitt[ed] stereotypical attitudes towards women to play a significant, though unquantifiable, role in its decision not to invite her to become a partner."

At this point Ann Hopkins had taken her proof as far as it could go. She had proved discriminatory input into the decisional process, and had proved that participants in the process considered her failure to conform to the stereotypes credited by a number of the decisionmakers had been a substantial factor in the decision. It is as if Ann Hopkins were sitting in the hall outside the room where partnership decisions were being made. As the partners filed in to consider her candidacy, she heard several of them make sexist remarks in discussing her suitability for partnership. As the decisionmakers exited the room, she was *told* by one of those privy to the decisionmaking process that her gender was a major reason for the rejection of her partnership bid.  * * * [O]ne would be hard pressed to think of a situation where it would be more appropriate to require the defendant to show that its decision would have been justified by wholly legitimate concerns.

\* \* \*

In my view, in order to justify shifting the burden on the issue of causation to the defendant, a disparate treatment plaintiff must show by direct evidence that an illegitimate criterion was a substantial factor in the decision.  * * *

Thus, stray remarks in the workplace, while perhaps probative of sexual harassment, cannot justify requiring the employer to prove that its hiring or promotion decisions were based on legitimate criteria.  Nor can statements by nondecisionmakers, or statements by decisionmakers unrelated to the decisional process itself suffice to satisfy the plaintiff's burden in this regard.  * * * Race and gender always "play a role" in an employment decision in the benign sense that these are human characteristics of which decisionmakers are aware and may comment on in a perfectly neutral and nondiscriminatory fashion.  For example, in the context of this case, a mere reference to "a lady candidate" might show that gender "played a role" in the decision, but by no means could support a rational factfinder's inference that the decision was made "because of" sex.  What is required is what Ann Hopkins showed here:  direct evidence that decisionmakers placed substantial negative reliance on an illegitimate criterion in reaching their decision.

\* \* \*

In this case, I agree with the plurality that petitioner should be called upon to show that the outcome would have been the same if respondent's professional merit had been its only concern.  On remand, the District Court should determine whether Price Waterhouse has shown by a preponderance of the evidence that if gender had not been part of the process, its employment decision concerning Ann Hopkins would nonetheless have been the same.

■ JUSTICE KENNEDY, with whom the CHIEF JUSTICE AND JUSTICE SCALIA join, dissenting.  * * *

We established the order of proof for individual Title VII disparate treatment cases in McDonnell Douglas Corp. v. Green, and reaffirmed this allocation in Texas Dept. of Community Affairs v. Burdine.  Under *Burdine,* once the plaintiff presents a prima facie case, an inference of discrimination arises.  The employer must rebut the inference by articulating a legitimate nondiscriminatory reason for its action.  The final burden of persuasion, however, belongs to the plaintiff. *Burdine* makes clear that the "ultimate burden of persuading the trier of fact that the defendant intentionally discriminated against the plaintiff remains at all times with the plaintiff." I would adhere to this established evidentiary framework, which provides the appropriate standard for this and other individual disparate treatment cases. Today's creation of a new set of rules for "mixed-motive" cases is not mandated by the statute itself. The Court's attempt at refinement provides limited practical benefits at the cost of confusion and complexity, with the attendant risk that the trier of fact will misapprehend the controlling legal principles and reach an incorrect decision.

\* \* \*

Although the District Court's version of Title VII liability is improper under any of today's opinions, I think it important to stress that Title VII creates no independent cause of action for sex stereotyping. Evidence of use by decisionmakers of sex stereotypes is, of course, quite relevant to the question of discriminatory intent. The ultimate question, however, is whether discrimination caused the plaintiff's harm. Our cases do not support the suggestion that failure to "disclaim reliance" on stereotypical comments itself violates Title VII. Neither do they support creation of a "duty to sensitize." As the dissenting judge in the Court of Appeals observed, acceptance of such theories would turn Title VII "from a prohibition of discriminatory conduct into an engine for rooting out sexist thoughts."

Employment discrimination claims require factfinders to make difficult and sensitive decisions. Sometimes this may mean that no finding of discrimination is justified even though a qualified employee is passed over by a less than admirable employer. In other cases, Title VII's protections properly extend to plaintiffs who are by no means model employees. As Justice Brennan notes, courts do not sit to determine whether litigants are nice. In this case, Hopkins plainly presented a strong case both of her own professional qualifications and of the presence of discrimination in Price Waterhouse's partnership process. Had the District Court found on this record that sex discrimination caused the adverse decision, I doubt it would have been reversible error. That decision was for the finder of fact, however, and the District Court made plain that sex discrimination was not a but-for cause of the decision to place Hopkins' partnership candidacy on hold. Attempts to evade tough decisions by erecting novel theories of liability or multi-tiered systems of shifting burdens are misguided.

The language of Title VII and our well-considered precedents require this plaintiff to establish that the decision to place her candidacy on hold was made "because of" sex. Here the District Court found that the "comments of the individual partners and the expert evidence of Dr. Fiske do not prove an intentional discriminatory motive or purpose," and that "[b]ecause plaintiff has considerable problems dealing with staff and peers, the Court cannot say that she would have been elected to partnership if the Policy Board's decision had not been tainted by sexually based evaluations." Hopkins thus failed to meet the requisite standard of proof after a full trial. I would remand the case for entry of judgment in favor of Price Waterhouse.

[The concurring opinion of Justice White is omitted.]

NOTES AND QUESTIONS

**1.** On remand, the district court found that Price Waterhouse had not established by a preponderance of the evidence that it would have refused a partnership to Hopkins notwithstanding the gender stereotyping that infected its consideration of her. As to remedy, the court ordered that she be offered a partnership effective July 1, 1990, with compensation and benefits as if she had been admitted to the partnership on July 1, 1983. Because she had not tried hard enough for equivalent work in the intervening years, she was awarded back pay (including interest) of only $371,175. Hopkins v. Price Waterhouse, 737 F.Supp. 1202 (D.D.C.1990), affirmed, 920 F.2d 967 (D.C.Cir.1990).

**2.** In 1996, Price Waterhouse named Frances C. Engoron the firm's first female senior partner. Ms. Engoron assumed a unique title in a Big Six accounting firm: Senior Partner, Intellectual Capital. Her duties are to oversee recruiting, human resources, career development, and training. Lee Berton, First Female Senior Partner is Named By Price Waterhouse For Recruiting, Wall St.J., February 2, 1996, at B13.

**3.** Until Hishon v. King & Spalding, 467 U.S. 69 (1984), courts had regarded partnership decisions as exempt from Title VII review. *Hishon* unanimously rejected that argument.

**4.** Can a collective decision-making process about a position (partner in accounting firm) for which different decision-makers apply different criteria ever be cleansed of considerations of race and gender? If not, then the burden of persuasion—the issue that divided the Court in *Price Waterhouse*—will be of great significance. Can the answer to this issue be found in the statutory language? How do you evaluate the social costs of putting the burden on the plaintiff versus the costs of placing it on the employer?

**5.** Ms. Hopkins brought a disparate treatment action. She (and the many other women who did not become partners at Price Waterhouse) might have brought a disparate impact challenge. After reading the next section, consider the *Price Waterhouse* facts against the standard for establishing disparate impact liability.

**6.** What would you tell Price Waterhouse to do to assure that its promotion procedures satisfy anti-discrimination law?

**7.** The Civil Rights Act of 1991 responded to *Price Waterhouse* by allowing an unlawful employment practice to be established "when the complaining party demonstrates that race, color, religion, sex, or national origin was a motivating factor for any employment practice, even though other factors also motivated the practice." 42 U.S.C. § 2000e–2(m). If, however, the employer demonstrates that it would have taken the same action even absent the impermissible motivating factor, the court may grant the plaintiff declaratory relief, certain types of injunctive relief, and partial attorney's fees, but it may not award damages. 42 U.S.C. § 2000e–5(g)(2)(B). Is this standard different from that proposed in earlier, unsuccessful legislation which would have established liability if the plaintiff could show that impermissible factors *contributed* to the employment practice?

Also, the Act made changes in Title VII procedures and remedies. For the first time, both compensatory and punitive damages are available, but only for intentional discrimination and subject to caps based on the size of the workforce (up to a cap of $300,000 for employers with more than 500 employees). Punitive damages are available only if the employer acted "with malice or with reckless indifference" to the plaintiff's statutory rights. In many Title VII cases, jury trial is now available.

For the most recent discussion of mixed motive cases and the Civil Rights Act of 1991, see Fuller v. Phipps, 67 F.3d 1137 (4th Cir.1995) (distinguishing between mixed-motive and pretext cases and holding that the procedural benefits of § 107 of the Civil Rights Act of 1991 are available only to plaintiffs in mixed-motive cases).

**8.**   In St. Mary's Honor Center v. Hicks, 509 U.S. 502 (1993), the Supreme Court held that a finding that an employer was not actually motivated by the reasons asserted for dismissal is not the equivalent of a finding of discriminatory animus. Melvin Hicks proved the existence of "a crusade to terminate him," but not that the crusade was racially rather than personally motivated. Justice Scalia wrote: "That the employer's proffered reason is unpersuasive, or even obviously contrived, does not necessarily establish that the plaintiff's proffered reason of race is correct. That remains a question for the fact finder to answer * * *." Justice Souter's dissent, joined by Justices White, Blackmun, and Stevens, called the result "unfair to plaintiffs, unworkable in practice, and inexplicable in forgiving employers who give false evidence in court."

**9.**   McKennon v. Nashville Banner Publishing Co., 513 U.S. 352 (1995), holding that a valid claim of discrimination is not defeated by after-acquired evidence of wrongdoing by the employee, is discussed in Chapter 10, infra.

**10.**   Consider the experiment, "Nonverbal Affect Responses to Male and Female Leaders: Implications for Leadership Evaluations," 58 J. Personality & Social Psychology 48 (1990). Social psychologists Doré Butler and Florence Geis studied perception of women and men in leadership roles to see if automatic expectations for women were still dominated by traditional stereotypes.

Male and female subjects participated in four-person discussions in which male or female confederates assumed leadership. The leadership roles were predetermined by a script which called either for "leader" and "non-leader" or "co-leader" roles. Male and female confederates would switch roles for consecutive trials, and the subjects' nonverbal responses were recorded from behind one-way mirrors during the discussions. Female leaders received more negative than positive non-verbal responses, in contrast to male leaders, who received at least as many positive as negative responses. In a survey following the discussion, female leaders received more negative ratings, such as being "bossy and dominating," than their male counterparts.

Butler and Geis found their results supported the premise that "intellectual assertiveness by women in mixed-sex discussions elicits visible cues of negative affect." They claim that this result has implications for hiring, salary, and promotion, which often depend on recognition of the individual as an emergent leader. The results suggest that training women to be "more assertive" (or less assertive, for that matter) in leadership will not eliminate discrimination.

Does this change your perception of the result in Price Waterhouse? How do you see Hopkins' evaluations and co-workers' comments about her technique and personality?

### Note on Physical Appearance and Gender Discrimination

While physical attractiveness is not a protected category, employers who discriminate on the basis of physical appearance may find their employees subsumed under one the several protected categories, such as race, age, or disability. A study by Jeff E. Biddle and Daniel S. Hamermesh demonstrated that lawyers, both male and female, who were considered "attractive" were more successful than those who were not considered to be attractive. Why should some immutable attributes, such as intelligence or physical prowess, be considered benign grounds for employer choice while positive attributes of appearance are not to be considered as assets in the employment field? A student note in the Harvard Law Review in 1987 argued that such "facial discrimination" ought to be prohibited under the same laws protecting against discrimination on the basis of disability. Note, Facial Discrimination: Extending Handicap Law to Employment Discrimination on the Basis of Physical Appearance, 100 Harv.L.Rev. 2035 (1987). In a satirical response to this note, an editor of The New Republic noted, "[T]he one citadel of prejudice we may be sure is free from storming by the battalions of Harvard Law School is our society's overwhelming bias in favor of smart people. They may be short, fat, and ugly up there, with protruding ears, unusual noses, jutting chins, and dyspeptic personalities. But they're not dumb." The Tyranny of Beauty, The New Republic, Oct. 12, 1987 at 4.

Given the empirical evidence in the Biddle and Hamermesh study, however, why should employers not be entitled to prefer the higher-achieving class of attractive workers? While mere "customer preference" has not been accepted by the courts, employers are justifying their hiring preferences using a combination of BFOQ and business justification theories. A recent judgment by the EEOC against the Hooters restaurant chain awarded male applicants denied jobs at the bar-restaurants individual awards totalling $22 million. The EEOC then announced its decision not to intervene in the private class-action lawsuit against the chain, citing a need to devote scarce litigation resources elsewhere, but asserting its position that "denying any American a job simply because of his or her sex is a serious issue which should be taken seriously." Hooters Chain Is Freed of Job Bias Inquiry, N.Y. Times, May 2, 1996 at B10. Hooters defends its women-only policy as sufficiently job-related by insisting that their primary business is not to run a restaurant serving burgers, beer, and chicken wings, but to present lightly-clad "Hooters girls" as entertainment, preferred by their clientele over male servers, and therefore more profit-able. Such a justification plays around the borders of the business justifi-cation and BFOQ theories, while also raising the question as to where the line is drawn between permissible art and entertainment and unacceptable exploitation of workers' bodies. While a Broadway revue may present dancers and actors selected on the basis of sex and even more lightly clad than Hooters waitresses, the imprimatur of art on such a presentation seems unequivocally permissible as an employment practice. Hooters and other establishments serving a similar clientele, however, are deemed by the EEOC to be exploitative and sexist in their employment practices. Is it possible that such a distinction is based on aesthetics determined in part by class, rather than by evenly-applied standards?

Following EEOC v. Sage Realty Corp., page 563 infra, and the South-west Airlines case, page 277 infra, it appears that requiring employees to dress in a sexually provocative manner is prohibited, or at least limited, on the ground that it exposes female employees to unwanted sexual harass-ment and illegally discriminates on the basis of sex. If employees are offered a choice between sexy and demure costumes, however, it is clear that some employees in the service fields, such as cocktail waitresses, will opt for the more revealing outfit since the tips will be higher if they are so clothed. Interestingly, the Hooters case has not been brought to reawaken the female employees' objections to their required uniform [see discussion of that case at page 568, infra], but by prospective male employees who allege that they are being denied, on the basis of their sex, opportunities to dress lightly and serve beer.

In her 1991 book on images of beauty and their effect on women, Naomi Wolf dedicates a chapter to a discussion of women's appearance in the workplace. Arguing that requirements of beauty and appearance function to prevent women from fully achieving in the workplace, Wolf surveys American and British case law and concludes that while statutory protection is not precluded, courts have been unwilling to protect women's jobs in the face of ambivalent cultural markers. She imagines the all-too-real absurdity of a woman trying to dress for work with her attorney present to advise her on what to wear, with little success. Women, Wolf argues, are trapped in competing and conflicting ideas of appropriate standards of female appearance in the professional world. If young and attractive, female employees are considered to be using inappropriate sexuality to achieve, while "asking for" harassment, and if old and less attractive, are no longer qualified for any job which brings contact with the public. Wolf defines this appearance requirement as the "PBQ," or professional beauty qualification.

Sex equality statutes single out the BFOQ ... as an *exceptional* instance in which sex discrimination in hiring is fair because the job itself demands a specific gender; as a conscious exception to the rule of equal opportunity law, it is extremely narrowly defined. What is happening now is that a parody of the BFOQ—what I'll call more specifically the PBQ, or professional beauty qualification—is being extremely *widely* institutionalized as a condition for women's hiring and promotion. By taking over in bad faith the good-faith language of the BFOQ, those who manipulate the professional beauty qualification can defend it as being nondiscriminatory with the disclaimer that it is a necessary requirement if the job is to be properly done. Since the ever-expanding PBQ has so far been applied overwhelmingly to women in the workplace and not to men, using it to hire and promote (and harass and fire) is in fact sex discrimination and should be seen as a violation of Title VII of the 1964 Civil Rights Act....

Naomi Wolf, The Beauty Myth 27–28 (1991).

Of interest to lawyers were the controversies surrounding the clothing and appearance of two female attorneys. Rosalie Osias, who represents mortgage brokers and mortgage companies in Great Neck, New York, drew the ire of the Nassau County Bar Association over her print advertisements. In the ads, Osias posed on her desk and on a motorcycle in high heels and low cut blouses in provocative poses, with such copy as, "Does this law firm have a reputation? You bet it does!!!" Osias reported that her business has quadrupled since the start of the campaign. D. Wise, Woman Lawyer's Suggestive Ads Stir Ire, N.Y.Law Journal, Oct. 23, 1995, p. 1. In Fulton County, Georgia, an assistant district attorney, Nancy A. Grace, confronted a motion to compel her "to wear appropriate trial attire" including skirts no shorter than one inch above the knee, no slits higher than one inch above the knee, and no low-cut blouses. In addition, her opponent wished the judge to order her not to "bend over in front of any and all jurors, thereby revealing cleavage." The defense counsel added that if Grace were not restrained, he would attend court in a tank top. Trisha Renaud, Fulton County Daily Report, Oct. 24, 1995.

### Note on Fisher v. Vassar College

70 F.3d 1420 (2d Cir.1995), affirmed en banc, 114 F.3d 1332 (1997).

Cynthia Fisher, an assistant professor at Vassar College denied tenure in the biology department, sued alleging violations of Title VII and the Age Discrimination in Employment Act. Fisher could not prove a claim of "simple" sex discrimination based solely on her status as a woman because Vassar had many women professors in its tenured faculty. She therefore alleged that Vassar had discriminated against her for being a married woman, thereby establishing a Title VII prima facie case of "sex plus" discrimination, which was recognized by the Supreme Court in Phillips v. Martin Marietta Corp., 400 U.S. 542 (1971).

Fisher had spent eight years away from the teaching profession while caring for her two children. She alleged that "it was her decision to be a wife, mother and a scientist before seeking tenure at Vassar that resulted in the denial of [her] tenure application" and "claim[ed] that despite her qualifications and her progress in becoming current in her field, her absence from academia was held against her as an insurmountable barrier."

The district court found for plaintiff and criticized Vassar's "acceptance of a stereotype and bias: that a married woman with an active and on-going family life cannot be a productive scientist and, therefore, is not one despite much evidence to the contrary."

A panel of the court of appeals for the second circuit reversed: "In making tenure decisions, it is perfectly reasonable to consider as a factor the candidate's prolonged absence from academia in making hiring and promotion decisions. The law does not prevent employers from considering such things. Moreover, the choice of remaining at home for an extended period following the birth of a child 'is not the inevitable consequence of a medical condition related to pregnancy.' A policy may discriminate between those employees who take off long periods of time in order to raise children and those who either do not have children or are able to raise them without an appreciable career interruption. That is not inherently sex specific and does not give rise to a claim under Title VII." Fisher v. Vassar College, 70 F.3d 1420, 1448 (2d Cir.), aff'd en banc, 114 F.3d 1332 (1995).

Who was right, the district or the circuit court? Compare Cynthia Fisher to Ann Hopkins. Is it possible that Professor Fisher was too "feminine" when she took a leave of absence from her career to raise a family, while Ms. Hopkins was too "masculine" because she was aggressive at work?

The court of appeals opinion reasoned that taking time off work to raise children was not "inherently sex specific" and therefore did not constitute a basis for a claim of sex discrimination. Similarly, the court of appeals for the eighth circuit in Piantanida v. Wyman Center, Inc., 116 F.3d 340 (8th Cir.1997), rejected plaintiff's Title VII claim of pregnancy discrimination. Plaintiff was demoted upon her return from maternity leave to a position "for a new mom to handle." The court found for employer because "an individual's choice to care for a child is not a 'medical condition' related to childbirth ... [but] is a social role chosen by all new parents who make the decision to raise a child."

Professor Christine Littleton rejects what she terms a "symmetrical" approach against sex discrimination, which assumes that there are no differences between men's and women's ability to perform in the workplace. Littleton instead argues in favor of an "asymmetrical" model of sexual equality, one which recognizes both biological and social differences between the sexes: "If women currently tend to assume primary responsibility for childrearing, we should not ignore that fact in an attempt to prefigure the rosy day when parenting is fully shared. We should instead figure out how to assure that equal resources, status, and access to social decision-making flow to those women (and few men) who engage in this socially female behavior." Christine A. Littleton, Reconstructing Sexual Equality, 75 Calif.L.Rev. 1279 (1987).

### Note on the Pregnancy Discrimination Act of 1978

In 1978, Congress amended Title VII by adding the Pregnancy Discrimination Act of 1978 ("PDA"), which provides in part:

> The terms "because of sex" or "on the basis of sex" include, but are not limited to, because of or on the basis of pregnancy, childbirth, or related medical conditions; and women affected by pregnancy, childbirth, or related medical conditions shall be treated the same for all employment-related purposes, including receipt of benefits under fringe benefit programs, as other persons not so affected but similar in their ability to work.

For a discussion of the PDA as it affects health benefits, see infra, Chapter 6.

**1.** Does the PDA either require or proscribe accommodations by an employer for pregnant employees? Compare *Piantanida*, supra, where the court held that the employer permissibly demoted the plaintiff to a "new mom" position, with Ilhardt v. Sara Lee Corp., 118 F.3d 1151 (7th Cir. 1997), in which the court held that the employer did not violate the PDA when, as part of a reduction in force, it fired a pregnant employee because she was the only part-time attorney in her department.

**2.** Loyal American Life Insurance Company offered Margaret Ahmad employment as a medical claims examiner but withdrew its offer two days later when it learned that she was four months pregnant. Loyal American contended that Ms. Ahmad's anticipated leave of absence would interfere with her four to five month long training program. Ms. Ahmad sued alleging pregnancy discrimination. The court found for the employer and held that the insurance company had a legitimate concern in only hiring employees who could begin processing claims immediately after training. Ahmad v. Loyal American Life Insurance Co., 767 F.Supp. 1114 (S.D.Ala. 1991). Do you agree that a company may consider a pregnant applicant's anticipated maternity leave in denying her employment? Could an employer also inquire about an applicant's plans to raise a family? What if the employee changes her mind?

### b. ADVERSE IMPACT

Proof of discrimination in adverse impact cases takes a much different form from disparate treatment cases. Intent is relatively unimportant: since the challenged selection criteria—like the high school diploma requirement in *Griggs*—apply equally to all employees or applicants for employment, any discrimination which occurs may be unintentional in nature. This is the importance of *Griggs;* it recognizes even unintentional discrimination as unlawful. In contrast to disparate treatment cases, the critical questions in disparate impact cases are: What constitutes an "adverse impact" sufficient to be considered discrimination? What constitutes "job relatedness" or "business necessity," the defenses mentioned by the Supreme Court in *Griggs?*  And finally, what level of proof must the parties establish in order to prevail at trial?

An employer's selection process must be shown to have an adverse impact on a protected class under Title VII before any liability can be found.  While the concept is an easy one to understand, what actually constitutes adverse impact has been the subject of considerable litigation.  The Equal Employment Opportunity Commission has issued official Guidelines for its agents to follow in conducting compliance checks of large employers.

## Uniform Guidelines on Employee Selection Procedures (1978)

29 C.F.R. § 1607.4D.

*Adverse impact and the "four-fifths rule."*  A selection rate for any race, sex, or ethnic group which is less than four-fifths (⅘) will generally be regarded by the Federal enforcement agencies as evidence of adverse impact, while a greater than four-fifths rate will generally not be regarded by Federal enforcement agencies as evidence of adverse impact.  Smaller differences in selection rate may nevertheless constitute adverse impact, where they are significant in both statistical and practical terms or where a user's actions have discouraged applicants disproportionately on grounds of race, sex, or ethnic group.  Greater differences in selection rate may not constitute adverse impact where the differences are based on small numbers and are not statistically significant, or where special recruiting or other programs cause the pool of minority or female candidates to be atypical of the normal pool of applicants from that group.  Where the user's evidence concerning the impact of a selection procedure indicates adverse impact but is based upon numbers which are too small to be reliable, evidence concerning the impact of the procedure over a longer period of time and/or evidence concerning the impact which the selection procedure had when used in the same manner in similar circumstances elsewhere may be considered in determining adverse impact.

While the EEOC Guidelines have received deference from the courts as an interpretation of the law from the agency charged by Congress with enforcing the statute, they are not binding on the federal courts, nor is the Commission's finding of reasonable cause to believe that discrimination has or has not occurred.

## Wards Cove Packing Co. v. Atonio

490 U.S. 642 (1989).

■ Justice White delivered the opinion of the Court.

Title VII of the Civil Rights Act of 1964 makes it an unfair employment practice for an employer to discriminate against any individual with repect to hiring or the terms and condition of employment because of such individual's race, color, religion, sex, or national origin; or to limit, segregate or classify his employees in ways that would adversely affect any employee because of the employee's race, color, religion, sex, or national origin.  Griggs v. Duke Power Co. construed Title VII to proscribe "not only overt discrimination but also practices that are fair in form but discriminatory in practice."  Under this basis for liability, which is known as the "disparate impact" theory and which is involved in this case, a facially neutral employment practice may be deemed violative of Title VII without evidence of the employer's subjective intent to discriminate that is required in a "disparate treatment" case.

* * *

The claims before us are disparate-impact claims, involving the employment practices of petitioners, two companies that operate salmon canneries in remote and widely separated areas of Alaska.  The canneries operate only during the salmon runs in the summer months.  They are inoperative and vacant for the rest of the year.  In May or June of each year, a few weeks before the salmon runs begin, workers arrive and prepare the equipment and facilities for the canning operation.  Most of these workers possess a variety of skills.  When salmon runs are about to begin, the workers who will operate the cannery lines arrive, remain as long as there are fish to can, and then depart.  The canneries are then closed down, winterized, and left vacant until the next spring.  During the off season, the companies employ only a small number of individuals at their headquarters in Seattle and Astoria, Oregon, plus some employees at the winter shipyard in Seattle.

The length and size of salmon runs vary from year to year and hence the number of employees needed at each cannery also varies.  Estimates are made as early in the winter as possible; the necessary employees are hired, and when the time comes, they are transported to the canneries.  Salmon must be processed soon after they are caught, and the work during the canning season is therefore intense.  For this reason, and because the canneries are located in remote regions, all workers are housed at the canneries and have their meals in company-owned mess halls.

Jobs at the canneries are of two general types: "cannery jobs" on the cannery line, which are unskilled positions; and "noncannery jobs," which fall into a variety of classifications.  Most noncannery jobs are classified as skilled positions.  Cannery jobs are filled predominantly by nonwhites, Filipinos and Alaska Natives.  The Filipinos are hired through and dispatched by Local 37 of the International Longshoremen Workers Union pursuant to a hiring hall agreement with the Local.  The Alaska Natives primarily reside in villages near the remote cannery locations.  Noncannery jobs are filled with predominantly white workers, who are hired during the winter months from the companies' offices in Washington and Oregon.  Virtually all of the noncannery jobs pay more than cannery positions.  The predominantly white noncannery workers and the predominantly nonwhite cannery employees live in separate dormitories and eat in separate mess halls.

In 1974, respondents, a class of nonwhite cannery workers who were (or had been) employed at the canneries, brought this Title VII action against petitioners.  Respondents alleged that a variety of petitioners' hiring/promotion practices—e.g., nepotism, a rehire preference, a lack of objective hiring criteria, separate hiring channels, a practice of not promoting from within—were responsible for the racial stratification of the work force, and had denied them and other nonwhites employment as noncannery workers on the basis of race.  Respondents also complained of petitioners' racially segregated housing and dining facilities.  * * * [4]

In holding that respondents had made out a prima facie case of disparate impact, the court of appeals relied solely on respondents' statistics showing a high percentage of nonwhite workers in the cannery jobs and a low percentage of such workers in the noncannery positions.  Although statistical proof can alone make out a prima facie case, the Court of Appeals' ruling here misapprehends our precedents and the purposes of Title VII, and we therefore reverse.

"There can be no doubt," * * * "that the * * * comparison * * * fundamentally misconceived the role of statistics in employment discrimination cases."  The "proper comparison [is] between the racial composition of [the at-issue jobs] and the racial composition of the qualified * * * population in the relevant labor market."  It is such a comparison—between the racial composition of the qualified persons in the labor market and the persons holding at-issue jobs—that generally forms the proper basis for the initial inquiry in a disparate impact case.  Alternatively, in cases where such labor market statistics will be difficult if not impossible to ascertain, we have recognized that certain other statistics—such as measures indicating the racial composition of "otherwise-qualified applicants" for at-issue jobs—are equally probative for this purpose.

---

**4.**  The fact that neither the District Court, nor the Ninth Circuit *en banc,* nor the subsequent Court of Appeals panel ruled for respondents on their disparate treatment claims—i.e., their allegations of intentional racial discrimination—warrants particular attention in light of the dissents' comment that the canneries "bear an unsettling resemblance to aspects of a plantation economy."

Whatever the "resemblance," the unanimous view of the lower courts in this litigation has been that respondents did not prove that the canneries practice intentional racial discrimination.  Consequently, Justice Blackmun's hyperbolic allegation that our decision in this case indicates that this Court no longer "believes that race discrimination * * *

against nonwhites . . . is a problem in our society," is inapt.  Of course, it is unfortunately true that race discrimination exists in our country.  That does not mean, however, that it exists at the canneries—or more precisely, that it has been proven to exist at the canneries.

Indeed, Justice Stevens concedes that respondents did not press before us the legal theories under which the aspects of cannery life that he finds to most resemble a "plantation economy" might be unlawful.  Thus, the question here is not whether we "approve" of petitioners' employment practices or the society that exists at the canneries, but rather, whether respondents have properly established that these practices violate Title VII.

It is clear to us that the Court of Appeals' acceptance of the comparison between the racial composition of the cannery work force and that of the noncannery work force, as probative of a prima facie case of disparate impact in the selection of the latter group of workers, was flawed for several reasons. Most obviously, with respect to the skilled noncannery jobs at issue here, the cannery work force in no way reflected "the pool of *qualified* job applicants" or the "*qualified* population in the labor force." Measuring alleged discrimination in the selection of accountants, managers, boat captains, electricians, doctors, and engineers—and the long list of other "skilled" noncannery positions found to exist by the District Court— by comparing the number of nonwhites occupying these jobs to the number of nonwhites filling cannery worker positions is nonsensical. If the absence of minorities holding such skilled positions is due to a dearth of qualified nonwhite applicants (for reasons that are not petitioners' fault), petitioners' selection methods or employment practices cannot be said to have had a "disparate impact" on nonwhites.

Such a result cannot be squared with our cases or with the goals behind the statute. The Court of Appeals' theory, at the very least, would mean that any employer who had a segment of his work force that was—for some reason—racially imbalanced, could be haled into court and forced to engage in the expensive and time-consuming task of defending the "business necessity" of the methods used to select the other members of his work force. The only practicable option for many employers will be to adopt racial quotas, insuring that no portion of his work force deviates in racial composition from the other portions thereof; this is a result that Congress expressly rejected in drafting Title VII. The Court of Appeals' theory would "leave the employer little choice * * * but to engage in a subjective quota system of employment selection. This, of course, is far from the intent of Title VII." * * *

Consequently, we reverse the Court of Appeals' ruling that a comparison between the percentage of cannery workers who are nonwhite and the percentage of noncannery workers who are nonwhite makes out a prima facie case of disparate impact. Of course, this leaves unresolved whether the record made in the District Court will support a conclusion that a prima facie case of disparate impact has been established on some basis other than the racial disparity between cannery and noncannery workers. This is an issue that the Court of Appeals or the District Court should address in the first instance.

Since the statistical disparity relied on by the Court of Appeals did not suffice to make out a prima facie case, any inquiry by us into whether the specific challenged employment practices of petitioners caused that disparity is pretermitted, as is any inquiry into whether the disparate impact that any employment practice may have had was justified by business considerations. Because we remand for further proceedings, however, on whether a prima facie case of disparate impact has been made in defensible fashion in this case, we address two other challenges petitioners have made to the decision of the Court of Appeals.

First is the question of causation in a disparate-impact case. * * *

Our disparate-impact cases have always focused on the impact of *particular* hiring practices on employment opportunities for minorities. Just as an employer cannot escape liability under Title VII by demonstrating that, "at the bottom line," his work force is racially balanced (where particular hiring practices may operate to deprive minorities of employment opportunities), a Title VII plaintiff does not make out a case of disparate impact simply by showing that, "at the bottom line," there is racial *imbalance* in the work force. As a general matter, a plaintiff must demonstrate that it is the application of a specific or particular employment practice that has created the disparate impact under attack. Such a showing is an integral part of the plaintiff's prima facie case in a disparate-impact suit under Title VII.

Here, respondents have alleged that several "objective" employment practices (e.g., nepotism, separate hiring channels, rehire preferences), as well as the use of "subjective decision making" to select noncannery workers, have had a disparate impact on nonwhites. Respondents base this claim on statistics that allegedly show a disproportionately low percentage of nonwhites in the at-issue positions. However, even if on remand respondents can show that nonwhites are underrepresented in the at-issue jobs in a manner that is acceptable under the standards set forth in Part II, this alone will *not* suffice to make out a prima facie case of disparate impact. Respondents will also have to demonstrate that the disparity they complain of is the result of one or more of the employment practices that they are attacking here, specifically showing that each challenged practice has a significantly disparate impact on employment opportunities for whites and nonwhites. To hold otherwise would result in employers being potentially liable for "the myriad of innocent causes that may lead to statistical imbalances in the composition of their work forces." * * *

Consequently, on remand, the courts below are instructed to require, as part of respondents' prima facie case, a demonstration that specific elements of the petitioners' hiring process have a significantly disparate impact on nonwhites.

If, on remand, respondents meet the proof burdens outlined above, and establish a prima facie case of disparate impact with respect to any of petitioners' employment practices, the case will shift to any business justification petitioners offer for their use of these practices. This phase of the disparate-impact case contains two components: first, a consideration of the justifications an employer offers for his use of these practices; and second, the availability of alternate practices to achieve the same business ends, with less racial impact. We consider these two components in turn.

Though we have phrased the query differently in different cases, it is generally well-established that at the justification stage of such a disparate impact case, the dispositive issue is whether a challenged practice serves, in a significant way, the legitimate employment goals of the employer. The touchstone of this inquiry is a reasoned review of the employer's justification for his use of the challenged practice. A mere insubstantial justification in this regard will not suffice, because such a low standard of review would permit discrimination to be practiced through the use of spurious, seemingly neutral employment practices. At the same time, though, there is no requirement that the challenged practice be "essential" or "indispensable" to the employer's business for it to pass muster: this degree of scrutiny would be almost impossible for most employers to meet, and would result in a host of evils we have identified above. In this phase, the employer carries the burden of producing evidence of a business justification for his employment practice. The burden of persuasion, however, remains with the disparate-impact plaintiff. * * *

Finally, if on remand the case reaches this point, and respondents cannot persuade the trier of fact on the question of petitioners' business necessity defense, respondents may still be able to prevail. To do so, respondents will have to persuade the factfinder that "other tests or selection devices, without a similarly undesirable racial effect, would also serve the employer's legitimate [hiring] interest[s];" by so demonstrating, respondents would prove that "[petitioners were] using [their] tests merely as a 'pretext' for discrimination." If respondents, having established a prima facie case, come forward with alternatives to petitioners' hiring practices that reduce the racially-disparate impact of practices currently being used, and petitioners refuse to adopt these alternatives, such a refusal would belie a claim by petitioners that their incumbent practices are being employed for nondiscriminatory reasons.

Of course, any alternative practices which respondents offer up in this respect must be equally effective as petitioners' chosen hiring procedures in achieving petitioners' legitimate employment goals. Moreover, "[f]actors such as the cost or other burdens of proposed alternative selection devices are relevant in determining whether they would be equally as effective as the challenged practice in serving the employer's legitimate business goals." "Courts are generally less competent than employers to restructure business practices;" consequently, the judiciary should proceed with care before mandating that an employer must adopt a plaintiff's alternate selection or hiring practice in response to a Title VII suit.

For the reasons given above, the judgment of the Court of Appeals is reversed, and the case is remanded for further proceedings consistent with this opinion.

It is so ordered.

■ JUSTICE STEVENS, with whom JUSTICE BRENNAN, JUSTICE MARSHALL, and JUSTICE BLACKMUN join, dissenting.

Fully 18 years ago, this Court unanimously held that Title VII of the Civil Rights Act of 1964 prohibits employment practices that have discriminatory effects as well as those that are intended to discriminate. Griggs v. Duke Power Co. Federal courts and agencies consistently have enforced that interpretation, thus promoting our national goal of eliminating barriers that define economic opportunity not by aptitude and ability but by race, color, national origin, and other traits that are easily identified but utterly irrelevant to one's qualification for a particular job. Regrettably, the Court retreats from these efforts in its review of an interlocutory judgment respecting the "peculiar facts" of this lawsuit. Turning a blind eye to the meaning and purpose of Title VII, the majority's opinion perfunctorily rejects a longstanding rule of law and underestimates the probative value of evidence of a racially stratified work force.[4]  I cannot join this latest sojourn into judicial activism.

\* \* \*

In a disparate treatment case there is no "discrimination" within the meaning of Title VII unless the employer intentionally treated the employee unfairly because of race. Therefore, the employee retains the burden of proving the existence of intent at all times.  \* \* \*

In contrast, intent plays no role in the disparate impact inquiry. The question, rather, is whether an employment practice has a significant, adverse effect on an identifiable class of workers—regardless of the cause or motive for the practice. The employer may attempt to contradict the factual basis for this effect; that is, to prevent the employee from establishing a prima facie case. But when an employer is faced with sufficient proof of disparate impact, its only recourse is to justify the practice by explaining why it is necessary to the operation of business. Such a justification is a classic example of an affirmative defense.  \* \* \*

Also troubling is the Court's apparent redefinition of the employees' burden of proof in a disparate impact case. No prima facie case will be made, it declares, unless the employees " 'isolat[e] and identif[y] the specific employment practices that are allegedly responsible for any observed statistical disparities.' "  This additional proof requirement is unwarranted. It is elementary that a plaintiff cannot recover upon proof of injury alone; rather, the plaintiff must connect the injury to an act of the defendant in order to establish prima facie that the defendant is liable.

---

**4.** Respondents comprise a class of present and former employees of petitioners, two Alaskan salmon canning companies. The class members, described by the parties as "nonwhite," include persons of Samoan, Chinese, Filipino, Japanese, and Alaska Native descent, all but one of whom are United States citizens. Fifteen years ago they commenced this suit, alleging that petitioners engage in hiring, job assignment, housing, and messing practices that segregate nonwhites from whites, in violation of Title VII. Evidence included this response in 1971 by a foreman to a college student's inquiry about cannery employment:

"We are not in a position to take many young fellows to our Bristol Bay canneries as they do not have the background

for our type of employees. Our cannery labor is either Eskimo or Filipino and we do not have the facilities to mix others with these groups."

Some characteristics of the Alaska salmon industry described in this litigation—in particular, the segregation of housing and dining facilities and the stratification of jobs along racial and ethnic lines—bear an unsettling resemblance to aspects of a plantation economy. Indeed the maintenance of inferior, segregated facilities for housing and feeding nonwhite employees, strikes me as a form of discrimination that, although it does not necessarily fit neatly into a disparate impact or disparate treatment mold, nonetheless violates Title VII. Respondents, however, do not press this theory before us.

Although the causal link must have substance, the act need not constitute the sole or primary cause of the harm. Thus in a disparate impact case, proof of numerous questionable employment practices ought to fortify an employee's assertion that the practices caused racial disparities. Ordinary principles of fairness require that Title VII actions be tried like "any lawsuit." The changes the majority makes today, tipping the scales in favor of employers, are not faithful to those principles.

\* \* \*

Evidence that virtually all the employees in the major categories of at-issue jobs were white, whereas about two-thirds of the cannery workers were nonwhite, may not by itself suffice to establish a prima facie case of discrimination. But such evidence of racial stratification puts the specific employment practices challenged by respondents into perspective. Petitioners recruit employees for at-issue jobs from outside the work force rather than from lower-paying, overwhelmingly nonwhite, cannery worker positions. Information about availability of at-issue positions is conducted by word of mouth; therefore, the maintenance of housing and mess halls that separate the largely white noncannery work force from the cannery workers, coupled with the tendency toward nepotistic hiring, are obvious barriers to employment opportunities for nonwhites. Putting to one side the issue of business justifications, it would be quite wrong to conclude that these practices have no discriminatory consequence. Thus I agree with the Court of Appeals that when the District Court makes the additional findings prescribed today, it should treat the evidence of racial stratification in the work force as a significant element of respondents' prima facie case.

The majority's opinion begins with recognition of the settled rule that "a facially neutral employment practice may be deemed violative of Title VII without evidence of the employer's subjective intent to discriminate that is required in a 'disparate treatment' case." It then departs from the body of law engendered by this disparate impact theory, reformulating the order of proof and the weight of the parties' burdens. Why the Court undertakes these unwise changes in elementary and eminently fair rules is a mystery to me.

I respectfully dissent.

■ JUSTICE BLACKMUN, with whom JUSTICE BRENNAN and JUSTICE MARSHALL join, dissenting.

I fully concur in Justice Stevens' analysis of this case. \* \* \*

The harshness of these results is well demonstrated by the facts of this case. The salmon industry as described by this record takes us back to a kind of overt and institutionalized discrimination we have not dealt with in years: a total residential and work environment organized on principles of racial stratification and segregation, which, as Justice Stevens points out, resembles a plantation economy. This industry long has been characterized by a taste for discrimination of the old-fashioned sort: a preference for hiring nonwhites to fill its lowest-level positions, on the condition that they stay there. The majority's legal rulings essentially immunize these practices from attack under a Title VII disparate-impact analysis.

Sadly, this comes as no surprise. One wonders whether the majority still believes that race discrimination—or, more accurately, race discrimination against nonwhites—is a problem in our society, or even remembers that it ever was.

## NOTES AND COMMENTS

**1.** See the discussion in Chapter 3, of EEOC v. Consolidated Service Systems, dealing with use of word-of-mouth recruiting in a way that produced a workforce largely composed of Korean Americans.

**2.** On the strongest reading of *Griggs,* an employer with a smaller minority or female workforce than the appropriate labor pool had to show a business necessity for its selection processes. Thus companies had to "validate" their procedures or else demonstrate numerically satisfactory results. *Wards Cove* rejected (or, according to some commentators, changed) that statement of Title VII law:

a) The plaintiff must specify a particular selection practice, and show its relevance to the numerical results;

b) The employer must show a "business justification," and not that a challenged practice is "essential" or "indispensable";

c) The plaintiff bears the burden of showing that alternative selection practices would work just as well and produce more jobs for minorities or women.

The argument between the two positions was rehearsed, and in some ways more effectively joined, in Watson v. Fort Worth Bank and Trust, 487 U.S. 977 (1988), where each side had four votes (because Justice Kennedy had not yet been seated). *Watson* held unanimously that subjective or discretionary employment practices are subject to attack under disparate impact analysis. Justice O'Connor's opinion in *Watson* said that an employer seeking to justify a selection method (even one that has a statistical impact on the race or gender distribution of those hired) need only show "a manifest relationship to the employment in question." She said that formal validation studies are not required.

**3.** If the *Wards Cove* burden of proof had been applied in *Griggs,* would the plaintiffs have prevailed?

**4.** According to Professor Cass Sunstein:

Although the issue is complex, one might start by observing that discriminatory purpose is exceptionally difficult to show even when it exists. A test that makes discriminatory effects probative of discriminatory purpose might invalidate some practices that should, given perfect implementing devices, be upheld. *Wards Cove,* however, will validate many practices that should, given such devices, be struck down. Moreover, discrimination exists when an employer has been nonneutral in the sense that it has adopted a practice having a discriminatory effect on blacks that it would not have adopted if the burden had been imposed on whites; *Wards Cove* will not reach this form of discrimination. For these reasons, *Wards Cove* will produce substantial underenforcement of the law. By contrast, systemic barriers to the implementation of antidiscrimination statutes make any concern about overenforcement highly speculative. No approach is perfect in this situation, but *Griggs* was probably a better method of implementing the statutory proscription.

Cass R. Sunstein, Interpreting Statutes in the Regulatory State, 103 Harv.L.Rev. 405, 485 (1989). Do you agree?

**5.** Is the result in *Wards Cove* consistent with *Price Waterhouse,* supra p. 248? There, Justice O'Connor cast the decisive vote for requiring employers to demonstrate in a mixed-motive case that the improper consideration did not influence the hiring result. In *Wards Cove,* she supported the majority result that the plaintiff must prove that alternatives are available to a selection process that results in a numerically unbalanced labor force. Is it easier for Supreme Court justices to identify with a worker denied a partnership at an accounting firm than with Asian cannery workers in Alaska?

Why not analyze *Wards Cove* (and perhaps all disparate impact cases) as mixed-motive cases, similar to *Price Waterhouse?* If *Wards Cove* is approached that way, who wins?

**6.** The two-tier structure at Wards Cove arguably represents job channeling at a fairly obvious level. If the difference in wages and benefits between the cannery and noncannery jobs (i.e., between white and nonwhite workers) is not sufficient to establish a prima facie case of disparate impact, what would be? What is the evidentiary significance of the racial stratification at Wards Cove?

**7.** In light of the majority opinion, what is the role of statistics in proving violations of Title VII? How has it changed? Would statistics other than internal work force statistics suffice to establish a prima facie case of discrimination? As a practical matter, where would one find "relevant labor market" statistics for the seasonal salmon industry in Alaska?

**8.** What does the majority mean when it states that "specific causation" must be established? One possible approach is illustrated in Holder v. Raleigh, 867 F.2d 823 (4th Cir.1989) (nepotism does not, per se, constitute discrimination). The Fourth Circuit held that nepotism could be relevant evidence of disparate treatment, but that the plaintiff, who was passed over for promotion in favor of the son of a white crew supervisor, had failed to show that the practice of nepotism had worked to the disadvantage of black applicants.

**9.** See Lynch v. Freeman, 817 F.2d 380 (6th Cir.1987) (holding that furnishing unsanitary toilets to both men and women is unlawful sex discrimination because biology makes clean toilets more important to women). See also EEOC v. Warshawsky & Co., 768 F.Supp. 647 (N.D.Ill.

1991) (concluding that it is differential impact discrimination against females to require employees to work at least one year before becoming eligible for sick leave because of the effect of the policy on pregnant women).

**10.**   Courts are split on the issue of whether supervisors should be individually liable for claims of discrimination in the workplace.  Some have held that no individual liability exists under Title VII.  See, e.g., Miller v. Maxwell's International, Inc., 991 F.2d 583 (9th Cir.1993), cert. denied, 510 U.S. 1109 (1994).  Others have held that supervisors, as agents of employers, are themselves "employers" for purposes of Title VII liability.  The Supreme Court has yet to resolve the debate.

**11.**   The Civil Rights Act of 1991 overturned *Wards Cove*'s formulation of the burden of proof and the types of proof necessary to show disparate impact discrimination.  Under the Act, an employee must still attempt to show which employment practice has caused the disparate impact.  If, however, the practices are impossible to disaggregate, courts must analyze the decisionmaking process as one practice.  In addition, Congress increased the burden on the employer in demonstrating that a challenged practice is job-related.  Now, the employer must show that "the challenged practice is job-related for the position in question and consistent with business necessity."  The burden of persuasion remains with the employer to prove business necessity.  See Kingsley R. Browne, The Civil Rights Act of 1991: A "Quota Bill," A Codification of *Griggs,* A Partial Return to *Wards Cove,* or All of the Above?, 43 Case W. Reserve L.Rev. 287 (1993).

### Note on the Civil Rights Act of 1991

The Civil Rights Act of 1991 was enacted in substantial part as a response to the Supreme Court's decision in *Wards Cove*.  The preamble states: "The purposes of this Act are . . . (2) to codify the concepts of 'business necessity' and 'job related' enunciated by the Supreme Court in Griggs v. Duke Power Co., and in the other Supreme Court decisions prior to Wards Cove Packing Co. v. Atonio;  (3) to confirm statutory authority and provide statutory guidelines for the adjudication of disparate impact suits under title VII . . .;  (4) to respond to recent decisions of the Supreme Court by expanding the scope of relevant civil rights statutes . . ."

The 1991 Act overturned *Wards Cove's* formulation of the burden of proof and the types of proof necessary to show disparate impact discrimination.  Under the Act, an employee must still attempt to show which employment practice has caused the disparate impact.  If, however, the practices are impossible to disaggregate, courts must analyze the decisionmaking process as one practice.  In addition, Congress increased the burden on the employer in demonstrating that a challenged practice is job-related.  Now, the employer must show that "the challenged practice is job-related for the position in question and consistent with business necessity."  The burden of persuasion remains with the employer to prove business necessity.  See Kinglsey R. Browne, The Civil Rights Act of 1991: A

"Quota Bill," A Codification of *Griggs,* A Partial Return to *Wards Cove,* or All of the Above?, 43 Case W.Reserve.L.Rev. 287 (1993).

In Landgraf v. USI Film Products, 507 U.S. 908 (1993), the Supreme Court held that the Civil Rights Act of 1991 did not apply to a Title VII case that was pending on appeal when the law was enacted.  In a companion case, Rivers v. Roadway Express, Inc., 508 U.S. 937 (1993), the Court held non-retroactive the provision of the 1991 Civil Rights Act permitting actions for damages under 42 U.S.C. § 1981 for a racially discriminatory dismissal.  The 1991 provision overturned Patterson v. McLean Credit Union, 491 U.S. 164 (1989), which had held § 1981 inapplicable to discriminatory conduct which occurred after the formation of an employment relationship.

In Bradley v. Pizzaco of Nebraska, Inc., 7 F.3d 795 (8th Cir.1993), the court struck down Domino's Pizza's no-beard policy because the policy had a differential impact on black males, half of whom suffer from the skin condition pseudofolliculitis barbae ("PFB").  The district court had found for defendant on the question of business justification under *Wards Cove.* It was reversed by the court of appeals which applied the 1991 Act rather than *Wards Cove* because the EEOC sought only prospective relief to enjoin Domino's no-beard policy.  The court rejected Domino's claim that it was "common sense" that "the better our people look, the better our sales will be," as speculative and conclusory.  The court also rejected the relevance of a consumer preference for smooth-shaven pizza delivery persons, even if such consumer preference could be shown.

## PROBLEM

The employer, a construction company, periodically needs bricklayers, but does not maintain a permanent force of bricklayers as its employees;  it hires them on an as-needed basis for specific projects.  It is important in its work to insure that only experienced and highly qualified individuals are hired.  The company delegates responsibility for hiring bricklayers to a supervisor;  his practice has been to hire only individuals with whom he has worked in the past or who have been recommended to him as experienced and competent.  He refuses to accept applications at the job site, an otherwise common practice in the construction industry.  On the company's most recent project, the supervisor initially hired 13 bricklayers, two of whom were black.  Two weeks later, he had hired another 24 bricklayers, two of whom were black.  A month later, he hired an additional six bricklayers, all of whom were black.  Ultimately, 13 percent of the total man-days worked on the job were worked by black bricklayers.  Two qualified black bricklayers applied at the job site for positions, but they were turned down.  Can they establish a prima facie case of discrimination?  Can the construction company successfully rebut any prima facie case?  How?  See Furnco Construction Corp. v. Waters, 438 U.S. 567 (1978) (employer's word of mouth hiring process not discriminatory because no adverse impact on blacks).

## 3.  THE BONA FIDE OCCUPATIONAL QUALIFICATION DEFENSE

Section 703(e) of Title VII provides that it is not unlawful for an employer to differentiate in hiring on the basis of religion, sex, or national origin "in those certain instances where religion, sex, or national origin is a bona fide occupational qualification reasonably necessary to the normal operation of that particular business or enterprise."

According to the EEOC's guidelines on sex as a BFOQ, 29 C.F.R. § 1604.2, the following situations do *not* warrant the application of the BFOQ exception: (1) refusal to hire a woman is based on the assumption of employment characteristics of women in general (e.g., turnover rate higher among women); (2) refusal to hire is based on sex stereotypes (e.g., women cannot be aggressive salespersons); (3) refusal to hire is based on the preferences of co-workers, clients, customers, or the employer; and (4) the fact that the employer may have to provide separate facilities.

State laws prohibiting women from working certain hours or lifting certain weights ("women's protective laws") are deemed to conflict with Title VII and, under the supremacy clause, have been struck down. See Rosenfeld v. Southern Pacific Co., 444 F.2d 1219 (9th Cir.1971).

The leading Supreme Court case is Dothard v. Rawlinson, 433 U.S. 321 (1977), in which plaintiff claimed that Alabama's height (5' 2") and weight (120 pounds) requirements for correctional officers and its rule forbidding women from "contact positions" in maximum security male penitentiaries were unlawful under Title VII. The Court held that Alabama's height and weight requirements discriminated impermissibly, but also held that the state could refuse to hire women for "contact positions" even though the rule excluded women from 75 percent of the correctional counselor jobs in the Alabama prison system.

It said "the bfoq exception was in fact meant to be an extremely narrow exception to the general prohibition of discrimination on the basis of sex," but that Alabama met that test because "a woman's relative ability to maintain order in a male, maximum-security, unclassified penitentiary of the type Alabama now runs could be directly reduced by her womanhood. There is a basis in fact for expecting that sex offenders who have criminally assaulted women in the past would be moved to do so again if access to women were established within the prison. There would also be a real risk that other inmates, deprived of a normal heterosexual environment, would assault women guards because they were women. In a prison system where violence is the order of the day, where inmate access to guards is facilitated by dormitory living arrangements, where every institution is understaffed, and where a substantial portion of the inmate population is composed of sex offenders mixed at random with other prisoners, there are a few visible deterrents to inmate assaults on women custodians."

\* \* \*

Justice Marshall, in a dissent shared by Justice Brennan, said that "what would otherwise be considered unlawful discrimination against women is justified by the Court, however, on the basis of the 'barbaric and inhumane' conditions in Alabama prisons, conditions so bad that state officials have conceded that they violate the Constitution. To me, this analysis sounds distressingly like saying two wrongs make a right. * * * The effect of the decision, made I am sure with the best of intentions, is to punish women because their very presence might provoke sexual assaults. It is women who are made to pay the price in lost job opportunities for the threat of depraved conduct by prison inmates. Once again, '[t]he pedestal upon which women have been placed has * * *, upon closer inspection, been revealed as a cage.' Sail'er Inn, Inc. v. Kirby, 5 Cal.3d 1, 20, 485 P.2d 529, 541 (1971). It is particularly ironic that the cage is erected here in response to feared misbehavior by imprisoned criminals."

# Wilson v. Southwest Airlines Co.

517 F.Supp. 292 (N.D.Tex.1981).

■ Patrick E. Higginbotham, District Judge.

This case presents the important question whether femininity, or more accurately female sex appeal, is a bona fide occupational qualification ("BFOQ") for the jobs of flight attendant and ticket agent with Southwest Airlines. Plaintiff Gregory Wilson and the class of over 100 male job applicants he represents have challenged Southwest's open refusal to hire males as a violation of Title VII of the Civil Rights Act of 1964. The class further alleges that Southwest's published height-weight requirement for flight attendants operates to exclude from eligibility a greater proportion of male than female applicants.

At the phase one trial on liability, Southwest conceded that its refusal to hire males was intentional. The airline also conceded that its height-weight restrictions would have an adverse impact upon male applicants, if actually applied. Southwest contends, however, that the BFOQ exception to Title VII's ban on sex discrimination justifies its hiring only females for the public contact positions of flight attendant and ticket agent. The BFOQ window through which Southwest attempts to fly permits sex discrimination in situations where the employer can prove that sex is a "bona fide occupational qualification reasonably necessary to the normal operation of that particular business or enterprise." Southwest reasons it may discriminate against males because its attractive female flight attendants and ticket agents personify the airline's sexy image and fulfill its public promise to take passengers skyward with "love." Defendant claims maintenance of its females-only hiring policy is crucial to the airline's continued financial success.

Since it has been admitted that Southwest discriminates on the basis of sex, the only issue to decide is whether Southwest has proved that being female is a BFOQ reasonably necessary to the normal operation of its particular business. * * *

Barely intact, Southwest, in early 1971, called upon a Dallas advertising agency, the Bloom Agency, to develop a winning marketing strategy. Planning to initiate service quickly, Southwest needed instant recognition and a "catchy" image to distinguish it from its competitors.

The Bloom Agency evaluated both the images of the incumbent competitor airlines as well as the characteristics of passengers to be served by a commuter airline. Bloom determined that the other carriers serving the Texas market tended to project an image of conservatism. The agency also determined that the relatively short haul commuter market which Southwest hoped to serve was comprised of predominantly male businessmen. Based on these factors, Bloom suggested that Southwest break away from the conservative image of other airlines and project to the traveling public an airline personification of feminine youth and vitality. A specific female personality description was recommended and adopted by Southwest for its corporate image:

> This lady is young and vital * * * she is charming and goes through life with great flair and exuberance * * * you notice first her exciting smile, friendly air, her wit * * * yet she is quite efficient and approaches all her tasks with care and attention. * * *

From the personality description suggested by The Bloom Agency, Southwest developed its now famous "Love" personality. Southwest projects an image of feminine spirit, fun and sex appeal. Its ads promise to provide "tender loving care" to its predominantly male, business passengers.[3] The first advertisements run by the airline featured the slogan, "AT LAST THERE IS SOMEBODY ELSE UP THERE WHO LOVES YOU." Variations on this theme have continued through newspaper, billboard, magazine and television advertisements during the past ten years.[4] Bloom's "Love" campaign was given a boost in 1974–1975 when the last of Southwest's competitors moved its operations to the new Dallas/Fort Worth Regional Airport, leaving Southwest as the only heavy carrier flying out of Dallas' convenient and fortuitously named, Love Field.

Over the years, Southwest gained national and international attention as the "love airline." Southwest Airlines' stock is traded on the New York Stock Exchange under the ticker symbol "LUV". During 1977 when Southwest opened five additional markets in Texas, the love theme was expanded to "WE'RE SPREADING LOVE ALL OVER TEXAS."

---

**3.** According to an October, 1979 onboard marketing survey commissioned before this lawsuit was filed, 69.01% of the respondents were male, while 58.41% of all respondents listed their occupation as either professional/technical, manager/administrator, or sales. Only 49.75% of the passengers surveyed, however, gave "business" as the reason for their trip.

**4.** Unabashed allusions to love and sex pervade all aspects of Southwest's public image. Its T.V. commercials feature attractive attendants in fitted outfits, catering to male passengers while an alluring feminine voice promises in-flight love. On board, attendants in hot-pants (skirts are now optional) serve "love bites" (toasted almonds) and "love potions" (cocktails). Even Southwest's ticketing system features a "quickie machine" to provide "instant gratification."

As an integral part of its youthful, feminine image, Southwest has employed only females in the high customer contact positions of ticket agent and flight attendant.  From the start, Southwest's attractive personnel, dressed in high boots and hot-pants, generated public interest and "free ink."  Their sex appeal has been used to attract male customers to the airline.  Southwest's flight attendants, and to a lesser degree its ticket agents, have been featured in newspaper, magazine, billboard and television advertisements during the past ten years.  Some attendants assist in promotional events for other businesses and civic organizations.  Southwest flight attendants and ticket agents are featured in the company's in-flight magazine and have received notice in numerous other national and international publications.  The airline also encourages its attendants to entertain the passengers and maintain an atmosphere of informality and "fun" during flights.  According to Southwest, its female flight attendants have come to "personify" Southwest's public image.

Southwest has enjoyed enormous success in recent years.  * * *

In evaluating Southwest's BFOQ defense, the Court proceeds on the basis that "love," while important, is not everything in the relationship between Defendant and its passengers.  Still, it is proper to infer from the airline's competitive successes that Southwest's overall "love image" has enhanced its ability to attract passengers.  To the extent the airline has successfully feminized its image and made attractive females an integral part of its public face, it also follows that femininity and sex appeal are qualities related to successful job performance by Southwest's flight attendants and ticket agents.  The strength of this relationship has not been proved.  It is with this factual orientation that the Court turns to examine Southwest's BFOQ defense.

* * *

To date, the [EEOC] has steadfastly adhered to its position that customer preference gives rise to a bona fide occupational qualification for sex in one instance only, "[w]here it is necessary for the purpose of authenticity or genuineness * * * e.g. an actor or actress."  This exception is analogous to the example of a BFOQ for a French Cook in a French restaurant suggested by the Senate Floor Managers in their Interpretative Memorandum.  * * *

Those courts which have analyzed Title VII's BFOQ exception, however, have broadened its sweep.  Consistent with the language of § 703(e), courts have held, or stated, that customer preference for one sex may be taken into account in those limited instances where satisfying customer preference is "reasonably necessary to the normal operation of the particular business or enterprise."

This Circuit's decisions in Weeks v. Southern Bell Tel. & Tel. Co., 408 F.2d 228 (5th Cir.1969) and Diaz v. Pan American World Airways, Inc., 442 F.2d 385 (5th Cir.) cert. denied 404 U.S. 950 (1971) have given rise to a two step BFOQ test:  (1) does the particular *job* under consideration require that the worker be of one sex only;  and if so, (2) is that requirement reasonably necessary to the "essence" of the employer's business. The first level of inquiry is designed to test whether sex is so essential to job performance that a member of the opposite sex simply could not do the same job. The second level is designed to assure that the qualification being scrutinized is one so important to the operation of the business that the business would be undermined if employees of the "wrong" sex were hired.

Southwest concedes with respect to the *Weeks* test that males are able to perform safely and efficiently all the basic, mechanical functions required of flight attendants and ticket agents.   * * *

Southwest's position, however, is that females are required to fulfill certain non-mechanical aspects of these jobs: to attract those male customers who prefer female attendants and ticket agents, and to preserve the authenticity and genuineness of Southwest's unique, female corporate personality.

A similar, though not identical, argument that females could better perform certain non-mechanical functions required of flight attendants was rejected in *Diaz*. There, the airline argued and the trial court found that being female was a BFOQ because women were superior in "providing reassurance to anxious passengers, giving courteous personalized service and, in general, making flights as pleasurable as possible within the limitations imposed by aircraft operations." Although it accepted the trial court findings, the Court of Appeals reversed, holding that femininity was not a BFOQ, because catering to passengers' psychological needs was only "tangential" to what was "reasonably *necessary* " for the business involved (original emphasis). Characterizing the "essence" or "primary function" of Pan American's business as the safe transportation of passengers from one point to another, the court explained:

> While a pleasant environment, enhanced by the obvious cosmetic effect that female stewardesses provide as well as, according to the findings of the trial court, their apparent ability to perform the non-mechanical functions of the job in a more effective manner than most men, may all be important, they are tangential to the essence of the business involved. No one has suggested that having male stewards will so seriously affect the operation of the airline as to jeopardize or even minimize its ability to provide safe transportation from one place to another.

Similar reasoning underlay the appellate court's rejection of Pan American's claim that its customers' preference for female attendants justified its refusal to hire males. Because the non-mechanical functions that passengers preferred females to perform were tangential to the airline's business, the court held, "the fact that customers prefer [females] cannot justify sex discrimination." The Fifth Circuit in *Diaz* did not hold that customer preference could never give rise to a sex BFOQ. Rather, consistent with the EEOC's exception for authenticity and genuineness, the Court allowed that customer preference could "be taken into account only when it is based on the company's inability to perform the primary function or service it offers," that is, where sex or sex appeal is itself the dominant service provided.

*Diaz* and its progeny establish that to recognize a BFOQ for jobs requiring multiple abilities, some sex-linked and some sex-neutral, the sex-linked aspects of the job must predominate. Only then will an employer have satisfied *Weeks'* requirement that sex be só essential to successful job performance that a member of the opposite sex could not perform the job. An illustration of such dominance in sex cases is the exception recognized by the EEOC for authenticity and genuineness. In the example given in § 1604.–2(a)(2), that of an actor or actress, the primary function of the position, its essence, is to fulfill the audience's expectation and desire for a particular role, characterized by particular physical or emotional traits. Generally, a male could not supply the authenticity required to perform a female role. Similarly, in jobs where sex or vicarious sexual recreation is the primary service provided, e.g. a social escort or topless dancer, the job automatically calls for one sex exclusively; the employee's sex and the service provided are inseparable. Thus, being female has been deemed a BFOQ for the position of a Playboy Bunny, female sexuality being reasonably necessary to perform the dominant purpose of the job which is forthrightly to titillate and entice male customers. One court has also suggested, without holding, that the authenticity exception would give rise to a BFOQ for Chinese nationality where necessary to maintain the authentic atmosphere of an ethnic Chinese restaurant. Consistent with the language of *Diaz,* customer preference for one sex only in such a case would logically be so strong that the employer's ability to perform the primary function or service offered would be undermined by not hiring members of the authentic sex or group exclusively.

The Court is aware of only one decision where sex was held to be a BFOQ for an occupation not providing primarily sex oriented services. In Fernandez v. Wynn Oil Co., 20 FEP Cases 1162 (C.D.Cal.1979), the court approved restricting to males the job of international marketing director for a company with extensive overseas operations. The position involved primarily attracting and transacting business with Latin American and Southeast Asian customers who would not feel comfortable doing business with a woman. The court found that the customers' attitudes, customs, and mores relating to the proper business roles of the sexes created formidable obstacles to successful job performance by a woman. South American distributors and customers, for example, would have been offended by a woman conducting business meetings in her hotel room. Applying the *Diaz* test, the court concluded that hiring a female as international marketing director "would have totally subverted any business [defendant] hoped to accomplish in those areas of the world." Because hiring a male was *necessary* to the Defendant's ability to continue its foreign operations, sex was deemed a BFOQ for the marketing position.

Applying the first level test for a BFOQ, with its legal gloss, to Southwest's particular operations results in the conclusion that being female is not a qualification required to perform successfully the jobs of flight attendant and ticket agent with Southwest. * * *

While possession of female allure and sex appeal have been made qualifications for Southwest's contact personnel by virtue of the "love" campaign, the functions served by employee sexuality in Southwest's operations are not dominant ones. * * * Accordingly, the ability of the airline to perform its primary business function, the transportation of passengers, would not be jeopardized by hiring males.

It is also relevant that Southwest's female image was adopted at its discretion, to promote a business unrelated to sex. Contrary to the unyielding South American preference for males encountered by the Defendant company in *Fernandez,* Southwest exploited, indeed nurtured, the very customer preference for females it now cites to justify discriminating against males. Moreover, the fact that a vibrant marketing campaign was necessary to distinguish Southwest in its early years does not lead to the conclusion that sex discrimination was then, or is now, a business *necessity.* Southwest's claim that its female image will be tarnished by hiring males is, in any case, speculative at best.

* * *

One final observation is called for. This case has serious underpinnings, but it also has disquieting strains. These strains, and they were only that, warn that in our quest for non-racist, non-sexist goals, the demand for equal rights can be pushed to silly extremes. The rule of law in this country is so firmly embedded in our ethical regimen that little can stand up to its force—except literalistic insistence upon one's rights. And such inability to absorb the minor indignities suffered daily by us all without running to court may stop it dead in its tracks. We do not have such a case here—only warning signs rumbling from the facts.

## NOTES AND QUESTIONS

**1.** Recently, Southwest Airlines published an advertisement capitalizing on the notoriety of its approach in the 1970s to flight attendant dress and behavior. The full page ad, which shows a kickline of comely flight attendants dressed in hot pants and knee-high boots, makes reference to the good old days of "luv bites" served by hiply clad stewardesses, who were likely to leap out of overhead compartments or wear bunny tails at Easter time. While the ad sheepishly admits "the hot pants had to go," the ad clearly intends to attract patrons to the sexy image of the airline.

**2.** One issue posed by the BFOQ defense is individualized determination. Consider the following situation: An employer has a job opening on its loading dock and the workers need to be able to lift and load 150 pound boxes. Could the employer interview only men for the job or would the employer be required to test each female applicant (as well as male) to see if she could lift the 150 pounds? Would there be any obligation to use 50 pound boxes so that more women could lift them? Suppose an employer has a 50 pound lifting requirement, which a woman applicant can meet.

She is then refused employment because the dock foreman says: "Big deal, she can lift one box. There's no way she can do it all day long." In a Title VII case, what result? Suppose that a woman of small stature applies for a job on the loading dock, attempts to lift a heavy box, and injures her back. Is the employer liable? See Legault v. aRusso, 842 F.Supp. 1479 (D.N.H. 1994) (granting preliminary injunction in favor of plaintiff because a fire department testing procedure which included a physical agility test that no woman applicant could pass was discriminatory).

**3.** The second issue raised by BFOQ cases is "essence of the job." Are you persuaded by the court's conclusion that attracting airline passengers with sex-linked ads is not the essence of the job Southwest Airlines is filling? Is the court invalidating use of sex (and appearance) in hiring models, cocktail waitresses, and Las Vegas hostesses? If not, is the court second-guessing the airline's judgment about how to survive in its competitive market?

**4.** Jean Rae Sutton, a woman, worked as a security guard at a distillery in Cincinnati, Ohio. To prevent the theft of tools and small bottles of liquor ("miniatures") the company began having the security guards conduct pat-down searches of employees as they left the distillery. Some of the 500 male workers and their wives objected to the searches by a woman guard and she was transferred. Has the employer violated Title VII? See Sutton v. National Distillers Products Co., 445 F.Supp. 1319 (S.D.Ohio 1978), affirmed, 628 F.2d 936 (6th Cir.1980) (held: no violation).

**5.** In Healey v. Southwood Psychiatric Hospital, 78 F.3d 128 (3d Cir. 1996), the Third Circuit found that a psychiatric hospital treating emotionally disturbed and sexually abused children had established that gender is a bona fide occupational qualification necessary for normal business operation. If members of both sexes were not present on a shift, the court found, Southwood's ability to provide therapeutic care to sexually abused patients who feel comfortable talking only to a staff member of the same sex would be hindered, disrupting the normal operation of its particular business. Thus, although the night shift was a less desirable shift because of added housekeeping duties and less patient contact, the court held that the hospital did not discriminate unlawfully against a female employee by assigning her to that shift. The Third Circuit has not yet decided whether concern for the privacy needs of the patients justifies the use of sex as a BFOQ.

The job of "counselor" at a chain of weight loss centers includes taking tape measurements of customers every two weeks and taking body-fat measurements with calipers every six. Can the employer refuse to hire males for the position because its mostly female clientele has, in the past, refused to accept counseling services from males? See EEOC v. Hi 40 Corp., 953 F.Supp. 301 (W.D.Mo.1996) (held: no).

Cf. Hernandez v. University of St. Thomas, 793 F.Supp. 214 (D.Minn. 1992) (court finds fact question as to whether sex is a BFOQ for custodial work in women's dorm precludes summary judgment).

**6.**  The court distinguishes Fernandez v. Wynn Oil Co., allowing selection of a male to work with Latin American and Asian customers.  The *Fernandez* decision was reversed, 653 F.2d 1273 (9th Cir.1981).  Could we have a rule that the discriminatory preferences of foreigners are more worthy of legal respect than the preferences of American customers?  Would this mean that an overseas airline could hire only female cabin attendants?  What about refusing to assign a Jewish anesthesiologist to work at a hospital in Saudi Arabia?  See Abrams v. Baylor College of Medicine, 805 F.2d 528 (5th Cir.1986) (held: illegal discrimination on the basis of religion).  See also Kern v. Dynalectron Corp., 577 F.Supp. 1196 (N.D.Tex.1983), affirmed, 746 F.2d 810 (5th Cir.1984), which upheld a BFOQ defense for an employer's requirement that helicopter pilots hired to fly into Mecca be Moslem.  The court wrote: "Dynalectron has proven a factual basis for believing that *all* non-Moslems would be unable to perform this job safely.  Specifically, non-Moslems flying into Mecca are, if caught, beheaded.  * * * Thus, the essence of Dynalectron's business would be undermined by the beheading of all the non-Moslem pilots based in Jeddah."

**7.**  In *Dothard* the Court struck down the use of height and weight requirements because of the disparate impact on women.  Roadway Express would not hire anyone taller than 6′4″ as a truckdriver.  Plaintiff, a 6′7″ male, sued, saying that .9% of adult men are taller than 6′4″ and only .3% of adult women are 6′ or taller.  The court decided for the employer, saying height rules should be scrutinized carefully on behalf of historically disfavored groups but not on behalf of a formerly preferred group.  The court noted that under the allegedly anti-male system Roadway had hired 189 male drivers and 2 females.  Livingston v. Roadway Express, Inc., 802 F.2d 1250 (10th Cir.1986).

**8.**  What about cultural differences between men and women?

A) American Airlines required cabin attendants who became mothers to switch to ground duty positions but imposed no such rule on fathers.  This was held to violate Title VII, In re Consolidated Pretrial Proceedings, 582 F.2d 1142 (7th Cir.1978).  The court said, "[A]ttributes that are culturally more common to one sex than the other are an insufficient basis for a BFOQ.  Cultural stereotypes should not be employed to justify sex discrimination * * * To accept [the view that a mother would be preoccupied with her parental duties and so be deficient in assisting safe transport] requires acquiescence in assumptions steeped in cultural stereotypes, such as that female parents have a more intense concern for their children than male parents, assumptions that are inconsistent with the purposes of the Act."  Did the Supreme Court disagree when it upheld special treatment for pregnancy in California Federal Savings & Loan v. Guerra, infra p. 515.

B) Defendant company violates Title VII by requiring male employees but not female employees to keep their hair a certain length, "since this disparate treatment is based on the sex stereotype that men should have short hair."  Longo v. Carlisle DeCoppett & Co., 403 F.Supp. 692 (S.D.N.Y. 1975), reversed, 537 F.2d 685 (2d Cir. 1976).  But see Willingham v. Macon

Telegraph Pub. Co., 507 F.2d 1084 (5th Cir.1975), holding that Title VII does not bar different hair lengths for males and females because such a rule is discrimination "based not upon sex, but rather upon grooming standards," and because Title VII does not bar distinctions between men and women "on the basis of something other than immutable or protected characteristics." (Macon community disapproval of long-haired males had recently been exacerbated by an "International Pop Festival" at Byron, Georgia.)

C) Devine v. Lonschein, 621 F.Supp. 894 (S.D.N.Y.1985), affirmed without opinion, 800 F.2d 1127 (2d Cir.1986), upheld a rule requiring male attorneys before a court (and not female attorneys) to wear neckties. Concerning uniforms and other sex-differentiated dress requirements see infra pages 563–570.

**9.** A major test of the intersection between culture and anti-discrimination law arose when the Equal Employment Opportunity Commission sued Sears, Roebuck, asserting that women did not hold their share of better paid commission sales positions. The litigation took many procedural turns, but in the end a court of appeals accepted, as a legally sufficient explanation for statistical disparity between men and women, Sears' argument that "women were not as interested in commission sales positions as were men. * * * [W]omen were generally more interested in product lines like clothing, jewelry, and cosmetics that were usually sold on a noncommission basis, than they were in product lines involving commission selling like automobiles, roofing, and furnaces." Judge Cudahy, dissenting in part, said that "the stereotype of women as less greedy and daring than men is one that the sex discrimination laws were intended to address. * * * There are abundant indications that women lack neither the desire to compete strenuously for financial gain nor the capacity to take risks." EEOC v. Sears, Roebuck & Co., 839 F.2d 302 (7th Cir.1988).

For insightful discussion of the *Sears* litigation, see Lucinda Finley, Choice and Freedom: Elusive Issues in the Search for Gender Justice, 96 Yale L.J. 914, 937–40 (1987):

> The statement of qualifications for [the higher paid positions at Sears] reads like a description of the stereotypical male: someone who is aggressive, competitive, has lots of drive, physical vigor, and social dominance, someone with technical knowledge and fluency, someone who could frequently work odd evening or weekend hours. People with prior experience selling technical product lines were preferred, and personnel interviewers often evaluated candidates according to how closely they matched those already doing the job, a comparison group that was almost totally male. Perhaps recognizing how unlike their conceptions of themselves these very male job descriptions were, most women who did apply to be sellers for Sears stated a preference for selling noncommissioned and very female products—jewelry, lingerie, cosmetics, and women's apparel. * * *

The court finds that women also do not like to accept financial risk as much as men; this is perhaps because their economic dependence and their principal responsibility for children can make monetary risk a suicidal course. Women's education makes it less likely that they will have the requisite technical background, comfort, or confidence in their ability to master technical information. For all these reasons, it was not surprising that Sears encountered difficulties in attempting to convince women to apply for positions selling machinery, home improvement devices, and automotive products.

[According to some commentators,] the argument based on women's nature ends the inquiry. Men and women simply are different, and that means they have different interests. Government should do nothing to disturb these natural preferences. But instead of satisfying these choice advocates, these supposedly preference-based disparities between men and women could lead to profoundly important inquiries about liberty. These inquiries would suggest how men and women could be liberated from the powerful constraints set by the social construction of gender roles. First, rather than blaming women and their nature for their underrepresentation in the high paying jobs, why not reexamine the jobs and their values? It may not be necessary for a salesperson to be an aggressive hustler willing to pester the customer to sell the commissioned items successfully. * * * Second, is the qualifications personality profile really geared to the needs of the job, or does it merely describe those who have been doing the job and the way they have been doing it? * * * Finally, should it be of any concern to an equal liberty advocate that when a woman sees the male bias in the job itself, she may sense that she is not wanted or would suffer isolation and hazing on the job, and instead may cope with the odds against her by convincing herself that she really does not want what she probably would not get? A woman's "choice" to accept a traditionally female sales position may not be such a free one, after all. * * *

On the assumption that people exposed to new possibilities begin to change their attitudes, government might require employers to grant parenting leave and create incentives for men to take it. Employers might need to restructure their advancement tracks, so that those of either sex who assume parenting obligations need not sacrifice their careers. Employers might need to reevaluate the skills or traits currently considered desirable for certain jobs. Government could provide incentives to try things in new ways. It might even inaugurate affirmative action for men in traditionally female jobs, as well as for women in traditionally male jobs. Such significant departures from existing practices would be much more likely to result in * * * a world in which men and women can exercise the full range of options previously available primarily to the other sex, without risking undue economic loss or social disapprobation for nontraditional choices, and a world in which one's gender is not as determinative as it is now of what one can do or wants to do.

In *Sears,* the defendant prevailed by arguing that women lack interest in "male" jobs. Gender plaintiffs have been less likely to prevail against the lack of interest defense than race plaintiffs. A comparison of the content and strength of race and sex discrimination cases concluded that sex discrimination cases are not weaker than race cases to a degree sufficient to explain the disparity in success rates of plaintiffs. Vicki Schultz, Race, Gender, Work, and Choice: An Empirical Study of the Lack of Defense in Title VII Cases Challenging Job Segregation, 59 U.Chi.L.Rev. 1073 (1992). Professor Schultz found that judges regularly accepted the premise that a woman's work aspirations have been shaped through socialization or innate predisposition and not artificially limited because of a discriminatory market.

But cultural stereotypes of women are not always detrimental to plaintiffs in gender discrimination cases. In fact, some courts have recently accepted expert testimony on sexual stereotyping that provides a credible theoretical framework to support claims of gender discrimination and sexual harassment. In Robinson v. Jacksonville Shipyards, 760 F.Supp. 1486 (M.D.Fla.1991), a female welder sued her employer for relief against a hostile work environment. Pictures of nude and partially nude women from magazines and on plaques and calendars were displayed throughout the workplace. The plaintiff also testified to lewd comments and ridicule in front of co-workers. The court concluded that the incidents were so prevalent that the employer had violated Title VII. The employer had a rule against posting unauthorized material, but did not enforce it.

The plaintiff in *Robinson* introduced testimony from a sociologist who described "sex role spill over," the tendency to regard women in terms of their sexuality and their worth as sex objects rather than their worth as co-workers.

> The sexualization of the workplace imposes burdens on women that are not borne by men. Women must constantly monitor their behavior to determine whether they are eliciting sexual attention. They must conform their behavior to the existence of the sexual stereotyping either by becoming sexy and responsive to the men who flirt with them or by becoming rigid, standoffish, and distant so as to make it clear that they are not interested in the status of sex object.

For a further discussion of sexual harassment, see Chapter 7 infra.

In Stender v. Lucky Stores, Inc., 803 F.Supp. 259 (N.D.Cal.1992), plaintiffs introduced statistical evidence to show a significant disparity in job distribution and job promotion between male and female employees. Expert testimony showed that ambiguous job qualifications coupled with the secrecy of the decision-making process led test subjects to recommend candidates of their own sex. When evaluative criteria were clear and the decision-making process public, sex was less likely to be a factor in selection.   Defendants used the lack of interest defense to explain the statistical disparity.   This argument was rejected by the court:

> Even in a situation where gender stereotypes about work interest patterns reflect reality, it is unlawful for an employer to discriminate against those whose work interests deviate from the stereotype. Therefore, the court holds that job interest surveys cannot be used as a defense in disparate treatment cases.   Defendant's survey only has evidentiary weight as a rebuttal to plaintiff's statistical argument in its disparate impact claim.   In rebuttal, interest surveys may be used to explain the statistical disparities between men and women which plaintiff alleges.   However, anecdotal evidence of disparate treatment or of disparate impact cannot be rebutted by job interest surveys. Generalizations about women's job interests cannot be used to trump the testimony of individual women about their job interests.

**10.**   Section 703(e) of Title VII does *not* include race among those classifications for which a BFOQ defense may be raised.   Can race ever be a BFOQ?   Consider the following case:   A county's civil service commission assigned a black personnel specialist to minority recruitment against his wishes.   The commission argued that it was trying to attract more minority applicants to the civil service and it believed that a black personnel specialist would be better able to develop a rapport with potential black applicants.   Is the county's rationale a valid defense to a charge of race discrimination?   See Knight v. Nassau County Civil Service Commission, 649 F.2d 157 (2d Cir. 1981), cert. denied, 454 U.S. 818 (1981) (held:  no). Does this mean that a police department in assigning officers partners and "beats" could not consider the race of the officers?   Are there valid interests served by assuring that at least some minority officers are assigned to patrol in minority neighborhoods?

**11.**   Illinois opened a "boot camp" for young criminals.   Although 68 percent of the inmates were black, the correctional officers, lieutenants, and captains were overwhelmingly white.   Is it permissible for the state to use race as a factor in the promotion of correctional officers on the belief that they will be more effective?   See Wittmer v. Peters, 87 F.3d 916 (7th Cir.1996), cert. denied, 117 S.Ct. 949 (1997) (held:  promotion of black officer over higher ranked white officers was unconstitutional).

**12.**   On February 27, 1997, the Vienna Philharmonic Orchestra ended its men-only policy and voted to accept women as members.   The first woman to be admitted was a female harpist who had played for the Vienna Philharmonic for 26 years.

Just one week prior to the announcement, the orchestra director argued that an orchestra containing women would be paralyzed by mass pregnancy and long maternity leaves.   According to the new rules, any player absent more than 24 months will have to audition for his or her place again.

Some of the musicians have complained that admitting women will change the dynamic of the orchestra, which is its traditional deep strings.

Perhaps they should consider blind auditions, a technique that has become popular with United States orchestras.

Economists Claudia Goldin of Harvard and Cecelia Rouse of Princeton conducted a study of auditions for American orchestras.   They found that when judges could not see auditioners, and musicians auditioned behind a heavy cloth suspended from the ceiling, the odds of a woman getting the job were boosted by 50 percent.

With the switch to blind auditions, the percentage of female musicians in the top five orchestras in the United States increased from five percent in 1970 to 25 percent in 1996.   Thirty-five percent of the new hires for the Boston and Chicago symphonies were women, while less than 10 percent of the new hires in years prior to the use of blind auditions were women. Wall Street Journal, March 7, 1997, B6B.

**13.**   Issues of fetal vulnerability (employer arguments that women of child-bearing age must be excluded from certain jobs because of health risks to unborn or unconceived children) are considered in Chapter 8.

————

The employer's selection process usually is not based on the results of a single test or other measure of an applicant's ability or suitability for a job.   Instead, the employer will use several factors in combination to decide who to hire or promote.   What happens when one of those factors has an adverse impact, but the employer's selection decisions reveal no adverse impact on a protected group?   Connecticut v. Teal, 457 U.S. 440 (1982) (5–4), held that an employer cannot use a "bottom-line" defense (at the end of the process an appropriate number of blacks or females has been hired) to save the use of one criterion (in *Teal* a written test) that has an adverse impact and is not shown to be job-related.

PROBLEM FOR DISCUSSION:  EVALUATING BIASED SELECTION CRITERIA

A department store has ten sales clerk openings at its store located in a suburban mall.   Ten whites and ten blacks apply.   Their experience and other qualifications are virtually identical.   Because of the mall location, the personnel manager (an afficionado of trivia games) decides to ask all of the applicants 100 questions from his favorite game: Trivial Pursuit—The All Preppy Edition.   The questions all ask about non-job-related middle and upper class white culture.   The white applicants get scores ranging between 57 and 82.   The black applicants get scores ranging between 15 and 33.   The personnel manager then selects the top five whites and the top five blacks.   Is this discriminatory?   Suppose it is an urban department store and the applicants are asked 100 questions from Trivial Pursuit—The Inner City Edition?   Suppose all 20 applicants at the mall location were white and all 20 applicants at the urban location were black?

## 4.   Affirmative Action

In addition to the legal standards which employers are required to meet in hiring employees and the obligations which may be imposed on employers who violate those standards, there are numerous instances where an employer undertakes voluntarily to alter the mix of employees which its applicant pool and existing selection methods would otherwise produce.   Usually such a change takes the form of an affirmative action program under which the employer seeks to recruit minorities or sets aside a specific number or percentage of job vacancies for blacks, women or some other group.   Such plans have been challenged by individuals (usually white males) who claim that the program shuts them out of employment opportunities as a result of their race or sex, and that they are the victims of reverse discrimination under § 703(j) of Title VII, which states:

> Nothing contained in this title shall be interpreted to require any employer, employment agency, labor organization, or joint labor-management committee subject to this title to grant preferential treatment to any individual or to any group because of the race, color, religion, sex, or national origin of such individual or group.
> * * *

## Taxman v. Board of Education

91 F.3d 1547 (3d Cir.1996) (en banc), cert. dismissed, 118 S.Ct. 595 (1997)

■ Mansmann, Circuit Judge.

In this Title VII matter, we must determine whether the Board of Education of the Township of Piscataway violated that statute when it made race a factor in selecting which of two equally qualified employees to lay off.   Specifically, we must decide whether Title VII permits an employer with a racially balanced work force to grant a non-remedial racial preference in order to promote "racial diversity".

It is clear that the language of Title VII is violated when an employer makes an employment decision based upon an employee's race.   The Supreme Court determined in United Steelworkers v. Weber, 443 U.S. 193 (1979), however, that Title VII's prohibition against racial discrimination is not violated by affirmative action plans which first, "have purposes that mirror those of the statute" and second, do not "unnecessarily trammel the interests of the [non-minority] employees."

We hold that Piscataway's affirmative action policy is unlawful because it fails to satisfy either prong of *Weber*.   Given the clear antidiscrimination mandate of Title VII, a non-remedial affirmative action plan, even one with a laudable purpose, cannot pass muster.   We will affirm the district court's grant of summary judgment to Sharon Taxman.

Sharon Taxman.  Photo by New Jersey Law Journal.

In 1975, the Board of Education of the Township of Piscataway, New Jersey, developed an affirmative action policy applicable to employment decisions.  The Board's Affirmative Action Program, a 52–page document, was originally adopted in response to a regulation promulgated by the New Jersey State Board of Education.  That regulation directed local school boards to adopt "affirmative action programs," to address employment as well as school and classroom practices and to ensure equal opportunity to all persons regardless of race, color, creed, religion, sex or national origin. In 1983 the Board also adopted a one page "Policy", entitled "Affirmative Action—Employment Practices."  It is not clear from the record whether the "Policy" superseded or simply added to the "Program," nor does it matter for purposes of this appeal.

**Debra Williams**. (AP Photo/Daniel Hulshizer, File)

The 1975 document states that the purpose of the Program is "to provide equal educational opportunity for students and equal employment opportunity for employees and prospective employees," and "to make a concentrated effort to attract ... minority personnel for all positions so that their qualifications can be evaluated along with other candidates." The 1983 document states that its purpose is to "ensure[ ] equal employment opportunity ... and prohibit [ ] discrimination in employment because of[, inter alia,] race...."

The operative language regarding the means by which affirmative-action goals are to be furthered is identical in the two documents. "In all cases, the most qualified candidate will be recommended for appointment. However, when candidates appear to be of equal qualification, candidates meeting the criteria of the affirmative action program will be recommended." The phrase "candidates meeting the criteria of the affirmative action program" refers to members of racial, national origin or gender groups identified as minorities for statistical reporting purposes by the New Jersey State Department of Education, including Blacks. The 1983 document also clarifies that the affirmative action program applies to "every aspect of employment including ... layoffs...."

The Board's affirmative action policy did not have "any remedial purpose"; it was not adopted "with the intention of remedying the results of any prior discrimination or identified underrepresentation of minorities within the Piscataway Public School System." At all relevant times, Black teachers were neither "underrepresented" nor "underutilized" in the Piscataway School District work force. Indeed, statistics in 1976 and 1985 showed that the percentage of Black employees in the job category which included teachers exceeded the percentage of Blacks in the available work force.

### A.

In May, 1989, the Board accepted a recommendation from the Superintendent of Schools to reduce the teaching staff in the Business Department at Piscataway High School by one. At that time, two of the teachers in the department were of equal seniority, both having begun their employment with the Board on the same day nine years earlier. One of those teachers was intervenor plaintiff Sharon Taxman, who is White, and the other was Debra Williams, who is Black. Williams was the only minority teacher among the faculty of the Business Department.

Decisions regarding layoffs by New Jersey school boards are highly circumscribed by state law; nontenured faculty must be laid off first, and layoffs among tenured teachers in the affected subject area or grade level must proceed in reverse order of seniority. Seniority for this purpose is calculated according to specific guidelines set by state law. Thus, local boards lack discretion to choose between employees for layoff, except in the rare instance of a tie in seniority between the two or more employees eligible to fill the last remaining position.

The Board determined that it was facing just such a rare circumstance in deciding between Taxman and Williams. In prior decisions involving the layoff of employees with equal seniority, the Board had broken the tie through "a random process which included drawing numbers out of a container, drawing lots or having a lottery." In none of those instances, however, had the employees involved been of different races.

In light of the unique posture of the layoff decision, Superintendent of Schools Burton Edelchick recommended to the Board that the affirmative action plan be invoked in order to determine which teacher to retain.

Superintendent Edelchick made this recommendation "because he believed Ms. Williams and Ms. Taxman were tied in seniority, were equally qualified, and because Ms. Williams was the only Black teacher in the Business Education Department."

While the Board recognized that it was not bound to apply the affirmative action policy, it made a discretionary decision to invoke the policy to break the tie between Williams and Taxman. As a result, the Board "voted to terminate the employment of Sharon Taxman, effective June 30, 1988 . . . ."

At her deposition, Paula Van Riper, the Board's Vice President at the time of the layoff, described the Board's decision-making process. According to Van Riper, after the Board recognized that Taxman and Williams were of equal seniority, it assessed their classroom performance, evaluations, volunteerism and certifications and determined that they were "two teachers of equal ability" and "equal qualifications."

At his deposition Theodore H. Kruse, the Board's President, explained his vote to apply the affirmative action policy as follows:

A.   Basically I think because I had been aware that the student body and the community which is our responsibility, the schools of the community, is really quite diverse and there—I have a general feeling during my tenure on the board that it was valuable for the students to see in the various employment roles a wide range of background, and that it was also valuable to the work force and in particular to the teaching staff that they have—they see that in each other.

Asked to articulate the "educational objective" served by retaining Williams rather than Taxman, Kruse stated:

A.   In my own personal perspective I believe by retaining Mrs. Williams it was sending a very clear message that we feel that our staff should be culturally diverse, our student population is culturally diverse and there is a distinct advantage to students, to all students, to be made—come into contact with people of different cultures, different background, so that they are more aware, more tolerant, more accepting, more understanding of people of all background.

Q.   What do you mean by the phrase you used, culturally diverse?

A.   Someone other than—different than yourself. And we have, our student population and our community has people of all different background, ethnic background, religious background, cultural background, and it's important that our school district encourage awareness and acceptance and tolerance and, therefore, I personally think it's important that our staff reflect that too.

### B.

Following the Board's decision, Taxman filed a charge of employment discrimination with the Equal Employment Opportunity Commission. Attempts at conciliation were unsuccessful, and the United States filed suit under Title VII against the Board in the United States District Court for the District of New Jersey.[5]  Taxman intervened, asserting claims under both Title VII and the New Jersey Law Against Discrimination (NJLAD).

Following discovery, the Board moved for summary judgment and the United States and Taxman cross-moved for partial summary judgment only as to liability.  The district court denied the Board's motion and granted partial summary judgment to the United States and Taxman, holding the Board liable under both statutes for discrimination on the basis of race.

A trial proceeded on the issue of damages.  By this time, Taxman had been rehired by the Board and thus her reinstatement was not an issue. The court awarded Taxman damages in the amount of $134,014.62 for backpay, fringe benefits and prejudgment interest under Title VII.  A jury awarded an additional $10,000 for emotional suffering under the NJLAD. The district court denied the United States' request for a broadly worded injunction against future discrimination, finding that there was no likelihood that the conduct at issue would recur, but it did order the Board to give Taxman full seniority reflecting continuous employment from 1980. Additionally, the court dismissed Taxman's claim for punitive damages under the NJLAD.

\* \* \*

## II.

In relevant part, Title VII makes it unlawful for an employer "to discriminate against any individual with respect to his compensation, terms, conditions, or privileges of employment" or "to limit, segregate, or classify his employees ... in any way which would deprive or tend to deprive any individual of employment opportunities or otherwise affect his status as an employee" on the basis of "race, color, religion, sex, or national origin."

\* \* \*

In 1979, [the Supreme Court held] in the seminal case of United Steelworkers v. Weber, 443 U.S. 193 (1979), that Title VII's prohibition against racial discrimination does not condemn all voluntary race-conscious affirmative action plans.  In *Weber,* the Court considered a plan implemented by Kaiser Aluminum & Chemical Corporation.  Prior to 1974, Kaiser hired as craftworkers only those with prior craft experience.  Because they had long been excluded from craft unions, Blacks were unable to present the credentials required for craft positions.  Moreover, Kaiser's hiring practices, although not admittedly discriminatory with regard to minorities, were questionable.  As a consequence, while the local labor force was about 39% Black, Kaiser's labor force was less than 15% Black and its crafts-work force was less than 2% Black.  In 1974, Kaiser entered into a collective

---

**5.** The suit did not assert a Fourteenth Amendment Equal Protection claim.  By the time suit was filed, the statute of limitations had run for claims based on 42 U.S.C. § 1983.

bargaining agreement which contained an affirmative action plan. The plan reserved 50% of the openings in an in-plant craft-training program for Black employees until the percentage of Black craft-workers in the plant reached a level commensurate with the percentage of Blacks in the local labor force. During the first year of the plan's operation, 13 craft-trainees were selected, seven of whom were Black and six of whom were White.

Thereafter, Brian Weber, a White production worker, filed a class action suit, alleging that the plan unlawfully discriminated against White employees under Title VII.

\* \* \*

The Supreme Court [held] that although the plaintiffs' argument was not "without force", it disregarded "the significance of the fact that the Kaiser–USWA plan was an affirmative action plan voluntarily adopted by private parties to eliminate traditional patterns of racial segregation." The Court then embarked upon an exhaustive review of Title VII's legislative history and identified Congress' concerns in enacting Title VII's prohibition against discrimination—the deplorable status of Blacks in the nation's economy, racial injustice, and the need to open employment opportunities for Blacks in traditionally closed occupations. Against this background, the Court concluded that Congress could not have intended to prohibit private employers from implementing programs directed toward the very goal of Title VII—the eradication of discrimination and its effects from the workplace.

\* \* \*

In 1987, the Supreme Court decided a second Title VII affirmative action case, Johnson v. Transportation Agency, 480 U.S. 616 (1987). There, the Santa Clara County Transit District Board of Supervisors implemented an affirmative action plan stating that " 'mere prohibition of discriminatory practices [was] not enough to remedy the effects of past discriminatory practices and to permit attainment of an equitable representation of minorities, women and handicapped persons.' " The plan noted that women were represented in numbers far less than their proportion of the available work force in the Agency as a whole and in the skilled craft worker job category relevant to the case, and observed that a lack of motivation in women to seek training or employment where opportunities were limited partially explained the underrepresentation. The plan authorized the Agency to consider as one factor the gender of a qualified candidate in making promotions to positions with a traditionally segregated job classification in which women were significantly underrepresented. The plan did not set quotas, but had as its long-term goal the attainment of a work force whose composition reflected the proportion of women in the area labor force. Acknowledging the practical difficulties in attaining the long-term goal, including the limited number of qualified women, the plan counseled that short range goals be established and annually adjusted to serve as realistic guides for actual employment decisions.

On December 12, 1979, the Agency announced a vacancy for the promotional position of road dispatcher. At the time, none of the 238 positions in the applicable job category was occupied by a woman. The Agency Director, authorized to choose any of seven applicants who had been deemed eligible, promoted Diane Joyce, a qualified woman, over Paul Johnson, a qualified man. As the Agency Director testified: " 'I tried to look at the whole picture, the combination of her qualifications and Mr. Johnson's qualifications, their test scores, their expertise, their background, affirmative action matters, things like that ... I believe it was a combination of all those.' "

\* \* \*

Declaring its prior analysis in *Weber* controlling, the [Supreme] Court examined whether the employment decision at issue "was made pursuant to a plan prompted by concerns similar to those of the employer in *Weber*" and whether "the effect of the [p]lan on males and nonminorities [was] comparable to the effects of the plan in that case." The first issue the Court addressed, therefore, was whether "consideration of the sex of applicants for Skilled Craft jobs was justified by the existence of a 'manifest imbalance' that reflected underrepresentation of women in 'traditionally segregated job categories.' " Although the Court did not set forth a quantitative measure for determining what degree of disproportionate representation in an employer's work force would be sufficient to justify affirmative action, it made clear that the terms "manifest imbalance" and "traditionally segregated job category" were not tantamount to a prima facie case of discrimination against an employer since the constraints of Title VII and the Federal Constitution on voluntarily adopted affirmative action plans are not identical. *Johnson.* In this regard, the Court further reasoned that requiring an employer in a Title VII affirmative action case to show that it had discriminated in the past "would be inconsistent with *Weber's* focus on statistical imbalance, and could inappropriately create a significant disincentive for employers to adopt an affirmative action plan".

\* \* \*

## IV.

### A.

Title VII was enacted to further two primary goals: to end discrimination on the basis of race, color, religion, sex or national origin, thereby guaranteeing equal opportunity in the workplace, and to remedy the segregation and underrepresentation of minorities that discrimination has caused in our Nation's work force.

\* \* \*

Title VII's first purpose is set forth in section 2000e–2's several prohibitions, which expressly denounce the discrimination which Congress sought to end. 42 U.S.C. § 2000e–2(a)–(d), (1); *McDonnell Douglas,* 411 U.S. at 800 ("The language of Title VII makes plain the purpose of

Congress to assure equality of employment opportunities and to eliminate those discriminatory practices and devices which have fostered racially stratified job environments to the disadvantage of minority citizens.'').

\* \* \*

Title VII's second purpose, ending the segregative effects of discrimination, is revealed in the congressional debate surrounding the statute's enactment.

The significance of this second corrective purpose cannot be overstated. It is only because Title VII was written to eradicate not only discrimination per se but the consequences of prior discrimination as well, that racial preferences in the form of affirmative action can co-exist with the Act's antidiscrimination mandate.

Thus, based on our analysis of Title VII's two goals, we are convinced that unless an affirmative action plan has a remedial purpose, it cannot be said to mirror the purposes of the statute, and, therefore, cannot satisfy the first prong of the *Weber* test.

\* \* \*

Accordingly, it is beyond cavil that the Board, by invoking its affirmative action policy to lay off Sharon Taxman, violated the terms of Title VII. While the Court in *Weber* and *Johnson* permitted some deviation from the antidiscrimination mandate of the statute in order to erase the effects of past discrimination, these rulings do not open the door to additional non-remedial deviations.  Here, as in *Weber* and *Johnson,* the Board must justify its deviation from the statutory mandate based on positive legislative history, not on its idea of what is appropriate.

\* \* \*

## B.

In *Johnson,* the Court held that the legality of the Santa Clara County Transportation Agency's plan under Title VII must be guided by the Court's determination in *Weber* that affirmative action is lawful if an employer can point to a " 'manifest imbalance . . . in traditionally segregated job categories.' "  In Wygant v. Jackson Board of Education, 476 U.S. 267 (1986), by contrast, the Court determined that under the Constitution a public employer's remedial affirmative action initiatives are valid only if crafted to remedy its own past or present discrimination;  that is, societal discrimination is an insufficient basis for "imposing discretionary legal remedies against innocent people."  In the plurality's words, affirmative action must be supported by "a factual determination that the employer had a strong basis in evidence for its conclusion that remedial action was necessary."

\* \* \*

## V.

Since we have not found anything in the Board's arguments to convince us that this case requires examination beyond statutory interpretation, we return to the point at which we started: the language of Title VII itself and the two cases reviewing affirmative action plans in light of that statute. Our analysis of the statute and the caselaw convinces us that a non-remedial affirmative action plan cannot form the basis for deviating from the antidiscrimination mandate of Title VII.

\* \* \*

Finally, we are convinced that the harm imposed upon a nonminority employee by the loss of his or her job is so substantial and the cost so severe that the Board's goal of racial diversity, even if legitimate under Title VII, may not be pursued in this particular fashion. This is especially true where, as here, the nonminority employee is tenured. In *Weber* and *Johnson,* when considering whether nonminorities were unduly encumbered by affirmative action, the Court found it significant that they retained their employment. We, therefore, adopt the plurality's pronouncement in *Wygant* that "[w]hile hiring goals impose a diffuse burden, often foreclosing only one of several opportunities, layoffs impose the entire burden of achieving racial equality on particular individuals, often resulting in serious disruption of their lives. That burden is too intrusive."

Accordingly, we conclude that under the second prong of the *Weber* test, the Board's affirmative action policy violates Title VII. In addition to containing an impermissible purpose, the policy "unnecessarily trammel[s] the interests of the [nonminority] employees."

\* \* \*

## VIII.

While we have rejected the argument that the Board's non-remedial application of the affirmative action policy is consistent with the language and intent of Title VII, we do not reject in principle the diversity goal articulated by the Board. Indeed, we recognize that the differences among us underlie the richness and strength of our Nation. Our disposition of this matter, however, rests squarely on the foundation of Title VII. Although we applaud the goal of racial diversity, we cannot agree that Title VII permits an employer to advance that goal through non-remedial discriminatory measures.

Having found that the district court properly concluded that the affirmative action plan applied by the Board to lay off Taxman is invalid under Title VII, and that the district court did not err in calculating Taxman's damages or in dismissing her claim for punitive damages, we will affirm the judgment of the district court.

■ SLOVITER, CHIEF JUDGE, dissenting, with whom JUDGES LEWIS and McKEE join.

In the law, as in other professions, it is often how the question is framed that determines the answer that is received. Although the divisive issue of affirmative action continues on this country's political agenda, I do not see this appeal as raising a broad legal referendum on affirmative action policies. Indeed, it is questionable whether this case is about affirmative action at all, as that term has come to be generally understood—i.e. preference based on race or gender of one deemed "less qualified" over one deemed "more qualified." Nor does this case even require us to examine the parameters of the affirmative action policy originally adopted in 1975 by the Board of Education of the Township of Piscataway (School Board or Board) in response to a state regulation requiring affirmative action programs or the Board's concise 1983 one-page affirmative action policy.

## NOTES AND QUESTIONS

**1.** At least at the moment, the law seems to be that race-conscious affirmative action plans can benefit minority applicants for new jobs who were not themselves the individual victims of prior discrimination, but that such race-conscious relief cannot cause layoffs of white workers who relied on a "bona fide" seniority system. Compare *Taxman* and Wygant v. Jackson Board of Education, 476 U.S. 267 (1986) with Johnson v. Transportation Agency, 480 U.S. 616 (1987) and United Steelworkers v. Weber, 443 U.S. 193 (1979). The explanation for this doctrinal distinction is the perceived importance of seniority, and a judicial sense that losing the benefits of earned seniority is a much more serious deprivation than being passed over initially for an open position. The significance of seniority in the American labor market is discussed at pp. 658–661 infra. The clearest statement in favor of the current state of the law on this question is Richard H. Fallon & Paul C. Weiler, Firefighters v. Stotts: Conflicting Models of Racial Justice, 1984 Sup.Ct.Rev. 1, 57:

> Employers are not irrational in adopting seniority rules, nor are employees irrational in welcoming them. From the employer's perspective, this compensation arrangement enhances productivity by reducing turnover within its work force and reinforcing the employees' commitment to a career with the firm. By the same token, the employee has an interest in attaining the security afforded by the implicit promise of gradual upward progress in earnings, as well as in achieving the stability in his personal life associated with secure employment.

> Seniority is the glue that holds together this mutually beneficial arrangement for stable career employment. To the worker, seniority guarantees that his employer, having obtained the benefit of a higher performance/compensation ratio during the early years of employment, will not replace its older employees when that ratio becomes unfavorable. At the same time, a strong commitment to seniority serves the long-run interest of employers, by allowing them to make credible promises of de facto tenure to

their newer employees in order to obtain their consent to an overall compensation package.

**2.**   The dispute in *Taxman* ended abruptly in a settlement on November 21, 1997.   The settlement was prompted by a coalition of civil rights groups which, fearing an adverse ruling by the Supreme Court, provided a major share of the settlement payment by the school board to Ms. Taxman. Although the Supreme Court did not render an opinion in *Taxman,* other lower court cases are raising similar issues, and the Court may decide to hear one of them.   For example, in University & Community College System of Nevada v. Farmer, 930 P.2d 730 (Nev.1997), the Nevada Supreme Court held that because it satisfied *Weber*'s two-pronged test the university's voluntary affirmative action program did not violate Title VII. In that case, Yvette Farmer was denied employment as a professor in favor of a male immigrant from Africa, Johnson Makoba.   Although she was hired a year later, she received a smaller salary than did Makoba.

**3.**   In United States v. Paradise, 480 U.S. 149 (1987), the Alabama Department of Public Safety had been found guilty by a federal district court of "pervasive, systematic, and obstinate" discrimination in the hiring and promotion of blacks in the state trooper system.   The court ordered 50 percent black promotions until each rank was 25 percent black, but only if there were qualified black candidates, if a particular rank were less than 25 percent black, and if the Department had not developed and implemented a promotion plan that did not have an adverse impact on blacks.   The Supreme Court held, five to four, that the order did not violate the equal protection clause of the fourteenth amendment:   there is a compelling governmental interest in eradicating stubborn discrimination against blacks, and the one-for-one promotion requirement was sufficiently narrowly tailored to withstand even strict scrutiny analysis.   Specifically, the plan was temporary in nature, it did not require gratuitous promotions, it could be (and had been) waived by the court if there were no qualified black candidates, the numerical relief ordered bore a proper relationship to the percentage of nonwhites in the relevant labor force, and it did not impose an unacceptable burden on innocent white candidates for promotion.   The Court noted that the plan did not bar the advancement of whites, but only postponed their promotion, and concluded that the plan represented an informed attempt to balance the rights and interests of the plaintiffs, the Department, and white state troopers.

**4.**   In Local 93, International Association of Firefighters v. Cleveland, 478 U.S. 501 (1986), the Supreme Court held that § 706(g) did not prohibit the entry of a consent decree which contained an affirmative action program requiring the hiring or promotion of individuals who were not themselves actual victims of discrimination.   Similarly, in Local 28, Sheet Metal Workers' v. EEOC, 478 U.S. 421 (1986), the Court held that § 706(g) did not prohibit a court, in appropriate circumstances, from ordering race-conscious relief that benefitted nondiscriminatees where the conduct of the employer or union was egregious.

**5.** In Martin v. Wilks, 490 U.S. 755 (1989) (5–4), the Supreme Court allowed white Birmingham, Alabama, firefighters to challenge a consent decree agreed to ten years earlier by the city and the local branch of the NAACP. For the majority, Chief Justice Rehnquist said the white workers were not parties to the consent decree and cannot be barred by it from bringing their lawsuit now. Justice Stevens, dissenting, said the result would inhibit voluntary efforts to overcome discrimination. He wrote: "There is nothing unusual about the fact that litigation between adverse parties may, as a practical matter, seriously impair the interests of third persons who elect to sit on the sidelines." The Civil Rights Act of 1991 responded to this decision by making consent decrees much more difficult to challenge.

**6.** Officers for Justice v. Civil Service Comm'n, 979 F.2d 721 (9th Cir. 1992), cert. denied, 507 U.S. 1004 (1993), held that the San Francisco Police Department could "band" scores (as an alternative to rank ordering the candidates according to their scores) in an attempt to choose more minority and female sergeants and assistant inspectors, even though there had been "an undisputed history of discrimination." The city established that differences within the "bands" were statistically insignificant. The court rejected a challenge based on the Civil Rights Act of 1991, holding that "the 1991 Act does not alter existing affirmative action law."

**7.** Sharon Taxman did not assert an equal protection claim against the Piscataway School District. Federal, state, and local affirmative action programs, however, raise special constitutional problems under the Fifth and Fourteenth Amendments. In Adarand Constructors, Inc. v. Pena, 515 U.S. 200 (1995), a white-owned subcontractor who was the low bidder on a government road project but lost the job to a certified minority-owned contractor under the Small Business Law requirements sued the government claiming that its affirmative action program violated the Fifth Amendment. The Court held, in a plurality opinion by Justice O'Connor, that government race-based classifications, even if created for "benign" purposes such as making up for past inequality, are subject to strict scrutiny. Under such a standard, the classification must be related to a "compelling government interest" and be "narrowly tailored" to achieve that end. A strenuous dissent by Justice Stevens noted that no race based classification has ever survived strict scrutiny.

Adarand's tightening of allowable affirmative action seems part of an overall trend, both in the United States and abroad. Recently, the Fifth Circuit invalidated the University of Texas Law School's affirmative action program for admitting students, Hopwood v. Texas, 78 F.3d 932 (5th Cir.1996), cert. denied, 116 S.Ct. 2581. The European Court of Justice issued a preliminary ruling in an affirmative action case where a male candidate denied the post of Section Manager in the Bremen, Germany Parks Department challenged the German labor law which required that "women who have the same qualifications as men applying for the same post are to be given priority in sectors where they are under-represented." Both the plaintiff and the female employee held diplomas in landscape gardening and both had been horticultural employees of the Parks Department for roughly the same period of time. The plaintiff, however, had also served as permanent assistant to the Section Manager. The Court found that "implementation of the principle of equal treatment for men and women" in employment "precludes national rules such as those in the present case which, where candidates of different sexes shortlisted for promotion are equally qualified, automatically give priority to women in sectors where they are under-represented, under-representation being deemed to exist when women do not make up at least half of the staff in the individual pay brackets in the relevant personnel group or in the function levels provided for in the organization chart." Kalanke v. Freie Hansestadt Bremen, 1996 ECR I–3051 (1995).

The European Court of Justice, however, later clarified that not all affirmative action programs are impermissible. In Marschall v. Land Nordrhein–Westfalen, a male teacher sued a German School district when it denied him a promotion in favor of a woman. The German law on Civil Servants of the state of North Rhine–Westfalia provides that "[w]here . . . there are fewer women than men in the particular higher grade post in the career bracket, women are to be given priority for promotion in the event of equal suitability, competence and professional performance, unless reasons specific to an individual [male] candidate tilt the balance in his favour." The Court of Justice held that this law did not violate its earlier ruling in Kalanke because unlike the labor law in that case, it contained a "saving clause," allowing for case-by-case judgments in favor of men. Case C–409/95, Marschall v. Land Nordrhein–Westfalen,—ECR—(1997).

PROBLEM

The Devonshire School, an exclusive, co-educational, nonresidential preparatory school in Poloville, was founded in 1960 by James St. John–Smythe. The 10 original faculty members were all friends of St. John–Smythe, and all were white males. The first students were all white, although a small but growing number of minority students began enrolling in the 1970s. By 1985, when St. John–Smythe retired and was replaced as headmaster by James Stock, the faculty has grown to 25, and was still all white males. There was no intentional discrimination against women and minorities; they simply did not apply or were not recommended by current faculty.

As headmaster, Mr. Stock decided to diversify the faculty and hired several well qualified women and minority faculty members between 1985 and 1998, bringing the total faculty to 40. In 1998, because of declining enrollment, the school was forced to lay off 10 faculty members. Stock realized that, even though faculty members expected layoffs to be made on the basis of seniority, if only seniority were used, all of the women and minority faculty members would be laid off, and the faculty would become all white male again. To avoid this result, Stock put the names of all 40 faculty members in a hat and selected the 10 for layoff. One of the 10 selected was Percy Chalmers, a 63 year old member of the original faculty.

Chalmers sues under Title VII.  He alleges that the random selection method is unlawful, because it was adopted for the impermissible purpose of promoting race and gender diversity on the faculty.  What result under *Taxman?*

---

## B.   DISCRIMINATION BASED ON FACTORS OTHER THAN RACE OR SEX

### 1.   RELIGION

## Tucker v. California Department of Education

97 F.3d 1204 (9th Cir.1996).

■ REINHARDT, CIRCUIT JUDGE:

Monte Tucker, the plaintiff-appellant, is a deeply religious man who works as a computer analyst in the California State Department of Education.  He contends that orders promulgated by his supervisors that forbid employees in his division from engaging in any oral or written religious advocacy in the workplace and displaying any religious artifacts, tracts or materials outside their offices or cubicles violate his rights to freedom of speech guaranteed by the First Amendment.  Although the government may have legitimate interests in preventing a number of the activities in which Tucker has engaged or wants to continue to engage, the challenged orders are overbroad and impermissibly infringe on First Amendment rights.  Accordingly we reverse the district court order granting summary judgment for the government and direct that summary judgment be issued in favor of Tucker.

### FACTS AND PROCEDURAL HISTORY

Tucker has worked as a computer analyst for the State Department of Education since 1977.  He is currently employed in the Child Nutrition and Food Distribution Division.  His religious beliefs command him to give credit to God for the work he performs.  In 1988, he decided to comply with this command by placing the phrase "Servant of the Lord Jesus Christ" and the acronym "SOTLJC" after his name on the label of a software program he was working on.  The program, with the acronym, was distributed within the department.  Tucker began placing the acronym on other material he was working on.  Shortly thereafter, his supervisor, James Phillips, instructed him not to use the acronym.  After a series of orders and warnings, Tucker was suspended for five days in May 1988.

On June 9, 1988 Tucker met with a number of his supervisors, including Phillips and Maria Balakshin, who gave him the following orders:

1.  You are to refrain from using a name, acronym, or symbol with religious connotations on any document in the work place.  This prohibition of the use of religious names, acronyms or symbols in the work place applies but is not limited to:

a).  all written correspondence (letters/memorandums) [sic] prepared in either draft or final format on State letterhead or plain paper.

b).  any written correspondence circulated within your work unit, division, branch or department.

c).  all data keyed into the computer (including logos on computer software applications)

2.  You are to refrain from initiating or promoting religious discussions during the course of your work day.  Breaks and lunch periods are excluded, provided such prohibited activity takes place outside the work place.

3.  You are to refrain from displaying or promoting religious books, pamphlets, tracts, brochures, pictures, etc., outside the inner perimeter surfaces of the partitions that define your office space.

On February 7, 1989 Balakshin issued the following orders to all employees of the Child Nutrition and Food Distribution Division, including Tucker, which provide that they may not:

1.  Store or display any religious artifacts, tracts, information or other materials in any part of the workplace other than in their own closed offices or defined cubicles;

2.  Engage in any religious advocacy, either written or oral, during the work hours or in the workplace.

3.  Place any personal acronym, title, symbol, logo, or declaration unrelated to the business of the Department on any official communication or work product.

In May 1989 Tucker filed an action in federal district court against the California Department of Education and his supervisors alleging both constitutional and statutory (Title VII) causes of action.  In 1990 the district court denied Tucker's motion for a preliminary injunction.  In April 1991 the court granted partial summary judgment for the defendants on the question of Tucker's facial challenge to the constitutional validity of the department's orders and denied summary judgment on the Title VII claim.  In 1994, the parties stipulated to the dismissal of Tucker's remaining unadjudicated claims under Federal Rule of Civil Procedure 41(a), and the court directed the clerk to enter judgment for the defendants.  Tucker filed a timely appeal in which he challenges the validity of two of the February 7, 1989 orders.

## I.  THE ORDER BANNING RELIGIOUS ADVOCACY

We consider first the order banning religious advocacy, written or oral, in the workplace.  Both in their briefs and at oral argument the parties disagreed as to the relevant cases and doctrinal framework to be applied to the issues before us.  The parties both discuss areas of First Amendment jurisprudence that are of no relevance in addition to those that are directly applicable.  Although we must look to the most appropriate precedent and doctrine, we are also aware of the dangers of reducing the First Amendment to a series of doctrinal cubbyholes and of warping different fact situations to fit into the boxes we have created. "First Amendment doctrines are manifold, and their diverse facts and analyses may reveal but one consistent truth with respect to the amendment—each case is decided on its own merits."

Our first step is to try to separate the doctrines that are applicable here from those that are not. Tucker contends that the orders must pass strict scrutiny because the government has created a limited purpose public forum in its offices by allowing its employees both to discuss "public questions when they assemble informally at their desks, drinking fountains, lunch rooms, copy machines, etc." and to display written materials in and around their offices and cubicles. We reject that argument. In Cornelius v. NAACP Legal Defense Fund, 473 U.S. 788, 802 (1985), the Court stated, "[t]he government does not create a public forum by inaction or by permitting limited discourse, but only by *intentionally* opening a nontraditional forum for public discourse." (emphasis added). Assuming that Tucker and his co-workers talked about whatever they wanted to at work (before the passage of the challenged order), and that they posted all sorts of materials on the walls, that still would not show that the government had intentionally opened up the workplace for public discourse.

We also reject the state's argument that the orders should be considered time, place and manner restrictions. The time, place and manner test is only applicable to speech regulations that are content neutral. Because the orders here regulate only a certain type of expression, based on its *content*—religious expression—they are not content neutral.

The state also cites cases that concern the Free Exercise Clause and appears to argue that we should analyze the orders as generally applicable restrictions that incidentally restrict Tucker's religious practice. This argument is also obviously wrong. These orders are no more "generally applicable" regulations that incidentally burden Tucker's exercise of religion than they are content neutral speech regulation: they specifically target religious speech and no other.

Finally, we reject the state's contention, which it makes without citing any supporting cases, that employee speech about religion is not on matters of public concern and thus is not protected workplace speech. This circuit and other courts have defined public concern speech broadly to include almost *any* matter other than speech that relates to internal power struggles within the workplace. The Supreme Court has also made it clear that an employee need not address the public at large, for his speech to be deemed to be on a matter of public concern. Here, the speech is religious expression and it is obviously of public concern.

Casting these red herrings aside, we look instead to applicable doctrine, which is found in the case law governing employee speech in the workplace. In Pickering v. Board of Education, 391 U.S. 563 (1968), the Court made it clear that employees could not be forced to relinquish their First Amendment rights simply because they had received the benefit of public employment. Nevertheless, the Court recognized that "the State has interests as an employer in regulating the speech of its employees that differ significantly from those it possesses in connection with regulation of the speech of the citizenry in general." Despite the government's greater interest in regulating workplace speech, when it restricts such speech it bears the burden of justifying its action, and its interests must outweigh those of the employee.

Most of the workplace speech cases involve disciplinary action taken by an employer in response to statements by employees. Here, however, Tucker challenges the validity of orders that apply to all the employees of the division and ban all speech on a broad and important topic. It is clear that the government's burden when seeking to justify a broad deterrent on speech that affects an entire group of its employees is greater than when it is defending an individual disciplinary decision. In cases involving a broad ban on group speech, "[t]he Government must show that the interests of both potential audiences and a vast group of present and future employees in a broad range of present and future expression are outweighed by that expression's 'necessary impact on the actual operation' of the Government." This is indeed an exacting standard.

### The State's Asserted Interests

The state asserts a number of interests to justify its order prohibiting religious advocacy: (i) promoting the efficiency of the workplace, (ii) protecting the "liberty interests" of other employees not to be subjected to religious advocacy, (iii) "meeting the expectations of the taxpayers that their tax dollars are being used to support legitimate State business and not to promote religion,"; (iv) fulfilling its duty to comply with the Establishment Clause of the United States Constitution; and (v) fulfilling its duty to comply with the religion clauses of the California Constitution. We conclude that the state has failed to demonstrate that its "interests" are substantial, individually or in combination, or that they outweigh the employees' interests in free expression. Nor has it made any showing that the expression to be prohibited has a "necessary [adverse] impact on the actual operation of the government."

### i. The State's Asserted Efficiency Interest

We first consider the state's asserted interest in "efficiency." The government has failed to show that its broad ban on religious advocacy is necessary to further its interest in discipline and efficiency. In the first place, it makes at most only a minimal showing that one individual's speech has disrupted the workplace, or threatens to do so. The district court based its efficiency decision in large part if not entirely on the fact that Phillips, Tucker's immediate supervisor, "has had to devote" "hundreds of hours to plaintiff's religious conduct," principally to the acronym issue. The only other evidence in the record going to real or threatened disruption in the workplace is Phillips' statements that only he had "been impacted" by Tucker's use of a religious acronym and that the orders were handed down in response to "what might occur in the future, what Monte [Tucker] might do."

We conclude that the time spent by Tucker's supervisor trying to restrict his religious speech does not constitute disruption.  It affected only the supervisor himself, did not threaten morale in the department generally and for the most part did not concern the issues involved in the two orders before us.  The separate order regarding acronyms remains in effect and is not challenged in this appeal.  In addition, it was part of the supervisor's regular functions to deal with problems of this nature.  In any event, the time Phillips spent dealing with Tucker's expressive behavior cannot justify imposing a ban on religious advocacy by all employees.  There is not only no evidence of disruption in general, but there is no evidence that any employee other than Tucker ever engaged in any kind of "religious advocacy."  In short, the government has utterly failed to justify its broad prohibition on efficiency grounds.

### ii.   The State's Asserted Interest in Protecting Its Employees' Interests

The state asserts that it has an interest in protecting the liberty interests of its employees, but it never explains exactly what these liberty interests are.  Nor does the state cite cases that speak to the existence of such an interest, much less cases that support its claim that this interest justifies restricting employee speech in advance by a flat ban against an entire category of speech.  Moreover, there is no evidence in the record that any of his co-employees have complained about Tucker's speech, that any have complained about religious advocacy generally, or that any have asserted that their liberty interests have been affected in any way.

### iii.   The State's Asserted Interest in Protecting the Taxpayers

There is no basis in the record or otherwise for the state's asserted interest in protecting the public weal.  Nor is there any evidence that the taxpayers' expectations that government money will be spent on the government's business, not on supporting religion, have been frustrated.  There is no showing that any members of the public have been exposed to any religious speech or displays or expressed any concern or complained about Tucker or any other employee's conversations about religion or display of religious materials.  Only Phillips, a supervisor, has spent any significant amount of the government's time dealing with Tucker's activities (and he, of course, was dealing mainly with the acronym issue.)  Therefore, as in the case of the other assertions of the state's interests, the government has failed to meet its burden of showing that there is anything more than speculation or fancy to support its order banning religious advocacy.

### iv.   The State's Asserted Interest in Avoiding the Establishment of Religion

The state primarily relies on its contention, which the district court found persuasive, that the order serves the state's compelling interest in remaining neutral on religious matters and avoiding the establishment of religion.  It also argues that because the order concerns the Department of Education it is justified in light of the Supreme Court's special concern for maintaining church-state separation in public schools. The last point, which the state pressed vigorously at oral argument, is entirely specious.

While the Supreme Court has not considered the constitutionality of a flat ban on religious speech by and among employees who work in a government office, we have little doubt as to how it would rule. In a far more difficult case, the Court rejected the argument that allowing all student groups, including religious groups, to hold meetings on the campus of a public university has a primary effect of advancing religion. The Court stated such an "open-forum" policy does not confer any "imprimatur of state approval on religious sects or practices." In Rosenberger v. University of Virginia, 515 U.S. 819 (1995), the Court said that there must be a "plausible fear" that the speech in question would be attributed to the state, and rejected an Establishment Clause argument because there was "no real likelihood" that the speech would seem to be "either endorsed or coerced by the State." The challenged regulation here prohibits all sorts of employee speech that could in no way create the impression that the state has taken a position in support of a religious sect or of religion generally. For example, if one employee suggested to another during the course of a private conversation at the office that he should consider being baptized or circumcised, or, while at his work station, wrote a letter to his sister suggesting that she enter a convent or convert to Judaism, his conduct would not carry or give the impression of carrying the impermissible "imprimature of state approval on religious sects or practices." In fact, most of the conduct covered by the orders is speech that could in no way cause anyone to believe that the government endorsed it.

The state contends that as a result of the Supreme Court's particular concern about church-state separation in schools, the order is justified because it applies to employees in the Department of Education. The truth is that the state has adopted a rule that might have some basis in reason if it applied to teachers acting in their role as teachers, or to department employees addressing the public in their official capacities; instead the state has made it applicable exclusively to the employees of a division that performs no educational function whatsoever. Quite plainly, the order does not apply to those persons in the department whose performance of their official duties has the most potential for creating public misperception of the state's role.

A teacher appears to speak for the state when he or she teaches; therefore, the department may permissibly restrict such religious advocacy. Similarly, the department may, at least under some circumstances, prevent at least some of its employees from advocating religion in the course of making public speeches on education. However, as the Fifth Circuit has recognized, speech by a public employee, even a teacher, does not always represent, or even appear to represent, the views of the state. Texas State Teachers Assoc. v. Garland Indep. Sch. Dist., 777 F.2d 1046 (5th Cir.1985), aff'd 479 U.S. 801 (1986). In *Garland,* the court struck down a policy that prevented teachers from discussing the teachers' organization during non-class time. The court found no merit in the government's contention that the restriction was necessary to uphold the Texas Education Code's policy of "neutrality" towards groups and organizations.

What Tucker, a computer analyst in the Child Nutrition and Food Distribution Division, discusses in his cubicle or in the hallway with other computer analysts, clearly would not appear to any reasonable person to represent the views of the state. Certainly, nothing Tucker says about religion in his office discourse is likely to cause a reasonable person to believe that the state is speaking or supports his views. Allowing employees of the Child Nutrition and Food Distribution Division to discuss whatever subject they choose at work, be it religion or football, may incidentally benefit religion (or football), but it would not give the appearance of a state endorsement. There is simply no legitimate basis for the state's singling out the employees of the Child Nutrition and Food Distribution Division and subjecting them alone to an order prohibiting all advocacy of religion in the workplace on the ground that it is necessary to avoid the appearance that the state is favoring religion.

### v.   The State's Asserted Interest in Complying with the Religion Clauses of the California Constitution

The government also contends that its interest in meeting the California Constitution's command of "strict neutrality by public officials on matters of religion" justifies the orders. If the California courts had held that limitations on speech such as those challenged here are necessary in order to insure compliance with the California Constitution, we might be required to address the question whether a state interest derived from its constitution provides a legitimate justification to restrict employee speech protected under the First Amendment, or whether the Supremacy Clause precludes reliance on the state constitution. We do not need to reach that issue, however, because we conclude that the state constitution neither requires nor justifies the ban at issue.

* * *

### Conclusion

Because the state's justifications for the ban are meritless, we hold that its asserted interests do not outweigh "the interests of both potential audiences and a vast group of present and future employees in a broad range of present and future expression". Nor does the banned expression have a " 'necessary [adverse] impact on the actual operation of the Government.' " Accordingly, we hold that the order violates the free speech clause of the Constitution.

### II.   THE ORDER BANNING THE STORAGE OR DISPLAY OF ANY RELIGIOUS ARTIFACTS, TRACTS, INFORMATION, AND MATERIALS

Our analysis of the second challenged order, which prevents the display of religious materials outside employees' cubicles or offices, is similar to our analysis of the restrictions on religious advocacy. There are, however, important distinctions between restricting employees' speech at the workplace and prohibiting employees from using the state's walls, tables or other space to post messages or place materials. The government has a greater interest in controlling what materials are posted on its property than it does in controlling the speech of the people who work for it, especially when its employees are engaged in private conversation among themselves. There is a greater likelihood that materials posted on the walls of the corridors of government offices would be interpreted as representing the views of the state than would private speech by individual employees walking down those same corridors.

The interior walls of the offices of the Child Nutrition and Food Distribution Division are neither a public forum, nor a limited purpose public forum.

"Control over access to a non-public forum can be based on subject matter and speaker identity so long as the distinctions drawn are reasonable in light of the purposes served by the forum and are viewpoint neutral." We have applied the "reasonableness" test on a number of occasions. The test requires more of a showing than does the traditional rational basis test; i.e., it is not the same as "establish[ing] that the regulation is rationally related to a legitimate governmental objective, as might be the case for the typical exercise of the government's police power."

We conclude that it is not reasonable to allow employees to post materials around the office on all sorts of subjects, and forbid only the posting of religious information and materials. The challenged ban not only prevents employees from posting non-controversial information that might interest some or all employees—such as bulletins announcing the time and location of church services, invitations to children of employees to join a church youth group, and newspaper clippings praising Billy Graham, Mother Theresa or Cardinal Bernardin—it would also ban religious messages on controversial subjects such as abortion, abstinence of various types, family values, and the v-chip. Material that addresses controversial topics from a non-religious viewpoint would, however, be permissible, as would signs inviting employees to motorcycle rallies, swap meets, x-rated movies, beer busts, burlesque shows, massage parlors or meetings of the local militia. The prohibition is unreasonable not only because it bans a vast amount of material without legitimate justification but also because its sole target is religious speech.

The state's strongest argument is that allowing the posting of religious material on the interior space of the building in question would give the appearance of government endorsement of religious messages. Such endorsement would, of course, be unconstitutional. Even considering the government's greater interest in its wall-space, we find the rationale it offers for the order unpersuasive. Although the government states that "CDE's [California Department of Education's] facilities are public facilities," there is nothing in the record that would indicate that the public has access to or ever goes into the office areas where Tucker and the other employees of the Child Nutrition and Food Distribution Division do their work. Even if there were, the sweeping ban on the posting of all religious information would clearly be unreasonable. Reasonable persons are not likely to consider all of the information posted on bulletin boards or walls in government buildings to be government-sponsored or endorsed. Certainly a total ban on posting religious information of any kind is an unreasonable means of obviating such a concern. This case is different from Monterey Cty. Democratic Central Comm. v. U.S. Postal Serv., 812 F.2d 1194 (9th Cir.1987), where we upheld a narrow ban on partisan political activity on the walkway area around a post office—an area we determined was a non-public forum, although it was widely used by the public. There, we had reason to be concerned that the public might believe that the government endorsed the particular activity sought to be carried on. Here, that is simply not the case.

The government need not choose the least restrictive alternative when regulating speech in a nonpublic forum. However, "its failure to select ... simple available alternative[s] suggests" that the ban it has enacted is not reasonable. The state has simpler and far less restrictive alternatives available to it, such as setting up employee bulletin boards and limiting all employee postings to those sites, or permitting postings generally in the parts of the building not ordinarily visited by the public. Reasonable content-neutral restrictions on the space to be used and the duration of the posting would not be inconsistent with the first amendment. Any regulations would of course be subject to the principles governing content and viewpoint discrimination. The state might also, in a properly drawn order, ban the exhibition of religious symbols, artifacts or other similar items, which might reasonably convey an impression of state endorsement—or at least it might do so in areas outside of the employees' private office space. The constitutionality of any such order would depend of course on all of the circumstances involved in the particular case. Nevertheless, the availability of simple alternatives which infringe much less on the First Amendment rights of employees further supports our conclusion that the challenged order is unreasonable.

Finally, although the line between content and viewpoint discrimination is a difficult one to draw, we are also concerned that the order may constitute viewpoint discrimination because it has the effect of preventing not only messages that discuss religion generally, but also of silencing religious perspectives on controversial subjects in general. For example, as we have suggested above, the ban would appear to prevent a sign stating that "gay marriage is a sin," and quoting passages from the Bible to support that position. However, an employee could post a sign advocating a person's right to choose whatever mate he or she wishes, if he omitted any reference to biblical or other religious support for that position. While we hold the order unreasonable for other reasons, we note that Tucker has raised a colorable claim that it constitutes impermissible viewpoint based discrimination.

We should note that there is a legitimate state interest in preventing displays of religious objects that might suggest state endorsement of religion.  The state has a legitimate interest, for example, in preventing the posting of Crosses or Stars of David in the main hallways, by the elevators, or in the lobbies, and in other locations throughout its buildings.  Such a symbol could give the impression of impermissible government support for religion.  For the same reasons, the state may have a legitimate interest in regulating, or perhaps banning displays of religious artifacts and symbols in various parts of its office buildings.  However, banning the posting of *all* religious materials and information in *all* areas of an office building except in employees' private cubicles simply goes too far.  It is not a reasonable means of achieving the state's legitimate ends.

## OVERBREADTH

Tucker contends that the order banning religious advocacy and the order banning religious postings are overbroad.  We will not hold provisions facially overbroad where a suitable limiting construction is possible or where the overbreadth is not both "real, [and] substantial as well, judged in relation to the [provision's] plainly legitimate sweep."

We will discuss each order in turn, briefly.  In the case of the order banning religious advocacy, we conclude that the overbreadth is real and substantial.  The order prevents free expression by employees, whenever they are in the workplace, even during lunch breaks, coffee breaks, and after-hours.  Moreover, the undefined term "religious advocacy" encompasses a wide range of speech, much of it permissible.  We need not repeat the illustrations here.

\* \* \*

Our analysis as to the second order is similar;  the order covers the posting on bulletin boards of a wide range of materials, from notices of church services to articles about all sorts of topics from a religious perspective.  There appears to be no possible narrowing construction, and were we to attempt to sever the order in a manner that might minimize its constitutional deficiencies—so that, for example, it prohibited only the posting or display of religious artifacts—we would inevitably strip it of a substantial part of its purpose and effect.  The state has not asked us to take any such step and we question whether it would be appropriate for us to do so.  Here, unlike a case in which a statute is declared overbroad, the state can easily promulgate a new order that complies with the Constitution if it so wishes.

## CONCLUSION

Although we recognize that the state has a legitimate interest in avoiding the appearance of supporting religion and in furthering the efficiency of the workplace, the state interests here are insufficient to support the ban on religious advocacy, and the order prohibiting the posting of religious materials is clearly unreasonable.  Moreover, both orders are overbroad.  The order granting summary judgment for the defendant-appellees is reversed with directions to enter summary judgment for plaintiff-appellant and to afford such relief as may be appropriate.

REVERSED AND REMANDED.

## NOTES AND QUESTIONS

**1.** Tucker was a public employee and therefore was able to assert constitutional claims against his employer. Section 703(a) of Title VII prohibits discrimination in employment on the basis of religion, and § 701(j) establishes a duty on the part of employers to "reasonably accommodate . . . an employee's or prospective employee's religious observance or practice [unless it would result in] undue hardship on the conduct of the employer's business." Has the court in *Tucker* applied a similar approach in its constitutional analysis? If so, how? Would the result of the case be the same if it were brought against a private employer under Title VII? Should it?

**2.** Based on *Tucker,* would it be lawful for a public employer to prohibit bible study and evangelism at work? See Brown v. Polk County, 61 F.3d 650 (8th Cir.1995), cert. denied, 116 S.Ct. 1042 (1996) and Kelly v. Municipal Court, 97 F.3d 902 (7th Cir.1996) (held: no).

**3.** Charita Chalmers is an evangelical Christian who believed that God required her to write letters to two of her coworkers in which she urged them to confess their sins and seek forgiveness. The letters greatly upset the employees, one of whom was convalescing at home after giving birth to a child out of wedlock. After being discharged from her job, Chalmers brought an action alleging religious discrimination under Title VII. What result? See Chalmers v. Tulon Co. of Richmond, 101 F.3d 1012 (4th Cir.1996) (held: no violation).

**4.** Section 701(j) protects "all aspects of religious observance and practice, *as well as belief* * * * " (emphasis added). Thus, even highly personal and idiosyncratic beliefs may be protected, as long as they fall under the umbrella of a religious belief. The issue often involves whether employees can refuse to perform certain job requirements on the ground that they violate the individual's religion. For example, a high school biology teacher refused to teach evolution. He argued that evolutionism was part of the religion of "secular humanism," and therefore to require him to teach this "religion" violated the First Amendment. Has the school district violated the Establishment Clause of the First Amendment? See Peloza v. Capistrano Unified School District, 37 F.3d 517 (9th Cir.1994), cert. denied, 515 U.S. 1173 (1995) (held: no).

**5.** Some issues of a secular nature that arise in the workplace may be so closely tied to religious beliefs as to implicate Title VII religious discrimination. For example, in Turic v. Holland Hospitality, Inc., 842 F.Supp. 971 (W.D.Mich.1994), when a pregnant waitress told some coworkers that she was considering having an abortion, some of the "very Christian" staff became upset and she was later discharged for allegedly poor performance. The trial court denied the defendant's motion for summary judgment and held that the plaintiff had alleged sufficient facts to establish Title VII religious discrimination as well as a violation of the Pregnancy Discrimination Act. In another abortion-related case, Wilson v. U.S. West Communications, Inc., 58 F.3d 1337 (8th Cir.1995), the court held that the discharge of an information specialist who refused to stop wearing or cover up an anti-abortion pin depicting a fetus did not violate Title VII because it was disturbing, disruptive, and offensive to other employees. On the other hand, in Rodriguez v. City of Chicago, 69 FEP Cases 993 (N.D.Ill.1996), the court refused to dismiss a claim of religious discrimination filed by a Roman Catholic police officer who asserted that protecting an abortion clinic conflicted with his religious beliefs.

**6.** A related issue is whether employer efforts to *promote* religion violate the Title VII (or comparable state law) rights of employees. The results have varied. Where religious observance plays an ancillary part in a business activity, the activity may still be lawful. For example, in Kolodziej v. Smith, 588 N.E.2d 634 (Mass.1992), it was lawful for an employer to require that management employees attend a week-long seminar on "interpersonal relationships," which drew heavily on the scriptures. On the other hand, if employee religious concerns may be easily accommodated, the employer may be required to do so. An employer who forced an employee to answer the telephone "Merry Christmas" against her religious beliefs, when it would have been easy to accommodate her, was found in violation of Title VII. Kentucky Commission on Human Rights v. Lesco Manufacturing & Design Co., Inc., 736 S.W.2d 361 (Ky.App.1987).

Restrictions on the right of an employer to exercise *its* rights with regard to religion may involve constitutional issues. For example, in Meltebeke v. Bureau of Labor & Industries, 852 P.2d 859 (Or.App.1993), affirmed, 903 P.2d 351 (Or. 1995), the Bureau determined that the employer, the sole proprietor of a painting business, had committed unlawful religious harassment by proselytizing on religious subjects and making statements such as: "[H]e was a sinner and was going to hell because he lived with his girlfriend and did not attend church, and * * * a person had to be a good Christian to be a good painter." The court held that the Bureau's rule, by applying a "reasonable person" standard to determine whether religious conduct is harassment is not the least restrictive means of eliminating religious harassment and therefore violates the free exercise clause of the Oregon Constitution.

**7.** An apprentice electrician, a devout Roman Catholic, believed that commercial nuclear power threatens the environment and future generations. Did an apprenticeship training council have an obligation to accommodate his beliefs by not assigning him to work at a nuclear power plant? See Best v. California Apprenticeship Council, 207 Cal.Rptr. 863 (Cal.App. 1984) (held: yes). Why? Is opposition to nuclear power part of Catholic theology? Would the same holding be applied to an agnostic or atheist? Suppose the apprentice belonged to a religion that *did* oppose nuclear power as a part of its religious tenets? Is there a difference between religious beliefs and moral beliefs? Would it violate Title VII for an employer to force an employee to resign because of his membership in and presidency of a church-affiliated organization that advocated equal rights for homosexuals?

**8.** Title VII prohibits invidious, overt discrimination in employment based on religion. See e.g., Shapolia v. Los Alamos National Laboratory, 992 F.2d 1033 (10th Cir. 1993). Much of the case law, however, focuses on the duty of reasonable accommodation. Frequently, the cases involve adjusting work schedules to permit religious observances. In the leading case, Trans World Airlines, Inc. v. Hardison, 432 U.S. 63 (1977), the Supreme Court construed the employer's obligations quite narrowly and held that requiring employers to bear more than a de minimis cost to accommodate an employee would impose an undue hardship. Similarly, in Ansonia Board of Education v. Philbrook, 479 U.S. 60 (1986), the Court held that an employer must offer an employee reasonable accommodation but need not show that each of the employee's proposed alternatives would result in undue hardship. Only where the employer refuses to make de minimis efforts at accommodation will there be a violation, such as in Smith v. Pyro Mining Co., 827 F.2d 1081 (6th Cir.1987), cert. denied, 485 U.S. 989 (1988), where the employer required the employee to find his own replacement when it could have done so without undue hardship by placing a notice in the company newspaper or on its bulletin board.

**9.** To what extent do you think that the minimal duty of reasonable accommodation to religious beliefs imposed on employers by Title VII is an effort to avoid violating the Establishment Clause of the First Amendment? See Protos v. Volkswagen of America, Inc., 797 F.2d 129 (3d Cir.1986), cert. denied, 479 U.S. 972 (1986). Compare this duty of reasonable accommodation with the duty of reasonable accommodation imposed under disability discrimination laws, infra pp. 337–347.

**10.** In *Hardison,* the plaintiff sought preferential scheduling to accommodate his Saturday sabbath beliefs. In other cases, the courts have found violations of Title VII where employers failed to revise an employee's schedule to accommodate an employee's regular religious observance, EEOC v. Arlington Transit Mix, Inc., 957 F.2d 219 (6th Cir.1991), or specific holidays or observances, EEOC v. Ilona of Hungary, Inc., 97 F.3d 204 (7th Cir.1996); Heller v. Ebb Auto Co., 8 F.3d 1433 (9th Cir.1993).

**11.** Reasonable accommodation to an individual's religion may involve personal appearance and grooming standards on the job (discussed in Chapter 7). Consider the following problem: Sally Smith applies for a job as a flight attendant with Intercontinental Airlines. She is a Muslim and is required by her religion to wear a headdress which covers her hair whenever she is in public. Smith is qualified for the job, but the company refuses to hire her because she would not conform to its dress code, which specifies uniform clothing for its flight crews and attendants. Intercontinental flight attendants currently wear a beret-type hat that does not meet Smith's religious needs. The company is not willing to permit her to wear anything else. If Smith filed a claim of discrimination on the basis of religion against Intercontinental, would she be successful? What arguments would you raise on her behalf or on behalf of the company? Cf. Goldman v. Weinberger, 475 U.S. 503 (1986) (Air Force's refusal to permit a psychologist who was an ordained rabbi to wear a yarmulke with his Air

Force uniform did not violate the First Amendment); Cooper v. Eugene School District No. 4J, 708 P.2d 1161 (Or.App.1985) (revocation of teaching certificate excessive penalty for Sikh teacher who violated state statute prohibiting wearing of religious attire when teaching in public school). For a further discussion of grooming and dress regulations, see Chapter 7.

**12.**  An applicant for the position of truck driver, who was a member of the Native American Church, was denied a position because his occasional (twice within the six-month period before applying for the job) use of peyote in religious ceremonies precluded him from safely driving for 24 hours after ingestion. Does the employer have a duty to accommodate the applicant's religious use of peyote? See Toledo v. Nobel–Sysco, Inc., 892 F.2d 1481 (10th Cir.1989), cert. denied, 495 U.S. 948 (1990) (held: yes).

**13.**  If an individual quits or is discharged because performing certain work activities would violate his or her religion, what effect does this have on eligibility for unemployment insurance? In Employment Division v. Smith, 494 U.S. 872 (1990), a county employee whose job was an alcohol abuse counselor was discharged because of his off-duty use of peyote. The Supreme Court, six-to-three, found no violation of the free exercise clause of the First Amendment in denying him unemployment compensation for work-related misconduct. *Smith* was overruled by the Religious Freedom Restoration Act of 1993, 107 Stat. 1488, 42 U.S.C. § 2000bb et seq., but the statute was held to be unconstitutional in City of Boerne v. Flores, 117 S.Ct. 2157 (1997). This issue is further discussed in Chapter 12.

**14.**  Section 702 of Title VII exempts religious institutions from the ban on discrimination on the basis of religion. Thus, religious institutions may favor members of their own religion in all employment. Does the exemption extend to all activities of the institution? For example, is the Christian Science Monitor newspaper permitted to hire only Christian Scientists? See Feldstein v. Christian Science Monitor, 555 F.Supp. 974 (D.Mass.1983) (held: yes). See also Little v. Wuerl, 929 F.2d 944 (3d Cir. 1991).

## 2.   NATIONAL ORIGIN

### Fragante v. City & County of Honolulu

888 F.2d 591 (9th Cir.1989), cert. denied, 494 U.S. 1081 (1990).

■ TROTT, CIRCUIT JUDGE:

Manuel Fragante applied for a clerk's job with the City and County of Honolulu (Defendants). Although he placed high enough on a civil service eligible list to be chosen for the position, he was not selected because of a perceived deficiency in relevant oral communication skills caused by his "heavy Filipino accent." Fragante brought suit, alleging that the defendants discriminated against him on the basis of his national origin, in violation of Title VII of the Civil Rights Act. At the conclusion of a trial, the district court found that the oral ability to communicate effectively and clearly was a legitimate occupational qualification for the job in question.

This finding was based on the court's understanding that an important aspect of defendant's business—for which a clerk would be responsible—involved the providing of services and assistance to the general public. The court also found that defendant's failure to hire Fragante was explained by his deficiencies in the area of oral communication, not because of his national origin. Finding no proof of a discriminatory intent or motive by the defendant the court dismissed Fragante's complaint, and he appeals. We have jurisdiction under 28 U.S.C. § 1291, and we affirm.

In April 1981, at the age of sixty, Fragante emigrated from the Philippines to Hawaii. In response to a newspaper ad, he applied in November of 1981 for the job at issue in this appeal—an entry level Civil Service Clerk SR–8 job for the City of Honolulu's Division of Motor Vehicles and Licensing. The SR–8 clerk position involved such tasks as filing, processing mail, cashiering, orally providing routine information to the "sometimes contentious" public over the telephone and at an information counter, and obtaining supplies. Fragante scored the highest of 721 test takers on the written SR–8 Civil Service Examination which tested, among other things, word usage, grammar and spelling. Accordingly, he was ranked first on a certified list of eligibles for two SR–8 clerk positions, an achievement of which he is understandably quite proud.

Fragante then was interviewed in the normal course of the selection process—as were other applicants—by George Kuwahara, the assistant licensing administrator, and Kalani McCandless, the division secretary. Both Kuwahara and McCandless were personally familiar with the demands of the position at issue, and both had extensive experience interviewing applicants to the division. During the interview, Kuwahara stressed that the position involved constant public contact and that the ability to speak clearly was one of the most important skills required for the position.

Both Kuwahara and McCandless had difficulty understanding Fragante due to his pronounced Filipino accent, and they determined on the basis of the oral interview that he would be difficult to understand both at the information counter and over the telephone. Accordingly, both interviewers gave Fragante a negative recommendation. They noted he had a very pronounced accent and was difficult to understand. It was their judgment that this would interfere with his performance of certain aspects of the job. As a consequence, Mr. Fragante dropped from number one to number three on the list of eligibles for the position.

Under the city's civil service rules, the Department of Motor Vehicles and Licensing, as the appointing authority, is allowed discretion in selecting applicants for the clerk vacancies. City Civil Service Rule 4.2(d) allows the defendants to select any of the top five eligibles without regard to their rank order. The essence of this rule was clearly stated in the employment announcement posted for the SR–8 position:

> The names of the "top five" qualified applicants with the highest examination grades will be referred to the employing agency in the order of their examination grade and availability for employment

according to Civil Service Rules.  The employing agency may select any one of the eligibles referred.  Those not selected will remain on the list for at least one year for future referrals.

In accord with this process, the two other applicants who were judged more qualified than Fragante and who therefore placed higher than he on the final list got the two available jobs, and he was so notified by mail.

After exhausting administrative remedies, Fragante filed a claim under Title VII of the Civil Rights Act against the City and County of Honolulu, alleging he was discriminated against because of his accent.  The district court relied on the results of the oral interview and found that Fragante's oral skills were "hampered by his accent or manner of speaking."  The court found no evidence of unlawful discrimination in violation of Title VII, concluding that Fragante lacked the "bona fide occupational requirement" of being able to communicate effectively with the public, and dismissed his claim.

* * *

Title VII prohibits employment discrimination on the basis of race, color, sex, religion and national origin.  42 U.S.C. § 2000e–2(a)(1) (1982). A plaintiff may bring an action against an employer under a disparate treatment and/or disparate impact theory.  Fragante's action was brought under the disparate treatment theory.

* * *

Defendants first argue Fragante failed to meet his burden of proving a prima facie case because he failed to show he was actually qualified for the SR–8 clerk position, a position which requires the applicant to be able to communicate clearly and effectively.  Fragante, on the other hand, contends he was qualified for the position.  As proof he points to his exceptional score on the objective written examination, and he argues that his speech, though heavily accented, was deemed comprehensible by two expert witnesses at trial.  Fragante's position is supported by the approach taken by the Equal Employment Opportunity Commission which submits that a plaintiff who proves he has been discriminated against solely because of his accent does establish a prima facie case of national origin discrimination. This contention is further supported by EEOC guidelines which define discrimination to include "the denial of equal employment opportunity * * * because an individual has the * * * linguistic characteristics of a national origin group."  29 C.F.R. § 1606.1 (1988).  Furthermore, Fragante was never advised that he was not qualified for the job; he was only told that he was less-qualified than his competition.

Because we find that Fragante did not carry the ultimate burden of proving national origin discrimination, however, the issue of whether Fragante established a prima facie case of discrimination is not significant, and we assume without deciding that he did.

Preliminarily, we do well to remember that this country was founded and has been built in large measure by people from other lands, many of whom came here—especially after our early beginnings—with a limited knowledge of English.   This flow of immigrants has continued and has been encouraged over the years.   From its inception, the United States of America has been a dream to many around the world.   We hold out promises of freedom, equality, and economic opportunity to many who only know these words as concepts.   It would be more than ironic if we followed up our invitation to people such as Manuel Fragante with a closed economic door based on national origin discrimination.   It is no surprise that Title VII speaks to this issue and clearly articulates the policy of our nation: unlawful discrimination based on national origin shall not be permitted to exist in the workplace.   But, it is also true that there is another important aspect of Title VII: the "preservation of an employer's remaining freedom of choice."

* * *

We turn our discussion to whether defendants articulated a legitimate, nondiscriminatory reason for Fragante's nonselection.   We find that they did, but to this finding we add a note of caution to the trial courts.   Accent and national origin are obviously inextricably intertwined in many cases. It would therefore be an easy refuge in this context for an employer unlawfully discriminating against someone based on national origin to state falsely that it was not the person's national origin that caused the employment or promotion problem, but the candidate's inability to measure up to the communications skills demanded by the job.   We encourage a very searching look by the district courts at such a claim.

An adverse employment decision may be predicated upon an individual's accent when—but only when—it interferes materially with job performance.   There is nothing improper about an employer making an *honest* assessment of the oral communications skills of a candidate for a job when such skills are reasonably related to job performance.

The defendants advertised for applicants to fill SR–8 vacancies.   The initial job announcement listed the ability to "deal tactfully and effectively with the public" as one of the areas to be tested.   There is no doubt from the record that the oral ability to communicate effectively in English is reasonably related to the normal operation of the clerk's office.   A clerk must be able to respond to the public's questions in a manner which the public can understand.   In this regard, the district court in its Findings of Fact and Conclusions of Law and Order made the following significant observations:

> The job is a difficult one because it involves dealing with a great number of disgruntled members of the public.   The clerk must deal with 200–300 people a day, many of whom are angry or complaining and who do not want to hear what the clerk may have to explain concerning their applications or an answer to their questions.   It is a high turnover position where people leave quickly because of the high stress involving daily contact with contentious people.

What must next be determined is whether defendants established a factual basis for believing that Fragante would be hampered in performing this requirement. Defendants submit that because his accent made Fragante difficult to understand as determined by the interview, he would be less able to perform the job than other applicants. Fragante, on the other hand, contends he is able to communicate effectively in English as established by two expert witnesses at trial and by his responses in open court. In essence, he argues his non-selection was effectively based upon national origin discrimination.

After the interview, Kuwahara and McCandless scored Fragante on a rating sheet that was used for all applicants. Applicants were scored in the categories of appearance, speech, self-confidence, emotional control, alertness, initiative, personality, attitude, work experience, and overall fitness for the job. A scale of 1–10 was used. Kuwahara gave Fragante a score of 3 for speech, and noted: "very pronounced accent, difficult to understand." Although McCandless did not enter a score in the speech category, she noted: "Heavy Filipino accent. Would be difficult to understand over the telephone."

After the interviews were scored, Kuwahara and McCandless reviewed the scores, discussed the applicants, and decided on their hiring recommendation to finance director Peter Leong. In making the recommendation, written examination scores were given no consideration. Kuwahara prepared the written recommendation to Leong, dated April 13, 1982, recommending two others for selection. Fragante in his position as Number 3 on the final list was described as follows:

> 3. Manuel Fragante—Retired Phillippine (sic) army officer. Speaks with very pronounced accent which is difficult to understand. He has 37 years of experience in management administration and appears more qualified for professional rather than clerical work. However, because of his accent, I would not recommend him for this position.

McCandless then notified Fragante that he was not selected for either of the clerk position vacancies. Pursuant to a request from Fragante, Kuwahara then reduced the matter to writing. In a letter, dated June 28, 1982, the reasons why he was not selected were articulated as follows:

> As to the reason for your non-selection, we felt the two selected applicants were both superior in their verbal communication ability. As we indicated in your interview, our clerks are constantly dealing with the public and the ability to speak clearly is one of the most important skills required for the position. Therefore, while we were impressed with your educational and employment history, we felt the applicants selected would be better able to work in our office because of their communication skills.

Thus, the interviewers' record discloses Fragante's third place ranking was based on his "pronounced accent which is difficult to understand." Indeed, Fragante can point to no facts which indicate that his ranking was based on factors other than his inability to communicate effectively with the public. This view was shared by the district court.

Although the district court determined that the interview lacked some formality as to standards, instructions, guidelines, or criteria for its conduct and that the rating sheet was inadequate, the court also found that these "insufficiencies" were irrelevant with respect to plaintiff's complaint of unlawful discrimination. A review of the record reveals nothing that would impeach this assessment. Kuwahara and McCandless recorded their evaluation of Fragante's problem in separate written remarks on their rating sheets. As such, a legitimate factual basis for this conclusion that Fragante would be less able than his competition to perform the required duties was established.

Fragante argues the district court erred in considering "listener prejudice" as a legitimate, nondiscriminatory reason for failure to hire. We find, however, that the district court did not determine defendants refused to hire Fragante on the basis that some listeners would "turn off" a Filipino accent. The district court after trial noted that: "Fragante, in fact, has a difficult manner of pronunciation and the Court further finds as a fact from his general testimony that he would often not respond directly to the questions as propounded. He maintains much of his military bearing." We regard the last sentence of the court's comment to be little more than a stray remark of no moment.

We do not find the court's conclusion clearly erroneous. We find support for our view in Fernandez v. Wynn Oil, 653 F.2d 1273, 1275 (9th Cir.1981), where this court held inability to communicate effectively to be one valid ground for finding a job applicant not qualified.

Having established that defendants articulated a legitimate reason for Fragante's non-selection, our next inquiry is whether the reason was a mere pretext for discrimination. Fragante essentially argues that defendant's selection and evaluation procedures were so deficient as to render the proffered reason for non-selection nothing more than a pretext for national origin discrimination. The problem with this argument, however, is that on examination it is only a charge without substance. The process may not have been perfect, but it reveals no discriminatory motive or intent. Search as we have, we have not been able to find even a hint of a mixed motive such as existed in *Price Waterhouse*. Instead, it appears that defendants were motivated exclusively by reasonable business necessity.

Fragante's counsel attempts to cast this case as one in which his client was denied a job simply because he had a difficult accent. This materially alters what actually happened. Fragante failed to get the job because two competitors had superior qualifications with respect to a relevant task performed by a government clerk. Insofar as this implicates "the interest of the State, as an employer, in promoting the efficiency of the public services it performs through its employees * * *," it is not something we are permitted to ignore. Title VII does not stand for the proposition that a person in a protected class—or a person with a foreign accent—shall enjoy a position of advantage thereby when competing for a job against others not similarly protected. And, the record does not show that the jobs went to persons less qualified than Fragante: to the contrary.

Under our holding in Ward v. Westland Plastics, Inc., 651 F. 1266, 1269 (9th Cir.1980), "[a]n employer's decision may be justified by the hired employee's superior qualifications unless the purported justification is a pretext for invidious discrimination." In this case, there is simply no proof whatsoever of pretext, and we do not find the district court's finding of "no discrimination" to be clearly erroneous.

In sum, the record conclusively shows that Fragante was passed over because of the deleterious *effect* of his Filipino accent on his ability to communicate orally, not merely because he had such an accent.

The district court is

AFFIRMED.

## NOTES AND QUESTIONS

**1.** According to the court, must the defendant prove that customers or the public would not want to listen to the plaintiff's accent or that they would not be able to understand it?

**2.** Should the same standard be applied to coworkers as is applied to customers or the public in determining whether they can understand the plaintiff? What steps did the court take to make sure that its holding is limited to the facts of this case?

**3.** Professor Mari Matsuda, who served as volunteer appellate counsel for Mr. Fragante, writes critically of the level of scrutiny given by the trial court to the employer's assertion that Fragante could not be understood.

> The evaluation of Fragante was shoddy. Given the care and effort put into the civil service examination process, the cursory interview by untrained office workers seems an irrational allocation of resources. The interviewers who found Fragante's accent "difficult" did not identify any incidences of misunderstanding during the interview. The lack of standard interview questions, the irrationality of the rating sheet, and the absence in the interview process of training or instruction in either speech assessment or the obligation of nondiscrimination, reveal a weak system of evaluation. This weakness is unjustified given the size and the resources of the employer, and the regular turnover in the job. Significantly, the evaluation process did not include a functional component. That is, Fragante's speech was never tested in a real or simulated job setting. There was no evidence other than presumption that Fragante could not communicate with customers at the DMV.
>
> The evaluation process invited discretion and subjective judgment. As the sociolinguistic evidence would have predicted, a candidate with an accent identified as foreign and inferior is unlikely to survive such a subjective process. The interviewers concluded that a person with a heavy Filipino accent could not

function in the job.  The expert/linguist concluded the opposite. He testified that the unprejudiced listener would have no trouble understanding Fragante.  There is significant evidence on the record that every listener in the courtroom could understand Mr. Fragante during direct and cross-examinations, which required speech more complex than that described by the employer as necessary for the job.  A reviewing court could easily find, on this record, an absence of fair evaluation.  At a minimum, a reviewing court should require that trial courts scrutinize the fairness of the evaluation process.

Professor Matsuda further raises the issue of the role of accent in the "culture of domination."

Unmasking the false neutrality of accent discrimination raises a deeper set of questions:  Why are employers so willing to discriminate on the basis of accent, and why are courts so willing to allow this?  Why does accent discrimination seem like an employer's entitlement, such that employers willingly confess to intentional discrimination on the basis of accent?  The answer may be that we are acculturated to domination.  As a student once wrote in response to an exam question on the rights of aliens, "What would be the point of being a citizen" if noncitizens had equal rights?  In thinking about accents, we come up against the inside/outside culture of dominance that is so fundamental to our understanding of the universe that we don't see it as ideology.  In trying to name and see the ideology, I ask how accent is situated in the structures of domination.  * * *

When certain accents are deemed inappropriate for the workplace, for political life, for use in schools and boardrooms, a policing of public and private boundaries occurs.  Who may speak, when, and where, is a typical mechanism for distributing power. Who is competent to testify in court, who may speak at political meetings, who is an expert authority—answers to these questions stand at the border between the public realm of power and the private realm of the personal.  * * *

Class boundaries, as well, are maintained by accent.  Linguists have found that, while all accents are subject to natural drift and change over time, upper-class accents tend to resist blending into middle-class accents, even when this requires awkward phonological maneuvers.  Upper-class speech will even borrow from foreign accents in order to maintain distance from other speech.  Accent serves an ideological function:  it helps elites to stand apart from—superior to—the masses.

Accents thus construct social boundaries, and social boundaries reinforce accents.  The circumstances that perpetuate accents—including residential segregation, tracking systems in schools, and social distancing—are socially created.  In distributing social standing according to accent, we distribute according to accents we have, in part, created.

Mari J. Matsuda, Voices of America: Accent, Antidiscrimination Law, and a Jurisprudence for the Last Reconstruction, 100 Yale L.J. 1329, 1384–85, 1397–98 (1991).

**4.** In Xieng v. Peoples National Bank, 844 P.2d 389 (Wash.1993), the Washington Supreme Court affirmed the holding that a Seattle bank committed national origin discrimination by refusing to promote an employee because of his Cambodian accent. The employee, a bank teller, successfully completed a management training program and also took additional English classes. He was told that he could not be promoted because he could not speak "American." The court rejected the bank's argument that it acted in good faith belief that the plaintiff's lack of communication skills would materially interfere with his job performance. The court stated that such a subjective standard "could easily become a refuge for unlawful national origin discrimination."

For an interesting article arguing that Title VII should be amended to prohibit discrimination based on "ethnicity" rather than "national origin," see Juan F. Perea, Ethnicity and Prejudice: Reevaluating "National Origin" Discrimination Under Title VII, 35 Wm. & Mary L.Rev. 805 (1994).

**5.** In Jiminez v. Mary Washington College, 57 F.3d 369 (4th Cir.1995), cert. denied, 516 U.S. 944 (1995), a black, Trinidad-born economics professor was denied tenure in part because of poor student evaluations, which complained of the professor's thick accent. The Fourth Circuit reversed the trial court's finding of discrimination. In rejecting the argument that white students were engaged in a conspiracy to drive Jiminez from the school because of his race and national origin, the court noted that student criticism included complaints that he spoke too softly, spoke into the chalk board, covered material too fast, and had poorly worded questions. He also failed to meet the school's requirements for scholarly publication. Suppose a number of the students, for racial and ethnic reasons, refused to enroll in his elective courses. Is low enrollment in courses a basis for refusal to grant tenure?

**6.** The term "national origin" has been held to include the country of one's ancestors, even if that country no longer exists. See Pejic v. Hughes Helicopters, 840 F.2d 667 (9th Cir.1988) (employee of Serbian ancestry filed Title VII action after his discharge). At the time of the case, Serbia, had not existed as a separate political entity in more than 70 years. The court found that animosity based on national origin can outlast political boundaries and held that statutory protection is not limited to nations with modern boundaries or nations that have existed for a set period of time. See Janko v. Illinois State Toll Highway Authority, 704 F.Supp. 1531 (N.D.Ill.1989) ("Gypsy" is a national origin for Title VII purposes).

**7.** *Fragante* held that if the ability to speak English is job related, the employer may require it of prospective employees. But may an employer forbid employees from speaking their native tongue on the job? One court of appeals upheld a rule forbidding sales personnel from speaking their native tongue (Spanish) while at work. Garcia v. Gloor, 618 F.2d 264 (5th Cir.1980), cert. denied, 449 U.S. 1113 (1981). The employer's justifications for the rule included customer preference for employees to speak English even when speaking to other employees about the customer's order and making it easier for non-bilingual supervisors to supervise. Another court of appeals disagreed, holding that a rule adopted by a Los Angeles district court requiring bilingual translator employees to communicate with each other during office hours only in English violated Title VII because it had a differential impact on Hispanic workers. Gutierrez v. Municipal Court, 838 F.2d 1031 (9th Cir.1988). See also Judge Kozinski's dissent from the refusal of en banc review, Gutierrez v. Municipal Court, 861 F.2d 1187 (9th Cir.1988). After plaintiff accepted a cash settlement, a petition for certiorari was dismissed as moot. Municipal Court v. Gutierrez, 490 U.S. 1016 (1989). See generally Juan Perea, English–Only Rules and the Right to Speak One's Primary Language in the Workplace, 23 U.Mich.J.L.Ref. 265 (1990).

**8.** In Arizonans for Official English v. Arizona, 117 S.Ct. 1055 (1997), the Ninth Circuit, in a 6–5 en banc decision, held that an amendment to the Arizona Constitution, which prohibits state employees from using languages other than English in performing their duties, violated the First Amendment. According to Judge Reinhardt's majority opinion, "the adverse impact of [the amendment's] overbreadth is especially egregious because it is not uniformly spread over the population, but falls almost entirely upon Hispanics and other national origin minorities." The Supreme Court vacated the Ninth Circuit's judgment on grounds of mootness, because the plaintiff had resigned her state job. The merits of the case will now be decided by the Arizona Supreme Court in a separate challenge.

**9.** EEOC's regulations on national origin indicate that Title VII protection extends to the following:

(1) Marriage or association with a person of a specific national origin;

(2) Membership in, or association with, an organization identified with or seeking to promote the interests of national groups;

(3) Attendance at, or participation in, schools, churches, temples, or mosques generally used by persons of a national origin group;

(4) Use of an individual's or spouse's name which is associated with a national origin group.

29 C.F.R. § 1606.1.

**10.** Because they adversely affect Asians and Hispanics, height and weight requirements have been held to constitute disparate impact national origin discrimination. See Craig v. Los Angeles, 626 F.2d 659 (9th Cir.1980), cert. denied, 450 U.S. 919 (1981).

**11.** Section 703(e) provides that BFOQ is a defense to national origin discrimination. There are few cases. The legislative history suggests that

BFOQ would permit a restaurant to advertise for or hire only a French or Italian chef. If so, this is a more expansive definition of BFOQ than has been used in religion and sex cases and one that may not be job related. Should a French restaurant be permitted to refuse to hire Julia Child because she is not French? Can you think of a more justifiable national origin BFOQ?

**12.** Title VII applies to the United States operations of foreign companies. If a foreign company discriminates against United States citizens (usually this has involved senior level positions), does this discrimination violate Title VII? See Chaiffetz v. Robertson Research Holding, Ltd., 798 F.2d 731 (5th Cir.1986) (held: yes). See generally Note, Title VII, United States Citizenship, and American National Origin, 60 N.Y.U.L.Rev. 245 (1985). In EEOC v. Arabian American Oil Co., 499 U.S. 244 (1991), the Supreme Court held that Title VII does not apply extraterritorially to regulate employment practices of U.S. employers that employ U.S. citizens abroad. This decision was overturned by the Civil Rights Act of 1991. Both Title VII and the Americans with Disabilities Act now apply to American citizens working for American businesses abroad.

**13.** A number of states have enacted statutes that restrict access to certain jobs to citizens and, in some instances, lawfully admitted aliens who have applied for citizenship. In a series of cases, the Supreme Court has held that the U.S. Constitution prohibits many such laws. In Application of Griffiths, 413 U.S. 717 (1973), invalidated a state statute which excluded aliens from eligibility for membership in the state bar. In Sugarman v. Dougall, 413 U.S. 634 (1973), the Court held that the fourteenth amendment prohibited barring aliens from a broad range of state jobs. A similar holding in Hampton v. Mow Sun Wong, 426 U.S. 88 (1976), based on the due process clause of the fifth amendment, invalidated across-the-board bans on hiring aliens for permanent positions in the civil service, while recognizing that there is a compelling governmental interest in barring aliens from some positions. In Foley v. Connelie, 435 U.S. 291 (1978), the Court held that a state could require citizenship for "important nonelective positions" held by "officers who participate directly in the formulation, execution, or review of broad public policy." Subsequent cases have further defined the parameters of *Foley,* generally limiting the broad holdings of *Sugarman* and *Hampton.* In Ambach v. Norwick, 441 U.S. 68 (1979), the Court upheld a Connecticut statute prohibiting aliens from teaching in the public schools, although they could teach in private schools or be elected to the School Board. In Cabell v. Chavez-Salido, 454 U.S. 432 (1982), the Court upheld a California statute requiring probation officers and their deputies to be citizens, although an alien could be appointed as chief probation officer, could serve as attorney in a case before the probation board, or could serve as a state Superior Court judge or Supreme Court justice. In Bernal v. Fainter, 467 U.S. 216 (1984), the Court struck down a Texas statute which prohibited aliens from becoming notaries public.

### A Note on National Origin Discrimination Under IRCA

Section 102 of the Immigration Reform and Control Act, 8 U.S.C. § 1324b, makes it an "unfair immigration-related employment practice" to discriminate in hiring, recruitment, or discharge against a lawfully admitted alien because of the individual's national origin, or in the case of a citizen or "intending citizen," because of the individual's citizenship status. "Intending citizen" includes aliens who are lawfully admitted and who complete a Declaration of Intention to Become a Citizen. 12 C.F.R. § 268.3001. IRCA does not prohibit discrimination in wages, promotions, fringe benefits, or other terms and conditions of employment, although Title VII may afford additional protection to some individuals.

IRCA applies to all employers that employ four or more employees. 8 U.S.C. § 1324b(a)(2)(A). Thus, it provides additional and exclusive protection for applicants or employees of small employers not covered by Title VII. EEOC, however, has exclusive jurisdiction of any case in which an individual alleges national origin discrimination and the employer is covered under Title VII. 8 U.S.C. § 1324b(a)(2)(B).

IRCA contains two exceptions to the nondiscrimination provision. It is not unlawful to prefer a U.S. citizen over an alien if the two individuals are equally qualified. 28 C.F.R. § 44.200(b)(2). Nevertheless, such a policy may constitute national origin discrimination under Title VII if the purpose or effect is discriminatory. In addition, an employer may hire only citizens or may otherwise discriminate in favor of citizens if required to do so by a law or governmental contract. 28 C.F.R. § 44.200(b)(1)(iii).

IRCA provides that "immigration-related unfair employment practices" are investigated by a "special counsel" in the Department of Justice. 28 C.F.R. § 0.53. There is a 180–day statute of limitations. 8 U.S.C. § 1324b(d)(3). If the special counsel fails to resolve the matter or bring a complaint within 120 days, the individual may file a complaint directly with an administrative law judge of the INS. After a hearing, as provided for in the regulations, the ALJ is authorized to award, among other things, hiring, reinstatement, back pay for up to two years, and attorney fees. Civil penalties of $100 to $1,000 for each individual discriminated against (or $2,000 to $5,000 each for repeat offenders) also may be assessed. 8 U.S.C. § 1324b(g)(2)(B). Appeals from ALJ decisions go to the United States Court of Appeals for the circuit in which the violation occurred or in which the employer resides or transacts business.

## 3. AGE

### EEOC v. Francis W. Parker School

41 F.3d 1073 (7th Cir.1994), cert. denied, 515 U.S. 1142 (1995).

■ BAUER, CIRCUIT JUDGE.

The United States Equal Employment Opportunity Commission ("EEOC") brought an action against the Francis W. Parker School ("Parker") alleging that in its 1989 hiring of a drama teacher, the school violated the Age Discrimination in Employment Act ("ADEA"), 29 U.S.C. §§ 621–634. The district court granted summary judgment in favor of Parker. We affirm.

Parker is a private primary and secondary school located in Chicago's Lincoln Park area. The principal of the school has ultimate authority as to decisions on hiring and firing of teachers. Incumbent teachers' salaries are determined by a twenty-two-step system which links salary to work experience. As a matter of policy, Parker has also used the step system to determine the salaries it will pay new teachers by crediting them for prior teaching experience they have had elsewhere.

When a teacher left Parker's drama department in the fall of 1988, Paul Druzinsky, the head of the department, was asked to search for a replacement. Because of fiscal constraints, Parker's principal, John Cotton, told Druzinsky that the position would pay an annual salary of no more than $28,000. The list of candidates was narrowed to three, all of whom were interviewed between March 14 and March 24 of 1989. On March 27, Parker hired Nancy Bishop as the school's new full-time drama teacher. Bishop had at the time a year of experience and was to start at an annual salary of $22,000.

In the meantime, on March 13, after Druzinsky had announced the three finalists for the position, one of Parker's music teachers asked Druzinsky if he would review the resume of a drama teacher named Harold Johnson. Johnson was sixty-three years old and claimed to have thirty years of experience. Druzinsky called Johnson a week later to inform him that he would not be hired. One of the reasons given for the decision was that Johnson qualified for a salary higher than Parker could afford. Druzinsky claims that he also told Johnson that he was not considered for the position because Druzinsky had received Johnson's resume after the search process was over and the final candidates had been chosen. Johnson denies that Druzinsky ever mentioned this.

On Johnson's behalf, the EEOC filed this lawsuit alleging that Parker's conduct constituted disparate treatment and disparate impact in violation of the ADEA. Parker's first motion for summary judgment was denied on August 27, 1992. In light of the Supreme Court's decision in Hazen Paper Co. v. Biggins, ___ U.S. ___, 113 S.Ct. 1701 (1993), Parker requested that the court reconsider its ruling. The court granted the request, and on June 14, 1993, granted Parker's motion for summary judgment on the EEOC's disparate treatment claim. Parker followed up with a motion for summary judgment on the EEOC's disparate impact claim, and again relying on *Hazen Paper,* the court granted this motion. The EEOC appeals only the decision on its claim of disparate impact.

\* \* \*

Disparate treatment occurs when an employee is treated less favorably simply because of race, color, sex, national origin, or in our case, age. This is the most obvious form of discrimination. To be successful on this type of claim, proof of discriminatory motive is critical.

Disparate impact is the result of more subtle practices, which on their face are neutral in their treatment of different groups but which in fact fall more harshly on one group than another. No proof of discriminatory motive is necessary, but if the practice is found to be justified by business necessity, the claim will fail. The EEOC claims that due to the statistically significant relationship between age and work experience, by setting a low maximum salary limit, Parker excluded a disproportionate percentage of applicants over the age of forty from consideration for the teaching position. Because no business justification was offered in defense of this policy, the EEOC concludes that Parker's process in hiring a new drama teacher violated the dictates of the ADEA.

We begin our analysis with a brief discussion of the Supreme Court's decision in *Hazen Paper*. Walter Biggins, a sixty-two year old technical director for the Hazen Paper Company was fired from his position in 1986. Hazen Paper's pension liability vested after an employee completed ten years of service. Biggins's pension benefits would have vested had he worked a few more weeks. As an alternative to his release, Hazen Paper offered to retain Biggins as a consultant, a position which would not have allowed Biggins's pension benefits to vest. Biggins brought an ERISA and ADEA claim against Hazen Paper. The jury held in his favor on both counts, and the Court of Appeals affirmed both findings of liability. The Supreme Court granted certiorari to decide whether discharge of an employee motivated by the employer's desire to avoid the vesting of pension benefits is sufficient to state a disparate treatment claim under the ADEA. Because the evidence did not show that Hazen Paper's decision was based on Biggins's age, the Court held that his disparate treatment claim was deficient.

*Hazen Paper* was, by its own terms, a disparate treatment case only. Nevertheless, the Court's examination of the ADEA is instructive here. Critical to the Court's analysis was its belief that inaccurate stereotyping of the elderly was, "the essence of what Congress sought to prohibit in the ADEA." The ADEA "requires the employer to ignore an employee's age . . . it does not specify further characteristics that an employer must also ignore." Hence, when an employer denies a worker an employment opportunity based on the belief that older employees are less efficient or less productive, the ADEA provides the worker with a cause of action. On the other hand, "[w]hen the employer's decision is wholly motivated by factors other than age, the problem of inaccurate and stigmatizing stereotypes disappears. This is true even if the motivating factor is correlated with age, as pension status typically is." Nevertheless, "[b]ecause age and years of service are analytically distinct, an employer can take account of one while ignoring the other, and thus it is incorrect to say that a decision based on years of service is necessarily 'age-based.' "

Because the decision to fire Biggins was not based on misperceptions about the competence of older workers, Hazen Paper did not violate the ADEA. The Court's discussion makes clear that the ADEA prevents employers from using age as a criterion for employment decisions. On the other hand, decisions based on criteria which merely tend to affect workers over the age of forty more adversely than workers under forty are not prohibited.

Our reading of *Hazen Paper* and the ADEA is supported by subsection (f) which reads:

> It shall not be unlawful for an employer, employment agency or labor organization—
>
> > (1) to take any action otherwise prohibited under subsection [ ](a), . . . of this section where age is a bona fide occupational qualification reasonably necessary to the normal operation of the particular business, or where the differentiation is based on reasonable factors other than age.

29 U.S.C. § 623(f).

The exception for differentiation based on "reasonable factors other than age" is particularly noteworthy. It suggests that decisions which are made for reasons independent of age but which happen to correlate with age are not actionable under the ADEA. A similar provision in the Equal Pay Act which permits discrepancies in wages paid to male and female workers for "factors other than sex," has been construed to preclude disparate impact claims. A sensible interpretation of this provision is that it is further evidence of the ADEA's focus on eliminating decisions made based on stereotypes about age.

Our dissenting colleague insists that the EEOC's claim can be reconciled with the Court's decision in *Hazen Paper*. In his view, disparate impact theory is designed to bring scrutiny on actions which, although not invidiously discriminatory, might perhaps be the product of unconscious or lingering stereotypes. In this case, however, this approach is of limited applicability.

Perhaps most problematic is Judge Cudahy's reliance on Title VII jurisprudence which, though not unprecedented, seems inappropriate on the facts of this case. He concludes that because Title VII's prohibitions mirror those of the ADEA and Title VII permits disparate impact relief, "similar acceptance in ADEA cases" is required.

In the relevant statutory provisions, however, Title VII and the ADEA differ in a significant way. Subsection (2) of Title VII's prohibitions, which was the basis for the Supreme Court's holding in Griggs v. Duke Power Co., 401 U.S. 424 (1971), proscribes any actions by employers which "limit, segregate, or classify [their] employees or *applicants for employment* in any way which would deprive or tend to deprive any individual of employment opportunities or otherwise adversely affect his status as an employee, because of such individual's race, color, religion, sex, or national origin." The "mirror" provision in the ADEA omits from its coverage, "applicants for employment." In light of the ADEA's nearly verbatim adoption of Title VII language, the exclusion of job applicants from subsection (2) of the ADEA is noteworthy. Hence, while the dissent may find our decision creates a "practical difficulty," it is a result dictated by the statute itself.

Moreover, disparate impact theory does not relieve the EEOC of its obligation to prove the error of the employer's ways. Parker's policy of linking wages to experience is an economically defensible and reasonable means of determining salaries. This is borne out by the ADEA's "safe harbor" provision which permits an employer to "observe the terms of a bona fide seniority system ... which is not a subterfuge to evade the purposes of [the ADEA's prohibitions]." Though years of service may be age-correlative, *Hazen Paper* holds that "it is incorrect to say that a decision based on years of service is necessarily age-based," unless the plaintiff can demonstrate that the reason given was a pretext for a stereotype-based rationale.

Ultimately, the EEOC must show that Parker's rationale is pretextual and that the salary system is predicated on some stereotype, conscious or unconscious. Otherwise, summary judgment in favor of Parker is proper. The EEOC has not alleged how Parker's salary system might be a subterfuge for the belief that older teachers are less effective than younger teachers. The EEOC contends only that Parker's system disproportionately affects older applicants. As the district court held, this statistical correlation alone is insufficient to sustain a finding of ADEA liability. For these reasons, the decision of the lower court granting summary judgment in favor of Parker is

AFFIRMED.

■ CUDAHY, CIRCUIT JUDGE, dissenting.

The majority affirms the district court's grant of summary judgment on the apparent theory that Hazen Paper Co. v. Biggins, 507 U.S. 604, 113 S.Ct. 1701 (1993), precludes the use of the disparate impact theory of liability under the ADEA. The disparate impact theory as applied here would concern the school's employment policy in refusing to depart from its practice of raising salaries for years of experience even when an older and more experienced teacher is willing to work for less. Such a policy disproportionately burdens older workers. I say "apparent theory" because the majority stops ever so slightly short of announcing this conclusion with perfect clarity. But that is the unmistakable import of the majority approach.

The majority's analysis begins with the premise that the decision not to hire Johnson was not based on misperceptions about the competence of older workers. If this characterization is accurate, then the majority is correct in saying that *Hazen Paper* precludes ADEA liability. My difficulty with the majority's approach is that its analysis begins with its conclusion: that the decision to pass Johnson by had nothing to do with stereotypical views of older workers. But, as I understand the use of disparate impact analysis in the age discrimination context, one of its important purposes is to answer this very question. Hence, disparate impact analysis should be allowed to proceed to determine whether the refusal to hire did really arise from stereotypical views of older workers. Not to do so is to say that "overqualified" (i.e. overage) music teachers need not apply.

Metz v. Transit Mix, Inc., 828 F.2d 1202 (7th Cir.1987), held that employers violate the ADEA when they make employment decisions based on factors that correlate with age in an obvious manner, like salary, the proximity of pension benefits' vesting or gray hair. The Supreme Court's recent opinion in *Hazen Paper* rejects part of that framework. *Hazen Paper* focuses the scrutiny of the ADEA on discrimination on the basis of age *qua* age. The ADEA's purpose under *Hazen Paper* is to prohibit discrimination against older workers "on the basis of inaccurate and stigmatizing stereotypes." An "employer cannot rely on age as a proxy for an employee's remaining characteristics, such as productivity, but must instead focus on those factors directly."

So where an employer is *in fact* motivated by a desire to reduce salaries, it is permissible to fire higher-paid older workers and replace them with younger ones who will work for less. And perhaps if the employer *actually* has an aversion to gray hair, she can make her employment decisions accordingly. But, even so, *Hazen Paper* does not spell the end of the ADEA. It remains unlawful to invoke pretextually an ostensibly neutral factor that tends to correlate with age, while actually laboring under forbidden "inaccurate and stigmatizing stereotypes."

All of this tells us about the underlying theory of ADEA liability, not the method of proof. Even before *Hazen Paper* there was substantial disagreement about the permissibility of premising ADEA liability on a showing of disparate impact. And while the three concurring justices in *Hazen Paper* believed that "there are substantial arguments that it is improper to carry over disparate impact analysis from Title VII to the ADEA," there is no suggestion that *Hazen Paper* itself answers the question.

So the question presented by this appeal is whether a plaintiff may endeavor to prove that an employer discriminated on the basis of age *qua* age by implementing a particular employment practice that disproportionately burdens older workers.

The answer to that question depends mostly on what one thinks are the purposes of disparate impact liability. Implicit in the majority's approach is the view that employers are held liable under a disparate impact theory even where the practice or policy they have implemented isn't *really* discriminatory. As I have indicated, the employment policy at issue in this case is the school's refusal to depart from its policy of escalating salaries in relation to years of experience, where an older and more experienced teacher is willing to work for less.

The majority says that "there is no allegation that Francis Parker's salary system is a subterfuge for its belief that older teachers are less effective than younger teachers." But it would not appear to me that such a conscious and invidious scheme would need to be alleged in order to state a claim under the ADEA.

The basic prohibition of the ADEA makes it unlawful to "discriminate against any individual ... because of such individual's age." This language mirrors the anti-discrimination provision of Title VII. In the Title VII context, the disparate impact method of proving "discrimination ...

because of [membership in a protected class]" is well-established (codified, in fact, by the Civil Rights Act of 1991).

The *Griggs* disparate impact method recognizes that not all discrimination is apparent and overt. It is sometimes subtle and hidden. It is at times hidden even from the decisionmaker herself, reflecting perhaps subconscious predilections and stereotypes. The disparate impact method therefore requires employers to determine which of their employment practices and policies burden a protected class in a disproportionate way.

But such practices need not *necessarily* be abandoned. They are nonetheless permissible, despite their disparate impact, where they are supported by a "business necessity." The point of that defense is to rebut the inference of discrimination (even unconscious discrimination) that the disparate impact tends to demonstrate. If business necessity is shown, we can assume that the practice in question was established *because* of that necessity, not merely as a product of stereotyping.

## NOTES AND QUESTIONS

**1.** To what degree should circuit courts defer to the dictum in a concurring opinion of three justices? How much deference is given by the majority and dissenting opinions in this case?

**2.** Lower court decisions after *Hazen Paper* have disagreed on whether disparate impact is a viable approach under the ADEA, although most courts seem to have taken their lead from the justices in rejecting this theory. See, e.g., Ellis v. United Airlines, Inc., 73 F.3d 999 (10th Cir.1996), cert. denied, 116 S.Ct. 2500 (1996).

**3.** Professor Alfred Blumrosen adds another criticism based on the perceived effects of using disparate impact analysis under the ADEA.

> [T]he prime beneficiaries of the ADEA are white males in their fifties and sixties. They are also the beneficiaries of traditional discrimination against minorities and women. To give them the benefit of the *Griggs* principle will inevitably slow the process of affirmative action for minorities and women.

Book Review, 12 Seton Hall L.Rev. 186, 192 (1981). Do you agree? See generally Steven J. Kaminshine, The Cost of Older Workers, Disparate Impact, and the Age Discrimination in Employment Act, 42 Fla.L.Rev. 229 (1990).

**4.** The Age Discrimination in Employment Act (ADEA), 29 U.S.C. §§ 621–634, originally enacted in 1967, prohibits age discrimination in the employment, discharge, promotion, or treatment of persons over the age of 40. (As originally enacted, persons were protected between age 40 and 65.) A 1986 amendment to the Act prohibits all mandatory retirement. Retirement is considered in Chapter 13.

See generally Howard C. Eglit, The Age Discrimination in Employment Act at Thirty: Where It's Been, Where It Is Today, Where It's Going, 31 U.Richmond L.Rev. 579 (1997).

**5.**   The ADEA applies to every employer engaged in an enterprise affecting commerce that has 20 or more employees for each working day in each of 20 or more calendar weeks in the current or preceding calendar year.   The ADEA also applies to employment agencies, unions, state and local political subdivisions, and the federal government.   Although the ADEA was passed as an amendment to the Fair Labor Standards Act, with enforcement vested in the Department of Labor, since 1978 responsibility for enforcing the ADEA has been assigned to the EEOC.   Private actions also may be brought by aggrieved individuals.   In addition to the ADEA, most states have laws prohibiting age discrimination in employment.   Procedures under the ADEA are similar to those under Title VII, except that there is a right to a jury trial under the ADEA.   There is also a wide range of relief available, including reinstatement, injunctive and declaratory relief, and attorney fees.

**6.**   Generally speaking, the courts have applied the *McDonnell Douglas* test to disparate treatment age discrimination cases.   See, e.g., Sutton v. Atlantic Richfield Co., 646 F.2d 407 (9th Cir.1981).   The burden then shifts to the defendant to prove a lawful, nondiscriminatory reason for the plaintiff's adverse treatment.

Section 4(f) of the ADEA sets forth five affirmative defenses:

It shall not be unlawful for an employer, employment agency or labor organization—

(1) to take any action otherwise prohibited * * * where age is a bona fide occupational qualification reasonably necessary to the normal operation of the particular business.   * * *

(2) to take any action otherwise prohibited * * * where the different action is based on reasonable factors other than age. * * *

(3) to observe the terms of a bona fide seniority system. * * *

(4) to observe the terms of * * * any bona fide employee benefit plan.   * * *

(5) to discharge or otherwise discipline an individual for good cause.

With regard to BFOQ, EEOC has issued the following interpretive regulation, 29 C.F.R. § 1625.6(b):

An employer asserting a BFOQ defense has the burden of proving that

(1) the age limit is reasonably necessary to the essence of the business, and either

(2) that all or substantially all individuals excluded from the job involved are in fact disqualified or

(3) that some of the individuals so excluded possess a disqualifying trait that cannot be ascertained except by reference to age.

If the employer's objective in asserting a BFOQ is the goal of public safety, the employer must prove that the challenged practice does indeed effectuate that goal and that there is no acceptable alternative which would better advance it with less discriminatory impact.

**7.** In O'Connor v. Consolidated Coin Caterers Corp., 517 U.S. 308 (1996), a 56 year-old employee was fired and replaced by a 40 year-old. The Fourth Circuit held that there was no violation of the ADEA because the employee was replaced by another individual in the protected class. The Supreme Court unanimously reversed. According to Justice Scalia:

> [The ADEA] does not ban discrimination against employees because they are aged 40 or older; it bans discrimination against employees because of their age, but limits the protected class to those who are 40 or older. * * * [T]he fact that a replacement is substantially younger than the plaintiff is a far more reliable indicator of age discrimination than is the fact that the plaintiff was replaced by someone outside the protected class.

Id. at 1310. How should the lower courts determine when the replacement is "substantially younger"? Is this a question of fact or a question of law?

**8.** Employers refusing to hire older workers because of concerns for public safety have more often found the courts to be sympathetic. For example, in Usery v. Tamiami Trail Tours, Inc., 531 F.2d 224 (5th Cir.1976), the employer refused to consider applications from individuals over age 40 to be intercity bus drivers. In sustaining the employer's BFOQ defense the court stated: "[S]afety to fellow employees is of such humane importance that the employer must be afforded substantial discretion in selecting specific standards which, if they err at all, should err on the [side of] preservation of life and limb." Id. at 238.

**9.** Punker's Paradise is a large, way-out punk rock bar. Its customers are almost exclusively 18–25 year-old punk rockers, many of whom have taken to outlandish dress and grooming styles. The bar has several openings for bartenders, food servers, receptionists, and other positions. Several of the applicants are over 40 years of age. Although these people are qualified, the bar does not want to hire them because it will destroy the image the bar is trying to project. Can the bar restrict its hiring to people under the age of 25? Is it unlawful for a "gentleman's club" to refuse to promote a waitress to the position of topless dancer because she is over 40? See Lindsey v. Prive Corp., 987 F.2d 324 (5th Cir.1993) (reversing summary judgment for defendant and remanding for trial).

**10.** Is salary a "reasonable factor other than age"? The replacement of an older, higher paid employee with a younger, lower paid one may be in violation of the ADEA, even though the employer was motivated solely by a desire to save costs, whether the employer replaces a group of older workers, Leftwich v. Harris–Stowe State College, 702 F.2d 686 (8th Cir. 1983), or a single individual, Metz v. Transit Mix, Inc., 828 F.2d 1202 (7th Cir.1987). Cf. EEOC v. Chrysler Corp., 733 F.2d 1183 (6th Cir.1984) (the "prospect of imminent bankruptcy" may constitute a reasonable factor other than age and justify a forced retirement policy). How else can the employer in financial difficulty cut payroll costs without violating the statute?

Can an employer be liable for age discrimination based on its refusal to hire an applicant because he was "overqualified"? See Taggart v. Time Inc., 924 F.2d 43 (2d Cir.1991) (held: yes). But see Stein v. National City Bank, 942 F.2d 1062 (6th Cir.1991) (no violation of ADEA for bank to refuse to consider college graduates for customer service representative position).

## 4.   DISABILITY

## Vande Zande v. State of Wisconsin Department of Administration

44 F.3d 538 (7th Cir.1995).

■ POSNER, CHIEF JUDGE.

In 1990, Congress passed the Americans with Disabilities Act, 42 U.S.C. §§ 12101 et seq. The stated purpose is "to provide a clear and comprehensive national mandate for the elimination of discrimination against individuals with disabilities," said by Congress to be 43 million in number and growing. "Disability" is broadly defined. It includes not only "a physical or mental impairment that substantially limits one or more of the major life activities of [the disabled] individual," but also the state of "being regarded as having such an impairment." The latter definition, although at first glance peculiar, actually makes a better fit with the elaborate preamble to the Act, in which people who have physical or mental impairments are compared to victims of racial and other invidious discrimination. Many such impairments are not in fact disabling but are believed to be so, and the people having them may be denied employment or otherwise shunned as a consequence. Such people, objectively capable of performing as well as the unimpaired, are analogous to capable workers discriminated against because of their skin color or some other vocationally irrelevant characteristic. (The Act is not limited to employment discrimination, but such discrimination, addressed by Subchapter I of the Act, is the only kind at issue in this case and we limit our discussion accordingly.)

The more problematic case is that of an individual who has a vocationally relevant disability—an impairment such as blindness or paralysis that limits a major human capability, such as seeing or walking. In the common case in which such an impairment interferes with the individual's ability to perform up to the standards of the workplace, or increases the cost of employing him, hiring and firing decisions based on the impairment are not "discriminatory" in a sense closely analogous to employment discrimination on racial grounds. The draftsmen of the Act knew this. But they were unwilling to confine the concept of disability discrimination to cases in which the disability is irrelevant to the performance of the disabled person's job.  Instead, they defined "discrimination" to include an employer's "not making reasonable accommodations to the known physical or mental limitations of an otherwise qualified individual with a disability who is an applicant or employee, unless . . . [the employer] can demonstrate that the accommodation would impose an undue hardship on the operation of the . . . [employer's] business."

The term "reasonable accommodations" is not a legal novelty, even if we ignore its use (arguably with a different meaning, however,) in the provision of Title VII forbidding religious discrimination in employment. It is one of a number of provisions in the employment subchapter that were borrowed from regulations issued by the Equal Employment Opportunity Commission in implementation of the Rehabilitation Act of 1973, 29 U.S.C. §§ 701 et seq.  Indeed, to a great extent the employment provisions of the new Act merely generalize to the economy as a whole the duties, including that of reasonable accommodation, that the regulations under the Rehabilitation Act imposed on federal agencies and federal contractors.  We can therefore look to the decisions interpreting those regulations for clues to the meaning of the same terms in the new law.

It is plain enough what "accommodation" means.  The employer must be willing to consider making changes in its ordinary work rules, facilities, terms, and conditions in order to enable a disabled individual to work.  The difficult term is "reasonable."  The plaintiff in our case, a paraplegic, argues in effect that the term just means apt or efficacious.  An accommodation is reasonable, she believes, when it is tailored to the particular individual's disability.  A ramp or lift is thus a reasonable accommodation for a person who like this plaintiff is confined to a wheelchair.  Considerations of cost do not enter into the term as the plaintiff would have us construe it.  Cost is, she argues, the domain of "undue hardship"—a safe harbor for an employer that can show that it would go broke or suffer other excruciating financial distress were it compelled to make a reasonable accommodation in the sense of one effective in enabling the disabled person to overcome the vocational effects of the disability.

These are questionable interpretations both of "reasonable" and of "undue hardship."  To "accommodate" a disability is to make some change that will enable the disabled person to work.  An unrelated, inefficacious change would not be an accommodation of the disability at all.  So "reasonable" may be intended to qualify (in the sense of weaken) "accommodation," in just the same way that if one requires a "reasonable effort" of someone this means less than the maximum possible effort, or in law that the duty of "reasonable care," the cornerstone of the law of negligence, requires something less than the maximum possible care.  It is understood in that law that in deciding what care is reasonable the court considers the cost of increased care.  (This is explicit in Judge Learned Hand's famous formula for negligence.  United States v. Carroll Towing Co., 159 F.2d 169, 173 (2d Cir.1947).)  Similar reasoning could be used to flesh out the meaning of the word "reasonable" in the term "reasonable accommodations."  It would not follow that the costs and benefits of altering a workplace to enable a disabled person to work would always have to be quantified, or even that an accommodation would have to be deemed unreasonable if the cost exceeded the benefit however slightly. But, at the very least, the cost could not be disproportionate to the benefit. Even if an employer is so large or wealthy—or, like the principal defendant in this case, is a state, which can raise taxes in order to finance any accommodations that it must make to disabled employees—that it may not be able to plead "undue *hardship*," it would not be required to expend enormous sums in order to bring about a trivial improvement in the life of a disabled employee. If the nation's employers have potentially unlimited financial obligations to 43 million disabled persons, the Americans with Disabilities Act will have imposed an indirect tax potentially greater than the national debt. We do not find an intention to bring about such a radical result in either the language of the Act or its history. The preamble actually "markets" the Act as a cost saver, pointing to "billions of dollars in unnecessary expenses resulting from dependency and nonproductivity." The savings will be illusory if employers are required to expend many more billions in accommodation than will be saved by enabling disabled people to work.

The concept of reasonable accommodation is at the heart of this case. The plaintiff sought a number of accommodations to her paraplegia that were turned down. The principal defendant as we have said is a state, which does not argue that the plaintiff's proposals were rejected because accepting them would have imposed undue hardship on the state or because they would not have done her any good. The district judge nevertheless granted summary judgment for the defendants on the ground that the evidence obtained in discovery, construed as favorably to the plaintiff as the record permitted, showed that they had gone as far to accommodate the plaintiff's demands as reasonableness, in a sense distinct from either aptness or hardship—a sense based, rather, on considerations of cost and proportionality—required. On this analysis, the function of the "undue hardship" safe harbor, like the "failing company" defense to antitrust liability, is to excuse compliance by a firm that is financially distressed, even though the cost of the accommodation to the firm might be less than the benefit to disabled employees.

This interpretation of "undue hardship" is not inevitable—in fact probably is incorrect. It is a defined term in the Americans with Disabilities Act, and the definition is "an action requiring significant difficulty or expense." The financial condition of the employer is only one consideration in determining whether an accommodation otherwise reasonable would impose an undue hardship. The legislative history equates "undue hardship" to "unduly costly." These are terms of relation. We must ask, "undue" in relation to what? Presumably (given the statutory definition and the legislative history) in relation to the benefits of the accommodation to the disabled worker as well as to the employer's resources.

So it seems that costs enter at two points in the analysis of claims to an accommodation to a disability. The employee must show that the accommodation is reasonable in the sense both of efficacious and of proportional to costs. Even if this prima facie showing is made, the employer has an opportunity to prove that upon more careful consideration the costs are excessive in relation either to the benefits of the accommodation or to the employer's financial survival or health. In a classic negligence case, the idiosyncrasies of the particular employer are irrelevant. Having above-average costs, or being in a precarious financial situation, is not a defense to negligence. Vaughan v. Menlove, 3 Bing. (N.C.) 468, 132 Eng.Rep. 490 (Comm.Pl.1837). One interpretation of "undue hardship" is that it permits an employer to escape liability if he can carry the burden of proving that a disability accommodation reasonable for a normal employer would break him.

Lori Vande Zande, aged 35, is paralyzed from the waist down as a result of a tumor of the spinal cord. Her paralysis makes her prone to develop pressure ulcers, treatment of which often requires that she stay at home for several weeks. The defendants and the amici curiae argue that there is no duty of reasonable accommodation of pressure ulcers because they do not fit the statutory definition of a disability. Intermittent, episodic impairments are not disabilities, the standard example being a broken leg. But an intermittent impairment that is a characteristic manifestation of an admitted disability is, we believe, a part of the underlying disability and hence a condition that the employer must reasonably accommodate. Often the disabling aspect of a disability is, precisely, an intermittent manifestation of the disability, rather than the underlying impairment. The AIDS virus progressively destroys the infected person's immune system. The consequence is a series of opportunistic diseases which (so far as relevant to the disabilities law) often prevent the individual from working. If they are not part of the disability, then people with AIDS do not have a disability, which seems to us a very odd interpretation of the law, and one expressly rejected in the regulations. We hold that Vande Zande's pressure ulcers are a part of her disability, and therefore a part of what the State of Wisconsin had a duty to accommodate—reasonably.

Vande Zande worked for the housing division of the state's department of administration for three years, beginning in January 1990. The housing division supervises the state's public housing programs. Her job was that of a program assistant, and involved preparing public information materials, planning meetings, interpreting regulations, typing, mailing, filing, and copying. In short, her tasks were of a clerical, secretarial, and administrative-assistant character. In order to enable her to do this work, the defendants, as she acknowledges, "made numerous accommodations relating to the plaintiff's disability." As examples, in her words, "they paid the landlord to have bathrooms modified and to have a step ramped; they bought special adjustable furniture for the plaintiff; they ordered and paid for one-half of the cost of a cot that the plaintiff needed for daily personal care at work; they sometimes adjusted the plaintiff's schedule to perform backup telephone duties to accommodate the plaintiff's medical appointments; they made changes to the plans for a locker room in the new state office building; and they agreed to provide some of the specific accommodations the plaintiff requested in her October 5, 1992 Reasonable Accommodation Request."

But she complains that the defendants did not go far enough in two principal respects. One concerns a period of eight weeks when a bout of pressure ulcers forced her to stay home. She wanted to work full time at home and believed that she would be able to do so if the division would provide her with a desktop computer at home (though she already had a laptop). Her supervisor refused, and told her that he probably would have only 15 to 20 hours of work for her to do at home per week and that she would have to make up the difference between that and a full work week out of her sick leave or vacation leave. In the event, she was able to work all but 16.5 hours in the eight-week period. She took 16.5 hours of sick leave to make up the difference. As a result, she incurred no loss of income, but did lose sick leave that she could have carried forward indefinitely. She now works for another agency of the State of Wisconsin, but any unused sick leave in her employment by the housing division would have accompanied her to her new job. Restoration of the 16.5 hours of lost sick leave is one form of relief that she seeks in this suit.

She argues that a jury might have found that a reasonable accommodation required the housing division either to give her the desktop computer or to excuse her from having to dig into her sick leave to get paid for the hours in which, in the absence of the computer, she was unable to do her work at home. No jury, however, could in our view be permitted to stretch the concept of "reasonable accommodation" so far. Most jobs in organizations public or private involve team work under supervision rather than solitary unsupervised work, and team work under supervision generally cannot be performed at home without a substantial reduction in the quality of the employee's performance. This will no doubt change as communications technology advances, but is the situation today. Generally, therefore, an employer is not required to accommodate a disability by allowing the disabled worker to work, by himself, without supervision, at home. This is the majority view, illustrated by Tyndall v. National Education Centers, Inc., 31 F.3d 209, 213–14 (4th Cir.1994), and Law v. United States Postal Service, 852 F.2d 1278 (Fed.Cir.1988) (per curiam). The District of Columbia Circuit disagrees. Langon v. Dept. of Health & Human Services, 959 F.2d 1053, 1060–61 (D.C.Cir.1992); Carr v. Reno, 23 F.3d 525, 530 (D.C.Cir.1994). But we think the majority view is correct. An employer is not required to allow disabled workers to work at home, where their productivity inevitably would be greatly reduced. No doubt to this as to any generalization about so complex and varied an activity as employment there are exceptions, but it would take a very extraordinary case for the employee to be able to create a triable issue of the employer's failure to allow the employee to work at home.

And if the employer, because it is a government agency and therefore is not under intense competitive pressure to minimize its labor costs or maximize the value of its output, or for some other reason, bends over backwards to accommodate a disabled worker—goes further than the law requires—by allowing the worker to work at home, it must not be punished for its generosity by being deemed to have conceded the reasonableness of so far-reaching an accommodation. That would hurt rather than help disabled workers. Wisconsin's housing division was not required by the Americans with Disabilities Act to allow Vande Zande to work at home; even more clearly it was not required to install a computer in her home so that she could avoid using up 16.5 hours of sick leave. It is conjectural that she will ever need those 16.5 hours; the expected cost of the loss must, therefore, surely be slight. An accommodation that allows a disabled worker to work at home, at full pay, subject only to a slight loss of sick leave that may never be needed, hence never missed, is, we hold, reasonable as a matter of law.

Vande Zande complains that she was reclassified as a part-time worker while she was at home, and that this was gratuitous. She was not reclassified. She received her full pay (albeit with a little help from her entitlement to sick leave), and full benefits, throughout the period. It is true that at first her supervisor did not think he would have full-time work for her to do at home. Had that turned out to be true, we do not see on what basis she could complain about being reclassified; she would be working on a part-time basis. It did not turn out to be true, so she was not reclassified, and we therefore do not understand what she is complaining about.

Her second complaint has to do with the kitchenettes in the housing division's building, which are for the use of employees during lunch and coffee breaks. Both the sink and the counter in each of the kitchenettes were 36 inches high, which is too high for a person in a wheelchair. The building was under construction, and the kitchenettes not yet built, when the plaintiff complained about this feature of the design. But the defendants refused to alter the design to lower the sink and counter to 34 inches, the height convenient for a person in a wheelchair. Construction of the building had begun before the effective date of the Americans with Disabilities Act, and Vande Zande does not argue that the failure to include 34–inch sinks and counters in the design of the building violated the Act. She could not argue that; the Act is not retroactive. But she argues that once she brought the problem to the attention of her supervisors, they were obliged to lower the sink and counter, at least on the floor on which her office was located but possibly on the other floors in the building as well, since she might be moved to another floor. All that the defendants were willing to do was to install a shelf 34 inches high in the kitchenette area on Vande Zande's floor. That took care of the counter problem. As for the sink, the defendants took the position that since the plumbing was already in place it would be too costly to lower the sink and that the plaintiff could use the bathroom sink, which is 34 inches high.

Apparently it would have cost only about $150 to lower the sink on Vande Zande's floor; to lower it on all the floors might have cost as much as $2,000, though possibly less. Given the proximity of the bathroom sink,

Vande Zande can hardly complain that the inaccessibility of the kitchenette sink interfered with her ability to work or with her physical comfort. Her argument rather is that forcing her to use the bathroom sink for activities (such as washing out her coffee cup) for which the other employees could use the kitchenette sink stigmatized her as different and inferior; she seeks an award of compensatory damages for the resulting emotional distress. We may assume without having to decide that emotional as well as physical barriers to the integration of disabled persons into the workforce are relevant in determining the reasonableness of an accommodation. But we do not think an employer has a duty to expend even modest amounts of money to bring about an absolute identity in working conditions between disabled and nondisabled workers. The creation of such a duty would be the inevitable consequence of deeming a failure to achieve identical conditions "stigmatizing." That is merely an epithet. We conclude that access to a particular sink, when access to an equivalent sink, conveniently located, is provided, is not a legal duty of an employer. The duty of reasonable accommodation is satisfied when the employer does what is necessary to enable the disabled worker to work in reasonable comfort.

In addition to making these specific complaints of failure of reasonable accommodation, Vande Zande argues that the defendants displayed a "pattern of insensitivity or discrimination." She relies on a number of minor incidents, such as her supervisor's response, "Cut me some slack," to her complaint on the first day on which the housing division moved into the new building that the bathrooms lacked adequate supplies. He meant that it would take a few days to iron out the bugs inevitable in any major move. It was clearly a reasonable request in the circumstances; and given all the accommodations that Vande Zande acknowledges the defendants made to her disability, a "pattern of insensitivity or discrimination" is hard to discern. But the more fundamental point is that there is no separate offense under the Americans with Disabilities Act called engaging in a pattern of insensitivity or discrimination. The word "pattern" does not appear in the employment subchapter, and the Act is not modeled on RICO. As in other cases of discrimination, a plaintiff can ask the trier of fact to draw an inference of discrimination from a pattern of behavior when each individual act making up that pattern might have an innocent explanation. The whole can be greater than the sum of the parts. But in this case all we have in the way of a pattern is that the employer made a number of reasonable and some more than reasonable—unnecessary—accommodations, and turned down only requests for unreasonable accommodations. From such a pattern no inference of unlawful discrimination can be drawn.

AFFIRMED.

## NOTES AND QUESTIONS

**1.** The Americans with Disabilities Act of 1990 (ADA), 42 U.S.C. §§ 12101–12213, is the first comprehensive federal law to prohibit discrimination in employment against the estimated 43 million Americans with physical or mental disabilities. The employment provisions of the ADA apply to employers with 15 or more employees.

The coverage of the ADA is intended to be broad. Besides most private employers, the ADA applies to state and local government employers. It also does not preempt existing federal and state discrimination laws (such as a state law that covers small employers). The enforcement procedures and remedies are the same as exist under Title VII of the Civil Rights Act of 1964.

Congress drew heavily from the Rehabilitation Act in fashioning the framework of the ADA. The term "disability" is defined in § 3 of the ADA as "(A) a physical or mental impairment that substantially limits one or more of the major life activities of such individual; (B) a record of such an impairment; or (C) being regarded as having such an impairment." Certain conditions, however, are excluded by § 511: homosexuality, bisexuality, transvestism, transsexualism, pedophilia, exhibitionism, voyeurism, gender identity disorders not resulting from physical impairments, other sexual behavior disorders, compulsive gambling, kleptomania, pyromania, and psychoactive substance use disorders resulting from current illegal use of drugs.

Section 104 of the ADA also excludes from coverage any employee or applicant who is currently engaging in the illegal use of drugs. Individuals who are not currently engaged in the illegal use of drugs are covered if they have been rehabilitated, are currently participating in rehabilitation, or are erroneously regarded as engaging in drug use. It is not clear when individuals are no longer engaging in drug use (i.e., for how long do they have to be "clean"). It is also unclear whether individuals with a false-positive drug test are "erroneously regarded" as engaging in the illegal use of drugs.

**2.** Many of the principles embodied in the ADA are based on the Rehabilitation Act of 1973, 29 U.S.C. §§ 701–796. The Rehabilitation Act is applicable to federal government employers (§ 501), federal government contractors (§ 503), and recipients of federal financial assistance (§ 504). The limited coverage of the Rehabilitation Act and the lack of effective remedies against violators were two of the main reasons behind the passage of the ADA. The ADA does not preempt the Rehabilitation Act, which continues to be valuable because it provides the only source of coverage for federal government employees, requires government contractors to engage in affirmative action to hire and promote qualified individuals with disabilities, and because the remedies under the Rehabilitation Act include debarment of contractors and the termination of federal payments to grantees.

**3.** The ADA does not preempt any state or local law that provides protection to individuals with disabilities at least as stringent as the ADA. Every state except for Arkansas and Mississippi has such a law. State laws also remain important because many of them extend protection to employers with fewer employees than the federal minimum of 15, and some state laws have been construed to cover a broader range of disabilities than the federal law.

**4.** Numerous ADA cases have considered the threshold issue of whether the plaintiff is an "individual with a disability," and therefore covered by the ADA. In general, the courts have been restrictive of ADA coverage. Some of the most common reasons for denying coverage are the following: (a) "minor" impairments are not disabilities, e.g., Roth v. Lutheran General Hospital, 57 F.3d 1446 (7th Cir.1995) (strabismus); Lawrence v. Metro–Dade Police Department, 872 F.Supp. 950 (S.D.Fla.1993) ("hammer toes"); (b) temporary impairments are not disabilities, e.g., Rogers v. International Marine Terminals, Inc., 87 F.3d 755 (5th Cir.1996) (ankle injury); Kramer v. K & S Associates, 942 F.Supp. 444 (E.D.Mo.1996) (broken leg); (c) personality traits and environmental, cultural, or economic factors are not impairments, e.g., Greenberg v. New York State, 919 F.Supp. 637 (E.D.N.Y. 1996) (inability to perform under stress); Holt v. Northwest Pennsylvania Training Partnership Consortium, 694 A.2d 1134 (Pa.Cmwlth.1997) (transsexualism not a disability under state law); and (d) pregnancy and related medical conditions, absent unusual situations, are not impairments, e.g., Wenzlaff v. NationsBank, 940 F.Supp. 889 (D.Md.1996); Gudenkauf v. Stauffer Communications, Inc., 922 F.Supp. 465 (D.Kan.1996).

In Bragdon v. Abbott, 118 S.Ct. ___, 1998 WL 332958 (1998), the Supreme Court held that asymptomatic HIV infection is a disability under the ADA. "In light of the immediacy with which the virus begins to damage the infected person's white blood cells and the severity of the disease, we hold it is an impairment from the moment of infection." The Court further held that HIV infection was a substantial limitation on the major life activity of reproduction. Although *Bragdon* was a Title III ADA case involving the public accommodation of a dentist's services, it undoubtedly applies to employment.

**5.** In *Vande Zande*, the court held that the plaintiff's minor symptoms of paraplegia (pressure ulcers) were a part of her disability. Other courts, however, have rejected this approach in reaching highly questionable results. For example, in Sanders v. Arneson Products, Inc., 91 F.3d 1351 (9th Cir.1996), cert. denied, 117 S.Ct. 1247 (1997), the Ninth Circuit held that an employee who took a four-month leave of absence to recover from a psychological impairment caused by his colon cancer surgery did not have a covered disability because the psychological condition was only temporary.

**6.** Individualized determination of fitness is one of the core concepts of both federal and state disabilities laws. The courts have been reluctant to permit the exclusion of entire groups of individuals with certain impairments without an individual consideration of ability to perform the job. For example, a hospital could not exclude all individuals with epilepsy from direct patient care positions, Silverstein v. Sisters of Charity, 614 P.2d 891 (Colo.App.1979), and a school for the blind could not refuse to hire teachers' aides with impaired vision, Connecticut Institute for the Blind v. Connecticut Commission on Human Rights & Opportunities, 405 A.2d 618 (Conn.1978). Individual assessments, however, are very expensive. Is such a determination required in every case?

**7.** Determining "reasonable accommodations" is often fact-specific. Based on *Vande Zande,* should the same standard be used to determine whether an accommodation is reasonable when it directly relates to the job (e.g. ability to work at home) as when it applies to other conditions of employment (e.g. kitchenettes used for lunch and coffee breaks)?

**8.** An employer's duty of accommodation only extends to *reasonable* accommodations. The accommodation need not be ideal. McAdams v. United Parcel Service, 30 F.3d 1027 (8th Cir.1994). The burden of proof is on the individual to prove that an accommodation exists that will permit him or her to perform the essential functions of the job. White v. York International Corp., 45 F.3d 357 (10th Cir.1995).

**9.** Accommodations that pose an undue hardship or expense are not required. For example, a medical group had no duty to hire an assistant to help an internist with reflex sympathetic dystrophy perform the physical tasks related to practicing medicine. Reigel v. Kaiser Foundation Health Plan, 859 F.Supp. 963 (E.D.N.C.1994).

**10.** One frequently requested accommodation is unpaid leave to obtain medical treatment. In general, courts have held that leaves of absence are reasonable accommodations. See Schmidt v. Safeway, Inc., 864 F.Supp. 991 (D.Or.1994); Eisfelder v. State of Michigan Department of Natural Resources, 847 F.Supp. 78 (W.D.Mich.1993). On the other hand, an employer did not have a duty to grant an employee indefinite leave at half salary while he recovered from chronic heart disease, hypertension, phlebitis, and diabetes. Myers v. Hose, 50 F.3d 278 (4th Cir.1995).

**11.** A contentious issue in reasonable accommodation is the employer's duty to reassign an individual to another position. There is no duty to reassign an individual where there is no vacant position. Fedro v. Reno, 21 F.3d 1391 (7th Cir.1994). Where there is only one vacant position, does an employer have a duty to reassign the employee with a disability or the employee with the most seniority, based on the terms of a collective bargaining agreement? See Aka v. Washington Hospital Center, 116 F.3d 876 (D.C.Cir.1997) (held: no per se rule; conflict with collective bargaining agreement should be considered as one factor in evaluating reasonableness of accommodation).

**12.** What defenses are available? Some of the most common defenses asserted in disability discrimination cases are the following:

(a) *Employee misconduct.* Employee discharges have been upheld where they were the result of misconduct, such as shoplifting, Harris v. Polk County, 103 F.3d 696 (8th Cir.1996), fighting, Johnson v. New York Hospital, 96 F.3d 33 (2d Cir.1996), and making threats, Palmer v. Circuit Court of Cook County, 117 F.3d 351 (7th Cir.1997).

(b) *Customer/coworker preference.* In race, sex, and other discrimination cases this defense has failed. The courts may not reject it out of hand in disability cases, however. Does a gourmet restaurant have to hire "Elephant Man" to be head waiter? Cf. Chico

Dairy Co. v. West Virginia Human Rights Commission, 382 S.E.2d 75 (W.Va.1989) (employee who had prosthetic eye and disfigured eye socket did not have a handicap, and Human Rights Commission lacked authority to interpret state law to cover "perceived handicaps," thus employer's refusal to promote employee to manager at a food store because of her "unsavory appearance" was not unlawful).

In EEOC v. Kinney Shoe Corp., 104 F.3d 683 (4th Cir.1997), a shoe salesperson had uncontrolled epileptic seizures, which caused him to lose consciousness.  When this occurred, he would fall to the floor, causing coworkers to rush to his assistance and customers to become upset.  After 16 seizures in a six-month period, he was discharged.  The court held that there was no violation of the ADA, that the employer did not discriminate because of the employee's epilepsy but because of the effects of the epilepsy.  It cautioned, however, that its holding was limited to the facts and was not an endorsement of a "customer preference" defense.

(c) *Direct threat.*  Section 103(b) of the ADA provides that qualification standards may include a requirement that the individual may not pose a direct threat to the individual, coworkers, customers, or the public.  For example, the direct threat defense was upheld where a United States marshal with a paranoid personality disorder would create a risk if he carried a firearm.  Lassiter v. Reno, 885 F.Supp. 869 (E.D.Va.1995), affirmed mem., 86 F.3d 1151 (4th Cir.1996), cert. denied, 117 S.Ct. 766 (1997).

**13.**   Another contentious issue is whether employees who assert that they are totally disabled in applying for Social Security disability benefits and other forms of compensation are barred from bringing actions for disability discrimination under the ADA.  The defendants' assertion is that if the individuals were "totally disabled" and unable to work, this would prevent them from being qualified under the ADA.  A substantial number of courts have applied the doctrine of judicial estoppel to bar the ADA action, often without regard to the outcome of the other proceeding.  See, e.g., McNemar v. Disney Store, Inc., 91 F.3d 610 (3d Cir.1996), cert. denied, 117 S.Ct. 958 (1997). See Maureen C. Weston, The Road Best Traveled: Removing Judicial Roadblocks That Prevent Workers From Obtaining Both Disability Benefits and ADA Civil Rights Protection, 26 Hofstra L. Rev. 377 (1997).

## 5.  SEXUAL ORIENTATION

## Shahar v. Bowers

114 F.3d 1097 (11th Cir.1997) (en banc), cert. denied, 118 S.Ct. 693 (1998).

■ EDMONDSON, CIRCUIT JUDGE:

In this government-employment case, Plaintiff–Appellant contends that the Attorney General of the State of Georgia violated her federal constitutional rights by revoking an employment offer because of her purported "marriage" to another woman.   The district court concluded that Plaintiff's rights had not been violated.   We affirm.

* * *

While a law student, Shahar spent the summer of 1990 as a law clerk with the Department.   In September 1990, the Attorney General offered Shahar the position of Staff Attorney when she graduated from law school. Shahar accepted the offer and was scheduled to begin work in September 1991.

In the summer of 1990, Shahar began making plans for her "wedding."   Her rabbi announced the expected "wedding" to the congregation at Shahar's synagogue in Atlanta.   Shahar and her partner invited approximately 250 people, including two Department employees, to the "wedding." The written invitations characterized the ceremony as a "Jewish, lesbian-feminist, out-door wedding."   The ceremony took place in a public park in South Carolina in June 1991.

In November 1990, Shahar filled out the required application for a Staff Attorney position.   In response to the question on "marital status," Shahar indicated that she was "engaged."   She altered "spouse's name" to read "future spouse's name" and filled in her partner's name: "Francine M. Greenfield."   In response to the question "Do any of your relatives work for the State of Georgia?" she filled in the name of her partner as follows: "Francine Greenfield, future spouse."

Sometime in the spring of 1991, Shahar and her partner were working on their "wedding" invitations at an Atlanta restaurant.   While there, they ran into Elizabeth Rowe and Susan Rutherford.   Rowe was employed by the Department as a paralegal, Rutherford as an attorney.   Rowe was invited to, and did attend, Shahar's ceremony.   The four women had a brief conversation, which included some discussion of the "wedding" preparations.

In June 1991, Shahar told Deputy Attorney General Robert Coleman that she was getting married at the end of July, changing her last name, taking a trip to Greece and, accordingly, would not be starting work with the Department until mid-to-late September.   At this point, Shahar did not say that she was "marrying" another woman.   Senior Assistant Attorney General Jeffrey Milsteen, who had been co-chair of the summer clerk committee, was in Coleman's office at the time and heard Coleman congratulate Shahar.   Milsteen later mentioned to Rutherford that Shahar was getting married.   Rutherford then told Milsteen that Shahar was planning on "marrying" another woman.   This revelation caused a stir.

Senior aides to the Attorney General became concerned about what they viewed as potential problems in the office resulting from the Department's employment of a Staff Attorney who purported to be part of a same-sex "marriage."   As the Attorney General was out of the office that week, the five aides held several meetings among themselves to discuss the situation.

Upon the Attorney General's return to the office, he was informed of the situation.   He held discussions with the senior aides, as well as a few other lawyers within the Department.   After much discussion, the

Robin Shahar.
© John Disney, Fulton County Daily Reporter

Attorney General decided, with the advice of his senior lawyers, to withdraw Shahar's job offer. In July 1991, he did so in writing. The pertinent letter stated that the withdrawal of Shahar's offer:

has become necessary in light of information which has only recently come to my attention relating to a purported marriage between you and another woman. As chief legal officer of this state, inaction on my part would constitute tacit approval of this purported marriage and jeopardize the proper functioning of this office.

\* \* \*

Shahar brought the present action against the Attorney General, individually and in his official capacity, seeking both damages and injunctive relief (including "reinstatement"). She said revoking her offer violated her free exercise and free association rights and her rights to equal protection and substantive due process.

Bowers moved for summary judgment on all causes of action. On that same day, Shahar moved for partial summary judgment. The district court granted the Attorney General's motion for summary judgment and denied Shahar's.

\* \* \*

We must decide whether Shahar's interests outweigh the disruption and other harm the Attorney General believes her employment could cause. *Pickering* balancing is never a precise mathematical process: it is a method of analysis by which a court compares the *relative* values of the things before it. A person often knows that "x" outweighs "y" even without first determining exactly what either "x" or "y" weighs. And it is this common experience that illustrates the workings of a *Pickering* balance.

To decide this case, we are willing to accord Shahar's claimed associational rights (which we have assumed to exist) substantial weight. But, we know that the weight due intimate associational rights, such as, those involved in even a state-authorized marriage, can be overcome by a government employer's interest in maintaining the effective functioning of his office.

In weighing her interest in her associational rights, Shahar asks us also to consider the "non-employment related context" of her "wedding" and "marriage" and that "[s]he took no action to transform her intimate association into a public or political statement." In addition, Shahar says that we should take into account that she has affirmatively disavowed a right to benefits from the Department based on her "marriage."

To the extent that Shahar disclaims benefits bestowed by the State based on marriage, she is merely acknowledging what is undisputed, that Georgia law does not and has not recognized homosexual marriage. We fail to see how that technical acknowledgment counts for much in the balance.

If Shahar is arguing that she does not hold herself out as "married," the undisputed facts are to the contrary. Department employees, among many others, were invited to a "Jewish, lesbian-feminist, out-door wedding" which included exchanging wedding rings: the wearing of a wedding ring is an outward sign of having entered into marriage. Shahar listed her "marital status" on her employment application as "engaged" and indicated that her future spouse was a woman. She and her partner have both legally changed their family name to Shahar by filing a name change petition with the Fulton County Superior Court. They sought and received the married rate on their insurance. And, they, together, own the house in which they cohabit. These things were not done secretly, but openly.

Even if Shahar is not married to another woman, she, for appearance purposes, might as well be. We suppose that Shahar could have done more to "transform" her intimate relationship into a public statement. But after (as she says) "sanctifying" the relationship with a large "wedding" ceremony by which she became—and remains for all to see—"married," she has done enough to warrant the Attorney General's concern. He could conclude that her acts would give rise to a likelihood of confusion in the minds of members of the public: confusion about her marital status and about his attitude on same-sex marriage and related issues.

As for disruption within the Department, Shahar argues that we may discount the potential harm based on (what she sees as) the weakness of the Attorney General's predictions. Shahar overstates the Attorney General's "evidentiary burden."

\* \* \*

As we have already written, the Attorney General's worry about his office being involved in litigation in which Shahar's special personal interest might appear to be in conflict with the State's position has been borne out in fact. This worry is not unreasonable. In addition, the Department, when the job offer was withdrawn, had already engaged in and won a recent battle about homosexual sodomy—highly visible litigation in which its lawyers worked to uphold the lawful prohibition of homosexual sodomy. This history makes it particularly reasonable for the Attorney General to worry about the internal consequences for his professional staff (for example, loss of morale, loss of cohesiveness and so forth) of allowing a lawyer, who openly—for instance, on her employment application and in statements to coworkers—represents herself to be "married" to a person of the same sex, to become part of his staff. Doubt and uncertainty of purpose can undo an office; he is not unreasonable to guard against that potentiality.

Shahar also argues that, at the Department, she would have handled mostly death penalty appeals and that the *Pickering* test requires evidence of potential interference with these particular duties. Even assuming Shahar is correct about her likely assignment within the Department, a particularized showing of interference with the provision of public services is not required. In addition, the Attorney General must be able to reassign his limited legal staff as the needs of his office require.

* * *

As we have already touched upon, the Attorney General, for balancing purposes, has pointed out, among other things, his concern about the public's reaction—the public that elected him and that he serves—to his having a Staff Attorney who is part of a same-sex "marriage." Shahar argues that he may not justify his decision by reference to perceived public hostility to her "marriage." We have held otherwise about the significance of public perception when law enforcement is involved. In McMullen v. Carson, 754 F.2d 936 (11th Cir.1985), we held that a sheriff's clerical employee's First Amendment interest in an off-duty statement that he was employed by the sheriff's office and also was a recruiter for the Ku Klux Klan was outweighed by the sheriff's interest in esprit de corps and credibility in the community the sheriff policed. More important, we relied, in large part, on public perceptions of the employee's constitutionally protected act.

In *McMullen*, both public perception and the anticipated effect that the employee's constitutionally protected activity would have on cohesion within the office were crucial in tipping the scales in the sheriff's favor. Nothing indicates that the employee had engaged in a criminal act or that he had joined an organization (he had joined the Invisible Empire) that had engaged in any criminal act. Given that it was additionally undisputed that neither the employee's statements nor his protected expressive association hindered his ability to perform his clerical duties and that the specific clerk "performed his duties in exemplary fashion," the two factors—public perception and anticipated effect—seemed to be the only ones weighing on the sheriff's side of the scale. But that was enough.

This case is different from *McMullen* in some ways, but *McMullen* guides us about the significance of "public perception." In this case, the Attorney General was similarly entitled to consider any "deleterious effect on [his] ability to enforce the law of the community," and that "[u]nder our system of Government, that duty [law enforcement] can be performed only with the consent of the vast majority.... Efficient law enforcement requires mutual respect, trust and support."

The Attorney General was also entitled to conclude that the public may think that employment of a Staff Attorney who openly purports to be part of a same-sex "marriage" is, at best, inconsistent with the other positions taken or likely to be taken by the Attorney General as the state's chief legal officer. The Attorney General has a right to take steps to protect the public from confusion about his stand and the Law Department's stand on controversial matters, such as same-sex marriage.

Public perception is important; but, at the same time, it is not knowable precisely. That the public (which we know is rarely monolithic) would not draw the Attorney General's anticipated inferences from Shahar's "marriage" or, at least, would not attribute such perceptions to the

Department or the Attorney General is a possibility. But assessing what the public perceives about the Attorney General and the Law Department is a judgment for the Attorney General to make in the day-to-day course of filling his proper role as the elected head of the Department, not for the federal judiciary to make with hindsight or from a safe distance away from the distress and disturbance that might result if the decision was mistaken. We must defer to Georgia's Attorney General's judgment about what Georgians might perceive unless his judgment is definitely outside of the broad range of reasonable views.

\* \* \*

Shahar says that by taking into account these concerns about public reaction, the Attorney General impermissibly discriminated against homosexuals; and she refers us to the Supreme Court's recent decision in Romer v. Evans, 116 S.Ct. 1620 (1996). In *Romer,* the Supreme Court struck down an amendment to a state constitution as irrational because the amendment's sole purpose was to disadvantage a particular class of people and because the government engaged in "classification of persons undertaken for its own sake, something the Equal Protection Clause does not permit."

*Romer* is about people's condition; this case is about a person's conduct. And, *Romer* is no employment case. Considering (in deciding to revoke a job offer) public reaction to a future Staff Attorney's conduct in taking part in a same-sex "wedding" and subsequent "marriage" is not the same kind of decision as an across-the-board denial of legal protection to a group because of their condition, that is, sexual orientation or preference.

This case is about the powers of government as an employer, powers which are far broader than government's powers as sovereign. In addition, the employment in this case is of a special kind: employment involving access to the employer's confidences, acting as the employer's spokesperson, and helping to make policy. This kind of employment is one in which the employer's interest has been given especially great weight in the past. Furthermore, the employment in this case is employment with responsibilities directly impacting on the enforcement of a state's laws: a kind of employment in which appearances and public perceptions and public confidence count a lot.

Particularly considering this Attorney General's many years of experience and Georgia's recent legal history, we cannot say that he was unreasonable to think that Shahar's acts were likely to cause the public to be confused and to question the Law Department's credibility; to interfere with the Law Department's ability to handle certain controversial matters, including enforcing the law against homosexual sodomy; and to endanger working relationships inside the Department. We also cannot say that the Attorney General was unreasonable to lose confidence in Shahar's ability to make good judgments as a lawyer for the Law Department.

\* \* \*

AFFIRMED.

■ BARKETT, CIRCUIT JUDGE, dissenting:

* * *

While overemphasizing the Attorney General's concerns in the Pickering balance, the majority also discounts Shahar's interests. The majority never expressly identifies Shahar's claims that she has kept her relationship with her partner a largely private and decidedly low-key matter, and that she has not engaged in any conduct which is at odds with Georgia law. Given the fact that it is not illegal in Georgia for two women to own a house in common, purchase insurance together or even exchange rings, it is difficult to understand how the fact that someone might discover these things could possibly affect the ability of the Attorney General to do his job effectively; the Attorney General is simply not charged with ensuring that his employees refrain from obtaining the blessing of their religious leaders prior to co-habitating in Georgia (which is essentially all Shahar has done).

Finally, I believe that the Attorney General has an evidentiary burden to offer credible predictions of harm or disruption based on more than mere speculation. The Attorney General's "worry about his office being involved in litigation in which Shahar's special personal interest might appear to be in conflict with the State's position" is simply not a reasonable basis upon which to expect disruption. First, the record contains no evidence that homosexual issues in general constitute a "special personal interest" for Shahar. Indeed, Shahar was intended for an assignment involving the review of death penalty cases. Moreover, even if Shahar has a "special personal interest" in homosexual rights, such an interest tells us nothing about its disruptiveness to her work environment. Surely the Attorney General's office has lawyers who have a "special interest" in any number of topics: abortion, school desegregation, affirmative-action or rights for the disabled, for instance. When those issues arise and the Attorney General is forced to take a view, some attorneys may personally disagree with that view and may even ask not to work on the matter, but that does not establish that those views have been disruptive to the office as a whole. Absent hard evidence, it is difficult to imagine a court upholding, for example, an Attorney General's assertion that he fired a black attorney because he believed (assumed?) that attorney's "special interest" in desegregated schools would prove disruptive to the office.

For these reasons, I respectfully dissent.

NOTES AND QUESTIONS

**1.** In *Shahar,* both the majority and dissenting opinions refer to the Supreme Court's decision in Pickering v. Board of Education, 391 U.S. 563 (1968). In *Pickering,* the Supreme Court said that the determination whether a public employer has properly discharged an employee for engaging in speech requires "a balance between the interests of the [employee], as a citizen, in commenting upon matters of public concern and the interest of the State, as an employer, in promoting the efficiency of the public services it performs through its employees." Id. at 568. For a further discussion, see Rankin v. McPherson, infra p. 613.

In *Shahar,* the same principle is applied to freedom of association under the First Amendment. Has the court appropriately allocated the burden of proof? Has it correctly identified and balanced the interests?

**2.** After the court's en banc decision, the plaintiff submitted a petition for rehearing. She submitted two newspaper articles reporting that former Attorney General Michael J. Bowers had admitted having an adulterous affair in the past with a woman employed in the Department of Law. In addition to seeking a rehearing, she also requested that this information be added to the record, asserting that it was relevant to the issue of whether his asserted fear of adverse public reaction to perceived sexual misconduct by the Georgia Department of Law was a bona fide reason. A majority of the en banc panel voted to deny the petition, over the dissent of three judges. Shahar v. Bowers, 120 F.3d 211 (10th Cir.1997).

**3.** *Shahar* involved government employment and therefore constitutional protections were applicable. For similar holdings, see United States Information Agency v. Krc, 989 F.2d 1211 (D.C.Cir.1993), cert. denied, 510 U.S. 1109 (1994); Doe v. Gates, 981 F.2d 1316 (D.C.Cir.1993), cert. denied 510 U.S. 928 (1993). In the private sector, however, individuals do not have such protections. The term "sex" in Title VII has been held not to include sexual orientation and therefore Title VII may not be used by individuals claiming discrimination based on sexual orientation. DeSantis v. Pacific Telephone & Telegraph Co., 608 F.2d 327 (9th Cir.1979). Similarly, common law theories, such as invasion of privacy, breach of contract, and wrongful discharge, are unlikely to afford relief against discrimination in private employment. See, e.g., Madsen v. Erwin, 481 N.E.2d 1160 (Mass. 1985).

**4.** Although not used in *Shahar,* a frequent argument used by employers in sexual orientation cases is a concern about possible blackmail. For example, in Padula v. Webster, 822 F.2d 97 (D.C.Cir.1987), the FBI successfully argued that the refusal to hire a lesbian woman was justified by the concern that the employee, who would have access to classified information, might be subject to blackmail. Employees who are not openly gay are subject to the blackmail argument; those who are openly gay, such as Shahar, are assertedly an embarrassment to the agency.

**5.** Ten states (Cal., Conn., Haw., Mass., Minn., N.H., N.J., R.I., Vt., and Wis.), the District of Columbia, and at least 50 cities have enacted laws prohibiting discrimination in private employment on the basis of sexual orientation. In Underwood v. Archer Management Services, Inc., 857 F.Supp. 96 (D.D.C.1994), the court held that the District of Columbia's law prohibiting discrimination based on sexual orientation did not extend to transsexuals, although a discharge based on the plaintiff's masculine appearance stated a claim for discrimination based on the D.C. statute prohibiting discrimination based on personal appearance, see infra p. 562, note 8.

**6.** In Romer v. Evans, 517 U.S. 620 (1996), the Supreme Court, 6–3, held that Colorado's "Amendment 2" was unconstitutional. The amendment invalidated all existing and *future* state and local legislative, executive, or judicial action in Colorado, including those dealing with employment, that protect homosexuals from discrimination. In holding that Amendment 2 violated Equal Protection, Justice Kennedy wrote that Amendment 2 "seems inexplicable by anything but animus toward the class it affects."

# PART III

# TERMS AND CONDITIONS OF EMPLOYMENT

# CHAPTER 5

# WAGES AND HOURS

## A. STATE AND FEDERAL WAGE AND HOUR REGULATION

Direct government regulation of wages, hours, and other working conditions has existed in America since colonial times; in 1630, the Massachusetts General Court placed a wage cap of two shillings a day on the work of carpenters, bricklayers, thatchers, and other craftsmen, and under threat of a heavy fine, forbade them to charge, or anyone to pay, more. The shortage of skilled workers in the colonies had resulted in high wages, with colonial craftsmen earning up to 100 percent above what their peers in England received for the same work. Even common laborers typically earned a wage premium of 30 percent over contemporary English wages. Concern over protective working conditions surfaced as early as the eighteenth century, when Philadelphia carpenters advocating a ten-hour day engaged in a work stoppage. Regulating working hours was also a way of limiting workers' exposure to hazardous conditions early associated with certain industries and of protecting women and children from overwork. Government interference with the private right of contract, however, was subject to challenge and, in many cases, judicial hostility, despite the progressive ends usually sought by such legislation.

## Lochner v. New York

198 U.S. 45 (1905).

■ MR. JUSTICE PECKHAM delivered the opinion of the court:

The indictment, it will be seen, charges that the plaintiff in error violated the 110th section of article 8, chapter 415, of the Laws of 1897, known as the labor law of the state of New York, in that he wrongfully and unlawfully required and permitted an employee working for him to work more than sixty hours in one week. * * * The mandate of the statute, that "no employee shall be required or permitted to work," is the substantial equivalent of an enactment that "no employee shall contract or agree to work," more than ten hours per day; and, as there is no provision for special emergencies, the statute is mandatory in all cases. It is not an act merely fixing the number of hours which shall constitute a legal day's work, but an absolute prohibition upon the employer permitting, under any circumstances, more than ten hours' work to be done in his establishment. The employee may desire to earn the extra money which would arise from his working more than the prescribed time, but this statute forbids the employer from permitting the employee to earn it.

The statute necessarily interferes with the right of contract between the employer and employees, concerning the number of hours in which the latter may labor in the bakery of the employer. The general right to make a contract in relation to his business is part of the liberty of the individual protected by the 14th Amendment of the Federal Constitution. Under that provision no state can deprive any person of life, liberty, or property without due process of law. The right to purchase or to sell labor is part of the liberty protected by this amendment, unless there are circumstances which exclude the right. There are, however, certain powers, existing in the sovereignty of each state in the Union, somewhat vaguely termed police powers, the exact description and limitation of which have not been attempted by the courts. Those powers, broadly stated, and without, at present, any attempt at a more specific limitation, relate to the safety, health, morals, and general welfare of the public. Both property and liberty are held on such reasonable conditions as may be imposed by the governing power of the state in the exercise of those powers, and with such conditions the 14th Amendment was not designed to interfere.

The state, therefore, has power to prevent the individual from making certain kinds of contracts, and in regard to them the Federal Constitution offers no protection. If the contract be one which the state, in the legitimate exercise of its police power, has the right to prohibit, it is not prevented from prohibiting it by the 14th Amendment.

\* \* \*

It must, of course, be conceded that there is a limit to the valid exercise of the police power by the state. There is no dispute concerning this general proposition. \* \* \* In every case that comes before this court, therefore, where legislation of this character is concerned, and where the protection of the Federal Constitution is sought, the question necessarily arises: Is this a fair, reasonable, and appropriate exercise of the police power of the state, or is it an unreasonable, unnecessary, and arbitrary interference with the right of the individual to his personal liberty, or to enter into those contracts in relation to labor which may seem to him appropriate or necessary for the support of himself and his family? Of course the liberty of contract relating to labor includes both parties to it. The one has as much right to purchase as the other to sell labor.

\* \* \*

The question whether this act is valid as a labor law, pure and simple, may be dismissed in a few words. There is no reasonable ground for interfering with the liberty of person or the right of free contract, by determining the hours of labor, in the occupation of a baker. There is no contention that bakers as a class are not equal in intelligence and capacity to men in other trades or manual occupations, or that they are not able to assert their rights and care for themselves without the protecting arm of the state, interfering with their independence of judgment and of action. They are in no sense wards of the state. Viewed in the light of a purely labor law, with no reference whatever to the question of health, we think that a law like the one before us involves neither the safety, the morals, nor the welfare, of the public, and that the interest of the public is not in the slightest degree affected by such an act. The law must be upheld, if at all, as a law pertaining to the health of the individual engaged in the occupation of a baker. It does not affect any other portion of the public than those who are engaged in that occupation. Clean and wholesome bread does not depend upon whether the baker works but ten hours per day or only sixty hours a week.

* * *

We think the limit of the police power has been reached and passed in this case. There is, in our judgment, no reasonable foundation for holding this to be necessary or appropriate as a health law to safeguard the public health, or the health of the individuals who are following the trade of a baker. * * * It might be safely affirmed that almost all occupations more or less affect the health. There must be more than the mere fact of the possible existence of some small amount of unhealthiness to warrant legislative interference with liberty. It is unfortunately true that labor, even in any department, may possibly carry with it the seeds of unhealthiness. But are we all, on that account, at the mercy of legislative majorities? A printer, a tinsmith, a locksmith, a carpenter, a cabinetmaker, a dry goods clerk, a bank's, a lawyer's, or a physician's clerk, or a clerk in almost any kind of business, would all come under the power of the legislature, on this assumption. No trade, no occupation, no mode of earning one's living, could escape this all-pervading power, and the acts of the legislature in limiting the hours of labor in all employments would be valid, although such limitation might seriously cripple the ability of the laborer to support himself and his family. In our large cities there are many buildings into which the sun penetrates for but a short time in each day, and these buildings are occupied by people carrying on the business of bankers, brokers, lawyers, real estate, and many other kinds of business, aided by many clerks, messengers, and other employees. Upon the assumption of the validity of this act under review, it is not possible to say that an act, prohibiting lawyers' or bank clerks, or others, from contracting to labor for their employers more than eight hours a day would be invalid. It might be said that it is unhealthy to work more than that number of hours in an apartment lighted by artificial light during the working hours of the day; that the occupation of the bank clerk, the lawyer's clerk, the real-estate clerk, or the broker's clerk, in such offices is therefore unhealthy, and the legislature, in its paternal wisdom, must, therefore, have the right to legislate on the subject of, and to limit, the hours for such labor; and, if it exercises that power, and its validity be questioned, it is sufficient to say, it has reference to the public health; it has reference to the health of the employees condemned to labor day after day in buildings where the sun never shines; it is a health law, and therefore it is valid, and cannot be questioned by the courts.

* * *

It is manifest to us that the limitation of the hours of labor as provided for in this section of the statute under which the indictment was found, and the plaintiff in error convicted, has no such direct relation to, and no such substantial effect upon, the health of the employee, as to justify us in regarding the section as really a health law. It seems to us that the real object and purpose were simply to regulate the hours of labor between the master and his employees (all being men, sui juris), in a private business, not dangerous in any degree to morals, or in any real and substantial degree to the health of the employees. Under such circumstances the freedom of master and employee to contract with each other in relation to their employment, and in defining the same, cannot be prohibited or interfered with, without violating the Federal Constitution.

Reversed.

■ Mr. Justice Harlan (with whom Mr. Justice White and Mr. Justice Day concurred) dissenting:

\* \* \*

It is plain that this statute was enacted in order to protect the physical well-being of those who work in bakery and confectionery establishments. It may be that the statute had its origin, in part, in the belief that employers and employees in such establishments were not upon an equal footing, and that the necessities of the latter often compelled them to submit to such exactions as unduly taxed their strength. Be this as it may, the statute must be taken as expressing the belief of the people of New York that, as a general rule, and in the case of the average man, labor in excess of sixty hours during a week in such establishments may endanger the health of those who thus labor. \* \* \* I find it impossible, in view of common experience, to say that there is here no real or substantial relation between the means employed by the state and the end sought to be accomplished by its legislation. \* \* \*

Professor Hirt in his treatise on the "Diseases of the Workers" has said: "The labor of the bakers is among the hardest and most laborious imaginable, because it has to be performed under conditions injurious to the health of those engaged in it. It is hard, very hard, work, not only because it requires a great deal of physical exertion in an overheated workshop and during unreasonably long hours, but more so because of the erratic demands of the public, compelling the baker to perform the greater part of his work at night, thus depriving him of an opportunity to enjoy the necessary rest and sleep,—a fact which is highly injurious to his health." Another writer says: "The constant inhaling of flour dust causes inflammation of the lungs and of the bronchial tubes. The eyes also suffer through this dust, which is responsible for the many cases of running eyes among the bakers. The long hours of toil to which all bakers are subjected produce rheumatism, cramps, and swollen legs. The intense heat in the workshops induces the workers to resort to cooling drinks, which, together with their habit of exposing the greater part of their bodies to the change in the atmosphere, is another source of a number of diseases of various organs.   Nearly all bakers are pale-faced and of more delicate health than the workers of other crafts, which is chiefly due to their hard work and their irregular and unnatural mode of living, whereby the power of resistance against disease is greatly diminished.   The average age of a baker is below that of other workman; they seldom live over their fiftieth year, most of them dying between the ages of forty and fifty.   During periods of epidemic diseases the bakers are generally the first to succumb to the disease, and the number swept away during such periods far exceeds the number of other crafts in comparison to the men employed in the respective industries.   When, in 1720, the plague visited the city of Marseilles, France, every baker in the city succumbed to the epidemic, which caused considerable excitement in the neighboring cities and resulted in measures for the sanitary protection of the bakers.''

* * *

We judicially know that the question of the number of hours during which a workman should continuously labor has been, for a long period, and is yet, a subject of serious consideration among civilized peoples, and by those having special knowledge of the laws of health.   Suppose the statute prohibited labor in bakery and confectionery establishments in excess of eighteen hours each day.   No one, I take it, could dispute the power of the state to enact such a statute.   * * *

* * * We cannot say that the state has acted without reason, nor ought we to proceed upon the theory that its action is a mere sham.   Our duty, I submit, is to sustain the statute as not being in conflict with the Federal Constitution, for the reason—and such is an all-sufficient reason—it is not shown to be plainly and palpably inconsistent with that instrument.   Let the state alone in the management of its purely domestic affairs, so long as it does not appear beyond all question that it has violated the Federal Constitution.   This view necessarily results from the principle that the health and safety of the people of a state are primarily for the state to guard and protect.

## NOTES AND QUESTIONS

**1.**   The majority in *Lochner* recognized that there were circumstances under which the state could legitimately regulate private contracts.   Can you think of any employment setting in which the *Lochner* majority would have upheld such legislation?   Suppose the state had tried to limit the number of hours worked by underground miners or steelworkers?   Hospital workers?   Airline pilots?   Why?   See Holden v. Hardy, 169 U.S. 366 (1898).

**2.**   If, as Justice Harlan pointed out, the Court would not have overturned a statute prohibiting an 18–hour day, why did it overturn the New York statute?   What about a 16–hour day?   14?   12?

**3.**   Nominally, *Lochner* is a case about maximum working hours in the baking industry.   It has also been characterized as the paradigm constitutional law case, for its holding on the permissible reach of state action, for the extent of judicial activism engaged in by the majority in striking down the New York statute, and for its unspoken, but unquestioning, approval of the existing distribution of wealth and entitlements. For a discussion of the larger constitutional issues, see, for example, Cass R. Sunstein, Lochner's Legacy, 87 Colum.L.Rev. 873 (1987).

———

Until the Depression, the state legislatures were much more successful than the federal government in regulating working conditions, largely because of constitutional problems similar to those posed by *Lochner*. As *Lochner* illustrates, the rationale most frequently cited for government interference with the employment relationship was public health. If state regulation was an impermissible infringement on freedom of contract, federal regulation was seen as even worse. The widespread unemployment of the 1930s, however, cast a new perspective on wage and hour laws in which minimum wage regulation was perceived as necessary to guarantee "the minimum standard of living necessary for health, efficiency, and general well-being of workers," and hour regulation as an important way to spread a scarce commodity—employment—among distressed American workers. After several unsuccessful attempts to establish a comprehensive legislative scheme, Congress finally passed the Fair Labor Standards Act (FLSA) in 1938. In passing the FLSA, however, Congress did not preempt the states' ability to regulate employment as well, and to this day state law plays an important role in protecting workers' rights. For example, state minimum wage laws may be higher than the federal standard and may apply to workers not covered by the federal law. In addition, it is state law that provides the means for employees who have not been paid their full wages, regardless of how much they earn, to recover unpaid compensation from their employers.

## 1. FEDERAL WAGE AND HOUR REGULATION: THE FAIR LABOR STANDARDS ACT

### a. LEGISLATIVE HISTORY

## Bernard Schwartz, Statutory History of the United States: Labor Organization

(Robert F. Koretz ed. 1970) 396–399.*

The Wagner Act, of course, was but one of a number of statutes passed during the New Deal focusing on labor conditions. But, in a sense, it was a culmination of years of employee attempts to establish minimum wages and maximum hours. As early as 1868, Congress had established a ten-hour day for employees on public works. Subsequently, the government's efforts to establish labor standards related largely to work conditions under public

* Reprinted by permission of Chelsea House Publishers.

contract and to interstate mail transportation, although Congress did attempt to control child labor through its commerce and taxing powers. The idea was for the government to set an example for private employers to follow. But the inability to establish minimum working conditions through Congress also reflected labor's national political weakness. Workingmen's organizations were often much more successful at the state level. Child labor laws, for example, were enacted in the six New England states by the mid-nineteenth century, and by 1900 some twenty-eight states had at least minimal protection for child workers. Today, there exists in every state a considerable body of law covering the employment of women and children, sanitation, and safety. Much of this sort of legislation, both state and federal, was challenged in the courts by employers and often declared unconstitutional. Thus, the Supreme Court upheld in 1898 a state statute fixing maximum hours for male miners (Holden v. Hardy, 169 U.S. 366), but subsequently decided in 1905 that it was unconstitutional for a state to limit work hours in bakeries (Lochner v. New York, 198 U.S. 45). The Court similarly struck down in 1923 state legislation fixing minimum wages in Adkins v. Children's Hospital, 261 U.S. 525. Federal regulation fared no better. An effort to control child labor was nullified by the Court in 1922 (Bailey v. Drexel Furniture Company, 259 U.S. 20). Further, the early efforts of the New Deal to regulate labor standards through the National Industrial Recovery Act [A.L.A. Schechter Poultry Corporation v. United States, 295 U.S. 495 (1935)] and the Bituminous Coal Conservation Act [Carter v. Carter Coal Company, 298 U.S. 238 (1936)] suffered the same fate. But in 1937, the Court sustained the constitutionality of the Wagner Act and upheld a state minimum wage law, in West Coast Hotel Company v. Parrish, 300 U.S. 379. Decisions such as these quite plainly forecast Court approval of federal legislation in the area of wages and hours. * * *

On May 24, 1937, President Roosevelt, whose Administration consistently urged wage and hour legislation as an anti-depression measure, sent Congress a special message: "To conserve our primary resources of manpower, Government must have some control over maximum hours, minimum wages, the evil of child labor, and the exploitation of unorganized labor." The President argued that Congress' power to act in these matters rested on the Constitution's commerce clause. On the same day, Senator Eugene Black (Dem., Tex.) and Representative Lawrence Connery (Dem., Mass.) introduced bills to implement the Presidential request. But more than a year of legislative activity passed before a law was enacted. * * *

The new statute created a Wage and Hour Division in the Department of Labor under the supervision of an administrator. The statute regulated wages, hours, and child labor. More specifically, it provided for a minimum hourly wage of twenty-five cents for the first year, and thirty cents for the second year. A minimum of forty cents was to become effective after seven years, and a wage between thirty and forty cents could be ordered during the first seven years. As to hours, it sought to spread employment by overtime penalties: for the first year maximum straight-time hours were forty-four; for the second year, forty-two; and thereafter forty. The child labor provisions, similar to those previously declared unconstitutional by the Supreme Court, prohibited the interstate shipment of goods produced in an establishment employing child labor.

Consistent with the constitutional philosophy exhibited in the Supreme Court's decisions to uphold the Wagner and Railway Labor Acts, the Court, in United States v. Darby, 312 U.S. 100 (1941), sustained the constitutionality of the act against attacks based upon the commerce clause and due process clause of the Fifth Amendment.

[Following several Supreme Court interpretations of the FLSA which extended substantial benefits to employees, employers lobbied for amendment of the Act; other proposals to amend the Act were designed to tidy up loose ends that had surfaced in the first decade of its existence.]

In the meantime, a number of proposals had been made for revision of the act. These culminated in what was called the "Fair Labor Standards Amendments of 1949." * * * It has been pointed out that "the Amendments of 1949 were a compromise between President Truman's desire for a broader law to cover all employees of employers engaged in covered business, raise standards, and restrict exemptions, and the aims of those who wished to narrow the coverage, broaden the exemptions, and tie the minimum wage to the cost-of-living index." In brief, the 1949 amendments narrowed the coverage of the statute, strengthened the child labor prohibitions, set forth in greater detail the overtime standards, revised certain exemptions, made certain administrative changes, and increased the minimum wage to seventy-five cents.

There have been a number of amendments since 1949, the most important of which have increased the minimum wage and broadened statutory coverage. Coverage was extended by the 1961 amendments through a new concept, the covering of specified business enterprises as well as the activities of individual employees; in 1966 the enterprise concept was utilized to further broaden coverage. In 1963 equal pay provisions were added to the act for the purpose of eliminating wage differentials based upon sex.

––––––––

b. BASIC PROVISIONS OF THE FAIR LABOR STANDARDS ACT

The basic scheme of the FLSA is quite simple: it establishes a minimum wage applicable to all employees of covered employers and it provides for mandatory overtime payment for covered employees who work more than 40 hours a week. The statutory scheme has remained practically unchanged since its original passage, except for updates to bring the minimum wage into parity with wage inflation. Currently, the Act covers approximately 85 percent of the nonsupervisory workforce, or about 69 million employees.

The Fair Labor Standards Act Amendments of 1989, the first substantive modifications to the Act in nine years, increased the minimum wage from $3.35 an hour to $3.80 an hour, effective April 1, 1990, with a further increase to $4.25 an hour effective April 1, 1991. In August 1996, Congress passed and President Clinton signed into law a minimum wage increase to $5.15 an hour effective September 1, 1997. In contrast, the national average hourly wage was $11.76 in 1996. The protection of the statute's minimum wage provisions has its greatest impact on wage rates for low-level, unskilled jobs; the national economic shift from manufacturing to services has resulted in larger numbers of such jobs.

The overtime provisions of the FLSA, which do not limit the number of hours employees may work but merely require overtime pay after a certain number of hours, have more general applicability than the wage provisions. The child labor provisions of the Act regulate employment of children. Generally, the statute prohibits employing children under the age of 12, with special exceptions for certain types of agricultural work and for actors and performers. The Department of Labor has also issued regulations that limit the kinds of work children over 12 may perform as well as the hours they may work.

One might assume that the relative stability of the law and the fairly low profile it commands indicate that there is currently no significant compliance problem with the Act. The Wage and Hour Division of the Department of Labor, the federal agency responsible for enforcing the FLSA, however, remains active in policing violations. In fiscal year 1988, the Wage and Hour Division of the Department of Labor conducted 75,656 compliance actions. In fiscal year 1988, the FLSA enforcement program indicated that $30 million was due 154,000 workers as a result of minimum wage violations, and $113 million was due 324,000 employees for overtime pay violations. Further, violators are not limited to sweat shops and day labor camps. In October 1982, the United States Postal Service entered into a settlement agreement with the Department of Labor under which it agreed to pay $400 million for overtime and premium pay violations committed during the period 1974–1978. Approximately 550,000 current and former employees were entitled to receive amounts up to $765 each to resolve their claims; the settlement was the largest ever achieved in an FLSA case.

Section 206(a) of the FLSA is the basic minimum wage provision. It provides:

> Every employer shall pay to each of his employees who in any workweek is engaged in commerce or in the production of goods for commerce, or is employed in an enterprise engaged in commerce or in the production of goods for commerce, wages at the following rates: (1) * * * not less than $3.35 an hour after December 31, 1980, [increased to $3.80 an hour April 1, 1990] except as otherwise provided in this section. * * *

The balance of § 206 illustrates the particularized nature of some sections of the statute, enumerating special provisions for domestic workers, seamen on American vessels, and other workers. Section 206(d) prohibits sex discrimination in wages for male and female employees performing equal work (See Part B., infra.).

Section 6 of the 1989 Amendments also introduced a temporary subminimum "training wage" of "not less than $3.35 an hour or 85 percent of the [basic minimum wage]" for employees under the age of 20 who are engaged in on-the-job training, for a period of 90 days, renewable for another 90 days.   Employers may not displace regular employees in order to create training wage positions, and no more than one-quarter of all hours paid in any month may be paid at the training wage rate.   The training wage provision automatically expires April 1, 1993.

Section 207(a)(1) concerns maximum hours:

> Except as otherwise provided in this section, no employer shall employ any of his employees who in any workweek is engaged in commerce or in the production of goods for commerce, or is employed in an enterprise engaged in commerce or in the production of goods for commerce, for a workweek longer than forty hours unless such employee receives compensation for his employment in excess of the hours above specified at a rate not less than one and one-half times the regular rate at which he is employed.

The rest of § 207 addresses special conditions for hours worked pursuant to a collective bargaining agreement, piece workers, hospital workers, police and firefighters, and transit workers, many of whose traditional work days or work weeks do not fit the typical "eight hours a day/40 hours a week" configuration.   The 1989 amendments added § 207(q), a maximum hour exemption for up to ten hours in any workweek for remedial education offered by the employer to employees who lack a high school diploma or education at the eighth-grade level.

For further information about the minimum wage, see the Department of Labor's internet web site and "Minimum Wage" hot button at www.dol.gov.

### c.  COVERAGE

#### (i) Who Is a Covered Employer?

Coverage of the Act is extensive.   A business is covered if it has only two employees and meets the commerce test.   Goods or services produced by the business must cross state lines in order for an employer to be engaged in "commerce" within the meaning of the statute, but this requirement has been broadly construed (e.g., a laundry facility using soap that has been shipped across state lines is a covered employer).   (A business that does not meet the interstate "commerce" test for coverage under the FLSA may, however, be regulated by similar state legislation.)

Section 203, the definitions section of the Act, defines an enterprise so as to exempt from the Act's coverage certain types of small businesses according to their gross sales.   The 1989 Amendments streamlined the § 203(s) definition of an "enterprise engaged in commerce or in the production of goods for commerce," by replacing a diversity of industry-specific gross annual sales limits with a more uniform coverage floor of $500,000 annual gross volume of sales made or business done.  Hospitals, schools, and public agencies are covered regardless of their financial size; any business that employs only members of the immediate family of the owner are exempted regardless of size.  Under § 203(r), the gross sales of separate businesses having unified operations or under common control may be aggregated to bring a business within the Act's coverage.

To determine whether companies are an enterprise, courts apply a three-part test.  The company must (1) perform related activities (2) under unified operations or common control (3) for a common business purpose.  See Martin v. Deiriggi, 985 F.2d 129, 133 (4th Cir.1992).

NOTES AND QUESTIONS

**1.**   The proportionality of the minimum wage to the national average has not been constant.  When originally enacted, the minimum wage was set at about half the national average wage.  When the minimum wage was amended in 1989, it dropped to about one-third the national average wage.  After legislation in 1996, the minimum wage increased to $5.15—almost half the national average wage of $11.76.  Prior to the legislation in 1996, the minimum wage adjusted for inflation was approaching a 40 year low.  How should the appropriate level of the minimum wage be determined?  How frequently should Congress consider changes to the minimum wage, and based on what factors?

**2.**   Consider the effect of the statute's coverage scheme.  A large real estate agency might not be covered (no interstate goods or services), while the corner newsstand probably is.  Under what circumstances, if any, would the FLSA cover an organic truck farm?  A building maintenance service?  A nonprofit charitable foundation?

**3.**   In 1976, the Supreme Court held that the application of the provisions of the FLSA to state and local governments constituted a violation of the tenth amendment.  National League of Cities v. Usery, 426 U.S. 833 (1976).  Nine years later, in Garcia v. San Antonio Metropolitan Transit Authority, 469 U.S. 528 (1985), the Court overruled *National League of Cities* and held, five-to-four that nothing in the minimum wage and overtime provisions of the Act violated any constitutional provision.  Congress promptly passed the Fair Labor Standards Amendments of 1985, permitting state and local government employers to substitute compensatory time off for the mandatory overtime provisions of the FLSA, eliminating volunteers and state and local legislative employees from coverage, and minimizing employers' liability for unpaid wages prior to April 15, 1986 (the effective date of the Amendments).  "Comp time" in lieu of overtime must accrue at the time-and-a-half rate for overtime set forth in the Act, however.  The 1985 Amendments were upheld in Rhinebarger v. Orr, 839 F.2d 387 (7th Cir.1988), cert. denied, 488 U.S. 824 (1988).

**4.**   The Ventana Foundation is a nonprofit religious organization whose primary purposes are to "establish, conduct and maintain an Evangelistic

Church." Ventana does not seek contributions from the public in order to conduct its ministry; instead, it relies on the income from a number of commercial activities staffed by church volunteers or "associates," most of whom were drug addicts, derelicts, or criminals before they were rehabilitated by the Foundation. Ventana's businesses include service stations, retail clothing and grocery outlets, hog farms, construction companies, a motel, and a candy company. The volunteers are not paid by Ventana. They do receive room and board, clothing, transportation, and medical benefits. The Secretary of Labor sued Ventana for violations of the wage and overtime provisions of the FLSA. At trial, the "associates" testified that they worked voluntarily for religious and evangelical purposes. Ventana claimed that it was not an "enterprise" within the meaning of the Act, that its volunteers were not employees, and that extension of the FLSA to its operations would be a violation of the free exercise and establishment clauses of the first amendment. How should the court rule? See Tony & Susan Alamo Foundation v. Secretary of Labor, 471 U.S. 290 (1985) (no unconstitutional burden on free exercise by individuals to require employer to keep records and pay cash wages to employees).

**5.** The judiciary has liberally interpreted the "enterprise" definition of the FLSA in favor of coverage, particularly where "separate" businesses which individually are too small to be covered by the Act are owned and operated by the same individual or parent corporation. In Donovan v. Grim Hotel Co., 747 F.2d 966 (5th Cir.1984), cert. denied, 471 U.S. 1124 (1985), the court found that five separate hotel corporations were a single "enterprise" where they were all virtually controlled by a single individual, members of his family owned the shares that he did not, the corporations shared the same officers, and a related company provided bookkeeping and financial services for the group.

### (ii) Who Is a Covered Employee?

Even though an enterprise may be covered by the FLSA, not all of its employees may be. The definition of "employee" in § 203(e)(1) is broad, but § 213 spells out a patchwork of exemptions. Excluded from the Act's coverage are such diverse types of employees as summer camp counselors (seasonal recreational establishments), professional crabbers (employees engaged in fishing), the Saturday night babysitter (casual babysitters and companions to the elderly and infirm), and journalists on local newspapers with circulation less than 4,000. The Act also exempts from its overtime provisions certain occupations whose hours do not traditionally fit a standard eight-hour working day, such as taxi drivers, employees at movie theatres, radio or television news announcers, local agricultural workers, and a variety of employees engaged in transportation. Other types of employees are partially exempted from the overtime pay provisions: for instance, certain retail employees paid on a commission basis, private hospital and nursing home employees, and law enforcement and firefighting personnel. Independent contractors are also exempt from coverage, because they are not considered employees.

Prisoners may be "employees" under the FLSA, depending on their employers. Prisoners working under prison programs are not subject to the FLSA. McMaster v. State of Minn., 30 F.3d 976 (8th Cir.1994), cert. denied, 513 U.S. 1157 (1995). However, some work performed by private employers may fall within the scope of FLSA. See Henthorn v. Department of Navy, 29 F.3d 682 (D.C.Cir.1994) (voluntary work for a private employer is subject to FLSA unless wages are paid by prison). Thus prisoners are not entirely excluded from the FLSA. Vanskike v. Peters, 974 F.2d 806 (7th Cir.1992), cert. denied, 507 U.S. 928 (1993).

The single most significant exemption from the statute's general coverage, however, is for executive, administrative and professional employees. In order to be exempt, such employees must be paid on a salary basis. But who is an executive? How do you distinguish an administrative employee from a clerical employee? What are the hallmarks of a professional?

## Dalheim v. KDFW–TV

918 F.2d 1220 (5th Cir.1990).

■ ALVIN B. RUBIN, CIRCUIT JUDGE:

\* \* \*

Plaintiffs are nineteen present and former general-assignment reporters, producers, directors, and assignment editors employed in the news and programming departments of television station KDFW–TV (KDFW). As its call letters imply, KDFW serves the Dallas–Fort Worth area which, with approximately 3.5 million viewers, is the eighth largest television market in the nation. The news and programming departments are responsible for producing KDFW's local news broadcasts and its public affairs programming.

KDFW's general-assignment reporters usually receive a new coverage assignment each day. The assignment manager or an assignment editor tells the reporter the story to be covered, what she is expected to "shoot," and the intended angle or focus of the story. After the reporter interviews the persons that she or another KDFW employee has arranged to interview, she obtains pertinent video footage, and then writes and records the text of the story, subject to review by the producer. Some reporters help assemble the video and text narration; others rely on a video editor to put the final package together. General-assignment reporters are only infrequently assigned to do a series of reports focusing on a single topic or related topics. Successful reporters usually have a pleasant physical appearance and a strong and appealing voice, and are able to present themselves as credible and knowledgeable.

Producers are responsible for determining the content of the ten-to-twelve minute news portion of KDFW's thirty-minute newscast. They participate in meetings to decide which stories and story angles will be covered; they also decide the amount of time to be given a particular story, the sequence in which stories will be aired, and when to take commercial breaks. Producers have the authority to revise reporters' stories. All of the producers' actions are subject to approval by the executive producer.

Directors review the script for the newscast in order to prepare technical instructions for "calling" the show. The director decides which camera to use and on which machine to run videotaped segments or preproduction graphics. During the broadcast, the director cues the various technical personnel, telling them precisely when to perform their assigned tasks. The overall appearance of KDFW's newscasts, however, is prescribed by station management. The director therefore has no discretion concerning lighting, camera-shot blocking, closing-shot style, or the sequence of opening and closing graphics. KDFW's directors also direct some public affairs programming, which have no prescribed format but involve only simple camera work and a basic set. In addition, KDFW's directors screen commercials to be aired by the station to ensure that they meet the standards set by KDFW's parent, Times Mirror Corporation.

Assignment editors are primarily responsible for pairing reporters with both photographers and videotape editors. They also monitor the wire services, police and fire department scanners, newspapers, and press releases for story ideas that conform to KDFW's general guidelines. Assignment editors have no authority to decide the stories to be covered, but they may reassign reporters if they learn of a story requiring immediate action. Assignment editors operate under the supervision of the assignment manager.

Plaintiffs brought this suit in May, 1985, alleging that KDFW's reporters, producers, directors, and assignment editors were required to work more than forty hours per week without overtime pay, in willful violation of § 7 of the FLSA, and seeking to recover back wages from May, 1982 to the present. After an eight-day bench trial, the district court concluded that none of the plaintiffs was exempt from § 7 as a bona fide executive, administrative, or professional employee under § 13(a)(1) and that KDFW had violated the FLSA by failing to pay overtime. The court further concluded, however, that KDFW's violation was not willful, and that KDFW therefore was not liable for damages outside the FLSA's two-year statute of limitations for nonwillful violations.

Section 7 of the FLSA requires employers to pay overtime to employees who work more than forty hours per week. Section 13(a)(1) exempts from the maximum hour provision employees occupying "bona fide executive, administrative, or professional" positions. That same section empowers the Secretary of Labor to define by regulation the terms "executive," "administrative," and "professional." She has done so at 29 C.F.R. § 541.0 et seq., setting out "long" tests for employees earning more than $155 per week but less than $250 per week, which include specific criteria, and "short" tests, described in less detail, for employees earning more than $250 per week. In addition, the Secretary has issued interpretations of those regulations, which are codified at 29 C.F.R. § 541.100 et seq. The § 13(a)(1) exemptions are "construed narrowly against the employer seeking to assert them," and the employer bears the burden of proving that employees are exempt.

The short test for the executive exemption requires that an employee's "primary duty" consist of the "management of the enterprise" in which she is employed "or a customarily recognized subdivision thereof." In addition, the executive employee's work must include "the customary and regular direction of the work" of two or more employees. The regulations define an exempt administrative employee as one whose "primary duty" consists of "office or nonmanual work directly related to management policies or general business operations" that "includes work requiring the exercise of discretion and independent judgment." The exemption for creative professionals requires that the employee's "primary duty" consist of work that is "original and creative in character in a recognized field of artistic endeavor," the result of which depends "primarily on the invention, imagination, or talent of the employee."

KDFW challenges the holding of the district court on four distinct grounds, claiming that the district court (1) erroneously construed the term "primary duty" to mean duties occupying more than half of an employee's time; (2) erroneously concluded that reporters' work is not "original and creative" as those terms are used in the regulations; (3) misconstrued the requirement that administrative work be "directly related to management policies and general business operations," in that it (a) erroneously applied the concept of "production," as that term is used in the Secretary's interpretations, to the work of white-collar employees like producers, directors, and assignment editors, and (b) erroneously concluded that the work of producers, directors, and assignment editors should not be deemed "directly related" to business operations because they "carr[y] out major assignments in conducting the operations of the business," within the meaning of the interpretations; and (4) erroneously failed to "tack" exemptions for producers, directors, and assignment editors as provided for in the regulations.

\* \* \*

## IV

### A.   *KDFW's General–Assignment Reporters*

KDFW argues that its general-assignment reporters are exempt artistic professionals. Under the regulations, KDFW must prove that the reporter's "primary duty" consists of work that is "original and creative in character in a recognized field of artistic endeavor," the result of which depends "primarily on the invention, imagination, or talent of the employee."

The regulations and interpretations at issue here, §§ 541.3(a)(2) and 541.303(e) and (f), have not changed in any material respect since 1949, long before broadcast journalism evolved into its modern form. To apply the Secretary's interpretation literally to the plaintiffs would be to assume that those occupations exist today as they did forty years ago. No one disputes that the technological revolution that has swept this society into the so-called Information Age has rendered that assumption untenable. The question is what role, if any, § 541.303(e) and (f) may have in determining the exempt status of modern broadcast journalists.

KDFW argues that the district court gave the interpretation undue weight, thus blinding itself to the realities of modern broadcast journalism. Rather than focusing on the "essential nature" of reporters' duties, KDFW contends, the district court "pigeonholed" reporters according to standards that are decades out of date. Amicus National Association of Broadcasters (NAB) goes even further, contending that the Secretary's interpretation is based on "erroneous, outmoded assumptions about journalism and journalists," and that "[i]nsofar as the District Court took these 1940 assumptions about print journalists and applied them to the present-day duties of KDFW television reporters, [it] erred as a matter of law."

* * *

The Secretary's interpretations make it abundantly clear that § 541.3(a)(2) was intended to distinguish between those persons whose work is creative in nature from those who work in a medium capable of bearing creative expression, but whose duties are nevertheless functional in nature. The factual inquiry in this case was directed precisely at determining on which side of that line KDFW's reporters stand. The district court found that, at KDFW, the emphasis was on "good reporting, in the aggregate," and not on individual reporters with the "presence" to draw an audience. The district court found that the process by which reporters meld sound and pictures relies not upon the reporter's creativity, but upon her skill, diligence, and intelligence. More importantly, the district court found that "[r]eporters are told the story that the station intends they cover, what they are expected to shoot, and the intended angle or focus of the story."

In essence, the district court found that KDFW failed to prove that the work constituting its reporters' primary duty is original or creative in character. The district court recognized, and we think correctly, that general-assignment reporters may be exempt creative professionals, and that KDFW's reporters did, from time to time, do original and creative work. Nevertheless, at KDFW, the approach reporters take to their day-to-day work is in large part dictated by management, and the stories they daily produce are neither analytic nor interpretive nor original. In neither form nor substance does a reporter's work "depend[ ] primarily on [her] invention, imagination, or talent." Those inferences, while not compelled by the evidence, are certainly supported by it. Based on those inferences and the underlying historical facts, which we review only for clear error, we think the legal conclusion that reporters are nonexempt follows as a matter of course. We therefore conclude that the district court did not err in holding that KDFW's general-assignment reporters are not exempt professionals.

B.   *KDFW's News Producers*

KDFW argues that its news producers are exempt either as creative professionals, administrators, executives, or a combination thereof.   We address each argument in turn.

1.   *Producers as Creative Professionals.*—KDFW does not press this argument much, for good reason.   The district court found that KDFW failed to prove that the work producers do in rewriting reporters' copy and in formatting the newscast are products of their "invention, imagination, and talent."   Rather, producers perform their work within a well-defined framework of management policies and editorial convention.   To the extent that they exercise discretion, it is governed more by skill and experience than by originality and creativity.   Because the district court's findings are supported by the record, we find no error.

2.   *Producers as Administrators.*—The argument KDFW pursues most vigorously with respect to producers is that they are exempt administrative employees.   Section 541.2 of the regulations requires that an exempt administrator perform (1) office or nonmanual work (2) that is directly related to the employer's management policies or general business operations and (3) involves the exercise of discretion and independent judgment. The Secretary's interpretation, § 541.205(a), defines the "directly related" prong by distinguishing between what it calls "the administrative operations of a business" and "production."   Administrative operations include such duties as "advising the management, planning, negotiating, representing the company, purchasing, promoting sales, and business research and control."   Work may also be "directly related" if it is of "substantial importance" to the business operations of the enterprise in that it involves "major assignments in conducting the operations of the business, or * * * affects business operations to a substantial degree."   KDFW argues that the district court erred in finding that producers' work failed the "directly related" requirement because it is neither related to the administrative operations of KDFW, nor is it of "substantial importance" to the enterprise.   Whether an employee's work is or should be deemed "directly related" to business operations is an inference drawn from the historical facts;   we review such inferences for clear error.

\* \* \*

That is not the case with KDFW's news producers.   Their responsibilities begin and end with the ten-to-twelve minute portion of the newscast they are working on.   They are not responsible for setting business policy, planning the long- or short-term objectives of the news department, promoting the newscast, negotiating salary or benefits with other department personnel, or any of the other types of "administrative" tasks noted in § 541.205(b).   The district court determined, based on the facts before it, that "[t]he duties of a producer clearly relate to the production of a KDFW news department product and not to defendant's administrative operations."   That determination was not erroneous.

KDFW next asserts that the district court erred in holding that producers' work does not consist of carrying out "major assignments" of "substantial importance" to KDFW's business. Again, KDFW disputes the district court's factual conclusions and inferences, and again, its contention is without merit. KDFW was charged with proving that its producers are exempt employees. The only record evidence KDFW points to in support of its contention that producers' work is of "substantial importance," other than the evidence of what producers do, is that KDFW operates in the nation's eighth largest television market, and that local news is an important source of revenue for the station. The "importance" of producers' work we are left to infer is that, if a producer performs poorly, KDFW's bottom line might suffer.

As a matter of law, that is insufficient to establish the direct relationship required by § 541.2 by virtue of the "substantial importance" contemplated by § 541.205(c). The Secretary's interpretations specifically recognize that the fact that a worker's poor performance may have a significant profit-and-loss impact is not enough to make that worker an exempt administrator. "An employee's job can even be 'indispensable' and still not be of the necessary 'substantial importance' to meet the 'directly related' element." In assessing whether an employee's work is of substantial importance, it is necessary yet again to look to "the *nature* of the work, not its ultimate consequence." The nature of producers' work, the district court found, is the application of "techniques, procedures, repetitious experience, and specific standards" to the formatting of a newscast. KDFW was obliged to demonstrate how work of that nature is so important to KDFW that it should be deemed "directly related" to business operations. It did not do so. Indeed, the evidence shows that the work one would think of as being "substantially important"—such as setting news department policy and designing the uniform "look" of the newscast—is done by employees who seem clearly to be exempt administrators: the executive producer and the news director, for example. We therefore conclude that the district court did not err in holding that producers are not exempt administrators.

3. *Producers as Executives.—*

\* \* \*

To qualify for an executive exemption under the short test, an employee's primary duty must consist of the "management of the enterprise" in which she is employed "or a customarily recognized subdivision thereof." In addition, the employee must customarily and regularly direct the work of two or more employees. The district court found that management was not the producers' primary duty, and that producers do not customarily direct the work of two or more employees.

We agree with the district court. The evidence establishes that, while the producer plays an important role in coordinating and formatting a portion of the newscast, the other members of the ensemble—that is, the reporters, technicians, assignment editors, and so on—are actually supervised by other management personnel. Producers perform none of the executive duties contemplated by the regulations, such as training, supervising, disciplining, and evaluating employees. Indeed, this court previously upheld a determination by the National Labor Relations Board that neither producers nor directors nor assignment editors are "supervisors" within § 2(11) of the National Labor Relations Act. Producers, therefore, do not "manage," and are not exempt executives.

\* \* \*

### C. *KDFW's Directors and Assignment Editors*

For the same reasons it asserts with respect to its producers, KDFW claims that the district court erred in concluding that its directors and assignment editors are not exempt either as executives or administrators or a combination thereof. KDFW's arguments with respect to directors and assignment editors thus fail for the reasons set out above. First, the evidence wholly fails to establish that the work of either directors or assignment editors is "directly related" to management policies or business operations, as required by § 541.2. Second, the evidence does not demonstrate that either directors or assignment editors "manage" anything, as required by § 541.1. KDFW's directors are, as the district court found, highly skilled coordinators, but they are not managers. Assignment editors have no real authority, and participate in no decisions of consequence. Finally, because neither directors nor assignment editors do any exempt work, the district court did not err in failing to consider a combination exemption under § 541.600.

For the reasons stated above, the judgment of the district court is AFFIRMED.

### NOTES AND QUESTIONS

**1.** Sherwood v. Washington Post, 871 F.Supp. 1471 (D.D.C.1994), held that a *Post* reporter is not entitled to overtime pay because the work requires "inventions, imaginations, and talents." Thus, the reporter is an "artistic professional," exempt from FLSA protection since the Act does not apply to "any employee employed in a bona fide ... professional capacity." But see Nordquist v. McGraw–Hill Broadcasting Co., 38 Cal. Rptr.2d 221 (Ct.App.1995), holding that a television station's sports director/newscast anchor had a legal right to overtime pay because his responsibilities were not primarily intellectual or creative, but instead were mundane and routine. The artistic professional exemption has also been applied to book editors. See Shaw v. Prentice Hall, 977 F.Supp. 909 (S.D.Ind.1997) (giving exempted status to computer guide editors).

**2.** The Second Circuit decided that television newswriters and producers have no legal right to overtime pay because they are "artistic professionals." Overtime protection "may still apply to small-town reporters whose responsibilities don't differ much from those of [earlier] journalists, [but] it is anachronistic, even irrational, to continue to impose those guidelines on journalists in major news organizations." Freeman v. National Broadcasting Co., Inc., 80 F.3d 78 (2d Cir.1996).

**3.** Functionally, the bona fide executive, administrative, or professional employee exemption operates to deny those employees overtime payment under the Act, rather than minimum wages. Why should executives, administrators, or professionals be exempted from coverage of the Act?

**4.** Under the Department of Labor's regulations, 29 C.F.R. § 541.1, the "short test" for the bona fide executive or administrative employee exemption applies to anyone earning $250 per week or more. The "long test" is applied to anyone earning between $155 and $200 per week. In 1996, average hourly earnings for all non-agricultural workers were over $11.00 per hour. Is $250 a week too low to be an effective indicator of presumptive exempt status? The U.S. economy is increasingly based on provision of services rather than production of goods. What are the implications, if any, for revision of the "executive, administrative or professional" employee standard?

In O'Dell v. Alyeska Pipeline Service Co., 856 F.2d 1452 (9th Cir.1988), the Ninth Circuit held, quoting from the regulations and adding emphasis, that under the long test, an administrative employee would only qualify as exempt if his job required that he "*customarily and regularly* exercised discretion and independent judgment," while under the short test, the job would only have to "*include* . . . work requiring the exercise of discretion and independent judgment." In reviewing the exempt status of a field inspector for an oil pipeline, the Ninth Circuit reversed the district court's application of the long test and found that under the short test, the district court "could only have come to the ultimate conclusion that O'Dell exercised some discretion and independent judgment during the course of his job" and was therefore exempt. In his job, O'Dell had represented the company in contacts with state inspectors, offered assistance to contractors in interpreting codes, issued reports which included opinions as to safety and recommendations for action, and conferred with company clients and tried to persuade them to make changes. Determining whether an employee falls within the FLSA exemption for executive or administrative employees is not as simple as distinguishing between blue-collar and white-collar jobs. Consider that insurance claims investigators have been held non-exempt. Gusdonovich v. Business Information Co., 705 F.Supp. 262 (W.D.Pa.1985) (job concerned primarily with production of information and not exercise of judgment or discretion), as have "department managers" for a market (while some job duties were normally recognized as managerial in nature, actual examination of job duties led to holding that employees were nothing more than "working foremen").

**5.** Under the Department of Labor's regulations, 29 C.F.R. § 541.3, the "short test" for professional exemption applies to anyone whose primary duty is work which requires the consistent exercise of discretion and judgment and "knowledge of an advance type in a field of science or learning customarily acquired by a prolonged course of specialized intellectual instruction study, as distinguished from a general academic education and from an apprenticeship, and from training in the performance of routine, mental, manual, or physical processes ..." See Szarnych v. Theis–Gorski Funeral Home, 1997 WL 452681 (N.D.Ill.) (giving professional exemption status to an embalmer/funeral director).

**6.** The Office of Personnel Management established a rebuttable presumption that any federal employee classified in grade GS–11 or higher would be ineligible for overtime pay, as an executive, administrative or professional employee under § 213(a)(1) of the Act. Is this permissible under the Act? See American Federation of Government Employees v. OPM, 821 F.2d 761 (D.C.Cir.1987) (GS–11 requirement invalidated).

**7.** Courts use the "economic realities test" to determine an individual's status as an independent contractor or an employee. The "economic realities test" typically relied on by the courts derives from United States v. Silk, 331 U.S. 704 (1947), in which the Supreme Court set forth the factors to be considered in determining employee status: (1) the degree of control exercised by the alleged employer over the workers, (2) the workers' opportunity for profit or loss and their investment in the business, (3) the degree of skill and independent initiative required to perform the work, (4) the performance or duration of the working relationship, and (5) the extent to which the work is an integral part of the employer's business. The factors are applied in a "totality of the circumstances" test. Using the Silk factors, what would be the employee status in the following case? Mr. W owns 100 fireworks stands located and operated across south Texas. Texas law permits the sale of fireworks only during a 13–day season ending January 1 and during an 11–day season ending July 4 each year. Mr. W. Fireworks operates an office and warehouse in Somerset, Texas, from which it buys and imports from Asia the fireworks it sells, recruits operators, acquires land for fireworks stands, constructs the stands and paints them in uniform colors with a standard Mr. W logo, employs 5 or 6 routemen to supply the stands with fireworks, and advertises. Mr. W procures licenses and insurance for all the stands; it also pays for electrical service at all the stands, and it pays a commission to the operators of the stands. The operators are responsible for trash collection, pay for renting portable toilets (the stands are permanent), and pay for various devices to improve business conditions, security, and the personal living environment at the stands. All operators sign standard form contracts with Mr. W that set stand hours and prices, and prohibit the sale of other merchandise by the operators. The contracts, however, refer to the stand operators as independent contractors and give them sole control over day-to-day operations of their stands. Are the operators employees or independent contractors? See Brock v. Mr. W Fireworks, 814 F.2d 1042 (5th Cir.), cert. denied, 484 U.S. 924 (1987) (stand operators are "employees" due to owners' control and investment); cf. Brock v. Superior Care, 840 F.2d 1054 (2d Cir.1988). See also Secretary of Labor v. Lauritzen, 835 F.2d 1529 (7th Cir.1987), cert. denied, 488 U.S. 898 (1988).

**8.** The FLSA was enacted in 1938, under an entirely different set of assumptions about how people work than pertains today. For example, the number of telecommuters increased 30% between 1995 and 1997, when there were 11 million Americans telecommuting at least one day each month. Does the FLSA provide adequate minimum working conditions today? Are there adequate protections against exploitation of telecommuting employees? As you read, consider what changes, if any, should be made to update the statute.

**9.** The Immigration Reform and Control Act of 1986 (IRCA), supra p. 121 made it unlawful to hire undocumented aliens and provides sanctions against employers who do so. Is an undocumented alien who has been unlawfully hired under IRCA an "employee" within the meaning of the Fair Labor Standards Act and entitled to its protection? See Patel v. Quality Inn South, 846 F.2d 700 (11th Cir.1988), cert. denied, 489 U.S. 1011 (1989) (undocumented alien was "employee" under FLSA and can sue for unpaid wages); Cf. Sure–Tan, Inc. v. NLRB, 467 U.S. 883 (1984) (undocumented aliens were "employees" under the NLRA, but were not entitled to back pay during any period when they were not lawfully entitled to be present and employed in the United States.) Undocumented alien workers are included in Title VII's definition of "employee." 42 U.S.C. §§ 2000e(f, i). See EEOC v. Tortilleria "La Mejor," 758 F.Supp. 585, 586 (E.D.Cal.1991).

**10.** Some courts in the past found migrant workers not to be employees of the farms where they worked, but employees instead of their crew leaders, who were classified as independent contractors to the farms. This resulted in large numbers of agricultural workers not being covered by the statute. Recent cases have focused more stringently on the "economic realities" test, specifically in finding crew leaders and farms to be joint employers within the meaning of the Act. See Secretary of Labor v. Lauritzen, 835 F.2d 1529 (7th Cir.1987), cert. denied, 488 U.S. 898 (1988) (migrant cucumber pickers not independent contractors; see Judge Easterbrook's concurrence, advocating abandonment of fact-bound factors test in favor of more focused statutory test). Cf. Donovan v. Brandel, 736 F.2d 1114 (6th Cir.1984). See also Real v. Driscoll Strawberry Associates, Inc., 603 F.2d 748 (9th Cir.1979) (expansive definition of employer and employee); Haywood v. Barnes, 109 F.R.D. 568 (E.D.N.C.1986) (owners and operators are joint employers); Mendez v. Brady, 618 F.Supp. 579 (W.D.Mich.1985) (blueberry harvesters employees). See also Frank Diehl Farms v. Secretary of Labor, infra, p. 682.

In Alfred L. Snapp & Son v. Puerto Rico, 458 U.S. 592 (1982), the Supreme Court permitted the Commonwealth of Puerto Rico to sue Virginia apple growers, alleging violations of the statutory job rights of Puerto Rican migrant workers. The relevant statutes in effect grant job preferences to United States citizens, including Puerto Ricans. The lawsuit alleged that jobs were going to Jamaicans that, under the statutory scheme, should have gone to Puerto Ricans.

In two separate actions, the Migrant and Seasonal Agricultural Worker Protection Act and the Farm Labor Contractor Registration Act were held to apply to forestry work. Bracamontes v. Weyerhaeuser Co., 840 F.2d 271

(5th Cir.1988), cert. denied, 488 U.S. 854 (1988); Bresgal v. Brock, 833 F.2d 763 (9th Cir.1987).

**11.** The FLSA only applies to about 38 percent of all agricultural workers; the Migrant and Seasonal Agricultural Workers Protection Act, 29 U.S.C. § 1801 et seq. (formerly the Farm Labor Contractor Registration Act, 7 U.S.C. §§ 2041 to 2055), provides additional regulation of working conditions, requiring employers of migrant workers to post notices of wage rates, provide pay statements, maintain records of hours worked and pay deductions, and maintain adequate housing, where housing is provided. That statute protects against substandard, "sweatshop," working conditions, such as those in a New York garment district factory where workers were paid below the minimum wage for sewing and pressing clothing for up to 60 hours per week in rooms with exposed wiring, no fire exits and only three small fans for ventilation. Employees who missed a day of work were fired, and those who made mistakes were beaten. One employee was fired for yawning on the job.

The word "sweatshops" conjures images of industrial revolution factories where destitute immigrants and young children struggled to earn a few dollars a day, cringing at their sewing machines under abusive supervision.[1] Today, sweatshops are a reality in the United States, where it is estimated that more than half of the country's 22,000 sewing shops violate minimum wage and overtime laws and three quarters of U.S. garment shops violate safety and health laws. The exploitative conditions and abuse of sweatshops is illustrated by the 1995 El Monte, California incident, where 72 Thai immigrant workers labored an average of 115 hours per week for 69 cents an hour in a seven-unit sewing factory in which they worked and lived, surrounded by razor wire fences and armed guards to prevent escape. The factory was without air-conditioning, and in some cases up to sixteen workers shared one bedroom. Following a Department of Labor investigation and raid of the El Monte facility, workers recovered back wages and civil fines were imposed.

Enforcing labor laws at sweatshops like the one at El Monte reflects problems in protecting workers' rights and well-being. Legislation aimed at ensuring safe and adequate work conditions is enforced through Department of Labor investigations and industry monitors, which may result in closing sweatshop factories and dissolving jobs. In 1997, the Department of Labor developed a new approach hinging on cooperation and publicity, with lists of complying and non-complying corporations published on the internet at www.dol.gov/dol/esa/public/nosweat/garment7.htm.

Is there a better way to enforce safe and adequate work conditions? Enforcement frequently results in the dislocation of workers. Are you comfortable leaving people unemployed? The subject of dislocated workers can be found in Chapter 12. Another question to consider is sweatshop

---

**1.** The General Accounting Office definition of a sweatshop is an employer "that violates more than one federal or state labor, industrial homework, occupational safety and health, worker's compensation, or industry regulation."

immigrant worker conditions.  In 1996 alone, INS agents arrested 1,824 undocumented aliens during investigations of 150 New York garment shops.  See pp. 121–128 for a further discussion of immigrant worker issues.  With more than one million garment industry laborers working in roughly 22,000 sewing shops nationwide, is enforcement practical?

## d.  WAGES

Beginning September 1, 1997, the statutory minimum wage increased from $4.25 an hour to $5.15 an hour.  The Act itself and regulations issued by the Department of Labor specify how the wage actually received by employees should be computed.  Employees need not actually be paid on an hourly basis.  For example, piece work rates, such as are common in the garment industry, are permissible as long as employees in fact receive at least the minimum wage for time worked.  Similarly, fixed weekly or monthly salaries are permissible, as long as the average weekly salary equals or exceeds the minimum wage.  Minimum wage compliance is determined on a weekly basis; employers who pay on a semi-monthly or monthly basis may not pay more in one week to make up for a prior underpayment, unless a statutory exception exists.

Wages need not be in cash.  Noncash payments may be credited toward the minimum wage if certain conditions are met.  Employers may credit toward the minimum wage the reasonable cost (not retail value) to the employer of meals, lodging, and other facilities provided by the employer for the employees' benefit—not the employer's.  The facility must be of a kind typically provided by the employer (e.g., meals from a restaurant), employees must be told that the value is being deducted from their wages, and acceptance by employees must be voluntary.  The cost of facilities which are provided primarily for the employer's benefit may not be included in computing wages; this would include the cost of uniforms which the employer requires employees to wear, safety equipment required by law, or medical services and hospitalization that the employer is required by law to furnish.  Offsets for debts owed to the employer by the employee may not be applied if the resulting wage would be below the statutory minimum.

The employee's "regular rate of pay" is important for purposes of determining how much must be paid when overtime is due.  Under § 207(e) of the Act, exclusions from regular rates of pay include gifts or bonuses; vacation, holiday or sick pay, when no work is performed; irrevocable contributions to pension or insurance plans; premium pay for hours worked in excess of the employee's normal or regular working hours or pursuant to a collective bargaining agreement.  Such premium rate compensation may also be credited toward overtime payment under the Act.

## NOTES AND QUESTIONS

**1.**  The employer may be able to deduct from wages the cost of meals even where the employee does not take advantage of them.  Melton v. Roundtable Restaurants, Inc., 20 Wage & Hour Cases (BNA) 532 (N.D.Ga.1971).

Furthermore, the employer need not give employees a choice between cash and meals or board.  See Davis Brothers v. Donovan, 700 F.2d 1368 (11th Cir.1983);  Morrison, Inc. v. Donovan, 700 F.2d 1374 (11th Cir.1983) (cafeterias may credit toward minimum cash wages the cost of meals provided to employees; "customarily furnished" language of statute means "regularly provided" by employer, not "voluntarily accepted" by employee).

**2.**   The Second Circuit ruled that housing furnished to migrant farmworkers was presumptively for the benefit of the workers rather than the employer and thus includable as wages under the FLSA.  Soler v. G. & U., Inc., 833 F.2d 1104 (2d Cir.1987), cert. denied, 488 U.S. 832 (1988).  But see Osias v. Marc, 700 F.Supp. 842 (D.Md.1988) (employer not entitled to housing credit where facilities provided were substandard).

**3.**   Special provisions apply to the wages of "tipped employees," who customarily and regularly receive more than $30 a month in tips.  Section 207(m) of the FLSA allows employers to take a credit against the minimum wage for tips earned by employees.  The credit may not exceed the amount of tips actually received by employees, nor may the credit exceed 50 percent, even if employers have received more than that amount in tips.  If employee tips plus the base amount paid by the employer do not meet the minimum wage, the employer must pay the difference.  To receive a tip credit, employers must give employees notice.  See Martin v. Tango's Restaurant, Inc., 969 F.2d 1319 (1st Cir.1992) (tip credit eliminated where restaurant failed to give waiter employees notice of tip credit).

**4.**   The Seventh Circuit has held that service charges added by hotels and restaurants for banquets and distributed to banquet waiters are commissions under the FLSA, rather than tips or regular wages. Mechmet v. Four Seasons Hotels, Ltd., 825 F.2d 1173 (7th Cir. 1987).  This ruling exempts such work from the overtime requirements of the Act since overtime payment is one and one-half times the employee's "regular rate."  Other exclusions to the regular rate include discretionary bonuses, pay for time not worked (vacation, sick leave, jury duty, etc.), and profit-sharing plan contributions.  Does the Seventh Circuit's decision seem fair to the waiters who will not be paid overtime for what could easily be more than 40 hours of work a week?

**5.**   Setoffs against any back pay due as a result of an action to enforce the Act are prohibited.  In Brennan v. Heard, 491 F.2d 1, 7 (5th Cir.1974), the court held that such offsets were impermissible in an action to enforce the Act:

> Congress has determined that the individual worker should have both the freedom and the responsibility to allocate his minimum wage among competing economic and personal interests.  Defendants succeeded below in preventing the full exercise of that employee discretion, which has been mandated by the FLSA and specifically recognized by this Court.  The FLSA decrees a minimum unconditional payment and the commands of that Act are not to be vitiated by an employer, either acting alone or through

the agency of a federal court. The federal courts were not designated by the FLSA to be either collection agents or arbitrators for an employee's creditors. Their sole function and duty under the Act is to assure to the employees of a covered company a minimum level of wages. Arguments and disputations over claims against those wages are foreign to the genesis, history, interpretation, and philosophy of the Act. The only economic feud contemplated by the FLSA involves the employer's obedience to minimum wage and overtime standards. To clutter these proceedings with the minutiae of other employer-employee relationships would be antithetical to the purpose of the Act. Set-offs against back pay awards deprive the employee of the "cash in hand" contemplated by the Act, and are therefore inappropriate in any proceeding brought to enforce the FLSA.

Suppose employees of an employer that has been found guilty of violating the Act owe the employer money for goods purchased at a company store. If the employer is not entitled to set off against its penalties the amount of money owed to it by its employees, how will it recover the money owed to it? Under what circumstances may an employer properly set off debts owed it by an employee? Why should it make a difference if, for instance, food is furnished to employees by the employer as meals, which are a proper offset against wages, or if the employer permits employees to select food of their choice at a company-owned store? In Blanton v. City of Murfreesboro, 856 F.2d 731 (6th Cir.1988), the court found that the city's downward adjustment of firefighters' base wage rate to offset the increased cost imposed by the Act violated the FLSA regardless of the city's good faith.

**6.** Prior to entering into an employment relationship, an employer and a prospective employee enter into an agreement under which the employee agrees to give up her entitlement to statutory overtime compensation in exchange for fringe benefits—paid vacations and holidays and biannual bonuses—the value of which would exceed the amount of overtime compensation otherwise due. What result in an action by the Secretary of Labor to enforce the overtime provisions of the Act? See Dunlop v. Gray–Goto, 528 F.2d 792 (10th Cir.1976) (held: arrangement violated FLSA).

**7.** Employers may not shift the burden of business losses to their employees by deducting them from pay. A California appellate court held illegal Neiman Marcus's practice of deducting from sales associates' commissions a percentage of merchandise returns. Hudgins v. Neiman Marcus Group, 41 Cal.Rptr.2d 46 (Ct.App.1995).

### e. HOURS

The FLSA requires that employees be paid for all hours worked, at minimum wage for the first 40 hours worked in a week and at time and a half their regular rate of pay for all hours in excess of 40 per week. What constitutes compensable hours is subject to debate. Employees must be paid for all time they are engaged in "principal" job activities, as well as "incidental" activities which are an integral part of their work. However, the Portal-to-Portal Act excludes preliminary and postliminary activity ("waiting to be engaged") from compensable time. Generally, time spent in such activities as coffee breaks, waiting, staff meetings, fire drills, and grievance adjustment during working hours ("engaged to be waiting") are compensable. Meal periods longer than one-half hour, scheduled maintenance shutdowns, union meetings for internal union affairs, voting time (unless compensation required by state law), and absences for illness, holiday, or vacation are examples of noncompensable time.

## Halferty v. Pulse Drug Co.

864 F.2d 1185 (5th Cir.1989).

■ SNEED, CIRCUIT JUDGE:

Pulse Drug Co., Inc., ("Pulse") appeals a judgment awarding damages and an attorney's fee to Irma Ruth Halferty under the Fair Labor Standards Act. Pulse argues that the judgment impermissibly conflicts with an earlier order in the case and that Halferty's recovery is not proper under the FLSA. We reverse on the latter ground.

Pulse provides nonemergency ambulance care to disabled individuals. Halferty worked for Pulse as a telephone dispatcher in her home from December 1981 to May 1984. She generally was on duty from 5:00 p.m. to 8:00 a.m. five nights per week. Halferty's work required her to answer a small number of telephone calls each night, but otherwise allowed her to pursue personal, social, and business activities. For example, she could and did eat, sleep, watch television, entertain guests, babysit, and do laundry. Halferty also could leave her home so long as she could have her calls forwarded or could find someone else to answer them.

Pulse initially paid Halferty $2.50 per night plus $1.00 per ambulance run, but later paid her a flat rate of $230.00 per month. Pulse also reimbursed her for some of her telephone expenses. Halferty, however, became dissatisfied with her compensation. In 1984, Halferty filed a complaint with the Wage and Hour Division of the Department of Labor alleging that Pulse had failed to pay her the minimum wage and the overtime compensation required by the FLSA. When the Department of Labor informed Halferty that Pulse had refused to pay any back wages, she sued Pulse in the United States district court below.

The district court, with former Chief Judge Sessions presiding, held that Halferty was an "employee" of Pulse under 29 U.S.C. § 216(a) (1982), and concluded that Pulse should have paid her the minimum wage and the overtime compensation required by §§ 206(a)(1) & 207(a)(1)....

Halferty submitted proposed findings of fact and conclusions of law to the court. A slightly modified version of these were included in a final order issued on November 5, 1987, and amended on November 18, 1987. The order awarded Halferty $19,607.88 in damages and a $28,184.00 attorney's fee. The order did not reduce Halferty's compensation under either the homeworker's or the waiting to be engaged exceptions to the FLSA. The court ruled that Halferty did not have complete freedom while on duty and that she spent her waiting time predominantly for the benefit of Pulse. . . .

Pulse contends fundamentally that the district court erred in requiring it to pay Halferty for each and every hour that she was on duty. Pulse argues that Halferty did not work for all of these hours and that the FLSA does not require it to compensate her to that extent.

The FLSA's minimum wage and overtime requirements, set forth in 29 U.S.C. § 206(a)(1) and § 207(a)(1) (1982), are designed to apply readily and easily to workers whose jobs require them to show up at specific hours and to work more or less continuously while on their employers' premises. Like Halferty, however, not all workers have jobs that conform to such a pattern. As a result, the courts have fashioned the so-called "waiting to be engaged" and "homeworker's" doctrines to make it possible to determine the compensation that such workers deserve under the FLSA.

These doctrines operate in different ways. The waiting to be engaged doctrine may entitle workers to receive compensation for periods of inactivity when they spend such periods waiting on their employers. The homeworker's exception, by contrast, may allow an employer to pay an employee according to a reasonable compensation agreement instead of the FLSA's specific hourly rate requirements when the employer cannot determine the exact hours that the employee works. In this case, we conclude that Halferty should not receive compensation for her inactive time under the waiting to be engaged exception. Moreover, we hold that Pulse properly paid Halferty under a reasonable compensation agreement because Halferty's duties made it difficult to determine the exact number of hours she worked.

In explaining the waiting to be engaged doctrine, we stated earlier that when idle time is spent predominantly for the benefit of the employer, not the employee, the employee is engaged to be waiting, not waiting to be engaged, and is entitled to compensation. Conversely, if the time primarily benefits the employee, the employee can be considered to be waiting to be engaged, and should receive compensation only for actual work time. . . .

Department of Labor regulations make clear that the critical issue in determining whether an employee should receive compensation for idle time is whether the employee can use the time effectively for his or her own purposes. The facts show that Halferty could visit friends, entertain guests, sleep, watch television, do laundry, and babysit. We, therefore, conclude that she could use the time for her own purposes and that she is not entitled to compensation for her idle time under the waiting to be engaged doctrine. . . .

The district court refused to permit Halferty's employment agreement to determine her compensation under the homeworker's exception for two reasons. First, the district court found that Halferty "did not have periods of complete freedom from her duties." Second, the district court found that Halferty and Pulse had reached an agreement that Halferty worked seventy-five hours per week. We must disagree with each of these reasons.

When deciding whether Halferty had the "periods of complete freedom" that the regulation requires, the district court should not have focused only on Halferty's on-duty time. The regulation does not require employees to have complete freedom during on duty time; the courts have looked to both on-duty time and off-duty time when evaluating an employee's freedom. This must be done because Halferty did not reside on her employer's premises. The work premises were her home. Halferty had complete freedom during the day and, even while on duty at night, she had enough time for eating, sleeping, and entertaining. This is all the freedom that the homeworker's exception requires.

Section 785.23 makes clear that when an employee has such freedom, and when it is "difficult to determine the exact hours worked," an employer can pay the employee according any reasonable agreement that takes into consideration all of the pertinent facts. In this case, Pulse could not have determined, except in an intrusive manner, the exact amount of time that Halferty spent dealing with telephone calls and dispatching ambulances. Moreover, it would be clearly erroneous to conclude that Halferty's compensation was not reasonable. Her pay far exceeded the price of comparable services. The record shows that Halferty collected an average of $230.00 each month when paid a flat rate and only somewhat less when paid a fixed amount per night and a small sum per ambulance run. Comparable telephone answering services were available in the area for $35 to $50 per month. Pulse, in addition, allowed Halferty to augment her personal freedom and income by permitting her to arrange for relief from friends and to pursue personal business endeavors such as babysitting and doing laundry. We thus hold that the FLSA does not require that Halferty receive compensation greater than the amount she already has received.

We note, finally, that the district court erred when it concluded that Pulse agreed to pay Halferty for seventy-five hours per week. Although the Department of Labor opinion states that parties may make a reasonable agreement for determining the number of hours worked, the parties in this case never made such an agreement. As noted above, they agreed only that Halferty would receive a certain compensation and that she would be, or have someone be, available to answer the telephone for seventy-five hours each week. They did not hypothesize any specific number of working hours for the purposes of the FLSA. The case therefore does come within the specific facts contemplated by the Department of Labor opinion.

NOTES AND QUESTIONS

1. Do you agree with the decision in Halferty v. Pulse Drug Co.? How should employees who are "on call" in their own homes be treated? See also Bright v. Houston Northwest Medical Center Survivor, Inc., 888 F.2d 1059 (5th Cir.1989), affirmed on rehearing, 934 F.2d 671 (5th Cir.1991),

cert. denied, 502 U.S. 1036 (1992) (repair technician on call 24 hours a day, 365 days a year).

**2.**  For what nonwork activities performed during normal working hours, if any, should employees be compensated?  OSHA allows a representative authorized by employees to accompany an inspector during the walkaround inspection of the workplace.  Employees participated in some phase of such an inspection on a major oil plant's property during their regular working hours.  When the employer discontinued compensating employees for the time spent in the inspection, the employees brought suit.  Their complaint alleged that the OSHA statutory scheme envisions placing the economic burden of industrial safety on employers and that the nonfrivolous nature of employees' participation in the inspection benefitted the employer in meeting its statutory duty to provide safe working conditions.  The employees claimed that they were thus entitled to compensation under the FLSA.  Should this inspection time be considered "hours worked," and thus compensable?  If so, by what standard should they be paid: their regular contract rate of pay or the FLSA minimum wage?  Should the time spent in the walkaround count toward overtime if it puts the employees over 40 hours of work for the week?  What factors should the court consider in formulating an "hours worked" test?  See Leone v. Mobil Oil Corp., 523 F.2d 1153 (D.C.Cir.1975). See also Marshall v. Partida, 613 F.2d 1360 (5th Cir.1980) (laundromat attendants were entitled to compensation for time spent performing random tasks for the employer's benefit).

**3.**  While meal times over one-half hour are generally considered noncompensable, the employer may put so many restrictions on employees' right to take a meal break that it is in fact considered compensable time, either under the FLSA or equivalent state laws, since the meal time benefits the employer.  In Avery v. City of Talladega, 24 F.3d 1337 (11th Cir.1994), police officers were not compensated for meal breaks since they could spend the breaks however they wanted so long as they were in uniform, left radios on, and gave forwarding numbers if they left the station.  Voluntary payment for meals does not transfer non-work time into work time under the FLSA.  Barefield v. Village of Winnetka, 81 F.3d 704 (7th Cir.1996) (holding that FLSA provides a floor, not a ceiling, for compensation).

**4.**  What is the difference between incidental work performed at the beginning or end of the work day, which is compensable under the FLSA, and preliminary or postliminary work which is noncompensable?  Consider the following facts:

Employees are electricians employed to install and repair electrical wiring.  Their daily wage rate is calculated on the basis of a workday beginning at 8:00 a.m.  On a typical day, however, the employees arrive between 15 and 20 minutes early in order to perform tasks preparatory to departing for various job sites.  These tasks include filling out various time and material sheets, checking job locations, removing the previous day's trash, loading and fueling trucks, and picking up plans for the day's job.

Should this work be compensable under the FLSA as work performed in excess of 40 hours a week? Can it be considered to be "of consequence," enabling the employer to derive significant benefit from its performance, or is the work more appropriately characterized as activity "preliminary to * * * [an employee's] principal activity," which is exempt from coverage under § 4(a)(2) of the Portal-to-Portal Act of 1947? What factors should be considered in formulating the appropriate distinguishing test? See Dunlop v. City Electric, Inc., 527 F.2d 394 (5th Cir.1976) (work similar to that cited above is performed as part of employer's principal activities and is therefore compensable); Marshall v. Gerwill, Inc., 495 F.Supp. 744 (D.Md.1980) (time spent by taxi drivers in returning cabs to garage and parking after dropping off last fare is compensable). Travel time to and from work is not compensable. Vega v. Gasper, 36 F.3d 417 (5th Cir. 1994).

**5.** In Owens v. Local No. 169, Association of Western Pulp & Paper Workers, 971 F.2d 347 (9th Cir.1992), the Ninth Circuit ruled that off-duty time spent on-call by pulp mill mechanics was not compensable. The court, under the standard articulated in Armour & Co. v. Wantock, 323 U.S. 126 (1944), looked to see if employees had freedom to engage in personal activities while on call and whether there was an agreement between the parties. Answering both questions in the affirmative, the court reversed the grant of summary judgment for the plaintiffs and remanded for summary judgment for the defendants.

**6.** A court recently awarded overtime pay to police officers assigned to the canine detachment for time spent feeding, exercising, and transporting the dogs. The court found that caring for the dogs constituted "an integral and indefeasible" part of the officer's work-related responsibilities. Levering v. District of Columbia, 869 F.Supp. 24 (D.D.C.1994).

But the Second Circuit ruled that police department dog handlers are not entitled to compensation for time spent commuting with their dogs, who live with them. The handlers' duties in that time are de minimis, and the mere presence of a dog "quietly occupying the back of the car" does not make the time compensable. Reich v. New York City Transit Authority, 45 F.3d 646 (2d Cir.1995).

**7.** Operating room employees in a hospital are required to work "on-premises-on-call" overtime, during which they have to remain at the hospital, although they are not on active duty until called. When they are on active duty, they perform their regular jobs and are paid one and one-half their regular shift rate. During waiting periods, employees have no assigned duties and are free to sleep, watch television, and otherwise occupy themselves. Employees are paid one and one-half times the federal minimum wage for waiting periods, an amount considerably less than their usual rate. Does the employer violate the FLSA with this two-rate wage structure? Not necessarily, held the Third Circuit in Townsend v. Mercy Hospital, 862 F.2d 1009 (3d Cir.1988). Under § 7(g)(2) of the FLSA, an employer and employee may agree to a "bona fide rate" that is different from the employee's regular rate of pay and is applicable to work performed only during overtime hours. Typically, the parties agree to two rates when the employee performs two or more kinds of work in the ordinary course of working, with the two-rate structure being carried over to overtime.  In *Townsend,* the employer did not pay two different wages for active duty and waiting periods during employees' regular hours;  the two-rate structure applied only to "on-call-on-premises" overtime.  The Third Circuit held no violation, finding that in addition to there being agreement between the parties, there was a qualitative difference between "idle time" during regular shift hours, when employees were constrained in what they could do (e.g., no sleeping or watching television), and the separately compensable "waiting time" that occurred during the on-call shifts.

In Bouchard v. Regional Governing Board, 939 F.2d 1323 (8th Cir. 1991), cert. denied, 503 U.S. 1005 (1992), the court held employees of a Nebraska institution for the mentally retarded, who were required to sleep on the premises, were not entitled to overtime compensation for sleep time. A somewhat different result was reached in Johnson v. Columbia, 949 F.2d 127 (4th Cir.1991), where the court held that an "express agreement" to exclude sleep and meal time from compensable work hours is not enforceable under the FLSA when the "agreement" was extracted under threat of termination.  Such exclusions must be consensual. In Armour & Co. v. Wantock, 323 U.S. 126 (1944), the Supreme Court held that where an employee is on duty for 24 hours or more, up to eight hours may be excluded from compensable time by agreement of the employer and employee if the employee's sleep time is not interrupted for at least five hours and the employer provides adequate sleeping facilities.

**8.**  A 1907 statute, the Hours of Service Act, restricts railroad crew members to 12 consecutive hours of work, after which the employee must be given at least 10 consecutive hours off duty.

**9.**  In a case of first impression, the Eighth Circuit held that an employer policy that forces employees to use accrued compensatory time at intervals determined by the employer violates the FLSA, so long as an employee's decision to "cash in" does not "unduly disrupt" the employer's operations. Heaton v. Moore, 43 F.3d 1176 (8th Cir.1994), cert. denied, 515 U.S. 1104 (1995).

**10.**  Work sharing and flextime have been suggested as possible ways to enhance the quality of work life for some employees, especially women with small children.  What special modifications, if any, would need to be made in the FLSA's wage and hour provisions to accommodate and to promote such nontraditional working conditions?

## f.  CHILD LABOR

In addition to the minimum wage and overtime provisions of the FLSA, the Act also restricts the employment of children under the age of 18 and limits the conditions under which they may work.  A significant number of young people are employed. Nearly half of 16 and 17 year olds are employed, though more than three-quarters of them hold part-time jobs. In 1997, the Secretary of Labor estimated that over three million teens will work summer jobs. (See also Chapter 2.)

Intolerable and abusive working conditions for children in the late nineteenth and early twentieth centuries led to some of the first legislative efforts, at both the state and federal level, to regulate "freedom of contract" between employer and employee through the enactment of protective legislation. While child labor problems are not as extensive today, they still exist. A 1989 study by the General Accounting Office showed that the number of violations of the FLSA's child labor provisions increased 250 percent from 1983 (9,000) to 1989 (more than 22,500). The Wage and Hour Division of the Department of Labor has only about 800 inspectors to monitor the working conditions of all of the 125 million workers.

Child labor violations not only disrupt school and other opportunities of children, they are responsible for death, injury, and illness. Children often are given the dirtiest and least safe and healthful jobs to perform, they may be too small to work with tools properly, or they may lack the experience and judgment to work with machinery. According to the National Institute for Occupational Safety and Health (NIOSH), approximately 70 adolescents (16 and 17 year olds) die of workplace injuries each year, and another 64,000 require emergency medical treatment. Agriculture and restaurant work have the most reported injuries, illnesses, and fatalities, although the lack of good data remains a problem.

### Peter J. McGovern, *Children's Rights and Child Labor: Advocacy on Behalf of the Child Worker*

28 S.D.L.Rev. 293 (1983).

In July 1982, while making a movie at 2:30 A.M., scores of actors and movie technicians watched a helicopter fall out of control and plunge into the Santa Clara River. The main rotors of the helicopter instantly killed three actors, Victor Morrow and two children, ages six and seven. Immediately, questions were raised as to whether the children should have been working during that pre-dawn filming session.

Substandard child labor conditions have become more prevalent in recent years. The United States Secretary of Labor, in his 69th Annual Report to Congress, reported that 13,825 minors were employed in violation of the child labor provisions of the Fair Labor Standards Act in 1981. This was an increase of almost forty percent over the previous year's violations of 9,968. The Secretary's report reflected that of the total violations: "[t]wo-thirds of the minors were employed in retail trades; 3,781 were in nonagricultural occupations declared hazardous, and 131 in agricultural occupations declared hazardous. Six hundred and fifty-two minors were found employed contrary to other agricultural provisions of the FLSA [Fair Labor Standards Act]."

\* \* \*

Employment questions concerning children constantly arise. Consider the following typical child labor issues:  May a contractor building single dwelling homes hire a twelve year-old this summer to mow lawns on the houses that have been built and are for sale?  Should a sixteen year-old be allowed to operate a forklift truck?  Must one pay minimum wages to children?  Can the manager of the fast food restaurant down the street really ask a fourteen year-old to come to work at six in the morning and stay until midnight?  A seventeen year-old was injured on the job.  Is he covered by workers' compensation?  Can a farmer hire a neighbor's fifteen year-old son to drive a farm tractor while the farmer works in the fields?  Are ten and eleven year-old children of migratory farmers allowed to work in the fields?  Can children be used in a cast of a theatrical production if the play will be presented in the evening during a normal school semester?

# Reich v. Shiloh True Light Church of Christ

85 F.3d 616 (4th Cir.1996).

■ PER CURIAM:

Appellant Shiloh True Light Church of Christ's members hold a religious belief that their children should receive meaningful vocational training.  This belief is effectuated through the Shiloh Vocational Training Program (SVTP).  The issue in this case is whether SVTP participants under the age of sixteen are "employees" entitled to the protections of the Fair Labor Standards Act.  The Church argues that those children are not employees, and that at any rate, application of the FLSA would violate both the Free Exercise Clause and Department of Labor administrative policy.

The district court entered partial summary judgment against the Church, rejecting its free exercise and administrative defenses.  Then, following a two-day bench trial, the court concluded that the under-sixteen participants in the SVTP qualified as employees under the FLSA.  Finding no error, we affirm the judgment of the district court.

Church youth perform a variety of construction projects through the SVTP, and customers pay the Church for the work.  We have upheld application of the FLSA to the SVTP once before.  Brock v. Wendell's Woodwork, Inc., 867 F.2d 196 (4th Cir.1989).  After the trial in Wendell's Woodwork, the Church reorganized the program.  A principal modification was that children under the age of 16 would no longer receive a wage for their work.  The SVTP also decided to segregate its work crews by age, but has since discontinued that practice—children under and over 16 now work together in combined work crews, performing largely the same tasks.

The SVTP's projects formerly consisted mostly of subcontract work at construction sites.  Representative projects include installing a fireplace, constructing a carport, adding a room, laying a foundation under a garage, and building concrete retainer walls.  Since 1990, the program has also been in the business of constructing entire new houses—the SVTP built 15 new homes between 1990 and 1993.  Children under 16 participate in all aspects of new home construction, including roofing, building the foundation, mixing mortar, laying bricks, and installing drywall.

The SVTP charges labor costs, material costs, other general expenses, and also administrative fee and an interest fee for its new home construction. The labor charge does not include the work of children under the age of 16, in furtherance of the policy barring payment of wages to under 16 participants. But while children under 16 do not receive a wage, they have not been completely free of financial inducement. They have received lump sum payments in the past, with the amount depending on the child's degree of experience and achievement in the program—the Church characterizes these awards as "gifts." The under 16 participants also earn "imaginary" raises on top of "imaginary" wages as a mechanism for determining their actual wage upon turning 16.

The Department of Labor filed suit against the SVTP on December 3, 1992, contending that the program violates FLSA provisions governing child labor, minimum wage, and record-keeping. The SVTP initially admitted that all of the children were employees subject to the FLSA, but then adopted a position that the children under 16 were not employees under the Act. It also challenged application of the FLSA on free exercise grounds. Finally, it asserted defenses based on the Department of Labor's no-enforcement policy with respect to some vocational programs and the Department's failure to promulgate regulations under 29 U.S.C. § 214(d) exempting certain student employment.

The district court held a bench trial to answer that question on May 15 and 16, 1995. Based on the evidence presented at trial and on the 154 findings of fact set forth in its opinion, the court determined that SVTP participants under 16 were employees subject to the protections of the FLSA. As a result, the court concluded, the Church had violated the Act's child labor, minimum wage, and record-keeping requirements with respect to those employees. This appeal followed.

The SVTP contends that the district court erred in concluding that the children under 16 are employees under the Act. We do not agree. The district court's ruling was based on extensive factual findings developed with the benefit of a two-day bench trial, findings that we must not lightly second-guess on appeal.

The FLSA defines an "employee" as "any individual employed by an employer," 29 U.S.C. § 203(e)(1), and "employ" as "to suffer or permit to work," 29 U.S.C. § 203(g). In some circumstances, trainees are not considered employees. In this circuit, "the general test used to determine if an employee is entitled to the protections of the Act is whether the employee or the employer is the primary beneficiary of the trainees' labor." The inquiry is by nature a fact-intensive one.

The SVTP agrees that the "primary beneficiary" test should govern this case, but disputes the district court's application of it. In our view, however, the district court's conclusion that the Church is the primary beneficiary of the under 16 labor finds support in the factual record.

Although the under 16 participants may not receive wage compensation, they have received substantial lump sum awards in the past (as high as $5,500). While the Church evidently has discontinued these payments, the record suggests that it has continued to seek ways to compensate the children without running afoul of the FLSA. Moreover, workers under the age of 16 still receive "imaginary" raises that directly translate into a higher rate of pay upon turning 16. And the SVTP expert who testified as to the non-financial benefits of the program was viewed by the district court as lacking credibility. Given all of this, we cannot question the district court's finding "as a fact that the . . . church policy to not pay the minors under 16 is an attempt to label them students rather than employees."

The court also concluded that the Church benefits greatly from the work of children under 16. In the past, although the under 16 labor was not charged, the SVTP informed customers that they could make a "donation" in an amount approximating the value of the work; such a donation normally was made. While the donation practice has been discontinued, the Church still gains significant financial benefit from projects in which under 16 children participate. Between 1990 and 1993, the SVTP finished 97 construction projects and 15 complete houses with the help of children under the age of 16, producing substantial financial returns. Three of the houses, for instance, were sold for $134,000, $124,000, and $213,456. By using children under 16 to complete these projects, the district court found, the SVTP enjoyed the benefit of experienced labor without incurring any cost in wages. "Clearly," the court concluded, "the program has been converted into a commercial enterprise competing with other contractors."

In short, substantial evidence in the record supports the district court's conclusion that the Church was the primary beneficiary of the under 16 labor, and that the children under 16 are thus employees entitled to the protections of the FLSA.

* * *

## NOTES AND QUESTIONS

**1.** For earlier discussion of employee status, see *Microsoft*, supra, p. 93.

**2.** If the children's parents agreed to the Shiloh Vocational Training Program (SVTP) and the children did not complain about the labor, why should the church's activities be illegal?

**3.** If the children participating in the SVTP had not received any form of compensation, either imaginary or otherwise, would the church have been in violation of the statute?

**4.** Is there any way for the SVTP to restructure its operations to continue to employ children between the ages of 14 and 16 without violating the FLSA?

**5.** Under the FLSA, children between the ages of 14 and 16 may be employed if employment takes place outside of school hours. While school is in session, children may not work more than 18 hours a week and no more than three hours a day. While school is out of session, children may not work more than 40 hours a week and no more than 8 hours a day. In addition, employment must be between 7 a.m. and 7 p.m., or until 9 p.m. when school is not in session. See Thomas v. Brock, 617 F.Supp. 526 (W.D.N.C.1985), modified and remanded to correct order, 810 F.2d 448 (4th Cir. 1987)(regulations violated where children between the ages of 14 and 16 sold candy door to door until 11:30 p.m. or midnight). See also Echaveste v. Q & D, 2 Wage & Hour Cases 2d (BNA) 726 (E.D.Pa.1994).

**6.** The FLSA not only regulates the hours that children may work, but also protects them from dangerous working conditions. Regulations issued by the Department of Labor cover 17 hazardous occupations plus agriculture and prohibit all work in certain occupations, such as mining, roofing, and excavation, as well as work with such equipment as power saws, metal presses, and meat slicers and grinders in groceries, delicatessens, and fast food restaurants. Minors are also prohibited from operating freight elevators and hoisting apparatuses such as forklift trucks. See Breitwieser v. KMS Industries, Inc., 467 F.2d 1391 (5th Cir.1972), cert. denied, 410 U.S. 969 (1973), where a 16 year-old boy hired to drive a forklift for a construction company was killed when the forklift flipped over.

**7.** Section 213(c) of the FLSA provides exemptions from the Act's coverage, such as for children who are employed by their parents in agriculture, except in situations declared hazardous by the Secretary of Labor. Other exemptions include minors employed as actors or as newspaper deliverers. State laws may provide coverage in these areas, however, for instance, where state law prohibits the selling of alcoholic beverages or employment in a tavern by anyone under age 21.

**8.** While the employment of children under the age of 12 is generally forbidden under the Act, § 213(c)(4)(A) permits employers to apply for a waiver from the Secretary of Labor for children age 10 and 11 to work as hand harvesters for not more than eight weeks in a calendar year to pick what are known as "short season" crops (e.g., strawberries). The Secretary of Labor may not grant any waivers unless certain statutorily specified conditions are met, and any waivers granted are subject to other limitations, such as no employment during school hours.

Controversy has arisen over the Secretary's right to issue waivers where certain chemicals and pesticides have been used on crops shortly before harvest. A waiver may issue only where the Secretary has found, "based on objective data," that employment will not be "deleterious" to the health and well-being of the children. Because of the lack of specific data on the health effects on children of certain commonly used agricultural chemicals, the Department of Labor in 1978 proposed a rule that would apply the EPA, OSHA, and NIOSH standards to establish safe exposure levels for minors entering sprayed fields. Following bitter litigation against the Department by both state farm bureaus and child advocacy representatives, the rule was ultimately modified to provide that waivers could only be issued to growers who do not use pesticides or those who provide sufficient data to the Secretary to establish safe reentry times. See Washington State Farm Bureau v. Marshall, 625 F.2d 296 (9th Cir.1980); National Association of Farmworkers Organizations v. Marshall, 628 F.2d 604 (D.C.Cir.1980); 29 C.F.R. § 575.5(d) (1982).

**9.** Every state also regulates child labor; in enacting the FLSA, Congress provided that the federal law would not preempt state law but that whichever standard provided greater protection to the child would apply. There is no clear pattern of state regulation: some states have higher standards than the FLSA and others have lower ones. Local conditions are often reflected in state regulations: Maine has special laws regarding the employment of children in the ski industry, while Nevada has specific restrictions on employment in casinos.

**10.** For a thorough discussion of the history of child labor laws in the United States and the pattern of violations since 1980, see Michael A. Pignatella, Note, The Recurring Nightmare of Child Labor Abuse—Causes and Solutions for the 90s, 15 B.C.Third World L.J. 171 (1995).

g. ENFORCEMENT OF THE FLSA

## Stephan G. Wood & Mary Anne Q. Wood, *The Fair Labor Standards Act: Recommendations to Improve Compliance*

1983 Utah L.Rev. 529.

Five enforcement actions are possible under the FLSA: The Secretary of Labor may commence either an action for civil liability, an action for civil money penalties for making use of oppressive child labor or an action for an injunction; one or more employees may seek civil damages; and the Department of Justice may bring an action for criminal penalties.

The Secretary of Labor may bring an action for civil liability to recover the amount of back wages and an additional equal amount as liquidated damages. Any sums recovered by the Secretary are held in a special deposit account and are paid directly to the affected employee or employees. Any sums not paid to an employee because the Department of Labor is unable to locate him or her within a period of three years are paid into the Treasury of the United States.

The Secretary of Labor may bring an action for civil money penalties against any person who violates the provisions prohibiting oppressive child labor. The Secretary of Labor determines the amount of the civil penalty. That amount is final unless the person charged with the violation takes exception. If that person protests, a final determination of the civil penalty is made in a Department of Labor administrative proceeding before an administrative law judge. The Secretary of Labor also may seek an injunction to restrain violations of section 215, and to order the payment of back wages found by the court to be due to employees under the FLSA.

Employees can seek back pay and damages for minimum wage or overtime compensation violations through a civil action against their employer. An action for civil liability also can be brought against any employer who discharges an employee in retaliation for instituting an FLSA suit. In that action, the employer is liable for such legal or equitable relief as may be appropriate, including, without limitation, employment reinstatement, promotion, back wages and an additional equal amount as liquidated damages. Either of those actions for civil liability can be maintained in any federal or state court of competent jurisdiction. The employee's right to bring such an action, however, terminates upon the filing of (1) a complaint by the Secretary of Labor in an action for an injunction in which either restraint is sought of any further delay in the payment of back wages or legal or equitable relief is sought as a result of an alleged attempt by an employer to discharge or in any other manner discriminate against any employee (section 217 action) or (2) a complaint by the Secretary in which recovery is sought of back wages or liquidated or other damages due such employees, unless such action is dismissed without prejudice on motion of the Secretary of Labor (section 216(c) action).

An action for criminal penalties brought by the Department of Justice is another enforcement tool available under the FLSA. That action can be brought against any person who willfully violates any of the provisions in section 215. If convicted, the person is subject to a fine of not more than $10,000, imprisonment for not more than six months or both.

———

The statute of limitations for filing an action under the Act presents a recurrent enforcement issue for the courts. Ordinarily, the limitations period is two years, unless the employer's violation is "wilful," in which case a three-year period applies. But what is "wilful" conduct under the Act?

## McLaughlin v. Richland Shoe Co.

486 U.S. 128 (1988).

■ JUSTICE STEVENS delivered the opinion of the Court.

The question presented concerns the meaning of the word "willful" as used in the statute of limitations applicable to civil actions to enforce the Fair Labor Standards Act (FLSA). The statute provides that such actions must be commenced within two years "except that a cause of action arising out of a willful violation may be commenced within three years after the cause of action accrued." 61 Stat. 88, 29 U.S.C. § 255(a).

Respondent, a manufacturer of shoes and boots, employed seven mechanics to maintain and repair its equipment. In 1984, the Secretary of Labor (Secretary) filed a complaint alleging that "in many work weeks" respondent had filed to pay those employees the overtime compensation required by the FLSA. As an affirmative defense, respondent pleaded the 2–year statute of limitations. The District Court found, however, that the 3–year exception applied because respondent's violations were willful, and entered judgment requiring respondent to pay a total of $11,084.26, plus interest, to the seven employees.

In resolving the question of willfulness, the District Court followed Fifth Circuit decisions that had developed the so-called *Jiffy June* standard. The District Court explained:

> The Fifth Circuit has held that an action is willful when "there is substantial evidence in the record to support a finding that the employer knew or suspected that his actions might violate the FLSA. Stated most simply, we think the test should be: Did the employer know the FLSA was in the picture?" Coleman v. Jiffy June Farms, Inc., 458 F.2d 1139, 1142 (5th Cir.)[, cert. denied, 409 U.S. 948 (1972) ].
>
> This standard requires nothing more than that the employer has an awareness of the possible application of the FLSA. "An employer acts willfully and subjects himself to the three year liability if he knows, or has reason to know, that his conduct is *governed* by the FLSA." 623 F.Supp., at 670–671.

On appeal respondent persuaded the Court of Appeals for the Third Circuit "that the *Jiffy June* standard is wrong because it is contrary to the plain meaning of the FLSA." Adopting the same test that we employed in Trans World Airlines, Inc. v. Thurston, 469 U.S. 111, 125–130 (1985), the Court of Appeals held that respondent had not committed a willful violation unless "it knew or *showed reckless disregard for the matter of whether* its conduct was prohibited by the FLSA." Accordingly, it vacated the District Court's judgment and remanded the case for reconsideration under the proper standard.

The Secretary filed a petition for certiorari asking us to resolve the post–*Thurston* conflict among the Circuits concerning the meaning of the word "willful" in this statute. The petition noted that the statute applies not only to actions to enforce the overtime and recordkeeping provisions of the FLSA, but also to the Equal Pay Act, the Davis–Bacon Act, the Walsh–Healey Act, and the Age Discrimination in Employment Act (ADEA). Somewhat surprisingly, the petition did not endorse the *Jiffy June* standard that the Secretary had relied on in the District Court and the Court of Appeals, but instead invited us to adopt an intermediate standard.

Because no limitations period was provided in the original 1938 enactment of the FLSA, civil actions brought thereunder were governed by state statutes of limitations. In the Portal–to–Portal Act of 1947, 61 Stat. 84, 29 U.S.C. §§ 216, 251–262, however, as part of its response to this Court's expansive reading of the FLSA, Congress enacted the 2–year statute to place a limit on employers' exposure to unanticipated contingent liabilities. As originally enacted, the 2–year limitations period drew no distinction between willful and nonwillful violations.

In 1965, the Secretary proposed a number of amendments to expand the coverage of the FLSA, including a proposal to replace the 2–year statute of limitations with a 3–year statute. The proposal was not adopted, but in 1966, for reasons that are not explained in the legislative history, Congress enacted the 3–year exception for willful violations.

The fact that Congress did not simply extend the limitations period to three years, but instead adopted a two-tiered statute of limitations, makes it obvious that Congress intended to draw a significant distinction between ordinary violations and willful violations. It is equally obvious to us that the *Jiffy June* standard of willfulness—a standard that merely requires that an employer knew that the FLSA "was in the picture"—virtually obliterates any distinction between willful and nonwillful violations. As we said in Trans World Airlines, Inc. v. Thurston, "it would be virtually impossible for an employer to show that he was unaware of the Act and its potential applicability." Under the *Jiffy June* standard, the normal 2–year statute of limitations would seem to apply only to ignorant employers, surely not a state of affairs intended by Congress.

In common usage the word "willful" is considered synonymous with such words as "voluntary," "deliberate," and "intentional." The word "willful" is widely used in the law, and, although it has not by any means been given a perfectly consistent interpretation, it is generally understood to refer to conduct that is not merely negligent. The standard of willfulness that was adopted in *Thurston*—that the employer either knew or showed reckless disregard for the matter of whether its conduct was prohibited by the statute—is surely a fair reading of the plain language of the Act.

The strongest argument supporting the *Jiffy June* standard is that it was widely used for a number of years. The standard was not, however, consistently followed in all Circuits. In view of the fact that even the Secretary now shares our opinion that it is not supported by the plain language of the statute, we readily reject it.

We also reject the intermediate alternative espoused by the Secretary for the first time in this Court. Relying on the opinion of the Court of Appeals for the District of Columbia in Laffey v. Northwest Airlines, Inc., 567 F.2d 429, 461–462 (1976), cert. denied, 434 U.S. 1086 (1978), she argues that we should announce a two-step standard that would deem an FLSA violation willful "if the employer, recognizing it might be covered by the FLSA, acted without a reasonable basis for believing that it was complying with the statute." This proposal differs from *Jiffy June* because it would apparently make the issue in most cases turn on whether the employer sought legal advice concerning its pay practices. It would, however, permit a finding of willfulness to be based on nothing more than negligence, or, perhaps, on a completely good-faith but incorrect assumption that a pay plan complied with the FLSA in all respects. We believe the Secretary's new proposal, like the discredited *Jiffy June* standard, fails to give effect to the plain language of the statute of limitations.[13]

Ordinary violations of the FLSA are subject to the general 2–year statute of limitations. To obtain the benefit of the 3–year exception, the Secretary must prove that the employer's conduct was willful as that term is defined in both *Thurston* and this opinion.

The judgment of the Court of Appeals is affirmed.

■ JUSTICE MARSHALL, with whom JUSTICE BRENNAN and JUSTICE BLACKMUN join, dissenting.

The Court today imports into a limitations provision of the Fair Labor Standards Act (FLSA) the "knowing or reckless" definition of "willful" that we previously adopted in construing a liquidated damages provision of the Age Discrimination in Employment Act of 1967, 81 Stat. 602, as amended, 29 U.S.C. § 621 et seq., (ADEA). In doing so, the Court departs from our traditional contextual approach to the definition of the term "willful," ignores significant differences between the relevant provisions of the two Acts, and fails to accommodate the remedial purpose of civil actions under the FLSA. For these reasons, I would accept the slightly more expansive definition of "willful" urged by the Secretary of Labor. Under this latter standard, a violation of the FLSA is "willful" and therefore subjects an employer to a 3–year rather than a 2–year statute of limitations if the employer knew that there was an appreciable possibility that it was covered by the Act and failed to take steps reasonably calculated to resolve the doubt.

I have no quarrel with the opinion of the Court to the extent that it rejects the "in the picture" standard of willfulness elaborated in Coleman v. Jiffy June Farms, Inc. * * * But the Court's focus on the shortcomings of the *Jiffy June* standard is disingenuous, because neither party in the instant case urged the adoption of that standard before this Court. Rather, the dispute in this case pits the *Thurston* "knowing or reckless" standard, adopted by the Third Circuit in this case and urged by respondent Richland Shoe, against the *Laffey* standard, adopted by the D.C. Circuit in an earlier case and urged by petitioner the Secretary of Labor. The Court does not address this dispute until the penultimate page of its opinion, and its reasons for embracing the former standard over the latter are not convincing.

The Court seems to rely in part on "common usage" of the word "willful" in adopting the "knowing or reckless" standard. The Court fails to acknowledge, however, that the dictionary includes a wide variety of

---

**13.** We recognize that there is some language in *Trans World Airlines v. Thurston* not necessary to our holding, that would seem to permit a finding of unreasonableness to suffice as proof of knowing or reckless disregard, and thus that would render petitioner's standard an appropriate statement of the law. Our decision today should clarify this point: If an employer acts reasonably in determining its legal obligation, its action cannot be deemed willful under either petitioner's test or under the standard we set forth. If an employer acts unreasonably, but not recklessly, in determining its legal obligation, then, although its action would be considered willful under petitioner's test, it should not be so considered under *Thurston* or the identical standard we approve today.

definitions of "willful," ranging from "malicious" to "not accidental," and including precisely the intermediate definition urged by the Secretary—under which an act is willful if it is "done without ground for believing it is lawful." By refusing to recognize the various meanings that the term "willful" has come to bear in different legal settings, the Court today departs from our previous contextual approach to defining that term. In Spies v. United States, 317 U.S. 492, 497 (1943), this Court explained that "willful" is a word "of many meanings, its construction often being influenced by its context." Since *Spies,* we consistently have looked to the statutory context in which the word appears in order to determine its proper meaning. The Court's apparent abandonment of this approach in favor of a nonexistent "plain language" definition of "willful" is unprecedented and unwise.

Had the Court properly applied the traditional contextual approach, I believe it would have adopted the willfulness standard urged by the Secretary. Such an approach would have revealed that the definition of "willful" adopted previously in the context of the ADEA in Trans World Airlines, Inc. v. Thurston, does not transplant easily to the context of the FLSA. In *Thurston,* this Court explicitly acknowledged that its choice of the "knowing or reckless" definition of "willful" was influenced by the "punitive" nature of the double damages that flow from a finding of willfulness under the ADEA. In the instant case, a finding of willfulness leads not to a punitive sanction, but merely to an extended period during which an unlawfully underpaid employee may recover compensatory damages. What is at stake here is the applicability of the remedial provisions of the FLSA in the first instance. Perhaps recognizing this crucial distinction, the Court in *Thurston* expressly left open the possibility that the "knowing or reckless" definition of "willful" adopted for the ADEA might not be appropriate for the FLSA statute of limitations. The answer that the Court provides today may have an attractive tidiness, but it fails to recognize the contextual differences that call for different standards of willfulness in varying provisions of the two Acts. As a result, the Court has adopted a definition of "willful" that is improperly narrow in light of its effect on the remedial scope of the FLSA.

## NOTES AND QUESTIONS

**1.** Does the majority opinion give full weight to the congressional intent regarding "wilful" violations of the FLSA? Why should an employer who acts "unreasonably, but not recklessly" be subject to the same (shorter) statute of limitations as the reasonable employer? The majority interprets "wilful" not only for the FLSA, but also for the ADEA, Equal Pay Act, Davis–Bacon Act, and Walsh–Healey Act. What considerations under each statute might suggest different standards of wilfulness?

**2.** As Wood and Wood point out, actions under the Fair Labor Standards Act may be brought in a number of ways. The right to a private action under § 216(b) terminates when the Secretary of Labor files suit. Actions by the Secretary are usually brought either under § 216(c), which provides for civil damages, or § 217, which authorizes injunctive relief. Suits under

§ 216 may be brought before a jury, while § 217 actions proceed before a judge. Court delays and administrative limitations are such that the Department of Labor almost routinely files under § 217 rather than § 216. Does this make any difference in the enforcement or effectiveness of the Act?

Technically, monetary remedies under the FLSA are broader than the limited "make whole" remedies of Title VII, because § 216(b) of the FLSA provides that employers who violate the wage and hour provisions of the Act are liable to employees for their unpaid wages or overtime compensation *plus* an equal amount in liquidated damages, in the discretion of the trial judge. Liquidated damages, however, are not available in § 217 actions; because § 217 actions are the type most frequently filed by DoL, employees rarely receive liquidated damages. Wages which remain unpaid because employees entitled to them cannot be found revert to the Treasury Department in actions brought under § 216; under § 217 actions, the employer is permitted to keep them.

Section 15(a)(3) is the nonretaliation provision of the FLSA; it prohibits discharge or any other discrimination against an employee who has filed a complaint or instituted any proceeding under the Act. An employer discharged employees who insisted on compensation for overtime work. Is such a discharge unlawful under the statute? See Brock v. Casey Truck Sales, Inc., 839 F.2d 872 (2d Cir.1988). In Martin v. Gingerbread House, Inc., 977 F.2d 1405 (10th Cir.1992), a discharge was not held not to be retaliatory, despite the employer's statement that "people who are loyal don't call the labor department," since other valid reasons would have led to the same result.

**3.** What effect does the existence of a collective bargaining agreement have on the employees' FLSA claim? Can a union, bargaining in good faith on behalf of employees, agree to wage or hour terms different from those specified in the Act? For instance, instead of time and a half for overtime, could the union instead agree that overtime would be compensated by single time pay and double compensatory time off (for each hour of overtime, the employee would receive his regular rate of pay plus two hours time off)?

Could an employer and union foreclose employees' access to FLSA enforcement procedures by providing in a collective bargaining agreement for submission of any wage and hour claims to the binding arbitration procedures of that agreement? On petition for rehearing in *Jiffy June,* the employer argued that the employees had entered into a collective bargaining agreement under which all disputes were to be resolved by binding arbitration and that the employees should be bound by their agreement to process claims through the grievance machinery. The court found that resorting to the contractual grievance procedure would have been "a hopeless charade" since the union and the employer had previously agreed that the time worked would not be compensated as overtime.

In Barrentine v. Arkansas–Best Freight System, Inc., 450 U.S. 728 (1981), the Supreme Court applied the rationale of Alexander v. Gardner–

Denver Co., 415 U.S. 36 (1974), to disputes which were arguably a violation of both a collective bargaining agreement and the FLSA. *Alexander* had held that a victim of discrimination under Title VII could file both a charge at the EEOC and a grievance under a collective bargaining agreement and that neither cause of action was preempted or foreclosed by resort to the other. In *Barrentine*, the contract between Arkansas–Best and the Teamsters provided for grievances arising under the contract to be submitted to a joint union-employer committee for resolution. When the company refused to pay truckers for time spent conducting required pre-trip safety inspections and transporting trucks failing inspection to the company's repair facility, the truckers filed a grievance, which was rejected by the joint committee without explanation. The grievants then filed suit under the FLSA, alleging that the time spent performing the pre-trip inspection was compensable under the Act and that the union had breached its duty of fair representation by entering into a side deal with the company regarding compensability. The Supreme Court held that prior submission of the claim to arbitration did not foreclose the employees' statutory cause of action:

> While courts should defer to an arbitral decision where the employee's claim is based on rights arising out of the collective bargaining agreement, different considerations apply where the employee's claim is based on rights arising out of the statute designed to provide minimum substantive guarantees to individual workers.

450 U.S. at 737. The Court determined that the right to minimum wage and overtime pay was an individually guaranteed statutory right, and that employees could pursue redress through both a collective bargaining agreement, for contractually guaranteed rights, and through the statutory enforcement mechanism for statutory rights. Is this an effective means of accommodating the twin goals of our national labor policy of fostering collective bargaining and simultaneously protecting individual rights? Allowing employees to pursue both contractual and statutory rights, as permitted by cases like *Alexander* and *Barrentine* has been equated with giving employees "two bites at the apple." Is this fair to employers? Should employees have to exhaust internal contractual remedies before filing a statutory claim?

**4.** The Act also provides for both civil and criminal penalties, although the criminal penalties are almost never used. A study by the Government Accounting Office of DoL's FLSA enforcement practices indicated that regional directors in at least four regions could not recall having filed a criminal suit under the Act in more than ten years. Imprisonment is available only after a second criminal conviction, and the maximum prison term is six months.

**5.** It is open to question whether the Department of Labor is enforcing the Fair Labor Standards Act effectively. A U.S. Government Accounting Office (GAO) report issued in September 1985, updated a 1981 report which had concluded that noncompliance with minimum wage, overtime and record-keeping provisions of the FLSA was a serious and continuing problem, and that the Department of Labor was not seeking maximum compensation permitted for employees who were due wages. The 1985 Report found that most of the problems identified four years earlier still existed, and in several cases, were even worse. Recidivism is a problem. Because fines for first-time offenders under the FLSA are a maximum of $10,000, the Justice Department does not consider them serious, and other cases take priority. The Department of Labor has instructed regional directors to pursue liquidated damages more routinely, but personnel shortages make it unlikely that major shifts in enforcement will be forthcoming, absent any changes in the law which would make enforcement easier. What changes in the Act's enforcement provisions would you suggest? See U.S. General Accounting Office, The Department of Labor's Enforcement Of The Fair Labor Standards Act (1985).

Econometric analysis has borne out the GAO's conclusions. One study showed that noncompliance with the minimum wage provisions of the FLSA is higher in lower wage sectors, in nonmanufacturing, in the South, among females, among nonwhites, among teenagers, among employees over 55, and among part-time workers. The study found noncompliance to be greater for low-paid salaried workers than for hourly paid workers. Noncompliance varies positively with increases in the minimum wage rate and in the unemployment rate, and negatively with increases in inflation. Apparently, enforcement is not a significant deterrent. See Brigitte H. Sellekaerts & Stephen W. Welch, An Econometric Analysis of Minimum Wage Noncompliance, 23 Ind.Rel. 244 (1984).

In a survey taken to estimate noncompliance with the overtime provisions of the Act, at least 9.6 percent and as many as 20 percent of covered employees received *no* premium pay for overtime worked, and another 16 percent received less than time-and-a-half. As the authors somewhat drily concluded, "The evidence * * * strongly suggests that noncompliance with the overtime pay provisions of the FLSA is a nontrivial problem." See Ronald G. Ehrenburg & Paul L. Schumann, Compliance with the Overtime Pay Provisions of the Fair Labor Standards Act, 25 J.L. & Econ. 159 (1982).

## h. THE ECONOMICS OF MINIMUM WAGE LAWS

The purpose of the minimum wage, according to the FLSA's drafters, was to provide a "minimum standard of living necessary for health, efficiency and general well-being of workers * * *" Does the law accomplish what Congress originally intended? At the time of its passage more than 50 years ago, the minimum wage was 25 cents an hour. Beginning September 1, 1997, the minimum wage increased to $5.15 an hour. At that rate, an individual working full-time (40 hours a week, 50 weeks a year) would earn $10,300. In 1996, the federal poverty level for a family of three was $12,980. Is it appropriate to say that the minimum wage currently provides that minimum decent standard of living originally envisioned by Congress?

For years, economists have also questioned the efficiency of the Act, for entirely different reasons:

## Charles Brown, Curtis Gilroy, & Andrew Kohen, *The Effect of the Minimum Wage on Employment and Unemployment*

20 J.Econ.Lit. 487 (1982).

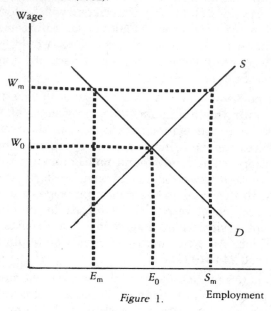

*Figure* 1.

### A.   Simple Supply-Demand Model

The most basic model of minimum wage effects on employment and unemployment focuses on a single competitive labor market with homogeneous workers whose wage $W_0$ would otherwise fall below the legally set minimum wage $W_m$.   Employers minimize costs both before and after the minimum wage law, workers' skills and level of effort are identical and given exogenously, and all workers in the market are covered by the minimum wage.   Adjustment to the new equilibrium is not considered.   In this model, initial employment $E_0$ is determined by supply and demand; once the minimum wage is introduced, employment falls to $E_m$, the level demanded at wage $W_m$ (Figure 1).   The proportional reduction in employment ($ln\ E_m - ln\ E_0$) is equal to the proportional wage increase ($ln\ W_m - ln\ W_0$) times the elasticity of demand.

If employment would otherwise increase, the "reduction" in employment predicted by the model may take the form of a lower rate of employment growth rather than an actual decline in the number employed. If employment actually declines, it may take the form of not replacing workers who quit rather than discharging workers.

While the model determines an excess supply of labor at the new minimum wage, $S_m - E_m$, this excess supply does not correspond to the official measure of unemployment, or even to the increase in such unemployment above some "frictional" level. $S_m$ represents the number (or work-hours) of those persons willing to work at $W_m$, but some of the $S_m - E_m$ who are not employed may decide that prospects of finding work are too dim to make actively searching for work worthwhile. Those not actively looking for work are not included in the official unemployment count.

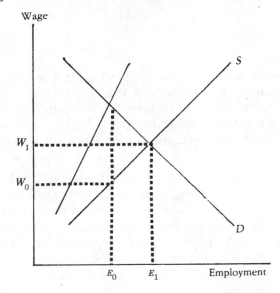

*Figure 2.*

## B.  *Monopsony*

A well-known exception to the conclusion that the minimum wage reduces employment is the monopsony case. Without a minimum wage, the monopsonistic employer's marginal cost of labor everywhere exceeds the supply price; labor is hired until marginal cost and demand are equal (Figure 2). A minimum wage makes the employer a pricetaker, up to the level of employment $S(W_m)$. Thus, a minimum wage between the original monopsony wage $W_0$ and the competitive wage $W_1$ will increase employment; choosing $W_m = W_1$ brings employment to its competitive level, $E_1$. Once $W_m$ equals $W_1$, further increases would reduce employment below the competitive level. The monopsony model has not motivated much recent work, perhaps because there is little evidence that it is important in modern-day low-wage labor markets.

## C.  *"Shock" Effects*

If employers do not minimize costs, there is the possibility that they will respond to a minimum wage increase by raising the productivity of their operation to offset the increase. This possibility is often labeled a "shock" effect—the minimum "shocks" employers into greater productivity.

Such a shock effect might reduce the disemployment from a minimum wage (increase) but is unlikely to eliminate it.  First, while some firms may be in a position to take advantage of previously unrealized economies, other firms may not be so fortunate.  Surveys of employers find reports of such responses from some but not all firms.  Second, firms may have failed to minimize costs by using *too much* labor at the previous wage $W_0$; cost-cutting would then take the form of discharging (or not replacing) the extra workers.

\* \* \*

H.   *Welfare Effects*

The effect of the minimum wage in the simplest competitive market is straight-forward:  employment is reduced, and the efficiency of the labor market is impaired, because some individuals whose marginal product exceeds their reservation wage are unable to work.  Under monopsony, a minimum wage could increase employment and enhance the efficiency of the labor market.

The remaining models often identify factors that could reduce the disemployment effects of a minimum wage—improved managerial efficiency (or additional worker effort), movement from the covered to the uncovered sector, or (partially) offsetting increases in employment of better-paid workers.  Each of these mitigating factors, however, has a welfare cost of its own.  For example, workers displaced into the uncovered sector end up working in jobs where their marginal product is less than it was in the covered sector.  Thus, a zero employment loss would not imply that welfare costs were negligible.  \* \* \*

NOTES AND QUESTIONS

**1.**  In addition to creating unemployment, the minimum wage has also been charged with fueling inflation.  If the minimum wage has the unemployment and inflation effects that economists predict, why is it so popular?  One reason may be simple politics.  Another suggestion is that the perforce rudimentary models economists are able to build may make assumptions which are unwarranted or untrue when tested against reality.  The Simple Supply-Demand Model assumes that no employer is able to alter demand or restrict supply, that all workers are maximizing their individual productivity, that productivity is measurable, and that wages can be based on productivity.  Do these assumptions accurately describe the world in which we live?

John Dunlop, economist and former Secretary of Labor, has written:

[E]fficiency is not the only test that a society applies to its labor markets, and particularly to internal markets, which are asked to meet tests of equity, security, equal employment opportunity, and other goals.  In brief, I do not believe that microeconomic theory is adequate to provide a useful understanding of internal labor markets and their effects on internal and external movements of labor, on internal wage structures for job classifications in enterprises of size, and for on-the-job training. * * *

It is a well established fact that wage rates or average hourly earnings for a defined job classification, such as maintenance electrician or keypunch operator, show very wide variations in a locality, particularly in a community with a variety of industries. * * * Neoclassical economics has sought to live with these large differences by proposing that they are related to the quality of the labor force in the different enterprises; compensating differences in working conditions, safety, distances, and the like; differences in information; and by the fact that there are longer-run competitive forces in labor markets tending to eliminate these differences. * * * My experience teaches that this view of wage rate differentials is simply grossly inadequate to the reality, granted that some persistent differentials arise from the sources stressed by microeconomics, although they are virtually impossible to measure satisfactorily. * * *

John Dunlop, Industrial Relations and Economics: The Common Frontier of Wage Determination, Proceedings of the 37th Annual Meeting, IRRA, 9, 17–18 (1985).

How do Dunlop's comments on determining relative wage rates apply to microeconomic theory on minimum wages? See also Nancy K. Kubasek, The Artificiality of Economic Models as a Guide for Legal Evolution, 33 Cleveland St.L.Rev. 505 (1985).

Another response to the neoclassical microeconomists suggests that the income and work-incentive effects of the minimum wage outweigh the unemployment effects. Yet another tack is to analyze the minimum wage in the context of those who are actually affected by it (i.e., the marginally employed individuals most likely to be benefitted by an increase or put out of work by it) and the network of social welfare resources at their disposal if they are indeed unemployed as a result of an increase in minimum wage. See Keith B. Leffler, Minimum Wages, Welfare, and Wealth Transfers to the Poor, 21 J. Law & Econ. 345 (1978).

For a general analysis of the economics of legislated minimum employment standards that is critical of the traditional neoclassical model, see Steven L. Willborn, Individual Employment Rights and the Standard Economic Objection: Theory and Empiricism, 67 Neb.L.Rev. 101 (1988).

**2.** One possible alternative to a minimum wage would be a wage subsidy for individuals who earned less than a certain wage. What economic effect would a wage subsidy have? Would it be preferable to a mandatory minimum wage?

**3.** Studies measuring the unemployment effects of the minimum wage show that it hits hardest at teenagers, one estimate being that a ten percent increase in the minimum wage induces a one percent increase in teenage unemployment (and less than half that for adults). The teenage unemployment rate is already considerably higher than any older segment of the workforce.  One proposed solution to the unemployment effect of the minimum wage would be a subminimum wage for youth, which would establish a new, lower minimum wage rate for teenagers.  Proponents of the youth subminimum argue that it would encourage employers to hire teenagers, who tend to be unskilled and in need of substantial job training, and thus enable teenagers to escape the Catch–22 cycle of "employers won't hire you if you don't have experience, and how will you get experience if no one will hire you?"  What are the potential dangers of the subminimum wage?  See David H. Solomon, Note: A Model Youth Differential Amendment:  Reducing Youth Unemployment Through A Lower Minimum Wage for the Young, 19 Harv.J. on Legis. 143 (1982).

Such a subminimum wage was enacted as part of the 1989 Amendments to the FLSA.  Section 6 of the Amendments established a "training wage" of $3.35 an hour effective April 1, 1990;  beginning April 1, 1991, the training minimum wage will change to "not less than $3.35 an hour or 85 percent of the [standard minimum wage]."  What are the potential problems with a subminimum wage?  How well do the provisions of the 1989 training wage address those concerns?

## 2.  MISCELLANEOUS FEDERAL STATUTES

In addition to the Fair Labor Standards Act, other federal statutes govern wage rates in specific industries, primarily for government contractors.  All of these statutes attempt to guarantee wage rates for employees on government projects at a level commensurate with prevailing local wage rates. Employment at 85 percent of the minimum wage may be permitted for students in retail or service establishments, agriculture or in their schools.  § 214(b)(1–3).  This subminimum wage rate may be applied if approved by the Wage–Hour Administrator.

The Walsh-Healey Public Contracts Act, 41 U.S.C. §§ 35–45, establishes basic labor standards for work done on U.S. government contracts in excess of $10,000 in value for materials, supplies, articles, equipment, or naval vessels.  All persons engaged in the manufacture or furnishing of contracted items are covered, except those in executive, administrative, or professional positions, or those performing office, custodial, or maintenance work.

The Davis-Bacon Act, 40 U.S.C. §§ 276a to 276a–5, covers construction, alteration, or repair of federal buildings or other public works for contracts in excess of $2000.  It applies to all agencies of the federal government and the District of Columbia.  Davis-Bacon requires federal contractors to pay wages on construction work that are equivalent to the prevailing wages for corresponding types of workers on similar construction in the locality where the work is performed.  It also provides for the determination of prevailing fringe benefits.  The Secretary of Labor is charged with making the determination of what are prevailing wages.  Employee complaints may be filed with the contracting agency or with the Department of Labor.  The Miller Act of 1935, 40 U.S.C. §§ 270 et seq., is an important adjunct to the Davis-Bacon Act;  it requires construction contractors to execute a payment bond to protect the wages of employees providing labor before any contract covered by its provisions is awarded. The law applies to contracts over $2000 for the construction, alteration, or repair of any public building or public work of the United States; it does not apply to federal aid projects but only to direct federal contracts.

The Service Contract Act of 1965, 41 U.S.C. §§ 351–358, establishes labor standards for federal contracts in excess of $2500 for the provision of services through the use of service employees. This includes employees in a wide variety of occupations: cafeteria and food service, maintenance and guard service, linen supply services, warehousing or storage services, laundry and drycleaning, and secretarial services. As with the Walsh-Healey Act, executive, administrative, and professional employees are exempted.

## NOTES AND QUESTIONS

**1.** The "prevailing wage" acts have been criticized by both politicians and economists for their inflationary economic effects, and numerous unsuccessful attempts have been made to modify or eliminate the Davis-Bacon Act particularly. See Robert S. Goldfarb & John F. Morrell, The Davis-Bacon Act: An Appraisal of Recent Studies, 34 Industrial & Lab.Rel.Rev. 191 (1981); John Warner, Congressional and Administrative Efforts to Modify or Eliminate the Davis-Bacon Act, 10 Western St.U.L.Rev. 1 (1982).

Why enact such legislation? The economic efficiency arguments are weak. One possible rationale is to prevent the government from abusing its tremendous economic power, but government effectively competes with private employers for employees. Another is to eliminate any incentive for contractors bidding on government contracts to cut costs ("wage busting" particularly) to the point where project quality deteriorates. The most likely rationale is that it is designed to redistribute or stabilize income in the construction trades. The Department of Labor has stated that the Davis-Bacon Act's purpose is "to protect prevailing living standards of the construction workers, to provide equality of opportunity for contractors, and to prevent the disturbance of the local economy." Comments in U.S. General Accounting Office, Report: The Davis-Bacon Act Should Be Repealed 203 (1979).

Recent studies indicate that the inflationary effect of the Davis-Bacon Act is much less than earlier thought. See Steven G. Allen, Much Ado About Davis-Bacon: A Critical Review and New Evidence, 26 J. Law & Econ. 707 (1983).

**2.** The Walsh-Healey and Service Contract Acts have been subject to the same criticisms as the Davis-Bacon Act, but have exhibited a similar political resilience. For a thorough cost-benefit analysis of the Service Contract Act, see Robert G. Goldfarb & John S. Heywood, An Economic Evaluation of the Service Contract Act, 36 Ind. & Lab.Rel.Rev. 56 (1982).

**3.** The Walsh-Healey Act and the Contract Work Hours and Safety Standards Act were amended in December 1985 by P.L. 99-145. Effective January 1, 1986, employees of government contractors no longer have to be paid a daily overtime premium for work over eight hours a day; instead, overtime will be due only after 40 hours a week.

## 3.   STATE WAGE AND HOUR PROTECTION

In addition to the wage and hour provisions of the Fair Labor Standards Act, every state has enacted wage and hour laws.  Many have passed state equivalents of the FLSA, which exist concurrent with the federal statute, with state-mandated minimum wages ranging from a low of $1.60 an hour in Wyoming to a high of $6.25 in Missouri.  Where state minimum wages are higher than the federal minimum, the state minimum controls; state law may also cover individuals not covered by the FLSA.  State law may specify how wages are to be paid and establish timetables for payment. An important component of state wage protection law is the state wage collection statute, which generally provides a means by which employees may recover unpaid wages, regardless of amount, from employers, by filing a claim with a state agency or going to court.

## Ressler v. Jones Motor Co.

487 A.2d 424 (Pa.Super.1985).

■ JOHNSON, JUDGE:

Appellants Ressler and Hertwig brought suit on behalf of themselves and a class of non-union employees of appellee Jones Motor Company's now defunct General Commodities Division ("GCD"), seeking recovery of sums withheld from their wages as "contributions" to an Earnings Participation Plan ("EPP" or "Plan").  The Plan placed salaries on a sliding scale varying as a function of the employer's profit or loss ratio, and was instituted by Jones Motor during a period of significant financial hardship. The trial court found no violation of the Commonwealth's Wage Payment and Collection Law ("WPCL") and granted summary judgment on behalf of Jones Motor upon a determination that the "contributions" to the Plan were wage reductions.  * * *

In 1979, the GCD began to suffer serious financial losses, which continued through 1980 and into 1981.  In a desperate effort to reduce these losses, the EPP was instituted, which placed salaries on a sliding scale varying according to the GCD's ratio of total expenses to total revenues.  According to the Plan proposal, when this ratio equals 95%, employees would draw their regular salaries.  If the ratio is 96% or above, employees would "contribute" to the Plan based upon a figure related to the ratio and their wage brackets, with the amount withheld varying at each expense ratio.  The proposal indicates further that if the expense ratio falls below 100%, "a lump sum adjustment payment will be made to plan participants."  Even where the expense ratio falls to 94% or below, all employees, regardless of wage bracket, receive the same percentage bonus, calculated at each expense ratio.

Prior to implementation of the Plan, Jones Motor's management, including the named appellants, met with employees and explained the EPP, promoting it in terms of the company's ultimate survival. A key to the Plan's effectiveness was obtaining 100% participation by all employees, union and non-union alike. Approximately 97% of the GCD employees signed authorization forms agreeing to participate and stating they would be legally bound to "make contributions or receive benefits under the Plan." The EPP was implemented on June 14, 1981, at which time the expense ratio was 112%, resulting in smaller paychecks for all employees.

After approximately three months, a Delaware Teamster's Union local filed a grievance claiming the Plan violated their collective bargaining agreement. Jones Motor agreed to discontinue the Plan for its union employees, and paid back the "contributions" they had already made.

Jones Motor continued the EPP with its non-union employees, but it proved to be an insufficient cost-cutting mechanism, and the GCD ceased operations on October 29, 1982. Appellants brought suit * * * for recovery of their "contributions," claiming they were withheld in violation of the WPCL. The amended complaint alleged breach of contract under the terms of the EPP agreement, and appellants further sought certification of a class action.

* * *

The trial judge determined the EPP to be "nothing more than a program of wage reductions (or increases should the company reenter a period of prosperity) dressed up in a fancy name to be more acceptable to the employees; * * * " and found no provisions "which, by any interpretation, would infer that the Defendant's employees could expect a return of the reduction which they realized in their paychecks." The court granted Jones Motor's motion for summary judgment, and denied appellants' motion for certification of a class action without discussion. Upon careful examination of the record, however, we believe the "contributions" withheld by Jones Motor from its employees' paychecks were wage deductions, thus raising a genuine issue of material fact as to conformity with the law of this Commonwealth.

Viewing the EPP in its entirety, it is clear to us that the sums withheld from employees' paychecks were deductions from earnings rather than reductions in salary. As noted previously, the "contributions" or "benefits" were to be calculated at each expense ratio level. There appears to be no fixed or easily ascertainable sum which would be withheld or paid out, and we find such indefinite, unpredictable amounts to more closely resemble deductions than reductions as held by the trial court. Furthermore, Jones Motor's President Sheehy, in a letter dated September 25, 1981, stated: "In order to avoid a possible strike action while we attempt to resolve the E.P.P. issue, I am temporarily suspending the *payroll deductions* for E.P.P. contributions from union personnel. The non-union personnel will be required to continue the participation." [Emphasis added].

Finally, and perhaps most persuasive, we find a letter dated July 22, 1982, from the Director of the Department of Labor and Industry's Bureau of Labor Standards.  Responding to a request by Jones Motor's Vice President and General Counsel for clarification of a claim by a former terminal manager, the director states:

> [The employee] advised us that $85.80 was deducted from his earned wages each pay period for a total of 20 pay periods from June 20 through October 30, 1981; a total of $1716.
>
> Our claimant maintains he signed no authorization for the deduction in question which is identified on his pay slip as EPP contribution.
>
> Unless Jones Motor can produce an authorization signed by [the employee] to permit this deduction we must consider said deduction illegal under the Wage Payment and Collection Law.

This letter is significant at this point in our analysis because it is the only indication we find in the record that the contributions were *identified* on employees' pay slips as an amount presumably subtracted from gross pay. Common sense dictates that salary reductions would not be so designated. This supports a conclusion that we are here dealing with deductions, much like any other type of deduction which would be noted on a pay slip.  We must therefore turn to the WPCL to determine whether the amounts in question were lawfully withheld from employees' wages.

The Wage Payment and Collection Law states, in pertinent part:

260.3   Regular payday

(a) Wages other than fringe benefits and wage supplements. Every employer shall pay all wages, other than fringe benefits and supplements, due to his employes on regular paydays designated in advance by the employer.  * * * The wages shall be paid in lawful money of the United States or check, except that *deductions provided by the law, or as authorized by regulation of the Department of Labor and Industry for the convenience of the employe, may be made including deductions of contributions to employe benefits plans,* which are subject to the Employee Retirement Income Security Act of 1974, 29 U.S.C. § 1001 et seq.  [Emphasis added].

(b) Fringe benefits and wage supplements.  Every employer who by agreement deducts union dues from employes' pay or agrees to pay or provide fringe benefits or wage supplements, must remit the deductions or pay or provide the fringe benefits or wage supplements, as required, within 10 days after such payments are required to be made to the union in case of dues or to a trust or pooled fund, or within 10 days after such payments are required to be made directly to the employe, or within 60 days of the date when proper claim was filed by the employe in situations where no required time for payment is specified.

43 P.S. § 260.3.

Pursuant to this provision, 34 Pa.Code § 9.1 sets forth those deductions from wages authorized by law as promulgated by the Department of Labor and Industry.  The first twelve provisions delineate such deductions as, for example, contributions to employee welfare and pension plans, payments to credit unions and savings funds, contributions for charitable purposes, deductions for social security and taxes, labor organization dues, and other specified deductions.  Deductions which are not listed under 34 Pa.Code § 9.1 (1–12) may fall under 34 Pa.Code § 9.1(13): "Such other deductions authorized in writing by employes as *in the discretion of the Department is proper and in conformity with the intent and purpose of the Wage Payment and Collection Law* (43 P.S. §§ 260.1–260.12)." [Emphasis added].

Although Jones Motor obtained written authorizations from its employees, the record does not establish that the Department evaluated the EPP and determined the Plan to be in conformity with the WPCL. Appellee directs us to the Department's July 22, 1982 letter, referred to supra, claiming this establishes departmental approval of the Plan.  We do not find this letter controlling in construing the entire EPP program as lawful.  Absent departmental approval, the Plan was invalid, and Jones Motor wrongfully withheld wages due to its employees.  An inquiry is therefore necessary on the factual issue of whether the Department of Labor and Industry evaluated and authorized the EPP as in conformity with the intent and purpose of the WPCL, and summary judgment was inappropriately granted.

Pa.R.C.P. 1035(b) provides that summary judgment will be granted only "if the pleadings, depositions, answers to interrogatories, and admissions on file, together with the affidavits, if any, show that there is no genuine issue as to any material fact and that the moving party is entitled to judgment as a matter of law."  It is well established that the moving party has the burden of showing that there is no genuine issue of material fact, and the record must be viewed in the light most favorable to the non-moving party.

The [trial court] found neither a significant dispute nor the raising of a genuine issue as to any material fact.  Our examination of the relevant materials, however, indicates the existence of a genuine issue of material fact.  We therefore reverse the granting of summary judgment, finding a significant dispute regarding departmental approval of the EPP.

Department of Labor and Industry evaluation of a proposed deduction would necessarily analyze conformity with the "intent and purpose" of the WPCL.  We find it helpful here to consider what those purposes might be.

In Weingrad v. Fischer & Porter Company, 47 D. & C.2d 244 (C.C.P. Bucks Co. 1968), the court provided a thoughtful analysis of the Wage Payment and Collection Law (in denying recovery to plaintiff by holding said statute to provide only for wages earned prior to termination of employment).  Finding no cases directly bearing upon the question presented, the court turned to authority pertaining to the purpose for enacting similar statutes in other jurisdictions.  The court quoted from the Supreme

Court of Oregon in State ex rel. Nilsen v. Oregon State Motor Assn., 248 Or. 133, 138, 432 P.2d 512, 515 (1967):

> "The policy of the statute is to aid an employe in the prompt collection of compensation due him and to discourage an employer from using a position of economic superiority as a lever to dissuade an employe from promptly collecting his agreed compensation * * *. The smaller the amount of the unpaid compensation the greater is the need for assistance in effecting collection."

* * *

The *Weingrad* court was obviously concerned with the aspect of "wages due," but we believe the notion of economic superiority exercised by an employer in the payment (or non-payment) of wages is of equal import. If Jones Motor instituted a plan at will to allow for deductions from its employees' wages, we view this as the type of economic coercion which the statute addresses, and which the Department of Labor and Industry is empowered to regulate. Moreover, the Department, in promulgating the Act, has carefully delineated those deductions which are permitted. Provisions 1 through 12 of 34 Pa.Code § 9.1 specifically set forth acceptable deductions and we believe public policy, and no less common sense, dictates that the Department have equal, if not greater, concern for those deductions which are not enumerated, but fall under 34 Pa.Code § 9.1(13) ("other deductions"). An earnings plan which affects wage payments deserves close scrutiny by the state agency empowered to assure that the interests of employees are protected. We therefore hold that a deduction from wages as herein described in the case before us is unlawful absent a showing of Department of Labor and Industry approval and written authorizations by employees.

This decision is not in any way intended to impair the ability of an employer or employee to modify the terms of an employment contract. Indeed, the law of this Commonwealth permits an employer to reduce the salary of an employee hired at will where the employee acquiesces in or agrees to the change. 320 Pa. 414, 183 A. 40 (1936). However, when an employer establishes a so-called earnings participation plan such as the EPP herein described, there is an obligation to analyze the plan to determine exactly what is involved. Our examination of Jones Motor's plan indicates that it is not an acceptable means of modifying salaries, and it therefore does not rise to the level of lawful wage reductions.

* * *

Reversed and remanded.

## NOTES AND QUESTIONS

**1.** Why does the court conclude that withheld earnings under the EPP were a wage deduction rather than a reduction?

**2.** What was the effect of the permissions Jones got from its employees agreeing to the EPP?

**3.** What else could Jones Motor Company have done to effect the cost savings it required?

**4.** Jones Motor Company went bankrupt. How likely is it that the employees will be able to collect their unpaid wages? See Chapter 12.

**5.** Pennsylvania's Wage Payment and Collection Law is typical of state wage collection statutes, in that it sets up a framework for employees to collect unpaid wages within a set period of time through a fairly informal proceeding at the state Department of Industry. The statute defines what are permissible deductions and withholdings from an individual's paycheck. Setoff of claimed debts to the employer is usually not permitted, although deductions for loss or damage resulting from gross negligence, willful misconduct, or dishonesty generally are. Agency decisions are usually appealable de novo in state or municipal court; if a recalcitrant employer refuses to pay, the agency's final decision is enforceable in court. Attorney's fees are sometimes provided for, but not always, and there may be a statutory penalty assessed against employers.

**6.** Garnishment of wages is also subject to regulation by state law. A relatively new use of garnishment is to permit automatic wage withholding from individuals who have failed to make court-ordered child support payments. Congress has stepped in to encourage states to take such action with the Child Support Enforcement Amendments of 1984 to the Child Support Enforcement Act of 1975, 42 U.S.C. §§ 651–662 (1982). The Amendments required states to enact conforming legislation by October 1, 1985, or suffer losses in federal welfare funding. See Note, Kansas Enacts New Provisions for Child Support Enforcement—Mandatory Wage Withholding, 25 Washburn L.J. 91 (1985) for background on the federal legislation and a detailed description of one state's response. The Kansas Department of Social and Rehabilitation Services (SRS) acts as the public agency which assumes the function of wage withholding. The Kansas statute requires all support orders or modifications after January 1, 1986, to include a conditional order for income withholding, to eliminate the necessity to file an application with SRS for withholding services. Wage withholding is automatically triggered thereafter the tenth day after a one-month arrearage develops. Federal law requires the state agency to charge an application fee of up to $25; in Kansas the fee is one dollar, while Missouri charges ten cents. The procedure is initiated by giving notice of the proposed withholding to the obligor, who has an opportunity to contest. There are specific and limited statutory grounds upon which to contest the withholding: due process or mistakes of fact in the notice of delinquency on the amount due, the amount to be withheld, or the identity of the obligor. The federal act specifies that inappropriateness of amount, changed financial circumstances of obligor, or lack of visitation are not subjects to be addressed through the wage withholding process. The federal statute establishes employer responsibilities and tries to make them as straightforward and simple as possible. See 42 U.S.C. § 666(b)(6). After receiving an order for wage withholding, the employer must initiate withholding no later than the first pay period that occurs 14 days after the service date of the order.  Wages withheld must be sent to the requesting court clerk or trustee.  The clerk or trustee must be promptly notified when the obligor terminates his employment, along with the last known address of the obligor and the name and address of his new employer.  If there is more than one withholding order, satisfaction must be apportioned among them.  Wage withholding may not exceed the maximum allowed by the Consumer Credit Protection Act, 15 U.S.C. § 1673(b) (up to 65 percent of disposable earnings and may include such income as retirement benefits).  The employer may collect a small fee (not to exceed ten dollars a month) to cover administrative costs.  Finally, the federal law requires that support orders have priority over any other legal process against the same wages.  See 42 U.S.C. § 666(b)(7).

7.  State law may also provide for wages and benefits to continue for employees called to serve on jury duty.  But see Frolic Footwear, Inc. v. State, 683 S.W.2d 611 (Ark.1985), where the Arkansas Supreme Court held that § 39–103 of the Arkansas Statutes, which provides in part: "No employer shall subject an employee to discharge, loss of sick leave, loss of vacation time, or any other form of penalty on account of his or her absence from employment by reason of jury duty," did not require an employer to make up the employee's net loss in pay arising from jury duty.

8.  What effect, if any, does an arbitration clause in an employment contract have on an individual's ability to pursue a wage claim through state administrative channels?  In Perry v. Thomas, 482 U.S. 483 (1987), the Supreme Court held that the U.S. Arbitration Act preempted provisions of the California wage statute that permitted actions for the collection of wages without regard to the existence of a private agreement to arbitrate.  Should arbitration clauses that effectively waive the individual's statutory rights be subject to the same standards for enforcement as releases?  What standards should apply?

9.  California's prevailing wage law sets pay levels for workers on public-works projects.  The law, which allows contractors to pay apprentices in approved programs lower wages, was upheld by the Supreme Court against an ERISA preemption challenge brought by a contractor who subcontracted work through a non-approved apprentice program.  California Division of Labor Standards Enforcement v. Dillingham Construction, N.A., Inc., 117 S.Ct. 832 (1997).

---

## B.   What Is a Job Worth?

### 1.   The Economics of Wage Determination

Whether an individual is paid minimum wage or more than a million dollars a year is determined by some measure of the value of the individual's labor.  But what is a job "worth"?  To some extent, that depends on whose perspective is used to determine the worth or value of a job.  Some employers set wages by looking externally at the "market rate" for similar work at other enterprises.  Others engage industrial engineers to conduct sophisticated internal job evaluations, which peg the relative value to the employer of different jobs within the same enterprise. From the employee's perspective, both monetary and nonmonetary factors affect individual determinations of what a job is "worth."

## Robert J. Flanagan, *The Price of Labor and Its Value,* The Park City Papers—Papers Presented at the Labor Law Group Conference on Labor and Employment Law in Park City, Utah

293–303 (1985).

It will come as no surprise to you if I reveal at the outset that the price of labor is determined by supply and demand. So, in some important but sometimes subtle ways is the value. The answer is of no help, nor are the subtleties obvious, however, until one explores the meaning of that well-worn phrase, "the forces of supply and demand," in the labor market. Nevertheless, I believe that there are only three basic ideas, which, once understood, give the fundamental analytical power to labor market analysis. These three ideas pertain to (a) the employer's side of the market (demand), (b) the worker's side of the market (supply), and (c) the interaction of the two sides of the market (equilibrium).

*The Employer's Side: The Tradeoff Between Wages and Employment*

The first basic idea is that on the demand side of the market there is a tradeoff between the rate of compensation and the level of employment. An increase in the wage rate induces a reduction in employment (other things held equal) and conversely. Technically, this is sometimes referred to as the "law of downward sloping demand for labor." This is a proposition of fundamental importance and one for which there is considerable empirical support. Consider two of the most obvious implications. Increases in the wage rate via collective bargaining or minimum wage statutes will induce reductions in employment. (This behavioral response is behind the skepticism of most economists concerning the efficacy of minimum wages as a device to reduce poverty.) Conversely, a wage subsidy policy may be a good way to expand the employment opportunities of the unemployed.

Where does this scientific "law" come from? What is its behavioral basis? We are dealing with the employer side of the market, so we must begin with the employer's objectives. This is usually taken to be profit maximization. Profit maximization yields one important decision rule: Take any action that adds more to revenues than it does to costs—i.e., any action that increases profits. The corollary is: Stop taking any action (e.g., the hiring of workers) at the point at which the additional revenues obtained from the action just equal the additional costs incurred. It is the application of this decision rule that is implied by the profit maximization objective that yields the tradeoff between the wage rate and the level of employment on the employer's side of the market.

To see this, simply apply the decision rule to the labor hiring decision. Initially, assume that the additional (marginal) cost of hiring another worker is the wage rate. What is the additional (marginal) revenue from hiring another worker? The additional revenue consists of the additional production that is attributable to the hiring of another employee multiplied by the price at which the new output can be sold. A profit-maximizing firm will hire workers up to the point at which the revenue received from hiring one more worker just equals the wage of the worker. But—getting back to the basic question—why does the application of the decision rule of a profit-maximizing firm result in a tradeoff between wages and employment? In a competitive labor market, the wage paid will not vary as a firm hires more workers. Likewise, in a competitive product market, the price at which the product is sold will remain constant as the firm sells more output (produced by additional workers). The key question, then, is how the output per worker changes as more workers are hired. Here we run into the law of diminishing returns: As more and more workers are added to a fixed capital stock or plant, their productivity (although positive) will begin to diminish at some point. It is usually easiest to think of this as the problem of not enough machines and equipment to use labor resources efficiently. With each new worker producing less, the additional revenue to hiring workers is falling. When it falls to the wage rate, the firm stops hiring labor.

From an employer's point of view, the "value" of labor is the market value of the additional output produced by adding the last worker (technically referred to as the value of the marginal product of labor), and this is the same as the wage rate. Thus, the value and the price of labor are the same.

Now consider the dynamics of this situation. Initially, an employer applies the decision rule discussed above to maximize profits. Then a wage increase (e.g., as the result of a minimum wage increase or collective bargaining settlement) raises the employer's marginal costs above the value of labor's marginal product. Profits are no longer maximized. In order to set marginal revenue equal to marginal costs again (as the decision rule requires) the employer must raise the marginal productivity of labor, and the only way to do this is to reduce employment (relative to capital, materials, etc.). Thus, it is the technical relationships that induce diminishing marginal productivity that produce the tradeoff between wages and employment.

### The Worker Side: Compensating Wage Differentials

The second basic idea is that the wage rates that we observe in the labor market tend to compensate for variations in the nonmonetary conditions of jobs. This idea goes back to Adam Smith over 200 years ago—a relatively long period of time for a scientific idea to survive. It is important to note at the outset that the nonmonetary working conditions can be good or bad (e.g., a very safe or a very unsafe work environment).

The key fact that differentiates labor from other productive resources is the fact that it can have preferences concerning the work environment, and any serious analysis of the labor market must cope with this. Adam Smith's durable theory was deceptively simple, and it involves both a *process* and a *result*. The process is this: Workers select jobs that maximize their "net advantage" (i.e., the combination of monetary and nonmonetary aspects of a job). Therefore, they move between jobs until the net advantage of different jobs is equalized—i.e., there is no job change worth making.

The result of this process is a system of "compensating" or "equalizing" wage differentials between jobs. To see that this is the result, recall that (a) if net advantage (the sum of wage and nonwage job elements) is equalized and (b) the nonwage characteristics of jobs differ across jobs, then (c) the wage of the jobs must also differ in offsetting directions. In effect, a worker "buys" agreeable working conditions by accepting a relatively low wage (other factors, including skill, held constant). Alternatively, a worker is bribed to accept relatively poor working conditions by being offered a relatively high wage. Thus, for a given skill, there will be a spectrum of wages and working conditions, reflecting the dispersion of tastes among workers for the mix of pecuniary and nonpecuniary compensation.

What does this imply for our discussion of the value and price of labor? Obviously, the notion of compensation that is appropriate for labor supply decisions is much broader than the "price" of labor that is commonly reported in wage and fringe benefit statistics. When benefits are relatively congenial, the value of a job will exceed the observed price (because some of the worker's potential money wage has been "spent" on good working conditions). When job conditions are very poor, the value of the job may be less than the observed wage—i.e., the nonmonetary aspects are effectively negative.

\* \* \*

*Both Sides of the Labor Market: Equilibrium*

Economic analysis is distinguished from most other work in the social sciences by the notion of *equilibrium*—there are forces that drive the system toward a resting point. These forces are the supply and demand factors discussed above. This is the third basic idea in discussing the price and value of labor. In the context of a labor market, equilibrium is the rate of compensation and level of employment from which there is no tendency for the system to move in the absences of some disturbance on the demand or supply side. It is the outcome of the interaction of the two sets of motivations discussed above: the employer's drive to maximize profits and the worker's drive to maximize net advantage.

A key feature of the equilibrium notion is that there are two sets of motivations operating simultaneously—i.e., on the two sides of the market. Some of the most persistent economic fallacies arise from arguments that address the response on one side of the market while ignoring the simultaneous responses on the other side of the market. Consider the earlier minimum wage example. Those who argue that increasing the minimum wage is desirable because it will draw individuals off of welfare and into the labor force are more or less correct about the supply response if there was a certain prospect of employment, but are completely overlooking the demand side of the market, where the effect of an increased minimum wage would be to reduce the probability that new labor force entrants would find a job.

The presence of an equilibrium greatly simplifies the study of the effect of institutional impacts (e.g., statutes or collective bargaining) on the price and value of labor, because the effect of such an impact is normally to change the equilibrium wage and employment levels.

\* \* \*

My first examples come from EEO law. When applied to wage discrimination in a class action context, these laws raise the following question: Is the work of some groups undervalued in comparison to that of other groups? A standard of value is needed to answer this question, and the touchstone for developing the standard is the compensating differentials idea that each aspect of a job has a price. This has two roles in employment discrimination litigation, one apparently much less obvious than the other.

The more obvious role is the statistical implementation of the idea that there is a specific monetary return to education, training, stable job attendance, etc. Every class action begins with a showing that the average wage of racial minorities or women is less than the average wage of whites or men that is countered by the defendant's claim that there are skill differences or other "business necessity" explanations for the average wage differences. Who is right? With a large sample of individuals, one can implement the compensating differentials idea by estimating a statistical relationship that effectively describes the "price" of each job or personal attribute *and* also permits a test of whether the plaintiff's class is disadvantaged *after* controlling for the effects of the factors that the defendant claims explain the average wage difference.

Suppose a statistically significant wage difference associated with race or sex remains? Does this reflect discrimination? Absent additional evidence, many judges presumably would accept this as evidence of "adverse impact"—it would be seen as the result of something the employer is doing to the worker. Often that is exactly what is going on. But is it always? This is where a more subtle implication of the compensating differential idea may be important. Suppose that the group with the relatively low average wage has chosen jobs with relatively attractive nonmonetary working conditions more frequently than the group with the relatively high average wage. The observed wage differential may be nothing more than compensation for unobserved differences in nonmonetary compensation. Absent some demonstration that the two groups do systematically make different job choices in this manner (a showing that might require data from a job bidding system), the "adverse impact" interpretation might erroneously be accepted, solely because the overly limited measure of monetary compensation was used.

NOTES AND QUESTIONS

**1.** If, as Professor Flanagan suggests, individuals value working conditions as well as monetary reward, why are menial jobs, which very few individuals would choose to work, so low-paid, while jobs with better working conditions are higher paid?   If Flanagan is correct, should we not expect the opposite economic effect?

**2.** What does the economic theory of the price and value of labor suggest for labor and employment *law*?   Elsewhere in the article, Flanagan states:

> [T]here is nothing inherently desirable from a distributional perspective about the structure of wages or income that results from the unfettered operation of a market economy.   Whatever the efficiency attributes of such a system, the resulting distribution of income and degree of inequality will depend in important ways on the initial endowments of assets.

> Second, while there is nothing inherently desirable about the income distribution that results from a market wage structure, direct action against the wage structure is often an inefficient way to attain distributional objectives.   * * * Precisely because direct action against (relative) wages tends to induce opposite employment reactions, the correlation between policy-induced changes in wages and policy-induced changes in income is weak and, under certain circumstances, can be negative.

**3.** The traditional neoclassical model of the labor market posited by Professor Flanagan has been criticized as unrealistic.   What real-life impediments to free functioning of the market exist?   What are their implications for employment law and policy?

## 2.   WAGE COMPARABILITY FOR INDIVIDUALS: THE QUEST FOR PAY EQUITY

Even where employees perform the same job, different employees are paid different wages, no matter how one determines the abstract "value" of the job.   As Professor Flanagan suggests, a number of factors are used to justify wage differentials:   seniority, qualifications, education, prior experience, better bargaining power, and a host of others.   But there are questions whether legitimate factors account for the entire earnings gap between men and women, whites and blacks. Figures from the Bureau of Labor Statistics reveal that the median weekly earnings for full-time wage and salary workers in 1996 were: $586 for white males; $413 for black males;   $364 for Hispanic males;   $438 for white females;   $362 for black females;   and $316 for Hispanic females.   Bureau of Labor Statistics, Employment and Earnings, January 1997, Table 37 (1997).   On average, women who work full-time earn roughly 70 percent of what their male counterparts earn.  That percentage has remained relatively constant for several decades, although it has shown some upward movement in recent years.  Women continue to be concentrated disproportionately in the lowest paying occupations.  The apparent existence of such a significant sex-based wage gap has resulted in substantial litigation, as women have sought to redress perceived discrimination in salaries paid to women and in occupations traditionally dominated by women.

a.   THE EQUAL PAY ACT

The Equal Pay Act of 1963, passed as an amendment to the Fair Labor Standards Act, prohibits sex-based wage discrimination.  29 U.S.C. § 206(d)(1) provides:

> No employer having employees subject to any provisions of this section shall discriminate, within any establishment in which such employees are employed, between employees on the basis of sex by paying wages to employees in such establishment at a rate less than the rate at which he pays wages to employees of the opposite sex in such establishment for equal work on jobs the performance of which requires equal skill, effort, and responsibility, and which are performed under similar working conditions, except where such payment is made pursuant to (i) a seniority system; (ii) a merit system; (iii) a system which measures earnings by quantity or quality of production; or (iv) a differential based on any other factor other than sex: *Provided,* That an employer who is paying a wage rate differential in violation of this subsection shall not, in order to comply with the provisions of this subsection, reduce the wage rate of any employee.

But what are "equal" jobs?  Must they be absolutely identical?  What are "equal skill, effort and responsibility" and "similar working conditions"?

## Corning Glass Works v. Brennan

417 U.S. 188 (1974).

■ MR. JUSTICE MARSHALL delivered the opinion of the Court.

These cases arise under the Equal Pay Act of 1963, which added to § 6 of the Fair Labor Standards Act of 1938 the principle of equal pay for equal work regardless of sex.  The principal question posed is whether Corning Glass Works violated the Act by paying a higher base wage to male night shift inspectors than it paid to female inspectors performing the same tasks on the day shift, where the higher wage was paid in addition to a separate night shift differential paid to all employees for night work.  [Corning operated plants in Corning, New York, and Wellsboro, Pennsylvania.  The Second Circuit had held that Corning's practices violated the Act, while the

Third Circuit, in a separate lawsuit against the Company, reached the opposite conclusion.]

## I.

Prior to 1925, Corning operated its plants in Wellsboro and Corning only during the day, and all inspection work was performed by women. Between 1925 and 1930, the company began to introduce automatic production equipment which made it desirable to institute a night shift. During this period, however both New York and Pennsylvania law prohibited women from working at night. As a result, in order to fill inspector positions on the new night shift, the company had to recruit male employees from among its male dayworkers. The male employees so transferred demanded and received wages substantially higher than those paid to women inspectors engaged on the two day shifts. During this same period, however, no plant-wide shift differential existed and male employees working at night, other than inspectors, received the same wages as their day shift counterparts. Thus a situation developed where the night inspectors were all male, the day inspectors all female, and the male inspectors received significantly higher wages.

In 1944, Corning plants at both locations were organized by a labor union and a collective-bargaining agreement was negotiated for all production and maintenance employees. This agreement for the first time established a plant-wide shift differential, but this change did not eliminate the higher base wage paid to male night inspectors. Rather, the shift differential was superimposed on the existing difference in base wages between male night inspectors and female day inspectors.

Prior to June 11, 1964, the effective date of the Equal Pay Act, the law in both Pennsylvania and New York was amended to permit women to work at night. It was not until some time after the effective date of the Act, however, that Corning initiated efforts to eliminate the differential rates for male and female inspectors. Beginning in June 1966, Corning started to open up jobs on the night shift to women. Previously separate male and female seniority lists were consolidated and women became eligible to exercise their seniority, on the same basis as men, to bid for the higher paid night inspection jobs as vacancies occurred.

On January 20, 1969, a new collective-bargaining agreement went into effect, establishing a new "job evaluation" system for setting wage rates. The new agreement abolished for the future the separate base wages for day and night shift inspectors and imposed a uniform base wage for inspectors exceeding the wage rate for the night shift previously in effect. All inspectors hired after January 20, 1969, were to receive the same base wage, whatever their sex or shift. The collective-bargaining agreement further provided, however, for a higher "red circle" rate for employees hired prior to January 20, 1969, when working as inspectors on the night shift. This "red circle" rate served essentially to perpetuate the differential in base wages between day and night inspectors.

The Secretary of Labor brought these cases to enjoin Corning from violating the Equal Pay Act and to collect back wages allegedly due female employees because of past violations. Three distinct questions are presented: (1) Did Corning ever violate the Equal Pay Act by paying male night shift inspectors more than female day shift inspectors? (2) If so, did Corning cure its violation of the Act in 1966 by permitting women to work as night shift inspectors? (3) Finally, if the violation was not remedied in 1966, did Corning cure its violation in 1969 by equalizing day and night inspector wage rates but establishing higher "red circle" rates for existing employees working on the night shift?

## II.

Congress' purpose in enacting the Equal Pay Act was to remedy what was perceived to be a serious and endemic problem of employment discrimination in private industry—the fact that the wage structure of "many segments of American industry has been based on an ancient but outmoded belief that a man, because of his role in society, should be paid more than a woman even though his duties are the same." S. Rep. No. 176, 88th Cong., 1st Sess., 1 (1963). The solution adopted was quite simple in principle: to require that "equal work will be rewarded by equal wages."

The Act's basic structure and operation are similarly straightforward. In order to make out a case under the Act, the Secretary must show that an employer pays different wages to employees of opposite sexes "for equal work on jobs the performance of which requires equal skill, effort, and responsibility, and which are performed under similar working conditions." Although the Act is silent on this point, its legislative history makes plain that the Secretary has the burden of proof on this issue, as both of the courts below recognized.

The Act also establishes four exceptions—three specific and one a catchall provision—where different payment to employees of opposite sexes "is made pursuant to (i) a seniority system; (ii) a merit system; (iii) a system which measures earnings by quantity or quality of production; or (iv) a differential based on any other factor other than sex." Again, while the Act is silent on this question, its structure and history also suggest that once the Secretary has carried his burden of showing that the employer pays workers of one sex more than workers of the opposite sex for equal work, the burden shifts to the employer to show that the differential is justified under one of the Act's four exceptions. All of the many lower courts that have considered this question have so held, and this view is consistent with the general rule that the application of an exemption under the Fair Labor Standards Act is a matter of affirmative defense on which the employer has the burden of proof.

The contentions of the parties in this case reflect the Act's underlying framework. Corning argues that the Secretary has failed to prove that Corning ever violated the Act because day shift work is not "performed under similar working conditions" as night shift work. The Secretary maintains that day shift and night shift work are performed under "similar working conditions" within the meaning of the Act.   Although the Secretary recognizes that higher wages may be paid for night shift work, the Secretary contends that such a shift differential would be based upon a "factor other than sex" within the catchall exception to the Act and that Corning has failed to carry its burden of proof that its higher base wage for male night inspectors was in fact based on any factor other than sex.

\* \* \*

The most notable feature of the history of the Equal Pay Act is that Congress recognized early in the legislative process that the concept of equal pay for equal work was more readily stated in principle than reduced to statutory language which would be meaningful to employers and workable across the broad range of industries covered by the Act.   As originally introduced, the Equal Pay bills required equal pay for "equal work on jobs the performance of which requires equal skills."   There were only two exceptions—for differentials "made pursuant to a seniority or merit increase system which does not discriminate on the basis of sex.   \* \* \* "

In both the House and Senate committee hearings, witnesses were highly critical of the Act's definition of equal work and of its exemptions. Many noted that most of American industry used formal, systematic job evaluation plans to establish equitable wage structures in their plants. Such systems, as explained coincidently by a representative of Corning Glass Works who testified at both hearings, took into consideration four separate factors in determining job value—skill, effort, responsibility and working conditions—and each of these four components was further systematically divided into various subcomponents.   Under a job evaluation plan, point values are assigned to each of the subcomponents of a given job, resulting in a total point figure representing a relatively objective measure of the job's value.

In comparison to the rather complex job evaluation plans used by industry, the definition of equal work used in the first drafts of the Equal Pay Act was criticized as unduly vague and incomplete.   Industry representatives feared that as a result of the Act's definition of equal work, the Secretary of Labor would be cast in the position of second-guessing the validity of a company's job evaluation system.   They repeatedly urged that the bill be amended to include an exception for job classification systems, or otherwise to incorporate the language of job evaluation into the bill.

\* \* \*

We think it plain that in amending the Act's definition of equal work to its present form, the Congress acted in direct response to these pleas. Spokesmen for the amended bill stated, for example, during the House debates:

> "The concept of equal pay for jobs demanding equal skill has been
> expanded to require also equal effort, responsibility, and similar
> working conditions.   These factors are the core of all job classifica-

tion systems.  They form a legitimate basis for differentials in pay."

Indeed, the most telling evidence of congressional intent is the fact that the Act's amended definition of equal work incorporated the specific language of the job evaluation plan described at the hearings by Corning's own representative—that is, the concepts of "skill," "effort," "responsibility," and "working conditions."

Congress' intent, as manifested in this history, was to use these terms to incorporate into the new federal act the well-defined and well-accepted principles of job evaluation so as to ensure that wage differentials based upon bona fide job evaluation plans would be outside the purview of the Act.

\* \* \*

It is in this light that the phrase "working conditions" must be understood, for where Congress has used technical words or terms of art, "it [is] proper to explain them by reference to the art or science to which they [are] appropriate."  This principle is particularly salutary where, as here, the legislative history reveals that Congress incorporated words having a special meaning within the field regulated by the statute so as to overcome objections by industry representatives that statutory definitions were vague and incomplete.

While a layman might well assume that time of day worked reflects one aspect of a job's "working conditions," the term has a different and much more specific meaning in the language of industrial relations.  As Corning's own representative testified at the hearings, the element of working conditions encompasses two subfactors: "surroundings" and "hazards."  "Surroundings" measures the elements, such as toxic chemicals or fumes, regularly encountered by a worker, their intensity, and their frequency.  "Hazards" takes into account the physical hazards regularly encountered, their frequency, and the severity of injury they can cause.  This definition of "working conditions" is not only manifested in Corning's own job evaluation plans but is also well accepted across a wide range of American industry.

Nowhere in any of these definitions is time of day worked mentioned as a relevant criterion.  The fact of the matter is that the concept of "working conditions," as used in the specialized language of job evaluation systems, simply does not encompass shift differentials.  Indeed, while Corning now argues that night inspection work is not equal to day inspection work, all of its own job evaluation plans, including the one now in effect, have consistently treated them as equal in all respects, including working conditions.  And Corning's Manager of Job Evaluation testified that time of day worked was not considered to be a "working condition."  Significantly, it is not the Secretary in this case who is trying to look behind Corning's bona fide job evaluation system to require equal pay for jobs which Corning has historically viewed as unequal work.  Rather, it is Corning which asks us to differentiate between jobs which the company itself has always equated.  We agree with the Second Circuit that the inspection work at issue in this case, whether performed during the day or night, is "equal work" as that term is defined in the Act.

This does not mean, of course, that there is no room in the Equal Pay Act for nondiscriminatory shift differentials.  Work on a steady night shift no doubt has psychological and physiological impacts making it less attractive than work on a day shift.  The Act contemplates that a male night worker may receive a higher wage than a female day worker, just as it contemplates that a male employee with 20 years' seniority can receive a higher wage than a woman with two years seniority.  Factors such as these play a role under the Act's four exceptions—the seniority differential under the specific seniority exception, the shift differential under the catch-all exception for differentials "based on any other factor other than sex."

The question remains, however, whether Corning carried its burden of proving that the higher rate paid for night inspection work, until 1966 performed solely by men, was in fact intended to serve as compensation for night work, or rather constituted an added payment based upon sex.  We agree that the record amply supports the District Court's conclusion that Corning had not sustained its burden of proof.  As its history revealed, "the higher night rate was in large part the product of the generally higher wage level of male workers and the need to compensate them for performing what were regarded as demeaning tasks."  The differential in base wages originated at a time when no other night employees received higher pay than corresponding day workers and it was maintained long after the company instituted a separate plant-wide shift differential which was thought to compensate adequately for the additional burdens of night work.  The differential arose simply because men would not work at the low rates paid women inspectors, and it reflected a job market in which Corning could pay women less than men for the same work.  That the company took advantage of such a situation may be understandable as a matter of economics, but its differential nevertheless became illegal once Congress enacted into law the principle of equal pay for equal work.

### III.

We now must consider whether Corning continued to remain in violation of the Act after 1966 when, without changing the base wage rates for day and night inspectors, it began to permit women to bid for jobs on the night shift as vacancies occurred.  It is evident that this was more than a token gesture to end discrimination, as turnover in the night shift inspection jobs was rapid.  Relying on these facts the company argues that it ceased discriminating against women in 1966, and was no longer in violation of the Equal Pay Act.

But the issue before us is not whether the company, in some abstract sense, can be said to have treated men the same as women after 1966.  Rather, the question is whether the company remedied the specific violation of the Act which the Secretary proved.  We agree with the Second Circuit, as well as with all other circuits that have had occasion to consider this issue, that the company could not cure its violation except by equalizing the base wages of female day inspectors with the higher rates paid the night inspectors. This result is implicit in the Act's language, its statement of purpose, and its legislative history.

\* \* \*

To achieve this end, Congress required that employers pay equal pay for equal work and then specified:

> "*Provided*, That an employer who is paying a wage rate differential in violation of this subsection shall not, in order to comply with the provisions of this subsection, reduce the wage rate of any employee." 29 U.S.C. § 206(d)(1).

The purpose of this proviso was to ensure that to remedy violations of the Act, "[t]he lower wage rate must be increased to the level of the higher." H.R. Rep. No. 309, supra, at 3. Comments of individual legislators are all consistent with this view. Representative Dwyer remarked, for example, "The objective of equal pay legislation \* \* \* is not to drag down men workers to the wage levels of women, but to raise women to the levels enjoyed by men in cases where discrimination is still practiced." \* \* \*

By proving that after the effective date of the Equal Pay Act, Corning paid female day inspectors less than male night inspectors for equal work, the Secretary implicitly demonstrated that the wages of female day shift inspectors were unlawfully depressed and that the fair wage for inspection work was the base wage paid to male inspectors on the night shift. The whole purpose of the Act was to require that these depressed wages be raised, in part as a matter of simple justice to the employees themselves, but also as a matter of market economics, since Congress recognized as well that discrimination in wages on the basis of sex "constitutes an unfair method of competition." § 2(a)(5).

The Equal Pay Act is broadly remedial, and it should be construed and applied so as to fulfill the underlying purposes which Congress sought to achieve. If, as the Secretary proved, the work performed by women on the day shift was equal to that performed by men on the night shift, the company became obligated to pay the women the same base wage as their male counterparts on the effective date of the Act. To permit the company to escape that obligation by agreeing to allow some women to work on the night shift at a higher rate of pay as vacancies occurred would frustrate, not serve, Congress' ends.

The company's final contention—that it cured its violation of the Act when a new collective-bargaining agreement went into effect on January 20, 1969—need not detain us long. While the new agreement provided for equal base wages for night or day inspectors hired after that date, it continued to provide unequal base wages for employees hired before that date, a discrimination likely to continue for some time into the future because of a large number of laid-off employees who had to be offered re-employment before new inspectors could be hired.

\* \* \*

We therefore conclude that on the facts of this case, the company's continued discrimination in base wages between night and day workers, though phrased in terms of a neutral factor other than sex, nevertheless operated to perpetuate the effects of the company's prior illegal practice of paying women less than men for equal work.

NOTES AND QUESTIONS

**1.** Why was it not sufficient for Corning to cure the statutory violation by opening night shift jobs to women?  Why was it unlawful for the company to red circle individuals who had been receiving the higher rate of pay?

**2.** *Corning* illustrates the concept of "similar working conditions" under the Equal Pay Act.  What are "equal skill, effort and responsibility"?  Consider the following case: An employer had previously hired Female Selector-Packers to pack glassware it manufactured, at $2.14 an hour.  Snap-up Boys were males who performed lifting, errands, and clean-up tasks in the same department, at $2.16 an hour.  Male Selector-Packers performed the same work as the Female Selector-Packers, plus occasional snap-up work, at $2.36 an hour.  The employer's justification for the difference in the male and female selector-packer rates was that the males performed additional tasks and that the extra flexibility that the employer had in assigning them work was a differential based on "a factor other than sex" under the Act.  Is this permissible under the Act?  See Shultz v. Wheaton Glass Co., 421 F.2d 259 (3d Cir.), cert. denied, 398 U.S. 905 (1970) (held:  flexibility factor did not justify wage differential of 22 cents per hour when snap-up work paid only two cents more per hour than female selector-packer).  What standards should be used to determine what constitutes "equal" work?

In EEOC v. Madison Community Unit School District No. 12, 818 F.2d 577 (7th Cir.1987), the employer school district had paid female athletic coaches of girls' sports teams less than it had male athletic coaches of boys' teams.  In upholding the district court's finding that the school district had violated the Equal Pay Act, Judge Posner addressed the problem of determining similarity of jobs:

> \* \* \* [T]he jobs that are compared must be in some sense the same to count as "equal work" under the Equal Pay Act; and here we come to the main difficulty in applying the Act; whether two jobs are the same depends on how fine a system of job classification the courts will accept.  If coaching an athletic team in the Madison, Illinois school system is considered a single job rather than a congeries of jobs, the school district violated the Equal Pay Act prima facie by paying female holders of this job less than male holders \* \* \*  If on the other hand coaching the girls' tennis team is considered a different job from coaching the boys' tennis team,

and a fortiori if coaching the girls' volleyball or basketball team is considered a different job (or jobs) from coaching the boys' soccer team, there is no prima facie violation. So the question is how narrow a definition of job the courts should be using in deciding whether the Equal Pay Act is applicable.

We can get some guidance from the language of the Act. The Act requires that the jobs compared have "similar working conditions," not the same working conditions. This implies that some comparison of different jobs is possible. It is true that the similarity of working conditions between the jobs being compared is not enough to bring the Act into play—the work must be "equal" and the jobs must require "equal" skill, effort, and responsibility, as well as similar working conditions. But since the working conditions need not be "equal," the jobs need not be completely identical * * *.

818 F.2d at 580. See also Brock v. Georgia Southwestern College, 765 F.2d 1026 (11th Cir.1985)(need to show that jobs are "substantially equal," not the skills and qualifications of the individual employees holding those jobs). Cf. Stanley v. University of Southern California, 13 F.3d 1313 (9th Cir. 1994) (additional revenues from men's basketball justified finding that coaching positions not equal).

**3.** A clothing store employs only men as sales clerks in the men's department and women as sales clerks for women's clothing. The male sales clerks are paid more than the female clerks; the employer's justification is that the men's department is more profitable than the women's. Is this a violation of the Equal Pay Act? See Hodgson v. Robert Hall Clothes, Inc., 473 F.2d 589 (3d Cir.), cert. denied, 414 U.S. 866 (1973) (held: no violation; exception for "any other factor other than sex" included greater profits earned in men's department). Cf. Bence v. Detroit Health Corp., 712 F.2d 1024 (6th Cir. 1983), cert. denied, 465 U.S. 1025 (1984) (male and female managers of health spas received substantially equal total compensation, but female managers were paid lower membership commissions; held: lower commissions not justified, because female managers generated more profit than male counterparts.) See also EEOC v. Hay Associates, 545 F.Supp. 1064 (E.D.Pa.1982) (violation of Equal Pay Act for employer to base different starting salaries for male and female employees solely on expectation that male's work would be more profitable than female's.) Cf. Hein v. Oregon College of Education, 718 F.2d 910 (9th Cir.1983) (different male and female starting salaries no violation of Equal Pay Act if difference can be justified under one of the four exceptions to the Act). Peters v. Shreveport, 818 F.2d 1148 (5th Cir.1987) (no violation of Equal Pay Act where employer paid male-dominated fire communications officers 40% more than female-dominated police communications officers for substantially equal work because sex was not a significant factor).

**4.** One of the most difficult elements of an Equal Pay Act case is determining what constitutes a legitimate "factor other than sex." For example, in Kouba v. Allstate Insurance Co., 691 F.2d 873 (9th Cir.1982), the employer computed the minimum salary guaranteed to new sales agents on the basis of ability, education, experience, and prior salary.  As a result of its practice, female sales agents, on average, made less than their male counterparts.  Lola Kouba, a female sales agent, sued under Title VII, alleging that the company's use of prior salaries, in particular, caused the wage differential and constituted unlawful sex discrimination, because of historic sex-based wage discrimination against women in the labor market.  In rejecting Kouba's claim, the Ninth Circuit addressed the company's "factor other than sex" defense, incorporated into Title VII wage discrimination claims by the Bennett Amendment (infra, p. 439:

> * * * Kouba insists that in order to give the Act its full remedial force, employers cannot use any factor that perpetuates historic sex discrimination.  * * * But while Congress fashioned the Equal Pay Act to help cure long-standing societal ills, it also intended to exempt factors such as training and experience that may reflect opportunities denied to women in the past.  * * *

> * * * The Equal Pay Act concerns business practices.  It would be nonsensical to sanction the use of a factor that rests on some consideration unrelated to business.  An employer thus cannot use a factor which causes a wage differential between male and female employees absent an acceptable business reason.  Conversely, a factor used to effectuate some business policy is not prohibited simply because a wage differential results.

>     * * *

691 F.2d at 876.  But see Glenn v. General Motors Corp., 841 F.2d 1567 (11th Cir.1988)(employer's reliance on market force theory failed to justify pay disparity between male and female clerks), cert. denied, 488 U.S. 948 (1988); Price v. Lockheed Space Operations Co., 856 F.2d 1503 (11th Cir.1988) (prior salary alone insufficient to justify pay differential).  See generally, Note, When Prior Pay Isn't Equal Pay:  A Proposed Standard for the Identification of "Factors Other than Sex" under the Equal Pay Act, 89 Colum.L.Rev. 1085 (1989).

**5.**  Consider in the following hypotheticals whether the distinguishing factors used by the employers to justify different salaries for males and females warrant an exception to the Act, keeping in mind that, by definition, the males and the females are performing essentially the same job.

    a.  A municipal employer calculates starting salaries according to a standardized pay classification system, resulting in different starting salaries for individual male and female employees.  See Maxwell v. Tucson, 803 F.2d 444 (9th Cir.1986)(employer's pay classification system did not establish a merit system defense to the Equal Pay Act); Parker v. Burnley, 693 F.Supp. 1138 (N.D.Ga.1988)(employer violated Equal Pay Act by paying female employee less than male predecessor for substantially equal work).

    b.  A female employee is hired at a salary less than her male predecessor, or a male replacement is hired at a higher salary than the female who just retired from the position.  See Parker v. Burnley, supra; Ciardella v.

Carson City School District, 671 F.Supp. 699 (D.Nev.1987). Is the size of the differential important? Suppose it is an increase for the male of $5,000 over a salary of $60,000. Is an increase of $12,000 over a salary of $24,000 qualitatively different?

c. The employer uses a "head of the household" eligibility test for medical and dental benefits. (Benefits are considered "compensation" under the Act.) See EEOC v. J.C. Penney Co., 843 F.2d 249 (6th Cir.1988) (" 'factor other than sex' defense does not include literally *any* other factor, but a factor that, at a minimum, was adopted for a legitimate business reason").

d. An employer pays women less than men because hiring females increases its costs for unemployment compensation, workers' compensation, and group health insurance. See Wirtz v. Midwest Manufacturing Corp., 9 FEP Cases 483 (S.D.Ill.1968) (held: unlawful). Why would this case be decided differently from *Robert Hall Clothes,* supra note 3? Both cases involve an "economic benefit" for the employer, don't they? (For a discussion of differential insurance rates in the context of retirement annuities, see City of Los Angeles Department of Water & Power v. Manhart, infra, p. 1234.)

e. A federal employer hires a man with disabilities and four women and proceeds to pay the male employee significantly more. The male employee's eligibility for a special exception to normal Civil Service hiring criteria was found to be a factor other than sex. Girdis v. EEOC, 688 F.Supp. 40 (D.Mass.1987), affirmed, 851 F.2d 540 (1st Cir.1988).

**6.** The employer justifies a higher salary to a male employee, John, because "he's married with a new baby"; Mary, a female employee, is single, with no family. Would this be a violation of the Act if John and Mary perform the same job? What if there are three individuals performing the same job—John, Mary and Elmer, who is also single and without family responsibilities—and Mary and Elmer are paid the same salary. Violation of the Act? Should the employer's liability under the Act depend on the composition of its work force? On the other hand, should Mary have a cause of action for wage discrimination while Elmer has none?

**7.** The employer offers two openings for similar jobs to Robert and Sally, both at a starting salary of $40,000 per year. Sally accepts the offer immediately. Robert says, "I'd like to work for you, but I think I'm worth $50,000." They bargain, and agree on a salary for Robert of $45,000. Must the employer now raise Sally's salary to match Robert's? Same situation, but Robert says, "I have an outstanding offer from another firm for $40,000, and you'll have to pay me $45,000 for me to accept your offer rather than theirs." The company complies.

### b. TITLE VII OF THE CIVIL RIGHTS ACT OF 1964

The Equal Pay Act requires equal pay for equal work. In addition, it is unlawful under Title VII of the Civil Rights Act of 1964 to discriminate in wage rates on the basis of Title VII's protected categories. Section

703(a)(1) provides: "It shall be an unlawful employment practice for an employer * * * to discriminate against any individual with respect to his compensation * * * because of such individual's race, color, religion, sex, or national origin."

The Equal Pay Act only applies to circumstances in which employees are performing "substantially equal" work, as interpreted by the Supreme Court in *Corning;* it does not apply to situations where men and women perform work *similar* in "skill, effort, and responsibility" and are not paid equally. Nor can it be used to attack an employer's decision to pay a female-dominated occupation less than it would pay a male-dominated occupation; this common situation is the target of "comparable worth" advocates.

The "comparable worth" or "pay equity" movement has engendered substantial debate between employee advocates and feminists, on the one hand, and management representatives on the other. The debate has largely centered on whether pervasive sex-based wage discrimination in the workplace actually exists, its sources in the economics and politics of the labor market, and the appropriateness of legal efforts to change practices so deeply rooted in social and cultural norms.

Arguments have been made that application of disparate impact analysis, see Griggs v. Duke Power Co., supra page 232, would lead to a conclusion that gender-based pay scales violate Title VII's ban on discrimination on the basis of sex, but the legislative history of the Civil Rights Act of 1991 specifically disclaimed such arguments. See H.R.Rep. No. 40(1), 102d Cong., 1st Sess., 1991 U.S.C.C.A.N. 549 (1991): "Additionally, concerns have been raised that applying disparate impact analysis to terms and conditions of employment somehow implicates 'comparable worth' claims. That concern is unfounded. The legislation does not provide any basis for challenges based on disparate impact that did not exist prior to Wards Cove."

National gross earnings data clearly indicate, at an aggregate level, the existence of a substantial earnings gap between men and women. At the level of specific occupations, however, the differences are smaller. Studies by the Bureau of Labor Statistics and by the National Academy of Sciences conclude that while some of the differential in gross earnings is due to recognized distinguishing factors, such as differences in education levels, not all of it can be explained by such factors. Others have attempted to control for occupation and job tenure and have concluded that women occupying the same jobs as men for the same length of time earn approximately the same wage or salary, undercutting the notion of a serious "earnings gap" problem.

*Sources of the Wage Gap*

What are the sources of the earnings gap? Figure 5–1 illustrates the wage gap between men and women conceptually.

FIGURE 5-1

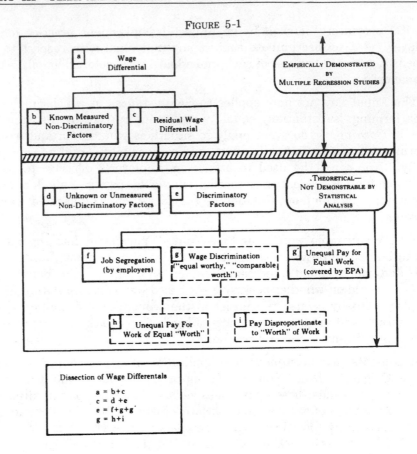

From Bruce A. Nelson, Edward M. Opton, & Thomas E. Wilson, Wage Discrimination and the "Comparable Worth" Theory in Perspective, 13 Mich. J. L. Ref. 231 (1980)

The "wage differential" (a) in Figure 5–1 is the gross difference in wages between men and women. Econometric studies have separated the differential into two components: Known measured nondiscriminatory factors (b) and the residual wage difference (c). Known measured nondiscriminatory factors include seniority, education, and experience, all of which men tend to have more of than women. The residual wage difference can be divided into two more components, unknown or unmeasured nondiscriminatory factors (d) and discriminatory factors (e).

Unknown and unmeasured nondiscriminatory factors (d) include, for instance, voluntary job segregation by employees: how many women with children choose lower level, less demanding jobs in order to have time and energy for family responsibilities? Or refuse to work voluntary overtime for the same reason? The more demanding a job is, the more it tends to pay. Alternatively, studies on occupational preferences show that women in general prefer jobs that are not as dirty or risky as some traditionally male jobs which pay better than traditionally female jobs such as secretary.

Also, parents and schools may encourage young women to pursue educational programs different from those toward which they push young men, with the result that men have educational backgrounds more highly valued in the employment market. Societal sex typing conventions play a role in individual choice here, but it is not clear that it is possible or practical to measure their effect. And because such choices are voluntary, they are categorized as nondiscriminatory factors, not subject to "correction" by the law.

Discriminatory factors (e) can be broken down into job segregation by employers (f) and wage discrimination (g) and (g'). Women may be in lower paying jobs because of unequal access to high-paying jobs. Job segregation may be voluntary or involuntary; furthermore, job segregation alone does not necessarily produce wage discrimination. For example, in baseball, only about 9 percent of all pitchers are black, while 53 percent of outfielders are black. There would appear to be job segregation, but statistics show that there is no wage discrimination which accompanies the job segregation: many outfielders make as much as or more than pitchers, depending on their batting and fielding skills. Job channelling, as it is also known, may give rise to a cause of action under Title VII, however, so that women who are routinely assigned to low level (and legitimately low-paid) jobs without regard to their qualifications could sue, not for direct wage discrimination, but for discriminatory job assignment. If successful, they would be entitled to back pay and increased future wages as part of their remedy.

Wage discrimination takes two forms: unequal pay for equal work (g'), which is unlawful under the Equal Pay Act, and wage discrimination in jobs which are not readily identifiable as "equal" (g). Category (g) represents the target of pay equity litigation, and it subsumes two different forms of discrimination: unequal pay for jobs which are comparable but not, strictly speaking, equal (h), and disproportionately low pay for jobs which are in some sense "worth" more than what they are paid (i).

## How Real Is the Wage Gap?

Depending on what set of data one uses, estimates are that women earn, on average, somewhere between 60 and 65 percent of what men earn. The measure of actual sex-based wage differentials is probably somewhere between the no-gap proponents who claim that the entire differential is due to such known, identifiable nondiscriminatory factors as education and experience, and those who claim that all women only earn two-thirds what men earn, because of deliberate discrimination against women. Recent studies show that over the past decade, occupational sex-segregation has decreased, primarily because the proportion of both men and women in sex-neutral occupations like sales has increased. The largest percentage occupational increase for women has been in the category of executive, administrative, and managerial occupations. The proportion of women in many formerly male-dominated occupations is rising, albeit slowly in most areas.

Women in both the formerly male-dominated and sex-neutral fields, at least at entry levels, earn about the same as similarly situated males.

More sobering are the data which indicate that women are not achieving upper-level positions in these occupations at the same rate as their male cohorts. In addition, while some "male" occupations are being "feminized" by the entry of women, there is no significant comparable "masculinization" of such traditionally female—and low-paid—occupations as secretary, private household services, and nursing. Consequently, both *inter*-occupational and *intra*-occupational segregation still account for some amount of the male-female wage gap. The mere existence of a gap is not necessarily unlawful, but given the statutory prohibitions against sex-based wage discrimination, the persistence of the earnings gap is troubling.[1]

### Pay Equity

A certain amount of doctrinal confusion pervades discussion of pay equity. There are actually two distinct types of alleged wage discrimination which arise in the workplace, both of which pay equity advocates would like to eliminate. (See boxes (h) and (i) in Figure 5–1.) The first is where male and female employees are performing what is essentially "comparable work" and being paid different wages. This situation is typified by the *Gunther* case, below, where Washington County had separate job categories for male jail wardens and female jail wardens. Even though the work performed by both was comparable, it did not meet the "substantially equal" standard of the Equal Pay Act and was not actionable under that statute.

The second type of problem presented in pay equity cases is more subtle and complex, and presents a more fundamental challenge to the economics and wage structure of the workplace as we know it. Women occupy eight out of ten jobs in the lowest paying occupations and only three out of ten in the highest. Is the concentration of women in low-paying jobs an accident, or does it reflect wage discrimination against various occupations, not because of their intrinsic value or "worth" to an employer but because they are female-dominated and our society undervalues women and their work? This theory of sex-based wage discrimination takes the first theory a step further, in looking less at "comparable work" than at "comparable worth."

### NOTE

Annual data from the Bureau of Labor Statistics reveal that librarians—a highly skilled occupation requiring higher education—earned, on average in 1996, $697 a week; the occupation is 83 percent female. Computer analysts, on the other hand, (an occupation 72 percent male)

---

**1.** Sources: Rytina & Bianchi, Occupational Reclassification and Changes in Distribution by Gender, Monthly Labor Rev., March 1984, at 11; Mellor, Investigating the Differences in Weekly Earnings of Women and Men, Monthly Labor Rev., June 1984, at 17 (especially Table 2, at 20–22, detailing male-female wage differentials in a number of specific occupations); Seiling, Staffing Patterns Prominent in Female-Male Earnings Gap, id., at 29.

earned an average of $891 per week for work which is arguable comparable to the systems analysis and data manipulation, tracking, and retrieval performed by librarians. In its purest form, comparable worth theory asks whether librarians are paid less not because their work is in any real sense "worth" less than that of computer analysts, but solely because most librarians are women. The same data show registered nurses (93 percent female) earned $697 per week; pharmacists (57 percent male) earned $992 per week. Such occupations are at least tangentially related to one another in terms of function and education requirements; what about less direct comparisons? For example, elementary school teachers (83 percent female) earned $662 weekly; plumbers and pipe fitters (98 percent male), $586. Secretaries (99 percent female): $406 weekly; truck drivers (95 percent male): $481. What do these differences suggest about the existence of wage discrimination? Source: BLS, Handbook of Labor Statistics, Employment and Earnings, January 1997, Tables 11 and 39.

As noted by the Supreme Court in its *Corning* decision, many employers use formal job evaluation systems to determine wage scales; evaluation systems attempt to measure the "value" of a job based on a number of factors. But measures of "value" as determined by such a system are only as good as the system itself. The following excerpt both describes and questions the operation of common job evaluation techniques.

Michele Andrisin Wittig & Gillian Turner, Implementing Comparable Worth: Some Measurement and Conceptual Issues in Job Evaluation, Comparable Worth, Pay Equity, and Public Policy 143–145 (Rita Mae Kelly & Jane Bayes, eds. 1988).

\* \* \*

**JOB EVALUATION**

The tool of comparable worth is job evaluation, which attempts to compare dissimilar jobs and rank them hierarchically in a particular firm or industry. Critics disparage comparable worth job evaluation as an attempt to compare "apples and oranges," either because it involves comparing jobs of dissimilar content on each of several compensable factors and/or because it usually gives equal weight to each of these compensable factors. However, the practice of establishing common criteria by which to compare jobs of different content and structure, then weighing and summing the respective point values for each job, is an inherent aspect of job evaluation systems. Such procedures, originally developed by industrial-organization psychologists during World War II, have been widely accepted in the public and private sectors since that time (Ferraro, 1984).

In job evaluation, jobs are assessed on a set of compensable factors (usually including skill, responsibility, effort, and working conditions) to produce a total job-worth score. The Equal Pay Act of 1963 stipulates that for two jobs to be considered similar, they must have the same score on each of the compensable factors. In contrast, according to the comparable worth approach, two jobs are similar if their composite scores are the same (Campbell, 1983).

Because job evaluation involves judgments about which compensable factors to use and how to weight them, discriminatory elements may be incorporated (Treiman and Hartmann, 1981; Remick, 1978; Thomsen, 1978). Even guidelines that have been developed to reduce such discriminatory elements (Remick, 1978; Thomsen, 1978) cannot remove the subjectivity inherent in job evaluation. For example, if most women, but few men, know how to sew, then female-dominated jobs requiring this skill may be weighted low on "need for training." However, the same job, if male-dominated, may be scored higher on need for training simply because men ordinarily have not already acquired this skill. Ferraro (1984) reports just such a case of job evaluation bias concerning bookbinder in the U.S. Government Printing Office.

## MEASUREMENT ISSUES

A number of measurement and statistical problems arise in modeling the relationship between various worker characteristics, job requirements, and wages. One problem concerns gender and race differences in the fit between operational definitions and their theoretical constructs. For example, when seniority is used as the measure of on-the-job experience, it may be defined as the number of continuous days worked at a particular job. However, an alternative measure of the same theoretical construct is the total number of days worked at the job, regardless of continuity. Both measures are useful proxies for theoretical construct "on-the-job experience," but the "fit" of the former measure to men's actual job experience is likely to be greater than to women's, and the reverse is likely for the latter definition. Continuous days worked and total number of days worked may each contribute positively to on-the-job experience. However, the two measures may introduce distinct biases, causing the regression lines relating job experience to salary to be displaced for different groups of workers. Measures of continuous service may underestimate the actual experience of workers who have interrupted their labor force participation for childrearing or military duty. On the other hand, total number of days worked may overestimate the useful experience of such workers relative to their continuously working counterparts because of the disruptive effect of suspension of labor force participation in job categories for which start-up time is a factor in performance.

Furthermore, the reasons for a worker's labor force interruption can introduce secondary effects apart from the actual time lost. For example, while some types of military duty are more life-threatening than is childbearing, the former is paid work and the free training associated with it is more likely to increase the worker's later civilian employability than does maternity. Such differential spin-offs undermine simplistic interpretations of the role of seniority as a predictor of wages.

A second type of measurement problem involves statistical interactions between gender or race and measures of worker characteristics. Specifically, when the direction of the relationship between a given predictor and salary is equal for the two sex or race groups, but opposite in direction, the importance of that variable may be completely obscured when the respective effects of sex and race are combined in a common regression equation. For example, the relationship of marital status to wages may be opposite in direction for men and women workers, such that being married contributes positively to wage increments for males, but negatively for females.  In such a case, with approximately equal numbers of males and females in a sample, combining the data for both genders and attempting to fit one regression equation could result in these two effects cancelling each other out, so that marital status does not contribute significantly to the prediction of wages.  However, separate regression equations by gender would show a significant weight or "effect" of marital status, opposite in direction for each sex, for these same data.  * * *

NOTES AND QUESTIONS

**1.**  The importance of job evaluations in proving wage discrimination cannot be overstated.  In some wage discrimination cases, employers are forced to attack their own previously conducted studies; in others, a battle of the experts develops over plaintiffs' independently conducted evaluation. The courts have shown a definite disinclination to examine competing evaluations, on the grounds that they are complicated (and, implicitly, beyond the court's expertise) and that it is inappropriate for the judiciary to second-guess the employer.  It should be kept in mind, however, that courts routinely evaluate very complex matters in a variety of cases: antitrust, other race and sex discrimination cases, rate-fixing in a number of regulated industries, and the like.  What is different about a case of wage discrimination, especially given the availability, familiarity, and near-universal use in industry of job evaluation systems?

**2.**  In its first important case on pay equity, COUNTY OF WASHINGTON v. GUNTHER, 452 U.S. 161 (1981), the Supreme Court was faced with the question whether Title VII of the Civil Rights Act of 1964 provided a cause of action for sex-based wage discrimination separate from the Equal Pay Act, or whether § 703(h) of Title VII limited Title VII's applicability in such cases.  The relevant portion of § 703(h), also known as the Bennett Amendment, had been inserted into Title VII to harmonize that statute with the Equal Pay Act, which had been passed a year earlier.  The Bennett Amendment states:

> It shall not be an unlawful employment practice under this title for any employer to differentiate upon the basis of sex in determining the amount of the wages or compensation paid to employees of such employer if such differentiation is authorized by the provisions of Section 6(d) of the Fair Labor Standards Act of 1938 as amended (29 U.S.C. § 206(d)) [the Equal Pay Act].

The County of Washington, Oregon, paid female guards in the female section of the county jail substantially lower wages ($525–$668 per month in 1973) than it paid male guards in the male section ($701–$940 per month).  State law required that female prisoners be guarded solely by women, and women were not employed to guard male prisoners.  The plaintiffs sued, alleging that they were paid unequal wages for work substantially equal to that performed by male guards and, in the alternative, that because of intentional discrimination, the county set the pay scale for female guards, but not for male guards, at a level lower than that warranted by its own wage survey. According to the plaintiffs, the survey indicated that the female guards' job was worth approximately 95 percent of the male guard's job. It was paid 70 percent as much, while male guards received the full amount indicated in the survey. The two jobs were not identical: the males guarded ten times more prisoners than the women, and the women performed more clerical duties than the males. The plaintiffs' Equal Pay Act claim was rejected under the "equal skill, effort, and responsibility" standard. The county further argued that a sex-based wage discrimination claim under Title VII also had to satisfy the equal work standard of the Equal Pay Act, because the Bennett Amendment, which read into Title VII all of the provisions of the Equal Pay Act, limited Title VII claims to those which could also be brought under the Equal Pay Act.

In a five to four decision, the Court held that the Bennett Amendment was a "technical amendment" intended only to harmonize potential conflicts between Title VII and the Equal Pay Act. Thus, § 703(h)'s effect was to incorporate only the affirmative defenses of the Equal Pay Act (seniority system, merit system, quantity or quality of production system, and "any other factor other than sex"); it did not usurp an independent claim for sex-based wage discrimination that could arise under Title VII. In its opinion, the majority was clearly concerned about undermining Title VII:

> Our interpretation of the Bennett Amendment draws additional support from the remedial purposes of Title VII and the Equal Pay Act. Section 703(a) of Title VII makes it unlawful for an employer "to fail or refuse to hire or to discharge any individual, or *otherwise to discriminate* against any individual with respect to his compensation, terms, conditions, or privileges of employment" because of such individual's sex. As Congress itself has indicated, a "broad approach" to the definition of equal employment opportunity is essential to overcoming and undoing the effect of discrimination. We must therefore avoid interpretations of Title VII that deprive victims of discrimination of a remedy, without clear congressional mandate.

> Under petitioner's reading of the Bennett Amendment, only those sex-based wage discrimination claims that satisfy the "equal work" standard of the Equal Pay Act could be brought under Title VII. In practical terms, this means that a woman who is discriminatorily underpaid could obtain no relief—no matter how egregious the discrimination might be—unless her employer also employed a man in an equal job in the same establishment, at a higher rate of pay. Thus, if an employer hired a woman for a unique position in the company and then admitted that her salary would have been higher had she been male, the woman would be

unable to obtain legal redress under petitioner's interpretation. Similarly, if an employer used a transparently sex-biased system for wage determination, women holding jobs not equal to those held by men would be denied the right to prove that the system is a pretext for discrimination.  * * * Congress surely did not intend the Bennett Amendment to insulate such blatantly discriminatory practices from judicial redress under Title VII.

In the majority opinion, Justice Brennan emphasized the "narrowness" of the question before the Court, noting that "respondents' suit does not require a court to make its own subjective assessment of the value of the male and female guard jobs, or to attempt by statistical technique or other method to quantify the effect of sex discrimination on the wage rates."  In fact, the Court rejected the notion that *Gunther* was a "comparable worth" case, "under which plaintiffs might claim increased compensation on the basis of a comparison of the intrinsic worth or difficulty of their job with that of other jobs in the same organization or community."

In a strong dissent, Justice Rehnquist rejected the majority's opinion as a misinterpretation of the legislative history of Title VII and the political compromises which were made to ensure the passage of Title VII:

> In rejecting [the County's] argument, the Court ignores traditional canons of statutory construction and relevant legislative history.  Although I had thought it well settled that the legislative history of a statute is a useful guide to the intent of Congress, the Court today claims that the legislative history "has no bearing on the meaning of the Act," "does not provide a solution to our present problem," and is simply of "no weight."  Instead, the Court rests its decision on its unshakable belief that any other result would be unsound public policy.  It insists that there simply *must* be a remedy for wage discrimination beyond that provided in the Equal Pay Act.  The Court does not explain *why* that must be so, nor does it explain *what* the remedy might be.  And, of course, the Court cannot explain why it and not Congress is charged with determining what is and what is not sound public policy.  [Emphasis in original.]

While *Gunther* was viewed as a victory for the advocates of pay equity, it did not address how the lower federal courts should treat other pay equity cases, particularly the application of Title VII theory to such cases. Perhaps the most problematic issue has been the appropriateness of the employer's "market rate" defense.

# AFSCME v. Washington
578 F.Supp. 846 (W.D.Wash.1983).

[Two unions representing 15,500 state employees in jobs primarily held by females initiated a class action against the state of Washington for discriminatory implementation and application of its compensation system.

In 1973, the state had conducted a study of male and female compensation that suggested the existence of a wage gap between job classes held predominately by men and those filled predominately by women, a gap that could not be explained solely by "job worth." Subsequently, in 1974 the state engaged an independent consulting firm to perform a more complete study. "Men's" or "women's" jobs were defined as jobs with 70% men or women. The study concluded that there was a tendency for women's job classes to be paid less than men's job classes for jobs of comparable worth; overall, the disparity was about 20 percent, and the amount of disparity increased as the job value increased. In December 1976, then-Governor Evans included a $7 million budget appropriation to begin the process of eradicating sex-based wage discrimination in state employment. That same month, the State Personnel Board adopted a resolution stating its support for the correction of disparities identified by the study. In 1977, a new Governor eliminated the appropriation from that year's budget, even though the state had a budget surplus; the state legislature authorized continuing study of compensation differentials and instructed two state agencies to furnish the governor with supplementary data on compensation differentials, in the form of a separate salary schedule.

District Judge Jack Tanner concluded that the state was guilty of intentional discrimination against employees in predominately female job classifications. The evidence established a pattern of sex discrimination in employment by the state, in that it historically failed to pay predominately female jobs their full evaluated worth as established by the state's own job evaluation studies; further, the state failed to rebut the plaintiffs' prima facie case by producing credible evidence demonstrating a legitimate and overriding business justification.]

The Defendant, State of Washington, has set forth a number of reasons injunctive relief should not be formulated and enforced by this Court: (1) the tremendous costs involved; (2) lack of revenue because of the depressed economy nationally, and more particularly in the State of Washington (i.e., high unemployment and recession in the forest industry which provides much of the State tax revenues); (3) prior State revenue commitments to education, prisons, and social services; (4) the State Constitution's mandated balanced budget; (5) disruption in the State's work force, and of the State's compensation scheme; (6) the State Legislature has already initiated a remedy which will eliminate the sex discrimination by no later than 1993; and (7) the Tenth Amendment to the United States Constitution. This Court finds that Defendant's reasons are without merit and unpersuasive, for the following reasons:

First, Title VII does not contain " * * * a cost-justification defense comparable to the affirmative defense available in a price discrimination suit. (footnote omitted) * * * neither Congress nor the Courts have recognized such a defense under Title VII. (footnote omitted)." Los Angeles Dept. of Water and Power v. Manhart, 435 U.S. 702, 716–17 (1978).

Second, Defendant's shortage of revenue, prior revenue commitments, and constitutionally mandated balanced budget defenses, cannot withstand the evidence produced at trial herein. It was uncontroverted that in the 1976–77 biennium the State of Washington had a surplus budget, was cognizant of the disparity which is the subject of this lawsuit, and did not consider the acknowledged discrimination enough of a priority to divert the surplus to the victims of the discrimination. The bad faith of Defendant's action is patent, and cannot be overcome at this late date with arguments that sound in equity.

Third, any disruption full implementation of the proposed injunctive relief would effect, is a direct result of the discrimination Defendant created and has maintained. Sound reasoning dictates that in any cause-effect analysis one cannot be heard to argue the effect is the evil to be eradicated.

Fourth, the belated May 1983 appropriation did not purport to eliminate discrimination. At best, it indicated a change in attitude by the Defendant.

Further, were the Court to adopt the May 1983 act of the Washington legislature as the injunctive remedy herein, this Court would be endorsing a compensation plan that works a grave injustice to the discriminatees. Injunctive orders couched in terms of "with all deliberate speed" result in non-action. This Court sees no credible distinction between endorsing a remedy to be phased in over a ten (10) year period and an injunction ordering compliance "with all deliberate speed."

It is time, *right now* for a remedy. Defendant's preoccupation with its budget constraints pales when compared with the invidiousness of the impact ongoing discrimination has upon the Plaintiffs herein.

* * *

There is little doubt that had the State produced evidence that the unlawful discrimination was other than in "bad faith", the *Manhart* and *Norris* decisions would have persuaded this court that back pay would not have been an appropriate remedy. The devastating cost to a Defendant who did not act in bad faith would then, and only then, become relevant. However, the record herein does not lend itself to a finding that the State was acting in good faith by not paying Plaintiffs their evaluated worth. Rather, the persistent and intransigent conduct of Defendant in refusing to pay Plaintiffs indicates "bad faith." * * *

This Court finds that the State had knowledge of the sex discrimination in employment before and after the March 24, 1972 amendment to Title VII; that the evidence shows the discrimination is pervasive and intentional and is still being practiced by the State; and that the State is adhering to a practice of sex discrimination in violation of the terms of Title VII with full knowledge of, and indifference to, its effect upon the Plaintiffs.

# AFSCME v. Washington

770 F.2d 1401 (9th Cir.1985).

■ KENNEDY, CIRCUIT JUDGE:

In this class action affecting approximately 15,500 of its employees, the State of Washington was sued in the United States District Court for the Western District of Washington. The district court found the State discriminated on the basis of sex in violation of Title VII of the Civil Rights Act of 1964, 42 U.S.C. § 2000e–2(a) (1982), by compensating employees in jobs where females predominate at lower rates than employees in jobs where males predominate, if these jobs, though dissimilar, were identified by certain studies to be of comparable worth. The State appeals. We conclude a violation of Title VII was not established here, and we reverse.

The State of Washington has required salaries of state employees to reflect prevailing market rates. Throughout the period in question, comprehensive biennial salary surveys were conducted to assess prevailing market rates. The surveys involved approximately 2,700 employers in the public and private sectors. The results were reported to state personnel boards, which conducted hearings before employee representatives and agencies and made salary recommendations to the State Budget Director. The Director submitted a proposed budget to the Governor, who in turn presented it to the state legislature. Salaries were fixed by enactment of the budget.

In 1974 the State commissioned a study by management consultant Norman Willis to determine whether a wage disparity existed between employees in jobs held predominantly by women and jobs held predominantly by men. The study examined sixty-two classifications in which at least seventy percent of the employees were women, and fifty-nine job classifications in which at least seventy percent of the employees were men. It found a wage disparity of about twenty percent, to the disadvantage of employees in jobs held mostly by women, for jobs considered of comparable worth. * * * The State of Washington conducted similar studies in 1976 and 1980, and in 1983 the State enacted legislation providing for a compensation scheme based on comparable worth. The scheme is to take effect over a ten-year period. * * *

AFSCME alleges sex-based wage discrimination throughout the state system, but its explanation and proof of the violation is, in essence, Washington's failure as early as 1979 to adopt and implement at once a comparable worth compensation program. The trial court adopted this theory as well. The comparable worth theory, as developed in the case before us, postulates that sex-based wage discrimination exists if employees in job classifications occupied primarily by women are paid less than employees in job classifications filled primarily by men, if the jobs are of equal value to the employer, though otherwise dissimilar. * * *

We must determine whether comparable worth, as presented in this case, affords AFSCME a basis for recovery under Title VII.

* * *

In the instant case, the district court found a violation of Title VII, premised upon both the disparate impact and the disparate treatment theories of discrimination. Under the disparate impact theory, discrimination may be established by showing that a facially neutral employment practice, not justified by business necessity, has a disproportionately adverse impact upon members of a group protected under Title VII. Proof of an employer's intent to discriminate in adopting a particular practice is not required in a disparate impact case. The theory is based in part on the rationale that where a practice is specific and focused we can address whether it is a pretext for discrimination in light of the employer's explanation for the practice. Under the disparate treatment theory, in contrast, an employer's intent or motive in adopting a challenged policy is an essential element of liability for a violation of Title VII. It is insufficient for a plaintiff alleging discrimination under the disparate treatment theory to show the employer was merely aware of the adverse consequences the policy would have on a protected group. The plaintiff must show the employer chose the particular policy because of its effect on members of a protected class.

\* \* \*

The trial court erred in ruling that liability was established under a disparate impact analysis. The precedents do not permit the case to proceed upon that premise. AFSCME's disparate impact argument is based on the contention that the State of Washington's practice of taking prevailing market rates into account in setting wages has an adverse impact on women, who, historically, have received lower wages than men in the labor market. Disparate impact analysis is confined to cases that challenge a specific, clearly delineated employment practice applied at a single point in the job selection process. Atonio v. Wards Cove Packing Co., 768 F.2d 1120, 1130 (9th Cir.1985); see also *Dothard*, 433 U.S. at 328–29 (height and weight requirement disproportionately excluded women); *Griggs,* 401 U.S. at 430–31 (requirement of high school diploma or satisfactory performance on standardized tests disproportionately affected minorities). The instant case does not involve an employment practice that yields to disparate impact analysis. As we noted in an earlier case, the decision to base compensation on the competitive market, rather than on a theory of comparable worth, involves the assessment of a number of complex factors not easily ascertainable, an assessment too multifaceted to be appropriate for disparate impact analysis. In the case before us, the compensation system in question resulted from surveys, agency hearings, administrative recommendations, budget proposals, executive actions, and legislative enactments. A compensation system that is responsive to supply and demand and other market forces is not the type of specific, clearly delineated employment policy contemplated by *Dothard* and *Griggs;* such a compensation system, the result of a complex of market forces, does not constitute a single practice that suffices to support a claim under disparate impact theory. Such cases are controlled by disparate treatment analysis. Under these principles and precedents, we must reverse the district court's determination of liability under the disparate impact theory of discrimination.

We consider next the allegations of disparate treatment. Under the disparate treatment theory, AFSCME was required to prove a prima facie case of sex discrimination by a preponderance of the evidence. Our review of the record, however, indicates failure by AFSCME to establish the requisite element of intent by either circumstantial or direct evidence.

AFSCME contends discriminatory motive may be inferred from the Willis study, which finds the State's practice of setting salaries in reliance on market rates creates a sex-based wage disparity for jobs deemed of comparable worth. AFSCME argues from the study that the market reflects a historical pattern of lower wages to employees in positions staffed predominantly by women; and it contends the State of Washington perpetuates that disparity, in violation of Title VII, by using market rates in the compensation system. The inference of discriminatory motive which AFSCME seeks to draw from the State's participation in the market system fails, as the State did not create the market disparity and has not been shown to have been motivated by impermissible sex-based considerations in setting salaries.

The requirement of intent is linked at least in part to culpability. That concept would be undermined if we were to hold that payment of wages according to prevailing rates in the public and private sectors is an act that, in itself, supports the inference of a purpose to discriminate. Neither law nor logic deems the free market system a suspect enterprise. Economic reality is that the value of a particular job to an employer is but one factor influencing the rate of compensation for that job. Other considerations may include the availability of workers willing to do the job and the effectiveness of collective bargaining in a particular industry. We find nothing in the language of Title VII or its legislative history to indicate Congress intended to abrogate fundamental economic principles such as the laws of supply and demand or to prevent employers from competing in the labor market.

While the Washington legislature may have the discretion to enact a comparable worth plan if it chooses to do so, Title VII does not obligate it to eliminate an economic inequality that it did not create. Title VII was enacted to ensure equal opportunity in employment to covered individuals, and the State of Washington is not charged here with barring access to particular job classifications on the basis of sex.

We have recognized that in certain cases an inference of intent may be drawn from statistical evidence. We have admonished, however, that statistics must be relied on with caution. Though the comparability of wage rates in dissimilar jobs may be relevant to a determination of discriminatory animus, job evaluation studies and comparable worth statistics alone are insufficient to establish the requisite inference of discriminatory motive critical to the disparate treatment theory. The weight to be accorded such statistics is determined by the existence of independent corroborative evidence of discrimination. We conclude the independent evidence of discrimination presented by AFSCME is insufficient to support an inference of the requisite discriminatory motive under the disparate treatment theory.

AFSCME offered proof of isolated incidents of sex segregation as evidence of a history of sex-based wage discrimination. The evidence consists of "help wanted" advertisements restricting various jobs to members of a particular sex. These advertisements were often placed in separate "help wanted—male" and "help wanted—female" columns in state newspapers between 1960 and 1973, though most were discontinued when Title VII became applicable to the states in 1972. * * * However, none of the individually named plaintiffs in the action ever testified regarding specific incidents of discrimination. The isolated incidents alleged by AFSCME are insufficient to corroborate the results of the Willis study and do not justify an inference of discriminatory motive by the State in the setting of salaries for its system as a whole. * * * We also reject AFSCME's contention that, having commissioned the Willis study, the State of Washington was committed to implement a new system of compensation based on comparable worth as defined by the study. Whether comparable worth is a feasible approach to employee compensation is a matter of debate. Assuming, however, that like other job evaluation studies it may be useful as a diagnostic tool, we reject a rule that would penalize rather than commend employers for their effort and innovation in undertaking such a study. The results of comparable worth studies will vary depending on the number and types of factors measured and the maximum number of points allotted to each factor. A study that indicates a particular wage structure might be more equitable should not categorically bind the employer who commissioned it. The employer should also be able to take into account market conditions, bargaining demands, and the possibility that another study will yield different results. * * * We hold there was a failure to establish a violation of Title VII under the disparate treatment theory of discrimination, and reverse the district court on this aspect of the case as well. The State of Washington's initial reliance on a free market system in which employees in male-dominated jobs are compensated at a higher rate than employees in dissimilar female-dominated jobs is not in and of itself a violation of Title VII, notwithstanding that the Willis study deemed the positions of comparable worth. Absent a showing of discriminatory motive, which has not been made here, the law does not permit the federal courts to interfere in the market-based system for the compensation of Washington's employees.

REVERSED.

NOTES AND QUESTION

**1.** For other post-*Gunther* decisions, illustrating the mixed results in pay equity cases, see: Spaulding v. University of Washington, 740 F.2d 686 (9th Cir.), cert. denied, 469 U.S. 1036 (1984) (no discrimination where members of nursing faculty paid less than faculty in other departments); Plemer v. Parsons-Gilbane, 713 F.2d 1127 (5th Cir.1983) (court refused to assess subjectively the value of two jobs); Lanegan-Grimm v. Library Association,

560 F.Supp. 486 (D.Or.1983) (library discriminated when it paid female driver of mobile library less than male delivery truck driver); Briggs v. City of Madison, 536 F.Supp. 435 (W.D.Wis.1982) (plaintiffs failed to establish prima facie case of discrimination when their proof did not eliminate "most common nondiscriminatory reason for wage disparity: differences in the jobs' requirements of skill, effort and responsibility"); Power v. Barry County, 539 F.Supp. 721 (W.D.Mich.1982) (plaintiffs failed to establish that their salaries were lower solely because they were women).

**2.** The Ninth Circuit firmly rejected the use of the disparate impact theory to prove the existence of sex-based wage discrimination. Is the disparate impact model in fact limited only to employer selection processes, as the opinion stated? (Hint: see City of Los Angeles Department of Water & Power v. Manhart, infra, p. 1234.) Disparate impact analysis is typically used in other systemic discrimination cases. Why did the court reject its use in *AFSCME II?*

Following *AFSCME II,* comparable worth litigation has almost uniformly met with failure in the federal courts. See UAW v. Michigan, 886 F.2d 766 (6th Cir.1989); EEOC v. Sears, Roebuck & Co., 839 F.2d 302 (7th Cir.1988), discussed supra p. 285; American Nurses' Association v. Illinois, 783 F.2d 716 (7th Cir.1986) (particularly notable for its discussion of the labor market defense by Judge Posner); California State Employees' Association v. State of California, 724 F.Supp. 717 (N.D.Cal.1989); Manuel v. WSBT, Inc., 706 F.Supp. 654 (N.D.Ind.1988); Beard v. Whitley County REMC, 656 F.Supp. 1461 (N.D.Ind.1987), affirmed 840 F.2d 405 (7th Cir. 1988). But in Denny v. Westfield State College, 669 F.Supp. 1146 (D.Mass. 1987), 880 F.2d 1465 (1st Cir.1989), female faculty members successfully sued for sex-based wage discrimination under Title VII when they proved that they received significantly lower salaries than male faculty members and the college failed to provide a legitimate nondiscriminatory reason for the difference; the court rejected explanations for the difference based on departmental affiliation and exceptional performance.

**3.** In trying to prove a case of disparate treatment, how can plaintiffs establish an employer's intent to discriminate in wages? In *AFSCME I,* Judge Tanner looked at direct and circumstantial evidence of historical discrimination against women, job segregation, and overtly discriminatory behavior and statements by state officials. Why is that not enough for the Court of Appeals? What additional evidence would support a finding of "intent"? In deciding the question of "intent" in favor of plaintiffs, the court in Taylor v. Charley Brothers, 25 F.E.P. Cases 602 (W.D.Pa.1981), noted the following: the employer's failure to conduct a job evaluation; its practice of segregating women within one department in the company (a large warehousing operation); its practice of only considering women job applicants for openings in that department; and discriminatory remarks made by company officials. In general, what *minimal* evidence would be necessary to establish intent?

**4.** The failure of the legal system to recognize comparable worth as a viable theory has not meant its death. Pay equity has been the focus of negotiations between public employers and public sector employee unions in a number of jurisdictions. According to *Pay Equity Activity in the Public Sector, 1979–1989,* a report published by the National Committee on Pay Equity, pay equity initiatives in the public sector during that decade resulted in more than $450 million in pay equity adjustments at state, county, and municipal levels, almost exclusively in organized workplaces.

In addition, some states have enacted statutes designed to eliminate pay inequity. See Minn.Stat. §§ 471.991–.999 and Iowa Code § 602.1401. In addressing Minnesota's experience with its statute, the Minnesota Commissioner of Employee Relations stated:

> What did *not* happen when we implemented pay equity in Minnesota is probably more significant than what did happen, in view of the dire consequences predicted by opponents. * * *
>
> No employees have had wages reduced or frozen, and no employees have been laid off as a result of the pay equity program. There have been no strikes or lawsuits. There has been no creation of a new bureaucracy to manage the process. There has been no change in the State's ability to attract and retain qualified workers or to meet its fiscal responsibilities. The costs have been reasonable.
>
> Opponents of pay equity have suggested that women would lose jobs, or that women would be discouraged from seeking nontraditional jobs. Again, our experience shows that these fears are unfounded. Since we started implementing pay equity, the number of women in nontraditional state jobs has increased by nineteen percent.
>
> It has also been suggested that pay equity will cause disruption and low morale in the work force. Again, this has not happened. An independent study of Minnesota state employees showed that over eighty percent strongly supported pay equity— men as well as women, and those who received pay equity increases as well as those who did not.

Nina Rothchild, Pay Equity—The Minnesota Experience, 20 U.Mich. J.L.Ref. 209 (1986).

Does the voluntary implementation by a state of a comparable worth program designed to raise wages in female-dominated jobs present any problems as unlawful sex discrimination in favor of women?

**5.** The Ninth Circuit relied heavily on the defendant's "market rate" theory to hold that the plaintiffs failed to establish intent, a requisite part of their prima facie disparate treatment case. Review the burdens of proof for establishing discrimination under Title VII. Given the inference of intent that can be drawn from the employer's wage statistics, should not the court have recognized that plaintiffs established a prima facie case and then evaluated the market rate argument as the employer's defense to the prima facie case? What difference would this make?

The market rate defense has proved powerful in post-*Gunther* litigation. Opponents of legal intervention on behalf of pay equity argue that any intrusion into the free workings of the labor market is unwarranted. This same argument can be made about almost any statute, however; Title VII constitutes a deliberate intrusion into the "free market", as do the Fair Labor Standards Act, OSHA, and other statutes establishing minimum working standards. Similarly, antitrust or environmental laws interfere with the free operation of the market in areas outside employment. What role should "the market" play in cases of alleged wage discrimination?

Further, is it not true that the Supreme Court rejected a market rate defense under the Equal Pay Act in *Corning*, supra p. 422? The Equal Pay Act defenses apply to Title VII cases such as *AFSCME I* and *II*. If the market rate is not a good defense under the Equal Pay Act, why should it be available in Title VII cases, especially when cost is not a defense to a discrimination claim under Title VII? The following article suggests a response to proponents of the market rate defense.

**6.** The comparable worth movement has been criticized as attempting to establish that the secretaries of one employer should be paid the same as truck drivers at a different company, or without regard to real differences in jobs at the same company. There have been fears that if the advocates of pay equity were successful, the entire American economy would be restructured, undermining the operation of the market in determining wages, as employers would be ordered to pay wage rates that bore little relation to competitive rates. The resulting distortion of the labor market would lead to serious dislocations and chaos. Such an outcome would indeed be cause for concern.

In actuality, the wage discrimination suits which have been brought have been tightly focused, with narrower likely effects. Cases to date have involved specific individuals working for the same employer and performing demonstrably equivalent (or comparable) jobs, measured either by job content or by the usual standards of experience, skill, effort, and responsibility. Nor have comparable worth cases addressed the issues of job access and job segregation; instead, they have focused on females who were already employed but were being paid less for jobs demonstrably similar to those held by males. The Equal Pay Act defenses—seniority or merit system, production quotas, or "any other factor other than sex"—are available to employers in cases brought under that Act or under Title VII. In no instance would the law require, for instance, an employer to pay individuals with different experience the same wage.

**7.** If comparable worth theories were successfully used to increase wages in traditionally female-dominated jobs, wouldn't those higher wages encourage women to stay in (or enter) those jobs and thus perpetuate occupational segregation? Is that a result we want to encourage?

**8.** What applicability, if any, does comparable worth analysis have for eliminating race discrimination?

**9.** Not surprisingly, the comparable worth debate has spawned considerable scholarly interest. See generally, Jeanne M. Dennis, The Lessons of Comparable Worth: A Feminist Vision of Law and Economic Theory, 4 UCLA Women's L.J. 1 (1993); Mayer G. Freed & Daniel D. Polsby, Comparable Worth in the Equal Pay Act, 51 U.Chi.L.Rev. 1078 (1984); Levit & Kathleen E. Mahoney, The Future of Comparable Worth Theory, 56 U.Colo.L.Rev. 99 (1984); Sandra J. Libeson, Reviving the Comparable Worth Debate in the United States: A Look Toward the European Community, 16 Comp.Lab.L.J. 358 (1995); Pamela L. Perry, Let Them Become Professionals: An Analysis of the Failure to Enforce Title VII's Pay Equity Mandate, 14 Harv. Women's L.J. 127 (1991); Deborah L. Rhode, Occupational Inequality, 1988 Duke L.J. 1207; George Schatzki, An Observation About Comparable Worth, 9 U. Puget Sound L.Rev. 491 (1986); Paul C. Weiler, The Wages of Sex: The Uses and Limits of Comparable Worth, 99 Harv.L.Rev. 1728 (1986); Symposium, The Gender Gap in Compensation, 82 Geo.L.J. 27 (1993).

For economic analysis, both theoretical and empirical, see the exchange: Richard A. Posner, An Economic Analysis of Sex Discrimination Laws, 56 U.Chi.L.Rev. 1311 (1989), and John J. Donohue, Prohibiting Sex Discrimination in the Workplace: An Economic Perspective, 56 U.Chi. L.Rev. 1337 (1989). See also George Johnson & Gary Solon, The Attainment of Pay Equity Between the Sexes by Legal Means: An Economic Analysis, 20 U.Mich.J.L. Reform 183 (1986) (entire issue devoted to comparable worth).

## Carin Clauss, *Comparable Worth—The Theory, Its Legal Foundation, and the Feasibility of Implementation*

20 U.Mich.J.L.Ref. 7 (1986).

A major difficulty in discussing the legal status of comparable worth, as well as its economic cost and administrative feasibility, is that the phrase "comparable worth" is used interchangeably to refer to many different concepts. Comparable worth may mean (1) a requirement that compensation be proportional to the intrinsic worth of the job, (2) a pay system under which all jobs of equal value are paid the same, (3) a procedure that permits the comparison of job content and compensation across job families (i.e., work that is dissimilar), (4) evidence used in a wage discrimination case to demonstrate that the difference in wages is due to sex and not to any difference in job value, (5) a requirement that female-dominated jobs be paid the same as male-dominated jobs of equal value, (6) a requirement that the wage rates for female-dominated jobs be established using the same criteria as are used in establishing the wage rates for male-dominated jobs, and (7) a requirement that wage disparities based on sex (or race) be eliminated.

The important distinction in these various meanings is between an equal value concept (items (1), (2), and (5) above), under which the employer is required to pay the same wage rate for all jobs of equal or comparable value, and a nondiscrimination concept (items (3), (4), (6), and (7)), under which the employer is prohibited from using different standards in establishing the rates for male- and female-dominated jobs, or from otherwise basing wages on sex. Unlike an equal value concept, nondiscrimination does not mandate equal wages for work of equal value but instead prohibits disparate wage treatment on the basis of sex or race.

The legal and moral justifications for these two distinct concepts vary considerably. Most people would probably agree that wage discrimination offends a basic civil liberty and is thus properly dealt with by our legal system—as witnessed by the widespread support for the Equal Pay Act and the nondiscrimination in pay provisions of Title VII of the Civil Rights Act. By the same token, there are probably very few people who would agree that equal pay for work of equal value (without regard to discrimination) is a basic civil liberty—whatever their view might be as to the fairness of such a system. Indeed, there are a great many compensation systems in both the private and public sectors that do not pay all jobs of equal or comparable value at the same rate, regardless of whether those jobs are male or female. In these systems, male-dominated jobs are paid less than other male-dominated jobs even though the work content of the jobs might be of "equal" or "comparable" value. For example, the average wage for architects is less than the average wage for engineers, although the educational and skill requirements for the two jobs are very much the same. Similar disparities also exist among female jobs.

The reasons for such disparities could be several: individual employers, or society as a whole, may reward certain skills more than others (e.g., managerial skills over artistic skills, or technical skills over administrative skills); wages may be inflated by the unionization of specific occupations, or by restrictions on entry into particular occupations; or wages may be influenced by tradition and custom. Whatever the reason, such disparities are commonplace. It is not the wage disparity in jobs of equal value that invokes the charge of discrimination; rather, it is the use of different standards—i.e., disparate treatment—in establishing the wage rates for the male- and female-dominated jobs.

This distinction between an equal value concept and a theory of nondiscrimination is critical, not only because it establishes the legal and moral justification for comparable worth, but also because it answers three of the more common criticisms directed at comparable worth. First, comparable worth does not mandate an "equality of results" for employees in male- and female-dominated jobs. Those individuals who make this argument suggest that comparable worth proponents want to eliminate the earnings gap between men and women by compelling employers to increase the wage rates for female-dominated jobs even if these jobs are less skilled or are located in the more marginal firms or industries—what the chairman of the United States Civil Rights Commission calls "reparations for middle-class white women" or a "financial quota system."

But comparable worth, as defined here, and as used by litigators and legislators, does not seek to raise the wage rates of less skilled or less productive female jobs to equal those of higher skilled or more productive male jobs, or to ensure that women obtain the same economic benefits from a day's labor as do men. It may be that the high concentration of women in less skilled and less productive jobs is the result of discrimination, but discrimination in employment, not pay. Comparable worth is only concerned with pay discrimination. So, for example, if it were shown that a publishing company had channeled women college graduates into clerical jobs and men college graduates into editorial positions, or that a bank had assigned women applicants to teller positions and men with equivalent education and experience to officer trainee positions, the remedy would be to allow women to transfer into the "male" positions, not to increase the wage rates for clerical and teller positions to equal the wage rates for editorial assistants and officer trainees. On the other hand, if it were shown that the clerical jobs and teller positions were paid less than male-dominated jobs of comparable or lesser value, the remedy would be to reassess the wage rates for the female-dominated jobs using the same criteria as were used in establishing the wage rates for the male-dominated jobs—i.e., equal treatment, not equal results.

Second, because comparable worth is based on a theory of discrimination (disparate treatment) and not on some ill-defined notion of public justice, it does not attempt to eliminate all wage disparities existing within an employing unit, but only those resulting from the application of different standards in establishing the wage rates for female-dominated jobs. Thus, it would not affect any differentials existing between male-dominated jobs, where certain male-dominated jobs are paid more than others of comparable or equal value. Nor would comparable worth affect any disparities existing between female-dominated jobs of equal value. Such disparities may be the result of market forces or of long-standing custom, or they may just be the result of a random wage structure. But they are not the result of prohibited disparate treatment. The fact that disparate treatment must be based on sex, race, color, religion, or national origin—and not just on custom or chance—should satisfy the frequently expressed concern that comparable worth will open the floodgates to large numbers of suits challenging the relative ranking of jobs.

And finally, because comparable worth is not concerned with just any wage disparity, but only those disparities that are the result of sex-based wage discrimination, the degree of government or judicial intervention into an employer's wage practice will be much more limited than the critics suggest. Bureaucrats and judges would not, for example, be authorized to determine what the fair wage should be for any male-dominated or integrated job. These decisions would all be made by the employer. Nor would the government or courts be able to alter the ranking of these jobs. Comparable worth does not require an employer to pay more to those who perform work of greater value, or less to those who perform work of lesser value; the employer is free to pay all employees the same rate, or to pay different rates for work of equal value. The employer can choose to give greater monetary weight to artistic or creative skills than to managerial skills, or it can give little or no weight to such skills. Similarly, it can give greater weight to responsibility than to skill, or, alternatively, greater weight to skill than to responsibility. The only requirement of comparable worth is that the employer use the same standards in establishing the pay rates for female-dominated jobs, and for black and Hispanic jobs, as it uses in establishing the pay rates for male-dominated and integrated jobs. Where it can be shown that the employer has used different standards, the doctrine of comparable worth requires that the employer adjust the wage rates for the female-dominated jobs so that these jobs will occupy the same relative position that they would have occupied had they been male-dominated or integrated jobs.

# CHAPTER 6

# HEALTH INSURANCE AND OTHER FRINGE BENEFITS

## A. INTRODUCTION

The debate over health insurance reform in the United States, begun in earnest in the 1992 Presidential election campaign, is in many respects a debate about the role of employers in funding, controlling access to, administering, and containing the costs of employer-sponsored health insurance. Under any of the sweeping reforms currently under serious consideration, it is likely that employers will continue to play an important role in health insurance. Regardless of the merits of such a system in the abstract, the fact is that this is the way the system has developed, there are powerful interests with a stake in its perpetuation, and there is inadequate political support for any system that is not dependent, at least financially, on employers.

The magnitude of the fringe benefit obligations of employers is staggering and continues to grow. Employee benefits represent about 40 percent of total payroll costs. Health insurance is the fastest growing expense. It accounts, on average, for about $4,000 per year per employee. At some companies the annual per employee cost of health benefits is over $6,000 per year. Indeed, wage levels have remained virtually unchanged for over two decades, with almost all of the increased compensation costs going to health benefits. Thus, in a real sense, supposedly employer-funded health insurance is really employee-funded health insurance. Efforts by employers to reduce their health insurance costs (e.g., by increasing the employees' contributions) have resulted in health insurance issues becoming the most common reason for strikes by the early 1990s.

This chapter will explore the economic, social, and legal framework of health insurance and other fringe benefits. It will discuss in some detail the Employee Retirement Income Security Act (ERISA) and its effect on welfare benefits. It will also consider discrimination in benefits, other benefits such as child care and elder care, and the consequences of placing increasing requirements for social welfare programs on employers. This chapter focuses on an area of employment law that is front-page news on a daily basis, and that will continue to be extremely important for the foreseeable future.

## UNITED STATES CHAMBER OF COMMERCE
## 1997 EMPLOYEE BENEFITS REPORT

| Growth of Employee Benefits, 1929 to 1996 | | | | | | | | | | | | |
|---|---|---|---|---|---|---|---|---|---|---|---|---|
| | 1929 | 1955 | 1965 | 1975 | 1986 | 1988 | 1989 | 1991 | 1992 | 1993 | 1994 | 1995 | 1996 |
| Type of Payment | | | | | | (Percent of wages and salaries) | | | | | | | |
| 1. Legally required | 0.8 | 3.3 | 5.3 | 8.4 | 11.1 | 11.6 | 12.2 | 12.2 | 12.1 | 11.8 | 11.8 | 12.0 | 11.7 |
| Old–Age, Survivors, Disability, and Health Insurance (FICA taxes) | 0.0 | 1.4 | 2.3 | 4.6 | 5.9 | 6.1 | 6.5 | 6.3 | 6.4 | 6.2 | 6.4 | 6.4 | 6.3 |
| Unemployment Compensation | 0.0 | 0.7 | 1.0 | 0.8 | 1.2 | 1.0 | 0.9 | 0.7 | 0.9 | 0.9 | 0.9 | 0.9 | 0.8 |
| Workers' compensation | 0.6 | 0.5 | 0.7 | 1.0 | 1.0 | 1.6 | 1.7 | 1.7 | 1.8 | 1.6 | 1.6 | 1.6 | 1.4 |
| Government employees retirement | 0.2 | 0.5 | 1.0 | 1.7 | 2.8 | 2.7 | 2.9 | 3.2 | 2.7 | 3.1 | 2.9 | 3.1 | 3.0 |
| Other | 0.0 | 0.2 | 0.3 | 0.3 | 0.2 | 0.2 | 0.2 | 0.3 | 0.3 | 0.2 | 0.2 | 0.2 | 0.2 |
| Agreed-upon | 0.4 | 3.6 | 4.6 | 7.4 | 9.7 | 10.6 | 11.0 | 12.7 | 13.1 | 15.1 | 15.6 | 16.5 | 15.5 |
| Pensions | 0.2 | 2.2 | 2.3 | 3.6 | 2.8 | 4.1 | 4.0 | 5.1 | 5.3 | 5.8 | 6.0 | 6.7 | 5.8 |
| Insurance | 0.1 | 1.1 | 2.0 | 3.4 | 5.6 | 5.9 | 6.4 | 6.7 | 7.2 | 8.3 | 8.3 | 8.3 | 8.1 |
| Other | 0.1 | 0.3 | 0.3 | 0.4 | 1.3 | 0.6 | 0.6 | 0.9 | 0.6 | 1.0 | 1.3 | 1.6 | 1.6 |
| Rest Periods | 1.0 | 3.0 | 3.1 | 3.7 | 3.3 | 2.9 | 3.0 | 2.5 | 3.1 | 2.6 | 2.2 | 2.2 | 3.7 |
| Time not Worked | 0.7 | 5.9 | 7.3 | 9.4 | 10.2 | 10.4 | 10.2 | 9.9 | 10.2 | 9.7 | 9.7 | 10.2 | 10.2 |
| Vacations | 0.3 | 3.0 | 3.8 | 4.8 | 5.2 | 5.5 | 5.4 | 5.2 | 5.4 | 5.2 | 5.1 | 5.4 | 5.3 |
| Holidays | 0.3 | 2.0 | 2.5 | 3.2 | 3.1 | 3.2 | 3.2 | 3.1 | 3.2 | 2.9 | 3.1 | 3.3 | 3.1 |
| Sick leave | 0.1 | 0.8 | 0.8 | 1.2 | 1.4 | 1.3 | 1.2 | 1.2 | 1.2 | 1.2 | 1.2 | 1.2 | 1.2 |
| Other | 0.0 | 0.1 | 0.2 | 0.2 | 0.5 | 0.4 | 0.4 | 0.4 | 0.4 | 0.4 | 0.3 | 0.4 | 0.6 |
| Bonuses profit-sharing, etc. | 0.1 | 1.2 | 1.2 | 1.1 | 1.2 | 1.1 | 1.1 | 0.9 | 0.6 | 0.6 | 0.7 | 0.8 | 0.8 |
| Total benefit payments | 3.0% | 17.0% | 21.5% | 30.0% | 35.5% | 36.7% | 37.5% | 38.2% | 39.1% | 39.6% | 4.0% | 41.8% | 41.9 |
| Wages and Salaries (billions $) | $50.50 | $212.10 | $363.70 | $814.70 | $2,093.00 | $2,431.10 | $2,573.30 | $2,827.00 | $2,985.40 | $3,090.60 | $3,241.10 | $3,419.7 | $3,633.60 |
| Total benefit payments (billions $) | $1.50 | $36.10 | $78.20 | $244.40 | $743.00 | $813.90 | $964.98 | $1,080.14 | $1,164.31 | $1,223.88 | $1,296.44 | $1,429.22 | $1,522.47 |

Source: Estimated by U.S. Chamber of Commerce from U.S. Department of Commerce data and U.S. Chamber of Commerce Survey.

Reprinted with permission of the Chamber of Commerce of the United States from the 1997 edition of *Employee Benefits*.

| Employee Benefits, By Type of Benefit: All Employees, 1996 | | | |
|---|---|---|---|
| Type of Benefit | Total, All Companies | Total, All Manufacturing | Total, All Nonmanufacturing |
| Total employees benefits as percent of payroll | 41.3 | 44.1 | 40.7 |
| 1. Legally required payments (employer's share only) | 8.8 | 9.7 | 8.7 |
|   a. Old–Age, Survivors, Disability, and Health Insurance (employer FICA taxes) and Railroad Retirement Tax | 7.0 | 7.3 | 7.0 |
|   b. Unemployment compensation | 0.7 | 1.0 | 0.6 |
|   c. Workers' compensation (including estimated cost of self-insured) | 1.1 | 1.4 | 1.1 |
|   d. State sickness benefit insurance and other | 0.1 | 0.0 | 0.1 |
| 2. Retirement and savings plan payments (employer's share only) | 6.3 | 6.2 | 6.3 |
|   a. Defined benefit pension plan contributions | 3.4 | 4.0 | 3.2 |
|   b. Defined contribution plan payments (401K type) | 1.5 | 1.3 | 1.6 |
|   c. Profit sharing | 0.5 | 0.6 | 0.4 |
|   d. Stock bonus and employee stock ownership plans (ESOP) | 0.1 | 0.1 | 0.1 |
|   e. Pension plan premiums (net) under insurance and annuity contracts (insured and trusted) | 0.5 | 0.0 | 0.6 |
|   f. Administrative and other costs | 0.3 | 0.2 | 0.4 |
| 3. Life insurance and death benefit payments (employers' share only) | 0.4 | 0.4 | 0.3 |
| 4. Medical & medically related benefit payments (employers' share only) | 9.6 | 10.4 | 9.5 |
|   a. Hospital, surgical, medical, and major medical insurance share only (net) | 7.0 | 7.7 | 6.9 |
|   b. Retiree (payments for retired employees) hospital, surgical, medical, and major medical insurance premiums (net) | 1.0 | 1.1 | 0.9 |
|   c. Short-term disability, sickness or accident insurance (company plan or insured plan) | 0.4 | 0.6 | 0.4 |
|   d. Long-term disability or wage continuation (insured, self-administered, or trusts) | 0.3 | 0.3 | 0.3 |
|   e. Dental insurance premiums | 0.5 | 0.3 | 0.6 |
|   f. Other (vision care, physical and mental fitness benefits for former employees) | 0.4 | 0.5 | 0.4 |
| 5. Paid rest periods, coffee breaks, lunch periods, wash-up time, travel time, clothes-change time, get ready time, etc. | 3.7 | 4.6 | 3.5 |
| 6. Payments for time not worked | 10.2 | 10.2 | 10.2 |
|   a. Payment for or in lieu of vacations | 5.3 | 5.1 | 5.3 |
|   b. Payment for or in lieu of holidays | 3.1 | 3.7 | 3.0 |
|   c. Sick leave pay | 1.2 | 0.3 | 1.4 |
|   d. Parental leave (maternity and paternity leave payments) | 0.0 | 0.0 | 0.0 |
|   e. Other | 0.6 | 1.1 | 0.5 |
| 7. Miscellaneous benefit payments | 2.3 | 2.6 | 2.2 |
|   a. Discounts on goods and services purchased from company by employees | 0.4 | 0.0 | 0.4 |
|   b. Severance Pay | 0.3 | 0.1 | 0.4 |
|   c. Employee education expenditures | 0.4 | 0.9 | 0.3 |
|   d. Child care | 0.0 | 0.0 | 0.0 |
|   e. Other | 1.2 | 1.5 | 1.1 |
| Total employee benefits as cents per hour | 679.9¢ | 887.8¢ | 646.4¢ |
| Total employee benefits as dollars per year per employee | $14,086 | $19,217 | $13,299 |

## B.  HEALTH BENEFITS

## 1.  INTRODUCTION

## Mark A. Rothstein, Medical Screening and the Employee Health Cost Crisis *
195–98 (1989).

Employer-provided group health insurance became common during World War II because such fringe benefits were not subject to wartime wage and price controls.  Thus, employees (often union members bargaining collectively) were given health insurance coverage when increasing wages was not possible.  Perhaps the most attractive feature to employees of health insurance as an employer-provided fringe benefit was the tax-favored treatment of benefits.  Employer contributions to a group plan were and still are deductible to the employer as a business expense and, more important, are excluded from the taxable income of the employee.  Consequently, health insurance provides a greater after-tax gain to employees than comparable (taxable) wage payments.

From the 1950s through the 1970s, the scope of coverage of health benefits expanded from hospital care to a wide range of medical, dental, and other benefits.  Coverage also was extended to retirees and workers' family members.  In his book, *America's Health Care Revolution*, Joseph A. Califano, Jr., former Secretary of Health, Education and Welfare, chronicled the growth of employee health benefits funded by Chrysler Corporation.  This growth, representative of many large corporations, is illustrated in Table 10–1.

| Table 10–1 |
|---|
| The Growth of Chrysler Corporation's Health Benefits Plan, 1941–1979 |

|  |  |
|---|---|
| 1941 | Hospitalization plan with employees paying all costs through payroll deductions |
| 1950 | Chrysler pays half the costs and extends coverage to cover physicians' fees |
| 1953 | Retirees added to plan, but they pay all costs |
| 1961 | Chrysler pays all costs for employees and their dependents; half the costs for retirees and their dependents |
| 1964 | Full health coverage for retirees and their dependents; first-dollar coverage for employee outpatient psychiatric care |
| 1967 | Prescription drug plan added for employees and dependents |
| 1973 | Dental coverage for employees and dependents |
| 1976 | Dental coverage for retirees and dependents; eyeglasses for employees; hearing aids for employees and retirees |
| 1979 | Eyeglasses for retirees |

*Source:* Adapted from J. Califano, America's Health Care Revolution 13–15 (1986). Copyright 1986, Random House, Inc.  Reprinted by permission.

* Reprinted by permission of the Bureau of National Affairs, Inc., Washington, D.C.

Although Chrysler has been in the forefront of efforts to reduce health care costs, the general trend of increasing the scope of employee health benefits has continued in the 1980s. For example, between 1980 and 1986 the percentage of medium and large companies providing vision care benefits nearly doubled—from 21 percent to 40 percent.

Today, 85 to 90 percent of Americans covered by health insurance are covered by group health insurance and 68 percent are covered under employer-provided plans. The availability of health insurance through an employer not only represents a tax saving to employees, but, for many workers, it is their only opportunity to obtain health insurance. Without employer-funded or employer-subsidized group health insurance, many lower paid workers would be unable to afford the premiums on an individual health insurance policy or would be uninsurable because of their medical condition.

\* \* \*

It is also important to consider the changing method of funding employer health benefits. During the 1970s many larger corporations with rising health costs realized that, with a stable work force, increases in experience-rated premiums were predictable by simply applying an inflation factor. Insurers actually were eliminating very little risk. "In effect, the employee groups covered by large corporations had grown to such a size as to render of little value the essential function of insurance—i.e., reducing the risk by pooling independent exposures."

The result was a growing use of self-insurance, whereby employers directly assume responsibility for health care expenses rather than by purchasing health insurance. Some self-insured companies still contract with commercial insurers or other service companies for claims processing or to purchase "stop loss" insurance to limit their liability for large claims.

Employers obtain several advantages from self-insurance. They save the profits of the commercial insurers; they are able to use and retain earnings on amounts paid to insurers and held as claims reserves; and they pay no taxes on premiums. Most important, in an era of increasing state regulation of health insurance, self-insured plans are exempt from state insurance laws and regulations, including state high-risk insurance pools. These latter laws, enacted in at least 15 states in the 1980s, provide a fund to enable medically uninsurable individuals to obtain health insurance at subsidized rates.

## Institute of Medicine, National Academy of Sciences, Employment and Health Benefits: A Connection at Risk

82–85, 98–102 (1993).

### FEDERAL REGULATION AND THE EMPLOYER'S GROWING ROLE *

#### Federal and State Roles Before 1974

The federal structure of the U.S. political system has produced a particularly complex and uneven mix of state and national regulation of health insurance and related matters. Before 1974, states generally regulated private health insurance, whether it was individual or employment-based, insured or self-insured. State insurance regulation began in the mid–1800s and was upheld by a Supreme Court decision in 1868, which ruled that insurance contracts were not part of interstate commerce and therefore were subject to state and not federal regulation. In 1944 the Court reversed its decision, holding that insurance transactions did involve interstate commerce and were subject to federal antitrust and other laws. This decision, in turn, was overruled in 1945, when Congress passed the McCarran–Ferguson Act. The act returned to the states many regulatory powers but left the option of national regulation of insurance if states did not act. In order to promote systematic state action and avoid federal regulation, the National Association of Insurance Commissioners was formed to assist in the development and passage of model state legislation.

Until the 1970s the national government largely confined its attention to employment-based health benefits to two policy issues: collective bargaining and taxation. Faced with rising Medicare and Medicaid costs in the 1970s, the federal government instituted an array of cost management initiatives, including federal wage-price controls, health resource planning, HMO promotion, and quality and utilization review of health care services. With the exception of the HMO Act of 1973, which mandated that most employers offer their employees a federally qualified HMO if one was available, these initiatives did not touch employment-based health benefits very directly. (Legislation adopted in 1988 calls for the HMO mandate provision to expire in 1995.)

#### The Employee Retirement Income Security Act of 1974

In 1974 the division of federal and state regulatory authority with respect to employee benefits changed fundamentally with the passage of the Employee Retirement Income Security Act (ERISA). Since then, the relevance of state regulation to employment-based health plans has declined dramatically—without any significant expansion in substantive federal regulation of plan operations and characteristics.

ERISA was aimed primarily at private employer pension plans, and most of its provisions and implementing regulations are directed at such pension plans with little explicit attention to health plans. As interpreted by the courts over the years since its passage, however, ERISA has preempted an increasing number of state regulations affecting employment-based health plans. Despite some pressure to do so, Congress has refused to enact legislation that would overrule these interpretations.

States can indirectly reach some employers through their regulation of insured health plans, including insured HMO plans, but the group of insured employers has grown smaller every year as more employers—including quite small employers—have seen the advantages of self-insuring to avoid such regulation. Multistate employers are free to establish uniform health benefit programs across state lines and no longer have to modify their programs to conform to the myriad different details of state laws.

For self-insured employers the major regulatory consequences of ERISA are that such plans are exempt from several requirements: state taxes on insurance premiums; state mandates that certain types of benefits be provided; state limits on certain kinds of utilization management and provider contracting arrangements; solvency and prefunding requirements; defined claims settlement procedures; state law claims for various kinds of damages; and mandatory participation in state risk pools or uncompensated care plans. The last protection is now one of the most controversial, as many states try to maintain or establish these kinds of programs. * * *

Although ERISA precludes state regulation of self-insured employer-sponsored health benefits, it does not replace diverse state policies with an equivalent set of consistent national standards. The requirements it imposes on employers are quite limited. They primarily involve information reporting and disclosure, prudent exercise of fiduciary responsibilities, limits on disproportionate benefits for highly compensated employees, and (since 1985) continued coverage for certain former workers and others. There is no provision for waivers from ERISA requirements, and only one state, Hawaii, has obtained a statutory waiver.

The point that ERISA preempts state regulation without substituting explicit federal regulation of some basic dimensions of health benefit plans can be illustrated with several specific examples. Unlike many or all state laws, ERISA

• sets no solvency, reserve, funding, financial management, or backup insurance requirements for health plans to protect employees in the event of employer bankruptcy;

• specifies no standards for health coverage or minimum benefits;

• establishes no requirements that certain categories of employees or family members be generally eligible for coverage (except for the continued coverage requirements described below); and

• contains no prohibitions against unilateral reduction or termination of benefits by an employer during the plan year nor any limits on medical underwriting practices such as exclusions of coverage for preexisting conditions.

With respect to this last point, although ERISA did not set funding and vesting requirements for health benefit plans as it did for pension plans, other statutes and the general law of contracts may limit employers' freedom to reduce or terminate benefits in some cases. For example, employers may need to prove that their right to terminate retiree benefits was specifically stated and widely known to employees. This constraint is particularly significant for employers considering their options given recent nongovernmental rules established by the Financial Accounting Standards Board (FASB). These rules require that benefits promised to retirees be recognized as liabilities on a firm's financial statements.

ERISA did establish somewhat more extensive regulatory provisions for one type of employment-based health benefits involving multiple employers, but the results have not been satisfactory to many. *Multiple employer plans* were originally defined as plans to which more than one employer contributes but which are not collectively bargained. Then in 1982, Congress redefined this category as multiple employer welfare arrangements (MEWAs), and made such plans subject to special regulations intended to control abuses fostered by the lack of applicable federal or state regulation. Fully insured MEWAs are subject to direct state insurance regulation related to the adequacy of contribution and reserve levels. MEWAs that are not fully insured are subject to all state insurance regulations, to the extent that they are not inconsistent with ERISA. Abuses and outright fraud by some third parties marketing MEWAs have led to calls for further legislation to strengthen regulation of such plans at the state or federal level or both.

Further complicating the regulatory picture are *multiemployer plans,* which, as defined by statute, are plans to which more than one employer contributes pursuant to collective bargaining agreements. They generally have joint labor-management boards, are regulated under the 1947 Taft–Hartley Act, and are explicitly excluded from coverage under the ERISA amendments related to multiple employer welfare arrangements.

Federal laws enacted since ERISA have imposed a limited number of mandates on employers. The most important emerged from the Consolidated Omnibus Budget Reconciliation Act (COBRA) of 1985. That act requires employers with 20 or more employees who offer health benefits to offer continued coverage to most former employees, their dependents, and certain others for 18 or 36 months or until coverage under another plan begins. Employers can charge no more than 102 percent of the average cost to the employer of providing coverage to all its employees. An earlier federal law, the Tax Equity and Fiscal Responsibility Act of 1982, requires employers with 20 or more workers to cover certain employees (those aged 65 to 69, the disabled, and those with end-stage renal disease) who would otherwise be eligible for Medicare coverage.

Overall, ERISA gave a powerful boost to employer discretion and involvement in the management of health benefits. It diminished the position and influence of states and insurers and eliminated some protections for insured individuals but provided little in the way of explicit national standards for employee health benefits.  As states' concern about the uninsured and the financial problems of health care institutions providing uncompensated care has grown, ERISA has also limited states' efforts to develop state risk pools, set minimum standards for certain kinds of health benefit programs, and act generally in areas in which the federal government has not taken the initiative.

\* \* \*

## WHAT TYPES OF COVERAGE ARE OFFERED?

### Types of Health Plans

If the typical health plan offering of 20 years ago could be described as a "plain vanilla" plan with some limited variations in ingredients, health plans today come in a multitude of flavors that are not easily categorized. The following discussion distinguishes simply between conventional and network plans on the basis of whether the plans impose restrictions on the participant's choice of health care provider.

Both conventional and network plans are evolving so rapidly that general characterizations and comparisons can become quickly outdated. In addition, behind this dichotomy lies much variability, particularly among network health plans.  Moreover, because a network plan that is more restrictive on one variable (such as coverage for out-of-network services or the extent to which access to specialists and other care is controlled by a primary care "gatekeeper") may be less so on others, it is difficult to array different types of network plans along a simple continuum.  These caveats notwithstanding, group and staff model health maintenance organizations (HMOs) are generally considered to be more restrictive than independent practice associations (IPAs), and the latter are assumed to be more restrictive than preferred provider organizations (PPOs) and point-of-service (POS) plans (see glossary for definitions).

### Conventional Plans

Conventional plans (which may also be called indemnity, fee-for-service, open panel, or freedom-of-choice plans) place few if any restrictions on the participant's choice of the health care practitioners and providers whose services are otherwise covered.  They may and increasingly do incorporate managed care features such as prior review of proposed hospital care, but they continue to pay health care practitioners and providers largely or entirely on a fee-for-service basis.

Conventional plans have a long history in the United States, are familiar to most employees, and are often the only type of plan offered by employers.  For purposes of this discussion, the category includes Blue Cross and Blue Shield plans that have very broad-based participating hospital and physician programs that may include up to 100 percent of area providers.  Depending on specific plan practices in contracting with and paying providers, some plans could be categorized as weak network plans. The border separating conventional and network plans thus contains a "gray area." * * *

*Network Plans*

Network plans, as the name implies, restrict coverage in whole or part to services provided by a specified network or group of physicians, hospitals, and other health care providers. Some network plans, such as various kinds of HMOs, limit nonemergency coverage entirely to network providers. Other plans, such as PPOs, POS plans, and open-ended HMOs, cover enrollees for some nonemergency services received from nonnetwork providers but typically impose higher deductibles, coinsurance, and other employee cost sharing for such care. In essence, employees can choose between network and nonnetwork services when they seek care rather than once a year when choices among health plans are made. A few employers have established their own networks, either by providing certain health services through company clinics and hospitals or by contracting directly with health care providers.

Network plans are sometimes termed *closed* or *exclusive provider panels* (if they exclude out-of-network coverage for nonemergency care), *alternative delivery systems,* or *managed care plans,* although each of these terms may be used in narrower, broader, or different ways. In particular, the term *managed care* may be applied to conventional plans that include certain utilization management strategies such as preadmission review and case management.

Network plans may pay physicians on a salaried, capitated, or modified fee-for-service basis. The modifications to fee-for-service payments may involve discounts to normal fees or acceptance by the provider of some risk for levels of use or expenses that are higher than planned. In addition to their payment arrangements, many network plans require members to designate a primary care physician who serves as "gatekeeper" for referrals to specialists and other services.

In the last decade, network-based health plans have grown greatly in numbers, enrollments, and variety (Table 3.4), partly because federal law required many employers to offer HMOs, partly because employers have seen these plans as vehicles for limiting increases in their health benefit costs, and partly because employers have considered choice of health plan attractive to employees. Across all firms surveyed by HIAA in 1990, 20 percent of covered employees were enrolled in HMOs, 13 percent in PPOs, and 5 percent in other network-based plans such as POS plans. More recent data suggest that POS plans are growing rapidly. Only 123 HMOs offered such plans in 1990, compared with 256 in 1991.

**TABLE 3.4**  Percentage Distribution of Employees Across Types of Health Benefit Plans, 1987 to 1990

|  | 1987 | 1988 | 1989 | 1990 |
|---|---|---|---|---|
| Conventional without utilization management | 41 | 28 | 18 | 5 |
| Conventional with utilization management | 32 | 43 | 49 | 57 |
| Health maintenance organization | 16 | 18 | 17 | 20 |
| Preferred provider organization | 11 | 11 | 16 | 13 |
| Point-of-service plan | — | — | — | 5 |
| Total network-based managed care | 27 | 29 | 33 | 38 |
| Total nonnetwork plans | 73 | 71 | 67 | 62 |

SOURCE: Hoy et al., 1991, p. 19.  Based on Health Insurance Association of America surveys, 1989 to 1991.  Reprinted by permission of *Health Affairs* Winter 1991.

Larger employers have been considerably more likely than smaller employers to offer HMOs and PPOs, but the differential is smaller for PPOs.  Regional differences and urban-rural differences contribute to additional variation in employers' offerings.  These differences involve the availability of network plans (which can be difficult to establish in less populated areas), regional attitudes of physicians and others toward such plans, and state laws that may encourage or discourage such plans.

### Covered Services

\* \* \*

Today, virtually all those covered by employment-based health plans are covered for inpatient hospital care (including prescription drugs), outpatient surgery, physician hospital and office services, and outpatient prescription drugs (DOL, 1990, 1991).  In this last respect, most employment-based plans are more generous than Medicare, which does not cover outpatient drugs.  A substantial majority of covered workers have some coverage for extended care facilities and home health services; fewer than half are covered for hospice care.  Dental benefits are available to about two-thirds of health plan participants in medium and large private establishments but less than one-third of participants in small organizations.

## 2.   EMPLOYER LIABILITY

## Dawes Mining Co. v. Callahan

272 S.E.2d 267 (Ga.1980).

■ HILL, JUSTICE.

Certiorari was granted to review Dawes Mining Co. v. Callahan, 154 Ga.App. 229, 267 S.E.2d 830 (1980), in which the Court of Appeals held that when an employer changes its group health insurance policy on employees and the employees are incorrectly advised that the coverage under the new policy is the same as under the old policy, an employee can sue his employer for breach of an implied contract to continue the same insurance coverage, and can recover such damages as result from the difference in coverage.  The facts are set forth in the Court of Appeals' opinion and are restated here for convenience.

The evidence shows that appellee Callahan was first employed by appellant Dawes Mining Co. in 1957 as an hourly wage earner. A few years later Callahan started participating in Dawes' group health insurance program. The insurance paid for medical and hospital expenses incurred by Callahan and his dependents, with half the premiums paid for by Callahan by deductions from his pay and the other half by Dawes. Dawes processed employee claims under the policy to the insurer.

In 1975, without consulting the employees, Dawes changed coverage from the existing insurer to another insurance company.[1] The employees were told of the change and to come to the office to sign up with the new insurer. The local representative of Dawes and a representative of the new insurer were present in the office. The insurer's representative said the coverage was the same as under the former policy and said nothing about exclusion of coverage for pre-existing illnesses.[2]

Callahan, who could not read but could sign his name, signed an application for insurance as directed by the insurer's representative. Some weeks later he received an insurance card as evidence of the insurance. Unknown to Callahan at the time, the new insurance master policy had a provision which prohibited payment of medical expenses incurred as a result of pre-existing illnesses until the policy had been in effect a certain period of time.[3] Within that excluded period, Callahan's wife was hospitalized for a pre-existing illness and, after six months and several hospitalizations, died. After mistakenly paying some of the expenses and demanding repayment, the new insurer invoked the pre-existing illness exclusion and refused payment of any of the medical and hospital expenses, which were in excess of $14,000.

Having no recourse against the insurer, Callahan brought this suit against Dawes. The jury returned a verdict for Callahan for an amount equal to the medical and hospital expenses incurred, Dawes' motions for judgment notwithstanding the verdict and new trial were denied, and Dawes appealed. The Court of Appeals affirmed and we granted certiorari. As the Court of Appeals noted, this is a case of first impression in this state.

Our first inquiry is as to the relationships between employee, employer and the insurer issuing a group insurance policy. Without undertaking to be fully comprehensive, it can be said that group insurance is insurance

---

1. The employer had changed coverage on several prior occasions. Callahan's claims had always been promptly paid.

2. The employees were not told they could continue their existing group life insurance on an individual basis (Code Ann. § 56–2704(9)) or whether they could continue their group health insurance on the same basis.

3. The policy excludes expenses incurred "for an injury or sickness for which the insured person received medical care, treatment, or recommended treatment within 90 days preceding the effective date of his insurance hereunder; this provision will apply until the insured person completes a period of 90 consecutive days ending after the effective date of his insurance hereunder, during which he has received no medical care, treatment, or recommended treatment or until his insurance hereunder has been in effect for twenty-four (24) months, whichever is earlier."

coverage for a number of individuals by means of a single or blanket policy usually at a lower rate than for individuals.  Employee groups are frequently covered by group insurance.

There is disagreement among the states as to whether an employee insured under a group contract is a party to the contract, or a third party beneficiary of the contract between the employer and the insurer.  Some jurisdictions decide this question on the basis of whether the employee contributes toward payment of the premium.

\* \* \*

Where, as here, the employee contributes toward payment of the premium either the employee is a party to the insurance contract or has a contract with the employer by which the employer agrees, for the consideration paid by the employee, to provide insurance coverage to the employee. We need not finally resolve the status of a contributing employee because we find that the relationship of the employee to the insurer is not controlling here.  Rather, it is the status of the employer and the relationship between the employer and the employee which is controlling.

The Court of Appeals has held that for some purposes the employer is an agent of the group insurer.  That court has held that for other purposes the employer is an agent of the employee.

\* \* \*

The dividing line appears to be this:  Once the group policy has been issued, the employer is the agent of the insurer in determining which persons are its employees and are thereby eligible to participate as a member of the group, in determining which of its employees are regularly performing their duties and are thereby eligible to receive certificates of increased insurance, and in determining which of its employees are employed full time.  These cases are governed by the rule that the employer who obtains a group insurance policy covering its employees is the agent of the insurance company for every purpose necessary to make effective the group policy, and thus the insurance company has imputed knowledge of facts which the employer knows.  \* \* \*

However, in selecting a group insurer, in selecting a policy, in selecting coverages to be afforded by the insurer, the employer is negotiating with the prospective insurer;  there is no contract in force;  and the employer cannot be the agent of the insurer.  It has been said that " 'When procuring the policy [and] obtaining applications of employees \* \* \* employers act not as agents of the insurer but for their employees or for themselves.' "

Hence we find that the relationship which is decisive in this case is that in procuring the group policy and obtaining employee applications, the employer acts as an agent of the employees where the employees will be contributing toward payment of the premium.[4]  Some of the cases and

---

**4.** Whether the employee is to become a party to the insurance contract, or a contract

authorities (see below), suggest that the employer should be found to be a trustee, but the duty of the trustee would be the same as the duty of the agent as will appear hereinafter.

The duties of an agent to his principal are fairly well defined. "The duties of an agent depend initially on his contract with the principal, but in every agency relationship the law imposes certain duties whether they are expressly included in the contract or not." "As a fiduciary the agent is required to act primarily for the benefit of the principal in matters connected with the agency. Among the agent's fiduciary duties is * * * to act with proper skill and diligence, and not to make a personal profit from the agency. Moreover, the agent is subject to the duty of loyalty to his principal and must deal fairly with him at all times." "The principal has the right to expect from his agent 'a full revelation of all pertinent facts which might jeopardize their rights in the property entrusted to the defendant (agent),' * * * Thus it has been held that an agent having made a contract for his principal must pass on to him, 'all the evidence and information in reference to such contract in his possession.' * * * The general rule is that all material facts within the agent's knowledge concerning the subject matter of the agency or any transaction into which he enters in his representative capacity must be communicated to the principal." One reason an agent is under a duty to communicate to his principal all pertinent and material facts concerning any transaction entered into on behalf of the principal is that knowledge of an agent is imputed to the principal by law and only by the agent's performance of this duty can the principal acquire actual knowledge and govern or protect himself accordingly.

Notwithstanding our recognition of the employer as the agent of the employee for purposes of this case, the employer seeks to defend on grounds the employee could have discovered the change had he read the policy as required by law. However, Code Ann. § 37–707 provides that "Any relations shall be deemed confidential, arising from nature or created by law, or resulting from contracts, where one party is so situated as to exercise a controlling influence over the will, conduct, and interest of another; or where, from similar relation of mutual confidence, the law requires the utmost good faith; such as partners, *principal and agent,* etc." (Emphasis supplied.) Where a confidential relationship is found to exist between employer and employee or principal and agent, the duty to read does not bar recovery against the employer or agent. We are persuaded by these decisions and find that the employer owed the employee a duty which cannot be ignored simply because the employee, pursuant to instruction, signed the application for insurance without reading the new master policy.

We therefore hold that when changing a group policy insuring contributing employees and obtaining the applications of those employees, the employer acts as an agent of the employees, and as such is under a duty to

with the employer to provide insurance (see above), is thus immaterial; the result would be the same in either event.

notify the employees of differences between the old and new policies and of any rights the employees may have to continue the old insurance on an individual basis.   We hold further that where this duty is breached, an employee can recover such damages as result from the difference in coverage.

Cases from other jurisdictions show that the issue of whether an employee is entitled to notice of policy modification or cancellation remained unsettled for many years.   The weight of authority now is that notice is required.   We hold that an employer policyholder of a group health and accident policy is obligated to inform the "insured employee of the termination or modification of benefits under the policy."   * * *

Although we disagree with the Court of Appeals that the employer is bound by an implied agreement to maintain the same group insurance coverage when it changes insurers, that court did not err in affirming the judgment in favor of the employee.

*Judgment affirmed.*

## NOTES AND QUESTIONS

**1.**   Why is it important to determine if Dawes Mining was an agent of the insurer, the employee, or neither? Was the employee's action preempted by ERISA?   See infra pp. 470–485.

**2.**   What duties do employers have to inform employees of the nature of their health benefits plans?   Arkansas enacted a law in 1995 requiring employers to disclose whether the health benefits are "self-insured, fully insured, or ERISA-qualified."   Ark.Code Ann. § 11–2–122.

**3.**   What effect should employer statements, employer silence, handbook provisions, or other factors have on the employee's reliance on health insurance coverage?   See Bice v. Indurall Chemical Coating Systems, Inc., 544 So.2d 948 (Ala.1989) (employer had no duty to explain insurance coverage to employee where eligibility was set out in employee handbook).

**4.**   When an employer terminates an employee's medical coverage, and prior to notifying the employee, a member of the employee's family is injured, is the employer liable for the medical expenses?   See Bushman v. Pure Plant Food International, Ltd., 330 N.W.2d 762 (S.D.1983) (held: yes).

**5.**   Does an employer have a duty to inform an employee leaving employment that state insurance law permits an employee to convert the group plan to an individual policy?   Compare Schnabel v. Philadelphia American Life Insurance Co., 795 F.Supp. 816 (S.D.Tex.1992) (yes) with Jakobsen v. Wilfred Laboratories, Inc., 471 N.Y.S.2d 306 (App.Div.1984) (no).

**6.**   After Blue Cross canceled the employer's group medical policy, the employer's director of personnel secured a replacement insurer.   Premiums for the new policy were deducted by the employer, but the employer made no contribution.   When the insurance company became insolvent and failed to pay claims, was the employer liable for not using due care in recommending the insurer?  See Passman v. Common Market Employee Benefit Association, 447 So.2d 1198 (La.App.1984) (held: no).

## 3.   ERISA—PREEMPTION OF STATE ACTIONS

The Employee Retirement Income Security Act (ERISA), 29 U.S.C. §§ 1001–1461, is the primary federal law of employee benefits.  Although much of the legislative history deals with abuses in the administration and investment of private pension plans, ERISA also applies to fringe benefits.  ERISA does not require employers to provide pensions or any other benefit, nor does it mandate any specific level of benefits if employers choose to offer them.  Instead, it establishes minimum standards to protect employees from breach of benefit promises made by employers.

Under ERISA, there are two main types of benefit plans.  First, pension benefit plans are discussed in Chapter 13.  Second, welfare benefit plans are broadly defined under ERISA and include the following: medical, surgical, or hospital care or benefits;  benefits in the event of sickness, accident, disability, death, or unemployment;  vacation benefits;  apprenticeship or training programs;  day care centers;  scholarship funds;  pre-paid legal services;  and other benefits allowed under section 302(c) of the Labor Management Relations Act.

ERISA contains an extremely broad preemption provision.  It bars state regulation of benefit plans, both pension and welfare.  ERISA, however, contains substantive federal standards only for pension plans.  Nevertheless, ERISA preempts state regulation of welfare plans, even though there is no comparable federal regulation.  Section 514(a) of ERISA, 29 U.S.C. § 1144(a), preempts "any and all State laws insofar as they may now or hereafter relate to any employee benefit plan" covered by the Act.  Among the exceptions to this provision include state laws that regulate insurance, banking, or securities;  generally applicable criminal laws;  and qualified domestic relations orders.  Because of the breadth of the preemption provisions of ERISA, numerous cases have raised this issue.

### a.   STATE MANDATE LAWS

## Metropolitan Life Insurance Co. v. Massachusetts

471 U.S. 724 (1985).

■ JUSTICE BLACKMUN delivered the opinion of the Court.

A Massachusetts statute requires that specified minimum mental-health-care benefits be provided a Massachusetts resident who is insured under a general insurance policy, an accident or sickness insurance policy, or an employee health-care plan that covers hospital and surgical expenses.  The first question before us in these cases is whether the state statute, as applied to insurance policies purchased by employee health-care plans regulated by the federal Employee Retirement Income Security Act of 1974, is pre-empted by that Act.  The second question is whether the state statute, as applied to insurance policies purchased pursuant to negotiated collective-bargaining agreements regulated by the National Labor Relations Act, is pre-empted by the Labor Act.

General health insurance typically is sold as group insurance to an employer or other group. Group insurance presently is subject to extensive state regulation, including regulation of the carrier, regulation of the sale and advertising of the insurance, and regulation of the content of the contracts. Mandated-benefit laws, that require an insurer to provide a certain kind of benefit to cover a specified illness or procedure whenever someone purchases a certain kind of insurance, are a subclass of such content regulation.

While mandated-benefit statutes are a relatively recent phenomenon, statutes regulating the substantive terms of insurance contracts have become commonplace in all 50 States over the last 30 years. Perhaps the most familiar are those regulating the content of automobile insurance policies.

The substantive terms of group-health insurance contracts, in particular, also have been extensively regulated by the States. For example, the majority of States currently require that coverage for dependents continue beyond any contractually imposed age limitation when the dependent is incapable of self-sustaining employment because of mental or physical handicap; such statutes date back to the early 1960's. And over the last 15 years all 50 States have required that coverage of infants begin at birth, rather than at some time shortly after birth, as had been the prior practice in the unregulated market. Many state statutes require that insurers offer on an optional basis particular kinds of coverage to purchasers. Others require insurers either to offer or mandate that insurance policies include coverage for services rendered by a particular type of health-care provider.

Mandated-benefit statutes, then, are only one variety of a matrix of state laws that regulate the substantive content of health-insurance policies to further state health policy. Massachusetts Gen.Laws Ann., ch. 175, § 47B (West Supp.1985), is typical of mandated-benefit laws currently in place in the majority of States. With respect to a Massachusetts resident, it requires any general health-insurance policy that provides hospital and surgical coverage, or any benefit plan that has such coverage, to provide as well a certain minimum of mental-health protection. In particular, § 47B requires that a health-insurance policy provide 60 days of coverage for confinement in a mental hospital, coverage for confinement in a general hospital equal to that provided by the policy for nonmental illness, and certain minimum outpatient benefits. * * *

The federal Employee Retirement Income Security Act of 1974, 88 Stat. 829, as amended, 29 U.S.C. § 1001 et seq. (ERISA), comprehensively regulates employee pension and welfare plans. An employee welfare-benefit plan or welfare plan is defined as one which provides to employees "medical, surgical, or hospital care or benefits, or benefits in the event of sickness, accident, disability [or] death," whether these benefits are provided "through the purchase of insurance or otherwise." § 3(1), 29 U.S.C. § 1002(1). Plans may self-insure or they may purchase insurance for their

participants.   Plans that purchase insurance—so-called "insured plans"—
are directly affected by state laws that regulate the insurance industry.

ERISA imposes upon pension plans a variety of substantive requirements relating to participation, funding, and vesting.   It also establishes
various uniform procedural standards concerning reporting, disclosure, and
fiduciary responsibility for both pension and welfare plans.   It does not
regulate the substantive content of welfare-benefit plans.

ERISA thus contains almost no federal regulation of the terms of
benefit plans.   It does, however, contain a broad pre-emption provision
declaring that the statute shall "supersede any and all State laws insofar as
they may now or hereafter relate to any employee benefit plan."   Appellant
Metropolitan argues that ERISA pre-empts Massachusetts' mandated-benefit law insofar as § 47B restricts the kinds of insurance policies that benefit
plans may purchase.

While § 514(a) of ERISA broadly pre-empts state laws that relate to an
employee-benefit plan, that pre-emption is substantially qualified by an
"insurance saving clause," which broadly states that, with one exception,
nothing in ERISA "shall be construed to exempt or relieve any person from
any law of any State which regulates insurance, banking, or securities."
The specified exception to the saving clause is found in § 514(b)(2)(B), 29
U.S.C. § 1144(b)(2)(B), the so-called "deemer clause," which states that no
employee-benefit plan, with certain exceptions not relevant here, "shall be
deemed to be an insurance company or other insurer, bank, trust company,
or investment company or to be engaged in the business of insurance or
banking for purposes of any law of any State purporting to regulate
insurance companies, insurance contracts, banks, trust companies, or investment companies."   Massachusetts argues that its mandated-benefit
law, as applied to insurance companies that sell insurance to benefit plans,
is a "law which regulates insurance," and therefore is saved from the effect
of the general pre-emption clause of ERISA.

In deciding whether a federal law pre-empts a state statute, our task is
to ascertain Congress' intent in enacting the federal statute at issue.   Pre-
emption may be either express or implied, and "is compelled whether
Congress' command is explicitly stated in the statute's language or implicitly contained in its structure and purpose."   The narrow statutory ERISA
question presented is whether Mass.Gen.Laws Ann., ch. 175, § 47B (West
Supp.1985), is a law "which regulates insurance" within the meaning of
§ 514(b)(2)(A), 29 U.S.C. § 1144(b)(2)(A), and so would not be pre-empted
by § 514(a).

Section 47B clearly "relate[s] to" welfare plans governed by ERISA so
as to fall within the reach of ERISA's pre-emption provision, § 514(a).
The broad scope of the pre-emption clause was noted recently in Shaw v.
Delta Air Lines, Inc., [463 U.S. 85 (1983)] where we held that the New
York Human Rights Law and that State's Disability Benefits Law "relate[d] to" welfare plans governed by ERISA.   The phrase "relate to" was
given its broad common-sense meaning, such that a state law "relate[s] to"
a benefit plan "in the normal sense of the phrase, if it has a connection

with or reference to such a plan." 463 U.S., at 97. The pre-emption provision was intended to displace all state laws that fall within its sphere, even including state laws that are consistent with ERISA's substantive requirements. Id., at 98–99. "[E]ven indirect state action bearing on private pensions may encroach upon the area of exclusive federal concern." Alessi v. Raybestos–Manhattan, Inc., 451 U.S. 504, 525 (1981).

Though § 47B is not denominated a benefit-plan law, it bears indirectly but substantially on all insured benefit plans, for it requires them to purchase the mental-health benefits specified in the statute when they purchase a certain kind of common insurance policy. The Commonwealth does not argue that § 47B as applied to policies purchased by benefit plans does not relate to those plans, and we agree with the Supreme Judicial Court that the mandated-benefit law as applied relates to ERISA plans and thus is covered by ERISA's broad pre-emption provision set forth in § 514(a).

Nonetheless, the sphere in which § 514(a) operates was explicitly limited by § 514(b)(2). The insurance saving clause preserves any state law "which regulates insurance, banking, or securities." The two pre-emption sections, while clear enough on their faces, perhaps are not a model of legislative drafting, for while the general pre-emption clause broadly pre-empts state law, the saving clause appears broadly to preserve the States' lawmaking power over much of the same regulation. While Congress occasionally decides to return to the States what it has previously taken away, it does not normally do both at the same time.

Fully aware of this statutory complexity, we still have no choice but to "begin with the language employed by Congress and the assumption that the ordinary meaning of that language accurately expresses the legislative purpose." We also must presume that Congress did not intend to pre-empt areas of traditional state regulation.

To state the obvious, § 47B regulates the terms of certain insurance contracts, and so seems to be saved from pre-emption by the saving clause as a law "which regulates insurance." This common-sense view of the matter, moreover, is reinforced by the language of the subsequent subsection of ERISA, the "deemer clause," which states that an employee-benefit plan shall not be deemed to be an insurance company "for purposes of any law of any State purporting to regulate insurance companies, *insurance contracts,* banks, trust companies, or investment companies." § 514(b)(2)(B), 29 U.S.C. § 1144(b)(2)(B) (emphasis added). By exempting from the saving clause laws regulating insurance contracts that apply directly to benefit plans, the deemer clause makes explicit Congress' intention to include laws that regulate insurance contracts within the scope of the insurance laws preserved by the saving clause. Unless Congress intended to include laws regulating insurance contracts within the scope of the insurance saving clause, it would have been unnecessary for the deemer clause explicitly to exempt such laws from the saving clause when they are applied directly to benefit plans.

The insurers nonetheless argue that § 47B is in reality a health law that merely operates on insurance contracts to accomplish its end, and that it is not the kind of traditional insurance law intended to be saved by § 514(b)(2)(A). We find this argument unpersuasive.

Initially, nothing in § 514(b)(2)(A), or in the "deemer clause" which modifies it, purports to distinguish between traditional and innovative insurance laws. The presumption is against pre-emption, and we are not inclined to read limitations into federal statutes in order to enlarge their pre-emptive scope. Further, there is no indication in the legislative history that Congress had such a distinction in mind.

Appellants assert that state laws that directly regulate the insurer, and laws that regulate such matters as the way in which insurance may be sold, are traditional laws subject to the clause, while laws that regulate the substantive terms of insurance contracts are recent innovations more properly seen as health laws rather than as insurance laws, which § 514(b)(2)(A) does not save. This distinction reads the saving clause out of ERISA entirely, because laws that regulate only the insurer, or the way in which it may sell insurance, do not "relate to" benefit plans in the first instance. Because they would not be pre-empted by § 514(a), they do not need to be "saved" by § 514(b)(2)(A). There is no indication that Congress could have intended the saving clause to operate only to guard against too expansive readings of the general pre-emption clause that might have included laws wholly unrelated to plans. Appellants' construction, in our view, violates the plain meaning of the statutory language and renders redundant both the saving clause it is construing, as well as the deemer clause which it precedes, and accordingly has little to recommend it.

Moreover, it is both historically and conceptually inaccurate to assert that mandated-benefit laws are not traditional insurance laws. As we have indicated, state laws regulating the substantive terms of insurance contracts were commonplace well before the mid–70's, when Congress considered ERISA. The case law concerning the meaning of the phrase "business of insurance" in the McCarran–Ferguson Act, 15 U.S.C. § 1011 et seq., also strongly supports the conclusion that regulation regarding the substantive terms of insurance contracts falls squarely within the saving clause as laws "which regulate insurance." * * *

Nor is there any contrary case authority suggesting that laws regulating the terms of insurance contracts should not be understood as laws that regulate insurance. In short, the plain language of the saving clause, its relationship to the other ERISA pre-emption provisions, and the traditional understanding of insurance regulation, all lead us to the conclusion that mandated-benefit laws such as § 47B are saved from pre-emption by the operation of the saving clause.

Nothing in the legislative history of ERISA suggests a different result. There is no discussion in that history of the relationship between the general pre-emption clause and the saving clause, and indeed very little discussion of the saving clause at all. In the early versions of ERISA, the general pre-emption clause pre-empted only those state laws dealing with subjects regulated by ERISA. The clause was significantly broadened at the last minute, well after the saving clause was in its present form, to include all state laws that relate to benefit plans. The change was made with little explanation by the Conference Committee, and there is no indication in the legislative history that Congress was aware of the new prominence given the saving clause in light of the rewritten pre-emption clause, or was aware that the saving clause was in conflict with the general pre-emption provision. There is a complete absence of evidence that Congress intended the narrow reading of the saving clause suggested by appellants here. Appellants do call to our attention a few passing references in the record of the floor debate to the "narrow" exceptions to the pre-emption clause, but these are far too frail a support on which to rest appellants' rather unnatural reading of the clause.

We therefore decline to impose any limitation on the saving clause beyond those Congress imposed in the clause itself and in the "deemer clause" which modifies it. If a state law "regulates insurance," as mandated-benefit laws do, it is not pre-empted. Nothing in the language, structure, or legislative history of the Act supports a more narrow reading of the clause, whether it be the Supreme Judicial Court's attempt to save only state regulations unrelated to the substantive provisions of ERISA, or the insurers' more speculative attempt to read the saving clause out of the statute.

We are aware that our decision results in a distinction between insured and uninsured plans, leaving the former open to indirect regulation while the latter are not. By so doing we merely give life to a distinction created by Congress in the "deemer clause," a distinction Congress is aware of and one it has chosen not to alter. We also are aware that appellants' construction of the statute would eliminate some of the disuniformities currently facing national plans that enter into local markets to purchase insurance. Such disuniformities, however, are the inevitable result of the congressional decision to "save" local insurance regulation. Arguments as to the wisdom of these policy choices must be directed at Congress. * * *

We hold that Massachusetts' mandated-benefit law is a "law which regulates insurance" and so is not pre-empted by ERISA as it applies to insurance contracts purchased for plans subject to ERISA. We further hold that the mandated-benefit law as applied to a plan negotiated pursuant to a collective-bargaining agreement subject to the NLRA is not pre-empted by federal labor law.

The judgment of the Supreme Judicial Court of Massachusetts is therefore affirmed.

It is so ordered.

## NOTES AND QUESTIONS

**1.** The Massachusetts statute at issue in the *Metropolitan Life* case is quite typical. Since the early 1970s, laws enacted in every state have mandated the inclusion of various substantive terms in group health insurance contracts. There are now over 1000 such mandates. Alcoholism, drug abuse, home health care, maternity, mental health, newborn care, outpatient surgery, and nursing home benefits are some of the more common provisions. While the Supreme Court's decision may have been a reasonable statutory interpretation of ERISA, the result is to create a tripartite health benefits system. Large companies are the most likely to be self-insured and not subject to state regulation; medium-sized companies are the most likely to purchase a group health insurance contract regulated by state law; and small companies are the most likely not to offer any health insurance.

**2.** In New York State Conference of Blue Cross & Blue Shield Plans v. Travelers Insurance Co., 514 U.S. 645 (1995), the Supreme Court reviewed a New York statute requiring hospitals to collect surcharges from patients covered by a commercial insurer or HMO, but not from patients insured by a Blue Cross/Blue Shield plan. The exemption for Blue Cross/Blue Shield is based on their open enrollment policies, whereby individuals rejected by commercial insurers are often covered by the blues. Significantly, the law makes no distinction for employers' self-insured plans. The Court held that the "surcharge" provision does not "relate to" an employee benefit plan within the meaning of § 514(a) of ERISA and therefore is not preempted. "While Congress' extension of preemption to all 'state laws relating to benefit plans' was meant to sweep more broadly than 'state laws dealing with the subject matters covered by ERISA ...,' nothing in the language of the Act or the context of its passage indicates that Congress chose to displace general health care regulation, which historically has been a matter of local concern."

**3.** If ERISA was enacted to protect employees' entitlements to various benefits, why is it that *employers* rather than employees attempt to invoke ERISA by using preemption as a tool to divest state courts of jurisdiction? One management representative has stated:

> * * * ERISA preemption defenses, when available, present extraordinary advantages: (1) the complete bar to all state law claims, including allegations of "bad faith" conduct, (2) certain "deep pocket" defendants, such as the plan sponsor and claims review agents, cannot even be sued under federal law, (3) the participant has no cause of action for delay in processing claims, (4) the participant cannot recover extracontractual compensatory damages or punitive damages, (5) the participant must generally exhaust administrative remedies as a prerequisite to filing suit, (6) the defendants have a statutory right to remove cases to federal court, (7) ERISA bars a jury trial, (8) the courts do not conduct de novo hearings on a participant's [claim] for benefits, and instead uphold the fiduciary's decision unless "arbitrary or capricious," and (9) ERISA permits an award of attorneys' fees and costs.

5 Labor & Employment Law News (State Bar of California Labor and Employment Law Section) 15 (Fall 1986).

**4.** Under Department of Labor "safe harbor" provisions, a group insurance program offered by an insurer to employees is not an ERISA welfare plan if the employer does not contribute premiums or make a profit from the program, if the employer does not endorse the program in any manner other than permitting the insurer to publicize the program to employees, collecting premiums from employees, and remitting them to the insurer, and if employee participation is voluntary. 29 C.F.R. § 2510.3–1(j). See Taggart Corp. v. Life & Health Benefits Administration, Inc., 617 F.2d 1208 (5th Cir.1980), cert. denied, 450 U.S. 1030 (1981) (an employer's "bare purchase" of health insurance does not establish an ERISA plan).

**5.** In Pilot Life Insurance Co. v. Dedeaux, 481 U.S. 41 (1987), the Supreme Court held that state common law causes of action asserting improper processing of benefits claims under an employee benefit plan would be preempted by ERISA unless, as in *Metropolitan Life,* the state common law cause of action regulated insurance. In Metropolitan Life Insurance Co. v. Taylor, 481 U.S. 58 (1987), the Supreme Court also held that these state common law claims were displaced by ERISA's civil enforcement provision and thus were removable to federal court.

**6.** Preemption is an issue not only under ERISA, but also under the National Labor Relations Act for employees covered by collective bargaining agreements. See Keystone Consolidated Industries v. McNeil, 784 F.2d 817 (7th Cir.1986), in which the court held that the Illinois Wage Payment and Collection Act was preempted by § 301 of the LMRA; the court expressly refused to address the issue of ERISA preemption. But see Mackey v. Lanier Collections Agency, 486 U.S. 825 (1988) (Georgia statute prohibiting garnishment of plan benefits preempted by ERISA, even though Congress did not intend to preempt state-law garnishment of ERISA welfare benefit plan).

b.   MEDICAL MALPRACTICE

# Kuhl v. Lincoln National Health Plan of Kansas City, Inc.

999 F.2d 298 (8th Cir.1993).

■ BEAM, CIRCUIT JUDGE.

This consolidated appeal arises from the district court's orders resolving two actions brought against Lincoln National Health Plan of Kansas City, Inc. (Lincoln National) as a result of the death of its insured, Buddy Kuhl. The district court held that the plaintiffs' state law claims against Lincoln National were preempted by the Employee Retirement Income Security Act of 1974 (ERISA), and that ERISA did not authorize the recovery of monetary damages for Lincoln National's alleged misconduct. We affirm both orders of the district court.

Lincoln National is an "independent physician" HMO, which means that it pays independent physicians, hospitals, and other health care providers to render medical services for its members. Pursuant to a contract between Lincoln National and Belger Cartage Services, Inc. (Belger), Lincoln National pays for medical services provided to Belger employees under Belger's Group Health Plan. Belger's Group Health Plan is an "employee welfare benefit plan" regulated under ERISA. Under the Belger Plan, Lincoln National is not contractually obligated to pay for medical services rendered outside the "Service Area" of the Lincoln National network or for medical services rendered by personnel not participating in the Lincoln National network. All decisions concerning the payment of claims under the Belger Plan are the responsibility of Lincoln National. Lincoln National makes advance decisions regarding payment for medical services rendered outside of its service area through "precertification review," a process by which it determines whether a particular procedure or hospitalization is covered by the Belger Plan.

Buddy Kuhl was an employee of Belger, and had opted to receive medical benefits under the Belger Plan administered by Lincoln National as of March 1, 1989. On April 29, 1989, Buddy Kuhl suffered a heart attack. Dr. Grimes, Buddy Kuhl's designated primary care physician, placed Buddy Kuhl in the care of Dr. Levi, a heart specialist at Menorah Medical Center. Dr. Levi concluded that heart surgery was necessary, including open heart LV aneurysmectomy and a coronary by-pass. Lincoln National arranged for a second opinion by Dr. Ahuja. In a letter dated May 23, 1989, Dr. Ahuja confirmed that surgery was necessary, stating that Buddy Kuhl was "at high risk of sudden death" and needed the recommended surgery "in the next few weeks."

Buddy Kuhl underwent extensive tests at Menorah between June 13, 1989, and June 16, 1989, to determine the extent of his heart damage and the proper course of treatment. On June 20, 1989, Dr. Levi determined that Buddy Kuhl had inducible ventricular tachycardia and would need formal electrophysiologically guided left ventricular aneurysm resection and subendocardial resection, as well as his bypass surgery. Because the Kansas City area hospitals did not have the equipment to perform the necessary surgery, Dr. Levi concluded that Buddy Kuhl would have the best chance of survival if the surgery were performed at Barnes Hospital in St. Louis, Missouri. Dr. Levi also noted that the surgeons at Barnes Hospital had more experience and success with this type of surgery than any doctor in Kansas City. Dr. Hannah, a cardiac surgeon at Menorah and a participating provider under the Belger Plan, concurred in Dr. Levi's conclusions. Therefore, arrangements were made for Dr. Cox, a heart surgeon specializing in computerized cardiac mapping and bypass surgery, to perform the surgery at Barnes Hospital on July 6, 1989.

On June 20, 1989, Dianne Long, a utilization review coordinator for Lincoln National, received a call from Barnes Hospital requesting precertification for the surgery. On June 23, 1989, Lincoln National refused to precertify payment for the surgery because Barnes Hospital is outside the Lincoln National service area. The surgery scheduled for July 6, 1989, was cancelled. Lincoln National then scheduled an appointment for Buddy Kuhl to see Dr. Brodine at Research Medical Center in Kansas City on July 6, 1989, to determine whether the surgery could be performed in Kansas City rather than in St. Louis. After examining Buddy Kuhl, Dr. Brodine immediately informed Lincoln National that he agreed with the recommendations of Dr. Levi and Dr. Hannah that the surgery should be performed at Barnes Hospital.

Two weeks later, on July 20, 1989, Lincoln National informed Buddy Kuhl that it would authorize the surgery at Barnes Hospital. Buddy Kuhl immediately attempted to schedule the surgery, but was informed that the surgery team was unavailable until September 1989. On September 2, 1989, Dr. Cox examined Buddy Kuhl in anticipation of surgery and found that his heart had deteriorated to such an extent that the proposed surgery was no longer a viable option. Dr. Cox recommended that Buddy Kuhl be evaluated for cardiac transplantation and asked that he be placed on a heart transplant waiting list at Barnes Hospital. Lincoln National refused to precertify payment of these medical costs. However, Buddy Kuhl was placed on a heart transplant waiting list at Kansas University Medical Center.

Buddy Kuhl died as a result of ventricular tachycardia on December 28, 1989, while waiting for a heart transplant.

On March 15, 1991, Mary Kuhl, Buddy Kuhl, Jr., and Marnie K. Kuhl (the Kuhls) filed a petition in the Circuit Court of Jackson County, Missouri, asserting four claims against Lincoln National: medical malpractice, emotional distress, tortious interference with Buddy Kuhl's right to contract for medical care, and breach of a contract through Buddy Kuhl as a third-party beneficiary. Lincoln National filed a Notice of Removal pursuant to 28 U.S.C. § 1441(b), asserting that ERISA provides federal question jurisdiction over each of the Kuhls' claims. The Kuhls sought remand, arguing that ERISA did not apply. Lincoln National opposed the motion to remand and filed a motion for summary judgment on the grounds of ERISA preemption. The district court determined that the Kuhls' state law claims arise from the administration of the Belger Plan and therefore are preempted as claims that "relate to" an ERISA plan. The court also examined the possible remedies under ERISA, and concluded that the Kuhls could not state a claim under ERISA. Accordingly, the district court denied the Kuhls' motion to remand and granted summary judgment in favor of Lincoln National.

The Kuhls then moved to amend the judgment, moved to amend their complaint to include a cause of action under ERISA, and filed a second suit in the district court alleging that Lincoln National breached its fiduciary duty under ERISA. Lincoln National opposed the Kuhls' motions and filed a motion to dismiss the second complaint. The district court denied the Kuhls' motion to amend the original complaint because the action had been dismissed and the Kuhls' proffered no reason why the amendments were not made before the action was dismissed. Additionally, the court concluded that the Kuhls' state law claims could not be recharacterized as ERISA claims and thus, reaffirmed its grant of summary judgment in favor of Lincoln National. Finally, the court granted Lincoln National's motion to dismiss the second complaint on three grounds: (1) the court's grant of summary judgment in favor of Lincoln National was res judicata as to the allegations in the second complaint; (2) under the reasoning in the court's order granting summary judgment, the Kuhls could not state a cause of action under ERISA for breach of a fiduciary duty; and (3) the "other equitable relief" clause in 29 U.S.C. § 1132(a)(3)(B)(i) does not include monetary damages.

On appeal, the Kuhls argue that the district court erred in granting Lincoln National's motion for summary judgment and in denying the Kuhls' motion to remand because their state law claims are not preempted by ERISA. In the alternative, the Kuhls contend that the district court erred in not recharacterizing their state law claims under ERISA, in denying their motion to amend the original complaint to include a cause of action under ERISA, and in dismissing their second complaint.

ERISA is a comprehensive statute designed to promote the interests of employees and their beneficiaries by regulating the creation and administration of employee benefit plans. Pilot Life Ins. Co. v. Dedeaux, 481 U.S. 41, 44 (1987). "The statute imposes participation, funding, and vesting requirements on pension plans. It also sets various uniform standards, including rules concerning reporting, disclosure, and fiduciary responsibility, for both pension and welfare plans." Shaw v. Delta Air Lines, Inc., 463 U.S. 85, 91 (1983). Consistent with the decision to create a comprehensive, uniform federal scheme for regulation of employee benefit plans, Congress drafted ERISA's preemption clause in broad terms. Ingersoll–Rand Co. v. McClendon, 498 U.S. 133 (1990).

Under section 514(a) of ERISA, Congress preempted "all State laws insofar as they may now or hereafter relate to any employee benefit plan." Statutory mandates, court decisions, and state law from all other sources are included in the preemption clause. The question of whether a certain state law is preempted by ERISA is necessarily a question of legislative intent, and the Supreme Court has left no doubt that Congress intended the preemption clause to be construed extremely broadly.

The key to determining whether a state law is preempted is whether the state law in question "relates to" an ERISA plan. "A law [clearly] 'relates to' an employee benefit plan, in the normal sense of the phrase, if it has a connection with or reference to such a plan." Moreover, ERISA's preemption clause is not limited to laws which relate to the specific provisions of ERISA. A state law may "relate to" an employee benefit plan, and therefore be preempted, even though the state law was not designed to affect benefit plans and its effect on such plans is only incidental.

Despite Congress' intention that ERISA cut a wide swath of preemption through state laws, the Supreme Court has recognized that not every cause of action that might be brought against an ERISA plan is preempted. "Some state actions may affect employee benefit plans in too tenuous, remote, or peripheral a manner to warrant a finding that the law 'relates to' the plan." In Mackey v. Lanier Collection Agency & Serv., Inc., 486 U.S. 825 (1988), the Court held that ERISA did not preempt a state's general garnishment statute as applied to collect judgments against plan participants.  The Court noted that although collection might burden the administration of the plan, this fact was not dispositive on the question of whether the state law "relates to" the benefit plan.  Thus, the Court's decisions do not provide a clear-cut method for determining whether a state law which merely has some unintended effects on ERISA-governed plans will be preempted.

We have no difficulty in concluding that the Kuhls' three state law claims that rely on Buddy Kuhl's status as a beneficiary of the Belger Plan are preempted by ERISA.  The Kuhls' claims are all based on Lincoln National's alleged misconduct in delaying Buddy Kuhl's heart surgery in St. Louis.  The Kuhls contend that Lincoln National tortiously interfered with the contractual relationship between Buddy Kuhl and his doctors, that Lincoln National committed medical malpractice because it assumed the role of Buddy Kuhl's physician by making decisions about proper medical treatment and made decisions that constitute medical malpractice, and that Lincoln National breached its contract with Belger, to which Buddy Kuhl was a third-party beneficiary, by delaying the surgery in St. Louis.  The district court found that all of these state law claims arise from the administration of benefits under the Belger Plan and are therefore preempted by ERISA.  We agree.

In *Pilot Life,* the Supreme Court held that ERISA preempts state common-law causes of action arising from the alleged improper processing of a claim for benefits under an ERISA-regulated plan.  In that case, the beneficiary of an ERISA-regulated plan brought state common law tort and contract claims against the insurer for failure to pay benefits under the insurance policy.  The Court held that these state law claims "relate to" the employee benefit plan and thus, the comprehensive civil enforcement scheme detailed in the provisions of section 502(a) of ERISA provides the exclusive remedies for claims involving the administration of plan benefits.  "The policy choices reflected in the inclusion of certain remedies and the exclusion of others under the federal scheme would be completely undermined if ERISA-plan participants and beneficiaries were free to obtain remedies under state law that Congress rejected in ERISA."

The Kuhls attempt to avoid ERISA preemption by suggesting that Lincoln National's actions with respect to Buddy Kuhl went beyond the mere administration of benefits.  They assert that Lincoln National not only refused to precertify payment for Buddy Kuhl's operation, but "cancelled" the operation and undertook treatment of Buddy Kuhl according to its own medical opinions.  The Kuhls rely heavily on Lincoln National's admission for the purpose of its motion for summary judgment that it "cancelled" the surgery scheduled for July 6, 1989, in St. Louis.  The district court rejected the Kuhls' arguments, concluding that the Kuhls' "claims are based on the manner in which Lincoln National responded to the request for 'pre-certification' of Buddy Kuhl's heart surgery.  Artful pleading by characterizing Lincoln National's actions in refusing to pay for the surgery as 'cancellation' or by characterizing the same administrative decisions as 'malpractice' does not change the fact that plaintiffs' claims are based on the contention that Lincoln National improperly processed Kuhl's claim for medical benefits.''

Taking the facts in the light most favorable to the Kuhls, as we must for purposes of Lincoln National's motion for summary judgment, we are compelled to agree with the district court.   Lincoln National became involved in the cancellation of the St. Louis surgery only after the Barnes Hospital staff requested a precertification review.   Lincoln National's admission that it "cancelled" the surgery cannot be stretched to imply that Lincoln National went beyond the administration of benefits and undertook to provide Buddy Kuhl with medical advice.  Although the surgery in St. Louis was unquestionably cancelled as a result of Lincoln National's decision not to precertify payment, the decision not to precertify payment relates directly to Lincoln National's administration of benefits.

We do not imply that how the surgery was cancelled would be immaterial in every case.  In a different case, the cancellation of a beneficiary's surgery by an ERISA benefits provider may lay the basis for non-preempted state law claims.  Here, however, the Kuhls have failed to allege that there was a practical difference between Lincoln National "cancelling" the surgery and simply denying precertification.  The Kuhls make no allegations that Buddy Kuhl would have had the surgery even if Lincoln National refused to pay for it;  that Buddy Kuhl was thwarted in his efforts to arrange other financing for the surgery upon Lincoln National's "cancellation;"  or that the timing of the "cancellation" made it impossible for Buddy Kuhl to have the surgery on July 6, 1989, if payment could be otherwise arranged.  The July 18, 1989, letter that Buddy Kuhl wrote to Dr. Grimes requesting her assistance in persuading Lincoln National to certify payment for his surgery makes it clear that he was not under the misconception that Lincoln National had taken the place of his treating physicians.

Under *Pilot Life,* any state law claim that Buddy Kuhl may have had against Lincoln National for its conduct in delaying the surgery scheduled for July 6, 1989, arose from Lincoln National's denial of benefits under the Belger Plan.   The Kuhls' attempt to invoke *Mackey* and to characterize their claims as merely tangentially related to the Plan is unpersuasive. Accordingly, the Kuhls' state law claims through Buddy Kuhl "relate to" the Belger plan and are preempted by ERISA.

Mary Kuhl, Buddy Kuhl's wife, also asserts a claim for intentional infliction of emotional distress, alleging that she was aware that Lincoln National "cancelled" Buddy Kuhl's surgery;  that she was present when he was informed in September 1989 that his heart could no longer withstand surgery and transplantation was his only remaining option;  and that she was present when Buddy Kuhl collapsed and died while waiting for a heart to become available.  Mary Kuhl relies on dicta in Drinkwater v. Metro Life Ins. Co., 846 F.2d 821, 826 (1st Cir.), cert. denied, 488 U.S. 909 (1988) for the proposition that claims for emotional distress are not preempted by ERISA.   She attempts to distinguish the persuasive precedent to the contrary, on the grounds that her underlying vicarious malpractice claim is not preempted by ERISA.

As we previously indicated, Mary Kuhl is mistaken in her contention that her underlying state law claim for medical malpractice is not preempted. Mary Kuhl's claim for emotional distress, like the Kuhls' other state law claims, is based upon Lincoln National's failure to expeditiously precertify payment for the St. Louis surgery. We conclude that Mary Kuhl's claim for emotional distress "relates to" Lincoln National's administration of the Belger Plan within the broad meaning of the ERISA preemption clause. Accordingly, Mary Kuhl's claim for emotional distress is also preempted under section 514(a) of ERISA.

We recognize the obvious salutary effect that imposing state law liability on Lincoln National might have on deterring poor precertification decisions. However, this is precisely the type of state regulation of plan administration that ERISA was designed to replace. "Section 514(a) was intended to ensure that plans and plan sponsors would be subject to a uniform body of benefits law; the goal was to minimize the administrative and financial burden of complying with conflicting directives among States or between States and the Federal Government." Other courts have speculated that Congress could not have foreseen the precertification review process when it enacted a preemption clause so broad that it relieves ERISA-regulated plans of most tort liability. Although this may well be true, modification of ERISA in light of questionable modern insurance practices must be the job of Congress, not the courts.

The Kuhls' argue that even if their state law claims are preempted by ERISA, the district court erred by not recharacterizing their state law claims under ERISA, by denying the Kuhls' motion to amend the complaint to allege a cause of action under ERISA, and by dismissing their subsequent complaint alleging a breach of fiduciary duty under ERISA. Although the Kuhls apparently did not ask the district court to recharacterize their state law claims under ERISA, the court examined the civil remedies available under section 502(a) of ERISA, and concluded that the Kuhls' factual allegations do not state a claim under ERISA. The Kuhls suggest that section 502(a)(3)(B)(i) permits them to recover monetary damages for Lincoln National's alleged breach of its fiduciary duty. They argue that we should follow the Sixth Circuit's determination that monetary damages constitute "other appropriate equitable relief."

We have previously held that monetary damages are not available under section 502(a)(3)(B)(i). [W]e [have] expressly rejected the [Sixth Circuit's] reasoning and held that an award of monetary damages is a legal remedy, not an equitable one.

This interpretation has recently been vindicated by the Supreme Court. Mertens v. Hewitt Assocs., 113 S.Ct. 2063 (1993). After an extensive review of the history of equitable remedies and the statutory language of section 502(a)(3), the Court concluded that damages do not constitute "other equitable relief." The district court properly held that the Kuhls' claim for monetary damages was not cognizable under section 502(a)(3)(B)(i).

For the reasons discussed above, the orders of the district court are affirmed.

NOTES AND QUESTIONS

**1.** The increased use of "managed care" by large, self-insured employers as a way of controlling health care costs has led to two main types of legal claims. First, as in *Kuhl*, plaintiffs have alleged that the failure to authorize a medical procedure, the delay in authorizing a procedure, or the authorization of a substandard procedure has caused a physical harm to the patient. In general, the third-party payers have been successful in raising the ERISA preemption defense. The second type of claim is one in which the medical services already have been rendered and the subscriber or the provider is seeking reimbursement under the health benefit plan. These actions are authorized under ERISA but, as discussed in the *Salley* case infra, there are substantive hurdles for the plaintiffs to overcome.

**2.** In Corcoran v. United Healthcare, Inc., 965 F.2d 1321 (5th Cir.1992), cert. denied, 506 U.S. 1033 (1992), an employee of South Central Bell telephone company had several medical problems that placed her in the category of a "high risk pregnancy." Near the end of her pregnancy, her obstetrician recommended that she be hospitalized for the rest of her pregnancy so that the fetus could be monitored constantly. The defendant, however, against the recommendation of its own medical consultant, refused to approve the hospitalization, but merely authorized 10 hours of home nursing care. During a period when no nurse was on duty, the fetus went into distress and died. The Fifth Circuit affirmed the district court's granting of summary judgement for the defendant on the ground that the Louisiana statutory negligence action was preempted by ERISA. According to the court, even though the defendant was performing a medical function when it refused to authorize the hospitalization, the decision was incident to its claims administration function.

**3.** In Prudential Health Care Plan, Inc. v. Lewis, 77 F.3d 493 (10th Cir.1996), the Tenth Circuit held that medical malpractice claims against a health maintenance organization (HMO) were not preempted by ERISA. The physicians allegedly negligently failed to diagnose a malignancy, and the plaintiff sued the HMO under a theory of vicarious liability. According to the court: "Just as ERISA does not preempt the malpractice claim against the doctor, it should not preempt the vicarious liability claim against the HMO if the HMO has held out the doctor as its agent."

**4.** In Shea v. Esensten, 107 F.3d 625 (8th Cir.1997), the plaintiff's decedent consulted his family physician complaining of chest pain, shortness of breath, muscle tingling, and dizziness. Despite these warning signs, his family physician did not refer him to a cardiologist, and he later died of heart failure. Unknown to the patient, his HMO provided financial incentives to its participating physicians to limit referrals to specialists. The Eighth Circuit rejected the claim of the HMO that an action against it was preempted by ERISA. The court held that the incentive plan to the physician was "material information," and the failure to disclose the arrangement was a breach of fiduciary duty under ERISA.

**5.** In Doe v. Southeastern Pennsylvania Transportation Authority (SEPTA), 72 F.3d 1133 (3d Cir.1995), cert. denied, 117 S.Ct. 51 (1996), the defendant allegedly violated the plaintiff's constitutional right to privacy by disclosing among management employees the fact that the plaintiff was taking AZT and therefore was HIV-positive. The defendant learned the information through an audit of prescription drug records submitted through the employer's self-insured health benefits plan and despite providing assurances to the plaintiff that prescription drug information was not disclosed in an individually-identifiable form. In reversing a jury award of $125,000, the Third Circuit held that the defendant's need to know justified the "minimal intrusion."

## 4. ERISA—Substantive Provisions

### a. DENIAL OF BENEFITS

## Salley v. E.I. DuPont de Nemours & Co.

966 F.2d 1011 (5th Cir.1992).

■ JERRE S. WILLIAMS, CIRCUIT JUDGE:

Danielle Salley was a psychiatric patient at DePaul Hospital. DuPont paid for her treatment under an ERISA plan it had established. DuPont concluded that Danielle's treatment was no longer medically necessary and terminated the benefits. Salley and her father brought suit to recover the costs of Danielle's hospitalization. The district court ruled in their favor. DuPont appeals the decision, claiming the district court erred both in holding that the plan administrators abused their discretion and in applying the treating physician rule. DuPont also appeals the court's decision to award attorney's fees, and the Salleys contest the court's calculation of the fees. We affirm the district court's ruling.

DuPont established its Hospital Medical–Surgical Coverage Policy (the "Plan") in accordance with the Employee Retirement Income Security Act of 1974, 29 U.S.C. § 1001, et seq. ("ERISA"). At all relevant times, Connecticut General administered the Plan, and DuPont reimbursed Connecticut General the full costs of medical claims. DuPont also contracted with Preferred Health Care ("Preferred") to manage the individual cases.

Danielle Salley is a fifteen-year-old girl with a history of emotional disabilities, drug abuse, and depression. Her father, Jack Salley, is a retired DuPont employee and continues to participate in the Plan under which Danielle is covered as his dependent. Danielle has been an inpatient three times at DePaul Northshore Hospital in Covington, Louisiana. Each time, she has been under the care of Dr. Gordon Blundell, a psychiatrist in charge of the hospital's adolescent unit. The present litigation concerns DuPont's termination of benefits during the third admission in the hospital.

During her first two visits, Danielle was an extremely troubled child. She displayed suicidal tendencies, attempted to escape, and experienced episodes of head-banging. She, however, improved during each visit, but as soon as she was released, she "recompensated"—i.e. reverted back to her previous behavior. Dr. Blundell thus determined that Danielle could not live with her parents and attend public schools.

Dr. Blundell was concerned about Danielle's continual admissions and releases from the hospital, a problem he referred to as her "revolving door admissions." In an attempt to eliminate the revolving door admissions, Dr. Blundell worked with Plan administrators to "flex" the benefits. A "benefits flex" is a health insurance industry practice in which the parties amend or modify the policy's coverage benefits in order to accommodate a contingency that the original contract did not address specifically. Although the policy does not in terms permit the treatment provided, the treatment is mutually beneficial because the insured receives the coverage desired while the insurer reduces its payout expense through less expensive treatment.

Beginning in Danielle's second admission at DePaul Hospital, the Salleys and hospital employees attempted to locate a less restrictive treatment for Danielle, including several boarding schools. They, however, were unable to find a facility capable to meet Danielle's particular needs. Unable to find such a facility, the hospital released Danielle to attend public school. She subsequently recompensated.

On September 10, 1990, Danielle was readmitted to DePaul Hospital. As the hospital's records evidence, she quickly restabilized. In fact, Dr. Blundell wrote in his October 5, 1990 Progress Notes that Danielle was beginning "to function at the highest level she ever has in life."

On September 28, 1990, Dr. Blundell conversed on the telephone with Ron Schlegel, a Preferred case manager, regarding Danielle's condition. Schlegel was knowledgeable about Danielle's case because he had been involved with it since her first admission. Dr. Blundell apprised Schlegel of Danielle's dramatic improvement but also informed Schlegel that although Danielle was currently stable, he did not think he could release her because she would quickly regress. Schlegel advised Dr. Blundell that Dr. Satwant Ahluwalia, in accordance with Preferred procedures, would review the case to determine medical necessity. The Plan pays only for expenses that are "medically necessary," although the Plan never defines the phrase.

Dr. Ahluwalia, a psychiatrist and regional director at Preferred, also had been involved with the case since Danielle's first admission. She, however, never had examined Danielle nor reviewed the medical records from the second or third admission. She had reviewed the records from Danielle's first admission.

Dr. Blundell and Dr. Ahluwalia discussed Danielle's treatment on the telephone on October 2, 1990. Dr. Blundell told Dr. Ahluwalia that

Danielle was stabilizing and would be able to leave the hospital soon, but he did not want to repeat the revolving door of admissions. Dr. Ahluwalia instructed Dr. Blundell that DuPont would terminate the benefits for in-patient hospitalization on October 11, 1990. She testified at trial that she knew Dr. Blundell did not agree with this date for release.

The Salleys brought suit challenging DuPont's termination of benefits from October 11, 1990 through January 25, 1991.[1] Dr. Blundell discharged Danielle on January 25, 1991. She has since enrolled in the Darrow School in New York.

The district court concluded that DuPont abused its discretion when it terminated benefits for Danielle's in-patient hospitalization. Consequently, the court found DuPont liable for Danielle's hospital bills from October 11, 1990 through January 25, 1991. * * * DuPont appeals the district court's ruling.

We first address the standard of review we employ in evaluating DuPont's decision to terminate benefits under the terms of the ERISA benefit plan. The Supreme Court holds that the denial of benefits "is to be reviewed under a de novo standard unless the benefit plan gives the administrator or fiduciary discretionary authority to determine eligibility for benefits or to construe the terms of the plan." Firestone Tire and Rubber Co. v. Bruch, 489 U.S. 101, 115 (1989). If the plan gives the administrator or fiduciary discretionary authority, then we apply an abuse of discretion standard. In applying the abuse of discretion standard, we analyze whether the plan administrator acted arbitrarily or capriciously.

The Policy states "The [DuPont] Employee Relations Department shall be responsible for development of procedures to implement the policy, for interpretation of policy, and for coordination of administration." Similar language has led this Court to apply the abuse of discretion standard.

The Salleys assert two reasons why we should not apply the abuse of discretion standard. First, DuPont contracted with Preferred Health Care for medical necessity reviews. DuPont, therefore, was not exercising its discretion as the Plan envisioned. We disagree. The contract between DuPont and Preferred explicitly states, "DUPONT reserves final authority to authorize or deny payment for services to beneficiaries of a Plan." Moreover, counsel for DuPont stated that DuPont exercised final authority in the case at hand. As long as a company maintains the ultimate decision on denial of benefits, it can be beneficial for it to have experienced agents assist in the determination.

DuPont's conflict of interest also concerns the Salleys. DuPont funds the Plan from current operating revenues, giving it an apparent incentive to deny benefits. The alleged conflict, however, does not change the standard of review. "[I]f a benefit plan gives discretion to an administrator or fiduciary who is operating under a conflict of interest, that conflict

---

1. In accordance with an agreement between the parties, DuPont paid Danielle's hospitalization expenses through November 20, 1990, although DuPont challenges whether the Plan required it to make the payments.

must be weighed as a 'factor[ ] in determining whether there is an abuse of discretion.' " Firestone, 489 U.S. at 115 (citation omitted). Accordingly, we apply an abuse of discretion standard to DuPont's benefits termination decision.

Analyzing the record before us, we conclude the district court correctly ruled that DuPont abused its discretion when it terminated benefits for Danielle's in-patient hospitalization. DuPont argues that this Court's decision whether the Plan administrator abused his discretion must be based upon the facts known to the administrator at the time the decision was made. Although we generally decide abuse of discretion based upon the information known to the administrator at the time he made the decision, the administrator can abuse his discretion if he fails to obtain the necessary information. In the present case, neither Schlegel nor Dr. Ahluwalia ever examined Danielle, nor had either one obtained the records from the second or third admissions to DePaul Hospital.

The Plan administrators may rely on the treating physician's advice, or it can independently investigate the treatment's medical necessity. In the present case, the Plan administrators apparently relied on Dr. Blundell's description that Danielle was no longer suicidal or out of control. The administrators, however, cannot rely on part of Dr. Blundell's advice and ignore his other advice. Dr. Blundell also warned Dr. Ahluwalia that he could release Danielle only if there was an "iron-clad plan in hand that would assure her structure, safety, and well being." Such a plan had not been found.

The hospital records from the third admission would have demonstrated to the administrators the medical necessity of Danielle's in-patient hospitalization. Danielle was stable when she was in the hospital, but as soon as she was released into her former environment, she began to deteriorate. The doctors who examined Danielle and carefully evaluated her case were confident release into the improper environment would lead to recompensation.

DuPont maintains that options other than just hospitalization or release to her former environment existed. It suggests, for example, that a residential care treatment would have satisfied Danielle's needs. In reality, hospitalization and release to her former environment were the only options available at the time in question. Dr. Blundell agreed a less restrictive environment could be beneficial to Danielle, but he felt releasing Danielle was inappropriate until a proper program and environment was found. Such a program had not been discovered at the time in question. Therefore, if Dr. Blundell had released Danielle, of necessity she would have returned to her former environment.

Both the Salleys and the hospital spent significant time trying to find a less restrictive environment for Danielle. The evidence indicates they acted in good faith and without any unnecessary delay. In fact, the Salleys eventually found an appropriate environment for Danielle at Darrow School, where she enrolled in January 1991.

We further note that the issue of a less restrictive environment has nothing to do with money.  One of the issues the district court addressed was whether DuPont would pay for the alternative treatment.  The district court held DuPont did not have to pay for the costs of Darrow School, and the Salleys have not appealed this issue.  Whether DuPont would pay for the alternative treatment, however, is irrelevant.  If the requisite facility had been found, then hospitalization would not have been medically necessary.  On the other hand, until the facility was found, hospitalization was medically necessary.

We hold that although DuPont followed the prescribed procedures, it abused its discretion in relying upon the Schlegel and Dr. Ahluwalia recommendation to terminate Danielle's benefits.  Because they chose to follow Dr. Blundell's diagnosis, Schlegel and Dr. Ahluwalia were required, absent independent inquiry, to follow all his advice, not just part of it.  If they decided to deviate from his diagnosis, they were required to investigate further the medical necessity of in-patient hospitalization.  Whether this investigation included an examination of Danielle or an analysis of hospital records depended on the particulars of each case.  At the very least, however, administrators relying on hospital records obviously must review the most recent records.  The case administrator and the physician conceded at trial that they did not do so.

During the trial, the judge stated, "I am certainly going to give deference to the treating physician."  Moreover, the court's opinion stated, "In light of Dr. Blundell's testimony in this matter, and the deference to be shown him as the patient's treating physician, the Court concludes that the continued inpatient psychiatric hospitalization * * * was 'medically necessary' * * * "  DuPont maintains that applying the "treating physician rule" is improper in ERISA cases.

The "treating physician rule" requires the court, in appropriate circumstances, to defer to a patient's treating physician's testimony unless substantial evidence contradicts the testimony.  We have recognized the use of the rule in cases involving termination of social security benefits.  Courts have also applied the rule in suits brought under the Federal Tort Claims Act.  But we declined to apply the rule when a handicapped child's treating physician testified regarding the appropriate education for the child.

This Court has not addressed the propriety of the "treating physician rule" in ERISA cases.  We have considerable doubt about holding the rule applicable in ERISA cases.  Under it, the treating physician would stand to profit greatly if the court were to find benefits should not be terminated.  There is a clear and strong conflict of interest, and we are doubtful that a court should defer automatically to his or her testimony.

The district court did apply the "treating physician rule."  But even assuming this was error, the error was harmless.  Although the court announced it was applying the "treating physician rule," it later stated in its opinion that "of all the witnesses heard, the one most interested in the welfare of this patient, and not in the insurer's pocketbook, was the treating physician." Assuming it is error to grant a presumption in favor of the treating physician in an ERISA case, the district court nevertheless may properly assess each case's individual circumstances and evaluate the witnesses' credibility. If a court believes the treating physician is more credible than other witnesses, it is entitled to give greater weight to his or her testimony. The record here is clear that the court made the decision as to credibility and properly relied heavily upon the testimony of the treating physician.

\* \* \*

AFFIRMED.

## NOTES AND QUESTIONS

**1.** The basis of the denial of the claim in *Salley* was that the hospitalization was "not medically necessary." Who has the burden of proving medical necessity? What should the standard be for making the determination? What should the standard be for reviewing determinations by plan administrators?

**2.** Another line of cases addresses the other main reason for denial of medical benefits under ERISA-qualified plans—that the treatment was "experimental." A number of cases have concerned the issue of high dose chemotherapy with autologous bone marrow transplants, a procedure used for advanced cases of breast cancer and that may cost upwards of $150,000. Most of the cases have held that the procedure is experimental. See, e.g., Harris v. Mutual of Omaha Cos., 992 F.2d 706 (7th Cir.1993); Holder v. Prudential Insurance Co. of America, 951 F.2d 89 (5th Cir.1992). Some cases, however, have held that the treatment is not experimental. See, e.g., Kekis v. Blue Cross & Blue Shield, 815 F.Supp. 571 (N.D.N.Y.1993); Wilson v. Group Hospitalization & Medical Services, Inc., 791 F.Supp. 309 (D.D.C.1992). Other procedures held to be experimental include a Jarvik–7 artificial heart, Loyola University of Chicago v. Humana Insurance Co., 996 F.2d 895 (7th Cir.1993), hyperbaric oxygen therapy for quadriplegia, Washington v. Winn–Dixie of Louisiana, Inc., 736 F.Supp. 1418 (E.D.La.1990), and radial keratotomy, Stringfield v. Prudential Insurance Co. of America, 732 F.Supp. 69 (E.D.Tenn.1989).

**3.** Procedurally, the cases may be brought as actions for injunctive relief, in which the plaintiff is seeking a court order directing the approval of certain treatment. They also may be brought after the treatment already has been provided, in which the action seeks reimbursement. In the latter action, what relevance, if any, should evidence that the procedure was successful (or unsuccessful) have on whether it was "not medically necessary" or "experimental"?

### b. DISCRIMINATION

## Phelps v. Field Real Estate Co.

991 F.2d 645 (10th Cir.1993).

■ WESLEY E. BROWN, SENIOR DISTRICT JUDGE.

Plaintiff–Appellant John Phelps (Phelps) sought recovery for an alleged violation of Section 510 of ERISA, 29 U.S.C. § 1140, which prohibits discrimination against participants of any employee benefit plan for the purpose of interfering with rights under such plan. He also sought damages for alleged discrimination under a Colorado statute prohibiting employer discrimination against those with handicaps, C.R.S. § 24–34–402(1)(a).

Phelps began work as a commercial real estate division manager for defendant Field Real Estate Company in February, 1985. In November, 1986, he learned that he had tested positive for the virus which causes the disease Acquired Immuno–Deficiency Syndrome (AIDS). On August 4, 1989, Phelps was discharged from his employment, and this resulted in his loss of insurance benefits.

The district court found that Phelps had failed to prove the requisite intent to violate 29 U.S.C. § 1140 and that he had likewise failed to prove that he was discharged or discriminated against in violation of Colorado law. Phelps v. Field Real Estate, 793 F.Supp. 1535 (D.Colo.1991).

Phelps contends that the district court misconstrued the nature of the showing required for liability under ERISA § 510, and that under the facts found by the trial court, Phelps met his statutory burden of proof under the Colorado handicap discrimination statute. In this respect, Phelps accepts the findings of fact as found by the district court, but contends that its conclusions of law from those facts are erroneous.

A summary of the district court's findings of fact establishes this sequence of events:

Prior to February, 1985, when he began working for defendant Field Real Estate, Phelps had obtained an M.B.A. from Arizona State University, served two years in Vietnam, and began work as a real estate salesman in Pueblo, Colorado, in 1974. In 1979, he began work with Fuller & Company in Denver, selling commercial real estate, including undeveloped land. He obtained a real estate broker's license in 1983 but wanted to move into management; and, following an interview with Ray Stanley, then president of Field Real Estate Company, in February, 1985, he entered the Field organization as vice president of the commercial real estate division at $60,000 per year plus 3.5% commission with a guarantee of $82,000 during the first two years. At this time, W. Douglas Poole was chairman of the board and chief executive officer of Field.

When Phelps began work, a job specification was created for the commercial real estate division manager. Under this, the position was described as general management of the division without any direct selling, in accordance with Phelps' wishes.

The commercial real estate division was divided into a commercial sales division and a commercial leasing division. Phelps was manager of commercial sales and reported directly to Poole, while Ray Stanley was manager of commercial leasing.

At the outset, there was some conflict with Poole as to the expected volume of business which would be generated. Phelps believed that each sales agent could be expected to generate $2 million in sales per year, while Poole stated he expected $8 million per agent in each year. Poole's background was in retail sales, and he had had no experience in the real estate business. However, the two appeared to get along well; and Poole felt that Phelps did a good job in 1986 and 1987.

In November, 1986, Phelps learned that he was infected with the AIDS virus; but he was not ill, he had no symptoms of disease, and his condition did not interfere with his ability to perform his job. He kept his infection secret and did not disclose his medical condition to anyone.

By letter dated January 22, 1987, Poole extended Phelps' employment letter with the same compensation and benefits except that Phelps was to be granted listing agreements, beginning with the "Midland Building." Additional listing agreements were to be selected by Poole.

Annual performance evaluations were made by Poole, rating employees from 5 down. Poole gave Phelps mostly 3's for the 1986 evaluation. The only written comment under "areas for growth" was "needs to take a more hands-on approach to job."

On May 8, 1987, Phelps and Norman Marsh, manager of accounting, administration and personnel and assistant to Poole, were made senior vice presidents of Field.

In the annual review for 1987, Phelps was given mostly 4's, with note that Phelps needed "more personal involvement in development of third party business," and that he needed to reduce his outside activities in order to concentrate on developing the commercial sales division. Poole resented the time that Phelps spent away from the office, but he and Phelps continued to have a good working relationship.

In March, 1988, Poole found an anonymous note on his desk from "Members of the Staff," advising that Phelps had a fatal blood disease and requesting that he be transferred. When Phelps was shown the note, he told Poole that the note was true, that he had kept his condition a secret, and that he was concerned about his job and keeping his insurance. Poole assured Phelps that the matter would be kept in confidence and that, so long as Phelps was at Field, he had nothing to worry about.

Poole was concerned about Phelps' condition; the matter was discussed at a board meeting on May 3, 1988, and Poole and Phelps had another meeting on May 24, 1988. Phelps spoke of his disease as "diminished lymphoma," a phrase with no medical meaning, and told Poole that it involved a dormancy period of 8 to 10 years, and that when the disease became active, there would be 2 to 3 years of productivity and then death. Poole was concerned with corporate liability; and, because there was a possibility Field might be sold, there could be a problem about securing "key man" insurance for Phelps.

In June, 1988, Phelps went to see Dr. Kerr about the problem of obtaining insurance and obtained a letter from him which concealed more than it revealed.[4]  The doctor's letter stated in pertinent part that:

> The tests for which I am aware of in (Phelps') case indicate that, although currently able to perform all the duties of your occupation, owing to your past exposure to potentially injurious agents, you are at increased risk for certain types of cancers and other conditions.  It is my opinion that the agents detected by the tests which I am aware of are likely to be discovered in the course of the routine tests that are generally administered to determine an individual's insurability, and that it is highly likely that an insurer would decline to issue a policy to you on this basis.

> Again, I would wish to emphasize that, from a medical standpoint, you are presently able to satisfactorily perform all of the duties of your current position, and that your condition does not pose any health threat to anyone whom you may encounter in the workplace.

The doctor's letter was given to Poole, and Poole stated that he was "completely satisfied" that Phelps was capable of doing his job.

On July 10, 1988, Poole placed a blind classified ad for a "real estate commercial division manager."  The job description was applicable to Phelps' position, and also to Stanley's position, the leasing manager. Other anonymous notes appeared; there was some conflict between Poole and Phelps, and on July 23 and 24, Poole met with managers and real estate agents and informed them he was considering a new division to handle "REO properties," properties with defaulted loans.  One agent asked Poole why he had called the meeting.  Poole stated "that some people thought Phelps' job was in jeopardy, but it wasn't."

In January, 1989, there was another annual evaluation of employees. Phelps was given 4's on all categories, but under "performance" Poole wrote the following:

> The Commercial Sales division's development over the past three years has been very poor—both from the standpoint of recruiting productive agents as well as meeting Company objectives growth-wise.

Phelps was allowed to write and place a rebuttal of this evaluation in his file.  In this rebuttal, Phelps admitted that the Commercial Division had lost money in 1988, but he attributed the loss to three external causes—a decline in Denver's overall economy;  market prices declining below Bank Western's inventory prices;  and loss of confidence by the sales

---

**4.**  At the doctor's request, Phelps drafted this letter and, after making some changes, the doctor signed it.  There was no mention of the AIDS virus, and all references to future risk were related to an example based upon blood tests relating to the presence of "Agent Orange".

force due to the classified ad for a "commercial division manager," which resulted in the loss of two sales agents.

\* \* \*

Marsh and Poole met with Phelps on August 4, 1989, to tell him he was being discharged because of poor performance of the division and because of the reorganization.   Phelps asked if they knew they were firing someone with AIDS and that terminating his job would also terminate his insurance benefits.   Poole's response was that he was sorry, and Poole and Marsh both stated that they did not know that Phelps had AIDS.   Marsh suggested that Phelps could stay on as a real estate agent, working on commissions, and then he could continue his insurance at his own expense. Phelps declined to do so.   This offer was repeated by letter of August 17, 1989, but it was rejected and Phelps filed this action on November 21, 1989.

### The ERISA Claim

Section 510 of ERISA, 29 U.S.C. § 1140, provides in part that:

> It shall be unlawful for any person to discharge, fine, suspend, expel, discipline, or discriminate against a participant or beneficiary for exercising any right to which he is entitled under the provisions of an employee benefit plan \* \* \* *for the purpose of interfering with the attainment of any right to which such participant may become entitled under the plan* \* \* \*.   (Emphasis supplied)

As noted by the district court, Phelps was required to prove, by a preponderance of the evidence, that his discharge was motivated by an intent to interfere with employee benefits protected by ERISA.   In order to establish this intent, the courts have looked to circumstantial evidence surrounding the employment decision because there is rarely direct evidence of wrongful intent.

Since Poole was the one who personally made the decision to discharge Phelps, the question thus was whether Poole fired Phelps because "at least in part," Poole wanted to protect the benefit plans from the effect of Phelps' health condition.   As noted by the district court, "(p)ut bluntly, was Poole motivated to save the costs of health care, disability and death benefits as the expected consequences of the plaintiff's developing AIDS?"

Phelps contends that his appeal "is based entirely, and only, upon the facts found and accepted by the trial court".   As a part of its findings, the district court determined that Poole in fact was aware that Phelps had AIDS, but that this was not the motivating factor for Phelps' discharge.   In this respect, the district court found that "sales performance was a serious problem in the summer of 1988," and that placement of the ad for a new manager on July 12, 1988, "was an awkward effort to motivate Phelps to resign."   The court found that "(f)or whatever reason, Poole failed to confront Phelps directly about his health.   The lack of candor between these two men affected the working relationship between them.   Yet, a failure of leadership or ineffective management of this difficult situation is not equivalent to discriminatory treatment for the purpose of protecting the assets of the employee plans."

While there was evidence concerning the possible effect of an AIDS patient on benefit plans, the record supports the district court's conclusion that there was "no evidence that Poole, Marsh or anyone else in Field's management made any such calculations or even expressed any awareness of such consequences," and we agree that it is also significant that Phelps' termination was not made until more than fourteen months after he first disclosed his medical condition.   In addition, the evidence was that the commercial sales division failed to meet the expectations of Poole and his board of directors.   Whether or not this was in fact Phelps' fault, the fact remains that the commercial sales and leasing department was completely reorganized into three divisions, with new employees heading the industrial and office divisions, with Ray Stanley in charge of the retail division.   It is significant that Stanley was warned that his future was limited and that he, too, left the company soon after the reorganization.

Under this evidence, the district court's conclusion that Phelps had failed to prove the intent required by Section 510 of ERISA was correct.

## NOTES AND QUESTIONS

**1.**   What factors in the case most strongly suggest that the employer did not engage in discrimination?   Suppose that the employee had an 18–year record of excellent evaluations, he was discharged for allegedly poor performance shortly after notifying the employer that he had multiple sclerosis, the employer failed to follow its normal procedure of probation before discharge, and the employer had a strong financial incentive to fire him because its medical and disability plans were self-funded.   Would these facts create an inference of discrimination?   See Folz v. Marriott Corp., 594 F.Supp. 1007 (W.D.Mo.1984) (held: defendant violated § 510).

**2.**   Discrimination under § 510 is broadly defined to include not only the discharge of an employee to prevent benefit accrual, but discrimination against any beneficiary for asserting rights under ERISA, as well as retaliating against an employee for exercising rights under the statute. See, e.g., Fleming v. Ayers & Associates, 948 F.2d 993 (6th Cir.1991) (discharge of employee because of expected high medical costs of her infant child).

**3.**   In InterModal Rail Employees Association v. Atchison, Topeka & Santa Fe Railway Co., 117 S.Ct. 1513 (1997), the Supreme Court held § 510 prohibits interference with *both* pension plans and welfare plans.

**4.**   An employee with nine years and eight months of service alleges that he was discharged by his employer four months before his retirement and pension benefits vested so that his employer could avoid its obligation to contribute to his pension fund.   In a wrongful discharge action based on the public policy exception to the at-will doctrine, the employer argues that the action is preempted by § 510 of ERISA.   Is it?   See Ingersoll–Rand Co. v. McClendon, 498 U.S. 133 (1990) (held: yes).

**5.** Does it violate § 510 to amend the benefit plan to prevent the payment of health benefits to a particular employee or a class of employees? Consider the following case.

c.   CHANGES IN THE PLAN

# McGann v. H & H Music Co.

946 F.2d 401 (5th Cir.1991), cert. denied, 506 U.S. 981 (1992).

■ GARWOOD, CIRCUIT JUDGE:

Plaintiff-appellant John McGann (McGann) filed this suit under section 510 of the Employee Retirement Income Security Act of 1974 (ERISA), against defendants-appellees H & H Music Company (H & H Music), Brook Mays Music Company (Brook Mays) and General American Life Insurance Company (General American) (collectively defendants) claiming that they discriminated against McGann, an employee of H & H Music, by reducing benefits available to H & H Music's group medical plan beneficiaries for treatment for acquired immune deficiency syndrome (AIDS) and related illnesses.   The district court granted defendants' motion for summary judgment on the ground that an employer has an absolute right to alter the terms of medical coverage available to plan beneficiaries.   We affirm.

## FACTS AND PROCEEDINGS BELOW

McGann, an employee of H & H Music, discovered that he was afflicted with AIDS in December 1987.   Soon thereafter, McGann submitted his first claims for reimbursement under H & H Music's group medical plan, provided through Brook Mays, the plan administrator, and issued by General American, the plan insurer, and informed his employer that he had AIDS.   McGann met with officials of H & H Music in March 1988, at which time they discussed McGann's illness.   Before the change in the terms of the plan, it provided for lifetime medical benefits of up to $1,000,000 to all employees.

In July 1988, H & H Music informed its employees that, effective August 1, 1988, changes would be made in their medical coverage.   These changes included, but were not limited to, limitation of benefits payable for AIDS-related claims to a lifetime maximum of $5,000.[1]   No limitation was placed on any other catastrophic illness.   H & H Music became self-insured under the new plan and General American became the plan's administrator.   By January 1990, McGann had exhausted the $5,000 limit on coverage for his illness.

In August 1989, McGann sued H & H Music, Brook Mays and General American under section 510 of ERISA, which provides, in part, as follows:

"It shall be unlawful for any person to discharge, fine, suspend, expel, discipline, or discriminate against a participant or

---

**1.** Other changes included increased individual and family deductibles, elimination of coverage for chemical dependency treat-ment, adoption of a preferred provider plan and increased contribution requirements.

John McGann.   Photo courtesy of Dr. Frank Greenberg.

beneficiary for exercising any right to which he is entitled under the provisions of an employee benefit plan, * * * or for the purpose of interfering with the attainment of any right to which such participant may become entitled under the plan * * * "

McGann claimed that defendants discriminated against him in violation of both prohibitions of section 510.[2]  He claimed that the provision limiting coverage for AIDS-related expenses was directed specifically at him in retaliation for exercising his rights under the medical plan and for the

---

**2.** McGann also asserted various state law claims which the district court dismissed without discussion.  McGann's brief in this court states that he "does not appeal from that part of the [district] court's order."

purpose of interfering with his attainment of a right to which he may become entitled under the plan.

Defendants, conceding the factual allegations of McGann's complaint, moved for summary judgment.[3] These factual allegations include no assertion that the reduction of AIDS benefits was intended to deny benefits to McGann for any reason which would not be applicable to other beneficiaries who might then or thereafter have AIDS, but rather that the reduction was prompted by the knowledge of McGann's illness, and that McGann was the only beneficiary then known to have AIDS.[4] On June 26, 1990, the district court granted defendants' motion on the ground that they had an absolute right to alter the terms of the plan, regardless of their intent in making the alterations. The district court also held that even if the issue of discriminatory motive were relevant, summary judgment would still be proper because the defendants' motive was to ensure the future existence of the plan and not specifically to retaliate against McGann or to interfere with his exercise of future rights under the plan.

## DISCUSSION

McGann contends that defendants violated both clauses of section 510 by discriminating against him for two purposes: (1) "for exercising any right to which [the beneficiary] is entitled," and (2) "for the purpose of interfering with the attainment of any right to which such participant may become entitled." In order to preclude summary judgment in defendants' favor, McGann must make a showing sufficient to establish the existence of a genuine issue of material fact with respect to each material element on which he would carry the burden of proof at trial.

At trial, McGann would bear the burden of proving the existence of defendants' specific discriminatory intent as an essential element of either of his claims. Thus, in order to survive summary judgment McGann must make a showing sufficient to establish that a genuine issue exists as to defendants' specific intent to retaliate against McGann for filing claims for AIDS-related treatment or to interfere with McGann's attainment of any right to which he may have become entitled.

Although we assume there was a connection between the benefits reduction and either McGann's filing of claims or his revelations about his illness, there is nothing in the record to suggest that defendants' motivation was other than as they asserted, namely to avoid the expense of paying for AIDS treatment (if not, indeed, also for other treatment), no more for

---

3. General American claimed that the district court should have dismissed it as a defendant with respect to McGann's ERISA claim because ERISA does not create a cause of action against a nonemployer and McGann has never been employed by General American. Because of our disposition of this appeal on alternative grounds, we do not find it necessary to address this issue.

4. We assume, for purposes of this appeal that the defendants' knowledge of McGann's illness was a motivating factor in their decision to reduce coverage for AIDS-related expenses, that this knowledge was obtained either through McGann's filing of claims or his meetings with defendants, and that McGann was the only plan beneficiary then known to have AIDS.

McGann than for any other present or future plan beneficiary who might suffer from AIDS.  McGann concedes that the reduction in AIDS benefits will apply equally to all employees filing AIDS-related claims and that the effect of the reduction will not necessarily be felt only by him.  He fails to allege that the coverage reduction was otherwise specifically intended to deny him particularly medical coverage except "in effect."  He does not challenge defendants' assertion that their purpose in reducing AIDS benefits was to reduce costs.

Furthermore, McGann has failed to adduce evidence of the existence of "any right to which [he] may become entitled under the plan."  The right referred to in the second clause of section 510 is not simply any right to which an employee may conceivably become entitled, but rather any right to which an employee may become entitled pursuant to an existing, enforceable obligation assumed by the employer.  "Congress viewed [section 510] as a crucial part of ERISA because, without it, employers would be able to circumvent the provision of *promised* benefits."

McGann's allegations show no *promised* benefit, for there is nothing to indicate that defendants ever promised that the $1,000,000 coverage limit was permanent.  The H & H Music plan expressly provides: "Termination or Amendment of Plan: The Plan Sponsor may terminate or amend the Plan at any time or terminate any benefit under the Plan at any time."  There is no allegation or evidence that any oral or written representations were made to McGann that the $1,000,000 coverage limit would never be lowered.  Defendants broke no promise to McGann.  The continued availability of the $1,000,000 limit was not a right to which McGann may have become entitled for the purposes of section 510.[5]  To adopt McGann's contrary construction of this portion of section 510 would mean that an employer could not effectively reserve the right to amend a medical plan to reduce benefits respecting subsequently incurred medical expenses, as H & H Music did here, because such an amendment would obviously have as a purpose preventing participants from attaining the right to such future benefits as they otherwise might do under the existing plan absent the amendment.  But this is plainly not the law, and ERISA does not require such "vesting" of the right to a continued level of the same medical benefits once those are ever included in a welfare plan.

McGann appears to contend that the reduction in AIDS benefits alone supports an inference of specific intent to retaliate against him or to interfere with his future exercise of rights under the plan.  McGann characterizes as evidence of an individualized intent to discriminate the fact that AIDS was the only catastrophic illness to which the $5,000 limit was applied and the fact that McGann was the only employee known to have AIDS.  He contends that if defendants reduced AIDS coverage because they learned of McGann's illness through his exercising of his rights

---

**5.** McGann does not claim that he was not fully reimbursed for all claimed medical expenses incurred on or prior to August 1, 1988; or that the full $5,000 has not been made available to him in respect to AIDS related medical expenses incurred by him on or after July 1, 1988.

under the plan by filing claims, the coverage reduction therefore could be "retaliation" for McGann's filing of the claims.[6]   Under McGann's theory, any reduction in employee benefits would be impermissibly discriminatory if motivated by a desire to avoid the anticipated costs of continuing to provide coverage for a particular beneficiary.   McGann would find an implied promise not to discriminate for this purpose; it is the breaking of this promise that McGann appears to contend constitutes interference with a future entitlement.

McGann cites only one case in which a court has ruled that a change in the terms and conditions of an employee-benefits plan could constitute illegal discrimination under section 510.   Vogel v. Independence Federal Sav. Bank, 728 F.Supp. 1210 (D.Md.1990).   In *Vogel,* however, the plan change at issue resulted in the plaintiff and only the plaintiff being excluded from coverage.   McGann asserts that the *Vogel* court rejected the defendant's contention that mere termination of benefits could not constitute unlawful discrimination under section 510, but in fact the court rejected this claim not because it found that mere termination of coverage could constitute discrimination under section 510, but rather because the termination at issue affected only the beneficiary.   Nothing in *Vogel* suggests that the change there had the potential to then or thereafter exclude any present or possible future plan beneficiary other than the plaintiff.   *Vogel* therefore provides no support for the proposition that the alteration or termination of a medical plan could alone sustain a section 510 claim.   Without necessarily approving of the holding in *Vogel,* we note that it is inapplicable to the instant case.   The post-August 1, 1988 $5,000 AIDS coverage limit applies to any and all employees.

McGann effectively contends that section 510 was intended to prohibit any discrimination in the alteration of an employee benefits plan that results in an identifiable employee or group of employees being treated differently from other employees.   The First Circuit rejected a somewhat similar contention in Aronson v. Servus Rubber, Div. of Chromalloy, 730 F.2d 12 (1st Cir.), cert. denied, 469 U.S. 1017 (1984).   In *Aronson,* an employer eliminated a profit sharing plan with respect to employees at only one of two plants.   The disenfranchised employees sued their employer under section 510, claiming that partial termination of the plan with respect to employees at one plant and not at the other constituted illegal discrimination.   The court rejected the employees' discrimination claim, stating in part:

> "[Section 510] relates to discriminatory conduct directed against individuals, not to actions involving the plan in general.   The problem is with the word 'discriminate.'   An overly literal interpretation of this section would make illegal any partial termination, since such terminations obviously interfere with the at-

---

**6.** We assume that discovery of McGann's condition—and realization of the attendant, long-term costs of caring for McGann—did in fact prompt defendants to reconsider the $1,000,000 limit with respect to AIDS-related expenses and to reduce the limit for future such expenses to $5,000.

tainment of benefits by the terminated group, and, indeed, are expressly intended so to interfere * * *. This is not to say that a plan could not be discriminatorily modified, intentionally benefitting, or injuring, certain identified employees or a certain group of employees, but a partial termination cannot constitute discrimination per se. A termination that cuts along independently established lines—here separate divisions—and that has a readily apparent business justification, demonstrates no invidious intent." Id. at 16 (citation omitted).

The Supreme Court has observed in dictum: "ERISA does not mandate that employers provide any particular benefits, and does not itself proscribe discrimination in the provision of employee benefits." To interpret "discrimination" broadly to include defendants' conduct would clearly conflict with Congress's intent that employers remain free to create, modify and terminate the terms and conditions of employee benefits plans without governmental interference.

* * *

As persuasively explained by the Second Circuit, the policy of allowing employers freedom to amend or eliminate employee benefits is particularly compelling with respect to medical plans:

"With regard to an employer's right to change medical plans, Congress evidenced its recognition of the need for flexibility in rejecting the automatic vesting of welfare plans. Automatic vesting was rejected because the costs of such plans are subject to fluctuating and unpredictable variables. Actuarial decisions concerning fixed annuities are based on fairly stable data, and vesting is appropriate. In contrast, medical insurance must take account of inflation, changes in medical practice and technology, and increases in the costs of treatment independent of inflation. These unstable variables prevent accurate predictions of future needs and costs." Moore v. Metropolitan Life Ins. Co., 856 F.2d 488, 492 (2d Cir.1988).

In *Metropolitan Life*, the court rejected an ERISA claim by retirees that their employer could not change the level of their medical benefits without their consent. The court stated that limiting an employer's right to change medical plans increased the risk of "decreas[ing] protection for future employees and retirees."

McGann's claim cannot be reconciled with the well-settled principle that Congress did not intend that ERISA circumscribe employers' control over the content of benefits plans they offered to their employees. McGann interprets section 510 to prevent an employer from reducing or eliminating coverage for a particular illness in response to the escalating costs of covering an employee suffering from that illness. Such an interpretation would, in effect, change the terms of H & H Music's plan. Instead of making the $1,000,000 limit available for medical expenses on an as-incurred basis only as long as the limit remained in effect, the policy would make the limit *permanently* available for all medical expenses as they might thereafter be incurred because of a single event, such as the contracting of AIDS. Under McGann's theory, defendants would be effectively proscribed from reducing coverage for AIDS once McGann had contracted that illness and filed claims for AIDS-related expenses. If a federal court could prevent an employer from reducing an employee's coverage limits for AIDS treatment once that employee contracted AIDS, the boundaries of judicial involvement in the creation, alteration or termination of ERISA plans would be sorely tested.

As noted, McGann has failed to adduce any evidence of defendants' specific intent to engage in conduct proscribed by section 510. A party against whom summary judgment is ordered cannot raise a fact issue simply by stating a cause of action where defendants' state of mind is a material element.

Proof of defendants' specific intent to discriminate among plan beneficiaries on grounds not proscribed by section 510 does not enable McGann to avoid summary judgment. ERISA does not broadly prevent an employer from "discriminating" in the creation, alteration or termination of employee benefits plans; thus, evidence of such intentional discrimination cannot alone sustain a claim under section 510. That section does not prohibit welfare plan discrimination between or among categories of diseases. Section 510 does not mandate that if some, or most, or virtually all catastrophic illnesses are covered, AIDS (or any other particular catastrophic illness) must be among them. It does not prohibit an employer from electing not to cover or continue to cover AIDS, while covering or continuing to cover other catastrophic illnesses, even though the employer's decision in this respect may stem from some "prejudice" against AIDS or its victims generally. The same, of course, is true of any other disease and its victims. That sort of "discrimination" is simply not addressed by section 510. Under section 510, the asserted discrimination is illegal only if it is motivated by a desire to retaliate against an employee or to deprive an employee of an existing right to which he may become entitled. The district court's decision to grant summary judgment to defendants therefore was proper. Its judgment is accordingly

AFFIRMED.

NOTES AND QUESTIONS

**1.** Following *McGann,* Texas amended its insurance laws to prohibit the cancellation of an accident or sickness policy during its term because the insured has been diagnosed with HIV infection or AIDS. Tex.Ins.Code § 3.70–3A. Even if the amendment had been in effect at the time of Mr. McGann's illness, however, it still would not have prohibited H & H, as a self-insured employer, from curtailing his benefits. See generally Lorraine Schmall, Toward Full Participation and Protection of the Worker with Illness: The Failure of Federal Law After *McGann v. H & H Music Co.,* 29 Wake Forest L.Rev. 781 (1994).

**2.** ERISA distinguishes between welfare benefit plans and pension plans, providing more stringent protections for the latter. The statute expressly excludes welfare plans from the stringent minimum vesting, participation, and funding standards imposed on pension plans. ERISA §§ 201(1), 301(a)(1), 29 U.S.C. §§ 1051(1), 1081(a)(1).

**3.** Does this differentiation between welfare plans and pension plans seem fair? One commentator has recommended that Congress amend ERISA to provide more protection for medical plans.

> Retiree insurance should be presumed a lifetime benefit which vests at retirement unless the employer includes in plan documents and employee handbooks an explicit and unambiguous termination clause indicating otherwise. Even if such a clause is included, it should not be enforced unless it permits reductions or termination only in the event that the company is in severe financial distress. Finally, to ensure that retirees receive their benefits, . . . retiree insurance plans [should] be funded in ways similar to those in which pension plans are funded.

Joan Vogel, Until Death Do Us Part: Vesting of Retiree Insurance, 9 Indus.Rel.L.J. 183, 240 (1987).

Does this seem like a good solution?

**4.** Sometimes courts have been faced with welfare plans which have no explicit provision reserving the right to the employer to reduce or eliminate benefits. In the case of collectively bargained benefits, the court will look to the intent of the parties to determine if the benefits are to continue beyond the agreement's termination. When the language is ambiguous and the company's actions and statements indicate it did not consider the benefits to be limited to the duration of the collective bargaining agreement, the court will treat the benefits as guaranteed for the retiree's lifetime. See International Union (UAW) v. Yard–Man, Inc., 716 F.2d 1476 (6th Cir.1983), cert. denied, 465 U.S. 1007 (1984). In construing ambiguous terms, the court may look to extrinsic evidence or to other sections in the contract.

**5.** In Stiltner v. Beretta U.S.A. Corp., 74 F.3d 1473 (4th Cir.1996) (en banc), cert. denied, 117 S.Ct. 54 (1996), the plaintiff was an employee who was disabled by a heart condition. The employer threatened to cut off his free health insurance unless he dropped his lawsuit seeking $332,000 in long-term disability benefits. The plaintiff then sued under § 510 of ERISA, asserting that the threat to terminate his health insurance was an "interference" with his benefits. The Fourth Circuit held, eight-to-five, that ERISA does not prevent employers from revoking gratuitous benefits. The dissent argued that § 510 bars all retaliation, regardless of whether the benefits are gratuitous.

**6.** Section 501(c)(3) of the Americans with Disabilities Act provides that the employment discrimination title of the Act shall not be construed to prohibit an employer "from establishing, sponsoring, observing or administering the terms of a bona fide benefit plan that is not subject to State laws that regulate insurance." In other words, the ADA does not appear to regulate the terms of the health benefits plans of self-insured employers, so long as the plan was not a "subterfuge" to avoid the ADA. A June 1993 statement by the EEOC, however, asserts that it will violate the ADA for an employer to offer any health benefit plan that discriminates on the basis of disability or fails to afford equal access to health benefits unless justified by actuarial considerations. "Employees with disabilities must be accorded 'equal access' to whatever health insurance the employer provides to employees without disabilities." Employers may not set lower benefit levels for particular conditions, such as AIDS, cancer, or heart disease, although broad distinctions applying to numerous disorders may be permissible. EEOC Interim Guidance on Application of the ADA to Health Insurance (1993).

**7.** In Henderson v. Bodine Aluminum, Inc., 70 F.3d 958 (8th Cir.1995), a breast cancer patient insured under an ERISA plan sought a preliminary injunction compelling the plan to provide coverage for high-dose chemotherapy (HDCT) and autologous bone marrow transplant on the ground that the denial violated the ADA. In reversing the district court's denial of the injunction, the Eighth Circuit held that because HDCT was approved for other types of cancer, the denial of the treatment for breast cancer was disability-based discrimination in violation of the ADA. On the other hand, in Krauel v. Iowa Methodist Medical Center, 95 F.3d 674 (8th Cir.1996), the Eighth Circuit held that an employer's medical benefits plan, which contained an exclusion for infertility treatments, did not violate the ADA. Can you distinguish *Henderson?*

**8.** The Health Insurance Portability and Accountability Act (HIPAA), discussed infra p. 546, provides that individuals in a group health plan may not be subject to discrimination based on health status in their eligibility, enrollment, or premium contributions. If HIPAA had been in effect at the time of *McGann,* H & H Music could not have reduced the benefits only for AIDS. Nevertheless, it could have reduced benefits across the board or even eliminated all benefits. This illustrates the principle that making optional benefits more expensive will result in more employers dropping benefits altogether.

## 5.   CONTINUATION COVERAGE UNDER COBRA

### McDowell v. Krawchison

125 F.3d 954 (6th Cir.1997).

■ MOORE, CIRCUIT JUDGE.

Defendants–Appellants John Raymond Krawchison and Winton Road Chiropractic Center, Inc. appeal from the district court's order entering judgment in favor of Plaintiff–Appellee Terry McDowell[1] in this action for failure to provide health insurance benefits under ERISA, as amended by

---

**1.** McDowell appears before this court on his own behalf and as the Executor of the Last Will of Sharon Sidovar, who died during the pendency of the district court litigation.

the Comprehensive Omnibus Budget Reconciliation Act of 1986, § 10002, Pub.L. No. 99–272, 100 Stat. 227–32 (codified as amended at 29 §§ 1161–1168) ("COBRA").

## I.  BACKGROUND

At the times relevant to this case, Krawchison held an ownership interest in and operated several chiropractic clinics in Ohio, Kentucky, and Indiana.  He owned half of the shares in each of three clinics, and owned all of the shares in the others, including Winton Road Chiropractic Center, Inc.  Most of the clinics, including Winton Road, were separately incorporated.  Krawchison also wholly owned Michiana Corporation, which provided management services for all of his clinics, such as paying bills (using the separate clinics' own funds), and provided patient transportation for the Indiana clinics.  Krawchison followed corporate formalities with respect to each incorporated clinic and did not commingle their funds.  The clinics provided health insurance to their employees through Medical Benefits Mutual Life Insurance Company; the plan under which employees of all the separate clinics were covered was obtained under the name "John R. Krawchison Corporation" (that name appeared on the employees' insurance cards).  Krawchison obtained the insurance under a single plan for all the clinics in order to receive a lower rate (by aggregating the numbers of employees); there was no actual John R. Krawchison Corporation.

In late 1991, Krawchison asked McDowell to work for him at the Winton Road clinic in Cincinnati.  McDowell accepted and began work in early January 1992.  In September 1992, Dr. Dennis Anderson, who had previously worked at the Winton Road clinic, returned to buy the clinic from Krawchison.  He terminated McDowell's employment, effective two days later.  McDowell, whose wife, Sidovar, had breast cancer, wanted to continue his and Sidovar's health insurance.  Although McDowell claimed that Anderson had assured him that "we" would take care of the insurance, Krawchison disputed Anderson's authority to act on behalf of either Krawchison or the Winton Road corporation at that point.  McDowell later asked Susan Porter, the office manager for the Winton Road clinic, if he could continue on the health insurance plan.  Porter told him that she believed it was possible, but that she would check with Krawchison, which she did.  On McDowell's last day of employment, Porter told him that his health insurance would be continued; the parties dispute whether Porter told McDowell that he would have to pay the premiums.  Porter stated in her deposition that she had so told him, and that she also had told him that he should contact Trisha Kincer, an employee of Michiana Corporation who handled the health insurance plan, to find out the amount of the premiums.  McDowell never contacted Kincer.

Porter also gave McDowell a release to sign, waiving all claims related to his employment against Winton Road Chiropractic Center, Inc. or Krawchison individually.  After consulting with counsel, McDowell signed the release.

Neither McDowell nor Sidovar sought coverage for any medical treatment from September 1992 until early June 1993. At that time, Sidovar sought pre-approval for medical treatment and learned that she had no insurance coverage. McDowell and Sidovar filed suit against Krawchison in early 1994 alleging violation of COBRA in addition to several state claims; they later added the Winton Road corporation as a defendant. In July 1995, the district court issued an order denying Krawchison's motion for summary judgment with regard to his individual liability on the COBRA claim, denying the corporation's motion for summary judgment based on its contention that it was exempt from COBRA requirements, denying the defendants' motion for summary judgment based on the signed release, granting the plaintiffs' motion for partial summary judgment based on failure to provide notice of COBRA rights, and granting the defendants' motion for summary judgment as to the allegation of an oral promise to provide continued benefits and as to the state law claims. After a hearing and stipulations, the court issued a final order in March 1996 entering judgment for the plaintiffs against both defendants. On appeal, the defendants base their challenge on the issues of COBRA notice, Krawchison's liability, and the effect of the release.

## II. ANALYSIS

\* \* \*

### A. COBRA Notice

COBRA imposes a statutory requirement that a plan administrator notify "any qualified beneficiary" of his or her right to continue health insurance coverage for up to eighteen months after a "qualifying event" (here, McDowell's termination). *See* 29 U.S.C. § 1166(a)(4) (notice requirement); 29 U.S.C. § 1162 (continuation coverage); 29 U.S.C. § 1163(2) (termination of covered employee as qualifying event). "Providing appropriate notice is a key requirement under COBRA.... If the administrator fails to provide that notice [of triggering of COBRA rights] to the qualified beneficiary, it may be bound to provide coverage to her." Both plaintiffs in this case were qualified beneficiaries as defined by COBRA. 29 U.S.C. § 1167(3)(A) (defining "qualified beneficiary" as including the spouse of a covered employee, if the spouse was a beneficiary under the plan as of the day before the qualifying event); 29 U.S.C. § 1167(3)(B) (including a covered employee as a qualified beneficiary in the case of a termination other than for gross misconduct or reduction of hours).

\* \* \*

COBRA rights include the option to continue health insurance coverage equivalent to other qualified beneficiaries for at least eighteen months, at a cost of no more than 102 percent of the premium; the beneficiary must elect coverage within sixty days after the qualifying event, and may not be required to make the first premium payment before forty-five days after election. 29 U.S.C. §§ 1162, 1165. The statute itself does not prescribe the contents of the required notice. *See* 29 U.S.C. § 1166(a)(4) (In the case of a qualifying event, "the administrator shall notify ... any qualified beneficiary ... of such beneficiary's rights under this [part]."). Nevertheless, the notice given must be sufficient to allow the qualified beneficiary to make an informed decision whether to elect coverage.

Although the defendants contend that oral notice should be deemed sufficient, we need not decide that issue in this case. Even if the notice to McDowell by way of his conversation with Porter was legally sufficient, it did not meet the statutory requirement as to Sidovar. She was entitled by statute to *her own notice* of her rights. The statute explicitly requires notice to be given to any qualified beneficiary, and defines a covered spouse to be a qualified beneficiary. 29 U.S.C. §§ 1166(a)(4), 1167(3)(A)(i). A covered spouse has his or her own rights under COBRA, which are *not* dependent on the covered employee's rights. For example, a covered spouse might choose to elect coverage while the covered employee does not, or they might choose different plans. 29 U.S.C. § 1165(2). The covered spouse often may be a qualified beneficiary where the covered employee is not: a covered spouse is specifically defined as a qualified beneficiary, 29 U.S.C. § 1167(3)(A)(i); a covered employee, on the other hand, is a qualified beneficiary only when he or she is terminated other than for gross misconduct or experiences a reduction in hours, 29 U.S.C. § 1167(3)(B). In fact, the definition of "qualifying event" focuses largely on the resulting loss of coverage to other family members; COBRA coverage for qualified beneficiaries is triggered not only when the covered employee is terminated, but also when he or she dies or becomes covered by Medicare, when the covered spouse is divorced or legally separated from the covered employee, when a dependent child ceases to be a dependent child, or when an employer from whom the covered employee retired files for bankruptcy.

Other COBRA provisions belie the defendants' contention that notice to the covered employee satisfies the administrator's obligation as to a covered spouse. For instance, § 1166(c) states that notification by the administrator "to an individual who is a qualified beneficiary as the spouse of the covered employee shall be treated as notification to all other qualified beneficiaries residing with such spouse at the time such notification is made." In other words, the administrator is not required to notify each covered dependent child living at home, provided that the nonemployee parent, the spouse of the covered employee, is notified. If the statute eliminates the need to notify certain qualified beneficiaries, but does *not* explicitly except notification of the spouse—and, in fact, relies upon such notification to provide notice to covered dependents—then we cannot read the statute to eliminate the need to notify a covered spouse.

The statute also provides that "any election of continuation coverage by a qualified beneficiary ... shall be deemed to include an election of continuation coverage on behalf of any other qualified beneficiary who would lose coverage under the plan by reason of the qualifying event. If there is a choice among types of coverage under the plan, each qualified beneficiary is entitled to make a separate selection among such types of coverage." 29 U.S.C. § 1165(2). Perhaps significantly, this provision acts only to preserve coverage for other qualified beneficiaries; it does not, for instance, treat one beneficiary's decision not to continue coverage as eliminating the other beneficiaries' option to elect, and in fact it allows beneficiaries to elect different types of coverage. This election provision is useful as an analogy—it allows one beneficiary to be deemed to have acted on others' behalf only in order to maintain coverage, and it explicitly provides for a separate election by each beneficiary; it does not allow beneficiaries to be treated as a unit for purposes of denying coverage. Similarly, we do not interpret the statute's notice provisions as treating the covered employee and his or her spouse as a unit for notice purposes, such that the plan administrator is absolved of its duty to notify the spouse.

Taken together, §§ 1165(2) and 1166(c) indicate that qualified beneficiaries are to be treated separately for COBRA purposes except in these specifically-defined exceptions, both of which operate in favor of coverage. Moreover, these two provisions strongly suggest that had Congress intended notice to a covered employee to serve as notice to that employee's covered spouse as well, it would have so provided. Therefore, we hold that the plan administrator was required to provide Sidovar with sufficient notice of her rights, and that failure to do so violated COBRA.

\* \* \*

Defendants urge this court that to require actual notice to Sidovar would turn COBRA into "a technical labyrinth"; to the contrary, we believe that the clear language of the statute not only mandates actual notice, but establishes a simple requirement that will not mire plan administrators and courts in fact-specific inquiries as to whether a covered employee actually notified the covered spouse, whether that notification adequately informed the spouse of his or her rights, and so on.

## C.  The Effect of the Release

The defendants contend that the plaintiffs' COBRA claims are barred by the release that McDowell signed, which waived all claims against the Winton Road corporation and Krawchison "directly or indirectly relating" to his employment. We need not decide that issue, however, because we hold that the release signed by McDowell could not have waived Sidovar's COBRA rights.[12] The defendants argue that the release barred Sidovar's COBRA claim as well as McDowell's, since her right to coverage was dependent on his right to coverage, because there was no "qualifying event" as to Sidovar. A simple reading of the statute shows that the defendants are clearly mistaken. A rule by which the spouse's COBRA rights would derive from the employee's rights could apply, if at all, only to cases where the covered employee himself or herself was a qualified beneficiary. For that reason, the defendants' reading of the statute is nonsensical; it would eradicate all COBRA coverage for nonemployees (i.e.,

12. The damages in this action were based entirely on Sidovar's medical costs, and not on any damages resulting from McDo-well's lack of coverage, as defendants' counsel conceded at oral argument.

spouses and families) triggered by the qualifying events listed in 29 U.S.C. § 1163(1), (3)–(5)—all but § 1163(2) and (6).  Under the clear language of the statute, Sidovar, as a spouse of an employee, and as a beneficiary under the plan as of the day before the qualifying event of McDowell's termination, was a qualified beneficiary entitled to COBRA coverage.  See 29 U.S.C. § 1167(3)(A).  Her rights were in no way contingent on McDowell's.  Therefore, even if McDowell did waive his COBRA rights, he did not—and could not—waive Sidovar's.

### III.  CONCLUSION

For the reasons discussed above, we AFFIRM the judgment of the district court awarding damages to the plaintiffs against Defendant Krawchison, and REVERSE the judgment against Defendant Winton Road Chiropractic Center, Inc.  We REMAND to the district court for further proceedings consistent with this opinion.

NOTES AND QUESTIONS

**1.**  The court in *McDowell* follows the general rule that the burden of proving that proper notice was given following a qualifying event is on the plan administrator, not on the qualified beneficiary.  See Stanton v. Larry Fowler Trucking, Inc., 52 F.3d 723 (8th Cir.1995).

**2.**  The courts are in disagreement over whether the qualifying event is the date of termination or reduction of hours leading to the loss of coverage or the actual loss of coverage.  Compare Gaskell v. Harvard Cooperative Soc'y, 3 F.3d 495 (1st Cir.1993) (qualifying event was event leading to loss of coverage) with Mlsna v. Unitel Communications, Inc., 41 F.3d 1124 (7th Cir.1994) (qualifying event was day employee stopped working).

**3.**  In Geissal v. Moore Medical Corp., 118 S.Ct. 1869 (1998), the Supreme Court held that an employer may not deny COBRA continuation coverage under its health plan to an otherwise eligible beneficiary because he was covered under his wife's plan at the time he elected COBRA coverage.

**4.**  In In re Appletree Markets, Inc., 19 F.3d 969 (5th Cir.1994), a multiemployer employee welfare benefit plan brought an action claiming that an employer that withdrew from membership in the plan and established a new plan for its current employees had an obligation to extend coverage under its new plan to its COBRA-qualified former employees who were receiving benefits under the multiemployer plan.  The court held that COBRA defines the multiemployer health insurance plan as the "sponsor" of the plan and therefore the plan is responsible for the coverage of COBRA-qualifying former employees.

**5.**  COBRA contains an exemption for employers with fewer than 20 employees.  29 U.S.C. § 1161(b).  In Kidder v. H & B Marine, Inc., 932 F.2d 347 (5th Cir.1991), the court held that in computing whether an employer has 20 or more employees, closely-related corporations with the same ownership may be considered as a single employer.

**6.** The Health Insurance Portability and Accountability Act of 1996 (HIPAA), discussed infra p. 546, amended COBRA in the following four significant aspects:

a) Under COBRA, the 18–month maximum benefit was extended to 29 months if, at the time of the qualifying event, the beneficiary was disabled.  HIPAA clarifies that this extended maximum coverage applies to a disabled qualified beneficiary of a covered employee.

b) Under HIPAA, if the beneficiary becomes disabled within the first 60 days of COBRA coverage, the 29–month benefit also is available.

c) Under HIPAA, COBRA coverage may be terminated before 18 months if the qualified beneficiary becomes covered under another group health plan with no preexisting condition limitation or exclusion.

d) HIPAA modifies the definition of "qualified beneficiary" to include a child born to or adopted by the covered employee during the period of COBRA coverage.

## 6.   NONDISCRIMINATION IN BENEFITS

### a.   PREGNANCY LEAVE

Title VII of the Civil Rights Act of 1964 prohibits discrimination with respect to all terms and conditions of employment, including benefits.  One of the most controversial and heavily litigated subjects under Title VII's prohibition against sex discrimination in benefits has been the provision of pregnancy benefits for female employees.  The Supreme Court first held in Geduldig v. Aiello, 417 U.S. 484 (1974), that a state law which excluded from disability benefits a temporary disability arising from a normal pregnancy did not violate the equal protection clause of the fourteenth amendment.  Then in General Electric Co. v. Gilbert, 429 U.S. 125 (1976), the Court held that an employer's disability plan which covered all disabilities except those associated with or arising out of pregnancy was not a violation of Title VII.  The Court reasoned that discrimination on the basis of pregnancy was not sex-based discrimination, since at any given time there were both men and (non-pregnant) women who benefitted fully from the disability plan.

A year later, in Nashville Gas Co. v. Satty, 434 U.S. 136 (1977), the Court reviewed an employer policy which required pregnant women to take a formal leave of absence during pregnancy but provided no disability benefits to them, and then stripped them of their accrued company seniority for competitive bidding purposes upon their return from maternity leave.  The company did not hold jobs for women on maternity leave nor did it guarantee them a job when they returned.  A woman who wanted to return to work had to apply for a new job, and permanent positions were not always available.  The Court upheld the disability exclusion under its reasoning in *Gilbert,* but distinguished the mandatory forfeiture of seniority:

In *Gilbert,* there was no showing that General Electric's policy of compensating for all non-job-related disabilities except pregnancy favored men over women.   No evidence was produced to suggest that men received more benefits from General Electric's disability insurance fund than did women;   both men and women were subject generally to the disabilities covered and presumably drew similar amounts from the insurance fund.   We therefore upheld the plan under Title VII.

* * *

Here, by comparison, petitioner has not merely refused to extend to women a benefit that men cannot and do not receive, but has imposed on women a substantial burden that men need not suffer.   The distinction between benefits and burdens is more than one of semantics.   We held in *Gilbert* that § 703(a)(1) did not require that greater economic benefits be paid to one sex or the other "because of their differing roles in 'the scheme of human existence,'" 429 U.S. at 139 n. 17.   But that holding does not allow us to read § 703(a)(2) to permit an employer to burden female employees in such a way as to deprive them of employment opportunities because of their significant role.

434 U.S. at 139–42.   The Court pointed out that the employer had the opportunity to establish the existence of a business necessity which would justify its policy, but that Nashville Gas Company had not submitted such proof.

Following *Gilbert* and *Satty,* Congress amended Title VII by adding the Pregnancy Discrimination Act of 1978, codified as § 701(k) of Title VII.   It provides:

The terms "because of sex" or "on the basis of sex" include, but are not limited to, because of or on the basis of pregnancy, childbirth, or related medical conditions, and women affected by pregnancy, childbirth, or related medical conditions shall be treated the same for all employment-related purposes, including receipt of benefits under fringe benefit programs, as other persons not so affected but similar in their ability or inability to work, and nothing in section 703(h) of this title shall be interpreted to permit otherwise.   * * *

Section 701(k) "undoes" *Gilbert* by making it clear that an employer must treat pregnant employees the same as nonpregnant employees.   That is, the employer may not maintain a policy that adversely affects pregnant employees relative to other employees, unless it can establish a business necessity or BFOQ defense.

As a result of the passage of § 701(k), a number of employers amended their health insurance plans to cover pregnancy-related conditions of female employees to the same extent as other medical conditions.   In Newport News Shipbuilding & Dry Dock Co. v. EEOC, 462 U.S. 669 (1983), a male employee alleged that his employer unlawfully refused to provide full insurance coverage for the hospitalization costs associated with his wife's pregnancy.  The Supreme Court held that the employer's plan was a violation of Title VII, since under the plan, married male employees received less comprehensive coverage than married female employees.

## Lang v. Star Herald

107 F.3d 1308 (8th Cir.1997), cert. denied, 118 S.Ct. 114 (1997).

■ HANSEN, CIRCUIT JUDGE.

Jodee Lang appeals from the district court's grant of summary judgment to the *Star Herald* in this Title VII case, in which Lang alleges gender discrimination on the basis of her pregnant status.  We affirm.

Viewed in the light most favorable to Lang, the record reveals the following facts.  Jodee Lang began working as a part-time employee for the *Star Herald* in April of 1991 and moved to full-time status in November of 1992.  Under the *Star Herald* 's employee benefits policy, which is outlined in an employee handbook, Lang accumulated vacation time and sick leave based upon the number of hours she worked.

In early May 1993, Lang informed her supervisor, Scott Walker, that she was pregnant.  She continued working during her pregnancy until she took one week of vacation from June 7 through 11.  During her vacation, Lang experienced some bleeding associated with her pregnancy and was advised by her physician not to return to work until it stopped.

On Monday, June 14, 1993, Lang left a message for Walker, stating that she would not be in because she had a medical appointment.  The next day, Lang phoned Walker and read him a note from her doctor, which recommended rest for two weeks.  During this conversation, she asked Walker whether the *Star Herald* had a short-term disability policy; he replied that he would find out for her.  Lang was absent from work the entire week of June 14–18 and was paid with the balance of her accrued sick leave and vacation time.

Walker phoned Lang on June 23 and informed her that her sick leave had expired and she had no remaining paid vacation time.  He also reported that the *Star Herald* did not have a short-term disability policy.  Walker said he would have to let her go but agreed not to take any action until after Friday, June 25.

That Friday, Lang told Walker that her doctor had told her not to resume work because she was still incurring pregnancy-related problems.  Lang said she would know after her medical appointment on Monday, June 28, when she could return to work.  Walker promised not to take any action until after that time.

On June 28, Lang's doctor recommended that she take additional time off from her job and said he could not predict when she could resume work.  When Lang informed Walker of the doctor's recommendation, Walker explained the *Star Herald* 's policy for unpaid leaves of absence.  The policy provides that an employee who has exhausted her paid leave time can apply for an unpaid leave of absence, but the *Star Herald* does not guarantee that it will hold open the employee's position during her absence. Walker asked Lang to apply for an indefinite leave of absence, but Lang refused to do so because she would not be guaranteed re-employment. As a result of her refusal, her employment with the *Star Herald* was terminated.

Lang filed a charge of discrimination with the Equal Employment Opportunity Commission and then timely filed this suit. The *Star Herald* filed a motion for summary judgment, which was eventually granted by the district court. This appeal followed.

Title VII makes it "an unlawful employment practice for an employer to fail or refuse to hire or to discharge any individual, or otherwise to discriminate against any individual with respect to his compensation, terms, conditions, or privileges of employment, because of such individual's ... sex." 42 U.S.C. § 2000e–2(a) (1994). In 1978, Congress enacted the Pregnancy Discrimination Act (PDA), amending the definitional provision of Title VII to clarify that discrimination "on the basis of pregnancy, childbirth, or related medical conditions" is sex discrimination under Title VII. *Id.* § 2000e(k).

Lang claims that the *Star Herald* illegally discriminated against her on the basis of her pregnancy by denying her an indefinite leave of absence with a guarantee that she could return to her position. Lang appeals the district court's grant of the *Star Herald*'s motion for summary judgment, arguing that her Title VII claim should survive under the theories of disparate treatment and disparate impact.

\* \* \*

Lang argues that the policy was in fact discriminatory. She first points to a nonpregnant coworker, Peggy Carbojol, who allegedly was given indefinite time off for personal reasons. The benefit Carbojol received was quite different, however, from the one Lang sought. Carbojol's absence, which amounted to only one day, was covered by her accrued paid leave time. The evidence of Carbojol's leave does not show that Carbojol or any employee was granted unpaid leave time with a guarantee of re-employment as Lang sought, nor does it establish that Lang was qualified to receive that benefit.

Lang also makes a comparison to another nonpregnant coemployee, Teresa Martinez, who was granted a variance from the leave policy. According to Lang's brief, Martinez asked for and received three to four days off without pay at the commencement of her employment period. The benefit Martinez received differs significantly from the one Lang sought in that Martinez's period of unpaid leave was definite in duration—four days at the most. Like the Carbojol evidence, this evidence of Martinez's leave does not advance Lang's case.

Because Lang has produced no evidence to show that the *Star Herald*'s indefinite-leave-of-absence policy was different for her than it was for nonpregnant employees, we conclude that Lang failed to establish a prima facie case.  Lang has not submitted evidence showing that she is qualified to receive an unpaid indefinite leave of absence with a guarantee of returning to her position or that the *Star Herald* has ever granted such a benefit to other employees.

Lang maintains that the fact that she asked for indefinite leave is unimportant, because coworkers could have covered for her.  The relevant question, however, is whether the *Star Herald* treated Lang differently than nonpregnant employees on an indefinite leave of absence, not whether the *Star Herald* could have made more concessions for Lang.  We emphasize again that Title VII does not create rights to preferential treatment.

Finally, Lang contends that she actually had five remaining unpaid vacation days to use at the time she was discharged.  She points to a policy provision in the employee handbook, which states: "All employees eligible for vacation who have not earned two weeks of vacation during the year may take unpaid time off in addition to their paid vacation time off up to a total of two weeks off during the year."  Lang contends that because she had only accumulated 40 hours (5 days) of vacation time at the time she was terminated (June), she could have taken 5 unpaid days under this provision.

We agree with the district court that this provision applies only to newly hired employees who have not yet worked for the *Star Herald* for one year.  At the time Lang was discharged, she had worked for the *Star Herald* for more than two years.  The provision is therefore inapplicable here.

We do not address Lang's arguments that the *Star Herald*'s proffered reason for its employment decision was pretext for discrimination, because her failure to establish her prima facie case means that the burden of production of the employer's allegedly nondiscriminatory reason never arises.

Lang also argues her case under the theory of disparate impact.  The district court dismissed Lang's disparate impact claim because she had not specifically alleged in her pleadings that the *Star Herald*'s unpaid leave policy has a disproportionate impact on pregnant women.  Because Lang's disparate impact claim fails as a matter of law, we decline to address the pleading issue.  To establish a prima facie case of disparate impact, Lang must show that the *Star Herald*'s facially neutral policy is in fact unjustifiably more harsh on pregnant women than on other people.  To prove this, Lang "must offer 'statistical evidence of a kind and degree sufficient to show that the practice in question has caused the exclusion' of benefits because the beneficiaries would be women."  Lang has provided no statistical support for her claim, and in fact concedes in her brief that "there is no evidence of statistical imbalance with this small [of] an employer."  As a result, there is no evidence in this record of a disproportionately adverse impact on pregnant women, and we affirm the district court's judgment because Lang cannot establish a prima facie case of disparate impact.

For the above reasons, we affirm the judgment of the district court.

## NOTES AND QUESTIONS

**1.** Could Nebraska enact a law mandating more generous leave policies for pregnant employees than other nonpregnant employees? See California Federal Savings & Loan Association v. Guerra, 479 U.S. 272 (1987) (upholding California law). In the absence of a statutory requirement, would it be lawful for an employer to treat pregnant employees more favorably? See Harness v. Hartz Mountain Corp., 877 F.2d 1307 (6th Cir.1989) (upholding employer's preferential leave policy).

**2.** Employers are not required to provide pregnant employees with light duty work, Ensley–Gaines v. Runyon, 100 F.3d 1220 (6th Cir.1996), nor to engage in reasonable accommodation for their pregnancy. For a discussion of occupational safety and health issues related to fertile and pregnant women employees, see Chapter 8, infra.

## THE FAMILY AND MEDICAL LEAVE ACT OF 1993

The Family and Medical Leave Act of 1993, 29 U.S.C. §§ 2601–2654, for the first time requires as a matter of federal law that employers provide leaves of absence for childbirth or the care of children or other family members. Employers of 50 or more employees must permit eligible workers to take up to 12 weeks of unpaid leave in any 12–month period for the birth or adoption of a child, to care for a child, spouse, or parent with a serious health condition, or for the worker's own serious health condition that makes him or her unable to perform the job. Only workers who have been employed by the employer for at least 12 months and have at least 1,250 hours of service during that period are eligible for statutory leave. "Serious health condition" is defined as an illness, injury, impairment, or physical or mental condition that involves inpatient care or continuing treatment by a health care provider. An employer may require medical certification, including a second or third opinion at its expense, of the need for a leave to care for a sick relative or for the employee's own illness.

An employee may elect, or the employer may require the employee to substitute, any accrued paid vacation leave, personal or family leave, or medical or sick leave for any part of the 12–week leave provided by the Act. When leave for childbirth or adoption is foreseeable, the employee must give at least 30 days' notice of his or her intention to take a leave; when medical leave is foreseeable because of a planned treatment, the employee must make a reasonable effort to schedule the treatment in a manner that will not unduly disrupt the employer's operations, and the employee must give 30 days' notice if possible. If a husband and wife work for the same employer, the employer may limit their aggregate number of weeks of leave for birth, adoption, or care of a sick parent to 12 in a 12–month period.

During the leave the employer must continue to provide health care benefits at the same level and under the same conditions as if the employee were actively at work. If the employee fails to return from leave for a reason other than the continuation, recurrence, or onset of a serious health condition that would entitle the employee to leave under the Act, or for some other reason beyond the employee's control, the employer may recover any premium it paid to maintain the employee's coverage during the leave. When the employee returns from leave, the employer must restore him or her to the same or an equivalent position, with no loss of employment benefits accrued before the date the leave began. The employer may, however, deny restoration of employment to a salaried employee who is among the highest paid ten percent of its workforce, if the denial is "necessary to prevent substantial and grievous economic injury" to its operations, and the employer notifies the employee of its determination.

The enforcement mechanisms of the Act are similar to those under the Fair Labor Standards Act. The Act may be enforced through suit in either federal or state court by employees individually or on behalf of themselves and other similarly situated employees, or by the Secretary of Labor. An employee's right to bring suit terminates if the Secretary brings an action on his or her behalf. The statute of limitations is two years from the last event constituting a violation and three years for willful violations. The Department of Labor may receive and investigate employee complaints, but, as under the FLSA, there is no administrative prerequisite to suit.

Remedies for violations of the Act include lost wages and benefits plus interest, or, if the employee has not lost any wages or benefits, any actual monetary losses the employee sustained as a direct result of the violation, plus interest. The statute mentions the cost of providing care as an example of these non-wage losses. In addition, plaintiffs may recover an amount equal to the monetary recovery as liquidated damages, subject to reduction by the court if the employer proves it acted in good faith and with reasonable grounds for believing it was not in violation of the Act. The court must award a victorious plaintiff reasonable attorney's fees, reasonable witness fees, and costs. Because the statute speaks only of fee awards from defendants to plaintiffs, fee awards under the Act are not available to prevailing defendants.

There are currently 26 states with such laws, 14 applicable to the public and private sector and 12 applicable only in the public sector. The states vary in whether they require leave for the birth of a child, adoption, family illness (including the employee's own illness), or some combination of the three. The duration of the leave ranges from six weeks to two years. Most state laws provide that employees on leave can continue group health and other benefits at their own expense, while some states also specify which benefits must be extended and at what cost to the employee.

For examples of judicial construction of state family leave laws, see e.g., Portland General Electric Co. v. Bureau of Labor & Industries, 859 P.2d 1143 (Or.1993) (state parental leave statute allowed employee to use accrued leave during parental leave, even if employee did not meet eligibility criteria under collective bargaining agreement); Butzlaff v. Wisconsin Personnel Commission, 480 N.W.2d 559 (Wis.App.1992) (employee need not work for same employer for 52 consecutive weeks prior to leave).

# Manuel v. Westlake Polymers Corp.

66 F.3d 758 (5th Cir.1995).

■ PATRICK E. HIGGINBOTHAM, CIRCUIT JUDGE:

June Manuel appeals a summary judgment in favor of Westlake Polymers Corporation.  The district court held that Manuel did not satisfy the notice requirements of the Family and Medical Leave Act of 1993, 29 U.S.C. § 2601 et seq., because she did not expressly invoke the statute's protection when she notified her employer of her need for leave.  We reverse and remand.

June Manuel began working for Westlake Polymers Corporation in July 1986.  Manuel missed a substantial number of days of work each year.  In 1987, for example, she was absent seventeen days.  As a result, Westlake's supervisors advised Manuel that her employment would be in jeopardy if her attendance did not improve.  Despite the warning, she missed forty-nine days in 1988 and thirty days in 1990.  In June, 1991, Bryan Taylor, Westlake's Human Resources Coordinator, informed Manuel that her attendance record was unacceptable.

In 1992 Westlake established a "no fault" employment policy designed to ensure that its employees met reasonable attendance standards.  Under the terms of the policy, every absence was counted regardless of the cause of the absence.  The policy established a four-step system of progressive warnings and disciplinary measures calculated to apprise employees of attendance problems.  Step one was an oral reprimand; step two was a written warning; step three was a one-week suspension and final warning; and step four was termination.

Manuel was warned in February, July, and September of 1992, the last of which informed her that "failure to immediately correct this problem will result in more severe disciplinary action, up to and including termination."  Manuel continued to miss days of work.  On December 30, 1992, Westlake sent Manuel a formal warning letter notifying her that, since the last warning three months earlier, she had missed approximately 14 days of work.  This letter again advised her that her continued absenteeism could result in suspension or termination.

On October 6, 1993, two months after the FMLA went into effect, Manuel visited Dr. Frank Robbins seeking treatment for an ingrown toenail.  Dr. Robbins advised her that her toenail needed to be removed and that, if the procedure were performed on a Friday, she could return to work the following Monday.  Manuel notified her supervisor, Sheldon Cooley, who immediately gave her permission to take Friday, October 8th off from work.

Dr. Robbins performed the procedure that Friday, but complications developed.  Due to infection and swelling of her toe, Manuel was unable to walk without crutches.  On the following Monday, Manuel contacted Cooley and notified him that she could not return to work due to her toe.  Keeping in constant contact with Westlake, she remained absent from work for over a month. During this time, Manuel did not mention the FMLA, nor did she expressly invoke its protection. In fact, Manuel did not know the Act existed.

On November 29, 1993 at the request of Westlake, Manuel saw Dr. White, the Westlake company physician. After examining Manuel, Dr. White pronounced her able to return to work and advised her to report for work. The following day she returned to work, but Westlake promptly suspended her for four days and issued its "Final Warning/Suspension Letter for Unsatisfactory Attendance." The letter stated that "unless you are able to and actually do report for work regularly and as scheduled, your employment will be terminated."

Less than two months later, on January 25, 1994, Manuel became ill while at work and went home. She returned to work after three days, but this absence was one too many. On February 7, Westlake fired her because of her persistent attendance problem.

On April 14, 1994, Manuel sued Westlake in the United States District Court for the Western District of Louisiana, alleging that Westlake violated the Family and Medical Leave Act of 1993, 29 U.S.C. § 2601 et seq., by counting her October–November, 1993 absence as an additional step in its "no fault" policy. After conducting limited discovery, both Manuel and Westlake moved for summary judgment.

The district court granted Westlake's motion for summary judgment. The court found that Manuel notified her supervisor of the need to miss work for medical reasons but did not expressly invoke the FMLA or its protection when requesting leave. Examining the Department of Labor's interim regulations, the court noted that the regulations specified different notice requirements depending upon the foreseeability of the need for leave. Although in the case of foreseeable leave the employee "need not express certain rights under the FMLA or even mention the FMLA," 29 C.F.R. § 825.302(b), the regulation governing unforeseeable leave omitted this language and required an employee to give notice to her employer "of the need for the FMLA leave."

Noting that Manuel's extended absence in October–November, 1993 was unforeseeable, the district court determined that her ingrown toenail was not such "an obviously serious injury, such as a broken leg, cancer, or heart attack, which would trigger an employer inquiry into whether the employee intended to use FMLA leave." The court concluded that when the need for leave is unforeseeable "and when the serious medical condition alleged is not the type which would normally require an employer to inquire whether FMLA leave is needed, it is not inconvenient nor unduly burdensome to require an employee in some manner to refer, or attempt to refer, to the Act." Because Manuel did not make such an attempt, the court held that Manuel's notice to Westlake was insufficient to trigger the protection of the FMLA and granted Westlake's motion for summary judgment.

The FMLA provides eligible employees such as June Manuel twelve weeks of unpaid leave each year for "a serious health condition that makes the employee unable to perform the functions of the position of such employee." Where that leave is *foreseeable,* the Act requires that the employee:

> (B) shall provide the employer with not less than 30 days' notice, before the date the leave is to begin, of the employee's intention to take leave under such subparagraph, except that if the date of the treatment requires leave to begin in less than 30 days, the employee shall provide such notice as is practicable.

29 U.S.C. § 2612(e)(2)(B). Significantly, the Act does not specify the form of notice required for foreseeable leave, nor does it mention any notice requirement for *unforeseeable* leave.

Similarly, the legislative history of the FMLA does not mention the content of the notice that an employee must give. The Senate Report accompanying the Act explains that 30–day advance notice is required for foreseeable leave but that "[e]mployees who face emergency medical conditions or unforeseen changes will not be precluded from taking leave if they are unable to give 30 days' advance notice." The House Report is more vague, stating only that "30–day advance notice is not required in cases of medical emergency or other unforeseen events." However, neither report mentions whether an employee must expressly invoke the FMLA when taking leave.

More helpfully, the Secretary of Labor, pursuant to his statutory authority, promulgated interim regulations specifying what notice an employee must give. The interim regulations provide that, when the need for leave is foreseeable, the employee must give "at least verbal notice sufficient to make the employer aware that the employee needs FMLA-qualifying leave, and the anticipated timing and duration of the leave." Significantly, the regulation continues, providing that an employee "need not expressly assert rights under the FMLA or even mention the FMLA, but may only state that leave is needed for an expected birth or adoption, for example."

When the need for leave is unforeseeable, however, the interim regulations contain no disclaimer of notice expressly invoking the FMLA's protection. The regulation requires that an employee "should give notice to the employer of the need for FMLA leave as soon as practicable under the facts and circumstances of the particular case." Westlake interprets this difference in regulatory language as denoting that, when the need for leave is unforeseeable, an employee must mention the FMLA in order to provide sufficient notice to the employer. We disagree.

First, the regulation governing notice for unforeseeable leave does not, on its face, require express invocation of the FMLA. Rather, the regulation requires "notice of the need for FMLA leave." The reference to "FMLA leave" is ambiguous at best; it does not compel the conclusion that an employee seeking "FMLA leave" must mention the statute by name. The district court itself doubted that the phrase "FMLA leave" denotes a substantive requirement that an employee mention the FMLA when requesting leave.

Second, the absence of the disclaimer does not impose a requirement that the leave be expressly invoked by employees who could not foresee their need for leave. To the contrary, other provisions in the interim regulations suggest that the Secretary did not intend employees, including those who could not foresee their need for FMLA leave, to expressly invoke the FMLA to satisfy their notice obligation. § 825.208(a)(1) iterates:

> As noted in section 825.302(c), an employee giving notice of the need for unpaid FMLA leave does not need to expressly assert rights under the Act or even mention the FMLA to meet their [sic] obligation to provide notice, though they would need to state a qualifying reason for the needed leave.

Moreover, this regulation provides that "*[i]n all circumstances,* it is the employer's responsibility to designate leave, paid or unpaid, as FMLA-qualifying, based on information provided by the employee." If the employer does not have sufficient information about the employee's reason for taking leave, "the employer should inquire further to ascertain whether the paid leave is potentially FMLA-qualifying." To require the employee to designate her leave as pursuant to the FMLA would render these provisions meaningless, if not directly contradict them.

Any doubt as to the Secretary's intention is resolved by the final regulations, which confirm that an employee seeking leave for unforeseen medical treatment need not expressly invoke the Act's protection. Resolving the ambiguity lying at the heart of this case, the final regulation governing notice requirements for unforeseeable leave incorporates the disclaimer of express notice. 29 C.F.R. § 825.303(b) now provides that "[t]he employee need not expressly assert rights under the FMLA or even mention the FMLA, but may only state that leave is needed."

Westlake argues that this change in regulatory language confirmed that the interim regulation did require express mention of the FMLA. We disagree. The Department of Labor's explanation of the amendments to the interim regulations does not even discuss its addition. This treatment suggests that the Department of Labor was attempting to clarify the law as it existed under the interim regulation, not to remove a pre-existing duty to mention the FMLA when requesting leave.

Westlake's argument ultimately rests on a perceived regulatory error. It offers no practical reason for its proposed reading. Westlake does not explain why the Secretary would impose such a stringent requirement upon employees who cannot foresee their need for leave but not upon employees who can foresee their need for leave. Congress added the notice requirement to assist employers plan around their employees' absences. That goal is not advanced by requiring employees to expressly mention the FMLA by name: an absent employee is an absent employee.

Westlake argues that requiring express mention of the FMLA furthers the employers' ability to invoke their rights under the Act. We disagree. The FMLA grants no rights to employers that they did not possess prior to the Act. Nor do we believe that Congress added the notice provision to apprise employers of their right to pursue their statutory safeguards.

Meanwhile, requiring employees unable to foresee their need for leave to expressly invoke the FMLA's protection would significantly burden the employees. Employees often cannot foresee their need for medical or family leave. Even more than employees who can foresee their need for leave, those who cannot foresee such need are ill-equipped to identify the statutory source of their right. We do not believe that Congress, in enacting the FMLA, intended to impose such an onerous requirement on employees, particularly where employers receive no benefit from it.

We are persuaded that the interim regulations do not require employees to expressly mention the FMLA when notifying their employer of their need for FMLA leave.

Westlake argues that if the regulations permit employees to invoke the FMLA's protection without expressly mentioning the Act, they are contrary to the FMLA. We disagree. Where a statute is silent or ambiguous, we limit our inquiry to "whether the agency's answer is based on a permissible construction of the statute." Administrative regulations promulgated in response to express delegations of authority, like the one at issue here, "are given controlling weight unless they are arbitrary, capricious, or manifestly contrary to the statute."

Neither the statutory language nor the Act's legislative history disclose congressional will regarding the content of the required notice. We are unable to say that the regulations challenged here are so patently at odds with the legislative scheme as to render them invalid. To the contrary, their disclaimer of any requirement that notice must expressly invoke the FMLA is a reasonable interpretation of the statutory scheme created by Congress.

Westlake points to the "express mandate" of the statute requiring notice of the employee's intention "to take leave under such subparagraph." 29 U.S.C. § 2612(e)(2)(B). We reject the contention that the FMLA requires employees not only to invoke the statute's protection by name, but to refer to the specific subparagraph of the FMLA under which they claim protection. These are workers, not lawyers.

Congress enacted the FMLA in order *"to entitle employees* to take reasonable leave for medical purposes." Its legislative history discloses that it "is based on the same principle as the child labor laws, the minimum wage, Social Security, the safety and health laws, the pension and welfare benefit laws, and other labor laws that establish minimum standards for employment." Significantly, none of these other federal labor laws granting benefits to employees requires those employees to refer to the specific statute, much less the specific statutory subsection, in order to avail themselves of its benefits. We do not believe Congress intended to depart from this practice and require employees to consult attorneys before notifying their employer of their need for FMLA leave.

Furthermore, contrary to Westlake's suggestion, permitting employees to avail themselves of the FMLA's protection without expressly invoking the statute does not leave employers such as Westlake without protection from abuse of the Act's generous provisions, nor does it require employers to engage in intrusive inquiries to determine whether the FMLA applies. The Act permits employers notified of an employee's intent to take leave due to a serious health condition to require the employee to provide certification from a physician. If the employer has reason to doubt the validity of the certification, it may ask for a second opinion from a different physician. If the second opinion differs from the first, the employer may require a third opinion. Moreover, the employer may require recertification on a reasonable, on-going basis. In short, the FMLA provides safeguards from delinquent employees, but express notice by an employee that she takes leave pursuant to the FMLA is not one of those safeguards.

We hold that the Family and Medical Leave Act of 1993 does not require an employee to invoke the language of the statute to gain its protection when notifying her employer of her need for leave for a serious health condition.

We decline to announce any categorical rules for the content of the notice by an employee. When an employee cannot give 30–days advance notice of the need for FMLA leave, the FMLA requires notice "as is practicable." What is practicable, both in terms of the timing of the notice and its content, will depend upon the facts and circumstances of each individual case. The critical question is whether the information imparted to the employer is sufficient to reasonably apprise it of the employee's request to take time off for a serious health condition.

Congress, in enacting the FMLA, did not intend employees like June Manuel to become conversant with the legal intricacies of the Act. The district court erred by requiring such knowledge. We leave to the district court the question of whether Manuel gave Westlake sufficient notice under the FMLA.[3]

REVERSED and REMANDED.

NOTES AND QUESTIONS

**1.** Did Manuel attempt to take advantage of her employer? According to company lawyers, Manuel missed an average of 300 hours a year during her seven-year tenure at the company, including four days when her cat died. See Joann S. Lublin, Family–Leave Law Can Be Excuse for a Day Off, Wall St.J., July 7, 1995, at B1.

**2.** The Wage and Hour Division of the Labor Department issued final regulations implementing the Family and Medical Leave Act in early 1995. 60 Fed.Reg. 2180, codified at 29 C.F.R. Part 825. The regulations provide

---

**3.** We express no opinion regarding whether the complications arising from Manuel's surgery for her ingrown toenail constitute a "serious health condition."

that to be a "serious health condition," there must be a period of incapacity of more than three days. According to the Labor Department, the FMLA was not intended to cover short-term conditions for which treatment and recovery are very brief because Congress expected that such conditions would be covered by "even the most modest of employer sick leave policies." Some critics of the "more than three day" rule argued unsuccessfully that it encourages employees to remain absent from work longer than necessary in order to qualify for statutory protection. Other critics, however, have contended that "more than three days" is too short and that the FMLA was not intended to cover short-term absences caused by routine illnesses, but only long-term absences caused by serious health conditions.

**3.** Several cases have been decided on the issue of what is a "serious illness." See, e.g., Oswalt v. Sara Lee Corp., 74 F.3d 91 (5th Cir.1996) (food poisoning not a serious illness); Bauer v. Dayton–Walther Corp., 910 F.Supp. 306 (E.D.Ky.1996) (rectal bleeding not a serious illness); Brannon v. Oshkosh B'Gosh, 897 F.Supp. 1028 (M.D.Tenn.1995) (gastroenteritis and upper respiratory infection not a serious illness).

**4.** If the employee fails to return to work at the end of the leave, the employee loses protection under the FMLA. In Brown v. J.C. Penney Corp., 924 F.Supp. 1158 (S.D.Fla.1996), the employee took 12 weeks of leave to care for her terminally ill father. The employee did not return to work until five days after the 12–week period had ended, some 30 days after the death of her father. The court held that the employee lost the protection of the FMLA.

**5.** The courts are divided over whether supervisors may be individually liable under the FMLA. See Frizzell v. Southwest Motor Freight, Inc., 906 F.Supp. 441 (E.D.Tenn.1995) (no individual liability); Freemon v. Foley, 911 F.Supp. 326 (N.D.Ill.1995) (individual liability).

**6.** The next wave of leave laws may be those requiring employers to provide a certain number of unpaid "personal leave" hours or days per year. The employee could use this time off to attend to personal matters such as medical appointments, court appearances, weddings, funerals, and parent conferences at school. Some states already provide such leave for state employees. See, e.g., Ohio Rev.Code Ann. § 124.386.

b. MARITAL STATUS

# Braatz v. Labor & Industry Review Commission

496 N.W.2d 597 (Wis.1993).

■ STEINMETZ, JUSTICE.

The issue in this case is whether the Labor and Industry Review Commission ("LIRC") properly concluded that the marital status provisions of the Wisconsin Fair Employment Act ("WFEA") permit the school district of Maple's health insurance nonduplication policy. The circuit court answered in the negative, and LIRC appealed from the judgment.

The court of appeals affirmed the circuit court's judgment in Braatz v. LIRC, 168 Wis.2d 124, 483 N.W.2d 246 (Ct.App.1992).

We affirm the court of appeals reversal of LIRC's decision. The school district of Maple's nonduplication policy constitutes marital status discrimination which is prohibited under the WFEA. Health insurance is not excepted from this prohibition, expressly or implicitly.

The facts of this case are not in dispute. The plaintiffs are teachers employed by the Maple School District. Each teacher is married; each teacher's spouse is employed; and each spouse's employer offers health insurance benefits to the spouse.

The 1986–87 collective bargaining agreement between the Maple Federation of Teachers and the Maple Board of Education provides as follows:

Article V–A. Insurance. Health, Life, Dental and Long Term Disability.

Section 1. Health and Hospitalization Insurance Coverage:

Hospital, medical and major medical coverage for the employees and their family will be provided if requested by the employee through the existing contract with the insurance company presently providing coverage to district employees. All requests for hospital, medical, and major medical will be subjected to the limitations outlined in a, b, c and d below:

a. All single employees may request single coverage under this plan.

b. Unmarried person who has the care custody or support of any minor children of said unmarried person is eligible for family coverage if the policy so warrants.

c. A married employee is entitled to family coverage.

d. A married teacher who [sic] spouse is eligible for family coverage at his/her place of work shall have the option of carrying either the district's policy or the spouse's policy but not both. If the spouse carries a single plan, the employee of the district shall be eligible for a single plan through the district.

(1) Employees who are presently duplicating insurance coverage who do not fall into the above guidelines would be allowed to do so if they notify the school district that they wish to have the premium for health insurance deducted from their paycheck. Employees who do not fall into the above guidelines who are duplicating insurance and do not wish to have the premium deducted from their paycheck will have to notify the school district that they wish to have their health coverage with the district terminated.

(2) The Board would allow duplicate coverage if the employee's other insurance policy provided significantly less coverage than the School District of Maple's policy. This would be determined by the school administration.

The LIRC describes this condition of employment as simply a "health insurance non-duplication policy." However, it is a non-duplication policy applicable only to married employees. Married employees, with employed spouses who are covered by comparable employer provided health insurance, are forced to elect the district's policy or the spouse's policy. The plaintiffs in this case were forced to make this election.

The WFEA prohibits employers from "discriminat[ing] against any individual in promotion, compensation or in terms, conditions or privileges of employment" on the basis of marital status. Section 111.322(1); sec. 111.321, Stats. Section 111.32(12) defines marital status as "the status of being married, single, divorced, separated or widowed."

There is only one express exception to this prohibition against marital status discrimination. It provides as follows: "Notwithstanding 111.322, it is not employment discrimination because of marital status to prohibit an individual from directly supervising or being directly supervised by his or her spouse." Section 111.345, Stats.

The declaration of policy in sec. 111.31(3), Stats., mandates liberal construction of the WFEA:

> In the interpretation and application of this subchapter, and otherwise, it is declared to be the public policy of the state to encourage and foster to the fullest extent practicable the employment of all properly qualified individuals regardless of * * * marital status * * *. This subchapter shall be liberally construed for the accomplishment of this purpose.

LIRC argues that the school district of Maple's policy does not discriminate based on marital status. Instead, application of the policy is triggered by the conduct of an employee's spouse (choosing to work, accepting health insurance benefits from an employer, etc.) rather than marital status. Because LIRC did not rely on this rationale in its decision, we review this interpretation of the school district's policy de novo.

We disagree with LIRC's interpretation. The school district's policy constitutes marital status discrimination. It is only married employees with duplicate coverage who must make a choice between the district's policy or the policy provided by their spouse's employer. Single employees who have health insurance coverage from another source are not forced to choose between that coverage and the district's coverage.

Moreover, the choice required by the district's policy does not account for an employee's death or divorce, which may terminate the former spouse's coverage through the district and leave him or her unable to obtain a single or family policy elsewhere, especially if not qualifying healthwise. This problem would not exist if spouses were allowed to accept their employer-provided health insurance in addition to the district's coverage.

Also, insurance companies consider double policies within a family by allowing coverage only by a primary carrier. The policy can state that it is secondary to any other coverage and therefore the premium can be lower. This, of course, will raise an issue of which policy is primary coverage.

In its decision, LIRC concluded that the school district's policy did not violate the WFEA because health insurance benefits are implicitly excepted from the WFEA's prohibition against marital status discrimination. In support of its implied exception theory, LIRC argues that the fact that the state of Wisconsin, as an employer and by statute, offers different health insurance benefits to married and single employees evinces a legislative intent to allow employers in general to do the same.

LIRC specifically refers to two state practices. First, the state offers dependent health insurance benefits to an employee's spouse but not to an employee's adult companion, although dependant in fact. See sec. 40.02(20), Stats.; Phillips v. Wisconsin Personnel Commission, 167 Wis.2d 205, 482 N.W.2d 121 (Ct.App.1992). Second, if both spouses are state employees and one spouse elects family coverage, the state provides coverage to the other spouse as a dependant but prohibits that spouse from electing other coverage.

Because LIRC's decision was based on this implied exception theory, this court will uphold LIRC's interpretation of the WFEA if it is reasonable and not clearly contrary to legislative intent. Interpretation of a statute and application of that statute to undisputed facts presents a question of law. Generally, an agency's conclusion of law is reviewed *de novo*. However, in this case we give deference to LIRC's conclusion because LIRC has experience in interpreting the marital status discrimination provision of the WFEA.

Health insurance benefits are not implicitly excepted from the WFEA's prohibition against marital status discrimination. There is no reasonable basis to support LIRC's conclusion. LIRC's conclusion is simply contrary to the intent of the legislature.

The fact that the state offers dependant health insurance benefits to an employee's spouse but not to an employee's adult companion does not support LIRC's implied exception theory. *Phillips* held that this practice does not constitute marital status discrimination. The court reasoned that "[i]t is only where similarly situated persons are treated differently that discrimination is an issue." Even though an employee and an adult companion may "have a committed relationship that partakes of many of the attributes of marriage in the traditional sense," a spouse and a companion are not similarly situated. This is so because Wisconsin law imposes a mutual duty of general support upon married couples, but there is no comparable duty of support imposed upon adult companions.

In effect, the plaintiff in *Phillips* wanted something not even married employees got: reimbursement for medical expenses that she had no obligation to pay. *Phillips* and the policy reviewed therein are not relevant to this case.

The state's policy of prohibiting duplication of health insurance by married couples employed by the state also does not support LIRC's position.   Even if we assume *arguendo* that this policy indicates that there is an implied exception to the WFEA's prohibition against marital status discrimination, the school district of Maple's policy would not fall within this exception.   The state's policy is not the same as the Maple policy.   The state's policy only applies where both spouses are employed by the state.   Maple's policy applies no matter where the employee's spouse is employed.

Further support for our conclusion that health insurance benefits are not excepted from the WFEA's prohibition against marital status discrimination is found in sec. 111.33(2)(d), Stats.   That section excepts health insurance from the WFEA's prohibition against age discrimination.   It states that it is not age discrimination "[t]o apply varying insurance coverage according to an employe's age."   This exception indicates that the legislature considered the WFEA's effect on health insurance issues, chose to create an exception for age discrimination, but chose not to create an exception for marital status discrimination.

Finally, our conclusion is supported by the WFEA's liberal construction clause, referred to above.   Limiting the reach of the WFEA's prohibition against marital status discrimination with an implied exception is certainly not liberal construction.

We hold that the district's policy violates the WFEA.   The policy constitutes marital status discrimination and does not fall within an exception, express or implied, to the WFEA's prohibition against such discrimination.

The decision of the court of appeals is affirmed.

NOTE

**1.** In Tumeo v. University of Alaska, 1995 WL 238359 (Alaska Super.1995), the court held that the defendant's health benefits plan, which provides benefits to employees' spouses, but not to employees' cohabiting "partners" violates a state law prohibiting discrimination on the basis of marital status.   In 1996, *Tumeo* was legislatively overruled.   Alaska Stat. § 18.80.220 allows employers to provide greater health and retirement benefits for workers who are married or who have dependent children than for unmarried or childless workers.   See University of Alaska v. Tumeo, 933 P.2d 1147 (Alaska 1997).

c.   SEXUAL ORIENTATION

# Rovira v. AT & T

817 F.Supp. 1062 (S.D.N.Y.1993).

■ PATTERSON, DISTRICT JUDGE.

This is an action for declaratory relief and damages alleging violations of the Employee Retirement Income Security Act ("ERISA"), 29 U.S.C. § 1001 et seq.   Plaintiffs allege that Defendant American Telegraph & Telephone Company ("AT & T"), in its administration of the AT & T

Management Pension Plan (the "Plan"), discriminates against its employees on the basis of marital status and sexual orientation in determining beneficiary eligibility for Sickness Death Benefits under the Plan. Defendant AT & T moves for summary judgment pursuant to Rule 56(b) of the Federal Rules of Civil Procedure, and Plaintiffs cross move for partial summary judgment. For the reasons set forth below, Defendant's motion for summary judgment is granted, and Plaintiffs' motion for partial summary judgment is denied.

Marjorie Forlini, an AT & T employee, died of cancer in 1988. Plaintiff Sandra Rovira was her gay life partner, and plaintiffs Frank and Alfred Morales (the "Moraleses") are Rovira's biological adult children from a prior marriage who lived with Rovira and Forlini for ten of the twelve years the two women lived together.

In 1976, Forlini and Rovira entered into what proved to be a long and committed relationship. The couple formalized their relationship on March 7, 1977, in a ceremony "during which they exchanged rings and vows. Though as a lesbian couple (residing in New York) they were not entitled to marry, Sandra [Rovira] and Marjorie [Forlini] utilized the same symbolic ceremony usually associated with marriage to commit themselves to each other for the rest of their lives." On March 7, 1987, Rovira and Forlini signed an unofficial certificate attesting to their commitment and relationship.

In 1978, the Moraleses, then aged 11 and 8, came to live with Rovira and Forlini. Although Rovira was the biological mother of the Moraleses, their tuition, medical bills, food, clothing, housing, entertainment and other expenses were paid from the joint financial resources of Forlini and Rovira. From 1979 to 1984, Forlini claimed one or both of the Moraleses as "dependents" on her tax returns and described them therein as her "godchild[ren]." Indeed, throughout their relationship, Rovira and Forlini "pooled their [financial] resources, shared responsibility for making the important decisions affecting their lives, jointly owned their home [and] took vacations together."

In 1988, Rovira was named the beneficiary of Forlini's life insurance policy, which was provided to Forlini as a benefit of her employment with AT & T. Forlini listed Rovira as her "friend" under the relationship column of the life insurance designation form. In Forlini's Last Will and Testament, Rovira was named the residuary legatee and executor of Forlini's estate. As the residuary legatee of Forlini's estate, Rovira received between $20,000 and $30,000 in cash and Forlini's car. Forlini's will did not, however, refer to Rovira as her spouse, and did not mention the Moraleses. Pursuant to a right of survivorship, Rovira also received Forlini's share of the house they co-owned and which was worth $300,000.

As an AT & T sales manager, Forlini was covered under the Plan, an employee benefit plan governed by ERISA that provides for payment of a Sickness Death Benefit to the eligible beneficiaries of deceased employees who participated in the Plan. The Plan limits eligible beneficiaries for

Sickness Death Benefits to three categories of persons: "the spouse and the dependent children and other dependent relatives of the deceased."

The Plan further creates two categories of beneficiaries: mandatory and discretionary. With respect to the mandatory beneficiary category, the Plan states that "the maximum benefit shall be paid to the spouse, dependent children, or a dependent parent living with or in a household in the vicinity that is provided by the employee." With regard to the discretionary beneficiary category, the Plan states that "a Sickness Death Benefit * * * may be paid to other dependent relatives," and it grants AT & T's Employees' Benefit Committee, the "final review committee" on all decisions involving benefit claims, "full authority to determine to whom payments shall be paid and the amount of the payments, taking into consideration the degree of dependency and such other facts as it may deem pertinent."

Under section 3(2)(e)(i) of the Plan, the Employees' Benefit Committee "shall grant or deny claims for benefits under the Plan with respect to employees of each Participating Company, respectively, and authorize disbursements according to this Plan." The Employees' Benefit Committee are trustees of the Plan pursuant to the provisions of ERISA.

* * *

Pursuant to its legal obligations under ERISA, AT & T created and gave its salaried employees, including Forlini, a Summary Plan Description ("SPD") that summarizes the provisions of the Plan. The eligible beneficiary categories listed in the SPD mirror the beneficiary categories contained in the Plan. * * *

Pursuant to ERISA, AT & T distributed copies of the SPD and the interpretive Death Benefit Guidelines, but not the Plan, to its employees.

AT & T also published an AT & T Personnel Guide and the AT & T Equal Employment Opportunity/Affirmative Action Employee Reference Guide (the "E.O. Reference Guide"). Both Guides contain guidelines opposing discrimination against employees. Neither the Plan, the SPD, nor the interpretive Death Benefit Guidelines are referred to in the Personnel Guide or the E.O. Reference Guide.

In the Personnel Guide, AT & T defines equal opportunity in general to mean "that all employment decisions are made and personnel policies are administered without discrimination on the basis of * * * sexual preference or orientation [or] marital status * * *." The Personnel Guide then explains that it is AT & T's particular policy to "[p]rohibit unlawful discrimination * * * because of race, color, religion, national origin, sex, age * * * in any employment decision or in the administration of any personnel policy." "The use of a person's sexual preference or orientation, or marital status," on the other hand, is prohibited "as a criterion in personnel decisions." While the Personnel Guide does not elaborate on the distinctions between "employment decisions," "administration of any personnel policy" and "personnel decisions," it states that the equal opportunity policy "applies to all aspects of employment at AT & T, specifically including benefits * * *."

The E.O. Reference Guide contains similar guidelines for non-discrimination toward AT & T's employees, although its legal effect is limited by a "Notice" on the first page of the Reference Guide stating:

> This guide is not a contract of employment but a set of guidelines for the implementation of personnel policies. It should not be interpreted to create any expressed [sic] or implied contractual rights between AT & T and any employee. AT & T explicitly reserves the right to modify or rescind the provisions in this guide at any time and without notice within the limits permitted by law.

* * *

In October 1988, Rovira submitted a claim to AT & T as a mandatory beneficiary for the Sickness Death Benefits provided as part of Forlini's AT & T employment benefits plan, alleging that she stood in the position of spouse of Forlini. AT & T's Employee Benefits Department denied the claim orally. On January 9, 1989, the Moraleses also claimed a benefit as mandatory beneficiaries and as discretionary beneficiaries under the Plan, alleging that they stood in the position of dependent children or dependent relatives of Forlini. That claim too was denied orally by the Employee Benefits Department.

On April 26, 1989, Plaintiffs appealed both denials of Sickness Death Benefits to the AT & T Benefit Committee, which, as the intermediate review committee below the Employees' Benefit Committee, makes initial reviews of denials of benefits by the Employee Benefits Department. The Plaintiffs' appeal to the Benefit Committee relied in part upon AT & T's equal opportunity policy contained in the AT & T Personnel Guide. On June 19, 1989, the AT & T Benefit Committee considered the Plaintiffs' claims for Sickness Death Benefits totalling $53,000. "Two members voted in favor of paying the benefit * * *. Two members voted against paying any benefit to the plaintiffs."

* * *

The AT & T benefit committee's decision was appealed to the Employees' Benefit Committee, the final review committee, which reviewed Plaintiffs' applications at its meeting on November 14, 1989. In voting to deny Plaintiffs' benefits claims pursuant to the Plan, the Committee stated:

> The Committee determined that because Ms. Forlini and Ms. Rovira's relationship is not recognized as a valid marriage in the state in which they resided, Ms. Rovira does not meet the eligibility criteria to qualify as a beneficiary under the provisions of the [Plan]. Dependent children must be either the natural or adopted children of the employee, or the natural or adopted children of the employee's legal spouse. The Committee determined that because Frank and Alfred Morales are not the natural or adopted children of Ms. Forlini or of her legal spouse, they also do not qualify as

beneficiaries under the provisions of the [Plan]. The Committee also noted that the provisions of the [Plan] are administered uniformly to all employees without discrimination on the basis of race, color, religion, national origin, sex, sexual preference or orientation.

On August 20, 1990, Plaintiffs filed the present complaint, in which they allege that the Employees' Benefit Committee's denial of their claims for death benefits was arbitrary and capricious.

\* \* \*

The AT & T Employees' Benefit Committee's denial of Plaintiffs' Sickness Death Benefits challenged under 29 U.S.C. § 1132(a)(1)(B) is to be "reviewed under a de novo standard unless the benefit plan gives the administrator or fiduciary discretionary authority to determine eligibility for benefits or to construe the terms of the plan."

\* \* \*

Certain provisions of the Plan appear to give the Employees' Benefit Committee discretionary authority to determine eligibility for benefits.

\* \* \*

The Plan does not, however, expressly confer upon the Committee the power to interpret or construe the terms or provisions of the Plan, nor does it state that the Committee's eligibility determinations are to be given deference. Furthermore, some Plan provisions regarding Sickness Death Benefits contain categorical language that evidence no grant of discretion to the Committee under the present circumstances with regard to mandatory death beneficiaries.

Accordingly, since the Plan does not indicate unambiguously that the Plan administrator, AT & T, shall wield discretionary authority over benefits decisions, the Court will subject the AT & T Employees' Benefits Committee's denial of the claimed benefits to a de novo standard of review.

The Plan is a contract between private parties—AT & T and its employees. Defining a beneficiary as "a person designated by a participant, or by the terms of an employee benefit plan, who is or may become entitled to a benefit thereunder," ERISA "provides for enforcement of the terms of a plan agreement and gives a participant or beneficiary the right to bring a civil action."

To establish that they have standing to bring this case under ERISA, Plaintiffs must make out a "colorable" claim that they are beneficiaries under the Plan because they are or will become eligible for Sickness Death Benefits under the terms of the Plan. This Plaintiffs have not done. First, there is no showing on the record that Forlini, as an AT & T Plan participant, designated Rovira as a Sickness Death Benefit beneficiary or a beneficiary of any sort under the Plan or referred to Rovira as her spouse or life partner in any employment or benefit-related document. There is also no showing on the record that Forlini specifically designated or intended the Moraleses to receive Sickness Death Benefits, or that she referred to either of the Moraleses in any employment or benefit-related documents as her adopted children, step-children or relatives.

Second, the terms of the Plan documents, especially the interpretive Death Benefit Guidelines, plainly limit eligible beneficiaries to legal spouses, and persons who are either the dependent adopted children, step-children, or dependent relatives of the participant.

* * *

Under the terms of the Plan documents, therefore, Rovira is not a designated mandatory beneficiary because she is not Forlini's legal spouse.

Plaintiffs argue, relying on New York law, that Rovira is the functional equivalent of a spouse and therefore should be eligible as a mandatory beneficiary under the Plan, that the Moraleses are the functional equivalent of Forlini's children and therefore should qualify as mandatory beneficiaries, and that for all functional purposes they are Forlini's "relatives" who qualify as discretionary beneficiaries.

With regard to Rovira's claim for benefits as a mandatory beneficiary, the plain words of the SPD and the Plan, which bind the Employees' Benefits Committee in its interpretations of the Plan and determinations thereunder, require a legal marriage rather than a putative or functional one.  In this case, the Committee members who voted to deny Rovira's claim for benefits construed "spouse" as stated under the Plan and "legal spouse" in the SPD by its plain meaning to require a marriage valid under state law.  There is no evidence that as trustees under the Plan they had ever interpreted the term in any other way.

As for the Moraleses' claim for benefits as mandatory beneficiaries on the ground that they are Forlini's dependent children, the plain meaning of the term "children" requires that the beneficiary be the natural, adopted or step-child of Forlini, the Plan participant.  The Moraleses fall into none of these categories: The record indicates that Forlini did not adopt them, nor are they the children of Forlini's spouse by a previous marriage.

Therefore, the Moraleses are not mandatory beneficiaries, nor, under the plain meaning of the term, are they "relatives" of Forlini either by birth or by marriage who may qualify as discretionary beneficiaries.

Plaintiffs contend, however, that by limiting the class of eligible beneficiaries to legal spouses and dependent children and relatives, AT & T breached its promises, contained in its equal opportunity policy, not to discriminate on the basis of marital status or sexual orientation in the administration of benefits.  They argue that where an employer adopts a non-discrimination policy which it states is applicable to the administration of employees' benefits, that policy must be followed with regard to the administration of plan benefits, and that, without such application, the policy has no meaning and in failing to fulfill its promises to its employees the employer violates ERISA.

The SPD and the interpretive Death Benefit Guidelines, copies of which AT & T furnished to Forlini, as well as the Plan itself, are the only controlling documents that form part of the terms of the Plan agreement, and that apply to the administration of the Plan. They are the only documents upon which the Employees' Benefits Committee, trustees of the Plan, as fiduciaries can rely in making eligibility determinations and discharging their duties under the Plan.

AT & T's equal opportunity policy not to discriminate on the basis of marital status or sexual orientation is addressed to personnel, i.e., employees, and there is no showing that it was "intended to apply to any person other than the employee herself."

In fact, the E.O. Reference Guide contains a notice that it does not confer any contractual rights at all. In short, the policy contained in the E.O. Reference Guide, and presumably the Personnel Guide, is disaffirmed as conferring contractual rights on AT & T's employees. Thus, AT & T's equal opportunity policy does not create third party beneficiary rights on Plaintiffs allowing them to recover Plan benefits pursuant to ERISA.

\* \* \*

In addition, Plaintiffs have not pointed to any evidence on the record that Forlini relied to her detriment on the representations contained in the equal opportunity policy, or that the equal opportunity policy's general non-discrimination provisions misled Forlini about her Sickness Death Benefits or defeated her reasonable expectations concerning the administration of the Sickness Death Benefits.

Plaintiffs also fail to make out a "colorable" claim for discrimination cognizable under ERISA. Plaintiffs point to several New York state law cases to argue that AT & T's denial of benefits to them is based on discrimination against unmarried couples and gays and lesbians. Where ERISA is involved, however, these state cases cannot provide guidance as to the outcome. "ERISA's preemption provision is very broad: ERISA 'shall supersede any and all State laws insofar as they may now or hereafter relate to any employee benefit plan described in section 1003(a) of this title.' Under this provision, pension plan regulation is made an exclusively federal concern."

Of course, discrimination "constitutes a fiduciary breach for purposes of ERISA." But provisions within governing documents of ERISA-covered pension plans limiting the class of eligible beneficiaries to actual spouses and defining the term "spouse" to require a marriage valid under state law, as is the case here, are not per se unreasonable or discriminatory under ERISA.

In sum, based on a de novo review, the decision of AT & T's Employees' Benefits Committee to deny Rovira and the Moraleses Sickness Death Benefits under AT & T's Management Pension Plan was not incorrect, and Plaintiffs are not entitled to damages. Accordingly, AT & T's motion for summary judgment is granted, and Plaintiffs' motion for partial summary judgment is denied.

NOTES AND QUESTIONS

**1.**  In Ross v. Denver Department of Health & Hospitals, 883 P.2d 516 (Colo.App.1994), cert. denied (Colo.1994), the court held that a city-employed social worker was not eligible for family sick leave benefits while she took care of her injured same-sex life partner.  The court held that the plaintiff's application was not denied because of her sexual orientation, but because her life partner is not a member of her "immediate family," which was defined to include spouses, parents, siblings, and in-laws, but which excludes nonmarried lovers.  "Ross is thus in the same situation, and was treated the same, as all unmarried heterosexual men and women."  Do you agree?

**2.**  In Rutgers Council of AAUP Chapters v. Rutgers, 689 A.2d 828 (N.J.Super.1997), the court held that denial of health insurance coverage to same-sex domestic partners did not violate state discrimination law, equal protection, order an executive order of the governor prohibiting discrimination on the basis of sexual orientation.

**3.**  Although not required to do so by law, many companies have extended health insurance benefits to same-sex partners of employees.  Among the companies offering such benefits are American Express, Barnes & Noble, Chevron, Coors, Disney, Eastman Kodak, Microsoft, and Shell.  These companies generally extend benefits to homosexual partners but not heterosexual partners.  Why?  Do these policies raise any problems?

## 7.  RETIREE BENEFITS

### Curtiss–Wright Corp. v. Schoonejongen

514 U.S. 73 (1995).

■ JUSTICE O'CONNOR delivered the opinion of the Court.

Section 402(b)(3) of the Employee Retirement Income Security Act of 1974 (ERISA), 88 Stat. 875, 29 U.S.C. § 1102(b)(3), requires that every employee benefit plan provide "a procedure for amending such plan, and for identifying the persons who have authority to amend the plan."  This case presents the question whether the standard provision in many employer-provided benefit plans stating that "The Company reserves the right at any time to amend the plan" sets forth an amendment procedure that satisfies § 402(b)(3).  We hold that it does.

For many years, petitioner Curtiss–Wright voluntarily maintained a postretirement health plan for employees who had worked at certain Curtiss–Wright facilities; respondents are retirees who had worked at one such facility in Wood–Ridge, New Jersey.  The specific terms of the plan, the District Court determined, could be principally found in two plan documents; the plan constitution and the Summary Plan Description (SPD), both of which primarily covered active employee health benefits.

In early 1983, presumably due to the rising cost of health care, a revised SPD was issued with the following new provision: "TERMI-NATION OF HEALTH CARE BENEFITS. . . . Coverage under this Plan will cease for retirees and their dependents upon the termination of business operations of the facility from which they retired." The two main authors of the new SPD provision, Curtiss–Wright's director of benefits and its labor counsel, testified that they did not think the provision effected a "change" in the plan, but rather merely clarified it. Probably for this reason, the record is less than clear as to which Curtiss–Wright officers or committees had authority to make plan amendments on behalf of the company and whether such officers or committees approved or ratified the new SPD provision. In any event, later that year, Curtiss–Wright announced that the Wood–Ridge facility would close. Shortly thereafter, an executive vice president wrote respondents a series of letters informing them that their post-retirement health benefits were being terminated.

Respondents brought suit in federal court over the termination of their benefits, and many years of litigation ensued. The District Court ultimately rejected most of respondents' claims, including their contention that Curtiss–Wright had bound itself contractually to provide health benefits to them for life. The District Court agreed, however, that the new SPD provision effected a significant change in the plan's terms and thus constituted an "amendment" to the plan; that the plan documents nowhere contained a valid amendment procedure, as required by § 402(b)(3); and that the proper remedy for the § 402(b)(3) violation was to declare the new SPD provision void *ab initio*. The court eventually ordered Curtiss–Wright to pay respondents $2,681,086 in back benefits.

On appeal, Curtiss–Wright primarily argued that the plan documents did contain an amendment procedure, namely, the standard reservation clause contained in the plan constitution and in a few secondary plan documents. The clause states: "The Company reserves the right at any time and from time to time to modify or amend, in whole or in part, any or all of the provisions of the Plan." In Curtiss–Wright's view, this clause sets forth an amendment procedure as required by the statute. It says, in effect, that the plan is to be amended by *"[t]he Company."*

The Court of Appeals for the Third Circuit rejected this argument, as well as all other arguments before it, and affirmed the District Court's remedy. It explained: "A primary purpose of § 402(b)(3) is to ensure that all interested parties [including beneficiaries] will know how a plan may be altered and who may make such alterations. Only if they know this information will they be able to determine with certainty at any given time exactly what the plan provides." And the court suggested that § 402(b)(3) cannot serve that purpose unless it is read to require that every amendment procedure specify precisely "what individuals or bodies within the Company c[an] promulgate an effective amendment." In the court's view, then, a reservation clause that says that the plan may be amended "by the Company," without more, is too vague.

* * *

In a footnote, the court related the concurring views of Judge Roth. According to the court, Judge Roth thought that the notion of an amendment "by the Company" should be read in light of traditional corporate law principles, which is to say amendment "by the board of directors or whomever of the company has the authority to take such action." And read in this more specific way, "by the Company" indicates a valid amendment procedure that satisfies § 402(b)(3). She concurred rather than dissented, however, because, in the court's words, "neither [Curtiss–Wright's] board nor any other person or entity within [Curtiss–Wright] with the power to act on behalf of 'the Company' ratified [the new SPD provision]."

Curtiss–Wright petitioned for certiorari on the questions whether a plan provision stating that "[t]he Company" reserves the right to amend the plan states a valid amendment procedure under § 402(b)(3) and, if not, whether the proper remedy is to declare this or any other amendment void *ab initio*. We granted certiorari on both.

In interpreting § 402(b)(3), we are mindful that ERISA does not create any substantive entitlement to employer-provided health benefits or any other kind of welfare benefits. Employers or other plan sponsors are generally free under ERISA, for any reason at any time, to adopt, modify, or terminate welfare plans. Nor does ERISA establish any minimum participation, vesting, or funding requirements for welfare plans as it does for pension plans. Accordingly, that Curtiss–Wright amended its plan to deprive respondents of health benefits is not a cognizable complaint under ERISA; the only cognizable claim is that the company did not do so in a permissible manner.

The text of § 402(b)(3) actually requires *two* things: a "procedure for amending [the] plan" *and* "[a procedure] for identifying the persons who have authority to amend the plan." With respect to the second requirement, the general "Definitions" section of ERISA makes quite clear that the term "person," wherever it appears in the statute, includes companies. The Curtiss–Wright reservation clause thus appears to satisfy the statute's identification requirement by naming "[t]he Company" as "the perso[n]" with amendment authority.

The text of § 402(b)(3) speaks, somewhat awkwardly, of requiring a *procedure* for identifying the persons with amendment authority, rather than requiring identification of those persons outright. Be that as it may, a plan that simply identifies the persons outright necessarily indicates a procedure for identifying the persons as well. With respect to the Curtiss–Wright plan, for example, to identify "[t]he Company" as the person with amendment authority is to say, in effect, that the procedure for identifying the person with amendment authority is to look always to "[t]he Company." Such an identification procedure is more substantial than might first appear.  To say that one must look always to "[t]he Company" is to say that one must look *only* to "[t]he Company" and *not* to any other person— that is, not to any union, not to any third-party trustee, and not to any of the other kinds of outside parties that, in many other plans, exercise amendment authority.

The more difficult question in this case is whether the Curtiss–Wright reservation clause contains a "procedure for amending [the] plan."  To recall, the reservation clause says in effect that the plan may be amended "by the Company."  Curtiss–Wright is correct, we think, that this states an amendment procedure and one that, like the identification procedure, is more substantial than might first appear.  It says the plan may be amended by a unilateral company decision to amend, and only by such a decision—and not, for example, by the unilateral decision of a third-party trustee or upon the approval of the union.  Moreover, to the extent that this procedure *is* the barest of procedures, that is because the Curtiss– Wright plan is the simplest of plans: a voluntarily maintained single-employer health plan that is administered by the employer and funded by the employer.  More complicated plans, such as multiemployer plans, may have more complicated amendment procedures, and § 402(b)(3) was designed to cover them as well.

In any event, the literal terms of § 402(b)(3) are ultimately indifferent to the level of detail in an amendment procedure, or in an identification procedure for that matter.  The provision requires only that there *be* an amendment procedure, which here there is.  A "procedure," as that term is commonly understood, is a "particular way" of doing something, Webster's Third New International Dictionary 1807 (1976), or "a manner of proceeding," The Random House Dictionary of the English Language 1542 (2d ed. 1987).  Certainly a plan that says it may be amended only by a unilateral company decision adequately sets forth "a particular way" of making an amendment.  Adequately, that is, with one refinement.

In order for an amendment procedure that says the plan may be amended by "[t]he Company" to make any sense, there must be some way of determining what it means for "[t]he Company" to make a decision to amend or, in the language of trust law, to "sufficiently manifest [its] intention" to amend.  Restatement (Second) of Trusts § 331, Comment *c* (1957).  After all, only natural persons are capable of making decisions.  As Judge Roth suggested, however, principles of corporate law provide a ready-made set of rules for determining, in whatever context, who has authority to make decisions on behalf of a company.  Consider, for example, an ordinary sales contract between "Company X" and a third-party.  We would not think of regarding the contract as meaningless, and thus unenforceable, simply because it does not specify on its face exactly who within "Company X" has the power to enter into such an agreement or carry out its terms.  Rather, we would look to corporate law principles to give "Company X" content.  So too here.

In the end, perhaps the strongest argument for a textual reading of § 402(b)(3) is that to read it to require specification of individuals or bodies within a company would lead to improbable results. That is, it might lead to the invalidation of myriad amendment procedures that no one would think violate § 402(b)(3), especially those in multiemployer plans—which, as we said, § 402(b)(3) covers as well. For example, imagine a multi-employer plan that says "This Plan may be amended at any time by written agreement of two-thirds of the participating Companies, subject to the approval of the plan Trustees." This would seem to be a fairly robust amendment procedure, and we can imagine numerous variants of it. Yet, because our hypothetical procedure does not specify who within any of "the participating Companies" has authority to enter into such an amendment agreement (let alone what counts as the "approval of the plan Trustees"), respondents would say it is insufficiently specific to pass muster under § 402(b)(3). Congress could not have intended such a result.

Curtiss–Wright's reservation clause thus satisfies the plain text of both requirements in § 402(b)(3). Respondents nonetheless argue that, in drafting § 402(b)(3), Congress intended amendment procedures to convey enough detail to serve beneficiaries' interest in knowing the terms of their plans. Ordinarily, we would be reluctant to indulge an argument based on legislative purpose where the text alone yields a clear answer, but we do so here because it is the argument the Court of Appeals found persuasive.

Section 402(b)(3)'s primary purpose is obviously functional: to ensure that every plan *has* a workable amendment procedure. This is clear from not only the face of the provision but also its placement in § 402(b), which lays out the requisite functional features of ERISA plans.

Requiring every plan to have a coherent amendment procedure serves several laudable goals. First, for a plan *not* to have such a procedure would risk rendering the plan forever unamendable under standard trust law principles. Second, such a requirement increases the likelihood that proposed plan amendments, which are fairly serious events, are recognized as such and given the special consideration they deserve. Finally, having an amendment procedure enables plan administrators, the people who manage the plan on a day-to-day level, to have a mechanism for sorting out, from among the occasional corporate communications that pass through their offices and that conflict with the existing plan terms, the bona fide amendments from those that are not. In fact, plan administrators may have a statutory responsibility to do this sorting out. That Congress may have had plan administrators in mind is suggested by the fact that § 402(b)(3), and § 402(b) more generally, is located in the "fiduciary responsibility" section of ERISA.

Respondents argue that § 402(b)(3) was intended not only to ensure that every plan has an amendment procedure, but also to guarantee that the procedure conveys enough detail to enable beneficiaries to learn their rights and obligations under the plan at any time. Respondents are no doubt right that one of ERISA's central goals is to enable plan beneficiaries to learn their rights and obligations at any time.  But ERISA already *has* an elaborate scheme in place for enabling beneficiaries to learn their rights and obligations at any time, a scheme that is built around reliance on the face of written plan documents.

The basis of that scheme is another of ERISA's core functional requirements, that "[e]very employee benefit plan shall be established and maintained *pursuant to a written instrument.*"  § 1102(a)(1) (emphasis added). In the words of the key congressional report, "[a] written plan is to be required in order that every employee may, *on examining the plan documents,* determine exactly what his rights and obligations are under the plan."  ERISA gives effect to this "written plan documents" scheme through a comprehensive set of "reporting and disclosure" requirements, of which § 402(b)(3) is not part.  One provision, for example, requires that plan administrators periodically furnish beneficiaries with a Summary Plan Description, the purpose being to communicate to beneficiaries the essential information about the plan.  Not surprisingly, the information that every SPD must contain includes the "name and address" of plan administrators and other plan fiduciaries, but not the names and addresses of those individuals with amendment authority.  The same provision also requires that plan administrators furnish beneficiaries with summaries of new amendments no later than 210 days after the end of the plan year in which the amendment is adopted.  Under ERISA, both Summary Plan Descriptions and plan amendment summaries "shall be written in a manner calculated to be understood by the average plan participant."

More important, independent of any information automatically distributed to beneficiaries, ERISA requires that every plan administrator make available for inspection in the administrator's "principal office" and other designated locations a set of all currently operative, governing plan documents, see § 1024(b)(2), which necessarily includes any new, bona fide amendments.  As indicated earlier, plan administrators appear to have a statutory responsibility actually to run the plan in accordance with the currently operative, governing plan documents and thus an independent incentive for obtaining new amendments as quickly as possible and for weeding out defective ones.

This may not be a foolproof informational scheme, although it is quite thorough.  Either way, it is the scheme that Congress devised.  And we do not think Congress intended it to be supplemented by a far-away provision in another part of the statute, least of all in a way that would lead to improbable results.

In concluding that Curtiss–Wright's reservation clause sets forth a valid amendment procedure, we do not mean to imply that there is anything wrong with plan beneficiaries trying to prove that unfavorable plan amendments were not properly adopted and are thus invalid.  This is exactly what respondents are trying to do here, and nothing in ERISA is designed to obstruct such efforts. But nothing in ERISA is designed to facilitate such efforts either.

* * *

The judgment of the Court of Appeals is reversed, and the case is remanded for further proceedings consistent with this opinion.

*It is so ordered.*

NOTES AND QUESTIONS

**1.** With increasing health care costs and a growing ratio of retirees to current employees in many industries, many companies have reduced or eliminated health care benefits for retirees. From a policy standpoint, is the discontinuation of retiree benefits better or worse than the discontinuation of benefits for current employees?

**2.** Should the right to health insurance benefits vest on the date of retirement in the same way that pension benefits vest? What would be the legal and economic consequences of such a policy?

**3.** In Varity Corp. v. Howe, 516 U.S. 489 (1996), former employees of Massey–Ferguson, Inc., a wholly-owned subsidiary of Varity Corporation sued to recover their benefits under an employer welfare plan and to obtain other relief. To rid itself of debts, including its obligations to pay medical and other nonpension benefits to employees of Massey–Ferguson's money-losing divisions, Varity created a new separately incorporated subsidiary called Massey Combines. Rather than terminate the benefits of the Massey–Ferguson employees directly (as it had a right to do), Varity attempted to avoid the undesirable fallout by inducing the employees of the failing divisions to switch employers and thereby relieve Massey–Ferguson of its obligations. To persuade the employees to switch employers and benefit plans, Varity called a special meeting at which it assured the employees that the benefits would remain secure. Varity knew, however, that Massey Combines had a negative net worth of $46 million on the day it was formed. Varity persuaded 1,500 current Massey–Ferguson employees to switch, and it unilaterally assigned 4,000 retired Massey–Ferguson employees to the new company. Massey Combines ended its first year of operations with a loss of $88 million and ended its second year in receivership.

The former employees sued under ERISA, seeking to recover the benefits they would have been owed under the old plan had they not been misled into transferring employers and benefit plans. The Supreme Court, 6–3, held that Varity was acting as a fiduciary when it significantly and deliberately misled the employees. In so doing, Varity violated § 404 of ERISA, which sets out the obligations of plan administrators. The Court held that this breach was actionable under § 502(a)(3), which authorizes individual relief for breach of fiduciary obligations.

**4.** Are cases such as *Curtiss–Wright* and *Varity* aberrant? Would other employers be tempted to engage in similar conduct? Consider the following commentary.

## Uwe E. Reinhardt, *Employer–Based Health Insurance: R.I.P. in the Future U.S. Healthcare System: Who Will Care for the Poor and Uninsured?*\*

342–43 (Stuart H. Altman, Uwe E. Reinhardt & Alexandra E. Shields, eds. 1998).

Until the early 1990s, private employers did not have to recognize on their income statements or on their balance sheets the liability that is incurred in a given year when workers are promised future health benefits in retirement. This huge gap in the Generally Accepted Accounting Principles that govern business accounting in the United States, literally allowed corporations to pay their workers partially with funny money. For decades, the managers of these private corporations kept the ever mounting liability that was incurred in this way perfectly secret from their shareholders and from the investing community. Naturally, they also did not then, and even do not now, have set-aside funds for the future day when these promises will have to be honored. Only in 1992, when FASB–106 forced private employers to recognize on their income statements the expense of these promises *when they are made,* and to show the associated cumulative liability openly on their balance sheets, did the world learn of the staggering mortgages past management had written stealthily, year after year, on the future cash flows and net worth of their enterprises.

General Motors furnishes a dramatic illustration of this stealth approach to health insurance. Between 1991 and 1992, in one year, the net worth of General Motors shrank by $21 billion, from $27 billion to approximately $6 billion, as that firm was finally forced by FASB–106 to report to shareholders the cumulative pre-tax tax liability of $33 billion that it had incurred through promised retiree health benefits (General Motors 1992). More ominously, in the footnotes of its annual report the firm announced that, while being forced to put this liability on the balance sheet, General Motors' compliance with that new rule did not amount to an acknowledgment on the firm's part of any *legal* liability actually to own up to the promises it had made earlier to its current and former workers (General Motors 1993). To appreciate the temptation that future managers of General Motors will face to welsh on these promises, one need only imagine how many automobiles the company would have to sell to cover a pre-tax liability of $33 billion. Although General Motors' predicament in this respect is dramatic, many other companies with large, aging work forces face similarly burdensome and hitherto unacknowledged liabilities for promised retiree health benefits.

It is remarkable that Americans have been content for so long to anchor an important part of their families' financial security in particular firms whose financial strength is contingent on the managerial acumen of a handful of future managers, whose very existence can be threatened by the vagaries of the dynamic global market, whose management can change its ethical precepts over time with changing circumstances, and who can at any time marshall the legal prowess to break promises made to employees

---

\* Reprinted with the permission of Health Administration Press.

decades earlier.  In no other industrialized nation is the economic security of citizens during retirement that closely tied to the economic fortunes of a particular business enterprise and to the personal integrity of the few managers who control that enterprise.  Workers should worry how long this brittle, private social security system can survive in the global market economy of the late twentieth and the early twenty-first centuries.  Sooner or later, the public sector may well have to step into the breach to assume some of the mortgages that were recklessly and stealthily written years ago by private employers.

## 8.  HEALTH CARE REFORM

### a.  COMPREHENSIVE REFORM

## Cathie Jo Martin, *Stuck in Neutral:  Big Business and the Politics of National Health Care Reform**

20 J. Health Politics, Pol'y & L. 431 (1995)

In retrospect, the failure of national health care reform seems over-determined:  It is rather amazing that a minority president (elected with 43 percent of the vote) would even attempt policy change of such scope and with such a history of near misses.  Compounded by a Republican leadership refusal to entertain serious bipartisan compromise and by full-scale mobilization against the bill by vested interests, health care reform once again floundered on the shoals of divided government and interest group liberalism, the age-old villains in the story of American governance.  That we ever thought it could be different reminds me of Oscar Wilde's definition of second marriages:  the triumph of hope over experience.

For many of us, hope for health care reform rested with the interests and actions of corporate employers, although others remained skeptical.  As major losers in the cost-shifting game, firms anxiously watched their profits being eroded by double-digit inflation of health care costs.  Reform promised to impose equal costs on the competitors of those already offering benefits and to cap the escalation of health care costs.  Throughout the 1980s, corporate activists struggled to put health care reform on the public agenda.  Repeated survey data showed that most big business managers supported employer mandates and radical health system restructuring.  Political mobilization by big business conceivably could overcome the entrenched opposition of providers, insurers, and other natural enemies of reform.

But big business was the big no-show in the health care reform saga.  Understanding why large employers failed to support their self-described interests and opinions provides a clue to the failure of health care reform in particular and of American social policy innovation in general.  In this essay, I relate the disappointed business showing to three interrelated

---

* Copyright 1995, Duke University Press.
Reprinted with permission.

factors: economic interests, business organization, and politicians' strategies.

First, some large employers were concerned whether the bill would meet their economic interests. This seems surprising, because the Clinton administration worked hard to develop a proposal designed to bring corporate purchasers into the reform coalition. Reform was packaged to "level the playing field" between U.S. and foreign firms (which have much lower health care costs) and between current providers of health care benefits and their competitors who do not offer benefits. The health alliances on the purchaser side resembled the Enthovan-inspired purchasing coalitions already being advocated by many local business groups. The accountable health plans on the provider side seemed to be a continuation of managed care networks, already the intervention of choice for many firms. The big insurers seemed well positioned to administer the new health alliances, because they were primary organizers of private managed care networks. Employer mandates were not an especially big leap for the large employers, because many already provided health care benefits. In fact, some firms believed that a defined minimum benefit package with tax caps on employee deductions could even help them to curb their health care benefit commitments to their unions.

Yet business managers also had serious economic concerns about the bill, especially about the health alliances. Managed competition was sold as a mechanism to control costs and still to preserve the employer-based system, yet the shape of the health alliances in the administration's original proposal made many firms fear that they would be pushed into these regional entities (a firm had to have more than 5,000 employees to opt out). Because health alliances were to span entire regions, companies worried that they would lose their considerable purchasing power relative to the public pools and would receive very poor rates from providers. Company executives also thought the original minimum benefits package was excessive, worrying that they would no longer control their own plans and would be transformed into "check writers." Business managers thought that the administration engaged in a fiscal slight of hand by suggesting that health care reform could be achieved without any tax increase, and some believed the cost-control mechanisms were excessively weak in the president's plan. In addition, as the bill moved through the legislative process, it gave increasingly enormous subsidies to small business and placed heavier burdens on large employers.

A second factor in the relative absence of large employers from the political debate was the failure of business organization. If a piece of legislation does not meet our interests, the all-American response is to work to change it; indeed, many corporate managers conveyed their concerns about the bill to the administration. But these corporate concerns were not embedded in group support for the larger aims of the legislation. Business associations could not express the preferences of most of their members for health reform, because these groups were crippled by the objections of a vocal minority (usually insurers and pharmaceutical companies). Advocates of health system restructuring struggled within each of the major business organizations to secure endorsement for the reform proposal, yet none of the umbrella organizations overcame the divisions within their ranks and supported reform (or in the case of the Chamber of Commerce, remained in favor of support). Instead, they catered to minority interests, ignored the sentiment of most of their members, and engaged in least-common-denominator politics.

The inability of business groups to endorse the parts of the reform proposal favored by most of their members made the administration and Congress less willing to take seriously big business objections to some aspects of reform. Politicians wanted active help in getting votes in exchange for attention to corporate concerns. As it became more and more apparent that big business groups were incapacitated by minority opposition and could not act as a countervailing force, increasingly legislators granted concessions to the much better organized small business community to try to buy off its opposition. Thus the weakness of big business moved the legislation away from its interests.

Political leaders' counterproductive strategies represented the final factor that contributed to the disappointing showing of big business. Although the president developed a product designed to appeal to business, he neglected the process of bringing corporate leaders into the reform coalition. Because labor organization and party discipline are weak in the United States, fundamental policy change usually requires a centrist politics, such as that used by Lyndon Johnson to sell the Great Society. The circumstances of Clinton's rise to power, his slim victory, and the conservative tenor of the times added to the logic of constructing a centrist, bipartisan coalition for health care reform.

Instead the Clinton administration pursued a politics of exclusion and a language of conflict. The administration suffered in general from confusion about the distinction between campaigning and governing. Governance requires building broad support beyond the electoral coalition, and the administration's tendency to reward loyalists and to punish former enemies made it miss the opportunity to build this broader coalition. For example, Clinton's Office of Public Liaison reduced access to groups perceived as hostile on other issues. As one trade association representative said, "Outreach to them means access to those who have been with them from the beginning and shutting out everyone else".

The task force process was a manifestation of the politics of exclusion. Whereas Johnson used task forces to build consensus and to pursue a centrist politics of inclusion, the Clintons used the task force to keep out special interests (which they defined as almost everyone). Although the administration (primarily Ira Magaziner) met with business groups, potential corporate constituents of reform believed the administration was not interested in having their input. One staff member at the Chamber of Commerce (before it reversed its pro-mandate position) believed that the Clinton administration's stance helped to defeat the reformist struggle within the organization.

The campaign sentiment and neglect of governance was also reflected in the language of class warfare.  The administration likes stories of good and evil, heroes and villains; in health reform the villains were drug and insurance companies.  Although deserved in many cases, the language of heroes and villains elicited emotional, ideological responses that transformed the debate from one of technical fixes to ideological class conflict and undercut the ability of business policy experts to portray the issue in technocratic terms.  The Clintons' language of class warfare worked against the policy wonks within the firms.

If the Democrats engaged in politics of exclusion, the Republicans engaged in a politics of obstruction, believing that only marginal adjustments to the health system were necessary.  They dramatically tried to prevent business from supporting reform, threatening retaliation in future policy areas.  For example, pressure from the congressional Republicans contributed in large part to the dramatic policy reversal at the Chamber of Commerce.  The Chamber's endorsement of an employer mandate and a standardized benefits package angered conservative congressional Republicans.  The Conservative Opportunity Society in the House demanded a meeting with Chamber President Richard Lesher and Vice–President Bill Archey and "read them the riot act."  At the meeting, Jim Bunning (R–KY) gave a speech against big government, big labor, and big business.  John Boehner (R–OH and chairman of the group) sent letters on congressional letterhead to Chamber constituents saying that they should cancel their Chamber memberships.

What does this episode in the history of business and social reform teach us?  American social policy seems to have reached a dead end:  There has been no real innovation since the 1960s.  This failure of government response may have crippled our ability to cope with a rapidly changing world.  Business support for welfare initiatives may become increasingly important in our postindustrial future as the labor movement becomes more fragmented.  Although centrist coalitions may produce policy with conservative hues, there may be no alternative for building support for social modernization.

Yet, as the health care reform case illustrates, generating corporate support for social innovation requires that we revamp our institutions of interest representation.  Much has been made of U.S. companies' short-term strategies in capital investment; one might argue that business has a similar short-term perspective regarding investment in social infrastructure.  We live in a society with little space between left and right, but rather enormous institutional conflict in the private and public spheres.  Ginsberg and Shefter describe with alarm the stalemate brought on by divided government.  A similar fragmentation and limited policy capacity within the corporate sphere also contribute to our inability as a society to modernize our social institutions.

NOTE

There have been numerous books and articles written about the failure of health care reform.  Among them are the following: Theda Skocpol,

Boomerang: Clinton's Health Security Effort and the Turn Against Government in U.S. Politics (1996); W. John Thomas, The Clinton Health Care Reform Plan: A Failed Dramatic Presentation, 7 Stan.L. & Pol'y Rev. 83 (1995–96); Symposium, The Failure of Health Care Reform, 20 J. Health Politics, Pol'y & L. 271 (1995).

b.   INCREMENTAL REFORM

## THE HEALTH INSURANCE PORTABILITY
## AND ACCOUNTABILITY ACT OF 1996

In the first important step of incremental health care reform, the Kassebaum–Kennedy Health Insurance Portability and Accountability Act of 1996 (HIPAA), codified at 42 U.S.C. § 300gg et seq., was enacted by the 104th Congress and signed into law on August 21, 1996.

The law applies to employer-based group health plans (ERISA qualified, self-insured, employee welfare plans) and commercially issued group health insurance (previously the exclusive subject of state insurance regulation). HIPAA curtails the use of exclusions for preexisting conditions. Employers and insurers may apply a maximum, one-time 12–month exclusion to illnesses that were diagnosed or treated within the six months prior to enrollment, but individuals must be given a credit for time they were covered under another plan. Therefore, an individual with at least one year's continuous coverage who changes jobs is eligible immediately for all benefits. No exclusions at all may be applied for pregnancy, newborns, or adopted children. Genetic information may not be treated as a preexisting condition in the absence of a diagnosis of the condition.

An individual who is leaving a group health plan must first use COBRA continuation coverage. Thereafter, the individual is eligible for individual insurance without an exclusion for preexisting conditions. Although the individual insurance is "guaranteed issue," there is no limitation on the premiums that may be charged.

Individuals in a group health plan may not be subject to discrimination based on health status in their eligibility, enrollment, or premium contributions. Individuals cannot be charged higher premiums than other "similarly situated individuals," which refers to full-time/part-time status or geographic location.

An insurer that issues group health plans to the small employer market must accept all applying small employers and all eligible employees. The insurer also must renew insurance coverage to small and large employers.

The law is not comprehensive. It does not apply to individuals who are unemployed. It does not require that employers provide health insurance coverage or any specific benefits package. Employers may place restrictions or limitations on the amount, level, or nature of the benefits. There are no restrictions on the amount an insurer may charge an employer or the premiums that may be charged employees.

Although the HIPAA does not resolve many of the issues related to "health care reform," it is notable in two respects. First, it is the first substantive regulation of self-insured employer welfare plans. Second, it is the first congressional foray into commercial health insurance since the McCarron–Ferguson Act gave states the exclusive responsibility to regulate insurance. Additional reform measures, therefore, are likely to build on the structure of HIPAA.

## Robert Kuttner, *The Kassebaum–Kennedy Bill—The Limits of Incrementalism*

337 New.Eng.J.Med. 64 (1997).

When Senators Nancy Kassebaum (R–Kans.) and Edward M. Kennedy (D–Mass.) proposed the legislation that became the 1996 Health Insurance Portability and Accountability Act, "portability" became a catch phrase for the bridging of gaps in our fragmented health insurance system. Since about two thirds of Americans are insured through their employers, the loss of a job has often meant the loss of a health plan. And with the rise of medical underwriting and the widespread practice of denying new insurance to people with preexisting conditions, that loss may be permanent.

At the Kassebaum–Kennedy hearings, there were accounts of people suddenly deemed uninsurable merely because they had changed employers, and others who retained undesired jobs mainly to keep their health insurance. A detailed study prepared for Senator Kassebaum by the General Accounting Office found that 18 percent of people seeking new individual policies were flatly turned down because of their health status. Insurers often charge two or three times the standard rate to subscribers they consider medical risks and exclude from coverage particular conditions that they know afflict the person seeking insurance. Moreover, since insurance plans increasingly limit the choices of doctor and hospital, a less extreme but still burdensome problem is that people who change jobs may abruptly find themselves dealing with new, unfamiliar teams of health professionals.

When the Kassebaum–Kennedy bill was signed into law by President Bill Clinton last August 21, both political parties congratulated themselves on having solved the portability problem. President Clinton declared that the bill "seals the cracks that swallow as many as 25 million Americans" who cannot get insurance when they change or lose jobs. In reality, the new law falls far short of mandating secure insurance coverage. An examination of its limitations sheds useful light on how a fragmented health insurance system resists fixing. The messy blend of federal and state regulation mirrors the fragmentation of the insurance system itself and compounds the complexity.

\* \* \*

At bottom, our system may be such a patchwork that government regulation cannot efficiently compensate for its multiple anomalies and inequities. Yet public policy is clearly evolving in the direction of more piecemeal regulation, in response to public dissatisfaction with the gaps in the present system. Recently, Congress required health plans to allow new mothers to remain at least 48 hours in the hospital, and seven states have prohibited plans from requiring that mastectomies be performed as outpatient procedures. Some critics have termed this approach "regulation, one organ at a time."

Out of frustration with the gaps in insurance, we are superimposing ever more baroque regulatory overlays. The McCarran–Ferguson Act says that states regulate insurance. But ERISA partly preempts McCarran–Ferguson. And Kassebaum–Kennedy partly preempts ERISA. Each overlay necessitates an explicit interpretation of what is exempt and how regulation is to be shared; it requires ever more elaborate attention to contingencies, ever more prudent lawyering, and ever more pages in the *Federal Register*. More of the same is in store, as Congress and the states wrestle with such issues as how to mandate standards for managed care; whether to regulate physician-operated health networks as insurance companies; and how to insure children from families too rich to be eligible for Medicaid and too poor to afford private health insurance.

In a system in which health insurance is mostly provided by employers, but voluntarily, too much regulation raises costs and leads employers to drop their coverage, or water it down. It adds to the bureaucratic aspects of a system that is already far too burdened with public and private bureaucracies. Ironically, by maintaining a largely private health insurance system aimed at limiting the reach of government regulation, we reap ever more complex regulation to compensate for the inadequacies of that very system. Oddly, too, there is evidently a political consensus favoring the kind of piecemeal regulation that nobody really likes, but no political majority favors more streamlined basic reform.

A universal system, of course, has no portability problem, because everyone is in one group. Hence, there is no regulatory need to resolve issues of continuity and eligibility, let alone interminable certifications, appeals, and adjudications. A universal system requires no taxonomy to parse issues of transitions between groups, as compared with transitions from small group to large group, group to individual, and individual to group. There are no questions of rate-banding, cross-subsidies, guaranteed issues, or permissible exclusions for various categories of applicants and conditions, and no lawyers, lobbyists, and consumer advocates tilting with regulators over such arcana. But the United States continues to resist a universal system, because adopting one would mean giving too large a role to government.

NOTE

Congress has continued to embrace incremental health care reform. In 1996, it enacted two new laws mandating certain coverage for individuals with health insurance. The Mental Health Parity Act of 1996, 29 U.S.C. § 1185a, 42 U.S.C. § 300gg–5, provides that effective January 1,

1998, group health plans of employers with more than 50 employees must provide mental health benefits comparable to those offered for other medical conditions.  The Newborns' and Mothers' Health Protection Act of 1996, 29 U.S.C. § 1185, 42 U.S.C. § 300gg–4, provides that a group health plan and a group health insurer may not restrict benefits for the mother or newborn child to less than 48 hours for a normal vaginal delivery or 96 hours following a cesarian section.

In 1997, the budget bill established a $24 billion program to provide health insurance for uninsured children.  States are allocated block grants to use in providing insurance for children through private insurance plans, Medicaid expansion, direct services, or any combination of the three so long as no more than 10 percent of the funds are spent on direct services.

## C.   CHILD CARE, ELDER CARE, AND OTHER BENEFITS

According to a 1993 study, American workers receive a wide range of benefits beyond the traditional benefits such as health benefits, life and disability insurance, and paid sick leave and vacations.  These "other" benefits, listed by the percentage of workers who receive them, include the following:  continuing education courses (55%), long-term care (44%), wellness programs (33%), health education courses (33%), dependent care reimbursement (24%), and group legal services (21%).  Colonial Life and Accident Company and Employers Council on Flexible Compensation, Workplace Pulse National Survey 8 (1993).

The availability of nontraditional benefits often depends on the size of the employer.  Large employers tend to offer a wider range of benefits.  In addition, certain types of benefits, such as child care assistance, are most common.  A 1996 study of 1,050 large U.S. employers indicated that 86% of the employers offered child care benefits, 30% of the companies offered elder care benefits, and 23% offered adoption benefits.  Hewitt Associates, Work and Family Benefits Provided by Major U.S. Employers in 1996, Medical Benefits, May 30, 1997, at 1.

## Nancy E. Dowd, *Family Values and Valuing Family:  A Blueprint for Family Leave*

30 Harv.J. on Legis. 335, 359–62 (1993).

Child-care policy is an obvious area that needs coordination with family leave.  Yet child-care and family-leave legislation have evolved separately, with separate sets of advocates, each espousing separate agendas.  Child-care policy has prioritized poor families, although indirect subsidy of child care through the tax system primarily benefits middle- and upper-class families.

In contrast to the long struggle to enact leave legislation, a child-care bill was enacted by Congress in 1990.[75] The legislation combined tax credits and grant funding to support expanded child-care facilities and assistance with the cost of child care for low-income families. The tax credit expanded the earned income tax credit for working, low-income families, with additional credit for children under age one. This credit is available as long as one person in the household works, regardless of whether income tax is paid. In the event no tax is due, a refund will be given. The funding provision is designed to be used in several ways, including providing direct subsidies for the poorest families to pay for child care; funding expanded care for low-income families not poor enough for welfare; and improving the quality of care. The legislation represents a compromise among several legislative initiatives that began in 1988. One issue that pervaded the political process concerned whether to mandate the quality of care by imposing federal health and safety standards on child-care providers. Some argued that quality standards would make it harder to maintain and expand available child care. There was also debate on whether to subsidize (in money or vouchers) poor families' child-care expenses, provide tax credits for child-care and insurance costs, increase funding of Head Start to reach a greater proportion of preschoolers, and fund after-school programs for school-age children in addition to preschool programs.

Although geared to providing child-care support to low-income families, this package serves only a fraction of those families. The tax credit, for example, requires low-income families to file a tax return. Without massive public education on the availability of the credit, many low-income families will not utilize it. Furthermore, with a maximum credit of $2,013 by 1994, the amount of care that can be bought with this credit is far below the estimated $6,000 per year that child care actually costs. The dependent-care tax credit, by contrast, is the largest single program of child-care assistance. However, because it provides no refund, it is useless to families with insufficient income to pay tax.

The funding programs attempt to address a broad range of child-care issues without fully addressing any of them. For instance, available funding for latchkey children would serve only 300,000 of the over ten million latchkey children. Child-care funding for families who needed such care to stay at work and off welfare was limited to $300 million. Head

---

**75.** Omnibus Budget Reconciliation Act of 1990, Pub.L. No. 101–508, §§ 5081–5082, 104 Stat. 1388–1, 1388–233 to –250. This was the first major child-care legislation since 1971, when President Nixon vetoed a measure to provide child-care programs out of fear that it would encourage women to work outside of the home. See 1990 Cong. Q. Almanac 547 (citing 1971 Cong. Q. Almanac 504).

The other significant child-care legislation enacted since 1988 was the child-care provisions of the welfare reform overhaul of 1988. The Family Support Act of 1988, Pub.L. No. 100–485, § 301, 102 Stat. 2343, 2382, required states to provide child-care and medical benefits to families leaving welfare for jobs, along with training programs to move welfare mothers from welfare to work. See 1989 Cong. Q. Almanac 224 (citing 1988 Cong. Q. Almanac 347). The states have found it difficult to provide these child-care services.

Start funding, although enormously increased due to the popularity of the program and because of the political battle between Congress and the Bush administration to claim credit for supporting the program, still serves less than half of the eligible children.

It is striking that child care and family leave have not been considered together. Child care is essential for parents to return to wage work. In addition, child care provides essential backup care for sick children, again allowing their parents to be able to go to work.

The interconnection also relates to how family leave should be structured now, as opposed to how it might be structured in view of a better child-care system. For instance, wage replacement during leave is further mandated by the immediate, significant expense of infant care. On the other hand, it may make more sense developmentally, as well as financially, both to extend the financial support and the time frame for leave. Then we could concentrate child-care resources on programs for children over one year old, which are less expensive.

We are quite a distance from closing the gap between the need and the reality of quality child care. The hesitancy to develop a national child-care policy coordinated with family leave is tied to the individualistic ideology that so permeates the family-policy area. It is connected strongly to ideas of appropriate mothering. Finally, it may stem from an aversion to scrutinizing the structure of existing child care. Gender and class interests may be subtle brakes on evaluation of the need and cost of quality universal child care because child care depends so strongly on underpaid, mostly female, wage workers.

Beyond these ideological hurdles, we need to address other issues. Should family policy be centralized or decentralized? How can diversity in the provision of care be maximized without hurting quality? Should child care be connected solely to wage work? As with family leave, gender, race, and class concerns must be kept in the forefront, particularly where the structural issues are framed as "choice" versus "equality." The primary focus, however, must always remain what system produces the best quality care for all children.

## D.  RETHINKING THE EMPLOYER'S ROLE IN BENEFITS

## Craig J. Cantoni, *The Case Against Employee Benefits**
Wall St.J., Aug. 18, 1997, at A14.

The American system of employer-provided health and retirement benefits has become an anachronism. Employers and employees would be better off if medical coverage and retirement programs were independent of the employment relationship.

* Reprinted by permission.

To understand why, consider some history.  In 1940 only 10% of the U.S. work force, or 12 million people, were covered by health insurance, primarily through such plans as Blue Cross and Kaiser Permanente, which grew in response to the hardships of the Depression.  In 1942 Congress passed the Stabilization Act, which limited wage increases in order to keep prices in check during wartime.  The act permitted the adoption of employer-paid insurance plans in lieu of wage increases.  In 1945 the War Labor Board ruled that it was illegal to modify or terminate group insurance plans during the life of a labor contract.  Later, the National Labor Relations Board ruled that insurance and pension benefits fell under the legal definition of "wages."  Employer-paid benefits had been institutionalized.

The Liberty Mutual Insurance Co. led the way in 1949 by introducing major-medical coverage, a new insurance product that coupled comprehensive coverage with the new features of deductibles and coinsurance.  By 1951, 100,000 people were covered by major-medical insurance;  by 1960, 32 million;  and by 1986, 156 million.

In 1979, 97% of full-time employees in medium-to-large companies had employer-sponsored health insurance.  But by 1991, that percentage had declined to 83%.  What happened?  Employment declined in durable goods manufacturing, in which 93% of workers are covered, and rose in retail, in which only 62% are.  And people started changing jobs more often.  Even with mandated coverage for departing employees at their own expense (known as Cobra benefits), waiting periods and exclusions for pre-existing illnesses often leave job switchers without coverage at least for a time.  Less than half of all workers, meanwhile, are covered by private retirement plans.

The most significant cause of the decline in health and retirement coverage has been the growth in the contingent work force.  Often companies are using part-time and contract workers for the express purpose of avoiding the costs—both direct and administrative—of providing benefits.  Who can blame them?

From 1971 to 1991, the cost of medical care rose almost 70% faster than inflation.  Although medical costs have leveled off, the cost of all fringe benefits has soared to 40% of total compensation, compared with 17% in 1955.  Corporations spend almost 12% of total revenues on employee benefits, vs. 4.4% in the 1950s.  The average employee's benefits package (including payroll taxes) costs just under $15,000.

Add to this the costs of administering benefits and complying with ever-more-complex regulations.  The 1974 Employee Retirement Income Security Act alone has spawned regulations that are two feet thick;  complying with these rules takes an army of attorneys and benefits consultants, in addition to in-house benefits administrators (about one for every 1,000 employees).  Such costs hit small businesses especially hard: The annual cost to a midsize or smaller business of administering a "simple" 401(k) retirement plan is $475 per participant.

What do companies get for this trouble and money? Black eyes—not only from the usual adversaries in the media and government, but also from the recipients of their generosity. Except for the largest and richest companies, which can afford gold-plated programs, benefits are often a source of employee dissatisfaction and distrust, and rarely a source of motivation or productivity. This is particularly true of medical insurance.

Company-sponsored medical insurance creates a paternalistic relationship. The employer plays the role of the munificent parent, who protects the employee-child from the vagaries of life—a role at odds with the economic decisions of running a business. It also gives employers reasons to intrude on the most personal aspects of their employees' lives, from a family's medical history to a worker's sexual orientation (in the case of domestic partner coverage). Once involved with such personal matters, it seems perfectly natural for employers to devote precious time and energy to matters of health and lifestyle, by offering smoking cessation programs, stress reduction classes, cholesterol screenings, health awareness lectures and newsletters about diet and nutrition. But whatever goodwill such nannyism might generate, it evaporates as soon as the employer increases premiums, switches managed care networks or denies a claim.

Noncash benefits corrupt the employer-employee relationship in other important ways. When 40% of total compensation is in the form of benefits, it is difficult for employees to put a true market value on their compensation package or to walk away from a job they don't like. From management's point of view, it is difficult to have true pay-for-performance when employees see 40% of their compensation as an entitlement.

NOTES AND QUESTIONS

**1.** Do you agree that employers and employees would both be better off if employers were no longer responsible for benefits? Who or what entity should be responsible? What obstacles exist to such a transfer? Consider the Martin article, supra p. 542.

**2.** For a further discussion of other obligations of employers beyond benefits, including law enforcement and remedial education, see Mark A. Rothstein, Arbitration in the Employer Welfare State, in Arbitration 1991: The Changing Face of Arbitration in Theory and Practice 94–98 (1992).

# CHAPTER 7

# CONDITIONS OF EMPLOYMENT

Wages, hours, and fringe benefits—the subjects of the preceding two chapters—are often thought to be the most important aspects of the employment relationship. Although certainly important, these elements are merely the starting points in assessing the employment setting. From an employee perspective, the "conditions of employment" greatly affect the quality of working life. From an employer perspective, the "conditions of employment" define the workplace atmosphere and management prerogatives.

In a unionized workplace, the collective bargaining agreement negotiated between an employer and union representing the employees typically includes contractual provisions limiting the employer's authority to run the business as it sees fit. Such matters as job assignments, probation periods, seniority rights, promotion procedures, and discipline are covered in the contract, and arbitrary actions by the employer in breach of the contract are subject to its grievance and arbitration procedure. The collective bargaining agreement acts as a constitution or bill of rights for employees covered by it, with private arbitration available to enforce the agreement. For nonunionized employees, however, there was traditionally no legal restriction on the employer's right to act freely except for the limited protection provided by statutes. In 1964 Title VII of the Civil Rights Act prohibited discrimination in terms or conditions of employment on the basis of race, color, religion, sex, and national origin. In 1970 the Occupational Safety and Health Act required employers to provide a safe workplace. More recently, the judiciary has begun to recognize additional sources of protection in common law torts and contracts and, for public employees, in the United States Constitution.

The first two parts of the chapter, "Work Environment" and "Regulation of Off-Work Activity," focus on aspects of work that are of particular importance to individual employees. In many ways, these elements of work are the conditions which give meaning and dignity to their worklife or make it intolerably intrusive. For employers, control over these same elements may mean the difference between a disciplined, productive operation and a chaotic, inefficient one. The final part of the chapter, "Seniority and Promotion," addresses a subject normally found in collective bargaining agreements, but which greatly affects the employment opportunities of nonunion employees as well.

The issues addressed in this chapter exemplify a recurring theme in the field of employment law: the struggle for control of the workplace.

554

Traditionally, the employer could freely dictate any and all working conditions. Above all else, the law protected the employer's property rights, managerial prerogatives, and right to direct the workforce as it saw fit. Today, society recognizes the value of other individual rights, such as privacy and freedom of expression. Employee gains in the area of working conditions epitomize changing perceptions of the proper relationship between employers and employees. This is particularly true with respect to the readjustment and redefinition of rights for nonunion employees, whose gains in this area have been achieved not through the use of economic strength but through legislative and judicial changes in policy, which have in turn caused employers to reassess their internal employment policies.

As you read the cases and materials in this chapter, notice how the method of analysis and the outcome are affected by whether the employer is public or private, by whether the employees are union or nonunion, and by whether the source of the relevant law is constitutional, statutory (federal or state), regulatory, or common law. Try to assess whether the outcomes and doctrines are consistent, what the appropriate level of legal intervention is in a particular setting, and what is the most appropriate means for achieving desired ends.

## A.  WORK ENVIRONMENT

This section contains a diverse collection of cases with a single theme: what is the appropriate level of employer control of the personal affairs of employees while they are on the job?

The first part of this section, "Grooming and Dress," deals with the relationship among sex roles, sex stereotypes, and sex discrimination. A similar set of issues is raised in the second part, "Harassment," where sexual harassment is addressed.

Parts three and four, "Privacy" and "Freedom of Expression," address the concern of employees to be free of employers' intrusion into their personal lives. Constitutional and tort principles form the main legal bases of protection.

The final part, "Collective Action," looks to the National Labor Relations Act as a source of protection for the group actions of nonunion employees.

It is sometimes said that "the Bill of Rights stops at the plant gate." Assuming this is true, at least with regard to the private sector, should the freedom of expression, the right of privacy, and other similar concepts be applied in the workplace? If so, what is the legal authority for these rights? What are the limits? What procedures should be used in their enforcement? What is the cost of establishing them?

## 1. GROOMING AND DRESS

### Kelley v. Johnson

425 U.S. 238 (1976).

■ MR. JUSTICE REHNQUIST delivered the opinion of the Court.

\* \* \*

In 1971 respondent's predecessor, individually and as president of the Suffolk County Patrolmen's Benevolent Association, brought this action under the Civil Rights Act of 1871, 42 U.S.C. § 1983, against petitioner's predecessor, the Commissioner of the Suffolk County Police Department. The Commissioner had promulgated Order No. 71–1, which established hair-grooming standards applicable to male members of the police force. The regulation was directed at the style and length of hair, sideburns, and mustaches; beards and goatees were prohibited, except for medical reasons; and wigs conforming to the regulation could be worn for cosmetic reasons. The regulation was attacked as violative of respondent patrolman's right of free expression under the First Amendment and his guarantees of due process and equal protection under the Fourteenth Amendment, in that it was "not based upon the generally accepted standard of grooming in the community" and placed "an undue restriction" upon his activities therein.

\* \* \*

Section 1 of the Fourteenth Amendment to the United States Constitution provides in pertinent part:

"No State shall \* \* \* deprive any person of life, liberty, or property, without due process of law."

This section affords not only a procedural guarantee against the deprivation of "liberty," but likewise protects substantive aspects of liberty against unconstitutional restrictions by the State.

The "liberty" interest claimed by respondent here, of course, is distinguishable from the interests protected by the Court in Roe v. Wade, Eisenstadt v. Baird, Stanley v. Illinois, Griswold v. Connecticut, and Meyer v. Nebraska. Each of those cases involved a substantial claim of infringement on the individual's freedom of choice with respect to certain basic matters of procreation, marriage, and family life. But whether the citizenry at large has some sort of "liberty" interest within the Fourteenth Amendment in matters of personal appearance is a question on which this Court's cases offer little, if any, guidance. We can, nevertheless, assume an affirmative answer for purposes of deciding this case, because we find that assumption insufficient to carry the day for respondent's claim.

Respondent has sought the protection of the Fourteenth Amendment, not as a member of the citizenry at large, but on the contrary as an employee of the police department of Suffolk County, a subdivision of the State of New York. While the Court of Appeals made passing reference to this distinction, it was thereafter apparently ignored. We think, however, it is highly significant.  In Pickering v. Board of Education, 391 U.S. 563 (1968), after noting that state employment may not be conditioned on the relinquishment of First Amendment rights, the Court stated that "[a]t the same time it cannot be gainsaid that the State has interests as an employer in regulating the speech of its employees that differ significantly from those it possesses in connection with regulation of the speech of the citizenry in general."  More recently, we have sustained comprehensive and substantial restrictions upon activities of both federal and state employees lying at the core of the First Amendment.  If such state regulations may survive challenges based on the explicit language of the First Amendment, there is surely even more room for restrictive regulations of state employees where the claim implicates only the more general contours of the substantive liberty interest protected by the Fourteenth Amendment.

The hair-length regulation here touches respondent as an employee of the county and, more particularly, as a policeman.  Respondent's employer has, in accordance with its well-established duty to keep the peace, placed myriad demands upon the members of the police force, duties which have no counterpart with respect to the public at large.  Respondent must wear a standard uniform, specific in each detail.  When in uniform he must salute the flag.  He may not take an active role in local political affairs by way of being a party delegate or contributing or soliciting political contributions.  He may not smoke in public.  All of these and other regulations of the Suffolk County Police Department infringe on respondent's freedom of choice in personal matters, and it was apparently the view of the Court of Appeals that the burden is on the State to prove a "genuine public need" for each and every one of these regulations.

This view was based upon the Court of Appeals' reasoning that the "unique judicial deference" accorded by the judiciary to regulation of members of the military was inapplicable because there was no historical or functional justification for the characterization of the police as "para-military."  But the conclusion that such cases are inapposite, however correct, in no way detracts from the deference due Suffolk County's choice of an organizational structure for its police force.  Here the county has chosen a mode of organization which it undoubtedly deems the most efficient in enabling its police to carry out the duties assigned to them under state and local law.  Such a choice necessarily gives weight to the overall need for discipline esprit de corps, and uniformity.

The county's choice of an organizational structure, therefore, does not depend for its constitutional validity on any doctrine of historical prescription.  Nor, indeed has respondent made any such claim.  His argument does not challenge the constitutionality of the organizational structure, but merely asserts that the present hair-length regulation infringes his asserted liberty interest under the Fourteenth Amendment.  We believe, however, that the hair-length regulation cannot be viewed in isolation, but must be rather considered in the context of the county's chosen mode of organization for its police force.

The promotion of safety of persons and property is unquestionably at the core of the State's police power, and virtually all state and local governments employ a uniform police force to aid in the accomplishment of that purpose.  Choice of organization, dress, and equipment for law enforcement personnel is a decision entitled to the same sort of presumption of legislative validity as are state choices designed to promote other aims within the cognizance of the State's police power.  Having recognized in other contexts the wide latitude accorded the government in the "dispatch of its own internal affairs," Cafeteria Workers v. McElroy, 367 U.S. 886 (1961), we think Suffolk County's police regulations involved here are entitled to similar weight.  Thus the question is not, as the Court of Appeals conceived it to be, whether the State can "establish" a "genuine public need" for the specific regulation.  It is whether respondent can demonstrate that there is no rational connection between the regulation, based as it is on the county's method of organizing its police force, and the promotion of safety of persons and property.

We think the answer here is so clear that the District Court was quite right in the first instance to have dismissed respondent's complaint.  Neither this Court, the Court of Appeals, nor the District Court is in a position to weigh the policy arguments in favor of and against a rule regulating hairstyles as a part of regulations governing a uniformed civilian service.  The constitutional issue to be decided by these courts is whether petitioner's determination that such regulations should be enacted is so irrational that it may be branded "arbitrary," and therefore a deprivation of respondent's "liberty" interest in freedom to choose his own hairstyle.  The overwhelming majority of state and local police of the present day are uniformed.  This fact itself testifies to the recognition by those who direct those operations, and by the people of the States and localities who directly or indirectly choose such persons, that similarity in appearance of police officers is desirable.  This choice may be based on a desire to make police officers readily recognizable to the members of the public, or a desire for the esprit de corps which such similarity is felt to inculcate within the police force itself.  Either one is a sufficiently rational justification for regulations so as to defeat respondent's claim based on the liberty guarantee of the Fourteenth Amendment.

\* \* \*

The regulation challenged here did not violate any right guaranteed respondent by the Fourteenth Amendment to the United States Constitution, and the Court of Appeals was therefore wrong in reversing the District Court's original judgment dismissing the action.  The judgment of the Court of Appeals is

*Reversed.*

\* \* \*

■ MR. JUSTICE MARSHALL, with whom MR. JUSTICE BRENNAN joins, dissenting.

The Court today upholds the constitutionality of Suffolk County's regulation limiting the length of a policeman's hair. While the Court only assumes for purposes of its opinion that "the citizenry at large has some sort of 'liberty' interest within the Fourteenth Amendment in matters of personal appearance * * *," I think it clear that the Fourteenth Amendment does indeed protect against comprehensive regulation of what citizens may or may not wear. And I find that the rationales offered by the Court to justify the regulation in this case are insufficient to demonstrate its constitutionality. Accordingly, I respectfully dissent.

As the Court recognizes, the Fourteenth Amendment's guarantee against the deprivation of liberty "protects substantive aspects of liberty against unconstitutional restriction by the State." And we have observed that "[l]iberty under law extends to the full range of conduct which the individual is free to pursue." It seems to me manifest that that "full range of conduct" must encompass one's interest in dressing according to his own taste. An individual's personal appearance may reflect, sustain, and nourish his personality and may well be used as a means of expressing his attitude and lifestyle. In taking control over a citizen's personal appearance, the government forces him to sacrifice substantial elements of his integrity and identity as well. To say that the liberty guarantee of the Fourteenth Amendment does not encompass matters of personal appearance would be fundamentally inconsistent with the values of privacy, self-identity, autonomy, and personal integrity that I have always assumed the Constitution was designed to protect.

To my mind, the right in one's personal appearance is inextricably bound up with the historically recognized right of "every individual to the possession and control of his own person," Union Pacific R. Co. v. Botsford, 141 U.S. 250, 251 (1891), and, perhaps even more fundamentally, with "the right to be let alone—the most comprehensive of rights and the right most valued by civilized men." Olmstead v. United States, 277 U.S. 438, 478 (1928) (Brandeis, J., dissenting). In an increasingly crowded society in which it is already extremely difficult to maintain one's identity and personal integrity, it would be distressing, to say the least, if the government could regulate our personal appearance unconfined by any constitutional strictures whatsoever.

Acting on its assumption that the Fourteenth Amendment does encompass a right in one's personal appearance, the Court justifies the challenged hair-length regulation on the grounds that such regulations may "be based on a desire to make police officers readily recognizable to the members of the public, or a desire for the esprit de corps which such similarity is felt to inculcate within the police force itself." While fully accepting the aims of "identifiability" and maintenance of esprit de corps, I find no rational relationship between the challenged regulation and these goals.

As for the first justification offered by the Court, I simply do not see how requiring policemen to maintain hair of under a certain length could rationally be argued to contribute to making them identifiable to the public as policemen. Surely, the fact that a uniformed police officer is wearing his hair below his collar will make him no less identifiable as a policeman. And one cannot easily imagine a plainclothes officer being readily identifiable as such simply because his hair does not extend beneath his collar.

As for the Court's second justification, the fact that it is the president of the Patrolmen's Benevolent Association, in his official capacity, who has challenged the regulation here would seem to indicate that the regulation would if anything, decrease rather than increase the police force's esprit de corps. And even if one accepted the argument that substantial similarity in appearance would increase a force's esprit de corps, I simply do not understand how implementation of this regulation could be expected to create any increment in similarity of appearance among members of a uniformed police force. While the regulation prohibits hair below the ears or the collar and limits the length of sideburns, it allows the maintenance of any type of hairstyle, other than a ponytail. Thus, as long as their hair does not go below their collars, two police officers, with an "Afro" hairstyle and the other with a crewcut could both be in full compliance with the regulation.

The Court cautions us not to view the hair-length regulation in isolation, but rather to examine it "in the context of the county's chosen mode of organization for its police force." While the Court's caution is well taken, one should also keep in mind, as I fear the Court does not, that what is ultimately under scrutiny is neither the overall structure of the police force nor the uniform and equipment requirements to which its members are subject, but rather the regulation which dictates acceptable hair lengths. The fact that the uniform requirement, for instance, may be rationally related to the goals of increasing police officer "identifiability" and the maintenance of esprit de corps does absolutely nothing to establish the legitimacy of the hair-length regulation. I see no connection between the regulation and the offered rationales and would accordingly affirm the judgment of the Court of Appeals.

## NOTES AND QUESTIONS

**1.** The police department argued that the hair length and grooming regulations were needed to protect the police officers, to achieve esprit de corps, and to maintain uniformity. Which of these arguments is the strongest? Why? What else could have been argued?

**2.** If you agree with the dissent that the police department failed to justify the need for the regulation, would there be a justification for prohibiting officers from wearing jewelry, using excessive makeup or cosmetics, or wearing unusual eyeglasses? What about the police department's prohibition on officers smoking in public?

**3.** *Kelley* was brought under a First Amendment theory. Most hair length cases in private employment have been brought under a Title VII sex discrimination theory. The plaintiffs have argued that employer rules prohibiting men but not women from having long hair discriminate on the basis of sex. Generally, plaintiffs have been unsuccessful for two reasons. First, it has been held that Title VII was designed only to prohibit discrimination based on *immutable* characteristics. Fagan v. National Cash Register Co., 481 F.2d 1115 (D.C.Cir.1973). Second, the cases have declared that hair length regulations do not inhibit employment *opportunity*. Willingham v. Macon Telegraph Publishing Co., 507 F.2d 1084 (5th Cir.1975) (en banc). Implicit in both theories are the ideas that differential hair length is a social norm, that grooming regulations seek to project a favorable company image to the public, and that "Congress sought only to give all persons equal access to the job market, not to limit an employer's right to exercise his informed judgment as to how best to run his shop." *Willingham,* supra. See Tavora v. New York Mercantile Exchange, 101 F.3d 907 (2d Cir.1996), cert. denied, 117 S.Ct. 1821 (1997) (hair length restriction applied only to male employees does not violate Title VII).

**4.** A number of cases have been brought challenging employer "no-beard" rules. Although the obvious ground for attack would appear to be alleged sex discrimination, e.g. Rafford v. Randle Eastern Ambulance Service, Inc., 348 F.Supp. 316 (S.D.Fla.1972) (holding for defendant), other theories also have been asserted. For example, in Keys v. Continental Illinois National Bank & Trust Co., 357 F.Supp. 376 (N.D.Ill.1973), the plaintiff argued that long sideburns, beards, and mustaches are symbols of black pride and therefore the employer's prohibition of facial hair was race discrimination. The court rejected this argument.

**5.** Sing Sing Prison in New York had a grooming rule that prohibited prison guards from having spikes, tails, or names shaved into their hair. Two prison guards became members of the Rastafarian religion and started wearing their hair in dreadlocks. The prison ordered them to cut their hair because it allegedly was unprofessional and created a risk to safety. Has the prison violated Title VII? See Francis v. Keane, 888 F.Supp. 568 (S.D.N.Y.1995) (held: yes).

**6.** A black man applied for a job as a bus driver. The bus company had a no-beard policy for its bus drivers. The man asserted that he suffered from pseudofolliculitis barbae, a skin disorder resulting from ingrown hair which is aggravated by shaving. He demonstrated that this condition affects 25 percent of black males but less than one percent of white males. In a Title VII race discrimination action, what result? See EEOC v. Trailways, Inc., 530 F.Supp. 54 (D.Colo.1981) (held: employer failed to rebut prima facie case). See Bradley v. Pizzaco of Nebraska, Inc., 7 F.3d 795 (8th Cir.1993) (employer failed to accommodate workers with pseudofolliculitis barbae). See also EEOC v. United Parcel Service, 94 F.3d 314 (7th Cir.1996) (no-beard rule may constitute religious discrimination). But see Fitzpatrick v. City of Atlanta, 2 F.3d 1112 (11th Cir.1993) (upholding no-beard rule for firefighters because beard interfered with respirator use).

**7.** A hotel maid applied for a promotion to the job of secretary. Her hotel-casino employer refused to promote her because she failed to satisfy the appearance criteria for "public contact" positions. At her interview, it was noted that "her hair was not clean, neat, or combed, she was slightly overweight, and her clothing was not neat or tidy or coordinated." Has the employer violated Title VII? See Mannikko v. Harrah's Reno, Inc., 630

F.Supp. 191 (D.Nev.1986). (held: no violation of Title VII). Does it violate a state disability discrimination law for a "four star" ski resort to discharge a chambermaid because she was toothless and she did not wear her dentures to work because they were too painful to wear? See Hodgdon v. Mt. Mansfield Co., 624 A.2d 1122 (Vt.1992) (held: plaintiff had an impairment under Vermont law; remanded on issue of whether her contact with hotel guests made her unfit to perform the job).

**8.** A female receptionist was constantly criticized by her female supervisor for, among other things, wearing low cut and tight blouses, sitting with her legs open, being rude and boisterous at parties, and having disheveled hair. One male company official, commenting about her to another male official, said "if he had not known better, he would have thought she was a prostitute." After repeated harassment about her appearance and behavior, the woman resigned. She then brought an action alleging constructive discharge in violation of the District of Columbia Human Rights Act, D.C.Code §§ 1–2501 et seq., which prohibits discrimination based on personal appearance, defined as:

> the outward appearance of any person, irrespective of sex, with regard to bodily condition or characteristics, manner or style of dress, and manner or style of personal grooming, including, but not limited to, hair style and beards. It shall not relate, however, to the requirement of * * * prescribed standards * * * when uniformly applied to a class of employees for a reasonable business purpose. * * *

D.C.Code § 1–2502(22). Has the employer violated the statute? See Atlantic Richfield Co. v. District of Columbia Commission on Human Rights, 515 A.2d 1095 (D.C.App.1986) (held: yes). Is a statutory approach to personal appearance discrimination desirable? What problems do you envision? In Kennedy v. District of Columbia, 654 A.2d 847 (D.C.App.1994), the court held that the fire department violated the Human Rights Act by discharging a firefighter with a beard and handlebar mustache. The fire department failed to prove its purported safety reason for the regulation.

**9.** An employer had a rule prohibiting male employees from wearing facial jewelry, including earrings; female employees were permitted to wear facial jewelry that was not "unusual or overly large." Does this rule constitute sex discrimination in violation of a state fair employment law? See Lockhart v. Louisiana–Pacific Corp., 795 P.2d 602 (Or.App.1990) (held: no).

**10.** In 1991, American Airlines settled a lawsuit brought by its flight attendants, which alleged that the airline's weight standards discriminated on the basis of age and sex. Under the airline's former standards, any woman 5–foot–5 could weigh no more than 129 pounds. Under the new standards, a 25–year–old who is 5–foot–5 can weigh up to 136 pounds; a 55–year–old who is 5–foot–5 can weigh up to 154 pounds. For a general discussion of this issue, see Pamela Whitesides, Note, Flight Attendant Weight Policies: A Title VII Wrong Without a Remedy, 64 S.Cal.L.Rev. 175 (1990).

# EEOC v. Sage Realty Corp.

507 F.Supp. 599 (S.D.N.Y.1981).

■ ROBERT J. WARD, DISTRICT JUDGE.

\* \* \*

Plaintiff Hasselman's job as a lobby attendant included security, safety, maintenance and information functions. For instance, as a lobby attendant Hasselman kept an eye on the elevators to make sure they were in working order and reported any elevator problems to maintenance personnel. She offered assistance and information to people entering the building and kept those who did not belong in the building from loitering. Hasselman's duties required her to replace defective light bulbs and to report any conditions in the lobby requiring the attention of cleaning personnel.

Sage furnished uniforms to all lobby attendants working in the buildings it managed. The uniforms were selected and paid for by Sage and after use remained Sage's property. During the period of Hasselman's employment, new uniforms were issued approximately every six months, each spring and fall.

\* \* \*

In February or March 1976 Sage commissioned a graphic design firm, Pamela Waters Studio Inc., to develop a design concept for the uniforms to be worn by Sage's lobby attendants during the following spring and summer seasons. The Waters Studio presented Kaufman, Sage's president, with several designs. Kaufman approved a uniform known as the Bicentennial uniform, apparently developed to celebrate the nation's bicentennial year. The outfit resembled an American flag. It consisted of broad stripes of red, white and blue material sewn together. Each stripe was approximately 13 inches wide, and the uniform bore three stars across the front.

The Bicentennial uniform was constructed in the shape of a red-white-and-blue octagon with an opening in the center for the lobby attendant's head. This spring 1976 outfit was to be worn as a poncho, or cape, draped over the shoulders, with snaps at each wrist and stitching in the form of tacks, one tack at each side. The uniform was otherwise open at the sides. Underneath the poncho the lobby attendants wore blue dancer pants and sheer stockings. The Bicentennial uniform was to be worn with white, low-heeled shoes. The lobby attendants were not permitted to wear a shirt or blouse, a Danskin, pants or a skirt under the outfit.

The Pamela Waters Studio retained a seamstress to manufacture the uniforms. Although Sage's female lobby attendants were of different sizes, the uniforms were supposed to be made in one size only. Moreover, the outfits were poorly made, had uneven hems, and contained little additional fabric that could be used to enlarge the garments to fit different individuals.

The first Bicentennial uniforms were delivered to the lobby attendants on or about May 12, 1976. When Hasselman tried on her uniform, she found it short and revealing on both sides. Her thighs and portions of her buttocks were exposed, and understandably she was concerned about wearing the outfit in the 711 Third Avenue lobby.

Hasselman had been told by Sage that if she had any problems with her uniform she was to call the Pamela Waters Studio. She did so, complaining that her uniform did not fit properly. Shortly thereafter, Joan Petruska, an employee of the Waters Studio, came to 711 Third Avenue to inspect the fit of Hasselman's garment. Petruska observed that the uniform was open above the thighs and that the blue dancer pants, worn underneath the outfit, were revealed when Hasselman assumed certain positions (positions she would likely be required to assume on the job). In addition, Petruska discovered, when Hasselman raised either of her arms the side of her body above the waist was visible. After inspecting the uniform and listening to Hasselman's complaints about it, Petruska promised to report the problem to the Waters Studio to see what could be done.

A few days after Petruska's visit, another Pamela Waters employee, Meta Shaw, visited Hasselman at 711 Third Avenue. Shaw observed the uniform on Hasselman, and she also found it to be too short. Hasselman had not as yet worn the Bicentennial uniform on the lobby floor.

Following the inspections by Petruska and Shaw, some alterations were made on Hasselman's uniform and it was lengthened slightly. The altered uniform, however, was uneven and remained as revealing as it had been in its unaltered form. Hasselman returned the outfit once again to the Pamela Waters Studio and requested that further alterations be made. The Bicentennial uniform was returned to Hasselman on May 26, 1976. Hasselman tried it on, found that it was still too revealing, and again complained to the Pamela Waters Studio. She was told, however, that at this point no further alterations would be made.

Following this conversation with the Waters Studio, and knowing Sage's uniform policy, Hasselman wore the uniform in the lobby of 711 Third Avenue on May 27 and May 28, 1976. While wearing the Bicentennial uniform and as a result of wearing it, Hasselman was subjected to repeated harassment. She received a number of sexual propositions and endured lewd comments and gestures. Humiliated by what occurred, Hasselman was unable to perform her duties properly.

Although Hasselman complained to Baxter, Sage's building manager for 711 Third Avenue, about the fit of her uniform and the harassment to which she was being subjected, Baxter took no steps to remedy the situation. As a result Hasselman determined not to wear the Bicentennial uniform and, presumably beginning on June 1, 1976 (the Tuesday following the 1976 Memorial Day holiday), wore the previously issued uniform, the fall 1975 beige jumper outfit.

\* \* \*

[After being observed wearing her old uniform, Hasselman was offered and accepted, in lieu of discharge, a "lay-off letter" stating that she had lost her job because of a lack of work.]

The Court has viewed photographs of Hasselman in the Bicentennial uniform and finds that on Hasselman the uniform was short, revealing and sexually provocative. It could reasonably be expected that were such an outfit to be worn by plaintiff Hasselman in the lobby at 711 Third Avenue, as it was for two days, she would be subjected to sexual harassment.

Apparently conceding, at least arguendo, that the uniform was short on Hasselman, defendant Sage contends that a new and larger uniform was made for her. The Court has been unable to determine whether any new or larger uniform was in fact sewn for Hasselman. In any event, however, the Court finds that no such new or larger uniform was ever delivered to Hasselman and that she was never told a new uniform was being made and would be delivered to her at some future time.

There is no question that defendants Sage and Monahan Cleaners required Hasselman to wear the Bicentennial uniform because she is a woman. Due to its revealing nature, the uniform caused Hasselman to endure harassment in the performance of her job. The wearing of the uniform was made a condition of Hasselman's employment, and her employment was terminated when she refused to continue wearing the garment.

Plaintiffs assert that, in issuing and requiring Hasselman to wear the Bicentennial uniform as a term and condition of her employment, and in firing her for refusing to wear the outfit, defendants violated section 703(a) of the Civil Rights Act of 1964. 42 U.S.C. § 2000e–2(a). The section provides:

It shall be an unlawful employment practice for an employer—

(1) to fail or refuse to hire or to discharge any individual, or otherwise to discriminate against any individual with respect to his compensation, terms, conditions, or privileges of employment, because of such individual's race, color, religion, sex, or national origin; or

(2) to limit, segregate, or classify his employees or applicants for employment in any way which would deprive or tend to deprive any individual of employment opportunities or otherwise adversely affect his status as an employee, because of such individual's race, color, religion, sex, or national origin.

To prevail on their claim that defendants committed an unlawful employment practice pursuant to section 703(a), plaintiffs must prove that a term or condition of employment was imposed on Hasselman and that this term or condition was imposed on the basis of sex. Plaintiffs have the burden of establishing a prima facie case of sex discrimination. Although the ultimate burden of persuasion remains with plaintiffs, once plaintiffs present evidence sufficient to make their prima facie showing, the burden of production shifts to defendants to rebut the prima facie case by articulating a legitimate, nondiscriminatory reason for their actions.

The Court finds that plaintiffs established their prima facie case by demonstrating, first, that as a condition of her employment Hasselman was required to wear the Bicentennial uniform; second, that Sage and Monahan Cleaners imposed this condition; and, third, that but for her womanhood Hasselman would not have been required to appear on her job in the lobby of 711 Third Avenue in a uniform that subjected her to sexual harassment. Sage and Monahan Cleaners required Hasselman to wear, as a condition of her employment, a uniform that was revealing and sexually provocative and could reasonably be expected to subject her to sexual harassment when worn on the job—and a uniform that Sage and Monahan Cleaners knew did subject her to such harassment. Defendants, on the other hand, have not offered any legitimate, nondiscriminatory explanation for imposing this condition, and thus have failed to rebut plaintiffs' prima facie showing.

\* \* \*

There is no dispute that as a condition of her employment as a lobby attendant Hasselman was required to wear a uniform selected and issued by Sage and, in the summer of 1976, to wear the Bicentennial uniform. Defendants, however, maintain that Hasselman was never required to wear a sexually revealing and sexually provocative garment. They claim that Hasselman was only required to wear the properly fitted, nonrevealing second uniform that they say was made for her after she complained about how poorly her original uniform fit her. The evidence reveals otherwise. The Court finds that even if a new uniform was made for her—as defendants contend—Hasselman was never told that she would only be required to wear this new, allegedly nonrevealing outfit.

Sage maintains that requiring Hasselman to wear the Bicentennial uniform was a proper exercise of its right to require an employee to work in company-prescribed attire. The Court does not question an employer's prerogative to impose reasonable grooming and dress requirements on its employees, even where different requirements are set for male and female employees, when those requirements have a negligible effect on employment opportunities and present no distinct employment disadvantages. The prerogative to impose reasonable grooming and dress requirements, however, as this Court ruled in denying defendants' motion for summary judgment, does not mean that "an employer has the unfettered discretion \* \* \* to require its employees to wear *any* uniform the employer chooses, including uniforms which may be characterized as revealing and sexually provocative." EEOC v. Sage Realty Corp., 87 F.R.D. 365, 371 (S.D.N.Y. 1980).

Sage's and Monahan Cleaners' requirement that Hasselman wear the Bicentennial uniform, when they knew that the wearing of this uniform on the job subjected her to sexual harassment, constituted sex discrimination of the same nature as that found by the Third and District of Columbia

Circuits in Tomkins v. Public Service Electric & Gas Co., 568 F.2d 1044 (3d Cir.1977), and Barnes v. Costle, 561 F.2d 983 (D.C.Cir.1977).

Although in *Tomkins* and *Barnes* the victims of sex discrimination were subjected to the direct sexual advances of their supervisors, the reasoning of those courts is entirely apposite here, where Sage and Monahan Cleaners knowingly allowed Hasselman, a female employee, to remain, as a condition of her employment, in a position where she would be subjected to sexual harassment on the job. Indeed, the *Tomkins* court, in holding the corporate employer responsible for the conduct of the supervisor of its complaining female employee, grounded its ruling on the allegation that the corporate defendant knowingly or constructively made Tomkins' acquiescence in her supervisor's advances a job prerequisite. The situation here is directly analogous. In requiring Hasselman to wear the revealing Bicentennial uniform in the lobby of 711 Third Avenue, defendants made her acquiescence in sexual harassment by the public, and perhaps by building tenants, a prerequisite of her employment as a lobby attendant.

Contending that its uniform requirement constitutes artistic expression, Sage argues that to the extent Title VII as applied in the instant case prohibits this employer from dressing its lobby attendants in an outfit such as the Bicentennial uniform, Title VII is an unconstitutional affront to freedom of expression in violation of the first amendment. Whatever merit this argument may have in other instances, it has no merit here. The issue before the Court in this case is not whether defendant Sage could permissibly outfit its lobby attendants in a Bicentennial costume, or in any other employer-designed uniform, but whether Sage could require plaintiff Hasselman, a female lobby attendant, to wear a uniform which subjected her to sexual harassment on the job. Sage has disclaimed any intention to express itself artistically by dressing its lobby personnel in sexually revealing outfits.

Similarly without merit is any contention that the wearing of a sexually revealing Bicentennial uniform is a bona fide occupational qualification ("bfoq") pursuant to section 703(d). While it may well be a bfoq for Sage to require female lobby attendants in its buildings to wear certain uniforms designed to present a unique image, in accordance with its philosophy of urban design, it is beyond dispute that the wearing of sexually revealing garments does not constitute a bfoq. Indeed, the evidence establishes that wearing the uniform interfered with Hasselman's ability to perform her job.

Accordingly, the Court finds that Sage and Monahan Cleaners, in discriminating against plaintiff Hasselman on the basis of sex, committed an unlawful employment practice in violation of section 703(a).

## NOTES AND QUESTIONS

**1.** The court relied on the fact that Hasselman was subjected to harassment by customers. Suppose there were no lewd comments or gestures.

Should this affect the outcome of the case? Should Hasselman's humiliation and embarrassment be judged on a subjective or objective basis?

**2.** Suppose the uniform had been short, but not open at the sides and sexually provocative. Could Sage have refused to hire Hasselman because it did not think her legs were attractive enough? What is the relationship between dress requirements and appearance requirements?

**3.** Suppose Sage Realty had required that a provocative Bicentennial costume be worn by both male and female employees. Would the result in *Sage* have been the same?

**4.** In some occupations a sexually provocative appearance is the "essence of the business" and therefore it would not violate Title VII to require "exotic dancers" or Playboy "bunnies" to wear revealing costumes. What about a requirement that cocktail waitresses and restaurant employees wear provocative clothing? In 1993, the EEOC and the Sands Hotel Casino in Atlantic City settled a Title VII action brought by female cocktail servers who complained about the costumes they were required to wear. Female employees were required to wear sexually revealing and provocative costumes, while male servers wore tuxedo pants and shirts. According to the settlement, the casino agreed to provide female cocktail servers with "gender appropriate" costumes that will be "neither revealing nor provocative." Daily Lab.Rep. (BNA), Oct. 18, 1993, at A–10. The settlement allows female cocktail servers to choose between continuing to wear their current costumes or the new, more modest, attire. Are any problems created by giving employees a choice of uniform?

**5.** Suppose that some female employees (such as cocktail servers) preferred to wear the challenged outfit (perhaps on a theory that they get better tips). How should the court rule in a *Sage*-type suit brought by a more modest employee?

Six female, former waitresses at the Hooters restaurant in Minneapolis filed a lawsuit in 1993 alleging sex discrimination and sexual harassment in violation of the Minnesota Human Rights Act. The suit alleges, among other things, that the plaintiffs were required to wear sexually provocative outfits (see photo below) and that they had to endure sexually offensive remarks and contact. The suit claims that the employer deliberately promoted a sexually-charged and hostile environment, which included the name of the restaurant (slang for breasts) and sign over the door which read: "Men: no shirt, no shoes: no service. Women: no shirt: free food." Both customers and supervisors were alleged to have made numerous unwelcome remarks of a sexual nature as well as unwelcome touching.

Have the women "assumed the risk" of this conduct by going to work for such an employer? See Kelly Ann Cahill, Hooters: Should There Be an Assumption of Risk Defense to Some Hostile Work Environment Sexual Harassment Claims?, 48 Vand.L.Rev. 1107 (1995). What is the essence of

## PROBLEM FOR DISCUSSION:  DEFINING ESSENCE OF THE BUSINESS

Plaintiffs' attorney Lori Peterson shows one of the T-shirts that
female Hooters employees were required to wear at one time.

the business?   Compare the *Wilson* (supra p. 277 and *Sage* (supra p. 563
cases.   If you think that the conduct of Hooters is unlawful, would it be
unlawful if the employer were a topless bar?   Should it matter if Hooters
calls itself a "family restaurant?"   Can you formulate some workable legal
doctrine to cover "mixed essence" businesses?

## PROBLEM FOR DISCUSSION:  IS THE REQUIREMENT THAT EMPLOYEES WEAR UNIFORMS A FORM OF DISCRIMINATION?

The women in the above photograph are bank employees wearing their required "career ensemble," which consists of a color-coordinated skirt or slacks and a choice of a jacket, tunic, or vest.   The dress requirement applies to all female tellers, office, and managerial employees; male employees need wear only customary business attire.   Does this dress requirement violate Title VII?   See Carroll v. Talman Federal Savings & Loan Association, 604 F.2d 1028 (7th Cir.1979), cert. denied, 445 U.S. 929 (1980) (held: Title VII violation).   Accord, Department of Civil Rights v. Edward W. Sparrow Hospital Association, 377 N.W.2d 755 (Mich.1985) (state fair employment practice law violation for hospital to require female, but not male, technologists to wear uniform under white lab coat). See generally Marc Linder, Smart Women, Stupid Shoes, and Cynical Employers: The Unlawfulness and Adverse Health Consequences of Sexually Discriminatory Workplace Footwear Requirements for Female Employees, 22 J.Corporation L. 295 (1997).

Suppose the employer had a dress requirement applicable to all male and female employees in clerical and teller positions, but not managers, with the effect that mostly female employees were subject to the dress code. Would this rule be discriminatory?

**1.**   In O'Donnell v. Burlington Coat Factory Warehouse, Inc., 656 F.Supp. 263 (S.D.Ohio 1987), the employer required female sales clerks to wear a smock while allowing male sales clerks to wear a shirt and tie.   Despite a lack of discriminatory motive, the court held that the dress rule had the "blatant effect" of perpetuating sexual stereotypes.   "[I]t is demeaning for one sex to wear a uniform when members of the other sex holding the same positions are allowed to wear professional business attire.   * * * [T]he smock rule creates disadvantages to the conditions of employment of female sales clerks and hence, is a violation of Title VII."

**2.**   Is it sex discrimination for a state court judge to require that male attorneys appear in court wearing neckties without a similar requirement for female attorneys?   See Devine v. Lonschein, 621 F.Supp. 894 (S.D.N.Y. 1985), affirmed, 800 F.2d 1127 (2d Cir.1986) (held: no).

**3.**   Would an employer violate Title VII by prohibiting women employees from wearing pants in the executive offices?   See Lanigan v. Bartlett & Co. Grain, 466 F.Supp. 1388 (W.D.Mo.1979) (held: no). In 1994, California enacted a law that makes it illegal for an employer to prohibit female employees from wearing pants to work, unless special clothing is required as a uniform or costume.   Cal. Gov't Code § 12947.5. See generally Nadine Taub, Keeping Women in Their Place: Stereotyping Per Se as a Form of Discrimination, 21 B.C.L.Rev. 345 (1980).

**4.**   Apart from claims of sex discrimination, are uniforms per se discriminatory, in that they institutionalize dominant-subordinate status relationships?   Do employers have legitimate business justifications for uniform requirements?   See generally Mary Whisner, Gender Specific Clothing Regulation: A Study in Patriarchy 4–5 Harv. Women's L.J. 73 (1981–82).

## 2.   HARASSMENT

### Daniel Goleman, *Sexual Harassment: About Power, Not Lust*

N.Y. Times, Oct. 22, 1991, at C1.*

Consider the case of a male supervisor who, in the midst of a conversation with a female employee about an assignment, asked her out of the blue, "Are you wearing panties?" and then blithely continued the conversation seemingly pleased that he had left her rattled.

Years later, the woman says she is still outraged by the incident, though she said nothing at the time. One of a flood of tales that have surfaced in the wake of Anita F. Hill's accusations of sexual harassment in hearings on Clarence Thomas's Supreme Court nomination, the story underscores a picture that is emerging from extensive research on such harassment: it has less to do with sex than with power. It is a way to keep women in their place; through harassment men devalue a woman's role in the work place by calling attention to her sexuality.

"Sexual harassment is a subtle rape, and rape is more about fear than sex," said Dr. John Gottman, a psychologist at the University of Washington. "Harassment is a way for a man to make a woman vulnerable."

While sexual harassment may on first glance be taken as simple social ineptness or as an awkward expression of romantic attraction, researchers say that view is wrong and pernicious because it can lead women who suffer harassment to blame themselves, believing that something in their dress or behavior might have brought the unwanted attention.

In fact, only about 25 percent of cases of sexual harassment are botched seductions, in which the man "is trying to get someone into bed," said Dr. Louise Fitzgerald, a psychologist at the University of Illinois. "And in less than 5 percent of cases the harassment involves a bribe or threat for sex, where the man is saying, 'If you do this for me, I'll help you at work, and if you don't, I'll make things difficult for you.' " The rest, she said, are assertions of power.

The use of harassment as a tactic to control or frighten women, researchers say, explains why sexual harassment is most frequent in occupations and work places where women are new and are in the minority. In fact, no matter how many men they encounter in the course of their work, women who hold jobs traditionally held by men are far more likely to be harassed than women who do "women's work."

For example, a 1989 study of 100 women working in a factory found that those who were machinists, not a job traditionally held by women, reported being harassed far more than those on the assembly line, where more women work. Women in both groups encountered about the same number of men at work.

* Copyright © 1991 by the New York Times Company. Reprinted by permission.

"On all 28 items of a sexual harassment scale, ranging from lewd remarks to sexual assault, the women machinists had the highest scores," said Dr. Nancy Baker, a psychologist in Los Angeles who conducted the study. "Among women in white-collar jobs, the same holds true. The more nontraditional the job for women, the more sexual harassment. Women surgeons and investment bankers rank among the highest for harassment."

The style of harassment also is likely to differ among professionals and blue-collar workers. "In the blue-collar work place, there's often a real hostility to women," said Dr. Fitzgerald. "Men see women as invading a masculine environment. These are guys whose sexual harassment has nothing whatever to do with sex. They're trying to scare women off a male preserve."

Dr. Fitzgerald added, "Professional men don't go around putting used condoms in your desk, as can happen in a blue-collar setting. It's more likely to be something like what happened to a woman lawyer I know at a large international firm. As she was sitting at a conference table with other executives, all men, she said, 'I have two points,' and one of the men interrupted, 'Yes you do, and they look wonderful.'"

Some harassment simply seems to result from what Dr. Fitzgerald calls a "cultural lag." "Many men entered the work place at a time when sexual teasing and innuendo were common-place," she said. "They have no sense there's anything wrong with it. All they need is some education."

But genuine harassers, Dr. Fitzgerald said, "continue to do offensive things even when a woman tells them it is obnoxious."

In a 1981 study of 10,648 women working for the Federal Government, 42 percent said they had been harassed. In a third of cases the harassment took the form of unwanted sexual remarks; 28 percent involved leers and suggestive looks, and a quarter involved being touched. About 15 percent of women complained of being pressured for dates, and 9 percent said they had been pressured for sexual favors. One percent reported being assaulted or raped at work.

Sexual harassment of men is much less common and is little studied by researchers.

To be sure, there is a gulf in men's and women's perceptions, a gray zone that may itself lead to some instances of harassment. For instance, in a random telephone survey of 1,000 men and women in Los Angeles, Dr. Barbara Gutek, a psychologist at the University of Arizona business school, found that 67 percent of men said they would be complimented if they were propositioned by a woman at work. Seventeen percent of women said so. The same survey found that 10 percent of women had left a job because of sexual harassment.

\* \* \*

While the current uproar about sexual harassment may make some men feel uneasy that some of their own behavior could be construed by women as sexual harassment, the best guess is that fewer than 1 percent of men are chronic harassers, said Dr. Gutek.

* * *

Several studies have found that only 3 percent of women who have been sexually harassed make a formal complaint. "We find that close to 90 percent of women who have been sexually harassed want to leave, but can't because they need their job," said Dr. Paludi.

Despite company policies forbidding harassment, many victims say they believe that reporting it will simply lead to more trouble. In a study of 2,000 women working at large state universities, Dr. Fitzgerald found that most had not reported sexual harassment because they feared they would not be believed, that they would suffer retaliation, would be labeled as troublemakers, or would lose their jobs. Some women say they stay silent because they fear that reporting an incident may cost the harasser his job or his marriage.

Another reason most women who are sexually harassed remain silent is that "women feel a responsibility to be emotional managers of relationships and often want to keep things friendly," said Antonio Abbey, a psychologist at Wayne State University.

In research with victims of sexual harassment, Dr. Paludi has found that the emotional aftermath can be similar to that found in victims of traumas like rape or assault.

## Ellison v. Brady

924 F.2d 872 (9th Cir.1991).

■ BEEZER, CIRCUIT JUDGE:

Kerry Ellison appeals the district court's order granting summary judgment to the Secretary of the Treasury on her sexual harassment action brought under Title VII of the Civil Rights Act of 1964. This appeal presents two important issues: (1) what test should be applied to determine whether conduct is sufficiently severe or pervasive to alter the conditions of employment and create a hostile working environment, and (2) what remedial actions can shield employers from liability for sexual harassment by co-workers. The district court held that Ellison did not state a prima facie case of hostile environment sexual harassment. We reverse and remand * * *.

I.

Kerry Ellison worked as a revenue agent for the Internal Revenue Service in San Mateo, California. During her initial training in 1984 she met Sterling Gray, another trainee, who was also assigned to the San Mateo office. The two co-workers never became friends, and they did not work closely together.

Gray's desk was twenty feet from Ellison's desk, two rows behind and one row over. Revenue agents in the San Mateo office often went to lunch in groups. In June of 1986 when no one else was in the office, Gray asked Ellison to lunch. She accepted. Gray had to pick up his son's forgotten lunch, so they stopped by Gray's house. He gave Ellison a tour of his house.

Ellison alleges that after the June lunch Gray started to pester her with unnecessary questions and hang around her desk. On October 9, 1986, Gray asked Ellison out for a drink after work. She declined, but she suggested that they have lunch the following week. She did not want to have lunch alone with him, and she tried to stay away from the office during lunch time. One day during the following week, Gray uncharacteristically dressed in a three-piece suit and asked Ellison out for lunch. Again, she did not accept.

On October 22, 1986 Gray handed Ellison a note he wrote on a telephone message slip which read:

> I cried over you last night and I'm totally drained today. I have never been in such constant term oil (sic). Thank you for talking with me. I could not stand to feel your hatred for another day.

When Ellison realized that Gray wrote the note, she became shocked and frightened and left the room. Gray followed her into the hallway and demanded that she talk to him, but she left the building.

Ellison later showed the note to Bonnie Miller, who supervised both Ellison and Gray. Miller said "this is sexual harassment." Ellison asked Miller not to do anything about it. She wanted to try to handle it herself. Ellison asked a male co-worker to talk to Gray, to tell him that she was not interested in him and to leave her alone. The next day, Thursday, Gray called in sick.

Ellison did not work on Friday, and on the following Monday, she started four weeks of training in St. Louis, Missouri. Gray mailed her a card and a typed, single-spaced, three-page letter. She describes this letter as "twenty times, a hundred times weirder" than the prior note. Gray wrote, in part:

> I know that you are worth knowing with or without sex * * *. Leaving aside the hassles and disasters of recent weeks. I have enjoyed you so much over these past few months. Watching you. Experiencing you from O so far away. Admiring your style and elan * * *. Don't you think it odd that two people who have never even talked together, alone, are striking off such intense sparks * * * I will [write] another letter in the near future.[1]

---

1. In the middle of the long letter Gray did say "I am obligated to you so much that if you want me to leave you alone I will * * *. If you want me to forget you entirely, I can not do that."

Explaining her reaction, Ellison stated: "I just thought he was crazy. I thought he was nuts. I didn't know what he would do next. I was frightened."

She immediately telephoned Miller. Ellison told her supervisor that she was frightened and really upset. She requested that Miller transfer either her or Gray because she would not be comfortable working in the same office with him. Miller asked Ellison to send a copy of the card and letter to San Mateo.

Miller then telephoned her supervisor, Joe Benton, and discussed the problem. That same day she had a counseling session with Gray. She informed him that he was entitled to union representation. During this meeting, she told Gray to leave Ellison alone.

At Benton's request, Miller apprised the labor relations department of the situation. She also reminded Gray many times over the next few weeks that he must not contact Ellison in any way. Gray subsequently transferred to the San Francisco office on November 24, 1986. Ellison returned from St. Louis in late November and did not discuss the matter further with Miller.

After three weeks in San Francisco, Gray filed union grievances requesting a return to the San Mateo office. The IRS and the union settled the grievances in Gray's favor, agreeing to allow him to transfer back to the San Mateo office provided that he spend four more months in San Francisco and promise not to bother Ellison. On January 28, 1987, Ellison first learned of Gray's request in a letter from Miller explaining that Gray would return to the San Mateo office. The letter indicated that management decided to resolve Ellison's problem with a six-month separation, and that it would take additional action if the problem recurred.

After receiving the letter, Ellison was "frantic." She filed a formal complaint alleging sexual harassment on January 30, 1987 with the IRS. She also obtained permission to transfer to San Francisco temporarily when Gray returned.

Gray sought joint counseling. He wrote Ellison another letter which still sought to maintain the idea that he and Ellison had some type of relationship.

The IRS employee investigating the allegation agreed with Ellison's supervisor that Gray's conduct constituted sexual harassment. In its final decision, however, the Treasury Department rejected Ellison's complaint because it believed that the complaint did not describe a pattern or practice of sexual harassment covered by the EEOC regulations. After an appeal, the EEOC affirmed the Treasury Department's decision on a different ground. It concluded that the agency took adequate action to prevent the repetition of Gray's conduct.

Ellison filed a complaint in September of 1987 in federal district court. The court granted the government's motion for summary judgment on the ground that Ellison had failed to state a prima facie case of sexual harassment due to a hostile working environment. Ellison appeals.

## II.

Congress added the word "sex" to Title VII of the Civil Rights Act of 1964 at the last minute on the floor of the House of Representatives. Virtually no legislative history provides guidance to courts interpreting the prohibition of sex discrimination. In Meritor Savings Bank v. Vinson, the Supreme Court held that sexual harassment constitutes sex discrimination in violation of Title VII.

Courts have recognized different forms of sexual harassment. In "quid pro quo" cases, employers condition employment benefits on sexual favors. In "hostile environment" cases, employees work in offensive or abusive environments. This case, like *Meritor,* involves a hostile environment claim.

\* \* \*

## III.

The parties ask us to determine if Gray's conduct, as alleged by Ellison, was sufficiently severe or pervasive to alter the conditions of Ellison's employment and create an abusive working environment. The district court, with little Ninth Circuit case law to look to for guidance, held that Ellison did not state a prima facie case of sexual harassment due to a hostile working environment. It believed that Gray's conduct was "isolated and genuinely trivial." We disagree.

\* \* \*

Although *Meritor* and our previous cases establish the framework for the resolution of hostile environment cases, they do not dictate the outcome of this case. Gray's conduct falls somewhere between forcible rape and the mere utterance of an epithet. \* \* \*

The government asks us to apply the reasoning of other courts which have declined to find Title VII violations on more egregious facts. In Scott v. Sears, Roebuck & Co., 798 F.2d 210, 212 (7th Cir.1986), the Seventh Circuit analyzed a female employee's working conditions for sexual harassment. It noted that she was repeatedly propositioned and winked at by her supervisor. When she asked for assistance, he asked "what will I get for it?" Co-workers slapped her buttocks and commented that she must moan and groan during sex. The court examined the evidence to see if "the demeaning conduct and sexual stereotyping cause[d] such anxiety and debilitation to the plaintiff that working conditions were 'poisoned' within the meaning of Title VII." The court did not consider the environment sufficiently hostile.

Similarly, in Rabidue v. Osceola Refining Co., 805 F.2d 611 (6th Cir.1986), cert. denied, 481 U.S. 1041, 107 S.Ct. 1983, 95 L.Ed.2d 823 (1987), the Sixth Circuit refused to find a hostile environment where the workplace contained posters of naked and partially dressed women, and where a male employee customarily called women "whores," "cunt," "pussy," and "tits," referred to plaintiff as "fat ass," and specifically stated, "All that bitch needs is a good lay." Over a strong dissent, the majority held that the sexist remarks and the pin-up posters had only a de minimis effect and did not seriously affect the plaintiff's psychological well-being.

We do not agree with the standards set forth in *Scott* and *Rabidue*, and we choose not to follow those decisions. Neither *Scott's* search for "anxiety and debilitation" sufficient to "poison" a working environment nor *Rabidue's* requirement that a plaintiff's psychological well-being be "seriously affected" follows directly from language in *Meritor*. It is the harasser's conduct which must be pervasive or severe, not the alteration in the conditions of employment. Surely, employees need not endure sexual harassment until their psychological well-being is seriously affected to the extent that they suffer anxiety and debilitation. Although an isolated epithet by itself fails to support a cause of action for a hostile environment, Title VII's protection of employees from sex discrimination comes into play long before the point where victims of sexual harassment require psychiatric assistance.

We have closely examined *Meritor* and our previous cases, and we believe that Gray's conduct was sufficiently severe and pervasive to alter the conditions of Ellison's employment and create an abusive working environment. We first note that the required showing of severity or seriousness of the harassing conduct varies inversely with the pervasiveness or frequency of the conduct.

Next, we believe that in evaluating the severity and pervasiveness of sexual harassment, we should focus on the perspective of the victim. If we only examined whether a reasonable person would engage in allegedly harassing conduct, we would run the risk of reinforcing the prevailing level of discrimination. Harassers could continue to harass merely because a particular discriminatory practice was common, and victims of harassment would have no remedy.

We therefore prefer to analyze harassment from the victim's perspective. A complete understanding of the victim's view requires, among other things, an analysis of the different perspectives of men and women. Conduct that many men consider unobjectionable may offend many women.

We realize that there is a broad range of viewpoints among women as a group, but we believe that many women share common concerns which men do not necessarily share.[9] For example, because women are dispropor-

---

**9.** One writer explains: "While many women hold positive attitudes about uncoerced sex, their greater physical and social vulnerability to sexual coercion can make women wary of sexual encounters. Moreover, American women have been raised in a society where rape and sex-related violence have reached unprecedented levels, and a vast pornography industry creates continuous images of sexual coercion, objectification and violence. Finally, women as a group tend to hold more restrictive views of both the situation and type of relationship in which sexual conduct is appropriate. Because of the inequality and coercion with which it is so frequently associated in the minds of women, the appearance of sexuality in an unexpected context or a setting of ostensible equality can be an anguishing experience." Abrams, Gender Discrimination and the Transformation

tionately victims of rape and sexual assault, women have a stronger incentive to be concerned with sexual behavior. Women who are victims of mild forms of sexual harassment may understandably worry whether a harasser's conduct is merely a prelude to violent sexual assault. Men, who are rarely victims of sexual assault, may view sexual conduct in a vacuum without a full appreciation of the social setting or the underlying threat of violence that a woman may perceive.

In order to shield employers from having to accommodate the idiosyncratic concerns of the rare hyper-sensitive employee, we hold that a female plaintiff states a prima facie case of hostile environment sexual harassment when she alleges conduct which a reasonable woman [11] would consider sufficiently severe or pervasive to alter the conditions of employment and create an abusive working environment.[12]

We adopt the perspective of a reasonable woman primarily because we believe that a sex-blind reasonable person standard tends to be male-biased and tends to systematically ignore the experiences of women. The reasonable woman standard does not establish a higher level of protection for women than men. Instead, a gender-conscious examination of sexual harassment enables women to participate in the workplace on an equal footing with men. By acknowledging and not trivializing the effects of sexual harassment on reasonable women, courts can work towards ensuring that neither men nor women will have to "run a gauntlet of sexual abuse in return for the privilege of being allowed to work and make a living."

We note that the reasonable victim standard we adopt today classifies conduct as unlawful sexual harassment even when harassers do not realize that their conduct creates a hostile working environment. Well-intentioned compliments by co-workers or supervisors can form the basis of a sexual harassment cause of action if a reasonable victim of the same sex as the plaintiff would consider the comments sufficiently severe or pervasive to alter a condition of employment and create an abusive working environment.[13] That is because Title VII is not a fault-based tort scheme. "Title VII is aimed at the consequences or effects of an employment practice and not at the * * * motivation" of co-workers or employers. To avoid liability under Title VII, employers may have to educate and sensitize their work-

of Workplace Norms, 42 Vand.L.Rev. 1183, 1205 (1989).

**11.** Of course, where male employees allege that co-workers engage in conduct which creates a hostile environment, the appropriate victim's perspective would be that of a reasonable man.

**12.** We realize that the reasonable woman standard will not address conduct which some women find offensive. Conduct considered harmless by many today may be considered discriminatory in the future. Fortunately, the reasonableness inquiry which we adopt today is not static. As the views of reasonable women change, so too does the Title VII standard of acceptable behavior.

**13.** If sexual comments or sexual advances are in fact welcomed by the recipient, they, of course, do not constitute sexual harassment. Title VII's prohibition of sex discrimination in employment does not require a totally desexualized work place.

force to eliminate conduct which a reasonable victim would consider unlawful sexual harassment.

The facts of this case illustrate the importance of considering the victim's perspective. Analyzing the facts from the alleged harasser's viewpoint, Gray could be portrayed as a modern-day Cyrano de Bergerac wishing no more than to woo Ellison with his words. There is no evidence that Gray harbored ill will toward Ellison. He even offered in his "love letter" to leave her alone if she wished. Examined in this light, it is not difficult to see why the district court characterized Gray's conduct as isolated and trivial.

Ellison, however, did not consider the acts to be trivial. Gray's first note shocked and frightened her. After receiving the three-page letter, she became really upset and frightened again. She immediately requested that she or Gray be transferred. Her supervisor's prompt response suggests that she too did not consider the conduct trivial. When Ellison learned that Gray arranged to return to San Mateo, she immediately asked to transfer, and she immediately filed an official complaint.

We cannot say as a matter of law that Ellison's reaction was idiosyncratic or hyper-sensitive. We believe that a reasonable woman could have had a similar reaction. After receiving the first bizarre note from Gray, a person she barely knew, Ellison asked a co-worker to tell Gray to leave her alone. Despite her request, Gray sent her a long, passionate, disturbing letter. He told her he had been "watching" and "experiencing" her; he made repeated references to sex; he said he would write again. Ellison had no way of knowing what Gray would do next. A reasonable woman could consider Gray's conduct, as alleged by Ellison, sufficiently severe and pervasive to alter a condition of employment and create an abusive working environment.

Sexual harassment is a major problem in the workplace. Adopting the victim's perspective ensures that courts will not "sustain ingrained notions of reasonable behavior fashioned by the offenders." Congress did not enact Title VII to codify prevailing sexist prejudices. To the contrary, "Congress designed Title VII to prevent the perpetuation of stereotypes and a sense of degradation which serve to close or discourage employment opportunities for women." We hope that over time both men and women will learn what conduct offends reasonable members of the other sex. When employers and employees internalize the standard of workplace conduct we establish today, the current gap in perception between the sexes will be bridged.

### IV.

We next must determine what remedial actions by employers shield them from liability under Title VII for sexual harassment by co-workers. * * *

We * * * believe that remedies should be "reasonably calculated to end the harassment." An employer's remedy should persuade individual harassers to discontinue unlawful conduct. We do not think that all harassment warrants dismissal; rather, remedies should be "assessed proportionately to the seriousness of the offense." Employers should impose sufficient penalties to assure a workplace free from sexual harassment. In essence, then, we think that the reasonableness of an employer's remedy will depend on its ability to stop harassment by the person who engaged in harassment.[17] In evaluating the adequacy of the remedy, the court may also take into account the remedy's ability to persuade potential harassers to refrain from unlawful conduct. Indeed, meting out punishments that do not take into account the need to maintain a harassment-free working environment may subject the employer to suit by the EEOC.

Here, Ellison's employer argues that it complied with its statutory obligation to provide a workplace free from sexual harassment. It promptly investigated Ellison's allegation. When Ellison returned to San Mateo from her training in St. Louis, Gray was no longer working in San Mateo. When Gray returned to San Mateo, the government granted Ellison's request to transfer temporarily to San Francisco.

We decline to accept the government's argument that its decision to return Gray to San Mateo did not create a hostile environment for Ellison because the government granted Ellison's request for a temporary transfer to San Francisco. Ellison preferred to work in San Mateo over San Francisco. We strongly believe that the victim of sexual harassment should not be punished for the conduct of the harasser. We wholeheartedly agree with the EEOC that a victim of sexual harassment should not have to work in a less desirable location as a result of an employer's remedy for sexual harassment.

Ellison maintains that the government's remedy was insufficient because it did not discipline Gray and because it allowed Gray to return to San Mateo after only a six-month separation. Even though the hostile environment had been eliminated when Gray began working in San Francisco, we cannot say that the government's response was reasonable under Title VII. The record on appeal suggests that Ellison's employer did not express strong disapproval of Gray's conduct, did not reprimand Gray, did not put him on probation, and did not inform him that repeated harassment would result in suspension or termination. Apparently, Gray's employer only told him to stop harassing Ellison. Title VII requires more than a mere request to refrain from discriminatory conduct. Employers send the wrong message to potential harassers when they do not discipline employees for sexual harassment. If Ellison can prove on remand that Gray knew or should have known that his conduct was unlawful and that the government failed to take even the mildest form of disciplinary action,

---

**17.** We do not think that the appropriate inquiry is what a reasonable employer would do to remedy the sexual harassment. Although employers are statutorily obligated to provide a workplace free from sexual harassment, they may be reluctant, for business reasons, to punish high ranking and highly productive employees for sexual harassment. In addition, asking what a reasonable employer would do runs the risk of reinforcing any prevailing level of discrimination by employers and fails to focus directly on the best way to eliminate sexual harassment from the workplace.

the district court should hold that the government's initial remedy was insufficient under Title VII. At this point, genuine issues of material fact remain concerning whether the government properly disciplined Gray.

Ellison further maintains that her employer's decision to allow Gray to transfer back to the San Mateo office after a six-month cooling-off period rendered the government's remedy insufficient. She argues that Gray's *mere presence* would create a hostile working environment.

We believe that in some cases the mere presence of an employee who has engaged in particularly severe or pervasive harassment can create a hostile working environment. To avoid liability under Title VII for failing to remedy a hostile environment, employers may even have to remove employees from the workplace if their mere presence would render the working environment hostile. Once again, we examine whether the mere presence of a harasser would create a hostile environment from the perspective of a reasonable woman.

The district court did not reach the issue of the reasonableness of the government's remedy. Given the scant record on appeal, we cannot determine whether a reasonable woman could conclude that Gray's mere presence at San Mateo six months after the alleged harassment would create an abusive environment. Although we are aware of the severity of Gray's conduct (which we do not consider to be as serious as some other forms of harassment), we do not know how often Ellison and Gray would have to interact at San Mateo.

Moreover, it is not clear to us that the six-month cooling-off period was reasonably calculated to end the harassment or assessed proportionately to the seriousness of Gray's conduct. There is evidence in the record which suggests that the government intended to transfer Gray to San Francisco permanently and only allowed Gray to return to San Mateo because he promised to drop some union grievances. We do know that the IRS did not request Ellison's input or even inform her of the proceedings before agreeing to let Gray return to San Mateo. This failure to even attempt to determine what impact Gray's return would have on Ellison shows an insufficient regard for the victim's interest in avoiding a hostile working environment. On remand, the district court should fully explore the facts concerning the government's decision to return Gray to San Mateo.

V.

We reverse the district court's decision that Ellison did not allege a prima facie case of sexual harassment due to a hostile working environment, and we remand for further proceedings consistent with this opinion. Although we have considered the evidence in the light most favorable to Ellison because the district court granted the government's motion for summary judgment, we, of course, reserve for the district court the resolution of all factual issues.

■ STEPHENS, DISTRICT JUDGE, dissenting:

This case comes to us on appeal in the wake of the granting of a summary judgment motion. There was no trial, therefore no opportunities for cross examination of the witnesses. In addition, there are factual gaps in the record that can only lead by speculation. Consequently, I believe that it is an inappropriate case with which to establish a new legal precedent which will be binding in all subsequent cases of like nature in the Ninth Circuit. I refer to the majority's use of the term "reasonable woman," a term I find ambiguous and therefore inadequate.

Nowhere in section 2000e of Title VII, the section under which the plaintiff in this case brought suit, is there any indication that Congress intended to provide for any other than equal treatment in the area of civil rights. The legislation is designed to achieve a balanced and generally gender neutral and harmonious workplace which would improve production and the quality of the employees' lives. In fact, the Supreme Court has shown a preference against systems that are not gender or race neutral, such as hiring quotas. While women may be the most frequent targets of this type of conduct that is at issue in this case, they are not the only targets. I believe that it is incumbent upon the court in this case to use terminology that will meet the needs of all who seek recourse under this section of Title VII. Possible alternatives that are more in line with a gender neutral approach include "victim," "target," or "person."

The term "reasonable man" as it is used in the law of torts, traditionally refers to the average adult person, regardless of gender, and the conduct that can reasonably be expected of him or her. For the purposes of the legal issues that are being addressed, such a term assumes that it is applicable to all persons. Section 2000e of Title VII presupposes the use of a legal term that can apply to all persons and the impossibility of a more individually tailored standard. It is clear that the authors of the majority opinion intend a difference between the "reasonable woman" and the "reasonable man" in Title VII cases on the assumption that men do not have the same sensibilities as women. This is not necessarily true. A man's response to circumstances faced by women and their effect upon women can be and in given circumstances may be expected to be understood by men.

It takes no stretch of the imagination to envision two complaints emanating from the same workplace regarding the same conditions, one brought by a woman and the other by a man. Application of the "new standard" presents a puzzlement which is born of the assumption that men's eyes do not see what a woman sees through her eyes. I find it surprising that the majority finds no need for evidence on any of these subjects. I am not sure whether the majority also concludes that the woman and the man in question are also reasonable without evidence on this subject. I am irresistibly drawn to the view that the conditions of the workplace itself should be examined as affected, among other things, by the conduct of the people working there as to whether the workplace as existing is conducive to fulfilling the goals of Title VII. In any event, these are unresolved factual issues which preclude summary judgment.

The focus on the victim of the sexually discriminatory conduct has its parallel in rape trials in the focus put by the defense on the victim's conduct rather than on the unlawful conduct of the person accused. Modern feminists have pointed out that concentration by the defense upon evidence concerning the background, appearance and conduct of women claiming to have been raped must be carefully controlled by the court to avoid effectively shifting the burden of proof to the victim. It is the accused, not the victim who is on trial, and it is therefore the conduct of the accused, not that of the victim, that should be subjected to scrutiny. Many state legislatures have responded to this viewpoint, and rules governing the presentation of evidence in rape cases have evolved accordingly.

It is my opinion that the case should be reversed with instructions to proceed to trial. This would certainly lead to filling in the factual gaps left by the scanty record, such as what happened at the time of or after the visit of Ellison to Gray's house to cause her to be subsequently fearful of his presence. The circumstances existing in the work place where only men are employed are different than they are where there are both male and female employees. The existence of the differences is readily recognizable and the conduct of employees can be changed appropriately. This is what Title VII requires. Whether a man or a woman has sensibilities peculiar to the person and what they are is not necessarily known. Until they become known by manifesting themselves in an obvious way, they do not become part of the circumstances of the work place. Consequently, the governing element in the equation is the work place itself, not concepts or viewpoints of individual employees. This does not conflict with existing legal concepts.

The creation of the proposed "new standard" which applies only to women will not necessarily come to the aid of all potential victims of the type of misconduct that is at issue in this case. I believe that a gender neutral standard would greatly contribute to the clarity of this and future cases in the same area.

Summary judgment is not appropriate in this case.

## NOTES AND QUESTIONS

**1.** Although the Ninth Circuit's decision in Ellison v. Brady has attracted much attention for its application of a "reasonable woman standard" in a Title VII sexual harassment case, this case was not the first to hold that the crucial issue is the perspective of the victim. See also Andrews v. City of Philadelphia, 895 F.2d 1469 (3d Cir.1990); Harris v. International Paper Co., 765 F.Supp. 1509 (D.Me.1991), vacated in part on other grounds, 765 F.Supp. 1529 (D.Me.1991) (applying "reasonable black person standard," finding authority in earlier First Circuit case); Robinson v. Jacksonville Shipyards, Inc., 760 F.Supp. 1486 (M.D.Fla.1991); Barbetta v. Chemlawn Services Corp., 669 F.Supp. 569 (W.D.N.Y.1987).

**2.** Other courts continue to follow a "reasonable person" standard. In Rabidue v. Osceola Refining Co., 805 F.2d 611 (6th Cir.1986), cert. denied, 481 U.S. 1041 (1987), the court held that the "trier of fact ... must adopt the perspective of a reasonable person's reaction to a similar environment under essentially like or similar circumstances." It is worth noting, however, that the Sixth Circuit seems a bit confused about the appropriate standard to apply in such cases. For instance, in Yates v. Avco Corp., 819 F.2d 630 (6th Cir.1987), the court applied a "reasonable woman" standard without refuting the holding of the *Rabidue* court. While citing to the dissent in *Rabidue,* the *Yates* court nonetheless included the employer's intent in its inquiry. Later Sixth Circuit cases, however, seem to ignore *Yates.* See, e.g., Dabish v. Chrysler Motors Corp., 902 F.2d 32 (6th Cir.1990) (citing *Rabidue's* holding). The Seventh Circuit has followed the Sixth Circuit in applying a "reasonable person" standard. See Scott v. Sears, Roebuck & Co., 798 F.2d 210 (7th Cir.1986); Brooms v. Regal Tube Co., 881 F.2d 412 (7th Cir.1989).

**3.** Many courts seem unsure of which standard they are applying. For example, in Lipsett v. University of Puerto Rico, 864 F.2d 881 (1st Cir. 1988), the court held that the trier of fact must look to the perspective of both the victim and the perpetrator. Citing to the dissent in *Rabidue,* however, the court's decision has been held to constitute an affirmance of the "reasonable woman" standard. Similarly, the Fifth Circuit's finding in Bennett v. Corroon & Black Corp., 845 F.2d 104 (5th Cir.1988), cert. denied, 489 U.S. 1020 (1989), that "[a]ny reasonable person would have to consider these cartoons highly offensive to a woman * * *" leaves open the question of whether this is truly an application of a "reasonable person" standard. See generally Robert S. Adler & Ellen R. Peirce, The Legal, Ethical, and Social Implications of the "Reasonable Woman" Standard in Sexual Harassment Cases, 61 Fordham L.Rev. 773 (1993); Susan Estrich, Sex at Work, 43 Stan.L.Rev. 813 (1991).

A related issue is whether sexual harassment may be established where a hostile environment is created for members of both sexes. For example, in Steiner v. Showboat Operating Co., 25 F.3d 1459 (9th Cir.1994), cert. denied, 513 U.S. 1082 (1995), a casino supervisor had verbally abused both male and female employees. The Ninth Circuit held that there was sexual harassment because the supervisor's abuse of women was different because it relied on sexual epithets and explicit references to women's bodies and sexual conduct. In applying the reasonable woman standard, the court said that the supervisor cannot cure his conduct by equally degrading men.

**4.** Another pervasive question is what kind of emphasis to place on obscene language and pornographic pictures. The tendency of courts using a "reasonable person" standard is to hold that such evidence alone will not constitute a hostile environment. According to the *Rabidue* court, "[t]he sexually oriented poster displays had a de minimis effect on the plaintiff's work environment when considered in the context of a society that condones and publicly features and commercially exploits open displays of written and pictorial erotica at the newsstands, on prime-time television, at the cinema, and in other public places." Thus, such courts emphasize overt propositions, offensive touching, and similarly persuasive evidence. Moreover, courts relying on the "reasonable person" standard consider whether the workplace in question was always a place of lewd language and obscene behavior. Thus, if these men had always put up pornographic pictures or used offensive language, then their conduct would not be discriminatory. "The presence of actionable sexual harassment would be different depending upon the personality of the plaintiff and the prevailing work environment." These courts seem therefore to incorporate a fault-based standard into Title VII.

In Burns v. McGregor Electronic Industries, Inc., 989 F.2d 959 (8th Cir.1993), a female employee alleged hostile environment sexual harassment. The district court found that while a reasonable person would consider the complained of conduct to constitute sexual harassment, it did not constitute sexual harassment as to the plaintiff. It further stated that because the plaintiff had posed nude for *Easyriders* magazine, the uninvited sexual advances and crude behavior toward her were not offensive to her. The Eighth Circuit reversed. "The plaintiff's choice to pose nude for a magazine outside work hours is not material to the issue of whether plaintiff found her employer's work-related conduct offensive. * * * Her private life, regardless of how reprehensible the trier of fact might find it to be, did not provide lawful acquiescence to unwanted sexual advances at her workplace by her employer."

**5.** Where an employee had been sexually abused when she was younger and sexual harassment at work brings back memories of the abuse, should the employee's heightened response to the harassment affect the employer's liability? See Poole v. Copland, Inc., 481 S.E.2d 88 (N.C.Ct.App.1997) (in action for intentional infliction of emotional distress, standard is the employee of ordinary sensibilities unless the employer knew of the employee's peculiar susceptibility).

**6.** Whether sexual overtures or sexual horseplay were "unwelcome" often involves close questions of fact. See, e.g., Pascual v. Anchor Advanced Products, Inc., 819 F.Supp. 728 (E.D.Tenn.1993) (no Title VII violation where employees participated in sexual horseplay); Kouri v. Liberian Services, Inc., 55 FEP Cases 124, 1991 WL 50003 (E.D.Va.1991), affirmed mem., 960 F.2d 146 (4th Cir.1992) (no Title VII violation where plaintiff sent "mixed signals" by, among other things, exchanging gifts and notes with her supervisor).

**7.** One commentator has raised the question of whether a claim of hostile work environment, resulting from offensive speech alone, can withstand First Amendment arguments.

> The one circumstance in which expression might be relied upon consistent with the first amendment to support a claim of hostile environment is when expression is used to show motive, but the expression may not be used to add weight to the assertion that the environment was hostile. Because Title VII prohibits harassment only on the basis of protected status, an employee must show that harassment taking a nonsexual or nonracial form was the product of sexual or racial animus. What is said in the context of the harassment may well shed light on the motivation. If so, it should be admissible for that purpose. However, the trier of fact should

not be permitted to consider the offense engendered by the expression in determining whether the environment was a hostile one.

Kingsley R. Browne, Title VII as Censorship: Hostile Environment and the First Amendment, 52 Ohio St.L.J. 481 (1991). For contrary analyses of the issue of freedom of expression, compare Deborah Epstein, Can a "Dumb Ass Woman" Achieve Equality in the Workplace? Running the Gauntlet of the Hostile Environment Harassing Speech, 84 Geo.L.J. 399 (1996) with Eugene Volokh, What Speech Does "Hostile Work Environment" Harassment Law Restrict?, 85 Geo.L.J. 627 (1997).

**8.**  The first Supreme Court case to recognize sexual harassment was Meritor Savings Bank v. Vinson, 477 U.S. 57 (1986). The Court unanimously recognized that unwelcome sexual advances and other forms of hostile and intimidating behavior can create an abusive environment. Regardless of whether adverse economic consequences result from the harassment or the employee's reaction to the harassment, hostile environment sexual harassment is actionable as sex discrimination under Title VII. Title VII also forbids quid pro quo sexual harassment in which acquiescence to sexual demands is made a condition of employment or advancement.

In Faragher v. City of Boca Raton, 118 S.Ct. ___, 1998 WL 336322 (1998) and Burlington Industries, Inc. v. Ellerth, 118 S.Ct. ___, 1998 WL 336326 (1998), the Supreme Court delineated the burden of proof in cases of hostile environment sexual harassment by supervisors. An employer is vicariously liable for the sexual harassment of a supervisor. When the supervisor's action culminates in a tangible employment action, such as discharge, demotion, or undesirable reassignment, there is no defense available to the employer. When the employee suffers no tangible, adverse employment action, the employer may defend by showing that it exercised reasonable care to prevent and correct promptly any sexually harassing behavior and the employee unreasonably failed to take advantage of the preventive or corrective opportunity provided by the employer or to avoid harm otherwise. These decisions emphasize the importance of employers establishing, disseminating, and enforcing sexual harassment policies. See generally David Benjamin Oppenheimer, Exacerbating the Exasperating: Title VII Liability of Employers for Sexual Harassment Committed by their Supervisors, 81 Cornell L.Rev. 66 (1995).

**9.**  In Nichols v. Frank, 42 F.3d 503 (9th Cir.1994), the court reiterated *Meritor*'s holding that an employee's acquiescence in the sexual demands of a supervisor is not inconsistent with a finding that the employee's participation was "unwilling." The employee, a postal worker with total hearing and speech impairments, who communicated through sign language and notes, "was sexually harassed by her night-shift supervisor and, as a result, repeatedly but unwillingly performed oral sex on him over a period of approximately six months." The court used both objective and subjective tests to determine that the employee had a well-founded belief that failure to comply would result in loss of employment.

**10.** If the relationship is truly consensual, an action for hostile environment sexual harassment will not lie. See Herman v. Western Financial Corp., 869 P.2d 696 (Kan.1994). Nevertheless, many companies have adopted policies which forbid even consensual relationships among employees, especially where one of the employees has supervisory authority over the other.

**11.** If a supervisor gives preferential treatment to an employee with whom he is romantically involved, does this amount to sex discrimination against the other employees? See Thomson v. Olson, 56 F.3d 69 (8th Cir.1995) (held: no). For a further discussion, see, p. 670, note 6.

**12.** For a proposed new paradigm to deal with sexual harassment, in which "reasonableness" is replaced with the standard of a "respectful person," see Anita Bernstein, Treating Sexual Harassment with Respect, 111 Harv.L.Rev. 446 (1997).

## Harris v. Forklift Systems, Inc.

510 U.S. 17 (1993).

■ JUSTICE O'CONNOR delivered the opinion of the Court.

In this case we consider the definition of a discriminatorily "abusive work environment" (also known as a "hostile work environment") under Title VII of the Civil Rights Act of 1964.

Teresa Harris worked as a manager at Forklift Systems, Inc., an equipment rental company, from April 1985 until October 1987. Charles Hardy was Forklift's president.

The Magistrate found that, throughout Harris' time at Forklift, Hardy often insulted her because of her gender and often made her the target of unwanted sexual innuendos. Hardy told Harris on several occasions, in the presence of other employees, "You're a woman, what do you know" and "We need a man as the rental manager"; at least once, he told her she was "a dumb ass woman." Again in front of others, he suggested that the two of them "go to the Holiday Inn to negotiate [Harris'] raise." Hardy occasionally asked Harris and other female employees to get coins from his front pants pocket. He threw objects on the ground in front of Harris and other women, and asked them to pick the objects up. He made sexual innuendos about Harris' and other women's clothing.

In mid-August 1987, Harris complained to Hardy about his conduct. Hardy said he was surprised that Harris was offended, claimed he was only joking, and apologized.  He also promised he would stop, and based on this assurance Harris stayed on the job.  But in early September, Hardy began anew: While Harris was arranging a deal with one of Forklift's customers, he asked her, again in front of other employees, "What did you do, promise the guy * * * some [sex] Saturday night?"  On October 1, Harris collected her paycheck and quit.

Harris then sued Forklift, claiming that Hardy's conduct had created an abusive work environment for her because of her gender.  The United States District Court for the Middle District of Tennessee, adopting the report and recommendation of the Magistrate, found this to be "a close case," but held that Hardy's conduct did not create an abusive environment.  The court found that some of Hardy's comments "offended [Harris], and would offend the reasonable woman," but that they were not

> "so severe as to be expected to seriously affect [Harris'] psychological well-being.  A reasonable woman manager under like circumstances would have been offended by Hardy, but his conduct would not have risen to the level of interfering with that person's work performance.
>
>    "Neither do I believe that [Harris] was subjectively so offended that she suffered injury * * *.  Although Hardy may at times have genuinely offended [Harris], I do not believe that he created a working environment so poisoned as to be intimidating or abusive to [Harris]."

In focusing on the employee's psychological well-being, the District Court was following Circuit precedent.  See Rabidue v. Osceola Refining Co., 805 F.2d 611, 620 (CA6 1986), cert. denied, 481 U.S. 1041 (1987).  The United States Court of Appeals for the Sixth Circuit affirmed in a brief unpublished decision.

We granted certiorari to resolve a conflict among the Circuits on whether conduct, to be actionable as "abusive work environment" harassment (no *quid pro quo* harassment issue is present here), must "seriously affect [an employee's] psychological well-being" or lead the plaintiff to "suffe[r] injury."  Compare *Rabidue* (requiring serious effect on psychological well-being); Vance v. Southern Bell Telephone & Telegraph Co., 863 F.2d 1503, 1510 (CA11 1989) (same); and Downes v. FAA, 775 F.2d 288, 292 (CA Fed.1985) (same), with Ellison v. Brady, 924 F.2d 872, 877–878 (CA9 1991) (rejecting such a requirement).

Title VII of the Civil Rights Act of 1964 makes it "an unlawful employment practice for an employer * * * to discriminate against any individual with respect to his compensation, terms, conditions, or privileges of employment, because of such individual's race, color, religion, sex, or national origin."  As we made clear in Meritor Savings Bank v. Vinson, 477 U.S. 57 (1986), this language "is not limited to 'economic' or 'tangible' discrimination.  The phrase 'terms, conditions, or privileges of employment' evinces a congressional intent 'to strike at the entire spectrum of disparate treatment of men and women' in employment," which includes requiring people to work in a discriminatorily hostile or abusive environment. When the workplace is permeated with "discriminatory intimidation, ridicule, and insult," that is "sufficiently severe or pervasive to alter the conditions of the victim's employment and create an abusive working environment," Title VII is violated.

This standard, which we reaffirm today, takes a middle path between making actionable any conduct that is merely offensive and requiring the conduct to cause a tangible psychological injury. As we pointed out in *Meritor,* "mere utterance of an * * * epithet which engenders offensive feelings in a employee," does not sufficiently affect the conditions of employment to implicate Title VII. Conduct that is not severe or pervasive enough to create an objectively hostile or abusive work environment—an environment that a reasonable person would find hostile or abusive—is beyond Title VII's purview. Likewise, if the victim does not subjectively perceive the environment to be abusive, the conduct has not actually altered the conditions of the victim's employment, and there is no Title VII violation.

But Title VII comes into play before the harassing conduct leads to a nervous breakdown. A discriminatorily abusive work environment, even one that does not seriously affect employees' psychological well-being, can and often will detract from employees' job performance, discourage employees from remaining on the job, or keep them from advancing in their careers. Moreover, even without regard to these tangible effects, the very fact that the discriminatory conduct was so severe or pervasive that it created a work environment abusive to employees because of their race, gender, religion, or national origin offends Title VII's broad rule of workplace equality. The appalling conduct alleged in *Meritor,* and the reference in that case to environments " 'so heavily polluted with discrimination as to destroy completely the emotional and psychological stability of minority group workers,' " merely present some especially egregious examples of harassment. They do not mark the boundary of what is actionable.

We therefore believe the District Court erred in relying on whether the conduct "seriously affect[ed] plaintiff's psychological well-being" or led her to "suffe[r] injury." Such an inquiry may needlessly focus the factfinder's attention on concrete psychological harm, an element Title VII does not require. Certainly Title VII bars conduct that would seriously affect a reasonable person's psychological well-being, but the statute is not limited to such conduct. So long as the environment would reasonably be perceived, and is perceived, as hostile or abusive, there is no need for it also to be psychologically injurious.

This is not, and by its nature cannot be, a mathematically precise test. We need not answer today all the potential questions it raises, nor specifically address the EEOC's new regulations on this subject, see 58 Fed.Reg. 51266 (1993) (proposed 29 CFR §§ 1609.1, 1609.2); see also 29 CFR § 1604.11 (1993). But we can say that whether an environment is "hostile" or "abusive" can be determined only by looking at all the circumstances. These may include the frequency of the discriminatory conduct;

its severity; whether it is physically threatening or humiliating, or a mere offensive utterance; and whether it unreasonably interferes with an employee's work performance. The effect on the employee's psychological well-being is, of course, relevant to determining whether the plaintiff actually found the environment abusive. But while psychological harm, like any other relevant factor, may be taken into account, no single factor is required.

Forklift, while conceding that a requirement that the conduct seriously affect psychological well-being is unfounded, argues that the District Court nonetheless correctly applied the *Meritor* standard. We disagree. Though the District Court did conclude that the work environment was not "intimidating or abusive to [Harris]," it did so only after finding that the conduct was not "so severe as to be expected to seriously affect plaintiff's psychological well-being," and that Harris was not "subjectively so offended that she suffered injury," *ibid.* The District Court's application of these incorrect standards may well have influenced its ultimate conclusion, especially given that the court found this to be a "close case."

We therefore reverse the judgment of the Court of Appeals, and remand the case for further proceedings consistent with this opinion.

■ Justice Scalia, concurring.

Meritor Savings Bank v. Vinson, 477 U.S. 57 (1986), held that Title VII prohibits sexual harassment that takes the form of a hostile work environment. The Court stated that sexual harassment is actionable if it is "sufficiently severe or pervasive 'to alter the conditions of [the victim's] employment and create an abusive work environment.'" Today's opinion elaborates that the challenged conduct must be severe or pervasive enough "to create an objectively hostile or abusive work environment—an environment that a reasonable person would find hostile or abusive."

"Abusive" (or "hostile," which in this context I take to mean the same thing) does not seem to me a very clear standard—and I do not think clarity is at all increased by adding the adverb "objectively" or by appealing to a "reasonable person's" notion of what the vague word means. Today's opinion does list a number of factors that contribute to abusiveness, but since it neither says how much of each is necessary (an impossible task) nor identifies any single factor as determinative, it thereby adds little certitude. As a practical matter, today's holding lets virtually unguided juries decide whether sex-related conduct engaged in (or permitted by) an employer is egregious enough to warrant an award of damages. One might say that what constitutes "negligence" (a traditional jury question) is not much more clear and certain than what constitutes "abusiveness." Perhaps so. But the class of plaintiffs seeking to recover for negligence is limited to those who have suffered harm, whereas under this statute "abusiveness" is to be the test of whether legal harm has been suffered, opening more expansive vistas of litigation.

Be that as it may, I know of no alternative to the course the Court today has taken. One of the factors mentioned in the Court's nonexhaustive list—whether the conduct unreasonably interferes with an employee's work performance—would, if it were made an absolute test, provide greater guidance to juries and employers. But I see no basis for such a limitation in the language of the statute. Accepting *Meritor*'s interpretation of the term "conditions of employment" as the law, the test is not whether work has been impaired, but whether working conditions have been discriminatorily altered. I know of no test more faithful to the inherently vague statutory language than the one the Court today adopts. For these reasons, I join the opinion of the Court.

■ JUSTICE GINSBURG, concurring.

Today the Court reaffirms the holding of Meritor Savings Bank v. Vinson, 477 U.S. 57, 66 (1986): "[A] plaintiff may establish a violation of Title VII by proving that discrimination based on sex has created a hostile or abusive work environment." The critical issue, Title VII's text indicates, is whether members of one sex are exposed to disadvantageous terms or conditions of employment to which members of the other sex are not exposed. As the Equal Employment Opportunity Commission emphasized, the adjudicator's inquiry should center, dominantly, on whether the discriminatory conduct has unreasonably interfered with the plaintiff's work performance. To show such interference, "the plaintiff need not prove that his or her tangible productivity has declined as a result of the harassment." It suffices to prove that a reasonable person subjected to the discriminatory conduct would find, as the plaintiff did, that the harassment so altered working conditions as to "ma[k]e it more difficult to do the job."
* * *

The Court's opinion, which I join, seems to me in harmony with the view expressed in this concurring statement.

## NOTES AND QUESTIONS

**1.** The Court in *Harris* resolved only one of the unsettled issues from *Ellison*—whether the plaintiff must show severe psychological distress in a sexual harassment case. The more vexing issue is whether the "reasonable person" or the "reasonable victim" standard is applied. All three opinions in *Harris* refer to the "reasonable person." Is this an implicit repudiation of *Ellison?*

**2.** A former employee brought an action against her former employer alleging sexual harassment and retaliation. The employee claimed damages for both past and ongoing emotional distress. Is the employer entitled to conduct a psychological examination of her? See Jansen v. Packaging Corp. of America, 158 F.R.D. 409 (N.D.Ill.1994) (held: yes, but it did not have the right to use an expert of its own choice). How far should the employer's right of discovery extend? What are the dangers?

**3.** Justice Ginsburg's concurring opinion, her first opinion as a member of the Court, suggests that the focus should be on "whether the discriminatory conduct has unreasonably interfered with the plaintiff's work performance." This does not require a loss of productivity; it can be established by an alteration of working conditions that simply makes it "more difficult to do the job." How is the court to determine when a job has been made more difficult?

**4.** The EEOC guidelines on sex discrimination include a section on sexual harassment. 29 C.F.R. § 1604.11(a) provides:

Unwelcome sexual advances, requests for sexual favors, and other verbal or physical conduct of a sexual nature constitute sexual harassment when (1) submission to such conduct is made either explicitly or implicitly a term or condition of an individual's employment, (2) submission to or rejection of such conduct by an individual is used as the basis for employment decisions affecting such individual, or (3) such conduct has the purpose or effect of unreasonably interfering with an individual's work performance or creating an intimidating, hostile, or offensive working environment.

**5.** In addition to defining sexual harassment, the EEOC Guidelines define employer responsibility for the harassment of agents, supervisory employees, and coworkers. They also state that an employer "may also be responsible for the acts of non-employees, with respect to sexual harassment of employees in the workplace, where the employer (or its agents or supervisory employees) knows or should have known of the conduct and fails to take immediate and appropriate corrective action." 29 C.F.R. § 1604.11(e). In *Sage Realty,* supra p. 563, the employer was found guilty of sex discrimination on this theory when it ordered a female employee to wear a provocative costume. How far does this responsibility go? Kelly Services provides temporary office help to other businesses. Kelly is not an employment agency; the workers it sends to other businesses are Kelly employees. The large majority of Kelly's workforce is female. If a Kelly employee informs her supervisor that she has been sexually harassed by someone to whom Kelly provides services, what should Kelly do to avoid being held responsible?

**6.** In addition to Title VII remedies the victim of sexual harassment may be able to proceed on a breach of contract theory, see Monge v. Beebe Rubber Co., 316 A.2d 549 (N.H.1974), or a tort theory, see Phillips v. Smalley Maintenance Services, 435 So.2d 705 (Ala.1983). Sexual harassment also may support tort actions for assault, battery, and intentional infliction of emotional distress. See Rojo v. Kliger, 801 P.2d 373 (Cal. 1990); Ford v. Revlon, Inc., 734 P.2d 580 (Ariz.1987); Johnson v. Ramsey County, 424 N.W.2d 800 (Minn.App.1988). See generally Regina Austin, Employer Abuse, Worker Resistance, and the Tort of Intentional Infliction of Emotional Distress, 41 Stan.L.Rev. 1 (1988).

**7.** To what extent can factors external to the actual working environment help to establish hostile environment sexual harassment?

The Swedish Bikini Team originally appeared in three television commercials for Old Milwaukee Beer, a product of the Stroh Brewery Company of Detroit ("Stroh"). The commercials begin like many others of their genre: A group of men is outside engaging in stereotypically manly behavior—hiking, canoeing, and, of course, drinking beer—and believing that things could not be any better.  The twist, however, is that they *do* get better when several bikini-clad and identical-looking blond women—the Swedish Bikini Team—appear from out of the blue *with even more beer!* The Bikini Team has itself become very popular outside of the beer commercials and has even gone so far as to capture a Playboy cover and a "900" number.  The advertising campaign, however, also received a great deal of negative publicity, including a Time magazine award for being one of the worst advertising campaigns of the year.  * * *  The campaign has now been canceled.

More importantly, these commercials are the subject of several sexual harassment lawsuits in a state court in St. Paul, Minnesota, filed by eight factory workers at Stroh's St. Paul brewery.  In *Haston v. The Stroh Brewery Co.* and related cases, the women allege that they have been subjected to obscene and threatening behavior in the workplace ranging from the display of pornographic materials to physical fondling and sexist and racist comments. One woman claims that obscenities were written on the bathroom wall about her.  Another claims that a male employee "displayed his pubic hair and grabbed [her] head and pushed it down to his crotch."  The women allege that they had to eat lunch in a secluded corner in order to avoid the hostility in the lunchroom. In general, the women allege "sexual harassment, assault, battery, sexual battery, reprisal, defamation, and intentional and negligent infliction of emotional distress."

What is unique about the case is that the women claim that Stroh's Swedish Bikini Team advertising campaign contributed to the harassment by creating an "overall atmosphere of hostility" to women.  George Kuehn, General Counsel for Stroh, insists that the commercials were intended to parody typical beer commercials; advertisers claim that to force them off the air would be censorship.  The plaintiffs' attorney, Lori Peterson, responds that "if one man in the workplace says women are T & A [tits and ass], the law says that's sexual harassment.  If it's multiplied by a $19 million ad campaign, then it's considered a free-speech right."  Peterson insists the commercials are relevant because "it's a statement by this company about what women are for * * *.  [T]his company is saturated with sexism from top to bottom and * * * the employees are just following the employer's lead."

Stacy J. Cooper, Sexual Harassment and the Swedish Bikini Team: A reevaluation of the "Hostile Environment" Doctrine, 26 Colum.J.L. & Soc. Problems 387 (1993).  The state trial court judge ruled that the advertising campaign could not be used as evidence of a corporate culture that allegedly demeaned female workers.  The case was later settled.  In re Stroh Litigation, 63 FEP Cases (BNA) 258 (Minn.Dist.Ct.1993), summarized at Daily Lab.Rep., Dec. 2, 1993, at A–6.

**8.** Employers who pursue claims of sexual harassment too aggressively may be sued by the individual accused of doing the harassing. In Foley v. Polaroid Corp., 508 N.E.2d 72 (Mass.1987), an employee who was acquitted on charges of sexual assault of a coemployee sued his employer for malicious prosecution, false arrest, defamation, and outrageous conduct. The court held, however, that the employer acted with probable cause in instituting prosecution.

**9.** Harassment may be based on a variety of factors other than sex. It may be based on race, Snell v. Suffolk County, 782 F.2d 1094 (2d Cir.1986), national origin, Erebia v. Chrysler Plastic Products Corp., 772 F.2d 1250 (6th Cir.1985), cert. denied, 475 U.S. 1015 (1986), religion, Weiss v. United States, 595 F.Supp. 1050 (E.D.Va.1984), age, Crawford v. Medina General Hospital, 96 F.3d 830 (6th Cir. 1996), or other factors. These other forms of harassment are invariably of the "abusive environment" variety. The EEOC guidelines on these other forms of harassment appear at 58 Fed.Reg. 51,266 (1993).

## Oncale v. Sundowner Offshore Services, Inc.

118 S. Ct. 998 (1998).

■ JUSTICE SCALIA delivered the opinion of the Court.

This case presents the question whether workplace harassment can violate Title VII's prohibition against "discriminat[ion] ... because of ... sex," 42 U.S.C. § 2000e–2(a)(1), when the harasser and the harassed employee are of the same sex.

I

The District Court having granted summary judgment for respondent, we must assume the facts to be as alleged by petitioner Joseph Oncale. The precise details are irrelevant to the legal point we must decide, and in the interest of both brevity and dignity we shall describe them only generally. In late October 1991, Oncale was working for respondent Sundowner Offshore Services on a Chevron U.S.A., Inc., oil platform in the Gulf of Mexico. He was employed as a roustabout on an eight-man crew which included respondents John Lyons, Danny Pippen, and Brandon Johnson. Lyons, the crane operator, and Pippen, the driller, had supervisory authority. On several occasions, Oncale was forcibly subjected to sex-related, humiliating actions against him by Lyons, Pippen and Johnson in the presence of the rest of the crew. Pippen and Lyons also physically assaulted Oncale in a sexual manner, and Lyons threatened him with rape.

Oncale's complaints to supervisory personnel produced no remedial action; in fact, the company's Safety Compliance Clerk, Valent Hohen, told Oncale that Lyons and Pippen "picked [on] him all the time too," and called him a name suggesting homosexuality. Oncale eventually quit—

asking that his pink slip reflect that he "voluntarily left due to sexual harassment and verbal abuse."  When asked at his deposition why he left Sundowner, Oncale stated "I felt that if I didn't leave my job, that I would be raped or forced to have sex."

Joseph Oncale (center) at press conference in Baton Rouge, Louisiana, March 4, 1998, the day of the Supreme Court's decision. With him are his lawyers Andre LaPlace (left) and Nick Canady (right). AP Photo/Bill Haber.

Oncale filed a complaint against Sundowner in the United States District Court for the Eastern District of Louisiana, alleging that he was discriminated against in his employment because of his sex.  Relying on the Fifth Circuit's decision in Garcia v. Elf Atochem North America, 28 F.3d 446, 451–452 (C.A.5 1994), the district court held that "Mr. Oncale, a male, has no cause of action under Title VII for harassment by male co-workers." On appeal, a panel of the Fifth Circuit concluded that *Garcia* was binding Circuit precedent, and affirmed.  We granted certiorari.

## II

Title VII of the Civil Rights Act of 1964 provides, in relevant part, that "[i]t shall be an unlawful employment practice for an employer ... to discriminate against any individual with respect to his compensation, terms, conditions, or privileges of employment, because of such individual's race, color, religion, sex, or national origin." We have held that this not only covers "terms" and "conditions" in the narrow contractual sense, but "evinces a congressional intent to strike at the entire spectrum of disparate treatment of men and women in employment." Meritor Savings Bank, FSB v. Vinson, 477 U.S. 57, 64 (1986) (citations and internal quotation marks omitted). "When the workplace is permeated with discriminatory intimidation, ridicule, and insult that is sufficiently severe or pervasive to alter the condition of the victim's emplyment and create an abusive working environment, Title VII is violated." Harris v. Forklift Systems Inc., 510 U.S. 17, 21 (1993) (citations and internal quotation marks omitted.)

Title VII's prohibition of discrimination "because of .... sex" protects men as well as women, and in the related context of racial discrimination in the workplace we have rejected any conclusive presumption that an employer will not discriminate against members of his own race. "Because of the many facets of human motivation, it would be unwise to presume as a matter of law that human beings of one definable group will not discriminate against other members of that group." In Johnson v. Transportation Agency, Santa Clara Cty., 480 U.S. 616 (1987), a male employee claimed that his employer discriminated against him because of his sex when it preferred a female employee for promotion. Although we ultimately rejected the claim on other grounds, we did not consider it significant that the supervisor who made that decision was also a man. If our precedents leave any doubt on the question, we hold today that nothing in Title VII necessarily bars a claim of discrimination "because of ... sex." merely because the plaintiff and the defendant (or the person charged with acting on behalf of the defendant) are of the same sex.

Courts have had little trouble with that principle in cases like *Johnson,* where an employee claims to have been passed over for a job or promotion. But when the issue arises in the context of a "hostile environment" sexual harassment claim, the state and federal courts have taken a bewildering variety of stances. Some, like the Fifth Circuit in this case, have held that same-sex sexual harassment claims are never cognizable under Title VII. Other decisions say that such claims are actionable only if the plaintiff can prove that the harasser is homosexual (and thus presumably motivated by sexual desire). Still others suggest that workplace harassment that is sexual in content is always actionable, regardless of the harasser's sex, sexual orientation, or motivations.

We see no justification in the statutory language or our precedents for a categorical rule excluding same-sex harassment claims from the coverage of Title VII. As some courts have observed, male-on-male sexual harassment in the workplace was assuredly not the principal evil Congress was concerned with when it enacted Title VII. But statutory prohibitions often go beyond the principal evil to cover reasonably comparable evils, and it is ultimately the provisions of our laws rather than the principal concerns of our legislators by which we are governed. Title VII prohibits "discriminat[ion] ... because of ... sex" in the "terms" or "conditions" of employment. Our holding that this includes sexual harassment must extend to sexual harassment of any kind that meets the statutory requirments.

Respondents and their amici contend that recognizing liability for same-sex harassment will transform Title VII into a general civility code for the American workplace. But that risk is no greater for same-sex than for opposite-sex harassment, and is adequately met by careful attention to the requirements of the statute. Title VII does not prohibit all verbal or physical harassment in the workplace; it is directed only at *"discrimi-nat[ion] . . . because of . . . sex."* We have never held that workplace harassment, even harassment between men and women, is automatically discrimination because of sex merely because the words used have sexual content or connotations. "The critical issue, Title VII's text indicates, is whether members of one sex are exposed to disadvantageous terms or conditions of employment to which members of the other sex are not exposed."

Courts and juries have found the inference of discrimination easy to draw in most male-female sexual harassment situations, because the challenged conduct typically involves explicit or implicit proposals of sexual activity; it is reasonable to assume those proposals would not have been made to someone of the same sex. The same chain of inference would be available to a plaintiff alleging same-sex harassment, if there were credible evidence that the harasser was homosexual. But harassing conduct need not be motivated by sexual desire to support an inference of discrimination on the basis of sex. A trier of fact might reasonably find such discrimination, for example, if a female victim is harassed in such sex-specific and derogatory terms by another woman as to make it clear that the harasser is motivated by general hostility to the presence of women in the workplace. A same-sex harassment plaintiff may also, of course, offer direct comparative evidence about how the alleged harasser treated members of both sexes in a mixed-sex workplace. Whatever evidentiary route the plaintiff chooses to follow, he or she must always prove that the conduct at issue was not merely tinged with offensive sexual connotations, but actually constituted *"discrimina[tion] . . . because of . . . sex."*

And there is another requirement that prevents Title VII from expanding into a general civility code: As we emphasized in *Meritor* and *Harris,* the statute does not reach genuine but innocuous differences in the ways men and women routinely interact with members of the same sex and of the opposite sex. The prohibition of harassment on the basis of sex requires neither asexuality nor androgyny in the workplace; it forbids only behavior so objectively offensive as to alter the "conditions" of the victim's employment. "Conduct that is not severe or pervasive enough to create an objectively hostile or abusive work environment—an environment that a reasonable person would find hostile or abusive—is beyond Title VII's purview." We have always regarded that requirement as crucial, and as sufficient to ensure that courts and juries do not mistake ordinary socializing in the workplace—such as male-on-male horseplay or intersexual flirtation—for discriminatory "conditions of employment."

We have emphasized, moreover, that the objective severity of harassment should be judged from the perspective of a reasonable person in the plaintiff's position, considering "all the circumstances." In same-sex (as in all) harassment cases, that inquiry requires careful consideration of the social context in which particular behavior occurs and is experienced by its target. A professional football player's working environment is not severely or pervasively abusive, for example, if the coach smacks him on the buttocks as he heads onto the field—even if the same behavior would reasonably be experienced as abusive by the coach's secretary (male or female) back at the office. The real social impact of workplace behavior often depends on a constellation of surrounding circumstances, expectations, and relationships which are not fully captured by a simple recitation of the words used or the physical acts performed. Common sense, and an appropriate sensitivity to social context, will enable courts and juries to distinguish between simple teasing or roughhousing among members of the same sex, and conduct which a reasonable person in the plaintiff's position would find severely hostile or abusive.

Because we concluded that sex discrimination consisting of same-sex sexual harassment is actionable under Title VII, the judgment of the Court of Appeals for the Fifth Circuit is reversed, and the case is remanded for further proceedings consistent with this opinion.

It is so ordered.

■ Justice Thomas, concurring.

I concur because the Court stresses that in every sexual harassment case, the plaintiff must plead and ultimately prove Title VII's statutory requirement that there be discrimination "because of . . . sex."

## 3.  Privacy

### Bodewig v. K–Mart, Inc.

635 P.2d 657 (Or.App.1981).

■ Buttler, Presiding Judge.

In this tort action for outrageous conduct, plaintiff seeks damages against her former employer, K–Mart, and a K–Mart customer, Mrs. Golden. Both defendants moved for summary judgment, which the trial court granted. Plaintiff appeals from the resulting final judgments entered. We reverse and remand.

* * * On the evening of March 29, 1979, plaintiff was working as a part-time checker at K–Mart. Defendant Golden entered plaintiff's checkout lane and plaintiff began to ring up Golden's purchases on the cash register. When plaintiff called out the price on a package of curtains, Golden told plaintiff the price was incorrect because the curtains were on sale. Plaintiff called a domestics department clerk for a price check. That clerk told plaintiff the curtains in question were not on sale. Upon hearing this, Golden left her merchandise on plaintiff's counter and returned with the clerk to the domestics department to find the "sale" curtains.

After Golden left, plaintiff moved Golden's merchandise to the service counter, voided the register slip containing the partial listing of Golden's items and began to check out other customers. Three to ten minutes later, Golden returned to plaintiff's checkstand, where another customer was being served. Golden "looked around" that customer and asked what plaintiff had done with her money. When plaintiff replied, "What money?", Golden said that she had left four five-dollar bills on top of the merchandise she was purchasing before she left with the domestics clerk. Plaintiff told Golden she had not seen any money. Golden continued in a loud, abrupt voice to demand her money from plaintiff and caused a general commotion. Customers and store personnel in the area began to look on curiously.

The K–Mart manager, who had been observing the incident from a nearby service desk, walked over to plaintiff's counter. After a short discussion with Golden, he walked up to plaintiff, pulled out her jacket pockets, looked inside and found nothing. Then he, plaintiff and two or three other store employees conducted a general search of the area for the money. When this effort proved fruitless, the manager explained there was nothing more he could do except check out plaintiff's register. Golden said, "Well, do it." The manager and an assistant manager locked plaintiff's register and took the till and the register receipt to the cash cage. While the register was being checked, Golden continued to glare at plaintiff while plaintiff checked out customers at another register. The register balanced perfectly. When the manager so advised Golden, Golden replied that she still believed plaintiff took her money and continued to "cause commotion" and glare at plaintiff. A further general search of the surrounding area was conducted without success. Golden still would not leave; another employee was trying to calm her down.

The manager then told [1] plaintiff to accompany a female assistant manager into the women's public restroom for the purpose of disrobing in order to prove to Golden that she did not have the money. As plaintiff and the assistant manager walked to the restroom, the manager asked Golden if she wanted to watch the search; Golden replied: "You had better believe I do, it is my money." In the restroom, plaintiff took off all her clothes except her underwear while Golden and the assistant manager watched closely. When plaintiff asked Golden if she needed to take off more, Golden replied that it was not necessary because she could see through plaintiff's underwear anyway.

Plaintiff put on her clothes and started to leave the restroom when the assistant manager asked Golden how much money she had in her purse. Golden replied that she did not know the exact amount, but thought she

---

**1.** In her deposition, plaintiff stated that the manager "asked" her to disrobe. Plaintiff stated in a later affidavit that the manager "told" her to disrobe. Given plaintiff's youthful age and subservient position as an employee, her consistent statements in both her deposition and her affidavit that she believed she had no choice but to disrobe outweighs the semantic inconsistency of the two words. Whether she truthfully believed that, and, if so, whether it was a reasonable belief, is for the jury.

had between five and six hundred dollars. She did not attempt to count it at that time.

Plaintiff then returned to her checkstand. Golden followed plaintiff to the counter and continued to glare at her as she worked. Finally, the manager told Golden nothing more could be done for her, and after more loud protestations, Golden left the store.

Upon arriving home, Golden counted the money in her purse. She had $560. She called plaintiff's mother, whom she knew casually, and related the entire incident to her, stating that she had told K–Mart that plaintiff had taken her money. She described the strip search to plaintiff's mother and stated that when she was asked if she wanted to watch the strip, she responded, "Damn right." The mother expressed concern that plaintiff would lose her job; Golden said she would call the store and ask them not to let her go. Golden did make that call. After the conversation with Golden, plaintiff's mother, father and sister went to K–Mart to see if plaintiff was all right and to take her home.

Plaintiff returned to work the next day and was told that the keys to the cash register were lost and she was to work on a register with another employee. That procedure is known as "piggy-backing," and plaintiff had been told three months earlier that the store would no longer "piggy-back" checkers. Plaintiff believed the store was monitoring her by the "piggy-back" procedure; she quit at the end of her scheduled shift that day.

Each defendant, as the party moving for summary judgment, has the burden of showing that there is no genuine issue of material fact and that each of them is entitled to judgment as a matter of law. Because the questions relating to each defendant differ, we consider the trial court's ruling as to each of them separately.

## K–MART

K–Mart contends that the trial court properly granted its motion, because the facts presented do not constitute outrageous conduct as a matter of law. Its principal argument is that plaintiff consented to the strip search, either expressly as its manager stated, or tacitly by not expressly objecting. Plaintiff stated, variously, that she was told or asked by the manager to disrobe, but, whether asked or told, she did not consider that she had a choice. She thought she would lose her job if she refused, and she needed the job. The issue of lack of consent to that search is an issue of fact, but whether it is an issue of material fact depends upon whether, assuming plaintiff's version to be true, the facts are sufficient to submit the case to the jury on the outrageous conduct theory.

The relatively short history and development of the tort of outrageous conduct, at least in Oregon, is summarized by the court in Brewer v. Erwin, 287 Or. 435, 454–58, 600 P.2d 398 (1979). As the court pointed out, the exact elements of the tort are still in process of clarification. There are at least two versions of the tort. One is represented by Turman v. Central Billing Bureau, 279 Or. 443, 568 P.2d 1382 (1977), and involves intentional conduct, the very purpose of which is to inflict psychological and emotional distress on the plaintiff.  The other is represented by Rockhill v. Pollard, 259 Or. 54, 485 P.2d 28 (1971), where the wrongful purpose was lacking, but "the tortious element can be found in the breach of some obligation, statutory or otherwise, that attaches to defendant's relationship to plaintiff * * *."  287 Or. 435, at 457, 600 P.2d 398.  The court concluded its discussion as follows:

"* * * This court has not had occasion to consider whether in the absence of such a relationship a recovery for solely emotional distress can be based on a defendant's conduct, not otherwise tortious, that a jury may find to be beyond the limits of social toleration, though the conduct is not deliberately aimed at causing such distress but only reckless of the predictable effect.

In *Brewer,* the court did not consider the question posed in the foregoing quote, because it found the defendant's conduct was intentional. Here, we are faced with the issue, unless there was the type of special relationship between plaintiff and K–Mart justifying recovery for emotional distress based on that defendant's conduct, which was not deliberately aimed at such distress but was reckless of the predictable effect of that conduct.

Neither the Supreme Court nor this court has been presented with the question of whether the employer-employee relationship falls into that special category.  This court, however, has treated the landlord-tenant relationship as a "prime consideration" in evaluating the defendant's conduct.  We reached that conclusion because landlords were in a position of authority with respect to tenants and could affect the tenants' interest in the quiet enjoyment of their leasehold.  An employer has even more authority over an employee, who, by the nature of the relationship, is subject to the direction and control of the employer and may be discharged for any or no reason, absent an agreement restricting that authority. Clearly, that relationship is not an arm's length one between strangers. Accordingly, we conclude that the relationship between plaintiff and K–Mart was a special relationship, based on which liability may be imposed if K–Mart's conduct, though not deliberately aimed at causing emotional distress, was such that a jury might find it to be beyond the limits of social toleration and reckless of the conduct's predictable effects on plaintiff.

We conclude that a jury could find that the K–Mart manager, a 32-year-old male in charge of the entire store, after concluding that plaintiff did not take the customer's money, put her through the degrading and humiliating experience of submitting to a strip search in order to satisfy the customer, who was not only acting unreasonably, but was creating a commotion in the store;  that the manager's conduct exceeded the bounds of social toleration and was in reckless disregard of its predictable effects on plaintiff.

### GOLDEN

Because there was no special relationship between plaintiff and Golden, the evidence must be such that a jury could find Golden's conduct not only socially intolerable, but that it was deliberately aimed at causing plaintiff emotional distress.  Golden contends the evidence does not permit those findings, because she was merely trying to get her money back from plaintiff.  To sustain that position, it would be necessary to resolve the disputed facts relating to Golden's conduct in her favor.  As in the case against K–Mart, those factual issues are material only if, after resolving them in plaintiff's favor, the evidence would permit a jury to find for plaintiff.

We conclude that the facts, viewed most favorably to plaintiff, would permit a jury to find that Golden's entire course of conduct was intended to embarrass and humiliate plaintiff in order to coerce her into giving Golden $20, whether rightfully hers or not;  that Golden did not know how much money she had in her purse, variously stated to be between $300 and $600, made no effort to determine if she was, in fact, missing four five dollar bills until she returned home, at which time she found she was mistaken;  that Golden's insistence on a check of plaintiff's cash register, her insistence that plaintiff still had her money after the register checked out perfectly, her eager participation in the strip search of plaintiff and her continuing to stare angrily at plaintiff over an extended period, even after all efforts to find her money failed, would permit a jury to find Golden's conduct deliberately calculated to cause plaintiff emotional distress and exceeded the bounds of social toleration.

A jury could also find in Golden's favor, but the mere fact that her stated ultimate objective was to get her money back is not sufficient to defeat plaintiff's claim.  In Turman v. Central Billing Bureau, supra, the defendant's objective was to collect a bill, but its methods of achieving that objective were held actionable as outrageous conduct.  There are lawful (socially tolerable) ways to collect money from another, and there are unlawful (socially intolerable) ways to do so.

## EMOTIONAL DISTRESS

Common to her claims against both defendants is the requirement that plaintiff prove that she suffered severe emotional distress.  If the facts presented are believed, plaintiff suffered shock, humiliation and embarrassment, suffering that was not merely transient.  Plaintiff characterized herself as a shy, modest person, and said that she had two or three sleepless nights, cried a lot and still gets nervous and upset when she thinks about the incident.  Concededly, this element of the tort has been, and still is, troublesome to courts.  K–Mart contends there is no objective evidence of the distress, such as medical, economic or social problems.  In Rockhill v. Pollard, supra, plaintiff became nervous and suffered from sleeplessness and a loss of appetite over a period of about two years.  The court said:

> " * * * Defendant belittles these symptoms, but it is the distress which must be severe, not the physical manifestations. * * * " 259 Or. at 63, 485 P.2d 28.

Defendant Golden contends that the purpose of requiring proof of severe emotional distress is to guard against fraudulent or frivolous claims and that some degree of transient and trivial distress is a part of the price of living among people.  Here, however, it is not unreasonable to expect that a shy, modest, young woman put in plaintiff's position would suffer the effects she claims to have suffered from the incident, and that her distress was more than that which a person might be reasonably expected to pay as the price of living among people.

We cannot say as a matter of law that plaintiff's evidence of severe emotional distress is insufficient to go to a jury.

\* \* \*

Because neither defendant was entitled to judgment as a matter of law, neither motion for summary judgment should have been granted.

The judgment for each of the defendants is reversed.  The case is remanded for trial.

NOTES AND QUESTIONS

**1.**  Suppose the plaintiff refused to disrobe and was fired.  Would she have any legal recourse?  Would it matter if she quit rather than acquiesce in the strip search?

**2.**  Is the strip search of an employee *ever* justified?  If so, when?  What degree of suspicion is needed?  See McDonell v. Hunter, 809 F.2d 1302 (8th Cir.1987) (strip search of correctional facility employee requires "reasonable suspicion based on specific objective facts and rational inferences").  For what other public or private employees would a strip search be reasonable?

**3.**  Does it violate the constitutional right to privacy in California for a women's health center to require that all health workers perform cervical self-examinations in front of other women?  See Feminist Women's Health Center v. Superior Court, 61 Cal.Rptr.2d 187 (Ct.App.1997) (held:  no).

**4.**  During her afternoon break a retail store employee returned to her locker and found the lock hanging open and the personal items from her purse in disarray.  Four store officials had opened locked employee lockers to search for a stolen watch and missing price-marking guns.  Does this employee have any possible action against the store?  See K–Mart Corp. v. Trotti, 677 S.W.2d 632 (Tex.App.1984) (recognizing a cause of action for invasion of privacy), writ denied, 686 S.W.2d 593 (Tex.1985).

**5.**  When an employer suspects an employee has stolen merchandise, what may the employer do?  May the employer interrogate the employee?  If so, for how long, where, and in what manner?  Would it be actionable for a department store to interrogate a 19 year-old woman for three hours in a small, windowless room?  See Smithson v. Nordstrom, Inc., 664 P.2d 1119 (Or.App.1983) (held:  yes).  Suppose security guards grabbed an employee and took him to a glass-enclosed guard house, where he was detained for 35 minutes for questioning and was observed by 5000 employees as they were entering and leaving the plant. Would this conduct be actionable? See General Motors Corp. v. Piskor, 381 A.2d 16 (Md.1977) (held: yes). See also Mansfield v. American Telephone & Telegraph Corp., 747 F.Supp. 1329 (W.D.Ark.1990) (claim for the tort of outrage stated where employer allegedly subjected the plaintiff to six hours of questioning, laughed at her and accused her of lying, accused her of having a lesbian relationship with a co-worker, and did not permit her to leave until she signed a statement).

**6.** Federal Express was given an expensive wristwatch for delivery. When the watch disappeared, Federal Express launched a security investigation of its own employees. Two Federal employees were separately confined in a room for interrogation and, during the course of the interrogation, a security employee pulled back his jacket to reveal a firearm that he was carrying. The two employees were very upset at the investigation and sued Federal Express for false imprisonment and intentional infliction of emotional distress. What result? See Leahy v. Federal Express Corp., 613 F.Supp. 906 (E.D.N.Y.1985) (held: no recovery).

# Vega–Rodriguez v. Puerto Rico Telephone Co.

110 F.3d 174 (1st Cir.1997).

■ Selya, Circuit Judge.

As employers gain access to increasingly sophisticated technology, new legal issues seem destined to suffuse the workplace. This appeal raises such an issue. In it, plaintiffs-appellants Hector Vega–Rodriguez (Vega) and Amiut Reyes–Rosado (Reyes) revile the district court's determination that their employer, the Puerto Rico Telephone Company (PRTC), may monitor their work area by means of continuous video surveillance without offending the Constitution. Because the red flag of constitutional breach does not fly from these ramparts, we affirm.

## I. FACTUAL SURVEILLANCE

\* \* \*

The Executive Communications Center (the Center) is located in the penthouse of the PRTC's office complex in Guaynabo, Puerto Rico. It maintains communication between the company's various operating units and the senior executive on duty, but it does not have primary corporate responsibility for security and it does not house communication switching centers, cables, transmission lines, or kindred equipment. For security reasons, access to the Center is restricted; both the elevator foyer on the penthouse floor and the doors to the Center itself are inaccessible without a control card.

PRTC employs Vega, Reyes, and others as attendants (known colloquially as "security operators") in the Center. They monitor computer banks to detect signals emanating from alarm systems at PRTC facilities throughout Puerto Rico, and they alert the appropriate authorities if an alarm sounds. Although individual employees work eight-hour shifts, the Center is staffed around the clock.

The work space inside the Center consists of a large L-shaped area that contains the computers, the monitors, and assorted furniture (e.g., desks, chairs, consoles). The work space is completely open and no individual employee has an assigned office, cubicle, work station, or desk.

PRTC installed a video surveillance system at the Center in 1990 but abandoned the project when employees groused. In June of 1994, the company reinstated video surveillance. Three cameras survey the work space, and a fourth tracks all traffic passing through the main entrance to the Center. None of them cover the rest area. The surveillance is exclusively visual; the cameras have no microphones or other immediate eavesdropping capability. Video surveillance operates all day, every day; the cameras implacably record every act undertaken in the work area. A video monitor, a switcher unit, and a video recorder are located in the office of the Center's general manager, Daniel Rodriguez–Diaz, and the video-tapes are stored there. PRTC has no written policy regulating any aspect of the video surveillance, but it is undisputed that no one can view either the monitor or the completed tapes without Rodriguez–Diaz's express permission.

Soon after PRTC installed the surveillance system (claiming that it was desirable for security reasons), the appellants and several fellow employees protested. They asserted, among other things, that the system had no purpose other than to pry into employees' behavior. When management turned a deaf ear, the appellants filed suit in Puerto Rico's federal district court. They contended that the ongoing surveillance constitutes an unreasonable search prohibited by the Fourth Amendment, violates a constitutionally-conferred entitlement to privacy, and abridges rights secured by the First Amendment. After the parties had taken considerable discovery, PRTC moved for dismissal and/or summary judgment, and the individual defendants moved for summary judgment. The district court found merit in these submissions and entered judgment accordingly. The appellants then prosecuted this appeal.

In the pages that follow, we deal first with a problem of how best to characterize the district court's ruling. We then address the appellants' illegal search and invasion of privacy claims. Because the appellants have neither briefed nor argued their First Amendment claim in this venue, we deem it waived and do not pursue it.

\* \* \*

## III. THE FOURTH AMENDMENT

PRTC is a quasi-public corporation. It is, therefore, a government actor, subject to the suasion of the Fourth Amendment. Building on this foundation, the appellants allege that PRTC's continuous video surveillance contravenes the "right of the people to be secure in their persons ...

against unreasonable searches." U.S. Const. amend. IV. We consider that allegation.

### A. *Privacy Rights and the Fourth Amendment.*

Intrusions upon personal privacy do not invariably implicate the Fourth Amendment. Rather, such intrusions cross the constitutional line only if the challenged conduct infringes upon some reasonable expectation of privacy. To qualify under this mantra, a privacy expectation must meet both subjective and objective criteria: the complainant must have an actual expectation of privacy, and that expectation must be one which society recognizes as reasonable. Determining the subjective component of the test requires only a straightforward inquiry into the complainant's state of mind, and, for purposes of this appeal, we are willing to assume *arguendo* that the appellants, as they profess, had some subjective expectation of privacy while at work. We turn, then, to the objective reasonableness of the asserted expectation of privacy.

In previous cases, the Supreme Court has answered this type of question by examining such diverse factors as the Framers' intent, the uses to which an individual has put a location, and society's understanding that certain areas (say, a person's home) deserve heightened protection from government intrusions. But the Court has not developed a routinized checklist that is capable of being applied across the board, and each case therefore must be judged according to its own scenario. With this in mind, we proceed by first surveying the legal principles that relate to searches of business premises and then narrowing our focus to the facts of this case and the appellants' asseverational array.

### B. *Privacy Rights and Business Premises.*

Generally speaking, business premises invite lesser privacy expectations than do residences. The Fourth Amendment protections that these expectations entail are versatile; they safeguard individuals not only against the government *qua* law enforcer but also *qua* employer.

The watershed case in this enclave of Fourth Amendment jurisprudence is O'Connor v. Ortega, 480 U.S. 709 (1987). *O'Connor's* central thesis is that a public employee sometimes may enjoy a reasonable expectations of privacy in his or her workplace vis-à-vis searches by a supervisor or other representative of a public employer. Withal, *O'Connor* recognized that "operational realities of the workplace," such as actual office practices, procedures, or regulations, frequently may undermine employees' privacy expectations. The four dissenting Justices shared this belief, and subsequent case law confirms it. In the last analysis, the objective component of an employee's professed expectation of privacy must be assessed in the full context of the particular employment relation.

*O'Connor* is a typical case in which a public employee's workplace-based privacy interests were vindicated. Dr. Ortega was on administrative leave from his post at a state hospital when hospital personnel, investigating misconduct charges, entered his office and removed personal items from his desk and file cabinets.  The Court held that Dr. Ortega had a reasonable expectation of privacy in his desk and file cabinets because he did not share them with other workers, he used them to store personal materials, and the hospital had no policy discouraging employees from stashing personal items there.  Moreover, although the plurality eschewed the issue, a majority of the Justices believed that Dr. Ortega maintained a reasonable privacy expectation in his private office as well.

Applying *O'Connor* in various work environments, lower federal courts have inquired into matters such as whether the work area in question was given over to an employee's exclusive use, the extent to which others had access to the work space, the nature of the employment, and whether office regulations placed employees on notice that certain areas were subject to employer intrusions.

## C.  *Privacy Interests in the Appellants' Workplace.*

We begin with first principles.  It is simply implausible to suggest that society would recognize as reasonable an employee's expectation of privacy against being viewed while toiling in the Center's open and undifferentiated work area.  PRTC did not provide the work station for the appellants' exclusive use, and its physical layout belies any expectation of privacy.  Security operators do not occupy private offices or cubicles.  They toil instead in a vast, undivided space—a work area so patulous as to render a broadcast expectation of privacy unreasonable.

The precise extent of an employee's expectation of privacy often turns on the nature of an intended intrusion.  In this instance the nature of the intrusion strengthens the conclusion that no reasonable expectation of privacy attends the work area.  Employers possess a legitimate interest in the efficient operation of the workplace, and one attribute of this interest is that supervisors may monitor at will that which is in plain view within an open work area.  Here, moreover, this attribute has a greater claim on our allegiance because the employer acted overtly in establishing the video surveillance: PRTC notified its work force in advance that video cameras would be installed and disclosed the cameras' field of vision.  Hence, the affected workers were on clear notice from the outset that any movements they might make and any objects they might display within the work area would be exposed to the employer's sight.

The appellants concede that, as a general matter, employees should expect to be under supervisors' watchful eyes while at work.  But at some point, they argue, surveillance becomes unreasonable.  In their estimation, when surveillance is electronic and, therefore, unremitting—the camera, unlike the human eye, never blinks—the die is cast.  In constitutional terms, their theory reduces to the contention that the Fourth Amendment precludes management from observing electronically what it lawfully can see with the naked eye.  This sort of argument has failed consistently under the plain view doctrine, and it musters no greater persuasiveness in the present context.  When all is said and done, employees must accept some circumscription of their liberty as a condition of continued employment.

Once we put aside the appellants' theory that there is something constitutionally sinister about videotaping, their case crumbles. If there is constitutional parity between observations made with the naked eye and observations recorded by openly displayed video cameras that have no greater range, then objects or articles that an individual seeks to preserve as private may be constitutionally protected from such videotaping only if they are not located in plain view. In other words, persons cannot reasonably maintain an expectation of privacy in that which they display openly. Justice Stewart stated the proposition in no uncertain terms three decades ago: "What a person knowingly exposes to the public, even in his own home or office, is not a subject of Fourth Amendment protection." Katz v. United States, 389 U.S. 347, 351 (1967). Consequently, no legitimate expectation of privacy exists in objects exposed to plain view as long as the viewer's presence at the vantage point is lawful. And the mere fact that the observation is accomplished by a video camera rather than the naked eye, and recorded on film rather than in a supervisor's memory, does not transmogrify a constitutionally innocent act into a constitutionally forbidden one.

The bottom line is that since PRTC could assign humans to monitor the work station continuously without constitutional insult, it could choose instead to carry out that lawful task by means of unconcealed video cameras not equipped with microphones, which record only what the human eye could observe.

### D. *The Appellants' Other Fourth Amendment Arguments.*

The appellants trot out a profusion of additional asseverations in their effort to convince us that continuous video surveillance of the workplace constitutes an impermissible search. First, invoking Orwellian imagery, they recite a catechism pasted together from bits and pieces of judicial pronouncements recognizing the intrusive nature of video surveillance. These statements are taken out of context. Without exception, they refer to cameras installed surreptitiously during the course of criminal investigations. Concealed cameras which infringe upon the rights of criminal defendants raise troubling constitutional concerns—concerns not implicated by the employer's actions in this case.

By like token, the appellants' attempts to analogize video monitoring to physical searches are unavailing. The silent video surveillance which occurs at the Center is less intrusive than most physical searches conducted by employers. PRTC's stationary cameras do not pry behind closed office doors or into desks, drawers, file cabinets, or other enclosed spaces, but, rather, record only what is plainly visible on the surface. Sounds are not recorded; thus, the cameras do not eavesdrop on private conversations between employees. And while the Court occasionally has characterized the taking of pictures as a search, it is a constitutionally permissible activity if it does not transgress an objectively reasonable expectation of privacy.

Next, the appellants complain that while at work under the cameras' unrelenting eyes they cannot scratch, yawn, or perform any other movement in privacy. This complaint rings true, but it begs the question. "[T]he test of legitimacy is not whether a person chooses to conceal assertedly 'private' activity," but whether the intrusion is objectively unreasonable.

Finally, the appellants tout the potential for future abuse, arguing, for example, that PRTC might expand video surveillance "into the restrooms." Certainly, such an extension would raise a serious constitutional question. But present fears are often no more than horrible imaginings, and *potential* privacy invasions do not constitute searches within the purview of the Fourth Amendment.

We have said enough on this score. The appellants have failed to demonstrate the existence of an issue of material fact sufficient to withstand summary judgment on their Fourth Amendment claim. Because they do not enjoy an objectively reasonable expectation of privacy against disclosed, soundless video surveillance while at work, they have no cause of action under the Fourth Amendment.

\* \* \*

## VI. CONCLUSION

We need go no further. Because the appellants do not have an objectively reasonable expectation of privacy in the open areas of their workplace, the video surveillance conducted by their employer does not infract their federal constitutional rights. PRTC's employees may register their objections to the surveillance system with management, but they may not lean upon the Constitution for support.

*Affirmed.*

## NOTES AND QUESTIONS

**1.** According to the court, whether a public employee has a reasonable expectation of privacy depends on whether the employee has exclusive use of the work area, the nature of the employment, and whether office regulations placed the employee on notice of possible employer intrusions. Do these factors go to whether the employee has an expectation of privacy or a reasonable expectation of privacy? How would the analysis differ if the employee worked for a private sector employer?

**2.** Surveillance of workers on the job is increasing in an effort to improve efficiency and reduce theft. Does the use of TV cameras, microphones, metal detectors, mirrors, one-way mirrors, and other devices invade any legitimate interests of employees? Does the reasonableness of such measures depend on the employer's justifications, the consent of the workers, or some other factors? See Thomas v. General Electric Co., 207 F.Supp. 792 (W.D.Ky.1962) (holding that employer's photographing employee to increase efficiency of his operations and promote safety of employees did not violate employee's right to privacy); Sacramento County Deputy Sheriffs' Association v. Sacramento County, 59 Cal.Rptr.2d 834 (Ct.App.1996) (placement of video camera in county jail's release office did not violate deputy sheriff's Fourth Amendment rights).

**3.** One area in which employee rights may be protected directly is wiretapping and electronic surveillance. Title III of the Omnibus Crime Control and Safe Streets Act of 1968, 18 U.S.C. §§ 2510–2522, prohibits the interception of oral and electronic communications, even by private citizens. There are several exceptions to the law and its application in the workplace is still not settled. See, e.g., Briggs v. American Air Filter Co., 630 F.2d 414 (5th Cir.1980) (eavesdropping on extension phone during business call exempt); Simmons v. Southwestern Bell Telephone Co., 452 F.Supp. 392 (W.D.Okl.1978), affirmed, 611 F.2d 342 (10th Cir.1979) (telephone company permitted to monitor employee phone calls); United States v. Harpel, 493 F.2d 346 (10th Cir.1974) (tape recording conversation on extension telephone illegal). See generally Julie A. Flanagan, Note, Restricting Electronic Monitoring in the Private Workplace, 43 Duke L.J. 1256 (1994).

**4.** An emerging area of workplace privacy involves the practice of computer monitoring of employees. For example, some airline-reservation computers closely measure how long individual clerks take to handle each customer, the amount of time between calls, lunch hours, coffee breaks, and even trips to the bathroom. In 1986 about ten million workers were computer monitored and this number is expected to double in five years. Besides monitoring work efficiency, computers can check the telephone numbers dialed by employees at work. Computers also can be used to match employment records with child support payments, tax records, and other government information. Employees complain about the increased stress of working while being monitored. Employers have a legitimate interest in measuring productivity. Can employer and employee interests be accommodated? What legal issues are raised by computer monitoring?

**5.** An employee was fired when his (presumably) private E-mail message was intercepted by his employer. The message contained pledges or threats to "kill the backstabbing bastards." Has the employer committed an invasion of privacy? See Smyth v. Pillsbury Co., 914 F.Supp. 97 (E.D.Pa.1996) (held: no; employee has no reasonable expectation of privacy in E-mail). See generally Frances A. McMorris, Is Office Voice Mail Private? Don't Bet on It, Wall St.J., Feb. 28, 1995, at B1, col. 3.

**6.** Some privacy issues have arisen after an employee has suffered an injury on the job. For example, in Lambert v. Dow Chemical Co., 215 So.2d 673 (La.App.1968), an employee was badly lacerated in the upper inside portion of his left thigh. He was rushed to a nearby hospital and during surgery, unbeknownst to him, photographs were taken of his wounds. The company later used the photographs at its safety meetings to demonstrate the consequences of poor safety practices. The employee was awarded $250 in damages in his action for invasion of privacy. Could the employer have required all employees, as a condition of employment, to sign a release form allowing the employer to use accident pictures such as those taken in *Lambert?* Could the employer have demanded such a release from Mr. Lambert after the pictures were taken? What about similar releases for medical records or personnel files?

**7.** An employee was awarded workers' compensation for a back strain. After receiving a report from a medical consultant that the employee was malingering, the employer hired a surveillance company, which took 18 rolls of movie film of the employee as he was mowing his lawn, rototilling his garden, and fishing from a bridge near his home. Some of the movies were taken from the employee's property. He only learned of the film when it was shown at the workers' compensation hearing. Does the employee have an action for trespass, invasion of privacy, or some other tort? See McLain v. Boise Cascade Corp., 533 P.2d 343 (Or.1975) (affirming award of $250 for trespass, but nothing for invasion of privacy).

**8.** When an employee of the Grand Gulf Nuclear Power Station was hospitalized, rumors began to circulate that she was suffering from radiation exposure. To squelch these rumors, her coworkers were informed that the employee's illness was related to a recent hysterectomy. In an action for invasion of privacy, what result? See Young v. Jackson, 572 So.2d 378 (Miss.1990) (held: disclosure was privileged and therefore no liability). See generally Scott L. Fast, Comment, Breach of Employee Confidentiality: Moving Toward a Common–Law Tort Remedy, 142 U.Pa.L.Rev. 431 (1993).

## A NOTE ON EMPLOYMENT RECORDS

An individual's employment record or personnel file is important to that person's present and future employment opportunities. With the computer age, these records are even more important because of the ease with which the information can be compiled, sorted, stored, and disseminated.

From a legal standpoint, two main questions have arisen. First, what rights do individuals have to inspect and correct their own files? Second, are there any restrictions on an employer's freedom to communicate or use employment record information?

Most of the regulation of employment records involves state law. About one-fourth of the states have enacted laws giving employees such rights as access to their files, the right to correct their files, the right to receive notice prior to release of information, and the right to have employers refrain from maintaining records about their nonemployment activities. See, e.g., Cal.Lab.Code § 1198.5 (right to see personnel files); Ohio Rev.Code Ann. § 4113.23 (right to see medical records); Mich.Comp. Laws Ann. § 423.501 (prohibition on collecting information about off-duty political activities of employees).

Employees also have certain access rights under federal statutes and regulations. For example, under OSHA employees exposed to toxic substances or harmful physical agents have a right of access to their exposure and medical records. 29 C.F.R. § 1910.20. For a further discussion, see Chapter 8.

The Privacy Act of 1974, 5 U.S.C. § 522a, requires federal agencies to keep their records with due regard for the privacy of the subjects of the records. Among other things, the law requires the agencies to: (1) keep only relevant and necessary information; (2) give individuals an opportunity to examine their own files; (3) permit individuals to request amendment of the files; and (4) limit disclosure of the records without consent. A number of proposals have been made to extend these rights to private sector records, but as yet there has been no action. See Comment, Employee Privacy Rights: A Proposal, 47 Fordham L.Rev. 155 (1978). A number of states, however, have enacted privacy laws regulating records collected and maintained by the state government. See, e.g., Minn.Stat. Ann. § 13.02; Utah Code Ann. § 63–2–101 through –909. Would it violate the Privacy Act for a federal agency to release personnel records to the union? See Andrews v. Veterans Administration, 838 F.2d 418 (10th Cir.1988) (held: no violation absent willful or intentional conduct).

The Family Educational Rights and Privacy Act of 1974, 20 U.S.C. § 1232g ("the Buckley Amendment"), and its implementing regulations, 34 C.F.R. Part 99, provide, among other things, that students at educational institutions receiving federal funds have a right of access to their educational records and have a right to challenge the contents of their records. Should employees have a similar right? What about applicants?

Three common law theories have been used by employees who believe their employment records have been misused: defamation, invasion of privacy, and negligence. Defamation is discussed in Chapter 4. The common law tort of invasion of privacy is comprised of four separate kinds of tortious acts: (1) appropriation, for the defendant's benefit or advantages, of the plaintiff's name or likeness; (2) unreasonable and highly offensive intrusion upon the seclusion of another; (3) public disclosure of embarrassing private facts about the plaintiff; and (4) publicity which places the plaintiff in a false light in the public eye. W. Page Keeton, et al., Prosser and Keeton on the Law of Torts ch. 20 (5th ed. 1984). A theory commonly used in invasion of privacy actions is that there has been a public disclosure of private facts. Thus, issues often arise as to whether certain facts are "private" and whether they have been disclosed publicly.

In one litigated case, a woman employee of the Nabisco bakery was supposed to work the 11:30 p.m. to 7:30 a.m. shift. Instead of reporting to work, and unbeknownst to her husband, she spent the night at the home of her paramour. When the woman's husband called the bakery to talk to his wife he was told that she had not reported to work and the assistant personnel manager later told him that his wife had not reported the night before and several other evenings. The man then committed suicide. Is Nabisco liable for invasion of privacy and wrongful death for disclosing the woman's attendance record to her husband? See Kobeck v. Nabisco, Inc., 305 S.E.2d 183 (Ga.App.1983) (held: no).

Another theory for a tort action in this area is negligence; specifically, the allegation that the employer negligently maintained personnel files. The tort encompasses the failure to maintain accurate records and the failure to prevent unauthorized dissemination of the information. This theory has been accepted in a few cases: e.g., Quinones v. United States, 492 F.2d 1269 (3d Cir.1974); Bulkin v. Western Kraft East, Inc., 422 F.Supp. 437 (E.D.Pa.1976).

## 4.   FREEDOM OF EXPRESSION

Legal regulation of employee speech, inside the workplace or out, depends to a large extent on whether the employer is private or public: where government is the employer, the U.S. Constitution protects employees from arbitrary "state action" adversely affecting their job status. The Fourteenth Amendment ensures government employees "due process" protection against discipline or discharge, while the first amendment provides at least limited substantive protection. In Perry v. Sindermann, 408 U.S. 593 (1972), the Supreme Court stated:

> For at least a quarter century, this Court has made clear that even though a person has no "right" to a valuable governmental benefit and even though the government may deny him the benefit for any number of reasons, there are some reasons upon which the government may not rely. It may not deny a benefit to a person on a basis that infringes his constitutionally protected interests— especially, his interest in freedom of speech. For if the government could deny a benefit to a person because of his constitutionally protected speech or associations, his exercise of those freedoms would in effect be penalized and inhibited.  * * * Such interference with constitutional rights is impermissible.

Id. at 597. As developed by the courts, however, the individual's freedom to speak out on the job is not unlimited.

(The procedural limits on the government employer's ability to discharge employees are discussed infra at pp. 974–981.)

# Rankin v. McPherson

483 U.S. 378 (1987).

■ JUSTICE MARSHALL delivered the opinion of the Court.

The issue in this case is whether a clerical employee in a county constable's office was properly discharged for remarking, after hearing of an attempt on the life of the President, "If they go for him again, I hope they get him."

On January 12, 1981, respondent Ardith McPherson was appointed a deputy in the office of the constable of Harris County, Texas. The constable is an elected official who functions as a law enforcement officer. At the time of her appointment, McPherson, a black woman, was 19 years old and had attended college for a year, studying secretarial science. Her appointment was conditional for a 90–day probationary period.

Although McPherson's title was "deputy constable," this was the case only because all employees of the constable's office, regardless of job function, were deputy constables. She was not a commissioned peace officer, did not wear a uniform, and was not authorized to make arrests or permitted to carry a gun. McPherson's duties were purely clerical. Her work station was a desk at which there was no telephone, in a room to which the public did not have ready access. Her job was to type data from court papers into a computer that maintained an automated record of the status of civil process in the county. Her training consisted of two days of instruction in the operation of her computer terminal.

On March 30, 1981, McPherson and some fellow employees heard on an office radio that there had been an attempt to assassinate the President of the United States. Upon hearing that report, McPherson engaged a co-worker, Lawrence Jackson, who was apparently her boyfriend, in a brief conversation, which according to McPherson's uncontroverted testimony went as follows:

"Q: What did you say?

"A: I said I felt that that would happen sooner or later.

"Q: Okay. And what did Lawrence say?

"A: Lawrence said, yeah, agreeing with me.

"Q: Okay. Now, when you—after Lawrence spoke, then what was your next comment?

"A: Well, we were talking—it's a wonder why they did that. I felt like it would be a black person that did that, because I feel like most of my kind is on welfare and CETA, and they use medicaid, and at the time, I was thinking that's what it was.

" * * * But then after I said that, and then Lawrence said, yeah, he's cutting back medicaid and food stamps. And I said, yeah, welfare and CETA. I said, shoot, if they go for him again, I hope they get him."

McPherson's last remark was overheard by another deputy constable, who, unbeknownst to McPherson, was in the room at the time. The remark was reported to Constable Rankin, who summoned McPherson. McPherson readily admitted that she had made the statement, but testified that she told Rankin, upon being asked if she made the statement, "Yes, but I didn't mean anything by it." After their discussion, Rankin fired McPherson.

McPherson brought suit in the United States District Court for the Southern District of Texas under 42 U.S.C. § 1983, alleging that petitioner Rankin, in discharging her, had violated her constitutional rights under color of state law. She sought reinstatement, back pay, costs and fees, and other equitable relief.

\* \* \*

It is clearly established that a State may not discharge an employee on a basis that infringes that employee's constitutionally protected interest in freedom of speech. Even though McPherson was merely a probationary employee, and even if she could have been discharged for any reason or for no reason at all, she may nonetheless be entitled to reinstatement if she was discharged for exercising her constitutional right to freedom of expression.

The determination whether a public employer has properly discharged an employee for engaging in speech requires "a balance between the interests of the [employee], as a citizen, in commenting upon matters of public concern and the interest of the State, as an employer, in promoting the efficiency of the public services it performs through its employees." Pickering v. Board of Education, 391 U.S. 563, 568 (1968); Connick v. Myers, 461 U.S. 138, 140 (1983). This balancing is necessary in order to accommodate the dual role of the public employer as a provider of public services and as a government entity operating under the constraints of the First Amendment. On one hand, public employers are *employers,* concerned with the efficient function of their operations; review of every personnel decision made by a public employer could, in the long run, hamper the performance of public functions. On the other hand, "the threat of dismissal from public employment is \* \* \* a potent means of inhibiting speech." Vigilance is necessary to ensure that public employers do not use authority over employees to silence discourse, not because it hampers public functions but simply because superiors disagree with the content of employees' speech.

The threshold question in applying this balancing test is whether McPherson's speech may be "fairly characterized as constituting speech on a matter of public concern." "Whether an employee's speech addresses a matter of public concern must be determined by the content, form, and context of a given statement, as revealed by the whole record." The District Court apparently found that McPherson's speech did not address a matter of public concern. The Court of Appeals rejected this conclusion, finding that "the life and death of the President are obviously matters of public concern." Our view of these determinations of the courts below is limited in this context by our constitutional obligation to assure that the record supports this conclusion: " 'we are compelled to examine for ourselves the statements in issue and the circumstances under which they [were] made to see whether or not they \* \* \* are of a character which the principles of the First Amendment, as adopted by the Due Process Clause of the Fourteenth Amendment, protect.' "

Considering the statement in context, as *Connick* requires, discloses that it plainly dealt with a matter of public concern. The statement was made in the course of a conversation addressing the policies of the President's administration. It came on the heels of a news bulletin regarding what is certainly a matter of heightened public attention: an attempt on the life of the President. While a statement that amounted to a threat to kill the President would not be protected by the First Amendment, the District Court concluded, and we agree, that McPherson's statement did not amount to a threat punishable under 18 U.S.C. § 871(a) or 18 U.S.C. § 2385, or, indeed, that could properly be criminalized at all. The inappropriate or controversial character of a statement is irrelevant to the question whether it deals with a matter of public concern. "[D]ebate on public issues should be uninhibited, robust, and wide-open, and * * * may well include vehement, caustic, and sometimes unpleasantly sharp attacks on government and public officials." New York Times Co. v. Sullivan, 376 U.S. 254, 270 (1964); see also Bond v. Floyd, 385 U.S. 116, 136 (1966): "Just as erroneous statements must be protected to give freedom of expression the breathing space it needs to survive, so statements criticizing public policy and the implementation of it must be similarly protected."

Because McPherson's statement addressed a matter of public concern, *Pickering* next requires that we balance McPherson's interest in making her statement against "the interest of the State, as an employer, in promoting the efficiency of the public services it performs through its employees." The state bears a burden of justifying the discharge on legitimate grounds.

In performing the balancing, the statement will not be considered in a vacuum; the manner, time, and place of the employee's expression are relevant, as is the context in which the dispute arose. We have previously recognized as pertinent considerations whether the statement impairs discipline by superiors or harmony among coworkers, has a detrimental impact on close working relationships for which personal loyalty and confidence are necessary, or impedes the performance of the speaker's duties or interferes with the regular operation of the enterprise.

These considerations, and indeed the very nature of the balancing test, make apparent that the state interest element of the test focuses on the effective functioning of the public employer's enterprise. Interference with work, personnel relationships, or the speaker's job performance can detract from the public employer's function; avoiding such interference can be a strong state interest. From this perspective, however, petitioner fails to demonstrate a state interest that outweighs McPherson's First Amendment rights. While McPherson's statement was made at the workplace, there is no evidence that it interfered with the efficient functioning of the office. The Constable was evidently not afraid that McPherson had disturbed or interrupted other employees—he did not inquire to whom respondent had made the remark and testified that he "was not concerned who she had made it to." In fact, Constable Rankin testified that the possibility of interference with the functions of the Constable's office had *not* been a consideration in his discharge of respondent and that he did not even inquire whether the remark had disrupted the work of the office.

Nor was there any danger that McPherson had discredited the office by making her statement in public.  McPherson's speech took place in an area to which there was ordinarily no public access;  her remark was evidently made in a private conversation with another employee.  There is no suggestion that any member of the general public was present or heard McPherson's statement.  Nor is there any evidence that employees other than Jackson who worked in the room even heard the remark.  Not only was McPherson's discharge unrelated to the functioning of the office, it was not based on any assessment by the constable that the remark demonstrated a character trait that made respondent unfit to perform her work.

While the facts underlying Rankin's discharge of McPherson are, despite extensive proceedings in the District Court, still somewhat unclear, it is undisputed that he fired McPherson based on the content of her speech.  Evidently because McPherson had made the statement, and because the constable believed that she "meant it," he decided that she was not a suitable employee to have in a law enforcement agency.  But in weighing the State's interest in discharging an employee based on any claim that the content of a statement made by the employee somehow undermines the mission of the public employer, some attention must be paid to the responsibilities of the employee within the agency.  The burden of caution employees bear with respect to the words they speak will vary with the extent of authority and public accountability the employee's role entails.  Where, as here, an employee serves no confidential, policymaking, or public contact role, the danger to the agency's successful function from that employee's private speech is minimal.  We cannot believe that every employee in Constable Rankin's office, whether computer operator, electrician, or file clerk, is equally required, on pain of discharge, to avoid any statement susceptible of being interpreted by the Constable as an indication that the employee may be unworthy of employment in his law enforcement agency.  At some point, such concerns are so removed from the effective function of the public employer that they cannot prevail over the free speech rights of the public employee.

This is such a case.  McPherson's employment-related interaction with the Constable was apparently negligible.  Her duties were purely clerical and were limited solely to the civil process function of the constable's office.  There is no indication that she would ever be in a position to further—or indeed to have any involvement with—the minimal law enforcement activity engaged in by the constable's office.  Given the function of the agency, McPherson's position in the office, and the nature of her statement, we are not persuaded that Rankin's interest in discharging her outweighed her rights under the First Amendment.

Because we agree with the Court of Appeals that McPherson's discharge was improper, the judgment of the Court of Appeals is

Affirmed.

■ JUSTICE POWELL, concurring.

\* \* \*

If a statement is on a matter of public concern, as it was here, it will be an unusual case where the employer's legitimate interests will be so great as to justify punishing an employee for this type of private speech that routinely takes place at all levels in the workplace. The risk that a single, off-hand comment directed to only one other worker will lower morale, disrupt the work force, or otherwise undermine the mission of the office borders on the fanciful. To the extent that the full constitutional analysis of the competing interests is required, I generally agree with the Court's opinion.

In my view, however, the case is hardly as complex as might be expected in a dispute that now has been considered five separate times by three different federal courts. The undisputed evidence shows that McPherson made an ill-considered—but protected—comment during a private conversation, and the Constable made an instinctive, but intemperate, employment decision on the basis of this speech. I agree that on these facts, McPherson's private speech is protected by the First Amendment.

I join the opinion of the Court.

■ JUSTICE SCALIA, with whom THE CHIEF JUSTICE, JUSTICE WHITE, and JUSTICE O'CONNOR join, dissenting.

I agree with the proposition, felicitously put by Constable Rankin's counsel, that no law enforcement agency is required by the First Amendment to permit one of its employees to "ride with the cops and cheer for the robbers." The issue in this case is whether Constable Rankin, a law enforcement official, is prohibited by the First Amendment from preventing his employees from saying of the attempted assassination of President Reagan—on the job and within hearing of other employees—"If they go for him again, I hope they get him." The Court, applying the two-prong analysis of Connick v. Myers, 461 U.S. 138 (1983), holds that McPherson's statement was protected by the First Amendment because (1) it "addressed a matter of public concern," and (2) McPherson's interest in making the statement outweighs Rankin's interest in suppressing it. In so doing, the Court significantly and irrationally expands the definition of "public concern"; it also carves out a new and very large class of employees—i.e., those in "nonpolicymaking" positions—who, if today's decision is to be believed, can never be disciplined for statements that fall within the Court's expanded definition. Because I believe the Court's conclusions rest upon a distortion of both the record and the Court's prior decisions, I dissent.

\* \* \*

Even if I agreed that McPherson's statement was speech on a matter of "public concern," I would still find it unprotected. It is important to be clear on what the issue is in this part of the case. It is not, as the Court suggests, whether "Rankin's interest *in discharging [McPherson]* outweighed her rights under the First Amendment." Rather, it is whether his interest *in preventing the expression of such statements in his agency* outweighed her First Amendment interest in making the statement. We are not deliberating, in other words, (or at least should not be) about whether the sanction of dismissal was, as the concurrence puts it, "an * * * intemperat[e] employment decision." It may well have been—and personally I think it was. But we are not sitting as a panel to develop sound principles of proportionality for adverse actions in the state civil service. We are asked to determine whether, given the interests of this law enforcement office, McPherson had a *right* to say what she did—so that she could not only not be fired for it, but could not be formally reprimanded for it, or even prevented from repeating it endlessly into the future. It boggles the mind to think that she has such a right.

The Constable testified that he "was very concerned that this remark was made." Rightly so. As a law enforcement officer, the Constable obviously has a strong interest in preventing statements by any of his employees approving, or expressing a desire for, serious, violent crimes—regardless of whether the statements actually interfere with office operations at the time they are made or demonstrate character traits that make the speaker unsuitable for law enforcement work. In *Connick,* we upheld the dismissal of an assistant district attorney for circulating among her co-workers a questionnaire implicitly criticizing her superiors. Although we held that one of the questions—dealing with pressure in the office to participate in political campaigns—satisfied the "public concern" requirement, we held that the discharge nonetheless did not violate the First Amendment because the questionnaire itself "carrie[d] the clear potential for undermining office relations." Statements like McPherson's obviously carry a similar potential in an office devoted to law enforcement. Although that proposition is in my view evident on its face, we have actual evidence of it in the present record: The only reason McPherson's remark was brought to the Constable's attention was that one of his deputies, Captain Levrier, had overheard the remark and, according to the Constable, "was very upset because of [it]."

Statements by the Constable's employees to the effect that "if they go for the President again, I hope they get him" might also, to put it mildly, undermine public confidence in the Constable's office. A public employer has a strong interest in preserving its reputation with the public. We know—from undisputed testimony—that McPherson had or might have had some occasion to deal with the public while carrying out her duties.

The Court's sweeping assertion (and apparent holding) that where an employee "serves no confidential, policymaking, or public contact role, the danger to the agency's successful function from that employee's private speech is minimal," is simply contrary to reason and experience. Nonpolicymaking employees (the assistant district attorney in *Connick,* for example) can hurt working relationships and undermine public confidence in an organization every bit as much as policymaking employees. I, for one, do not look forward to the new First Amendment world the Court creates, in which nonpolicymaking employees of the Equal Employment Opportunity Commission must be permitted to make remarks on the job approving of racial discrimination, nonpolicymaking employees of the Selective Service

System to advocate noncompliance with the draft laws, and (since it is really quite difficult to contemplate anything more absurd that the present case itself), nonpolicymaking constable's deputies to express approval for the assassination of the President.

In sum, since Constable Rankin's interest in maintaining both an esprit de corps and a public image consistent with his office's law enforcement duties outweighs any interest his employees may have in expressing on the job a desire that the President be killed, even assuming that such an expression addresses a matter of public concern it is not protected by the First Amendment from suppression.  I emphasize once again that that is the issue here—and *not*, as both the Court's opinion and especially the concurrence seem to assume, whether the means used to effect suppression (viz., firing) were excessive.  The First Amendment contains no "narrow tailoring" requirement that speech the government is entitled to suppress must be suppressed by the mildest means possible.  If Constable Rankin was entitled (as I think any reasonable person would say he was) to admonish McPherson for saying what she did on the job, within hearing of her co-workers, and to warn her that if she did it again a formal censure would be placed in her personnel file, then it follows that he is entitled to rule that particular speech out of bounds in that particular work environment—and that is the end of the First Amendment analysis.  The "intemperate" manner of the permissible suppression is an issue for another forum, or at least for a more plausibly relevant provision of the Constitution.

NOTES AND QUESTIONS

**1.**  In *Rankin,* is the proper focus on the setting in which the statement was made, the effect of the statement on the governmental entity, the nature of the statement itself, or other factors?

**2.**  The facts in *Rankin* are unique.  How would you describe in general terms to a public employee what his or her rights are regarding expression in the workplace?  How does this answer affect your analysis in question 1?  If the dissent had prevailed, how would you explain the right of free expression?

**3.**  In Waters v. Churchill, 511 U.S. 661 (1994), a nurse working at a public hospital was fired because of statements she made to coworkers during a dinner break that were critical of the hospital.  It was disputed whether the statements were "disruptive."  The district court granted summary judgment for the hospital and the Seventh Circuit reversed.  The Supreme Court, seven-to-two, vacated the judgment and remanded the case for trial.  Writing for a four-justice plurality, Justice O'Connor, relying on Connick v. Myers, 461 U.S. 138 (1983), held that the government's interests are greater when it acts as an employer than when it acts as a sovereign.  Therefore, it may restrict more of employee speech in the interest of efficiency.  In reviewing the facts, the key is what the employer reasonably believed was said, rather than what the trier of fact ultimately determines was said.  The public employer must merely proceed with reasonable care to determine the facts and act in good faith.  In a concurring opinion for three justices, Justice Scalia asserted that a public employer's disciplining of an employee violates the First Amendment only if it is in retaliation for the employee's speech on a matter of public concern.  An investigation is not necessary before taking disciplinary action.  Thus, only the employer's motive is relevant.  In dissent, Justices Stevens and Blackmun argued that nondisruptive speech on a matter of public concern is protected, and whether it is protected should not turn on whether the employer believed the speech was protected.

**4.**  Should a different standard of "public concern" be used for matters of public concern generally (as in *Rankin* ) than for matters of public concern involving the employer?  Consider the following case: Kenneth Dixon was a maintenance worker for the Indiana Department of Highways (DOH).  One day after work, Dixon visited the home of Mark Hardaman, a summer DOH employee, and told him about a possible job opening.  Dixon said, however, that he had heard DOH supervisors imply that Hardaman would not be hired because he had filed a racial discrimination claim with the NAACP against DOH.  When DOH management heard about this conversation, they considered Dixon's statement harmful to DOH and fired him.  Is Dixon's speech protected?  See Indiana Department of Highways v. Dixon, 541 N.E.2d 877 (Ind.1989) (held:  yes).

**5.**  The County of Los Angeles Fire Department, in attempting to prevent sexual harassment, adopted a policy of prohibiting sexually-oriented magazines in dormitories, rest rooms, and lockers.  Does this policy, as applied to the private possession, reading, and consensual sharing of *Playboy* violate the First Amendment?  See Johnson v. Los Angeles County Fire Department, 865 F.Supp. 1430 (C.D.Cal.1994) (held:  yes).  The court rejected the argument that permitting the presence of sexually-oriented magazines would inevitably lead to sexual harassment.  According to the court, even if the men who read *Playboy* might entertain sexually degrading thoughts, "mere thoughts are outside the scope of Title VII."

**6.**  A bank teller refused to cash the state payroll check of a probationary corrections officer because the officer had no account with the bank.  After the officer obtained authorization from a service representative, the teller cashed the check.  As the officer was leaving the bank, from a distance of about 20 feet, the officer loudly said:  "Hitler should have gotten rid of all you Jews."  The teller was Egyptian.  After the incident was reported to the officer's supervisor, he was discharged.  He sued and argued that the discharge violated the First Amendment.  What result?  See Hawkins v. Department of Public Safety & Correctional Services, 602 A.2d 712 (Md. 1992) (held:  off-duty ethnic slur not a matter of public concern and therefore no duty to balance employee's interest against the state's interest in maintaining order in prison).

**7.**  The limits of the First Amendment's protection extend beyond employee criticism of employer policies to such matters as political activity.  Although most government employees are limited in the kinds of political activity in which they may actively engage by the Hatch Act, 5 U.S.C.

§§ 1501–1508, 7321–7326, and state "little Hatch Acts," employment decisions may not be made on the basis of party affiliation alone except for confidential or policymaking positions.   Branti v. Finkel, 445 U.S. 507 (1980); Elrod v. Burns, 427 U.S. 347 (1976); Goodwin v. LaPolla, 589 F.Supp. 1423 (N.D.N.Y.1984).

It has been held that statements on matters of public concern before the legislature may not serve as the basis for discharge where the statements do not pertain to a political party.   See State v. Haley, 687 P.2d 305 (Alaska 1984).

**8.**   Freedom of association and the right to privacy also protect certain extra-employment activities for public employees, although the employer's interest is often found to outweigh the individual's rights where other employees or clients are also involved.   See Barry v. City of New York, 712 F.2d 1554 (2d Cir.), cert. denied, 464 U.S. 1017 (1983) (family financial disclosure law for public employees upheld); Shawgo v. Spradlin, 701 F.2d 470 (5th Cir.1983), cert. denied, 464 U.S. 965 (1983) (12-day suspension for two police officers found to be living together upheld, even though no rule expressly prohibited cohabitation); Naragon v. Wharton, 572 F.Supp. 1117 (M.D.La.1983), affirmed, 737 F.2d 1403 (5th Cir.1984) (demotion of teacher having lesbian affair with pupil upheld); Briggs v. North Muskegon Police Department, 563 F.Supp. 585 (W.D.Mich.1983) (dismissal of married police officer who was flirting with married woman struck down), affirmed, 746 F.2d 1475 (6th Cir.1984), cert. denied, 473 U.S. 909 (1985); Baron v. Meloni, 556 F.Supp. 796 (W.D.N.Y.1983), remanded without opinion, 742 F.2d 1439 (2d Cir.1983), on remand, 602 F.Supp. 614 (W.D.N.Y.1985), affirmed mem., 779 F.2d 36 (2d Cir.1985) (policeman validly ordered to stop seeing wife of organized crime figure); Dronenburg v. Zech, 741 F.2d 1388 (D.C.Cir.1984), rehearing denied en banc, 746 F.2d 1579 (D.C.Cir.1984) (Navy policy of mandatory discharge for homosexual conduct does not violate right of privacy).

**9.**   The exercise of First Amendment rights does not protect employees who would have been legitimately discharged anyway.   See Mt. Healthy City School District Board of Education v. Doyle, 429 U.S. 274 (1977).

**10.**   In Bush v. Lucas, 462 U.S. 367 (1983), the Supreme Court held that where Congress has provided a comprehensive and meaningful scheme to protect civil servants against arbitrary action by supervisors, it would not interfere with that scheme by creating a separate judicial remedy for an employee who was demoted for exercising his first amendment rights.

The statutory scheme for dismissals under the federal Merit Systems Protection Board, 5 U.S.C. § 7513(a), requires an agency to make two determinations before removing an employee for off-duty conduct: that the employee actually committed the conduct and that the removal will promote the efficiency of the service.   In D.E. v. Department of the Navy, 721 F.2d 1165 (9th Cir.1983), D.E. was removed from his job following a plea of nolo contendere to charges of sexual abuse of a minor.   The court held that the Navy could not presume a nexus between D.E.'s off-duty conduct and his agency performance in the absence of evidence of actual adverse impact.

# Novosel v. Nationwide Insurance Co.

721 F.2d 894 (3d Cir.1983).

■ ADAMS, CIRCUIT JUDGE.

This appeal presents us with the task of determining under what circumstances a federal court sitting in diversity under Pennsylvania law may intercede in a non-union employment relationship and limit the employer's ability to discharge employees. In his suit against Nationwide Insurance Company, John Novosel brought two separate claims, one sounding in tort, the other in contract. The tort claim turns on whether a cause of action is created by a discharge that contravenes either important public policies or rights conferred on employees as members of the citizenry at large. The contract claim raises the question whether an enforceable contractual right to longterm employment may be read into what has traditionally been termed an employment-at-will position. The district court, concluding that no cause of action was stated, granted the employer's motion to dismiss both claims. Finding jurisdiction over this appeal under 28 U.S.C. § 1291, we vacate the district court's judgment and remand for further proceedings.

Novosel was an employee of Nationwide from December 1966 until November 18, 1981. He had steadily advanced through the company's ranks in a career unmarred by reprimands or disciplinary action. At the time his employment was terminated, he was a district claims manager and one of three candidates for the position of division claims manager.

In late October 1981, a memorandum was circulated through Nationwide's offices soliciting the participation of all employees in an effort to lobby the Pennsylvania House of Representatives. Specifically, employees were instructed to clip, copy, and obtain signatures on coupons bearing the insignia of the Pennsylvania Committee for No–Fault Reform. This Committee was actively supporting the passage of House Bill 1285, the "No–Fault Reform Act," then before the state legislature.

The allegations of the complaint charge that the sole reason for Novosel's discharge was his refusal to participate in the lobbying effort and his privately stated opposition to the company's political stand. Novosel contends that the discharge for refusing to lobby the state legislature on the employer's behalf constituted the tort of wrongful discharge on the grounds it was willful, arbitrary, malicious and in bad faith, and that it was contrary to public policy. Alternatively, the complaint avers a breach of an implied contract promising continued long-term employment so long as Novosel's job performance remained satisfactory. Novosel sought damages, reinstatement and declaratory relief. Nationwide did not file an answer to the complaint; instead it presented a motion to dismiss. Following the submission of briefs on the motion to dismiss, and without benefit of either affidavits or oral argument, the district court granted the motion on January 14, 1983. * * *

In a landmark opinion, the Pennsylvania Supreme Court acknowledged that such a situation could give rise to a legal cause of action:

> It may be granted that there are areas of an employee's life in which his employer has no legitimate interest. An intrusion into one of these areas by virtue of the employer's power of discharge might plausibly give rise to a cause of action, particularly where some recognized facet of public policy is threatened. The notion that substantive due process elevates an employer's privilege of hiring and discharging his employees to an absolute constitutional right has long since been discredited.

Geary v. United States Steel Corp., 456 Pa. 171, 184, 319 A.2d 174, 180 (1974). Under the particular facts of *Geary,* the court held:

> this case does not require us to define in comprehensive fashion the perimeters of this privilege [to employ-at-will], and we decline to do so. We hold only that where the complaint itself discloses a plausible and legitimate reason for terminating an at-will employment relationship and no clear mandate of public policy is violated thereby, an employee at will has no right of action against his employer for wrongful discharge.

456 Pa. at 184–85, 319 A.2d at 180. Despite the actual holding, *Geary* stands for the availability of legal remedies in private employer wrongful discharge cases and has been so interpreted by this Court.

Two subsequent Pennsylvania Superior Court cases upheld wrongful discharge causes of action under the theory that "where a clear mandate of public policy is violated by the [employee's] termination, the employer's right to discharge may be circumscribed * * *" Reuther v. Fowler & Williams, Inc., 255 Pa.Super. 28, 31, 386 A.2d 119, 120 (1978). The *Reuther* court held that "the law of this Commonwealth recognizes a cause of action for damages resulting when an employee is discharged for having performed his obligation of jury service." Similarly in Yaindl v. Ingersoll–Rand Co., 281 Pa.Super. 560, 572, 422 A.2d 611, 617 (1980), the Superior Court recognized "an interest of the public in seeing to it that the employer does not act abusively." See also Hunter v. Port Authority of Allegheny County, 277 Pa.Super. 4, 419 A.2d 631 (1980) (non-statutory wrongful discharge claim of public employee). In addition, other state courts have used public policy standards as the benchmark for wrongful discharge cases.

Thus, on the issue whether such a suit may go forward, it was incorrect as a matter of law to declare that "no cause of action for wrongful discharge is stated under Pennsylvania law * * *." The district court's assertion that "there occurs an express or implied waiver or relinquishment of otherwise valid constitutional rights when an employee voluntarily engages in employment * * *" must consequently be rejected as a ruling that "simply persists from blind imitation of the past."

Applying the logic of *Geary,* we find that Pennsylvania law permits a cause of action for wrongful discharge where the employment termination abridges a significant and recognized public policy. The district court did not consider the question whether an averment of discharge for refusing to support the employer's lobbying efforts is sufficiently violative of such public policy as to state a cause of action. Nationwide, however, now proposes that "the only prohibition on the termination of an employee is that the termination cannot violate a *statutorily* recognized public policy."

This Court has recognized that the "only Pennsylvania cases applying public policy exceptions have done so where no statutory remedies were available." Moreover, both *Reuther* and *Hunter* allowed causes of action to be implied directly from the Pennsylvania Constitution. *Hunter* further noted that Pennsylvania courts allow direct causes of action under the Constitution regardless of legislative action or inaction. Given that there are no statutory remedies available in the present case and taking into consideration the importance of the political and associational freedoms of the federal and state Constitutions, the absence of a statutory declaration of public policy would appear to be no bar to the existence of a cause of action. Accordingly, a cognizable expression of public policy may be derived in this case from either the First Amendment of the United States Constitution or Article I, Section 7 of the Pennsylvania Constitution.[6]

The key question in considering the tort claim is therefore whether a discharge for disagreement with the employer's legislative agenda or a refusal to lobby the state legislature on the employer's behalf sufficiently implicate a recognized facet of public policy. The definition of a "clearly mandated public policy" as one that "strikes at the heart of a citizen's social right, duties and responsibilities," set forth in Palmateer v. International Harvester Co., 85 Ill.2d 124, 52 Ill.Dec. 13, 421 N.E.2d 876 (1981), appears to provide a workable standard for the tort action. While no Pennsylvania law directly addresses the public policy question at bar, the protection of an employee's freedom of political expression would appear to involve no less compelling a societal interest than the fulfillment of jury service or the filing of a workers' compensation claim.

\* \* \*

We further note that the Pennsylvania Supreme Court has similarly voiced its concern over the threat posed by discharges to the constitutionally protected rights of employees. In Sacks v. Commonwealth of Pennsylvania, Department of Public Welfare, 502 Pa. 201, 465 A.2d 981 (Pa.Sup.Ct. 1983), the court ordered a state employee reinstated following a discharge for public comments critical of his agency employer. The court reasoned,

> there is a calculus of injury required in First Amendment government employee cases in which as the First Amendment interest in the speech rises, so does the government's obligation to react with caution, disciplining an employee, if at all, only when injury to the agency is more than speculative.

---

**6.** The relevant portion of Article I, Section 7 of the Pennsylvania Constitution states:

The free communication of thoughts and opinions is one of the invaluable rights of man, and every citizen may freely speak, write and print on any subject, being responsible for the abuse of that liberty.

Id., 502 Pa. at 215, 465 A.2d at 988.

Although Novosel is not a government employee, the public employee cases do not confine themselves to the narrow question of state action. Rather, these cases suggest that an important public policy is in fact implicated wherever the power to hire and fire is utilized to dictate the terms of employee political activities. In dealing with public employees, the cause of action arises directly from the Constitution rather than from common law developments. The protection of important political freedoms, however, goes well beyond the question whether the threat comes from state or private bodies. The inquiry before us is whether the concern for the rights of political expression and association which animated the public employee cases is sufficient to state a public policy under Pennsylvania law. While there are no Pennsylvania cases squarely on this point, we believe that the clear direction of the opinions promulgated by the state's courts suggests that this question be answered in the affirmative.

Having concluded thereby that an important public policy is at stake, we now hold that Novosel's allegations state a claim within the ambit of *Geary* in that Novosel's complaint discloses no plausible and legitimate reason for terminating his employment, and his discharge violates a clear mandate of public policy. The Pennsylvania Supreme Court's rulings in *Geary* and *Sacks* are thus interpreted to extend to a non-constitutional claim where a corporation conditions employment upon political subordination.

\* \* \*

Because this case is to be remanded, and taking into consideration the relative novelty of wrongful discharge actions, we proceed to a consideration of the factual bases a plaintiff would have to establish in order to prevail. It appears that the same factors to which the Pennsylvania Supreme Court referred in *Sacks* for evaluating the evidentiary sufficiency of Sacks' claim would be just as applicable to the case at hand. Thus, on remand the district court should employ the four part inquiry the *Sacks* court derived from *Connick* [v. Myers, 461 U.S. 138 (1983)] and *Pickering* [v. Board of Education, 391 U.S. 563 (1968)]:

1. Whether, because of the speech, the employer is prevented from efficiently carrying out its responsibilities;

2. Whether the speech impairs the employee's ability to carry out his own responsibilities;

3. Whether the speech interferes with essential and close working relationships;

4. Whether the manner, time and place in which the speech occurs interferes with business operations.

*Sacks,* supra, 502 Pa. at 216, 465 A.2d at 988.

In weighing these issues, a court should employ the balancing test factors set forth for wrongful discharge cases by the Pennsylvania Superior Court in *Yaindl,* supra:

(a) the nature of the actor's conduct,

(b) the actor's motive,

(c) the interests of the other with which the actor's conduct interferes,

(d) the interests sought to be advanced by the actor,

(e) the social interests in protecting the freedom of action of the actor and the contractual interests of the other,

(f) the proximity or remoteness of the actor's conduct to the interference, and

(g) the relations between the parties.

281 Pa.Super. at 574, 422 A.2d at 618, quoting Restatement (Second) of Torts § 767 (1979).

\* \* \*

The judgment and order of the district court will be vacated and the case remanded for discovery and further proceedings consistent with this opinion.

## NOTES AND QUESTIONS

**1.** In effect, *Novosel* extends constitutional protections to private sector employees via the public policy exception to the at will doctrine. Does this abrogate the "state action" requirement for constitutional claims? See generally Lisa B. Bingham, Employee Free Speech in the Workplace: Using the First Amendment as Public Policy for Wrongful Discharge Actions, 55 Ohio St.L.J. 341 (1994).

**2.** Does it violate the First Amendment for a county to pay a police officer for time spent *voluntarily* participating in a demonstration supporting legislation to ban assault weapons? See Donaggio v. Arlington County, 880 F.Supp. 446 (E.D.Va.1995), affirmed without opinion, 78 F.3d 578 (4th Cir.1996) (held: no).

**3.** "Free speech" in the workplace encompasses speech that is made in the workplace as well as speech activity outside. Private sector employees' free speech rights often depend on the type of free speech at issue.

*Internal speech*—Employees who have been discharged because of internal speech have alleged that their discharge violated a public policy in favor of free speech or some more specific public policy based on the nature of the speech. Often, these cases have concerned complaints to management about certain practices in the company. Most courts have held for the employer. See Suchodolski v. Michigan Consolidated Gas Co., 316 N.W.2d 710 (Mich.1982) (complaints to management about internal accounting practices; discharge upheld); Keneally v. Orgain, 606 P.2d 127 (Mont.1980) (complaints to supervisors about inadequate service to customers; discharge upheld); Geary v. United States Steel Corp., 319 A.2d 174 (Pa.1974) (complaints to supervisors about defective products; discharge upheld).

For an interesting discussion of employee discipline for obscenity, see James B. Atleson, Obscenities in the Workplace: A Comment on Fair and Foul Expression and Status Relationships, 34 Buff.L.Rev. 693 (1985).

*External speech*—Employees are more likely to be protected when their speech is outside the workplace. As discussed in Chapter 11, infra, many of the early cases to recognize wrongful discharge actions involved the exercise of statutorily created rights by employees, such as the filing of workers' compensation claims. Whether other forms of external communications are protected usually depends on the public policy implicated by the speech activity. Compare Rozier v. St. Mary's Hospital, 411 N.E.2d 50 (Ill.App.1980) (reporting incidents at local hospital to newspaper; discharge upheld) with Palmateer v. International Harvester Co., 421 N.E.2d 876 (Ill.1981) (reporting suspected criminal activity of another employee to police; discharge unlawful).

**4.** Fuller development of the law of wrongful discharge, including tort actions based on a violation of public policy, is presented in Chapter 10.

## 5.   COLLECTIVE ACTION

### NLRB v. Washington Aluminum Co.

370 U.S. 9 (1962).

■ MR. JUSTICE BLACK delivered the opinion of the Court.

* * * The respondent company is engaged in the fabrication of aluminum products in Baltimore, Maryland, a business having interstate aspects that subject it to regulation under the National Labor Relations Act. The machine shop in which the seven discharged employees worked was not insulated and had a number of doors to the outside that had to be opened frequently. An oil furnace located in an adjoining building was the chief source of heat for the shop, although there were two gas-fired space heaters that contributed heat to a lesser extent. The heat produced by these units was not always satisfactory and, even prior to the day of the walkout involved here, several of the eight machinists who made up the day shift at the shop had complained from time to time to the company's foreman "over the cold working conditions."

January 5, 1959, was an extraordinarily cold day for Baltimore, with unusually high winds and a low temperature of 11 degrees followed by a high of 22. When the employees on the day shift came to work that morning, they found the shop bitterly cold, due not only to the unusually harsh weather, but also to the fact that the large oil furnace had broken down the night before and had not as yet been put back into operation. As the workers gathered in the shop just before the starting hour of 7:30, one of them, a Mr. Caron, went into the office of Mr. Jarvis, the foreman, hoping to warm himself but, instead, found the foreman's quarters as uncomfortable as the rest of the shop. As Caron and Jarvis sat in Jarvis' office discussing how bitingly cold the building was, some of the other machinists walked by the office window "huddled" together in a fashion that caused Jarvis to exclaim that "[i]f those fellows had any guts at all, they would go home." When the starting buzzer sounded a few moments later, Caron walked back to his working place in the shop and found all the other machinists "huddled there, shaking a little, cold." Caron then said to these workers, " * * * Dave [Jarvis] told me if we had any guts, we would go home. * * * I am going home, it is too damned cold to work." Caron asked the other workers what they were going to do and, after some discussion among themselves, they decided to leave with him. One of these workers, testifying before the Board, summarized their entire discussion this way: "And we had all got together and thought it would be a good idea to go home; maybe we could get some heat brought into the plant that way." As they started to leave, Jarvis approached and persuaded one of the workers to remain at the job. But Caron and the other six workers on the day shift left practically in a body in a matter of minutes after the 7:30 buzzer.

When the company's general foreman arrived between 7:45 and 8 that morning, Jarvis promptly informed him that all but one of the employees had left because the shop was too cold. The company's president came in at approximately 8:20 a.m. and, upon learning of the walkout, immediately said to the foreman, " * * * if they have all gone, we are going to terminate them." After discussion "at great length" between the general foreman and the company president as to what might be the effect of the walkout on employee discipline and plant production, the president formalized his discharge of the workers who had walked out by giving orders at 9 a.m. that the affected workers should be notified about their discharge immediately, either by telephone, telegram or personally. This was done.

On these facts the Board found that the conduct of the workers was a concerted activity to protest the company's failure to supply adequate heat in its machine shop, that such conduct is protected under the provision of § 7 of the National Labor Relations Act which guarantees that "Employees shall have the right * * * to engage in * * * concerted activities for the purpose of collective bargaining or other mutual aid or protection," and that the discharge of these workers by the company amounted to an unfair labor practice under § 8(a)(1) of the Act, which forbids employers "to interfere with, restrain, or coerce employees in the exercise of the rights guaranteed in section 7." Acting under the authority of § 10(c) of the Act, which provides that when an employer has been guilty of an unfair labor practice the Board can "take such affirmative action including reinstatement of employees with or without back pay, as will effectuate the policies of this Act," the Board then ordered the company to reinstate the discharged workers to their previous positions and to make them whole for losses resulting from what the Board found to have been the unlawful termination of their employment.

In denying enforcement of this order, the majority of the Court of Appeals took the position that because the workers simply "summarily left their place of employment" without affording the company an "opportunity to avoid the work stoppage by granting a concession to a demand," their walkout did not amount to a concerted activity protected by § 7 of the Act. On this basis, they held that there was no justification for the conduct of the workers in violating the established rules of the plant by leaving their jobs without permission and that the Board had therefore exceeded its power in issuing the order involved here because § 10(c) declares that the Board shall not require reinstatement or back pay for an employee whom an employer has suspended or discharged "for cause."

We cannot agree that employees necessarily lose their right to engage in concerted activities under § 7 merely because they do not present a specific demand upon their employer to remedy a condition they find objectionable.  The language of § 7 is broad enough to protect concerted activities whether they take place before, after, or at the same time such a demand is made.  To compel the Board to interpret and apply that language in the restricted fashion suggested by the respondent here would only tend to frustrate the policy of the Act to protect the right of workers to act together to better their working conditions.  Indeed, as indicated by this very case, such an interpretation of § 7 might place burdens upon employees so great that it would effectively nullify the right to engage in concerted activities which that section protects.  The seven employees here were part of a small group of employees who were wholly unorganized.  They had no bargaining representative and, in fact, no representative of any kind to present their grievances to their employer.  Under these circumstances, they had to speak for themselves as best they could.  As pointed out above, prior to the day they left the shop, several of them had repeatedly complained to company officials about the cold working conditions in the shop.  These had been more or less spontaneous individual pleas, unsupported by any threat of concerted protest, to which the company apparently gave little consideration and which it now says the Board should have treated as nothing more than "the same sort of gripes as the gripes made about the heat in the summertime."  The bitter cold of January 5, however, finally brought these workers' individual complaints into concert so that some more effective action could be considered.  Having no bargaining representative and no established procedure by which they could take full advantage of their unanimity of opinion in negotiations with the company, the men took the most direct course to let the company know that they wanted a warmer place in which to work.  So, after talking among themselves, they walked out together in the hope that this action might spotlight their complaint and bring about some improvement in what they considered to be the "miserable" conditions of their employment.  This we think was enough to justify the Board's holding that they were not required to make any more specific demand than they did to be entitled to the protection of § 7.

Although the company contends to the contrary, we think that the walkout involved here did grow out of a "labor dispute" within the plain meaning of the definition of that term in § 2(9) of the Act, which declares that it includes "any controversy concerning terms, tenure or *conditions of employment* * * *."  The findings of the Board, which are supported by substantial evidence and which were not disturbed below, show a running dispute between the machine shop employees and the company over the heating of the shop on cold days—a dispute which culminated in the decision of the employees to act concertedly in an effort to force the company to improve that condition of their employment. The fact that the company was already making every effort to repair the furnace and bring heat into the shop that morning does not change the nature of the controversy that caused the walkout. At the very most, that fact might tend to indicate that the conduct of the men in leaving was unnecessary and unwise, and it has long been settled that the reasonableness of workers' decisions to engage in concerted activity is irrelevant to the determination of whether a labor dispute exists or not. Moreover, the evidence here shows that the conduct of these workers was far from unjustified under the circumstances. The company's own foreman expressed the opinion that the shop was so cold that the men should go home. This statement by the foreman but emphasizes the obvious—that is, that the conditions of coldness about which complaint had been made before had been so aggravated on the day of the walkout that the concerted action of the men in leaving their jobs seemed like a perfectly natural and reasonable thing to do.

Nor can we accept the company's contention that because it admittedly had an established plant rule which forbade employees to leave their work without permission of the foreman, there was justifiable "cause" for discharging these employees, wholly separate and apart from any concerted activities in which they engaged in protest against the poorly heated plant. Section 10(c) of the Act does authorize an employer to discharge employees for "cause" and our cases have long recognized this right on the part of an employer. But this, of course, cannot mean that an employer is at liberty to punish a man by discharging him for engaging in concerted activities which § 7 of the Act protects. And the plant rule in question here purports to permit the company to do just that for it would prohibit even the most plainly protected kinds of concerted work stoppages until and unless the permission of the company's foreman was obtained.

It is of course true that § 7 does not protect all concerted activities, but that aspect of the section is not involved in this case. The activities engaged in here do not fall within the normal categories of unprotected concerted activities such as those that are unlawful, violent or in breach of contract. Nor can they be brought under this Court's more recent pronouncement which denied the protection of § 7 to activities characterized as "indefensible" because they were there found to show a disloyalty to the workers' employer which this Court deemed unnecessary to carry on the workers' legitimate concerted activities. The activities of these seven employees cannot be classified as "indefensible" by any recognized standard of conduct. Indeed, concerted activities by employees for the purpose of trying to protect themselves from working conditions as uncomfortable as the testimony and Board findings showed them to be in this case are unquestionably activities to correct conditions which modern labor-management legislation treats as too bad to have to be tolerated in a humane and civilized society like ours.

We hold therefore that the Board correctly interpreted and applied the Act to the circumstances of this case and it was error for the Court of Appeals to refuse to enforce its order. The judgment of the Court of Appeals is reversed and the cause is remanded to that court with directions to enforce the order in its entirety.

Reversed and remanded.

NOTES AND QUESTIONS

**1.** Is there any difference between employees refusing to work because it is too cold and employees refusing to work unless the employer raises wages?

**2.** Not all concerted activity by employees is protected. Violence, threats, insubordination, and disloyalty may constitute "discharge for cause" under § 10(c) of the NLRA. These standards are vague and the Board is required to consider the facts of each case and to balance employee rights under § 7 against an employer's right "to maintain order and respect" in the conduct of its business. See NLRB v. IBEW, Local 1229 (Jefferson Standard Broadcasting Co.), 346 U.S. 464 (1953). See generally Charles J. Morris, NLRB Protection in the Nonunion Workplace: A Glimpse at a General Theory of Section 7 Conduct, 137 U.Pa.L.Rev. 1673 (1989).

**3.** When employees engage in protected concerted activity, what can the employer do by way of response? If the employer cannot discharge the employees, can it hire temporary or permanent replacements? See NLRB v. MacKay Radio & Telegraph Co., 304 U.S. 333 (1938) (held: employer may hire permanent replacements for economic strikers).

**4.** Three employees refused to work because they feared that the metal they were required to use in their work was radioactive. In fact, the metal was not radioactive. Was their work refusal protected activity or was the employer free to discharge them? See NLRB v. Modern Carpet Industries, Inc., 611 F.2d 811 (10th Cir.1979) (held: good faith of employees made work refusal protected).

**5.** In order to be "protected" under § 8(a)(1) of the NLRA employee activity must be "concerted"—engaged in by more than one employee. In NLRB v. City Disposal Systems, Inc., 465 U.S. 822 (1984), the Supreme Court held, five to four, that an *individual* employee's honest and reasonable assertion of a right contained in a collective bargaining agreement was concerted activity.

> [W]hen an employee invokes a right grounded in the collective-bargaining agreement, he does not stand alone. Instead, he brings to bear on his employer the power and resolve of all his fellow employees. * * * [It] is, therefore, a concerted activity in a very real sense.

Id. at 832. This doctrine of "constructive concerted activity" is sometimes referred to as the Interboro rule. Interboro Contractors, Inc., 157 N.L.R.B. 110 (1966) enforced, 388 F.2d 495 (2d Cir.1967). In Meyers Industries, 268 N.L.R.B. 493 (1984), however, the NLRB overruled prior precedent and held that there could be no constructive concerted activity in the absence of a collective bargaining agreement.   Therefore, an individual nonunion employee's assertion of group rights will not be deemed concerted unless other employees have become directly involved in the dispute.   The Supreme Court in *City Disposal* refused to consider the validity of *Meyers.* The *Meyers* decision itself may be subject to question.   On appeal, the D.C. Circuit held that the Board's decision was erroneous and remanded the case for reconsideration in light of *City Disposal* and the court's own opinion.   Prill v. NLRB, 755 F.2d 941 (D.C.Cir.), cert. denied, 474 U.S. 971 (1985).   "*City Disposal* makes unmistakenly clear that, contrary to the Board's view in *Meyers,* neither the language nor the history of section 7 requires that the term 'concerted activities' be interpreted to protect only the most narrowly defined forms of common action by employees.   * * *" 755 F.2d at 952.   On remand, the Board reaffirmed its earlier holding.   281 N.L.R.B. No. 118 (1986).   In Prill v. NLRB, 835 F.2d 1481 (D.C.Cir.1987), cert. denied, 487 U.S. 1205 (1988), the Board's interpretation of "concerted activity" was affirmed.   See generally Robert A. Gorman & Matthew W. Finkin, The Individual and the Requirement of "Concert" Under the National Labor Relations Act, 130 U.Pa.L.Rev. 286 (1981).

**6.**   The election under the NLRA of an exclusive collective bargaining representative (union) may limit the ability of individual employees to seek redress of grievances from the employer.   In Emporium Capwell Co. v. Western Addition Community Organization, 420 U.S. 50 (1975), several black employees insisted on a meeting with top company officials to protest perceived discrimination against racial minorities in hiring and promotion. The employer refused to meet with the employees and asserted that the claims would have to be processed through the union.   The employees then held a press conference and distributed leaflets attacking the employer. Two of the protesting employees were discharged.   The Supreme Court upheld the discharge and said that the employees' protest was a "grievance" which could only be pursued by the union.   If a union acts arbitrarily, capriciously, or in bad faith in refusing to process a grievance (or in other representational matters), employees may bring an action for damages against the union under § 301 of the Labor-Management Relations Act for this breach of the "duty of fair representation."   See Vaca v. Sipes, 386 U.S. 171 (1967).

## B.   REGULATION OF OFF-WORK ACTIVITY

An employer's control over its employees extends even beyond the workplace.   In this section, the cases and materials address three areas of employer control: personal associations, political activity, and lifestyle.

The first limitations imposed upon employer control of off-work activities of employees were the constitutional protections afforded public employees.   Recently, certain protections have been given to private sector employees, but these are limited and depend on collective bargaining agreements, implied contract rights, and other sources.

As you read the cases and materials in this section try to decide when an employer may have a legitimate interest in regulating its employees' off-work activities and how the balance should be struck between employee and employer concerns.

## 1.  Personal Associations

## Rulon–Miller v. International Business Machines Corp.

208 Cal.Rptr. 524 (Cal.App.1984).

■ Rushing, Associate Justice.

International Business Machines (IBM) appeals from the judgment entered against it after a jury awarded $100,000 compensatory and $200,-000 punitive damages to respondent (Virginia Rulon-Miller) on claims of wrongful discharge and intentional infliction of emotional distress.  Rulon-Miller was a low-level marketing manager at IBM in its office products division in San Francisco.  Her termination as a marketing manager at IBM came about as a result of an accusation made by her immediate supervisor, defendant Callahan, of a romantic relationship with the manager of a rival office products firm, QYX.

\* \* \*

IBM knew about respondent's relationship with Matt Blum well before her appointment as a manager.  Respondent met Blum in 1976 when he was an account manager for IBM.  That they were dating was widely known within the organization.  In 1977 Blum left IBM to join QYX, an IBM competitor, and was transferred to Philadelphia.  When Blum returned to San Francisco in the summer of 1978, IBM personnel were aware that he and respondent began dating again.  This seemed to present no problems to respondent's superiors, as Callahan confirmed when she was promoted to manager.  Respondent testified: "Somewhat in passing, Phil said: I heard the other day you were dating Matt Blum, and I said: Oh. And he said, I don't have any problem with that.  You're my number one pick.  I just want to assure you that you are my selection."  The relationship with Blum was also known to Regional Manager Gary Nelson who agreed with Callahan.  Neither Callahan nor Nelson raised any issue of conflict of interest because of the Blum relationship.

Respondent flourished in her management position, and the company, apparently grateful for her efforts, gave her a $4,000 merit raise in 1979 and told her that she was doing a good job.  A week later, her manager, Phillip Callahan, left a message that he wanted to see her.

When she walked into Callahan's office he confronted her with the question of whether she was *dating* Matt Blum.  She wondered at the relevance of the inquiry and he said the dating constituted a "conflict of interest," and told her to stop dating Blum or lose her job and said she had a "couple of days to a week" to think about it.

The next day Callahan called her in again, told her "he had made up her mind for her," and when she protested, dismissed her. IBM and Callahan claim that he merely "transferred" respondent to another division.

Respondent's claims of wrongful discharge and intentional infliction of emotional distress were both submitted to the jury.   *  *  *

The initial discussion between Callahan and respondent of her relationship with Blum is important. We must accept the version of the facts most favorable to the respondent herein. When Callahan questioned her relationship with Blum, respondent invoked her right to privacy in her personal life relying on existing IBM policies. A threshold inquiry is thus presented whether respondent could reasonably rely on those policies for job protection. Any conflicting action by the company would be wrongful in that it would constitute a violation of her contract rights.

Under the common law rule codified in Labor Code section 2922, an employment contract of indefinite duration is, in general, terminable at "the will" of either party. This common law rule has been considerably altered by the recognition of the Supreme Court of California that implicit in any such relationship or contract is an underlying principle that requires the parties to deal openly and fairly with one another. * * * The duty of fair dealing by an employer is, simply stated, a requirement that like cases be treated alike. Implied in this, of course, is that the company, if it has rules and regulations, apply those rules and regulations to its employees as well as affording its employees their protection.

*  *  *

In this case, there is a close question of whether those rules or regulations permit IBM to inquire into the purely personal life of the employee. If so, an attendant question is whether such a policy was applied consistently, particularly as between men and women. The distinction is important because the right of privacy, a constitutional right in California, could be implicated by the IBM inquiry. Much of the testimony below concerned what those policies were. The evidence was conflicting on the meaning of certain IBM policies. We observe ambiguity in the application but not in the intent. The "Watson Memo" (so called because it was signed by a former chairman of IBM) provided as follows:

"TO ALL IBM MANAGERS:

"The line that separates an individual's on-the-job business life from his other life as a private citizen is at times well-defined and at other times indistinct. But the line does exist, and you and I, as managers in IBM, must be able to recognize that line.

"I have seen instances where managers took disciplinary measures against employees for actions or conduct that are not rightfully the company's concern. These managers usually justified their decisions by citing their personal code of ethics and morals or by quoting some fragment of company policy that seemed to support their position. Both arguments proved unjust on close examination. What we need, in every case, is balanced judgment which weighs the needs of the business and the rights of the individual.

"Our primary objective as IBM managers is to further the business of this company by leading our people properly and measuring quantity and quality of work and effectiveness on the job against clearly set standards of responsibility and compensation. This is performance—and performance is, in the final analysis, the one thing that the company can insist on from everyone.

"We have concern with an employee's off-the-job behavior only when it reduces his ability to perform regular job assignments, interferes with the job performance of other employees, or if his outside behavior affects the reputation of the company in a major way. When on-the-job performance is acceptable, I can think of few situations in which outside activities could result in disciplinary action or dismissal.

"When such situations do come to your attention, you should seek the advice and counsel of the next appropriate level of management and the personnel department in determining what action—if any—is called for. Action should be taken only when a legitimate interest of the company is injured or jeopardized. Furthermore the damage must be clear beyond reasonable doubt and not based on hasty decisions about what one person might think is good for the company.

"IBM's first basic belief is respect for the individual, and the essence of this belief is a strict regard for his right to personal privacy. This idea should never be compromised easily or quickly.

"/s/ Tom Watson, Jr."

It is clear that this company policy insures to the employee both the right of privacy and the right to hold a job even though "off-the-job behavior" might not be approved of by the employee's manager.

IBM had adopted policies governing employee conduct. Some of those policies were collected in a document known as the "Performance and Recognition" (PAR) Manual. IBM relies on the following portion of the PAR Manual:

"A conflict of interest can arise when an employee is involved in activity for personal gain, which for any reason is in conflict with IBM's business interests. Generally speaking, 'moonlighting' is defined as working at some activity for personal gain outside of your IBM job. If you do perform outside work, you have a special responsibility to avoid any conflict with IBM's business interests.

"Obviously, you cannot solicit or perform in competition with IBM product or service offerings. Outside work cannot be performed on IBM time, including 'personal' time off. You cannot use IBM equipment, materials, resources, or 'inside' information for outside work. Nor should you solicit business or clients or perform outside work on IBM premises.

"Employees must be free of any significant investment or association of their own or of their immediate family's [sic], in competitors or suppliers, which might interfere or be thought to interfere with the independent exercise of their judgment in the best interests of IBM."

This policy of IBM is entitled "Gifts" and appears to be directed at "moonlighting" and soliciting outside business or clients on IBM premises. It prohibits "significant investment" in competitors or suppliers of IBM. It also prohibits "association" with such persons "which might interfere or be thought to interfere with the independent exercise of their judgment in the best interests of IBM."

Callahan based his action against respondent on a "conflict of interest." But the record shows that IBM did not interpret this policy to prohibit a romantic relationship. Callahan admitted that there was no company rule or policy requiring an employee to terminate friendships with fellow employees who leave and join competitors.[4] Gary Nelson, Callahan's superior, also confirmed that IBM had no policy against employees socializing with competitors.

This issue was hotly contested with respondent claiming that the "conflict of interest" claim was a pretext for her unjust termination. Whether it was presented a fact question for the jury.

Do the policies reflected in this record give IBM a right to terminate an employee for a conflict of interest? The answer must be yes, but whether respondent's conduct constituted such was for the jury. We observe that while respondent was successful, her primary job did not give her access to sensitive information which could have been useful to competitors. She was, after all, a seller of typewriters and office equipment. Respondent's brief makes much of the concession by IBM that there was no evidence whatever that respondent had given any information or help to IBM's competitor QYX. It really is no concession at all; she did not have the information or help to give. Even so, the question is one of substantial evidence. The evidence is abundant that there was no conflict of interest by respondent.

It does seem clear that an overall policy established by IBM chairman Watson was one of no company interest in the outside activities of an employee so long as the activities did not interfere with the work of the employee. Moreover, in the last analysis, it may be simply a question for the jury to decide whether, in the application of these policies, the right was conferred on IBM to inquire into the personal or romantic relation-

**4.** An interesting side issue to this point is that Blum continued to play on an IBM softball team while working for QYX.

ships its managers had with others. This is an important question because IBM, in attempting to reargue the facts to us, casts this argument in other terms, namely: that it had a right to inquire even if there was no evidence that such a relationship interfered with the discharge of the employee's duties *because* it had the effect of diminishing the morale of the employees answering to the manager. This is the "Caesar's wife" argument; it is merely a recast of the principal argument and asks the same question in different terms.[5] The same answer holds in both cases: there being no evidence to support the more direct argument, there is no evidence to support the indirect argument.

Moreover, the record shows that the evidence of rumor was not a basis for any decline in the morale of the employees reporting to respondent. Employees Mary Hrize and Wayne Fyvie, who reported to respondent's manager that she was seen at a tea dance at the Hyatt Regency with Matt Blum and also that she was not living at her residence in Marin, did not believe that those rumors in any way impaired her abilities as a manager. In the initial confrontation between respondent and her superior the assertion of the right to be free of inquiries concerning her personal life was based on substantive direct contract rights she had flowing to her from IBM policies. Further, there is no doubt that the jury could have so found and on this record we must assume that they did so find.

The judgment is affirmed.

NOTES AND QUESTIONS

**1.** On what legal theory did the court uphold the verdict for the plaintiff? Was it contract, tort, or some other basis?

**2.** Ironically, IBM is a company well known for its commitment to employee rights and dignity—as evidenced in the "Watson memo." See also IBM's Guidelines on Employee Privacy, An Interview with Frank T. Cary, 54 Harv.Bus.Rev. No. 5, at 82 (1976). To what extent do you think IBM actually was disadvantaged in the case by its policy of tolerance of employee off-work activities? Would this fact tend to make IBM or other companies *less* tolerant in the future?

**3.** A romantic involvement with a competitor has the potential to be a conflict of interest for the employee and to have a negative effect on the company. At what point would a company be justified in attempting to regulate an employee's relationship with a competitor? What degree of proof of actual harm to the company is necessary before the employer can take action? See Salazar v. Furr's, Inc., 629 F.Supp. 1403 (D.N.M.1986) (employee failed to state claim of abusive discharge on ground that she was

---

**5.** What we mean by that is that if you charge that an employee is passing confidential information to a competitor, the question remains whether the charge is true on the evidence available to the person deciding the issue, in this case, the respondent's managers at IBM. If you recast this argument in the form of the "Caesar's wife" argument attempted by IBM, it will be seen that exactly the same question arises, namely, "is it true?" Indeed, the import of the argument is that the rumor, or an unfounded allegation, could serve as a basis for the termination of the employee.

discharged because she was married to employee of her employer's competitors).

**4.** A supervisory employee is discharged because of his continuing association with the former president of the company who had been discharged previously. Does the supervisor's discharge violate the public policy exception to the at will doctrine? See Ferguson v. Freedom Forge Corp., 604 F.Supp. 1157 (W.D.Pa.1985) (held: no). If not, how are the associational rights of private employees to be protected?

**5.** Is a private employer free to discharge an employee because he is a member of the Ku Klux Klan? Would it matter if the employee is a well publicized officer in the Klan or if other employees threatened a wildcat strike? See Bellamy v. Mason's Stores, Inc., 508 F.2d 504 (4th Cir.1974). Would your answer be different if the discharge were based on membership in the NAACP or Junior Chamber of Commerce?

**6.** Voluntary office romances, especially where one of the parties is a supervisor, create a dilemma for employers. An employer may be in violation of Title VII for sexual harassment or claims that the romance adversely affected the employment rights of other employees. On the other hand, does discharging a supervisor for dating a co-worker constitute outrageous conduct? See Federated Rural Electric Insurance Co. v. Kessler, 388 N.W.2d 553 (Wis.1986) (employer's rule prohibiting romantic association of employee with married co-employee did not discriminate on basis of marital status).

**7.** A former employee brought an action for breach of contract in which he alleged that he resigned as a result of humiliation and stress he suffered from working under the direct supervision of the company president. His wife, also an employee of the company, was known to be having a sexual relationship with the president of the company. Has the former employee stated a claim? See Kader v. Paper Software, Inc., 111 F.3d 337 (2d Cir.1997) (held: no; "uneasy and stressful environment" insufficient to establish constructive discharge).

**8.** A number of freedom of association cases have arisen in the public sector, where employees have alleged that adverse treatment based on off-work associations was unconstitutional under the First and Fourteenth Amendments. One series of cases involves cohabitation by an unmarried couple where neither individual was married or one or both individuals were married to other people. Are anticohabitation regulations for police officers and other public employees constitutional? Compare Shawgo v. Spradlin, 701 F.2d 470 (5th Cir.1983), cert. denied, 464 U.S. 965 (1983) and Hollenbaugh v. Carnegie Free Library, 436 F.Supp. 1328 (W.D.Pa.1977), affirmed, 578 F.2d 1374 (3d Cir.1978), cert. denied, 439 U.S. 1052 (1978) (upholding discharge) with Briggs v. North Muskegon Police Department, 563 F.Supp. 585 (W.D.Mich.1983), affirmed mem., 746 F.2d 1475 (6th Cir.1984), cert. denied, 473 U.S. 909 (1985) (reversing discharge). See also Shuman v. Philadelphia, 470 F.Supp. 449 (E.D.Pa.1979) (police officer need not answer questions about personal associations).

**9.** When would a public employer be justified in regulating the associational rights of its employees?  Would it be lawful for a sheriff to order his deputy to stop "associating" with the wife of a reputed mobster?  See Baron v. Meloni, 556 F.Supp. 796 (W.D.N.Y.1983), affirmed mem., 779 F.2d 36 (2d Cir.1985).  What about a police department regulation prohibiting fraternization with known felons?  See Morrisette v. Dilworth, 454 N.Y.S.2d 864 (App.Div.1982), affirmed, 452 N.E.2d 1222 (N.Y.1983).  Would it violate the First Amendment for a city to discipline a police officer who was a part owner of a video store that rented nonobscene, sexually explicit videotapes?  See Flanagan v. Munger, 890 F.2d 1557 (10th Cir. 1989) (held: yes).

**10.** A 30 year-old graduate assistant was having a lesbian affair with an 18 year-old university student who was not in any of her classes.  When university officials learned of the relationship, the graduate assistant's assignment was changed from teaching to research.  Does this action infringe upon her associational or privacy rights?  See Naragon v. Wharton, 572 F.Supp. 1117 (M.D.La.1983), affirmed, 737 F.2d 1403 (5th Cir. 1984) (held: no).

**11.** Tom Ward and Judy Johnson were not married and were living together.  They were both employees of Frito-Lay, Inc.  Johnson attempted to bid onto the same shift as Ward, and their relationship had caused "employee comment, insubordination, and the filing of a grievance." (Ward had a previous relationship with another female employee of Frito-Lay.  At that time, the woman's husband came to the plant armed with a gun, threatened Ward, and management had to call the police.)  The company had a rule against relatives working on the same shift.  Frito-Lay felt that Ward and Johnson should not continue working at the same plant and fired Ward.  What legal rights, if any, does or should Ward have?  See Ward v. Frito-Lay, Inc., 290 N.W.2d 536 (Wis.App.1980) (held: no wrongful discharge).

**12.** Arkansas enacted a law requiring all teachers in public schools to file affidavits giving names and addresses of all organizations to which they had belonged or contributed within the preceding five years.  What is the purpose of the law?  Is it valid?  See Shelton v. Tucker, 364 U.S. 479 (1960) (held: no).

**13.** The Department of Energy prepared a questionnaire requiring all employees to list the names of corporations, other business enterprises, partnerships, nonprofit organizations, and educational or other institutions with which they, their spouses, minor children, and dependents are connected as employee, officer, owner, director, trustee, partner, advisor, or consultant.  Can employees be required to complete the questionnaire? See American Federation of Government Employees, Local 421 v. Schlesinger, 443 F.Supp. 431 (D.D.C.1978) (held: no; questionnaire overbroad).

**14.** New York City enacted a financial disclosure law requiring annual financial reports from most elected and appointed officials, candidates for city office, and all civil service employees with an annual salary equal to or greater than $30,000.  Covered employees and their spouses must list, among other things, the identity of professional organizations from which the employee or spouse derives $1,000 or more in income during the preceding year; the source of capital gains of $1,000 or more, other than from the sale of a residence; the source of gifts or honoraria of $500 or more; indebtedness in excess of $500 that is outstanding for 90 days or more; and the nature of investments worth $20,000 or more. The reports must be filed with the city clerk and are available for public inspection. Is this law constitutional? See Barry v. New York, 712 F.2d 1554 (2d Cir.), cert. denied, 464 U.S. 1017 (1983) (held: yes). How does your analysis compare with the Department of Energy questionnaire? See also Walls v. City of Petersburg, 895 F.2d 188 (4th Cir.1990) (city employee's right to privacy not violated when she was discharged for failing to answer questions about her sexual relations, marital history, family's criminal record, and her financial background).

## 2.  POLITICAL ACTIVITY

### Nelson v. McClatchy Newspapers, Inc.

936 P.2d 1123 (Wash.1997).

■ SANDERS, JUSTICE.

\* \* \*

### *FACTS*

Sandra Nelson began working as a reporter for TNT in 1983, three years before McClatchy Newspapers, Inc., purchased it. When McClatchy acquired TNT in 1986 it retained Nelson as a reporter. Nelson covered the "education beat" and focused on Tacoma schools as well as regional and state educational issues and, by all accounts, did a good job.

A fundamental goal of TNT, as a news publication, is to appear objective in the eyes of its readers. As part of this effort, TNT management put forth an ethics code in 1987 regulating activity deemed to present apparent or actual conflicts of interest. The ethics code defines conflicts of interest to include all situations in which readers might be led to believe that the news reporting is biased, including situations in which reporters participate in high profile political activity. Nelson's admitted violation of this code of ethics led to her transfer and the present suit.

Journalistic codes of ethics are common. In fact, most newspapers in the country have some form of code of conduct to minimize conflicts of interest. A 1983 study indicates that 75 percent of news organizations have similar codes in place. For example, *The Washington Post* has a code nearly identical to TNT's stating in part that newsroom employees must " 'avoid active involvement in any partisan causes—politics, community affairs, social action, demonstrations—that could compromise or seem to compromise our ability to report and edit fairly.' " Similarly, the Associated Press has a code containing nearly identical provisions including "Involvement in politics, demonstrations and social causes that could cause a conflict of interest, or the appearance of such conflict should be avoided.'' The code of ethics of the Society of Professional Journalists is also similar.

Nelson is a self-professed lesbian who spends much of her off-duty hours serving as a political activist. She attends political fora, demonstrations, and classes for political causes including highly visible support for gay and lesbian rights, feminist issues, and abortion rights. Nelson is also a member of and organizer for Tacoma Radical Women, a feminist socialist organization, and the Freedom Socialist Party. Much of her political activism has been supported by this party and has been in support of its party platform. McClatchy knew of Nelson's political activities when it chose to retain her.

In 1987, Nelson was seen by a TNT reporter and photographer as she was picketing for abortion rights outside a local hospital. TNT management told her such activity compromised the paper's appearance of objectivity. Nelson responded she would continue her public political activity anyway.

In 1989, Nelson helped launch a ballot initiative to have an antidiscrimination ordinance reinstated following its repeal. Throughout 1990 she visibly promoted the initiative by organizing volunteers, soliciting support from various groups, arranging for community speakers, organizing rallies, and collecting signatures for the initiative. The initiative battle remained a major political story throughout the year and increasingly so as the fall election approached. On August 15, 1990, TNT's editors informed Nelson that she would be transferred from her position as education reporter to swing shift copy editor until after the November election. TNT stated that Nelson's activities violated the ethics code and raised concern about TNT's appearance of objectivity.

A swing shift copy editor is a nonmanagerial position requiring the same general qualifications as a reporter. Nelson maintained her salary, benefits, and seniority and edited a wide variety of local and national stories. However, she was required to work nights and weekends and was no longer a beat reporter investigating and writing stories. Nelson's transfer became permanent when she refused to promise future conformity with the ethics code.

Nelson remained politically active. For example in 1994 she actively opposed a ballot initiative which would have prevented municipalities from extending civil rights to gays and lesbians. Also in 1994 she testified before the state Legislature on behalf of the "Stonewall Committee" in support of a gay and lesbian civil rights bill. The story received front page coverage in TNT and most other state newspapers. TNT was initially alerted by a legislator who knew Nelson as a TNT employee and contacted TNT to ask if Nelson was lobbying the Legislature on TNT's behalf. TNT's editors wrote to Nelson that "We are dismayed and concerned that you have taken your political activism to a new and larger arena." The editors also wrote that such activity jeopardized the credibility of TNT in the eyes of its readers and the Legislature alike. They told Nelson that their discomfort had nothing to do with the content of her politics as, indeed, TNT has on several occasions adopted pro-gay positions in its editorial. TNT concluded by informing Nelson that if her political activism further compromised the paper's credibility, it would be forced to "further isolate" her and to "take appropriate disciplinary action."

Nelson requested TNT to reinstate her as reporter. In October 1993 she wrote to her supervisor requesting her reinstatement and she later applied for a position as reporter. In January 1995 she sent TNT a letter asking to be considered for what she asserted was an unannounced opening as education reporter. Since Nelson's transfer, TNT has hired nine reporters to cover various topics. Nelson alleged that it was made clear that the positions would remain closed to her so long as she continued her high profile political activism. TNT responded that Nelson never applied for any open position; however, for the purpose of this opinion we will assume the truth of Nelson's allegations.

After unsuccessfully pursuing redress in a federal forum, Nelson filed suit in Pierce County Superior Court alleging TNT improperly stripped her of her position as reporter. Nelson alleged TNT: (a) violated RCW 42.17.680(2) of the Fair Campaign Practices Act, which Nelson claims prohibits employers from discriminating against employees based on their support of initiatives, political parties or political committees; (b) violated several provisions of the state constitution including article I, section 5 (free speech), article I, section 4 (freedom to assemble and petition government), article I, section 19 (guarantee of free elections), and article II, section 1 (popular right to initiative); (c) breached her employment contract because she was transferred without good cause; and (d) wrongfully transferred her because it is against public policy to forbid employees from participating in off-duty political activity. The trial court granted summary judgment to TNT on Nelson's claim under RCW 42.17.680 and on all her constitutional claims. The remaining breach of employment and wrongful transfer claims survived and are scheduled for trial on remand. Thus, the issue before this court is the propriety of the trial court's summary judgment dismissal of Nelson's statutory and constitutional claims.

### DOES RCW 42.17.680(2) APPLY?

Nelson asserts that RCW 42.17.680(2) applies. We agree.

RCW 42.17.680(2) states in full:

> No employer or labor organization may discriminate against an officer or employee in the terms or conditions of employment for (a) the failure to contribute to, (b) the failure in any way to support or oppose or (c) *in any way supporting or opposing a candidate, ballot proposition, political party, or political committee.*

(Emphasis added.)

Nelson asserts the statute is clear on its face and applies in her case. A fundamental rule of construction is, absent ambiguity, the plain wording of the statute controls. Thus, the statute prohibits discrimination based on an employee's "supporting or opposing a candidate, ballot proposition, political party, or political committee."

The issue is whether an employee who is discriminated against for refusing to abstain from political involvement fits within the statutory language of someone removed for "supporting or opposing" a ballot initiative, political party or committee. There is little outside guidance on the meaning of the provision in question and there is no case law interpreting the statute. The original version of the initiative came out of the state senate as Engrossed Substitute Senate Bill 5864, and the legislative history of intent is scarce there as well. A staff memo circulated to the senate committee originally overseeing the bill stated that, amongst other things, the bill would prohibit employers from "discriminat[ing] against employees on the basis of their political activity." Newspaper articles and editorials published during the 1992 election season uniformly fail to mention this particular provision nor does the voter's pamphlet in its description of or the statements for and against the law. In all, the provision now before the court seems to have gone largely unnoticed.

Nelson urges that the plain language of the statute supports her position. And, in circumspect, one may also find support for her position in the subsection preceding the one at issue. Subsection (2)(b) states that no employer may discriminate against an employee for the "failure in any way to support or oppose" a candidate, ballot proposition, political party, or political committee. Subsection (2)(c), at issue here, states that no employer may discriminate against an employee for "in any way supporting or opposing a candidate, ballot proposition, political party, or political committee." Logically, subsection (2)(b) would apply when the employee fails to adopt and support the employer's political position, whereas subsection (2)(c) would apply when the employee refuses to abstain from political activity. It is difficult to imagine what subsection (2)(c) would mean if not what Nelson claims. Adopting TNT's reading that the statute does not apply when the employer merely requires political abstinence is contrary to the text of subsection (2)(c).

TNT, on the other hand, asserts that the provision should be read in context. TNT asserts that when read in context, the provision has a narrower meaning and will apply only when an employer attempts to strong-arm an employee into adopting its political position. The trial court agreed with TNT and held the statute applies only when the employer requires an employee to adopt its political position and does not apply when the employer merely requires political neutrality of its employees.

Initiative 134 which contains the provision in question was aimed at repairing the political process through campaign finance reform. The primary change proposed by the initiative was the imposition of contribution limits that individuals and entities could give per candidate per election. The initiative also sought to prohibit contributions from one candidate's campaign to another, forbid public funding of campaigns, limit the repayment of loans taken out while campaigning, and prohibit fundraising by legislators during session. The official ballot title asked:

Shall campaign contributions be limited;  public funding of state and local campaigns be prohibited;  and campaign related activities be restricted?

1992 Voters Pamphlet, *Initiative Measure 134,* at 8.

One of the stated purposes of the initiative was to prevent financially strong organizations from exercising a disproportionate or controlling influence on elections.  RCW 42.17.610(1).  In 1993, the initiative became codified under the heading of *Campaign Contribution Limitations* under chapter 42.17 RCW, the public disclosure act, the purpose of which is to inform the public of campaign and lobbying contributions and to help ensure, through disclosure, the integrity of government.

TNT argues the statutory provision in question was not intended to apply as Nelson asserts.  Washington already has a labor law statute forbidding discrimination against an employee on the basis of age, sex, marital status, race, creed, color, national origin, or physical handicap. Nelson's reading, TNT argues, in effect creates an additional category, that of political activist, but would locate it in the campaign finance reform law rather than in labor or other civil rights laws.  TNT argues if creation of such a broad right was intended, why was it quietly slipped into campaign finance reform?

But TNT's interpretation does not track the text of the act.  When read in context this law has a clear relation to the rest of the campaign finance reform act; it is meant to prevent employers from wielding their might to influence politics and elections.  The law is part of campaign finance, not civil rights or labor law.  Taken as a whole, the provision in question means that employers may not disproportionately influence politics by forcing their employees to support their position or by attempting to force political abstinence on politically active employees.  The law is designed to restrict organizations from wielding political influence by manipulating the political influence of their employees through employment decisions.  Moreover, TNT's reading essentially renders the provision in question meaningless as RCW 42.17.680(2)(b) already covers the interpretation urged by TNT.

We hold RCW 42.17.680(2) applies to the present case and substantial evidence supports its application.

We now turn to the constitutional issue which we find dispositive.

## DOES RCW 42.17.680(2) UNCONSTITUTIONALLY INFRINGE ON TNT'S RIGHT TO FREEDOM OF THE PRESS?

We hold that RCW 42.17.680(2) unconstitutionally infringes on TNT's right to freedom of the press.

TNT asserts that RCW 42.17.680(2) as applied to it violates the First Amendment to the United States Constitution and article I, section 5, of the state constitution.  In particular, TNT asserts that the free press clause of both constitutions guarantees it editorial discretion to control the content of its publication.  TNT further asserts that controlling the newspaper's credibility is an integral component of this. TNT argues its conflict of interest policies are designed to control its credibility and are a reflection of its content. TNT concludes that requiring its reporters to abide by its no-conflict-of-interest policy is necessary to uphold its editorial integrity, which TNT asserts is constitutionally protected. Accordingly, TNT claims that RCW 42.17.680(2) does not apply to it in this case. On the contrary, Nelson asserts that what TNT's reporters do on their own time has nothing to do with the content or credibility of the newspaper and accordingly the free press clauses of the federal and state constitutions are irrelevant. While the trial court dismissed Nelson's statutory claim holding the statute inapplicable, it redundantly ruled in TNT's favor on this point as well, reasoning:

> The First Amendment and the Washington Constitution protect Defendants' editorial discretion. Under the First Amendment and the Washington Constitution, Defendants have a right to protect the newspaper's unbiased content, both its facts and as perceived by its readers, its sources and its advertisers. In order to protect the newspaper's credibility, Defendants may enforce the political neutrality of reporters.

We agree with TNT and affirm the trial court on this ground.

The free speech clauses of the federal and state constitutions have always held a revered position in our society. Laurence Tribe, a preeminent constitutional law scholar, has characterized free speech as "the Constitution's most majestic guarantee." Free speech is a fundamental right on its own as well as a keystone right enabling us to preserve all other rights. As one federal judge has noted, "Free speech is the single most important element upon which this nation has thrived."

The Supreme Court has observed "the Founders ... felt that a free press would advance 'truth, science, morality, and arts in general' as well as responsible government." From the start we have acknowledged that active protection from governmental abridgment is essential. Upon presenting the Bill of Rights to Congress in 1789 James Madison declared "the liberty of the press is expressly declared to be *beyond the reach of this government....*"

\* \* \*

When addressing whether a governmental regulation or action affecting the press is violative of its constitutional free press protection, we begin by noting the two governing polar principles and then consider where the complained action falls. On one extreme is the general principle that a newspaper has "no special immunity from the application of general laws" simply because it is the press. Associated Press v. N.L.R.B., 301 U.S. 103 (1937). On the opposite side is the principle that the government absolutely may not regulate the content of a newspaper. Miami Herald Publishing Co. v. Tornillo, 418 U.S. 241 (1974).

*Miami Herald Publishing* is the seminal case on the issue. In *Miami Herald* the United States Supreme Court held that the state absolutely may not regulate the content of a newspaper. At issue was the constitutionality of a Florida "right-of-access" statute which forced newspapers to publish responses of politicians who had been criticized by the paper. At the heart of *Miami Herald* is the notion that in order to uphold the circulation of ideas the editors of a newspaper must be free to exercise editorial control and discretion. The court held that " '[l]iberty of the press is in peril as soon as the government tries to compel what is to go into a newspaper.' " The court concluded because the state law deprived the paper of its editorial discretion, it was necessarily unconstitutional as applied to the newspaper.

Thus, *Miami Herald* clearly establishes that editorial control is a necessary component of the free press and a state law infringing thereon will be unconstitutional as applied.

\* \* \*

Here, TNT implemented a code of ethics which it designed in good faith to foster the newspaper's integrity and credibility. Case law unambiguously allows a news publication to follow a code designed to limit conflicts of interest which may diminish publication credibility. TNT adopted such a code. Freedom of the press leaves such decisions to the press, not the legislature or the courts. The code is facially designed to uphold the appearance of impartiality. Indeed, the code seems representative of those in place at 75 percent of our nation's newspapers. In fact, as stated earlier, it is nearly identical to those employed by the Associated Press, *The Washington Post,* and the Society of Professional Journalists.

\* \* \*

### CONCLUSION

We recognize Nelson's statutory right to avoid workplace discrimination based on her politics. Since this right is established by the statute we need not consider whether it is also established by the state constitution. However, the First Amendment freedom of the press is the constitutional minimum regardless of the legal source of government abridgment. Choosing an editorial staff is a core press function, at least when that choice is based on editorial considerations. That is the case here. This statute has been unconstitutionally applied. The trial court's summary judgment dismissal of statutory claims is affirmed and McClatchy shall recover its costs on appeal. The case is remanded for further appropriate proceedings.

NOTES AND QUESTIONS

**1.** "Political expression laws" protecting private sector employees that have been enacted in slightly more than half of the states. California's law dates back to 1902. Cal.Lab.Code § 1102. Without statutory protection and before the erosion of the at will doctrine employers could not only refuse to permit employees to engage in their own political activities, but could insist on employees engaging in certain political activity. For example, in Bell v. Faulkner, 75 S.W.2d 612 (Mo.App.1934), an employee alleged that he was discharged because he would not vote for certain candidates in a city election and would not coerce family members to vote for them. Even though a specific Missouri statute prohibited coercion of workers to vote for political candidates the court held that the only remedy was imprisonment of offenders and therefore no private right of action for damages would lie.

Reconsider the facts of *Novosel,* supra p. 623. Would a statutory solution be preferable to the public policy approach used by the court? See Shovelin v. Central New Mexico Electric Cooperative, Inc., 850 P.2d 996 (N.M.1993) (dismissing employee for being elected mayor of city not a violation of public policy). Does *Nelson* suggest some problems with the statutory approach?

**2.** For public employees it is important to distinguish between partisan and nonpartisan political activities. While nonpartisan political activities are almost always protected under the first amendment, partisan activity may be regulated more closely.

The Hatch Act, 5 U.S.C. § 7324(a), prohibits federal employees from taking an active part in political campaigns. Similar state laws limit the political activities of state and local employees. In United States Civil Service Commission v. National Association of Letter Carriers, 413 U.S. 548 (1973), the Supreme Court spelled out the range of partisan political activities that can be regulated:

> We unhesitatingly reaffirm the *Mitchell* [United Public Workers v. Mitchell, 330 U.S. 75 (1947)] holding that Congress had, and has, the power to prevent Mr. Poole and others like him from holding a party office, working at the polls, and acting as party paymaster for other party workers. An Act of Congress going no farther would in our view unquestionably be valid. So would it be if, in plain and understandable language, the statute forbade activities such as organizing a political party or club; actively participating in fund-raising activities for a partisan candidate or political party; becoming a partisan candidate for, or campaigning for, an elective public office; actively managing the campaign of a partisan candidate for public office; initiating or circulating a partisan nominating petition or soliciting votes for a partisan candidate for public office; or serving as a delegate, alternate or proxy to a political party convention. Our judgment is that neither the First Amendment nor any other provision of the Constitution invalidates a law barring this kind of partisan political conduct by federal employees.

Id. at 556. See Developments in the Law—Public Employment, 97 Harv. L.Rev. 1611, 1651–57 (1984).

Based on the *Letter Carriers* case, could a city prohibit employees from being candidates in nonpartisan municipal elections? See Magill v. Lynch, 560 F.2d 22 (1st Cir.1977), cert. denied, 434 U.S. 1063 (1978). Could the Veterans Administration prohibit its employees from wearing political buttons? See American Federation of Government Employees v. Pierce, 586 F.Supp. 1559 (D.D.C.1984) (held: no).

**3.**  Political appointments (the hiring of non-civil service employees) raise a series of First Amendment issues.  In Elrod v. Burns, 427 U.S. 347 (1976), the Supreme Court held that patronage dismissals had to be limited to policymaking and confidential positions.  Thus, political party affiliation could not be used as the basis for hiring or retention for most non-civil service positions.  Is the job of assistant public defender policymaking or confidential?  See Branti v. Finkel, 445 U.S. 507 (1980) (held: no).

**4.**  Many governmental entities require employees to take or sign loyalty oaths, pledging loyalty to the United States.  Would an oath declaring that the individual is not a member of the Communist Party be valid?  In Baggett v. Bullitt, 377 U.S. 360 (1964), the Supreme Court held that such an oath was unconstitutionally vague.  To be valid, the oath must state that the individual did not have a specific intent to further illegal aims.  Would an oath be valid if it stated that the individual opposed the overthrow of the government of the United States by force, violence, or by any illegal or unconstitutional method?  See Cole v. Richardson, 405 U.S. 676 (1972) (held: yes).

**5.**  Could a state university refuse, solely on political grounds, to hire as chair of the department of government and politics a Marxist political science professor?  See Ollman v. Toll, 518 F.Supp. 1196 (D.Md.1981), affirmed, 704 F.2d 139 (4th Cir.1983) (holding that Professor Ollman had failed to establish that his Marxist beliefs were a substantial or motivating factor in the university president's decision to deny his appointment).

**6.**  Another approach to protecting political activity by private sector employees was attempted in Harrison v. KVAT Food Management, Inc., 766 F.2d 155 (4th Cir.1985), in which a discharged employee sued his former employer and two officials under 42 U.S.C. § 1985(3), alleging that they conspired in violation of his civil rights to prevent him from running for public office as a Republican, even though other employees had run for office as Democrats in the past.  The Fourth Circuit upheld dismissal of the case, on the ground that Republicans as a class are not protected by the statute.

**7.**  Section 501(b) of the Ethics in Government Act of 1978, as amended, prohibits a member of Congress, federal officer, or other federal government employee from accepting an honorarium for making an appearance or speech or writing an article.  In United States v. National Treasury Employees Union, 514 U.S. 1002 (1995), a class action of federal government employees below the grade of GS–16 who had previously received honoraria for speeches and articles on nongovernmental topics such as history, religion, and dance challenged the law.  The Supreme Court held that the statute was overbroad and violated the First Amendment.

## 3.  LIFESTYLE

## Chambers v. Omaha Girls Club, Inc.

834 F.2d 697 (8th Cir.1987).

■ WOLLMAN, CIRCUIT JUDGE.

Crystal Chambers appeals the district court's orders and judgment disposing of her civil rights, Title VII employment discrimination, and pendent state law claims. Chambers' claims arise from her dismissal as an employee at the Omaha Girls Club on account of her being single and pregnant in violation of the Club's "role model rule." The primary issue in this appeal is whether the Club's role model rule is an employment practice that is consistent with Title VII because it is justifiable as a business necessity or a bona fide occupational qualification.

The Omaha Girls Club is a private, nonprofit corporation that offers programs designed to assist young girls between the ages of eight and eighteen to maximize their life opportunities. Among the Club's many activities are programs directed at pregnancy prevention. The Club serves 1,500 members, ninety percent of them black, at its North Omaha facility and 500 members, fifty to sixty percent of them black, at its South Omaha facility. A substantial number of youngsters who are not Club members also participate in its programs. The Club employs thirty to thirty-five persons at its two facilities; all of the non-administrative personnel at the North Omaha facility are black, and fifty to sixty percent of the personnel at the South Omaha facility are black.

The Club's approach to fulfilling its mission emphasizes the development of close contacts and the building of relationships between the girls and the Club's staff members. Toward this end, staff members are trained and expected to act as role models for the girls, with the intent that the girls will seek to emulate their behavior. The Club formulated its "role model rule" banning single parent pregnancies among its staff members in pursuit of this role model approach.[2]

Chambers, a black single woman, was employed by the Club as an arts and crafts instructor at the Club's North Omaha facility. She became pregnant and informed her supervisor of that fact. Subsequently, she received a letter notifying her that because of her pregnancy her employment was to be terminated. Shortly after her termination, Chambers filed charges with the Nebraska Equal Opportunity Commission (NEOC) alleging discrimination on the basis of sex and marital status. The NEOC found no reasonable cause to believe that unlawful employment discrimination had occurred. Chambers then brought this action in the district court seeking injunctions and damages.

\* \* \*

A plaintiff seeking to prove discrimination under the disparate impact theory must show that a facially neutral employment practice has a

---

**2.** The Club's personnel policies state the rule as follows:

MAJOR CLUB RULES

All persons employed by the Girls Club of Omaha are subject to the rules and regulations as established by the Board of Directors. The following are not per-

mitted and such acts may result in immediate discharge:

. . . . . . . . . . . . . . . . . . . . . . . . . . . . . . . . . .

11. Negative role modeling for Girls Club Members to include such things as single parent pregnancies.

significant adverse impact on members of a protected minority group.  The burden then shifts to the employer to show that the practice has a manifest relationship to the employment in question and is justifiable on the ground of business necessity.  Even if the employer shows that the discriminatory employment practice is justified by business necessity, the plaintiff may prevail by showing that other practices would accomplish the employer's objectives without the attendant discriminatory effects.  The district court found that "because of the significantly higher fertility rate among black females, the rule banning single pregnancies would impact black women more harshly."  Thus, Chambers established the disparate impact of the role model rule.  The Club then sought to justify the rule as a business necessity.

Establishing a business necessity defense presents an employer with a "heavy burden."  Business necessity exists only if the challenged employment practice has " ' "a manifest relationship to the employment in question." ' "  The employer must demonstrate that there is a " 'compelling need * * * to maintain that practice,' " and the practice cannot be justified by " 'routine business considerations.' "  Moreover, the employer may be required to show that the challenged employment practice is " 'necessary to safe and efficient job performance,' " or that the employer's goals are "significantly served by" the practice.

The district court found that the role model rule is justified by business necessity because there is a manifest relationship between the Club's fundamental purpose and the rule.  Specifically, the court found:

> The Girls Club has established by the evidence that its only purpose is to serve young girls between the ages of eight and eighteen and to provide these women with exposure to the greatest number of available positive options in life.  The Girls Club has established that teenage pregnancy is contrary to this purpose and philosophy.  The Girls Club established that it honestly believed that to permit single pregnant staff members to work with the girls would convey the impression that the Girls Club condoned pregnancy for the girls in the age group it serves.  The testimony of board members * * * made clear that the policy was not based upon a morality standard, but rather, on a belief that teenage pregnancies severely limit the available opportunities for teenage girls.  The Girls Club also established that the policy was just one prong of a comprehensive attack on the problem of teenage pregnancy.  The Court is satisfied that a manifest relationship exists between the Girls Club's fundamental purpose and its single pregnancy policy.

The court also relied in part on expert testimony to the effect that the role model rule could be helpful in preventing teenage pregnancy.[14]  Chambers

---

**14.**  Chambers' expert witness testified that the only way to resolve the teenage pregnancy problem was through economic op- portunities such as education and jobs.  The Club's expert agreed that these factors were important, but also testified concerning the

argues, however, that the district court erred in finding business necessity because the role model rule is based only on speculation by the Club and has not been validated by any studies showing that it prevents pregnancy among the Club's members.

Business necessity determinations in disparate impact cases are reviewed under the clearly erroneous standard of review applied to factual findings.  Thus, we may reserve the district court's finding of business necessity only if we are " 'left with the definite and firm conviction that a mistake has been committed.' "

We believe that "the district court's account of the evidence is plausible in light of the record viewed in its entirety."  Therefore, we cannot say that the district court's finding of business necessity is clearly erroneous. The district court's conclusion on the evidence is not an impermissible one. Although validation studies can be helpful in evaluating such questions, they are not required to maintain a successful business necessity defense. Indeed, we are uncertain whether the role model rule by its nature is suited to validation by an empirical study.[15]

Chambers argues further, however, that the district court erred in discounting alternative practices that the Club could have used to ameliorate the discriminatory effects of the role model rule.  Chambers contends that the Club either could have granted her a leave of absence or transferred her to a position that did not involve contact with the Club's members.  The Club responds that neither of these alternatives was available in this case.  The Club has a history of granting leaves of up to six weeks, but the purposes of the role model rule would have required a five to six month leave for Chambers, given that the pregnancy would have become visually apparent probably within three or four months.  Moreover, employing a temporary replacement to take Chamber's position would itself have required six months of on-the-job training before the replacement would have been able to interact with the girls on the level that the Club's approach requires.  The use of temporary replacements would also disrupt the atmosphere of stability that the Club attempts to provide and would be inconsistent with the relationship-building and interpersonal interaction

value of role modeling and concluded that the role model rule "could be (and in her opinion is) another viable way to attack the problem of teenage pregnancy."

In addition to relying on the evidence concerning the Club's purpose and approach and expert testimony, the district court found that the rule was adopted in response to two incidents involving Club members' reactions to the pregnancies of single Club staff members.

**15.**  Ironically, at oral argument Chambers' counsel responded in the negative to the court's question concerning whether the rule could ever be empirically proven to prevent pregnancy among the Club's members. Counsel's response must be construed to mean either that it is impossible to perform a meaningful empirical study of such matters, or that counsel believes that no such study would ever show the rule to have the effect desired by the Club.  If we were to adopt the first construction it would be ludicrous for us to reverse for lack of validation studies. Moreover, the second construction presents nothing more than counsel's own belief concerning the role model rule, a belief rejected by the district court in favor of that held by the Club.

entailed in the Club's model approach. Furthermore, transfer to a "non-contact position" apparently was impossible because there are no positions at the Club that do not involve contact with Club members. The district court found that the Club considered these alternatives and determined them to be unworkable. We are unable to conclude that the district court's finding that there were no satisfactory alternatives to the dismissal of Chambers pursuant to the role model rule is clearly erroneous. Accordingly, we hold that the district court's finding that the role model rule is justified by business necessity and thus does not violate Title VII under the disparate impact theory is not clearly erroneous.

Unlike the disparate impact theory, the disparate treatment theory requires a plaintiff seeking to prove employment discrimination to show discriminatory animus. The plaintiff must first establish a prima facie case of discrimination. The burden of production then shifts to the employer to show a legitimate, nondiscriminatory reason for the challenged employment practice. If the employer makes such a showing, then the plaintiff may show that the reasons given by the employer were pretextual. No violation of Title VII exists, however, if the employer can show that the challenged employment practice is a bona fide occupational qualification (bfoq).

The district court found that Chambers had succeeded in establishing a prima facie case of discrimination but concluded that the Club's role model approach is a legitimate, nondiscriminatory reason for the role model rule. The court then found that Chambers was unable to show that the Club's reason for the rule was a pretext for intentional discrimination. The court also stated in passing that the role model rule "presumably" is a bfoq.

Chambers argues alternatively that the district court erred in failing to find a violation of Title VII under the disparate treatment theory, and that this case should not be analyzed under the disparate treatment theory because Chambers' discharge on account of her pregnancy constitutes intentional discrimination without further analysis. Chambers also argues that the role model rule cannot be justified as a bfoq. Because we are persuaded that the role model rule qualifies as a bfoq, we find it unnecessary to address Chambers' other arguments.

The bfoq exception is " 'an extremely narrow exception to the general prohibition of discrimination on the basis of sex.' " In Dothard v. Rawlinson, 433 U.S. 321 (1977), the Supreme Court found that a rule that prohibited employment of women in contact positions in all-male Alabama prisons was a bfoq under the particular circumstances of that case, which involved a prison system rife with violence. The statutory language, is, of course, the best guide to the content of the bfoq exception; however, the courts, including the Supreme Court in *Dothard*, have noted the existence of several formulations for evaluating whether an employment practice is a bfoq. The formulations include: whether " 'the *essence* of the business operation would be undermined' " without the challenged employment practice; whether safe and efficient performance of the job would be possible without the challenged employment practice; and whether the challenged employment practice has " 'a manifest relationship to the employment in question.' "

Although the district court did not clearly conclude that the role model rule qualified as a bfoq, several of the court's other findings are persuasive on this issue. The court's findings of fact, many of which are relevant to the analysis of a potential bfoq exception, are binding on this court unless clearly erroneous. The facts relevant to establishing a bfoq are the same as those found by the district court in the course of its business necessity analysis. As already noted, the district court found that the role model rule has a manifest relationship to the Club's fundamental purpose and that there were no workable alternatives to the rule. Moreover, the district court's finding of business necessity itself is persuasive as to the existence of a bfoq. This court has noted that the analysis of a bfoq "is similar to and overlaps with the judicially created 'business necessity' test." The various standards for establishing business necessity are quite similar to those for determining a bfoq. Indeed, this court has on different occasions applied the same standard—"manifest relationship"—to both business necessity and bfoq. Inasmuch as we already have affirmed the district court's finding of business necessity as not clearly erroneous, we feel compelled to conclude that "[i]n the particular factual circumstances of this case," the role model rule is reasonably necessary to the Club's operations. Thus, we hold that the role model rule qualifies as a bona fide occupational qualification.

* * *

In conclusion, we hold that the district court's finding that the Club's role model rule is justified by business necessity is not clearly erroneous, and we find further that the rule qualifies as a bona fide occupational qualification. Chambers' other allegations of error are without merit. Accordingly, the orders and judgment of the district court are affirmed.

■ McMILLIAN, CIRCUIT JUDGE, dissenting.

* * *

I agree with the majority that the district court's determination of business necessity or BFOQ in the present case is to be reviewed under the clearly erroneous standard. However, even under this very deferential standard, I would reject the BFOQ or business necessity exceptions offered by OGC because there is no evidence to support a relationship between teenage pregnancies and the employment of an unwed pregnant instructor, and therefore I am left with the definite and firm conclusion that the district court made a mistake.

The district court, and now this court, accepts without any proof OGC's assumption that the presence of an unwed pregnant instructor is related to teenage pregnancies. OGC failed to present surveys, school statistics or any other empirical data connecting the incidence of teenage pregnancy with the pregnancy of an adult instructor. OGC also failed to present evidence that other girls clubs or similar types of organizations employed such a rule. OGC instead relied on two or three highly questionable anecdotal incidents to support the rule.

The majority, while admitting to some uncertainty about whether the negative role model rule is subject to validation, places great weight on counsel's remarks during oral argument. Counsel's comments concerning the feasibility of such validation, however, are not a substitute for evidence demonstrating the validity or effectiveness of the role model rule. OGC had the burden of establishing a reasonable basis, that is a factual basis, for its belief, and in the absence of such proof, OGC may not implement the discriminatory rule.

NOTES AND QUESTIONS

**1.** Is the "role model" defense valid? Are there dangers in applying this defense? On the other hand, the Girls Club has a legitimate interest, does it not? Should it matter whether the Girls Club rule is applied to applicants instead of to current employees? Suppose the Omaha public school system adopted a similar "role model" rule. Valid? Suppose an obese person applied for a job as office manager at Weight Watchers. Could she be denied a job based on the "role model" defense? Does a type of public "role model" defense justify the drug testing of employees of the Customs Service? See *Von Raab*, supra p. 197.

**2.** See Regina Austin, Sapphire Bound!, 1989 Wis.L.Rev. 539:

Firing a young unmarried, pregnant black worker in the name of protecting other young black females from the limited options associated with early and unwed motherhood is ironic, to say the least. The Club managed to replicate the very economic hardships and social biases that, according to the district court, made the role model rule necessary in the first place. Crystal Chambers was not much older than some of the Club members and her financial and social status after being fired was probably not that much different from what the members would face if they became pregnant at an early age, without the benefit of a job or the assistance of a fully employed helpmate. On the other hand, she was in many respects better off than many teen mothers. She was in her early twenties and had a decent job. Chambers' condition became problematic *because of* the enforcement of the role model rule.

The material consequences that befell Crystal Chambers, and that plague other black women who have children despite their supposed role modeling responsibilities, are not inherent by-products of single pregnancy and motherhood. The condemnation and the economic hardships that follow in its wake are politically and socially contingent. Furthermore, they are not the product of a consensus that holds across race, sex, and class boundaries.

Judged by the values and behavior that are said to be indigenous to low-income, black communities of the sort from which the Club members came, sacking pregnant unmarried Crystal Chambers was not a "womanly" move. It was cold. The Club's actions stand in stark contrast to the tolerance pregnant teens and young single mothers report receiving from their female relatives and peers. Although disapproving of teenage pregnancy, black culture in general does not support abandoning the mothers or stigmatizing their offspring. Allowing for cultural heterogeneity, it is entirely possible that the black people of Omaha approved of the Club's actions. By and large, however, excluding young mothers and their children from good standing in the community would not strike most black women as being fair, feasible, or feminine.

This perspective is informed by a broader understanding of the exaggerated hostility that is generated by the pregnancies of poor, young, unmarried black females whose customs and conventions concerning childbearing and motherhood diverge from those of the mainstream. Because essentialist notions suggest that they cannot be harmed by those who are of the same gender and/or race, these females are vulnerable to the insidiously detrimental ministrations of do-good white women and "bougie" blacks. Moreover, middle-aged meddlers of every sort feel themselves entitled to heap upon these females a wisdom that has little to recommend it beyond the fact that its proponents have lived longer. If young unmarried black pregnant workers are to be adequately protected, the pregnancy discrimination law, in conjunction with provisions directed at racial and sexual oppression, must assure them working conditions that acknowledge the reproductive norms not only of females as opposed to males, but also of blacks as opposed to whites, of the young as opposed to the old, and of poor and working folks as opposed to the middle class.

Implicit in the *Chambers* decision, however, is an assumption that the actual cultural practices and articulated moral positions of the black females who know the struggles of early and single motherhood firsthand are both misguided and destructive. The older women are apparently so outrageous that they represent a grave threat to their own daughters. Yet, for some of us, their portrayal in the *Chambers* opinions is more flattering than the authors intended. Grounded in a culture that turns "bad" (pronounced "baaad") on its head and declares conduct that offends the white, male, and middle-class establishments, wily, audacious, and good, a black feminist scholar has to wonder whether the villainous black women one discerns lurking in the interstices of the opinions are not doing something right. A black feminist jurisprudential analysis of *Chambers* must seriously consider the possibility that young, single, sexually active, fertile, and nurturing black women are being viewed ominously because they have the temerity to attempt to break out of the rigid economic, social, and political categories that a racist, sexist, and class-stratified society would impose upon them.

**3.** Would it violate Title VII for a Roman Catholic high school in Dubuque, Iowa to fire an unmarried English teacher who became pregnant? See Dolter v. Wahlert High School, 483 F.Supp. 266 (N.D.Iowa 1980) (held: yes). Would it violate the due process clause of the Fourteenth Amendment for a state college to refuse to renew the contract of the director of residence halls for women because she bore a child out of wedlock? See Lewis v. Delaware State College, 455 F.Supp. 239 (D.Del.1978) (held: yes). Does it violate Title VII for a Catholic elementary school to refuse to renew the contract of a Protestant teacher because of her re-marriage? See Little v. Wuerl, 929 F.2d 944 (3d Cir.1991) (held: no). Can you distinguish these cases from *Chambers?*

**4.** Public employers are particularly concerned about off-duty conduct that might damage the reputation of the employer. For example, in Broderick v. Police Commissioner, 330 N.E.2d 199 (Mass.1975), cert. denied, 423 U.S. 1048 (1976), 90 off-duty Boston police officers went to Newport, Rhode Island to participate in a weekend Law Day celebration. While there, several of the officers committed larceny, assaults, and various forms of disorderly conduct and hooliganism. The police commissioner, attempting to determine the facts surrounding the Newport incident prepared a questionnaire for all police officers to complete. The Supreme Judicial Court of Massachusetts upheld the commissioner's right to demand completion of the questionnaire, holding that even if the activities were private, they reasonably related to the officers' ability and fitness to perform official duties.

**5.** Private employers also have been concerned about off-duty employee conduct that could damage the good will or reputation of the company. Most courts have upheld discharges made for this reason. See, e.g., United Transportation Union v. Union Pacific Railroad, 593 F.Supp. 1193 (D.Wyo. 1984), affirmed, 812 F.2d 630 (10th Cir.1987) (railroad employee convicted of possession of marijuana).

**6.** Both public and private employers have displayed a keen interest in the sex lives of their employees. In the private sector, unless there has been an invasion of privacy rising to the level of a public policy violation or there has been sex discrimination employers have been free to impose their sexual mores on employees. See Staats v. Ohio National Life Insurance Co., 620 F.Supp. 118 (W.D.Pa.1985) (employer did not violate public policy by discharging employee who appeared at convention with a woman who was not his wife). But cf. Jacobs v. Martin Sweets Co., 550 F.2d 364 (6th Cir.1977), cert. denied, 431 U.S. 917 (1977) (Title VII violation to discharge unwed mothers but not unwed fathers). In the public sector employees have been more successful in constitutional and statutory challenges to a variety of employer policies. See, e.g., Thorne v. El Segundo, 726 F.2d 459 (9th Cir.1983), cert. denied, 469 U.S. 979 (1984) (woman police officer refused to answer questions about her sex-life, such as the identity of her sex partners); Andrews v. Drew Municipal Separate School District, 507 F.2d 611 (5th Cir.1975), cert. dismissed 425 U.S. 559 (1976) (refusal to hire unwed mothers); Fisher v. Snyder, 476 F.2d 375 (8th Cir.1973) (middle-aged divorced school teacher had male guest stay overnight in her one bedroom apartment);  Morrison v. State Board of Education, 461 P.2d 375 (Cal.1969) (teacher could not be dismissed for a single, non-criminal homosexual episode with a fellow teacher).  In other cases, the discharges of public employees for gross immorality have been upheld.  See, e.g., Wishart v. McDonald, 500 F.2d 1110 (1st Cir.1974) (6th grade teacher dressed, undressed, and caressed a mannequin he kept in his yard);  Pettit v. State Board of Education, 513 P.2d 889 (Cal.1973) (48 year-old elementary school teacher who, with her husband, were members of a "swingers" club and had pleaded guilty to the misdemeanor of "outrageous public indecency");  In re Grossman, 316 A.2d 39 (N.J.Super.App.Div.1974) (teacher who had 10–12 year old students had sex-reassignment surgery);  Borges v. McGuire, 487 N.Y.S.2d 737 (App.Div.1985) (civilian employee of police department disciplined because she posed nude for Beaver magazine before she was hired).

**7.**  A New York statute prohibits employers from discriminating against employees for a range of off-duty recreational activities, including sports, games, hobbies, exercise, and movies.  Does the law prohibit an employer from discharging employees for violating the company's ban on dating between married employees and employees other than their spouses?  See State v. Wal–Mart Stores, Inc., 621 N.Y.S.2d 158 (App.Div.1995) (held: no—"To us, dating is entirely distinct from and, in fact, bears little resemblance to 'recreational activity' ").  But see Pasch v. Katz Media Corp., 1995 WL 469710 (S.D.N.Y.1995) (interpreting same statute to protect cohabitation).

**8.**  In Brunner v. Al Attar, 786 S.W.2d 784 (Tex.App.1990), an employee of an auto body shop who worked as a volunteer at the AIDS Foundation on the weekends, alleged that she was fired because the owner of the company feared that she could somehow become infected with HIV and then transmit it to him, his family, and other employees.  The Texas Court of Appeals, in affirming the grant of summary judgment for the defendant, held that the defendant's alleged conduct did not violate the limited public policy exception to the at-will rule recognized in Texas, and it did not violate the state disability discrimination law because the plaintiff had no disability.  Section 102(b)(4) of the Americans with Disabilities Act, which prohibits discrimination against individuals because the individuals associated with individuals with disabilities, would now apply to this situation.

**9.**  Discharge of employee for contemplating having an abortion was found to have violated the Pregnancy Discrimination Act in Turic v. Holland Hospitality, Inc., 85 F.3d 1211 (6th Cir.1996).  The Sixth Circuit held that an employee's pondered abortion, which precipitated controversy among other employees, was a motivating factor for her discharge.

---

## C.  SENIORITY AND PROMOTION

### 1.  SENIORITY

Numerous studies have shown that workers rank job security as their highest priority—far ahead of wages.  Indeed, often the most attractive feature of unionization and collective bargaining for unorganized workers is the promise of job security. In both union and nonunion workplaces job security is often based on seniority—the length of time the employee has worked for the particular company.

There are two main types of seniority. Benefits seniority refers to an employee's eligibility for benefits based on length of service and involves relations between the employee and the employer. Competitive seniority refers to a priority system for allocation of scarce employment conditions and involves relations among employees. Competitive seniority is the more contentious type, and is implicated in bidding systems for job transfers, in layoffs, and in other matters. For a discussion of the conflict between seniority and affirmative action, see Chapter 4.

For such a deeply ingrained concept in our employment system, seniority is frequently neither challenged nor well explained. There is no legal requirement for seniority; it is a matter of custom. Why is seniority honored? Are senior employees more able or more valuable? Is seniority such an easy standard to administer? Seniority often means higher wages. If junior employees are performing the same work as senior employees, perhaps it is not in an employer's economic interest to base layoffs on seniority. Why then do employers who are not obligated to do so use seniority? Consider the following explanation.

## Lester C. Thurow, The Zero–Sum Society *
56–57 (1980).

Upon examination, the basic assumptions about the nature of the labor market seem less than adequate. They ignore long-run employer-employee interests in a good mutual relationship.

They ignore the fact that much of our human capital is acquired on the job rather than in formal education. This can be seen in the analysis of the determinants of earnings or in the surveys of where working skills are acquired. The labor market is not primarily a market for allocating skills but a market for allocating training slots. Workers are only trained when job openings exist and an independent supply curve does not exist. But without independent supply and demand curves, wages must be determined in some fashion other than by a market correction.

\* \* \*

All industrial operations are subject to a substantial component of team as well as individual productivity. Evidence for this can be seen in the sharp learning curves of new industrial plants. As workers learn to work with each other, costs of production fall dramatically. They develop teamwork and team productivity that is over and above their individual skills and individual productivity.

* Reprinted by permission of Basic Books, New York, N.Y.

But under these circumstances, where does economic analysis lead? It leads to the two factors that are widely observed in the labor market: (1) Money wages exhibit downward rigidity; they do not fall when surplus labor exists; (2) Relative wages are rigid and change only in the long run.

Because skills are acquired on the job, in an informal process of one worker training another, every industrial operation needs workers willing to be trainers. But in a truly competitive world, no one wants to be an informal trainer. Every worker realizes that every additional worker trained will result in lower wages and a greater probability of being fired in any economic downturn. It is rational in a competitive world for each individual to seek a monopoly on local knowledge (how to run machine X) and then refuse to share his or her knowledge with anyone else. This preserves wage and job opportunities. To promote training and make workers willing to be trainers of other workers, employers essentially offer two guarantees. First, they promise not to lower wages if surplus workers become available. Second, they promise to hire and fire based on seniority. This means that each trainer's trainees will be fired before he is. Essentially the employer agrees not to be a short-run cost minimizer in the interests of long-run training and efficiency.

## NOTES AND QUESTIONS

**1.** Do you agree with Thurow's theory of the implied bargain in the use of seniority? If not, what explains the seniority system?

**2.** Section 703(h) of Title VII provides:

It shall not be an unlawful employment practice for an employer to apply different standards of compensation, or different terms, conditions, or privileges of employment pursuant to a bona fide seniority * * * system, * * * provided that such differences are not the result of an intention to discriminate * * *

Sometimes a threshold question is whether employment rules regarding benefits and length of service are a "seniority system" under Title VII. See California Brewers Association v. Bryant, 444 U.S. 598 (1980).

**3.** In general, seniority rights created by a collective bargaining agreement are not "vested" property rights, but may be revised or abrogated by later negotiations between the union and the employer. Suppose an employee transferred from full-time to part-time status for health reasons, in reliance on the union's promise that if she transferred she would not lose her seniority. When she later transferred back to full-time she learned that because of a new collective bargaining agreement she had lost her seniority. Does she have a valid claim against the union? See Hass v. Darigold Dairy Products Co., 751 F.2d 1096 (9th Cir.1985) (held: yes).

**4.** The Vietnam Era Veterans' Readjustment Assistance Act, 38 U.S.C. §§ 2021–2026, provides that persons who, as a consequence of being inducted into the United States military, must leave permanent positions of employment, have a right to be reinstated to their former positions, or to positions of like seniority, status, and pay, upon their return. In interpreting the Act, most courts have adopted an "escalator principle" which grants veterans the seniority and promotions they would have had if they occupied the same position continuously during their military service.  See Goggin v. Lincoln St. Louis, 702 F.2d 698 (8th Cir.1983).

## 2.  PROMOTIONS

The Horatio Alger story—that anyone through talent and effort can work his or her way up from stock clerk to president of the company—is more than a fairy tale.  It is, for many people, the driving force behind the American work ethic.  The promise of vertical social mobility makes the United States the land of opportunity.  But, is it true?  To be valid, promotions and employment opportunities should not be awarded for reasons other than merit.  Title VII prohibits discrimination in promotions based on race, color, religion, sex, or national origin.  Discrimination based on age, handicap, and other statutorily proscribed factors also is illegal. Unfairness in promotions, however, may not be the result of conscious, overt discrimination and this fact may pose difficult problems for the courts.  As you read the following cases, consider the appropriateness of legal regulation of promotion decisions.

## Namenwirth v. Board of Regents

769 F.2d 1235 (7th Cir.1985), cert. denied, 474 U.S. 1061 (1986).

■ CUDAHY, CIRCUIT JUDGE.

Appellant Namenwirth was denied tenure at the University of Wisconsin in Madison.  After the Department of Labor found that she had been denied tenure because of her sex, she brought this Title VII action in federal court; by agreement, the matter was heard by a magistrate, who found that the university had not discriminated against Namenwirth.  We affirm.

Marion Namenwirth was hired as an assistant professor by the Department of Zoology of the University of Wisconsin-Madison in September of 1971.  She was the first woman hired in a tenure-track position in thirty-five years, and apparently she was the first person in a tenure-track position ever to be denied tenure by the Department.

Her initial contract was for three years, and it was then to be renewed yearly until she was considered for tenure.  A faculty member in such a tenure-track position who is not promoted to the tenured rank of associate professor after the sixth year must ordinarily leave the University after her seventh year.

The University of Wisconsin has had a record of sex discrimination.  In 1970, prior to Namenwirth's hiring, only 150 of 2000 faculty members at the University of Wisconsin at Madison were female.  Of these, half were in traditionally female departments such as nursing and home economics. Nearly all were in the lower ranks.  Fifty academic departments had no women faculty members at all, even though between 10% and 38% of the

Ph.D.s being awarded in those disciplines were being awarded to women. Responding to a complaint from a campus action group, the Department of Health, Education and Welfare in July of 1970 began an investigation into sex discrimination at the University. HEW found that there was a pattern of discrimination against women, and found significant discrepancies between the salaries of males and females in the same positions. In spite of an affirmative action program adopted by the university under pressure from the federal government, the response of the science departments was slow. The magistrate found that in 1978, only six of 323 tenured faculty members in the science departments were women.

The record of the Zoology Department was apparently like that of the other science departments. Before Namenwirth was hired, the only woman to hold a tenure track position in the Zoology Department was Dr. Nellie Bilstad. Dr. Bilstad had received her Ph.D. from the University, and had been hired in 1931. The Department granted her tenure in 1942, and promoted her to associate professor in 1950. She remained an associate professor until 1969, the year of her retirement, when she was promoted to full professor. The magistrate found that Bilstad had been treated by her colleagues in a patronizing manner. He found that men who were junior to her and who had done little in the way of research rapidly moved beyond her in both salary and rank. He found that Dr. Bilstad was the victim of purposeful discrimination which reflected the discrimination prevalent in the University and in higher education in general in the time prior to the 1972 extension of Title VII to universities.

In 1971, Namenwirth was the only woman in a tenure track position in the Department. In 1976–77 she was considered for tenure. [After several votes, revotes, and reconsiderations by the Department and the Divisional Committee, the Dean of the College of Arts and Letters declined to recommend Namenwirth for tenure.]

A number of men were recommended for tenure in the years surrounding the Namenwirth decision. Perhaps the most pertinent case is that of Dr. Timothy Moermond, who was recommended for tenure in the 1978–79 academic year. Moermond's publication record was similar to Namenwirth's; like hers, it seemed to improve as the time for the tenure decision approached. Among his letters from outside evaluators, some were positive and some were critical. At the time the department first considered him for tenure, he had no outside grant support. The vote in the department was unanimous in favor of tenure, and he was recommended to the Division Executive Committee.

Namenwirth relies in part on the difference between the way she was treated and the way Moermond was treated to support her claim of discrimination. She points to these particular differences:

> The rate of publication for each of them increased toward tenure time. In the department's recommendation for Moermond, this was described as an expression of his meticulous approach to research. In the Namenwirth packet, it was described as the result of a last minute effort.

The supervision of graduate students is an important part of teaching. The number of graduate students reported as being supervised by Namenwirth was lower than the actual number; according to Namenwirth, the number reported for Moermond was inflated.

Each received critical comments from outside evaluators. Negative comments in the Moermond letters were minimized in the summary in his tenure packet sent to the Division. Negative comments about Namenwirth were highlighted.

In spite of the unanimous recommendation from the Department, the Division Executive Committee found Moermond's record to be weak, and it voted to deny him tenure. Three Zoology faculty members appeared before the committee to argue his case. They presented additional material in his favor, including evidence of a grant he had received after the tenure packet had first been sent on. The Executive Committee reconsidered and recommended Moermond for tenure. Shortly thereafter he was promoted to a tenured rank. The Department had made no such effort in the Namenwirth case.

\* \* \*

Namenwirth argues that she is qualified and ought to have been tenured. The magistrate found in fact that she was qualified; that was the basis on which he found that she had made a prima facie case. But it does not follow that she ought to have been awarded tenure. Mere qualification depends on objective measures—the terminal degree, the number of publications, and so on. Tenure requires something more; it requires that the department believe that the candidate have a certain amount of promise. The magistrate compared her record with the record of men who were awarded tenure and determined that the claim that the Department—and the University—found insufficient promise in Namenwirth's work was not pretextual. We have examined the records of Namenwirth and the various male candidates, and we cannot say that the magistrate's conclusion is in clear conflict with the evidence.

The evidence consists for the most part of comparative evidence of research quality and potential. That means that it consists in large part of the opinions of academics who serve not only as experts on qualifications but also as decision-makers in the tenure process. It is not our role, as federal courts have acknowledged, to consider merely the hard evidence of research output and hours spent on committee work, and reach tenure determinations *de novo*. A crucial part of the evidence we rely on is the esteem in which the candidate is held by the very persons making the tenure decision.

\* \* \*

We conclude that the magistrate's finding of no discrimination was supported by the evidence, and that in this case there was no convincing evidence of other sorts to counter that evidence.

The judgment of the district court is therefore affirmed.

■ SWYGERT, SENIOR CIRCUIT JUDGE, dissenting.

*  *  *

The majority wrestles with the problem of how to effectively review tenure decisions given that the dispositive factor in such decisions is the ability of the candidate to win the esteem of the very people whose sexual biases are in question.  It concludes that courts must generally defer to the expertise of academic peers in reaching subjective judgments about a candidate's academic standing and potential.  Consequently, "in a case of this sort, where it is a matter of comparing qualification against qualification, the plaintiff is bound to lose."

While I commend the majority for its frankness, I dissent from its defeatism.  The notion that tenure decisions must be accorded special deference was put to rest in 1972, when Congress, expressing concern about widespread discrimination against women in academia, removed academia's exemption from Title VII scrutiny.

*  *  *

In any event, I do not see a qualitative distinction between a tenure decision and any other employment decision.  The subjective esteem of colleagues and supervisors is often the key to any employment decision.  Yet, especially in the blue-collar context, the courts have not hesitated to review with great suspicion subjective judgments that adversely affect minorities.  Indeed, subjective esteem is more important in certain blue-collar contexts, where, for example, lives may depend on the employee's performance and good judgment.  And because all lawyers and judges are trained in academia, courts are better equipped to scrutinize academic decisionmaking than decisionmaking in the perhaps less familiar blue-collar context.

*  *  *

It is, of course, possible that some legitimate reason other than its perceptions of research output and potential caused the Department to grant tenure to the male candidate rather than the female candidate.  It is clear from the record that many members of the Department were fond of Moermond.  Even though personal popularity would be a poor reason to promote one candidate over another and even though such a criterion is not recognized by the University, this court does not review the wisdom of any particular tenure decision; we merely determine whether the decision was the product of invidious discrimination, not if it was wise.  Yet the University did not argue that it promoted Moermond on sexually-neutral popularity grounds.  It argues, instead, that it promoted Moermond solely because he possessed superior research output and potential.  Because the only legitimate, nondiscriminatory explanation of the tenure decisions proffered by the University is pretextual, Namenwirth is entitled to prevail on the merits.

In any event, it is difficult to believe that any factor other than sex explains the double-standard applied by the University in its reviews of Moermond and Namenwirth. Although many of the faculty members were clearly appalled by Namenwirth's allegations of sex bias, sex bias need not be conscious to be actionable. The most likely explanation for the events at bar is that Namenwirth was scrutinized by the Department because she was a woman breaking new ground. The Department wanted, at least consciously, to accept a woman as a peer, but it did not want to lower its standards for the sake of affirmative action. Accordingly, when Namenwirth turned out to be a marginal performer, many members of the Department refused to give Namenwirth the benefit of the doubt. But when a similarly-situated male turned out to be a marginal performer, i.e., Moermond, the entire Department was willing to give him the benefit of the doubt. In short, given Namenwirth's unhappy role as a pathbreaker, she had to perform better than a male to succeed. Such unequal treatment—however unconscious or subtle—violated Title VII.

## NOTES AND QUESTIONS

**1.** What effect, if any, should the University of Wisconsin's long history of sex discrimination have on the issue of whether Marion Namenwirth was discriminated against on the basis of sex?

**2.** Is it proper to permit faculty members to consider "collegiality" as a factor in tenure decisions or does this invite discrimination? Does the court place too much emphasis on "esteem?" Do collegiality and esteem make the promotion and tenure process overly subjective? For a further discussion of the use of subjective factors, see Chapter 4.

**3.** Was the majority too deferential to the university? Should different standards be applied to discrimination cases involving professionals? What factors make judicial scrutiny particularly difficult? For a further discussion, see Note, Namenwirth v. Board of Regents of the University of Wisconsin System: Proving Pretext in a Title VII Tenure Denial Case, 1987 Wis.L.Rev. 1041.

**4.** Do you agree with the dissent that, as a groundbreaking woman, Namenwirth was held to a higher standard? Compare *Price Waterhouse*, supra p. 248.

**5.** What effect do you think bringing this lawsuit will have on Namenwirth's career in academia? Is it likely that many incidents of discrimination go unredressed?

**6.** Many tenure votes are by secret ballot. Should faculty members be compelled to disclose their votes when a lawsuit is brought alleging discrimination? See University of Pennsylvania v. EEOC, 493 U.S. 182 (1990) (held: yes).

**7.** The dissent implies that personal popularity would be a poor reason for promotion, but would be sex-neutral and therefore not violative of Title VII. Do you agree? Consider the following case.

## Autry v. North Carolina Department of Human Resources

641 F.Supp. 1492 (W.D.N.C.1986), affirmed, 820 F.2d 1384 (4th Cir. 1987).

■ ROBERT D. POTTER, CHIEF JUDGE.

\* \* \*

The Plaintiff, Omega Autry, is a thirty-five year old black female citizen of the United States who resides in Mecklenburg County, North Carolina.  She has a high school diploma and earned a Bachelor of Arts degree in English and French at Johnson C. Smith University.

The Defendant is an agency of the State of North Carolina and operates the Charlotte-Mecklenburg Child Support Enforcement Agency ("the Agency").

The Plaintiff testified that she began working as a Child Support Enforcement Agent II ("Agent II") in the Agency's Union County office in March 1976 and transferred to the Charlotte office in that capacity on January 8, 1982.  She continues to be employed by the Defendant as an Agent II at the Agency in Charlotte.  Her performance as an Agent II has been consistently evaluated by her supervisors on their Work Performance Planning Reports as average or above average.

In July 1983, the Plaintiff and five other Agent IIs in Charlotte submitted applications for promotion to the position of Child Support Supervisor I ("Supervisor I").  The pool of applicants, who all met the minimum qualifications for the job, consisted of three black females, two white females, and one black male.

\* \* \*

Jean P. Bost, the white Child Support Supervisor IV and Director of the Mecklenburg and Union County offices of the Agency, was responsible for screening and interviewing applicants for the promotion and for determining which applicant should receive the position of Supervisor I.  Bost indicated \* \* \* that the selection criteria which she used for choosing a candidate to fill the position of Supervisor I were:  merit system education and experience requirements, good attitude toward others, and ability to make decisions and evaluate.

Ms. Bost testified as a hostile witness that she had worked with all of the applicants for years and had supervised directly all but one of the applicants.  She further testified that she had had a very close relationship with their supervisors and had a lot of background about their knowledge and abilities prior to her interviews with them.  Ms. Bost credibly testified, however, that she did not make a tentative selection of the successful candidate until after she interviewed the applicants.

The Plaintiff testified that her interview with Ms. Bost lasted approximately five minutes.  She further stated that Ms. Bost asked her only two questions, to wit, whether she had any previous supervisory experience and what she considered to be the hardest part of the supervisory job.  She maintained that she was not asked the questions on Plaintiff's Exhibit 5, page 2 (Ms. Bost's interview evaluation sheet for the Plaintiff) regarding any weaknesses she needed to strengthen to perform the job, the skills she believed the job required, whether she thought she had those skills, her ability to evaluate and determine trends and to appropriately represent them, or how her education and experience related to this job. The Plaintiff admitted that she did not initiate any discussion with Ms. Bost, but merely answered the questions by saying that she had no supervisory experience and that supervising former coworkers would be the hardest part of the job for her. Her only question of Ms. Bost was whether "that was all."

Ms. Bost testified that she did ask the Plaintiff all the questions on the interview evaluation sheet. She noted that the Plaintiff was very short with her answers and was generally cool in her attitude at the interview, as if she did not wish to be there. Bost explained that recorded responses appear after only two of the questions because there was not enough time between the Plaintiff's answers to write anything down. She further explained that the fact that there are no written responses next to certain questions does not mean she did not ask them, since her notation of responses was more a matter of "doodling" on her part than a matter of detailed recordation. The Court concludes that the Plaintiff has failed to show by a preponderance of the evidence that Ms. Bost did not ask her all the questions that appear on Plaintiff's Exhibit 5.

Harriet Grier, a black female applicant, testified that she interviewed with Ms. Bost for approximately ten minutes. Klydette Lowery, another black female applicant who was not selected for the subject promotion but who was subsequently promoted when another Supervisor I position opened, testified that she interviewed with Ms. Bost for approximately twenty minutes. Victoria Lipscomb, the successful white female applicant, testified that she interviewed with Ms. Bost for approximately forty-five minutes to one hour. The testimony of Otis Worthy, the black male applicant for the position, corroborated Ms. Lipscomb's estimation of the length of her interview. No evidence was presented as to the duration of Mr. Worthy's interview or the interview of the other white female applicant.

After the interviews, Ms. Bost formed a tentative opinion that Victoria Lipscomb was the strongest candidate for the position. She testified that to be sure, she thoroughly considered the performance criteria listed on Plaintiff's Exhibit 5, page 1, which she considered important to success in the Supervisor I position, and assigned point scores ranging from a low of one to a high of five to those criteria with respect to each applicant. The point totals confirmed Ms. Bost's tentative opinion, and she decided that Lipscomb should receive the promotion. She stated that the interview itself was a consideration but that it did not play a major role in her selection of the successful candidate or carry as much weight as other considerations.

\* \* \*

Having reviewed the evidence that the Plaintiff presented in an attempt to show that Lipscomb was less qualified than she for the Supervisor I position, the Court finds that she has failed to establish by a preponderance of the evidence (1) that Ms. Lipscomb was not qualified for the job, or (2) that the Plaintiff was more qualified for the job as a result of her more constant desk-sitting, higher level of education, or longer experience as an Agent II. While it is true that the Plaintiff had more education and more experience within the Agency, Ms. Lipscomb's credentials satisfied the education and experience requirements for the Supervisor I position. Further, nothing the Plaintiff presented shows that Lipscomb was not qualified or was less qualified than the Plaintiff with respect to the other selection criteria noted on the Defendant's Report of Applicant Selection/Rejection Data (i.e., good attitude toward others and ability to make decisions and evaluate).

The Plaintiff claims that Ms. Bost disregarded the relative qualifications of the applicants and decided to promote Ms. Lipscomb solely on the basis of her friendship with Lipscomb and the connections Lipscomb's mother allegedly had with state officials.

Ms. Lipscomb acknowledged that she and Ms. Bost were friendly to each other and that they went out to lunch a couple of times a month when she was an Agent II, usually with a group but sometimes alone. Ms. Bost testified that she did not remember going to lunch with Lipscomb as frequently as twice a month, but did state that she went to lunch with her on occasion.

Otis Worthy testified that when he saw Ms. Lipscomb after her interview, she told him that she thought her interview had been "pretty good," that she thought she had gotten the job, and that "it's not what you know, it's who you know." Ms. Lipscomb testified that she had no recollection of making the comment "it's not what you know, it's who you know," in July 1983. She stated that that was a cliche she has often heard and that she has probably said it at some point. She did not remember, however, saying it to anyone in particular with any particular intent. Lipscomb further testified that she has never said that her mother could help her in obtaining employment and promotions within the State bureaucracy.

\* \* \*

The Court is of the opinion that the Plaintiff has presented neither direct evidence of racial discrimination nor indirect evidence whose cumulative probative force supports as a reasonable probability the inference that race was a determining factor in Ms. Bost's decision not to promote her. The Court found above that the Plaintiff failed to establish that Lipscomb was not qualified or that she was not as qualified as the Plaintiff for the promotion. Nonetheless, the Plaintiff argues that the cumulative probative force of her evidence supports the inference that Ms. Bost, the white director of the program, promoted Ms. Lipscomb, also a white person, because of their friendship and because of her mother's connections with state officials, not because of her qualifications. She argues in turn that

> [w]hen friendship is used as a basis for promotion, and the promoting person is white, a [sic] inference of racial discrimination is raised since, in our society, white persons are much more likely to have white friends than friends of other races. Thus, race enters into a subjective selection procedure. When a person can make a comment such as that made by Lipscomb that "It's not what you know, but who you know," it destroys an objective promotion system. It also remains true in our society that white persons know officials who are higher up in government than black persons.

\* \* \*

While the Plaintiff's theory is quite novel, it fails to satisfy the Court that it is more likely than not that Bost would have promoted the Plaintiff instead of Lipscomb but for the fact that the Plaintiff was black. The Court grants the Plaintiff that there is too much hiring and promoting on the basis of who knows whom and who is friends with whom. Such an insidious practice should never decide who will get a job. Nonetheless, while the Court agrees that promotions should be based purely on a person's qualifications, the law unfortunately does not prohibit employment practices based on friendship or politics, but only those based on race.

## NOTES AND QUESTIONS

**1.** What is wrong with employers wanting to hire or promote individuals that they already know, like, and believe they can work well with? Can employees reasonably expect that they will be treated more fairly in promotions than in other employment decisions such as hiring, job assignment, working conditions, layoffs, or discharge? The law in many states permits employees to bring common law tort and contract actions for wrongful discharge. See Chapter 10. Should the law also permit actions for wrongful failure to promote?

**2.** If the courts were to review promotions and other employment actions where friendship or "connections" played a part, what practical problems might arise? Would it violate Title VII for an airline, in hiring pilots, to give a preference to the relatives of current employees? See Garland v. USAir, Inc., 767 F.Supp. 715 (W.D.Pa.1991) (held: yes). Compare this result with *Kotch,* p. 104. Would it violate Title VII to promote an employee's son instead of the minority plaintiff? See Holder v. City of Raleigh, 867 F.2d 823 (4th Cir.1989) (held: no). In Foster v. Dalton, 71 F.3d 52 (1st Cir.1995), a Navy commander hired an acquaintance, who also was the "fishing buddy" of another Navy official, for a civilian position, rather than the plaintiff, an African–American employee. The First Circuit held that there was no Title VII violation. According to the court, Title VII does not prohibit cronyism, and the plaintiff failed to prove disparate impact resulting from cronyism. For a further discussion, see Ann C. McGinley, The Emerging Cronyism Defense and Affirmative Action: A

Critical Perspective on the Distinction Between Colorblind and Race–Conscious Decision Making Under Title VII, 39 Ariz.L.Rev. 1003 (1997).

**3.** Autry's argument that whites are more likely to have white friends was, apparently, unsupported by any specific facts. What proof would satisfy the court? Is this a fact of which the courts could take judicial notice?

**4.** Suppose one white male is selected over another white male for promotion because the first male is a friend of the boss. Are the courts likely to intervene to prevent this unfairness? Would such an intervention invite review of the merits of millions of employment decisions made on the basis of various irrelevant but not statutorily proscribed criteria?

**5.** Not all of the courts to consider the issue have agreed with *Autry*. For example, in Roberts v. Gadsden Memorial Hospital, 835 F.2d 793 (11th Cir.1988), the court held that a "good ole boy appointment" of a manager's white drinking buddy instead of a better-qualified African–American employee violated Title VII.

**6.** Are there any situations in which friendship would be an impermissible factor in a promotion decision? Mabel King claimed that Norma Jean Grant was promoted rather than herself because Grant was having a sexual relationship with Dr. Francis Smith, their male supervisor. Is this a form of sexual harassment proscribed by Title VII? See King v. Palmer, 778 F.2d 878 (D.C.Cir.1985) (held: yes). Why? Suppose Smith promoted Grant because he was *hoping* to have a sexual relationship with her? Suppose their relationship were nonsexual? For a further discussion of the applicability of sexual harassment theory to voluntary relationships, see note 10 on p. 587.

**7.** Taken together, do *Namenwirth* and *Autry* suggest that some courts are unable or unwilling to deal with the employment effects of institutional and societal racism and sexism?

CHAPTER 8

# OCCUPATIONAL SAFETY AND HEALTH

The possibility of death, injury, or illness on the job is a stark reality to millions of American workers in a variety of jobs. This chapter is important, therefore, because of the gravity of its subject matter. Beyond that, however, it is important as a vehicle for studying the effectiveness of pervasive regulation of the workplace and a unique administrative framework established to implement national occupational safety and health policy.

As you read the cases and materials in this chapter, consider (1) whether the federal regulatory approach adopted under the Occupational Safety and Health Act, 29 U.S.C. §§ 651 et seq., is the most effective and efficient way of achieving the goal of occupational safety and health; (2) whether the economic and noneconomic costs of regulation are justified by gains in employee safety and health; and (3) whether the courts and administrative bodies possess the technical expertise and have adopted the appropriate procedural mechanisms to decide these complex scientific and regulatory issues.

## A. INTRODUCTION

### 1. BACKGROUND

### Joseph A. Page & Mary–Win O'Brien, Bitter Wages*
59–62 (1973).

As the economic crisis [of the Great Depression] worsened and unemployment mounted, workers became willing to face any kind of physical hazard in order to hang onto their jobs. This served only to diminish the already feeble pressures on industry to eliminate or reduce such hazards. Conditions were ripe for a disaster of the first magnitude, and it happened at Gauley Bridge, West Virginia, in 1930 and 1931.

In retrospect, it is incredible that the story of the digging of the tunnel near Gauley Bridge did not break until 1935. Although much controversy was to surround the calculation of the project's human cost, a U.S. Public Health Service official testifying before a Congressional committee in 1961

_____
* Reprinted by permission of Viking-Penguin, Inc., New York, N.Y.

put it at 476 dead and 1,500 disabled. Yet it took five years from the time construction began for nationwide attention to focus on the tragedy, and the full facts did not emerge until a year later in the course of a Congressional hearing.

The New Kanawha Power Co., a subsidiary of Union Carbide, secured a permit from the West Virginia legislature to build a hydroelectric plant in the southern part of the state, ostensibly for the purpose of supplying badly needed energy to the impoverished surroundings. In fact, the primary function of the plant was to power the nearby Electro-Metallurgical Co., another Union Carbide subsidiary engaged in the electro-processing of steel. Water from the New and Kanawha rivers was to be diverted through a tunnel to be built through a mountain near the town of Gauley Bridge. In 1929, the Rhinehart-Dennis Co. was chosen as the subcontractor on the tunnel construction project.

The original plan called for a tunnel width of thirty-two feet. But when the rock formation at the tunnel site was found to contain a high silica content, New Kanawha Power changed the specifications to allow a forty-six-foot width, so that silica excavated from the tunnel might be shipped to the Electro-Metallurgical Co. to be used in the processing of steel.

Actual construction began in 1930. Rhinehart-Dennis recruited its labor force from Pennsylvania, Georgia, North and South Carolina, Florida, Kentucky, Alabama, and Ohio, as well as from the surrounding hills of West Virginia. Most of the workers were black and unskilled. The pay scale began at fifty cents an hour, but as the Depression wore on, it dropped to as low as thirty cents an hour. Blacks paid fifty cents a week for their living quarters, ten-by-twelve-foot shacks, each of which housed twenty-five to thirty men, women, and children. They paid seventy-five cents a week for medical care, while whites paid fifty cents a week for the same service.

Working conditions strained credulity. Gasoline-powered trains filled the tunnel with carbon monoxide, poisoning the workers and making them drowsy. The dust was often so thick that workers couldn't see ten feet in front, even with the headlight of a train. (Indeed, occasionally trains collided with each other.) Though West Virginia mining law required a thirty-minute wait after blasting, workers were herded back into the tunnel immediately after a blast. The foremen at times had to beat them with pick handles to get them to return. The silica content of the rock being blasted was extremely high. Though New Kanawha Power warned its engineers to use masks when entering the tunnel, no one ever told the workers to take precautions.

Increasing numbers of workers became progressively shorter of breath and then dropped dead. Rhinehart-Dennis contracted with a local undertaker to bury the blacks in a field at fifty-five dollars per corpse. Three hours was the standard elapsed time between death in the tunnel and burial. In this way, the company avoided the formalities of an autopsy and death certificate.  It was estimated that 169 blacks ended up in the field, 2 or 3 to a hole.

Whenever the doctors did perform an autopsy, they concluded that the cause of death was tuberculosis, pneumonia, or "tunnelitis."  But the actual precipitating cause of most of the deaths was silicosis, which transformed lungs into a mass of scar tissues as a result of the inhalation of dust with a high silica content.  Before work on the tunnel began, it was a known fact that prolonged exposure to dust with a 25–30 percent silica content could cause silicosis.  The silica content of the dust in the tunnel was 90–95 percent.  There was little ventilation.  Men were dying from nine to eighteen months after brief exposures to the silica.  Toward the end of the project, some workers purchased their own respirators for $2.50.  The purchasing agent for Rhinehart-Dennis was overheard to say to a respirator salesman, "I wouldn't give $2.50 for all the niggers on the job."  The paymaster was also overheard to tell the superintendent, "I knew they was going to kill those niggers within five years, but I didn't know they was going to kill them so quick."

The deadly dust, however, was not color-conscious.  The foreman who herded the men into the tunnel died.  The assistant superintendent died.  White workers died.  Fifty percent of the tunnel workers died or were in the various stages of silicosis.  Gauley Bridge and surrounding towns became villages of the living dead.  In July, 1934, an official of the Federal Emergency Relief Administration visited the black community in one of the towns.  Of the 43 males in the community of 101, 33 were dying of terminal silicosis.  The official recommended relocation.  "It is unadvisable socially," he noted, "to keep a community of dying persons intact."

At the time of the Gauley Bridge disaster, the West Virginia workmen's compensation act did not cover silicosis, so that those workers who wanted to press claims had to sue at common law.  Under West Virginia law, as interpreted by that state's Supreme Court, lawsuits against Rhinehart-Dennis and New Kanawha Power had to be filed within one year of the harmful exposure to silica dust, a patently unfair rule because many of the workers did not become aware until much later that they had contracted the lung disease.  Some two hundred cases were thrown out of court because of the one-year rule.

The trials themselves were a macabre burlesque.  A Rhinehart-Dennis foreman testified in a wheezing voice that there had been no dust in the tunnel.  (He later died of silicosis.)  The chief of West Virginia's Mines Department testified that he had observed no dust in the tunnel in 1930 or 1931, yet in 1931 he had written letters urging the company to do something about the dust condition.  One of the jurors was held in contempt for riding home every evening in a company car.  Rumors of jury tampering abounded, and workers found themselves unable to win the necessary unanimous verdicts.  The juries consistently voted eleven-to-one or ten-to-two in favor of the workers, which meant that a new trial would be necessary.  Finally, 167 of the suits were settled out of court for $130,000, with one-half going to the workers' attorneys.  Payments were meager, with blacks receiving $80 to $250, and whites from $250 to $1,000. One law firm representing workers accepted a $20,000 payment on the side from the companies in order to make the lawyers more amenable to a settlement. When this bit of chicanery came to light, the lawyers were compelled to pay back half of this sum, which was then distributed among their clients.

NOTES

**1.** For a further discussion of the Gauley Bridge disaster, see Martin G. Cherniack, The Hawk's Nest Incident (1986).

**2.** Although workers' compensation laws and industrial safety laws were enacted in nearly every state by 1920, meaningful preventive action did not begin until the mid-1930s. It was not until 1970 that comprehensive national legislation was enacted. Despite major advancements, the human costs of workplace exposures remain high. According to 1985 government estimates, there are about 6,000 deaths annually due to injuries and between 5.6 million and 11.3 million nonfatal injuries. Occupational illness is harder to estimate, but the Bureau of Labor Statistics estimates there were 240,000 new cases of occupational illness in 1988, with 20,000 annual deaths from cancer alone.

**3.** Although Gauley Bridge-type disasters are rare, callous disregard for workers' lives, especially when the workers are members of vulnerable minorities, still occurs. In a celebrated trial in 1985, three former corporate officials were convicted of murder and reckless conduct in the 1983 death of an employee who inhaled lethal concentrations of cyanide at a silver-recovery plant in Elk Grove Village, Illinois. The company hired undocumented Mexican and Polish workers and had them working over open vats of a cyanide solution in removing silver from used film plates. The defendants were each sentenced to twenty-five years in prison and fined $10,000. The convictions were overturned in 1990 because different mens rea requirements for murder and reckless conduct made conviction for both offenses inconsistent.

Ironically, OSHA had inspected the company only days before the fatality, but the inspector simply checked the employer's injury and illness records and left without inspecting the actual working conditions. An insurance company's safety inspector, who had actually inspected the facility, had warned company officials that there were too many vats with no ventilation. The company's response was to bring in additional vats and move the business office elsewhere.

After the fatality, OSHA issued a citation against the company, Film Recovery Systems, and proposed a $4,000 penalty. The penalty was later reduced to $2,000, but OSHA made no effort to collect the money after the company assured OSHA that it was going out of business. The equipment was subsequently moved to Florida, where the company set up shop again, reportedly with conditions worse than ever.

In September 1993, three former company officials pleaded guilty to involuntary manslaughter before they were to be retried on murder charges. Daniel Rodriguez, former plant foreman, received 30 months probation, four months of home confinement, and 500 hours of community service. Charles Kirschbaum, former plant manager, was sentenced to two years in prison. Charles O'Neil, former president of the now-defunct company, was sentenced to three years in prison.

**4.** The 1984 leak of methyl isocyanate at Union Carbide's Bhopal, India plant, which killed an estimated 3400 people and injured another 200,000 is a reminder of the very great risks associated with modern industrial operations.

**5.** For further reading on the history of workplace safety and health hazards and their regulation, see Nicholas A. Ashford, Crisis in the Workplace (1976); Thomas O. McGarity & Sidney A. Shapiro, Workers at Risk (1993); Benjamin W. Mintz, OSHA: History, Law, and Policy (1984); U.S. Department of Labor, Protecting People at Work (1980).

### THE REGULATORY APPROACH TO OCCUPATIONAL SAFETY AND HEALTH

The U.S. government can approach the problem of workplace safety and health in any of three ways. First, it can leave the problem to employers and employees. This approach is supported by the following rationales: (a) under contract principles, employers with unsafe conditions would have to pay their employees higher wages; employees could "purchase" more safety by working for safer employers at presumably lower wages; (b) reliance should be placed on employers that, acting in their own enlightened self-interest, would improve safety and health; (c) safety and health issues should be resolved by collective bargaining; and (d) workers' compensation rates and the fear of personal injury litigation are adequate incentives in promoting occupational safety and health.

A second possible approach to the problem is to leave occupational safety and health regulation to the states. Although, in general, this approach was rejected by Congress in 1970 as having been tried and failed, OSHA allows states to adopt their own versions of OSHA—"state plans"— which preempt federal activity.

The third approach, adopted by Congress in 1970 with the enactment of OSHA, was enactment of federal legislation. Congress opted for a standards/enforcement model. The initial safety and health standards were industry-developed consensus standards and federal standards already established by other, less comprehensive laws. New standards were to be promulgated through informal notice and comment rulemaking by the Secretary of Labor, with only the vaguest statutory directions as to the level of protection to be afforded to workers and the costs to be imposed on the economy.

OSHA requires preinspection compliance by employers and provides penalties for noncompliance detected during an inspection. Thus, the Act contemplates an important role for safety and health inspectors (compliance officers). When the Act was passed, however, there was an acute shortage of trained inspectors. In fact, in 1970 there were twice as many fish and game wardens in the U.S. as safety and health inspectors. By 1973 there were still only about 500 inspectors to serve five million workplaces and 75 million workers. Even worse, many of the inspectors initially hired lacked a formal education in safety or industrial hygiene, were poorly trained by OSHA, and had a "traffic cop" mentality in which the more violations cited, the better. (Today there are about 3000 federal and state inspectors with better education and training.)

Poor quality initial standards (discussed infra) and often incompetent inspectors led to OSHA's negative image as nitpicking, harassing, and ineffective. Although most of these early problems have been resolved, there are three reasons why OSHA continues to be extremely unpopular with business. First, OSHA is pervasive. The FAA, FCC, ICC, and other agencies each regulate a particular industry. OSHA regulates all industries. Managers who are opposed to federal regulation will invariably have a common nemesis in OSHA. Second, OSHA is intrusive. Few business executives like the FTC, SEC, or IRS. But, generally speaking, these agencies do not show up at the door unannounced, demand to be let in, snoop about the workplace, and then require a company to change the way it has been doing business for years. Third, OSHA is costly and infringes upon management prerogatives. OSHA seemingly intrudes into labor-management relations on the side of labor and requires, among other things, that workers be allowed to see their medical records and be permitted to refuse to work when conditions are extremely hazardous.

## Mark A. Rothstein, Occupational Safety and Health Law *

2–10 (4th ed. 1998).

In 1936 Congress enacted the Walsh-Healey Public Contracts Act, which limited working hours, child and convict labor, and set mild standards for working conditions in factories. The Act required that contracts entered into by any agency of the United States for the manufacture or furnishing of materials in any amount exceeding $10,000 must contain a stipulation that the working conditions of the contractor's employees must not be unsanitary, hazardous, or dangerous to health and safety. The Walsh-Healey Act, however, had limited coverage and failed to provide and enforce strict industrial health and safety standards.

The Labor Management Relations Act (Taft-Hartley Act), passed in 1947 over President Truman's veto, contained a provision (§ 502) permitting employees to walk off a job if it was "abnormally dangerous." In 1948 President Truman attempted to remedy industrial accidents by calling the first Presidential Conference on Industrial Safety. Although these meetings continued to take place throughout the Eisenhower years, the only noticeable outcome of the conferences was a bill introduced by Senator

* Reprinted by permission of West Publishing Co.

Hubert Humphrey in 1951. The Humphrey Bill, which attempted to establish an accident prevention bureau, led Congresswoman Lenore K. Sullivan to ask Labor Secretaries James P. Mitchell and Willard Wirtz for their support of legislation to ensure proper standards for handling hazardous materials in industry.

In the area of mine safety, Congress was more inclined to take action after the occurrence of a tragic accident. For example, the death of 119 miners in West Frankfort, Illinois in December, 1951 led to the passage of a Coal Mine Safety Act in 1952. Six years later, the Maritime Safety Act was passed, which amended the Longshoremen's and Harbor Workers' Compensation Act.

During the mid and late 1960s Congress continued to enact specialized or limited safety statutes. In 1965 the McNamara-O'Hara Public Service Contract Act was passed to provide labor standards for the protection of employees of contractors who performed maintenance service for federal agencies. Also in 1965 the National Foundation on the Arts and Humanities Act was passed, conditioning receipt of federal grants on the maintenance of safe and healthful working conditions for performers, laborers, and mechanics.

Congress took its first significant step in job safety and health when it passed the Metal and Nonmetallic Mine Safety Act of 1966. In January, 1968, President Johnson proposed the nation's first comprehensive occupational safety and health program. Although this bill never reached a vote, a later version of the bill was reported out of the House Education and Labor Committee's Select Subcommittee on Labor.

Later in 1968, a coal mine explosion in Farmington, West Virginia, killed 78 men and shocked Congress into realizing the need for new job safety legislation. Congress reacted by passing the Coal Mine Health and Safety Act of 1969. The Contract Work Hours and Safety Standards Act of 1969 (also known as the Construction Safety Act) established federal standards for construction on public works. In 1970 Congress enacted the Federal Railway Safety Act, which was designed primarily for passenger safety, but also contained employee safety provisions.

By 1970, interest in job safety and health had reached new heights. The initial industry-specific legislation had already been passed and many members of Congress were ready to give serious consideration to more comprehensive federal regulations in industrial safety and health. The result was the passage of the Occupational Safety and Health Act of 1970 (OSHA).

* * *

The Act covers employment in every state, the District of Columbia, Puerto Rico, and all American territories, an estimated 6 million workplaces and 90 million employees. The Act does not apply to working conditions of employees over whom other state and federal agencies exercise statutory authority to prescribe or enforce standards or regulations affecting occupational safety or health.

Among other requirements, each employer must comply with two provisions of the Act. First, § 5(a)(1) requires the employer to keep its place of employment free from recognized hazards that are causing or likely to cause death or serious physical harm to its employees. Second, § 5(a)(2) requires the employer to comply with promulgated OSHA standards.

The Act provides for the promulgation of standards in three ways. Under § 6(a), the Secretary of Labor was authorized to adopt national consensus standards and established federal standards without lengthy rulemaking procedures for two years from the effective date of the Act. This authority ended April 27, 1973. Section 6(b) sets out the procedures to be followed in modifying, revoking, or issuing new standards. The Secretary may also promulgate an emergency temporary standard pursuant to § 6(c). An emergency temporary standard may be established if the Secretary determines that employees are subject to grave danger from exposure to substances or agents known to be toxic or physically harmful and that an emergency standard is necessary to protect employees from danger. These standards are effective upon publication in the Federal Register but remain in effect only for six months.

Pursuant to § 6(d), an employer may petition the Secretary for an order granting a variance from any standard promulgated under § 6. The main types of variances are temporary and permanent. A temporary variance may be issued if the employer is unable to comply with a standard because of unavailability of workers, facilities, or equipment; is taking all available steps to protect its employees from the hazards covered by the standard; and has an effective program for coming into compliance as soon as possible. A permanent variance will be issued only if the Secretary determines that the workplace is as safe and healthful as it would be by compliance with the established standard.

All enforcement functions of the Act rest with the Occupational Safety and Health Administration (OSHA) of the Labor Department. OSHA compliance officers (COs) are empowered by § 8(a) to inspect any workplace covered by the Act. The CO must present his or her credentials to the owner, operator, or agent in charge before proceeding with the inspection tour. The employer and an employee representative have a right to accompany the inspector. After the inspection a closing conference is held, during which the CO and employer representative discuss safety and health conditions and possible violations. Most COs cannot issue citations "on the spot," but must confer with the OSHA area director.

After the CO files a report, the area director decides whether to issue a citation, computes any penalties to be assessed, and sets the date for abatement of each alleged violation. If a citation is issued, it is mailed to the employer as soon as possible after the inspection, but in no event can it be more than six months after the alleged violation occurred. Citations must be in writing and must describe with particularity the violations alleged, including the relevant standards and regulations.

The Act provides for a wide range of penalties. As amended by the Omnibus Budget and Reconciliation Act of 1990, violations are categorized and penalties may be assessed as follows:

| | |
|---|---|
| De Minimis Notice | $0 |
| Nonserious | $0–$7,000 |
| Serious | $1–$7,000 |
| Repeated | $0–$70,000 |
| Willful | $5,000–$70,000 |
| Failure to abate | $0–$7,000 per day |
| Failure to Post | $0–$7,000 |

The good faith of the employer, the gravity of the violation, the employer's past history of compliance, and the size of the employer are all considered in penalty assessment. In addition to the above-mentioned civil penalties, there are criminal sanctions for willful violations that have caused the death of one or more employees.

Under the Act, an employer, an employee, or authorized employee representative (union) have 15 working days in which to file a notice of contest. If the employer does not contest the violation, abatement date, or proposed penalty, the citation becomes final and not subject to review by any court or agency. Contrarily, if a notice of contest is filed in good faith, the abatement requirement is tolled and a hearing is scheduled. An employer may also file a petition for modification of abatement (PMA), if unable to comply with any abatement requirement that has become a final order. If the Secretary or an employee contests the PMA, a hearing is held to determine whether any abatement requirement, even if part of an uncontested citation, should be modified.

The Secretary must immediately forward any notice of contest to the Occupational Safety and Health Review Commission (OSHRC). The Commission is a quasi-judicial, independent administrative agency comprised of three Presidentially-appointed Commissioners who serve staggered six year terms. In cases before the Commission, the Secretary is usually referred to as the complainant, and has the burden of proving the violation; the employer is usually called the respondent. The hearing is presided over by an administrative law judge (ALJ) of the Commission. After the hearing the ALJ renders a decision, affirming, modifying, or vacating the citation, penalty, or abatement date. The ALJ's decision then automatically goes before the OSHRC. An aggrieved party may file a petition for discretionary review (PDR), asking that the ALJ's decision be reviewed, but even without a PDR any Commission member may direct review of any part or all of the ALJ's decision. In this event, the Commission reconsiders the evidence and issues a new decision. If, however, no member of the Commission directs review within 30 days, the decision of the ALJ is final.

Any person adversely affected by a final order of the Commission may file a petition for review in the United States court of appeals for the circuit in which the violation is alleged to have occurred or in the United States Court of Appeals for the District of Columbia Circuit. The affected party must file within 60 days of the final order.

NOTES

**1.** The Occupational Safety and Health Act (OSHA) created three new government agencies: the National Institute for Occupational Safety and Health (NIOSH), located in the Department of Health and Human Services, is charged with scientific research on matters of occupational safety and health; the Occupational Safety and Health Administration (OSHA), located in the Department of Labor, is responsible for promulgating new standards and enforcement; and the Occupational Safety and Health Review Commission (OSHRC), an independent agency, adjudicates administrative cases arising under the Act. This compartmentalization of functions differs from the traditional administrative model and resulted from congressional concern about maintaining the separation of functions and assuring employers that these functions would, in fact, be separate and neutral.

**2.** Despite intense criticism of the Act and its enforcement, with the exception of penalty increases in 1990, there have been no substantive amendments. Congress has, however, enacted a series of enforcement limitations via riders to appropriations bills each year since fiscal 1977:

(1) OSHA is prohibited from inspecting employers with ten or fewer employees in industries with three digit Standard Industrial Classification (SIC) injury and illness rates of less than the current national average. There are several exceptions to the limitation, and inspections are still permitted in the following instances: in response to complaints, for failures to correct, for willful violations, to investigate accidents, for imminent dangers, for health hazards, and to investigate discrimination complaints.

(2) OSHA is prohibited from inspecting workplaces in states with approved plans for six months after a state inspection, except for investigation of employee complaints and fatalities, special studies, and accompanied monitoring visits.

(3) OSHA may not undertake any enforcement activity on the Outer Continental Shelf in excess of the authority granted to OSHA in the Outer Continental Shelf Lands Act or the Outer Continental Shelf Lands Act Amendments of 1978.

(4) The Secretary of Labor is prohibited from assessing penalties for first-instance nonserious violations of any employer unless the inspection discloses ten or more violations. OSHA is still permitted to issue citations for these violations which prescribe an abatement date. Second-instance violations of any nature can carry a penalty, even if fewer than ten violations are detected.

(5) Farms with ten or fewer employees at one time during the past year, except those with migrant labor camps, are exempt.

(6) OSHA may not promulgate or enforce any regulation restricting work activity in any recreational hunting, fishing, or shooting area.

(7) No penalties may be assessed against an employer with ten or fewer employees that had a prior on-site consultation and had made good faith efforts to abate the violative conditions prior to the inspection.

The Appropriations Act for 1998 prohibits OSHA from promulgating any proposed or final standard for ergonomic protection or from enforcing voluntary guidelines on ergonomic protection through the general duty clause of the Act.

**3.**  Before 1977, miners were protected by two separate laws: the Federal Metal and Nonmetallic Mine Safety Act of 1966 and the Federal Coal Mine Health and Safety Act of 1969.  Both laws were enforced by the Mining Enforcement and Safety Administration (MESA), part of the Department of the Interior.  Also within the Department of the Interior was the Bureau of Mines—charged with promoting mine production.  (Before 1973, when MESA was established, the Bureau of Mines also was responsible for safety.)  Besides this conflict of interest and a history of poor enforcement, neither act had provisions covering toxic substances and neither required specific training for inexperienced miners.  In addition, there were jurisdictional conflicts between OSHA and MESA.

To remedy these and other problems, Congress enacted the Federal Mine Safety and Health Act of 1977 (MSHA), 30 U.S.C. §§ 801–962.  All mining activity is now covered by one law, enforced by the Mine Safety and Health Administration (MSHA), within the Department of Labor.  The Mine Safety and Health Review Commission (MSHRC) was established to adjudicate contested mining cases.

MSHA was based on the OSHA model, but there are several differences reflecting the smaller number of sites covered (23,000 mines versus 5,000,-000 workplaces), the hazardous nature of mining, and the experience with some problem areas under OSHA.  Some of the unique features of MSHA are the following:

(1) All underground mines must be inspected at least four times a year and all surface mines must be inspected at least twice a year. § 103(a).

(2) All inexperienced miners must receive forty hours of training before working underground, § 115(a)(1), or twenty-four hours of training before working in a surface mine, § 115(a)(2).

(3) Inspectors may issue orders calling for the immediate withdrawal of miners.  § 104(b).

(4) There is no general duty clause.

(5) There are no state plans, but existing state laws are not automatically superceded.

(6) Miners may refuse to work if there are extremely hazardous conditions.  § 103(g).

(7) There is no difference between serious and nonserious violations.  Penalties up to $10,000 may be assessed for violations;

$25,000 and up to one year in jail for a willful violation; and $50,000 and up to five years in jail for a second willful violation.

(8) Employees filing nonfrivolous complaints alleging that they were discriminated against for exercising rights under MSHA are entitled to temporary reinstatement pending adjudication of the merits. § 105(c).

(9) Discrimination cases are heard initially by the Commission, with a right of appeal to district court. Miners may proceed on their own behalf if the Secretary declines to proceed. § 105(c).

(10) The MSHRC is comprised of five members, with two votes needed to direct review of an ALJ's decision. § 113(a).

## 2. Jurisdiction

## Frank Diehl Farms v. Secretary of Labor

696 F.2d 1325 (11th Cir.1983).

■ Vance, Circuit Judge:

This petition to review an order of the Occupational Safety and Health Review Commission challenges the Commission's and the Secretary of Labor's new interpretation of the statutory workplace as it relates to housing, provided in this case to seasonal farm workers.

The facts are not in dispute. Petitioners are four Hillsborough County, Florida farmers [1] each of whom employs seasonal workers and each of whom provides housing that is made available to the seasonal workers on a voluntary basis at little or no cost.[2] The workers are not required, either implicitly or explicitly, to live in the housing. Although petitioners presumably perceive the housing to be in their interest as an aid in maintaining a stable labor force, such housing is not essential to support such a labor pool. During the periods in question there has been a more than ample labor supply. The housing is not filled to capacity even during the peak of the harvest season. Some workers choose not to live in the housing provided. When work is available, the housed workers are required to

---

**1.** Frank Diehl Farms grows tomatoes on 125 acres and peppers on 25 to 30 acres. Diehl & Lee grows tomatoes on up to 125 to 140 acres and peppers on 30 to 40 acres. Villemaire Farms, Inc. grows tomatoes on approximately 100 acres. It also grows cucumbers and strawberries and has a lemon grove. V.V. Vogel & Sons Farms, Inc. raises tomatoes on up to 130 acres.

**2.** Frank Diehl Farms uses up to 120 temporary workers during the spring harvest. It provides free housing for up to 56 persons in a labor camp consisting of 13 mobile trailers. Diehl & Lee, MLC employs as many as 130 workers during harvest. It provides free housing in 12 trailers with a capacity of 54 persons. Villemaire Farms, Inc. utilizes as many as 70 temporary workers. It provides free housing for up to 60 persons in its labor camp. V.V. Vogel & Sons Farms, Inc. employs between 100 and 130 temporary workers during spring harvest. Between 70 and 85 of those workers generally reside in its camp consisting of a concrete block building, two army barracks and four houses for which each pays a fee of $10.00 per season.

work on the farm which provides the housing. At other times, however, they may continue to use the housing while working for other employers.

The issue raised on appeal is whether OSHA may regulate this housing. The evaluation of the OSHA regulations of housing provides the context for resolution of this issue. In 1971 acting under the authority of section 6(a) of the Occupational Safety and Health Act of 1970, the Secretary of Labor adopted Standard Z4.4–1968 of the American National Standards Institution (ANSI) as a consensus standard for temporary labor camps. The ANSI standard had a scope provision, but the scope provision was not incorporated into the standard as adopted by the Secretary.

Despite this initial silence on scope of jurisdiction, the Secretary in 1974 moved to clarify the issue. On September 23, 1974 the Secretary published a proposed new standard covering housing. The new standard contained many substantive revisions but stated that, insofar as the jurisdictional scope of the standard was concerned, its purpose was only "to more accurately describe the subject of the standard." The proposed rule stated that the Act applies "to housing furnished by employers to employees, to the extent that such housing constitutes a *condition of employment.*" Id. (emphasis added).[3] In 1976, after hearings the Secretary withdrew the proposed new standard stating that "[u]ntil such time as a single Departmental standard on employment related housing is promulgated, OSHA will continue to inspect temporary labor camps and enforce its *existing* standard, 29 C.F.R. § 1910.142." Ten days after the proposed regulation was withdrawn, the Secretary issued Field Information Memorandum No. 76–17 entitled "Clarification of Procedures for Inspection of Migrant Housing Facilities." This memorandum instructed field inspectors to apply a condition of employment test.[4] Cases brought by the Secretary have been decided consistently with the condition of employment test.

**3.** The proposed standard contained the following scope provisions:

   (a) General—(1) Scope. (i) This section is applicable to all housing sites, including those that utilize tents, that are owned, managed or controlled by employers and are furnished by them to employees as a condition of employment; however, facilities which because of the nature of the work are mobile, such as may be the case with trailers and railroad cars, are not subject to the requirements in this section unless such normally mobile facilities are permanently located and not utilized as mobile facilities.

   (ii) The furnishing of housing sites will be deemed a "condition of employment" only when the employees are required by the employer to utilize them, or are compelled by the practical or economic realities of the employment situation to utilize them. However, if housing made available by an employer is accepted by employees voluntarily, without contractual or practical compulsion, for example, on normal landlord-tenant bases, and in preference to other reasonably available facilities, such housing would not constitute a condition of employment.

39 Fed.Reg. 34,058–59 (1974).

   **4.** The following facts shall be carefully documented:

* * *

   (5) Determine if housing is provided as a condition of employment. Living in employer-provided housing is construed as a condition of employment if a) employers require employees to do so; or b) geographical circumstances require employees to do so, i.e., lack of comparable

On June 15, 1979 OSHA issued Instruction CPL 2.37.  This instruction replaced Field Memorandum No. 76–17.  The new instruction rejected the "condition of employment" test in favor of a "directly related to employment" standard: housing was deemed covered by the Act so long as it was in fact directly related to employment.[5]  Following this new standard, the Occupational Health and Safety Commission [sic] (OSHRC) overturned the decision of an administrative law judge who had dismissed, for lack of jurisdiction, OSHA citations against migrant housing in a case factually similar to this one.

The parties in this case agree that although the temporary workers' occupancy of the provided housing is not a "condition of employment," it is "directly related to employment."  The administrative law judge determined that the latter was the correct test and accordingly held that the temporary housing was a "workplace" within the meaning of the Act, and subject to the requirements of 29 C.F.R. §§ 1910.142f and 1903(1), for the violation of which petitioners were cited.  Because no member of the commission directed review, the administrative law judge's decision is a final order for purposes of our review.

The dispositive question presented is whether the Act may be construed to apply to this sort of housing which is work-related but which is not a condition of employment.  Regulations under the Act clearly embrace more than the actual physical area where employees perform their labor.  Petitioner concedes that OSHA has the statutory authority to enforce standards upon some temporary labor camps but argues that the authority extends only to those where residency is a condition of employment.  The Secretary argues that it is not material whether laborers are compelled to live in the camp as long as the camp is "directly beneficial, convenient, or advantageous to the employer."  Therefore, the Secretary argues, any housing provided by the employer for the purpose of guaranteeing a stable supply of labor is a "workplace" within the scope of the Act.

* * *

alternative housing in the area.  Notwithstanding an appearance of a landlord-tenant relationship, OSHA standards are applicable when housing is provided as a condition of employment.

Field Information Memorandum No. 76–17 at § 2(c)(5).

**5.** OSHA Instruction CPL 2.37 provides in pertinent part:

A "temporary labor camp" or "migrant housing facility" is defined as farm housing directly related to the seasonal or temporary employment of migrant farm workers.  In this context, "housing" includes both permanent and temporary structures located on or off the property of the employer, provided it meets the foregoing definition.

CPL 2.37 at § F(1).

Housing should be treated as employment-related if, a) employers require employees to live in the housing, or b) isolated location or lack of economically comparable alternative housing make it a practical necessity to do so, and/or c) the housing is provided or made available as a benefit to the employer.

Id. at § H(5).  The Instruction then listed five factors to be considered in making this determination.

Examination of the words of the statute, its legislative history and its underlying policies leads us to reject the reasons advanced by the agency to justify its interpretation. Our inquiry begins with the language of the statute. In the absence of clearly expressed contrary legislative intention, the plain language of the statute controls its construction. Since Congress left the term "workplace" undefined in the Act, it should be given its ordinary, common sense meaning. The term "workplace" connotes the place where one must be in order to do his job.

Nothing in the legislative history of the Act indicates that Congress intended it to apply to places which are not places of work. The terms used repeatedly throughout the legislative history, "working conditions," "work situations," "occupational safety and health" hazards, "work-related injuries," "place of employment," "work environment," "business or workplace," "job-related injuries," indicate that Congress' central concern was avoidance of safety and health hazards at the place where work is performed. With the workplace as the central focus of the legislation, we must determine whether OSHA has authority to extend its jurisdiction beyond the place where work is performed to encompass a residence.

The Secretary argues that the term "workplace" appearing in section 4(a) of the Act, read in conjunction with other provisions of the Act which reveal the Act's purpose as assuring safe and healthful "work situations," section 2(a) of the Act, "working conditions," section 2(b), and "work experience," section 2(b)(7), requires a broad reading of OSHA's grant of jurisdiction. But this argument, based on general policy considerations that lack self-limiting principles, proves too much. Migrant housing may well be unsafe and unhealthy, conditions that we deplore, but from that it does not follow that OSHA is the body authorized or even best suited to deal with these problems. OSHA does not possess a general mandate to solve the housing ills of America. It is true that the Act is remedial and should be construed liberally. For example, the Secretary should be able to extend the Act's coverage to certain employer provided means of transportation and certain employer provided housing even though such extension exceeds the plain language of the statute. This does not mean that coverage may be extended to any employer provided device or facility. In order for coverage under the Act to be properly extended to a particular area, the conditions to be regulated must fairly be considered *working* conditions, the safety and health hazards to be remedied *occupational,* and the injuries to be avoided *work-related.* The safety of the place where the employee has to be in order to work was central to Congress' concern. We think that the condition of employment standard best reflects that concern.

\* \* \*

Only if company policy or practical necessity force workers to live in employer provided housing is the degree of coercion such that the hazards of apartment living are sufficiently related to employment to come under the scope of the Act. OSHA may then impose additional duties upon the employer as mandatory landlord to comply with its housing regulations, even though these places would not otherwise be "workplaces" and even though the hazards associated with the housing are different in kind and quality from most occupational hazards. We find, therefore, that the condition of employment test previously used by OSHA is the essential bridge that links the residence to the workplace for the purpose of jurisdiction under the Act. Because OSHA assessed petitioners' farms for violations of 29 C.F.R. §§ 1903.2(a)(1), 1910.142, without jurisdiction, those assessments are

REVERSED.

■ JOHNSON, CIRCUIT JUDGE, dissenting:

\* \* \*

The evidence reflects that petitioners' business of growing tomatoes and vegetables depends on a workforce that necessarily exceeds the number of workers who live in the local area. Therefore, the success of their operation depends on the availability of migrant workers. The transitory nature of migrant workers' housing is characteristic to the work they perform. The employers in this case have stated that they supply housing to workers at no or little cost in order to assure an available supply of labor. In return the workers who live in the camp are expected to work for the employer when requested to do so. The camps, therefore, are an intrinsic part of the "work situation" or "working conditions." That the farmers also employ workers who do not live in the camps does not alter the fact that they depend on the core of workers who reside in the camp.

Given the Act's broad purpose to assure safe working conditions, OSHA not only has the authority but has a duty to regulate conditions in labor camps when the "operation of the camp is directly related to the employment of its occupants." OSHA Instruction CPL 2.37. Since the employers here have agreed that the provision of housing in this case meets the "directly related to employment" standard, I would deny the petitions for review and enforce the citations.

NOTES AND QUESTIONS

1. Farmworkers, particularly migrant farmworkers, have had a difficult time in securing occupational safety and health protection comparable to workers in other employment sectors. For example, in 1972 the National Congress of Hispanic American Citizens petitioned OSHA to issue a field sanitation standard requiring portable toilets, hand washing facilities, and drinking water. After 10 years of litigation, the case was settled in 1982 with OSHA agreeing to consider issuing a standard. A proposed standard was issued in 1984, but was withdrawn in 1985. In 1987, the D.C. Circuit held that the Secretary had acted contrary to law in withdrawing the proposed standard and ordered that the standard be issued within 30 days. Farmworker Justice Fund v. Brock, 811 F.2d 613 (D.C.Cir.1987).

Even with standards in place, enforcement has been difficult. Employers have raised various defenses, claiming that the workers are employed by the labor contractor rather than the grower, Griffin & Brand of McAllen, Inc., 6 OSHC 1702, 1978 OSHD ¶ 22,829 (1978), that the regulations are invalid because they go beyond workplaces, *Frank M. Diehl,* or that there is a conflict between federal and state jurisdiction, Five Migrant Farmworkers v. Hoffman, 345 A.2d 378 (N.J. Super. Law Div.1975). See generally Comment, Interpreting OSHA's Pre-emption Clause: Farmworkers as a Case Study, 128 U.Pa.L.Rev. 1509 (1980).

**2.** In *Diehl,* the court suggested that regulation of the housing conditions of migrant workers should be left to state law. The states, however, have a disappointing record in this area. There are essentially four categories of state laws: 17 states have no laws regulating migrant worker housing; 11 states with OSHA-approved state plans have laws that mirror OSHA in substance and scope; 11 states with OSHA-approved state plans have laws that go beyond OSHA in regulating migrant worker housing; and 11 states without state plans have enacted laws to regulate the housing of migrant workers. Nevertheless, even states in the last two categories often lack adequate funding, staffing, or legal authority to provide effective regulation. In addition, migrant workers are frequently too intimidated to file complaints.

**3.** OSHA is grounded constitutionally on the commerce clause and § 3(5) defines an employer as "a person engaged in a business affecting commerce who has employees, but does not include the United States or any State or political subdivision of a State." Although it is relatively easy to prove that an employer's business affects commerce (such as by using the mail or purchasing supplies from out of state), several cases have considered the burden of proof and the procedures for determining coverage. Usery v. Lacy, 628 F.2d 1226 (9th Cir.1980); Godwin v. OSHRC, 540 F.2d 1013 (9th Cir.1976); Brennan v. OSHRC (John J. Gordon Co.), 492 F.2d 1027 (2d Cir.1974).

**4.** Section 3(5) of the Act excludes states and political subdivisions of states from the definition of "employer." It is not always clear, however, whether a quasi-public entity is covered. For example, in Brock v. Chicago Zoological Society, 820 F.2d 909 (7th Cir.1987), the court held that the zoo was not a political subdivision of the state of Illinois. Even though over half of its funding was public, the zoo was operated by trustees who were private citizens and zoo employees were not covered by any laws applicable to public employees.

**5.** An important jurisdictional provision of the Act is § 4(b)(1), which provides that OSHA does not apply to "working conditions of employees with respect to which other Federal agencies * * * exercise statutory authority to prescribe or enforce standards or regulations affecting occupational safety and health." Congress sought to avoid duplication of enforcement by OSHA and other federal agencies, but § 4(b)(1) has posed a number of legal issues. Decisions of the OSHRC suggest a three-part test to determine whether OSHA is preempted from exercising authority by virtue of § 4(b)(1):

(1) The employer is covered by another federal act directed exclusively at employee safety and health or directed at public safety

and health and employees directly receive the protection the act is intended to provide.

(2) The other federal agency has exercised its statutory grant of authority.

(3) The other federal agency has acted in such a manner as to exempt the cited working conditions from OSHA jurisdiction.

See Northwest Airlines, Inc., 8 OSHC 1982, 1980 OSHD ¶ 24,751 (1980).

**6.**  A considerable controversy has developed over the proper interpretation of the words "working conditions" in § 4(b)(1).  In Southern Railway v. OSHRC, 539 F.2d 335 (4th Cir.), cert. denied, 429 U.S. 999 (1976), the Fourth Circuit defined "working conditions" as the "environmental area in which an employee customarily goes about his daily tasks."  In Southern Pacific Transportation Co. v. Usery, 539 F.2d 386 (5th Cir.1976), cert. denied, 434 U.S. 874 (1977), the Fifth Circuit held that "working conditions" "includes 'surroundings' (such as general problems of toxic liquids) and 'hazards' (a location, a category of items, or a specific item)."  Under which definition is preemption under § 4(b)(1) more likely?  Why?

**7.**  In § 4(b)(1) cases, employers typically argue that they are exempt from OSHA because they are regulated by another agency.  Cf. Old Dominion Power Co. v. Donovan, 772 F.2d 92 (4th Cir.1985) (in defending MSHA citation employer successfully argued that OSHA rather than MSHA applied).  Why would employers prefer to be regulated by an agency other than OSHA, such as the FAA, USDA, DOT, or FRA?

**8.**  The Act preempts all state occupational safety and health legislation.  Pursuant to § 18, however, if a state has an OSHA approved "state plan," with comparable standards, enforcement, and adjudicatory functions, jurisdiction may be ceded back to the state.  There are currently 23 approved state plans.

States without approved plans retain jurisdiction in certain areas.  States may enforce standards, such as state and local fire regulations, which are designed to protect a wider class of persons than employees.  They may conduct consultation, training, and safety information activities; and they may enforce standards to protect state and local government employees.  A variety of other state laws have been held not to be preempted by OSHA, including local zoning ordinances, drinking water and toilet facilities laws, injury reporting laws, criminal laws, and common law damage and indemnity actions.

## Illinois v. Chicago Magnet Wire Corp.

534 N.E.2d 962 (Ill. 1989), cert. denied sub nom., Asta v. Illinois, 493 U.S. 809 (1989).

■ JUSTICE WARD delivered the opinion of the court:

The issue we consider on this appeal is whether the Occupational Safety and Health Act of 1970 (OSHA) pre-empts the State from prosecuting the defendants, in the absence of approval from OSHA officials, for conduct which is regulated by OSHA occupational health and safety standards.

Indictments returned in the circuit court of Cook County charged the defendants, Chicago Magnet Wire Corporation, and five of its officers and agents, Anthony Jordan, Kevin Keane, Frank Asta, Gerald Colby and Alan Simon, with aggravated battery and reckless conduct. The individual defendants were also charged with conspiracy to commit aggravated battery. In substance, the indictments alleged that the defendants knowingly and recklessly caused the injury of 42 employees by failing to provide for them necessary safety precautions in the workplace to avoid harmful exposure to "poisonous and stupifying substances" used by the company in its manufacturing processes. On the defendants' motion, the trial court dismissed the charges, holding that OSHA has pre-empted the State from prosecuting the defendants for the conduct alleged in the indictments. The appellate court affirmed and we granted the State's petition for leave to appeal under Supreme Court Rule 315.

* * *

The circuit court dismissed the indictments, holding that OSHA pre-empts the States from prosecuting employers for conduct which is governed by Federal occupational health and safety standards, unless the State has received approval from OSHA officials to administer its own occupational safety and health plan. The court stated that because the conduct of the defendants set out in the indictments was governed by OSHA occupational health and safety standards, and the State had not received approval from OSHA officials to administer its own plan, it could not prosecute the defendants for such conduct.

The extent to which State law is pre-empted by Federal legislation under the supremacy clause of the Constitution of the United States is essentially a question of congressional intendment. Thus, if Congress, when acting within constitutional limits, explicitly mandates the pre-emption of State law within a stated situation, we need not proceed beyond the statutory language to determine that State law is pre-empted. Even absent an express command by Congress to pre-empt State law in a particular area, pre-emptive intent may be inferred where "the scheme of federal regulation is sufficiently comprehensive to make reasonable the inference that Congress 'left no room' for supplementary state regulation" or where the regulated field is one in which "the federal interest is so dominant that the federal system will be assumed to preclude enforcement of state laws on the same subject" Congressional intent to pre-empt State law may also be inferred where " 'the object sought to be obtained by the federal law and the character of obligations, imposed by it may reveal the same purpose.' "

The declared purpose of OSHA is "to assure so far as possible every working man and woman in the Nation safe and healthful working conditions and to preserve our human resources." To this end, Congress gave the Secretary of Labor the authority "to set mandatory occupational safety and health standards" for the workplace and to secure compliance with those standards by imposing civil and criminal sanctions for their violation. An "occupational health and safety standard" is defined as "a standard which requires conditions, or the adoption or use of one of more practices, means, methods, operations, or processes, reasonably necessary or appropriate to provide safe or healthful employment and places of employment." OSHA also imposes a duty on employers, separate and independent from specific standards set by the Secretary, to provide a workplace "free from recognized hazards that are causing or are likely to cause death or serious physical harm to his employees."

Congress also authorized the Secretary to conduct investigations and on-site inspections of workplaces and to institute enforcement proceedings for violations of OSHA standards. For violations of specific OSHA standards or section 654(a), OSHA authorizes the imposition of civil fines ranging from $1,000 to $10,000. Criminal fines of $10,000 may be imposed for giving unauthorized advanced notification of an OSHA inspection or knowingly making false statements on any OSHA filing. OSHA also provides for prison terms of up to six months for willful violations of OSHA standards that result in an employee's death.

The defendants read section 18(a) of OSHA to mean that under it Congress explicitly provided that the States are pre-empted from asserting jurisdiction over any occupational health and safety issue that is governed by OSHA occupational health and safety standards unless the State obtains approval from OSHA officials to administer its own occupational health and safety plan under section 18(b). Section 18 provides:

"(a) Nothing in this chapter shall prevent any State agency or court from asserting jurisdiction under State law over any occupational safety or health issue with respect to which no standard is in effect under section 655 of this title.

"(b) Any State which, at any time, desires to assume responsibility for development and enforcement therein of occupational safety and health standards relating to any occupational safety or health issue with respect to which a Federal standard has been promulgated under section 655 of this title shall submit a State plan for the development of such standards and their enforcement."

The defendants state that the conduct alleged in the indictments is governed by OSHA occupational health and safety standards. Specifically, they claim that OSHA standards define permissible exposure limits for the toxic substances which allegedly injured their employees and that OSHA also regulates the conduct that the prosecution says rendered the company's workplace unsafe. The defendants contend that therefore the trial court correctly held that, because the State had not received approval from OSHA officials pursuant to section 18(b) to prosecute the conduct set out in the indictments, the charges must be dismissed. We disagree.

Contrary to this argument, we cannot say that the language of section 18 of OSHA can reasonably be construed as explicitly pre-empting the enforcement of the criminal law of the States as to conduct governed by OSHA occupational health and safety standards.  The language of section 18 refers only to a State's development and enforcement of "occupational health and safety standards."  Nowhere in section 18 is there a statement or suggestion that the enforcement of State criminal law as to federally regulated workplace matters is pre-empted unless approval is obtained from OSHA officials.

The defendants argue, however, that because the charges set out in the indictments are based on conduct related to an alleged failure to maintain a safe work environment for their employees, in practical effect, the State is attempting to enforce occupational health and safety standards.  They contend that the primary purpose of punishing conduct under criminal law is to deter conduct that society deems harmful and to secure conformity with acceptable norms of behavior.  In that way, the criminal law establishes standards of care in society.  When applied to conduct in the workplace, the defendants argue, criminal law serves the same purpose as OSHA, i.e., to compel adherence to a particular standard of safety that will minimize the risk of injury.

It is the defendants' contention that in enacting OSHA, Congress intended to pre-empt all State laws to the extent that they regulate workplace safety.  They cite regulations promulgated by the Secretary which they say so interpret OSHA.  Specifically, they note that section 1901.2 provides:

> "Section 18(a) of [OSHA] is read as preventing any State agency or court from asserting jurisdiction under State law over any occupational safety or health issue to which a Federal standard has been issued."  29 C.F.R. § 1901.2 (1986).

They cite too this regulation promulgated by the Secretary:

> "[OSHA's pre-emption provisions] apply to all state or local laws which relate to an issue covered by a Federal standard, without regard to whether the state law would conflict with, complement, or supplement the Federal standard, and without regard to whether the state law appears to be 'at least as effective as' the Federal standard."  Hazard Communication Standard, 52 Fed.Reg. 31,852, 31,860 (1987).

We cannot accept the defendants' contention that it must be concluded that Congress intended to pre-empt the enforcement of State criminal laws in regard to conduct of employers in the workplace because the State criminal laws implicitly enforce occupational health and safety standards.

Although the imposition of sanctions under State penal law may effect a regulation of behavior as OSHA safety standards do, regulation through deterrence, however, is not the sole purpose of criminal law.  For example, it also serves to punish as a matter of retributive justice.  Too, whereas OSHA standards apply only to specific hazards in the workplace, criminal law reaches to regulate conduct in society in general. In contrast, occupational health and safety standards are promulgated under OSHA primarily as a means of regulating conduct to prevent injuries in the workplace.

It is to be observed also that for the most part OSHA imposes strict liability for violation of its standards, and that the criminal charges here allege that the defendants knowingly or recklessly injured several of their employees by unreasonably exposing them to toxic substances in the workplace. In order to be convicted of the charges, the State must establish that the defendants not only committed acts causing injury but that they also had the charged mental state, i.e., that they recognized the risk of injury and nevertheless willfully failed to take precautions to prevent injury. Thus, the criminal charges here do not set any new or other standards for workplace safety but rather seek to impose an additional sanction for an employer's conduct that, if proved, would certainly violate the duty set out in section 654(a) of OSHA.

There is nothing in the structure of OSHA or its legislative history which indicates that Congress intended to pre-empt the enforcement of State criminal law prohibiting conduct of employers that is also governed by OSHA safety standards. We would observe that the Supreme Court declared in Jones v. Rath Packing Co., (1977), 430 U.S. 519, 525 that "[w]here * * * the field which Congress is said to have pre-empted has been traditionally occupied by the States, * * * 'we start with the assumption that the historic police powers of the States were not to be superseded by the Federal Act unless that was the clear and manifest purpose of Congress.'"

Certainly, the power to prosecute criminal conduct has traditionally been regarded as properly within the scope of State superintendence. The regulation of health and safety has also been considered as "primarily, and historically" a matter of local concern. It cannot be said that it was the "clear and manifest" purpose of Congress to pre-empt the application of State criminal laws for culpable conduct of employers simply because the same conduct is also governed by OSHA occupational health and safety standards.

Although the provisions of OSHA are comprehensive, that Congress, in section 18, invited the States to administer their own occupational health and safety plans demonstrates that it did not intend to preclude supplementary State regulation. Indeed, section 651 of OSHA provides that the States are "to assume the fullest responsibility for the administration and enforcement of their occupational safety and health laws." It seems clear that the Federal interest in occupational health and safety was not to be exclusive.

Too, considering that until the recently increased interest in environmental safety charges were rarely brought under State law for conduct relating to an employer's failure to maintain a safe workplace, it would be unreasonable to say that Congress considered the pre-emption of State criminal law when enacting OSHA. Indeed, OSHA provides principally civil sanctions and only a few minor criminal sanctions for violations of its standards. Even for willful violations of OSHA standards which result in an employee's death an employer can be sentenced only to a maximum of six months' imprisonment. There is no penalty provided for conduct which causes serious injury to workers. It seems clear that the providing for appropriate criminal sanctions in cases of egregious conduct causing serious or fatal injuries to employees was not considered. Under these circumstances, it is totally unreasonable to conclude that Congress intended that OSHA's penalties would be the only sanctions available for wrongful conduct which threatens or results in serious physical injury or death to workers.

We judge that the purpose underlying section 18 was to ensure that OSHA would create a nationwide floor of effective safety and health standards and provide for the enforcement of those standards. It was not fear that the States would apply more stringent standards or penalties than OSHA that concerned Congress but that the States would apply lesser ones which would not provide the necessary level of safety. The comment has been made: "Congress * * * sought uniform national standards not to facilitate commerce but to prevent the 'race for the bottom' that occurred when each state set its own standards. Congress favored a federal law 'so that those states providing vigorous protection would not be disadvantaged by those that did not,' " (See Note, Getting Away With Murder: Federal OSHA Pre-emption of State Criminal Prosecutions for Industrial Accidents, 101 Harv.L.Rev. 535, 550 (1987).) While additional sanctions imposed through State criminal law enforcement for conduct also governed by OSHA safety standards may incidentally serve as a regulation for workplace safety, there is nothing in OSHA or its legislative history to indicate that Congress intended to pre-empt the enforcement of State criminal law simply because of its incidental regulatory effect.

\* \* \*

It is a contention of the defendants that it is irrelevant that the State is invoking criminal law jurisdiction as long as the conduct charged in an indictment or information is conduct subject to regulation by OSHA. The defendants argue that the test of pre-emption is whether the conduct for which the State seeks to prosecute is in any way regulated by Federal legislation. The defendants assert that because the conduct charged in the indictments is conduct regulated under OSHA, a State prosecution for that conduct is pre-empted by OSHA. The contention is not convincing.

Simply because the conduct sought to be regulated in a sense under State criminal law is identical to that conduct made subject to Federal regulation does not result in State law being pre-empted. When there is no intent shown on the part of Congress to pre-empt the operation of State law, the "inquiry is whether 'there exists an irreconcilable conflict between the federal and state regulatory schemes.' " A conflict arises where "compliance with both federal and state regulations is a physical impossibility", or when State law "stands as an obstacle to the accomplishment and execution of the full purposes and objectives of Congress."

The defendants argue that the prosecutions here would conflict with the purposes of OSHA. They say that Congress intended that under OSHA the Federal government was to have exclusive authority to set occupational health and safety standards. The standards were to be set only after extensive research to assure that the standards would minimize injuries in the workplace but at the same time not be so stringent that compliance would not be economically feasible. The defendants correctly point out that although the States are given the opportunity to enforce their own occupational health and safety standards, the plan submitted must contain assurances that the State will develop and enforce standards "at least as effective" as OSHA's. Even after a State plan is approved, the Occupational Safety and Health Administration retains jurisdiction to enforce its own standards until it determines, based on three years of experience, that the State's administration of the plan is "at least as effective" as OSHA's.

The defendants maintain that Federal supervision over State efforts to enforce their own workplace health and safety programs would be thwarted if a State, without prior approval from OSHA officials, could enforce its criminal laws for workplace conduct of employers which is also subject to OSHA standards. They say that the States would thus be permitted to impose standards so burdensome as to exceed the bounds of feasibility or so vague as not to provide clear guidance to employers.

We believe the concern of the defendants is unfounded. We cannot see that State prosecutions of employers for conduct which is regulated by OSHA standards would conflict with the administration of OSHA or be at odds with its goals or purposes. On the contrary, prosecutions of employers who violate State criminal law by failing to maintain safe working conditions for their employees will surely further OSHA's stated goal of "assur[ing] so far as possible every working man and woman in the Nation safe and healthful working conditions." State criminal law can provide valuable and forceful supplement to insure that workers are more adequately protected and that particularly egregious conduct receives appropriate punishment.

The defendants' statements that the State will now have the ability to enforce more stringent standards than OSHA's does not persuade. As stated, the charges here are based on the defendants' alleged willful failure to remove workplace hazards which create a substantial probability that they will cause injuries to their employees. Thus, employers are not left without guidance as to what standard of care they must meet. Too, in practical terms, if a defendant were in compliance with OSHA standards it is unlikely that the State would bring prosecutive action. Enforcement of State criminal law in the workplace will not "stand as an obstacle to the accomplishment and execution of the full purposes and objectives of Congress."

To adopt the defendants' interpretation of OSHA would, in effect, convert the statute, which was enacted to create a safe work environment for the nation's workers, into a grant of immunity for employers responsible for serious injuries or deaths of employees. We are sure that that would be a consequence unforeseen by Congress.

The question here has been considered by a few courts. The appellate court of Wisconsin in State ex rel. Cornellier .v. Black (Wis.App.1988), 144 Wis.2d 745, 425 N.W.2d 21, held that the State's authority to enforce its criminal laws in the workplace has not been pre-empted by OSHA. The court stated:

> "There is nothing in OSHA which we believe indicates a compelling congressional direction that Wisconsin, or any other state, may not enforce its homicide laws in the workplace. Nor do we see any conflict between the act and sec. 940.06, Stats. To the contrary, compliance with federal safety and health regulations is consistent, we believe, with the discharge of the state's duty to protect the lives of employees, and all other citizens, through enforcement of its criminal laws. Wisconsin is not attempting to impose a penalty for violation of any safety regulations. It is only attempting to impose the sanctions of the criminal code upon one who allegedly caused the death of another person by reckless conduct. And the fact that that conduct may in some respects violate OSHA safety regulations does not abridge the state's historic-power to prosecute crimes." (144 Wis.2d at 755, 425 N.W.2d at 25).

A divided court held to the contrary in People v. Hegedus (1988), 169 Mich.App. 62, 425 N.W.2d 729, leave to appeal granted in part (1988), 481 Mich. 870, 429 N.W.2d 598, citing the opinion of our appellate court in this case also held contra.

We would note that on September 27, 1988, the congressional committee on government operations approved and adopted a report on the question of whether State criminal prosecutions for workplace safety violations are pre-empted by OSHA. The committee concluded that inadequate use has been made of the criminal penalty provisions of the Act and recommended to Congress that "OSHA should take the position that the States have clear authority under the Federal OSH Act, as it is written, to prosecute employers for acts against their employees which constitute crimes under State law." Report of House Comm. on Government Operations, Getting Away with Murder in the Workplace: OSHA's Non-use of Criminal Penalties for Safety Violations, H.R.Rep. No. 1051, 100th Cong., 2d Sess. 9 (1988).

The People as supplemental authority cite a letter from the Department of Justice to the chairman of the committee. The letter of the Department of Justice, responding to the report, states in part that the Department shared the concerns of the committee as to the adequacy of the statutory criminal penalties provided for violations of OSHA and also observes:

> "As for the narrower issue as to whether the criminal penalty provisions of the OSH Act were intended to pre-empt criminal law

enforcement in the workplace and preclude the States from enforcing against employers the criminal laws of general application, such as murder, manslaughter, and assault, it is our view that no such general pre-emption was intended by Congress. As a general matter, we see nothing in the OSH Act or its legislative history which indicates that Congress intended for the relatively limited criminal penalties provided by the Act to deprive employees of the protection provided by State criminal laws of general applicability."

The defendants offered supplemental authorities also, arguing that the Department's view was not entitled to deference and was not binding on a court. It, of course, does not bind a court and, whether entitled to deference or not, it is certainly not inappropriate to note that the view of the governmental department charged with the enforcement of OSHA is also the view of this court.

In view of our holding that the State is not pre-empted from conducting prosecutions, we need not address the defendants' motion to strike portions of the State's brief and certain grand jury testimony.

For the reasons given, the judgments of the appellate court and circuit court are reversed and the cause is remanded to the circuit court of Cook County for further proceedings.

Judgments reversed; cause remanded.

## NOTES AND QUESTIONS

**1.** On remand, after an eight-month bench trial, the defendants were acquitted on the charges of aggravated battery, reckless conduct, and conspiracy. The court found that the defendants knew of the hazardous substances in the plant and the poor working conditions, but the state failed to prove beyond a reasonable doubt that workers' ailments were caused by conditions at the plant. The court also found inadequate evidence of reckless conduct or conspiracy.

**2.** What relevance, if any, is the fact that § 17(e) of the Occupational Safety and Health Act provides for criminal fines and imprisonment for any employer whose willful violation of the Act results in the death of an employee?

**3.** What are the policy considerations behind the issue of whether state criminal prosecutions are preempted? Are the purposes behind OSHA enforcement and criminal prosecutions the same? *Chicago Magnet* represents the majority rule that state criminal prosecutions are not preempted by OSHA. See, e.g., People v. Hegedus, 443 N.W.2d 127 (Mich.1989); People v. Pymm Thermometer Corp., 563 N.E.2d 1 (N.Y. 1990). See generally Kathleen F. Brickey, Death in the Workplace: Corporate Liability for Criminal Homicide, 2 Notre Dame J.L., Ethics & Pub. Pol'y (1987); Note, Getting Away with Murder: Federal OSHA Preemption of State Criminal Prosecutions for Industrial Accidents, 101 Harv.L.Rev. 534 (1987).

**4.**   There is an unmistakable irony surrounding the issue of OSHA pre-emption.  The federal law was enacted in large part because state efforts to protect employee safety and health were viewed as largely inadequate. State criminal prosecutions now are being brought in large part because of a perceived laxity in federal OSHA enforcement efforts.

## Gade v. National Solid Wastes Management Association

505 U.S. 88 (1992).

■ JUSTICE O'CONNOR announced the judgment of the Court and delivered an opinion, Parts I, III, and IV of which represent the views of the Court, and Part II of which is joined by THE CHIEF JUSTICE, JUSTICE WHITE, and JUSTICE SCALIA.

In 1988, the Illinois General Assembly enacted the Hazardous Waste Crane and Hoisting Equipment Operators Licensing Act, Ill.Rev.Stat., ch. 111, ¶¶ 7701–7717 (1989), and the Hazardous Waste Laborers Licensing Act, Ill.Rev.Stat., ch. 111, ¶¶ 7801–7815 (1989) (together, licensing acts). The stated purpose of the acts is both "to promote job safety" and "to protect life, limb and property."  In this case, we consider whether these "dual impact" statutes, which protect both workers and the general public, are pre-empted by the federal Occupational Safety and Health Act of 1970, 84 Stat. 1590, 29 U.S.C. § 651 et seq. (OSH Act), and the standards promulgated thereunder by the Occupational Safety and Health Administration (OSHA).

I.

The OSH Act authorizes the Secretary of Labor to promulgate federal occupational safety and health standards.  In the Superfund Amendments and Reauthorization Act of 1986 (SARA), Congress directed the Secretary of Labor to "promulgate standards for the health and safety protection of employees engaged in hazardous waste operations" pursuant to her author-ity under the OSH Act.  SARA, Pub.L. 99–499, Title I, § 126, 100 Stat. 1690–1692, codified at note following 29 U.S.C. § 655.  In relevant part, SARA requires the Secretary to establish standards for the initial and routine training of workers who handle hazardous wastes.

In response to this congressional directive, OSHA, to which the Secre-tary has delegated certain of her statutory responsibilities, promulgated regulations on "Hazardous Waste Operations and Emergency Response," including detailed regulations on worker training requirements.  51 Fed. Reg. 45654, 45665–45666 (1986) (interim regulations); 54 Fed.Reg. 9294, 9320–9321 (1989) (final regulations), codified at 29 CFR § 1910.120 (1991). The OSHA regulations require, among other things, that workers engaged in an activity that may expose them to hazardous wastes receive a mini-mum of 40 hours of instruction off the site, and a minimum of three days actual field experience under the supervision of a trained supervisor. Workers who are on the site only occasionally or who are working in areas that have been determined to be under the permissible exposure limits must complete at least 24 hours of off-site instruction and one day of actual field experience.  On-site managers and supervisors directly responsible for hazardous waste operations must receive the same initial training as general employees, plus at least eight additional hours of specialized training on various health and safety programs.  Employees and supervisors are required to receive eight hours of refresher training annually.  Those who have satisfied the training and field experience requirement receive a written certification; uncertified workers are prohibited from engaging in hazardous waste operations.

In 1988, while OSHA's interim hazardous waste regulations were in effect, the State of Illinois enacted the licensing acts at issue here.  The laws are designated as acts "in relation to environmental protection," and their stated aim is to protect both employees and the general public by licensing hazardous waste equipment operators and laborers working at certain facilities.  Both acts require a license applicant to provide a certified record of at least 40 hours of training under an approved program conducted within Illinois, to pass a written examination, and to complete an annual refresher course of at least eight hours of instruction.  In addition, applicants for a hazardous waste crane operator's license must submit "a certified record showing operation of equipment used in hazardous waste handling for a minimum of 4,000 hours."  Employees who work without the proper license, and employers who knowingly permit an unlicensed employee to work, are subject to escalating fines for each offense.

The respondent in this case, National Solid Waste Management Association (the Association), is a national trade association of businesses that remove, transport, dispose, and handle waste material, including hazardous waste.  The Association's members are subject to the OSH Act and OSHA regulations, and are therefore required to train, qualify, and certify their hazardous waste remediation workers.  For hazardous waste operations conducted in Illinois, certain of the workers employed by the Association's members are also required to obtain licenses pursuant to the Illinois licensing acts.  Thus, for example, some of the Association's members must ensure that their employees receive not only the three days of field experience required for certification under the OSHA regulations, but also the 500 days of experience (4,000 hours) required for licensing under the state statutes.

Shortly before the state licensing acts were due to go into effect, the Association brought a declaratory judgment action in United States District Court against Bernard Killian, the former Director of the Illinois Environmental Protection Agency (IEPA); petitioner Mary Gade is Killian's successor in office and has been substituted as a party pursuant to this Court's Rule 35.3.  The Association sought to enjoin IEPA from enforcing the Illinois licensing acts, claiming that the acts were pre-empted by the OSH Act and OSHA regulations and that they violated the Commerce Clause of the United States Constitution.  The District Court held that state laws that attempt to regulate workplace safety and health are not pre-empted by the OSH Act when the laws have a "legitimate and substantial purpose apart from promoting job safety." Applying this standard, the District Court held that the Illinois licensing acts were not preempted because each protected public safety in addition to promoting job safety. The court indicated that it would uphold a state regulation implementing the 4000–hour experience requirement, as long as it did not conflict with federal regulations, because it was reasonable to conclude that workers who satisfy the requirement "will be better skilled than those who do not; and better skilled means fewer accidents, which equals less risk to public safety and the environment." At the same time, the District Court invalidated the requirement that applicants for a hazardous waste license be trained "within Illinois" on the ground that the provision did not contribute to Illinois's stated purpose of protecting public safety. The court declined to consider the Association's Commerce Clause challenge for lack of ripeness.

On appeal, the United States Court of Appeals for the Seventh Circuit affirmed in part and reversed in part. National Solid Wastes Management Assn. v. Killian, 918 F.2d 671 (1990). The Court of Appeals held that the OSH Act pre-empts all state law that "constitutes, in a direct, clear and substantial way, regulation of worker health and safety," unless the Secretary has explicitly approved the state law. Because many of the regulations mandated by the Illinois licensing acts had not yet reached their final form, the Court of Appeals remanded the case to the District Court without considering which, if any, of the Illinois provisions would be pre-empted. The court made clear, however, its view that Illinois "cannot regulate worker health and safety under the guise of environmental regulation," and it rejected the District Court's conclusion that the State's 4000–hour experience requirement could survive pre-emption simply because the rule might also enhance public health and safety. Writing separately, Judge Easterbrook expressed doubt that the OSH Act pre-empts nonconflicting state laws. He concluded, however, that if the OSH Act does pre-empt state law, the majority had employed an appropriate test for determining whether the Illinois acts were superseded.

\* \* \*

## II.

In the OSH Act, Congress endeavored "to assure so far as possible every working man and woman in the Nation safe and healthful working conditions." To that end, Congress authorized the Secretary of Labor to set mandatory occupational safety and health standards applicable to all businesses affecting interstate commerce, and thereby brought the Federal Government into a field that traditionally had been occupied by the States. Federal regulation of the workplace was not intended to be all-encompassing, however. First, Congress expressly saved two areas from federal pre-emption. Section 4(b)(4) of the OSH Act states that the Act does not "supersede or in any manner affect any workmen's compensation law or \* \* \* enlarge or diminish or affect in any other manner the common law or statutory rights, duties, or liabilities of employers and employees under any law with respect to injuries, diseases, or death of employees arising out of, or in the course of, employment." Section 18(a) provides that the Act does not "prevent any State agency or court from asserting jurisdiction under State law over any occupational safety or health issue with respect to which no [federal] standard is in effect."

Congress not only reserved certain areas to state regulation, but it also, in § 18(b) of the Act, gave the States the option of pre-empting federal regulation entirely. That section provides:

> "Submission of State plan for development and enforcement of State standards to preempt applicable Federal standards.
>
> "Any State which, at any time, desires to assume responsibility for development and enforcement therein of occupational safety and health standards relating to any occupational safety or health issue with respect to which a Federal standard has been promulgated [by the Secretary under the OSH Act] shall submit a State plan for the development of such standards and their enforcement." 29 U.S.C. § 667(b).

About half the States have received the Secretary's approval for their own state plans as described in this provision. Illinois is not among them.

In the decision below, the Court of Appeals held that § 18(b) "unquestionably" pre-empts any state law or regulation that establishes an occupational health and safety standard on an issue for which OSHA has already promulgated a standard, unless the State has obtained the Secretary's approval for its own plan. Every other federal and state court confronted with an OSH Act pre-emption challenge has reached the same conclusion, and so do we.

Pre-emption may be either expressed or implied, and "is compelled whether Congress' command is explicitly stated in the statute's language or implicitly contained in its structure and purpose." Absent explicit pre-emptive language, we have recognized at least two types of implied pre-emption: field pre-emption, where the scheme of federal regulation is " 'so pervasive as to make reasonable the inference that Congress left no room for the States to supplement it,' " and conflict pre-emption, where "compliance with both federal and state regulations is a physical impossibility," or where state law "stands as an obstacle to the accomplishment and execution of the full purposes and objectives of Congress."

Our ultimate task in any pre-emption case is to determine whether state regulation is consistent with the structure and purpose of the statute as a whole. Looking to "the provisions of the whole law, and to its object and policy," we hold that nonapproved state regulation of occupational safety and health issues for which a federal standard is in effect is impliedly pre-empted as in conflict with the full purposes and objectives of the OSH Act. The design of the statute persuades us that Congress intended to subject employers and employees to only one set of regulations, be it federal or state, and that the only way a State may regulate an OSHA-regulated occupational safety and health issue is pursuant to an approved state plan that displaces the federal standards.

The principal indication that Congress intended to pre-empt state law is § 18(b)'s statement that a State "shall" submit a plan if it wishes to "assume responsibility" for "development and enforcement * * * of occupational safety and health standards relating to any occupational safety or health issue with respect to which a Federal standard has been promulgated." The unavoidable implication of this provision is that a State may not enforce its own occupational safety and health standards without obtaining the Secretary's approval, and petitioner concedes that § 18(b) would require an approved plan if Illinois wanted to "assume responsibility" for the regulation of occupational safety and health within the State. Petitioner contends, however, that an approved plan is necessary only if the State wishes completely to replace the federal regulations, not merely to supplement them. She argues that the correct interpretation of § 18(b) is that posited by Judge Easterbrook below: i.e., a State may either "oust" the federal standard by submitting a state plan to the Secretary for approval or "add to" the federal standard without seeking the Secretary's approval.

Petitioner's interpretation of § 18(b) might be plausible were we to interpret that provision in isolation, but it simply is not tenable in light of the OSH Act's surrounding provisions. "[W]e must not be guided by a single sentence or member of a sentence, but look to the provisions of the whole law." The OSH Act as a whole evidences Congress' intent to avoid subjecting workers and employers to duplicative regulation; a State may develop an occupational safety and health program tailored to its own needs, but only if it is willing completely to displace the applicable federal regulations.

Cutting against petitioner's interpretation of § 18(b) is the language of § 18(a), which saves from pre-emption any state law regulating an occupational safety and health issue with respect to which no federal standard is in effect. Although this is a saving clause, not a pre-emption clause, the natural implication of this provision is that state laws regulating the same issue as federal laws are not saved, even if they merely supplement the federal standard. Moreover, if petitioner's reading of § 18(b) were correct, and if a State were free to enact nonconflicting safety and health regulations, then § 18(a) would be superfluous: there is no possibility of conflict where there is no federal regulation. Because "[i]t is our duty 'to give effect, if possible, to every clause and word of a statute,' " we conclude that § 18(a)'s preservation of state authority in the absence of a federal standard presupposes a background pre-emption of all state occupational safety and health standards whenever a federal standard governing the same issue is in effect.

Our understanding of the implications of § 18(b) is likewise bolstered by § 18(c) of the Act, which sets forth the conditions that must be satisfied before the Secretary can approve a plan submitted by a State under subsection (b). State standards that affect interstate commerce will be approved only if they "are required by compelling local conditions" and "do not unduly burden interstate commerce." If a State could supplement federal regulations without undergoing the § 18(b) approval process, then the protections that § 18(c) offers to interstate commerce would easily be undercut. It would make little sense to impose such a condition on state programs intended to supplant federal regulation and not those that merely supplement it: the burden on interstate commerce remains the same.

Section 18(f) also confirms our view that States are not permitted to assume an enforcement role without the Secretary's approval, unless no federal standard is in effect. That provision gives the Secretary the authority to withdraw her approval of a state plan. Once approval is withdrawn, the plan "cease[s] to be in effect" and the State is permitted to assert jurisdiction under its occupational health and safety law only for those cases "commenced before the withdrawal of the plan." Under petitioner's reading of § 18(b), § 18(f) should permit the continued exercise of state jurisdiction over purely "supplemental" and nonconflicting standards. Instead, § 18(f) assumes that the State loses the power to enforce all of its occupational safety and health standards once approval is withdrawn.

The same assumption of exclusive federal jurisdiction in the absence of an approved state plan is apparent in the transitional provisions contained in § 18(h) of the Act. Section 18(h) authorized the Secretary of Labor, during the first two years after passage of the Act, to enter into an agreement with a State by which the State would be permitted to continue to enforce its own occupational health and safety standards for two years or until final action was taken by the Secretary pursuant to § 18(b), whichever was earlier. Significantly, § 18(h) does not say that such an agreement is only necessary when the State wishes fully to supplant federal standards. Indeed, the original Senate version of the provision would have allowed a State to enter into such an agreement only when it wished to enforce standards "not in conflict with Federal occupational health and safety standards," a category which included "any State occupational health and safety standard which provides for more stringent health and safety regulations than do the Federal standards." Although that provision was eliminated from the final draft of the bill, thereby allowing agreements for the temporary enforcement of less stringent state standards, it is indicative of the congressional understanding that a State was required to enter into a transitional agreement even when its standards were stricter than federal standards. The Secretary's contemporaneous interpretation of § 18(h) also expresses that understanding.

Looking at the provisions of § 18 as a whole, we conclude that the OSH Act precludes any state regulation of an occupational safety or health issue with respect to which a federal standard has been established, unless a state plan has been submitted and approved pursuant to § 18(b). Our review of the Act persuades us that Congress sought to promote occupational safety and health while at the same time avoiding duplicative, and possibly counter-productive, regulation. It thus established a system of uniform federal occupational health and safety standards, but gave States the option of pre-empting federal regulations by developing their own occupational safety and health programs. In addition, Congress offered the States substantial federal grant monies to assist them in developing their own programs. To allow a State selectively to "supplement" certain federal regulations with ostensibly nonconflicting standards would be inconsistent with this federal scheme of establishing uniform federal standards, on the one hand, and encouraging States to assume full responsibility for development and enforcement of their own OSH programs, on the other.

We cannot accept petitioner's argument that the OSH Act does not pre-empt nonconflicting state laws because those laws, like the Act, are designed to promote worker safety. In determining whether state law "stands as an obstacle" to the full implementation of a federal law, "it is not enough to say that the ultimate goal of both federal and state law" is the same. "A state law also is pre-empted if it interferes with the methods by which the federal statute was designed to reach th[at] goal." The OSH Act does not foreclose a State from enacting its own laws to advance the goal of worker safety, but it does restrict the ways in which it can do so. If a State wishes to regulate an issue of worker safety for which a federal standard is in effect, its only option is to obtain the prior approval of the Secretary of Labor, as described in § 18 of the Act.

### III.

Petitioner next argues that, even if Congress intended to pre-empt all nonapproved state occupational safety and health regulations whenever a federal standard is in effect, the OSH Act's pre-emptive effect should not be extended to state laws that address public safety as well as occupational safety concerns. As we explained in Part II, we understand § 18(b) to mean that the OSH Act pre-empts all state "occupational safety and health standards relating to any occupational safety or health issue with respect to which a Federal standard has been promulgated." We now consider whether a dual impact law can be an "occupational safety and health standard" subject to pre-emption under the Act.

The OSH Act defines an "occupational safety and health standard" as "a standard which requires conditions, or the adoption or use of one or more practices, means, methods, operations, or processes, reasonably necessary or appropriate to provide safe or healthful employment and places of employment." Any state law requirement designed to promote health and safety in the workplace falls neatly within the Act's definition of an "occupational safety and health standard." Clearly, under this definition, a state law that expressly declares a legislative purpose of regulating occupational health and safety would, in the absence of an approved state plan, be pre-empted by an OSHA standard regulating the same subject matter. But petitioner asserts that if the state legislature articulates a purpose other than (or in addition to) workplace health and safety, then the OSH Act loses its pre-emptive force. We disagree.

Although "part of the pre-empted field is defined by reference to the purpose of the state law in question, * * * another part of the field is defined by the state law's actual effect." English v. General Electric Co., 496 U.S. 72, 84 (1990). In assessing the impact of a state law on the federal scheme, we have refused to rely solely on the legislature's professed purpose and have looked as well to the effects of the law.

\* \* \*

Our precedents leave no doubt that a dual impact state regulation cannot avoid OSH Act pre-emption simply because the regulation serves several objectives rather than one. As the Court of Appeals observed, "[i]t would defeat the purpose of section 18 if a state could enact measures stricter than OSHA's and largely accomplished through regulation of worker health and safety simply by asserting a non-occupational purpose for the legislation." Whatever the purpose or purposes of the state law, pre-emption analysis cannot ignore the effect of the challenged state action on the pre-empted field. The key question is thus at what point the state regulation sufficiently interferes with federal regulation that it should be deemed pre-empted under the Act.

In *English* we held that a state tort claim brought by an employee of a nuclear-fuels production facility against her employer was not pre-empted by a federal whistle-blower provision because the state law did not have a "direct and substantial effect" on the federal scheme. In the decision below, the Court of Appeals relied on *English* to hold that, in the absence of the approval of the Secretary, the OSH Act pre-empts all state law that "constitutes, in a direct, clear and substantial way, regulation of worker health and safety." We agree that this is the appropriate standard for determining OSH Act pre-emption. On the other hand, state laws of general applicability (such as laws regarding traffic safety or fire safety) that do not conflict with OSHA standards and that regulate the conduct of workers and non-workers alike would generally not be pre-empted. Although some laws of general applicability may have a "direct and substantial" effect on worker safety, they cannot fairly be characterized as "occupational" standards, because they regulate workers simply as members of the general public. In this case, we agree with the court below that a law directed at workplace safety is not saved from pre-emption simply because the State can demonstrate some additional effect outside of the workplace.

In sum, a state law requirement that directly, substantially, and specifically regulates occupational safety and health is an occupational safety and health standard within the meaning of the Act. That such a law may also have a nonoccupational impact does not render it any less of an occupational standard for purposes of pre-emption analysis. If the State wishes to enact a dual impact law that regulates an occupational safety or health issue for which a federal standard is in effect, § 18 of the Act requires that the State submit a plan for the approval of the Secretary.

## IV.

We recognize that "the States have a compelling interest in the practice of professions within their boundaries, and that as part of their power to protect the public health, safety, and other valid interests they have broad power to establish standards for licensing practitioners and regulating the practice of professions." But under the Supremacy Clause, from which our pre-emption doctrine is derived, "any state law, however clearly within a State's acknowledged power, which interferes with or is contrary to federal law, must yield." We therefore reject petitioner's argument that the State's interest in licensing various occupations can save from OSH Act pre-emption those provisions that directly and substantially affect workplace safety.

We also reject petitioner's argument that the Illinois acts do not regulate occupational safety and health at all, but are instead a "pre-condition" to employment. By that reasoning, the OSHA regulations themselves would not be considered occupational standards. SARA, however, makes clear that the training of employees engaged in hazardous waste operations is an occupational safety and health issue, and that certification requirements before an employee may engage in such work are occupational safety and health standards. Because neither of the OSH Act's saving provisions are implicated, and because Illinois does not have an approved state plan under § 18(b), the state licensing acts are preempted by the OSH Act to the extent they establish occupational safety and health standards for training those who work with hazardous wastes. Like the Court of Appeals, we do not specifically consider which of the licensing acts' provisions will stand or fall under the pre-emption analysis set forth above.

The judgment of the Court of Appeals is hereby

*Affirmed.*

■ JUSTICE KENNEDY, concurring in part and concurring in the judgment.

\* \* \*

I do not believe that supplementary state regulation of an occupational safety and health issue can be said to create the sort of actual conflict required by our decisions. The purpose of state supplementary regulation, like the federal standards promulgated by the Occupational Safety and Health Administration (OSHA) is to protect worker safety and health. Any potential tension between a scheme of federal regulation of the workplace and a concurrent, supplementary state scheme would not, in my view, rise to the level of "actual conflict" described in our pre-emption cases. Absent the express provisions of § 18 of the Occupational Safety and Health Act of 1970 (OSH), 29 U.S.C. § 667, I would not say that state supplementary regulation conflicts with the purposes of the OSH Act, or that it "interferes with the methods by which the federal statute was designed to reach [its] goal."

\* \* \*

■ JUSTICE SOUTER, with whom JUSTICE BLACKMUN, JUSTICE STEVENS, and JUSTICE THOMAS join, dissenting.

\* \* \*

## IV.

In sum, our rule is that the traditional police powers of the State survive unless Congress has made a purpose to pre-empt them clear. The Act does not, in so many words, pre-empt all state regulation of issues on which federal standards have been promulgated, and respondent's contention at oral argument that reading subsections (a), (b), and (h) could leave no other "logical" conclusion but one of pre-emption is wrong. Each provision can be read consistently with the others without any implication of pre-emptive intent. They are in fact just as consistent with a purpose and objective to permit overlapping state and federal regulation as with one to guarantee that employers and employees would be subjected to only one regulatory regime. Restriction to one such regime by precluding supplemental state regulation might or might not be desirable. But in the absence of any clear expression of congressional intent to pre-empt, I can only conclude that, as long as compliance with federally promulgated standards does not render obedience to Illinois' regulations impossible, the enforcement of the state law is not prohibited by the Supremacy Clause. I respectfully dissent.

NOTES AND QUESTIONS

**1.** In *Gade,* the Court, in effect, overruled several lower court decisions which had construed the preemptive effect of § 18 much more narrowly. See, e.g., Associated Industries v. Snow, 898 F.2d 274 (1st Cir.1990); New Jersey State Chamber of Commerce v. Hughey, 774 F.2d 587 (3d Cir.1985).

**2.** Reconsider the *Diehl* case (p. 682). Based on *Gade,* would a state law regulating the housing (and perhaps other) conditions of migrant farm workers be preempted under OSHA? Would such a result be consistent with the congressional intent underlying OSHA?

**3.** In Industrial Truck Association, Inc. v. Henry, 125 F.3d 1305 (9th Cir.1997), the Ninth Circuit held that, based on *Gade,* the occupational safety regulations implemented as part of Proposition 65, the California Safe Drinking Water and Toxic Enforcement Act, were preempted.

## B. PROMULGATION OF STANDARDS

The Occupational Safety and Health Act does not describe the specific hazards to be regulated or the methods to reduce or eliminate the hazards. The responsibility for all rulemaking activity was delegated to the Secretary of Labor (and the administrator of OSHA). OSHA standards may be promulgated in three ways: (a) from 1971 to 1973, OSHA was empowered to adopt existing standards under other federal laws and privately developed standards; (b) OSHA can promulgate new standards or revise or revoke existing OSHA standards by following the rulemaking procedures set out in § 6(b); and (c) OSHA can promulgate emergency standards in accordance with § 6(c).

Numerous technical, policy, and legal issues have arisen under each of the rulemaking methods.   Under § 6(a), there have been questions of the applicability or scope of standards and the interpretation of vague language.   Under § 6(b), there have been questions about the certainty and severity of the risk needed to justify regulation, the adequacy of the evidence about the benefits to be achieved by the standards, and the economic and technological feasibility of the standards.   Under § 6(c), the question most commonly put has been whether an emergency temporary standard is needed to alleviate a "grave danger."

## 1.   INITIAL STANDARDS

### Mark A. Rothstein, *OSHA After Ten Years: A Review and Some Proposed Reforms*

34 Vand.L.Rev. 71 (1981).

Under section 6(a) of the Act the Secretary of Labor was initially authorized to adopt, as the agency's own regulations governing workplace conditions, "national consensus standards" [7] and "established federal standards" [8] without having first to comply with the lengthy rulemaking procedures of either section 6(b) or the Administrative Procedure Act. This special authority, which expired after two years, was included in the Act to assure that workers would be protected as soon as possible after the statute's effective date.   Because they were adopted without the burden of rulemaking procedures, the standards did provide immediate coverage to millions of employees across the nation.   Unfortunately, because the standards were adopted so quickly, they became the source of numerous problems and legal controversies.   This was especially true for the national consensus standards.

Most of the difficulties with national consensus standards can be traced to the fact that they were privately adopted, optional measures. Many of the standards were poorly drafted, extremely general, vague, redundant, contradictory, or hopelessly outdated.   The requirements were usually couched as specification standards [14] rather than as more flexible

---

**7.**  29 U.S.C. § 652(9) (1976) defines "national consensus standard" as follows:

The term "national consensus standard" means any occupational safety and health standard or modification thereof which (1), has been adopted and promulgated by a nationally recognized standards-producing organization under procedures whereby it can be determined by the Secretary that persons interested and affected by the scope of provisions of the standard have reached substantial agreement on its adoption, (2) was formulated in a manner which afforded an opportunity for diverse views to be considered and (3) has been designated as

such a standard by the Secretary, after consultation with other appropriate Federal agencies.

**8.**  29 U.S.C. § 652(10) (1976) defines "established federal standard" as follows:

The term "established Federal standard" means any operative occupational safety and health standard established by any agency of the United States and presently in effect, or contained in any Act of Congress in force on December 29, 1970.

**14.**  E.g., Ladder rungs must be made of wood and must be one inch in diameter.

performance standards.[15] Other standards were advisory, directory, or precatory and were never intended to be given binding effect.

In its haste to promulgate an initial standards package, OSHA did not review the standards carefully.[16] Consequently, some of the national consensus standards adopted under section 6(a) were trivial, outdated, and even ludicrous. For example, two of the more notorious standards adopted by OSHA were a prohibition on the use of ice in drinking water [17] and a requirement that all workplace toilet seats be "open-front." [18] Although these and similar questionable standards were not zealously enforced, they were the source of embarrassment to OSHA and contributed greatly to the Agency's developing image of over-enforcement of the Act and of nitpicking.

## Usery v. Kennecott Copper Corp.

577 F.2d 1113 (10th Cir.1977).

■ BARRETT, CIRCUIT JUDGE.

The Secretary of Labor (Secretary) petitions for review of an order of the Occupational Safety and Health Review Commission (Commission), which vacated an administrative law judge's decision that Kennecott Copper Company (Kennecott) had violated certain OSHA regulations. In reversing the decision of the administrative law judge, a divided Commission found that Kennecott had not failed to comply with occupational health and safety standards promulgated by the Secretary. Jurisdiction for review is derived from 29 U.S.C. § 660(b) of the Occupational Safety and Health Act (the Act).

The facts are basically undisputed. Kennecott, a large mineral mining and processing concern, employs some 1200 persons at its Magna, Utah, smelting plant. In addition to smelting copper ore at its Magna plant, Kennecott captures the fumes produced in the smelting process and, by passing them through "mist treaters," produces sulphuric acid. The "mist treaters," which are large cylindrical vats, several stories high, encircled by protruding horizontal ribs, occasionally spring leaks. When such difficul-

---

**15.** E.g., Ladder rungs must be capable of supporting 500 pounds.

**16.** On May 29, 1971, only a month and a day after the effective date of the Act, OSHA published its initial standards package. 36 Fed.Reg. 10,466–714 (1971). This package consisted of both national consensus standards—derived from the American National Standards Institute (ANSI) and the National Fire Protection Association (NFPA)—and established federal standards—based on the Walsh-Healey Act, 41 U.S.C. §§ 35–45 (1976); Service Contract Act, 41 U.S.C. §§ 351–357 (1976); Construction

Safety Act, 40 U.S.C. §§ 327–333 (1976); National Foundation on the Arts and Humanities Act, 20 U.S.C. §§ 951–953 (1976); and Longshoremen's and Harbor Workers' Compensation Act, 33 U.S.C. §§ 901–950 (1976).

**17.** 29 C.F.R. § 1910.141(b)(1)(iii) (1972), revised, 38 Fed.Reg. 10,932 (1973). The standard was directed at the nineteenth century practice of obtaining and storing ice cut from rivers and lakes that might be polluted.

**18.** 29 C.F.R. § 1910.141(c)(3)(iii) (1972), revised, 38 Fed.Reg. 10,933 (1973).

ties occur, skilled workmen, known as "leadburners," repair the leaks by standing on temporary scaffolds in order to reach the troublesome areas.

The citations issued against Kennecott grew out of an accident which occurred at the Magna plant in November of 1974.   Nick Laboa, a highly skilled and experienced "leadburner," constructed a makeshift scaffold to reach a leak 10 to 11 feet above the ground.   He took a six-foot long wooden plank with cleats in both ends and hooked it onto an angle-iron bracket attached to the inside of one of the "mist treaters."   There were no guard rails or toeboards on this scaffold and he did not use a ladder in order to gain access to the scaffold.   While either working on the scaffold or ascending to it, he fell.

After a routine investigation of the accident by a representative of the Secretary, Kennecott was cited for failing to comply with OSHA regulations relating to scaffolds:

> He had not been furnished with a scaffold which was erected in accordance with the promulgated standards.   The scaffold he used, which was approximately 11 feet 10 inches above the floor, was not provided with guardrails installed on the open side and across the two ends of the scaffold platform.

Further, Kennecott was cited for not providing a ladder for Laboa to use in gaining access to the scaffold:

> In addition, the employee gained access to the scaffold by unsafe means in that a ladder or equivalent safe access had not been provided.

Kennecott filed notice of intent to contest the citations and proposed penalty.   Following a hearing, the administrative law judge found that Kennecott had violated the Act by failing to comply with occupational safety and health standards.   He fined Kennecott $350.   The judge specifically found that standards requiring guardrails on scaffolds had been properly promulgated and that Kennecott should have required the use of access ladders when its employees were ascending to scaffolds.

Kennecott appealed to the Commission, which reversed the judge's decision.   In exonerating Kennecott, the Commission ruled that Kennecott had not violated the regulation requiring the use of guardrails on scaffolds because the regulation had been improperly promulgated and was, therefore, not binding on Kennecott.   The Commission also found that Kennecott had not violated the regulation dealing with providing access ladders.

In petitioning for review, the Secretary contends that:  (1) the Commission erroneously declared that the regulation dealing with guardrails was unenforceable because of improper promulgation and (2) the Commission erred in concluding that Kennecott had satisfied its OSHA obligations by providing its employees scaffold access ladders without requiring their use.

The Act was passed in 1970 to "assure so far as possible every working man and woman in the Nation safe and healthful working conditions."   To effect this objective the Secretary of Labor was empowered to promulgate mandatory occupational safety and health standards which would be applicable to any "person engaged in a business affecting commerce who has employees." In order to ensure that the Secretary would be able to swiftly promulgate safety and health standards, Congress empowered him to adopt existing industry standards for the first two years following enactment of the Act. These standards, known as "national consensus standards," could be promulgated by the Secretary without any rulemaking procedures if they:

> * * * had been adopted and promulgated by a nationally recognized standards-producing organization under procedures whereby it can be determined by the Secretary that persons interested and affected by the scope of provisions of the standard have reached substantial agreement on its adoption.

After the two year period allowed for promulgation of these interim standards any new standards or modification or revocation of standards could be enacted only by following the formal rulemaking procedure outlined in the Act.

## I.

The first citation charged Kennecott with failing to comply with a standard mandating the use of guardrails and toeboards in scaffolds:

> Guardrails and toeboards *shall* be installed on all open sides and ends of platforms more than 10 feet above the ground or floor. (Emphasis supplied.)

> 29 CFR 1910.28(a)(3).

This regulation was promulgated shortly after passage of the Act. Accordingly, the Secretary was not required to follow the Act's rulemaking procedures.

The Commission found that there had been no violation of this regulation by Kennecott because it had not been promulgated in accordance with the provisions of the Act and was, therefore, unenforceable. As noted above, the Secretary was granted broad powers to adopt necessary standards during the first two years of the Act's life so that safer working conditions would be provided American employees in a short time. In preparing the interim safety standards for scaffolds, the Secretary turned to standards which had been formulated by the American National Standards Institute (ANSI), which read:

> Guardrails and toeboards *should* be installed on all open sides and ends of platforms more than 10 feet above the ground or floor. (Emphasis supplied.) (*American National Standard Safety Requirements for Scaffolding*, American National Standards Institute, 1969, p. 9.)

In promulgating this standard the Secretary changed the language concerning guardrails on scaffolds so that it assumed a mandatory, rather than advisory, character:

Mandatory rules of this standard are characterized by the word *shall*. If a rule is of an advisory nature it is indicated by the word *should* or is stated as a recommendation. (Ibid, p. 7.)

It is the Secretary's adoption of the regulation by use of the word *shall* rather than the word *should* which poses the problem presented here. We must determine whether this usage constitutes such a substantial change that the regulation is not to be considered as a national consensus standard.

The Secretary contends that the change from *should* to *shall* is not significant, in that it is simply a pro forma change, having no substantive effect on the regulation. The Secretary points to the statute which requires an employer to follow health and safety standards promulgated by the Secretary:

Each employer shall comply with occupational safety and health standards promulgated under this chapter.

29 U.S.C. § 654(a)(2).

Because of the mandatory nature of the standards under the Act, the Secretary asserts that the substitution of mandatory for advisory language in the adoption of the guardrails and toeboards interim standards was valid. The Secretary argues that if the standards are to be complied with, it makes no difference whether the actual language is advisory or mandatory.

Employers are, of course, required to comply with standards properly established by the Secretary. The Act accords its special interim treatment exclusively to "any national consensus standard and any established Federal standard." The usual procedural due process safeguards accorded to persons who might be adversely affected by government regulations were relaxed only to the extent that standards, which had already been scrutinized and recognized by those to be affected and upon which there existed substantial agreement, would be considered acceptable for adoption as "national consensus standards." If, however, standards which were to be adopted during the two year interim involved modifications of established standards, then a formalized procedure had to be followed. This procedure included: recommendations to the Secretary from an advisory committee, publication of a proposed rule in the Federal Register, allowance of time for comments from interested persons, and public hearing if objections are raised. These procedures are designed to provide those who might be affected the opportunity to acquaint themselves with the proposed rule and to voice any possible opposition thereto. These procedural due process requisites have long been recognized as part of our system of jurisprudence.

We hold that the Secretary did not comply with the statute by reason of his failure to adopt the ANSI standard verbatim or by failure to follow the appropriate due process procedure. The promulgation of the standard with the use of *shall* rather than *should* did not constitute the adoption of a national consensus standard. It is, therefore, unenforceable. In order for the Secretary to have rendered the standard enforceable with the change in language, he was obliged to observe the rulemaking procedures contained in the Act. Administrative regulations are not absolute rules of law and should not be followed when they conflict with the design of the statute or exceed the administrative authority granted.

The Commission, in a decision which posed the same issue as that before us here, articulated the view that only standards which are national consensus standards are valid.

Further, we observe that the Secretary has recognized that only mandatory standards should be seen as national consensus standards:

> The national consensus standards contain only mandatory provisions of the standards promulgated by those two organizations. [ANSI and National Fire Protection Association.] The standards of ANSI and NFPA may also contain advisory provisions and recommendations the adoption of which by employers is encouraged, but they are not adopted in Part 1910.

> Fed.Register 36 No. 165, p. 10466.

We hold that the Secretary improperly promulgated the standard dealing with mandatory guardrails. We affirm the decision of the Commission that Kennecott could not be held to be in violation of an unenforceable standard.

## II.

Kennecott was also charged with violating an OSHA standard which required that when workers were on scaffolds, "An access ladder or equivalent safe access shall be provided." In holding that Kennecott had not violated this regulation, the Commission interpreted "provided" as being synonymous with "made available."

The Secretary contends that this interpretation is incorrect because it is in derogation of the underlying purpose of the Act. The Secretary maintains that the Commission erred in finding that Kennecott had complied with this regulation by simply providing its employees scaffold access ladders without *requiring* that they use them.

There is undisputed testimony that ladders were available to Kennecott's employees. It was also shown that some of the "leadburners" did not use them when ascending to their scaffolds and that Kennecott did not insist that such workers use the ladders for access to the scaffolds.

We hold that the Secretary's interpretation of the regulation is erroneous. Kennecott did comply with the regulation by providing ladders. It was not the purpose of the Act to make an employer the insurer of his employees' safety. The ultimate aim of the act was not to prevent all accidents, but to provide American employees with safe and healthful working conditions "so far as possible." Certainly the Act requires employers to be diligent in protecting the health and safety of its employees; however, it does not hold the employer responsible for the prevention of all accidents. In addition, the act does impose some responsibility for their safety on the employees, for "Each employee shall comply with occupational safety and health standards."

We do not agree that the Secretary may read "shall be provided" to mean "shall require use." In interpreting regulations, one must look at the plain meaning of the words used. The meaning usually attributed to the word provide is to furnish, supply or make available.

If the Secretary had determined to require that employees use ladders, he could have done so only by complying with the rulemaking procedure outlined in the Act. He did not do so. Accordingly, Kennecott was not required to assume the burden of guessing what the Secretary intended plain and unambiguous words employed in the safety regulations to mean. This is especially true when violation of a regulation subjects one to criminal or civil sanctions. A regulation cannot be construed to mean what an agency intended but did not adequately express. If the Secretary were to be permitted to interpret regulations by employing the unusual meaning of words, employers would be deprived of fair notice of that which is expected of them in violation of their due process rights.

\* \* \*

Kennecott did not violate the regulation. We affirm the Commission's decision. The relief prayed for is denied. We direct enforcement of the Commission Order.

## NOTES AND QUESTIONS

**1.** In 1984, OSHA revoked 153 "should" standards. Thus far, no efforts have been made to make any "should" standards mandatory.

**2.** The Commission has followed the Tenth Circuit's view that "provide" does not mean "require the use of." Pratt & Whitney Aircraft Group, 12 OSHC 1770, 1986 OSHD ¶ 27,564 (1986), affirmed, 805 F.2d 391 (2d Cir.1986).

**3.** On the effective date of OSHA the Secretary had two federal standards on chlorine exposure. A standard developed by the American Conference of Governmental Industrial Hygienists (ACGIH) and adopted by the Secretary in 1969 under the Walsh-Healey Act set a ceiling limit of one part per million (ppm). A second standard, adopted under the Construction Safety Act (CSA) in 1970, provided for a time-weighted average (TWA) of one ppm. It was not clear which of these established federal standards was adopted by OSHA and, in fact, it appears that both of them were adopted. This error was not discovered until December, 1978, when OSHA announced that the standard had been revised and that the more stringent ACGIH standard applied. In correcting the standard the Secretary did not use § 6(b) rulemaking procedures. Is the standard valid? See Chlorine Institute, Inc. v. OSHA, 613 F.2d 120 (5th Cir.1980), cert. denied, 449 U.S. 826 (1980) (held: yes).

**4.** The most troubling part of the § 6(a) standards controversy is that the § 6(a) health standards are not automatically updated. There are about 450 health standards adopted in 1971 as established federal standards which are based on 1968 American Conference of Governmental Industrial Hygienists (ACGIH) threshold limit values (TLVs). The standards set exposure levels, but do not require medical examinations, biological monitoring, or other compliance measures. The ACGIH revises its TLVs annually, but OSHA is required to use § 6(b) procedures to revise its standards, and since 1971 OSHA has promulgated only 23 new or revised health standards. As a result, many OSHA standards permitted exposures at levels no longer considered safe by experts. It was not until 1989 that new exposure levels were mandated for 376 substances, virtually all of which were based on the 1987 list of TLVs. See generally Grace E. Ziem & Barry I. Castleman, Threshold Limit Values: Historical Perspectives and Current Practice, 31 J. Occupational Med. 910 (1989).

## 2. NEW STANDARDS

### Industrial Union Department v. American Petroleum Institute (The Benzene Case)

448 U.S. 607 (1980).

[Benzene is a clear, highly flammable liquid hydrocarbon compound that is widely used in industry as a chemical intermediate, component of motor fuels, and solvent. While benzene had long been known to cause death within minutes at very high levels of concentration, studies in the early and mid–1970s demonstrated that lower concentration levels of benzene over an extended period of time caused leukemia.]

[In 1971 OSHA adopted the American National Standards Institute (ANSI) recommendation of a threshold limit value (TLV) of ten ppm After an earlier unsuccessful attempt to promulgate an emergency temporary standard (ETS), on May 27, 1977, OSHA proposed a new standard of one ppm and also called for extensive monitoring, medical examinations, labeling, record-keeping, and other requirements. After a three week hearing featuring 95 witnesses, 1400 comments and exhibits, and a transcript of 3500 pages, on February 3, 1978, OSHA promulgated a permanent standard with an effective date of March 13, 1978. The Fifth Circuit struck down the standard, holding that OSHA failed to prove by substantial evidence that a reduction in the permissible exposure limit (PEL) would result in appreciable benefits. American Petroleum Institute v. OSHA, 581 F.2d 493 (5th Cir.1978).]

■ MR. JUSTICE STEVENS announced the judgment of the Court and delivered an opinion in which THE CHIEF JUSTICE and MR. JUSTICE STEWART join and in Parts of which MR. JUSTICE POWELL joins.

\* \* \*

Our resolution of the issues in this case turns, to a large extent, on the meaning of and the relationship between § 3(8), which defines a health and safety standard as a standard that is "reasonably necessary and appropriate to provide safe or healthful employment," and § 6(b)(5), which directs the Secretary in promulgating a health and safety standard for toxic materials to "set the standard which most adequately assures, to the extent feasible, on the basis of the best available evidence, that no employee will suffer material impairment of health or functional capacity * * *."

In the Government's view, § 3(8)'s definition of the term "standard" has no legal significance or at best merely requires that a standard not be totally irrational. It takes the position that § 6(b)(5) is controlling and that it requires OSHA to promulgate a standard that either gives an absolute assurance of safety for each and every worker or that reduces exposures to the lowest level feasible. The Government interprets "feasible" as meaning technologically achievable at a cost that would not impair the viability of the industries subject to the regulation. The respondent industry representatives, on the other hand, argue that the Court of Appeals was correct in holding that the "reasonably necessary and appropriate" language of § 3(8), along with the feasibility requirement of § 6(b)(5), requires the Agency to quantify both the costs and the benefits of a proposed rule and to conclude that they are roughly commensurate.

In our view, it is not necessary to decide whether either the Government or industry is entirely correct. For we think it is clear that § 3(8) does apply to all permanent standards promulgated under the Act and that it requires the Secretary, before issuing any standard, to determine that it is reasonably necessary and appropriate to remedy a significant risk of material health impairment. Only after the Secretary has made the threshold determination that such a risk exists with respect to a toxic substance, would it be necessary to decide whether § 6(b)(5) requires him to select the most protective standard he can consistent with economic and technological feasibility, or whether, as respondents argue, the benefits of the regulation must be commensurate with the costs of its implementation. Because the Secretary did not make the required threshold finding in this case, we have no occasion to determine whether costs must be weighed against benefits in an appropriate case.

Under the Government's view, § 3(8), if it has any substantive content at all, merely requires OSHA to issue standards that are reasonably calculated to produce a safer or more healthy work environment. Apart from this minimal requirement of rationality, the Government argues that § 3(8) imposes no limits on the Agency's power, and thus would not prevent it from requiring employers to do whatever would be "reasonably necessary" to eliminate all risks of any harm from their workplaces. With respect to toxic substances and harmful physical agents, the Government takes an even more extreme position. Relying on § 6(b)(5)'s direction to set a standard "which most adequately assures * * * that no employee will suffer material impairment of health or functional capacity," the Government contends that the Secretary is required to impose standards that either guarantee workplaces that are free from any risk of material health impairment, however small, or that come as close as possible to doing so without ruining entire industries.

If the purpose of the statute were to eliminate completely and with absolute certainty any risk of serious harm, we would agree that it would be proper for the Secretary to interpret §§ 3(8) and 6(b)(5) in this fashion. But we think it is clear that the statute was not designed to require employers to provide absolutely risk-free workplaces whenever it is technologically feasible to do so, so long as the cost is not great enough to destroy an entire industry. Rather, both the language and structure of the Act, as well as its legislative history, indicate that it was intended to require the elimination, as far as feasible, of significant risks of harm.

By empowering the Secretary to promulgate standards that are "reasonably necessary or appropriate to provide safe or healthful employment and places of employment," the Act implies that, before promulgating any standard, the Secretary must make a finding that the workplaces in question are not safe. But "safe" is not the equivalent of "risk-free." There are many activities that we engage in every day—such as driving a car or even breathing city air—that entail some risk of accident or material health impairment; nevertheless, few people would consider these activities "unsafe." Similarly, a workplace can hardly be considered "unsafe" unless it threatens the workers with a significant risk of harm.

Therefore, before he can promulgate *any* permanent health or safety standard, the Secretary is required to make a threshold finding that a place of employment is unsafe—in the sense that significant risks are present and can be eliminated or lessened by a change in practices. This requirement applies to permanent standards promulgated pursuant to § 6(b)(5), as well as to other types of permanent standards. For there is no reason why § 3(8)'s definition of a standard should not be deemed incorporated by reference into § 6(b)(5). The standards promulgated pursuant to § 6(b)(5) are just one species of the genus of standards governed by the basic requirement. That section repeatedly uses the term "standard" without suggesting any exception from, or qualification of, the general definition; on the contrary, it directs the Secretary to select "*the* standard"—that is to say, one of various possible alternatives that satisfy the basic definition in § 3(8)—that is most protective. Moreover, requiring the Secretary to make a threshold finding of significant risk is consistent with the scope of the regulatory power granted to him by § 6(b)(5), which empowers the Secretary to promulgate standards, not for chemicals and physical agents generally, but for "*toxic* chemicals" and "*harmful* physical agents."

* * *

Given the conclusion that the Act empowers the Secretary to promulgate health and safety standards only where a significant risk of harm exists, the critical issue becomes how to define and allocate the burden of proving the significance of the risk in a case such as this, where scientific knowledge is imperfect and the precise quantification of risks is therefore impossible. The Agency's position is that there is substantial evidence in the record to support its conclusion that there is no absolutely safe level for a carcinogen and that, therefore, the burden is properly on industry to prove, apparently beyond a shadow of a doubt, that there *is* a safe level for benzene exposure. The Agency argues that, because of the uncertainties in this area, any other approach would render it helpless, forcing it to wait for the leukemia deaths that it believes are likely to occur before taking any regulatory action.

We disagree. As we read the statute, the burden was on the Agency to show, on the basis of substantial evidence, that it is at least more likely than not that long-term exposure to 10 ppm of benzene presents a significant risk of material health impairment. Ordinarily, it is the proponent of a rule or order who has the burden of proof in administrative proceedings. In some cases involving toxic substances, Congress has shifted the burden of proving that a particular substance is safe onto the party opposing the proposed rule. The fact that Congress did not follow this course in enacting OSHA indicates that it intended the Agency to bear the normal burden of establishing the need for a proposed standard.

In this case OSHA did not even attempt to carry its burden of proof. The closest it came to making a finding that benzene presented a significant risk of harm in the workplace was its statement that the benefits to be derived from lowering the permissible exposure level from 10 to 1 ppm were "likely" to be "appreciable." The Court of Appeals held that this finding was not supported by substantial evidence. Of greater importance, even if it were supported by substantial evidence, such a finding would not be sufficient to satisfy the Agency's obligations under the Act.

\* \* \*

Contrary to the Government's contentions, imposing a burden on the Agency of demonstrating a significant risk of harm will not strip it of its ability to regulate carcinogens, nor will it require the Agency to wait for deaths to occur before taking any action. First, the requirement that a "significant" risk be identified is not a mathematical straitjacket. It is the Agency's responsibility to determine, in the first instance, what it considers to be a "significant" risk. Some risks are plainly acceptable and others are plainly unacceptable. If, for example, the odds are one in a billion that a person will die from cancer by taking a drink of chlorinated water, the risk clearly could not be considered significant. On the other hand, if the odds are one in a thousand that regular inhalation of gasoline vapors that are two percent benzene will be fatal, a reasonable person might well consider the risk significant and take appropriate steps to decrease or eliminate it. Although the Agency has no duty to calculate the exact probability of harm, it does have an obligation to find that a significant risk is present before it can characterize a place of employment as "unsafe."

Second, OSHA is not required to support its finding that a significant risk exists with anything approaching scientific certainty. Although the Agency's findings must be supported by substantial evidence, § 6(b)(5) specifically allows the Secretary to regulate on the basis of the "best available evidence." As several courts of appeals have held, this provision requires a reviewing court to give OSHA some leeway where its findings must be made on the frontiers of scientific knowledge. Thus, so long as they are supported by a body of reputable scientific thought, the Agency is free to use conservative assumptions in interpreting the data with respect to carcinogens, risking error on the side of over-protection rather than under-protection.

Finally, the record in this case and OSHA's own rulings on other carcinogens indicate that there are a number of ways in which the Agency can make a rational judgment about the relative significance of the risks associated with exposure to a particular carcinogen.

It should also be noted that, in setting a permissible exposure level in reliance on less-than-perfect methods, OSHA would have the benefit of a backstop in the form of monitoring and medical testing. Thus, if OSHA properly determined that the permissible exposure limit should be set at 5 ppm, it could still require monitoring and medical testing for employees exposed to lower levels. By doing so, it could keep a constant check on the validity of the assumptions made in developing the permissible exposure limit, giving it a sound evidentiary basis for decreasing the limit if it was initially set too high. Moreover, in this way it could ensure that workers who were unusually susceptible to benzene could be removed from exposure before they had suffered any permanent damage.

Because our review of this case has involved a more detailed examination of the record than is customary, it must be emphasized that we have neither made any factual determinations of our own, nor have we rejected any factual findings made by the Secretary. We express no opinion on what factual findings this record might support, either on the basis of empirical evidence or on the basis of expert testimony; nor do we express any opinion on the more difficult question of what factual determinations would warrant a conclusion that significant risks are present which make promulgation of a new standard reasonably necessary or appropriate. The standard must, of course, be supported by the findings actually made by the Secretary, not merely by findings that we believe he might have made.

In this case the record makes it perfectly clear that the Secretary relied squarely on a special policy for carcinogens that imposed the burden on industry of proving the existence of a safe level of exposure, thereby avoiding the Secretary's threshold responsibility of establishing the need for more stringent standards. In so interpreting his statutory authority, the Secretary exceeded his power.

\* \* \*

The judgment of the Court of Appeals remanding the petition for review to the Secretary for further proceedings is affirmed.

*It is so ordered.*

■ [CHIEF JUSTICE BURGER filed a separate concurring opinion.]

■ [JUSTICE POWELL filed a separate opinion concurring in part and in the judgment.]

■ MR. JUSTICE REHNQUIST, concurring in the judgment.

\* \* \*

I believe that the legislative history demonstrates that the feasibility requirement, as employed in § 6(b)(5), is a legislative mirage, appearing to some members but not to others, and assuming any form desired by the beholder.   I am unable to accept MR. JUSTICE MARSHALL'S argument that, by changing the phrasing of § 6(b)(5) from "most adequately and feasibly assures" to "most adequately assures, to the extent feasible," the Senate injected into that section something that wasn't already there.

\* \* \*

We ought not to shy away from our judicial duty to invalidate unconstitutional delegations of legislative authority solely out of concern that we should thereby reinvigorate discredited constitutional doctrines of the pre-New Deal era.   If the nondelegation doctrine has fallen into the same desuetude as have substantive due process and restrictive interpretations of the Commerce Clause, it is, as one writer has phrased it, "a case of death by association[.]"   J.H. Ely, Democracy and Distrust, a Theory of Judicial Review 133 (1980).   Indeed, a number of observers have suggested that this Court should once more take up its burden of ensuring that Congress does not unnecessarily delegate important choices of social policy to politically unresponsive administrators.   Other observers, as might be imagined, have disagreed.

If we are ever to reshoulder the burden of ensuring that Congress itself make the critical policy decisions, this is surely the case in which to do it. It is difficult to imagine a more obvious example of Congress simply avoiding a choice which was both fundamental for purposes of the statute and yet politically so divisive that the necessary decision or compromise was difficult, if not impossible, to hammer out in the legislative forge.   Far from detracting from the substantive authority of Congress, a declaration that the first sentence of § 6(b)(5) of the OSHA constitutes an invalid delegation to the Secretary of Labor would preserve the authority of Congress.   If Congress wishes to legislate in an area which it has not previously sought to enter, it will in today's political world undoubtedly run into opposition no matter how the legislation is formulated.   But that is the very essence of legislative authority under our system.   It is the hard choices, and not the filling in of the blanks, which must be made by the elected representatives of the people.   When fundamental policy decisions underlying important legislation about to be enacted are to be made, the buck stops with Congress and the President insofar as he exercises his constitutional role in the legislative process.

I would invalidate the first sentence of § 6(b)(5) of the Occupational Safety and Health Act of 1970 as it applies to any toxic substance or harmful physical agent for which a safe level, that is a level at which "no employee will suffer material impairment of health or functional capacity even if such employee has regular exposure to [that hazard] for the period of his working life[,]" is, according to the Secretary, unknown or otherwise "infeasible."   Absent further congressional action, the Secretary would then have to choose, when acting pursuant to § 6(b)(5), between setting a safe standard or setting no standard at all.   Accordingly, for the reasons stated above, I concur in the judgment of the Court affirming the judgment of the Court of Appeals.

■ MR. JUSTICE MARSHALL, with whom MR. JUSTICE BRENNAN, MR. JUSTICE WHITE, and MR. JUSTICE BLACKMUN join, dissenting.

* * *

The plurality is insensitive to three factors which, in my view, make judicial review of occupational safety and health standards under the substantial evidence test particularly difficult.   First, the issues often reach a high level of technical complexity.   In such circumstances the courts are required to immerse themselves in matters to which they are unaccustomed by training or experience.   Second, the factual issues with which the Secretary must deal are frequently not subject to any definitive resolution. Often "the factual finger points, it does not conclude."   Causal connections and theoretical extrapolations may be uncertain.   Third, when the question involves determination of the acceptable level of risk, the ultimate decision must necessarily be based on considerations of policy as well as empirically verifiable facts.   Factual determinations can at most define the risk in some statistical way; the judgment whether that risk is tolerable cannot be based solely on a resolution of the facts.

The decision to take action in conditions of uncertainty bears little resemblance to the sort of empirically verifiable factual conclusions to which the substantial evidence test is normally applied.   Such decisions were not intended to be unreviewable; they too must be scrutinized to ensure that the Secretary has acted reasonably and within the boundaries set by Congress.   But a reviewing court must be mindful of the limited nature of its role.   It must recognize that the ultimate decision cannot be based solely on determinations of fact, and that those factual conclusions that have been reached are ones which the courts are ill-equipped to resolve on their own.

Under this standard of review, the decision to reduce the permissible exposure level to 1 ppm was well within the Secretary's authority.   The Court of Appeals upheld the Secretary's conclusions that benzene causes leukemia, blood disorders, and chromosomal damage even at low levels, that an exposure level of 10 ppm is more dangerous than one of 1 ppm, and that benefits will result from the proposed standard.   It did not set aside his finding that the number of lives that would be saved was not subject to quantification.   Nor did it question his conclusion that the reduction was "feasible."

In these circumstances, the Secretary's decision was reasonable and in full conformance with the statutory language requiring that he "set the standard which most adequately assures, to the extent feasible, on the basis of the best available evidence, that no employee will suffer material impairment of health or functional capacity even if such employee has regular exposure to the hazard dealt with by such standard for the period of his working life." 29 U.S.C. § 655(b)(5). On this record, the Secretary could conclude that regular exposure above the 1 ppm level would pose a definite risk resulting in material impairment to some indeterminate but possibly substantial number of employees. Studies revealed hundreds of deaths attributable to benzene exposure. Expert after expert testified that no safe level of exposure had been shown and that the extent of the risk declined with the exposure level. There was some direct evidence of incidence of leukemia, nonmalignant blood disorders, and chromosomal damage at exposure levels of 10 ppm and below. Moreover, numerous experts testified that existing evidence required an inference that an exposure level above 1 ppm was hazardous. We have stated that "well-reasoned expert testimony—based on what is known and uncontradicted by empirical evidence—may in and of itself be 'substantial evidence' when first-hand evidence on the question * * * is unavailable." Nothing in the Act purports to prevent the Secretary from acting when definitive information as to the quantity of a standard's benefits is unavailable. Where, as here, the deficiency in knowledge relates to the extent of the benefits rather than their existence, I see no reason to hold that the Secretary has exceeded his statutory authority.

The plurality avoids this conclusion through reasoning that may charitably be described as obscure. According to the plurality, the definition of occupational safety and health standards as those "reasonably necessary or appropriate to assure safe or healthful working conditions" requires the Secretary to show that it is "more likely than not" that the risk he seeks to regulate is a "significant" one. The plurality does not show how this requirement can plausibly be derived from the "reasonably necessary or appropriate" clause. Indeed, the plurality's reasoning is refuted by the Act's language, structure, and legislative history, and it is foreclosed by every applicable guide to statutory construction. In short, the plurality's standard is a fabrication bearing no connection with the acts or intentions of Congress.

At the outset, it is important to observe that "reasonably necessary or appropriate" clauses are routinely inserted in regulatory legislation, and in the past such clauses have uniformly been interpreted as general provisos that regulatory actions must bear a reasonable relation to those statutory purposes set forth in the statute's substantive provisions. The Court has never—until today—interpreted a "reasonably necessary or appropriate" clause as having a substantive content that supersedes a specific congressional directive embodied in a provision that is focused more particularly on an agency's authority. This principle, of course, reflects the common understanding that the determination of whether regulations are "reasonably necessary" may be made only by reference to the legislative judgment reflected in the statute; it must not be based on a court's own, inevitably subjective view of what steps should be taken to promote perceived statutory goals.

The plurality suggests that under the "reasonably necessary" clause, a workplace is not "unsafe" unless the Secretary is able to convince a reviewing court that a "significant" risk is at issue. That approach is particularly embarrassing in this case, for it is contradicted by the plain language of the Act. The plurality's interpretation renders utterly superfluous the first sentence of § 655(b)(5), which, as noted above, requires the Secretary to set the standard "which most adequately assures * * * that no employee will suffer material impairment of health." Indeed, the plurality's interpretation reads that sentence out of the Act. By so doing, the plurality makes the test for standards regulating toxic substances and harmful physical agents substantially identical to the test for standards generally—plainly the opposite of what Congress intended. And it is an odd canon of construction that would insert in a vague and general definitional clause a threshold requirement that overcomes the specific language placed in a standard-setting provision. The most elementary principles of statutory construction demonstrate that precisely the opposite interpretation is appropriate. In short, Congress could have provided that the Secretary may not take regulatory action until the existing scientific evidence proves the risk as issue to be "significant," but it chose not to do so.

The plurality's interpretation of the "reasonably necessary or appropriate" clause is also conclusively refuted by the legislative history. While the standard-setting provision that the plurality ignores received extensive legislative attention, the definitional clause received *none at all*. An earlier version of the Act did not embody a clear feasibility constraint and was not restricted to toxic substances or to "material" impairments. The "reasonably necessary or appropriate" clause was contained in this prior version of the bill, as it was at all relevant times. In debating this version, Members of Congress repeatedly expressed concern that it would require a risk-free universe. The definitional clause was not mentioned at all, an omission that would be incomprehensible if Congress intended by that clause to require the Secretary to quantify the risk he sought to regulate in order to demonstrate that it was "significant."

NOTES AND QUESTIONS

**1.** Section 3(8) defines the term "occupational safety and health standard" as "a standard which requires conditions, or the adoption or use of one or more practices, means, methods, operations, or processes, reasonably necessary *or* appropriate to provide safe or healthful employment and places of employment." (emphasis added). Justice Stevens misquotes this section as requiring that standards be "reasonably necessary *and* appropriate." How, if at all, does this interpretation affect the plurality's theory of significant risk?

**2.** What is the authority for Justice Stevens' "significant risk" and "more likely than not" requirements? Did Congress intend § 3(8) to have the importance Justice Stevens attributes to it?

**3.** When is a risk significant? Does Justice Stevens help to illustrate the concept?

Having ordered OSHA to apply a "significant risk" threshold test, the court gave very little indication of how the agency should go about meeting its burden, and the one example that the plurality opinion provided, demonstrated rather clearly that the author of the opinion did not understand the concept of environmental risk assessment. Justice Stevens, by way of explanation, offered the following example:

"Some risks are plainly acceptable and others are plainly unacceptable. If, for example, the odds are one in 1 billion that a person will die from cancer by taking a drink of chlorinated water, the risk clearly could not be considered significant. On the other hand, if the odds are one in a thousand that regular inhalation of gasoline vapors that are two percent benzene will be fatal, a reasonable person might well consider the risk significant and take appropriate steps to decrease or eliminate it."

The example is an ideal illustration of a confused approach to risk assessment in the public health context. Drinking chlorinated water is an activity engaged in by practically everyone in American society. If 250 million Americans drink 4 glasses of water a day and are exposed to a 1 in 1 billion risk each time, then an average of 1 cancer per day will result. This amounts to about 365 cancers per year, a number that reasonable people might find "significant." Justice Stevens's example of a significant risk is harder to address from a public health perspective, because he neglected to provide two important pieces of information: the length of exposure that would result in a cancer and the number of persons who regularly breath gasoline vapors. If we assume that exposure for a year presents the 1 in 1,000 risk and that 2 employees in each of the approximately 200,000 service stations in America are regularly exposed to benzene (an estimate that is, by the way, on the high side), then a 1 in 1,000 risk would yield 400 cancers per year, a number that is not meaningfully different from the 365 cancers per year that Justice Stevens found to be clearly insignificant.

Thomas O. McGarity & Sidney A. Shapiro, Workers at Risk 56–57 (1993).

**4.** The first step in the rulemaking process is risk assessment. Scientifically, there are three main ways in which this can be done:

(a) Short term *in vitro* tests, such as the Ames test, can estimate the carcinogenicity or toxicity of a substance. Existing technologies, however, are not sufficiently developed to permit detailed and precise risk assessments.

(b) *In vivo* tests or animal bioassay studies attempt to determine the effects of a substance on laboratory animals. These tests present a number of problems. First, the studies are costly (about $500,000 each) and take two to five years to complete. Each year about 150 chemicals are tested, but 1000 new chemicals are developed. Second, all species do not react to a substance in the same way. For example, rodents do not seem to be affected by benzene the way humans are. (This was a problem with the drug Thalidomide in the 1950s, which caused birth defects in humans.) Third, especially with carcinogens, disease may take years to develop. The studies need to determine whether exposure over a lifetime may cause disease, but the studies must be completed within a reasonable length of time. Scientists will expose the animals to high concentrations for a short period of time and then attempt to extrapolate the results to low concentrations over a long period of time.

(c) Epidemiological studies attempt to discover correlations between mortality (death) or morbidity (illness) rates and exposure to a certain environmental factor. Because direct experimentation on humans is not possible, statistical analyses of illnesses are the only way to quantify the observed effects on humans of a certain substance. Nevertheless, there are several problems with the use of this tool. To begin with, it takes many years to study whether exposures have effects over the lifetime of the subjects. In addition, it is often difficult to obtain information about exposures below the current standard. For example, there was evidence that the ten ppm standard for benzene was inadequate to protect workers. There was little concrete evidence, however, whether workers were at risk from exposures at five ppm, two ppm, or one ppm because they were below the legal standard. The plurality in the *Benzene* case criticized OSHA for not developing a dose-response curve, but this is often difficult to do. Other problems in epidemiology include multiple factor interactions and selection of proper cohorts.

**5.** Who should have the burden of proof when the health effects of occupational hazards are uncertain? Should OSHA have to prove that there are risks or should the industry have to prove the absence of risks? OSHA adopted the policy that there are no known safe levels at which humans can be exposed to a carcinogen and therefore exposures must be reduced to their lowest feasible levels. How did the plurality view this policy? What does Justice Marshall think about the burden of proof?

**6.** The *Benzene* case fills 118 pages of the U.S. Reports—an indication of the complexity of the issues and the divisions within the Court. Are the scientific questions raised in a case such as this beyond the expertise of the Court? Should the degree of deference afforded the administrative agency depend on the length and complexity of the case? Was the proper degree of deference shown in this case?

**7.** After the risk has been quantified, the regulator must then decide whether the risk is acceptable. What factors should be included in this calculation? Certain everyday risks (riding in an airplane, driving a car) are considered acceptable without much thought. What level of risk is acceptable in the workplace? Should workers be permitted to assume certain risks on the job?

**8.**   The two most important issues in the *Benzene* case are the interpretation of § 3(8) and the question of whether the Secretary proved the need for a new standard of one ppm.   On neither of these points is Justice Stevens' opinion the majority view of the Court.   Justice Rehnquist agreed with the four dissenters that § 3(8) was not a substantive limitation on § 6(b)(5).   Justice Rehnquist did not address the adequacy of the evidence issue, thus leaving the Court divided four to four.

**9.**   According to Justice Rehnquist, "feasible" in § 6(b)(5) is so vague as to be an unconstitutional delegation of legislative authority to the executive. Assuming that Congress did not intend to require *absolute* safety in exposure to toxic substances (such as appears in the Delaney Amendment to the Food and Drug Act absolutely prohibiting food additives if there is evidence of carcinogenicity at any level), how could you redraft § 6(b)(5) in terms that would not be vague?

**10.**   The OSHA rulemaking process is protracted, detailed, cumbersome, and adversarial.   As a result, few new health standards have been adopted. The stakes are high, in both economic and human terms.   No doubt this fact affects the length of the process.   A new standard takes years to promulgate and consumes millions of dollars.   (The transcript in OSHA's cancer policy rulemaking was 250,000 pages.)   Are there any ways to speed up the process while still preserving due process?   See Mark A. Rothstein, Substantive and Procedural Obstacles to OSHA Rulemaking:   Reproductive Hazards as an Example, 12 B.C. Envtl.Aff.L.Rev. 627 (1985); Sidney A. Shapiro & Thomas O. McGarity, Reorienting OSHA:   Regulatory Alternatives and Legislative Reform, 6 Yale J. on Reg. 1 (1989).

**11.**   In National Cottonseed Products Association v. Brock, 825 F.2d 482 (D.C.Cir.1987), cert. denied, 485 U.S. 1020 (1988), the D.C. Circuit held that the Secretary's failure to find that dust in cottonseed mills presents a significant risk of harm will not prevent the agency from requiring medical surveillance of employees.   The *Cottonseed* court acknowledged that the Supreme Court in the *Benzene* case had required that OSHA make a threshold finding of significant risk in promulgating standards for toxic substances.   The court, however, relied on dicta in *Benzene* that the agency may require medical monitoring as a backstop to ensure that workers will not be exposed to dangerous conditions.

**12.**   In order to perform epidemiological research to determine the health effects of various workplace exposures it is necessary to account for the role of such lifestyle factors as diet, smoking, drinking, hobbies, and sexual activity.   Are there any problems associated with making such sensitive inquiries of workers?   What safeguards are needed?   Do researchers (government or private) have a duty to notify individuals they identify as "high risk" about their research findings?

———

AMERICAN TEXTILE MANUFACTURERS INSTITUTE, INC. v. DONOVAN (THE COTTON DUST CASE), 452 U.S. 490 (1981).   In *The*

*Cotton Dust Case,* the Supreme Court addressed the issue of cost-benefit analysis it had avoided the year before when it decided *The Benzene Case.* In a five-to-three decision, the Court rejected the industry argument that the Act requires the use of cost-benefit analysis. Relying on the plain meaning of the word "feasible" in § 6(b)(5) as "capable of being done," the Court held that imposing a cost-benefit requirement would be inconsistent with the mandate of Congress.

> Congress itself defined the basic relationship between costs and benefits, by placing the "benefit" of worker health above all considerations save those making attainment of this "benefit" unachievable. * * * Thus, cost-benefit analysis by OSHA is not required by the statute because feasibility analysis is.

452 U.S. at 509 (footnote omitted).

The Court observed that when Congress has intended that an agency engage in cost-benefit analysis, it has clearly indicated such an intent on the face of the statute. Neither the language of the Act nor its legislative history indicate such a congressional intent. Moreover, the general definitional language of § 3(8) cannot be used to impose a cost-benefit requirement and thereby "eviscerate" the "to the extent feasible" language of § 6(b)(5).

According to the majority opinion of Justice Brennan, "feasible," as used in § 6(b)(5), includes economic feasibility. After reviewing the record, the Court concluded that the D.C. Circuit did not err in holding that the Secretary's finding that compliance with the cotton dust standard was economically feasible was supported by substantial evidence. Even though no specific economic studies were performed on the final standard, there were studies that showed that compliance with a stricter and more costly standard was feasible.

The five-Justice majority in *Cotton Dust* consisted of the four dissenters from *Benzene* and Justice Stevens. Justice Powell took no part in the decision. Justice Stewart filed a separate dissent. Justice Rehnquist, joined by Chief Justice Burger, dissented along the lines of his dissent in *Benzene.*

## NOTES AND QUESTIONS

**1.** Professor William Rodgers has suggested that economic cost consideration models exist on a continuum from the least to the most rigorous:

> (a) *cost-oblivious*—adoption of standards without regard for any cost-benefit consideration because of a moral and policy judgment that concerns about efficiency are inappropriate in some areas of regulation.

> (b) *cost-effective*—use of a formal analysis to determine the most efficient means for attaining a regulatory goal.

> (c) *cost sensitive*—costs, along with other economic factors, must be considered by the agency, but not necessarily with a formal cost-benefit analysis.

(d) *strict cost-benefit*—regulatory activity is limited to those areas where the calculable costs do not exceed the calculable benefits.

Based on the *Cotton Dust* case, which model, if any, is OSHA required to follow? Which of these models do you believe is most appropriate for OSHA? Why? See William H. Rodgers, Benefits, Costs, and Risks: Oversight of Health and Environmental Decisionmaking, 4 Harv.Envtl.L.Rev. 191 (1980).

**2.** In many instances the cost-benefit issue arises in the context of the method of compliance to be used. Engineering controls (e.g., ventilation systems) are much more expensive than personal protective equipment (e.g., respirators). According to the industrial hygiene principle of hierarchy of controls, however, engineering controls are preferred because they control a hazard at its source. Respirators often do not protect workers adequately; they may fit poorly and need frequent cleaning; they often are hot and uncomfortable, encouraging some workers to remove them.

**3.** The cost-benefit issue has been raised at the enforcement stage, as well as at the rulemaking stage. Thus, a cited employer may assert that compliance is economically infeasible. Atlantic & Gulf Stevedores, Inc. v. OSHRC, 534 F.2d 541, 548 (3d Cir.1976). In certain standards, the word "feasible" actually appears in the standard. (OSHA's noise standard is an example.) Should "feasible" in a standard be interpreted to require cost-benefit analysis or merely "capable of being achieved"? See Sherwin-Williams Co., 11 OSHC 2105, 1984 OSHD ¶ 26,986 (1984), petition for review withdrawn, No. 84–2587 (7th Cir.1984).

**4.** The term "feasible" in § 6(b)(5) also has been interpreted to mean "technologically feasible." Can the Secretary promulgate a standard that is "technology-forcing"? In other words, can the Secretary require employers to improve existing technologies or to develop new technologies? See Society of the Plastics Industry, Inc. v. OSHA, 509 F.2d 1301 (2d Cir.1975), cert. denied, 421 U.S. 992 (1975) (new standards may be technology-forcing).

# AFL–CIO v. OSHA

965 F.2d 962 (11th Cir.1992).

■ FAY, CIRCUIT JUDGE:

In 1989, the Occupational Safety and Health Administration ("OSHA"), a division of the Department of Labor, issued its Air Contaminants Standard, a set of permissible exposure limits for 428 toxic substances. Air Contaminants Standard, 54 Fed.Reg. 2332 (1989) (codified at 29 C.F.R. § 1910.1000). In these consolidated appeals, petitioners representing various affected industries and the American Federation of Labor and Congress of Industrial Organizations ("AFL–CIO" or "the union") challenge both the procedure used by OSHA to generate this multi-substance standard and OSHA's findings on numerous specific substances included in the new standard.  For the reasons that follow, we VACATE the Air Contaminants Standard and REMAND to the agency.

* * *

## III.   DISCUSSION

In challenging the procedure by which OSHA promulgated the Air Contaminants Standard, a group of industry petitioners complain that OSHA's use of generic findings, the lumping together of so many substances in one rulemaking, and the short time provided for comment by interested parties, combine to create a record inadequate to support this massive new set of PELs.  The union also challenges the rulemaking procedure utilized by OSHA for the Air Contaminants Standard.  Not surprisingly, however, the union claims that this procedure resulted in standards that are systematically underprotective of employee health.  The union further challenges OSHA's decision to limit the scope of the rulemaking to substances for which the ACGIH recommendation was more protective than the current PEL, and thereby to ignore both other air contaminant substances in need of regulation and standards for exposure monitoring and medical surveillance.  Moreover, the union argues that there is no record support for a four-year compliance period for these standards, given that OSHA itself found that the standards can be met by existing technology.

### A.   "GENERIC" RULEMAKING

Unlike most of the OSHA standards previously reviewed by the courts, the Air Contaminants Standard regulates not a single toxic substance, but 428 different substances.  The agency explained its decision to issue such an omnibus standard in its Notice of Proposed Rulemaking:

> OSHA has issued only 24 substance-specific health regulations since its creation.  It has not been able to review the many thousands of currently unregulated chemicals in the workplace nor to keep up with reviewing the several thousand new chemicals introduced since its creation.  It has not been able to fully review the literature to determine if lower limits are needed for many of the approximately 400 substances it now regulates.

> Using past approaches and practices, OSHA could continue to regulate a small number of the high priority substances and those of greatest public interest.  However, it would take decades to review currently used chemicals and OSHA would never be able to keep up with the many chemicals which will be newly introduced in the future.

53 Fed.Reg. at 20963.  For this reason, "OSHA determined that it was necessary to modify this approach through the use of *generic* rulemaking, which would simultaneously cover many substances."  54 Fed.Reg. at 2333 (emphasis added).

"Generic" means something "common to or characteristic of a whole group or class; typifying or subsuming; not specific or individual." Webster's Third New International Dictionary 945 (1966). Previous "generic" rulemakings by OSHA have all dealt with requirements that, once promulgated, could be applied to numerous different situations. For example, OSHA's Hazard Communication Standard, 29 C.F.R. § 1910.1200, mandates that employers inform employees of potentially hazardous materials. The regulation includes a basic list of substances which employers must treat as hazardous, but requires that the employers themselves also evaluate substances produced in their workplaces to determine if they are potentially hazardous based on available scientific evidence. United Steelworkers v. Auchter, 763 F.2d 728, 732 (3d Cir.1985). Similarly, OSHA has issued standards regulating employee access to medical and toxic substance exposure records, 29 C.F.R. § 1910.20, and setting forth uniform criteria for application in future regulation of exposure to carcinogens, 29 C.F.R. Part 1990.

By contrast, the new Air Contaminants Standard is an amalgamation of 428 unrelated substance exposure limits. There is little common to this group of diverse substances except the fact that OSHA considers them toxic and in need of regulation. In fact, this rulemaking is the antithesis of a "generic" rulemaking; it is a set of 428 specific and individual substance exposure limits. Therefore, OSHA's characterization of this as a "generic" rulemaking is somewhat misleading.

Nonetheless, we find nothing in the OSH Act that would prevent OSHA from addressing multiple substances in a single rulemaking. Moreover, because the statute leaves this point open and because OSHA's interpretation of the statute is reasonable, it is appropriate for us to defer to OSHA's interpretation. However, we believe the PEL for each substance must be able to stand independently, i.e., that each PEL must be supported by substantial evidence in the record considered as a whole and accompanied by adequate explanation. OSHA may not, by using such multi-substance rulemaking, ignore the requirements of the OSH Act. Both the industry petitioners and the union argue that such disregard was what in essence occurred. Regretfully, we agree.

## B.   SIGNIFICANT RISK OF MATERIAL HEALTH IMPAIRMENT

\* \* \*

### 1.   *Material Impairment*

In this rulemaking, OSHA grouped the 428 substances into eighteen categories by the primary health effects of those substances, for example, neuropathic effects, sensory irritation, and cancer. Industry petitioners charge that for several categories of substances OSHA failed to adequately justify its determination that the health effects caused by exposure to these substances are "material impairments." We disagree.

\* \* \*

OSHA is not required to state with scientific certainty or precision the exact point at which each type of sensory or physical irritation becomes a material impairment. Moreover, section 6(b)(5) of the Act charges OSHA with addressing all forms of "material impairment of health *or functional capacity*," and not exclusively "death or serious physical harm" or "grave danger" from exposure to toxic substances. Overall, we find that OSHA's determinations of what constitute "material impairments" are adequately explained and supported in the record.

### 2. *Significant Risk*

However, the agency's determination of the extent of the risk posed by individual substances is more problematic. "No one could reasonably expect OSHA to adopt some precise estimate of fatalities likely from a given exposure level, and indeed the Supreme Court has said that the agency has 'no duty to calculate the exact probability of harm.'" Nevertheless, OSHA has a responsibility to quantify or explain, at least to some reasonable degree, the risk posed by *each* toxic substance regulated. Otherwise, OSHA has not demonstrated, and this court cannot evaluate, how serious the risk is for any particular substance, or whether *any* workers will in fact benefit from the new standard for any particular substance. If each of these 428 toxic substances had been addressed in separate rulemakings, OSHA would clearly have been required to estimate in some fashion the risk of harm for each substance. OSHA is not entitled to take short-cuts with statutory requirements simply because it chose to combine multiple substances in a single rulemaking.

However, OSHA's discussions of individual substances generally contain no quantification or explanation of the risk from that individual substance. The discussions of individual substances contain summaries of various studies of that substance and the health effects found at various levels of exposure to that substance. However, OSHA made no attempt to estimate the risk of contracting those health effects. Instead, OSHA merely provided a conclusory statement that the new PEL will reduce the "significant" risk of material health effects shown to be caused by that substance, without any explanation of how the agency determined that the risk was significant. However, OSHA did make a generic finding that the Air Contaminants Standard as a whole would prevent 55,000 occupational illnesses and 683 deaths annually.

Moreover, a determination that the new standard is "reasonably necessary or appropriate," and that it is the standard that "most adequately assures * * * that no employee will suffer material impairment of health or functional capacity," necessarily requires some assessment of the level at which significant risk of harm is eliminated or substantially reduced. Yet, with rare exceptions, the individual substance discussions in the Air Contaminants Standard are virtually devoid of reasons for setting those individual standards. In most cases, OSHA cited a few studies and then established a PEL without explaining why the studies mandated the particular PEL chosen. For example, the PEL for bismuth telluride appears to be based on a single study that showed almost no effects of any kind in animals at several times that concentration.  Similarly, the PEL for ferrovanadium dust was based on pulmonary changes at exposure levels many hundreds of times higher than OSHA's new standard.  For some substances, OSHA merely repeated a boilerplate finding that the new limit would protect workers from significant risk of some material health impairment.  For example, OSHA did not cite any studies whatsoever for its aluminum welding fume standard, or its vegetable oil mist standard.

"While our deference to the agency is at a peak for its choices among scientific predictions, we must still look for *some* articulation of reasons for those choices."  * * *

Mere conclusory statements, such as those made throughout the Air Contaminants Standard, are simply inadequate to support a finding of significant risk of material health impairment.

On the other hand, OSHA established PELs for carbon tetrachloride and vinyl bromide, both carcinogens, at levels where OSHA itself acknowledged that the risk of material health impairment remained significant.  For carbon tetrachloride, OSHA stated that at the new level, "residual risk continues to be significant * * * 3.7 excess deaths per 1,000 workers exposed over their working lifetimes."  For vinyl bromide, OSHA stated that the new PEL "will not eliminate this significant risk, because * * * residual risk [at the new level] is 40 excess deaths per 1,000 exposed workers * * * [and thus] is clearly significant."  The only explanation given by OSHA in the final rule for setting its standard where a significant risk of material health impairment remains was that the time and resource constraints of attempting to promulgate an air contaminants standard of this magnitude prevented detailed analysis of these substances.  OSHA did not claim in the final rule that the PELs for these two substances were necessary because of feasibility concern.

The agency's response to this criticism is unpersuasive.  OSHA first contends that quantitative risk analysis using mathematical models like the ones developed for carcinogens was impossible for this rulemaking because no such models exist for noncarcinogens.

* * *

Yet, in several previous rulemakings, OSHA apparently succeeded in determining how many workers were exposed to a particular substance or how much risk would be alleviated by a new standard, even though those particular substances were *not* carcinogens.  It is therefore unclear whether the lack of a method to quantitatively assess the risk for noncarcinogens is a cause or a result of the agency's approach.  In this rulemaking, OSHA concluded that current exposure to 428 substances posed a "significant" risk of material health impairment, and that its new standards were required for most of these substances to eliminate or substantially reduce that risk.  It is not unreasonable to require that the agency explain how it arrived at that determination, and, indeed, this is precisely what Congress required.

The agency further claims that no quantification was required because OSHA's final standards " 'fall[ ] within a zone of reasonableness.' " However, without *any* quantification or *any* explanation, this court cannot determine what that "zone of reasonableness" is or if these standards fall within it.

OSHA also responds by noting that it incorporated "uncertainty" or "safety" factors into many PELs. However, OSHA did not use a uniform safety factor, but instead claims to have made a case-by-case assessment of the appropriate safety factor. "Studies are often of small size and, since there is a large variation in human susceptibility, a study because of its small size may not demonstrate an effect that actually exists * * *. For this reason, it is not uncommon to set a limit below that level which the study may have indicated showed no effect." OSHA claims that use of such uncertainty factors "has been the standard approach for recommending exposure limits for non-carcinogens by scientists and health experts in the field for many years." In this rulemaking, the difference between the level shown by the evidence and the final PEL is sometimes substantial. We assume, because it is not expressly stated, that for each of those substances OSHA applied a safety factor to arrive at the final standard. Nevertheless, the method by which the "appropriate" safety factor was determined for each of those substances is not explained in the final rule.

We find OSHA's use of safety factors in this rulemaking problematic. First, OSHA's use of safety factors in this rulemaking is very similar to the approach criticized by the Supreme Court in *Benzene*. Second, even assuming that the use of safety factors is permissible under the Act and *Benzene,* application of such factors without explaining the method by which they were determined, as was done in this case, is clearly not permitted.

From OSHA's description, safety factors are used to lower the standard below levels at which the available evidence shows no significant risk of material health impairment because of the *possibility* that the evidence is incorrect or incomplete; i.e., OSHA essentially makes an assumption that the existing evidence does not adequately show the extent of the risk. That may be a correct assumption, but beyond a general statement that the use of safety factors is common in the scientific community, OSHA did not indicate how the existing evidence for individual substances was inadequate to show the extent of the risk from those substances. Such a rationale is very reminiscent of the "benefits are likely to be appreciable" rationale rejected in *Benzene* as insufficient to satisfy the agency's obligations under the OSH Act.

* * *

Comparing OSHA's rationale for using safety factors in this rulemaking with the Court's discussion of their use in the *Benzene* case, we find little appreciable difference.

The Supreme Court in *Benzene* did recognize that absolute scientific certainty may be impossible when regulating on the edge of scientific knowledge, and that "so long as they are supported by a body of reputable scientific thought, the Agency is free to use conservative assumptions in interpreting the data * * *, risking error on the side of overprotection rather than underprotection." However, the Court also discussed the use of monitoring and medical testing as a "backstop," permitting the agency to "keep a constant check on the validity of the assumptions made in developing the permissible exposure limit, giving it a sound evidentiary basis for decreasing the limit if it was initially set too high."

The lesson of *Benzene* is clearly that OSHA may use assumptions, but only to the extent that those assumptions have some basis in reputable scientific evidence. If the agency is concerned that the standard should be more stringent than even a conservative interpretation of the existing evidence supports, monitoring and medical testing may be done to accumulate the additional evidence needed to support that more protective limit. *Benzene* does not provide support for setting standards below the level substantiated by the evidence. Nor may OSHA base a finding of significant risk at lower levels of exposure on unsupported assumptions using evidence of health impairments at significantly higher levels of exposure. Overall, OSHA's use of safety factors in this rulemaking was not adequately explained by this rulemaking record.

* * *

This implies that OSHA need no longer perform detailed analysis and explanation when promulgating PELs because the agency's analysis for other substances has been upheld in prior rulemakings. Besides displaying more than a touch of hubris, this passage reveals a fundamental misperception of the OSH Act and the caselaw interpreting that act.

While OSHA has probably established that most or all of the substances involved do pose a significant risk at some level, it has failed to establish that existing exposure levels in the workplace present a significant risk of material health impairment or that the new standards eliminate or substantially lessen the risk.

* * *

## IV.   CONCLUSION

It is clear that the analytical approach used by OSHA in promulgating its revised Air Contaminants Standard is so flawed that it cannot stand. OSHA not only mislabeled this a "generic" rulemaking, but it inappropriately treated it as such. The result of this approach is a set of 428 inadequately supported standards. OSHA has lumped together substances and affected industries and provided such inadequate explanation that it is virtually impossible for a reviewing court to determine if sufficient evidence supports the agency's conclusions. The individual substances discussed in this opinion are merely examples of what is endemic in the Air Contaminants Standard as a whole.

OSHA does have the authority to set priorities for establishing standards under the OSH Act. That priority-setting authority permits OSHA to combine rulemaking for multiple substances in one rulemaking, to limit the scope of this rulemaking in a rational manner, and to defer issuance of regulations for monitoring and medical surveillance until a later rulemaking. It does not, however, give OSHA blanket authority to pick and choose what statutory requirements it will follow. The OSH Act mandates that OSHA promulgate the standards that "most adequately" assure that workers will not be exposed to significant risks of material health impairment "to the extent feasible" for the affected industries. Further, section 6(e) and caselaw require OSHA to adequately explain its determinations. Section 6(b) of the Act does not provide an exception to these requirements for administrative convenience. The only exceptions to the strict statutory criteria are the start-up provisions of section 6(a), the applicability of which has long since passed, and the emergency provisions of section 6(c), neither of which are implicated in this case.

Therefore, although we find that the record adequately explains and supports OSHA's determination that the health effects of exposure to these 428 substances are material impairments, we hold that OSHA has not sufficiently explained or supported its threshold determination that exposure to these substances at previous levels posed a significant risk of these material health impairments or that the new standard eliminates or reduces that risk to the extent feasible. OSHA's overall approach to this rulemaking is so flawed that we must vacate the whole revised Air Contaminants Standard.

We have no doubt that the agency acted with the best of intentions. It may well be, as OSHA claims, that this was the only practical way of accomplishing a much needed revision of the existing standards and of making major strides towards improving worker health and safety. Given OSHA's history of slow progress in issuing standards, we can easily believe OSHA's claim that going through detailed analysis for each of the 428 different substances regulated was not possible given the time constraints set by the agency for this rulemaking. Unfortunately, OSHA's approach to this rulemaking is not consistent with the requirements of the OSH Act. Before OSHA uses such an approach, it must get authorization from Congress by way of amendment to the OSH Act. Legislative decisions on the federal level are to be made in the chambers of Congress. It is not for this court to undertake the substantial rewriting of the Act necessary to uphold OSHA's approach to this rulemaking.

Therefore, for the reasons stated above, we VACATE the revised Air Contaminants Standard, and REMAND to the agency.

NOTES AND QUESTIONS

1. The effect of the court's decision was to reinstate OSHA's prior air contaminant standard, which is based on 1968 scientific data.

2. Was the court constrained by the statutory language (and the *Benzene* case) to reach the result it did or was it overly rigid in its analysis,

insufficiently deferential to the Secretary of Labor, and unmindful of the remedial purpose of the statute?  If you were drafting an amendment to the Act to permit more expeditious updating of large numbers of standards, what language would you propose that accommodates the interests of scientific rigor, due process, and promptness?

**3.**  In American Dental Association v. Martin, 984 F.2d 823 (7th Cir.1993), cert. denied, 510 U.S. 859 (1993), the court upheld in most respects the OSHA standard for bloodborne pathogens.  Among other things, it rejected the argument that all health care providers should not be covered by the same standard and that the compliance costs (at least $813 million per year) were excessive.

## 3.   EMERGENCY TEMPORARY STANDARDS

Section 6(c)(1) provides that if the Secretary determines that employees are "exposed to grave danger from exposure to substances or agents determined to be toxic or physically harmful or from new hazards," an emergency temporary standard (ETS) may be issued.  These standards are effective immediately upon publication in the Federal Register without any detailed rulemaking.  Under § 6(c)(3) an ETS may remain in effect for only six months; thereafter, the Secretary must promulgate a permanent standard under § 6(b).  In this event the ETS serves as the proposed rule.

In 1983, OSHA promulgated an ETS for asbestos, lowering the permissible exposure limit (PEL) from 2.0 fibers per cubic centimeter (f/cc) to 0.5 f/cc.  The ETS was based on a new quantitative risk assessment showing that reducing the PEL for six months would save 40 to 80 lives.  OSHA had performed a detailed quantitative risk assessment and developed a dose-response curve from epidemiological studies of exposed workers rather than by relying on animal data.  This assessment was made specifically to satisfy the "significant risk" requirement of the Supreme Court's *Benzene* decision and the "grave danger" language of § 6(c).  A group of asbestos products manufacturers sought judicial review of the ETS in the Fifth Circuit.

In Asbestos Information Association/North America v. OSHA, 727 F.2d 415 (5th Cir.1984), the Fifth Circuit held that the ETS was invalid and stayed its enforcement.  The court's analysis focused on whether OSHA had proved the need to adopt an ETS for asbestos rather than modifying the existing standard after notice and comment rulemaking.  The Fifth Circuit was troubled by the possibility of inaccuracy in using risk assessment for a six-month exposure period.  Moreover, the court noted that the mathematical extrapolations had not been the subject of "peer reviews."  "Precisely because the data has not been scrutinized, however, the court has particular interest in having access to both favorable and unfavorable peer reviews."  Id. at 421 n. 15.

Did the court confuse "peer review" with "notice and comment" rulemaking?  All of the studies relied upon by OSHA were "peer reviewed"—they were scrutinized and analyzed by other scientific experts.

The type of peer review deemed essential by the court is the right of interested parties to comment upon and rebut OSHA's evidence. Such a procedure, specified under § 6(b), was specifically rejected by Congress in § 6(c). Indeed, the entire purpose of the ETS provision was to avoid the lengthy rulemaking that would preclude a swift, emergency regulation. Has the Fifth Circuit, in effect, written § 6(c) out of the statute?

Each year between 8200 and 9700 people die from asbestos exposure and the total will continue beyond the year 2000. By the end of this century, more than 200,000 people will have died from asbestos exposure since the 1940s. The court found that the Secretary's estimate that the ETS would save 80 lives in six months was too high. Should it matter whether the actual number is 60 or 40 or 35?

## C.   Employer Duties

The goal of OSHA is to prevent workplace hazards. Because the statute's coverage is so broad (about five million workplaces) and there are relatively few inspectors (between 1000 and 1500 federal inspectors), the Act establishes a preinspection duty to comply with specific standards (§ 5(a)(2)) and the general duty clause (§ 5(a)(1)). The possibility of inspection, citation, and penalty assessment is designed to encourage preinspection compliance.

In determining whether to cite an employer under § 5(a)(1) or § 5(a)(2), or under which particular standard under § 5(a)(2), the Commission and courts use the principle that the "specific" takes precedence over the "general." Thus, an employer may not be cited under § 5(a)(1) unless no specific standard applies. An employer may not be cited under the general industry standards unless none of the specific industry standards (construction, maritime and longshoring, agricultural) apply. And an employer may not be cited under a generally worded standard when a specific standard applies.

## 1.   Compliance With Standards

### a.   INTERPRETATION OF STANDARDS

## Brock v. City Oil Well Service Co.

795 F.2d 507 (5th Cir.1986).

■ Irving L. Goldberg, Circuit Judge:

Colorless, flammable, and with an odor like that of rotten eggs, hydrogen sulfide gas ($H_2S$) is a deadly byproduct of oil and gas production. On June 4, 1981, two employees of respondent City Oil Well Service Co. (City), a corporation engaged in the business of servicing oil wells, were swabbing a newly drilled oil well near Nixon, Texas. While on top of a tank, which was within one hundred feet of the well, the two workers were asphyxiated by $H_2S$.

Like the French and English soldiers in the First World War, the two workers were completely unprepared for deadly gas. City had not provided them with monitoring equipment, respirators, or safety instructions of any sort. While the workers could try to stand upwind of any gas, this common-sense precaution was unreliable at best, as $H_2S$ deadens the olfactory nerves, making its continued detection by smell problematic.

As a result of an inspection of the deaths by a compliance officer of the United States Department of Labor, Occupational Safety and Health Administration ("OSHA"), the Secretary of Labor cited City for violating section 5(a)(2) of the Occupational Safety and Health Act of 1970 (the "Act"), 29 U.S.C. § 654(a)(2), by failing to comply with the health standards found at 29 C.F.R. §§ 1910.134(a)(1) and (2), which relate to the provision of respirators to protect against toxic air contaminants. An Administrative Law Judge (ALJ) of the Occupational Safety and Health Review Commission (OSHRC) found that petitioner had failed to carry its burden of proof under the regulations and therefore vacated the citations. Anticipating the possibility that his legal conclusion as to the Secretary's burden of proof might not survive an appeal, the ALJ made alternative findings in order to avoid a remand. The short-handed two member OSHRC split, and therefore entered an order making the ALJ's decision the final, appealable order of the Commission. We reverse the order of the Commission and remand the case to the Commission for entry of judgment in favor of petitioner.

## DISCUSSION

The regulations with whose violation City has been charged read as follows:

**Respiratory protection.**

(a) *Permissible practice.* (1) In the control of those occupational diseases caused by breathing air contaminated with harmful dusts, fogs, fumes, mists, gases, smokes, sprays, or vapors, the primary objective shall be to prevent atmospheric contamination. This shall be accomplished as far as feasible by accepted engineering control measures (for example, enclosure or confinement of the operation, general and local ventilation, and substitution of less toxic materials). When effective engineering controls are not feasible, or while they are being instituted, appropriate respirators shall be used pursuant to the following requirements.

(2) Respirators shall be provided by the employer when such equipment is necessary to protect the health of the employee. The employer shall provide the respirators which are applicable and suitable for the purpose intended. The employer shall be responsible for the establishment and maintenance of a respiratory protective program

which shall include the requirements outlined in paragraph (b) of this section.

29 C.F.R. §§ 1910.134(a)(1) and (2) (1986). Among the ten listed requirements of a respiratory protective program outlined in paragraph (b) are the following:

(b) *Requirements for a minimal acceptable program.*

(1) Written standard operating procedures governing the selection and use of respirators shall be established.

(2) Respirators shall be selected on the basis of hazards to which the worker is exposed.

(3) The user shall be instructed and trained in the proper use of respirators and their limitations.

. . . .

(8) Appropriate surveillance of work area conditions and degree of employee exposure or stress shall be maintained.

(9) There shall be regular inspection and evaluation to determine the continued effectiveness of the program.

City failed to take *any* of these or other possible steps to protect its employees from the potential hazard of H₂S at this or any other well that it serviced. Nevertheless, the ALJ vacated the citations. City argued, and the ALJ agreed, that proof by the Secretary that effective engineering controls were "not feasible" was a prerequisite for requiring respirators, even if engineering controls were not in fact used. In other words, City convinced the ALJ that the regulation does not require the employer to take any steps to protect its employees as long as the employer can show that unused engineering controls were nonetheless feasible. City acknowledges that this interpretation of the regulation creates a situation in which the employee could be left without the protection of either engineering controls or respirators.

Whether or not we choose to accept this departure from common sense and the goals of the Act turns on the interpretation of the following sentence from section (a)(1) of the regulation:

When effective engineering controls are not feasible, or while they are being instituted, appropriate respirators shall be used. . . .

City contends that this sentence requires an employer to supply respirators in only two circumstances: (1) when effective controls are not feasible, or (2) when effective engineering controls are being instituted. In effect then, City argues that the regulation's failure to state explicitly that respirators shall be used when effective engineering controls *are* feasible but not in use—*i.e.,* the regulation's failure to state the obvious—should allow City to slip through the regulatory net.

This interpretation is contrary to both Commission and Court precedent. The interpretation was implicitly rejected, in a factual situation virtually identical to that of the instant case, in Secretary of Labor v.

Snyder Well Services, Inc., 1982 CCH OSHD ¶ 25,943 (1982).  In *Snyder* the employer argued, *inter alia,* that it had no duty to provide respirators so long as effective engineering controls were in use.  The Commission first held that, because the controls in use could not protect against sudden excursions of high concentrations of $H_2S$, the controls were not in fact effective.  Then, without even considering the feasibility *vel non* of effective controls, the Commission found that respirators were therefore "necessary" within the meaning of the standard and affirmed the citation, holding: "To the extent that engineering controls do not afford protection, *or are not used,* respirators must be used."

This court rejected a similar construction of 29 C.F.R. § 1926.105(a) in Brennan v. Southern Contractors Service, 492 F.2d 498 (5th Cir.1974), a case involving the whens and wherefores of safety nets.  The Commission argued that if the use of one of the safety devices listed as an alternative to safety nets was practical, then the employer need not supply safety nets even though the alternative device was not in fact utilized by the employer.

\* \* \*

We thus read 29 C.F.R. § 1910.134(a)(1) to require an employer to provide *either* effective engineering controls *or* respirators to its employees. The requirement is made even clearer by the regulation's command that the employer supply respirators "while [effective engineering controls] are being instituted," which necessarily subsumes the idea that an employer must supply respirators when effective engineering controls are not being instituted.  Proof that effective engineering controls are not feasible is not part of the Secretary's case.  Any other interpretation is absurd and ridiculous.  Any other conclusion would "eviscerate the import of the regulation and flout the purposes of the enabling legislation." *Southern Contractors Service,* supra.  We do not check our common sense at the courthouse door.

In this case, it is beyond dispute that effective engineering controls were not in place.  The record confirms that $H_2S$ could escape at the well head, at the open pit, and from the vent atop the frac tank during such operations.  The only remaining question is whether City had a duty to provide respirators to its employees.  The answer is clearly yes.

Section (a)(2) provides that "Respirators shall be provided by the employer when such equipment is necessary to protect the health of the employee."  Although the well here was not expected to produce $H_2S$, other wells within a few miles of the well had produced $H_2S$.  Thus City, had it exercised reasonable diligence, would have had notice of the risk of $H_2S$ emissions.  Moreover, even had the well in this case been the first in the area to emit $H_2S$, that fact would not have excused City's failure to provide respirators and a respiratory protection program to its employees.  The presence of hydrogen sulfide in oil and gas fields, while capricious, is nonetheless a constant risk, particularly while swabbing wells that have not yet been brought into production.  The Act and its regulations exist to prevent an employer from gambling with the health and safety of its employees, as City did here.  The well in this case, although expected to be free of H$_2$S, produced fatal levels of the gas, thereby confirming the risk. Under these circumstances, respirators were incontrovertibly necessary to protect the health of City's two employees.

City's only defense to its completely irresponsible behavior is a finger pointed at the well operator and the simultaneous incantation of industry custom.  City points to a line of cases in which industry custom has been used to flesh out generally worded regulations in order to avoid notice problems under the due process clause.  According to City and the record, the custom and practice of the industry is for the well servicer to rely on the well operator or owner to advise it if H$_2$S hazards are present and to provide respirators if necessary.

City's reliance on this line of cases is misplaced.  The regulation here is precise.  In City's case, it concerns only one hazard and two remedies. The hazard is hydrogen sulfide, which is listed as a dangerous substance in 29 C.F.R. § 1910.1000, where a permissible exposure to limit is set; the two remedies are effective engineering controls and respirators, the requirements for the selection, use, and maintenance of which are set out in detail.

In any event, City cannot use industry custom to shift its statutory responsibility for the health and safety of its employees to third parties. The Act and its regulations place the burden of compliance squarely on the employer: "Each *employer* ... shall comply with occupational safety and health standards promulgated under this chapter," 29 U.S.C. § 654(a)(2) (emphasis added); "Respirators shall be provided by the *employer* when such equipment is necessary to protect the health of the employee."  29 C.F.R. § 1910.134(a)(2) (emphasis added).  Under the Act, it is the employer's responsibility to ensure that its employees are protected.  It may accomplish this objective through others if it chooses, but the duty to provide the protection remains the employer's, and its agent's failure to comply with a standard constitutes a violation by the employer.

In Central of Georgia Railroad Company v. OSHRC, 576 F.2d 620 (5th Cir.1978), this court held that "an employer may not contract out of its statutory responsibilities under OSHA."

\* \* \*

This reasoning applies with even greater force to the instant case, where the shift of responsibility was purportedly accomplished, not by a formal contract, but by a vaguely defined industry custom.  Nor is there an issue, as in *Central of Georgia,* regarding City's ability to accomplish compliance.  Although the worksite was on someone else's property, City could have satisfied the standard simply by providing respirators and a respiratory protective program.  It needed no authority from the well operator or owner to do so.  Under these circumstances, City must "take the consequences" of its flagrant neglect of employee safety.

## CONCLUSION

This court can instruct the OSHRC to reinstate the citations, rather than remanding for further proceedings, if only one conclusion is supportable on the record before us. Only one conclusion is supportable on the record before us: City's failure to comply with the requirements of 29 C.F.R. §§ 1910.134(a)(1) and (2) created more than "a substantial probability that death or serious physical harm could result." Hydrogen sulfide kills, and does so quickly, yet City took not the feeblest step to safeguard its employees. Its blind conduct fell far below the statutory minimum. Accordingly, the citation vacated by the OSHRC is hereby remanded with directions that it be reinstated, and the petition for review is

GRANTED.

NOTE

The standard at issue in *City Oil Well Service* was imprecise, but the court had no difficulty in rejecting the "absurd and ridiculous" interpretation urged by the employer. Nevertheless, the case raises the broader issue of balancing the remedial interest of protecting worker health and safety against the employer's interest in due process.

In some cases the reviewing courts have rejected the broad interpretation of standard. For example, in Bethlehem Steel Corp. v. OSHRC, 573 F.2d 157, 161 (3d Cir.1978), the Third Circuit stated:

> In an adjudicatory proceeding, the Commission should not strain the plain and natural meaning of words in a standard to alleviate an unlikely and uncontemplated hazard. The responsibility to promulgate clear and unambiguous standards rests with the Secretary. The test is not what he might possibly have intended, but what he said. If the language is faulty, the Secretary has the means and the obligation to amend.

# Durez Division of Occidental Chemical Corp. v. OSHA

906 F.2d 1 (D.C.Cir.1990).

■ D.H. GINSBURG, CIRCUIT JUDGE:

Durez Division of Occidental Chemical Corporation petitions to review the way in which the Occupational Safety and Health Review Administration has interpreted the disclosure requirements of its Hazard Communications Standard and applied them to the petitioners' phenol-formaldehyde compound known as "Durez 153." We agree with the Secretary's contention that the decision of this court in General Carbon Co. v. OSHRC, 860 F.2d 479 (D.C.Cir.1979) forecloses the petitioner's attempt to challenge the Commission's interpretation of the HCS. We are therefore constrained to deny the petition for review.

## I. BACKGROUND

Durez 153, a compound containing phenol and formaldehyde, is used by Durez's customers to make a variety of heat-resistant products, including pot and pan handles and distributor caps. When it is molded by a downstream product manufacturer, it releases small quantities of phenol vapor into the atmosphere.

A manufacturer of phenol is required by the HCS to disclose to purchasers all potential health risks associated with that chemical. *See* 29 C.F.R. § 1910.1000, Table Z–1 (reference list of air contaminants); *id.* § 1910.1200(d)(3)(i) (coverage of HCS). The HCS imposes upon chemical manufacturers and upon other employers who expose their employees to chemical products at the workplace a variety of requirements intended to ensure that employers and employees alike receive the information necessary to anticipate and to protect against potential chemical hazards. The Standard applies to "any chemical which is known to be present in the workplace in such a manner that employees may be exposed under normal conditions of use or in a foreseeable emergency." It defines as "hazardous" any chemical "for which there is statistically significant evidence based on at least one study conducted in accordance with established scientific principles that acute or chronic health effects may occur in exposed employees." Phenol is a regulated air contaminant, *id.* § 1910.1000, Table Z–1–A, and is therefore subject to the Hazard Communications Standard, *id.* § 1910.1200(d)(3)(i).

The HCS requires every manufacturer of chemicals to investigate the potential hazards of each chemical it either produces or uses in production; to label containers of hazardous chemicals; and to distribute to downstream users a Material Safety Data Sheet (MSDS) disclosing the health hazards posed by exposure to such chemicals. The HCS requires the MSDS to list

> the health hazards of the hazardous chemical, including signs and symptoms of exposure, and any medical conditions which are generally recognized as being aggravated by exposure to the chemical. . . .

*Id.* § 1910.1200(g)(2)(iv). It further requires each downstream employer who uses these chemicals to instruct its employees, on the basis of the MSDS, in the appropriate methods for avoiding the hazards of exposure.

In 1988, OSHA inspected a chemical manufacturing facility operated by Durez, as a result of which the Secretary issued an "other-than-serious" citation alleging that the MSDS that Durez had prepared for Durez 153 violated the HCS. The MSDS disclosed the comparatively minor risks of irritation to the eyes, skin, and respiratory tract, but failed to disclose that overexposure to phenol may cause damage to the liver, the kidneys, or the heart.

Although Durez did not deny that overexposure to phenol may cause damage to the liver, the kidneys, and the heart, it contested the citation before the Occupational Safety and Health Review Commission on the ground that the amount of phenol residue that the compound will release under foreseeable conditions of use in downstream worksites is too insignificant to pose a realistic threat of such damage. After a hearing, an ALJ concluded, based upon the classification of phenol as a hazardous chemical, the Preamble to the HCS, and the decision of this court in *General Carbon,* that Durez must disclose the potential for heart, liver, and kidney damage regardless of employees' foreseeable levels of exposure to Durez 153. No member of the Commission having called for review of this decision, it became the final order of the Commission, per 29 C.F.R. § 2200.90(d).

## II.   INTERPRETATION OF THE HCS

The Company places considerable weight upon the Secretary's own distinction between mixtures and chemicals in putting forward its claim that the HCS, properly interpreted, does not require the MSDS for Durez 153 to disclose all potential health risks associated with phenol. Mixtures are chemicals composed of constituents that have not reacted chemically with each other; mixtures are for that reason presumed to retain the hazardous properties of their constituents. Because phenol reacts and bonds with formaldehyde, leaving only small amounts of phenol residue that have failed to react with the formaldehyde, Durez asserts that Durez 153 is a chemical rather than a mixture. Under the HCS, Durez contends, the presence in a chemical of a residuum of hazardous material does not require a health hazard warning if a reliable study has shown—as Durez claims here to be the case—that employees at downstream worksites will not be exposed to concentrations above the permissible exposure limits (PEL) for that ingredient in the conditions under which that chemical will foreseeably be used. In our view, however, this court's decision in *General Carbon* and the deference due the agency's reasonable interpretation of the HCS compel us to reject the claim that forms the core of the petitioner's argument.

*First.* In *General Carbon* we upheld a Commission order requiring a manufacturer to affix to containers of electrical brushes, which are mixtures, labels identifying the constituent chemicals and warning of all associated health risks. The brushes, made primarily of copper and graphite—both of which are hazardous chemicals for purposes of the HCS—emit small quantities of copper and graphite dust when they are handled by the employees of a downstream employer. This court considered and rejected the claim that the labeling requirements of the HCS, *id.* § 1910.1200(f)(1), do not apply where the foreseeable conditions under which such employees would handle the brushes would not expose them to concentrations in excess of the PELs for copper and graphite.

The court based its rejection of this argument upon the Preamble to the HCS, which provides that

> The hazard potential does not change even though the risk of experiencing health effects does vary with the degree of exposure.... The chemical manufacturer ... in making hazard determinations, should evaluate and communicate all the potential hazards associated with a chemical, whereas the [down-stream] employer may supplement this information by instructing employees on the specific nature and degree of hazard they are likely to encounter in their particular exposure situations.

48 Fed.Reg. 53,296 (1983). The import of this passage is clear: the likelihood, at a given level of exposure, of incurring any potential harm associated with a chemical ingredient is to be weighed and communicated by the downstream employer, rather than by the manufacturer of the chemical. The reason is equally obvious: the manufacturer of the chemical is less well positioned to foresee the full range of uses to which its product may be put and the full range of exposure levels to which downstream employees may be subjected. While *General Carbon* addressed the scope of the labeling requirement rather than that of the disclosures required in a MSDS, our deference to the agency's judgment that a downstream employer is better able than the manufacturer of a chemical to adjust health warnings to the needs of its own workplace applies equally in the present context. Indeed, we reached our conclusion about the scope of the labeling requirement in part by reference to the scope of the disclosure required for a MSDS.

Moreover, as we noted in *General Carbon,* "the MSDS is intended to set forth more detailed information than are the labels." Therefore, having interpreted the HCS to require container labels to list all potential health risks associated with hazardous constituents, regardless of expected exposure levels, it would be anomalous for us now to hold that the disclosures required on the corresponding MSDS need not cover health risks that the manufacturer concludes will not materialize at projected levels of exposure, and we decline to do so.

*Second.* Quite apart from the force of *General Carbon* as precedent, we are obliged to defer to the Secretary's interpretation of her own regulation, if it is reasonable. Here, the Secretary reasonably found that the rationale for allowing a downstream employer to determine the actual risks posed by a hazardous chemical, in light of the uses to which the chemical will be put, applies equally to mixtures and to chemicals; and that the presence in a chemical of a hazardous residue that retains its chemical identity implicates the same policy considerations as the presence in a mixture of hazardous constituent materials. The Commission agreed, noting that "Durez 153 resembles a mixture in that residual phenol retains its chemical identity as it is released"; and the Secretary, in her brief, adds the observation that "the hazards of phenol due to exposure to Durez 153 in the workplace are in no way diminished simply because phenol emissions represent unreacted raw material." Accordingly, recognizing that hazardous residue in pure form is no less dangerous when contained in a chemical than when contained in a mixture, the Secretary would interpret the HCS as attributing to the compound the hazardous properties of its unreacted ingredients. We find nothing in the petitioner's argument to cast doubt upon the reasonableness of this interpretation.

We pause only to notice, for we need not today address, another potential anomaly. The HCS provides that "[i]f a mixture has not been tested as a whole to determine whether the mixture is a health hazard, the mixture shall be assumed to present the same health hazards as do the components which comprise one percent (by weight or volume) or greater of the mixture." Because the Standard provides no such threshold for chemicals other than mixtures, however, it appears that the manufacturer of a chemical that is the product of a reaction is required to disclose all potential health hazards posed by hazardous raw materials that retain their chemical identity in the reaction product, regardless of how small a percentage of that product the raw material may be. The reason for such seemingly disparate treatment is not apparent, but we are not called upon to evaluate its reasonableness today, because in fact phenol comprises more than 1 percent of Durez 153.

### III. VALIDITY OF THE HCS

The Company's alternative argument is that if the Secretary's interpretation of the disclosure requirement, as applied to the MSDS, is correct, then she exceeded her statutory authority in promulgating the HCS (in 1983). Section 6(b) of the Occupational Safety and Health Act, 29 U.S.C. §§ 655 *et seq.*, authorizes the Secretary to promulgate a standard prescribing "the use of . . . appropriate forms of warning as are necessary to insure that employees are apprised of all hazards to which they are exposed. . . ." Durez contends that requiring disclosure of all potential health hazards of a chemical, regardless of foreseeable exposure levels, is not necessary to ensure "that employees are apprised of all hazards to which they are exposed."

This argument, while not addressed in and therefore not foreclosed by *General Carbon,* is not properly before us because it was not effectively raised before the Commission in the Company's Petition for Discretionary Review of the ALJ's decision. The PDR does list, as one of five issues raised, whether "the Standard exceed[s] the statutory authority granted," but it nowhere discusses this issue, nor does it cite any authority or otherwise put the Commission on notice of the nature of or basis for its challenge. Because 29 U.S.C. § 660(a) provides that "[n]o objection that has not been urged before the Commission shall be considered by the court, unless the failure or neglect . . . be excused by extraordinary circumstances," and because we find that the petitioner's abbreviated mention of its challenge to the validity of the Standard is "wholly inadequate to satisfy the requirement of § 660(a) that an objection be 'urged before the Commission,'" we conclude that the petitioner failed to preserve this challenge for judicial review.

### IV. MANUFACTURER'S TORT LAW DUTY TO WARN

Finally, we reject the Company's claim that the Secretary's interpretation of the HCS disclosure requirement interferes with its duty, under state tort law, to warn employees of the health hazards posed by its products. Specifically, the petitioner contends that the Secretary's construction of the Standard forces it to bury the warnings that properly belong in the MSDS amidst a mass of "obscure" and "unnecessary" information. This is overly dramatic, however. The MSDS for Durez 153 consists of four sparsely filled-in pages of a form, only a few entries on which would have to be elaborated to accommodate the risks to hearts, lungs, and kidneys. Realistically, therefore, OSHA's interpretation of the Standard does not force the manufacturer to choose between complying with the HCS and complying with the teachings of state tort law.

For these reasons, the petition for review is

*Denied.*

## NOTES AND QUESTIONS

**1.**  Why do you think the employer was so concerned about not informing employees about the possible harms to heart, lung, and kidneys?

**2.**  The hazard communication standard was upheld in United Steelworkers of America v. Auchter, 763 F.2d 728 (3d Cir.1985).

**3.**  In Martin v. American Cyanamid Co., 5 F.3d 140 (6th Cir.1993), the Sixth Circuit held that the hazard communication standard requires chemical manufacturers to include on shipping labels the "target organ" effects of exposure.

### b.   SAFETY TRAINING

## Superior Custom Cabinet Co.

18 OSHC 1019, (1997).

### BY THE COMMISSION:

Superior Custom Cabinet Co., Inc. ("Superior"), which is based in Garland, Texas, makes custom cabinets for new houses. A Superior delivery crew member carrying a cabinet upstairs in a house under construction was fatally injured in a fall. After its investigation of the accident, the Occupational Safety and Health Administration ("OSHA") issued a citation to Superior alleging four serious violations of the construction safety standards requiring instructions to employees in recognizing and avoiding hazards, regular inspections of the worksite by a competent person, and guardrails for landings and stairways. Administrative Law Judge Stanley M. Schwartz affirmed all four items in the citation and assessed a total penalty of $2,000. For the reasons that follow, we affirm the judge's decision.

### I.   Background

After a Superior salesperson takes the measurements for the cabinets at a house under construction, Superior's shop makes the cabinets to specifications in three to four weeks. One of four Superior delivery crews, each headed by a "leadman," then delivers the cabinets, usually following a call from the builder that the house is ready for them. Later, a different crew installs the cabinets. During all this time construction of the house is progressing, and the conditions are changing as the various subcontractors do their work. Generally by the time the delivery crew arrives there are railings on the stairs and landings.

On September 16, 1993, a delivery crew consisting of driver and leadman Tracy Sims and two "haulers" Larry Tiner and William Walton was assigned to deliver a custommade cabinet for the master bathroom in a house under construction in Rockwall, Texas.   The cabinet measured 5–½ feet tall, 2 feet wide, and 1–½ feet deep.   Sims checked the first floor of the house for obstructions that could cause the haulers to trip or fall.   He testified that he did not check upstairs because the delivery ticket did not show any cabinets to be delivered to the second floor.   After Sims' first-floor check, Tiner and Walton unloaded the cabinet, carried it into the house, and asked another person working in the house for the location of the "master bedroom."   They were told that it was upstairs.   They then proceeded up the stairs, with Tiner holding one end and walking backwards up the stairs followed by Walton holding the other end and walking forward.   The stairs, after a switchback point at a small landing midway up, led up to the top landing;  the exposed sides of the stairway and the top landing were not guarded by any railing or other protection.   When Tiner reached the second floor, he stepped backwards off the unguarded top landing and fell 10 feet 5 inches to the floor below.   He died after being hospitalized.

## II.   Lack of Adequate Instructions in Recognizing and Avoiding Fall Hazard

Item 2 alleges a serious violation of 29 C.F.R. § 1926.21(b)(2), which requires:

> The employer shall instruct each employee in the recognition and avoidance of unsafe conditions and the regulations applicable to his work environment to control or eliminate any hazards or other exposure to illness or injury.

Tom West, Superior's vice president, who had been with the company for twenty-three years, testified that the delivery crews are orally instructed that, if in trying to deliver a cabinet they see an "unsafe condition" that they cannot avoid, "like in this situation [where the cabinet goes] upstairs and there is no railing," they should leave the cabinet downstairs (unless the builder tells them not to) and call the office to speak with West, who has a pager if he is not in the office.   West testified that he had "personal knowledge" that Sims, Tiner, and Walton "were instructed on potential fall hazards when they delivered cabinets."   Superior had no written safety rules specifically addressing unguarded stairs or landings.

Leadman Sims testified that, prior to the accident, he had never been told not to go up stairs or walk on "floors" without guardrails.   However, he acknowledged that he had been told to watch out for "dangerous situations" including fall hazards.   Sims understood that, if he saw conditions at the worksite that were unsafe, he was supposed to call the shop and, if the conditions were upstairs, leave the cabinet downstairs.   Sims testified that he has left cabinets downstairs before but had never called West to notify him of the problem.   West confirmed this testimony, noting that he had been "chewed out" by builders because Sims had left cabinets downstairs.   According to Sims, there are some situations where unguarded stairs and landings do not pose a fall hazard because their configuration or width allows a person traversing them to stay far enough away from any unguarded edge.

Although hauler Walton did not testify at the hearing, a statement he made to the compliance officer ("CO") was admitted over objection. According to the CO, Walton told him that he would deliver cabinets upstairs where stairs and landings had no guardrails, as he tried to do the day of the accident, because the lack of guardrails "had never stopped [him] before."

The judge concluded from the evidence that Sims, Tiner, and Walton were inadequately trained in the avoidance of fall hazards. We agree.

Section 1926.21(b)(2) requires instructions to employees on (1) how to recognize and avoid unsafe conditions they may encounter on the job, and (2) the regulations applicable to those hazardous conditions. An employer's instructions are adequate under section 1926.21(b) if they are "specific enough to advise employees of the hazards associated with their work and the ways to avoid them" and are modeled on the applicable standards.

Because Superior's work rule was so general, employees developed their own different ideas about what was "unsafe." As noted above, according to Sims, a stairway without a railing could be safe depending on how it is constructed. This comports with his testimony that when ascending unguarded stairs he hugs the wall. Sims also thought that a landing without a railing could be safe if the landing was wide enough so that he did not need to get close to the unguarded edge. While the CO testified that he had seen landings (not necessarily in houses) where the unguarded end was 15 to 20 feet away from where employees worked or traveled, and that he agreed that in such instances that was a safe distance, Superior's instructions to its employees gave no guidance on a safe distance. In his capacity as a supervisor, Sims' decisions as to what is "unsafe" affect the employees on his crew.

Moreover, the decision to identify a condition as "unsafe" was left not just to leadman Sims, it was apparently also left to the interpretation of the haulers. When asked at the hearing whether hauler Walton indicated to him during his interview that the conditions (that is, the unguarded stairway and landing) at this house were unsafe, the CO responded that he did not. As noted, Walton told the CO that he would deliver cabinets upstairs despite the lack of any railing, as he had done in the past.

Rules such as Superior's that give employees too much discretion in identifying unsafe conditions have been found too general to be effective. As the Fourth Circuit noted in Tri–State Roofing & Sheet Metal, Inc. v. OSHRC, 685 F.2d 878, 881 (4th Cir.1982): "The particular views of workmen are not necessarily, and often times are not, the best determination as to what is safe and what is unsafe. Convenience rather than safety considerations often dictates a worker's perspective." We find that Superior's instructions to its employees to leave the cabinet downstairs and call the office if they encountered "unsafe" conditions were not specific enough to inform employees how to recognize and avoid the fall hazards posed by unguarded stairways and landings.

Moreover, Superior's instructions did not meet the other prong of the two-part test for adequate instructions under section 1926.21(b)(2): instructions should be modeled on applicable regulations. Under the applicable OSHA guardrail standards, 29 C.F.R. §§ 1926.500(d)(1) and 1926.1052(c)(1), which Superior was also cited for violating, railings are necessary with a few exceptions, none of which are the situations relied on by Sims. Section 1926.1052(c)(1) requires that a stairway have a guardrail system along each unprotected side and at least one handrail *unless* the stairway has less than four risers or rises 30 inches or less. Section 1926.500(d)(1) requires that a landing be guarded except where it is less than six feet above the adjacent floor or ground except where there is entrance to a ramp, stairway, or fixed ladder.

For the reasons above, we agree with the judge that Superior violated section 1926.21(b)(2).   * * *

## NOTES AND QUESTIONS

**1.** The standard at issue in *Superior Custom Cabinet,* 29 C.F.R. § 1916.21(b)(2), actually provides for instructing employees in hazard recognition. Even in the absence of such an explicit requirement, the Commission and courts have held that employers are required to train their employees to perform the job safely. The degree of training required depends on the obviousness of the hazard, the experience of the employee, the likelihood that an accident would occur, and the degree of harm likely to result from an accident. Pratt & Whitney Aircraft Group, 12 OSHC 1770, 1986 OSHD ¶ 27,564 (1986), aff'd, 805 F.2d 391 (2d Cir.1986).

**2.** The Commission has held that in formulating a safety training program the current industry practice is relevant, "but it is not dispositive if industry practice is shown to be inadequate." Baker Tank Co./Altech, 17 OSHC 1177, 1995 OSHD ¶ 30,734 (1995).

**3.** Some examples of cases in which the employer's safety training was held to be inadequate include the following: Ames Crane & Rental Service, Inc. v. Dunlop, 532 F.2d 123 (8th Cir.1976) (employer merely "made available" several hundred pages of written safety material which crane operators could read at their option); E.L. Davis Contracting Co., 16 OSHC 2046, 1994 OSHD ¶ 30,580 (1994) (oral direction to employees to leave a confined space if they felt they were getting dizzy or "smelled something a little different").

**4.** For a further discussion of safety training and the defense of unpreventable employee misconduct, see Brennan v. OSHRC (Republic Creosoting Co.), infra p. 762.

c.   BURDEN OF PROOF

## Syntron, Inc.

11 OSHC 1868, 1983–84 OSHD ¶ 26,841 (1984).

BY THE COMMISSION:

A decision of Administrative Law Judge Louis G. LaVecchia is before the Commission for review under 29 U.S.C. § 661(i). A citation was issued to Syntron, Inc. alleging that it violated 29 C.F.R. § 1910.212(a)(1) because the unused portion of the blade of its metal cut-off saw was not guarded. The record indicates that the operator of the saw positions the material to be cut in a vise while the machine is off, and then lowers the top portion of the saw until the blade is near the material. He then turns on the saw, which automatically makes the cut and shuts off. Both the compliance officer and Syntron's president testified that the operator stands about a foot from the unguarded blade. Judge LaVecchia vacated the citation on the ground that the evidence was insufficient to establish that during the operation of the saw employees were exposed to a "hazard" within the meaning of the standard.

We have examined the entire record—particularly a videotape showing the machine in operation—and we are unconvinced, as was the judge, that the operator's hands come, or would have reason to come, close enough to the unused portion of the blade to be exposed to a hazard.[1] Accordingly, the judge's decision is affirmed.

■ CLEARY, COMMISSIONER, dissenting:

The majority vacates this citation because it is not convinced that the operator's hands "come, or would have reason to come" close enough to an unguarded bandsaw blade to be exposed to a hazard. This holding simply ignores the purpose of the standard and long-standing Commission precedent by taking no account of the fact that the operator could be injured through inadvertence. Accordingly, I must dissent.

Section 1910.212(a)(1) provides that "[o]ne or more methods of machine guarding shall be provided to protect the operator and other employees in the machine area from hazards such as those created by point of operation...." This Commission has long held that "the standard is plainly intended to eliminate danger from unsafe operating procedures, poor training, or *employee inadvertence*." It is for this reason that the standard requires *physical* methods of guarding rather than methods of guarding that depend on correct human behavior. "The standard recognizes that men do not discard their personal qualities when they go to work."

Thus, it is beside the point that—as the majority essentially finds—it has not been shown that the operator would have reason to put his hands into the point of operation during its operating cycle. As stated above, our precedent unequivocally holds that the standard requires physical protec-

---

**1.** The dissent maintains that Syntron's president testified that the machine operator could inadvertently injure himself. The witness was asked, however, only whether inadvertent injury was *possible*. Given the range of the human imagination, it is understandable that he answered in the affirmative. The standard was not, however, intended to protect against the mere possibility of injury. Rather, whether a machine presents a hazard within the meaning of the standard must be determined by how the machine functions and how it is operated by the employees.

tion to guard against inadvertence. The facts in this case present precisely the conditions at which the machine guarding standards are directed.

It is undisputed that the operator stands only a foot away from the partially unguarded bandsaw blade. The operator is positioned with direct access to the point of operation and within reaching distance of it. The president of the company admitted that an employee could inadvertently injure himself. The videotape does not prove otherwise even though it is a staged presentation prepared by Syntron. Accordingly, I find that the operator is exposed to a hazard of injury from the partially guarded bandsaw blade.

Finally, there was testimony that a guard could have been secured or fabricated for no more than $20.00. If, indeed, the purpose of the Act is to provide safe working conditions and prevent injuries, twenty dollars is a small price to pay to protect against an inadvertent injury here.

## NOTES AND QUESTIONS

**1.** Are OSHA standards intended to protect employees only when they are operating machinery and equipment in accordance with the instructional video? See Fabricated Metal Products, Inc., 18 OSHC 1072, 1998 OSHD ¶ 31,463 (1997) (Secretary failed to establish reasonable predictability of employee access to the point of operation of unguarded machine).

**2.** Would the Commission have found a violation if the employee had lost his balance while operating the machine and had his arm chopped off by the saw blade?

**3.** How would a court analyze these facts if the case were a common law action based on products liability? See, e.g., Green v. Sterling Extruder Corp., 471 A.2d 15 (N.J.1984) (employee's inadvertence did not relieve manufacturer of liability). Is the low cost of prevention relevant to either the OSHA or products liability case?

**4.** To establish a prima facie violation of § 5(a)(2), the Secretary must prove by a preponderance of the evidence that (1) the cited standard applies; (2) there was a failure to comply with the standard; (3) an employee had access to the violative condition; and (4) the employer knew or could have known of the condition with the exercise of reasonable diligence. Dun–Par Engineered Form Co., 12 OSHC 1962, 1986–87 OSHD ¶ 27,651 (1986).

## 2. GENERAL DUTY CLAUSE

## Pepperidge Farm, Inc.

17 OSHC 1993, 1997 OSHD ¶ 31,301 (1997).

BY THE COMMISSION:

In this case, the Commission considers for the first time whether the Secretary may apply section 5(a)(1), the Act's general duty clause, to issues of "ergonomics." That term has been defined as the "science concerned with how to fit a job to a worker's anatomical, physiological, and psychological characteristics in a way that will enhance human efficiency and well-being." The lifting items here involve employees lifting 100–pound bags of sugar, 68–pound blocks of butter, roll stock weighing up to 165 pounds, and cookie tins weighing up to 38 pounds. The repetitive motion items involve employees performing in quick succession assembly line tasks, such as dropping paper cups from a stack with one hand and filling them with baked cookies with the other hand.

We find that the Secretary may utilize section 5(a)(1) to address lifting and repetitive motion hazards. In regard to the lifting tasks, Pepperidge did not seek review of the judge's finding that a hazard exists. Pepperidge did challenge his finding that it had recognized the hazard. We find that Pepperidge recognized the existence of numerous lifting hazards at the Downingtown plant, based on the memoranda and testimony of its corporate ergonomist, Ms. Jane Teed–Sparling, its own medical records of lifting injuries to employees, and memoranda from its workers' compensation carrier, Liberty Mutual Insurance Company. We reject the arguments that we should not consider that evidence in deciding the question.

\* \* \*

With regard to the alleged repetitive motion injuries, we find that the evidence shows that a substantial number of the alleged injuries, particularly carpal tunnel syndrome, did occur among the workers at Downingtown. This conclusion is supported by the medical records, the testimony of Pepperidge's own medical team regarding the medical records, and the views of outside medical professionals. As to the repetitive motion hazards, we have reviewed the testimony and scientific studies in evidence regarding whether the kinds of repetitive jobs at issue here substantially contribute to the development of carpal tunnel syndrome and other upper extremity musculo-skeletal disorders ("UEMSDs"). We find that such jobs can be a substantial contributing factor in these injuries. This view is supported by the clinical and epidemiological evidence discussed below, and by UEMSD incidence rate comparisons between Pepperidge's biscuit line workers and other populations. It is also supported by Pepperidge's own medical records, which contain reports of clinicians who examined and treated employees and reported a causal connection between the jobs and the development of their UEMSDs.

We find multiple bases for concluding that Pepperidge recognized the hazards at issue. These include memoranda by Pepperidge's corporate ergonomist and the medical records of injured employees, as well as testimony by both Pepperidge's medical director and its chief nurse at the plant. We also find that the hazards were causing serious physical harm up to and including disabling conditions requiring surgical correction and even termination of employment.

Finally, we find that abatement of the hazard here can be required under section 5(a)(1) but that the Secretary has failed to meet her burden of showing that further abatement action was required in light of what had already been undertaken. We conclude that the appropriate response to the hazard at Downingtown was a process that included actions selected from a menu of alternatives. The question of the appropriateness of the abatement here turns on the extent to which Pepperidge implemented the recommendations provided by its corporate ergonomist and the extent to which specific further actions urged by the Secretary were required to be undertaken. We conclude that the Secretary has not shown that the additional steps proposed by the Secretary and not taken by Pepperidge were feasible and that their efficacy in reducing the hazard was so compelling that the failure to have implemented them by the time of the inspection rendered Pepperidge's process inadequate.

\* \* \*

## III.  Upper Extremity Musculo–Skeletal Disorders

This item alleged 175 separate willful violations of section 5(a)(1), in that 175 employees "were required to perform tasks involving repetitive motions in postures resulting in stresses that had caused, were causing or were likely to cause cumulative trauma disorders." The proposed penalties were $5,000 per instance, for a total of $875,000. The employees worked beside conveyor belts in the Biscuit Division of the Downingtown plant. They assembled, packed, and packaged baked cookies.

A violation of section 5(a)(1) of the Act exists where: (1) a condition or activity in the employer's workplace presents a hazard to employees, (2) the cited employer or the employer's industry recognizes the hazard, (3) the hazard is causing or likely to cause death or serious physical harm, and (4) feasible means exist to eliminate or materially reduce the hazard.

\* \* \*

### B.  The Alleged Injuries

The kinds of ailments that Pepperidge's employees are alleged to have suffered are commonly referred to by various names including upper extremity musculo-skeletal disorders ("UEMSDs"), cumulative trauma disorders ("CTDs"), or repetitive strain injuries (RSIs). We will use the term UEMSDs because it describes the conditions without suggesting a cause.

A specific UEMSD that allegedly resulted in disability and surgery for numerous Pepperidge employees is carpal tunnel syndrome ("CTS"). As explained by the physicians in this case, CTS consists of a constellation of symptoms including numbness and tingling in fingers, loss of muscle strength in the hand, discomfort in the hand, wrist and arm (even the shoulder and neck in many patients). It is due to compression ("entrapment") of the median nerve, which runs through the carpal tunnel, including the wrist. In most cases it results in abnormal nerve conduction which may be measured by electrodiagnostic tests.

Other UEMSDs from which certain Pepperidge employees allegedly suffered were tendinitis (including epicondylitis), tenosynovitis (including DeQuervain's disease), trigger finger, and ganglionic cysts. As they relate to UEMSDs, those terms may be defined as follows. Tendinitis is the inflammation of a tendon. Webster's Third New Intl. Dictionary 2355 (1986). Epicondylitis is tendinitis at the elbow. Stedman's Medical Dictionary 470 (1976). Tenosynovitis is inflammation of a tendon sheath. *Webster's* at 2356. DeQuervain's disease is tenosynovitis of a thumb. *Stedman's* at 404. Trigger finger is a disorder in which a finger extends or flexes with a snap. *Webster's* at 2444. A ganglionic cyst is "a small cystic tumor containing viscid fluid and connected either with a joint membrane or tendon sheath," typically at the wrist. *Id.* at 934.

\* \* \*

### D.  Applicability of Section 5(a)(1) to Ergonomic Hazards

At the threshold, Pepperidge and supporting *amici* argue that the undefined nature of the hazard (assuming it exists) precludes regulation under section 5(a)(1). In a related vein, they argue that the hazard is so undefined and/or controverted that a finding of violation would defy constitutional requirements of notice and due process. Finally, they argue that the Secretary's evidence of hazard must be gauged by the "significant risk test" articulated in Kastalon, Inc., 12 OSHC 1928, 1986-87, OSHD ¶ 27,643 (1986).

Pepperidge argues that the hazard here cannot be regulated because, as it correctly points out, no one could testify as to when repetitive motion becomes a hazard or precisely how much Pepperidge should have reduced its employees' repetitive motion. While knowledge of the threshold for injury may be essential in some cases, however, the Commission has never held that certainty as to the threshold level for injury is a prerequisite to regulation under the general duty clause.

Pepperidge cites to our decision in *Kastalon*, which drew on the Supreme Court's decision in Industrial Union Dept. v. American Petroleum Inst., 448 U.S. 607 (1980) (*"Benzene"*) for the proposition that the Secretary must show that a condition poses a significant risk before it can be regulated under section 5(a)(1).

*Kastalon* addressed the issue of potential employee exposure to a suspected human carcinogen commonly called "MOCA." We noted that the Supreme Court's decision in *Benzene* held that to establish a significant risk of harm regarding an alleged carcinogen the Secretary seeks to regulate by rule, she must present "a body of reputable scientific thought," and that the Court "noted that animal studies, epidemiological evidence and worker mortality rates could be used to establish the existence of a significant risk."

The evidence of hazard in *Kastalon* was based on extrapolation from animal tests and concerned "potential" injury. In contrast, this case stems from allegations of actual injury to humans. The inability to quantify a threshold may be of great significance when there is little evidence that the putative hazard may cause injury to humans, or where the question is whether it should be presumed that the risk should be controlled to the full extent feasible. It is of less significance where, as here, human injury is allegedly manifest. Thus, where substantial injury is actually occurring, neither precedent nor common sense require that the finding of hazard be foresworn until there is determination of the threshold at which there occurs a substantial risk of injury.

Pepperidge further points out, however, and the Secretary's experts agree, that nonworkplace factors may cause or contribute to the illnesses at issue, and that individuals differ in their susceptibility to potential causal factors. However, such characteristics (and the inability to determine threshold of harm) are not unique to putative ergonomic hazards, but inhere in other workplace hazards as well. For example, some or all of these characteristics obtain for many chemical, toxic and other workplace hazards. Thus, to preclude the application of section 5(a)(1) to a hazard with the characteristics cited by Pepperidge would be to preclude the use of section 5(a)(1) for many occupational ills. To be clear, characteristics such as those identified by Pepperidge may (as discussed later) bear on questions of causation or feasibility of abatement. They do not, however, *ipso facto* preclude the possibility of regulation under section 5(a)(1).

Respondent and supporting *amici* correctly point out that a corner-stone of section 5(a)(1) is the principle that employers should not be penalized for failing to take actions for which they lacked reasonable notice. Thus, they note, citing our precedent, a "broad generic definition of the hazard" is unacceptable because it does not "identify conditions or practices over which the employer can reasonably be expected to exercise control." Pepperidge also cites *Diebold,* for the proposition that substantial dispute in the scientific community about whether jobs cause UEMSDs demonstrates that the general duty clause does not provide employers with the notice of ergonomic violations required by the Constitution. We agree with Pepperidge that the ability of an employer to identify a hazard and the state of scientific understanding are relevant to the question of notice. In the discussion that follows these factors play central roles.

### E.  Existence of a Hazard

The first element of a section 5(a)(1) violation is the existence of a hazard, which turns on two factors, first, actual or potential physical harm, and second, a sufficient causal connection between the harm and the workplace.

* * *

Pepperidge argues that the injuries alleged here may be essentially dismissed as questionable reports of soft tissue ills; however, carpal tunnel syndrome (a nerve disorder) was the single most identified injury at Pepperidge, representing almost half of the injured workers at issue. The experts appear to agree that CTS is susceptible to reliable diagnosis. The majority of those with carpal tunnel syndrome, Dr. Hadler acknowledged, "have a physiologically demonstrable abnormality. The nerve conducts normally until it goes to the wrist, and then it doesn't conduct normally across the wrist." Carpal tunnel syndrome, he explained, "can be defined by clinical and electrodiagnostic criteria of substantial sensitivity and specificity." At oral argument, Pepperidge agreed that "the diagnoses were generally accurate when it comes to carpal tunnel syndrome which required surgery." Pepperidge reported that 28 employees underwent 42 separate surgical procedures, including 32 carpal tunnel releases. These injuries, again, were diagnosed by Pepperidge's panel of doctors.

In light of the above, we find that the existence of carpal tunnel syndrome among the employees at Downingtown has been established on this record. Moreover, the existence of soft tissue ills at Downingtown is supported by the Downingtown medical records, by the testimony of Drs. Harrison and Snyder, and the testimony of the workers who reported injury. We additionally find the reservations raised by Drs. Hadler and Nathan about the reliability of soft tissue injury diagnoses inadequate to rebut the contemporaneous clinical evidence of injury here. (We note Dr. Nathan testified that generally he was not in a position to "second guess the Pepperidge Farm physicians and the physicians to whom the employees were referred as to whether the employees had the particular upper extremity musculo-skeletal disorders for which they were diagnosed.") We therefore conclude that injury, particularly carpal tunnel syndrome, existed among the Downingtown workers. This being the case, the question of the cause(s) of such injury, needs to be addressed.

* * *

We find that the weight of the clinical opinions here support the proposition that at least some of the UEMSDs were caused by the work. Testimony of three of the four expert clinicians supported the proposition that repetitive motion may cause some of the kinds of injuries at Downingtown. Further, Dr. Hadler's hypothesis that UEMSDs cannot be caused by customary and comfortable actions does not fit the case here where there is ample testimony by those on the scene—including Pepperidge's corporate ergonomist and workers—that the tasks at issue were not comfortable particularly in light of the high number of repetitions. Similarly, Dr. Hadler's view that reports of workplace related UEMSDs are typically claimed soft tissue ills that are a function of psychosocial factors does not fit a case such as this where many instances of carpal tunnel syndrome were diagnosed.

### F.  Recognition of the Hazards

The evidence of record in this case fully supports a finding that Pepperidge recognized the hazards alleged in this item. We summarize the evidence that supports this finding below. We must determine, however, whether it is appropriate to find recognition if Pepperidge's knowledge of the hazards was obtained, in part, through its own efforts toward achieving a safe workplace.

Turning first to the question of knowledge, we note that there is ample evidence that Pepperidge Farm was aware of both actual injury to employees and its causal connection to the workplace. That evidence includes records kept by Pepperidge's own medical department. Additionally, Dr. Snyder, Pepperidge's plant physician, testified that the cupping and capping jobs put the employees at increased risk of developing UEMSDs. Further, Pepperidge's chief nurse at the plant, Carol Moore, testified that "at our biscuit plant when they cupped cookies, that could give you tendinitis, especially if they were doing it either too fast or dropping the cups too fast or something." The physicians whom Pepperidge itself retained to examine and treat the 68 employees with UEMSDs generally concluded that those conditions were causally connected to their jobs and were the precipitating factor in the employees' disablement.

Evidence of Pepperidge's knowledge of the hazards further includes the reports submitted by Jane Teed–Sparling, the ergonomist for Pepperidge's parent company, Campbell Soup Co. She reported, following an investigation, that a causal connection between the biscuit line jobs at Downingtown (and other Pepperidge biscuit plants) and UEMSDs. She informed Pepperidge executives of her findings in her reports on the Downingtown and other plants.

* * *

## G.  Serious Physical Harm

Section 5(a)(1) requires the employer to abate only those recognized hazards "that are causing or are likely to cause death or serious physical harm to his employees." We find that at least some of the UEMSDs here constitute "serious physical harm."

* * *

There are nonserious UEMSDs. However, physical disorders that so adversely affect employees that they are disabled from doing their jobs are serious physical harm in our view—even if the disability is not permanent. Pepperidge's medical records show that about half of the 68 employees at issue became disabled from performing their regular jobs. Many were placed on disability and others were given restricted work. At least 33 employees were diagnosed with CTS, of which 16 underwent carpal tunnel release surgery (10 of them had more than one surgery). Those employees missed several weeks or months of work while recuperating. Employees with trigger finger and ganglion cysts also underwent surgery and lost time from work. All those UEMSDs clearly involved serious physical harm to the employees. In light of all of the above, we conclude that the hazards at issue were likely to cause serious physical harm to employees.

## H.  Feasibility of Abatement

### 1.  Introduction

As discussed, in order to prove a violation of section 5(a)(1), the Secretary also must show that feasible means exist to eliminate or materially reduce the hazards.

* * *

We conclude based on the entire record that here, where actual injury is present and substantial causation has been shown, the Secretary may require Pepperidge to engage in an abatement process, the goal of which is to determine what action or combination of actions will eliminate or materially reduce the hazard.

\* \* \*

Accordingly, the essential disagreement in this case does not relate to the nature of the Secretary's burden or the identification of core components of the abatement process.   Rather, the parties disagree on the extent to which Pepperidge actually implemented particular actions, and the extent to which it was obliged to pursue additional actions that would reduce repetitions.   For the reasons stated below, we find that the Secretary failed to meet her burden to demonstrate that: 1) Pepperidge failed to undertake the requisite abatement process, or 2) the specific actions allegedly not undertaken by Pepperidge were feasible and likely to materially reduce the hazard.

\* \* \*

In this regard we note, even when repetitions remain constant, reducing or eliminating a harmful work posture (*e.g.*, by training or new equipment) can reduce the number of *harmful* repetitions.   Also, the means of reducing repetition can take a number of forms.   Here, they include 1) automation, 2) the rotation of workers among tasks involving greater and lesser repetitions, 3) the reduction of conveyor belt speed or cookie drop rate, 4) work pauses (which reduce the number of repetitions per worker), and 5) the addition of workers to the assembly line (which also reduces the number of repetitions per worker).

\* \* \*

More specifically, Pepperidge took steps that had the effect of reducing certain repetitions.   First, Pepperidge installed an automatic case packer on the Institutional Goldfish line to eliminate manual packing of the institutional containers.   Pepperidge also made job rotation changes within the Biscuit Department.   Furthermore, it implemented Teed–Sparling's 1988 recommendations to: (1) limit cup dropping to every other station, thus allowing thumbs to rest 20 minutes between cup dropping, and (2) eliminate picking up the 5th Milano cookie with the left hand while clutching the cups.

Pepperidge made additional attempts to eliminate some forms of repetition through automation and better work methods.   Pepperidge tried to develop a method or mechanism to automatically drop the cups.   Pepperidge made significant efforts to automate the placement of cookies.   It also made many attempts to automate the capping of chocolate sandwich cookies—primarily at Downingtown.   \* \* \*

Thus, we find that the gravamen of the Secretary's criticism is not Pepperidge's general failure to address repetition but its failure to take specific actions advocated by the NIOSH ergonomists who testified for the

Secretary.  This requires us to consider under the *National Realty* test whether the Secretary established that these specific actions were feasible and likely to reduce risk.

### 4.  Further Steps Advocated by the Secretary

The Secretary presented the testimony of NIOSH ergonomists Daniel Habes and Dr. Vernon Putz–Anderson to establish that Pepperidge could have taken the following additional actions to abate the hazards:  (1) adding workers to each of the lines, (2) introducing micropauses into the conveyors to interrupt the work flow periodically, (3) reducing the line speeds, and (4) rotating employees out of highly repetitive jobs to less repetitive ones.

The judge accepted both Habes and Putz–Anderson as experts in ergonomics.  Dr. Putz–Anderson generally testified that "adding an individual to the line is one approach for reducing the repetition for each individual."  * * *

Teed–Sparling noted that Pepperidge had increased the number of employees working at the capping conveyors by early 1988.  Thus, Pepperidge considered the issue and had implemented a change for capping before the inspection.  * * *

Dr. Putz–Anderson further recommended that Pepperidge experiment with reducing line speeds in increments to assess whether employees' UEMSD–related symptoms abated.  He testified that a method used quite commonly by ergonomists is a "psychophysical method."  First, a questionnaire is used to determine the level of discomfort and symptoms that the employees experience working at the current speeds.  Then the line speed is reduced, normally in increments of about 10 percent.  After a week or two, the employees are questioned again to the amount of "reported symptoms of local muscle fatigue, tenderness or pain in the hands, arms, wrists or neck."  However, Dr. Putz–Anderson did not testify to any specific instance where that method had been tried successfully.  Nor did the Secretary present any evidence that slowing down the line by 10 percent or more would not effect the quality of the cookies.

* * *

Therefore, we conclude that with regard to three of the additional means of abatement which she sought, the Secretary has not established their feasibility at Pepperidge's Downingtown plant.  With respect to the addition of employees to the line, the Secretary has arguably met her burden of demonstrating feasibility by showing on occasion the company did add workers.  However, under all the circumstances and noting that Pepperidge has followed an incremental process approach, we cannot find that the Secretary has met her burden of showing that this measure would materially reduce the hazard.

### 5.  Conclusion

On this record, we conclude that the Secretary has failed to establish that the process engaged in by Pepperidge to abate the ergonomics hazards at Downingtown was insufficient.  Further, the Secretary has not shown that the additional steps not taken by Pepperidge were feasible and that their efficacy in reducing the hazard was so compelling that the failure to have implemented them by the time of the inspection rendered Pepperidge's process inadequate.  Accordingly, we uphold the judge's dismissal of this citation item.

NOTES AND QUESTIONS

**1.**  The general duty clause, § 5(a)(1), was included in the Act because Congress realized that it would be impossible to promulgate an OSHA standard dealing with every conceivable workplace hazard.  Therefore, alleged violations of the general duty clause originally tended to focus on distinct hazards, such as where an employee was suffocated by the cave-in of stored cottonseed, Southern Soya Corp., 1 OSHC 1412, 1973–4 OSHD ¶ 16,957 (1973), and where an employee was killed while cleaning the inside of cement mixer, Richmond Block, Inc., 1 OSHC 1505, 1973–74 OSHD ¶ 17,137 (1974).

In recent years, OSHA has attempted to use § 5(a)(1) to cite employers for more common hazards for which standards have not been promulgated for one reason or another.  The *Pepperidge Farm* case illustrates the difficulties of relying on the general duty clause.

**2.**  Because it is worded so broadly, Congress attempted to restrict the types of cases in which § 5(a)(1) could be used.  First, the hazard must be "recognized," which means that the cited employer or the employer's industry regards the condition as a hazard.  Second, § 5(a)(1) only applies to serious violations.  Third, the general duty clause may be cited only where the violation creates a risk of harm to employees of the cited employer.

**3.**  As discussed in *Pepperidge Farm,* the Secretary's burden of proof is greater in cases brought under § 5(a)(1) than those brought under § 5(a)(2).  In National Realty & Construction Co. v. OSHRC, 489 F.2d 1257 (D.C.Cir.1973), the D.C. Circuit held that to prove a violation of § 5(a)(1) the Secretary must prove:  (1) that the employer failed to render its workplace free of a hazard which was (2) recognized and (3) causing or likely to cause death or serious physical harm, and (4) the Secretary must specify the particular steps the cited employer should have taken to avoid citation and to demonstrate the feasibility and likely utility of these measures.

**4.**  Citation under § 5(a)(1) ordinarily is precluded if a specific standard applies.  The standards, compliance with which is mandated under § 5(a)(2), are deemed to provide employers with greater notice of their duties than the generally worded requirement of § 5(a)(1).  Brisk Waterproofing Co., 1 OSHC 1263, 1973–74 OSHD ¶ 16,345 (1973).  In International Union, UAW v. General Dynamics Land Systems Division, 815 F.2d 1570 (D.C.Cir.), cert. denied, 484 U.S. 976 (1987), however, the court held that even if the employer complies with the requirements of a specific standard it still may be in violation of § 5(a)(1) if it *knew* that the conditions at its place of employment are such that the safety standard will not adequately deal with the hazards to which its employees are exposed.

**5.** OSHA's attempts to regulate ergonomic hazards have been extremely controversial. OSHA's proposed ergonomics standard met with such vehement opposition from employers that Congress attached appropriations riders to OSHA's budget prohibiting it from issuing an ergonomics standard. In the appropriation act for fiscal 1998, OSHA was also prohibited from issuing citations for ergonomic hazards under § 5(a)(1). Why do you think this issue has aroused such widespread employer opposition? On ergonomics, see generally, David J. Kolesar, Cumulative Trauma Disorders: OSHA's General Duty Clause and the Need for an Ergonomics Standard, 90 Mich.L.Rev. 2079 (1992); Marc Linder, I Gave My Employer a Chicken That Had No Bone: Joint Firm–State Responsibility for Line–Speed–Related Occupational Injuries, 46 Case W.Res.L.Rev. 33 (1995).

**6.** In Megawest Financial, Inc., 17 OSHC 1337, 1995 OSHD ¶ 30,798 (ALJ 1995), the employer managed an apartment complex in a high crime area of Lauderhill, Florida. The four-person staff was continually subject to threats, belligerent conduct, and physical attack by tenants. Among the incidents, the property manager and assistant property manager had mace sprayed in their eyes by a woman who was upset about her security deposit; a tenant threw a telephone at the property manager's hand, causing injury; a tenant came into the office brandishing a 2–by–4 board; and an individual whose car was towed threatened to kill the night security officer. When the employer failed to respond to employee requests for a full-time security guard and other protections, the employees filed a complaint with OSHA. After an investigation, OSHA cited Megawest under § 5(a)(1) for failing to provide a safe workplace. The ALJ dismissed the citation on the ground that the Secretary failed to prove that the hazard of workplace violence is recognized by the employer or its industry. The case was not reviewed by the full Commission.

*Megawest* is the only reported OSHA case dealing with the issue of workplace violence, but the magnitude of the problem certainly suggests that the issue will surface again. Homicide is the second leading cause of death in the workplace (behind motor vehicle accidents), and it is the leading cause of death for women. See generally Leon J. Warshaw & Jacqueline Messite, Workplace Violence: Preventive and Interventive Strategies, 38 J.Occup. & Envt'l Med. 993 (1996).

Is workplace violence a proper subject for OSHA enforcement under either § 5(a)(1) or § 5(a)(2)? Do any of the arguments made in the *Frank Diehl* case, supra p. 682, have any relevance here?

**7.** In *Pepperidge Farm* the Secretary alleged 175 separate willful violations (at $5,000 per violation, for a total of $875,000), one for each employee exposed to the hazard of repetitive motion. This method of "instance-by-instance" or "egregious" penalties has been used by the Secretary since 1986 for willful violations with such aggravating factors as worker fatalities or multiple injuries, a persistently high rate of injury or illness, an extensive history of violations under the Act, and other indicators of bad faith or indifference to employee safety and health. In Reich v. Arcadian Corp., 110 F.3d 1192 (5th Cir.1997), the Fifth Circuit held that the Act does *not* permit the Secretary to assess penalties on this basis, at least as to violations of the general duty clause.

## 3.  DEFENSES

### Brennan v. OSHRC (Republic Creosoting Co.)

501 F.2d 1196 (7th Cir.1974).

■ PELL, CIRCUIT JUDGE.

The Secretary of Labor appeals from a decision of the Occupational Safety and Health Review Commission, which found that the respondent Republic Creosoting Company had not committed any violations of the Occupational Safety and Health Act. The underlying facts are not in dispute on appeal, these facts being either stipulated by the parties or testified to at the hearing before the administrative law judge.

Republic Creosoting Company (Republic), a division of Reilly Tar and Chemical Corporation, operated five railroad tie marshalling yards in southern Indiana, including one in Jeffersonville, Indiana. Despite its name, Republic did not at the Jeffersonville yard engage in the creosoting process but it did, upon the acquisition of newly cut or "green" ties, undertake the first step of seasoning or drying the wood for its eventual use. Republic ultimately resold the ties to railroad companies. These ties weighed approximately 150 to 235 pounds each.

The truckloads of ties arriving at the Jeffersonville yard were secured by chains to the transporting trucks. In twenty to twenty-five percent of the truckloads, the ties were bound together into packages, with each package held together by a single narrow steel band. Each package contained 25 to 45 ties, five ties high, five to nine ties across and one tie in length. The packaged ties were loaded lengthwise along the length of the truck, generally one package high and two packages across.

Republic unloaded the truckloads of banded ties in the following manner. The truckdriver ordinarily removed the chains holding the packages of ties onto the truck. The unloader operator (an employee of Republic) then moved the unloader (a forklift truck) into position so that it supported a package of banded ties. Only after the unloader was supporting a package, did the truckdriver, standing on an adjacent package, cut the band on the package to be unloaded. Under no circumstances would the band be cut before the unloader was in position. The unloader then removed the loosened ties from the truck. This process was repeated package by package until the truck was completely unloaded. During the entire operation, all Republic employees, other than the unloader operator, remained a safe distance from the truck.

On July 9, 1971, a truckload of banded ties was delivered to the Jeffersonville yard. Raymond Davis, a new employee working his fourth day for Republic, was present at the yard on that date. Davis had been hired to sort and stack ties after the completion of the unloading process. The unloader operator, James Wiseman, suggested to Davis on the day in question that he come to the unloading so that he could help sort the ties after they had been unloaded. Davis had never witnessed the unloading operation before nor had it been described to him. The field superintendent, Wallace Worley, however, when hiring Davis had told him "not to get around no trucks; the unloader done all the unloading."

Davis was originally standing some distance from the truck and Worley and Wiseman expected him to remain there until the unloading was completed. The chains had, at this time, already been removed from the truck but the unloader had not yet been moved into position. Without being ordered to do so and without informing anyone of what he intended to do, Davis went up to the truck and while standing on the ground next to the truck, cut the steel band on a package of ties with an ax. As a result, five of the ties fell on Davis, fatally injuring him.

On July 30, 1971, a compliance officer for the Secretary of Labor conducted an inspection of the Jeffersonville yard. On the basis of the inspection, the Secretary issued two citations to Republic for alleged violations of the Occupational Safety and Health Act: a "Citation for Serious Violation" based on the Davis accident; a "Citation" based on the lack of warning signs and barricades around the piles of ties in the yard.

Republic filed a notice of contest and a hearing was held before an administrative law judge, who affirmed both citations but raised the second citation from a nonserious to a serious violation. The total penalty imposed was $1300.

Republic petitioned for discretionary review by the Occupational Safety and Health Review Commission. The Commission (with one Commissioner dissenting) reversed the administrative law judge and vacated the citations.

\* \* \*

The citation issued to Republic on the basis of the Davis accident alleged a serious violation of the "general duty clause" of the Act, which provides:

> "Each employer (1) shall furnish to each of his employees employment and a place of employment which are free from recognized hazards that are causing or are likely to cause death or serious physical harm to his employees. \* \* \* \*"

A "serious violation" is present only where there is "a substantial probability that death or serious physical harm could result from a condition which exists or from one or more practices, means, methods, operations, or processes which have been adopted or are in use, in such place of employment unless the employer did not, and could not with the exercise of reasonable diligence, know of the presence of the violations." Republic does not dispute that the cutting of the band before the unloader was in place gave rise to "a substantial probability that death or serious physical harm could result." The issue on appeal is whether an employer, using reasonable diligence, would have foreseen the danger in question.

The Secretary contends that where an inexperienced, untrained employee is placed at the site of a potentially dangerous operation, the employer should foresee that the employee is likely, because of his ignorance of the safe procedures, to injure himself. Davis, the Secretary points out, was a new employee, working his fourth day for Republic. He had neither seen the unloading operation nor had it described to him. Davis was, nonetheless, asked by the unloader operator to be present at the place of the unloading. Since Davis did not know what the safe procedure for unloading the ties was, it was foreseeable, the Secretary argues, that Davis would do something unsafe and, thereby, injure himself—even if the exact nature of his unsafe actions, i.e., cutting the band, could not have been foreseen. The fact that Davis was not assigned to assist in the actual unloading operation itself is irrelevant, according to the Secretary, since Davis was requested to be present at the unloading site. In such a situation, it is argued, the employee should be instructed in the safe procedure for the operation which is going on in his presence.

The Commission rejected the Secretary's argument on the theory that the Act does not require that a new employee always be trained in proper procedures for a task simply because he is required to be present at the place of the operation in question in which he is not a participant. We agree with the Commission's interpretation of the Act. The Act clearly requires that, for a serious-violation citation to be sustained, the danger must be one of which the employer knew or, with reasonable diligence, could have known. Whether training is necessary and the amount of any training required will depend on a number of factors, such as the experience of the employee in the particular field of work, the extent of the employee's participation in the operation in question, and the complexity and danger involved in the operation. Where an employee is directly participating in a job, the employer may well, as the Commission noted, have a duty under the Act to instruct him on the safe procedure for handling the job. On the other hand, the Commission accurately recognized that training may be unnecessary for an employee who is wholly disassociated with the operation in question and who would not be foreseeably exposed to danger.

The instruction given to Davis was general but explicit and unambiguous. Worley testified: "I told him not to get around no trucks; the unloader done all the unloading." We find that, under these circumstances, this instruction was sufficient to satisfy the employer's duty under the Act. It is true that the unloading could be dangerous if the proper procedure was not followed. Davis' relationship with the trucks and the unloading, however, was very simple: he merely had to stay away from the trucks. This he was clearly told to do. The fact that he did not know the correct procedure for unloading a truck is immaterial since *his own* position with respect to the trucks had been stated in no uncertain terms: he was to stay away. In this situation, we agree with the Commission that a reasonably diligent employer would not have foreseen that Davis would injure himself.

## NOTES AND QUESTIONS

**1.** Would there have been a violation if Davis had been told nothing?

**2.** In what possible ways could Davis have construed the warning he was given?  In other words, aside from safety considerations, why might he be told not to do any unloading?

**3.** Should the employer be required to tell the employee *why* he should not get too close to the trucks?  How important a consideration is the employee's experience, training, skill, and degree of supervision?  What about the severity of the hazard?

**4.** In essence, the employer's position was that the warning was adequate and that it took all necessary steps to eliminate *preventable* hazards.  Therefore, the employee's act of cutting the bonds was unpreventable employee misconduct.  Although the issue was raised here in the context of a § 5(a)(1) violation, the identical defense is recognized under § 5(a)(2).  According to the Commission, an employer must satisfy a four-part test to invoke the unpreventable employee misconduct defense: (1) the employer has established work rules designed to prevent the violation; (2) it has adequately communicated these rules to its employees; (3) it has taken steps to discover violations; and (4) it has effectively enforced the rules when violations have been discovered.  Jensen Construction Co., 7 OSHC 1477, 1979 OSHD ¶ 23,664 (1979).

**5.** Unpreventable employee misconduct is the most important substantive defense, but there are many others, including vagueness of the standard, infeasibility of compliance, and the fact that compliance would cause a greater hazard.  For a discussion of these and other defenses, see Mark A. Rothstein, Occupational Safety and Health Law §§ 109–124 (4th ed. 1998).  Such common law defenses as contributory negligence and assumption of the risk do not apply to OSHA.  Why?

**6.** A laboratory technician with 21 years experience was electrocuted while conducting an experiment.  After an inspection, OSHA cited the employer under § 5(a)(1) for failing to use a system in which the technicians would work in teams of two and thereby reduce the risk of electrocution.  The evidence presented at the hearing showed that the decedent was extremely depressed and, in fact, may have committed suicide.  Assuming that is what happened, could the employer still be found in violation of OSHA?  See Brennan v. OSHRC (Hanovia Lamp Division), 502 F.2d 946 (3d Cir.1974).

**7.** During an OSHA inspection of a stevedoring company the compliance officer observed nearly all of the longshore workers without hard hats.  (OSHA requires hard hats to protect against serious head injuries from falling objects.)  In defending against the subsequent OSHA citation under § 5(a)(2), the employer claimed that it did all that it could to obtain compliance but the employees refused.  Specifically, the employer had furnished the required hard hats, had encouraged their use at regular safety meetings, had posted hard hat signs, had used payroll envelope stuffers to advocate hard hat wearing, and had placed hard hat safety messages on the hiring tapes.   The employer feared that sanctioning employees would cause a wildcat strike, which had already occurred at another port.  Is the employer in violation of OSHA?  What else should the employer have to do?  Is there any way for OSHA to cite the *employees?*  Should the workers be permitted to assume the risk?  See Atlantic & Gulf Stevedores, Inc. v. OSHRC, 534 F.2d 541 (3d Cir.1976).

---

## D.   EMPLOYEE RIGHTS

Section 5(b) of the Act provides that "Each employee shall comply with occupational safety and health standards and all rules, regulations, and orders issued pursuant to this Act which are applicable to his own actions and conduct."  This provision, however, is not enforceable by the government.  In Atlantic & Gulf Stevedores, Inc. v. OSHRC, 534 F.2d 541 (3d Cir.1976), the court held that neither OSHA nor the Commission could sanction disobedient employees nor order their compliance.  Employers have the duty to ensure the compliance of their employees.

Although enforcement action may not be directed at them, employees are the intended beneficiaries of the Act's protections.  Congress sought to ensure employee participation at all stages of OSHA proceedings.  At the rulemaking stage, employees may petition for adoption of a standard (§ 6(b)(1)), serve on standards advisory committees (§ 7(b)), and seek judicial review of new standards (§ 6(f)).  At the enforcement stage, employees may file a complaint with OSHA (§ 8(f)(1)), bring a mandamus action in district court to compel an inspection when there are imminent dangers (§ 13(d)), participate in the inspection tour (§ 8(e)), and have the employer post copies of all citations (§ 9(b)).  At the adjudicatory stage, employees may file a notice of contest to the abatement period in the citation (§ 10(c)), elect party status in contests initiated by the employer (§ 10(c)), and seek judicial review of Commission decisions (§ 11(a)).

The foregoing examples of employee rights include many rights that may be categorized as largely procedural.  Two important substantive rights—the right of access to certain information and the right to be free from employer discrimination for filing a complaint, testifying, or exercising other rights—are further explored in the following pages.

### 1.   ACCESS TO INFORMATION

## General Motors Corp.
14 OSHC 2064, 1991 OSHD ¶ 29,240 (1991).

BY THE COMMISSION:

 Certain employees of General Motors Corporation, Electro–Motive Division ("GM"), filed requests with GM for access to its medical and exposure records concerning them.  Those requests were made pursuant to the records access rule, 29 C.F.R. § 1910.20, promulgated by the Secretary of Labor's Occupational Safety and Health Administration ("OSHA").  GM denied the requests on the ground that they related to pending worker's compensation ("WC") claims that those employees had brought against it in Illinois.  We now review the merits of the Secretary's citations issued to GM based on those access denials.

GM claims that the access requests were invalid because they effectively change Illinois' WC law, in violation of § 4(b)(4) of the Occupational Safety and Health Act, 29 U.S.C. § 653(b)(4).  That section states, "[n]othing in this Act shall be construed to supersede or in any manner affect any workmen's compensation law...."  GM contends that the result of enforcing the employees' requests would be to give employees greater rights than GM has to pretrial disclosure of information relevant to their pending WC proceedings.  GM also argues that its refusal to provide access is at most a *de minimis* violation of the records access rule, warranting no penalty or abatement requirement.

Former Commission Administrative Law Judge Edward A. Bobrick rejected GM's arguments, found a willful and serious violation in all three cases, and assessed a $10,000 penalty in each case.  We affirm the judge's findings of violations, but find them non-willful and impose a $1000 penalty in each case, for the reasons that follow.

## I.   *Background*

The 1982 case involves William Havell, an employee at GM's La Grange, Illinois, facility.  Havell had filed a claim against GM in 1979 under the Illinois Worker's Compensation Act.  Ill.Rev.Stat. Ch. 48, ¶ 138.  The basis for that claim was that Havell "injured his body while working."

In March 1982, Havell submitted to GM, through the law firm that represented him in the WC claim, a signed request for access to "[a]ll medical and exposure records" concerning him.  The stated purpose of the request was "Investigation and legal representation."  Havell also specifically authorized release of the records to the law firm.

Upon receipt of the records access request, GM sought an opinion from its legal counsel about whether to comply.  GM's legal counsel advised that the request was invalid under § 4(b)(4) of the Act because the "obvious purpose of this request under OSHA is to gather information for use in the [WC] matter that cannot be gathered under the Illinois Compensation law."  In support, the counsel noted that the Illinois law allows no prehearing discovery regarding pending WC claims.  In denying the records access request, GM set forth the reasons supplied by its counsel.

The Secretary issued a one-item citation to GM in June 1982, with a single $480 proposed penalty.  Item 1A alleged a failure to provide Havell's designated representative with access to GM's medical records on him, contrary to § 1910.20(e)(1)(i). Item 1B alleged a failure to provide the representative with access to requested exposure records that GM kept concerning Havell, contrary to § 1910.20(e)(2)(i).

In June 1983, shortly before the hearing on the merits, the Secretary moved to amend the citation to allege that the item was both willful and serious, and to amend the proposed penalty to $4800. The judge granted the motion.

There is no dispute that GM failed to comply with the rule. Accordingly, the Secretary and GM submitted the case for resolution of only the following issues:

> ... the parties desire to limit this case to the questions of whether Mr. Havell's request for access to medical and exposure records can be valid in view of Section 4(b)(4) of the Occupational Safety and Health Act, the characteristization [sic] of the violation, if any, and the penalty, if any....

The two 1984 cases arose out of similar requests for records access, filed by, or on behalf of, two other employees at the same facility. The parties have agreed to be bound in those cases by the final decision in the 1982 case, except that GM has the option of presenting additional arguments on the alleged willfulness and proposed penalties in the 1984 cases.

## II. *Whether § 1910.20 violates § 4(b)(4), as applied here*

The language of § 4(b)(4) (quoted above at n. 2) is quite broad. However, we believe that the United States Court of Appeals for the D.C.Circuit properly interpreted that language in its comprehensive decision in the lead standard case. United Steelworkers of America v. Marshall, 647 F.2d 1189 (D.C.Cir.1980), cert. denied, 453 U.S. 913 (1981). It essentially held that § 4(b)(4) means only that the Act and OSHA regulations are not to be interpreted to alter the terms of any WC law.

The OSHA records access rule does not change the terms of either Illinois' WC Act or its Occupational Diseases Act. Ill.Rev.Stat. Ch. 48, ¶¶ 138, 172.36 et seq. ("Illinois Acts"). Nor must the Illinois Industrial Commission (IIC), which governs the adjudication of cases under both Acts, do anything inconsistent with their terms, as a result of § 1910.20. Thus, § 4(b)(4) has not been violated.

\* \* \*

There was testimony that pretrial "discovery" per se is not provided for under the Illinois Acts. However, those Acts provide ample opportunity for both WC claimants and their employers to obtain medical and exposure records for use in WC proceedings. For example, the Illinois Acts require that every person rendering treatment or services in connection with a claim must turn over their records to any party on written request. The IIC may permit pre-trial depositions of any person whose testimony is deemed necessary by either party, for use as evidence at trial. The IIC is required to issue subpoenas at the request of either party for the attendance of witnesses and production of documents.

Havell's effort to obtain information about his health through the records access rule violates neither the letter nor the spirit of the Illinois Acts. Procedures under those Acts are designed to minimize costs and to simplify and speed the process, so that an eligible employee may gain prompt and equitable compensation. Records access under § 1910.20, however, does not conflict with these objectives because such access does not slow down or otherwise interfere with Illinois WC proceedings. The Illinois Acts are not intended to negate information rights that employers or employees have under other laws.

It is also noteworthy that Congress did not anticipate that the required disclosure of employer records on toxic materials or harmful physical agents would violate § 4(b)(4). The Act instructs the Secretary to issue regulations requiring employers to maintain accurate records of all monitoring or measuring mandated under the Secretary's standards. § 8(c)(3) of the Act, 29 U.S.C. § 657(c)(3). It further states:

> Such regulations shall also make appropriate provision for *each* employee or former employee to have access to such records as will indicate his own exposure to toxic materials or harmful physical agents.

Id. (emphasis added). Section 8(c)(3) of the Act requires appropriate provisions for access by *each* employee to medical and exposure records.

Also, we agree with OSHA's formal interpretation that the rule is not rendered unenforceable by the mere fact that an access request is related to private litigation, including WC litigation. Access to Employee Exposure and Medical Records; Partial Stay; Interpretations, 46 Fed.Reg. 40,490 (Aug. 7, 1989). That interpretation was issued long before the citations in these cases, and it is consistent with the specific mandate of records access in the Act.

That interpretation shows that § 1910.20 was not intended to change WC discovery provisions. OSHA made clear that the rule does not require disclosure of records created by the employer in anticipation of litigation and which would be unavailable to the employee in WC proceedings for that reason. Here, GM does not claim that the requested records fall under that exception to discovery (the so-called "work product" doctrine), or under any other specific exemption from discovery. It merely claims that § 1910.20 unavoidably conflicts with § 4(b)(4), whenever there is a pending WC claim. Such a notion lacks merit.

Although the access required by the Act may have an indirect, practical impact on the timing of certain disclosures in WC proceedings, it has no legal effect on them. It does not change the terms of the Illinois Acts, or require actions inconsistent with those terms in WC proceedings. We therefore conclude that the rule does not violate § 4(b)(4).

\* \* \*

## III.  *Whether the violations were willful*

A willful violation is one committed with intentional, knowing or voluntary disregard for the requirements of the Act, or with plain indifference to employee safety.  It is differentiated from other types of violations by a "heightened awareness—of the illegality of the conduct or conditions—and by a state of mind—conscious disregard or plain indifference." However, a violation is not willful if the employer had a good faith belief that it was not in violation.  The test of good faith for these purposes is an objective one—whether the employer's belief concerning a factual matter, or concerning the interpretation of a rule, was reasonable, under the circumstances.

Based on the particular circumstances here, we find that GM had an objective, good faith basis for believing that it was not required to comply with the terms of the records access rule.  That basis includes, but is not limited to, its reasonable, although in our view incorrect, interpretation of § 4(b)(4).  We cannot find, on the state of these records, that GM's refusal to comply actually was based on an underlying, willful motive.  Thus, we find that the violations are not properly classified as willful.

\* \* \*

## IV.  *Whether the alleged violations should be termed de minimis*

The basis for GM's argument that these alleged violations are *de minimis* is certain *dicta* in a footnote to a Commission decision involving a similar records access request.  Johnson & Johnson Products, Inc., 11 OSHC 2097, 1984–85 OSHD ¶ 26,988 (1984).  There, the Commission vacated citations issued to two companies for denial of employee requests for access to exposure records on the ground that the employees had only requested access to medical records.  In the relevant footnote, the Commission majority apparently concluded that, even if the employees had included exposure records in their requests for access, the employers' failure to comply with these requests would only have been a de minimis violation of the Act, because the purpose of the requests was to obtain records for use in WC proceedings and WC proceedings are unrelated to the safety and health purposes of the Act.

\* \* \*

We cannot adopt a general classification of de minimis for noncompliance with records access requirements, although a particular departure from the rule's terms conceivably could be so minor as to qualify as *de minimis*.  The Act's recordkeeping requirements "play a crucial role in providing the information necessary to make workplaces safer and healthier."  Employee access to medical and exposure records also can play a crucial role in protecting the employee's health.  See, e.g., Amoco Chemicals Corp., 12 OSHC 1849, 1986 OSHD ¶ 27,621 (1986) (employer had medical records indicating that employee had pleural effusion—a symptom of possible cancer—but failed to inform employee of condition).

Lastly, we conclude that GM's argument lacks merit because the requests in these cases were not expressly limited to records relevant to the WC claims, and the parties' submissions do not show that only such records were covered by the requests. Havell had worked for GM for 20 years. GM does not dispute in this case that he was exposed to toxic substances and harmful physical agents within the scope of the records access rule. Its job descriptions for the positions held by Havell show that he would have been subject to exposure to carbon monoxide, welding smoke and fumes, dust from grinders, as well as noise from air hammers. Havell also told OSHA's inspector that he had been exposed to caustic chemical solutions in tanks near his work area. GM has not indicated that it attempted at any time to determine whether it has medical or exposure records relative to Havell that go beyond his lower back injury claim. For these reasons, the violations here are not properly classified as de minimis.

## NOTE

The purpose of the Access to Exposure and Medical Records rule, 29 C.F.R. § 1910.20, is "to enable workers to play a meaningful role in their own health management." The regulation applies to all covered general industry, maritime, and construction employers. It is, however, limited to employers having employees exposed to toxic substances or harmful physical agents. Unlike other OSHA recordkeeping requirements, the access regulation does not require that certain documents be prepared, but only that existing records be maintained and made available to employees and other parties designated in the regulation.

Any current or former employee or an employee being assigned or transferred to work where there will be exposure to toxic substances or harmful physical agents has a right of access to four kinds of exposure records: (1) environmental monitoring records; (2) biological monitoring results; (3) material safety data sheets; and (4) other records disclosing the identity of a toxic substance or harmful physical agent. Any worker who has a right of access to exposure records may designate a representative to exercise access rights. Recognized or certified collective bargaining agents (i.e., labor unions) are automatically considered "designated representatives" and have a right of access to employee exposure records without individual employee consent. OSHA also has a right of access to exposure records.

Access to employee medical records is more restricted. Employees have a right of access to their entire medical files regardless of how the information was generated or is maintained. Excluded from the definition of "employee medical record" are certain physical specimens, certain records concerning health insurance claims, and certain records concerning voluntary employee medical assistance programs. A limited discretion is also given physicians to deny access where there is a specific diagnosis of a terminal illness or psychiatric condition. Collective bargaining agents must obtain specific written consent before gaining access to employee medical records. OSHA has a right of access to employee medical records, but those records in a personally identifiable form are subject to detailed procedures and protections.

## 2. HAZARDOUS WORK REFUSAL

## Whirlpool Corp. v. Marshall

445 U.S. 1 (1980).

■ MR. JUSTICE STEWART delivered the opinion of the Court.

The Occupational Safety and Health Act of 1970 (Act) prohibits an employer from discharging or discriminating against any employee who exercises "any right afforded by" the Act. The Secretary of Labor (Secretary) has promulgated a regulation providing that, among the rights that the Act so protects, is the right of an employee to choose not to perform his assigned task because of a reasonable apprehension of death or serious injury coupled with a reasonable belief that no less drastic alternative is available.[3] The question presented in the case before us is whether this regulation is consistent with the Act.

The petitioner company maintains a manufacturing plant in Marion, Ohio, for the production of household appliances. Overhead conveyors transport appliance components throughout the plant. To protect employees from objects that occasionally fall from these conveyors, the petitioner has installed a horizontal wire mesh guard screen approximately 20 feet above the plant floor. This mesh screen is welded to angle-iron frames suspended from the building's structural steel skeleton.

Maintenance employees of the petitioner spend several hours each week removing objects from the screen, replacing paper spread on the screen to catch grease drippings from the material on the conveyors, and performing occasional maintenance work on the conveyors themselves. To perform these duties, maintenance employees usually are able to stand on the iron frames, but sometimes find it necessary to step onto the steel mesh screen itself.

---

**3.** The regulation, 29 CFR § 1977.12, 38 Fed.Reg. 2681, 2683 (1973), as corrected 38 Fed.Reg. 4577 (1973), provides in full:

\* \* \*

"(b)(2) However, occasions might arise when an employee is confronted with a choice between not performing assigned tasks or subjecting himself to serious injury or death arising from a hazardous condition at the workplace. If the employee, with no reasonable alternative, refuses in good faith to expose himself to the dangerous condition, he would be protected against subsequent discrimination. The condition causing the employee's apprehension of death or injury must be of such a nature that a reasonable person, under the circumstances then confronting the employee, would conclude that there is a real danger of death or serious injury and that there is insufficient time due to the urgency of the situation, to eliminate the danger through resort to regular statutory enforcement channels. In addition, in such circumstances, the employee, where possible, must also have sought from his employer, and been unable to obtain, a correction of the dangerous condition."

In 1973 the company began to install heavier wire in the screen because its safety had been drawn into question. Several employees had fallen partly through the old screen, and on one occasion an employee had fallen completely through to the plant floor below but had survived. A number of maintenance employees had reacted to these incidents by bringing the unsafe screen conditions to the attention of their foremen. The petitioner company's contemporaneous safety instructions admonished employees to step only on the angle-iron frames.

On June 28, 1974, a maintenance employee fell to his death through the guard screen in an area where the newer, stronger mesh had not yet been installed. Following this incident, the petitioner effectuated some repairs and issued an order strictly forbidding maintenance employees from stepping on either the screens or the angle-iron supporting structure. An alternative but somewhat more cumbersome and less satisfactory method was developed for removing objects from the screen. This procedure required employees to stand on power-raised mobile platforms and use hooks to recover the material.

On July 7, 1974, two of the petitioner's maintenance employees, Virgil Deemer and Thomas Cornwell, met with the plant maintenance superintendent to voice their concern about the safety of the screen. The superintendent disagreed with their view, but permitted the two men to inspect the screen with their foreman and to point out dangerous areas needing repair. Unsatisfied with the petitioner's response to the results of this inspection, Deemer and Cornwell met on July 9 with the plant safety director. At that meeting, they requested the name, address, and telephone number of a representative of the local office of the Occupational Safety and Health Administration (OSHA). Although the safety director told the men that they "had better stop and think about what [they] were doing," he furnished the men with the information they requested. Later that same day, Deemer contacted an official of the regional OSHA office and discussed the guard screen.

The next day, Deemer and Cornwell reported for the night shift at 10:45 p.m. Their foreman, after himself walking on some of the angle-iron frames, directed the two men to perform their usual maintenance duties on a section of the old screen. Claiming that the screen was unsafe, they refused to carry out this directive. The foreman then sent them to the personnel office, where they were ordered to punch out without working or being paid for the remaining six hours of the shift. The two men subsequently received written reprimands, which were placed in their employment files.

A little over a month later, the Secretary filed suit in the United States District Court for the Northern District of Ohio, alleging that the petitioner's actions against Deemer and Cornwell constituted discrimination in violation of § 11(c)(1) of the Act. As relief, the complaint prayed, inter alia, that the petitioner be ordered to expunge from its personnel files all references to the reprimands issued to the two employees, and for a permanent injunction requiring the petitioner to compensate the two employees for the six hours of pay they had lost by reason of their disciplinary suspensions.

Following a bench trial, the District Court found that the regulation in question justified Deemer's and Cornwell's refusals to obey their foreman's order on July 10, 1974. The court found that the two employees had "refused to perform the cleaning operation because of a genuine fear of death or serious bodily harm," that the danger presented had been "real and not something which [had] existed only in the minds of the employees," that the employees had acted in good faith, and that no reasonable alternative had realistically been open to them other than to refuse to work. The District Court nevertheless denied relief, holding that the Secretary's regulation was inconsistent with the Act and therefore invalid.

The Court of Appeals for the Sixth Circuit reversed the District Court's judgment.  * * *

The Act itself creates an express mechanism for protecting workers from employment conditions believed to pose an emergent threat of death or serious injury. Upon receipt of an employee inspection request stating reasonable grounds to believe that an imminent danger is present in a workplace, OSHA must conduct an inspection. In the event this inspection reveals workplace conditions or practices that "could reasonably be expected to cause death or serious physical harm immediately or before the imminence of such danger can be eliminated through the enforcement procedures otherwise provided by" the Act, the OSHA inspector must inform the affected employees and the employer of the danger and notify them that he is recommending to the Secretary that injunctive relief be sought. At this juncture, the Secretary can petition a federal court to restrain the conditions or practices giving rise to the imminent danger. By means of a temporary restraining order or preliminary injunction, the court may then require the employer to avoid, correct, or remove the danger or to prohibit employees from working in the area.

To ensure that this process functions effectively, the Act expressly accords to every employee several rights, the exercise of which may not subject him to discharge or discrimination. An employee is given the right to inform OSHA of an imminently dangerous workplace condition or practice and request that OSHA inspect that condition or practice. He is given a limited right to assist the OSHA inspector in inspecting the workplace, and the right to aid a court in determining whether or not a risk of imminent danger in fact exists. Finally, an affected employee is given the right to bring an action to compel the Secretary to seek injunctive relief if he believes the Secretary has wrongfully declined to do so.

In the light of this detailed statutory scheme, the Secretary is obviously correct when he acknowledges in his regulation that, "as a general matter, there is no right afforded by the Act which would entitle employees to walk off the job because of potential unsafe conditions at the workplace." By providing for prompt notice to the employer of an inspector's intention to seek an injunction against an imminently dangerous condition, the legislation obviously contemplates that the employer will normally respond by voluntarily and speedily eliminating the danger. And in the few instances where this does not occur, the legislative provisions authorizing prompt judicial action are designed to give employees full protection in most situations from the risk of injury or death resulting from an imminently dangerous condition at the worksite.

As this case illustrates, however, circumstances may sometimes exist in which the employee justifiably believes that the express statutory arrangement does not sufficiently protect him from death or serious injury. Such circumstances will probably not often occur, but such a situation may arise when (1) the employee is ordered by his employer to work under conditions that the employee reasonably believes pose an imminent risk of death or serious bodily injury, and (2) the employee has reason to believe that there is not sufficient time or opportunity either to seek effective redress from his employer or to apprise OSHA of the danger.

Nothing in the Act suggests that those few employees who have to face this dilemma must rely exclusively on the remedies expressly set forth in the Act at the risk of their own safety. But nothing in the Act explicitly provides otherwise. Against this background of legislative silence, the Secretary has exercised his rulemaking power under 29 U.S.C. § 657(g)(2) and has determined that, when an employee in good faith finds himself in such a predicament, he may refuse to expose himself to the dangerous condition, without being subjected to "subsequent discrimination" by the employer.

The question before us is whether this interpretative regulation constitutes a permissible gloss on the Act by the Secretary, in light of the Act's language, structure, and legislative history. Our inquiry is informed by an awareness that the regulation is entitled to deference unless it can be said not to be a reasoned and supportable interpretation of the Act.

The regulation clearly conforms to the fundamental objective of the Act—to prevent occupational deaths and serious injuries. The Act, in its preamble, declares that its purpose and policy is "to assure so far as possible every working man and woman in the Nation safe and healthful working conditions and to *preserve* our human resources * * *."

To accomplish this basic purpose, the legislation's remedial orientation is prophylactic in nature. The Act does not wait for an employee to die or become injured. It authorizes the promulgation of health and safety standards and the issuance of citations in the hope that these will act to prevent deaths or injuries from ever occurring. It would seem anomalous to construe an Act so directed and constructed as prohibiting an employee, with no other reasonable alternative, the freedom to withdraw from a workplace environment that he reasonably believes is highly dangerous.

Moreover, the Secretary's regulation can be viewed as an appropriate aid to the full effectuation of the Act's "general duty" clause. That clause provides that "[e]ach employer * * * shall furnish to each of his employees employment and a place of employment which are free from recognized hazards that are causing or are likely to cause death or serious physical harm to his employees." 29 U.S.C. § 654(a)(1). As the legislative history of this provision reflects, it was intended itself to deter the occurrence of occupational deaths and serious injuries by placing on employers a mandatory obligation independent of the specific health and safety standards to be promulgated by the Secretary. Since OSHA inspectors cannot be present around the clock in every workplace, the Secretary's regulation ensures that employees will in all circumstances enjoy the rights afforded them by the "general duty" clause.

The regulation thus on its face appears to further the overriding purpose of the Act, and rationally to complement its remedial scheme. In the absence of some contrary indication in the legislative history, the Secretary's regulation must, therefore, be upheld, particularly when it is remembered that safety legislation is to be liberally construed to effectuate the congressional purpose.

\* \* \*

For these reasons we conclude that 29 CFR § 1977.12(b)(2) was promulgated by the Secretary in the valid exercise of his authority under the Act. Accordingly, the judgment of the Court of Appeals is affirmed.

## NOTES AND QUESTIONS

**1.** The Court placed great reliance upon the fact that the OSHA regulation gave employees only a limited right to refuse work. Which of these limitations do you think is most important?

**2.** The Court in *Whirlpool* left open the question whether employees must be paid for "idle time" during a hazardous work refusal. On remand, the district court awarded back pay because the employees were not given a chance to perform safe, alternate work. Marshall v. Whirlpool Corp., 9 OSHC 1038, 1980 OSHD ¶ 24,956 (N.D.Ohio 1980). Accord, Marshall v. N.L. Industries, Inc., 618 F.2d 1220 (7th Cir.1980). Section 104(g)(2) of MSHA specifically provides that miners are entitled to up to one week's pay for idle time caused by an operator's failure to comply with MSHA standards. See Brock v. Metric Constructors, Inc., 766 F.2d 469 (11th Cir.1985).

**3.** Two other labor statutes have a direct bearing on the rights of employees to refuse to work under hazardous conditions. Section 8(a)(1) of the National Labor Relations Act (NLRA) makes it an unfair labor practice to, among other things, interfere with employees engaging in concerted activities for their mutual aid or protection. Section 8(a)(1) applies even if there is no collective bargaining agreement or union representation, but in the absence of a union contract employee actions must be concerted (engaged in by two or more employees) to be protected. NLRB v. City Disposal Systems, Inc., 465 U.S. 822 (1984); Meyers Industries, 268 N.L.R.B. No. 73 (1984), remanded sub nom. Prill v. NLRB, 755 F.2d 941 (D.C.Cir.1985), cert. denied, 474 U.S. 971 (1985). Employees covered under § 8(a)(1) may not be discriminated against if they are acting in good faith, even if they are erroneous in believing there are extremely hazardous conditions.   NLRB v. Modern Carpet, Inc., 611 F.2d 811 (10th Cir.1979).

Section 502 of the Taft-Hartley Amendments to the NLRA also applies to hazardous work refusals.   It provides that employees who quit work in good faith because of "abnormally dangerous conditions" are not deemed to be engaged in a strike.   In Gateway Coal Co. v. UMW, 414 U.S. 368 (1974), however, the Supreme Court held that to be protected under § 502 a union must present "ascertainable, objective evidence supporting its conclusion that an abnormally dangerous condition for work exists."   Id. at 386–87.

**4.**   Section 11(c) of OSHA, § 8(a)(1) of the NLRA, and § 502 of Taft-Hartley provide different standards for when a hazardous work refusal is protected.   Under § 8(a)(1) the employees must merely be acting in good faith.   Under § 502 the employees must be acting in good faith *and* their action must be supported by ascertainable, objective evidence of abnormally dangerous conditions.   Section 11(c) uses a middle standard—good faith plus some reasonable basis for the employee action.   What problems does this array of standards pose?   Would the implementation of a single standard be desirable?   Feasible?   See Note, Refusals of Hazardous Work Assignments: A Proposal for a Uniform Standard, 81 Colum.L.Rev. 544 (1981).

**5.**   Should an employee who is discharged for refusing to perform hazardous work be able to bring an action for wrongful discharge under the public policy exception to the at will doctrine?   Compare Trombetta v. Detroit, Toledo, & Ironton Railroad Co., 265 N.W.2d 385 (Mich.App.1978) and Walsh v. Consolidated Freightways, Inc., 563 P.2d 1205 (Or.1977) (no cause of action) with Wheeler v. Caterpillar Tractor Co., 485 N.E.2d 372 (Ill. 1985), cert. denied, 475 U.S. 1122 (1986) (cause of action permitted).   See Chapter 10.

## 3.   ANTI–RETALIATION

## Reich v. Hoy Shoe Co., Inc.
32 F.3d 361 (8th Cir.1994).

■ ELMO B. HUNTER, SENIOR DISTRICT JUDGE.

This case was filed by the Secretary of Labor complaining that Hoy Shoe Company, Inc. (Hoy Shoe), discharged Anita Godsey in retaliation for activities protected under the Occupational Safety and Health Act, 29 U.S.C.A. § 651 et seq (OSH Act).   The district court granted Hoy Shoe's summary judgment motion on the basis that the Secretary failed to set forth facts demonstrating that Hoy Shoe had actual knowledge that Anita Godsey engaged in statutorily protected activity.   As such, the district court concluded that the Secretary failed to make the requisite prima facie showing.   On appeal, the Secretary urges that: (1) the district court erred in requiring the Secretary to show that Hoy Shoe had actual knowledge that Anita Godsey had engaged in protected activity; (2) the district court improperly weighed the evidence and resolved a genuinely disputed factual issue regarding Hoy Shoe's motivation for discharging Anita Godsey; and (3) the district court erred in failing to consider Hoy Shoe's refusal to reinstate Anita Godsey as violative of the anti-discrimination provision of the OSH Act.  We REVERSE.

## BACKGROUND

Hoy Shoe is a family-owned business that manufactures and distributes sandals.  At all times relevant to this action, William Gebel was the President of Hoy Shoe.  He directed the company's manufacturing activities.  His son, Robert Gebel, was in charge of plant operations, including personnel matters.

Anita Godsey was hired by Hoy Shoe on January 4, 1990, and worked there for almost one year, until November 8, 1990.  Ms. Godsey, along with two other employees, operated the 1700 machine.  The 1700 machine molds polyurethane into shoes.

According to Anita Godsey, a few months after she began working at Hoy Shoe, she voiced certain health concerns to her co-operators related to the chemical spray used in the operation of the 1700 machine.  She also asked Robert Gebel whether the chemical spray in question was safe and whether employees should be wearing masks and/or gloves.

On October 8, 1990, Ms. Godsey made an informal complaint to the local office of the Occupational Safety and Health Administration (OSHA).  On October 20, 1990, Ms. Godsey filed a formal complaint with OSHA alleging hazardous conditions related to the use of the chemical spray at the 1700 machine.  On November 5, 1990, OSHA compliance officer, Thomas Briggs, conducted an on-site investigation of the Hoy Shoe plant.  Three days later, on November 9, 1990, Godsey reported to work late.  At that time she was informed by Robert Gebel that she was being laid off for excessive tardiness.  According to Godsey, Robert Gebel also told her that "if you don't think my father [William Gebel] knows what is going on in this factory, you're crazy."

As noted above, Thomas Briggs conducted an on-site inspection of Hoy Shoe.  During the inspection, he informed the President, William Gebel, that the inspection was pursuant to an employee complaint.  Briggs' report and notes related to the inspection indicate that William Gebel inquired regarding the identity of the complaining employee and appeared quite upset that Briggs could not reveal the employee's identity so he could "take care of the problem."  Briggs' notes further reflect his impression that William Gebel, "would harass the complainant if he knew who it was."  Finally, according to Briggs, W. Gebel indicated that he thought the employee who filed the OSHA complaint was a woman who had raised similar complaints to the company in the past.

Subsequent to her discharge, Godsey complained to OSHA that her discharge violated the anti-discrimination provision of the OSH Act.  The Secretary advised Hoy Shoe of the retaliation complaint and conducted an investigation.  After completing the investigation, the Secretary filed this lawsuit in the district court alleging that Hoy Shoe's discharge of and refusal to reinstate Godsey violated § 11(c) of the OSH Act.

On August 15, 1990, Hoy Shoe instituted an employee conduct policy, which, among other things, addressed employee attendance. The policy warned that excessive tardiness could provide a basis for suspension or termination. Hoy Shoe contends that it discharged Ms. Godsey for excessive tardiness, in violation of company policy.

The Secretary's investigation established that, prior to Godsey's discharge, no employee had been disciplined under the August 15th attendance policy. Godsey was the first person so disciplined, even though other employees had comparable or worse attendance records. The investigation further established that employees who continued to violate the policy, after Godsey's discharge, and whose instances of tardiness exceeded Godsey's, were not disciplined. The only other employee ever disciplined under the policy had a record significantly worse than Godsey's and was not disciplined until a point in time after Hoy Shoe had received notice of Godsey's retaliation complaint.

Pursuant to Hoy Shoe's motion, the district court granted summary judgment in favor of Hoy Shoe and dismissed the Secretary's complaint. The district court concluded that the Secretary was required to demonstrate that Hoy Shoe had actual knowledge of the identity of the complaining employee and that the evidence did not permit an inference that Hoy Shoe knew Ms. Godsey had filed the OSHA complaint giving rise to the inspection.

We disagree with the conclusion of the district court's analysis and its application of this Court's prior decisions. Accordingly, we now REVERSE.

* * *

In considering retaliation cases, this Court has adopted a three-pronged framework for analysis. First, the plaintiff must make a prima facie case by "showing participation in a protected activity, a subsequent adverse action by the employer, and some evidence of a causal connection between the protected activity ... and the subsequent adverse action." Second, once the plaintiff has established a prima facie case, the burden shifts to the employer to articulate an appropriate non-discriminatory reason for its action. Finally, if the employer satisfies this burden, the plaintiff must then demonstrate that the proffered reason is pretextual.

Here, the district court determined, as a matter of law, that the Secretary failed, in the first prong, to establish a causal link between Godsey's protected activity and the adverse employment action, thereby failing to make his prima facie case. In doing so, the district court opined that plaintiff has the burden of showing that the employer *knew* that the employee in question engaged in protected activity. Apparently, the district court would require in every case alleging retaliatory discharge that the plaintiff prove *actual knowledge* on the part of the defendant of the identity of the particular employee engaging in protected activity.  We do not read this Court's prior decisions as compelling such a rule.

\* \* \*

Taken in the light most favorable to the Secretary, the facts in this case are:  Ms. Godsey initially complained to co-workers and Robert Gebel about health concerns she had arising out of the use of certain chemical spray in operation of the 1700 machine she worked on.  Subsequent to these oral complaints, she informally complained to OSHA.  She followed her informal complaint with a formal complaint to OSHA that gave rise to an on-site inspection and investigation of the Hoy Shoe plant where Ms. Godsey worked.  During the on-site inspection, the OSHA compliance officer informed William Gebel that the inspection and investigation resulted from an employee complaint.  William Gebel pressed the compliance officer for the identity of the complaining employee and appeared quite upset when he was unable to get it.  William Gebel indicated that he thought the employee who filed the OSHA complaint was a woman who had made past complaints.  In his report, the compliance officer noted that it was his opinion William Gebel would harass the complaining employee if he attained her identity.

Three days after the on-site inspection, Ms. Godsey was discharged.  At that time, Robert Gebel told her that "if you don't think my father knows what is going on in this factory, you're crazy."  Hoy Shoe states that Godsey was fired for excessive tardiness, in violation of company policy.  A review of Hoy Shoe's personnel records, however, admits that employees with equivalent or worse records than Ms. Godsey were not discharged, and, in fact, prior to Ms. Godsey's discharge, no employee had ever been disciplined under the announced policy.  The district court concedes that the above-related evidence supports an inference that the Gebels suspected that Godsey might have filed the OSHA complaint.

The proper inquiry is whether the above-recited evidence suggests *a causal connection* between the protected activity and the subsequent adverse action sufficient to defeat summary judgment.  Subsumed in this inquiry is the question of whether, as a matter of law, a plaintiff may establish a causal connection between his or her protected activity and an adverse employment action by presenting evidence sufficient to establish that: a particular employee engaged in protected activity, in the form of lodging an OSHA complaint;  that the employer was aware that some employee had filed or made such a complaint;  that the employer suspected that employee of having made the complaint;  and that the employer took retaliatory action based on its suspicion.  We answer in the affirmative on both counts.

The key to establishing a causal connection focuses on the employer's motivation or intention with regard to the adverse employment action.  To establish a causal connection, the evidence should support a finding that retaliatory motive animated the adverse employment action.

It is beyond question that employers make employment decisions based upon what they actually know to be true. Likewise, common sense and experience establish that employers also make employment decisions on what they suspect or believe to be true. It would be a strange rule, indeed, that would protect an employee discharged because the employer actually *knew* he or she had engaged in protected activity but would not protect an employee discharged because the employer merely *believed* or *suspected* he or she had engaged in protected activity.

Construing § 11(c), the OSH Act's anti-retaliation provision, to protect employees from adverse employment actions because they are suspected of having engaged in protected activity is consistent with the general purposes of the Act and the specific purposes of the anti-retaliation provisions.

The announced purpose of the OSH Act is to "assure so far as possible every working man and woman in the Nation safe and healthful working conditions." The OSH Act is safety legislation that is remedial and preventative in nature and is to be liberally construed to effectuate its congressional purpose.

Congress recognized employees to be a valuable and knowledgeable source of information regarding work place safety and health hazards. "Congress was aware of the shortage of federal and state occupational safety inspectors, and placed great reliance on employee assistance in enforcing the Act." Marshall v. Whirlpool Corp., 593 F.2d 715, 722 (6th Cir.1979), aff'd, 445 U.S. 1 (1980). As such, Congress provided, among other things, a mechanism by which employees could file complaints. This provision allows a complaining employee to elect to file his or her complaint confidentially and prohibits the Secretary from disclosing the identity of such complaining employee. Id. Congress further included a broad anti-discrimination provision that prohibits employers from retaliating against a complaining employee. The primary purpose of this provision is to ensure that violations of the OSH Act are reported. The OSH Act's requirement that employers not retaliate against complaining employees, like the Act generally, should be read broadly, "otherwise the Act would be gutted by employer intimidation." As noted by the Sixth Circuit, in *Whirlpool Corp.*, "it is clear that without employee cooperation, even an army of inspectors could not keep America's work places safe."

It seems clear to this Court that an employer that retaliates against an employee because of the employer's *suspicion* or *belief* that the employee filed an OSHA complaint has as surely committed a violation of § 11(c) as an employer that fires an employee because the employer *knows* that the employee filed an OSHA complaint. Such construction most definitely furthers the purposes of the Act generally and the anti-retaliation provision specifically. To hold otherwise would allow an area of employer miscon-duct that would surely have a chilling effect on the meaningful filing of employee complaints under the Act.

NOTES AND QUESTIONS

**1.** Under § 11(c)(1), employers are prohibited from discriminating against employees who have filed complaints about unsafe or unhealthful working conditions. This provision has been broadly construed to include not only complaints made to OSHA, but also complaints to NIOSH and other federal agencies, complaints to state or local agencies, complaints to the employer, and complaints to other entities, such as a newspaper.

2. Pursuant to § 11(c)(2), employees who believe they have been subject to discrimination must file a complaint with the Secretary within 30 days of the alleged discrimination. After investigation, the Secretary is then authorized to file an action in United States District Court on behalf of the complainant. There is no private right of action, and the Secretary has unreviewable discretion in deciding whether to proceed on behalf of the complainant.

3. Is the § 11(c) procedure adequate to protect the rights of employees? If not, how would the uncertainty of statutory protection affect the advice you might give to an employee contemplating filing a complaint? For example, would you recommend filing an anonymous complaint?

4. Under the Mine Safety and Health Act, discrimination complaints are initially heard by the Mine Safety and Health Review Commission rather than the U.S. District Court and the complaining party may proceed even if the Secretary elects not to pursue the case. Is this a better statutory scheme?

## E.   ENFORCEMENT AND ADJUDICATION

The threat of an OSHA inspection and citation is intended to encourage employers to meet their preinspection duty to comply with the Act. For noncomplying employers, the enforcement process involves the government's effort to penalize prior dereliction and to require the prompt correction of existing hazards.

OSHA inspections may be divided into four categories, which have been assigned the following priority: (1) imminent dangers; (2) fatality and catastrophe investigations; (3) investigation of employee complaints; and (4) regional programmed inspections. The first three categories are referred to as unprogrammed inspections because they are scheduled quickly in response to a particular concern. The fourth category, programmed inspections, concentrates on establishments in high hazard industries and with large numbers of employees.

### 1.   INSPECTIONS

## Marshall v. Barlow's, Inc.

436 U.S. 307 (1978).

■ MR. JUSTICE WHITE delivered the opinion of the Court.

Section 8(a) of the Occupational Safety and Health Act of 1970 (OSHA) empowers agents of the Secretary of Labor (the Secretary) to search the work area of any employment facility within the Act's jurisdiction. The purpose of the search is to inspect for safety hazards and violations of OSHA regulations. No search warrant or other process is expressly required under the Act.

[A three-judge district court in Idaho ruled that OSHA's apparent statutory authority for warrantless inspections violated the fourth amendment.]

\* \* \*

This Court has already held that warrantless searches are generally unreasonable, and that this rule applies to commercial premises as well as homes. In Camara v. Municipal Court, 387 U.S. 523, 528–529. (1967), we held:

> "[E]xcept in certain carefully defined classes of cases, a search of private property without proper consent is 'unreasonable' unless it has been authorized by a valid search warrant."

On the same day, we also ruled:

> "As we explained in *Camara,* a search of private houses is presumptively unreasonable if conducted without a warrant. The businessman, like the occupant of a residence, has a constitutional right to go about his business free from unreasonable official entries upon his private commercial property. The businessman, too, has that right placed in jeopardy if the decision to enter and inspect for violation of regulatory laws can be made and enforced by the inspector in the field without official authority evidenced by a warrant." See v. City of Seattle, 387 U.S. 541, 543 (1967).

These same cases also held that the Fourth Amendment prohibition against unreasonable searches protects against warrantless intrusions during civil as well as criminal investigations. The reason is found in the "basic purpose of this Amendment \* \* \* [which] is to safeguard the privacy and security of individuals against arbitrary invasions by governmental officials." If the government intrudes on a person's property, the privacy interest suffers whether the government's motivation is to investigate violations of criminal laws or breaches of other statutory or regulatory standards. It therefore appears that unless some recognized exception to the warrant requirement applies, See v. City of Seattle, would require a warrant to conduct the inspection sought in this case.

The Secretary urges that an exception from the search warrant requirement has been recognized for "pervasively regulated business[es]," and for "closely regulated" industries "long subject to close supervision and inspection." These cases are indeed exceptions, but they represent responses to relatively unique circumstances. Certain industries have such a history of government oversight that no reasonable expectation of privacy could exist for a proprietor over the stock of such an enterprise. Liquor and firearms are industries of this type; when an entrepreneur embarks upon such a business, he has voluntarily chosen to subject himself to a full arsenal of governmental regulation.

Industries such as these fall within the "certain carefully defined classes of cases," referenced in *Camara*. The element that distinguishes these enterprises from ordinary businesses is a long tradition of close government supervision, of which any person who chooses to enter such a business must already be aware. "A central difference between those cases and this one is that businessmen engaged in such federally licensed and regulated enterprises accept the burdens as well as the benefits of their trade, whereas the petitioner here was not engaged in any regulated or licensed business. The businessman in a regulated industry in effect consents to the restrictions placed upon him."

The clear import of our cases is that the closely regulated industry is the exception. The Secretary would make it the rule. Invoking the Walsh-Healey Act of 1936, 41 U.S.C. § 35 et seq., the Secretary attempts to support a conclusion that all businesses involved in interstate commerce have long been subjected to close supervision of employee safety and health conditions. But the degree of federal involvement in employee working circumstances has never been of the order of specificity and pervasiveness that OSHA mandates. It is quite unconvincing to argue that the imposition of minimum wages and maximum hours on employers who contracted with the government under the Walsh-Healey Act prepared the entirety of American interstate commerce for regulation of working conditions to the minutest detail. Nor can any but the most fictional sense of voluntary consent to later searches be found in the single fact that one conducts a business affecting interstate commerce; under current practice and law, few businesses can be conducted without having some effect on interstate commerce.

\* \* \*

The Secretary nevertheless stoutly argues that the enforcement scheme of the Act requires warrantless searches, and that the restrictions on search discretion contained in the Act and its regulations already protect as much privacy as a warrant would. The Secretary thereby asserts the actual reasonableness of OSHA searches, whatever the general rule against warrantless searches might be. Because "reasonableness is still the ultimate standard," the Secretary suggests that the Court decide whether a warrant is needed by arriving at a sensible balance between the administrative necessities of OSHA inspections and the incremental protection of privacy of business owners a warrant would afford. He suggests that only a decision exempting OSHA inspections from the Warrant Clause would give "full recognition to the competing public and private interests here at stake."

The Secretary submits that warrantless inspections are essential to the proper enforcement of OSHA because they afford the opportunity to inspect without prior notice and hence to preserve the advantages of surprise. While the dangerous conditions outlawed by the Act include structural defects that cannot be quickly hidden or remedied, the Act also regulates a myriad of safety details that may be amenable to speedy alteration or disguise. The risk is that during the interval between an inspector's initial request to search a plant and his procuring a warrant following the owner's refusal of permission, violations of this latter type could be corrected and thus escape the inspector's notice. To the suggestion that warrants may be issued ex parte and executed without delay and without prior notice, thereby preserving the element of surprise, the Secretary expresses concern for the administrative strain that would be experienced by the inspection system, and by the courts, should ex parte warrants issued in advance become standard practice.

We are unconvinced, however, that requiring warrants to inspect will impose serious burdens on the inspection system or the courts, will prevent inspections necessary to enforce the statute, or will make them less effective. In the first place, the great majority of businessmen can be expected in normal course to consent to inspection without warrant; the Secretary has not brought to this Court's attention any widespread pattern of refusal. In those cases where an owner does insist on a warrant, the Secretary argues that inspection efficiency will be impeded by the advance notice and delay. The Act's penalty provisions for giving advance notice of a search, and the Secretary's own regulations indicate that surprise searches are indeed contemplated. However, the Secretary has also promulgated a regulation providing that upon refusal to permit an inspector to enter the property or to complete his inspection, the inspector shall attempt to ascertain the reasons for the refusal and report to his superior, who shall "promptly take appropriate action, including compulsory process, if necessary." [12] The regulation represents a choice to proceed by process where entry is refused; and on the basis of evidence available from present practice, the Act's effectiveness has not been crippled by providing those owners who wish to refuse an initial requested entry with a time lapse while the inspector obtains the necessary process. Indeed, the kind of process sought in this case and apparently anticipated by the regulation provides notice to the business operator. If this safeguard endangers the efficient administration of OSHA, the Secretary should never have adopted it, particularly when the Act does not require it. Nor is it immediately apparent why the advantages of surprise would be lost if, after being refused entry, procedures were available for the Secretary to seek an ex parte warrant and to reappear at the premises without further notice to the establishment being inspected. [15]

---

**12.** It is true, as the Secretary asserts, that § 8(a) of the Act, purports to authorize inspections without warrant; but it is also true that it does not forbid the Secretary from proceeding to inspect only by warrant or other process. The Secretary has broad authority to prescribe such rules and regulations as he may deem necessary to carry out his responsibilities under this chapter "including rules and regulations dealing with the inspection of an employer's establishment."

**15.** Insofar as the Secretary's statutory authority is concerned, a regulation expressly providing that the Secretary could proceed ex parte to seek a warrant or its equivalent would appear to be as much within the Secretary's power as the regulation currently in force and calling for "compulsory process."

Whether the Secretary proceeds to secure a warrant or other process, with or without prior notice, his entitlement to inspect will not depend on his demonstrating probable cause to believe that conditions in violation of OSHA exist on the premises.  Probable cause in the criminal law sense is not required.  For purposes of an administrative search such as this, probable cause justifying the issuance of a warrant may be based not only on specific evidence of an existing violation but also on a showing that "reasonable legislative or administrative standards for conducting an * * * inspection are satisfied with respect to a particular [establishment]."  A warrant showing that a specific business has been chosen for an OSHA search on the basis of a general administrative plan for the enforcement of the Act derived from neutral sources such as, for example, dispersion of employees in various types of industries across a given area, and the desired frequency of searches in any of the lesser divisions of the area, would protect an employer's Fourth Amendment rights.  We doubt that the consumption of enforcement energies in the obtaining of such warrants will exceed manageable proportions.

Finally, the Secretary urges that requiring a warrant for OSHA inspectors will mean that, as a practical matter, warrantless search provisions in other regulatory statutes are also constitutionally infirm.  The reasonableness of a warrantless search, however, will depend upon the specific enforcement needs and privacy guarantees of each statute.  Some of the statutes cited apply only to a single industry, where regulations might already be so pervasive that [an] exception to the warrant requirement could apply.  Some statutes already envision resort to federal court enforcement when entry is refused, employing specific language in some cases and general language in others.  In short, we base today's opinion on the facts and law concerned with OSHA and do not retreat from a holding appropriate to that statute because of its real or imagined effect on other, different administrative schemes.

Nor do we agree that the incremental protections afforded the employer's privacy by a warrant are so marginal that they fail to justify the administrative burdens that may be entailed.  The authority to make warrantless searches devolves almost unbridled discretion upon executive and administrative officers, particularly those in the field, as to when to search and whom to search.  A warrant, by contrast, would provide assurances from a neutral officer that the inspection is reasonable under the Constitution, is authorized by statute, and is pursuant to an administrative plan containing specific neutral criteria.  Also, a warrant would then and there advise the owner of the scope and objects of the search, beyond which limits the inspector is not expected to proceed.  These are important functions for a warrant to perform, functions which underlie the Court's prior decisions that the Warrant Clause applies to inspections for compliance with regulatory statutes.  We conclude that the concerns expressed by the Secretary do not suffice to justify warrantless inspections under OSHA or vitiate the general constitutional requirement that for a search to be reasonable a warrant must be obtained.

\* \* \*

We hold that Barlow was entitled to a declaratory judgment that the Act is unconstitutional insofar as it purports to authorize inspections without warrant or its equivalent and to an injunction enjoining the Act's enforcement to that extent.   The judgment of the District Court is therefore affirmed.

■ JUSTICE STEVENS, joined by JUSTICES BLACKMUN and REHNQUIST, dissented.

## NOTES AND QUESTIONS

**1.**   Do OSHA warrants add any meaningful protection that is not already afforded by the language of § 8?

**2.**   Why should a different standard of probable cause be used for criminal and administrative inspections?

**3.**   One of the main reasons why OSHA has been resented in the business community is that, unlike most other regulatory agencies (such as the FTC, SEC, and ICC), OSHA actually sends inspectors into the workplace and mandates the use of certain equipment and procedures.   Consequently, the inspection process symbolizes the intrusion of OSHA into the business world.   This helps to explain the significance of the *Barlow's* case itself and employer efforts to prevent OSHA inspections.

**4.**   *Barlow's* presented something of an ideological dilemma to both liberals and conservatives on the Court.   A broad reading of the Fourth Amendment translates into a pro-business, anti-regulation decision.   A narrow reading of the Fourth Amendment results in an anti-business, pro-regulation decision.   See generally Mark A. Rothstein, OSHA Inspections After Marshall v. Barlow's, Inc., 1979 Duke L.J. 63.

**5.**   The Court in *Barlow's* rejected the argument that the exception for pervasively regulated businesses should permit warrantless OSHA inspections.   In Donovan v. Dewey, 452 U.S. 594 (1981), however, the Court used this rationale to uphold warrantless inspections under MSHA.   In distinguishing *Barlow's,* the Court noted that MSHA "applies to industrial activity with a notorious history of serious accidents and unhealthful working conditions."   In addition, while periodic inspections are required by MSHA, the decision to inspect under OSHA lies within "the broad discretion of agency officials."   In dissent, Justice Stewart argued that the majority "conveniently discards" the other half of the exception, requiring that the business have a long history of regulation.   He also questioned the majority's assertion that MSHA can be distinguished from OSHA because it applies only to a specific industry.   He pointed out that MSHA applies to disparate industries such as limestone quarries, sand and gravel operations, surface mines, and various coal and metallic underground mines.

**6.**   A warrant is not required under OSHA if the inspection comes under one of the three relevant exceptions originally set out in Camara v.

Municipal Court, 387 U.S. 523 (1967) and See v. Seattle, 387 U.S. 541 (1967): consent, open view, and emergency.

**7.** The courts have had a difficult time deciding what is probable cause for the issuance of an OSHA warrant. The Supreme Court in *Barlow's* was vague about what would satisfy the standard of administrative probable cause. Lower courts have divided the cases into programmed and unprogrammed inspections. For programmed inspections, the Secretary must demonstrate simply that the scheduling plan was based on neutral criteria and that the particular establishment was appropriately selected under the plan. Brock v. Gretna Machine & Ironworks, Inc., 769 F.2d 1110 (5th Cir.1985). For unprogrammed inspections, however, where there is further evidence of the need to inspect, some courts have required a much higher standard of probable cause that approaches the criminal law standard. See Mark A. Rothstein, Occupational Safety and Health Law §§ 232–234 (4th ed. 1998).

**8.** An OSHA compliance officer read two articles in the Chicago *Sun-Times* describing an industrial accident in which an employee had his hands severed while operating a hydraulic punch press. The compliance officer took the two articles and a copy of a citation issued to the same employer four years earlier and sought to obtain an ex parte warrant. Is there probable cause for the United States Magistrate to issue the warrant? See Donovan v. Federal Clearing Die Casting Co., 655 F.2d 793 (7th Cir.1981) (held: no).

**9.** Another frequently litigated issue is the permissible scope of an OSHA warrant—especially for unprogrammed inspections. For example, if OSHA receives a complaint from Joe Smith alleging that the machine on which he works is unguarded, should the inspection be limited to Joe Smith's machine or can OSHA inspect other machines or the entire workplace? There are three lines of cases. The narrow view is that the scope of the inspection must be limited to the working conditions of the complaining employee. Marshall v. North American Car Co., 626 F.2d 320 (3d Cir. 1980). The broad view is that there is a presumption in favor of a comprehensive ("wall-to-wall") inspection after the filing of an employee complaint. Burkart Randall Division of Textron, Inc. v. Marshall, 625 F.2d 1313 (7th Cir. 1980). The middle standard permits a comprehensive inspection only if the Secretary makes "some showing" of why a broader search is needed. In re Inspection of Workplace (Carondelet Coke Corp.), 741 F.2d 172 (8th Cir. 1984). This middle standard seems to be emerging as the majority view of the courts and also seems to be followed by the Commission. Trinity Industries, Inc., 15 OSHC 1827, 1992 OSHD ¶ 29,211 (1992).

**10.** In McLaughlin v. Kings Island, Division of Taft Broadcasting, 849 F.2d 990 (6th Cir.1988), the Sixth Circuit held that OSHA regulations permitting warrantless searches of an employer's injury and illness records, required to be kept by OSHA, violate the Fourth Amendment. The court held that a business has a legitimate expectation of privacy in the records even though they are required by law to be kept. In McLaughlin v. A.B.

Chance Co., 842 F.2d 724 (4th Cir.1988), however, the Fourth Circuit declined to follow *Taft Broadcasting*. According to the court, there can be little expectation of privacy in information that is available to anyone observing the employee bulletin board.

**11.** The Commission has the authority to rule on the legality of OSHA inspections. Babcock & Wilcox Co. v. Marshall, 610 F.2d 1128 (3d Cir. 1979). Suppose the Commission concludes (in the course of a challenge to the validity of a subsequent citation) that there was a lack of probable cause to support the issuance of a warrant or that a warrantless search was unreasonable. Should the evidence be suppressed? Should a good faith exception apply? What ruling furthers public policy? Compare Donovan v. Sarasota Concrete Co., 693 F.2d 1061 (11th Cir.1982) (upholding use of exclusionary rule) with Donovan v. Federal Clearing Die Casting Co., 695 F.2d 1020 (7th Cir.1982) (rejecting use of exclusionary rule). See generally Charles E. Trant, OSHA and the Exclusionary Rule: Should the Employer Go Free Because the Compliance Officer Has Blundered?, 1981 Duke L.J. 667.

## 2. ADJUDICATORY PROCESS
### A Note on Commission Procedures

Section 9(a) of the Act provides that if the Secretary believes that an employer "has violated a requirement of section 5 of this Act, of any standard, rule or order promulgated pursuant to section 6 of this Act, or of any regulations prescribed pursuant to this Act, he shall with reasonable promptness issue a citation to the employer." Although a considerable controversy once surrounded the "reasonable promptness" language of § 9(a), it is now settled that a citation issued within six months of the occurrence of a violation (the statute of limitations contained in § 9(c)) will not be vacated on "reasonable promptness" grounds unless the employer was prejudiced by the delay.

Section 9(a) also requires that citations be in writing and "describe with particularity the nature of the violation, including a reference to the provision of the Act, standard, rule, regulation, or order alleged to have been violated." The Commission has adopted a fair notice test that will be satisfied if the employer is notified of the nature of the violation, the standard allegedly violated, and the location of the alleged violation.

The Act does not specifically provide for a method of service for citations. Section 10(a), however, authorizes service of notices of proposed penalties by certified mail and citations are usually sent together with the penalty notice by certified mail. With regard to the proper party to serve, the Commission has held that service is proper if it "is reasonably calculated to provide an employer with knowledge of the citation and notification of proposed penalty and an opportunity to determine whether to contest or abate." B.J. Hughes, Inc., 7 OSHC 1471, 1979 OSHD ¶ 23,675 (1979).

Under § 10 an employer or an employee or representative of employees may file a notice of contest within 15 working days. An employer may contest any part or all of the citation, proposed penalty, or abatement dates. Employee contests are limited to the reasonableness of the proposed abatement dates. Employees also have the right to elect party status after an employer has filed a notice of contest. Under § 10(a), the failure to file a notice of contest results in the citation and proposed penalty becoming a final order of the Commission "not subject to review by any court or agency." Notices of contest are not required to be in any particular form and are sent to the area director who issued the citation. The area director then forwards the notice to the Commission and the case is docketed.

Although the Commission's rules mandate the filing of a complaint by the Secretary and an answer by the respondent (usually the employer), pleadings are liberally construed and easily amended. About 90 percent of the cases are resolved without a hearing, either through settlement, withdrawal of the citation by the Secretary, or withdrawal of the notice of contest by the employer.

After pleadings, discovery, and other preliminary matters, a hearing will be scheduled before a Commission ALJ. Witnesses testify and are cross-examined under oath and a verbatim transcript is made. The Federal Rules of Evidence apply. In Atlas Roofing Co. v. OSHRC, 430 U.S. 442 (1977), the Supreme Court held that there is no Seventh Amendment right to a jury trial in OSHA cases.

Following the close of the hearing, parties have an opportunity to submit briefs to the ALJ. The ALJ's decision contains findings of fact and conclusions of law and affirms, vacates, or modifies the citation, proposed penalty, and abatement requirements. The ALJ's decision is filed with the Commission and within 30 days may be directed for review by any Commission member sua sponte or in response to a party's petition for discretionary review (PDR). The failure to file a PDR with the Commission will preclude subsequent judicial review.

When invoked, Commission review is de novo, but the factual determinations of the ALJ, especially with regard to credibility findings, are often afforded great weight. Briefs may be submitted to the Commission, but oral argument is within the Commission's discretion and is extremely rare.

Pursuant to § 11(a), "[a]ny person adversely affected or aggrieved by a final order of the Commission" may seek judicial review in the United States court of appeals for the circuit in which the alleged violation occurred, where the employer has its principal office, or in the Court of Appeals for the District of Columbia Circuit. Under § 11(b), the Secretary may seek review only in the circuit in which the alleged violation occurred or where the employer has its principal office. The courts apply the substantial evidence rule to factual determinations made by the Commission and its ALJs, but the courts vary on the degree of deference afforded the Commission's interpretations of the statute and standards.

In Martin v. OSHRC, 499 U.S. 144 (1991), the Supreme Court held that in judicial review of a contested citation, when the Secretary and the Commission both have reasonable but conflicting interpretations of an ambiguous standard, the reviewing court should defer to the Secretary's interpretation.

## Reich v. Sea Sprite Boat Co.

50 F.3d 413 (7th Cir.1995).

■ EASTERBROOK, CIRCUIT JUDGE.  Exercising its authority under the Occupational Safety and Health Act, the Department of Labor has required manufacturers to spray organic peroxides only within the confines of booths equipped with sprinkler systems.  29 C.F.R. sec. 1910.107(m)(1).  The Department concluded that organic peroxides burn at the slightest provocation, producing an intense fire that must be contained (hence the booth) and extinguished quickly (hence the sprinkler system) lest it spread and endanger everyone at the work site.

In January 1986 one of the Department's inspectors paid a call on Sea Sprite Boat Company in Crescent City, Illinois.  The firm builds recreational boats.  Sea Sprite molds the boats' hulls and sprays each hull with a mixture of styrene, fiberglass, and methyl ethyl ketone peroxide.  MEK–P, as this compound is abbreviated, is an organic peroxide that can ignite without a spark in the presence of other organic compounds.  Its combustion releases more oxygen than it consumes, so the fire is particularly hard to extinguish.  Sea Sprite knew about the combustion hazard and had plenty of water handy; it stored the spray applicator over a pail of water to prevent the mixture from igniting as it dripped; but Sea Sprite did not have a booth with a sprinkler system.  The inspector issued a citation in May 1986 requiring Sea Sprite to comply with the regulation within six months.  Sea Sprite did not contest this citation, which therefore automatically became a final order of the Occupational Safety and Health Review Commission.  Compliance should have been achieved by November 1986—failure to obey the Commission's orders carries civil penalties whether or not a court has enforced them—but Sea Sprite carried on its business without change.

In January 1987 another inspector visited the premises.  Sea Sprite was merrily spraying MEK–P without a sprinklered booth.  In April 1987 the Department of Labor issued another citation.  Sea Sprite did not contest this citation, which again became a formal order by operation of law.  The third inspection followed hard on the heels of the April 1987 order; the inspector found that Sea Sprite was still in violation.  Another citation followed.  This one was contested.  A year passed.  In May 1988 Sea Sprite promised, as part of a settlement, to install a sprinklered booth within 60 days.  Thus, two and a half years after the initial inspection, Sea Sprite had yet to comply and the Department of Labor had yet to levy a sanction of any kind.

Perhaps encouraged by the Department's forgiving nature to believe that it could thumb its nose at the law indefinitely, Sea Sprite ignored its settlement agreement.  When another inspector arrived in December 1988, the firm was still spraying MEK–P without benefit of a sprinklered booth.

Another citation for failure to abate an established violation followed; this time the inspector attached a price, proposing a penalty for $135,000. Sea Sprite did not contest the notification, which became a final and binding order on April 5, 1989.

Three years passed. Sea Sprite did not pay the penalty or install the required booth. The Occupational Safety and Health Administration then applied to this court for enforcement of the April 1989 order. Sea Sprite treated this application the same way it treated the regulation: by behaving as if it did not exist. Because Sea Sprite had not opposed the application, this court summarily enforced the administrative order and in May 1992 issued a decree providing in part that Sea Sprite must "[c]omply with the Commission's final orders ... requiring abatement of the enumerated violations of the OSH Act and payment of OSH Act penalties in the amount of $135,000.00".

Judicial order in hand, another inspector appeared at Sea Sprite's premises in July 1992. The firm was still spraying MEK–P on boat hulls and still lacked a sprinklered booth. By October 1992 Sea Sprite had not paid a penny (recall that the $135,000 had been due since April 1989) and had not conformed to the spraying regulation. Seven years of defiance were too much for the Department of Labor, which asked this court to hold Sea Sprite in contempt. Another two years of defiance were still to come— but let us not get ahead of the story.

We appointed Magistrate Judge Kauffman of the Central District of Illinois as our Special Master. Sea Sprite insisted that the Master could not require it to participate in discovery. Although Fed.R.App.P. 48 now presumptively gives appellate masters the power to compel the production of evidence, that rule did not come into force until December 1, 1994, and there was no comparable rule in 1992. We therefore delegated to the Master authority to oblige Sea Sprite to produce evidence. Among the items the Secretary sought was documentation of Sea Sprite's financial status and ability to pay the penalty—or a new, larger, penalty for contempt of court. Sea Sprite resisted turning over such evidence, and the Master declined to order its production. It therefore took the Department's lawyers a while longer to realize that in December 1992 Robert F. Smith, the president and sole stockholder of Sea Sprite, had drained the firm of assets and transferred boatbuilding operations to a newly formed corporation, Continental Marine, for which Smith occupied the same roles. Continental took up business on Sea Sprite's old premises and using its methods—spraying MEK–P without a sprinklered booth. The existence of Continental came to light for the first time during the evidentiary hearing before the Master in late April 1993. Smith explained that he formed Continental because Sea Sprite had too many unsatisfied judgments against it and was being hounded by creditors. Smith estimated the firm's debts at $9 million, demonstrating that the federal government is not the only creditor he was stiffing. Continental was to continue spraying MEK–P without the required sprinklered booth until the end of April 1994; the

Secretary believes that Continental has been in compliance since May 1, 1994.

Testifying at the hearing, Smith related that he had not complied with this court's order because he deemed it invalid.  He apparently thought the order ineffectual because, in his view, the Department's local officials were satisfied with a change the firm made in 1988 (of which more below), but he had no answer to the rule that one must obey even an invalid judicial order until the order is stayed or reversed by a higher court.  Smith conceded that Sea Sprite "probably" had the wherewithal to pay the $135,000 penalty in April 1989 and April 1992, but that he decided not to do so because the firm had better uses of its money.

Counsel for Sea Sprite contended that it did not need to comply with the regulation because our order is too vague and because the Department of Labor had promised not to enforce the regulation against it.  The Master thought both of these "defenses" preposterous, as do we.  Our order explicitly directs Sea Sprite to "[c]omply with the Commission's final orders ... requiring abatement of the enumerated violations of the OSH Act", and those orders explicitly direct Sea Sprite to install and use a sprinklered booth.  As for the idea that local agents of the Department of Labor had agreed not to enforce a regulation that the Department repeatedly had instructed Sea Sprite to obey: the best one can say is that the firm's "defense" reflects an inverted conception of the bureaucratic hierarchy.

Actually the firm's position is not inverted so much as it is invented. Witnesses for Sea Sprite testified that in 1988 the firm hired a consultant who reformulated the sprayed mixture to be less flammable.  The consultant testified that he advised local OSHA employees of this alteration and informed them that, in his view, a sprinklered booth was no longer necessary.  By this procedure, the consultant asserted, Sea Sprite obtained official approval to forego use of a booth.  Asked for evidence that any employee of the Department of Labor had approved this proposal, Sea Sprite came up empty handed.  Variances are available under 29 U.S.C. sec. 655(b)(6), but Sea Sprite did not apply for one and none of the procedures required by the statute was followed.  By the consultant's own description, moreover, the new procedure was legally identical to the old one.  For the regulation says that "[a]ll spraying operations involving the use of organic peroxides and other dual component coatings shall be conducted in approved sprinklered spray booths meeting the requirements of this section."  The reformulated spray included organic peroxides.  That Sea Sprite and its consultant thought the new mixture safer than the old one is beside the point, not only under the regulation but also under orders that post dated the reformulation.  Recall that Sea Sprite was cited for noncompliance after its supposedly "approved" modification—a citation that the firm ignored, that became administratively final in April 1989, and that we summarily enforced in 1992 when Sea Sprite disdained its opportunity to oppose the Secretary's application.  Sea Sprite might have presented its "approval" argument to the Commission in 1989 or to us in 1992.  It didn't. As a defense to a citation in contempt of court, Sea Sprite's position is six years late and $135,000 short.

Sea Sprite was and is in contempt of court, and it must pay a penalty reflecting the gravity of the violation. A substantial fine for completed contempt usually is a criminal sanction, and Sea Sprite has not been offered the protections of the criminal process. As it happens, however, this court possesses the power to impose not only a fine for contempt of court but also the daily penalty that the Department of Labor may use in administrative proceedings. See 29 U.S.C. sec. 660(b): "In any contempt proceeding brought to enforce a decree of a court of appeals . . . the court of appeals may assess the penalties provided by section 17, in addition to invoking any other available remedies." Section 17(d), 29 U.S.C. sec. 666(d), provides that "[a]ny employer who fails to correct a violation for which a citation has been issued . . . within the period permitted for its correction . . . may be assessed a civil penalty of not more than $7,000 for each day during which such failure or violation continues." Sea Sprite does not contend that the statutory description of the daily penalty as "civil" is impermissible * * *. True to form, Sea Sprite does not so much as mention sec. 17. We are not disposed to question, unbidden, the statutory designation of this penalty as "civil." Sea Sprite therefore faces under sec. 17 a daily penalty of $7,000 for the period between May 5, 1992, the date of this court's order, and the abatement of the violation on May 1, 1994, a total of 726 days.

Our Master recommended a penalty of $1,000 per day, aggregating $726,000. Sea Sprite contends that the daily penalty should not begin until November 8, 1993, the date of the Master's report concluding that it was in contempt of court. Unlike the common law dog, however, the litigant in federal court does not get one free bite. The contempt began in May 1992. Sea Sprite received our order and decided to flout it; it is answerable for this decision. The contempt was deliberate and enduring. It was the continuation of a pattern predating 1986. We do not know when Sea Sprite started spraying MEK–P, but it violated the regulation from the outset. Despite formal notices and demands commencing in January 1986, Sea Sprite refused to comply. Its justifications of this conduct are ludicrous, and the formation of Continental shows that Smith sought to get away with disobedience indefinitely, shuffling the assets among corporate shells to avoid liability. Since November 1986 Sea Sprite has been subject to a conclusive (because uncontested) order to abate, yet the entire penalty for noncompliance between November 1986 and May 1989 is only $135,000. No penalty of any kind has been imposed for violations before November 1986 or between May 1989 and this court's order of May 1992. The Department of Labor has shown undue forbearance toward this scofflaw, which has answered generosity with ingratitude by failing to pay even a dime of the modest penalty levied so far. The Master found that Sea Sprite receives royalty payments from Continental and owns real property; it could have paid even after December 1992 but chose not to. Even after the Master's report of November 1993 calling Sea Sprite's justifications of its conduct "specious," the firm (through Continental) went right on spraying MEK–P without a sprinklered booth. Additional lenity is unwarranted. Having resisted discovery into its financial condition, Sea Sprite is in no position to plead poverty. We choose a penalty of $2,000 per day, for a total of $1,452,000, and would be inclined to make the number higher if we thought that the Department could collect more. For any infractions after today, the penalty will be assessed at the statutory maximum rate of $7,000 per day.

Seven months after learning of Continental's existence, the Secretary sought to amend his pleading to accuse Smith and Continental, in addition to Sea Sprite, of contempt of court. We referred this motion to the Master, who recommended that it be denied, remarking that adding additional parties "would be ex post facto." If by this the Master meant that the effect of a judicial order is limited to the original litigants, the belief is incorrect. Federal injunctions and similar orders apply to the parties, their officers, their successors in interest, and other affiliated persons and entities who have actual notice. For orders issued by district courts, this principle appears in Fed.R.Civ.P. 65(d), which says that injunctions bind "the parties to the action, their officers, agents, servants, employees, and attorneys, and ... those persons in active concert or participation with them who receive actual notice of the order by personal service or otherwise." Smith and his creature Continental come within several of these categories. The rules of civil procedure do not apply to the courts of appeals, and Rule 65(d) lacks a counterpart in the Federal Rules of Appellate Procedure. Long ago, however, the Supreme Court held that Rule 65(d) simply restates a norm of federal equity practice and therefore is equally germane to orders enforcing decisions of administrative agencies.

Smith, the president and sole shareholder of Sea Sprite, received actual notice of this court's order and is no less bound by it than is Sea Sprite itself. An order issued to a corporation is identical to an order issued to its officers, for incorporeal abstractions act through agents. "A command to the corporation is in effect a command to those who are officially responsible for its affairs. If they, apprised of the writ directed to the corporation, prevent compliance or fail to take appropriate action within their power for the performance of the corporate duty, they, no less than the corporation itself, are guilty of disobedience and may be punished for contempt." Smith was obliged to secure Sea Sprite's compliance; instead he ensured its defiance. The formation of Continental for the admitted purpose of evading judgments against Sea Sprite was a further act of contempt. Continental, as successor in interest to Sea Sprite, acquired the business subject to this court's order. A sale of Sea Sprite's assets to an unrelated party would pose different, and potentially difficult, problems. A shuffle between two corporations, both wholly owned by Smith, cannot avoid the injunction. By applying MEK–P outside a sprinklered booth, Continental violated both the regulation and the judgment. There is nothing remotely "ex post facto" about penalizing Smith and Continental for disobeying an order that has bound Smith personally since May 5, 1992, and that bound Continental from the instant of its formation.

\* \* \*

Experience teaches, however, that Smith may resist collection by a combination of passive and active means. The more comprehensive the judgment against him and his creatures, the better. A formal adjudication in contempt also may set the stage for penalties beyond the collection, from Continental and Smith, of Sea Sprite's debts to the United States. Before reaching a conclusion on the Secretary's request to hold Continental and Smith in contempt of court, however, we must permit them to offer any defenses and evidence personal to themselves. So far Sea Sprite has been the only formal party. Although corporate officers and successors must obey an injunction against the corporation, any person charged with contempt is entitled to his own opportunity to defend. Unless Continental and Smith have evidence that was not offered in Sea Sprite's defense, the proceeding can be conducted with dispatch, but they are entitled to the opportunity. We therefore ask the Master to reopen the record and to offer Continental and Smith an opportunity to present any additional arguments and evidence bearing on the question whether they are in contempt of court. Decision in this case has too long been deferred. The Master should schedule the hearing within a month of this opinion and make his recommendations within a month of the hearing. An accelerated briefing schedule will follow.

To sum up: Sea Sprite is in contempt of court and must pay a penalty of $1,452,000 plus interest from today. We will assess $7,000 per day for any future noncompliance. Sea Sprite continues to owe the original $135,000, on which interest has been accumulating for years. Continental and Smith are added to the contempt proceeding as respondents and will have an opportunity to present arguments and evidence at a hearing to be held before the Master. Our conclusions about Sea Sprite are not subject to reexamination in these additional proceedings; Sea Sprite had a full opportunity to defend, the record concerning it is closed, and the penalty we have announced may be collected immediately. But everything we have said about Smith and Continental is provisional, reflecting the current record but not necessarily presaging the conclusions to be drawn from an enlarged record.

NOTES AND QUESTIONS

**1.** Is the contempt power of the federal courts an adequate remedy against recalcitrant employers or is a more fundamental change in the statutory enforcement mechanism necessary?

**2.** The Act places all of the enforcement responsibilities in the Secretary of Labor. In *Sea Sprite,* what remedies, if any, do employees have to prevent continued exposure to MEK–P? Does § 13(d) of the Act provide any help?

**3.** Sea Sprite finally abated the violation and paid both the $135,000 penalty and the $1,452,000 sanction for contempt of court. A dispute arose, however, as to whether interest on the $135,000 accrued from the 1992 order of the court or since the Secretary's citation in 1989. The court held that the defendants owed the additional interest (approximately $50,-

000), and also held that Robert F. Smith is individually liable.   Reich v. Sea Sprite Boat Co., 64 F.3d 332 (7th Cir.1995).

**4.**   OSHA and affected employees should be able to monitor employer abatement efforts more closely according to a new rule adopted in 1997. 62 Fed.Reg. 15,324.   Employers are now required to certify to OSHA that they have corrected workplace hazards cited by the agency, and they also must inform their employees of any abatement actions taken.

\* \* \*

## F.   NON-OSHA SAFETY AND HEALTH LAW

Section 4(b)(4) of the Act provides in pertinent part:

> Nothing in this Act shall be construed to supersede or in any manner affect any workmen's compensation law or to enlarge or diminish or affect in any manner the common law or statutory rights, duties, or liabilities of employers and employees.   \* \* \*

Despite this language, OSHA has had significant effects on a number of areas of employment law.   This section focuses on employment-related actions involving common law, labor law, and anti-discrimination law. OSHA's effects on workers' compensation and personal injury litigation are discussed in Chapter 8.

## 1.   COMMON LAW

## Shimp v. New Jersey Bell Telephone Co.

368 A.2d 408 (N.J. Super. Ch.Div.1976).

■ GRUCCIO, J.S.C.

This case involves a matter of first impression in this State:  whether a nonsmoking employee is denied a safe working environment and entitled to injunctive relief when forced by proximity to smoking employees to involuntarily inhale "second hand" cigarette smoke.

Plaintiff seeks to have cigarette smoking enjoined in the area where she works.   She alleges that her employer, defendant N. J. Bell Telephone Co., is causing her to work in an unsafe environment by refusing to enact a ban against smoking in the office where she works.   The company allows other employees to smoke while on the job at desks situated in the same work area as that of plaintiff.   Plaintiff contends that the passive inhalation of smoke and the gaseous by-products of burning tobacco is deleterious to her health.   Therefore her employer, by permitting employees to smoke in the work area, is allowing an unsafe condition to exist.   The present action is a suit to enjoin these allegedly unsafe conditions, thereby restoring to plaintiff a healthy environment in which to work.

The attorneys have submitted affidavits in lieu of oral testimony and it has been agreed that I will decide the issue upon submission of briefs by counsel. Plaintiff's affidavit clearly outlines a legitimate grievance based upon a genuine health problem. She is allergic to cigarette smoke. Mere passive inhalation causes a severe allergic reaction which has forced her to leave work physically ill on numerous occasions.

Plaintiff's representations are substantiated by the affidavits of attending physicians who confirm her sensitivity to cigarette smoke and the negative effect it is having upon her physical well-being. Plaintiff's symptoms evoked by the presence of cigarette smoke include severe throat irritation, nasal irritation sometimes taking the form of nosebleeds, irritation to the eyes which has resulted in corneal abrasion and corneal erosion, headaches, nausea and vomiting. It is important to note that a remission of these symptoms occurs whenever plaintiff remains in a smoke-free environment. Further, it appears that a severe allergic reaction can be triggered by the presence of as little as one smoker adjacent to plaintiff.

Plaintiff sought to alleviate her intolerable working situation through the use of grievance mechanisms established by collective bargaining between defendant employer and her union. That action, together with other efforts of plaintiff and her physician, resulted in the installation of an exhaust fan in the vicinity of her work area. This attempted solution has proven unsuccessful because the fan was not kept in continuous operation. The other employees complained of cold drafts due to the fan's operation, and compromises involving operation at set intervals have proven ineffective to prevent the onset of plaintiff's symptoms in the presence of smoking co-employees. The pleadings indicate plaintiff has tried every avenue open to her to get relief prior to instituting this action for injunctive relief.

It is clearly the law in this State that an employee has a right to work in a safe environment. An employer is under an affirmative duty to provide a work area that is free from unsafe conditions. This right to safe and healthful working conditions is protected not only by the duty imposed by common law upon employers, but has also been the subject of federal legislation. In 1970 Congress enacted the Occupational Safety and Health Act (OSHA), which expresses a policy of prevention of occupational hazards. The act authorizes the Secretary of Labor to set mandatory occupational safety and health standards in order to assure safe and healthful working conditions. Under the general duty clause, Congress imposed upon the employer a duty to eliminate all foreseeable and preventable hazards. OSHA in no way preempted the field of occupational safety. Specifically, 29 U.S.C.A. § 653(b)(4) recognizes concurrent state power to act either legislatively or judicially under the common law with regard to occupational safety.

In Canonico v. Celanese Corp. of America, [11 N.J.Super. 445, 778 A.2d 411 (App.Div.1951)], plaintiff was seeking to recover damages for illness allegedly contracted from the inhalation of cellulose acetate dust. The dust was a result of the manufacturing process in which plaintiff was employed. His job location was in the pulverizing room where as much as 400 pounds of dust could be present and circulating in the air in a single day. The court reiterated the common law premise that it is the master's duty to use reasonable care to provide a proper and safe place for the servant to work and that failure to use reasonable diligence to protect the employee from unnecessary risks will cause the employer to be answerable for the damages which ensue. The court upheld the trial judge's dismissal of the cause of action, emphasizing that cellulose acetate dust is a nontoxic result of the manufacturing process.

Two important distinctions are found between the *Canonico* decision and the present case. In *Canonico* the court was presented with a by-product which was a *necessary result* of the operation of the business. There is no way to pulverize cellulose acetate material without creating dust. The denial of recovery for an occupational disease where the nature of the risk is obvious or known to the employee is based on the theory that the employee assumes the risk as ordinarily incident to his employment. Plaintiff's complaint arises from the presence of cigarette smoke in the atmosphere of her work environment. Cigarette smoke, unlike cellulose dust, is not a natural by-product of N. J. Bell's business. Plaintiff works in an office. The tools of her trade are pens, pencils, paper, a typewriter and a telephone. There is no necessity to fill the air with tobacco smoke in order to carry on defendant's business, so it cannot be regarded as an occupational hazard which plaintiff has voluntarily assumed in pursuing a career as a secretary.

This case is further distinguishable from *Canonico* based on the nature of the substance which is being inhaled. In *Canonico* the trial judge found that the dust was a nontoxic substance. Evidence presented by a medical expert indicated that no one else he had ever seen had suffered disease or illness attributable to the inhalation of cellulose acetate dust. The Appellate Division upheld the trial court's determination that the dust was nontoxic. In the present case the substance being introduced into the air has a far more questionable record. The evidence against tobacco smoke is strong. I shall discuss the evidence presented to me later but note here that the smoke from burning cigarettes is toxic and deleterious to the health not only of smokers but also of nonsmokers who are exposed to "second hand" smoke, as plaintiff is here. It is evident that plaintiff is confronted with a work environment contaminated by the presence of a nonnecessary toxic substance.

Where an employer is under a common law duty to act, a court of equity may enforce an employee's rights by ordering the employer to eliminate any preventable hazardous condition which the court finds to exist. The courts of New Jersey have long been open to protect basic employees' rights by injunction. Although dealing with employee's collective bargaining rights, these cases establish the underlying principle that the powers of a court of equity are available in labor matters unless the subject matter is specifically withdrawn from its jurisdiction by the legislature.

The authority of this court has not been affected by the Workmen's Compensation Act.  The provisions of N.J.S.A. 34:15–8 cover the presumptively elective surrender by the parties of "their rights to any other method, form or amount of *compensation* or determination thereof  * * * "  (emphasis supplied).  This provision bars only the common law action in tort for damages resulting from work-related injury and make the workmen's compensation system the exclusive method of securing *money recoveries*.  The act is silent with respect to the question of injunctive relief against occupational hazards.  There is no provision in the act making it the exclusive method of protecting the worker against an occupational hazard.  The act becomes the exclusive remedy for the employee when the hazard has ripened to injury.

* * *

Since plaintiff has a common law right to a safe working environment, the issue remains whether the work area here is unsafe due to a preventable hazard which I may enjoin.  There can be no doubt that the by-products of burning tobacco are toxic and dangerous to the health of smokers and nonsmokers generally and this plaintiff in particular.

* * *

The evidence is clear and overwhelming.  Cigarette smoke contaminates and pollutes the air, creating a health hazard not merely to the smoker but to all those around her who must rely upon the same air supply.  The right of an individual to risk his or her own health does not include the right to jeopardize the health of those who must remain around him or her in order to properly perform the duties of their jobs.  The portion of the population which is especially sensitive to cigarette smoke is so significant that it is reasonable to expect an employer to foresee health consequences and to impose upon him a duty to abate the hazard which causes the discomfort.  I order New Jersey Bell Telephone Company to do so.

In determining the extent to which smoking must be restricted the rights and interests of smoking and nonsmoking employees alike must be considered.  The employees' right to a safe working environment makes it clear that smoking must be forbidden in the work area.  The employee who desires to smoke on his own time, during coffee breaks and lunch hours, should have a reasonably accessible area in which to smoke.  In the present case the employees' lunchroom and lounge could serve this function.  Such a rule imposes no hardship upon defendant New Jersey Bell Telephone Company.  The company already has in effect a rule that cigarettes may not be smoked around the telephone equipment.  The rationale behind the rule is that the machines are extremely sensitive and can be damaged by the smoke.  Human beings are also very sensitive and can be damaged by cigarette smoke.  Unlike a piece of machinery, the damage to a human is all too often irreparable.  If a circuit or wiring goes bad, the company can install a replacement part.  It is not so simple in the case of a human lung, eye or heart.  The parts are hard to come by, if indeed they can be found at all.

A company which has demonstrated such concern for its mechanical components should have at least as much concern for its human beings. Plaintiff asks nothing more than to be able to breathe the air in its clear and natural state.

Accordingly, I order defendant New Jersey Bell Telephone Company to provide safe working conditions for plaintiff by restricting the smoking of employees to the nonwork area presently used as a lunchroom. No smoking shall be permitted in the offices or adjacent customer service area.

It is so ordered.

NOTES AND QUESTIONS

**1.** *Shimp* has been followed in only one other case, Smith v. Western Electric Co., 643 S.W.2d 10 (Mo.App.1982). It has been rejected in two cases, Federal Employees for Non-Smokers' Rights v. United States, 446 F.Supp. 181 (D.D.C.1978), affirmed, 598 F.2d 310 (D.C.Cir.1979), cert. denied, 444 U.S. 926 (1979); Gordon v. Raven Systems & Research, Inc., 462 A.2d 10 (D.C.App.1983). See generally Alfred Blumrosen, et al., Injunctions Against Occupational Hazards: The Right to Work Under Safe Conditions, 64 Calif.L.Rev. 702 (1976); Comment, Injunctions Against Occupational Hazards: Toward A Safe Workplace Environment, 9 B.C.Envtl.Aff.L.Rev. 133 (1980–81).

In *Shimp* the plaintiff could not recover damages and would be limited to filing a workers' compensation claim. Suppose that an individual's pulmonary disease caused by passive inhalation of cigarette smoke is found to be noncompensable because it is not an occupational disease peculiar to a specific occupation. Would the individual then be able to maintain a common law action for negligence? See McCarthy v. State Department of Social & Health Services, 730 P.2d 681 (Wash. App.1986) (held: yes).

**2.** Suppose what the plaintiff complained about was the excess levels of asbestos, as to which OSHA has promulgated a specific standard? Would the result be the same?

**3.** Suppose that as a result of bringing this suit the plaintiff was discharged. Is she entitled to reinstatement under any federal statute? Under common law? In Hentzel v. Singer Co., 188 Cal.Rptr. 159 (Cal. App.1982), the court recognized tort causes of action for wrongful discharge and for intentional infliction of emotional distress for an employee who alleged he was terminated as a result of his efforts to obtain a smoke-free environment. The court concluded that the California Occupational Safety and Health provisions protecting complaining workers against dismissal are not exclusive and do not destroy the common law wrongful discharge action.

## 2.    COLLECTIVE BARGAINING

## NLRB v. American National Can Co.
924 F.2d 518 (4th Cir.1991).

■ ERVIN, CHIEF JUDGE:

The National Labor Relations Board petitions for enforcement of its order commanding American National Can Company, Foster Forbes Glass

Division (the Company) to grant representatives of the Glass, Pottery, Plastics and Allied Workers' Union, AFL–CIO (Local 193 and International, collectively the Unions) access to the Company's Wilson, North Carolina, plant to take heat measurements necessary for processing a heat relief grievance and for monitoring the Company's compliance with the on-job health protection provisions of the parties' collective bargaining agreement. Reviewing the Board's order under Section 10(e) of the National Labor Relations Act (the Act), as amended, 29 U.S.C. § 160(e), we conclude that there was substantial evidence to support the Board's finding that the Company committed an unfair labor practice. We also affirm the Board's refusal to defer the issue of union access to obtain heat information for resolution under the arbitration provision of the parties' collective bargaining agreement. Accordingly, we affirm the Board's findings and enforce the order against the Company.

I

The Company operates eight glass-container manufacturing plants, including a plant in Wilson, North Carolina. The Unions represent employees from two different bargaining units at the Wilson plant—a "hot end" unit consisting of employees in the forming department and a "cold end" unit consisting of employees in the production and maintenance departments. The relief sought by the complaint relates to the Unions' role as collective bargaining agent for cold end employees, who, despite the terminology, are often subjected to extreme heat. Each of these units is covered by a separate master contract between the International and its various local affiliates and the Company, covering comparable units in each of the other seven plants.

The Company acquired the Wilson plant in 1983 from Kerr Glass Company (Kerr). The Company succeeded to Kerr's bargaining relationship with the Unions and assumed its union contracts, due to expire in March 1986. The Kerr contracts provided additional relief time for hot end employees when heat conditions warranted, but not for cold end employees. These contracts also recognized the right of international and local union representatives to enter the plant to investigate complaints and grievances concerning the interpretation or application of contract terms.

In 1987 the parties agreed to extend the Company's master contracts to the Wilson plant, including the extension of the additional heat-relief provision to cover cold end employees. That provision, Article 18, Section 1(e) of the 1987 collective bargaining agreement, states that "[a]dditional relief shall be provided where heat or cold conditions warrant." At the Unions' initiative, the access provision in the Company's master contracts was renegotiated to afford access for grievance purposes to local union officials as well as to international representatives. Other pertinent provisions of the master contracts include an on-job health and safety provision and a four-step grievance provision culminating in binding arbitration.

On May 20, 1987, Local 193's president Sternfeld and other local union officials met with various plant managers to discuss their concern about heat conditions in the cold end and to clarify circumstances in which employees were entitled to heat relief under the contract.   Sternfeld discussed Local 193's interest in taking atmospheric measurements in the plant with a wet bulb globe thermometer or WBGT, a small instrument that measures atmospheric conditions such as ambient temperature, radiant heat, humidity, and wind velocity.   Upon Sternfeld's inquiry, the Company's plant manager, Ghegan, responded that the Company neither took heat measurements at the plant nor kept records of those measurements.   Ghegan stated that there were no established guidelines under the contract and that the Company reserved the responsibility to determine when conditions warranting additional heat relief were present.   Ghegan advised Sternfeld that the Company would not allow Local 193 access to take WBGT readings.

* * *

The Unions filed an unfair labor practice charge with the Board on November 18, 1987, alleging that the Company had refused to bargain in good faith as required by Sections 8(a)(1) and 8(a)(5) of the Act, 29 U.S.C. § 158(a)(1), (a)(5), by refusing to provide relevant requested information pursuant to the collective bargaining procedure.   After the Unions had filed this charge, the Company offered to arbitrate the question of the Unions' right of access to the plant together with its heat-relief grievance. A hearing was held before an Administrative Law Judge (ALJ) on March 15, 1988.   On May 29, 1988, the ALJ issued a recommended order that the issues raised by the complaint be deferred for resolution under the arbitration provisions of the parties' collective bargaining agreement.

The General Counsel and the Unions filed exceptions to the ALJ's decision.   After briefing, the Board entered a decision and order on April 28, 1989, in which the Board reversed the ALJ's decision to defer the case to arbitration and ruled that the Company had violated Sections 8(a)(1) and 8(a)(5) of the Act.   The Board ordered the Company to grant the Unions access to the Wilson plant "for reasonable periods of time at reasonable times," to take heat measurements necessary for processing Local 193's heat grievance and for monitoring the Company's compliance with the health protection provisions of the parties' collective bargaining agreement. In March 1990 the Board applied to this Court for enforcement of its order.

## II

The first issue before us is whether the Board abused its discretion by refusing to defer the issues relating to the taking of heat measurements for resolution under the arbitration provisions of the parties' collective bargaining agreement.   The Board's decision concerning deferral to arbitration is to be affirmed unless found to be an abuse of discretion.

The Company contends that the matters of access and heat relief are subjects governed by the collective bargaining agreement, and that by issuing an order on these matters instead of deferring them to arbitration the Board has improperly established a binding construction of a provision in the collective bargaining agreement.  The Company charges the Unions with trying to renegotiate the agreement and force the Company to comply with certain measurement criteria which were not negotiated over.

The Unions' complaint before the ALJ charged the Company with failing to provide the Unions access to the plant to gather information related to health and safety conditions.  Focussing on the issue of access, the ALJ found deferral appropriate primarily on the basis that the statutory right to access claimed by the Unions is paralleled by the parties' collective bargaining agreement and thus is not dependent on the Act.  The ALJ concluded that in such a case the existence of the contractual provision is controlling on the issue of deferral, which promotes a stated goal of the Act by encouraging the practice of voluntary collective bargaining.  Carey v. Westinghouse Electric Corp., 375 U.S. 261 (1964), quoted in Collyer Insulated Wire, 192 N.L.R.B. 837, 840 (1971).  The interpretation and extent of application of the access provision are matters within the province and expertise of arbitrators and not the Board.  See *Collyer,* supra, 192 N.L.R.B. at 841–42 (Board should defer to arbitration when it appears that arbitral interpretation of the contract will resolve both the unfair labor practice issue and the contract interpretation issue); Transport Service Co., 282 N.L.R.B. 111 (1986) (Board deferred to arbitration where collective bargaining agreement's grievance and arbitration provisions were sufficiently broad to encompass the issue of access and Company stated willingness to arbitrate).

The Board noted, however, that in *Transport Service,* even while deferring certain unfair labor practice issues to arbitration, the Board ordered the Company to comply with the Union's request to make available "all relevant *information* necessary to process the matters through the grievance and arbitration procedures."  Although the Board's guidelines have been less than clear as to when deferral is or is not appropriate in cases in which no arbitral award has yet issued, the Board has traditionally refused to defer in right-to-information cases.  This policy is based on the recognition that the Union's right to information that is relevant to the Union's performance of its responsibilities is statutory and not contractual, especially when it concerns health and safety conditions.

The Board found that the Unions' allegation did not primarily concern the issue of access—the Unions' concern was the obtaining of needed *information* which the Company had repeatedly refused to supply.  The Unions raised the issue of access only because the Company's refusal to cooperate made access necessary in order to obtain the information.  The Board held that the principles traditionally applied in refusing to defer request-for-information cases are equally applicable to the question whether to defer request-for-access-to-obtain-information cases.  Moreover, the Board expressed concern that deferral in such cases can lead to a two-tiered dispute resolution procedure, whereby the Union would have to file one grievance to obtain the needed information, followed by a second grievance concerning the access provision.  In the Board's view, such a procedure constitutes an "unacceptable impediment to the right of the Respondent's employees to be effectively represented by their collective bargaining representatives."

We agree with the Board's analysis.  The Company has a duty to supply information that is relevant and reasonably necessary to the performance of the Unions' responsibilities.  Yet the Company repeatedly refused to comply in any way with the Unions' request for information—not only the request for Union access to obtain such information, but also the Unions' requests for the Company to supply information as to what measurements and criteria it was using to deal with the heat relief problem.  Until the Unions filed the unfair labor practice charge with the Board, the Company was clearly not willing to negotiate its interpretation of the heat relief provision with the Unions, in spite of the fact that the duty to bargain extends beyond the period of contract negotiations to the arena of labor-management relations during the term of an agreement.

We find meritless the Company's contention that the Unions are attempting to bind the Company to an interpretation of the access provision which mandates the use of the NIOSH Criteria as the standard for measuring Company compliance.  At no stage in the proceedings have the Unions made the use of the NIOSH Criteria an issue, and they have acknowledged that these Criteria do not represent the only heat-stress standards that can be used with WBGT readings.  Moreover, the ALJ correctly pointed out that the Company would not be bound to the NIOSH Criteria by the fact that the Unions are permitted to take WBGT readings. If the Unions were to actually use the Criteria to determine that the Company was not complying with its duty under the heat-relief provision, the Company would then have the opportunity to press its own statutory interpretation claim, supported by its evidence of compliance according to whatever standard it has chosen to use.  An arbitrator's eventual finding in favor of the Company is not precluded by the Board's threshold determination of the relevance of the requested information.  385 U.S. at 438 (observing that refusal to defer a request-for-information case actually aids the functioning of the arbitration process by allowing evaluation of the merits of the claim before placing expenses of arbitration on the union).

### III

As a reviewing court, we must affirm the Board's findings of fact if they are supported by substantial evidence on the record considered as a whole.  We find that substantial evidence supports the Board's finding that the Company committed an unfair labor practice in refusing to allow the Unions access to obtain information relevant to heat relief.

The Unions were not required to present particularized evidence concerning the relevance of the information they wanted.  Information sought by a union concerning health and safety conditions is presumptively relevant because these are mandatory bargaining subjects.  A broad discovery-type standard applies to requests for the production of such information; it is only necessary that the requested information be of apparent aid in the investigation of an alleged contract violation. Only when faced with an "effective employer rebuttal" must the union show the precise relevance of the requested information. All the Company offered in rebuttal was its evidence on the parties' past interpretation and application of the collective bargaining agreement. This evidence is insufficient to forestall disclosure of presumptively relevant information concerning the health and safety of the Company's employees.

Having found that the Unions were entitled to obtain the heat-measurement information, the Board further determined, applying the analysis set forth in Holyoke Water Power Co., 273 N.L.R.B. 1369, enf'd, 778 F.2d 49 (1st Cir.1985), that the Unions were entitled to access to the Wilson plant to obtain this information.

*Holyoke* held that a union is not automatically entitled to access to an employer's premises to obtain information simply because the information has been shown to be relevant to the union's proper performance of its representational duties. The right of employees to be responsibly represented by a labor union must be balanced against the right of the employer to control its property and ensure that its operations are not interfered with. *Holyoke* thus requires that in a given case the Board determine whether responsible representation of employees can be achieved by any means other than entry onto the employer's premises. If the Board finds that alternative means exist, the union may properly be denied access. On the other hand, when it is found that responsible representation requires union access to the employer's premises, the employer's property rights must yield to the extent necessary to achieve this end without unwarranted interruption of the employer's operations.

The Board found nothing in the record to indicate that the Unions could obtain in-plant heat data without their representatives' actual entry into the plant. In fact, the Board concluded that the Company itself had rendered union access necessary by its refusal to provide the Unions requested heat-related information, to reveal what measures the Company was taking to monitor heat conditions, and to grant the Unions' conciliatory request to permit a third party access to take heat measurements.

Weighing the Company's interest in maintaining its operations unimpeded, the Board found the record likewise bare of evidence sufficient to show that granting the Unions access to take WBGT measurements for reasonable periods at reasonable times would necessarily undermine the Company's control of the plant or significantly interfere with the plant's operations. Thus, under *Holyoke,* the Company was required to grant the Unions access to take the necessary readings.

The Board's ultimate determinations concerning relevancy and the balance to be struck between competing interests are entitled to considerable deference because they fall "in an area of substantial Board expertise." We find no grounds for disturbing the Board's determination of the Unions' right to access. The Company's claim that extensive and disruptive testing of employees for metabolic heat information would be necessary in order to render atmospheric WBGT readings effective does not comport with information contained in the NIOSH Criteria. The metabolic heat values can be estimated, using tables of energy expenditure and task analysis provided by NIOSH. Hourly readings are needed only during periods of maximum heat. The Company failed to present sufficient evidence of potential disruption to deny the Unions access when the Board has determined that the Unions have no other means of responsibly representing the employees in this matter.

We have considered the other positions advanced by the Company and find them to be without merit. We hold that, on the record as a whole, the findings of the Board are supported by substantial evidence, and that the Board is therefore entitled to enforcement of its order.

ENFORCEMENT GRANTED.

NOTES AND QUESTIONS

**1.** Workplace safety and health issues are considered to be mandatory subjects of bargaining over which both the employer and the union must bargain in good faith. OCAW v. Shell Oil Co., 5 F.3d 960 (5th Cir.1993). As part of collective bargaining the parties have a duty to supply the other side with information relevant to its bargaining obligations. This duty extends beyond the period of contract negotiation to cover the entire term of the contract. NLRB v. Acme Industrial Co., 385 U.S. 432 (1967).

**2.** Access to company premises to measure workplace conditions is only one type of information access issue. In Minnesota Mining & Manufacturing Co., 261 N.L.R.B. No. 2 (1982), enforced 711 F.2d 348 (D.C.Cir.1983), the NLRB held that unions have a right to obtain individual employee medical records, the generic names of all substances used in the workplace, and other safety and health data. The Board held that even where supplying the union with statistical or aggregate medical data may result in identification of some individual employees, the important need for the data outweighs any minimal intrusion on employee privacy. The Board ordered the parties to bargain about a method of disclosing the requested information that would protect employer trade secrets.

**3.** Besides access to certain information, in what other ways do unions have rights relative to safety and health matters that individual employees do not?

3. ANTI-DISCRIMINATION LAWS

## International Union, UAW v. Johnson Controls, Inc.
499 U.S. 187 (1991).

■ JUSTICE BLACKMUN delivered the opinion of the Court.

In this case we are concerned with an employer's gender-based fetal-protection policy. May an employer exclude a fertile female employee from certain jobs because of its concern for the health of the fetus the woman might conceive?

### I.

Respondent Johnson Controls, Inc., manufactures batteries.  In the manufacturing process, the element lead is a primary ingredient.  Occupational exposure to lead entails health risks, including the risk of harm to any fetus carried by a female employee.

Before the Civil Rights Act of 1964 became law, Johnson Controls did not employ any woman in a battery-manufacturing job.  In June 1977, however, it announced its first official policy concerning its employment of women in lead-exposure work:

> "[P]rotection of the health of the unborn child is the immediate and direct responsibility of the prospective parents.  While the medical profession and the company can support them in the exercise of this responsibility, it cannot assume it for them without simultaneously infringing their rights as persons.

> \* \* \*

> " \* \* \* Since not all women who can become mothers wish to become mothers (or will become mothers), it would appear to be illegal discrimination to treat all who are capable of pregnancy as though they will become pregnant."

Consistent with that view, Johnson Controls "stopped short of excluding women capable of bearing children from lead exposure," but emphasized that a woman who expected to have a child should not choose a job in which she would have such exposure.  The company also required a woman who wished to be considered for employment to sign a statement that she had been advised of the risk of having a child while she was exposed to lead.  The statement informed the woman that although there was evidence "that women exposed to lead have a higher rate of abortion," this evidence was "not as clear \* \* \* as the relationship between cigarette smoking and cancer," but that it was, "medically speaking, just good sense not to run that risk if you want children and do not want to expose the unborn child to risk, however small \* \* \*."

Five years later, in 1982, Johnson Controls shifted from a policy of warning to a policy of exclusion.  Between 1979 and 1983, eight employees became pregnant while maintaining blood lead levels in excess of 30 micrograms per deciliter.  This appeared to be the critical level noted by the Occupational Health and Safety Administration (OSHA) for a worker who was planning to have a family.  The company responded by announcing a broad exclusion of women from jobs that exposed them to lead:

> " \* \* \* [I]t is [Johnson Controls'] policy that women who are pregnant or who are capable of bearing children will not be placed into jobs involving lead exposure or which could expose them to lead through the exercise of job bidding, bumping, transfer or promotion rights."

The policy defined "women \* \* \* capable of bearing children" as "[a]ll women except those whose inability to bear children is medically documented." It further stated that an unacceptable work station was one where, "over the past year," an employee had recorded a blood lead level of more than 30 micrograms per deciliter or the work site had yielded an air sample containing a lead level in excess of 30 micrograms per cubic meter.

## II.

In April 1984, petitioners filed in the United States District Court for the Eastern District of Wisconsin a class action challenging Johnson Controls' fetal-protection policy as sex discrimination that violated Title VII of the Civil Rights Act of 1964, as amended. Among the individual plaintiffs were petitioners Mary Craig, who had chosen to be sterilized in order to avoid losing her job, Elsie Nason, a 50–year–old divorcee, who had suffered a loss in compensation when she was transferred out of a job where she was exposed to lead, and Donald Penney, who had been denied a request for a leave of absence for the purpose of lowering his lead level because he intended to become a father. Upon stipulation of the parties, the District Court certified a class consisting of "all past, present and future production and maintenance employees" in United Auto Workers bargaining units at nine of Johnson Controls' plants "who have been and continue to be affected by [the employer's] Fetal Protection Policy implemented in 1982."

The District Court granted summary judgment for defendant-respondent Johnson Controls. Applying a three-part business necessity defense derived from fetal-protection cases in the Courts of Appeals for the Fourth and Eleventh Circuits, the District Court concluded that while "there is a disagreement among the experts regarding the effect of lead on the fetus," the hazard to the fetus through exposure to lead was established by "a considerable body of opinion"; that although "[e]xpert opinion has been provided which holds that lead also affects the reproductive abilities of men and women * * * [and] that these effects are as great as the effects of exposure of the fetus * * * a great body of experts are of the opinion that the fetus is more vulnerable to levels of lead that would not affect adults"; and that petitioners had "failed to establish that there is an acceptable alternative policy which would protect the fetus." The court stated that, in view of this disposition of the business necessity defense, it did not "have to undertake a bona fide occupational qualification's (BFOQ) analysis."

The Court of Appeals for the Seventh Circuit, sitting en banc, affirmed the summary judgment by a 7–to–4 vote. The majority held that the proper standard for evaluating the fetal-protection policy was the defense of business necessity; that Johnson Controls was entitled to summary judgment under that defense; and that even if the proper standard was a BFOQ, Johnson Controls still was entitled to summary judgment.

The Court of Appeals first reviewed fetal-protection opinions from the Eleventh and Fourth Circuits. See Hayes v. Shelby Memorial Hospital, 726 F.2d 1543 (CA11 1984), and Wright v. Olin Corp., 697 F.2d 1172 (CA4 1982). Those opinions established the three-step business necessity inquiry: whether there is a substantial health risk to the fetus; whether transmission of the hazard to the fetus occurs only through women; and whether there is a less discriminatory alternative equally capable of preventing the health hazard to the fetus. The Court of Appeals agreed with the Eleventh and Fourth Circuits that "the components of the business necessity defense the courts of appeals and the EEOC have utilized in fetal protection cases balance the interests of the employer, the employee and the unborn child in a manner consistent with Title VII."

\* \* \*

### III.

The bias in Johnson Controls' policy is obvious. Fertile men, but not fertile women, are given a choice as to whether they wish to risk their reproductive health for a particular job. Section 703(a) of the Civil Rights Act of 1964 prohibits sex-based classifications in terms and conditions of employment, in hiring and discharging decisions, and in other employment decisions that adversely affect an employee's status. Respondent's fetal-protection policy explicitly discriminates against women on the basis of their sex. The policy excludes women with childbearing capacity from lead-exposed jobs and so creates a facial classification based on gender. Respondent assumes as much in its brief before this Court.

Nevertheless, the Court of Appeals assumed, as did the two appellate courts who already had confronted the issue, that sex-specific fetal-protection policies do not involve facial discrimination. These courts analyzed the policies as though they were facially neutral, and had only a discriminatory effect upon the employment opportunities of women. Consequently, the courts looked to see if each employer in question had established that its policy was justified as a business necessity. The business necessity standard is more lenient for the employer than the statutory BFOQ defense. The Court of Appeals here went one step further and invoked the burden-shifting framework set forth in Wards Cove Packing Co. v. Atonio, 490 U.S. 642 (1989), thus requiring petitioners to bear the burden of persuasion on all questions. The court assumed that because the asserted reason for the sex-based exclusion (protecting women's unconceived offspring) was ostensibly benign, the policy was not sex-based discrimination. That assumption, however, was incorrect.

First, Johnson Controls' policy classifies on the basis of gender and childbearing capacity, rather than fertility alone. Respondent does not seek to protect the unconceived children of all its employees. Despite evidence in the record about the debilitating effect of lead exposure on the male reproductive system, Johnson Controls is concerned only with the harms that may befall the unborn offspring of its female employees. Accordingly, it appears that Johnson Controls would have lost in the Eleventh Circuit under Hayes because its policy does not "effectively and equally protec[t] the offspring of all employees." This Court faced a conceptually similar situation in Phillips v. Martin Marietta Corp., 400 U.S. 542 (1971), and found sex discrimination because the policy established "one hiring policy for women and another for men—each having preschool-age children." Johnson Controls' policy is facially discriminatory because it requires only a female employee to produce proof that she is not capable of reproducing.

Our conclusion is bolstered by the Pregnancy Discrimination Act of 1978 (PDA), 92 Stat. 2076, 42 U.S.C. § 2000e(k), in which Congress explicitly provided that, for purposes of Title VII, discrimination "on the basis of sex" includes discrimination "because of or on the basis of pregnancy, childbirth, or related medical conditions."[3] "The Pregnancy Discrimination Act has now made clear that, for all Title VII purposes, discrimination based on a woman's pregnancy is, on its face, discrimination because of her sex." In its use of the words "capable of bearing children" in the 1982 policy statement as the criterion for exclusion, Johnson Controls explicitly classifies on the basis of potential for pregnancy. Under the PDA, such a classification must be regarded, for Title VII purposes, in the same light as explicit sex discrimination. Respondent has chosen to treat all its female employees as potentially pregnant; that choice evinces discrimination on the basis of sex.

We concluded above that Johnson Controls' policy is not neutral because it does not apply to the reproductive capacity of the company's male employees in the same way as it applies to that of the females. Moreover, the absence of a malevolent motive does not convert a facially discriminatory policy into a neutral policy with a discriminatory effect. Whether an employment practice involves disparate treatment through explicit facial discrimination does not depend on why the employer discriminates but rather on the explicit terms of the discrimination.

\* \* \*

In sum, Johnson Controls' policy "does not pass the simple test of whether the evidence shows 'treatment of a person in a manner which but for that person's sex would be different.'" We hold that Johnson Controls' fetal-protection policy is sex discrimination forbidden under Title VII unless respondent can establish that sex is a "bona fide occupational qualification."

## IV.

Under § 703(e)(1) of Title VII, an employer may discriminate on the basis of "religion, sex, or national origin in those certain instances where religion, sex, or national origin is a bona fide occupational qualification reasonably necessary to the normal operation of that particular business or enterprise." We therefore turn to the question whether Johnson Controls'

---

**3.** The Act added subsection (k) to § 701 of the Civil Rights Act of 1964 and reads in pertinent part:

"The terms 'because of sex' or 'on the basis of sex' (in Title VII) include, but are not limited to, because of or on the basis of pregnancy, childbirth, or related medical con- ditions; and women affected by pregnancy, childbirth, or related medical conditions shall be treated the same for all employment-related purposes as other persons not so affected but similar in their ability or inability to work \* \* \*."

fetal-protection policy is one of those "certain instances" that come within the BFOQ exception.

The BFOQ defense is written narrowly, and this Court has read it narrowly. Our emphasis on the restrictive scope of the BFOQ defense is grounded on both the language and the legislative history of § 703.

\* \* \*

Johnson Controls argues that its fetal-protection policy falls within the so-called safety exception to the BFOQ. Our cases have stressed that discrimination on the basis of sex because of safety concerns is allowed only in narrow circumstances. In Dothard v. Rawlinson, 433 U.S. 321 (1977), this Court indicated that danger to a woman herself does not justify discrimination. We there allowed the employer to hire only male guards in contact areas of maximum-security male penitentiaries only because more was at stake than the "individual woman's decision to weigh and accept the risks of employment." We found sex to be a BFOQ inasmuch as the employment of a female guard would create real risks of safety to others if violence broke out because the guard was a woman. Sex discrimination was tolerated because sex was related to the guard's ability to do the job—maintaining prison security. We also required in Dothard a high correlation between sex and ability to perform job functions and refused to allow employers to use sex as a proxy for strength although it might be a fairly accurate one.

Similarly, some courts have approved airlines' layoffs of pregnant flight attendants at different points during the first five months of pregnancy on the ground that the employer's policy was necessary to ensure the safety of passengers. In two of these cases, the courts pointedly indicated that fetal, as opposed to passenger, safety was best left to the mother.

We considered safety to third parties in Western Airlines, Inc. v. Criswell, 472 U.S. 400 (1985), in the context of the ADEA. We focused upon "the nature of the flight engineer's tasks," and the "actual capabilities of persons over age 60" in relation to those tasks. Our safety concerns were not independent of the individual's ability to perform the assigned tasks, but rather involved the possibility that, because of age-connected debility, a flight engineer might not properly assist the pilot, and might thereby cause a safety emergency. Furthermore, although we considered the safety of third parties in Dothard and Criswell, those third parties were indispensable to the particular business at issue. In Dothard, the third parties were the inmates; in Criswell, the third parties were the passengers on the plane. We stressed that in order to qualify as a BFOQ, a job qualification must relate to the "essence," or to the "central mission of the employer's business."

The concurrence ignores the "essence of the business" test and so concludes that "the safety to fetuses in carrying out the duties of battery manufacturing is as much a legitimate concern as is safety to third parties in guarding prisons (Dothard ) or flying airplanes (Criswell )." By limiting its discussion to cost and safety concerns and rejecting the "essence of the business" test that our case law has established, the concurrence seeks to expand what is now the narrow BFOQ defense.   Third-party safety considerations properly entered into the BFOQ analysis in *Dothard* and *Criswell* because they went to the core of the employee's job performance.   Moreover, that performance involved the central purpose of the enterprise. *Dothard* ("The essence of a correctional counselor's job is to maintain prison security"); *Criswell* (the central mission of the airline's business was the safe transportation of its passengers).   The concurrence attempts to transform this case into one of customer safety.   The unconceived fetuses of Johnson Controls' female employees, however, are neither customers nor third parties whose safety is essential to the business of battery manufacturing.   No one can disregard the possibility of injury to future children;  the BFOQ, however, is not so broad that it transforms this deep social concern into an essential aspect of batterymaking.

Our case law, therefore, makes clear that the safety exception is limited to instances in which sex or pregnancy actually interferes with the employee's ability to perform the job.   This approach is consistent with the language of the BFOQ provision itself, for it suggests that permissible distinctions based on sex must relate to ability to perform the duties of the job.   Johnson Controls suggests, however, that we expand the exception to allow fetal-protection policies that mandate particular standards for pregnant or fertile women.   We decline to do so.   Such an expansion contradicts not only the language of the BFOQ and the narrowness of its exception but the plain language and history of the Pregnancy Discrimination Act.

The PDA's amendment to Title VII contains a BFOQ standard of its own:  unless pregnant employees differ from others "in their ability or inability to work," they must be "treated the same" as other employees "for all employment-related purposes."   This language clearly sets forth Congress' remedy for discrimination on the basis of pregnancy and potential pregnancy.   Women who are either pregnant or potentially pregnant must be treated like others "similar in their ability * * * to work."   In other words, women as capable of doing their jobs as their male counterparts may not be forced to choose between having a child and having a job.

The concurrence asserts that the PDA did not alter the BFOQ defense. The concurrence arrives at this conclusion by ignoring the second clause of the Act which states that "women affected by pregnancy, childbirth, or related medical conditions shall be treated the same for all employment-related purposes * * * as other persons not so affected but similar in their ability or inability to work."   Until this day, every Member of this Court had acknowledged that "[t]he second clause [of the PDA] could not be clearer:  it mandates that pregnant employees 'shall be treated the same for all employment-related purposes' as nonpregnant employees similarly situated with respect to their ability or inability to work."   The concurrence now seeks to read the second clause out of the Act.

The legislative history confirms what the language of the Pregnancy Discrimination Act compels.   Both the House and Senate Reports accompanying the legislation indicate that this statutory standard was chosen to protect female workers from being treated differently from other employees simply because of their capacity to bear children.

\* \* \*

This history counsels against expanding the BFOQ to allow fetal-protection policies. The Senate Report quoted above states that employers may not require a pregnant woman to stop working at any time during her pregnancy unless she is unable to do her work. Employment late in pregnancy often imposes risks on the unborn child, but Congress indicated that the employer may take into account only the woman's ability to get her job done. With the PDA, Congress made clear that the decision to become pregnant or to work while being either pregnant or capable of becoming pregnant was reserved for each individual woman to make for herself.

We conclude that the language of both the BFOQ provision and the PDA which amended it, as well as the legislative history and the case law, prohibit an employer from discriminating against a woman because of her capacity to become pregnant unless her reproductive potential prevents her from performing the duties of her job. We reiterate our holdings in *Criswell* and *Dothard* that an employer must direct its concerns about a woman's ability to perform her job safely and efficiently to those aspects of the woman's job-related activities that fall within the "essence" of the particular business.

## V.

We have no difficulty concluding that Johnson Controls cannot establish a BFOQ. Fertile women, as far as appears in the record, participate in the manufacture of batteries as efficiently as anyone else. Johnson Controls' professed moral and ethical concerns about the welfare of the next generation do not suffice to establish a BFOQ of female sterility. Decisions about the welfare of future children must be left to the parents who conceive, bear, support, and raise them rather than to the employers who hire those parents. Congress has mandated this choice through Title VII, as amended by the Pregnancy Discrimination Act. Johnson Controls has attempted to exclude women because of their reproductive capacity. Title VII and the PDA simply do not allow a woman's dismissal because of her failure to submit to sterilization.

Nor can concerns about the welfare of the next generation be considered a part of the "essence" of Johnson Controls' business. Judge Easterbrook in this case pertinently observed: "It is word play to say that 'the job' at Johnson [Controls] is to make batteries without risk to fetuses in the same way 'the job' at Western Air Lines is to fly planes without crashing."

Johnson Controls argues that it must exclude all fertile women because it is impossible to tell which women will become pregnant while working with lead. This argument is somewhat academic in light of our conclusion that the company may not exclude fertile women at all; it perhaps is worth noting, however, that Johnson Controls has shown no "factual basis for believing that all or substantially all women would be unable to perform safely and efficiently the duties of the job involved." Even on this sparse record, it is apparent that Johnson Controls is concerned about only a small minority of women. Of the eight pregnancies reported among the female employees, it has not been shown that any of the babies have birth defects or other abnormalities. The record does not reveal the birth rate for Johnson Controls' female workers but national statistics show that approximately nine percent of all fertile women become pregnant each year. The birthrate drops to two percent for blue collar workers over age 30. Johnson Controls' fear of prenatal injury, no matter how sincere, does not begin to show that substantially all of its fertile women employees are incapable of doing their jobs.

## VI.

A word about tort liability and the increased cost of fertile women in the workplace is perhaps necessary. One of the dissenting judges in this case expressed concern about an employer's tort liability and concluded that liability for a potential injury to a fetus is a social cost that Title VII does not require a company to ignore. It is correct to say that Title VII does not prevent the employer from having a conscience. The statute, however, does prevent sex-specific fetal-protection policies. These two aspects of Title VII do not conflict.

More than 40 States currently recognize a right to recover for a prenatal injury based either on negligence or on wrongful death. According to Johnson Controls, however, the company complies with the lead standard developed by OSHA and warns its female employees about the damaging effects of lead. It is worth noting that OSHA gave the problem of lead lengthy consideration and concluded that "there is no basis whatsoever for the claim that women of childbearing age should be excluded from the workplace in order to protect the fetus or the course of pregnancy." Instead, OSHA established a series of mandatory protections which, taken together, "should effectively minimize any risk to the fetus and newborn child." Without negligence, it would be difficult for a court to find liability on the part of the employer. If, under general tort principles, Title VII bans sex-specific fetal-protection policies, the employer fully informs the woman of the risk, and the employer has not acted negligently, the basis for holding an employer liable seems remote at best.

Although the issue is not before us, the concurrence observes that "it is far from clear that compliance with Title VII will preempt state tort liability."

\* \* \*

If state tort law furthers discrimination in the workplace and prevents employers from hiring women who are capable of manufacturing the product as efficiently as men, then it will impede the accomplishment of

Congress' goals in enacting Title VII. Because Johnson Controls has not argued that it faces any costs from tort liability, not to mention crippling ones, the pre-emption question is not before us. We therefore say no more than that the concurrence's speculation appears unfounded as well as premature.

The tort-liability argument reduces to two equally unpersuasive propositions. First, Johnson Controls attempts to solve the problem of reproductive health hazards by resorting to an exclusionary policy. Title VII plainly forbids illegal sex discrimination as a method of diverting attention from an employer's obligation to police the workplace. Second, the spectre of an award of damages reflects a fear that hiring fertile women will cost more. The extra cost of employing members of one sex, however, does not provide an affirmative Title VII defense for a discriminatory refusal to hire members of that gender. Indeed, in passing the PDA, Congress considered at length the considerable cost of providing equal treatment of pregnancy and related conditions, but made the "decision to forbid special treatment of pregnancy despite the social costs associated therewith."

We, of course, are not presented with, nor do we decide, a case in which costs would be so prohibitive as to threaten the survival of the employer's business. We merely reiterate our prior holdings that the incremental cost of hiring women cannot justify discriminating against them.

### VII.

Our holding today that Title VII, as so amended, forbids sex-specific fetal-protection policies is neither remarkable nor unprecedented. Concern for a woman's existing or potential offspring historically has been the excuse for denying women equal employment opportunities. Congress in the PDA prohibited discrimination on the basis of a woman's ability to become pregnant. We do no more than hold that the Pregnancy Discrimination Act means what it says.

It is no more appropriate for the courts than it is for individual employers to decide whether a woman's reproductive role is more important to herself and her family than her economic role. Congress has left this choice to the woman as hers to make.

The judgment of the Court of Appeals is reversed and the case is remanded for further proceedings consistent with this opinion.

It is so ordered.

■ Justice White, with whom The Chief Justice and Justice Kennedy join, concurring in part and concurring in the judgment.

The Court properly holds that Johnson Controls' fetal protection policy overtly discriminates against women, and thus is prohibited by Title VII unless it falls within the bona fide occupational qualification (BFOQ) exception, set forth at 42 U.S.C. § 2000e–2(e). The Court erroneously holds, however, that the BFOQ defense is so narrow that it could never justify a sex-specific fetal protection policy. I nevertheless concur in the judgment of reversal because on the record before us summary judgment in favor of Johnson Controls was improperly entered by the District Court and affirmed by the Court of Appeals.

* * *

The Court dismisses the possibility of tort liability by no more than speculating that if "Title VII bans sex-specific fetal-protection policies, the employer fully informs the woman of the risk, and the employer has not acted negligently, the basis for holding an employer liable seems remote at best." Such speculation will be small comfort to employers. First, it is far from clear that compliance with Title VII will pre-empt state tort liability, and the Court offers no support for that proposition. Second, although warnings may preclude claims by injured *employees,* they will not preclude claims by injured children because the general rule is that parents cannot waive causes of action on behalf of their children, and the parents' negligence will not be imputed to the children. Finally, although state tort liability for prenatal injuries generally requires negligence, it will be difficult for employers to determine in advance what will constitute negligence. Compliance with OSHA standards, for example, has been held not to be a defense to state tort or criminal liability. Moreover, it is possible that employers will be held strictly liable, if, for example, their manufacturing process is considered "abnormally dangerous."

Relying on Los Angeles Dept. of Water and Power v. Manhart, 435 U.S. 702 (1978), the Court contends that tort liability cannot justify a fetal protection policy because the extra costs of hiring women is not a defense under Title VII. This contention misrepresents our decision in *Manhart.* There, we held that a requirement that female employees contribute more than male employees to a pension fund, in order to reflect the greater longevity of women, constituted discrimination against women under Title VII because it treated them as a class rather than as individuals. We did not in that case address in any detail the nature of the BFOQ defense, and we certainly did not hold that cost was irrelevant to the BFOQ analysis. Rather, we merely stated in a footnote that "there has been no showing that sex distinctions are reasonably necessary to the normal operation of the Department's retirement plan." We further noted that although Title VII does not contain a "cost-justification defense comparable to the affirmative defense available in a price discrimination suit," "no defense based on the *total* cost of employing men and women was attempted in this case."

* * *

■ JUSTICE SCALIA, concurring in the judgment.

I generally agree with the Court's analysis, but have some reservations, several of which bear mention.

First, I think it irrelevant that there was "evidence in the record about the debilitating effect of lead exposure on the male reproductive system." Even without such evidence, treating women differently "on the basis of pregnancy" constitutes discrimination "on the basis of sex," because Congress has unequivocally said so.

Second, the Court points out that "Johnson Controls has shown no factual basis for believing that all or substantially all women would be unable to perform safely * * * the duties of the job involved," (internal quotations omitted). In my view, this is not only "somewhat academic in light of our conclusion that the company may not exclude fertile women at all," ibid.; it is entirely irrelevant. By reason of the Pregnancy Discrimination Act, it would not matter if all pregnant women placed their children at risk in taking these jobs, just as it does not matter if no men do so. As Judge Easterbrook put it in his dissent below, "Title VII gives parents the power to make occupational decisions affecting their families. A legislative forum is available to those who believe that such decisions should be made elsewhere."

Third, I am willing to assume, as the Court intimates, that any action required by Title VII cannot give rise to liability under state tort law. That assumption, however, does not answer the question whether an action *is* required by Title VII (including the BFOQ provision) even if it is subject to liability under state tort law. It is perfectly reasonable to believe that Title VII has *accommodated* state tort law through the BFOQ exception. However, all that need be said in the present case is that Johnson has not demonstrated a substantial risk of tort liability—which is alone enough to defeat a tort-based assertion of the BFOQ exception.

NOTES AND QUESTIONS

**1.** Based on the majority opinion, would it violate Title VII for a hospital to require that already-pregnant x-ray technicians be reassigned to other jobs in the hospital for the duration of their pregnancy?

**2.** Justice Blackmun's opinion relies on the principle of autonomy.

> The bias in Johnson Controls' policy is obvious. Fertile men, but not fertile women, are given a choice as to whether they wish to risk their reproductive health for a particular job.

To what extent should decisions about risk acceptability be left to employees? Does OSHA rely on autonomy or paternalism? What about the Americans with Disabilities Act?

**3.** A pregnant home health care nurse refused to treat a patient with AIDS and cryptococcal meningitis because of concern for the health of her unborn child. She challenged her subsequent discharge under the Pregnancy Discrimination Act. The court held for the employer.

> [A] pregnant employee, concerned about these increased risks yet still able to continue work, is faced with a difficult choice. It is precisely this choice, however difficult, that is reserved to the pregnant employee under the PDA and *Johnson Controls*.

Armstrong v. Flowers Hospital, Inc., 33 F.3d 1308, 1316 (11th Cir.1994).

**4.** Should employers have a duty to provide reasonable accommodation for pregnant employees? An airline had a policy of granting light-duty assignments only to workers who suffered from occupational injuries. Accordingly, it denied light-duty work to an employee whose pregnancy-related back problems prevented her from lifting over 20 pounds. Has the airline violated the Pregnancy Discrimination Act? See Urbano v. Continental Airlines, Inc., 138 F.3d 204 (5th Cir. 1998)(held: no). See generally D'Andra Millsap, Comment, Reasonable Accommodation of Pregnancy in the Workplace: A Proposal to Amend the Pregnancy Discrimination Act, 32 Hous.L.Rev. 1411 (1996).

**5.** How reassured are employers likely to be that their potential tort liability is "remote at best"? How would you address the issue of possible tort liability? See generally Jean Macchiaroli Eggen, Toxic Reproductive and Genetic Hazards in the Workplace: Challenging the Myths of the Tort and Workers' Compensation Systems, 60 Fordham L.Rev. 843 (1992); Susan S. Grover, The Employer's Fetal Injury Quandary After *Johnson Controls,* 81 Ky.L.J. 639 (1992–93).

**6.** The state courts have reached different results on the issue of whether personal injury claims may be brought by a child for prenatal harms allegedly caused by his or her mother's workplace exposure. Compare Namislo v. Akzo Chemicals, Inc., 620 So.2d 573 (Ala.1993) (action not barred by workers' compensation) with Widera v. Ettco Wire & Cable, 611 N.Y.S.2d 569 (App.Div.1994), appeal denied, 626 N.Y.S.2d 755 (1995) (employer owed no duty to child in utero).

**7.** Are the positions of labor and management in the *Benzene* case the same as in *Johnson?*

> [B]oth corporations and opponents of exclusionary practices seem to have reversed their characteristic positions on risk assessment and its implications for industrial policy. Typically, workers and their representatives have pressed management for the most extensive reductions in exposure levels to toxic substances. Further, they have maintained that uncertainty requires the most cautious assumptions about the possibility of harmful consequences. Corporations have responded by arguing that a risk-free environment is a chimerical notion and that the existence of uncertainty requires a willingness to tolerate levels of exposure that have not been proven harmful. Yet in relation to reproductive hazards and, more especially, danger to the fetus, it is labor and its allies that have viewed with some skepticism the data on potential risk. Corporations, on the other hand, have adopted an almost alarmist perspective.

Ronald Bayer, Reproductive Hazards in the Workplace: Bearing the Burden of Fetal Risk, 82 Milbank Fund Memorial Q. 633, 651–52 (1982). Can these positions be reconciled?

**8.** A great deal has been written about the problem of reproductive hazards. On regulatory policy, see Office of Technology Assessment,

United States Congress, Reproductive Health Hazards in the Workplace (1985); Mark A. Rothstein, Substantive and Procedural Obstacles to OSHA Rulemaking: Reproductive Hazards As An Example, 12 B.C.Envtl.Affairs L.Rev. 627 (1985). On employment discrimination issues, see Mary Becker, Reproductive Hazards After *Johnson Controls,* 31 Hous.L.Rev. 43 (1994); Laura Oren, Protection, Patriarchy, and Capitalism: The Politics and Theory of Gender–Specific Regulation in the Workplace, 6 U.C.L.A. Women's L.J. 321 (1996); Wendy W. Williams, Firing the Woman to Protect the Fetus: The Reconciliation of Fetal Protection with Employment Opportunity Goals Under Title VII, 69 Geo.L.J. 641 (1981).

**9.** Although the reproductive hazards problem is the best known of the seeming conflicts between OSHA and anti-discrimination laws, several potential conflicts involve other protected categories, including handicap, religion, and age. For example, an employer has a "no-beard" policy for all employees potentially exposed to toxic gases. The basis for the policy is that facial hair would prevent a tight "face seal" when wearing a respirator. An employee who is a member of the Sikh religion, which proscribes the cutting or shaving of hair, asserts that the employer's policy violates Title VII. What result? See Bhatia v. Chevron U.S.A., Inc., 734 F.2d 1382 (9th Cir.1984) (held: no violation).

## Moses v. American Nonwovens, Inc.

97 F.3d 446 (11th Cir.1996), cert. denied, 117 S.Ct. 964 (1997).

■ PER CURIAM:

Mark Moses has epilepsy. He brought a claim against American Nonwovens, Inc. alleging that it fired him in violation of the Americans with Disabilities Act. Moses appeals the district court's summary judgment. We have jurisdiction. We affirm.

\* \* \*

The ADA provides that an employer may not "discriminate against a qualified individual with a disability because of the disability ... in regard to ... [the] discharge of employees...." An employer may fire a disabled employee if the disability renders the employee a "direct threat" to his own health or safety. But there is no direct threat defense if the employer could have made "reasonable accommodation[s]." The employee retains at all times the burden of persuading the jury either that he was not a direct threat or that reasonable accommodations were available.

American admits that it fired Moses because of his epilepsy, and Moses does not deny that there was a significant risk that if he had continued working at American, he would have had seizures on the job. The issues are whether Moses produced evidence from which a reasonable jury could conclude (1) that he was not a direct threat or (2) that reasonable accommodations were available.

Moses failed to produce probative evidence that he was not a direct threat. Each of Moses's assigned tasks presented grave risks to an employee with a seizure disorder. As a product inspector, Moses sat on a platform above fast-moving press rollers. As a web operator, he sat underneath a conveyer belt with in-running pinch-points. And as a Hot Splicer Assistant, he worked next to exposed machinery that reached temperatures of 350 degrees Fahrenheit. Moses maintains that as long as he followed instructions and worked "downstream" from the equipment, there was no risk of harm. But the only supporting evidence to which he points is the deposition of Danny Avery, a manager at American, who stated that he always warned new employees that they should work "upstream" from the motion of the equipment so that it would "push you out of it rather than pull you into it." This testimony is insufficient: first, Avery suggests that it was more dangerous to work downstream, but he does not imply that it would be safe for epileptics to work upstream; second, Avery is referring to work on a specific machine, not to all of the tasks Moses was expected to perform.

Even though there is no genuine issue of material fact as to whether Moses was a direct threat, he could still defeat American's motion by producing probative evidence that reasonable accommodations were available. But Moses points to no probative evidence suggesting that American could have made his work sites safe.

Moses's primary arguments are that American failed to investigate his condition and failed to consider possible accommodations. Neither is persuasive. When American fired Moses, it knew he was taking medication for his epilepsy but that his medication was not controlling his seizures. This is not a case like *Kelley v. Bechtel Power Corp.,* 633 F.Supp. 927 (S.D.Fla.1986), in which the employee, although diagnosed as epileptic, had never suffered a seizure, and the employer had no basis for concluding that he was likely to suffer one. *Id.* at 933 (interpreting the Florida Human Rights Act).

We are more troubled by the evidence that American failed to investigate possible accommodations. No language in the ADA mandates a pretermination investigation, but the EEOC advises that "the employer must determine whether a reasonable accommodation would ... eliminate" the direct threat. We are persuaded that American's failure to investigate did not relieve Moses of his burden of producing probative evidence that reasonable accommodations were available. A contrary holding would mean that an employee has an ADA cause even though there was no possible way for the employer to accommodate the employee's disability. Stated differently: An employer would be liable for not investigating even though an investigation would have been fruitless. We are confident that although the ADA does not mandate a pretermination investigation, the possibility of an ADA lawsuit will, as a matter of practice, compel most employers to undertake such an investigation before terminating a disabled employee.

The district court did not err in granting American's motion for summary judgment.

AFFIRMED.

NOTES AND QUESTIONS

1. Section 103(b) of the ADA provides that "[t]he term 'qualification standards' may include a requirement that an individual shall not pose a direct threat to the health or safety of other individuals in the workplace." Although this language is narrow and does not include harm to the individual employee with a disability, the EEOC's interpretive regulation is broader. It defines a "direct threat" to include the affected individual, requires those determinations to be made on the basis of reasonable medical judgment, and lists four factors to consider. These factors are the duration of the risk, the nature and severity of the potential harm, the likelihood that the potential harm will occur, and the imminence of the potential harm.

Although at least one court has rejected the EEOC interpretation, holding that "direct threat" applies only to "other individuals," Kohnke v. Delta Airlines, Inc., 932 F.Supp. 1110 (N.D.Ill.1996), the court in *Moses* never addressed the issue.

2. Is the Supreme Court's treatment of autonomy and risk acceptability in *Johnson Controls* in accord with that of the ADA in *Moses?* Should it be? What weight, if any, should be given to OSHA considerations?

# CHAPTER 9

# DISABLING INJURY AND ILLNESS

The United States maintains a complicated and imperfectly coordinated system of income support for workers who become physically or mentally unable to continue working. Every state has a workers' compensation system (some still call it workmen's compensation). These systems require employers to obtain insurance (from private companies in some states and a state fund in others) or to self-insure against the economic consequences of certain workplace injuries and illnesses. If a worker becomes disabled, and the job was *not* the specific cause, he or she may or may not receive disability benefits from the employer depending on the coverage of the employer's disability plan. Workers' compensation presents important and complicated legal issues, and also poses challenging questions about what an American worker should be able to expect upon illness or injury, as well as about how to run a fair and efficient benefit program in heavily legalized America.

## A. INTRODUCTION TO WORKERS' COMPENSATION

## 1. HISTORY

### Arthur A. Larson, *The Nature and Origins of Workmen's Compensation*

37 Cornell L.Q. 206 (1952).

In 1838, one year after Lord Abinger announced the fellow-servant rule, and four years before Judge Shaw of Massachusetts popularized the defense of assumption of risk, Prussia enacted a law making railroads liable to their employees (as well as passengers) for accidents from all causes except act of God and negligence of the plaintiff. In 1854, Prussia required employers in certain industries to contribute one-half to the sickness association funds formed under various local statutes. In 1876 an unsuccessful voluntary insurance act was passed, and finally in 1884 Germany adopted the first modern compensation system, thirteen years before England, twenty-five years before the first American jurisdiction, and sixty-five years before the last American state.

It is interesting to inquire into the conditions which gave birth to the compensation idea. As to the intellectual origins: both philosophers and politicians played a part. Frederick the Great contributed both a profound conviction that "it is the duty of the state to provide sustenance and support of those of its citizens who cannot provide sustenance for themselves," and a completely uninhibited view of the state's power and right to bring this protection about by any means.  Among the philosophers, probably Fichte was most responsible for propounding the idea that many of the misfortunes, disabilities and accidents of individuals are ultimately social and not individual in origin, and that the state is therefore "not to be negative nor to have a mere police function, but to be filled with Christian concern, especially for the weaker members."  Lassalle, Sismondi, Winkelblech, Wagner and Schaeffle developed this general conception into insistent and eloquent arguments for the only mechanism which could effectively implement this ideal: industrial insurance.  At the same time, especially during the years following the war of 1870–71, Bismarck began to be concerned about the increasing strength shown in elections by the Marxian type of socialists as against the practical socialists of the school of Lassalle, who favored the cooperative association type of development.  Accordingly, in 1881 he met the situation by laying before the Reichstag his far-reaching plan for compulsory insurance, which was enacted in various measures between 1883 and 1887.  Thus, while Workmen's Compensation has a "socialistic" origin in the philosophical sense of the term associated with the views of Fichte and Hegel, it also has an anti-socialistic origin if the term is used in the Marxian sense.

The exact form taken by the German system should be specially noted, because it was significantly different from the English and American systems, and because it is continuing to exert a strong influence on the form taken by social legislation of all kinds.  The distinguishing feature of German insurance (apart from its much greater comprehensiveness) was that contributions by the workman himself were an integral part of the system.  Broadly, the German plan fell into three parts: the Sickness Fund (workers contributing two-thirds, employer one-third) paid benefits for the first thirteen weeks of either sickness or disability due to accident;  the Accident Fund (contributions by employers only) paid for disability after the first thirteen weeks;  and Disability Insurance (workers contribute one-half) provided for disability due to old age or other causes not specifically covered elsewhere.  The plan, though compulsory, was thus essentially based on mutual association.  The administration was placed in the hands of representatives of employers and employees under government supervision.  The striking resemblance of this plan to the present British system is at once apparent.

It seems paradoxical on the surface that Germany, with its more socialistic philosophical tradition, should produce a system which is more individualistic in the sense that the workman in effect purchases in his own right an insurance policy against sickness and disability, with the employer sharing the premium;  while America followed what might appear to be a more radical line by imposing unilateral liability without fault upon the employer, and by making him bear the entire burden of any insurance against that liability.  There are several reasons for this.  The choice of this mechanism in Germany was dictated largely by the existence of already successful schemes on this pattern within the German guilds

(Knappschaftskassen).   For hundreds of years these guilds had sponsored benefit societies and associations which provided disability, sickness and death benefits.   In a highly developed system, such as the miners' societies, there were benefits on the insurance principle for sickness, accident, and burial, and pensions for orphans, widows and invalids.   The system was administered by a committee made up half of employers and half of employees, and contributions were in the same proportion, with the employer paying the "premium" and deducting the employee's half from his next wage payment.

The New York Commission, whose report of March, 1910, was the basis for New York's Compensation Act, studied the German plan, and made the following report.

> Could we see a practical way to put a scheme of compensation in force in which the employer's share will be the 50 per cent. of earnings recommended in our bills, and the workmen's contribution say 25 per cent. above that, and the benefits insured to him thereby changed to three-fourths earnings during disability, we would recommend it.   The German system on some such lines seems admirable.   But practically we see no way to accomplish this by force of compulsory law.

The American pattern, then, became that of unilateral employer liability, with no contribution by employees.   The issue is by no means dead, however, what with the contributory principle appearing in the British comprehensive system, in the state non-occupational disability plans that have been adopted, and, of course, in old age and unemployment legislation.   It is most significant, therefore, to note that the New York Commission rejected the employee-contribution system only because of doubt that compulsory contributions could constitutionally be exacted, and that but for this doubt they would have recommended it.   No doubt the American pattern was also influenced by the fact that such recovery for industrial injury as the employee had obtained in the past had always taken the form of an adversary imposition of liability upon the employer, so that it was perhaps natural to conceive of even this totally new principle of employee protection in terms of the old mechanism of employer liability.

* * *

By the end of the nineteenth century, as shown above, the coincidence of increasing industrial injuries and decreasing remedies had produced in the United States a situation ripe for radical change, and when, in 1893, a full account of the German system written by John Graham Brooks was published, legislators all over the country seized upon it as a clue to the direction which efforts at reform might take.   Another stimulus was provided by the enactment of the first British Compensation Act in 1897 which later became the model of state acts in many respects.

A period of intensive investigation ensued, carried on by various state commissions, beginning with Massachusetts in 1904, Illinois in 1907, Connecticut in 1908 and a legislatively-created commission of representatives, industrialists and other experts in New York in 1909.  By 1910 the movement was in full swing, with commissions being created by Congress and the legislatures of Massachusetts, Minnesota, New Jersey, Connecticut, Ohio, Illinois, Wisconsin, Montana and Washington.  In 1910 also there occurred a conference in Chicago attended by representatives of all these commissions, at which a Uniform Workmen's Compensation Law was drafted.  Although the state acts which followed were anything but uniform, the discussions at this conference did much to set the fundamental pattern of legislation.

As to actual enactments, the story begins modestly with a rather narrow co-operative Accident Fund for miners passed by Maryland in 1902, which quietly expired when held unconstitutional in an unappealed lower court decision.  In 1909 another miners' compensation act was passed in Montana, and suffered the same fate.  In 1908 Congress passed a compensation Act covering certain federal employees.

In 1910 the first New York Act was passed, with compulsory coverage of certain "hazardous employments".  It was held unconstitutional in 1911 by the Court of Appeals in Ives v. South Buffalo Railway Co.,[76] on the ground that the imposition of liability without fault upon the employer was a taking of property without due process of law under the state and federal constitutions.  At the present time, with the constitutionality of all types of compensation acts firmly established, there is no practical purpose to be served by tracing out the elaborate and violent constitutional law arguments provoked by the early acts.  One important practical result did, however, flow from these preliminary constitutional setbacks: the very fear of unconstitutionality impelled the legislatures to pass over the ideal type of coverage, which would be both comprehensive and compulsory, in favor of more awkward and fragmentary plans whose very weakness and incompleteness might ensure their constitutional validity.  And so, beginning with New Jersey, "elective" or "optional" statutes became common, under which employers could choose whether or not they would be bound by the compensation plan, with the alternative of being subject to common-law actions without benefit of the three common-law defenses.

\* \* \*

In New York, the *Ives* decision was answered by the adoption in 1913 of a constitutional amendment permitting a compulsory law, and such a law was passed in the same year.  In 1917 this compulsory law, together with the Iowa elective-type and the Washington exclusive-state-fund-type law, was held constitutional by the United States Supreme Court, and, with fears of constitutional impediments virtually removed, the compensation system grew and expanded with a rapidity that probably has no parallel in any comparable field of law.

By 1920 all but eight states had adopted Compensation Acts, and on January 1, 1949, the last state, Mississippi, came under the system.

---

**76.**  201 N.Y. 271, 94 N.E. 431 (1911).

## Office of Technology Assessment, U.S. Congress, Preventing Illness and Injury in the Workplace

207–09 (1985).

Progressive Era Aims

In the early 1900s a number of Progressive Era humanitarian efforts underlined the plight of the injured worker and paved the way for workers' compensation programs.   Crystal Eastman conducted the now-famous "Pittsburgh Survey" of 1907–08.   She examined the economic conditions of the families of workers who had been killed or injured.   In over half the cases, she found that "the employers assumed absolutely no share of the inevitable income loss.   The costs of work accidents fell directly, almost wholly, and in likelihood finally, upon the injured workmen and their dependents."   She concluded that a system of compensation was necessary to achieve equity, social expediency, and prevention.

At about the same time, a State commission in Illinois reported that most court awards for industrial accidents were small, and that the families of the injured were often forced to live on charity.   Moreover, for employers who had liability insurance, only 42 percent of payments went to medical care.   The remaining 58 percent went for administration, claims investigation, and legal expenses.

Employers' Attitudes

The apparently small awards made to most workers was not the only reason for dissatisfaction with legal remedies.   Employers, who as a group supported workers' compensation legislation before labor unions did, also found advantages in compensation programs.   There is some evidence that just prior to the creation of workers' compensation laws, injured workers, at least in some circumstances, won a substantial portion of lawsuits against their employers.

Moreover, workers' compensation substituted a regular, fixed, and predictable compensation payment for uncertain, potentially ruinous liability judgments.   Employers also feared that without a workers' compensation system, the courts would start making more awards to injured employees, especially if a worker could show that his/her employer had violated one of the increasing number of State safety regulations.

Finally, employers advocated workers' compensation in order to remove one source of hostility from labor-management relations and possibly to prevent more fundamental changes in the worker-employer relationship. They specifically opposed the passage of liability law reforms that would have eliminated the common law defenses of employers.   Some large companies had already established company benefit plans that provided payments for work injuries.   Smaller manufacturers favored creation of such plans, but lacked the resources to do so privately.   Larger manufacturers feared that if such plans were not created, legislators might act to change employer and employee rights.   In the absence of changes, it was feared that the nascent unions would be given a boost.

For these reasons, some of the initial advocates of workers' compensation included groups like the National Association of Manufacturers, the National Civic Federation, the American Association for Labor Legislation, and a number of the leading industrialists of the day.

Labor Union Reactions

Unions, on the other hand, initially opposed workers' compensation. They generally wanted workers to retain the right to sue employers and advocated abolition of the three common law defenses. They held this position in part because they thought injured workers would receive larger payments under such a plan and because, at the time, they generally mistrusted the government and feared that governmental intervention would weaken unions.

Union opposition was also based on their perception that workers' compensation was "palliative and not preventive". The belief that workers' compensation could provide an economic incentive for prevention was, according to MacLaury, important in changing labor's position; it "seemed to tip the scales."

NOTE

For a further discussion, see Lawrence M. Friedman & Jack Ladinsky, Social Change and the Law of Industrial Accidents, 67 Colum.L.Rev. 50 (1967).

---

## 2. OVERVIEW

Workers' compensation programs require employers to provide cash benefits, medical care, and rehabilitative services for workers who suffer injuries or illnesses arising out of and in the course of their employment. All laws provide benefits for workers with occupational diseases, but they do not all cover every form of occupational disease.

Cash benefits compensate injured workers for lost income and earning capacity. These benefits are classified as: temporary total, temporary partial, permanent total, permanent partial, and death benefits. Temporary total benefits are paid for injuries that prevent an employee from working until he or she is fully recovered. Temporary partial benefits are paid during a period of reduced earnings and cease when the worker returns to full wages or is found eligible for permanent total or permanent partial benefits. Permanent total benefits are paid to workers who are completely disabled for an indefinite time. Permanent partial benefits are paid where the employee suffers an impairment that causes a permanent but partial loss of wages or wage-earning capacity. If the worker is fatally injured, the employer is required to provide burial expenses and to pay benefits to specified dependent survivors. For each category of benefits, all states prescribe a maximum weekly payment. Some states place limits on duration or total amount or both for certain classes of benefits.

Workers' compensation programs usually provide full medical benefits. Most states also pay for medical and vocational rehabilitation for workers who suffer severe disabilities.

Employers meet their statutory obligation to compensate injured workers through various forms of insurance. Private insurance carriers pay approximately two-thirds of all workers' compensation benefits. State-run insurance funds pay about 23 percent of all claims. The remainder are covered by employers through self-insurance.

In cases in which an injured worker's right to recovery is undisputed, benefit payments may be initiated by either agreement or direct payment. The agreement system operates in a majority of states. Under that system, the employer does not begin payments until it and the injured worker have reached an agreement in writing regarding the benefits to be paid. Because of the delays and potential bargaining disadvantages occasioned by the agreement system, many workers retain lawyers, even though their claims are uncontested. If an agreement cannot be reached, the claim is referred to the workers' compensation commission. In direct payment states, the employer must, within a prescribed number of days, begin paying benefits to the injured worker or file a notice with the state administrative agency of its intent to contest the claim.

After an employer's liability has been established, the extent or duration of that liability may be limited through compromise and release settlements. Under these settlements, the employer pays benefits to the injured worker in a lump sum in exchange for a release from further liability.

Workers' compensation costs have increased tremendously over the last 40 years, from $2.1 billion in 1960, to $4.9 billion in 1970, to $22.3 billion in 1980, to $56 billion in 1990, to $62 billion in 1992. John F. Burton, Jr., Workers' Compensation Costs, 1960–1992: The Increases, The Causes, and the Consequences, 6 Workers' Compensation Monitor, March/April 1993, at 1. In recent years, however, employer costs have declined, from $60.8 billion in 1993 to $57.1 billion in 1995. National Academy of Social Insurance, Workers' Compensation: Benefits, Coverage, and Costs, 1994–1995 (1997).

NOTE

According to the U.S. Chamber of Commerce, six objectives underlie workers' compensation laws:

1.  Provide sure, prompt, and reasonable income and medical benefits to work-accident victims, or income benefits to their dependents, regardless of fault;

2.  Provide a single remedy and reduce court delays, costs, and workloads arising out of personal-injury litigation;

3.  Relieve public and private charities of financial drains incident to uncompensated industrial accidents;

4. Eliminate payment of fees to lawyers and witnesses as well as time-consuming trials and appeals;

5. Encourage maximum employer interest in safety and rehabilitation through an appropriate experience-rating mechanism; and

6. Promote frank study of causes of accidents (rather than concealment of fault)—reducing preventable accidents and human suffering.

U.S. Chamber of Commerce, 1997 Analysis of Workers' Compensation Laws, at vi (1997).

As you read the rest of this chapter, consider whether these objectives are being met. Specifically, consider the viability of the basic workers' compensation "bargain": employees gave up the right to bring common law damage actions against their employer in exchange for a system of compensation that was to be prompt, certain, and reasonable in amount. Employers gave up the fault basis of liability and the common law defenses of contributory negligence, assumption of the risk, and the fellow servant rule in exchange for immunity from personal injury actions and relatively fixed costs that can be passed along to consumers.

In many ways, workers' compensation was a grand experiment—the first comprehensive no-fault system, an attempt to eliminate the all-or-nothing harshness of the tort system, and a recognition of the unacceptably high transaction costs of the courts. The following pages consider some of the many legal issues raised by this experiment.

## B.   Workers' Compensation Coverage

### 1.   "Employee"

### Eckis v. Sea World Corp.

134 Cal.Rptr. 183 (Cal.App.1976).

■ Ault, Presiding Justice.

Defendants Sea World and Kent Burgess have appealed from a judgment entered on a jury verdict awarding Anne E. Eckis $75,000 in compensatory damages. Plaintiff had sought both compensatory and punitive damages for personal injuries she sustained while riding "Shamu the Whale," framing her complaint on three theories: fraud, negligence, and liability for an animal with vicious or dangerous propensities. Before the case was submitted to the jury, the trial court denied Sea World's motion for a nonsuit on the fraud cause of action. Later its motions for judgment notwithstanding the verdict and for a new trial were also denied.

* * *

The major issue raised on appeal is the contention there was no substantial evidence to support the jury's finding that plaintiff's injuries did *not* occur in the course of her employment by Sea World. The facts which govern this issue are not in dispute.

When injured on April 19, 1971, plaintiff Anne E. Eckis, then 22 years old, was a full-time employee of Sea World. First hired by Sea World in 1967, she had worked variously as ticket sales girl, receptionist, in the accounting department, and in 1970 became the secretary for Kent Burgess, the director of Sea World's animal training department. From then on her job title was secretary, and that is what she considered herself to be, although from time to time she did other tasks at Burgess' request, such as taking the water temperature, doing research, and running errands. She worked five days a week, for which she was paid a salary of $450 per month. When first hired plaintiff, like all other Sea World employees, had signed an authorization for reproduction of her physical likeness. Plaintiff was also an excellent swimmer, with some scuba diving experience, and had occasionally worked as a model, sometimes for pay.

In April 1971 Gail MacLaughlin, Sea World's public relations director, and Kent Burgess asked plaintiff if she would like to ride Shamu, the killer whale, in a bikini for some publicity pictures for Sea World. Although the ride was not made a condition of her keeping her job, plaintiff eagerly agreed, thinking it would be exciting. Although warned in general terms that the ride involved dangers and aware that she might fall off, plaintiff was confident of her swimming ability and anxious to do it. She had never heard of whales pushing riders around.

Burgess had been responsible for training Shamu ever since Sea World first acquired the animal. He knew Shamu was conditioned to being ridden only by persons wearing wetsuits, and that Shamu had in the past attacked persons who attempted to ride her in an ordinary bathing suit: first a Catalina swimsuit model and then Jim Richards, one of the trainers at Sea World. In addition, Burgess had read training records which showed Shamu had been behaving erratically since early March 1971. This information he did not disclose to plaintiff.

Plaintiff was trained for the ride by Sea World trainers in the tank at Sea World during normal office working hours. First she practiced riding Kilroy, a smaller, more docile whale, while wearing a bathing suit. During her one practice session on Shamu, she wore a wetsuit, fell off, but swam to the edge of the tank without incident.

On April 19 plaintiff became apprehensive for the first time when one of Sea World's trainers said he was not going to watch her ride Shamu because it was "really dangerous." Plaintiff then went to Burgess and told him of her concern. He told her not to worry, said there was nothing to be concerned about, and that the ride was "as safe as it could be." He still did not tell her about the problems they had been having with Shamu or about the earlier incidents involving Richards and the swimsuit model. Thus reassured, plaintiff, wearing a bikini Sea World had paid for, then took three rides on Shamu. During the second ride one of the trainers noticed Shamu's tail was fluttering, a sign the animal was upset. During the third ride plaintiff fell off when Shamu refused to obey a signal. Shamu then bit her on her legs and hips and held her in the tank until she could be rescued.

Plaintiff suffered 18 to 20 wounds which required from 100 to 200 stitches and left permanent scars. She was hospitalized five days and out of work several weeks. She also suffered some psychological disturbance. Sea World paid all her medical expenses and continued to pay her salary as usual during this period. On advice of her counsel, she filed this civil action and a workers' compensation claim.

When an employee's injuries are compensable under the Workers' Compensation Act, the right of the employee to recover the benefits provided by the Act is his exclusive remedy against the employer.

Where a reasonable doubt exists as to whether an act of an employee is contemplated by the employment, or as to whether an injury occurred in the course of the employment, section 3202 requires courts to resolve the doubt against the right of the employee to sue for civil damages and in favor of the applicability of the Compensation Act. The importance of adhering to the rule requiring a liberal construction of the Act in favor of its applicability in civil litigation was emphasized by the court in *Scott*:

> "Though it may be more opportunistic for a particular plaintiff to seek to circumscribe the purview of compensation coverage because of his immediate interest and advantage, the courts must be vigilant to preserve the spirit of the act and to prevent a distortion of its purposes. That the question before us in this case arises out of litigation prosecuted in the superior court is all the more reason for care lest rules of doubtful validity, out of harmony with the objectives of the Act, be formulated." * * *

Governed by these legal principles, we examine the evidence to determine whether it supports the finding plaintiff was not acting within the course and scope of her employment at Sea World when she sustained her injuries.

The undisputed evidence shows: at the time she was injured plaintiff was an employee of Sea World; she was injured on the employer's premises during what were her regular working hours; she was injured while engaging in an activity which her employer had requested her to perform and for which it had provided her with the training and the means to perform; in riding Shamu the Whale for publicity pictures, plaintiff was not engaged in an activity which was personal to her, but rather one which was related to, furthered, and benefited the business of her employer.

Despite this formidable array of factors which indicate her injuries did arise out of and occurred in the course and scope of her employment plaintiff maintains substantial evidence supports the special finding to the contrary. She premises her position on the claim she was hired to be a secretary, not to ride a whale. Since her injuries were unrelated to the secretarial duties she was originally hired to perform, she argues her employment "had nothing whatsoever to do with her injury" and that her case does not come within the purview of the Compensation Act. Because of the highly unusual circumstances under which she was injured, she maintains the rules and formulas traditionally used to determine whether injuries have arisen out of or occurred in the course of employment are neither applicable nor helpful.

These arguments are without merit. The right to compensation is not limited to those cases where the injury occurs while the employee is performing the classical duties for which he was originally hired. Far less than a direct request by the employer operates to bring an injury-causing activity within the provisions of the Compensation Act. For example, in Lizama v. Workmen's Comp. Appeals Bd., 40 Cal.App.3d 363, 115 Cal.Rptr. 267, the employee was injured on the employer's premises after he had clocked out from work while using a table saw to construct a bench to sit on at lunch time. Although his assigned duties did not include use of the saw and he had never used it before, the injury was held compensable because the employer had expressly or impliedly permitted such use of equipment. At page 370, 115 Cal.Rptr. at page 271, the court stated:

> "Textwriters have long proposed and California courts have applied a 'quantum theory of work-connection' that seems peculiarly appropriate for application here. The theory merges the 'course of employment' and 'arising out of employment' tests, but does not dispense with a minimum 'quantum of work-connection.' There were at least these connections between petitioner's injury and his employment: the accident occurred on the employer's premises when petitioner was using the employer's equipment while constructing a bench for his personal comfort to be used on the employer's premises; and the employer expressly or impliedly permitted petitioner to use its equipment. * * *"

Where, as here, an employee is injured on the employer's premises during regular working hours, when the injury occurs while the employee is engaged in an activity which the employer has requested her to undertake, and when the injury-causing activity is of service to the employer and benefits the employer's business, the conditions imposing liability for compensation under Labor Code section 3600 are met as a matter of law, and it is immaterial that the activity causing the injury was not related to the employee's normal duties or that the circumstances surrounding the injury were unusual or unique.

It would be wholly incongruous and completely at variance with the long declared purposes and policies of the Workers' Compensation Law to say that an employee who sustained injuries under the circumstances of this case is not entitled to the benefits of the Workers' Compensation Act. Since her injuries fall within the scope of the Act, a proceeding under it constitutes plaintiff's exclusive remedy.

NOTES AND QUESTIONS

**1.** What facts in this case are most damaging to the plaintiff's claim that she was not injured during the course of her employment? If she was not an employee, what was she?  Is it her theory that she was an independent contractor?

**2.**  Why does the plaintiff want to be considered an independent contractor rather than an employee?  As an independent contractor the plaintiff is not entitled to workers' compensation, but she is not precluded from bringing a tort action in negligence.  Under workers' compensation, a claimant receives a percentage of lost income plus medical expenses.  In a common law action the plaintiff may recover compensatory damages for pain and suffering and may even be awarded punitive damages.  (The $75,000 the jury awarded the plaintiff in *Eckis* was undoubtedly much more than she would receive under workers' compensation.)  As long as workers' compensation benefit levels are relatively low, injured workers will attempt to "get out" of the workers' compensation system.  For a further discussion of this issue, see pp. 882–907, infra.

**3.**  Theoretically, independent contractors are excluded from coverage because they are not "employees."  Some classifications of employees excluded from coverage in one or more states include domestic servants, casual employees, real estate licensees, farmworkers, newspaper vendors, employees of public charities, professional athletes, and clergy.

## 2.   "Course of Employment"

### Weiss v. City of Milwaukee

559 N.W.2d 588 (Wis.1997).

Ann Walsh Bradley, Justice.

Holly Lynn Weiss seeks review of an unpublished court of appeals decision which affirmed a summary judgment dismissal of her complaint against the defendants, the City of Milwaukee and its employee, Yvette Marchan (together, "the City").  Weiss argues that the court of appeals erred in determining that the Worker's Compensation Act (WCA) provides the exclusive remedy for her claim of emotional distress resulting from the City's disclosure of her home address and telephone number to her abusive former spouse.  Because we conclude that Weiss has alleged injuries covered by the Worker's Compensation Act, and that the exclusive remedy provision of the WCA precludes her common law action against the defendants for negligent infliction of emotional distress, we affirm the decision of the court of appeals.

The relevant facts are not in dispute.  On July 31, 1990, Weiss obtained a temporary restraining order against her abusive husband, Osama Abughanim.  Shortly thereafter, she commenced a divorce action.  Abughanim, forced to vacate the marital residence, began a campaign of harassing telephone calls and personal visits during which he would threaten the lives of Weiss and their two children.  In October 1990, Weiss vacated the residence and moved in with her parents in order to escape her husband's harassment.  Abughanim persisted in making threatening telephone calls, both to Weiss's parents' residence and to her place of employment.   The calls to Weiss's employer were of such frequency that they resulted in her termination in December 1990.

In February 1991, Weiss obtained employment with the City of Milwaukee as an engineering technician.   As an employee, she was required to establish residence in Milwaukee within one month of hiring.   She therefore moved from her parents' residence in Waukesha County to an apartment located in Milwaukee.   At that time, Abughanim did not know Weiss's Milwaukee address or telephone number.

Weiss was instructed by her supervisor to provide her address and telephone number to the City's payroll department.   She contacted the payroll department, explained that she had an abusive former husband, and expressed her desire that her residential information remain confidential.   A City payroll clerk assured Weiss that the City had a policy prohibiting the disclosure of such employee information to private individuals.   Relying on the clerk's assurance, Weiss provided her address and telephone number to the payroll department.

On July 10, 1991, Abughanim contacted the City's Department of Employee Relations and spoke with Sheila Bowles, an employee of the department.   Abughanim falsely represented to Bowles that he was calling on behalf of a bank and needed to confirm Weiss's address and telephone number for credit purposes.   Bowles relayed the bogus inquiry to her supervisor, Yvette Marchan, who, without attempting to verify Abughanim's claimed credentials, authorized Bowles to disclose Weiss's residential information.

By this ruse, Abughanim obtained Weiss's home address and telephone number.   Thereafter, Abughanim regularly telephoned Weiss at work to inform her that he now knew her home address and telephone number, and that he would kill her and their two children.   Her awareness that Abughanim knew her address, and her then existing financial inability to change her residence, caused Weiss severe emotional distress arising from fear for her safety and that of their two children.

Weiss commenced a common law action in the circuit court against the City to recover damages for negligent infliction of emotional distress arising from the City's unwitting disclosure to Abughanim.   The City filed a motion for summary judgment, asserting that the WCA covered Weiss's injuries, and the statute's exclusive remedy provision therefore barred Weiss's suit.   The City also maintained that it had no duty to keep confidential Weiss's home address and telephone number, because such information was available to the public pursuant to Wisconsin's open records law.

The circuit court granted the City's motion for summary judgment, dismissing Weiss's complaint.   The court reasoned that the City had no duty to maintain the confidentiality of Weiss's home address and telephone number, since the open records law would have required disclosure had Abughanim filed a request for the information.   In addition, the court determined that the damages sought by Weiss were so difficult to ascertain that they were precluded on public policy grounds. The circuit court expressly declined to base its order on provisions of the WCA. Weiss appealed.

The court of appeals affirmed, on different grounds, the circuit court's grant of summary judgment. Concluding that Weiss stated a claim under the WCA, the court of appeals determined that her common law negligence action against the City was barred by the statute's exclusive remedy provision, Wis.Stat. § 102.03(2). The court did not squarely address the open records law issue, but did "detect grave faults in the trial court's application" of the statute. Weiss petitioned this court for review.

This court reviews a grant of summary judgment using the same methodology as the circuit court. If there are no material facts in dispute, as here, we must determine whether the movant is entitled to judgment as a matter of law. The question in this case is whether Weiss's common law negligence claim must be dismissed, as a matter of law, because it is precluded by the exclusive remedy provision of the WCA. Our task is to interpret the provisions of Chapter 102 of the Wisconsin Statutes. A question of law is therefore presented, which we review *de novo,* without deference to the decisions of the circuit court and court of appeals.

We have repeatedly stated that the provisions of Chapter 102 must be liberally construed to effectuate the WCA's goal of compensating injured workers. However, courts must also exercise care to avoid upsetting the balance of interests achieved by the WCA.

Generally, an employer's obligation to pay worker's compensation accrues under Chapter 102 when all of the following conditions are present: 1) the employee sustains an injury; 2) at the time of the injury, both the employer and the employee are subject to the provisions of the WCA; 3) at the time of the injury, the employee is performing service growing out of and incidental to his or her employment; 4) the injury is not intentionally self-inflicted; and 5) the accident or disease causing injury arises out of the employment. For purposes of our review of summary judgment in this case, our inquiry is limited to determining whether, at the time of her injury, Weiss was performing service growing out of and incidental to her employment, and whether the accident causing injury arose out of her employment.

It is well settled that when the § 102.03(1) conditions of liability for worker's compensation are satisfied, the exclusive remedy provision, precludes an injured employee from maintaining a negligence action against his or her employer and fellow employees. Thus, Weiss's common law action against the City is barred if her alleged injuries are covered by Chapter 102.

The City asserts that Weiss meets each of the five criteria set out in §§ 102.03(1)(a)–(e), and that the remedy for her injuries is therefore solely that which is provided under the WCA.[8] In attempting to establish that

**8.** The legal positions of the employer and employee in this instance are the reverse of those found in many worker's compensation cases. Often it is the employer who

her injury is not covered by Chapter 102, Weiss contends that at the time she was injured, she was not performing service growing out of and incidental to her employment. She also argues that the court of appeals erred when it determined that "the incident causing the injury arose out of Weiss's employment."

We deal first with Weiss's claim that her injury is not encompassed within the WCA because at the time of the injury, she was not "performing service growing out of and incidental to . . . her employment," as required by § 102.03(1)(c). In essence, Weiss's argument is that an employee cannot satisfy § 102.03(1)(c) when receiving a personal telephone call at work. We disagree.

The statutory clause "performing service growing out of and incidental to his or her employment" is used interchangeably with the phrase "course of employment." Both phrases refer to the "time, place, and circumstances" under which the injury occurred. Goranson v. DILHR, 94 Wis.2d 537, 549, 289 N.W.2d 270 (1980).

There is no dispute that Weiss's alleged injury occurred within the time and place of her employment. The question is whether receiving a personal phone call at work constitutes a "circumstance" of employment. We conclude that it does. Under the liberal construction given to Chapter 102, an employee acts within the course of employment when he or she is otherwise within the time and space limits of employment, and briefly turns away from his or her work to tend to matters "necessary or convenient to his [or her] own personal health or comfort." The personal comfort doctrine does not apply, and an employee is not within the course of employment, if the "extent of the departure is so great that an intent to abandon the job temporarily may be inferred, or . . . the method chosen is so unusual and unreasonable that the conduct cannot be considered an incident of the employment." Applying the doctrine to the facts of this case, we conclude that regardless of the contents of a brief personal telephone call, the act of taking such a call at work constitutes a momentary departure from work duties to attend to a matter of personal comfort. Thus, when Weiss answered the personal telephone call from Abughanim, she was engaged in an activity incidental to employment, and was therefore within the course of employment.

Weiss next contends that the accident causing her injury did not arise out of her employment. Weiss asserts that where, as here, an employee is injured at work by a non-employee for purely personal reasons, the injury is noncompensable under the WCA.

We agree with Weiss that *Goranson* stands for the proposition that injuries sustained in an assault occurring in the course of employment are

resists coverage under the WCA, and the employee who desires such coverage. As Weiss candidly admits, she has filed a common law action because she feels that a recovery under the WCA would be inadequate compared to a jury award on her tort claim. Conversely, the City invokes the WCA in this instance in order to limit Weiss's potential recovery for its allegedly wrongful disclosure of her residential information.

generally noncompensable under the WCA when the assailant is motivated purely by personal animus, and the employment in no way contributes to the incident. We also agree that Weiss's employment did not create the initial threat posed to her by Abughanim. We nevertheless conclude that the accident did arise out of Weiss's employment with the City, because the conditions of Weiss's employment facilitated her eventual injury.

The "arising out of" language of § 102.03(1)(3) refers to the causal origin of an employee's injury. However, "arising out of his or her employment" is not synonymous with the phrase "caused by the employment." In interpreting § 102.03(1)(e), we have adopted the "positional risk" doctrine:

> [A]ccidents arise out of employment if the conditions or obligations of the employment create a zone of special danger out of which the accident causing the injury arose. Stated another way, an accident arises out of employment when by reason of employment the employee is present at a place where he is injured through the agency of a third person, an outside force, or the conditions of special danger.

However, when the origin of the assault is purely private and personal, and the employment in no way contributes to the incident, the positional risk doctrine does not apply.

For example, in *Goranson*, a charter bus driver was injured after he drove a group of people to Green Bay. Upon arriving in Green Bay, the driver checked into a hotel along with his passengers. Later in the evening, he leaped from his third floor hotel room onto the roof of another section of the hotel two floors below, sustaining a broken hip and other injuries. There was evidence that the driver had been drinking throughout the evening with a woman, and that he had quarreled in his hotel room with the woman just prior to jumping from the hotel window.

This court upheld a denial of worker's compensation benefits. While there was no dispute that the driver was in the course of employment at the time of injury, the court determined that the accident did not arise out of the driver's employment, because the injuring force was purely personal to him.

The facts of this case are distinguishable from those in *Goranson*. In *Goranson*, the bus driver's employment did not contribute to or facilitate the accident causing the injury he suffered jumping from the hotel window. In this case, however, Weiss was required to provide her residential address and telephone number to the City as a condition of employment. If Weiss had never been required to provide the information to the City, the accident would not have occurred. The City's unwitting disclosure of that information to a private individual, Weiss's abusive former husband, was an accident that led to her injury. Because a condition of her employment facilitated the accident which caused her injury, we conclude that the accident arose out of her employment.

Weiss cites several cases from foreign jurisdictions for the proposition that when purely private animosity manifests itself in a workplace attack, the employment connection to the injury is so minimal that worker's compensation should be denied. Monahan v. United States Check Book Co., 4 Neb.App. 227, 540 N.W.2d 380 (1995); Ross v. Mark's, Inc., 120 N.C.App. 607, 463 S.E.2d 302 (1995). In both *Monahan* and *Ross,* a non-employee attacked and killed an ex-spouse at the ex-spouse's place of employment. Worker's compensation was denied in both cases, on the ground that assaults do not arise out of employment when they involve private quarrels imported into the workplace. In neither case did the court find evidence that the employment contributed to or facilitated the attacks.

We find unpersuasive the examples of worker's compensation denials cited by Weiss. Consistent with *Goranson,* we are of the view that in certain situations, "an injury from an admittedly private source should be compensable because it [is] facilitated or contributed to by the employment environment." For example, in Carter v. Penney Tire & Recapping Co., 261 S.C. 341, 200 S.E.2d 64 (1973), the claimant had previously quarreled with Crosby, a non-employee. On the date of the assault, Crosby threatened the claimant while the latter was engaged in repairing his employer's roof. Before returning to the roof, the claimant reported the threats to his employer, who responded that the claimant would be protected and should proceed with his work. Crosby later returned and shot the claimant, inflicting grievous injuries. The South Carolina Supreme Court determined that the claimant's injuries arose out of his employment, because:

> the employee was required to perform his duties under circumstances where he was endangered by a peril from a source outside of and unrelated to his actual work, which peril was known to the employer and against which the employer afforded no protection or relief.

*Id.* 200 S.E.2d at 67.

Similarly, in Raybol v. Louisiana State University, 520 So.2d 724 (La.1988), superseded by statute as stated in Guillory v. Interstate Gas Station, 653 So.2d 1152 (La.1995), the Supreme Court of Louisiana awarded worker's compensation to a dormitory worker who was assaulted at work by her estranged former boyfriend. The court concluded that the worker's injuries arose out of her employment, based in part on its determination that "the employer's custodial workers contributed to the danger of the assault by informing the assailant of the plaintiff's work location in the building and by assisting him in gaining access to her by unlocking a door to the dormitory."

In California Compensation & Fire Co. v. Workmen's Compensation Appeals Bd., 68 Cal.2d 157, 65 Cal.Rptr. 155, 436 P.2d 67 (1968), a worker at a table pad manufacturer was shot and killed by her ex-husband. The worker's employment required her to visit the homes of customers in order to measure the dimensions of tables. Upon learning that the worker intended to remarry, her ex-husband rented an apartment, ordered a table pad, and requested that someone be sent to measure the table. When his ex-wife arrived at the apartment, he murdered her and then committed suicide. The supreme court of California affirmed an award of death benefits in part on the grounds that the husband's elaborate plot was facilitated by the conditions of the worker's employment.

Finally, in Epperson v. Industrial Commission, 26 Ariz.App. 467, 549 P.2d 247 (1976), the claimant informed a security guard at her place of employment that she was having personal difficulties with her husband and did not wish to speak to him. Her husband later appeared at the building, observed the claimant, and proceeded unimpeded past the security guard's desk to confront the plaintiff. During the course of his ensuing conversation with the claimant, the husband shot her. The Arizona court of appeals concluded that the assault did not arise out of the course of her employment. However, it intimated that a different result would have been reached had the claimant informed the security guard of her fears and the dangers posed by her husband in a manner sufficient to justify reliance on the guard's protection.

None of the cited cases is on all fours with the one presently before us. However, each stands for the proposition that when an attack occurs during the course of employment and arises from personal animus imported from a private relationship, the incident arises out of the claimant's employment if employment conditions have contributed to or facilitated the attack. Weiss was required to provide her residential information to the City as a condition of employment. That condition of employment facilitated the City's subsequent accidental release of the information to a private individual, Weiss's abusive former spouse. The disclosure of the residential information in turn enabled Abughanim to threaten Weiss. We therefore conclude that the accident causing Weiss's injury arose out of her employment with the City.

In summary, Weiss has alleged an emotional injury which occurred in the course of employment and was caused by an accident arising out of that employment. Accordingly, we conclude that Weiss's complaint states a claim covered under § 102.03(1) of the WCA. Because the exclusive remedy provision of the WCA, § 102.03(2), bars Weiss's common law tort action against the City, the circuit court properly granted summary judgment dismissing the complaint, and the court of appeals correctly upheld the circuit court's decision.

The decision of the court of appeals is affirmed.

NOTES AND QUESTIONS

1.  In footnote 8, the court observes that the parties are asserting positions that are opposite their customary views. If the case were based on workers' compensation rather than tort, what would be the likely positions of the parties?

2.  Would the result of the case be different if Weiss' ex-husband physically assaulted her at work or at home? Should she be entitled to recover for the emotional distress inflicted on her at home, but not for the emotional distress she suffered as a result of being harassed at work?

**3.** Recovery for workplace assaults committed by customers and coworkers is often barred by workers' compensation. For example, Oscar Evans arrived at work at his usual time and was drinking coffee with fellow employees in a lounge area before work. Without any warning, a coworker in an alcoholic paranoid delusional state fatally shot him. Was the death in the course of employment for which workers' compensation is the exclusive remedy? See Evans v. Yankeetown Dock Corp., 491 N.E.2d 969 (Ind.1986) (held: yes). Accord, Fields v. Cummins Employees Federal Credit Union, 540 N.E.2d 631 (Ind.App.1989) (complaint against employer for sexual harassment and battery barred by workers' compensation).

**4.** The issue of "course of employment" frequently arises in the case of workers' compensation claims for recreational injuries. The claimants, who are often unable to assert a common law claim due to the lack of fault on the part of any party, seek to prove that the injury occurred in the course of employment. The courts have adopted several different approaches, including whether the employer benefitted from the employee's participation (such as through publicity or improved morale) and whether employees were reasonably expected to participate in the recreational activity. See, e.g., Ezzy v. Workers' Compensation Appeals Board, 194 Cal.Rptr. 90 (Cal.Ct.App.1983) (law student injured in law firm's summer softball game entitled to compensation because firm's partners expected her to play).

**5.** A sales agent for an insurance company won a promotional contest run by the company by selling a certain amount of insurance. The agent was given two tickets to see a Philadelphia Eagles football game and some money for expenses. While driving to the game with his son the man was killed in a car accident. Was his death compensable under workers' compensation? See Nationwide Insurance Co. v. Workmen's Compensation Appeal Board, 344 A.2d 756 (Pa.Cmwlth.1975) (held: no). Suppose the agent was taking a client to the game? See Brennan v. Joseph G. Brennan, 425 N.W.2d 837 (Minn.1988).

**6.** Another "course of employment" issue involves horseplay or "skylarking." Angel Diaz was hosing down with water certain frames lying on the floor. He playfully squirted water on the legs of Frank Waters, a coworker. Waters retaliated by throwing at Diaz a bucket of a clear liquid that he thought was water. Actually, the bucket contained lacquer, which was ignited by a nearby open flame, severely burning Diaz. Is Diaz entitled to compensation for his burns? See Diaz v. Newark Industrial Spraying, Inc., 174 A.2d 478 (N.J.1961) (held: yes). A factor often considered by the courts is whether the employer had prior knowledge or had previously condoned horseplay. See Bare v. Wayne Poultry Co., 318 S.E.2d 534 (N.C.App.1984) (chicken deboners were known to play with knives).

**7.** A coworker lowered the plaintiff's chair as part of a prank. When the plaintiff attempted to sit in the chair, she fell and injured her back. Although she was awarded workers' compensation benefits, she also sued her coworker in tort. The court held that because the employer condoned jokes and pranks on the job in order to maintain "harmonious working conditions," the injury was sustained within the scope of employment and therefore workers' compensation was the exclusive remedy. Oliva v. Heath, 41 Cal.Rptr.2d 613 (Cal.App.1995).

**8.** Thelma Grimes was injured at work when the brace on her right leg gave way, causing her to fall. Her ankle was fractured in the accident. She had polio as a child and was required to wear a full-length brace on her right leg that had to be locked each time she stood up. The brace had previously given way while she was at home. Is her fractured ankle compensable? See Leon County School Board v. Grimes, 548 So.2d 205 (Fla.1989) (held: no).

**9.** Vicky Forsythe, a 46–year–old mentally retarded woman lived in a group home and worked at a "sheltered workshop." Employees of the workshop brought food from home, but were required to remain on the premises during lunch and breaks. One day while eating lunch, she choked on a peanut butter sandwich and died. Is her estate entitled to workers' compensation death benefits? See Forsythe v. INCO, 384 S.E.2d 30 (N.C.App.1989) (held: no). Do cases such as *Grimes* and *Forsythe* discriminate against employees with disabilities or further public policy by encouraging their hiring? Compare *Turner* infra p. 853.

**10.** A lawyer in solo practice, whose specialty is workers' compensation law, was riding his bicycle to a CLE program when his bicycle tire got caught in the pavement, he lost his balance, fell, and broke his hip. He then used his cellular telephone to call his daughter to take him to the hospital. Is his injury compensable under workers' compensation? See McKeown v. SAIF Corp., 840 P.2d 1377 (Or.App.1992) (held: yes).

## C. OCCUPATIONAL DISEASE

### 1. OVERVIEW

### Elinor P. Schroeder & Sidney A. Shapiro, *Responses to Occupational Disease: The Role of Markets, Regulation, and Information*

72 Geo.L.J. 1231 (1984).

*Workers' Compensation.* Under state workers' compensation systems, recovery is made available on a no-fault basis once it is determined that an injury or disease is work related. Employer support for a no-fault approach was achieved by prohibiting workers covered by workers' compensation legislation from suing the employer for any remedy other than benefits under that system. Funds for compensation are obtained through charges levied on employers. Theoretically, employers are charged a premium based on the relative safety of their workplaces as measured by reported employee injuries and illnesses. Costs of work-related injuries and illnesses thus become costs to the firm. Employers will therefore engage in preventive safety efforts only as long as such efforts are less costly than the payments they must make to the workers' compensation fund.

In fact, few workers receive compensation for work-related illnesses. Studies estimate that only two to three percent of all workers' compensation payments compensate recipients for occupational disease. A 1980 U.S. Department of Labor report estimated that only about three percent of all workers severely disabled by occupational diseases received workers' compensation, and the payments they received replaced only about one-eighth of their lost wages. If these estimates are accurate, employers internalize little of the cost of occupational disease. The limited internalization occurs for six reasons.

First, there is little economic incentive for employers to spend money to prevent occupational disease. Decisions concerning how much to spend to prevent disease are not based on current workers' compensation expenses, which are the result of past actions, but on the likelihood that such efforts will prevent diseases in the future. Since future diseases may not occur until many years later, firms may heavily discount their consequences and spend little or nothing on prevention. Moreover, many firms are required to insure against the possibility of having to make workers' compensation payments. The structure of that insurance lessens their incentive to take preventive measures because premiums are based primarily on the experience of classes of employers rather than on the safety performance of individual employers.

Second, any employer liability for employee illness will be less than the social costs of the illness. Workers' compensation payments are controlled by a statutorily prescribed formula which often limits compensation to less than the direct wage losses of disabled employees. Further, payments do not cover such items as lost fringe benefits and the intangible costs of pain and suffering and the spouse's loss of consortium.

Third, there is little internalization because many workers fail to recognize that they have a claim when their illnesses occur long after the hazardous exposure. Asbestos insulation workers studied by Dr. Selikoff, for example, filed workers' compensation claims for only thirty-three percent of their asbestos-related disabilities, and their families filed claims for only thirty-six percent of the asbestos-related deaths. In the first seven years that brown lung disease (byssinosis) was compensable in North and South Carolina, only 1,000 disabled workers filed claims out of an estimated population of 30,000 disabled workers.

Fourth, there is little internalization because those workers who do file claims often fail to establish their eligibility for benefits. Some workers fail because there is insufficient information available about their disease to establish that it is work related. The long latency period of many illnesses means that the employee may have had no recent contact with the hazard that caused the disease. In such a case, the worker is without persuasive evidence that the illness is work related. Epidemiological data can establish that all workers exposed to a certain hazard will have a greater probability of contracting a disease than other workers, but this research alone cannot prove that a given worker became ill from contact with the hazardous substance rather than from a non-work-related cause. Worker ignorance is sometimes caused by employers who have withheld information needed to establish claims.

Fifth, workers also fail to obtain compensation because many states have established eligibility requirements that are difficult or impossible to satisfy. While few occupational diseases can be shown to result solely from workplace exposure, thirty-one states limit compensation to diseases that are "peculiar to" or "characteristic of" a worker's occupation. Many illnesses, like cancer, are widespread, but twenty-three states prohibit compensation for "diseases ordinary to life." Eighteen states have recent exposure rules that bar compensation to those workers who were exposed to a hazard more than a specified number of years earlier. Eighteen states have minimum exposure requirements for dust diseases and five states have the same requirement for all diseases. These types of restrictions ignore both the long latency periods associated with many diseases and the lack of knowledge about the relationship between the intensity and duration of exposure and adverse health effects. Realistic statutes of limitation must run from the date of discovery, because of the long latency periods, but twenty state statutes have chosen some point other than discovery.

Sixth, employers, or their insurance companies, litigate most occupational disease claims because the difficulty of proving causation and the existence of restrictive standards for recovery make employer victories in disease cases more likely than in accident cases. A 1980 study found that sixty percent of all such claims and ninety percent of dust disease claims were contested, as compared to only ten percent of accident claims. As a result, most workers making occupational disease claims required legal counsel (whose fees, of course, reduce any award). Further, there was an average of a year's delay between the time a claim was filed and the time an award was made. Finally, about one-half of the litigants found it attractive to settle their cases, often for amounts less than those for which they might have been eligible.

Workers' compensation has been no more effective than the tort system it replaced. For both the numerous accident claims and the relatively fewer disease claims, the system of administering workers' compensation is so costly that an average of forty percent of all taxes paid to support the system are spent for administrative costs, which do not include the lawyer's fees paid by many victims. Nevertheless, proposals for reform of the workers' compensation system have gone largely unheeded. The 1972 National Commission on Workmen's Compensation, for example, suggested that the system could be improved by eliminating requirements that a disease be "peculiar to or characteristic of" a worker's occupation and that a disease not be "ordinary to life." The Commission also recommended using expert panels to determine scientifically difficult issues of causation, and increasing the maximum allowable benefits for permanent disability to 200% of the average weekly wage within a state. A significant number of states have rejected the first recommendation, only seven have adopted the second recommendation, and only two states have adopted the third recommendation.

A 1977 Interdepartmental Report for Congress and the President recommended the elimination of both unrealistic statutes of limitation and minimum and recent exposure requirements, but many states have retained those restrictions. The 1977 report also suggested that a presumption in favor of workers be adopted. Under this proposal, if epidemiological data established that a hazard caused an occupational disease, the hazard would be presumed to have caused any individual case of the disease in an exposed worker. The burden of proof would then shift to the employer to establish that the disease was not work related. Only seven states have adopted this reform.

NOTE

As Professors Schroeder and Shapiro point out, occupational disease claims often are not filed, are usually contested, and are difficult to win. Even when they are successful the benefit levels may be reduced by application of legal rules totally inappropriate for disease cases. For example, in some jurisdictions the amount of compensation for occupational disease is based upon a percentage (usually two-thirds) of the claimant's average weekly wage at the time of the last exposure. For a disease with a long latency period the claimant may be compensated at a rate of two-thirds of his or her average wages 20 or 30 years ago. A similar problem exists where a gradually developed disease steadily reduces a claimant's earnings until the time of total disability. The amount of compensation will be based on this already-reduced earnings rate.

## 2.   BURDEN OF PROOF

## Mulcahey v. New England Newspapers, Inc.

488 A.2d 681 (R.I.1985).

■ KELLEHER, JUSTICE.

On Sunday, October 8, 1978, at approximately 10:30 a.m., Helen F. Mulcahey drove her husband, Edward F. Mulcahey, Jr., (Mulcahey) to his place of employment in Pawtucket, Rhode Island. There he picked up one of his employer's automobiles and drove to Schaeffer Stadium in nearby Foxboro, Massachusetts. Mulcahey's employer, New England Newspapers, Inc., was the publisher of a daily newspaper circulated in the Blackstone Valley area of this state and at that time called the Pawtucket Times (Times). For over a quarter of a century, Mulcahey was known to thousands of the Times readers as "Ted" Mulcahey, the paper's sports editor. Upon arriving at the stadium, Mulcahey parked his car in the "press parking lot." He then spent the better part of the afternoon in the press box watching two National Football League professional football teams, the New England Patriots and the Philadelphia Eagles, do battle with each other. Mulcahey returned to his Pawtucket residence at about 5:45 p.m. When he sat down to supper, he told his wife "something funny happened to me at the game today." When one of the Mulcahey sons asked his father who won the game, the reply was "That team." Soon Mulcahey became incoherent, and within a short time he was admitted to Pawtucket Memorial Hospital. Mulcahey died five days later, on October 13, and the cause of death was listed as cerebral hemorrhage.

The wife subsequently sought workers' compensation, alleging that the hemorrhage was attributable to her husband's job with the newspaper. At a hearing before a trial commissioner, a member of the Workers' Compensation Commission rejected the wife's claim. She then appealed to an appellate commission, which overturned the denial and entered a final decree granting the wife's petition. The employer appeals.

At the hearing before the trial commissioner, Mulcahey's widow described her husband's normal daily routine as follows: arise at 5 a.m.; arrive at the Times at 6 a.m.; work until 12 p.m.; return home until 6:30 p.m.; leave to observe the sporting scene until 11 p.m.; go to the paper to write a story until 1 a.m.; and then back to bed to arise once again at 5 a.m.

The Times sports department consisted of Mulcahey and two other individuals, all of whom were quite conscious of the competition for the reader's eye and money. The trio, in the widow's words, "did the job that the Providence Journal did with a much larger staff." Mrs. Mulcahey also explained that her spouse had been a diabetic for about six years and took a pill each day. He also took medication for high blood pressure.

One of Mulcahey's press-box companions, the sports editor of the Northampton [Massachusetts] Daily Gazette, testified that Mulcahey's Patriots-Eagles postgame behavior "was unusual." At the game's conclusion, the witness said, Mulcahey made no effort to visit the locker room to interview the coaches or the players. He made no effort to obtain a book furnished by the Patriots management to the press. The book contained a mimeographed play-by-play sheet for each of the four quarters of the game as well as a detailed analysis of the statistics for each team and the individual players. Such information, in the witness's opinion, was a "must" for an employee whose story was to be in a newspaper published on Monday morning.

At the hearing before the trial commissioner, three physicians testified on behalf of the widow: the family physician, a cardiologist who saw Mulcahey when he was admitted to the emergency room at Pawtucket Memorial Hospital, and a specialist in hypertension. The specialist in hypertension was the last witness to offer testimony on behalf of the widow's petition. Six months later, the Times, through its counsel, advised the trial commissioner that it would rest without presenting any evidence of its own. Subsequently, a change of mind occurred, and the employer's motion to reopen for the sole purpose of taking the deposition of a cardiologist, a member of the faculty of Brown University's medical school, was granted. The deposition is part of the record. The sum and substance of the deponent's testimony was that it was his opinion that Mulcahey's presence at the football game did not precipitate or aggravate his preexisting high blood pressure to the point where he suffered the cerebral hemorrhage that ultimately caused his death.

The trial commissioner in his decision discussed the testimony of the four physicians and was most impressed with the evidence given by the cardiologist who testified on behalf of the Times. The commissioner emphasized that there was no testimony that Mulcahey had exerted himself in any unusual manner while he was at Schaeffer Stadium on Sunday, October 8, 1978, or that the circumstances that day were any more or less exciting than any other events he had covered. In the commissioner's opinion, the fact that the hemorrhage began at the football game was "nothing more than happenstance."

Initially, we shall consider the appellate commission's rejection of the trial commissioner's reliance on the testimony presented by the cardiologist who testified by deposition. In Laganiere v. Bonte Spinning Co., 103 R.I. 191, 197, 236 A.2d 256, 259 (1967), and again in Davol, Inc. v. Aguiar, R.I., 463 A.2d 170, 173–74 (1983), we emphasized that even though G.L.1956 (1979 Reenactment) § 28–35–28 (1984 Cum.Supp.) purports to give the appellate commission the ability to reject factual findings made by a trial commissioner de novo, the commission, before disturbing findings based on credibility determinations, must first find that the trial commissioner was clearly wrong either because the commissioner was obviously mistaken in his or her judgment of the credibility of the witnesses or overlooked or misconceived material evidence in arriving at the conclusion reached.

As part of its investigation, a representative of the Times insurer interviewed a Providence Journal reporter who was present in the press box on the day of the Patriots-Eagles confrontation. The reporter told of talking to Mulcahey. According to the reporter, Mulcahey had no complaints of any illness. The reporter, when asked about any physical exertion, replied in the negative, agreeing that reporters were not required to run up and down to the playing field because interviews were held in the clubhouse after the game, at which time the coach was available for questioning. A reporter could view the game on closed-circuit TV, and each reporter was assigned a seat in the press box, which was situated high above the grandstand. Elevators took the reporters to and from the press-box area.

In direct examination the Times cardiologist expressed the opinion that Mulcahey's hemorrhage was in no way related to his presence at the Patriots-Eagles game, and that the hemorrhage could not be considered to be an incident of his occupation. The expert was then asked on cross-examination if the reporter's statement to the investigator played any part in the conclusions expressed during direct examination. The cardiologist replied, "I based my entire opinion on that." Consequently, the appellate commission properly rejected the commissioner's findings because the statement had never been properly admitted into evidence since the reporter had never been subject to cross-examination.

The Times does not challenge the commission's rejection of the trial commissioner's choice of experts, but it does argue that the other three physicians who did testify offered no competent evidence upon which the commission could base its conclusion.  In its appeal the Times faults the appellate commission's award of compensation because, in its words, "none of the experts who testified for petitioner could point to a single incident which occurred on October 8, 1978 which precipitated or contributed to the cerebral bleeding which caused [her husband's] death."  The employer also points to an absence of any evidence that the October 8, 1978 contest differed in any way from the many other sporting events that "Mulcahey covered" in his thirty-three-year career as an editor and scribe.

The Times's emphasis on the lack of evidence about any exciting event that might have occurred at the stadium ignores the fact that Rhode Island is one of the few states in which the workers' compensation statute since 1949 has not required proof of an accidental injury before compensation can be paid to an injured worker.  In fact, in heart-attack cases this court has said that it is immaterial whether the work performed by an employee involved unusual physical exertion.  Rather, the crucial issue is whether there is a causal relationship or nexus between the work and the attack.  It must be kept in mind that in workers' compensation cases we do not equate the term "causal relationship" with the term "proximate cause" as found in negligence actions.  Here, it is enough if the conditions and nature of the employment contribute to the injury.

In resolving the present controversy, the question is whether the principles involving heart attacks should be applied to other failures of the cardiovascular system.  The answer is unquestionably yes because an employer takes its workers as it finds them, and when the employee aggravates an existing condition and the result is an incapacity for work, the employee is entitled to compensation for such incapacity.

Our duty at this point is quite simple.  We must examine the record and determine whether there is any legally competent evidence to support the appellate commission's factual finding that Mulcahey's death was due to a cerebral hemorrhage resulting from the aggravation of his pre-existing hypertension.  Mulcahey's fellow editor spoke of the difficulty of meeting the deadline—the time at which the paper's sports section would have to be written, edited, and the pages "actually pasted up," and the presses were ready to roll.  All the time, the witness said, "the clock is staring at you and saying, you have to be out of here at X hour."

The hypertension expert had been engaged in this area for almost sixteen years, during which he engaged in the study, research, and treatment of this malady.  In response to a hypothetical question in which the specialist was asked his opinion about whether the incidents of Mulcahey's employment and his stressful work style caused or contributed to his hypertension, aggravating it to a point where he suffered a cerebral hemorrhage and died, the response was in the affirmative.  The specialist then pointed out that Mulcahey's blood pressure was of a type that would go up whenever he was under stress so that repeated episodes of meeting a deadline aggravated the blood pressure and certainly contributed to the hemorrhage that caused his death.

The certified cardiologist who examined Mulcahey shortly after his admittance to the hospital's emergency room attributed Mulcahey's death to a "massive intercerebral hemorrhage." This witness expressed the opinion that the stress of meeting numerous deadlines "probably aggravated" the deceased's hypertension; and, speaking in terms of reasonable medical certainty, the cardiologist expressed the opinion that the increased hypertension was responsible for the intracranial bleeding which the witness had previously described as "massive."

At one point in his cross-examination, the family physician, after expressing difficulty with understanding the cross-examiner's inquiry as to the absence of a "shall we say precipitating incident in this case," responded, "If you're referring to final event, I honestly believe that the precipitating cause of death was his being present at a Patriots game, with the atmosphere and the circumstances * * *." Later, the witness, in response to a further inquiry from the cross-examiner as to whether the family physician was saying that Mulcahey's work caused his death, answered, "I said the circumstances at the game caused his death, the workload, I'd say it's the probable cause of his death." Earlier, in direct examination, this witness made it clear that he was quite familiar with Mulcahey's work routine, particularly his working in "the wee hours of the morning, trying to make a deadline." Mulcahey's stressful employment, he said, aggravated both his hypertension and diabetes, "and the three of them escalate vascular disease." The commission obviously believed the medical testimony to which we have alluded, and this testimony is legally competent evidence that creates the requisite nexus between Mulcahey's job and his inability to meet the Columbus Day deadline.

[One other issue] raised by the Times [merits] a brief comment. The Times contends that the commission award is inconsistent with the dictates of Seitz v. L & R Industries, Inc., R.I., 437 A.2d 1345, 1347 (1981), in which an employee sought compensation benefits because she had become so mentally upset about work conditions that she terminated her employment. In *Seitz* it was noted that there are three types of psychic injury: the first is physical injury caused by mental stimulus, the second type is psychic injury caused by physical trauma, and the third type is mental injury produced by a mental stimulus where neither physical causes nor physical results exist. Seitz's injury fell within the third category, and a majority of this court ruled that Seitz could not prevail because the mental distress she suffered "did not exceed the intensity of stimuli encountered by thousands of other employees and management personnel every day. If psychic injury is to be compensable, a more dramatically stressful stimulus must be established." The holding of *Seitz* affords no support here because Mulcahey's disability falls within the first category—physical injury caused by mental stimulus, an area in which, *Seitz* notes, courts uniformly find compensability.

* * *

The employer's appeal is denied and dismissed, the decree appealed from is affirmed, and the case is remanded to the Workers' Compensation Commission.

NOTES AND QUESTIONS

**1.** The burden of proof in occupational disease cases is difficult enough in the ordinary cases. For cardiovascular disease it is especially troublesome. More than half the states have enacted "heart and lung" statutes applicable to firefighters and many of these states also include police officers. These laws provide that any respiratory or heart disease is presumed to be work related and compensable. In response to these laws, some municipalities have refused to hire cigarette smokers, because smoking-caused disabilities would be work related under the heart and lung statute. See discussion supra p. 181.

A bakery worker who developed a disabling lung disease after inhaling large amounts of flour dust filed a workers' compensation claim. Should he be barred from recovery because 85 percent of his problem was caused by cigarette smoking? See Fry's Food Stores v. Industrial Commission, 866 P.2d 1350 (Ariz.1994) (held: no).

**2.** In a growing number of compensation cases, claimants allege that emotional injuries were work related. For example, a worker was led to believe that he would be promoted. When his supervisor reneged on the promise the worker suffered an hysterical reaction. Is this a compensable illness? See Brown & Root Construction Co. v. Duckworth, 475 So.2d 813 (Miss.1985) (held: yes). Contra Cigna Property & Casualty Insurance Co. v. Sneed, 772 S.W.2d 422 (Tenn.1989) (emotional problem suffered by employee upon her termination *not* compensable). See also Livitsanos v. Superior Court, 828 P.2d 1195 (Cal.1992) (employee claims of emotional distress arising from employer misconduct preempted by workers' compensation in absence of physical injury).

An employee with 45 years of service was told by management that he would have to take early retirement. The employee was greatly agitated and the next day, while trimming trees in his yard, suffered a heart attack and died. Is his death compensable? See Ryan v. Connor, 28 Ohio St.3d 406, 503 N.E.2d 1379 (1986) (held: yes). In a similar case, an employee was told that he was being reassigned to different work and at a one-third pay cut. He fainted and struck his head on the tile-covered cement floor, which caused severe brain damage. Is the injury compensable? See Murphy v. Industrial Commission, 774 P.2d 221 (Ariz.1989) (held: yes).

**3.** In compensation cases based on stress, courts often require that the stress be either extreme (if based on a single precipitating cause) or beyond ordinary day-to-day stress. See Egeland v. Minneapolis, 344 N.W.2d 597 (Minn.1984) (ulcer compensable; depression not compensable). Is work-induced suicide compensable? See Martin v. Ketchum, Inc., 568 A.2d 159 (Pa.1990) (held: yes). See generally Comment, Workers' Compensation: Compensating Claimants Who Suffer Psychological Disabilities Caused Solely by Job-Related Mental Stress, 60 Tulane L.Rev. 651 (1986).

**4.** Taken together, what do *Nationwide* (note 5 on p. 841) and *Mulcahey* suggest about the wisdom of going to see the Philadelphia Eagles play?

**5.** An electronics manufacturing plant implemented a no-smoking rule throughout the plant except for the employee cafeteria. Sharon Kay Riddle had been smoking one to two packs of cigarettes a day for 24 years, and she was unable to stop smoking. As a result of the new rule, she developed a major depression, nicotine dependence, and post-traumatic stress disorder. Does she have a valid claim for workers' compensation? See Riddle v. Ampex Corp., 839 P.2d 489 (Colo.App.1992) (held: no).

**6.** Is Lyme disease (caused by a tick bite) an "accident" or a "disease"? In Foxbilt Electric v. Stanton, 583 So.2d 720 (Fla.App.1991), the court held that it was an accident rather than a disease. The effect was that the employee was not required to prove causation by "clear evidence," but only by normal causal connection standards.

**7.** Claims for repetitive stress (or cumulative trauma) disorders are increasingly common and in some jurisdictions now account for more than half of all workers' compensation claims for occupational illness. If a state workers' compensation law provides less compensation for these disorders than for the same impairment not caused by repetitive stress, does the statute violate equal protection under the Fourteenth Amendment? See Stephenson v. Sugar Creek Packing, 830 P.2d 41 (Kan.1992) (held: yes). But see Stenrich Group v. Jemmott, 467 S.E.2d 795 (Va.1996) (cumulative trauma disorders are not compensable under Virginia workers' compensation law).

---

## D. DETERMINING BENEFIT LEVELS

### 1. IMPAIRMENT AND DISABILITY

It is important to define the terms impairment and disability. Impairment is a medical conclusion based solely upon health status. Disability is a legal term representing the effects of impairment. According to the American Medical Association:

> It is particularly important to understand the distinction between a patient's *medical impairment,* which is an alteration of health status assessed by medical means, and the patient's *disability,* which is an alteration of the patient's capacity to meet personal, social, or occupational demands, or to meet statutory or regulatory requirements, which is assessed by nonmedical means. In a particular case, the existence of permanent medical impairment does not automatically support the presumption that there is disability as well. Rather, disability results when medical impairment leads to the individual's inability to meet demands that pertain to nonmedical fields and activities.

American Medical Association, Guides to the Evaluation of Permanent Impairment vii (3d ed. 1990).

The degree of impairment, its duration, and its effect on the claimant's ability to continue work are used to determine how the claimant's disability is classified and the level of benefits to which he or she is entitled.

## Mark A. Rothstein, *Legal Issues in the Medical Assessment of Physical Impairment by Third–Party Physicians*

5 J.Legal Med. 503 (1984).

From a medical standpoint, it may be difficult to determine when the period of temporary total disability has ended or, if a degree of impairment remains, when the temporary total disability becomes a permanent partial disability. The dates most frequently used for deciding that a temporary total disability has become a permanent partial disability are the date the claimant has reached maximum medical improvement, the date the impairment has become stationary, or the date the claimant is able to return to work.

Awards for permanent partial disability may be scheduled or unscheduled. Scheduled benefits are legislatively set and involve total loss or loss of use of specific body members, where wage loss is presumed. These scheduled benefits may be in addition to benefits received for temporary total disability and the claimant is entitled to a scheduled payment regardless of the economic consequences of the impairment. In other words, the basis of the award is medical impairment rather than wage loss.

For unscheduled permanent partial disability cases the wage loss principle generally is used. Degree of disability is calculated by comparing earnings before the injury or illness with earning capacity after the injury or illness. This latter estimate, of course, depends on the medical determination of impairment as well as other nonmedical factors relative to the claimant's employment opportunities.

Many workers' compensation laws and regulations are vague about the method to be used by examining physicians in calculating the claimant's level of impairment. Some states, such as Florida, use the American Medical Association's Guides to the Evaluation of Physical Impairment. Other states, such as Washington, have their own systems. Commonly, the physician will initially determine the degree of impairment caused by an injury or illness to a specific organ system or body part and then calculate the degree of impairment to the body as a whole.[126]

It is not necessary for a worker to be totally impaired to be considered totally disabled. For example, in West Virginia, a worker is considered totally disabled whenever the impairment rating is 85 percent or above.

---

**126.** Permanent partial disability awards usually are based on a percentage of the workers' average wage (60–70% with 66⅔% the most common), with a minimum amount and a maximum amount (usually based on a percentage of the statewide average weekly wage). The length of time that the claimant receives benefits depends on the percentage of disability.

But even with a percentage of impairment below the statutory total disability level a claimant may still be considered totally disabled where the impairment, in combination with non-medical factors, precludes the claimant from gainful employment. According to the Supreme Court of Tennessee: "In determining what may constitute permanent total disability, the concepts embodied in Workmen's Compensation take into account many pertinent factors, including skill, education, training, duration and job opportunity for the disabled."

## Turner v. American Mutual Insurance Co.

390 So.2d 1330 (La.1980).

■ DENNIS, JUSTICE.

The issue presented in this workers' compensation case is whether the plaintiff is unable "to engage in any gainful occupation for wages" and thus should be awarded compensation for permanent total disability. The court of appeal, affirming the trial court, held that the plaintiff, a mentally retarded woodcutter whose right foot had been crushed, was not permanently disabled because he could still perform "some type of gainful employment." We reverse and remand.

In Oster v. Wetzel Printing, Inc., 390 So.2d 1318 (La.1980) we held that the odd-lot doctrine should be used as the guiding concept in determining whether an injured employee is unable "to engage in any gainful occupation for wages" and is thus totally and permanently disabled. In the present case, the plaintiff's employment capabilities were severely restricted because of his mental and physical limitations, and the employer did not demonstrate the existence of an actual job in the employee's general locality at which he has a reasonable opportunity to be employed. Because the plaintiff established a prima facie showing of total and permanent disability, we reverse the holdings of the lower courts, but remand to allow the defendant a fuller opportunity to rebut by showing an actual job is available.

Silton Turner, a twenty year old black man, was employed as a sawhand for a logging contractor. His job required that he perform manual labor, including the operation of a power saw and, at times, a log skidder, in cutting and moving logs in the woods. On February 22, 1977, while riding on the front of a log skidder, plaintiff received serious injury to his right foot when the operator of the skidder raised the blade, pinning Turner's foot between the blade and the radiator of the skidder, breaking several bones. Turner was initially taken to Dr. LaCour in Oakdale and then transported to Rapides General Hospital where he was treated by Dr. Cedric Lowrey, an orthopedic specialist. After two operations conducted by Dr. Lowrey, plaintiff was ultimately released by the doctor with a residual disability of thirty to forty per cent in the right foot.

Turner was paid workers' compensation benefits until Dr. Lowrey notified the employer's insurer that he felt the plaintiff could resume work on a trial basis. Upon receiving this report, the insurer terminated compensation payments. Turner sued claiming that the payments were improperly discontinued because he was permanently disabled. * * *

Under the odd-lot test as announced in Oster v. Wetzel Printing, Inc., supra, an injured employee is entitled to total, permanent disability compensation if he can perform no services other than those which are so limited in quality, dependability, or quantity that a reasonably stable market for them does not exist. This determination is made after scrutiny of the evidence of the worker's physical impairment as well as his mental capacity, education, and training. If the worker establishes that he falls into the odd-lot category, he is entitled to total, permanent disability compensation unless the employer or his insurer is able to show that some form of suitable work is regularly and continuously available to the employee within reasonable proximity to the worker's residence.

In applying this analysis to the present case, we find that the concrete evidence is virtually undisputed. Turner sustained fractures of the second and third metatarsals of the right foot with a dislocation of all tarsometatarsal joints. He was required to undergo two surgical operations and wear a cast on his leg. His second metatarsal achieved questionable healing, resulting in a precarious union that makes him much more susceptible to injury than a normal person. Approximately one year after the accident, it was determined that he had lost virtually all motion of his great toe and 50% of the motion of his other toes. Atrophy of his right calf muscles had decreased the size of his limb by one inch in circumference. His doctors concluded that the 30 to 40% disability of his foot, and its added thickness, would require him to wear mismatched shoes.

Turner began working at the age of fifteen and labored primarily as a log cutter. He worked briefly in cannery and as a combination truck loader and driver for a pecan company. He attempted to go back to work as a log cutter as his doctor advised. He quit after three or four hours, however, when his foot became swollen and painful. He has attempted to exercise his foot by walking, but he experiences pain after standing or walking for long periods. Turner testified that he cannot perform any job that requires such use of his injured foot. He conceded that he could drive an automobile with an automatic transmission by applying the brake with his healthy left foot, but he testified that he could not operate a standard transmission truck or skidder, which would require manipulation of the brake with his injured foot.

Doctor Lowrey, the orthopedist who treated and performed surgery on Turner, testified the employee could eventually return full time to the job of log cutter. The doctor acknowledged that his patient had a 30–40% disability of the foot and a precarious union of one bone which could develop into a pseudo-arthrosis. He also acknowledged that Turner's foot could be reinjured easily if it was jerked up or down. The doctor did not doubt that Turner experiences pain and has a stiff forefoot, but the physician thought that the condition would improve if Turner forced himself to walk on it. The doctor was of the opinion that Turner could not do work that required him to put a great deal of weight or pressure on his toes.  Although the doctor confessed he was not too familiar with logging, he said he did not think it involved standing or pushing up on one's toes.

On the other hand, Dr. Joffrion, an orthopedist who saw Turner on one occasion for purposes of evaluation, testified that in his opinion the patient cannot perform the duties of a logger because he can no longer stand or walk for extended periods.  According to the doctor, Turner's disability results from a permanent stiffness of the midfoot which, together with the malunion of one bone, alters the mechanics of the foot, and causes excessive force at the ankle and toe area.  Dr. Joffrion testified that he was familiar with the physical requirements of the job of logger and that Turner could not perform them because his condition made prolonged walking, standing, stopping or climbing impossible.  Consequently, he recommended that the plaintiff be given rehabilitation and training for a sedentary occupation.

George Hearn, PhD, an industrial psychologist and vocational rehabilitationist, testified that he interviewed Turner and gave him a battery of intelligence, achievement, aptitude and psychological tests.  According to the tests, Turner has an intelligence quotient of 64, and has attained education grade levels of 4.6 in reading, 4.0 in spelling, and 2.3 in arithmetic.  He is mentally retarded, quite limited in academic skills, and his eye-hand motor coordination is consistent with his level of intellect, his achievement and his experience.  In the psychologist's opinion, however, Turner's job skills in these areas had not been further impaired because of the accident.

Over plaintiff's counsel's objection, Dr. Hearn was allowed to express his opinion of whether Turner can "work at any gainful occupation for wages" assuming that Turner has a "30 to 40 per cent impairment of function of his right foot as a whole;  * * * this limitation restricts him from doing work on his tip-toes; or in pushing up on his toes; * * * he has good motion [in] his ankle in and out, * * * up and down."  The psychologist testified that, since Turner had driven an automobile to his office for his interview, the injured employee could also drive a pulpwood truck and a skidder.  Dr. Hearn saw "no reason" why Turner could not perform assembly line work in a cannery or furniture factory, light janitorial or custodial work and a gasoline service station job which does not require him to handle money or credit cards.  The vocational psychologist testified that the state employment office had informed him of job openings for woodcutters and state civil service light custodial workers.  He also stated there were job opportunities at a cannery and a furniture factory.  Dr. Hearn did not testify, however, as to whether these employers would hire Turner despite his mental and physical limitations or whether the jobs were near his residence.  On cross-examination, in response to the direct question, "who has a job at this point, that would hire this man?", Dr. Hearn gave the qualified response that a cannery where Turner had worked before "should certainly consider hiring him, if it's the same kind of work, and under the assumption that he can do it."

Based on this evidence, the trial court found that Turner was not totally disabled because "he can perform work in the logging business as a truck driver and as operator of a skidder" as well as other occupations pointed out by the psychologist vocationalist. The court of appeal held that the trial court was not manifestly erroneous in rejecting Turner's claim of total permanent disability because he failed to prove to a legal certainty and by a reasonable preponderance of the evidence that he is unable to pursue any type of gainful employment as a result of the injury.

The trial court and court of appeal, of course, did not attempt to decide the case in accordance with the odd-lot doctrine. Although we mean no criticism of their failure to do so, in the absence of an expression by this Court on the subject, the result reached below illustrates the dangers of a simplistic or mechanical application of statutory rules in the field of workers' compensation. Turner, a mentally retarded, unskilled laborer, who sustained a permanent 30–40% disability of his foot, was denied either permanent partial disability or permanent total disability benefits. Both lower courts seemed to reject the opinion of the one doctor who said Turner could return to the work in which he was engaged at the time of the accident. But they based their decisions largely on the testimony of the vocational psychologist, who, in essence, stated that there were jobs available at various places in the state which a person with Turner's disability could perform. Thus, the trial court and court of appeal never focused on the question of whether Silton Turner, considering both his physical and mental limitations, can successfully obtain and hold regular employment in actual jobs available to him within reasonable proximity to his residence.

Under the proper interpretation of La.R.S. 23:1221(2), as set out by the odd-lot doctrine, the plaintiff's evidence makes a prima facie case for his classification in that category. It is agreed by all concerned that he is mentally and intellectually unable to do any work outside of manual labor. The plaintiff's evidence shows that he cannot do work which requires prolonged standing, walking, stooping, or climbing. It was also shown that increased activity affecting the injured foot will aggravate the arthritic condition and accelerate its effects.

The evidence regarding the plaintiff's ability to operate a skidder or drive a truck was conflicting though the trial judge decided that Turner possessed such ability. No evidence was introduced, however, that would establish that such work was actually available, nor that any employer would hire a person in Turner's condition over healthy competitors. The record is devoid of evidence that Turner's employer offered to rehire him either in his old job or at lighter work, such as operating a skidder or a truck. Turner is obviously at a substantial disadvantage in such competition especially when all his prior jobs contained at least some required tasks which he can no longer perform.

Turner lives in the small town of Simmesport. It is unknown how many jobs there were available to the plaintiff before he was injured, considering his mental capabilities. There is also no indication of whether there are any opportunities within a reasonable area for a person who can drive a truck or operate a skidder, but who cannot do other work which often is combined with those activities. Ultimately, it has not been shown that there is an occupation available within a reasonable area in which Turner can work considering his physical disability, education, and mental deficiencies.

We believe that a remand in this case is appropriate. We only recently announced in *Oster* that the odd-lot doctrine would be used to determine the extent of a worker's disability. We did not remand in *Oster* because the evidence showed that the injured elderly bookbinder could not engage in gainful employment even if a suitable job existed. Since it is possible that an actual job in Turner's vicinity exists that might afford the plaintiff gainful employment, we feel that the defendant should be allowed an opportunity to make this showing. On remand the plaintiff also will be allowed to introduce further evidence to support his case under the doctrine.

If the employer is successful in rebutting Turner's prima facie showing of total disability, the trial judge should reconsider the appropriateness of compensation for partial disability under La.R.S. 23:1221(3). If it is found that Turner can return to gainful employment, though not to the same or similar-work, then he would be entitled to an award of partial disability rather than the schedule loss under La.R.S. 23:1221(4)(g) and (o).

REVERSED AND REMANDED TO THE DISTRICT COURT.

NOTES AND QUESTIONS

**1.** Many employers are self-insured and others are experience-rated. This means that a workers' compensation claim for permanent disability may be quite costly. Would the *Turner* decision tend to discourage employers from hiring workers such as Silton Turner who, if they sustain ordinarily nondisabling injuries, are likely to be found totally disabled under the "odd lot" doctrine? If so, is there a solution to this problem?

**2.** The term "odd lot" was first used in the English case of Cardiff Corp. v. Hall, 1 K.B. 1009 (1911), where the court stated: "If I might be allowed to use such an undignified phrase, I should say that if the accident leaves the workman's labour in the position of an 'odd lot' in the labour market, the employer must shew that a customer can be found who will take it. * * *" The doctrine was first used in the United States by Judge Cardozo in Jordan v. Decorative Co., 130 N.E. 634 (N.Y.1921).

**3.** Should the burden of proof regarding employability rest with the claimant or the employer? Most jurisdictions hold that once the claimant proves inability to perform in the former job the burden shifts to the employer to show that there is other work available that the worker is capable of performing. See, e.g., Barrett v. Otis Elevator Co., 246 A.2d 668 (Pa.1968); Balczewski v. Department of Industry, Labor & Human Relations, 251 N.W.2d 794 (Wis.1977).

**4.** Cynthia Gettinger, an ambulance service employee, injured her back while lifting a patient on a stretcher and became a paraplegic. Under

Florida law, a paraplegic claimant is presumed to be totally disabled and the burden is on the employer to prove that the claimant possesses substantial earning capacity. The employer sought to rebut this presumption by showing that the claimant had become a successful wheelchair athlete and had earned a two-year college degree. Does this evidence rebut total disability? See Pinellas Ambulance Service, Inc. v. Gettinger, 504 So.2d 1386 (Fla.App.1987) (held: no). See also Hyman v. Farmland Feed Mill, 748 S.W.2d 151 (Ark.App.1988) (permanent disability not rebutted where claimant regularly engaged in square-dancing). The same issue arises under the Social Security disability program's requirement of "permanent and total disability," pp. 907–908 infra.

**5.** Is a worker entitled to permanent partial disability if, after the injury, the worker voluntarily retires and therefore suffers no wage loss? See Schroeder v. Highway Services, 403 N.W.2d 237 (Minn.1987) (held: yes). Is a worker who sustains a work-related injury and then becomes incarcerated eligible for temporary total disability compensation? See State ex rel. Ashcraft v. Industrial Commission, 517 N.E.2d 533 (Ohio 1987) (held: no; worker was no longer in a position to return to work).

**6.** After undergoing a corneal transplant, John Stover's work-related loss of vision was reduced from 80 percent to 25 percent in his right eye. Should his award for permanent partial disability consider the improvement in his vision caused by the transplant? See State ex rel. Kroger Co. v. Stover, 510 N.E.2d 356 (Ohio 1987) (held: no; because of prior rejections of grafts in his eye, the transplant was a "correction" and not a "restoration").

## A NOTE ON BENEFIT LEVELS

Benefits for total disability are based upon a percentage (usually two-thirds) of the worker's prior wages up to the statewide average weekly wage. This precludes very highly paid individuals from receiving exorbitant awards. Statutory maximum provisions, however, may also preclude workers from receiving enough money to live on. For example, in 1997 the maximum award for a totally disabled worker in Georgia was $275 per week. In some states a person receiving the maximum award is still below the poverty level. In several states, workers' compensation awards are offset by benefits received under Social Security or unemployment compensation. States also have minimum benefit levels. In 1997 in Arkansas and Florida the minimum benefit for a totally disabled worker was $20 per week.

Scheduled benefits for permanent partial disability are artificial and do not consider the effect of the scheduled injury on the particular individual. (Benefits for unscheduled injuries and illnesses are determined on an individual basis.) The benefit levels are often illogical in the distinctions drawn among injuries and the benefit levels vary dramatically among jurisdictions for identical injuries.

Scheduled benefit charts, sometimes called "meat charts," have been criticized as being dehumanizing. The following chart is a composite of the benefit levels for scheduled injuries as of January 1, 1997. Note the variations among jurisdictions for identical injuries.

# U.S. Chamber of Commerce, 1997 Analysis of Workers' Compensation Laws

34 (1997).

## CHART VII — INCOME BENEFITS FOR SCHEDULED INJURIES

| JURISDICTION | ARM AT SHOULDER | HAND | THUMB | FIRST FINGER | SECOND FINGER | THIRD FINGER | FOURTH FINGER | LEG AT HIP | FOOT | GREAT TOE | OTHER TOES | ONE EYE | HEARING ONE EAR | BOTH EARS |
|---|---|---|---|---|---|---|---|---|---|---|---|---|---|---|
| Alabama[2] | $48,840 | $37,400 | $13,640 | $9,460 | $6,820 | $4,840 | $3,520 | $44,000 | $30,580 | $7,040 | $2,420 | $27,280 | $11,660 | $35,860 |
| | | | *In this group of states, compensation for temporary disability is allowed in addition to allowance for scheduled injury.* | | | | | | | | | | | |
| Alaska[1] | No schedule. Benefits are $135,000 multiplied by the percent of whole person rating according to AMA *Guide to the Evaluation of Permanent Impairment.*[3] | | | | | | | | | | | | | |
| American Samoa[1] | PP disability benefits paid at 66⅔% of wages for specified number of weeks, no maximum.[4] | | | | | | | | | | | | | |
| Arizona[5] | 69,300 | 57,750 | 17,325 | 10,395 | 8,085 | 5,775 | 4,620 | 57,750 | 46,200 | 8,085 | 2,888 | 34,650 | 23,100 | 69,300 |
| Arkansas[6] | 54,810 | 41,238 | 16,443 | 9,657 | 8,352 | 5,481 | 4,176 | 48,024 | 34,191 | 8,352 | 2,871 | 27,405 | 10,962 | 41,238 |
| California[7] | 108,445[8] | 58,862.50[9] | 5,335 | 3,360 | 3,360 | 2,520 | 2,520 | 66,652.50[10] | 27,370[11] | 4,235 | 4,235[12] | 21,420[13] | 8,040 | 58,862.50 |
| Colorado[14] | 31,200 | 15,600 | 5,250 | 2,700 | 1,050 | 1,050 | 1,050 | 31,200 | 15,600 | 2,700 | 600 | 20,850 | 5,250 | 20,850 |
| Connecticut[15] | 122,512 | 98,952 | 37,107 | 21,204 | 17,081 | 12,369 | 10,013 | 91,295 | 73,625 | 16,492 | 5,301 | 92,473 | 20,615 | 61,256 |
| Delaware | 93,057.50 | 81,890.60 | 27,917.25 | 18,611.50 | 14,889.20 | 11,166.90 | 7,444.60 | 93,057.50 | 59,556.80 | 14,889.20 | 5,583.45 | 74,446 | 27,972.5 | 65,140.25 |
| District of Columbia | 233,635 | 182,672 | 56,150 | 34,439 | 22,460 | 18,717 | 11,230 | 215,613 | 153,475 | 28,449 | 11,979 | 45,265 | 38,930 | 149,731 |
| Florida | No schedule. Benefits paid according to degree of impairment.[16] | | | | | | | | | | | | | |
| Georgia | 67,500 | 48,000 | 18,000 | 12,000 | 10,500 | 9,000 | 7,500 | 67,500 | 40,500 | 9,000 | 6,000 | 45,000 | 22,500 | 45,000 |
| Guam[1] | 70,000 | 53,000 | 12,750 | 7,000 | 4,500 | 4,250 | 1,750 | 62,000 | 43,250 | 6,500 | 2,000 | 35,000 | 13,000 | 50,000 |
| Hawaii[17] | 156,312 | 122,244 | 37,575 | 23,046 | 15,030 | 12,525 | 7,515 | 144,288 | 102,705 | 19,038 | 8,016 | 80,160 | 26,052 | 100,200 |
| Idaho[18] | 64,350 | 57,915 | 23,595 | 15,015 | 11,797.50 | 5,362.50 | 3,217.50 | 42,900 | 30,030 | 9,009 | 1,501.50 | 32,175 | — | 37,537.50 |
| Illinois[19] | 234,351 | 148,422 | 54,682 | 31,247 | 27,341 | 19,529 | 15,623 | 214,822 | 121,081 | 27,341 | 9,374 | 124,987 | 42,149[20] | 84,318 |
| Iowa | 194,500 | 147,820 | 46,680 | 27,230 | 23,340 | 19,450 | 15,560 | 171,160 | 116,700 | 31,120 | 11,670 | 108,920 | 38,900 | 136,150 |
| Maine | Schedule is based on 80% of after-tax AWW for a number of weeks.[21] | | | | | | | | | | | | | |
| Maryland[22] | 166,000 | 138,195 | 18,500 | 7,400 | 6,425 | 5,550 | 4,625 | 166,000 | 138,195 | 7,400 | 1,850 | 138,195 | 23,125 | 138,195 |
| Massachusetts[23] | 25,183.38 | 19,912.44 | — | — | — | — | — | 22,840.74 | 16,984.14 | — | — | 22,840.74 | 16,984.14 | 45,095.82 |
| Minnesota | Benefits paid according to degree of impairment and loss of earnings, mostly set out in PPD schedule.[24] | | | | | | | | | | | | | |
| Mississippi | 54,134 | 40,600 | 16,240 | 9,473 | 8,120 | 5,413 | 4,060 | 47,367 | 33,833 | 8,120 | 2,706 | 27,067 | 10,826 | 40,600.50 |
| Missouri[25] | 62,343 | 47,026 | 16,123 | 12,092 | 9,405 | 9,405 | 5,912 | 55,125 | 41,652 | 10,748 | 3,762 | 37,621 | 11,824 | 45,145 |
| Montana | No schedule. Benefits paid according to degree of impairment, age, education, wage loss, and lifting restriction.[26] | | | | | | | | | | | | | |
| Nebraska[27] | 96,075 | 74,725 | 25,620 | 14,945 | 12,810 | 8,540 | 6,405 | 91,805 | 64,060 | 12,810 | 4,270 | 53,375 | 21,350 | [28] |
| Nevada | No schedule. Degree of disability determined in relation to whole person.[29] | | | | | | | | | | | | | |

| State | | | | | | | | | | | | | | |
|---|---|---|---|---|---|---|---|---|---|---|---|---|---|---|
| New Hampshire[30] | 158,760 | 12,884 | 57,456 | 35,532 | 28,728 | 14,364 | 6,804 | 105,840 | 74,088 | 13,608 | 2,268 | 63,504 | 22,680 | 92,988 |
| New Jersey[31] | 116,160 | 70,560 | 9,600 | 6,400 | 5,120 | 3,840 | 2,560 | 110,880 | 58,880 | 5,120 | 1,920 | 44,800 | 7,680 | 44,800 |
| New Mexico | 72,720 | 45,450 | 19,998 | 10,180.80 | 7,999.20 | 6,181.20 | 5,090.40 | 72,720 | 41,814 | 12,726 | 14,544[32] | 47,268 | 14,544 | 54,540 |
| North Carolina[33] | 122,880 | 102,400 | 38,400 | 23,040 | 20,480 | 12,800 | 10,240 | 102,400 | 73,728 | 17,920 | 5,120 | 61,440 | 35,840 | 76,800 |
| North Dakota[34] | 51,600 | 39,990 | 2,580 | 645[35] | 645[35] | 645[35] | 645[35] | 19,350 | 3,225 | 645[35] | 645[35] | 2,580 | 0 | 12,900 |
| Ohio[35] | 117,225 | 91,175 | 31,260 | 18,235 | 15,630 | 10,420 | 7,815 | 104,200 | 78,150 | 15,630 | 5,210 | 65,125 | 13,025 | 65,125 |
| Oregon[37] | 80,640 | 63,000 | 20,160 | 10,080 | 9,240 | 4,200 | 2,520 | 63,000 | 56,700 | 7,560 | 1,680 | 42,000 | 25,200 | 80,640 |
| Puerto Rico[38] | 12,000 | 12,000 | 4,875 | 2,600 | 1,950 | 1,625 | 1,300 | 12,000 | 11,375 | 1,950 | 975 | 39 | 3,250 | 12,000 |
| Rhode Island[40] | 28,080 | 21,960 | 6,750 | 4,140 | 2,700 | 2,250 | 1,800 | 28,080 | 18,450 | 3,420 | 900 | 14,400 | 5,400 | 18,000 |
| South Carolina | 99,136.40 | 83,364.70 | 29,290.30 | 18,024.80 | 15,771.70 | 11,265.50 | 9,012.40 | 87,870.90 | 63,086.80 | 15,771.70 | 4,506.20 | 63,086.80 | 36,049.60 | 74,352.30 |
| South Dakota | 75,000 | 56,250 | 18,750 | 13,125 | 11,250 | 7,500 | 5,625 | 60,000 | 46,875 | 11,250 | 3,750 | 56,250 | 18,750 | 56,250 |
| Tennessee[41] | 76,558 | 57,419 | 22,967 | 13,398 | 11,484 | 7,656 | 5,742 | 76,558 | 47,849 | 11,484 | 3,828 | 38,279 | 28,709 | 57,419 |
| Utah[42] | 65,637 | 58,968 | 23,517 | 14,742 | 11,934 | 5,967 | 2,808 | 43,875 | 30,888 | 9,126 | 1,404 | 42,120 | 17,550 | 35,100 |
| Vermont | No schedule. Benefits paid according to degree of impairment, *AMA Guide* 4th edition. | | | | | | | | | | | | | |
| Virgin Islands[43] | 65,560 | 53,640 | 23,840 | 23,840 | 23,840 | 23,840 | 22,350 | 53,640 | 35,768 | 23,840 | 22,350 | 58,110 | 35,760 | 53,640 |
| Virginia[44] | 93,000 | 69,900 | 27,960 | 16,310 | 13,980 | 9,320 | 6,990 | 81,550 | 58,250 | 13,980 | 4,660 | 46,600 | 23,300 | 46,600 |
| Washington[45] | 77,257 | 69,532 | 27,813 | 17,383 | 13,906 | 6,953 | 3,477 | 77,257 | 54,080 | 16,224 | 5,923 | 30,903 | 10,301 | 61,806 |
| West Virginia[46] | 106,706 | 88,922 | 35,569 | 17,784 | 12,449 | 8,892 | 8,892 | 107,706 | 62,245 | 17,784 | 7,114 | 58,689 | 40,015 | 97,814 |
| Wisconsin[47] | 87,000 | 69,600 | 27,840 | 10,440 | 7,830 | 4,524 | 4,872 | 87,000 | 43,500 | 14,500 | 4,352[48] | 47,850 | 9,570[49] | 57,420[49] |
| Wyoming | No schedule. Benefits paid by formula based on *AMA Guide to the Evaluation of Permanent Impairment.* | | | | | | | | | | | | | |
| F.E.C.A.[50] | 414,726 | 324,227 | 99,693.75 | 61,145.50 | 39,877.50 | 33,231.25 | 19,938.75 | 382,824 | 272,462.25 | 50,511.50 | 21,268 | 212,680 | 69,121 | 265,850 |
| Longshore Act | 249,930 | 195,459 | 60,080 | 36,849 | 24,032 | 20,027 | 12,016 | 230,705 | 184,217 | 30,440 | 12,817 | 128,170 | 41,656 | 160,212 |

*In this group of states, compensation for temporary disability is allowed in addition to scheduled injury with certain limitations as to period.*

| State | | | | | | | | | | | | | | |
|---|---|---|---|---|---|---|---|---|---|---|---|---|---|---|
| Indiana[51] | 48,000 | 34,000 | 6,400 | 4,000 | 3,500 | 3,000 | 2,000 | 41,000 | 27,000 | 6,400 | 3,000 | 27,000 | 8,500 | 34,000 |
| Kansas[52] | 73,350 | 48,900 | 19,560 | 12,062 | 9,780 | 6,520 | 4,890 | 65,200 | 40,750 | 9,780 | 3,260 | 39,120 | 9,780 | 35,860 |
| New York[53] | 124,800 | 97,600 | 30,000 | 18,400 | 12,000 | 10,000 | 6,000 | 115,200 | 82,000 | 15,200 | 6,400 | 64,000 | 24,000 | 60,000 |
| Pennsylvania[54] | 222,220 | 181,570 | 54,200 | 27,100 | 21,680 | 16,260 | 15,176 | 222,220 | 135,500 | 21,680 | 8,672 | 149,050 | 32,520 | 140,920 |

*In this group of states, compensation for temporary disability is deducted from the allowance for scheduled injury.*

| State | | | | | | | | | | | | | | |
|---|---|---|---|---|---|---|---|---|---|---|---|---|---|---|
| Kentucky[55] | No schedule. PP benefits paid at 66⅔% of wages up to 425 weeks according to degree of disability for 425 weeks if disability is 50% or less or 520 weeks if disability is greater than 50%.[57] | | | | | | | | | | | | | |
| Louisiana[56] | Schedule is based on 66⅔% of wages for a number of weeks. | | | | | | | | | | | | | |
| Michigan[58] | 143,377 | 114,595 | 34,645 | 20,254 | | 11,726 | 8,528 | 114,595 | 86,346 | 17,589 | 5,863 | 86,346 | 59 | 59 |
| Oklahoma[60] | 53,402.50 | 42,722 | 12,816.60 | 7,476.35 | 6,408.30 | 4,272.20 | 3,204.15 | 53,402.50 | 42,722 | 6,408.30 | 2,136.10 | 42,722 | 21,361 | 64,083 |
| Texas[61] | No schedule. Benefits paid according to degree of impairment. | | | | | | | | | | | | | |

Notes:  Explanatory notes deleted

## 2.  REHABILITATION AND OTHER SERVICES

# Squeo v. Comfort Control Corp.

494 A.2d 313 (N.J.1985).

■ GARIBALDI, J.

The primary issue in this workers' compensation case is whether the construction of a self-contained apartment attached to the home of an injured worker's parents may constitute "medical, surgical or other treatment * * * necessary to cure and relieve" or "other appliance" under N.J.S.A. 34:15–15 of the Workers' Compensation Act;  and if so, whether there is sufficient credible evidence in the record to support the finding that the construction of the apartment addition was necessary and that its cost was reasonable.

The petitioner, Eugene M. Squeo (Squeo), is a quadriplegic.  He was injured in 1978 when he fell from a roof while working for respondent, Comfort Control Corp. (Comfort Control).  He is totally and permanently disabled.  In 1979, a judgment ordering disability payments was entered by a judge of the Division of Workers' Compensation.

In February, 1982, Squeo filed an Application for Review or Modification of Formal Award seeking, inter alia, an order requiring Comfort Control to construct a self-contained apartment attached to the home of his parents.  The compensation court ordered that such construction be undertaken.

Squeo was 24 years old at the time of his accident in 1978.  He is a wheelchair-bound quadriplegic.  The compensation court concluded that his disability was orthopedic, neurologic, and neuropsychiatric involving residuals of multiple injuries including severance of the spinal cord.  Dr. Richard Sullivan, Medical Director of the Kessler Institute of Rehabilitation, treated Squeo for several months.  A witness on behalf of Comfort Control at the hearing, he testified that Squeo "had a terribly physical post injury course."  Usually after about eight weeks a quadriplegic is "well, though disabled;"  in contrast, Squeo was "unwell for probably about two, two and a half years after his injury."  Dr. Sullivan attributed Squeo's emotional problems to his protracted physical ailments.  He testified that Squeo

has had a terribly hard time.  The man has had just about every complication that God ever put on this earth for him.  Quadriplegic, the first year was devastating at the Veteran's Hospital and Hackensack because he went out of one problem into another and then when we saw him, immediately we had to do something to his urinary tract and surgery and then he came back and we had problems with skin breakdowns, rashes, you name the complications, this poor fellow had it.  Then he developed a curvature of the spine and we had to send him for corrective surgery to the spine and this was completed, and as I say he's had one medical difficulty after another.

For several years prior to his injury, Squeo had lived independently of his parents. Since 1980, he has been confined to a nursing home with predominantly elderly patients. The institutional living and the nursing home environment caused Squeo to become severely depressed. His depression was so great that on three occasions, while in the nursing home, he attempted suicide.

Because of the oppressive, institutional atmosphere that pervaded the nursing home, Squeo requested a modification of his disability award. Squeo testified at the compensation hearing that he wanted to "get on with life" which he "ha[d] not done in the last four years." He wanted to attend college and thereafter become gainfully employed. In order to do so, he felt it was necessary to be removed from the nursing home and "be rehabilitated into the world as a functional person again." He believed that the best way for him to be so rehabilitated was to live in a separate studio apartment attached to his parents' home.

* * *

Dr. Richard Sullivan, Medical Director of Kessler Institute of Rehabilitation, appeared as Comfort Control's main witness. He testified that in cases involving a quadriplegic, the usual practice at the Kessler Institute is a discussion between the employer or his insurance carrier and the patient about feasible housing plans for the patient. This practice was followed in this case. Dr. Sullivan spent a lot of time with Squeo's parents and his employer discussing plans to provide functional housing for Squeo. Among the alternatives considered were the conversion of the Squeos' basement to accommodate petitioner, a plan abandoned because the basement was considered to be too damp; a proposal to add a room and bath to the Squeos' house; and the attachment to their house of a mobile home, a plan unacceptable to the municipality. Unable to develop a feasible plan, Sullivan and Comfort Control advised the Squeos to meet with an architect to develop a plan. At that time, the Squeos were given a cost factor "that was compatible at that time with a room and bath addition to a home." He testified that the cost factor was based upon "the experience of the insurance company and ourselves as advisers in these conditions. We put many additions onto many homes for people."

Dr. Sullivan testified that the architect's recommendation surprised him. Instead of the usual addition of a room and bath, with ingress to and egress from the home, the plan contemplated a separate apartment attached to the home. The apartment would contain a bedroom, kitchen, living room, bathroom, carport, basement, and hydraulic lift, and would require its own electricity, plumbing, and heating. The architect estimated the cost to be in excess of $65,000.

When questioned by the compensation judge, Dr. Sullivan conceded that the addition of the separate apartment "is not that bad an idea." However, he expressed concern about the cost of such an addition.

* * *

The Appellate Division affirmed the order of the compensation court, finding that Squeo's injuries went beyond the paralysis of his limbs. It found that he was suffering from a severe mental depression that, on three occasions, had brought him to the brink of suicide. Providing Squeo with independent living quarters would relieve his depression and perhaps save his life. Accordingly, the apartment addition constituted "treatment" within the purview of the Act.

Medical treatment is given to preserve life and relieve the patient as much as possible from pain and disability whether physical or mental.

Mindful of the cost of the apartment addition, the Appellate Division instructed that the "cost of the apartment not go beyond providing for petitioner's basic need for independent living quarters." It ordered that the employer be secured by a mortgage executed by Squeo's parents so that if Squeo should no longer use the apartment, the employer would be compensated for any significant value the apartment may add to the property in the event it is sold, rented, or mortgaged.

N.J.S.A. 34:15–15 in pertinent part provides:

The employer shall furnish to the injured worker such medical, surgical and *other treatment,* and hospital service *as shall be necessary to cure and relieve the worker of the effects of the injury* and to restore the functions of the injured member or organ where such restoration is possible; * * * the Division of Workers' Compensation after investigating the need of the same and giving the employer an opportunity to be heard, shall determine that such physicians' and surgeons' treatment and hospital services *are or were necessary and that the fees for the same are reasonable* and shall make an order requiring the employer to pay for or furnish the same.

* * *

When an injured employee may be partially or wholly relieved of the effects of a permanent injury, by use of an artificial limb or *other appliance,* which phrase shall also include artificial teeth or glass eye, the Division of Workers' Compensation, *acting under competent medical advice, is empowered to determine the character and nature of such limb or appliance, and to require the employer or the employer's insurance carrier to furnish the same.*

[Emphasis added.]

Pursuant to N.J.S.A. 34:15–15, it is evident that an employer must provide an injured worker with "other treatment" or "other appliance" that serves to cure and relieve a worker of the effects of his work-connected injury. The employer contends, however, that "other treatment" or "appliance" under N.J.S.A. 34:15–15 is not intended to encompass the construction of a self-contained apartment.

* * *

Although this Court has liberally construed the Act to promote its beneficent purposes, we have always imposed the limitation that no expense incurred may be recovered that is not shown to be reasonable and necessary by sufficient competent medical evidence.

\* \* \*

Other jurisdictions have also liberally construed the terms "treatment" and "appliance" so as to allow such expenses as may be said to be reasonable and necessary for the cure of an ailment or relief of its symptoms. Courts have been generous in allowing recovery as "treatment" not only the cost of medical and hospital services, but also of necessary incidentals such as transportation, apparatus, and even nursing care furnished by a member of claimant's own family.

\* \* \*

In sum, courts in other jurisdictions governed by statutes similar to ours have been generous in their liberal construction of the language in question. The phrases "other treatment" and "appliance" have assumed various forms, ranging from permanent round-the-clock nursing care to the rent-free use of a modular home. Moreover, the relief provided has not been limited to physical amelioration but has encompassed psychological relief as well. This relief, however, has been allowed only after a determination that such expenses are "reasonable and necessary" to relieve the injured worker of the effects of his injuries.

\* \* \*

In view of the remedial nature of the New Jersey Workers' Compensation Act and the liberal construction accorded to it, we conclude that under certain unique circumstances, when there is sufficient and competent medical evidence to establish that the requested "other treatment" or "appliance" is reasonable and necessary to relieve the injured worker of the effect of his injuries, the construction of an apartment addition may be within the ambit of N.J.S.A. 34:15–15. We caution however that it is only the unusual case that may warrant such extraordinary relief.

We find this to be such an "unusual case," and, consequently, the apartment addition is to be considered "other treatment" within the intendment of N.J.S.A. 34:15–15. The facts before us support this conclusion.

\* \* \*

We agree with the restrictions on the cost of the construction of the apartment imposed by both the compensation judge and the Appellate Division. We find that within the limits of such restrictions the cost of the construction of the apartment will be reasonable.

The award also appears reasonable when viewed in comparison to the cost of the available alternatives which the employer was willing to pay.

Although the employer indicates that the cost of the apartment would be greater than that of the other alternatives, no such evidence was submitted. In fact, while the cost of the proposed addition initially may be greater, in the long run it is likely to be far less than the expense of maintaining a young man in a nursing home or rental unit for the rest of his life.

We affirm the judgment of the Appellate Division. At oral argument we learned that the Squeos have constructed the apartment. Accordingly, we remand to the Division of Workers' Compensation for a determination as to the portion of the cost of the construction of the apartment for which the employer will be liable, within the restrictions set forth by the Division and the Appellate Division.

NOTES AND QUESTIONS

**1.** Workers' compensation laws usually provide for the rehabilitation of individuals suffering from a work-related injury or illness. Medical services, nursing care, prosthetic devices, physical therapy, and vocational rehabilitation are customarily available. The case law differs on whether claimants are entitled to more unusual services.

**2.** Claimants have been awarded a wide range of "other" services. For example, a firm mattress, Izzi v. Royal Electric Corp., 216 A.2d 363 (R.I.1966), a hospital bed, City of Miami v. Harris, 452 So.2d 115 (Fla.App. 1984), a wheelchair-accessible van for a claimant with quadriplegia, Brawn v. Gloria's Country Inn, 698 A.2d 1067 (Me. 1997), and even a backyard swimming pool for a claimant with severe burns, Haga v. Clay Hyder Trucking Lines, 397 So.2d 428 (Fla.App.), review denied, 402 So.2d 609 (Fla.1981), have been held compensable. But see Davis v. Los Alamos National Laboratory, 775 P.2d 1304 (N.M.App.1989) (hot tub not compensable).

**3.** A laborer on a refuse-collecting truck suffered a work-related injury that left him able to be employed only in sedentary occupations. The claimant sought reimbursement for the costs of a four-year college education to study computer science and accounting. What result? See City of Salem v. Colegrove, 321 S.E.2d 654 (Va.1984) (held: not entitled). Accord, Beaver Valley Corp. v. Priola, 477 So.2d 408 (Ala.1985).

## 3. A NOTE ON DISPUTED CLAIMS

When an injured worker files a claim for benefits, the employer's insurer can contest it on one of two grounds. First, the insurer can argue that the injury is not compensable. Second, the insurer can admit liability, but challenge the extent of disability caused by the injury.

*Compensable Injuries.* The most frequently litigated question in the workers' compensation system involves whether a particular injury is compensable. The requirement that an injury "arise out of and in the course of employment'' can present difficult questions of causation.   For example, how can a worker prove that increased risk of heart attack or chronic nervousness arose out of employment?   Similarly, is a worker acting in the course of employment when injured during an altercation in the firm lunch room?   Occupational diseases, which originally were not covered by workers' compensation, pose special problems.   Not only is it difficult to establish a causal link between a worker's job and disease, but the employer's insurer may use the long latency period to question whether the injury occurred while the worker was employed by its insured.

*Extent of Disability.*   Even if the worker can prove that the injury is compensable, the insurer can still dispute the extent of disability.   Controversies frequently arise over the injured worker's medical record.   This record may be incomplete, inconclusive, or incorrect.   Where the record is sufficient, the insurer may challenge the worker's interpretation of it.   Some injuries, such as back pain, cannot be objectively determined and the medical record is of little help.   Beyond the uncertainty inherent in the medical record, a determination of how debilitating the injury is or how long the worker will be impaired is affected by a host of personal factors, including the worker's age, weight, and lifestyle.

The following table summarizes one study of the distribution of these two sources of disputes:

Percentage of Workers' Compensation Claims Contested by Case
Type and Reasons for Contesting

|  | Occupational Disease | Heart | Accident |
|---|---|---|---|
| % of Claims Contested | 62.7 | 55.2 | 9.8 |
| Primary Reason for Contesting Claims | | | |
| Work relatedness (%) | 72.5 | 76.0 | 20.6 |
| Extent of disability (%) | 12.0 | 11.6 | 55.8 |
| Other issues (%) | 15.5 | 12.4 | 23.6 |

(Reproduced from Linda Darling-Hammond & Thomas J. Kniesner, The Law and Economics of Workers' Compensation 33 (1980).)

Claim disputes create additional costs for the workers' compensation system.   According to a 1977 study, ''about 60 percent of the [Workers' Compensation] premium dollar [goes] for workers' compensation benefits, from which, however, must be deducted the amounts injured workers must pay their own lawyers.   The latter amounts have been estimated at about eight percent of the benefits so that it appears that about 52 percent of the premium dollar goes to the claimant as benefits.''   Interdepartmental Workers' Compensation Task Force, Workers' Compensation: Is There a Better Way?, at 9 (1977).   By statute, contingent fees are usually limited to about 10 to 20 percent.

## 4.   A NOTE ON HOW THE WORKERS' COMPENSATION SYSTEM WORKS—OR ADDING INSULT TO INJURY

### Mark Reutter, *Workmen's Compensation Doesn't Work or Compensate* *

35 Bus. & Soc'y Rev., Oct. 1980, at 39.

What has emerged, then, from seven decades of workmen's comp is a vast protection system for industry; one in which the enlightened self-interests of insurers and businessmen, lawyers and doctors, have meshed into a finely calibrated machine that rejects those most damaged by the workplace.   The statistics compiled by the Labor Department are instructive.   Although almost all severely disabled workers are theoretically eligible for compensation, only 94,000 (or 1 in 10) actually receive benefits. Not only are workers with occupational *diseases* deprived of benefits, but only 15 percent of the estimated 410,000 workers disabled by *injuries* get long-term compensation.   For injured workers who are awarded benefits, the average compensation to a man totally disabled for life is 30 percent of his lost wages—or less than half the amount specified by state laws.

The system's structure preordains this outcome by making it very easy for the insurer to pursue his economic interests.   First of all, the insurer has the right to contest any claim.   Accorded such a privilege, the insurer does what any businessman would do.   According to the Labor Department study, he contests severe disability (i.e., expensive claims) ten times more frequently than claims for minor or temporary injuries.

When a case is not contested, a worker usually receives prompt and adequate benefits.   A contested claim, however, sets off a series of procedures that help the insurer.   In a contested disease case (and all but minor disease cases are contested), the claimant is required to present indisputable evidence that his sickness was caused by a workplace condition.   That's next to impossible, given the thicket of legal restrictions against awards for occupational diseases.

On the other hand, a major injury claim often is delayed for months because of hearing backlogs.   Here an insurer's usual strategy is to seek a private settlement with the jobless, increasingly desperate worker.   In a typical "compromise and release" settlement, a disabled worker garners, say, $20,000 in return for signing away his future rights against the insurer.   Thus, thanks to the way the system is structured, a carrier is freed from the law's burdensome requirement that he pay a severely disabled worker lifelong "income maintenance" equivalent to two-thirds of lost wages.

Contesting a claim not only suits the self-interests of the insurer and employer, it is also the source of business for thousands of lawyers and doctors who specialize in comp work.  In this parody of no-fault insurance, lawyers are everywhere;  while defense lawyers spar with the seriously sick to reduce an insurer's liability, claimant lawyers make minor injuries into major cases to secure higher fees.  The worker who needs help the most is the worker whom comp attorneys are least likely to serve, because the economic incentives are elsewhere.

Another peculiarity of the system tends to distort medical judgments. Rather than basing disability awards on the income an employee will lose, workmen's comp sets benefits according to impairment ratings made by doctors.  In other words, a man who suffers a back injury is awarded compensation on the basis of the functional impairment of his back, regardless of the impairment's effect on his job or income.

* * *

Most comp lawyers and insurers have informal arrangements with certain physicians to examine their clients.  In a potentially costly case, an injured worker is shuffled from doctor to doctor as each side jockeys for ratings that suit its self-interest.  Doctor shopping not only delays benefits and raises the costs of the program, it encourages everyone to cheat.

NOTE

Workers' compensation sought to replace an inefficient tort system with a more efficient no-fault system.  With more than 40 percent of payments going to administrative expenses, it has failed in its goal of efficient delivery of benefits.

If doctors, lawyers, and insurers are the "winners" under the system, who are the losers?  Not only are claimants losers, but taxpayers are big losers in subsidizing the income of those not compensated by workers' compensation.

A number of studies have been conducted on the effects of asbestos disease on workers and their families.  One such study is the following:

### Economic Loss Replacement Following Deaths from Asbestos Diseases

| Source | Replacement Ratio (Total Cash Benefits: Total Net Loss) |
|---|---|
| Social Security Survivors' Benefits | 6.7% |
| Veterans' Widows' Benefits | 0.7% |
| Public Assistance | 0% |
| Government Sources, Subtotal | 7.4% |
| Private Pensions | 5.4% |
| Workers' Compensation | 6.4% |
| Tort Awards and Settlements | 3.6% |
| Total, All sources | 22.8% |

This table is from Barry I. Castleman, Asbestos:  Medical and Legal Aspects 796 (4th ed. 1996) (based on Johnson & Heler, Compensation for Death from Asbestos, 37 Indus. & Lab.Rel.Rev. 529 (1984)).

In reviewing the six objectives of workers' compensation, supra p. ____, how many of these are currently being met?

## Emily A. Spieler, *Perpetuating Risk?  Workers' Compensation and the Persistence of Occupational Injuries*

31 Hous.L.Rev. 119 (1994).

In 1992, state and federal workers' compensation programs consumed over 62 billion dollars.  This figure dwarfs (by a factor of over 100) the combined budgets of the three federal agencies whose primary focus is on the occupational safety and health of American workers.[3]  In fact, workers' compensation, designed to compensate victims of work-related injuries, illnesses, and fatalities, represents our primary allocation of publicly mandated funds to safety and health in the workplace.  Not surprisingly, the dramatic and persistent increases in these costs in recent years have not been welcomed by employers (who must pay them), by politicians (who must confront the political pressure which accompanies them), or by workers and labor unions (who must defend benefit levels in the political arena).

At the same time, available data appear to indicate that injury rates, and in particular injuries which result in lost work time, have not declined during this period of exploding costs.  There is no way to escape two essential and obvious facts:  the persistence of occupationally-induced morbidity and mortality continues to prevent substantial reduction in aggregate workers' compensation costs;  and the high cost of this social insurance program expends resources which might better be applied elsewhere.  Both American workers and enterprises are therefore paying a price for both the persistent levels of injury and disease and the growing costs of workers' compensation.

It would seem reasonable to expect that rising compensation costs would stimulate employers to engage in efforts to prevent occupational injury and disease.  There is no persuasive evidence that this is so, however.  Neither aggregate safety data nor more focused empirical studies give strong support to the notion that the high cost of workers' compensation in the aggregate, or enterprise-specific costs, have motivated large numbers of employers to take injury prevention activities seriously.  This is remarkable, in view of the fact that empirical studies do show that enterprises with aggressive safety programs often exhibit lower, sometimes substantially lower, workers' compensation costs, and that the reduction in these costs more than offsets the cost of safety initiatives.

\* \* \*

**3.** In 1992, the budgets for key federal occupational safety and health agencies were: Occupational Safety and Health Administration (OSHA), $297.08 million;  Mine Safety and Health Administration (MSHA), $182.04 million;  and National Institute for Occupational Safety and Health (NIOSH), $103.45 million, or a total of $582.57 million.

A substantial portion of the total benefits paid goes to health care providers and lawyers, not to injured workers, however. The medical component of workers' compensation benefits has risen from 33.6% in 1960, to 40.9% of total workers' compensation benefit costs in 1990, to 50% in 1993. The rate of inflation for medical costs within the workers' compensation programs has exceeded the already alarming rate of increase in U.S. health care expenditures generally in every recent year. This particular concern has led the Clinton Administration to indicate a preference for folding these health care costs into the general health care system as it is reformed.

Notably, while benefit costs have increased, the level of litigation over claims has also risen. Both the payment to health care providers and the payment to lawyers has therefore been increasing. The medical cost component can be easily quantified, since health care providers are paid directly. The cost of lawyers is more difficult to determine, however. Defense of claims is generally included in the administrative costs of insurance carriers, but the cost of legal representation to workers is almost always taken from the benefit amount paid directly to workers. States often regulate the fees that can be charged by claimants' representatives.

As litigation and medical costs have grown, the relative proportion of benefits paid to workers has declined and the component paid to others—including medical providers, lawyers, rehabilitation specialists, third party claims administrators—has increased. Thus, while the amount of total benefits paid has increased as a percent of payroll, the amount that is paid to individual workers may not be increasing—or may be doing so at a much slower pace.

* * *

Costs, not injury rates, drive the workers' compensation political debate. The explosion of costs over the past twenty years has heightened the chronic tension that characterizes the program. On the one hand, workers are accused of taxing the system through excessive filing of claims; as is often the case when the expansion of an entitlement program results in unanticipated levels of costs, applicants for benefits are blamed for ensuing financial woes. On the other hand, workers charge that the system still fails to provide adequate compensation to many injured workers. The political tug-of-war among insurers (seeking rate adequacy), employers (seeking cost reductions), and workers and unions (seeking benefit adequacy) has made workers' compensation into the politicians' most insoluble political conundrum. Workers' compensation "reform" is an annual exercise in political frustration in many states.

There is some sign of change, however. The political realities of workers' compensation require that its fundamental characteristic of compromise be maintained. Organized labor, as the putative voice of injured workers, therefore finds itself at the bargaining table when legislators debate mechanisms for decreasing cost. Political realities constrain labor's usual bargaining stance: the apparent consensus that costs are excessive has made the expansion of benefits in most states a politically untenable proposition.

\* \* \*

[S]tate legislatures are attempting to reduce the amount of delay and friction in the adjudicative system, to increase the speed at which injured workers with legitimate claims receive benefits, and to reduce the role of attorneys in the litigation of claims. Improved administration of claims has been a goal since before it was advanced by the National Commission on State Workmen's Compensation Laws over twenty years ago. Of course, there is not always consensus regarding the appropriate way to achieve administrative efficiency.

\* \* \*

States are responding to high costs in two ways. First, in reaction to employers' demands, legislatures have tightened the availability of benefits, heightened the consequences for fraud, and addressed the post injury costs of claims. In many instances, this recent legislation has attempted to turn back the clock, making claims non-compensable which had become compensable within the last twenty years.

This type of legislative response assumes that the critical goal is reduction in costs, not reduction in injuries. Undoubtedly, costs will fall as a result of more aggressive claims management or reduction in the numbers of claims that are viewed as compensable. This approach will not, however, change the underlying health and safety conditions for working people or reduce the number of injuries. Instead, it simply changes the number of injuries which are recognized by the system or the costs of those injuries which are compensated.

Second, mindful of the concerns voiced by organized labor and others, legislatures are adopting more pro-active approaches to occupational safety and health as a component of workers' compensation reform. This approach has significant political appeal. A successful campaign for safety will presumably result in reductions in costs without antagonizing workers through removal of benefits.

## John F. Burton, Jr., *Workers' Compensation Benefits, Costs, and Profits: An Overview of Developments in the 1990's*

1998 Workers' Compensation Year Book (1997).

This overview presents a summary of some general observations about workers' compensation developments in the 1990s.

A simplified summary of recent developments is provided in Figure A. Statutory benefits, as measured by actuarial evaluations of legislative changes in workers' compensation statutes and of changes in medical fees and hospital reimbursement rates, have declined by 0.3 percent per year during the 1990s. Benefits paid to workers, including cash and medical benefits, have increased 1.4 percent per year in this decade. Employers' costs of workers' compensation for all non-federal employees, measured in dollars per hour, have increased 3.6 percent per year since 1991. Profitability for workers' compensation insurers, measured in terms of the overall profitability ratio, has increased 4.7 percent per year during the 1990s.

The results shown in Figure A must be used with considerable caution, however, for several reasons. The annual rates of increase span different time periods because the latest year with available data varies among the four measures of workers' compensation performance from policy year 1992–93 (benefits paid), to 1995 (statutory benefits and insurers' profitability), to 1996 (employers' costs). Not only are the time spans different for the four measures, the patterns across individual years within the 1990s also differ among the measures as discussed below. Finally, as also discussed below, the scope of the employers and employees included in each of the four measures varies.

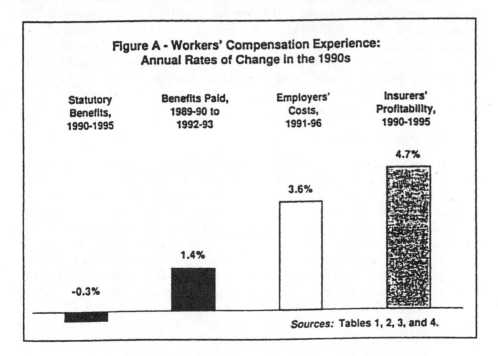

**Figure A - Workers' Compensation Experience: Annual Rates of Change in the 1990s**

*Sources:* Tables 1, 2, 3, and 4.

## Statutory Benefits

The countrywide changes in statutory benefits are calculated by the National Council on Compensation Insurance (NCCI), which is the organization that provides ratemaking and statistical services in most states with private workers' compensation insurance carriers. The NCCI publishes an *Annual Statistical Bulletin (NCCI Bulletin)* that includes information on the adjustments in workers' compensation premium levels due to statutory changes in cash benefits adopted by the various state legislatures, as well as medical fee and hospital rate changes. These benefits changes are evaluated by the NCCI using actuarial procedures. Data for 44 states and the District of Columbia are included in Exhibit III of the *NCCI Bulletin;* data are missing for the six states with exclusive state workers' compensation funds. Exhibit I of the *NCCI Bulletin* presents the countrywide annual averages of changes in statutory benefits for the 45 jurisdictions evaluated by the NCCI, which are used in Table 1 of this article.

These statutory benefit changes pertain to all employers and employees covered by the workers' compensation programs in these states, not just those employers (and their employees) who purchase workers' compensation insurance. Thus, the information on countrywide changes in benefits shown in Table 1 is a fairly comprehensive measure of what has been happening to the generosity of the workers' compensation cash benefits provided by statutes and of medical fees, with the only significant gap being information on the six exclusive fund states.

Figure A indicates that the average change in statutory benefits between 1990 and 1995 was a 0.3 percent annual rate of decline. The information in Table 1 and Figure B provides an interesting story of two subperiods in the 1990s: the first three years (1990–92), when statutory benefits increased in two out of the three years, and the next three years (1993–95), when statutory benefits declined sharply in two of the three years. The least volatile year was 1995, when statutory benefits increased by 0.1 percent countrywide.

## Benefits Paid to Workers

Another measure of workers' compensation benefits is the total benefits (cash benefits plus medical benefits) paid per 100,000 workers. This measure is examined in the companion article by Burton and Blum, and therefore will only be briefly described here. The data pertain to the cost of benefits that will ultimately be paid to workers for injuries that occur in specified policy periods. The data are limited to the experience in 45 jurisdictions for employers who purchase workers' compensation insurance from private carriers or, in some jurisdictions, from competitive state workers' compensation funds. Not encompassed by the data are employers who self-insure their workers' compensation risks or who purchase insurance from exclusive state funds or, in some jurisdictions, from competitive state workers' compensation funds.

The latest policy period with data available on the costs of benefits paid per 1000,000 workers is 1992–93. Over the four policy periods in the 1990s with available data, the total benefit payments per 100,000 workers had an average annual increase of 1.4 percent, as shown in Table 2 and Figure A. What the four-year average masks, however, is the significant downward trend in total benefits paid that is shown in Figure C. As demonstrated in the companion article by Burton and Blum, the trend of deceleration and then decline in benefits paid over the last four policy periods with data is found for both cash and medical benefits.

### Table 1 - Countrywide Changes in Statutory Benefits During the 1990s

| Year | Annual Change in Benefits (1) | Cumulative Change From 1989 (2) |
|------|------|------|
| 1990 | 1.3% | 1.3% |
| 1991 | -0.3% | 1.0% |
| 1992 | 0.9% | 1.9% |
| 1993 | -2.0% | -0.1% |
| 1994 | -1.9% | -2.0% |
| 1995 | 0.1% | -1.9% |
| Average | -0.3% | |

Note:  Data in column (2) calculated by Burton.

Source:  Exhibit I, "Countrywide Changes in Premium Level," National Council on Compensation Insurance, *Annual Statistical Bulletin, 1996 Edition.* The benefit change "refers to adjustments in premium level to account for statutory benefit changes, adopted by the various state legislatures, as well as medical fee and hospital rate changes."

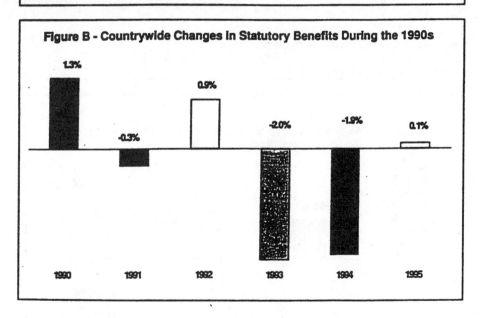

Figure B - Countrywide Changes in Statutory Benefits During the 1990s

### Employers' Costs of Workers' Compensation

The employers' costs of workers' compensation are measured each year by the Bureau of Labor Statistics (BLS), a unit within the U.S. Department of Labor.  This measure of the performance of the workers' compensation program is examined in the companion article by Burton and Yates, and will only be summarized here.

The BLS data include information on the cost of workers' compensation in dollars per hour worked for all non-federal employees. The private sector and state and local government sector employees who are included in

| Table 2 - National Changes in Total (Cash plus Medical) Benefits Paid Per 100,000 Workers During the 1990s | | |
|---|---|---|
| Policy Year | Annual Change In Benefits Paid (1) | Cumulative Change From 1988-89 (2) |
| 1989-90 | 14.6% | 14.6% |
| 1990-91 | 6.3% | 21.8% |
| 1991-92 | -4.8% | 16.0% |
| 1992-93 | -10.7% | 3.6% |
| Average | 1.4% | |

Note: Data in Column (2) calculated by Burton.

Source: Burton and Blum 1996, Table 3.

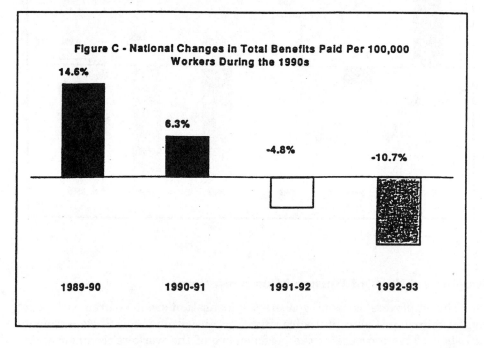

Figure C - National Changes in Total Benefits Paid Per 100,000 Workers During the 1990s

the data series include about 95 percent of all employees, which means this is a relatively inclusive measure.  The data are also timely, with data already published from the 1996 survey of employer expenditures.  However, the data series pertaining to all non-federal employees only began in 1991, and thus information for the entire period of the 1990s is unavailable.

| Table 3 - Changes in Employer Expenditures for Workers' Compensation Per Hour for All Non-Federal Employees During the 1990s | | | |
|---|---|---|---|
| Year | Cost in Dollars Per Hour (1) | Annual Change In Costs (2) | Cumulative Changes From 1991 (3) |
| 1991 | 0.32 | -- | -- |
| 1992 | 0.35 | 9.4% | 9.4% |
| 1993 | 0.38 | 8.6% | 18.8% |
| 1994 | 0.39 | 2.6% | 21.9% |
| 1995 | 0.38 | -2.6% | 18.8% |
| 1996 | 0.38 | 0.0% | 18.8% |
| Average | 0.37 | 3.6% | |

Note:  Data in Columns (2) and (3) calculated by Burton.

Source:  Burton and Yates 1996b, Table 1.

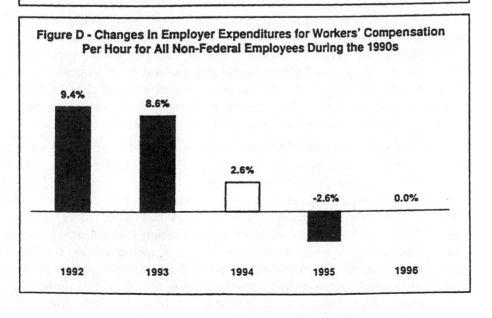

Figure D - Changes in Employer Expenditures for Workers' Compensation Per Hour for All Non-Federal Employees During the 1990s

Figure A indicates that the employers' costs of workers' compensation increased on average 3.6 percent per year during the period from 1991 to 1996. However, the data for individual years present an interesting pattern, as shown in Figure D and Table 3. The annual changes in employers' costs were up 9.4 percent from 1991 to 1992, and then up another 8.6 percent in 1993. From 1994 to 1996, however the changes were modest—indeed the employer's workers' compensation costs per hour in 1996 ($0.38) were exactly the same as the figure in 1993.

### Profitability for Workers' Compensation Insurers

The profitability of workers' compensation insurance can be measured by data produced by A.M. Best, a publisher of information on the insurance industry. The 1995 profit data for workers' compensation carriers is analyzed in another article in this issue by Yates. The 1995 data plus data from earlier years were used to construct Table 4.

A.M. Best publishes the overall operating ratio, which is shown in column (1) of Table 4. As explained in more detail in the article by Yates, the overall operating ratio essentially is (1) the total of expenses minus investment income on reserves, divided by (2) premiums.

Many people, including myself, find the overall operating ratio counter-intuitive because the insurance industry is more profitable with a lower ratio than a higher ratio, in contradiction of the notion that bigger is better. As a more intuitive measure of performance, I have calculated the overall profitability ratio (OPR) shown in column (2) of Table 4. The inverse of the overall operating ratio, the overall profitability ratio is (1) premium divided by (2) net expenses (the total of expenses minus investment income on reserves). Another way to understand the overall profitability ratio is this: the OPR indicates the amount of premiums in dollars per on hundred dollars of net expenses. An example is that in 1989, as shown in column 2 of Table 4, workers' compensation insurance carriers received $95.40 in premiums for every $100 in net expenses.

The 1990s has included subperiods of famine and feast for the workers' compensation insurance industry. From 1990 to 1992, the overall profitability ratio was less than 100 in every year, indicating continuing losses in workers' compensation insurance. But, as shown in Figure E, the OPR for the workers' compensation insurance industry has improved in every year since 1992. Moreover, the workers' compensation insurance industry has been profitable in every year since 1993 as measured by the overall profitability ratio. Indeed, as discussed in the companion article by Yates, when measured by the overall operating ratio, the workers' compensation insurance industry experienced record profitability in 1995. Restated in terms of the OPR, in 1995 the workers' compensation insurance industry received $124.70 in premiums for every $100 of net expenses.

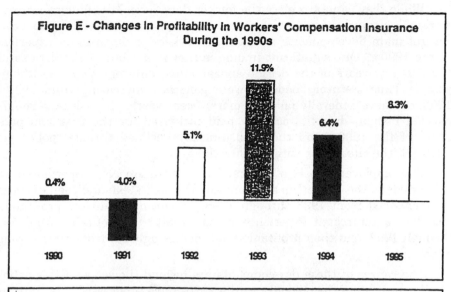

Figure E - Changes in Profitability in Workers' Compensation Insurance During the 1990s

Table 4 - Changes in Profitability in Workers' Compensation Insurance During the 1990s

| Year | Overall Operating Ratio (1) | Overall Profitability Ratio (OPR) (2) | Annual Change in OPR (3) | Cumulative Change in OPR From 1989 (4) |
|------|------|------|------|------|
| 1989 | 104.8 | 95.4 | – | – |
| 1990 | 104.4 | 95.8 | 0.4% | 0.4% |
| 1991 | 108.7 | 92.0 | -4.0% | -3.6% |
| 1992 | 103.4 | 96.7 | 5.1% | 1.4% |
| 1993 | 92.4 | 108.2 | 11.9% | 13.4% |
| 1994 | 86.9 | 115.1 | 6.4% | 20.6% |
| 1995 | 80.2 | 124.7 | 8.3% | 30.7% |
| Average | 97.3 | 104.0 | 4.7% | |

**Note:** Data in columns (2), (3), and (4) calculated by Burton.

**Source:** Overall Operating Ratios from Yates 1996b and Burton and Schmidle 1995, Table III.B.10.

## Conclusions

The only comprehensive data series for workers' compensation performance in the U.S. has been discontinued by the Social Security Administration, and pending the possible resuscitation of that series by another sponsor, the workers' compensation field is being forced to rely on fragmentary and inconsistent data in order to gain some sense of what is happening nationally.

While they cannot replace the former data series, the four measures of workers' compensation performance discussed in this article do reveal several main developments in national workers' compensation experience in the 1990s. One significant finding is that in all four of the data series, the first few years of the decade appear much different than the last few years. Thus statutory benefits were generally increasing from 1990 to 1992, but have generally fallen in more recent years. In at least a roughly parallel fashion, benefits actually paid increased for the first two policy years of the 1990s, and then substantially declined through policy year 1992–93 (the latest year with data for this series).

The employers' costs of workers' compensation also experienced two subperiods in the 1990s: up substantially through 1993, and then essentially unchanged from 1993 through 1996. Insurance industry profitability also had a bifurcated experience in the 1990s: unprofitable from 1990 through 1992, and then profitable (and increasingly so) from 1993 through 1995.

The causes of these developments are beyond the scope of this article. I will merely state the obvious; as the 1990s have progressed, the statutory protection and actual benefits paid to workers have deteriorated, while the costs for employers have stabilized and the profits for workers' compensation insurers have soared.

## E.  COMPENSATION SYSTEMS FOR SPECIAL INDUSTRIES

In addition to the state workers' compensation laws already discussed, there are important federal compensation laws applicable to federal employees and private sector employees in certain industries.

### Federal Employees' Compensation Act

The Federal Employees' Compensation Act (FECA), 5 U.S.C. §§ 8101–8193, provides compensation for the work-related injuries and illnesses of federal civilian employees. The FECA is similar in structure to state workers' compensation statutes.

FECA is a no-fault system. Compensation awards are based on loss of earning capacity. FECA awards, however, are much more generous than comparable awards under state workers' compensation laws. FECA is administered by the Office of Workers' Compensation Programs in the Department of Labor. Disputed claims are adjudicated by the Employees' Compensation Appeals Board.

### Federal Employers' Liability Act

The Federal Employers' Liability Act (FELA), 45 U.S.C. §§ 51–60, provides the exclusive remedy for the injury, illness, or death of railroad employees caused by the negligence of the employer where the employee and the railroad are engaged in interstate or foreign commerce. The Act supersedes all state laws.

Liability must be based on the employer's negligence, which is determined by federal law and is broadly construed. FELA case law has held that the injured employee must only prove that employer negligence played "any part, even the slightest" in producing the injury or death.

The employer's defenses are limited. Contributory negligence is the only defense and it will not bar recovery, but goes only to reduce the damages according to fault. Furthermore, where the injury or death was contributed to by the carrier's violation of a statute enacted for the safety of employees, contributory negligence does not apply at all.

The Act provides that the carrier is liable in damages to any employee suffering injury or death. It has been held that the employee may recover a sum that will compensate for pecuniary loss, both past and future, including loss of income, medical and other necessary expenses, as well as damages for pain and suffering. When death results, a claim also arises for the benefit of eligible dependents to recover their reasonable expectation of pecuniary benefits.

Actions may be brought in United States district court "in the district of the residence of the defendant, or in which the cause of action arose, or in which the defendant shall be doing business at the time of commencing such action" or in the state courts. Generally, once an action is initiated in state court it may not be removed.

### Jones Act

The Jones Act, 46 U.S.C. § 688, extends to "seamen" the same rights against their employers as are extended to railroad employees under the FELA. The term "seaman" is defined as "a master or member of a crew of any vessel."

### Longshoremen's and Harbor Workers' Compensation Act

The Longshoremen's and Harbor Workers' Compensation Act (LHWCA), 33 U.S.C. §§ 901–950, provides compensation to private employees working in maritime employment upon the navigable waters of the United States. The principal employments covered are stevedoring and ship service operations. The LHWCA is administered by the Office of Workers' Compensation Programs in the Department of Labor.

Benefits are provided to injured employees and, in case of death, to dependents. These benefits may not be waived, assigned, released, or commuted unless provided by the Act. Beyond compensation for injury, the employer must also furnish medical benefits for such period as the nature of the injury or the process of recovery requires. Death benefits are also available. If the injury is covered by the Act, the employer has no liability to the employees under other forms of legal action. All disputed LHWCA claims are resolved by the Benefits Review Board.

### Black Lung

The federal black lung program "was intended to rectify the historical lack of adequate state compensation schemes for miners suffering from pneumoconiosis." Hall v. Harris, 487 F.Supp. 535, 538 (W.D.Va.1980). When enacted in 1969, it was estimated that compensation would be awarded to 100,000 retired miners. Aided by some liberalizing amendments in 1972 and 1978, by the end of 1981, some 542,000 living miners, their spouses and dependents, and survivors of deceased miners, had collected more than $10 billion in benefits paid from general appropriations. A 1978 Trust Fund, financed by a producer's tonnage tax and designed to pay claims of former miners who had left mining before 1970, had a $1.4 billion deficit by 1981. See John S. Lopatto, The Federal Black Lung Program: A 1983 Primer, 85 W.Va.L.Rev. 677 (1983).

The Black Lung Benefits Amendments of 1981, 26 U.S.C. § 4121, were an attempt to restore the black lung program to solvency. They doubled the producers' tax on each ton of coal mined. They also significantly tightened the eligibility requirements for claims filed after January 1, 1982. Among other things, they deleted the presumptions of entitlement to benefits based on duration of coal mine employment and placed the burden of proving disability upon the claimant. See Robert L. Ramsey & Robert S. Habermann, The Federal Black Lung Program—The View From the Top, 87 W.Va.L.Rev. 575 (1985).

The black lung program is often cited as an example of a benefits program run amok, in which deserving claimants wait years, yet thousands of meritless claims are awarded. The problem that the program sought to address, however, is a real one, complicated by problems of causation and identifying the responsible employer. The black lung laws opted for a system of cost-sharing among employers and the public, and attempted to relieve adjudicatory problems through the use of medical presumptions. Despite the criticism of the federal black lung program, industry-specific and disease-specific compensation systems have been proposed for workers disabled by asbestos and other substances. It is unlikely that any single model can be used for more than one industry. For example, the black lung system is supported by taxes on coal. Without an ongoing industry to tax, funds must be derived from other sources. The need for such specific programs, however, can be traced directly to inadequate preventive measures and inadequate existing workers' compensation laws.

In Pittston Coal Group v. Sebben, 488 U.S. 105 (1988) (5–4), the Supreme Court invalidated interim Labor Department regulations because the Black Lung Benefits Reform Act of 1977 prohibited criteria more restrictive than those in force previously. The Department of Labor had attempted to impose a rule that only miners who had worked for ten years would be presumed to be totally disabled if afflicted by even the early stages of pneumoconiosis.

## F.   Tort Actions and "Exclusivity"

Workers' compensation laws were intended to supplant common law actions. In the language of many of the state statutes, resort to the compensation system is the "exclusive remedy" of workers and their families. An increasing number of exceptions, however, have been carved out of the exclusivity rule. These exceptions are of two main classes: actions against the employer and actions against third parties.

It is not difficult to understand why ill and injured workers, their dependents, and their lawyers would attempt to find an exception to the exclusivity rule. A 1980 study by the United States Department of Labor generated the following figures.

Comparison of Average Award for Product Liability
and Workers' Compensation

| Severity of Injury | Product Liability (Injury and Disease *) | Workers' Compensation (Injury) |
|---|---|---|
| Death | $133,000 | $57,000 |
| Permanent total | 255,000 | 23,000 |
| Permanent partial | 157,000 | 6,000 |
| Temporary total | 17,000 | 2,000 |

Source: U.S. Department of Labor, Assistant Secretary for Policy, Evaluation, and Research (ASPER), An Interim Report to Congress on Occupational Disease 94 (1980).

  * Includes a very small number of disease cases.

From the workers' perspective, tort actions are often uncertain, unfair, and protracted, but they offer the only chance for recovery of a reasonable amount of money. From the employers' perspective, tort actions are often uncertain, expensive to defend (win or lose), and undermine the viability of the entire compensation system.

## 1.  ACTIONS AGAINST THE EMPLOYER

### a.  DUAL CAPACITY

## Weinstein v. St. Mary's Medical Center

68 Cal.Rptr.2d 461 (Ct.App.1997).

■ WALKER, ASSOCIATE JUSTICE.

\* \* \*

### FACTUAL AND PROCEDURAL BACKGROUND

On October 14, 1994, [Beth] Weinstein sustained injuries to her left foot while acting in the course and scope of her duties as an employee of the Hospital. Weinstein had to use crutches due to her injury. Although still employed, she stopped working at the Hospital on November 7, 1994, and filed a workers' compensation claim. As a result of the injuries she sustained on October 14, Weinstein began drawing temporary disability and ongoing medical payments from the Hospital's workers' compensation administrator.

On January 10, 1995, while still on crutches, Weinstein went to the Hospital to receive medical treatment for her injury. After undergoing an MRI (magnetic resonance imaging) procedure on her foot, Weinstein was escorted from the MRI building to the radiology department by a medical technician employed by the Hospital. As this was happening, Weinstein slipped and fell on a watery liquid substance in one of the Hospital's hallways. The fall aggravated the previous injury to Weinstein's left foot, resulting in a condition of chronic intense pain.

On January 25, 1995, Weinstein was laid off from her job at the Hospital due to downsizing. Through Applied Risk Management, its worker's compensation carrier, the Hospital continues to pay the cost of medical treatment related to Weinstein's injuries sustained in the January 10 accident.

On December 12, 1995, Weinstein filed her complaint in this personal injury action against the Hospital. The form pleading, labeled "premises liability," seeks compensatory damages according to proof based on the January 10, 1995, accident. The Hospital filed an answer alleging as an affirmative defense the exclusivity of Weinstein's workers' compensation remedy under sections 3600, 3601, 3602 and 5300.

On May 21, 1996, the Hospital filed a motion for summary judgment based on the sole ground that Weinstein's "exclusive remedy is her ongoing Workers' Compensation action and the instant civil action is statutorily barred under Labor Code sections 3600 and 3602." In support of the motion, the Hospital argued that Weinstein was its employee at the time of the January 10, 1995, accident, and was present at the Hospital on that date in order to receive medical treatment for a previous injury suffered in the course of her employment, for which she was receiving workers' compensation benefits. On this basis, the Hospital contended that undisputed facts established the "conditions of compensation" existed between Weinstein and the Hospital at the time of her injury, her exclusive remedy was under the workers' compensation law, and her complaint against the Hospital was therefore barred under section 3602, subdivision (a). The Hospital specifically argued that the "dual capacity" doctrine is inapplicable to a premises liability action against an employer as owner or occupier of real property.

Weinstein opposed the motion for summary judgment on the grounds of the dual capacity doctrine. She argued that at the time of the accident on January 10, 1995, the Hospital was acting in its capacity as a medical facility rendering care to her as a member of the public, and not as Weinstein's employer. Thus the "conditions of compensation" were not met, and Weinstein was not restricted to the remedy of workers' compensation. At the hearing on the motion, Weinstein argued the dual capacity exception applied because she was at the Hospital as a patient rather than as an employee, and the Hospital was acting as a medical provider and not as an employer. The Hospital countered that it owed Weinstein the same duty to maintain safe premises whether she was there as a patient or an employee. Because Weinstein's claim was based on premises liability rather than professional malpractice, the Hospital argued she could not rely on the dual capacity "exception" to the rule of workers' compensation exclusivity.

The trial court agreed with the Hospital.  In its order granting the motion for summary judgment, the court stated: "[N]o triable issue of material fact exists as to the sole cause of action for premises liability against [the Hospital].  Specifically, [Weinstein] conceded that at the time of her alleged slip and fall accident on January 10, 1995, she was an employee of [the Hospital] and was receiving workers compensation benefits related to a prior industrial injury she sustained while employed by [the Hospital].  The doctrine of dual capacity is inapplicable under Labor Code section 3602[, subdivision] (a) since the [Hospital]'s duty to provide a safe premises pre-existed the injury."  The trial court entered judgment for the Hospital.  This appeal followed.

DISCUSSION

\* \* \*

Section 3852 is the origin of the "dual capacity" exception to the exclusive remedy of workers' compensation.  Under the dual capacity doctrine, an employee may recover in tort for negligent aggravation of an initial industrial injury against an employer who assumes the capacity of medical care provider by undertaking to treat the employee's injury itself. (Duprey v. Shane (1952) 249 P.2d 8)  The dual capacity doctrine is not necessarily limited to situations in which the employer's alternate second capacity toward the employer is that of medical care provider.  "[T]he decisive test of dual capacity is whether the nonemployer aspect of the employer's activity generates a different set of obligations by the employer toward the employee."

Dual capacity is thus legal shorthand for describing a situation in which a party has a duty of care that arises independently of any employment relationship.  It is based on the distinction between two entirely separate sets of duties: (1) the duties of an employer to an employee arising from the existence of an employment relationship under the workers' compensation law;  and (2) the common law (or other statutory) duties of care arising from other, nonemployment relationships, such as those of a medical care provider to a patient, or of a business or property owner to an invitee.  For example, an employer's duty to its employees requires it to provide, among other things, a safe place of employment.  This duty is distinct from the obligation of a property owner or business to an invitee, based on the common law tort duty of care.  The nature of an employer's duty in a given situation depends on the circumstances of the parties' relationship at the time of the incident.  Just because a person *is* an employee clearly does not mean he or she is *acting* as an employee under all circumstances.

In order to bear its burden of establishing the complete affirmative defense of workers' compensation exclusivity in this case, the Hospital was required to show that, at the time of her injury on January 10, 1995,

Weinstein was performing services growing out of and incidental to her employment, and was acting within the course of her employment. The fact Weinstein was an employee of the Hospital at the time of the accident is not controlling, since the nature of the Hospital's duty in this case depends not simply on whether Weinstein was an employee, but on the question whether she was acting within the course and scope of her employment at the time of her injury. Neither does the Hospital's duty to its employees to provide a safe work place have any relevance unless all the conditions of compensation were present at the time of the subject accident.

There is no dispute that Weinstein was performing employment-related services and acting within the course and scope of her employment with the Hospital at the time of her initial accidental injury on October 14, 1994. It is also undisputed Weinstein was still an employee of the Hospital at the time of her second injury on January 10, 1995. However, the Hospital had the burden on its motion for summary judgment of establishing that when Weinstein returned for treatment on January 10, 1995, she went *in her capacity as an employee.* It failed to do so. There was no evidence suggesting that any of Weinstein's actions during her visit to the Hospital on that date were within the course and scope of her employment with the Hospital, that she was performing any service growing out of or incidental to her employment, or that she was even working at all. In short, the Hospital did not bear its burden as the defendant moving for summary judgment of establishing that the "conditions of compensation" set out in section 3600, subdivision (a)(2) "concur[red]" in this case.

\* \* \*

The key distinguishing element is the distinction between an employer's duty to its employees arising from its contractual obligation as employer, and the common law duty of care of a business or property owner to an invitee. As an employer, the Hospital had a duty to provide compensation for Weinstein's injuries, but was under no duty or obligation to treat her personally. It is only when an employer imposes a contractual duty on the employee to obtain treatment from it, or itself undertakes a duty to provide such treatment as one of the direct benefits of employment, that any medical treatment it provides to the employee become a part of the employer-employee relationship. Where, as in this case, the employer simply accepts the employee as a patient and provides medical treatment separate from any of the conditions, obligations or benefits of employment, it acts in a different capacity toward the employee than that of employer.

This duty logically encompasses not only a professional duty of care in the provision of medical treatment, but a general duty of care to provide safe premises independent of any duty arising from the employment relationship.

\* \* \*

The judgment is reversed.

NOTES AND QUESTIONS

**1.** The court in *Weinstein* applied the dual capacity doctrine, which permits employees to recover from their employer if the employer "possesses a second persona so completely independent from and unrelated to his status as employer that by established standards the law recognizes it as a separate legal person." 2A Arthur Larson, Workers' Compensation Law § 72.81, at 14–290.88 (1995). See also Comment, The Dual Capacity Doctrine: Piercing the Exclusive Remedy of Workers' Compensation, 43 U.Pitt.L.Rev. 1013 (1982). The dual capacity doctrine remains the minority rule. Compare Guy v. Arthur H. Thomas Co., 378 N.E.2d 488 (Ohio 1978) (upholding rule) with Boyle v. Breme, 453 A.2d 1335 (N.J.Super.App.Div.1982) and McAlister v. Methodist Hospital, 550 S.W.2d 240 (Tenn.1977) (rejecting rule).

**2.** Most dual capacity actions are based on medical malpractice. Another minority line of cases permits employees to recover from their employer where the injury or illness was caused by a product manufactured by the employer for sale to the general public. For example, in Mercer v. Uniroyal, Inc., 361 N.E.2d 492 (Ohio 1976), an employee driving a truck for Uniroyal was injured when a Uniroyal tire on the truck blew out. In permitting the employee to maintain a dual capacity products liability action against Uniroyal the Ohio Court of Appeals stated: "It was only a matter of circumstance that the tire on the truck in which the plaintiff was riding was a Uniroyal tire rather than a Sears, Goodyear or Goodrich." 361 N.E.2d at 496. Contra, Wells v. Firestone Tire & Rubber Co., 364 N.W.2d 670 (Mich.1984). Most courts that have considered the issue of dual capacity products liability have rejected the doctrine. See, e.g., Horne v. General Electric Co., 716 F.2d 253 (4th Cir.1983) (N.C. law); Billy v. Consolidated Machine Tool Corp., 412 N.E.2d 934 (N.Y.1980). See generally Note, Dual Capacity Doctrine: Third-Party Liability of Employer-Manufacturer in Products Liability Litigation, 12 Ind.L.Rev. 553 (1979).

**3.** Injured workers and their estates have asserted a wide range of dual capacity or dual persona claims. For example, Veronica Soriano and her daughter Michelle were killed, and Soriano's coworker Sara Singhas was injured in an automobile accident. Allegedly, the accident was caused by the state's negligence in failing to properly stripe and place signs along the highway. At the time of the accident, Soriano and her husband were both public defenders employed by the state. Is a wrongful death action barred by workers' compensation because the decedent was a state employee and the complaint alleged negligence on the part of the state, or can the plaintiff use the dual capacity doctrine to sue the state because the state's negligence was in a capacity other than employer? See Singhas v. New Mexico State Highway Department, 946 P.2d 645 (N.M.1997) (held: action barred).

An employee who was injured when attacked by her employer's dog in the course of her employment sued her employer in his dual capacity as dog owner. Has she stated a cognizable exception to the exclusive remedy rule? See Barrett v. Rodgers, 562 N.E.2d 480 (Mass.1990) (held: no).

## b.  WILLFUL AND INTENTIONAL TORTS

In every jurisdiction workers' compensation is the exclusive remedy only for "accidental" injury or illness.  Thus, in cases where employees are punched, stabbed, or shot by employers, workers' compensation does not bar actions for assault and battery.  The courts, however, traditionally have required a plaintiff to prove that the employer had a specific intent to injure.

Conceptually, willful, wanton, and reckless misconduct lies between intentional and negligent conduct.  Should willful misconduct be considered an intentional act, for which workers' compensation is not a bar to recovery, or should it be considered a negligent act, for which workers' compensation is the exclusive remedy?

## Mandolidis v. Elkins Industries, Inc.

246 S.E.2d 907 (W.Va.1978).

■ McGRAW, JUSTICE:

\* \* \*

The workmen's compensation system completely supplanted the common law tort system only with respect to *negligently* caused industrial accidents, and employers and employees gained certain advantages and lost certain rights they had heretofore enjoyed.  Entrepreneurs were not given the right to carry on their enterprises without any regard to the life and limb of the participants in the endeavor and free from all common law liability.

The law of this jurisdiction recognizes a distinction between negligence, including gross negligence, and wilful, wanton, and reckless misconduct.  The latter type of conduct requires a subjective realization of the risk of bodily injury created by the activity and as such does not constitute any form of negligence.  As this Court said in Stone v. Rudolph, 127 W.Va. 335, 346, 32 S.E.2d 742, 748 (1944), citing 38 Am.Jur. 692:

> Wilfulness or wantonness imports premeditation or knowledge and consciousness that injury is likely to result from the act done or from the omission to act.  Wilful, malicious, or intentional misconduct is not, properly speaking, within the meaning of the term 'negligence.'  Negligence and wilfulness are mutually exclusive terms which imply radically different mental states.  'Negligence' conveys the idea of inadvertence as distinguished from premeditation or formed intention.  An act into which knowledge of danger and wilfulness enter is not negligence of any degree, but is wilful misconduct.

In our view when death or injury results from wilful, wanton or reckless misconduct such death or injury is no longer accidental in any meaningful sense of the word, and must be taken as having been inflicted with deliberate intention for the purposes of the workmen's compensation act.

In light of the foregoing discussion, the phrase "deliberate intent to produce such injury or death" must be held to mean that an employer loses immunity from common law actions where such employer's conduct constitutes an intentional tort [9] or wilful, wanton, and reckless misconduct. While wilful, wanton, and reckless misconduct are well-established concepts, we wish to make clear that we are using the words "wilful," "wanton," and "reckless" misconduct synonymously, and that the conduct removing the immunity bar must be undertaken with a knowledge and an appreciation of the high degree of risk of physical harm to another created thereby.  See Restatement (Second) of Torts § 500, Comment a at 587–88 (1965).[10]

Although liability is not simply a function of the degree of the risk created by the conduct without regard to the social utility of such conduct, the degree of the risk of physical harm necessary for a finding of reckless misconduct is greater than that which is necessary to make the conduct negligent.  Liability will require "a strong probability that harm may result."  Restatement (Second) of Torts § 500, Comment f at 590 (1965).

Having defined "deliberate intention" within the meaning of the Workmen's Compensation Act, we now consider the instant cases against that substantive law background.

On April 5, 1974, plaintiff Mandolidis was employed as a machine operator in the furniture manufacturing business of Elkins Industries, Inc. While operating a 10-inch table saw not equipped with a safety guard, his right hand came in contact with the saw blade resulting in the loss of two fingers and part of the hand itself.

On April 1, 1976, Mandolidis filed a complaint against Elkins Industries, Inc., in the Circuit Court of Randolph County, alleging that the table saw he was operating when he was injured was not equipped with a safety guard, although it was well known by the defendant that in the defendant's industry that this constituted a violation of federal and state safety laws and accepted industry standards; that the defendant had actual knowledge of the consequences of running such machinery without safety guards, because employees other than the plaintiff had previously suffered injuries as a result of the lack of such guards; that the plaintiff objected to operating the saw without a guard and was told by the defendant, through its agent, to operate the machine or be fired from his job; that this order

9. We adopt the Restatement Second of Torts definition of "intent," "Intentional * * * denote[s] that the actor desires to cause consequences of his act, or that he believes that the consequences are substantially certain to result from it." Restatement (Second) of Torts § 8A (1965).  See also W. Prosser, Handbook of the Law of Torts, 312 (4th ed. 1971).

10. Proof of the subjective realization of the risk may and must generally be proved by circumstantial evidence. For example, the defendant's knowledge of the existence and contents of federal and state safety laws and regulations is competent evidence.  Prior deaths or injuries as a result of the risk would certainly be relevant.

was issued by the defendant in wilful, wanton, malicious, and deliberate disregard for the well-being of the plaintiff with a deliberate intention to injure or kill him; that a short period of time before plaintiff's injury, federal inspectors had cited the defendant for violations of the Occupational Health and Safety Act because the table saw involved did not have a guard; that the inspectors put tags on the machine forbidding its use until equipped with a guard; that defendant installed a guard of the incorrect type and then shortly thereafter ordered it removed in wilful, malicious, and deliberate disregard of federal and state safety laws; that the defendant fired an employee who refused to operate the saw without a guard; that the defendant ordered employees to operate machines without guards in order to improve production speed and thus increase profits in utter and malicious disregard of the well-being of the plaintiff; that the aforesaid actions and inactions were taken by defendant with the deliberate intention to kill or injure plaintiff, and that the defendant had actual notice and knowledge of the dangerous condition of the unguarded saw and the injuries of other employees caused by that condition; that defendant wholly, wilfully, wrongfully, deliberately, maliciously and with intent to injure or kill plaintiff refused to provide plaintiff with reasonably safe equipment and a reasonably safe place to work; and that the conduct of the defendant was such as to constitute a wanton, wilful, and malicious disregard of the life and limb of its employees so as to warrant a specific finding of a deliberate intent to inflict bodily harm or injury upon its employees in general and the plaintiff in particular.

The defendant filed a motion to dismiss under R.C.P. 12(b) accompanied by affidavits denying any deliberate intent to injure the plaintiff, and contending that a subscriber to the Workmen's Compensation Fund, it was immune from a common law damage action. An affidavit by the President and General Manager of the defendant corporation stated that defendant was a subscriber to the Workmen's Compensation Fund, and denied both the allegation that the defendant deliberately intended to injure the plaintiff and the allegation that he, or anyone at his direction or in his presence, ever threatened or intimidated the plaintiff concerning the operation of his machine. In a second affidavit, defendant's foreman admitted there was no safety guard on the table saw at the time of plaintiff's injury but expressly denied that he or anyone in his presence had ever ordered the plaintiff to remove the safety guard, or to operate the saw without a safety guard. Similarly, he denied knowledge of the plaintiff being threatened with the loss of his job unless he operated the unguarded saw. The foreman's affidavit also asserted that just prior to the occurrence in question he had been assisting the plaintiff by acting as an "off bearer"; that he had to leave for a few minutes so he expressly instructed the plaintiff not to continue to operate the saw alone; and that plaintiff did operate the saw alone resulting in the injury complained of to his hand.

Plaintiff deposed seven former employees of Elkins Industries. Five of these employees, including the President and the steward of a union which once represented employees of Elkins Industries, Inc., indicated that they had complained on numerous occasions to the plant foreman and the plant manager regarding the lack of guards on the table saws. The steward indicated that on one occasion when he complained about the lack of saw guards, the plant foreman just "hee hawed around about it." The former union president indicated that she informed the plant manager that the absence of saw guards was a violation of law, but he "just shrugged his shoulders." Three former employees indicated that they had seen the plant foreman remove the guards from the saws. The former plant safety inspector indicated that he had shut down and placed an out-of-order sign on a guardless saw, but the foreman "tore off" the sign and placed the saw back in operation. Three of the former employees indicated that they had been told by the foreman that the guards slowed down production. In his deposition, the plaintiff contradicted the foreman's claim that he told the plaintiff not to continue to operate the saw alone. The plaintiff's version was corroborated by the deposition of another employee working near the plaintiff when the injury occurred.

Four of the former employees, including the plaintiff, indicated that the foreman's instructions via the plant manager were that anyone refusing to run a saw without a guard would be "sent home" or fired. One former employee indicated that he had been fired for refusing to run a saw without a guard. These assertions expressly contradicted the affidavits of the foreman and plant manager. Plaintiff's deposition expressly contradicted the assertion contained in the plant manager's affidavit that the allegation of deliberate intent in the plaintiff's complaint was made only to circumvent the immunity bar. The former union president indicated that she informed the plant manager that the plaintiff had been injured on a guardless saw and his reply was, "So what?" "He's getting compensation."

On August 17, 1976, the trial court, upon consideration of all matters presented to it, determined that "a deliberate intent to injure plaintiff was lacking," sustained the defendant's motion to dismiss, and dismissed the action with prejudice.

\* \* \*

Notwithstanding the style of defendant's motions to dismiss and the wording of the dismissal order \* \* \* the trial courts' consideration of affidavits and depositions converted the motions to dismiss to motions for summary judgment under Rule 56. Accordingly, the sole issue is whether the trial court \* \* \* erred in concluding there was no genuine issue of material fact and the defendants were entitled to judgment as a matter of law.

\* \* \*

The record in *Mandolidis* discloses that there were material facts in issue. Was the plaintiff told by a company agent that he would be discharged if he refused to run an unguarded saw? Did the foreman tell the plaintiff to wait until his return before continuing to run the saw? The circuit court's order unfortunately does not contain findings of fact or conclusions of law, but it is clear from the record that there were facts in issue. Accordingly, implicit in the court's ruling is the judgment that there were no material facts in issue. This Court cannot agree. The plaintiff is entitled to prove these facts in support of his case, because these facts render the desired inference, when taken together with other facts the plaintiff clearly intends to prove, i.e., that the defendant acted with deliberate intent, more probable than it would be without those facts.

We are of the view that complicated industrial "accidents," wherein the state of mind of company representatives is critical, seldom lend themselves to disposition by summary judgment, and where there is any doubt such a motion should be refused. Conclusory affidavits simply denying the existence of the requisite intent, obviously make no contribution to the factual development of the litigated event and, therefore, provide no assistance to the trial court in determining whether a genuine issue of material fact exists. It is for this reason that Rule 56(e) provides that affidavits "shall set forth such facts as would be admissible in evidence."

The trial court in *Mandolidis* "determine[d] that the deliberate intent to injure * * * is lacking." The Court thus found that even if all plaintiff's facts were taken as true plaintiff could not as a matter of law meet the evidentiary burden of proof with regard to a necessary element of his cause of action. The court determined that even if all of plaintiff's facts were taken as true, they would not support an inference that the defendant employer acted with "deliberate intent." In other words, reasonable men could not infer from all those facts the necessary intent. We do not believe that reasonable men could not infer the necessary intent from the facts in *Mandolidis*. Accordingly, the court's determination of this issue was erroneous. For these reasons the court's final order in *Mandolidis* was in error.

Accordingly, we hereby reverse and remand all three cases to the respective circuit courts for further proceedings consistent with this opinion.

## NOTES AND QUESTIONS

**1.** The court requires subjective intent and objective evidence that there was a strong probability that harm would result. Does the harm itself, the severity of consequences, have to be great?

**2.** *Mandolidis* remains a distinct minority rule. A more typical case in this area is Grillo v. National Bank of Washington, 540 A.2d 743 (D.C.1988). The plaintiff's decedent, a bank teller, was shot and killed by a bank robber during a holdup. The bank had safety glass enclosures around the tellers for security reasons, but when the bank was remodeled the glass was removed so that the bank would look the way it did at the turn of the century. Teller requests for bullet-proof glass were rejected by the bank. In affirming the dismissal of an action based on intentional tort, the court held that workers' compensation was the exclusive remedy. In order to proceed under the intentional tort exception, the plaintiff was required to prove that the defendant-employer acted with an intent to injure the plaintiff's decedent.

**3.** The plaintiff in *Mandolidis* actually spelled his name Manolidis. The court erroneously added an extra "d" to his name. Critics would no doubt assert that this was the least of the court's errors in the case. This was a highly controversial decision and in 1983 the West Virginia legislature amended the workers' compensation statute to restrict the kinds of cases that can be brought under this theory and to preclude the award of punitive damages. W.Va.Code § 23–4–2.

**4.** In footnote 10 the court indicates that knowledge of the existence and contents of federal and state safety laws and regulations is relevant to the issue of intent. What effect, if any, should the finding of a willful OSHA violation have? What about a criminal conviction under § 17(e) of OSHA? For a further discussion of the role of OSHA in tort litigation, see Teal v. E. I. Du Pont de Nemours & Co., infra p. 902.

**5.** Suppose that *Eckis,* supra p. 830, had arisen in West Virginia. Would Sea World be liable under *Mandolidis* because Burgess failed to disclose that Shamu was conditioned to be ridden only by persons wearing wetsuits, that Shamu had attacked other people who attempted to ride her in an ordinary bathing suit, and that Shamu had been behaving erratically?

**6.** Another intentional tort theory, fraudulent concealment, permits an employee to recover for injury or illness caused by the fraud or deceit of the employer. In Johns-Manville Products Corp. v. Contra Costa Superior Court, 612 P.2d 948 (Cal.1980), an asbestos worker died of work-related lung cancer. His heirs brought an action against the decedent's employer alleging that the employer fraudulently concealed from the decedent, doctors retained to treat the decedent, and the state government that the decedent was suffering from asbestos-related disease. The Supreme Court of California held that these allegations stated a valid cause of action for aggravation of the disease, although an action for contracting the disease would be barred by workers' compensation. See Teklinsky v. Ottawa Silica Corp., 583 F.Supp. 31 (E.D.Mich.1983); In re Johns-Manville Asbestosis Cases, 511 F.Supp. 1229 (N.D.Ill.1981).

## 2. ACTIONS AGAINST THIRD PARTIES

Even under such exceptions as dual capacity and intentional acts, tort actions against the employer of an injured or ill employee are difficult to maintain. Therefore, workers have frequently sued "third parties." There are three lines of cases.

First, actions may be brought against other employers that are not so closely connected with the primary employer as to be "co-employers." Some examples are as follows: (1) an action may be brought against an affiliated company, such as where a parent company assumed the duty of providing safety and health information and services; (2) although most states make general contractors liable for the workers' compensation of employees of subcontractors, thereby giving the general contractor immunity, some states permit damage actions against general contractors by employees of subcontractors; (3) some states also permit employees of a general contractor or a subcontractor to sue other subcontractors; (4) an action may lie against an architect, engineer, or safety and health consultant; (5) an action may be brought against a property owner, especially in states with scaffolding or structural work acts which create a nondelegable duty on the part of the owner to provide safe scaffolds; and (6) in a minority of jurisdictions a negligence action may be brought against a co-employee. The key to these actions is proof that a duty was owed to the worker by the defendant. See generally Mark A. Rothstein, Occupational Safety and Health Law § 507 (4th ed. 1998).

Second, actions have been brought against insurance companies, labor unions, and government agencies alleging that the negligent performance of a safety and health inspection at the worker's place of employment was the proximate cause of an injury or illness. About half the states permit actions against insurers, but actions against unions are rarely successful because of preemption by the federal labor laws and other defenses, and actions against federal and state governments are clouded by sovereign immunity and other doctrines. See generally Mark A. Rothstein, Occupational Safety and Health Law §§ 510–512 (4th ed. 1998).

In United Steelworkers of America v. Rawson, 495 U.S. 362 (1990), following a tragic fire that killed 91 miners in Kellogg, Idaho, the plaintiffs sued the union in state court on two theories. First, plaintiffs alleged that the union was negligent in performing inspections of the mine to identify safety violations. Second, plaintiffs claimed that the union breached its duty of fair representation. The Supreme Court of Idaho had held that the duty of fair representation claim was properly dismissed for failure to plead facts alleging more than mere negligence and the Supreme Court agreed. With regard to the common law negligence claim, the Supreme Court reversed the Supreme Court of Idaho and held that the common law negligence action was preempted by § 301 of the Labor Management Relations Act. The union's right to participate and its duties arising from that right came solely from the collective bargaining agreement.

Third, by far the most important third party actions are products liability suits brought against the manufacturers of defective products that caused an injury or illness in the workplace.

## York v. Union Carbide Corp.

586 N.E.2d 861 (Ind.Ct.App.1992).

■ STATON, JUDGE.

Denise York, administrator of the estate of her late husband Michael, appeals the trial court grant of summary judgment in favor of Union Carbide Corp. in York's wrongful death action. York filed a product liability claim against Union Carbide sounding in negligence and strict liability. To support her contention that summary judgment was not appropriate, York presents four issues for our consideration, which we consolidate and rephrase as:

  I. Whether Union Carbide fulfilled its duty to warn the decedent of the hazards associated with the use of its product.

  II. Whether York's cause of action is preempted by federal law.

Affirmed.

At the time of the accident that took his life, Michael York was employed as a millwright at U.S. Steel Corp. (USX). In March of 1986, USX shut down production of a 32–foot deep steel-making furnace known as the "Evelyn vessel" to reline its brick interior. The vessel is located in the No. 1 Basic Oxygen Process ("BOP") shop at USX's Gary, Indiana facility. As part of the "reline" procedure, scaffolding is erected to support an industrial elevator carrying workers from a repair platform, located about eight feet above the top of the vessel, to the vessel floor.

When the Evelyn vessel is in production, argon gas [2] supplied by Union Carbide flows through a main supply line, and then is injected into molten steel from the bottom of the chamber through 16 nozzles. Argon is pumped into the vessel to churn the molten steel, a process that causes impurities to rise to the top where they can be drawn off.

When the vessel is not in production, the flow of argon gas through the main supply line is automatically shut off and diverted to a small "bypass" supply line, also leading to the 16 nozzles. The purpose of the bypass line is to supply a small amount of argon gas to the chamber to keep the nozzles clear of debris. Union Carbide did not participate in the design, installation, maintenance, or operation of the piping system or its controls.

During the reline procedure, the pipelines carrying argon to the bottom of the vessel were disconnected. On March 29, 1986, the argon hoses were reconnected, though work on the reline was not completed until two days later. Immediately, argon gas began flowing through the bypass line into the chamber, but went undetected because air was circulated into the vessel by a high volume air mover. At 3:30 p.m. on March 31, the reline was completed and the air mover was disconnected and removed. About an hour later, a USX technician conducted an oxygen deficiency test by lowering a sensor into the vessel from the repair platform located some 40 feet above the vessel floor. The technician attempted to register the oxygen content at a "breathing zone" of five to six feet above the vessel floor, but apparently took a reading from the ten to twelve foot level. This test indicated that there was no oxygen deficiency.

Shortly thereafter, Michael York and a co-worker, Costas Lalios, took the elevator to the bottom of the vessel in order to prepare the scaffolding

---

 **2.** Argon is a colorless, odorless, non-toxic inert gas. However, because it is much heavier than oxygen and other gases found in the air we breathe, argon will displace oxygen when introduced into a confined space such as the Evelyn vessel, much like water poured into a pitcher will displace air. Thus, argon can cause rapid asphyxiation in a confined space that is not adequately ventilated.

for removal. Ten to fifteen minutes later, workers on the repair platform observed York and Lalios lying motionless on the vessel floor. It was later determined that argon gas had accumulated in the lower part of the vessel, displacing the oxygen and causing the deaths of York and Lalios by asphyxiation.

\* \* \*

## I.  FEDERAL PREEMPTION

\* \* \*

Whether federal law preempts state action in a particular case is a question of congressional intent. Federal preemption may be found if: (1) on the face of a federal law, Congress expressly stated an intent to preempt a state law; (2) the comprehensive and pervasive nature of the federal regulatory scheme indicates an implied intent to preempt state law; or (3) the state law stands as an obstacle to the accomplishment and execution of the full purposes and objectives of Congress. Administrative regulations promulgated pursuant to congressional authorization have the same preemptive effect as federal statutes.

Federal Hazard Communication Standards (FHCS) were promulgated under the authority of the Occupational Health and Safety Act of 1970 (The OSH Act, or OSHA), 29 U.S.C.A. § 651 *et seq.* (1985), for the stated purpose of ensuring

> that the hazards of all chemicals produced or imported are evaluated, and that information concerning their hazards is transmitted to employers and employees. This transmittal of information is to be accomplished by means of comprehensive hazard communication programs, which are to include container labeling and other forms or warning, material safety data sheets and employee training.

29 C.F.R. § 1920.1200(a)(1).

The FHCS further provides that:

> This occupational safety and health standard is intended to address *comprehensively* the issue of evaluating the potential hazards of chemicals, and communicating information concerning hazards and appropriate protective measures to employees, *and to preempt any legal requirements of a state, or political subdivision of a state, pertaining to the subject....* Under [29 U.S.C.A. § 667], *no state or political subdivision of a state may adopt or enforce, through any court or agency, any requirement relating to the issue addressed by this Federal standard, except pursuant to a Federally-approved state plan.*

29 C.F.R. § 1920.1200(a)(2) (emphasis added). This language would seem to indicate that strict liability and negligence claims predicated on a manufacturer's failure to provide adequate warnings have indeed been preempted by federal regulations.

One court facing a substantially similar question, however, came to the opposite result. In Pedraza v. Shell Oil Co. (1st Cir.1991), 942 F.2d 48, Cruz Pedraza filed a civil action alleging that he developed respiratory ailments from workplace exposure to epichlorohydrin (ECH), a toxic chemical manufactured by Shell Oil Company. Pedraza asserted various theories of negligence and strict liability, including allegations that Shell had failed to adequately warn of the dangers of exposure to ECH. The district court concluded that the OSH Act preempted Pedraza's failure to warn claims, but the First Circuit Court of Appeals reversed, holding that the OSH Act's "savings clause" evidences an intent to spare state tort laws from preemption.

The OSH Act's preemption language is expressed in the following provision:

> Nothing in this chapter shall prevent any State agency or court from asserting jurisdiction under State law over any occupational safety or health issue with respect to which no standard is in effect under [29 U.S.C.A. § 655].

29 U.S.C.A. § 667(a). By negative implication, if a federal standard for a particular occupational safety or health issue is in effect under the OSH Act, a state court may not assume jurisdiction over such an issue. The preemptive effect of this section is, however, tempered by the following language from the savings clause of 29 U.S.C.A. § 653:

> Nothing in this chapter shall be construed to supersede or in any manner affect any workmen's compensation law or to enlarge or diminish or affect in any other manner the common law or statutory rights, duties, or liabilities of employers and employees under any law with respect to injuries, diseases, or death of employees arising out of, or in the course of, employment.

29 U.S.C.A. § 653(b)(4).

The *Pedraza* court observed that there is a "solid consensus" that the savings clause operates to save state tort rules from preemption. Thus, although none of the cases cited by the first circuit dealt with product liability claims, much less those based on failure to warn theories, we agree with the *Pedraza* court's holding that the savings clause operates to exempt tort law claims from preemption. Because we find that state tort actions are expressly saved by the OSH Act, we will not address whether such actions are impliedly preempted.

## II. ADEQUACY OF WARNINGS

York next argues that a factual dispute exists regarding the adequacy of Union Carbide's warnings to the decedent of the potential dangers of argon gas. Union Carbide responds that the undisputed facts reveal that adequate warnings were given.

In Indiana, actions for strict liability in tort are governed by the Product Liability Act, IND.CODE 33–1–1.5–1 *et seq.* (1988).

\* \* \*

York contends that these provisions require Union Carbide to provide warnings and instructions directly to USX personnel, and that Union Carbide could not rely on USX to disseminate the information to its employees.

York relies chiefly on two cases for the general proposition that a manufacturer's duty to warn of the dangerousness of a product is nondelegable. In the first, Hoffman v. E.W. Bliss Co. (1983), Ind., 448 N.E.2d 277, our supreme court addressed trial court instructions on a manufacturer's duty to warn. The court found that the jury was correctly instructed that a manufacturer must provide warnings that will reach the ultimate user or consumer. Noting that the product in *Hoffman* had a latent defect, and did not operate as either the manufacturer or the plaintiff's employer intended, the court further held that, where a latent design or manufacturing defect becomes operable, "the manufacturer can *never* delegate to a second party the duty to warn...." Thus, argues York, Union Carbide was required to personally inform the decedent of the dangers of argon gas.

This argument relies on the mistaken assumption that the argon gas supplied by Union Carbide has a manufacturing or design defect. Argon is a chemical element, one of the more than 100 substances that constitute all matter. Union Carbide merely extracts the argon from other elements and supplies it in bulk to USX and other customers via pipeline. There is absolutely no evidence to warrant the inference that the argon was defective or contaminated, or anything other than that which USX had ordered or Union Carbide supplied. A manufacturer is legally bound to design and build products which are reasonably safe for the purpose for which they are intended. It was never intended for argon gas to come into contact with USX personnel. Stated in terms of the Product Liability Act, the argon gas was not in a condition "not contemplated by reasonable persons among those considered expected users or consumers" of the product, nor was it "unreasonably dangerous to the expected user or consumer *when used in reasonably expectable ways of handling or consumption.*" IC 33–1–1.5–2.5(a) (emphasis added). As a matter of law, the introduction of argon into the chamber at a time the vessel was shut down for repairs or maintenance was not a reasonably expected use of the product. Thus, the only manner in which argon could have been defective in this case, under Indiana's product liability law, is under the provision for a manufacturer's failure to warn, IC 33–1–1.5–2.5(b).

The court in *Hoffman* noted that cases involving design and manufacturing defects are distinguishable from failure to warn cases; in the latter case, a manufacturer can fulfill its duty to warn by informing employees responsible for receiving and setting up the product of dangers associated with the use of the product. This is so where, for instance, the product is one installed as a component of a multifaceted operation, and the manufacturer has no control over the work space, the instrumentality causing the injury or the hiring, instruction or placement of personnel. Thus, the manner of adequately warning employees in such a situation could be determined only *after* a given type of operation had been chosen and constructed.

\* \* \*

York also argues that Union Carbide was obligated to fully train USX technicians on the proper method of testing a confined space for oxygen deficiency, citing to the Product Liability Act requirement that the manufacturer give "reasonably complete instructions on proper use of the product." However, the "product" in this case is the argon gas; Union Carbide did not supply the gas testing equipment as York implies. Moreover, as Union Carbide points out, York offers no authority for the proposition that a manufacturer has a legal duty to train the employees of its buyers. Finally, it is undisputed that USX in fact instructed their technicians to take a reading in the normal breathing zone of five to six feet above the floor of the Evelyn vessel. The evidence leads solely to the conclusion that USX trained and certified gas testers took an oxygen reading from above the normal breathing zone. These facts have no bearing on Union Carbide's duty to warn.

\* \* \*

It is clear that USX had a great deal of knowledge concerning the effect of argon gas in a confined space. Thus, no additional warning or literature that could be furnished to USX by Union Carbide could have improved upon USX's understanding of the characteristics of the product. Because York does not raise a material issue of fact in this regard, we must conclude that the warnings issued by Union Carbide were adequate as a matter of law.

The trial court is affirmed.

NOTES AND QUESTIONS

**1.** The essential problem that York cannot escape is that the party with the primary or exclusive duty to the plaintiff's decedent was USX, and USX is not amenable to suit. As to Union Carbide, the argon gas itself was not defective, so the plaintiff's only basis for establishing liability is the alleged failure to warn. Where the product comes by pipeline, what degree of warnings must be placed on the pipe? Does the plaintiff expect Union Carbide to conduct warning sessions in person on USX property? Suppose Union Carbide knew that USX was not supplying adequate warnings, would the duty change? Would Union Carbide have a duty to stop supplying the argon gas until effective warnings were given to employees?

**2.** Failure to warn was the theory used by plaintiffs in the most important products liability cases involving workplace injuries and illnesses—the asbestos cases.

By 1982, the asbestos industry and its insurers had incurred costs of $1 billion in products liability suits. The principle theory of the plaintiffs is that the manufacturers knew that asbestos was dangerous but failed to warn the users. In the leading case of Borel v. Fibreboard Paper Products

Corp., 493 F.2d 1076 (5th Cir.1973), cert. denied, 419 U.S. 869 (1974), the Fifth Circuit stated: "This duty to warn extends to all users and consumers, including the common worker in the shop or in the field."

**3.**  On August 26, 1982, the Manville Corporation, the world's largest asbestos mining and manufacturing firm, filed a petition for reorganization under Chapter 11 of the Federal Bankruptcy Code.  Manville cited the fact that it was involved in more than 16,500 asbestos-related lawsuits and estimated an additional 32,000 lawsuits (with more than $2 billion in estimated potential liability) over the next 20 years.  At the time of the filing Manville had more than $2 billion in annual sales and more than $1 billion in assets.  Final disposition of the petition and all the cases stayed by the filing remains ongoing in the courts.

**4.**  The estates of three employees who died of cancer between 1979 and 1984 brought wrongful death actions against the supplier of chemical products handled by the decedents' employer.  The actions were not brought until 1989, but the plaintiffs alleged that they did not learn until 1987 that methylene chloride, to which the decedents had been exposed, could cause cancer.  They alleged, among other things, that the defendant had failed to warn about the danger of exposure.  The Georgia Supreme Court held that the actions were barred by the two-year statute of limitations, and it expressly refused to adopt a discovery rule that would have extended the limitations period.  Miles v. Ashland Chemical Co., 410 S.E.2d 290 (Ga.1991).

**5.**  Workers bringing products liability actions face a variety of scientific, procedural, and evidentiary problems.  Some of these problems are noted in the following article.

### Elinor P. Schroeder & Sidney A. Shapiro, *Responses to Occupational Disease: The Role of Markets, Regulation, and Information*

72 Geo.L.J. 1231 (1984).

One important obstacle to tort recovery is that the employer, who may be the most culpable party, is normally immune from the suit under the exclusive remedy provisions of workers' compensation.  Innovative plaintiffs have made some inroads into the exclusivity rule, but most jurisdictions have not created exceptions of any significance.  Therefore, injured workers must find some third party, such as a supplier or manufacturer of raw materials, who may be at least partially responsible for the injury.  In most states, a third-party manufacturer or supplier who is held liable to the plaintiff cannot seek contribution from the employer, even though the employer may also have been at fault.  Moreover, in all but three states the payor of workers' compensation benefits gains subrogation rights in the employee's third-party suit and will be reimbursed by any tort recovery the employee receives.  The existence of these subrogation rights can further reduce the incentive of the employer to eliminate workplace hazards and can impose costs on the third party which are disproportionate to its responsibility.

Statutes of limitation present a second obstacle to recovery. Although most tort statutes of limitation begin to run from the time the cause of action "accrues," jurisdictions differ about when that moment occurs. Several states follow a "last exposure rule," under which the cause of action accrues on the date of the last exposure to the harmful substance. Another approach is that the claim accrues when the damage is capable of ascertainment. The vast majority of jurisdictions adhere to some form of a third rule, the discovery rule, but there are various formulations as to when "discovery" occurs. The most common approach is that the statute begins to run when the plaintiff knew or reasonably should have known of the injury. Another formulation is that the statute starts to run when the plaintiff knew or should have known that the injury existed and that it was probably caused by the conduct of the defendant. Still another formulation is that the cause of action accrues when the disease actually manifests itself.

These variations in statute of limitation rules create great confusion, and the position a particular court will take is not always predictable. Further, even when a decision has been made, the court's formulation of its rule may not always be clear and capable of easy application to later cases. This legal uncertainty, coupled with the necessary factual determinations, requires extensive threshold litigation which can encourage defendants to resist claims and can deter plaintiffs from pursuing them.

The third obstacle is that many plaintiffs cannot meet the burden of proof assigned to them. Occupational disease claims generally proceed on a theory of strict liability, although claims of negligence and breach of warranty may be asserted as well. Most strict liability claims assert a duty to warn of hazards associated with the product. Since the disease-causing nature of most chemicals and dusts is inherent, these products are typically "unavoidably unsafe," and any manufacturer's liability results not from the dangers inherent in the products, but from the failure to give adequate warnings of those dangers. In most jurisdictions, manufacturers are required to warn only of reasonably foreseeable risks. Even though a defendant is held to the standard of an expert in its field, plaintiffs may not be able to show that knowledge of the risks was reasonably available at the time of manufacture, many years before the illness. Recently, however, a few courts have rejected this "state of the art" defense and have held that defendants could be liable for failure to warn of dangers that were undiscoverable at the time of manufacture. These decisions remove one of the major obstacles to a successful suit because most reported toxic substance cases have involved products for which no warning was given.

A fourth obstacle to tort suits is that plaintiffs may have no idea who manufactured the toxic substances to which they were exposed. In fact, workers often do not even know the names of the chemicals in the workplace, much less their manufacturer. * * *

Delay, the fifth obstacle, is perhaps the biggest problem faced by workers who wish to bring third-party tort suits. Defendants have a strong incentive to fight toxic substance suits, and vigorous and protracted defenses can be mounted because of the uncertainty of the law. For instance, the Chapter 11 bankruptcy filing of the Manville Corporation showed that the company had spent $24.5 million in legal fees defending tort claims of asbestos victims, as compared to payments of $24 million to claimants. Plaintiffs who need money desperately because of the death or disability of the principal wage earner in the family are often induced to accept relatively low settlements rather than litigate for years.

In spite of these obstacles, the number of tort suits appears to be growing, probably in large part because of the prospect, however slim, of a recovery greater than the meager amounts paid under workers' compensation. One important reaction to this increased litigation has been the Chapter 11 reorganization petitions filed by three currently healthy corporations, chief among them the Manville Corporation. Attacked as "fraudulent" and a "perversion" of the bankruptcy laws, these filings seek to have current and future liabilities to asbestos claimants consolidated and discharged. The petitions may ultimately be dismissed as filed in bad faith, or the bankruptcy courts may decide they lack the authority to terminate the claims of future plaintiffs. In the meantime, however, asbestos litigation against other co-defendants has proceeded. These companies, all smaller than Manville, must now bear the entire burden of defense in pending and future litigation, and in states which impose joint and several liability they must pay the entire amount of any judgments.

## 3.  EFFECT OF OSHA STANDARDS

## Teal v. E.I. DuPont de Nemours & Co.

728 F.2d 799 (6th Cir.1984).

■ CELEBREZZE, SENIOR CIRCUIT JUDGE.

Richard and Tina Teal brought this diversity action against E.I. DuPont deNemours and Company to recover for injuries sustained as a consequence of an accident that occurred at DuPont's plant in Old Hickory, Tennessee. At the conclusion of a five day jury trial, a verdict was returned in favor of DuPont. On appeal, appellants raise two issues which merit discussion. First, appellants claim that the trial court erred by instructing the jury that a landowner owes no duty to invitees to furnish protection against hazards on the landowner's premises. Second, appellants assert that the trial court erred by refusing to instruct the jury on the issue of negligence per se. Although the instruction concerning a landowner's duty to invitees is ambiguous, we conclude that such ambiguity is harmless. We hold, however, that the court's refusal to instruct the jury on the issue of negligence per se was improper and prejudicial. Accordingly, this case is affirmed in part, reversed in part and remanded for a trial solely on the issue of negligence per se.

The Daniel Construction Company (Daniel Construction) entered into a contract with DuPont to dismantle and remove hydraulic bailers from DuPont's plant.   The bailers occupied three floor levels within the plant and were used to compress synthetic Dacron® fiber.   Hydraulic "rams" provided the force necessary to compress the fiber.   The rams were located below the ground floor in a "bailer pit", access to which was provided by a straight and permanently affixed ladder.   On March 14, 1979, Richard Teal, an employee of Daniel Construction, fell approximately seventeen feet from the ladder to the floor of the bailer pit.   Richard Teal brought this action against DuPont alleging that his fall and injuries were the direct and proximate result of DuPont's negligence.[3]

One of appellant's negligence theories concerned DuPont's duty to invitees to "furnish protection against dangers" on DuPont's property. Initially, the trial court instructed the jury that a landowner's duty to invitees is "to give warning of, or use ordinary care to furnish protection against such dangers to employees of the contractor who are without actual or constructive notice of the dangers."   After the jury had retired for deliberations, it requested additional instructions.   Specifically, the jury asked the following question:

> Do DuPont employees wear safety belts on ladders: was it Du-
> Pont's responsibility to see that Richard Teal wore a safety belt?

The trial court again instructed the jury that a landowner owes a duty to invitees "to give warning of or use ordinary care to furnish protection against" dangers on the landowner's property.   The court further instructed the jury, however, that "an owner or occupant of land who has an independent contractor or who employs employees to perform work owes a duty to warn of hazards, but he is not under a duty to specify the manner in which those hazards should be avoided."   Appellants claim that the latter instruction is erroneous.

Appellants' second argument concerns their negligence per se claim. During the course of the trial, appellants introduced evidence which indicated that DuPont's ladder failed to conform to federal regulations promulgated pursuant to the Occupational Safety and Health Act of 1970.   Specifically, OSHA regulations require a clearance of not less than seven inches "from the centerline of the rungs, cleats or steps to the nearest permanent object in back of the ladder."   The uncontroverted testimony of Robert B. Taylor, a director of the Division of Occupational Safety and Health for the Tennessee Department of Labor, indicated that the ladder failed to conform with the seven inch clearance requirement.   Because DuPont had breached a regulatory obligation, appellants requested the trial court to instruct the jury on the issue of negligence per se.   The trial court refused; instead, it

---

**3.** In their complaint, appellants assert that DuPont acted negligently by failing to warn of latent dangers on DuPont's premises.   Alternatively, appellants claim that DuPont breached its duty to protect against dangers in its plant.   Additionally, appellants assert that DuPont failed to provide a safe place to work, failed to provide safe equipment and proper safety devices, and failed to inspect properly its equipment.   Finally, appellants allege that DuPont's breach of an OSHA regulation is negligence per se.

informed the jury that the OSHA regulation "may be considered * * * as some evidence * * * of the (appropriate) standard of care." Appellants claim that the district court's refusal to charge on the issue of negligence per se is reversible error.

* * *

The second issue on appeal concerns the trial court's refusal to instruct the jury on the issue of negligence per se. Pursuant to Tennessee case law, a breach of a duty imposed by statute or regulation is negligence per se if the party injured is a member of the class of persons the statute or regulation was intended to protect. In this case, the parties agree that Richard Teal was, at the time of the accident, an employee of Daniel Construction, an independent contractor, and that Teal fell from a permanently affixed ladder in DuPont's plant. Further, the parties agree that the OSHA regulation established a duty owed by DuPont and that DuPont breached its duty to conform with the specifications of the regulation.[4] Accordingly, the primary dispute is whether an employee of an independent contractor is a member of the class of persons that the OSHA regulation was intended to protect.

DuPont argues that the stated purposes for the Occupational Safety and Health Act of 1970 reveal that Congress did not intend to impose a duty upon employers to protect the safety of an independent contractor's employees who work in the employer's plant. In support of this proposition, DuPont relies upon the plain language of the Act which provides that "each employer shall furnish to each of *his* employees employment and a place of employment which are free from recognized hazards that are causing or are likely to cause death or serious physical harm to *his* employees." Although DuPont's legal position is not without support, we believe that an employer's duty to comply with OSHA regulations is broader than DuPont suggests.

---

**4.** DuPont concedes that it breached the regulatory obligation. DuPont argues, however, that its breach is "de minimus", and, thus, that the variance from the clearance specifications established by 29 C.F.R. Sec. 1910.27(c)(4) is not negligence per se. In contrast, appellants claim that even a slight variation from standards established by regulation is negligence per se. Furthermore, appellants argue that the trial court erred by permitting any testimony which characterized DuPont's breach of duty as "de minimus." We agree with appellants' assertion that even a de minimus breach of a statutory or regulatory duty is negligence per se. We disagree, however, with appellants' claim that the court permitted improperly testimony concerning the de minimus nature of DuPont's breach of duty.

If the plaintiff proves that the defendant breached a statutory or regulatory obligation, and that the statutory or regulatory duty was enacted for the plaintiff's benefit, then the defendant is considered negligent as a matter of law. A determination that the defendant is negligent per se, however, does not require necessarily an award of damages. Negligence per se only establishes a defendant's duty and breach thereof. The question whether the breach of the duty is a proximate cause of a plaintiff's injury and the question concerning the extent, if any, of injury are jury questions that survive a determination that the defendant is negligent per se. In our view, testimony that a defendant's breach of duty is de minimus concerns the issue of proximate cause, and thus, is admissible.

Congress' primary purpose for enacting the Occupational Safety and Health Act is "to assure so far as possible every working man and woman in the Nation safe and healthful working conditions." To further this primary goal, Congress imposed statutory duties on employers and employees.[5] Under the Act, an employer's duty is two-fold:

Each employer—

(1) Shall furnish to each of his employees employment and a place of employment which are free from recognized hazards that are causing or are likely to cause death or serious physical harm to his employees;

(2) Shall comply with Occupational Safety and Health standards promulgated under this chapter.

29 U.S.C. Sec. 654(a). The first duty is a "general duty" imposed on an employer to protect its employees from hazards that are likely to cause death or serious bodily injury. The second duty is a "specific duty" imposed on employers to comply with the OSHA regulations. These separate duty clauses have been subject to varying interpretations.

The difficulty which courts have experienced in attempting to define a particular employer's responsibilities under the Act is due primarily to the varying nature of the separate duty provisions. The general duty clause was intended by Congress to cover unanticipated hazards; Congress recognized that it could not anticipate all of the potential hazards that might affect adversely the safety of workers. Accordingly, it enacted the general duty clause to cover serious hazards that were not otherwise covered by specific regulations. Pursuant to Sec. 654(a)(1), every employer owes a duty of reasonable care to protect his employees from recognized hazards that are likely to cause death or serious bodily injury. The protection from *exposure* to serious hazards is the primary purpose of the general duty clause, and *every* employer owes this duty regardless of whether it controls the workplace, whether it is responsible for the hazard, or whether it has the best opportunity to abate the hazard. In contrast, Sec. 654(a)(2) is the specific duty provision. The class of employers who owe a duty to comply with the OSHA regulations is defined with reference to control of the workplace and opportunity to comply with the OSHA regulations. Accordingly, an employers' responsibilities under the Act depend upon which duty provision the employer is accused of breaching. Similarly, the class of persons for whom each of these duty provisions was enacted must be determined with reference to the particular duty in dispute.

In this case, DuPont is accused of breaching the specific duty imposed on employers by Sec. 654(a)(2). Accordingly, DuPont's reliance on the plain language of the general duty clause is misplaced. The very narrow question on appeal does not concern the scope of an employer's general duty to protect employees from exposure to recognized hazards, but rather,

---

**5.** Pursuant to 29 U.S.C. Sec. 654(b), every employee owes a duty to "comply with occupational safety and health standards and all rules, regulations, and orders issued pursuant to the Act which are applicable to his own actions and conduct."

the scope of an employer's duty to comply with the specific OSHA regulations. If the special duty provision is logically construed as imposing an obligation on the part of employers to protect *all* of the employees who work at a particular job site, then the employees of an independent contractor who work on the premises of another employer must be considered members of the class that Sec. 654(a)(2) was intended to protect. In other words, one cannot define the scope of an employer's obligation under Sec. 654(a)(2) as including the protection of another's employees and, at the same time, claim that these "other" employees are unintended beneficiaries.

We believe that Congress enacted Sec. 654(a)(2) for the special benefit of *all* employees, including the employees of an independent contractor, who perform work at another employer's workplace. The specific duty clause represents the *primary* means for furthering Congress' purpose of assuring "so far as possible every working man and woman in the Nation safe and healthful working conditions." The broad remedial nature of the Occupational Health and Safety Act of 1970 is the Act's primary characteristic. Consistent with the broad remedial nature of the Act, we interpret the scope of intended beneficiaries of the special duty provision in a broad fashion. In our view, once an employer is deemed responsible for complying with OSHA regulations, it is obligated to protect every employee who works at its workplace. Thus, Richard Teal, an employee of an independent contractor, must be considered a member of the class of persons that the special duty provision was intended to protect.

As we have indicated, Tennessee case law establishes that the breach of a duty imposed by regulation is negligence per se if the plaintiff is a member of the class of persons which the regulation was intended to protect. DuPont concedes that it owed a duty to comply with the OSHA regulation in question and that it breached this duty. Because Richard Teal is a member of the class of persons that the OSHA regulation was intended to protect, the appellants were entitled to a jury instruction on their negligence per se claim. Accordingly, we hold that the district court erred by refusing to give the requested instruction on the issue of negligence per se.

The district court's decision is affirmed in part, reversed in part and remanded for proceedings not inconsistent with this opinion.

NOTES AND QUESTIONS

**1.** The Tennessee rule applied in *Teal,* using the OSH Act to prove negligence per se, is in force in about one-fourth of the states. Most jurisdictions hold that OSHA standards are only "some evidence" of the standard of care. See, e.g., Knight v. Burns, Kirkley & Williams Construction Co., 331 So.2d 651 (Ala.1976); Kraus v. Alamo National Bank, 586 S.W.2d 202 (Civ.App.1979), affirmed, 616 S.W.2d 908 (Tex.1981). In a few jurisdictions, OSHA standards are inadmissible, either by statute, see Cal.Lab.Code § 6304.5, or by case law, see Hallmark v. Allied Products Corp., 646 P.2d 319 (Ariz.App.1982); Valdez v. Cillessen & Son, 734 P.2d

1258 (N.M.1987).  See generally Mark A. Rothstein, Occupational Safety and Health Law § 513 (4th ed. 1998).

**2.**  Section 4(b)(4) of OSH Act provides in pertinent part:

>   Nothing in this Act shall be construed to supersede or in any manner affect any workmen's compensation law or to enlarge or diminish or affect in any manner the common law or statutory rights, duties, or liabilities of employers and employees.  * * *

Despite this seemingly absolute language, the OSH Act *has* had some effects on workers' compensation and personal injury litigation.  It is well settled that the OSH Act does not create any causes of action (either by implication or under federal common law).  Jeter v. St. Regis Paper Co., 507 F.2d 973 (5th Cir.1975);  Byrd v. Fieldcrest Mills, Inc., 496 F.2d 1323 (4th Cir.1974).  Nevertheless, in those actions with another statutory or common law basis, OSH Act may be very important.

**3.**  Plaintiffs have been unsuccessful in attempts to introduce evidence of a defendant's violation of the OSH Act—that is, the actual citation or decision.  This evidence has been held to be inadmissible as irrelevant, prejudicial, and hearsay.  See, e.g., Swartz v. Dow Chemical Co., 326 N.W.2d 804 (Mich.1982).  What *is* admissible is any applicable OSHA standard, which may be used to prove the standard of conduct required.

**4.**  Some states provide for increases in workers' compensation payments (most only 10–15 percent) as penalties where the employer has failed to provide safety devices or to obey safety regulations.  Should a 15 percent penalty be assessed against an employer that has failed to comply with the OSH Act's general duty clause?  See Ryan v. Napa, 586 S.W.2d 6 (Ark. 1979) (held:  no).

**5.**  A worker suffering from a lung impairment filed a workers' compensation claim, alleging that his illness was caused by airborne contaminants at the employer's plant.  By way of a defense, the employer attempts to prove that exposure levels at the plant were in compliance with OSHA standards.  Is the worker entitled to workers' compensation?

## G.   SOCIAL SECURITY DISABILITY BENEFITS

Workers' compensation pays medical expenses and replaces wages for injuries and illnesses that arise on the job.  In addition, many Americans are eligible for income replacement payments if they become disabled away from the job but the consequence is that they cannot continue to work.  Disability payments are a "fringe benefit" in primary labor market jobs.  In several states including California, state government manages a program that provides income replacement for temporary disabilities.  But the major U.S. disability program is Social Security Disability, since 1956 a component of the federal Social Security system.  41 U.S.C. § 423 et seq.  This program pays more than $25 billion per year to about four million persons who have been found to be "permanently and totally disabled."

Social Security disability is important as an example of a "mass justice" system, imposing a vast decisionmaking burden on the Social Security Administration and on the federal courts.  See, e.g., Heckler v. Campbell, 461 U.S. 458 (1983);  Lance Liebman, The Definition of Disability in Social Security and Supplemental Security Income:  Drawing the Bounds of Social Welfare Estates, 89 Harv.L.Rev. 883 (1976).

# PART IV

# TERMINATING THE EMPLOYMENT RELATIONSHIP

# CHAPTER 10

# DISCHARGE

Discharge has been called the "capital punishment" of the workplace, and anyone who has ever been fired knows how apt that description is: loss of employment means not only loss of income but in our culture is often equated with loss of character and identity as well. Being fired, as opposed to quitting or being laid off due to economic circumstances, labels one a failure, unfit for employment. Justifiable causes for discharge include theft, dishonesty, falsification of records, fighting on company premises, possession or use of alcohol or drugs while on duty, insubordination, use of profane or abusive language to a supervisor, dangerous horseplay, sleeping on the job, excessive absenteeism, refusal to accept a work assignment, and disloyalty. There is also a wide range of unjustifiable or questionable reasons for discharge. Discharges lacking in good cause are at issue in several of the cases in this chapter.

Historically, management was entitled under common law to hire and fire whomever it pleased, as part of its right to run its business. The employer's position was, as stated by one early case, "May I not refuse to trade with any one? May I not dismiss my domestic servant for dealing, or even visiting, where I forbid? And if my domestic, why not my farm-hand, or my mechanic, or teamster? And, if one of them, then why not all four? And, if all four, why not a hundred or a thousand of them?" Payne v. Western & Atlantic Railway, 81 Tenn. 507, 518 (1884). To a great extent, this thinking still dominates employment law over a century later.

Theoretically, the at will rule operates on a principle of mutuality: both the employer and the employee are free to terminate their relationship at any time, without reason and without notice. From its inception, however, the rule has been criticized as unduly harsh on employees, whose inferior bargaining power relative to employers renders the mutuality of the "at will" principle illusory. Usually, the employer's threat of discharge is a serious one for employees, while the relative fungibility of workers in low level jobs means that the employee's threat of quitting places few constraints on the employer. In practice, it is usually easier for a company to replace employees than it is for an employee to find a new job. Approximately 60 million private sector employees are subject to the employment at will rule; at least 1.4 million of them are fired each year. It has been estimated that at least 150,000 of the discharges are unjust. See Jack Stieber & James R. Murray, Protection Against Unjust Discharge: The Need for a Federal Statute, 16 U.Mich.J.L.Ref. 319, 323 (1983).

The basic question posed in this chapter is what rights employers and employees should have in employment. To what extent should an essentially private relationship be governmentally regulated, by legislation or judicial rule?  Is it desirable to shift from a rule of employment at will to some other presumption governing the duration and termination of the employment relationship?  Should the law treat wrongs to this relationship as torts or breaches of contract?  Which cause of action is a preferable means of protecting employees' interests while still giving employers sufficient latitude to run their businesses?  Finally, what does the development of the wrongful discharge doctrine indicate about the concept of employment and the individual's "right" to a job?

## A.  FREEDOM OF CONTRACT/FAIRNESS IN EMPLOYMENT

One response to the perceived inequity of the employment at will rule was the institution, through unionization and collective bargaining, of a "for cause" standard for discharge, enforced through binding arbitration. During World War II, President Roosevelt forbade industrial strikes and created the War Labor Board, which used arbitration as a substitute for strikes in resolving labor disputes.  Widespread union organizing after the war resulted in the spread of both arbitration and the just cause standard. Today, 98 percent of all collective bargaining agreements provide for binding arbitration of grievances arising under the agreement between the parties, and a similar percent require an employer to have "cause" or "just cause" before disciplining or discharging an employee.

The definition of "just cause" has been the subject of considerable debate.  The seeming simplicity of the phrase and its intuitively obvious meaning mask the problem of applying the concept to individual circumstances.  One arbitrator stated: "Without attempting precisely to define 'cause', it is the arbitrator's view that the true test under a contract of the type involved here is whether a reasonable man, taking into account all relevant circumstances, would find sufficient justification in the conduct of the employee to warrant discharge."  RCA Communications, Inc., 29 LA 567, 571 (Harris, 1957).  Another arbitrator defined "just cause," "justifiable cause," "proper cause," and simply "cause" in terms of industry experience:

> There is no significant difference between these various phrases. These exclude discharge for mere whim or caprice.  They are, obviously, intended to include those things for which employees have traditionally been fired.  They include the traditional causes of discharge in the particular trade or industry, the practices which develop in the day-to-day relations of management and labor and most recently they include the decisions of courts and arbitrators.  They represent a growing body of "common law" that may be regarded either as the latest development of the law of "master and servant" or, perhaps, more properly as part of a new body of common law of "Management and labor under collective bargaining agreements."  They constitute the duties owed by employees to management and, in their correlative aspect, are part

of the rights of management. They include such duties as honesty, punctuality, sobriety, or, conversely, the right to discharge for theft, repeated absence or lateness, destruction of company property, brawling and the like. Where they are not expressed in posted rules, they may very well be implied, provided they are applied in a uniform, non-discriminatory manner.

Worthington Corp., 24 LA 1 (McGoldrick, 1955).

Another analysis of just cause starts by focusing on the shared interests of management and labor:

Management can have little objection to a fair and consistent system of discipline. Similarly, a union has no cause to object to disciplinary actions occasioned by employee conduct that significantly interferes with management's legitimate concern for production. Although the parties may differ as to whether a particular disciplinary system is fair or whether a given type of behavior warrants a certain measure of discipline, they can agree that the legitimate interests of management and labor provide the standards against which management's action must be judged.

In order to establish just cause for disciplinary action, management must first show that its interests were significantly affected by the employee's conduct. Alternatively, management may show that even though the employee is unlikely to repeat the wrongful conduct, it is important to deter other employees from such conduct and that discharge is the only effective form of deterrence. Either of these two explanations would establish a prima facie showing of just cause. In order to rebut this showing of just cause, a union must prove that management failed to give the employee industrial due process or industrial equal protection, or failed to consider mitigating factors. For example, the union may show that management took disciplinary action without adequate investigation, or singled out the employee for discipline when others had been excused for the same conduct, or ignored mitigating circumstances such as illness or provocation.

Roger Abrams & Dennis Nolan, Toward a Theory of "Just Cause" in Employee Discipline Cases, 1985 Duke L.J. 594, 610–12.

———

## B. JUDICIAL EROSION OF EMPLOYMENT AT WILL

### 1. PUBLIC POLICY

Initially, courts were reluctant to intervene in wrongful discharge cases, viewing the employment relationship as private and management rights as not amenable to outside intrusion. But the facts of some cases cried out for a legal remedy of some sort, and the judicial activism first encouraged by the employment discrimination laws ultimately spilled over into other aspects of employment.  The first successful assaults on the rule used tort theories of liability.  Contract law, with its doctrines of mutuality of obligation and consideration, was simply not sympathetic to the individual who had made a "bad bargain," unless fraud, duress, or coercion could be shown, and none of those applied in the typical employment relationship.  Tort law, more receptive to correcting wrongs otherwise without remedies, provided a vehicle for employees to attack the more blatant abuses of the at will rule, and the tort of wrongful discharge was created.

One of the first wrongful discharge cases was Petermann v. Teamsters Local 396, 344 P.2d 25 (Cal.App.1959).  The plaintiff, a business agent for the union, refused to perjure himself as instructed by his employer in testimony before a state legislative committee and was discharged the following day.  In recognizing a cause of action for wrongful discharge, the court noted that the right to discharge an employee under an at will contract could be limited by statute or public policy.  It further stated:

> The commission of perjury is unlawful (Pen.Code § 118).  It is also a crime to solicit the commission of perjury.  (Pen.Code, § 653f.)  * * * The threat of criminal prosecution would, in many cases, be a sufficient deterrent upon both the employer and employee, the former from soliciting and the latter from committing perjury.  However, in order to more fully effectuate the state's declared policy against perjury, the civil law, too, must deny the employer his generally unlimited right to discharge an employee whose employment is for an unspecified duration, when the reason for the dismissal is the employee's refusal to commit perjury. * * * The public policy of this state as reflected in the Penal Code sections referred to above would be seriously impaired if it were to be held that one could be discharged by reason of his refusal to commit perjury.  To hold that one's continued employment could be made contingent upon his commission of a felonious act at the instance of his employer would be to encourage criminal conduct upon the part of both the employee and employer and serve to contaminate the honest administration of public affairs.

344 P.2d at 27.

In *Petermann,* public policy was found in the state's penal code. Gradually, other states began to recognize limited public policy exceptions to the at will rule.  In Frampton v. Central Indiana Gas Co., 297 N.E.2d 425 (Ind.1973), the Indiana Supreme Court had no difficulty extending the reasoning of *Petermann* to an employee who had been discharged for filing a claim for an injury sustained on the job under the Indiana Workmen's Compensation Act: "We agree with the Court of Appeals that, under ordinary circumstances, an employee at will may be discharged without cause.  However, when an employee is discharged solely for exercising a statutorily conferred right an exception to the general rule must be recognized."

As the following cases illustrate, however, courts in general have found public policy a slippery concept to define satisfactorily, and several jurisdictions have refused to recognize the public policy exception to the at will rule altogether.

## Gantt v. Sentry Insurance

824 P.2d 680 (Cal.1992).

■ Arabian, Justice.

We granted review in this case to consider whether an employee who was terminated in retaliation for supporting a coworker's claim of sexual harassment may state a cause of action for tortious discharge against public policy and, if so, whether the exclusive remedy provisions of the Workers' Compensation Act bar the action. We hold that the claim is actionable * * * and is not preempted by the workers' compensation law.

\* \* \*

Viewing the record most strongly in favor of the judgment, as we must, the following pertinent chronology of facts appears: In September 1979, Sentry hired Gantt to serve as the sales manager of its Sacramento office. His mission was to develop the Sacramento sales force. How successfully he performed this task was the subject of conflicting evidence at trial. However, as explained below, the record amply supports the jury's specific finding that his demotion and constructive discharge were the product of his support for another employee's sexual harassment claim rather than the result of any legally valid business reason.

The specific circumstances which led to Gantt's estrangement from Sentry centered on Joyce Bruno, who was hired in January 1980 to be the liaison between trade associations and Sentry's Sacramento and Walnut Creek offices. In that capacity, Ms. Bruno reported to both Gantt and Gary Desser, the manager of the Walnut Creek office, as well as Brian Cullen, a technical supervisor at regional headquarters in Scottsdale, Arizona.

Shortly after she was hired, Ms. Bruno experienced sexual harassment at the hands of Desser. As the harassment continued, she complained to Gantt. He recommended she report it to Cullen in Scottsdale. Ultimately, Gantt himself contacted both Bonnie Caroline, who was responsible for receiving complaints of sexual discrimination, and Dave Berg, his immediate supervisor, about the problem. Despite these reports, the harassment continued. Accordingly, Gantt took it upon himself to speak a second time with both Berg and Ms. Caroline. Finally, in early 1981, Desser was demoted from sales manager to sales representative and replaced by Robert Warren. In March, Ms. Bruno was transferred to a sales representative position. A month later, however, she was fired.

Gantt stated that he was present at the April meeting in which Berg directed Warren to fire Bruno and ridiculed Gantt for supporting her. The following month, Berg himself resigned from Sentry following an investigation into claims that he had engaged in sexual harassment. Berg's replacement, Frank Singer, assumed the title "Director of Sales" and recruited John Tailby to assume Berg's old position supervising the various sales offices. According to one witness, Tailby said Singer told him that getting rid of Gantt was to be one of his first tasks. Tailby resisted, however, and in 1981 Gantt was ranked among Sentry's top district managers in premium growth.

Bruno, meanwhile, filed a complaint with the Department of Fair Employment and Housing (DFEH). She alleged harassment by Desser and failure by Sentry's higher management to act on her complaints. Caroline Fribance, Sentry's house counsel in charge of labor-related matters, undertook to investigate the matter. Gantt informed Fribance that he had reported Bruno's complaints to personnel in Scottsdale. However, Gantt gained the impression that he was being pressured by Fribance to retract his claim that he had informed Scottsdale of the complaints. Later, following the interview with Fribance, Tailby cautioned Gantt that Singer and others in the company did not care for Gantt. In a follow-up memorandum, Tailby cautioned Gantt that "it sometimes appears that you are involved in some kind of 'intrigue' and 'undercover' operation." In December 1982, Tailby rated Gantt's overall work performance for the year as "acceptable." Without directly informing Gantt, Singer changed the rating to "borderline acceptable/unacceptable."

Shortly thereafter, John Thompson, a DFEH investigator, contacted Fribance to arrange interviews with certain employees, including Gantt. Because of his growing unease about Fribance, Gantt arranged to meet secretly with Thompson before the scheduled interview. Gantt told him the facts of which he was aware, including his reporting of Bruno's complaints to Scottsdale, and Thompson assured him that he would be protected under the law from any retaliation for his statements. Thompson gained the impression that Gantt felt he was being pressured and was extremely fearful of retaliation because of his unfavorable testimony.

\* \* \*

Less than two months later, on March 3, 1983, Gantt attended an awards ceremony in Scottsdale to accept a life insurance sales award on behalf of his office. The following morning, Singer and Tailby informed him that he was being demoted to sales representative. Shortly thereafter, Gantt's new supervisor, Neil Whitman, warned him that he would be fired if he attempted to undermine Whitman's authority. Gantt was also informed that he would not be given a "book" of existing accounts to start his new job; according to Gantt, such a book was necessary to survive.

During the following month, Gantt was in the office only intermittently. He experienced a variety of illnesses and took vacation time and sick leave. In mid-April he was offered and accepted a position with another company. He left Sentry's payroll in early May. Two months later, he filed the instant lawsuit alleging that "as a result of the pressure applied by the defendants * * * he was forced to resign."

As noted earlier, the jury returned a special verdict in favor of Gantt, finding, inter alia, that Gantt had been constructively discharged; that Sentry lacked an "honest good faith belief the termination was warranted for legally valid business reasons"; that Gantt was discharged "in retaliation for his refusal to testify untruthfully or to withhold testimony"; that Gantt was further discharged in retaliation for his "actions or statements with respect to Joyce Bruno's sexual harassment allegations;" and that in committing these acts Sentry acted with malice, oppression or fraud.

* * * [F]ollowing the seminal California decision in Petermann v. International Brotherhood of Teamsters, the vast majority of states have recognized that an at-will employee possesses a tort action when he or she is discharged for performing an act that public policy would encourage, or for refusing to do something that public policy would condemn.

Yet despite its broad acceptance, the principle underlying the public policy exception is more easily stated than applied. The difficulty, of course, lies in determining where and how to draw the line between claims that genuinely involve matters of public policy, and those that concern merely ordinary disputes between employer and employee. This determination depends in large part on whether the public policy alleged is sufficiently clear to provide the basis for such a potent remedy. In Foley v. Interactive Data Corp., infra, we endeavored to provide some guidelines by noting that the policy in question must involve a matter that affects society at large rather than a purely personal or proprietary interest of the plaintiff or employer; in addition, the policy must be "fundamental," "substantial" and "well established" at the time of the discharge.

We declined in *Foley* to determine whether the violation of a statute or constitutional provision is invariably a prerequisite to the conclusion that a discharge violates public policy. A review of the pertinent case law in California and elsewhere, however, reveals that few courts have recognized a public policy claim absent a statute or constitutional provision evidencing the policy in question. Indeed, as courts and commentators alike have noted, the cases in which violations of public policy are found generally fall into four categories: (1) refusing to violate a statute; (2) performing a statutory obligation; (3) exercising a statutory right or privilege; and (4) reporting an alleged violation of a statute of public importance.

To be sure, those courts which have addressed the issue appear to be divided over the question whether nonlegislative sources may ever provide the basis of a public policy claim. Pierce v. Ortho Pharmaceutical Corp. (1980) 84 N.J. 58, 417 A.2d 505 is the leading case for a broad interpretation. As the New Jersey Supreme Court explained: "The sources of public policy [which may limit the employer's right of discharge] include legislation; administrative rules, regulation, or decision; and judicial decisions. In certain instances, a professional code of ethics may contain an expression of public policy." Several other states have adopted similarly broad views of the public policy exception.

Other courts have applied a stricter definition to public policy claims. The leading case is Brockmeyer v. Dun & Bradstreet (1983) 113 Wis.2d 561, 335 N.W.2d 834. There, the Wisconsin Supreme Court, while recognizing a public policy exception to the employment at-will doctrine, nevertheless limited plaintiffs to contract damages and confined such claims to statutory or constitutional violations. "Given the vagueness of the concept of public policy," the court explained, "it is necessary that we be more precise about the contours of the public policy exception. A wrongful discharge is actionable when the termination clearly contravenes the public welfare and gravely violates paramount requirements of public interest. The public policy must be evidenced by a constitutional or statutory provision." Other courts have adopted similarly restrictive views of the contours of the public policy exception.

Turning from other jurisdictions to California law, one finds the courts similarly divided. As we recently observed in *Foley:* "Several subsequent Court of Appeal cases have limited our holding [in *Tameny* ] to policies derived from statute." At least three other Court of Appeal decisions addressing the issue of where policy giving rise to an action may be found have concluded in dicta that public policy, as a basis for a wrongful discharge action, need not be policy rooted in a statute or constitutional provision.

Although we have not taken a position on this precise issue, it is true, as plaintiff notes, that this court has not previously confined itself to legislative enactments when determining the public policy of the state. We have, for example, long declined to enforce contracts inimical to law or the public interest, and long ago declared racial discrimination to be contrary to public policy under the common law duty of innkeepers and common carriers to furnish accommodations to all persons.

The analogy to illegal contracts has particular force. For at root, the public policy exception rests on the recognition that in a civilized society the rights of each person are necessarily limited by the rights of others and of the public at large; this is the delicate balance which holds such societies together. Accordingly, while an at-will employee may be terminated for no reason, or for an arbitrary or irrational reason, there can be no right to terminate for an unlawful reason or a purpose that contravenes fundamental public policy. Any other conclusion would sanction lawlessness, which courts by their very nature are bound to oppose. It is a very short and logical step, therefore, from declining to enforce contracts inimical to law or the public interest, to refusing to sanction terminations in contravention of fundamental public policy. Indeed, we expressly acknowledged the analogy in *Foley,* noting, in the context of our *Tameny* discussion: "A comparison of the manner in which contracts for illegal purposes are treated is useful."

Unfortunately, as we have also previously acknowledged, "[t]he term 'public policy' is inherently not subject to precise definition * * *. 'By "public" policy is intended that principle of law which holds that no citizen can lawfully do that which has a tendency to be injurious to the public or against the public good * * *.' " It was this rather open-ended definition on which the court relied in *Petermann,* the seminal decision articulating the public policy exception to the employment at-will doctrine.

Surveying the extensive and conflicting decisional law summarized above, several general observations are possible. First, notwithstanding the lively theoretical debate over the sources of public policy which may support a wrongful discharge claim, with few exceptions courts have, in practice, relied to some extent on statutory or constitutional expressions of public policy as a basis of the employee's claim.

Second, it is generally agreed that "public policy" as a concept is notoriously resistant to precise definition, and that courts should venture into this area, if at all, with great care and due deference to the judgment of the legislative branch, "lest they mistake their own predilections for public policy which deserves recognition at law." Indeed, one of the most frequently cited decisions favoring a broad interpretation, observed that courts "should proceed cautiously" if called upon to declare public policy absent some prior legislative expression on the subject.

These wise caveats against judicial policymaking are unnecessary if one recognizes that courts in *wrongful discharge actions* may not declare public policy without a basis in either the constitution or statutory provisions. A public policy exception carefully tethered to fundamental policies that are delineated in constitutional or statutory provisions strikes the proper balance among the interests of employers, employees and the public. The employer is bound, at a minimum, to know the fundamental public policies of the state and nation as expressed in their constitutions and statutes; so limited, the public policy exception presents no impediment to employers that operate within the bounds of law. Employees are protected against employer actions that contravene fundamental state policy. And society's interests are served through a more stable job market, in which its most important policies are safeguarded.

Here, we are *not* being asked to declare public policy. The issue as framed by the pleadings and the parties is whether there exists a clear constitutional or legislative declaration of fundamental public policy forbidding plaintiff's discharge under the facts and circumstances presented.

Initially, the parties dispute whether the discharge of an employee in retaliation for reporting a coworker's claim of sexual harassment to higher management may rise to the level of a *Tameny* violation. Sentry argues that such reporting inures only to the benefit of the employee in question rather than to the public at large, and questions the constitutional or statutory basis of such a claim. Plaintiff responds that the same constitutional provision (Cal. Const., art. I, § 8) that prohibits sexual discrimination against employees and demands a workplace free from the pernicious influence of sexual harassment also protects the employee who courageously intervenes on behalf of a harassed colleague.

Although Sentry did not discriminate against Gantt on account of his sex within the meaning of the constitutional provision, there is nevertheless direct statutory support for the jury's express finding that Sentry violated a fundamental public policy when it constructively discharged plaintiff "in retaliation for his refusal to testify untruthfully or to withhold testimony" in the course of the DFEH investigation. Indeed, *Petermann,* "one of the seminal California decisions in this area" presented the parallel situation of an employee who was dismissed from his position because he had refused to follow his employer's instructions to testify falsely under oath before a legislative committee. Such conduct, the court concluded, could not be condoned as a matter of "public policy and sound morality." "It would be obnoxious to the interests of the state and contrary to public policy and sound morality to allow an employer to discharge any employee * * * on the ground that the employee declined to commit perjury, an act specifically enjoined by statute * * *. The public policy of this state as reflected in the Penal Code sections referred to above would be seriously impaired if it were to be held that one could be discharged by reason of his refusal to commit perjury."

We endorsed the principles of *Petermann* in Tameny v. Atlantic Richfield Co., 610 P.2d 1330 (Cal.1980), holding that an employee who alleged that he was discharged because he refused to participate in an illegal price fixing scheme may subject his employer "to liability for compensatory and punitive damages under normal tort principles." As we explained: "[A]n employer's authority over its employee does not include the right to demand that the employee commit a criminal act to further its interests, and an employer may not coerce compliance with such unlawful directions by discharging an employee who refuses to follow such an order. An employer engaging in such conduct violates a basic duty imposed by law upon all employers, and thus an employee who has suffered damages as a result of such discharge may maintain a tort action for wrongful discharge against the employer."

The instant case fits squarely within the rubric of *Petermann* and *Tameny.* The FEHA specifically enjoins any obstruction of a DFEH investigation. Government Code section 12975 provides: "Any person who shall willfully resist, prevent, impede or interfere with any member of the department or the commission or any of its agents or employees in the performance of duties pursuant to the provisions of this part relating to employment discrimination, * * * is guilty of a misdemeanor" punishable by fine or imprisonment. Nowhere in our society is the need greater than in protecting well motivated employees who come forward to testify truthfully in an administrative investigation of charges of discrimination based on sexual harassment. It is self-evident that few employees would cooperate with such investigations if the price were retaliatory discharge from employment.

Thus, any attempt to induce or coerce an employee to lie to a DFEH investigator plainly contravenes the public policy of this State. Accordingly, we hold that plaintiff established a valid *Tameny* claim based on the theory of retaliation for refusal to withhold information or to provide false information to the DFEH.

* * *

In sum, we hold that the Workers' Compensation Act does not preempt plaintiff's *Tameny* action for tortious discharge in contravention of fundamental public policy.

The judgment of the Court of Appeal is affirmed.

## Murphy v. American Home Products

448 N.E.2d 86 (N.Y.1983).

■ JONES, JUDGE.

\* \* \*

Plaintiff, Joseph Murphy, was first employed by defendant, American Home Products Corp., in 1957. He thereafter served in various accounting positions, eventually attaining the office of assistant treasurer, but he never had a formal contract of employment. On April 18, 1980, when he was 59 years old, he was discharged.

Plaintiff claims that he was fired for two reasons: because of his disclosure to top management of alleged accounting improprieties on the part of corporate personnel and because of his age. As to the first ground, plaintiff asserts that his firing was in retaliation for his revelation to officers and directors of defendant corporation that he had uncovered at least $50 million in illegal account manipulations of secret pension reserves which improperly inflated the company's growth in income and allowed high-ranking officers to reap unwarranted bonuses from a management incentive plan, as well as in retaliation for his own refusal to engage in the alleged accounting improprieties. He contends that the company's internal regulations required him to make the disclosure that he did. He also alleges that his termination was carried out in a humiliating manner.

\* \* \*

With respect to his first cause of action, plaintiff urges that the time has come when the courts of New York should recognize the tort of abusive or wrongful discharge of an at-will employee. To do so would alter our long-settled rule that where an employment is for an indefinite term it is presumed to be a hiring at will which may be freely terminated by either party at any time for any reason or even for no reason. Plaintiff argues that a trend has emerged in the courts of other States to temper what is perceived as the unfairness of the traditional rule by allowing a cause of action in tort to redress abusive discharges. He accurately points out that this tort has elsewhere been recognized to hold employers liable for dismissal of employees in retaliation for employee conduct that is protected by public policy. Thus, the abusive discharge doctrine has been applied to impose liability on employers where employees have been discharged for disclosing illegal activities on the part of their employers, where employees have been terminated due to their service on jury duty, and where employees have been dismissed because they have filed workers' compensation claims. Plaintiff would have this court adopt this emerging view. We decline his invitation, being of the opinion that such a significant change in our law is best left to the Legislature.

Those jurisdictions that have modified the traditional at-will rule appear to have been motivated by conclusions that the freedom of contract underpinnings of the rule have become outdated, that individual employees in the modern work force do not have the bargaining power to negotiate security for the jobs on which they have grown to rely, and that the rule yields harsh results for those employees who do not enjoy the benefits of express contractual limitations on the power of dismissal. Whether these conclusions are supportable or whether for other compelling reasons employers should, as a matter of policy, be held liable to at-will employees discharged in circumstances for which no liability has existed at common law, are issues better left to resolution at the hands of the Legislature. In addition to the fundamental question whether such liability should be recognized in New York, of no less practical importance is the definition of its configuration if it is to be recognized.

Both of these aspects of the issue, involving perception and declaration of relevant public policy are best and more appropriately explored and resolved by the legislative branch of our government. The Legislature has infinitely greater resources and procedural means to discern the public will, to examine the variety of pertinent considerations, to elicit the views of the various segments of the community that would be directly affected and in any event critically interested, and to investigate and anticipate the impact of imposition of such liability. Standards should doubtless be established applicable to the multifarious types of employment and the various circumstances of discharge. If the rule of nonliability for termination of at-will employment is to be tempered, it should be accomplished through a principled statutory scheme, adopted after opportunity for public ventilation, rather than in consequence of judicial resolution of the partisan arguments of individual adversarial litigants.

Additionally, if the rights and obligations under a relationship forged, perhaps some time ago, between employer and employee in reliance on existing legal principles are to be significantly altered, a fitting accommodation of the competing interests to be affected may well dictate that any change should be given prospective effect only, or at least so the Legislature might conclude.

For all the reasons stated, we conclude that recognition in New York State of tort liability for what has become known as abusive or wrongful discharge should await legislative action.

## NOTES AND QUESTIONS

**1.** *Gantt* illustrates the most widely accepted formulations of the public policy exception to the at will rule, under which individuals may not be discharged for: (1) refusing to commit unlawful acts; (2) exercising statutory rights; (3) performing public functions; or (4) reporting an employer's unlawful conduct.

**2.**  A number of jurisdictions have upheld an employee's right to be free from discharge for exercising statutory rights.  See, e.g., Perks v. Firestone Tire & Rubber Co., 611 F.2d 1363 (3d Cir.1979) (discharge for refusal to take statutorily prohibited polygraph test);  Smith v. Atlas Off-Shore Boat Service, Inc., 653 F.2d 1057 (5th Cir.1981) (discharge for filing injury suit under Jones Act);  Savodnik v. Korvettes, Inc., 488 F.Supp. 822 (E.D.N.Y. 1980) (discharge to prevent pension from vesting);  Bowman v. State Bank, 331 S.E.2d 797 (Va.1985) (employee-stockholders discharged for refusing to vote in favor of merger to which they were opposed).  But see Martin v. Tapley, 360 So.2d 708 (Ala.1978) (contract "at will" means what it says;  where employee compensated for work-related injuries, employer has satisfied whatever implied contractual duty it owed to employee at will in regards to Workmen's Compensation Act).

In *Gantt,* the court refused to find a public policy basis for wrongful discharge that was not grounded in a constitutional or statutory provision.  However, a number of jurisdictions have recognized non-legislative sources of public policy.  See, e.g., Rocky Mountain Hospital & Medical Service v. Mariani, 916 P.2d 519 (Colo.1996) (rules of professional conduct for accountants have an important public purpose, and thus the discharge of an accountant for refusing to violate such rules was void as against public policy);  Boyle v. Vista Eyewear, Inc. 700 S.W.2d 859 (Mo.Ct.App.1985) (regulatory provisions, judicial decisions, and professional codes of ethics are acceptable).

A California court of appeals narrowed the scope of the public policy wrongful discharge tort in Sequoia Insurance Co. v. Superior Court, 16 Cal.Rptr.2d 888 (Cal.App.1993).  Interpreting *Gantt,* the court held that a public policy must be based on policies delineated by a statutory or constitutional provision and must be described "in detail ... with sharpness or vividness" to allow the employer to know the fundamental public policies expressed in that law.

**4.**  One state has legislated about the public policy exception to at-will employment.  The Arizona legislature, responding to Wagenseller v. Scottsdale Memorial Hospital, supra p. 10, with the Arizona Employment Protection Act in 1996, declared that "an employer may be held liable for civil damages of such employer discharges from employment an employee for a reason that is against the public of this state...  However, public policy is expressly determined by the legislature in the form of statutory provisions."

The only state with a comprehensive wrongful discharge statute is Montana.  The statute, enacted in 1987, prohibits employers from firing employees if the action was without "good cause" as defined in the statute or if the action was in violation of public policy or in violation of the express provisions of the employer's own written personnel policy.  Wrongfully discharged employees may be awarded up to four years lost wages and benefits, as well as punitive damages in limited cases.

By a 4–3 vote, the Montana Supreme Court upheld the constitutional validity of the state's Wrongful Discharge From Employment Act.  Meech

v. Hillhaven West, Inc., 776 P.2d 488 (Mont.1989). The act was challenged under the Montana constitutional provision assuring an individual "full legal redress", and also as a violation of equal protection of the laws because it denies full tort damages to some plaintiffs (dismissed employees) but not others. The majority opinion said that the legislature may alter the common law, and specifically that it may prescribe remedies and procedures for particular wrongs. Justice Sheehy, dissenting, wrote: "This is the blackest judicial day in the eleven years that I have sat on this Court. Indeed it may be the blackest judicial day in the history of the state. \* \* \* The decision today cleans the scalpel for the legislature to cut away unrestrainedly at the whole field of tort redress. \* \* \* The legislature, in effect, has converted the tort of wrongful discharge into a sort of contract action \* \* \*." See Cecil v. Cardinal Drilling Co., 797 P.2d 232 (Mont.1990) (executive discharged from oil drilling company during period of decline in oil prices was discharged for a legitimate business reason).

**5.** Some states have attempted to prevent the unfair treatment of employees by expanding the classes of persons protected by statutory anti-discrimination provisions or otherwise granting employees additional statutory rights in employment. For example, over half the states have laws providing that it is unlawful to discriminate against private sector employees who engage in political activity. See Nelson v. McClatchy Newspapers, Inc., supra p. 641. Other states prohibit discrimination based on status as a recipient of public assistance (e.g., Minn.), for filing a complaint alleging domestic violence (e.g., R.I.), or marital status. In Minnesota v. Floyd Wild, Inc., 384 N.W.2d 185 (Minn.Ct.App.1986), the court held that the state's marital status discrimination law did not apply to the discharge of the daughter-in-law of the employer's son following a contentious divorce.

**6.** Reporting an employer's unlawful conduct has been protected under the public policy exception to at-will employment. However, courts have distinguished cases where employees are discharged for reporting wrongdoing to law enforcement agencies or regulatory agencies, and those where the wrongdoing is reported internally, within the company. See McLauglin v. Gastrointestinal Specialists, Inc., 696 A.2d 173 (Pa.Super.1997) (an employee who was discharged after reporting OSHA violations to his employer, rather than to an outside agency, was not protected by the public policy exception.); Fox v. MCI Communications, 931 P.2d 857 (Utah 1997) (retaliatory discharge for reporting employee's fraudulent sales practices to employer does not contravene public policy, but discharge resulting from informing the police or authorities will support an action for wrongful discharge).

Thirty-seven states have enacted some form of statutory protection for whistleblowers. The scope of protected activity varies from jurisdiction to jurisdiction depending on the statute in question. The Whistleblower Protection Act of 1989, 5 U.S.C. § 2301(b)(9), expanded protection for federal employees who expose violations of law, gross mismanagement or waste of funds, abuse of authority, or substantial and specific danger to public health or safety in government agencies.

Legislation eliminates any question about there being a state policy against firing employees for opposing employer practices or protesting company safety or health standards. At least one court has refused to recognize a cause of action for whistleblowing absent a statutorily conferred right. Hostettler v. Pioneer Hi–Bred International, Inc., 624 F.Supp. 169 (S.D.Ind.1985). In some states, however, courts have ruled that the existence of statutory whistleblower remedies will preempt any common law claims, including the public policy exception to at-will employment. Dudewicz v. Norris–Schmid, Inc., 503 N.W.2d 645 (Mich.1993).

Courts have also held that whistleblowers' accusations must be true for statutory and common law protection to attach. See, e.g., Bard v. Bath Iron Works Corp., 590 A.2d 152 (Me.1991) (merely acting in good faith is not enough to protect an employee under the Maine Whistleblower Protection Act); Petrik v. Monarch Printing Corp., 493 N.E.2d 616 (Ill.App.1986) (employee who suspected, but could not prove, criminal wrongdoing related to discrepancies in corporate financial records was not protected by the public policy exception). For a different result, see Wichita County v. Hart, 917 S.W.2d 779 (Tex.1996). In order to qualify for protection under the Texas Whistleblower Act, a plaintiff must show he or she believes the conduct reported was a violation of the law and that the belief was reasonable in light of the employee's training and experience.

**7.** An employee's acquiescence in past illegal acts does not preclude a wrongful discharge claim as against public policy. In Jacobs v. Universal Development Corp., 62 Cal.Rptr.2d 446 (Ct.App.1997), an employee fearing a retaliatory discharge had initialed purchase orders including illegal rebates. The court noted that "an employee initially acquiescing in his employer's criminality should be encouraged to cease such activity and not left without recourse when he is consequently fired."

**8.** Courts have been reluctant to intervene in terminations resulting from "internal employment disputes," reasoning that such disputes are not sufficiently "public" to warrant the use of the public policy exception. In Beam v. IPCO Corp., 838 F.2d 242 (7th Cir.1988), the court held that it would not violate public policy for an employer to discharge an employee for consulting with an attorney after being reprimanded. For a different result, see Simonelli v. Anderson Concrete, 650 N.E.2d 488 (Ohio App. 1994), appeal denied, 648 N.E.2d 514 (Ohio 1995).

**9.** Courts have been reluctant to extend the public policy exception to in-house attorneys who are terminated after exposing client wrongdoing or refusing to violate laws or ethical obligations. The courts have reasoned that such claims will have a chilling effect on the attorney-client relationship, would violate attorney-client confidentiality, and are not necessary to prevent wrongdoing since attorneys are already professionally obligated to report unlawful conduct. Balla v. Gambro, Inc. 584 N.E.2d 104 (Ill.1991) (in-house attorney terminated after reporting the distribution of defective kidney dialysis equipment has no cause of action). For a similar result, see Willy v. Coastal States Management Co., 939 S.W.2d 193 (Tex.Ct.App.1996) (in-house attorney discharged after refusing to falsify environmental reports and conceal violations could not prove claim for wrongful discharge without violating his ethical duty of confidentiality).

However, courts in Massachusetts and California have held that under certain circumstances an in-house lawyer who loses his or her job for exposing wrongdoing may bring a claim for retaliatory discharge against an employer. Such claims are predicated on the ability of the attorney to prove the allegations without violating attorney-client confidentiality norms. See General Dynamics Corp. v. Superior Court, 876 P.2d 487 (Cal.1994); GTE Products Corp. v. Stewart, 653 N.E.2d 161 (Mass.1995).

**10.** What limits should be placed on the employer's right to discharge upper level employees—supervisors, managers, and professional employees?

> Compromise of the employer's power to make such judgments about professional, managerial, or other high-ranking employees * * * is especially undesirable. The higher ranking the employee, the more important to the success of the business is his effective performance. Compounding the potential for undue inhibition of the employer's judgment at the higher echelons of employment is the greater difficulty of articulating the basis for discharge at that level. Compared to the wage earner, whose routine duties can generally be measured against a mechanical standard, the value of a salaried employee is more likely to be measured in such intangible qualities as imagination, initiative, drive, and personality. The employer's evaluation of the higher ranking employee is usually a highly personalized, intuitive judgment, and, as such, is more difficult to translate into concrete reasons which someone else—a juryman—can readily understand and appreciate. Indeed, even if it is conceded that the protection from unwarranted discharges afforded rank and file employees by labor agreements is appropriate, it might still be argued that no intrusion of any kind upon the employer's subjective evaluation of higher echelon employees should be tolerated.

Lawrence Blades, Employment at Will v. Individual Freedom, 67 Colum.L.Rev. 1404, 1428–29 (1967). Should different standards be used in judging the propriety of managerial terminations? How would you articulate those standards for a judge or jury? Do the materials on selection procedures in Chapter 3 or on promotions in Chapter 7 suggest any solutions?

**11.** Public health and safety has been recognized by courts as an important non-statutory source for public policy exceptions. In Green v. Ralee Engineering Co., 61 Cal.Rptr.2d 352 (Ct.App.1997), modified, 52 Cal. App.4th 1534 (1997), an employee was discharged for objecting to the shipping of defective airline parts to airline manufacturers, although there was no express statutory provision dealing with such a situation. The California Court of Appeals recognized "in the hierarchy of public policies, safety from physical harm and death ranks at or near the top." The court then found that FAA administrative regulations were a sufficient public policy basis for a wrongful discharge claim.

See also Gardener v. Loomis Armored, Inc., 913 P.2d 377 (Wash.1996). An armored car delivery driver was waiting in the car while his partner made a scheduled delivery at a bank. The driver saw a knife-wielding man chasing a woman he recognized as the bank manager. He locked the armored car and chased the man into the bank. The assailant by then had taken another woman hostage at knife-point. The driver, with the help of a bank customer, tackled the assailant, disarmed him, and turned him over to the police. He was promptly fired for violating the company's absolute rule against leaving the car unattended. The Washington Supreme Court held that the discharge violated the public policy of encouraging citizens to rescue others from life-threatening situations.

In the absence of a direct nexus to the workplace, assertions of a general public policy in favor of safety and health have been rejected. For example, in Upton v. JWP Businessland, 682 N.E.2d 1357 (Mass.1997), a single mother was discharged for refusing to work newly-imposed long hours (8:15 A.M. to 10 P.M. six days a week), because it would prevent her from being with her young child. The court upheld the discharge, rejecting the argument that a purported public policy favoring care and protection of children supported a common law action for wrongful discharge.

**12.** Courts have recently extended the public policy exception to claims involving an employee's right to privacy. Nagy v. Whittlesey Automotive Group, 47 Cal.Rptr.2d 395 (Cal.App.1995) (unpublished) (employees who were terminated for refusing to permit their conversations to be taped without their permission may bring an action for wrongful termination in breach of public policy). Terminating employees based on information obtained through means which violate an employee's right to privacy can also be a basis for a wrongful discharge claim. See Greenwood v. Taft, Stettinius & Hollister, 663 N.E.2d 1030 (Ohio App.1995), appeal denied with dissenting opinion, 662 N.E.2d 22 (Ohio 1996) (homosexual employee fired after an employee benefits administrator wrongfully disclosed to others that the employee had amended his benefits form to designate his male life partner as a beneficiary could maintain a claim for violation of privacy).

However, employees who volunteer or otherwise publish information cannot later claim wrongful discharge against public policy grounded in a right to privacy. In Smyth v. Pillsbury Co., 914 F.Supp. 97 (E.D.Pa.1996), the termination of an employee for transmitting inappropriate and unprofessional comments over his employer's e-mail system did not violate public policy. The plaintiff claimed he had been promised that his e-mail transmissions would be held in confidence and that they could not be intercepted and used as grounds for termination or reprimand. The e-mails at issue between Smyth and his supervisor contained threats to "kill the backstabbing bastards" and referred to the office holiday party as the "Jim Jones Koolaid affair." The court found that Smyth, by voluntarily submitting e-mails on the company system, had no privacy interest in his e-mail and that even if he had, there was no offensive invasion of privacy in their interception. Similarly, in Green v. Bryant, 887 F.Supp. 798 (E.D.Pa.

1995), an employee fired after she confided to another employee that she had recently been raped and beaten at gunpoint by her estranged husband could not claim a violation of privacy.

**13.** Termination on the basis of discrimination has been recognized by courts as wrongful discharge in violation of public policy rooted both in constitutional and legislative sources. In Badih v. Myers, 43 Cal.Rptr.2d 229 (Cal.App.1995), an employee terminated on the basis of pregnancy was able to maintain an action for wrongful discharge in violation of public policy because pregnancy discrimination is prohibited by the Fair Employment and Housing Act and is a form of sex discrimination prohibited by the California Constitution.

The fact that an employer does not fall within the scope of an anti-discrimination statute does not necessarily preclude a wrongful discharge claim. A female veterinarian who worked for a medical practice with fewer than 15 employees was nevertheless able to pursue a sex discrimination claim in a common law action for wrongful discharge in violation of public policy. The court found that the legislature did not intend to permit employers with fewer than 15 employers to discriminate on the basis of sex, but rather intended to excuse small employers from the administrative burdens of the anti-discrimination statute. Therefore, the court found evidence of a "ubiquitous" public policy against termination because of sex. Molesworth v. Brandon, 672 A.2d 608 (Md.1996).

Some courts have refused to extend the public policy exception to cover claims that already exist under federal and state law. See List v. Anchor Paint Manufacturing Co., 910 P.2d 1011 (Okl.1996) (employee terminated because of age could not maintain a common law wrongful discharge claim where statutory relief is available). But see Stevenson v. Superior Court of Los Angeles, 941 P.2d 1157 (Cal.1997), in which the court held that the remedies provided for age discrimination in California's Fair Employment and Housing Act are nonexclusive and therefore do not preempt any common law wrongful discharge claim.

**14.** Courts have declined to extend the public policy exception to wrongful discharge in cases where the employee has not been terminated, but rather has been transferred, demoted, or reprimanded. In White v. State, 929 P.2d 396 (Wash.1997), the Supreme Court of Washington denied a retaliatory transfer claim where an employee was allegedly transferred for reporting abuse of patients in a nursing home. The court held that creating a tort of wrongful transfer would be an inappropriate intrusion by the judiciary on "the employer's right to run his business." See also Ludwig v. C & A Wallcoverings, Inc., 960 F.2d 40 (7th Cir.1992) (no cause of action for retaliatory demotion under Illinois law). On the other hand, a few courts have indicated their willingness to extend the public policy exception to employment at will to employer actions short of discharge, such as wrongful demotion or wrongful refusal to promote. See, e.g., Zimmerman v. Bucheit of Sparta, Inc., 615 N.E.2d 791 (Ill.Ct.App.1993); Bringham v. Dillon Cos., Inc., 935 P.2d 1054 (Kan.1997). See generally Michael D. Moberly & Carolann E. Doran, The Nose of the Camel: Extending the

Public Policy Exception Beyond the Wrongful Discharge Context, 13 Lab.Lawyer 371 (1997).

**15.** Under certain circumstances an employer's harassment of an employee resulting in a resignation by the employee may be deemed a "constructive discharge," a concept which predates the development of the wrongful discharge cause of action. In determining whether a quit is in fact a constructive discharge, the question for the courts is "whether [the employer] deliberately made * * * working conditions intolerable and drove [the employee] into an 'involuntary quit'" NLRB v. Tennessee Packers, Inc. 339 F.2d 203, 204 (6th Cir.1964). As stated by the Fifth Circuit:

> Constructive discharge occurs when the employer deliberately makes an employee's working conditions so intolerable that the employee is forced into an involuntary resignation. To find constructive discharge, the court determines whether or not a reasonable person in the employee's position and circumstances would have felt compelled to resign. The employee thus does not have to prove it was the employer's purpose to force the employee to resign.

Pittman v. Hattiesburg Municipal Separate School District, 644 F.2d 1071, 1077 (5th Cir.1981).

**16.** Damages in wrongful discharge claims can be considerable: awards of several hundred thousand dollars are not uncommon for those few plaintiffs who have successfully challenged their discharges. Typically awarded by juries, these large sums include not only compensatory damages but also punitive damages. In awarding punitive damages, some courts will consider the deterrent effect of the awards. Other courts will focus on the willful, wanton, malicious, reckless, or oppressive behavior by the employer.

## PROBLEMS

In which of the following circumstances should the employee have an action for wrongful discharge in violation of public policy? Why? What is the public policy at issue?

a. A doctor was discharged for refusing to violate the Hippocratic oath by performing experimental human research using a controversial drug she believed to be harmful. See Pierce v. Ortho Pharmaceutical Corp., 417 A.2d 505 (N.J.1980). Consider also the experienced nurse who was discharged for opposing her employer's proposed staffing cuts, which in her professional opinion would have left the hospital grossly understaffed. See Lampe v. Presbyterian Medical Center, 590 P.2d 513 (Colo.App.1978). Cf. Dabbs v. Cardiopulmonary Management Services, 234 Cal.Rptr. 129 (Cal.App.1987).

b. The wife and two-year-old daughter of a supermarket employee were shopping in the supermarket when a glass container exploded, causing a piece of glass to enter the child's eye. After rejecting a $200 settlement offer from the store's insurance company, the employee sued, on his daughter's behalf, the supermarket and the container manufacturer. He was discharged when he refused to withdraw the suit.  See DeMarco v. Publix Super Markets, Inc., 384 So.2d 1253 (Fla.App.1980).

c.  An employee got into a fight in the company parking lot with another employee who was drunk:  the sober employee had refused to return the drunk employee's car keys to him, to keep him from driving while drunk, and a fight broke out.  The company discharged both employees.  Is the sober employee's discharge a violation of the public policy against drunk driving?  See Stilphen v. Northrop Corp., 515 N.E.2d 154 (Ill.App.1987).

## 2.   BREACH OF CONTRACT

Following closely on the heels of the development of wrongful discharge as a tort cause of action, the courts began to scrutinize breach of contract claims in wrongful termination cases more carefully.  Most courts which had been faced with contract claims for wrongful discharge had treated the employment at will rule as inviolable.  Any other construction led to problems with two important tenets of traditional contract analysis:  mutuality of obligation and consideration.  Specifically, how could the employee be free to quit and the employer not be free to terminate?  What consideration beyond services for which the employer paid directly did the employee provide in order to secure a promise that termination would only occur for just cause?  The at will rule, however, represents only a rebuttable presumption, subject to modification by the parties either in writing or orally.

### a.   WRITTEN CONTRACTS

## Gordon v. Matthew Bender & Co.

562 F.Supp. 1286 (N.D.Ill.1983).

■ WILLIAM T. HART, DISTRICT JUDGE.

The plaintiff Joel Gordon ("Gordon"), a citizen of Illinois, has brought a twelve-count First Amended Complaint ("complaint") against Matthew Bender & Company, Inc. ("Matthew Bender"), a New York corporation with its principal place of business in New York.  * * *

Gordon began working for Matthew Bender on November 5, 1973, as one of its law book sales representatives in a territory which included parts of Chicago and the surrounding areas.  The employment agreement between Gordon and Matthew Bender stated no definite period during which the parties remained obligated to each other.  Gordon developed into a commendable employee who reached or exceeded the goals set for him by his employer.

On July 24, 1980, Gordon was informed by his superior at Matthew Bender that his territory would be reduced on September 1, 1980.  On October 7, 1980, he was told that he would be terminated if he failed to achieve in his new territory the same sales goals which had been set for the territory he worked in prior to the September 1 change.   Thus though Gordon's territory had been diminished, his sales goals remained the same. He did not meet the goals and was fired on January 8, 1981.

* * *

Gordon alleges that it was "Matthew Bender's policy and practice * * * to condition its sales representatives' continued employment on 'acceptable sales performance.'"   He refers to a letter from Matthew Bender to Gordon placing him on probationary status.   This letter states that if Gordon meets his goals, he will be "restored to the same status of acceptable sales performance as other Matthew Bender sales representatives."   Gordon alleges that this letter created a contract for continuous employment conditioned upon acceptable sales performance, which Matthew Bender breached by firing him even though he met or exceeded the requirement of acceptable sales performance.

Matthew Bender has moved to dismiss Count II on a variety of grounds, including:  (1) this was a contract terminable at will, and therefore Gordon's discharge is not actionable;  (2) the contract lacks mutuality and therefore is not actionable;  (3) the oral contract is unenforceable under the statute of frauds since it is for an indefinite period.   Since the Court finds that this was a contract terminable at will, the other arguments will not be addressed.

Gordon claims that though this was a contract for no definite period, it was not a contract without terms governing its duration.   Gordon's length of employment would depend on his "satisfactory performance" or "acceptable sales performance."   Therefore, the argument goes, so long as the condition of acceptable performance was being met—and this is a fact issue which precludes the granting of a motion to dismiss, since the Court must accept the plaintiff's allegations as true—the contract could not be terminated.   Gordon relies heavily on Scaramuzzo v. Glenmore Distilleries Co., 501 F.Supp. 727 (N.D.Ill.1980).

In *Scaramuzzo*, the fired plaintiff alleged that the defendant-employer had promised that Scaramuzzo "would be discharged only for good cause, and [that] he would retain all corporate responsibilities assigned to him as long as he competently executed such responsibilities."   Defendant moved for summary judgment on grounds that this was an employment agreement terminable at will.   The court denied the motion, stating that "[a] contract that fails to specify the length of the term of employment, but that does set conditions upon which termination may be based, is not terminable at will—it is terminated upon the existence of those conditions."   Since there existed a fact question as to whether such conditions existed—whether the plaintiff could be discharged only for good cause, and whether he would retain his responsibilities as long as he executed them competently— summary judgment could not be granted.

Gordon argues that there existed a condition to his employment contract with Matthew Bender—"acceptable sales performance"—so that, as in *Scaramuzzo,* a legal claim exists which at the very least precludes a dismissal of this count of the complaint.   But Gordon cannot distinguish two other cases precisely on point.   In Buian v. J.L. Jacobs and Company, 428 F.2d 531 (7th Cir.1970), the court found that the following contract language did not raise any fact issue, and that a contract terminable at will existed:  "It is scheduled that your assignment in Saudi Arabia will continue for a period of eighteen (18) months.  * * * It is intended that all staff associates assigned to the Saudi Arabia projects will remain in Saudi Arabia * * * throughout the duration of the specified assignments.   This of course presumes *satisfactory service* by each associate * * *."

In Payne v. AHFI/Netherlands, B.V., 522 F.Supp. 18 (N.D.Ill.1980), the court construed terms similar to those at issue in *Buian* and also found that a contract at will existed.   The duration of the *Payne* contract was to depend on factors such as "individual performance."

*Buian* and *Payne* clearly stand for the proposition that satisfactory or acceptable performance language does not transform a contract with no definite period—one at will—into a contract which cannot be terminated by either party at any time for any reason.   The Court finds that these cases control.   Further, *Scaramuzzo* is not contrary authority.   It is distinguishable on its facts—no discharge except "for good cause" (an objective criterion) has a different meaning, in this employment context, from an employment which lasts as long as performance is "acceptable" (a subjective decision).

Further, two Illinois cases hold that a "satisfactory performance" contract is terminable at will.   See Kendall v. West, 196 Ill. 221, 63 N.E. 683 (1902) (employment contract lasting as long as employee performed "satisfactory services" may be terminated at any time for any reason); Vogel v. Pekoc, 157 Ill. 339, 42 N.E. 386 (1895) (employment agreement "to continue only so long as satisfactory" may be terminated at any time for any reason).

Gordon disparages *Kendall* and *Vogel* as "turn-of-the-century cases." However, it is clear that at least *Kendall* has continuing vitality as it formed the basis of a recent decision of the Illinois appellate court.

In addition, the Illinois courts have shown no disposition to abandon the at will doctrine except in carefully defined areas.  * * *

A "condition" of satisfactory or acceptable performance theoretically could be implied in every employment contract.   Such an end-run around the at will doctrine would eviscerate it altogether, and the Illinois courts do not seem inclined to do so.   The motion to dismiss Count II is granted.

NOTES AND QUESTIONS

**1.**  In *Gordon,* the court distinguished contracts that continue as long as performance is "acceptable" or "satisfactory" from contracts that limit discharge to "good cause."   The court concluded that in the former, the employment remains at will because subjective criteria would be used in making a decision to discharge, whereas in the latter the employment is not at will because objective criteria would be used.   Do you agree with this reasoning?  In *Gordon,* how was "acceptable" performance to be determined?

**2.**   The general rule regarding written contracts is that if the contract is for a definite term the employee may be discharged before the expiration date only for breach of a contractual provision or other "good cause." When the employee establishes that he or she was discharged in violation of an employment contract, the burden of proof shifts to the employer to prove the existence of good cause for the discharge.  See Rosecrans v. Intermountain Soap & Chemical Co., 605 P.2d 963 (Idaho 1980).

**3.**   A sales representative has a written contract detailing the salary and commissions she is to receive as well as other terms and conditions of employment.  The contract is not for any definite term.  If the employer later reduces the amount of commission she is to receive, does the employee have a cause of action for breach of contract?  See Green v. Bettinger, 608 F.Supp. 35 (E.D.Pa.1984), affirmed, 791 F.2d 917 (3d Cir.1986), cert. denied, 479 U.S. 1069 (1987).

**4.**   When an employer notifies an at-will employee that the terms of employment are being changed, such as a reduction in salary, the employee has the option of accepting the new conditions or resigning.  "[T]he employer can terminate the old contract and make an offer for a unilateral contract under new terms."  Digiancinto v. Ameriko–Omserv Corp., 69 Cal.Rptr.2d 300, 304 (Cal.Ct.App.1997).  "If the employee continues working with knowledge of the changes, he has accepted the changes as a matter of law."  Hathaway v. General Mills, Inc., 711 S.W.2d 227, 229 (Tex.1986).

b.   IMPLIED TERMS OF AN ORAL CONTRACT

Unlike Joel Gordon, most employees have no individual written contract which sets out specific terms of employment or the parties' understandings.  In seeking a contract analysis solution to the problem of unfair terminations in these cases, the courts have had to look beyond the express terms of the contract to its implied ones.


## Pugh v. See's Candies, Inc.

171 Cal.Rptr. 917 (Cal.App.1981).

■ GRODIN, J.—After 32 years of employment with See's Candies, Inc., in which he worked his way up the corporate ladder from dishwasher to vice president in charge of production and member of the board of directors, Wayne Pugh was fired.  Asserting that he had been fired in breach of contract and for reasons which offend public policy he sued his former employer seeking compensatory and punitive damages for wrongful termination, and joined as a defendant a labor organization which, he alleged, had conspired in or induced the wrongful conduct.  The case went to trial before a jury, and upon conclusion of the plaintiff's case-in-chief the trial court granted defendants' motions for nonsuit, and this appeal followed.

\* \* \*

The defendant employer is in the business of manufacturing fresh candy at its plants in Los Angeles and South San Francisco and marketing the candy through its own retail outlets.

Pugh began working for See's at its Bay Area plant (then in San Francisco) in January 1941 washing pots and pans. From there he was promoted to candy maker, and held that position until the early part of 1942, when he entered the Air Corps. Upon his discharge in 1946 he returned to See's and his former position. After a year he was promoted to the position of production manager in charge of personnel, ordering raw materials, and supervising the production of candy. When, in 1950, See's moved into a larger plant in San Francisco, Pugh had responsibility for laying out the design of the plant, taking bids, and assisting in the construction. While working at this plant, Pugh sought to increase his value to the company by taking three years of night classes in plant layout, economics, and business law. When See's moved its San Francisco plant to its present location in South San Francisco in 1957, Pugh was given responsibilities for the new location similar to those which he undertook in 1950. By this time See's business and its number of production employees had increased substantially, and a new position of assistant production manager was created under Pugh's supervision.

In 1971 Pugh was again promoted, this time as vice president in charge of production and was placed upon the board of directors of See's northern California subsidiary, "in recognition of his accomplishments." In 1972 he received a gold watch from See's "in appreciation of 31 years of loyal service."

In May 1973 Pugh travelled with Charles Huggins, then president of See's, and their respective families to Europe on a business trip to visit candy manufacturers and to inspect new equipment. Mr. Huggins returned in early June to attend a board of director's meeting while Pugh and his family remained in Europe on a planned vacation.

Upon Pugh's return from Europe on Sunday, June 25, 1973, he received a message directing him to fly to Los Angeles the next day and meet with Mr. Huggins.

Pugh went to Los Angeles expecting to be told of another promotion. The preceding Christmas season had been the most successful in See's history, the Valentine's Day holiday of 1973 set a new sales record for See's, and the March 1973 edition of See's Newsletter, containing two pictures of Pugh, carried congratulations on the increased production.

Instead, upon Pugh's arrival at Mr. Huggins' office, the latter said, "Wayne, come in and sit down. We might as well get right to the point. I have decided your services are no longer required by See's Candies. Read this and sign it." Huggins handed him a letter confirming his termination and directing him to remove that day "only personal papers and possessions from your office," but "absolutely no records, formulas or other material"; and to turn in and account for "all keys, credit cards, et cetera." The letter advised that Pugh would receive unpaid salary, bonuses and accrued vacation through that date, and the full amount of his profit sharing account, but "No severance pay will be granted." Finally, Pugh was directed "not to visit or contact Production Department employees while they are on the job."

The letter contained no reason for Pugh's termination. When Pugh asked Huggins for a reason, he was told only that he should "look deep within [him]self" to find the answer, that "Things were said by people in the trade that have come back to us." Pugh's termination was subsequently announced to the industry in a letter which, again, stated no reasons.

When Pugh first went to work for See's, Ed Peck, then president and general manager, frequently told him: "if you are loyal to [See's] and do a good job, your future is secure." Laurance See, who became president of the company in 1951 and served in that capacity until his death in 1969, had a practice of not terminating administrative personnel except for good cause, and this practice was carried on by his brother, Charles B. See, who succeeded Laurance as president.

During the entire period of his employment, there had been no formal or written criticism of Pugh's work. No complaints were ever raised at the annual meetings which preceded each holiday season, and he was never denied a raise or bonus. He received no notice that there was a problem which needed correction, nor any warning that any disciplinary action was being contemplated.

Pugh's theory as to why he was terminated relates to a contract which See's at that time had with the defendant union. * * * [Pugh had objected in 1968 negotiations to a provision which permitted See's to pay seasonal employees at a lower rate. When asked in 1971 to be part of the company's negotiating team, Pugh responded that he would like to, but he was bothered by the possibility that See's had a "sweetheart" contract with the union, by which Pugh meant one that permitted the employer to get a competitive advantage over other employers by paying lower wages to some employees, with the collusion of the union.]

The union's alleged participation in Pugh's termination was in the form of a statement attributed to Mr. Button (the individual who succeeded Pugh as production manager) at a negotiating meeting between the company and the union in June 1973. According to one witness, Mr. Button stated at the commencement of the meeting, "Now we've taken care of Mr. Pugh. What are you going to do for us."

\* \* \*

In recent years, there have been established by statute a variety of limitations upon the employer's power of dismissal. Employers are precluded, for example, from terminating employees for a variety of reasons, including union membership or activities, race, sex, age or political affiliation. Legislatures in this country have so far refrained, however, from adopting statutes, such as those which exist in most other industrialized countries, which would provide more generalized protection to employees against unjust dismissal.   And while public employees may enjoy job security through civil service rules and due process, the legal principles which give rise to these protections are not directly applicable to employees in private industry.

Even apart from statute or constitutional protection, however, the employer's right to terminate employees is not absolute.   * * * Two relevant limiting principles have developed, one of them based upon public policy and the other upon traditional contract doctrine.   The first limitation precludes dismissal "when an employer's discharge of an employee violates fundamental principles of public policy" (Tameny v. Atlantic Richfield Co. (1980) 27 Cal.3d 167, 170), the second when the discharge is contrary to the terms of the agreement, express or implied.   * * *

The presumption that an employment contract is intended to be terminable at will is subject, like any presumption, to contrary evidence. This may take the form of an agreement, express or implied, that the relationship will continue for some fixed period of time.   Or, and of greater relevance here, it may take the form of an agreement that the employment relationship will continue indefinitely, pending the occurrence of some event such as the employer's dissatisfaction with the employee's services or the existence of some "cause" for termination.   Sometimes this latter type of agreement is characterized as a contract for "permanent" employment, but that characterization may be misleading.   In one of the earliest California cases on this subject, the Supreme Court interpreted a contract for permanent employment as meaning "that plaintiffs' employment * * * was to continue indefinitely, and until one or the other of the parties wish, *for some good reason,* to sever the relation."   (Lord v. Goldberg, 81 Cal. 596, 601–602, italics added.)

A contract which limits the power of the employer with respect to the reasons for termination is no less enforceable because it places no equivalent limits upon the power of the employee to quit his employment.   "If the requirement of consideration is met, there is no additional requirement of * * * equivalence in the values exchanged, or 'mutuality of obligation.' " (Rest.2d Contracts, § 81 (Tent. Draft No. 2, 1965); 1A Corbin on Contracts (1963) § 152, pp. 13–17).

Moreover, while it has sometimes been said that a promise for continued employment subject to limitation upon the employer's power of termination must be supported by some "independent consideration," i.e., consideration other than the services to be rendered, such a rule is contrary to the general contract principle that courts should not inquire into the adequacy of consideration.   "A single and undivided consideration may be bargained for and given as the agreed equivalent of one promise or of two promises or of many promises."   (1 Corbin on Contracts (1963) § 125, pp. 535–536.)   Thus there is no analytical reason why an employee's promise to render services, or his actual rendition of services over time, may not support an employer's promise both to pay a particular wage (for example) and to refrain from arbitrary dismissal.

* * *

In determining whether there exists an implied-in-fact promise for some form of continued employment courts have considered a variety of factors in addition to the existence of independent consideration. These have included, for example, the personnel policies or practices of the employer, the employee's longevity of service, actions or communications by the employer reflecting assurances of continued employment, and the practices of the industry in which the employee is engaged.

Here * * *, there were facts in evidence from which the jury could determine the existence of such an implied promise: the duration of appellant's employment, the commendations and promotions he received, the apparent lack of any direct criticism of his work, the assurances he was given, and the employer's acknowledged policies. While oblique language will not, standing alone, be sufficient to establish agreement, it is appropriate to consider the totality of the parties' relationship: Agreement may be " 'shown by the acts and conduct of the parties, interpreted in the light of the subject matter and of the surrounding circumstances.' " (Marvin v. Marvin (1976) 18 Cal.3d 660, 678, fn. 16). We therefore conclude that it was error to grant respondents' motions for nonsuit as to See's.

Since this litigation may proceed toward yet uncharted waters, we consider it appropriate to provide some guidance as to the questions which the trial court may confront on remand. We have held that appellant has demonstrated a prima facie case of wrongful termination in violation of his contract of employment. The burden of coming forward with evidence as to the reason for appellant's termination now shifts to the employer. Appellant may attack the employer's offered explanation, either on the ground that it is pretextual (and that the real reason is one prohibited by contract or public policy), or on the ground that it is insufficient to meet the employer's obligations under contract or applicable legal principles. Appellant bears, however, the ultimate burden of proving that he was terminated wrongfully.

By what standard that burden is to be measured will depend, in part, upon what conclusions the jury draws as to the nature of the contract between the parties. The terms "just cause" and "good cause," "as used in a variety of contexts * * * have been found to be difficult to define with precision and to be largely relative in their connotation, depending upon the particular circumstances of each case." (R.J. Cardinal Co. v. Ritchie (1963) 218 Cal.App.2d 124, 144.) Essentially, they connote "a fair and honest cause or reason, regulated by good faith on the part of the party exercising the power." (Id. at p. 145.) Care must be taken, however, not to interfere with the legitimate exercise of managerial discretion. "Good cause" in this context is quite different from the standard applicable in determining the propriety of an employee's termination under a contract for a specified term. And where, as here, the employee occupies a sensitive managerial or confidential position, the employer must of necessity be allowed substantial scope for the exercise of subjective judgment.

Evidence as to what appellant's successor told union representatives after his termination ("Now we've taken care of Mr. Pugh.  What are you going to do for us?"), while hardly in itself weighty, is nevertheless sufficient in context given principles applicable to nonsuits, to justify an inference that appellant was terminated in response to the union's insistence.   A union is privileged to induce a breach of contract between employer and employee in the pursuit of a legitimate labor objective; alternatively, a union's efforts to cause termination of a supervisory employee for reasons bearing upon his relationship to the union may constitute an unfair labor practice subject to the exclusive jurisdiction of the National Labor Relations Board (29 U.S.C. § 158(b)(1)(B)).   At this stage, however, the record is inadequate to support definitive application of either privilege or preemption.   We therefore conclude that the judgment of nonsuit was erroneously granted with respect to the union as well.

Reversed.

## NOTES AND QUESTIONS

**1.**   In concluding that Pugh's employment contract was not terminable at will, the court relied on statements made by See's former president Ed Peck that "If you are loyal to See's and do a good job, your future is secure."   Were these statements sufficient to establish an implied contract? Would the result have been the same if Pugh had only worked for See's for two years, instead of 29?   What factors does the court identify as determinants of employees' contract rights in employment?   Which ones were used to establish Pugh's right to his job?   What specific right does he have:  a right to "permanent" employment, not to be discharged at will, not to be discharged except for cause, or something else?

**2.**   How does the court treat the issue of consideration?   What consideration did Pugh offer in exchange for See's promise of future employment? How does mutuality of obligation fit into the court's analysis?

**3.**   The union representing production employees at See's arguably had a role in Pugh's termination.   Is there legal redress for such interference? How would you prove the union's culpability?   What effective remedy could be ordered?   Consider whether any state law claim in contract or tort would be preempted by an unfair labor practice claim under the National Labor Relations Act.

**4.**   Pugh sued in both tort and contract to challenge his discharge.   His tort claim was dismissed because the court concluded that the employer's actions, while morally reprehensible, did not fall within its narrow definition of the public policy exception.   Should the employer be potentially liable in both tort and contract?   See *Foley,* infra p. 953.   Alternatively, can an employer be liable in both tort and contract *automatically*?   Is not protecting the integrity of contracts an important "public policy" which the courts should want to include within the exception to the at will rule?   See Tameny v. Atlantic Richfield Co., 610 P.2d 1330, 1339 (Cal.1980) (Clark, J., dissenting).

**5.**   In Calleon v. Miyagi, 876 P.2d 1278 (Haw.1994), the Supreme Court of Hawaii declined to adopt the *Pugh* rationale, expressing doubt about "subjecting each discharge to judicial incursions into the amorphous concept of bad faith." Does *Pugh* really subject every discharge to a bad faith standard?

**6.** In Miller v. Pepsi–Cola Bottling Co., 259 Cal.Rptr. 56 (Ct.App.1989), and Davis v. Consolidated Freightways, 34 Cal.Rptr.2d 438 (Ct.App.1994), summary judgment for employers was granted where the only evidence of an implied contract was the employee's longevity of service, regular salary increases, and promotions. The court in *Miller* stated that these factors "should not change the status of an at-will employee to one that is dischargeable only for cause." Does this help to define the scope of *Pugh?*

**7.** Should *Pugh* apply to situations other than discharge, or is it the thin end of the wedge regarding the enforceability of oral promises from employers to employees? The New Hampshire Supreme Court held that an employer's promise to continue salary, pension, and insurance benefits for three months after possible layoffs could constitute an enforceable unilateral contract, if there was an offer that was accepted by an employee by continuing to perform his regular duties. Panto v. Moore Business Forms, Inc., 547 A.2d 260 (N.H.1988). Similarly, the Eighth Circuit held that laid-off employees could sue their employer for compensatory damages over failing to keep its promise of at will re-employment following a corporate restructuring. Bower v. AT & T Technologies, Inc., 852 F.2d 361 (8th Cir.1988).

### c. EMPLOYEE HANDBOOKS AND MANUALS

In addition to finding enforceable promises in oral statements made to employees during their term of employment, a number of courts have also been responsive to employees' claims that unilaterally issued personnel manuals can create binding obligations on employers.

## Woolley v. Hoffmann–La Roche, Inc.

491 A.2d 1257 (N.J.1985), modified, 499 A.2d 515 (N.J.1985).

■ Wilentz, C.J.

The issue before us is whether certain terms in a company's employment manual may contractually bind the company. We hold that absent a clear and prominent disclaimer, an implied promise contained in an employment manual that an employee will be fired only for cause may be enforceable against an employer even when the employment is for an indefinite term and would otherwise be terminable at will.

Plaintiff, Richard Woolley, was hired by defendant, Hoffmann-La Roche, Inc., in October 1969, as an Engineering Section Head in defendant's Central Engineering Department at Nutley. There was no written employment contract between plaintiff and defendant. Plaintiff began work in mid-November 1969. Some time in December, plaintiff received and read the personnel manual on which his claims are based.

In 1976, plaintiff was promoted, and in January 1977 he was promoted again, this latter time to Group Leader for the Civil Engineering, the Piping Design, the Plant Layout, and the Standards and Systems Sections. In March 1978, plaintiff was directed to write a report to his supervisors about piping problems in one of defendant's buildings in Nutley. This report was written and submitted to plaintiff's immediate supervisor on April 5, 1978. On May 3, 1978, stating that the General Manager of defendant's Corporate Engineering Department had lost confidence in him, plaintiff's supervisors requested his resignation. Following this, by letter dated May 22, 1978, plaintiff was formally asked for his resignation, to be effective July 15, 1978.

Plaintiff refused to resign. Two weeks later defendant again requested plaintiff's resignation, and told him he would be fired if he did not resign. Plaintiff again declined, and he was fired in July.

Plaintiff filed a complaint alleging breach of contract, intentional infliction of emotional distress, and defamation, but subsequently consented to the dismissal of the latter two claims. The gist of plaintiff's breach of contract claim is that the express and implied promises in defendant's employment manual created a contract under which he could not be fired at will, but rather only for cause, and then only after the procedures outlined in the manual were followed.[1] Plaintiff contends that he was not dismissed for good cause, and that his firing was a breach of contract.

Defendant's motion for summary judgment was granted by the trial court, which held that the employment manual was not contractually binding on defendant, thus allowing defendant to terminate plaintiff's employment at will.[2] The Appellate Division affirmed. We granted certification.[3]

---

**1.** According to the provisions of the manual, defendant could, and over the years apparently did, unilaterally change these provisions.

**2.** It may be of some help to point out some of the manual's general provisions here. It is entitled "Hoffmann-La Roche, Inc. Personnel Policy Manual" and at the bottom of the face page is the notation "issued to: [and then in handwriting] Richard Woolley 12/1/69." The portions of the manual submitted to us consist of eight pages. It describes the employees "covered" by the manual ("all employees of Hoffmann-La Roche"), the manual's purpose ("a practical operating tool in the equitable and efficient administration of our employee relations program"); five of the eight pages are devoted to "termination." In addition to setting forth the purpose and policy of the termination section, it defines "the types of termination" as "layoff," "discharge due to performance," "discharge, disciplinary," "retirement" and "resignation." As one might expect, layoff is a termination caused by lack of work, retirement a termination caused by age, resignation a termination on the initiative of the employee, and discharge due to performance and discharge, disciplinary, are both terminations for cause. There is no category set forth for discharge without cause. The termination section includes "Guidelines for discharge due to performance," consisting of a fairly detailed procedure to be used before an employee may be fired for cause. Preceding these definitions of the five categories of termination is a section on "Policy," the first sentence of which provides: "It is the policy of Hoffmann-La Roche to retain to the extent consistent with company requirements, the services of all employees who perform their duties efficiently and effectively."

**3.** Mr. Woolley died prior to oral argument before this Court. The claim for damages, while diminished, survives.

Hoffmann-La Roche contends that the formation of the type of contract claimed by plaintiff to exist—Hoffmann-La Roche calls it a permanent employment contract for life—is subject to special contractual requirements: the intent of the parties to create such an undertaking must be clear and definite; in addition to an explicit provision setting forth its duration, the agreement must specifically cover the essential terms of employment—the duties, responsibilities, and compensation of the employee, and the proof of these terms must be clear and convincing; the undertaking must be supported by consideration in addition to the employee's continued work.  Woolley claims that the requirements for the formation of such a contract have been met here and that they do not extend as far as Hoffmann-La Roche claims.  Further, Woolley argues that this is not a "permanent contract for life," but rather an employment contract of indefinite duration that may be terminated only for good cause and in accordance with the procedure set forth in the personnel policy manual. Both parties agree that the employment contract is one of indefinite duration;  Hoffmann-La Roche contends that in New Jersey, when an employment contract is of indefinite duration, the inescapable legal conclusion is that it is an employment at will;  Woolley claims that even such a contract—of indefinite duration—may contain provisions requiring that termination be only for cause.

\* \* \*

We are thus faced with the question of whether this is the kind of employment contract—a "long-range commitment"—that must be construed as one of indefinite duration and therefore at will \* \* \*, or whether ordinary contractual doctrine applies.  In either case, the question is whether Hoffmann-La Roche retained the right to fire with or without cause or whether, as Woolley claims, his employment could be terminated only for cause.  We believe another question, not explicitly treated below, is involved:  should the legal effect of the dissemination of a personnel policy manual by a company with a substantial number of employees be determined solely and strictly by traditional contract doctrine?  Is that analysis adequate for the realities of such a workplace?

\* \* \*

Given the facts before us and the common law of contracts interpreted in the light of sound policy applicable to this modern setting, we conclude that the termination clauses of this company's Personnel Policy Manual, including the procedure required before termination occurs, could be found to be contractually enforceable.  Furthermore, we conclude that when an employer of a substantial number of employees circulates a manual that, when fairly read, provides that certain benefits are an incident of the employment (including, especially, job security provisions), the judiciary, instead of "grudgingly" conceding the enforceability of those provisions, should construe them in accordance with the reasonable expectations of the employees.

The employer's contention here is that the distribution of the manual was simply an expression of the company's "philosophy" and therefore free of any possible contractual consequences. The former employee claims it could reasonably be read as an explicit statement of company policies intended to be followed by the company in the same manner as if they were expressed in an agreement signed by both employer and employees. From the analysis that follows we conclude that a jury, properly instructed, could find, in strict contract terms, that the manual constituted an offer; put differently, it could find that this portion of the manual (concerning job security) set forth terms and conditions of employment.

In determining the manual's meaning and effect, we must consider the probable context in which it was disseminated and the environment surrounding its continued existence. The manual, though apparently not distributed to all employees ("in general, distribution will be provided to supervisory personnel * * * "), covers all of them. Its terms are of such importance to all employees that in the absence of contradicting evidence, it would seem clear that it was intended by Hoffmann-La Roche that all employees be advised of the benefits it confers.

We take judicial notice of the fact that Hoffmann-La Roche is a substantial company with many employees in New Jersey. The record permits the conclusion that the policy manual represents the most reliable statement of the terms of their employment. At oral argument counsel conceded that it is rare for any employee, except one on the medical staff, to have a special contract. Without minimizing the importance of its specific provisions, the context of the manual's preparation and distribution is, to us, the most persuasive proof that it would be almost inevitable for an employee to regard it as a binding commitment, legally enforceable, concerning the terms and conditions of his employment. Having been employed, like hundreds of his co-employees, without any individual employment contract, by an employer whose good reputation made it so attractive, the employee is given this one document that purports to set forth the terms and conditions of his employment, a document obviously carefully prepared by the company with all of the appearances of corporate legitimacy that one could imagine. If there were any doubt about it (and there would be none in the mind of most employees), the name of the manual dispels it, for it is nothing short of the official *policy* of the company, it is the Personnel *Policy* Manual. As every employee knows, when superiors tell you "it's company policy," they mean business.

The mere fact of the manual's distribution suggests its importance. Its changeability—the uncontroverted ability of management to change its terms—is argued as supporting its non-binding quality, but one might as easily conclude that, given its importance, the employer wanted to keep it up to date, especially to make certain, given this employer's good reputation in labor relations, that the benefits conferred were sufficiently competitive with those available from other employers, including benefits found in collective bargaining agreements. The record suggests that the changes actually made almost always favored the employees.

Given that background, then, unless the language contained in the manual were such that no one could reasonably have thought it was intended to create legally binding obligations, the termination provisions of the policy manual would have to be regarded as an obligation undertaken by the employer.  It will not do now for the company to say it did not mean the things it said in its manual to be binding.  Our courts will not allow an employer to offer attractive inducements and benefits to the workforce and then withdraw them when it chooses, no matter how sincere its belief that they are not enforceable.

* * *

Having concluded that a jury could find the Personnel Policy Manual to constitute an offer, we deal with what most cases deem the major obstacle to construction of the terms as constituting a binding agreement, namely, the requirement under contract law that consideration must be given in exchange for the employer's offer in order to convert that offer into a binding agreement.  The cases on this subject deal with such issues as whether there was a promise in return for the employer's promise (the offer contained in the manual constituting, in effect, a promise), or whether there was some benefit or detriment bargained for and in fact conferred or suffered, sufficient to create a unilateral contract;  whether the action or inaction, the benefit or the detriment, was done or not done in reliance on the employer's offer or promise;  whether the alleged agreement was so lacking in "mutuality" as to be insufficient for contractual purposes—in other words, whether the fundamental requirements of a contract have been met.

We conclude that these job security provisions contained in a personnel policy manual widely distributed among a large workforce are supported by consideration and may therefore be enforced as a binding commitment of the employer.

In order for an offer in the form of a promise to become enforceable, it must be accepted.  Acceptance will depend on what the promisor bargained for:  he may have bargained for a return promise that, if given, would result in a bilateral contract, both promises becoming enforceable.  Or he may have bargained for some action or nonaction that, if given or withheld, would render his promise enforceable as a unilateral contract.  In most of the cases involving an employer's personnel policy manual, the document is prepared without any negotiations and is voluntarily distributed to the workforce by the employer.  It seeks no return promise from the employees.  It is reasonable to interpret it as seeking continued work from the employees, who, in most cases, are free to quit since they are almost always employees at will, not simply in the sense that the employer can fire them without cause, but in the sense that they can quit without breaching any obligation.  Thus analyzed, the manual is an offer that seeks the formation of a unilateral contract—the employees' bargained-for action needed to make the offer binding being their continued work when they have no obligation to continue.

The lack of definiteness concerning the other terms of employment—its duration, wages, precise service to be rendered, hours of work, etc., does not prevent enforcement of a job security provision.  The lack of terms (if the complete manual is similarly lacking) can cause problems of interpretation about these other aspects of employment, but not to the point of making the job security term unenforceable.  Realistically, the objection has force only when the agreement is regarded as a special one between the employer and an individual employee.  There it might be difficult to determine whether there was good cause for termination if one could not determine what it was that the employee was expected to do.  That difficulty is one factor that suggests the employer did not intend a lifetime contract with one employee.  Here the question of good cause is made considerably easier to deal with in view of the fact that the agreement applies to the entire workforce, and the workforce itself is rather large.  Even-handedness and equality of treatment will make the issue in most cases far from complex; the fact that in some cases the "for cause" provision may be difficult to interpret and enforce should not deprive employees in other cases from taking advantage of it.  If there is a problem arising from indefiniteness, in any event, it is one caused by the employer.  It was the employer who chose to make the termination provisions explicit and clear.  If indefiniteness as to other provisions is a problem, it is one of the employer's own making from which it should gain no advantage.  * * *

We therefore reverse the Appellate Division's affirmance of the trial court's grant of summary judgment and remand this matter to the trial court for further proceedings consistent with this opinion.  Those proceedings should have the benefit of the entire manual that was in force at the time Woolley was discharged.  The provisions of the manual concerning job security shall be considered binding unless the manual elsewhere prominently and unmistakably indicates that those provisions shall not be binding or unless there is some other similar proof of the employer's intent not to be bound.  * * * Woolley need not prove consideration—that shall be presumed.  Furthermore, it shall not be open to defendant to prove that good cause in fact existed on the basis of which Woolley could have been terminated.  If the court or jury concludes that the manual's job security provisions are binding, then, according to those provisions, even if good cause existed, an employee could not be fired unless the employer went through the various procedures set forth in the manual, steps designed to rehabilitate that employee in order to *avoid* termination.  On the record before us the employer's failure to do so is undeniable.  If that is the case, we believe it would be unfair to allow this employer to try now to recreate the facts as they might have existed had the employer given to Woolley that which the manual promised, namely, a set of detailed procedures, all for Woolley's benefit, designed to see if there was some way he could be retained by Hoffmann-La Roche.  * * *

We are aware that problems that do not ordinarily exist when collective bargaining agreements are involved may arise from the enforcement of employment manuals.  Policy manuals may not generally be as comprehensive or definite as typical collective bargaining agreements.  Further problems may result from the employer's explicitly reserved right unilaterally to change the manual. We have no doubt that, generally, changes in such a manual, including changes in terms and conditions of employment, are permitted. We express no opinion, however, on whether or to what extent they are permitted when they adversely affect a binding job security provision.

Our opinion need not make employers reluctant to prepare and distribute company policy manuals. Such manuals can be very helpful tools in labor relations, helpful both to employer and employees, and we would regret it if the consequence of this decision were that the constructive aspects of these manuals were in any way diminished. We do not believe that they will, or at least we certainly do not believe that that constructive aspect *should* be diminished as a result of this opinion.

All that this opinion requires of an employer is that it be fair. It would be unfair to allow an employer to distribute a policy manual that makes the workforce believe that certain promises have been made and then to allow the employer to renege on those promises. What is sought here is basic honesty: if the employer, for whatever reason, does not want the manual to be capable of being construed by the court as a binding contract, there are simple ways to attain that goal. All that need be done is the inclusion in a very prominent position of an appropriate statement that there is no promise of any kind by the employer contained in the manual; that regardless of what the manual says or provides, the employer promises nothing and remains free to change wages and all other working conditions without having to consult anyone and without anyone's agreement; and that the employer continues to have the absolute power to fire anyone with or without good cause.

Reversed and remanded for trial.

NOTES AND QUESTIONS

**1.** A number of jurisdictions have recognized employee rights grounded in employment handbooks or personnel manuals. See Toussaint v. Blue Cross & Blue Shield of Michigan, 292 N.W.2d 880 (Mich.1980); Pine River State Bank v. Mettille, 333 N.W.2d 622 (Minn.1983). Other courts have been reluctant to bind employers to the terms of an "agreement" which can hardly said to have been bargained for in any traditional sense, among them, Florida, Illinois, Indiana, and Texas. See also Note, Employee Handbooks and Employment-at-Will Contracts, 1985 Duke L.J. 196.

Courts have continued to divide on the question whether statements in a handbook or personnel manual give employees protection against at-will termination; not too surprisingly, the actual outcome in a number of cases depends on the exact nature of the statements in the handbook. See, e.g., Duldulao v. St. Mary of Nazareth Hospital Center, 505 N.E.2d 314 (Ill. 1987) (language in handbook that nonprobationary employee could be discharged only after written notice was sufficient to modify at-will nature of employment); Hoffmann–La Roche, Inc. v. Campbell, 512 So.2d 725 (Ala.1987) (provisions in handbook plus continued employment following receipt of handbook created unilateral contract that modified at-will relationship); Bauer v. American Freight System, Inc., 422 N.W.2d 435 (S.D. 1988) (statement in employee handbook that employment relationship "is firmly based on the foundation of fair play and just and equitable dealings" too general to create employment contract); Roy v. Woonsocket Institution for Savings, 525 A.2d 915 (R.I.1987) (bank vice-president at-will employee despite provisions of handbook and personnel manual).

**2.** In *Woolley,* what contract theory formed the legal basis for the court's finding a just cause right for Woolley: unilateral contract, bilateral contract, promissory estoppel, or something else? What would be the elements of each theory? The employer's defenses?

**3.** Employee handbooks are issued unilaterally by employers. May they be changed unilaterally as well, or do employee rights or benefits contained therein "vest" at some point? Would it make a difference whether the employer modified or eliminated a "right"—such as job security—or a "benefit"—such as severance pay? See Bankey v. Storer Broadcasting Co., 443 N.W.2d 112 (Mich.1989). Brodie v. General Chemical Corp., 934 P.2d 1263 (Wyo.1997), held that an employer cannot reduce contractual rights employees already retain without new consideration and continued employment is insufficient consideration for such a change. Other courts have held that remaining with an employer after receipt of a personnel manual promising job security supplies the necessary consideration to make the promise legally enforceable. Sisco v. GSA National Capital Federal Credit Union, 689 A.2d 52 (D.C.1997). See generally Stephen F. Befort, Employee Handbooks and the Legal Effect of Disclaimers, 13 Indus.Rel.L.J. 326 (1993).

**4.** If an employer may unilaterally change the terms of an employment handbook, how, if at all, must these changes be communicated to the employee? See Durtsche v. American Colloid Co., 958 F.2d 1007 (10th Cir.1992) (inconspicuous changes in a handbook were ineffective to notify an employee of change in his status from permanent employee to at-will employee). Cf. Adams v. Square D. Co., 775 F.Supp. 869 (D.S.C.1991) (new handbook, issued after employee was hired and which made employment at-will, superseded implied promises in prior handbook).

**5.** The rights employees may have under the terms of a handbook are not limited to substantive reasons for discharge, but may extend to procedural protection as well. In Mobil Coal Producing, Inc. v. Parks, 704 P.2d 702 (Wyo.1985), the discharge was held unlawful because the employer failed to follow the progressive discipline system it had established in its employee manual. Cf. Fiscella v. General Accident Insurance Co., 114 L.R.R.M. 2611 (W.D.Pa.1983), affirmed, 735 F.2d 1348 (3d Cir.1984).

**6.** The California Supreme Court ruled that employees can bring a breach-of-implied-contract action for wrongful demotion against their employer if they can show that the employer has violated its own employment policies. Because the employer intended to be bound by its policies, which were specific, detailed, and exhaustive, the policies created an implied contract not to demote except for just cause.   Scott v. Pacific Gas & Electric Co., 46 Cal.Rptr.2d 427 (Cal.1995).

For the opposite view, see Baragar v. State Farm Insurance Co., 860 F.Supp. 1257 (W.D.Mich.1994) (employee policy which gave rise to expectations of job security would not be extended to claims for wrongful demotions).

**7.**   In order to minimize the risk of a breach of contract claim following a termination, employers have been advised to avoid overselling job security at the time of initial hire.   One possible approach is for the employer to include a disclaimer in the application form or to require the successful job applicant to sign a waiver of job security as a condition of hire.   Sears, Roebuck & Company's employment application includes the following statement:   " * * * my employment and compensation can be terminated with or without cause, and with or without notice, at any time, at the option of either the Company or myself."   The company's employee handbook listed specific rules, the violation of which could result in discharge.   Several discharged employees contended that the handbook established an implied contract to discharge only for one of the listed causes or for some other good reason.   Sears argued that the provision in the application form constituted an effective waiver of any right not to be discharged except for cause.   What result?   See Reid v. Sears, Roebuck & Co., 790 F.2d 453 (6th Cir.1986).   See also Stone v. Mission Bay Mortgage Co., 672 P.2d 629 (Nev.1983);   Thompson v. St. Regis Paper Co., 685 P.2d 1081 (Wash.1984).

Personnel manuals, application forms, letters of hire, and the like are not the only possible sources of trouble for employers.   In Belknap, Inc. v. Hale, 463 U.S. 491 (1983), the employer had advertised in the newspaper for "permanent replacements" for striking workers.   When the strike was settled and the original employees returned to their jobs, the replacements were laid off.   The Supreme Court held that the replacements' suit against the employer in state court for breach of contract was not preempted by federal labor laws.

**8.**   Boilerplate language may not be enough to make a disclaimer effective. In Geldreich v. American Cyanamid Co., 691 A.2d 423 (N.J.Super.Ct.App.Div.1997), the court upheld a verdict against an employer for violation of termination provisions in an employee handbook.   The court held that where the handbook stated that the employer would attempt to find alternative employment for an employee who was downsized, it created an enforceable commitment necessitating more than a generalized disclaimer that the policy manual is not intended to create any contractual right.

**9.**   In New Jersey, juries will decide whether "an employee could reasonably expect that the [manual] provided for job security, thereby creating an implied contract of employment," and also whether the content of a disclaimer is effective.   Witkowski v. Thomas J. Lipton, Inc., 643 A.2d 546 (N.J.1994);   Nicosia v. Wakefern Food Corp., 643 A.2d 554 (N.J.1994).   For a discussion of the employee handbook issue more sympathetic to employers, see Mitchell v. Zilog, Inc., 874 P.2d 520 (Idaho 1994);   Gilmore v. Enogex, Inc., 878 P.2d 360 (Okl.1994).

**10.** The New York Court of Appeals held that "the existence of a private employer's written policy does not, in and of itself, limit the right to discharge an at-will employee." Because the plaintiff, the administrative director of a counseling center, had been employed long before the policy in question came into effect, he could not prove detrimental reliance, and so his wrongful discharge claim that the employer did not follow certain handbook procedures was dismissed. In the matter of De Petris v. Union Settlement Association, Inc., 657 N.E.2d 269 (N.Y.1995).

**11.** Implied-in-fact contract remedies are available against public sector employers. However, such employment agreements may not bind a public employer where the condition of employment is generally subject to statutory control. However, if the manual had been adopted by an act of the legislature, such contractual rights will be binding. Cooper v. Mayor of Hadden Heights, 690 A.2d 1036 (N.J.Super.Ct.App.Div.1997).

### d.  THE COVENANT OF GOOD FAITH AND FAIR DEALING

The third major approach used by courts to redress a wrongful discharge in the absence of express individual contractual rights is to find a covenant of good faith and fair dealing implicit in the employment contract. This covenant, which can be found in Restatement (Second) of Contracts, § 205, and which has traditionally been applied to commercial transactions, obligates each party to a contract to refrain from injuring in any way the other's right to receive the benefits of the contract. If such an obligation is appropriate to impose on impersonal commercial dealings, is it not equally applicable to the employment relationship? In the absence of any apparent reason to except employment from the covenant, the good faith and fair dealing theory has considerable intuitive appeal in its insistence that employment relations be characterized by fairness and good faith. In fact, it might seem at first to be a possible umbrella under which to collect all of the various causes of action which the judiciary has recognized in cases of wrongful discharge. However, as with the tort of wrongful discharge, the problems associated with defining and limiting the covenant of good faith and fair dealing are numerous.

## Fortune v. National Cash Register Co.

364 N.E.2d 1251 (Mass.1977).

■ ABRAMS, JUSTICE.

Orville E. Fortune (Fortune), a former salesman of The National Cash Register Company (NCR), brought a suit to recover certain commissions allegedly due as a result of a sale of cash registers to First National Stores Inc. (First National) in 1968. Counts 1 and 2 of Fortune's amended declaration claimed bonus payments under the parties' written contract of employment. The third count sought recovery in quantum meruit for the reasonable value of Fortune's services relating to the same sales transaction. Judgment on a jury verdict for Fortune was reversed by the Appeals

Court, and this court granted leave to obtain further appellate review. We affirm the judgment of the Superior Court. We hold, for the reasons stated herein, there was no error in submitting the issue of "bad faith" termination of an employment at will contract to the jury.

\* \* \*

Fortune was employed by NCR under a written "salesman's contract" which was terminable at will, without cause, by either party on written notice. The contract provided that Fortune would receive a weekly salary in a fixed amount plus a bonus for sales made within the "territory" (i.e., customer accounts or stores) assigned to him for "coverage or supervision," whether the sale was made by him or someone else. The amount of the bonus was determined on the basis of "bonus credits," which were computed as a percentage of the price of products sold. Fortune would be paid a percentage of the applicable bonus credit as follows: (1) 75% if the territory was assigned to him at the date of the order, (2) 25% if the territory was assigned to him at the date of delivery and installation, or (3) 100% if the territory was assigned to him at both times. The contract further provided that the "bonus interest" would terminate if shipment of the order was not made within eighteen months from the date of the order unless (1) the territory was assigned to him for coverage at the date of delivery and installation, or (2) special engineering was required to fulfil the contract. In addition, NCR reserved the right to sell products in the salesman's territory without paying a bonus. However, this right could be exercised only on written notice.

In 1968, Fortune's territory included First National. This account had been part of his territory for the preceding six years; he had been successful in obtaining several orders from First National, including a million dollar order in 1963. Sometime in late 1967, or early 1968, NCR introduced a new model cash register, Class 5. Fortune corresponded with First National in an effort to sell the machine. He also helped to arrange for a demonstration of the Class 5 to executives of First National on October 4, 1968. NCR had a team of men also working on this sale.

\* \* \* On November 29, 1968, First National signed an order for 2,008 Class 5 machines to be delivered over a four-year period at a purchase price of approximately $5,000,000. Although Fortune did not participate in the negotiation of the terms of the order, his name appeared on the order form in the space entitled "salesman credited." The amount of the bonus credit as shown on the order was $92,079.99.

On January 6, 1969, the first working day of the new year, Fortune found an envelope on his desk at work. It contained a termination notice addressed to his home dated December 2, 1968. Shortly after receiving the notice, Fortune spoke to the Boston branch manager with whom he was friendly. The manager told him, "You are through," but, after considering some of the details necessary for the smooth operation of the First National order, told him to "stay on," and to "[k]eep on doing what you are doing right now." Fortune remained with the company in a position entitled "sales support." In this capacity, he coordinated and expedited delivery of the machines to First National under the November 29 order as well as servicing other accounts.

Commencing in May or June, Fortune began to receive some bonus commissions on the First National order. Having received only 75% of the applicable bonus due on the machines which had been delivered and installed, Fortune spoke with his manager about receiving the full amount of the commission. Fortune was told "to forget about it." Sixty-one years old at that time, and with a son in college, Fortune concluded that it "was a good idea to forget it for the time being."

NCR did pay a systems and installations person the remaining 25% of the bonus commissions due from the First National order although contrary to its usual policy of paying *only* salesmen a bonus. * * *

Approximately eighteen months after receiving the termination notice, Fortune, who had worked for NCR for almost twenty-five years, was asked to retire. When he refused, he was fired in June of 1970. Fortune did not receive any bonus payments on machines which were delivered to First National after this date.

* * * By agreement of counsel, the case was sent to the jury for special verdicts on two questions:

"1. Did the Defendant act in bad faith * * * when it decided to terminate the Plaintiff's contract as a salesman by letter dated December 2, 1968, delivered on January 6, 1969?

"2. Did the Defendant act in bad faith * * * when the Defendant let the Plaintiff go on June 5, 1970?"

The jury answered both questions affirmatively, and judgment entered in the sum of $45,649.62.

The central issue on appeal is whether this "bad faith" termination constituted a breach of the employment at will contract. * * *

The contract at issue is a classic terminable at will employment contract. It is clear that the contract itself reserved to the parties an explicit power to terminate the contract without cause on written notice. It is also clear that under the express terms of the contract Fortune has received all the bonus commissions to which he is entitled. Thus, NCR claims that it did not breach the contract, and that it has no further liability to Fortune. According to a literal reading of the contract, NCR is correct.

However, Fortune argues that, in spite of the literal wording of the contract, he is entitled to a jury determination on NCR's motives in terminating his services under the contract and in finally discharging him. We agree. We hold that NCR's written contract contains an implied covenant of good faith and fair dealing, and a termination not made in good faith constitutes a breach of the contract.

We do not question the general principles that an employer is entitled to be motivated by and to serve its own legitimate business interests; that an employer must have wide latitude in deciding whom it will employ in the face of the uncertainties of the business world; and that an employer needs flexibility in the face of changing circumstances. We recognize the employer's need for a large amount of control over its work force. However, we believe that where, as here, commissions are to be paid for work performed by the employee, the employer's decision to terminate its at will employee should be made in good faith. NCR's right to make decisions in its own interest is not, in our view, unduly hampered by a requirement of adherence to this standard.

On occasion some courts have avoided the rigidity of the "at will" rule by fashioning a remedy in tort. We believe, however, that in this case there is remedy on the express contract. In so holding we are merely recognizing the general requirement in this Commonwealth that parties to contracts and commercial transactions must act in good faith toward one another. Good faith and fair dealing between parties are pervasive requirements in our law; it can be said fairly, that parties to contracts or commercial transactions are bound by this standard. See G.L. c. 106, § 1–203 (good faith in contracts under Uniform Commercial Code); G.L. c. 93B, § 4(3)(c) (good faith in motor vehicle franchise termination).

The requirement of good faith was reaffirmed in RLM Assocs. v. Carter Mfg. Corp., 356 Mass. 718, 248 N.E.2d 646 (1969). In that case the plaintiff (RLM), a manufacturer's representative of the defendant (Carter), was entitled to a commission on all of Carter's sales within a specified territory. Either party could terminate this arrangement on thirty days' notice. Carter cancelled the agreement shortly before being awarded a contract discovered and brought to Carter's attention by RLM. Because "[t]he evidence permitted the conclusion that Carter's termination of the arrangement was in part based upon a desire to avoid paying a commission to RLM", we held that the question of bad faith was properly placed before the jury. The present case differs from *RLM Assocs.,* in that Fortune was credited with the sale to First National but was fired immediately thereafter. NCR seeks to avoid the thrust of *RLM Assocs.* by arguing that bad faith is not an issue where it has been careful to protect a portion of Fortune's bonus commission under the contract. We disagree. The fact that the discharge was after a portion of the bonus vested still creates a question for the jury on the defendant's motive in terminating the employment.

Recent decisions in other jurisdictions lend support to the proposition that good faith is implied in contracts terminable at will. In a recent employment at will case, Monge v. Beebe Rubber Co., 114 N.H. 130, 133, 316 A.2d 549, 552 (1974), the plaintiff alleged that her oral contract of employment had been terminated because she refused to date her foreman. The New Hampshire Supreme Court held that "[i]n all employment contracts, whether at will or for a definite term, the employer's interest in running his business as he sees fit must be balanced against the interest of the employee in maintaining his employment, and the public's interest in maintaining a proper balance between the two. * * * We hold that a termination by the employer of a contract of employment at will which is motivated by bad faith or malice * * * constitutes a breach of the employment contract. * * * Such a rule affords the employee a certain stability of employment and does not interfere with the employer's normal exercise of his right to discharge, which is necessary to permit him to operate his business efficiently and profitably."

We believe that the holding in the *Monge* case merely extends to employment contracts the rule that " 'in *every* contract there is an implied covenant that neither party shall do anything which will have the effect of destroying or injuring the right of the other party to receive the fruits of the contract, which means that in *every* contract there exists an implied covenant of good faith and fair dealing' [emphasis supplied]."

In the instant case, we need not pronounce our adherence to so broad a policy nor need we speculate as to whether the good faith requirement is implicit in every contract for employment at will. It is clear, however, that, on the facts before us, a finding is warranted that a breach of the contract occurred. Where the principal seeks to deprive the agent of all compensation by terminating the contractual relationship when the agent is on the brink of successfully completing the sale, the principal has acted in bad faith and the ensuing transaction between the principal and the buyer is to be regarded as having been accomplished by the agent. Restatement (Second) of Agency § 454, and Comment a (1958). The same result obtains where the principal attempts to deprive the agent of any portion of a commission due the agent. Courts have often applied this rule to prevent overreaching by employers and the forfeiture by employees of benefits almost earned by the rendering of substantial services. In our view, the Appeals Court erroneously focused only on literal compliance with payment provisions of the contract and failed to consider the issue of bad faith termination.

NCR argues that there was no evidence of bad faith in this case; therefore, the trial judge was required to direct a verdict in any event. We think that the evidence and the reasonable inferences to be drawn therefrom support a jury verdict that the termination of Fortune's twenty-five years of employment as a salesman with NCR the next business day after NCR obtained a $5,000,000 order from First National was motivated by a desire to pay Fortune as little of the bonus credit as it could. The fact that Fortune was willing to work under these circumstances does not constitute a waiver or estoppel; it only shows that NCR had him "at their mercy."

NCR also contends that Fortune cannot complain of his firing in June, 1970, as his employment contract clearly indicated that bonus credits would be paid only for an eighteen-month period following the date of the order. As we have said, the jury could have found that Fortune was stripped of his "salesman" designation in order to disqualify him for the remaining 25% of the commissions due on cash registers delivered prior to the date of his first termination. Similarly, the jury could have found that Fortune was fired (or not assigned to the First National account) so that

NCR could avoid paying him *any* commissions on cash registers delivered after June, 1970.

\* \* \*

We think that NCR's conduct in June, 1970 permitted the jury to find bad faith.

\* \* \*

Judgment of the Superior Court affirmed.

## NOTES AND QUESTIONS

**1.** Why does the court recognize a new cause of action in the *Fortune* case? Would a simple suit in contract have sufficed to redress Fortune's loss? Although an implied covenant of good faith and fair dealing in employment contracts has not received as widespread acceptance as some other developments in wrongful discharge, it nonetheless has received support. See Savodnik v. Korvettes, Inc., 488 F.Supp. 822 (E.D.N.Y.1980); Reed v. Municipality of Anchorage, 782 P.2d 1155 (Alaska 1989); Cleary v. American Airlines, 168 Cal.Rptr. 722 (Cal.App.1980); Metcalf v. Intermountain Gas Co., 778 P.2d 744 (Idaho 1989); Prout v. Sears, Roebuck & Co., 772 P.2d 288 (Mont.1989); K Mart Corp. v. Ponsock, 732 P.2d 1364 (Nev.1987). Most jurisdictions have expressly rejected the doctrine, primarily on the theory that the doctrine of employment at will, under which an employer can discharge an employee for any reason, even a bad one, is inherently inconsistent with an implied covenant of good faith and fair dealing. See, e.g., McCormick v. Sears, Roebuck & Co., 712 F.Supp. 1284 (W.D.Mich.1989); Scholtes v. Signal Delivery Service, Inc., 548 F.Supp. 487 (W.D.Ark.1982); Jeffers v. Bishop Clarkson Memorial Hospital, 387 N.W.2d 692 (Neb.1986); Nelson v. Crimson Enterprises, 777 P.2d 73 (Wyo.1989).

**2.** Does a covenant of good faith and fair dealing exist in every contract? See Restatement (Second) of Contracts § 231 (Tent.Draft No. 5 (1970)); U.C.C. § 1–203 (1978); cf. Gram v. Liberty Mutual, 429 N.E.2d 21, 28 (Mass.1981). See also Note, Protecting At-Will Employees Against Wrongful Discharge: The Duty to Terminate Only in Good Faith, 93 Harv.L.Rev. 1816 (1980).

**3.** What does a covenant of good faith and fair dealing mean in terms of the employer's ability to discharge an employee? Does it mean that an employer must have good cause for discharge? That the employer has acted in good faith? Or that the employer has not acted in bad faith? What is the difference? See Magnan v. Anaconda Industries, Inc., 479 A.2d 781 (Conn.1984) (breach does not arise simply upon absence of good cause for discharge).

**4.** Would the result in *Fortune* have been the same if NCR had terminated Fortune at a time when it did not owe him a commission? See McKinney v. National Dairy Council, 491 F.Supp. 1108 (D.Mass.1980) (extending *Fortune* to "voluntary" retirement taken under duress).

**5.** Does the covenant of good faith and fair dealing impose procedural as well as substantive obligations on employers prior to terminating employees?

**6.** Before suing their employers, both Fortune and Monge failed to follow grievance procedures which existed either internally (Fortune) or through a union (Monge). How should that affect their claims?

**7.** What other aspects of the employment relationship are affected by the covenant of good faith and fair dealing? To the extent that there exists such a covenant in employment contracts, presumably it applies to both parties to that agreement. What are *employees'* obligations under the covenant? See Note, The Implied Covenant of Good Faith and Fair Dealing: Examining Employees' Good Faith Duties, 39 Hastings L.J. 483 (1988).

## Foley v. Interactive Data Corp.

765 P.2d 373 (Cal.1988).

■ Lucas, Chief Justice. After Interactive Data Corporation (defendant) fired plaintiff Daniel D. Foley, an executive employee, he filed this action seeking compensatory and punitive damages for wrongful discharge. In his second amended complaint, plaintiff asserted three distinct theories: (1) a tort cause of action alleging a discharge in violation of public policy, (2) a contract cause of action for breach of an implied-in-fact promise to discharge for good cause only, and (3) a cause of action alleging a tortious breach of the implied covenant of good faith and fair dealing.   * * * entered judgment for defendant.

The Court of Appeal affirmed on the grounds (1) plaintiff alleged no statutorily based breach of public policy sufficient to state a cause of action; (2) plaintiff's claim for breach of the covenant to discharge only for good cause was barred by the statute of frauds; and (3) plaintiff's cause of action based on breach of the covenant of good faith and fair dealing failed because it did not allege necessary longevity of employment or express formal procedures for termination of employees. We granted review to consider each of the Court of Appeal's conclusions.

We will hold that the Court of Appeal properly found that * * * plaintiff failed to allege facts showing a violation of a fundamental public policy. We will also conclude, however, that plaintiff has sufficiently alleged a breach of an "oral" or "implied-in-fact" contract, and that the statute of frauds does not bar his claim so that he may pursue his action in this regard. Finally, we will hold that the covenant of good faith and fair dealing applies to employment contracts and that breach of the covenant may give rise to contract but not tort damages.

* * *

According to the complaint, plaintiff is a former employee of defendant, a wholly owned subsidiary of Chase Manhattan Bank that markets computer-based decision-support services. Defendant hired plaintiff in June 1976 as an assistant product manager at a starting salary of $18,500. As a condition of employment defendant required plaintiff to sign a "Confidential and Proprietary Information Agreement" whereby he promised not to engage in certain competition with defendant for one year after the termination of his employment for any reason. The agreement also contained a "Disclosure and Assignment of Information" provision that obliged plaintiff to disclose to defendant all computer-related information known to him, including any innovations, inventions or developments pertaining to the computer field for a period of one year following his termination. Finally, the agreement imposed on plaintiff a continuing obligation to assign to defendant all rights to his computer-related inventions or innovations for one year following termination. It did not state any limitation on the grounds for which plaintiff's employment could be terminated.

Over the next six years and nine months, plaintiff received a steady series of salary increases, promotions, bonuses, awards and superior performance evaluations. In 1979 defendant named him consultant manager of the year and in 1981 promoted him to branch manager of its Los Angeles office. His annual salary rose to $56,164 and he received an additional $6,762 merit bonus two days before his discharge in March 1983. He alleges defendant's officers made repeated oral assurances of job security so long as his performance remained adequate.

Plaintiff also alleged that during his employment, defendant maintained written "Termination Guidelines" that set forth express grounds for discharge and a mandatory seven-step pretermination procedure. Plaintiff understood that these guidelines applied not only to employees under plaintiff's supervision, but to him as well. On the basis of these representations, plaintiff alleged that he reasonably believed defendant would not discharge him except for good cause, and therefore he refrained from accepting or pursuing other job opportunities.

The event that led to plaintiff's discharge was a private conversation in January 1983 with his former supervisor, vice president Richard Earnest. During the previous year defendant had hired Robert Kuhne and subsequently named Kuhne to replace Earnest as plaintiff's immediate supervisor. Plaintiff learned that Kuhne was currently under investigation by the Federal Bureau of Investigation for embezzlement from his former employer, Bank of America.[1] Plaintiff reported what he knew about Kuhne to Earnest, because he was "worried about working for Kuhne and having him in a supervisory position * * *, in view of Kuhne's suspected criminal conduct." Plaintiff asserted he "made this disclosure in the interest and for the benefit of his employer," allegedly because he believed that because defendant and its parent do business with the financial community on a

---

1. In September 1983, after plaintiff's discharge, Kuhne pleaded guilty in federal court to a felony count of embezzlement.

confidential basis, the company would have a legitimate interest in knowing about a high executive's alleged prior criminal conduct.

In response, Earnest allegedly told plaintiff not to discuss "rumors" and to "forget what he heard" about Kuhne's past. In early March, Kuhne informed plaintiff that defendant had decided to replace him for "performance reasons" and that he could transfer to a position in another division in Waltham, Massachusetts. Plaintiff was told that if he did not accept a transfer, he might be demoted but not fired. One week later, in Waltham, Earnest informed plaintiff he was not doing a good job, and six days later, he notified plaintiff he could continue as branch manager if he "agreed to go on a 'performance plan.' Plaintiff asserts he agreed to consider such an arrangement." The next day, when Kuhne met with plaintiff, purportedly to present him with a written "performance plan" proposal, Kuhne instead informed plaintiff he had the choice of resigning or being fired. Kuhne offered neither a performance plan nor an option to transfer to another position.

Defendant demurred to all three causes of action. After plaintiff filed two amended pleadings, the trial court sustained defendant's demurrer without leave to amend and dismissed all three causes of action. The Court of Appeal affirmed the dismissal as to all three counts. We will explore each claim in turn.

[The majority found that Foley had not alleged facts sufficient to establish that he had been discharged in violation of public policy. He alleged that he was discharged in violation of a "substantial public policy" imposing a legal duty on employees to report relevant business information to management. The court concluded that whether or not there was such a statutory duty, no *public* interest barred discharge of Foley for disclosing information of the sort he had: "When the duty of an employee to disclose information to his employer serves only the private interest of the employer, the rationale underlying the [public policy] cause of action is not implicated."

[With respect to Foley's breach of contract claim, the Court found that he had pleaded facts sufficient to establish, if proved, an implied-in-fact contract limiting the company's right to dismiss him arbitrarily.]

\* \* \*

We turn now to plaintiff's cause of action for tortious breach of the implied covenant of good faith and fair dealing. \* \* \* [P]laintiff asserts we should recognize tort remedies for such a breach in the context of employment termination.

The distinction between tort and contract is well grounded in common law, and divergent objectives underlie the remedies created in the two areas. Whereas contract actions are created to enforce the intentions of the parties to the agreement, tort law is primarily designed to vindicate "social policy." The covenant of good faith and fair dealing was developed in the contract arena and is aimed at making effective the agreement's promises. Plaintiff asks that we find that the breach of the implied covenant in employment contracts also gives rise to an action seeking an award of tort damages.

In this instance, where an extension of tort remedies is sought for a duty whose breach previously has been compensable by contractual remedies, it is helpful to consider certain principles relevant to contract law. First, predictability about the cost of contractual relationships plays an important role in our commercial system. Moreover, "Courts traditionally have awarded damages for breach of contract to compensate the aggrieved party rather than to punish the breaching party." With these concepts in mind, we turn to analyze the role of the implied covenant of good faith and fair dealing and the propriety of the extension of remedies urged by plaintiff.

"Every contract imposes upon each party a duty of good faith dealing in its performance and its enforcement." (Rest.2d Contracts, § 205.) This duty has been recognized in the majority of American jurisdictions, the Restatement, and the Uniform Commercial Code. Because the covenant is a contract term, however, compensation for its breach has almost always been limited to contract rather than tort remedies. As to the scope of the covenant, "[t]he precise nature and extent of the duty imposed by such an implied promise will depend on the contractual purposes." (Egan v. Mutual of Omaha Ins. Co. (1979) 24 Cal.3d 809, 818.) Initially, the concept of a duty of good faith developed in contract law as "a kind of 'safety valve' to which judges may turn to fill gaps and qualify or limit rights and duties otherwise arising under rules of law and specific contract language." As a contract concept, breach of the duty led to imposition of contract damages determined by the nature of the breach and standard contract principles.

An exception to this general rule has developed in the context of insurance contracts where, for a variety of policy reasons, courts have held that breach of the implied covenant will provide the basis for an action in tort.   * * *

In Egan v. Mutual of Omaha Ins. Co., supra, 24 Cal.3d 809, we described some of the bases for permitting tort recovery for breach of the implied covenant in the insurance context. "The insured in a contract like the one before us does not seek to obtain a commercial advantage by purchasing the policy—rather, he seeks protection against calamity." Thus, "As one commentary has noted, 'The insurers' obligations are * * * rooted in their status as purveyors of a vital service labeled quasi-public in nature. Suppliers of services affected with a public interest must take the public's interest seriously, where necessary placing it before their interest in maximizing gains and limiting disbursements. * * * [A]s a supplier of a public service rather than a manufactured product, the obligations of insurers go beyond meeting reasonable expectations of coverage. The obligations of good faith and fair dealing encompass qualities of decency and humanity inherent in the responsibilities of a fiduciary.' "

In addition, the *Egan* court emphasized that "the relationship of insurer and insured is inherently unbalanced; the adhesive nature of insurance contracts places the insurer in a superior bargaining position."

This emphasis on the "special relationship" of insurer and insured has been echoed in arguments and analysis in subsequent scholarly commentary and cases which urge the availability of tort remedies in the employment context.

The first California appellate case to permit tort recovery in the employment context was *Cleary,* 111 Cal.App.3d 443. To support its holding that tort as well as contract damages were appropriate to compensate for a breach of the implied covenant, the *Cleary* court relied on insurance cases without engaging in comparative analysis of insurance and employment relationships and without inquiring into whether the insurance cases' departure from established principles of contract law should generally be subject to expansion.

Similarly, *Cleary's* discussion of two previous California employment cases was insufficient. It found a "hint" in Coats v. General Motors Corp. (1934) 3 Cal.App.2d 340, to support the proposition that "on occasion, it may be incumbent upon an employer to demonstrate *good faith* in terminating an employee", but failed to acknowledge that in *Coats,* the employee sought recovery of only contract damages. Next, the *Cleary* court placed undue reliance on dictum in this court's *Tameny* decision, which suggested that tort remedies might be available when an employer breaches the implied covenant of good faith and fair dealing. The qualified *Tameny* dictum was based exclusively on precedent in insurance cases from this state, and two out-of-state employment cases. The out-of-state cases included Monge v. Beebe Rubber Company (N.H.1974) 316 A.2d 549, in which the court permitted an action for wrongful discharge but limited the plaintiff's recovery to contract damages, specifically excluding recovery for mental distress. Moreover, the New Hampshire Supreme Court thereafter confined *Monge* to cases in which the employer's actions contravene public policy. In the second case, Fortune v. National Cash Register Co. (Mass. 1977) 364 N.E.2d 1251, the court created a right of action based on breach of the implied covenant, but limited recovery to benefits the employee had already earned under the contract. Subsequent Massachusetts cases have pursued the same limited course.

In fact, although Justice Broussard asserts that the weight of authority is in favor of granting a tort remedy, the clear majority of jurisdictions have either expressly rejected the notion of tort damages for breach of the implied covenant in employment cases or impliedly done so by rejecting any application of the covenant in such a context.

\* \* \*

In our view, the underlying problem in the line of cases relied on by plaintiff lies in the decisions' uncritical incorporation of the insurance model into the employment context, without careful consideration of the fundamental policies underlying the development of tort and contract law in general or of significant differences between the insurer/insured and employer/employee relationships. When a court enforces the implied covenant it is in essence acting to protect "the interest in having promises performed"—the traditional realm of a contract action—rather than to protect some general duty to society which the law places on an employer without regard to the substance of its contractual obligations to its employee. Thus, in *Tameny*, as we have explained, the court was careful to draw a distinction between "ex delicto" and "ex contractu" obligations. An allegation of breach of the implied covenant of good faith and fair dealing is an allegation of breach of an "ex contractu" obligation, namely one arising out of the contract itself. The covenant of good faith is read into contracts in order to protect the express covenants or promises of the contract, not to protect some general public policy interest not directly tied to the contract's purposes. The insurance cases thus were a major departure from traditional principles of contract law. We must, therefore, consider with great care claims that extension of the exceptional approach taken in those cases is automatically appropriate if certain hallmarks and similarities can be adduced in another contract setting. With this emphasis on the historical purposes of the covenant of good faith and fair dealing in mind, we turn to consider the bases upon which extension of the insurance model to the employment sphere has been urged.

\* \* \*

After review of the various commentators, and independent consideration of the similarities between the two areas, we are not convinced that a "special relationship" analogous to that between insurer and insured should be deemed to exist in the usual employment relationship which would warrant recognition of a tort action for breach of the implied covenant. Even if we were to assume that the special relationship model is an appropriate one to follow in determining whether to expand tort recovery, a breach in the employment context does not place the employee in the same economic dilemma that an insured faces when an insurer in bad faith refuses to pay a claim or to accept a settlement offer within policy limits. When an insurer takes such actions, the insured cannot turn to the marketplace to find another insurance company willing to pay for the loss already incurred. The wrongfully terminated employee, on the other hand, can (and must, in order to mitigate damages) make reasonable efforts to seek alternative employment. Moreover, the role of the employer differs from that of the "quasi-public" insurance company with whom individuals contract specifically in order to obtain protection from potential specified economic harm. The employer does not similarly "sell" protection to its employees; it is not providing a public service. Nor do we find convincing the idea that the employee is necessarily seeking a different kind of financial security than those entering a typical commercial contract. If a small dealer contracts for goods from a large supplier, and those goods are vital to the small dealer's business, a breach by the supplier may have financial significance for individuals employed by the dealer or to the dealer himself. Permitting only contract damages in such a situation has ramifications no different from a similar limitation in the direct employer-employee relationship.

Finally, there is a fundamental difference between insurance and employment relationships. In the insurance relationship, the insurer's and insured's interest are financially at odds. If the insurer pays a claim, it diminishes its fiscal resources. The insured of course has paid for protection and expects to have its losses recompensed. When a claim is paid, money shifts from insurer to insured, or, if appropriate, to a third party claimant.

Putting aside already specifically barred improper motives for termination which may be based on both economic and noneconomic considerations [such as statutorily prohibited discrimination and wrongful discharge in violation of public policy], as a general rule it is to the employer's economic benefit to retain good employees. The interest of employer and employee are most frequently in alignment. If there is a job to be done, the employer must still pay someone to do it. This is not to say that there may never be a "bad motive" for discharge not otherwise covered by law. Nevertheless, in terms of abstract employment relationships as contrasted with abstract insurance relationships, there is less inherent relevant tension between the interests of employers and employees than exists between that of insurers and insureds. Thus the need to place disincentives on an employer's conduct in addition to those already imposed by law simply does not rise to the same level as that created by the conflicting interests at stake in the insurance context. Nor is this to say that the Legislature would have no basis for affording employees additional protections. It is, however, to say that the need to extend the special relationship model in the form of judicially created relief of the kind sought here is less compelling.

We therefore conclude that the employment relationship is not sufficiently similar to that of insurer and insured to warrant judicial extension of the proposed additional tort remedies in view of the countervailing concerns about economic policy and stability, the traditional separation of tort and contract law, and finally, the numerous protections against improper terminations already afforded employees.

\* \* \*

Plaintiff may proceed with his cause of action alleging a breach of an implied-in-fact contract promise to discharge him only for good cause. His cause of action for a breach of public policy pursuant to *Tameny* was properly dismissed because the facts alleged, even if proven, would not establish a discharge in violation of public policy. Finally, as to his cause of action for tortious breach of the implied covenant of good faith and fair dealing, we hold that tort remedies are not available for breach of the implied covenant in an employment contract to employees who allege they have been discharged in violation of the covenant.[42]

---

**42.** *Cleary,* 111 Cal.App.3d 443 and its progeny accordingly are disapproved to the extent that they permit a cause of action seeking tort remedies for breach of the implied covenant.

■ KAUFMAN, JUSTICE, concurring in part, dissenting in part:

\* \* \*

Thirty years ago, in Comunale v. Traders & General Ins. Co. (1958) 50 Cal.2d 654, this court first recognized that breach of the implied duty of good faith and fair dealing may give rise to a cause of action sounding in tort. I would not have thought, after these many years, that it was still necessary to defend and explain this basic principle. In purporting to trace its origins, however, the majority fundamentally misstates the nature of the tort, and thereby subverts the powerful impetus for its extension to the area of employment termination. A brief summary of familiar principles, therefore, may be useful.

In attempting to emphasize its contractual origins, the majority characterize the covenant of good faith and fair dealing as "a contract term" "aimed at making effective the agreement's promises." That characterization is simply incorrect under the decisions of this court and the authorities on which they relied. It is true that the law implies in every *contract* a duty of good faith and fair dealing. The duty to deal fairly and in good faith with the other party to a contract, however, "is a *duty imposed by law, not one arising from the terms of the contract itself.* In other words, this duty of dealing fairly and in good faith is nonconsensual in origin rather than consensual." While the nature of the obligations imposed by this duty is dependent upon the nature and purpose of the contract and the expectations of the parties, these obligations are not consensual, not agreed to in the contract; they are *imposed by law* and thus reflect the normative values of society as a whole. The interest which the duty of good faith and fair dealing is designed to preserve and protect is essentially not the *parties'* interest in having their promises performed, but *society's* interest in protecting its members from harm on account of nonconsensual conduct.

Because tort actions enforce "duties of conduct \* \* \* imposed by law, and are based primarily upon social policy, and not necessarily upon the will or intention of the parties \* \* \*", it was quite natural that courts would eventually approve the extension of tort remedies, in appropriate circumstances, to violations of the duty of good faith and fair dealing. Indeed, this court was among the first to recognize that the nature of the obligations, the purposes of the contract and the expectations of the parties all combine to impose a heightened duty upon insurers. As we explained in Egan v. Mutual of Omaha Ins. Co., supra, 24 Cal.3d 809, "The insured in a contract like the one before us does not seek to obtain a commercial advantage by purchasing the policy—rather, he seeks protection against calamity \* \* \*. [T]he major motivation for obtaining disability insurance is to provide funds during periods when the ordinary source of the insured's income—his earnings—has stopped. The purchase of such insurance provides peace of mind and security in the event the insured is unable to work." We also observed that "the relationship of insurer and insured is inherently unbalanced; the adhesive nature of insurance contracts places the insurer in a superior bargaining position."

In the classic tradition of the common law, which adapts functional principles from precedent as changing social and economic conditions require, a number of courts and commentators have distilled from our holdings in the insurance context a relatively narrow but serviceable "bad faith" doctrine for application in other areas: Breach of the duty of good faith and fair dealing may give rise to an action in tort where the contractual relation manifests elements similar to those which characterize the "special relationship" between insurer and insured, *i.e.* elements of public interest, adhesion, and financial dependency.

[R]ecent Court of Appeal decisions have unanimously recognized that willful and malicious discharge from employment may give rise to tort remedies.

The majority is not unmindful of these numerous authorities which have concluded that the criteria which make the relationship between insurer and insured suitable for tort remedies, apply with even greater force in the employment context. Indeed, the majority reviews the pertinent cases and authorities with considerable care. At the end of this lengthy prologue, however, the majority concludes that *all* of the arguments are deficient in comparative analysis, and proceeds to explain why it is "not convinced" that a relationship analogous to that between insurer and insured exists in the employment context. * * *

Such conclusions, in my view, expose an unrealistic if not mythical conception of the employment relationship. They also reveal a misplaced reluctance to define the minimal standards of decency required to govern that relationship. The delineation of such standards is not, as the majority strongly implies, judicial legislation, but rather constitutes this court's fundamental obligation.

It is, at best, naive to believe that the availability of the "marketplace," or that a supposed "alignment of interests," renders the employment relationship less special or less subject to abuse than the relationship between insurer and insured. Indeed, I can think of no relationship in which one party, the employee, places more reliance upon the other, is more dependent upon the other, or is more vulnerable to abuse by the other, than the relationship between employer and employee. And, ironically, the relative imbalance of economic power between employer and employee tends to increase rather than diminish the longer that relationship continues. Whatever bargaining strength and marketability the employee may have at the moment of hiring, diminishes rapidly thereafter. Marketplace? What market is there for the factory worker laid-off after 25 years of labor in the same plant, or for the middle-aged executive fired after 25 years with the same firm?

Financial security? Can anyone seriously dispute that employment is generally sought, at least in part, for financial security and all that that implies: food on the table, shelter, clothing, medical care, education for one's children. Clearly, no action for breach of the covenant of good faith and fair dealing will lie *unless* it has first been proved that, expressly or by implication, the employer has given the employee a reasonable expectation of continued employment so long as the employee performs satisfactorily. And that expectation constitutes a far greater and graver security interest than any which inheres in the insurance context. Most of us can live without insurance. Few of us could live without a job.

Peace of mind? One's work obviously involves more than just earning a living. It defines for many people their identity, their sense of self-worth, their sense of belonging. The wrongful and malicious destruction of one's employment is far more certain to result in serious emotional distress than any wrongful denial of an insurance claim.

If everything this court has written concerning the relation between insurer and insured has any deeper meaning; if we have created a living principle based upon justice, reason and common sense and not merely a fixed, narrow and idiosyncratic rule of law, then we must acknowledge the irresistible logic and equity of extending that principle to the employment relationship. We can reasonably do no less.

\* \* \*

[The concurring and dissenting opinion of Justice Broussard and the dissenting opinion of Justice Mosk have been omitted.]

## NOTES AND QUESTIONS

**1.** By addressing the question of remedies, *Foley* raises the issue of the nature of harm done when an individual is unjustly terminated from employment. While the majority did not eliminate the cause of action for a violation of the covenant of good faith and fair dealing, it undercut the vitality of litigation in the area by restricting remedies to contract damages. *Foley* was the first major employment law decision to issue from the California Supreme Court following the replacement of three liberal justices with more conservative individuals, and it probably signals the direction the court will take in subsequent employment cases. In K Mart Corp. v. Ponsock, 732 P.2d 1364 (Nev.1987), the Nevada Supreme Court held that the discharge of a tenured employee for the improper motive of defeating his contractual retirement benefits was a breach of the duty of good faith and fair dealing giving rise to tort liability because of the employer's bad faith.

Alabama, Alaska, Arizona, Idaho, Illinois, New Jersey, New Mexico, Texas and Wisconsin have concluded that remedies for a breach of the covenant of good faith and fair dealing are limited to contract damages. Decker v. Browning–Ferris Industries, of Colo., Inc., 931 P.2d 436 (Colo. 1997).

The wisdom of extending the tort cause of action is discussed in Thomas A. Diamond, The Tort of Bad Faith Breach of Contract: When, If At All, Should It Be Extended Beyond Insurance Transactions?, 64 Marq. L.Rev. 425 (1981). See also Michael H. Cohen, Note, Reconstructing Breach of the Implied Covenant of Good Faith and Fair Dealing as a Tort, 73 Calif.L.Rev. 1291 (1984).

**2.** In Wallis v. Superior Court, 207 Cal.Rptr. 123 (Cal.App.1984), a pre-*Foley* case, a senior employee entered into an agreement with his employer immediately prior to a permanent layoff in which the employer agreed to pay certain severance benefits until the employee reached age 65. When the employer breached the agreement and refused to pay, the employee sued for, among other things, breach of the covenant of good faith and fair dealing. Using the analogy to insurance cases, the court extended the reach of the covenant to the agreement between Wallis and his employer, to reverse the lower court's dismissal of Wallis' complaint. Following *Foley,* would *Wallis* be decided the same way?

**3.** Is a legislature better able than a court to make a judgment regarding proper remedies in wrongful discharge cases, as the majority asserts? Why or why not?

**4.** Why is the majority so concerned about the ability of lower courts to make decisions regarding good faith in determining whether tort damages are appropriate in individual cases? Isn't that a task routinely undertaken by courts? What is the importance of unpredictability regarding damages? If it is an undesirable trait in the judicial system, can it be eliminated or minimized? How?

**5.** In a footnote, the majority stated: "Unlike collective bargaining agreements that contain 'screening mechanisms' whereby 'unions sift out grievances that are viewed as unmeritorious or less important,' the proposed tort action essentially has no entry-level limitation." Is that true? If it is, what does it suggest about the majority's practical concerns in permitting tort actions? What weight should those concerns have in deciding whether to permit tort damages?

**6.** In comparing insurance and employment contracts, one common element that the majority discusses—and minimizes in the employment contest—is disparity of bargaining power. But California Labor Code Section 923 states "the individual unorganized worker is helpless to exercise actual liberty of contract and to protect his freedom of labor, and thereby to obtain acceptable terms and conditions of employment." What role should such a statutory finding play in the court's decisionmaking process?

**7.** Review the various contract law approaches to wrongful discharge. Which seems most effective? How can the tools of traditional contract analysis be used to prevent unfair or abusive discharges? The courts have not yet applied the doctrines of unconscionability, adhesion, standard forms, or illegality of provisions to wrongful discharge cases brought in contract. Is there something different about the employment relationship that makes it less amenable to standard contract analysis than, say, an agreement to buy a used car?

**8.** The California Supreme Court ruled 4–3 that an employee may not sue an employer for fraud arising out of the employee's wrongful termination. Since employment is fundamentally contractual, tort actions arising from the termination may not be maintained in the same case. Tort actions

may be brought if not connected with the termination itself, if not precluded by the Workers' Compensation Act.  Hunter v. Up–Right, Inc., 864 P.2d
88 (Cal.1993).  However, employer misrepresentations which induce a
future employee's reliance do support a tort claim for fraud, although any
wrongful termination claim would be limited to the contract claim.  Lazar
v. Superior Court, 909 P.2d 981 (Cal.1996).

## C.  OTHER PROTECTIONS FROM DISCHARGE

## 1.  COMMON LAW

In contrast to the relatively recent development of the wrongful
discharge cause of action, there are a number of torts for which employees
have traditionally been able to sue employers, other employees, or any
individuals who interfere with the employment relationship.  These actions
include intentional infliction of emotional distress;  invasion of privacy;
fraud and misrepresentation;  slander, defamation and libel;  negligence;
and tortious interference with contractual relations.  Although circumstances giving rise to such actions occurred relatively infrequently in the
past, developments in wrongful discharge law have resulted in an increase
in the number of these cases being filed as well.

## Wilson v. Monarch Paper Co.

939 F.2d 1138 (5th Cir.1991).

■ E. GRADY JOLLY, CIRCUIT JUDGE:

In this employment discrimination case, Monarch Paper Company, et
al., appeals a $3,400,000 jury verdict finding it liable for age discrimination
and retaliation under the Age Discrimination in Employment Act (ADEA),
29 U.S.C. § 621, and for intentional infliction of emotional distress under
Texas state law.  Monarch challenges the sufficiency of the evidence.  It
also challenges the district court's denial of their motions for directed
verdict, for judgment non obstante veredicto (JNOV), for new trial, and for
remittitur.  Upon review of the entire record, we affirm.

Because Monarch is challenging the sufficiency of the evidence, the
facts are recited in the light most favorable to the jury's verdict.  In 1970,
at age 48, Richard E. Wilson was hired by Monarch Paper Company.
Monarch is an incorporated division of Unisource Corporation, and Unisource is an incorporated group of Alco Standard Corporation.  Wilson
served as manager of the Corpus Christi division until November 1, 1977,
when he was moved to the corporate staff in Houston to serve as "Corporate Director of Physical Distribution."  During that time, he routinely
received merit raises and performance bonuses.  In 1980, Wilson received
the additional title of "Vice President."  In 1981, Wilson was given the
additional title of "Assistant to John Blankenship," Monarch's President at
the time.

While he was Director of Physical Distribution, Wilson received most of his assignments from Blankenship. Blankenship always seemed pleased with Wilson's performance and Wilson was never reprimanded or counseled about his performance. Blankenship provided Wilson with objective performance criteria at the beginning of each year, and Wilson's bonuses at the end of the year were based on his good performance under that objective criteria. In 1981, Wilson was placed in charge of the completion of an office warehouse building in Dallas, the largest construction project Monarch had ever undertaken. Wilson successfully completed that project within budget.

In 1981, Wilson saw a portion of Monarch's long-range plans that indicated that Monarch was presently advancing younger persons in all levels of Monarch management. Tom Davis, who was hired as Employee Relations Manager of Monarch in 1979, testified that from the time he started to work at Monarch, he heard repeated references by the division managers (including Larry Clark, who later became the Executive Vice President of Monarch) to the age of employees on the corporate staff, including Wilson.

In October 1981, Blankenship became Chairman of Monarch and Unisource brought in a new, 42–year–old president from outside the company, Hamilton Bisbee. An announcement was made that Larry Clark would be assuming expanded responsibilities in physical distribution. According to the defendants, one of Blankenship's final acts as President was to direct Clark (who was in his mid-forties at the time) to assume expanded responsibility for both the operational and physical distribution aspects of Monarch.

When Bisbee arrived at Monarch in November 1981, Wilson was still deeply involved in the Dallas construction project. Richard Gozon, who was 43 years old and the President of Unisource, outlined Blankenship's new responsibilities as Chairman of the company and requested that Blankenship, Bisbee, Wilson, and John Hartley of Unisource "continue to work very closely together on the completion of the Dallas project." Bisbee, however, refused to speak to Wilson or to "interface" with him. This "silent treatment" was apparently tactical; Bisbee later told another Monarch employee, Bill Shehan, "if I ever stop talking to you, you're dead." Shehan also testified that at a meeting in Philadelphia at about the time Bisbee became President of Monarch, Gozon told Bisbee, "I'm not telling you that you have to fire Dick Wilson. I'm telling you that he cannot make any more money."

\* \* \*

Blankenship was diagnosed with cancer in February 1982. In March 1982, Wilson was hospitalized for orthopedic surgery. Immediately after Blankenship's death in June 1982, Bisbee and Snelgrove gave Wilson three options: (1) he could take a sales job in Corpus Christi at half his pay; (2) he could be terminated with three months' severance pay; or (3) he could accept a job as warehouse supervisor in the Houston warehouse at the same salary but with a reduction in benefits. The benefits included participation in the management bonus plan, and the loss of the use of a company car, a company club membership, and a company expense account.

Wilson accepted the warehouse position. Wilson believed that he was being offered the position of Warehouse Manager, the only vacant position in the Houston warehouse at the time. When Wilson reported for duty at the warehouse on August 16, 1982, however, he was placed instead in the position of an entry level supervisor, a position that required no more than one year's experience in the paper business. Wilson, with his thirty years of experience in the paper business and a college degree, was vastly overqualified and overpaid for that position.

Soon after he went to the warehouse, Wilson was subjected to harassment and verbal abuse by his supervisor, Operations Manager and Acting Warehouse Manager Paul Bradley (who had previously been subordinate to Wilson). Bradley referred to Wilson as "old man" and admitted posting a sign in the warehouse that said "Wilson is old." In Bradley's absence, Wilson was placed under the supervision of a man in his twenties. Finally, Wilson was further demeaned when he was placed in charge of housekeeping but was not given any employees to assist him in the housekeeping duties. Wilson, the former vice-president and assistant to the president, was thus reduced finally to sweeping the floors and cleaning up the employees' cafeteria, duties which occupied 75 percent of his working time.

In the late fall of 1982, Wilson began suffering from respiratory problems caused by the dusty conditions in the warehouse and stress from the unrelenting harassment by his employer. On January 6, 1983, Wilson left work to see a doctor about his respiratory problems. He was advised to stay out of a dusty environment and was later advised that he had a clinically significant allergy to dust. Shortly after January 6, 1983, Wilson consulted a psychiatrist who diagnosed him as suffering from reactive depression, possibly suicidal, because of on-the-job stress. The psychiatrist also advised that Wilson should stay away from work indefinitely.

Wilson filed an age discrimination charge with the EEOC in January 1983. Although he continued being treated by a psychiatrist, his condition deteriorated to the point that in March 1983, he was involuntarily hospitalized with a psychotic manic episode. Prior to the difficulties with his employer, Wilson had no history of emotional illness.

Wilson's emotional illness was severe and long-lasting. He was diagnosed with manic-depressive illness or bipolar disorder. After his first hospitalization for a manic episode, in which he was locked in a padded cell and heavily sedated, he fell into a deep depression. The depression was unremitting for over two years and necessitated an additional hospital stay in which he was given electroconvulsive therapy (shock treatments). It was not until 1987 that Wilson's illness began remission, thus allowing him to carry on a semblance of a normal life.

On February 27, 1984, Wilson filed suit against the defendants, alleging age discrimination and various state law tort and contract claims. The defendants filed a counterclaim, seeking damages in excess of $10,000 for libel and slander, but later dismissed it. Before trial, the district court dismissed one of Wilson's claims on the basis of factual or legal insufficiency. The court also dismissed his emotional distress claim to the extent that "the alleged conduct occurred in the administration of [defendants'] disability plan" on grounds of ERISA preemption. On November 30 and December 28, 1988, the case was tried before a jury on Wilson's remaining claims that the defendants (1) reassigned him because of his age; (2) intentionally inflicted emotional distress; and (3) terminated his long-term disability benefits in retaliation for filing charges of age discrimination under the Age Discrimination in Employment Act (ADEA).

The district court denied the defendants' motions for directed verdict. The jury returned a special verdict in favor of Wilson on his age discrimination claim, awarding him $156,000 in damages, plus an equal amount in liquidated damages. The jury also found in favor of Wilson on his claim for intentional infliction of emotional distress, awarding him past damages of $622,359.15, future damages of $225,000, and punitive damages of $2,250,-000. The jury found in favor of the defendants on Wilson's retaliation claim. The district court entered judgment for $3,409,359.15 plus prejudgment interest. The district court denied the defendants' motions for judgment NOV, new trial, or, alternatively, a remittitur. The defendants appeal.

\* \* \*

Wilson's claim for intentional infliction of emotional distress is a pendent state law claim. As such, we are bound to apply the law of Texas in determining whether the defendant's motions should have been granted. The Texas Supreme Court has not expressly recognized the tort of intentional infliction of emotional distress. We, however, have nonetheless recognized on at least two prior occasions, see, e.g., Blankenship v. Kerr County, 878 F.2d 893, 898 (5th Cir.1989) and Dean v. Ford Motor Credit Co., 885 F.2d 300 (5th Cir.1989), that such a cause of action exists in Texas, based on the Texas Court of Appeals' decision in Tidelands Auto. Club v. Walters, 699 S.W.2d 939 (Tex.App.—Beaumont 1985, writ ref'd n.r.e.). To prevail on a claim for intentional infliction of emotional distress, Texas law requires that the following four elements be established:

(1) that the defendant acted intentionally or recklessly;

(2) that the conduct was 'extreme and outrageous';

(3) that the actions of the defendant caused the plaintiff emotional distress; and

(4) that the emotional distress suffered by the plaintiff was severe.

The sole issue before us is whether Monarch's conduct was "extreme and outrageous."

(1)

"Extreme and outrageous conduct" is an amorphous phrase that escapes precise definition.  In *Dean* however, we stated that

[l]iability [for outrageous conduct] has been found only where the conduct has been so outrageous in character, and so extreme in degree, as to go beyond all possible bounds of decency, and to be regarded as atrocious, and utterly intolerable in a civilized community * * *.  Generally, the case is one in which a recitation of the facts to an average member of the community would lead him to exclaim, "Outrageous."

885 F.2d at 306 (citing Restatement (Second) of Torts § 46, Comment d (1965)).  The Restatement also provides for some limits on jury verdicts by stating that liability "does not extend to mere insults, indignities, threats, annoyances, petty oppressions, or other trivialities * * *.  There is no occasion for the law to intervene in every case where someone's feelings are hurt."

The facts of a given claim of outrageous conduct must be analyzed in context, and ours is the employment setting.  We are cognizant that "the work culture in some situations may contemplate a degree of teasing and taunting that in other circumstances might be considered cruel and outrageous."  We further recognize that properly to manage its business, every employer must on occasion review, criticize, demote, transfer, and discipline employees.  We also acknowledge that it is not unusual for an employer, instead of directly discharging an employee, to create unpleasant and onerous work conditions designed to force an employee to quit, i.e., "constructively" to discharge the employee.  In short, although this sort of conduct often rises to the level of illegality, except in the *most* unusual cases it is not the sort of conduct, as deplorable as it may sometimes be, that constitutes "extreme and outrageous" conduct.

(2)

Our recent decision in *Dean* is instructive in determining what types of conduct in the employment setting will constitute sufficiently outrageous conduct so as to legally support a jury's verdict.  In *Dean,* the plaintiff presented evidence that (1) when she expressed interest in transferring to a higher paying position in the collection department, she was told that "women don't usually go into that department"; (2) she was denied a transfer to the collection department, and a lesser qualified man was selected; (3) the defendant's attitude toward the plaintiff changed after she complained about alleged discriminatory treatment; (4) management began to transfer her from desk to desk within the administrative department; (5) a coworker testified she believed management was trying to "set * * * [the plaintiff] up"; (6) she was called upon to do more work than the other clerks "and subjected to unfair harassment"; and (7) management used "special" annual reviews (that only the plaintiff received) to downgrade her performance.  Far more significant to the claim for intentional infliction of emotional distress, however, (8) the plaintiff proved that a supervisor, who had access to the employer's checks, intentionally placed checks in the plaintiff's purse in order to make it appear that she was a thief, or to put her in fear of criminal charges for theft. We expressly held that the "check incidents" were "precisely what [took] this case beyond the realm of an ordinary employment dispute and into the realm of an outrageous one." We concluded that without the "check incidents" the employer's conduct "would not have been outrageous."

Wilson argues that Monarch's conduct is sufficiently outrageous to meet the *Dean* standard; in the alternative, he argues that Monarch's actions are certainly more outrageous than the conduct in Bushell v. Dean, 781 S.W.2d 652 (Tex.App.—Austin 1989), writ denied in part, rev'd in part on other grounds, 803 S.W.2d 711 (Tex.1991), which is a recent pronouncement by the Texas courts on the subject. Monarch contends that Wilson's evidence of outrageous conduct, that is, his reassignment to a job he did not like, his strained relationship with the company president, and isolated references to his age, is the same evidence that he used to prove his age discrimination claim. According to Monarch, unless all federal court discrimination lawsuits are to be accompanied by pendent state law claims for emotional distress, this court must make it clear that ordinary employment disputes cannot support an emotional distress claim. We agree with Monarch that more is required to prove intentional infliction of emotional distress than the usual ADEA claim.

### (3)

In *Dean,* we found that the "check incidents" took the case beyond an ordinary discrimination case and supported the claim of infliction of emotional distress. Wilson contends that Monarch's conduct was equally outrageous as the "check incidents" in *Dean.* Generally, Wilson argues that an average member of the community would exclaim "Outrageous!" upon hearing that a 60–year–old man, with 30 years of experience in his industry, was subjected to a year-long campaign of harassment and abuse because his company wanted to force him out of his job as part of its expressed written goal of getting rid of older employees and moving younger people into management. More precisely, Wilson argues that substantial evidence of outrageous conduct supports the jury's verdict, including: (1) his duties in physical distribution were assigned to a younger person; (2) Bisbee deliberately refused to speak to him in the hallways of Monarch in order to harass him; (3) certain portions of Monarch's long-range plans expressed a desire to move younger persons into sales and management positions; (4) Bisbee wanted to replace Wilson with a younger person; (5) other managers within Monarch would not work with Wilson, and he did not receive his work directly from Bisbee; (6) he was not offered a fully guaranteed salary to transfer to Corpus Christi; (7) he was assigned to Monarch's Houston warehouse as a supervisor, which was "demeaning"; (8) Paul Bradley, the Warehouse Manager, and other Monarch managers, referred to Wilson as old; (9) Bradley prepared a sign stating "Wilson is old" and, subsequently, "Wilson is a Goldbrick"; and (10) Monarch filed a counterclaim against Wilson in this action. We are not in full agreement.

Most of Monarch's conduct is similar in degree to conduct in *Dean* that failed to reach the level of outrageousness. We hold that all of this conduct, except as explicated below, is within the "realm of an ordinary employment dispute," and, in the context of the employment milieu, is not so extreme and outrageous as to be properly addressed outside of Wilson's ADEA claim.

(4)

Wilson argues, however, that what takes this case out of the realm of an ordinary employment dispute is the degrading and humiliating way that he was stripped of his duties and demoted from an executive manager to an entry level warehouse supervisor with menial and demeaning duties. We agree. Wilson, a college graduate with thirty years experience in the paper field, had been a long-time executive at Monarch. His title was Corporate Director of Physical Distribution, with the added title of Vice–President and Assistant to the President. He had been responsible for the largest project in the company's history, and had completed the project on time and under budget. Yet, when transferred to the warehouse, Wilson's primary duty became housekeeping chores around the warehouse's shipping and receiving area. Because Monarch did not give Wilson any employees to supervise or assist him, Wilson was frequently required to sweep the warehouse. In addition, Wilson also was reduced to cleaning up after the employees in the warehouse cafeteria after their lunch hour. Wilson spent 75 percent of his time performing these menial, janitorial duties.

Monarch argues that assigning an executive with a college education and thirty years experience to janitorial duties is not extreme and outrageous conduct. The jury did not agree and neither do we. We find it difficult to conceive a workplace scenario more painful and embarrassing than an executive, indeed a vice-president and the assistant to the president, being subjected before his fellow employees to the most menial janitorial services and duties of cleaning up after entry level employees: the steep downhill push to total humiliation was complete. The evidence, considered as a whole, will fully support the view, which the jury apparently held, that Monarch, unwilling to fire Wilson outright, *intentionally and systematically* set out to humiliate him in the hopes that he would quit.[5] A reasonable jury could have found that this employer conduct was intentional and mean spirited, so severe that it resulted in institutional confinement and treatment for someone with no history of mental problems. Finally, the evidence supports the conclusion that this conduct was, indeed, so

---

**5.** Nevertheless, we are not unaware of the irony in this case: if Monarch had chosen only to fire Wilson outright, leaving him without a salary, a job, insurance, etc., it would not be liable for intentional infliction of emotional distress. There is some suggestion in the record, however, that Monarch was unwilling to fire Wilson outright because it had no grounds and perhaps feared a lawsuit. Although Monarch was willing to accept Wilson's resignation, Wilson was unwilling to resign. Once he was unwilling to resign, the evidence supports the inference that Monarch's efforts intensified to force his resignation.

outrageous that civilized society should not tolerate it.  *Dean,* 885 F.2d at 307.[6]  Accordingly, the judgment of the district court in denying Monarch's motions for directed verdict, JNOV and a new trial on this claim is affirmed.

\* \* \*

In conclusion, we express real concern about the consequences of applying the cause of action of intentional infliction of emotional distress to the workplace.  This concern is, however, primarily a concern for the State of Texas, its courts and its legislature.  Although the award in this case is astonishingly high, neither the quantum of damages, nor the applicability of punitive damages has been appealed.

For the reasons set forth above, the district court's denial of the motions for direct verdict, new trial and JNOV with respect to the intentional infliction of emotional distress verdict is AFFIRMED.  The denial of Monarch's motions with respect to the age discrimination and back pay is also AFFIRMED.

## NOTES AND QUESTIONS

**1.**  Wilson was an at-will employee.  Therefore, it would have been lawful for Monarch to tell him he was not needed in his former capacity and that the only available job was a menial job in the warehouse.  What was it in the case, beyond this, that results in liability?

**2.**  To what extent was the finding of liability affected by the magnitude of the psychological harm suffered by the plaintiff?  Who should have the burden of proving that Wilson would not have had the same health problems if he were simply discharged?

**3.**  In footnotes 5 and 6, the court points out the "irony" that the holding in *Wilson* could lead to more "civilized" firings of employees.  Is this ironical or the essence of the case?

**4.**  In a subsequent Fifth Circuit case, McCann v. Litton Systems, Inc., 986 F.2d 946 (5th Cir.1993), the court reversed a jury award for an employee in an age discrimination case.  The court held that an employee was not constructively discharged when he was asked to accept a 12 percent pay cut and to work for a supervisor half his age.  Unlike *Wilson,* in *McCann* the employee was not personally humiliated by the demotion.

**5.**  In Diamond Shamrock Refining & Marketing Co. v. Mendez, 844 S.W.2d 198 (Tex.1992), an employer allegedly publicized to the community that an employee, who had been discharged for inadvertently taking a handful of nails, was a thief.  The Texas Supreme Court held that the employer's conduct was not sufficiently outrageous to support a claim for intentional infliction of emotional distress.  It further held that, if the tort

---

**6.**  We suppose that the threat of an emotional distress claim also provides the irony of "civilizing" discrimination; or stated differently, employers will have to behave like ladies and gentlemen when discriminating.

of false light invasion of privacy exists in Texas, it requires a showing of actual malice for recovery.

**6.** In Wallis v. Superior Court, 207 Cal.Rptr. 123 (Cal.App.1984), the plaintiff sued for intentional infliction of emotional distress as well as breach of the covenant of good faith and fair dealing. Quoting an earlier decision, the *Wallis* court stated:

> The modern rule [defining outrageous conduct] is that there is liability for conduct exceeding all bounds usually tolerated by a decent society, of a nature which is especially calculated to cause, and does cause, mental distress. * * * Behavior may be considered outrageous if a defendant (1) abuses a relation or position which gives him power to damage the plaintiff's interest; (2) knows the plaintiff is susceptible to injuries through mental distress; or (3) acts intentionally or unreasonably with the recognition that the acts are likely to result in illness through mental distress.

**7.** In Harris v. Arkansas Book Co., 700 S.W.2d 41 (Ark.1985), the company discharged without severance pay or a pension an employee who had worked there for 49 years. The Arkansas Supreme Court rejected not only the employee's wrongful discharge claim but also his claim for intentional infliction of emotional distress, on the ground that since the employer has the right to discharge an at-will employee, it cannot be held liable for emotional distress based on the discharge itself. The employer could only be found liable if the *manner* in which the discharge was accomplished met the "extreme and outrageous" test, which was not the case here. See also Newberry v. Allied Stores, Inc., 773 P.2d 1231 (N.M.1989) (supervisor's yelling at employee on sales floor that he did not trust employee did not constitute extreme and outrageous conduct). But "outrageous conduct" was found where a supervisor intentionally placed company-endorsed checks in an employee's possession to make it appear that she was stealing from the company. Dean v. Ford Motor Credit Co., 885 F.2d 300 (5th Cir.1989).

**8.** In Mueller v. Union Pacific Railroad, 371 N.W.2d 732 (Neb.1985), plaintiffs were asked by company officials to participate in an investigation of internal theft and waste. They were told by the company that no retaliation or loss of employment would occur as a result of their cooperation. After having informed the company of alleged misappropriation of railroad funds by their immediate supervisors, plaintiffs were subjected to adverse changes in their working conditions and finally discharged. The Supreme Court of Nevada held that the plaintiffs had no cause of action against the railroad for wrongful discharge, but that they had stated a cause of action for fraud, the elements of which are: (1) a false representation of material fact [in *Mueller,* nonretaliation]; (2) knowledge that the representation was false or made in reckless disregard as to its truthfulness or falsity; (3) an intent to induce another to act; (4) a justifiable reliance on the representation; and (5) injury or damage resulting from such reliance. Employers have also been found liable for fraud or misrepresentation with respect to working conditions. The California Supreme Court has held that a cause of action exists when the employer fraudulently misrepresents or omits facts concerning job security, fair evaluation, health hazards, or never intends to live up to representations made. Johns-Manville Products Corp. v. Superior Court, 612 P.2d 948 (Cal.1980).

**9.** An employer may be liable for negligence in failing to inform an employee of all known performance deficiencies where the failure deprived the employee of notice and an opportunity to improve. See Chamberlain v. Bissell, Inc., 547 F.Supp. 1067 (W.D.Mich.1982). Similarly, an employer that undertakes to review an employee's performance owes that employee a duty of reasonable care, and liability for negligence may be imposed if the evaluation does not satisfy this standard. Schipani v. Ford Motor Co., 302 N.W.2d 307 (Mich.App.1981). Furthermore, the existence of just cause does not insulate the employer from liability for negligence. Damages under traditional negligence theory include emotional distress and humiliation.

**10.** An employer did not commit actionable defamation or negligent infliction of emotional distress when a supervisor escorted a terminated employee from the premises, ruled the Minnesota Supreme Court. The plaintiff had been terminated and was told to leave the premises immediately. A supervisor waited for him while he gathered his belongings and then escorted him off the grounds by walking silently behind him. The court held that mere conduct, without more, does not constitute defamation or negligent infliction of emotional distress. Bolton v. Department of Human Services, 540 N.W.2d 523 (Minn.1995).

**11.** Intentional infliction of emotional distress is also used as a doctrinal remedy for sexual harassment. However, the harassment must rise to the level of "extreme and outrageous" conduct. Courts have been reluctant to allow for the use of this tort, finding that the conduct is outrageous only if it "is atrocious and surpasses all possible bounds of decency such that it is utterly intolerable in a civilized community." In Gearhart v. Eye Care Centers of America, 888 F.Supp. 814 (S.D.Tex.1995), a female employee was told that she could get promoted only by sleeping with the boss and that she had to wear a specific type of pantyhose. Although her superior also touched her breasts, kicked her in the buttocks, and made numerous sexual comments, this did not constitute "extreme and outrageous conduct." Compare Bustamento v. Tucker, 607 So.2d 532 (La.1992), where sexual harassment rose to the level of "extreme and outrageous conduct" when over a two-year period, a male employee made numerous sexual comments to a female co-worker and threatened to run her over with a forklift, rape her, and run her out of the plant. Physically, the co-worker terrorized her by driving his forklift at her and pinning her against the wall. In one instance, he slapped her on the buttocks. Is there a problem in using the "civilized community standard" for cases of sexual harassment? Are the courts acknowledging that less severe sexual harassment is tolerable in a civilized community?

## 2. DISCHARGE IN PUBLIC SECTOR EMPLOYMENT: THE ROLE OF THE CONSTITUTION

Developments in discharge law in the public sector—which antedate those in the private sector—have indeed surrounded the status of employment "with the kind of safeguards once reserved for personality" in certain cases, because of limits placed on state action by the fourteenth amendment of the United States Constitution, which reads in part:

> No State shall abridge the privileges or immunities of citizens of the United States; nor shall any State deprive any person of life, liberty or property without due process of law; nor deny to any person within its jurisdiction the equal protection of the laws.

Adverse personnel action against an employee by government in its role as an employer is considered "state action" for purposes of invoking the protections of the fourteenth amendment. If an individual has a protected liberty or property interest, it cannot be taken away absent due process.

Due Process in Discharge: Property and Liberty Interests in Employment

## Goetz v. Windsor Central School District

698 F.2d 606 (2d Cir.1983).

■ CARDAMONE, CIRCUIT JUDGE:

Alleging a deprivation of property and liberty interests without due process of law, Dennis Goetz commenced this action under 42 U.S.C. § 1983 against the Windsor Central School District [School District] and four of its officials. The United States District Court for the Northern District of New York granted defendants' motion for summary judgment. We affirm as to the claimed deprivation of a property interest and reverse and remand to permit discovery on the claimed deprivation of a liberty interest.

### FACTS

In October 1979 the School District appointed Dennis Goetz to the position of "cleaner." One year later School District officials became aware of a series of thefts which had been occurring at the district offices. The New York State Police were notified and a formal investigation commenced. Shortly thereafter plaintiff was arrested and charged with third degree burglary.

On January 10, 1981 Goetz was suspended by the School District because of his alleged participation in these break-ins. Two days later [Ellen Skoviera, the School Business Executive] sent Goetz a letter requesting a full written explanation of his involvement in the matter. Goetz's application for an extension of time to respond was granted by Skoviera, but the record indicates that he never responded to Skoviera's letter. On January 19, 1981 plaintiff, through the attorney representing him in the

criminal proceedings, wrote Skoviera indicating that Goetz had been suspended without an opportunity to be heard, in violation of his constitutional rights, and requesting an opportunity to be heard. However, as a result
of not receiving a written explanation from Goetz, the School District
terminated his employment on January 22. No information regarding the
reasons for Goetz's termination from employment was placed in his personnel file.

On January 12, the same day that Skoviera wrote Goetz, she also
circulated a memo to Supervisors Decker and Mulcahy directing that they
and their staffs maintain the strictest confidentiality regarding the recent
events at the School. No direct mention of Goetz was contained in that
memo.

In March 1981 the burglary charge against plaintiff was reduced to a
misdemeanor and he was granted an adjournment in contemplation of
dismissal pursuant to New York Criminal Procedure Law § 170.55 (McKinney 1982).

On October 6, 1981 plaintiff instituted the present action charging that
defendants had deprived him of property and liberty interests without due
process of law.

\* \* \*

## PROPERTY INTEREST

Before one may be deprived of property the Fourteenth Amendment
mandates that the dictates of due process be satisfied. Some property
interest must exist in favor of the person seeking shelter under the
Amendment's broad umbrella. In deciding whether a person possesses a
property interest a court must carefully sift through abstract needs and
unilateral expectations until it locates a legitimate claim of entitlement.
Board of Regents v. Roth, 408 U.S. 564, 577 (1972). The source of such
interests are not to be found in the Constitution. Rather their existence
and dimensions are defined by "existing rules or understandings that stem
from an independent source such as state law—rules or understandings
that secure certain benefits and that support claims of entitlement to those
benefits." Thus, a property interest in employment can be created by local
ordinance or by implied contract. In either case, the sufficiency of the
claim of entitlement rests on state law.

Plaintiff concedes that he possesses no protectable property interest
under New York State's Civil Service Law. His position of "cleaner" is
classified in the regulations as an unskilled labor position covered by
section 42 of the Civil Service Law (McKinney 1973). New York law
provides that after five years of service such employees may only be
removed for incompetency or misconduct and must be afforded a hearing
before removal. As an unskilled laborer with less than five years of service
plaintiff's position was one terminable at will.

Supreme Court cases make clear that at will employees possess no
protectable property interest in continued employment. In *Roth*, the Court

noted that a person may possess a protected property interest in public employment if contractual or statutory provisions guarantee continued employment absent "sufficient cause" for discharge. Even a *de facto* system of tenure, if proved, is sufficient to create a property interest. See Perry v. Sindermann, 408 U.S. 593. * * * Plaintiff urges that a property interest arises from Article 9 of his collective bargaining agreement which provides that:

> In the case of employee release, at least one-day notice of release and reasons for such action to incorporate evaluation reports will be given to the employee. The employee, if he/she feels such reasons for release are essentially inadequate or inaccurate, may request an immediate audience with the Chief School Administrator, or his designee, to explain his/her reasons for contradicting the release order.

Goetz argues that where reasons for discharge must be provided to the employee, as here, the employer must come forward and justify the termination. He claims that the collective bargaining agreement changed his status from an employee who served at will to one who could be discharged solely for cause. For this contention plaintiff relies upon In re King v. Sapier, 17 A.D.2d 114, 364 N.Y.S.2d 652 (4th Dep't 1975), aff'd, 38 N.Y.2d 960, 384 N.Y.S.2d 152, 348 N.E.2d 609 (1976).

In our view neither *King* nor the collective bargaining agreement supports plaintiff's argument. *King* dealt with the requisite notice to be afforded a probationary state employee under New York's Civil Service regulatory scheme. The court found little justification for expanding the notice requirement of Section 4.5 of the Rules and Regulations of the Department of Civil Service to include notice of unsatisfactory performance "when, in the status which he then occupies, the probationer may not compel the appointing authority to justify the termination." As the court in *King* recognized, it is the employee's *status* which determines whether he has a legitimate expectation of future employment. The mere fact that an employer may be required to notify an employee of the reasons for discharge does not alter the employee's status. While a collective bargaining agreement may add to an employee's procedural rights, and even create a property interest in continued employment, nothing in the relevant agreement altered Goetz's status as an at will employee. Because he possessed no property interest in his employment, plaintiff's claim that he was denied due process of law for lack of a hearing must fail.

## LIBERTY INTEREST

Liberty as guaranteed by the Fourteenth Amendment denotes the right of the individual to engage in the common occupations of life and to enjoy privileges recognized as essential to the orderly pursuit of happiness. Under the Constitution its meaning must be "broad indeed." A liberty interest is therefore implicated and a name-clearing hearing required where an employer creates and disseminates a false and defamatory impression about an employee in connection with the employee's termination. See

Codd v. Velger, 429 U.S. 624, 628 (1977); cf. Bishop v. Wood, 426 U.S. at 348 (1976) (where defamatory information connected with a discharge is not made public it cannot form the basis of a liberty interest claim); Paul v. Davis, 424 U.S. 693, 709–10 (1976) (defamation by state official does not give rise to § 1983 claim where it did not occur in the course of termination of employment). In viewing this record there is no question but that the allegation that plaintiff is a thief is stigmatizing information which arose in connection with plaintiff's discharge. The factual issue as to whether this information is true or false cannot be resolved on a motion for summary judgment. Thus, plaintiff should be prevented from proceeding with his case at this stage of the litigation only if defendants have conclusively demonstrated that they did not disseminate the stigmatizing impression that plaintiff was fired because he is a thief.

In this connection defendants supplied affidavits attesting to their efforts to keep the defamatory information secret. Plaintiff, on the other hand, presented affidavits indicating that many of his fellow townspeople were fully aware of the allegation of thievery. Some of the information concerning thievery may have arisen from the public nature of plaintiff's arrest and handcuffing while on school premises. It may well turn out that the public in this small community came upon this stigmatizing impression from sources other than the defendants; but, alternatively, it may be established that school district employees or board members were in fact responsible for public awareness of the allegedly defamatory charge made against plaintiff. If so, notice and an opportunity to be heard are essential to protect his due process rights.

\* \* \*

We hold, finally, that plaintiff's failure to take advantage of the opportunity to provide an explanation for his alleged involvement in this affair does not constitute a waiver of his right to assert a due process claim. If it is found that Goetz was deprived of a liberty interest, he may well be entitled to more due process than the procedure under the collective bargaining agreement afforded him. Failure to take advantage of that procedure may not, therefore, be interpreted as a waiver of the full due process to which he would be entitled.

The matter is remanded therefore for further proceedings consistent with this opinion.

## NOTES AND QUESTIONS

**1.** The Supreme Court first recognized a property interest in employment for government employees sufficient to invoke the due process clause of the fourteenth amendment in Board of Regents v. Roth, 408 U.S. 564 (1972), and Perry v. Sindermann, 408 U.S. 593 (1972). In *Roth,* an assistant professor sued the University of Wisconsin when his one-year appointment was not renewed at the end of the academic year; in *Perry,* Sindermann, a ten-year veteran of the Texas state college system was not offered a new one-year contract after he became embroiled in a disagreement with his Board of Regents after having been elected president of the Texas Junior

College Teachers Association. The Supreme Court held that Roth was not entitled to any due process regarding the decision not to renew his contract because he had no property interest in his employment beyond the one-year contract, but that Sindermann was, because of the de facto tenure system in operation at his college. In *Roth,* the Court stated:

> To have a property interest in a benefit, a person clearly must have more than an abstract need or desire for it. He must have more than a unilateral expectation of it. He must, instead, have a legitimate claim of entitlement to it.

* * *

> Property interests, of course, are not created by the Constitution. Rather, they are created and their dimensions are defined by existing rules or understandings that stem from an independent source such as state law—rules or understandings that secure certain benefits and that support claims of entitlement to those benefits.

408 U.S. at 577.

In *Perry* the Court elaborated on its holding in *Roth:*

> We have made clear in *Roth* * * * that "property" interests subject to procedural due process protection are not limited by a few rigid, technical forms. Rather, "property" denotes a broad range of interests that are secured by "existing rules or under-standings." * * * A person's interest in a benefit is a "property" interest for due process purposes if there are such rules or mutually explicit understandings that support his claim of entitlement to the benefit and that he may invoke at a hearing.
>
> A written contract with an explicit tenure provision clearly is evidence of a formal understanding that supports a teacher's claim of entitlement to continued employment unless sufficient "cause" is shown. Yet absence of such an explicit contractual provision may not always foreclose the possibility that a teacher has a "property" interest in re-employment. For example, the law of contract in most, if not all, jurisdictions long has employed a process by which agreements, though not formalized in writing, may be "implied." 3 Corbin on Contracts, §§ 561–672A. Explicit contractual provisions may be supplemented by other agreements implied from "the promisor's words and conduct in the light of the surrounding circumstances."

408 U.S. at 601.

It is important to remember that the individual's property interest does not derive from the Constitution but from an independent source such as state law, municipal ordinance, or contractual agreement between the parties. A property interest can arise from written or unwritten state or local government policies or from mutually explicit understandings between the government employer and the employee. See Stana v. School District of Pittsburgh, 775 F.2d 122 (3d Cir.1985) (teacher's retention on eligibility list from which teaching positions filled considered property for due process purposes since School District's policy was to consider only names on the list for openings); Ashton v. Civiletti, 613 F.2d 923 (D.C.Cir.1979) (personnel handbook); Harkness v. City of Burley, 715 P.2d 1283 (Idaho 1986) (police policy manual and city council resolution).

Courts have refused to find a protected property interest in cases where there was merely a unilateral expectation on the employee's part of continued employment. See Batterton v. Texas General Land Office, 789 F.2d 316 (5th Cir.1986) (fact that one land office commissioner interpreted Texas Natural Resources Code in such a way as to discharge employees for "good cause" only did not confer property rights on employee where Code empowers commissioners to discharge any employee at will); Hadley v. County of Du Page, 715 F.2d 1238 (7th Cir.1983), cert. denied, 465 U.S. 1006 (1984); Malcak v. Westchester Park District, 754 F.2d 239 (7th Cir.1985) (verbal assurances of continued employment insufficient to establish property interest); Wells v. Doland, 711 F.2d 670 (5th Cir.1983) (subjective expectation of continued employment does not establish property interest); Jolly v. Listerman, 672 F.2d 935 (D.C.Cir.1982), rehearing denied, 675 F.2d 1308, cert. denied, 459 U.S. 1037 (1982).

How closely these cases are decided on the facts is illustrated by a more recent case which bears more than a passing factual resemblance to *Perry.* Sabet v. Eastern Virginia Medical Authority, 775 F.2d 1266 (4th Cir.1985), held that a state-operated medical school's practice of uniformly renewing faculty contracts during its nine-year existence could not alone support the conclusion that the medical school had fostered an implicit understanding that it would grant de facto tenure, where the contract renewals always contained explicit notice of the length of time of the appointment. How can you explain this difference in outcomes?

**2.** What is a "liberty," as opposed to "property," interest? In *Goetz,* the court indicated that a liberty interest is implicated "where an employer creates and disseminates a false and defamatory impression about an employee in connection with the employee's termination." As interpreted by the courts, a liberty interest is generally recognized in an individual's good name and his freedom to work, but the courts have had more difficulty pinning down the concept of liberty than they have in identifying property interests, particularly following the Supreme Court's decision in Paul v. Davis, 424 U.S. 693 (1976), holding that stigma alone resulting from defamatory statements is insufficient to invoke the liberty interest protection of the due process clause unless it accompanies discharge. In Wells v. Doland, 711 F.2d 670 (5th Cir.1983), the Fifth Circuit held that an employee's liberty interests are violated when: (1) he is stigmatized as a result of the discharge process, where charges made against the individual seriously damaged his standing and associations in his community or foreclosed his freedom to take advantage of other employment opportunities *and* were false; (2) the charges were made public; and (3) the individual was denied a meaningful name-clearing hearing. The charges typically include immorality, dishonesty, alcoholism or drug abuse, disloyalty, and subversion. Even where an individual's liberty interests have been violated, the remedy ordered is generally not reinstatement, but only an opportunity to refute the false charges.

The individual's interest in reputation alone, without a more tangible interest such as employment, has been found not to be a protected "liberty" interest within the meaning of the due process clause. See Hardiman v. Jefferson County Board of Education, 709 F.2d 635 (11th Cir.1983); In re Selcraig, 705 F.2d 789 (5th Cir.1983). Similarly, proof that an individual's termination has made him or her less attractive to other employers is not enough to establish a liberty interest; the individual must effectively be foreclosed from employment. See Martin v. Unified School District No. 434, 728 F.2d 453 (10th Cir.1984). Compare Lyons v. Barrett, 851 F.2d 406 (D.C.Cir.1988) (loss of job combined with injury to reputation arising from alleged sexual harassment of co-worker gives rise to liberty interest) with Brandt v. Board of Cooperative Educational Services, 845 F.2d 416 (2d Cir.1988) (liberty interest requires publication; where allegations of sexual harassment in terminated teacher's personnel file were removed from permanent file, fact that they might have been seen before removal by some members of the board insufficient to invoke liberty interest).

**3.** What "process" is "due" before an employee with a protected property or liberty interest in a job can be terminated? In *Roth,* the Supreme Court indicated that the rudimentary elements of due process include a statement of reasons for the termination and a hearing prior to the decision to terminate. In Cleveland Board of Education v. Loudermill, 470 U.S. 532 (1985), the Court elaborated on what constitutes due process for employees with protectable interests in their jobs. Specifically, the Court held that employees are entitled to notice and an explanation of the charges, as well as an opportunity to respond and to be heard *before* being discharged, even if the employer has elaborate post-discharge hearing procedures and even if there is no dispute that the individual has committed the acts for which he or she is being discharged.

**4.** Should the due process protections of notice and a prior hearing attach to employer actions less severe than discharge, e.g., disciplinary suspensions? Some courts—most notably the Seventh Circuit, and specifically Judge Posner—are concerned that extension of due process protection will result in the wholesale displacement of state contract law. See Lyznicki v. Board of Education, 707 F.2d 949 (7th Cir.1983); Brown v. Brienan, 722 F.2d 360 (7th Cir.1983). Accord, Hughes v. Whitmer, 714 F.2d 1407 (8th Cir.1983), cert. denied, 465 U.S. 1023 (1984). See also Vail v. Board of Education, 706 F.2d 1435 (7th Cir.1983), affirmed by equally divided court, 466 U.S. 377 (1984).

**5.** Suppose a government employer, after unilaterally establishing certain rules for employment, unilaterally changes them in such a fashion as to decrease job security or otherwise make employment less attractive. Does that constitute an unlawful taking of "property"? See Gabe v. Clarke

County, 701 F.2d 102 (9th Cir.1983) (per curiam) (changing status of secretary's employment without her knowledge and consent held an unlawful taking); Salerno v. O'Rourke, 555 F.Supp. 750 (D.N.J.1983) (subjecting employee to constant shift changes, transfers, undesirable shift assignments, and unsatisfactory performance ratings after years of commendable service constituted deprivation of property).

Do job "perks" like a limousine, preferential scheduling, and better work assignments become "property interests" protectable under the fourteenth amendment? See Mosrie v. Barry, 718 F.2d 1151 (D.C.Cir.1983) (held: no).

**6.** Governmental immunity does not protect a municipality from liability for the unconstitutional acts of its officials, where the city has adopted a policy of delegating authority to such officials to make certain final personnel decisions for the city. See, e.g., Williams v. Butler, 746 F.2d 431 (8th Cir.1984), affirmed on rehearing, 863 F.2d 1398 (8th Cir.1988), cert. denied, 492 U.S. 906 (1989).

**7.** Substantive protection against arbitrary dismissal for public sector employees is found in the first amendment, whose free speech provisions guarantee a measure of protection against dismissal for employees who speak out in the workplace on matters of public concern. Review Chapter 7 and Rankin v. McPherson, supra p. 613, on the reach of the free speech rights of public employees.

**8.** Who is a government employer or employee for purposes of Due Process clause protection? This question is important as it applies to employees of government contractors, i.e., private employees doing government work. In Milo v. Cushing Municipal Hospital, 861 F.2d 1194 (10th Cir.1988), the personnel actions of a private corporation hired by a municipal authority to operate a publicly funded hospital were held to constitute state action. If an individual is deprived of his employment in the private sector due to the actions of government officials, he or she is deemed protected by the Due Process clause to the extent that a public employee is (e.g., the individual must demonstrate a reasonable expectation in continued employment to establish a property interest). Merritt v. Mackey, 827 F.2d 1368 (9th Cir.1987).

### 3.   OVERLAPPING AND CONFLICTING REMEDIES

In one sense, the various causes of action which have lately been recognized by the judiciary as providing potential remedies for employees who have been wrongly discharged break new legal ground, in that individuals who had no legal redress in the past may now seek objective judicial evaluation of their right to employment. In another sense, however, these common law actions are not so much harbingers of a more pro-employee legal system as they are the newest arrivals to a legal landscape already populated with federal and state statutes that attempt to protect employees from unfair employer practices. In many instances, a wrongfully discharged individual may have several alternative courses of action, not all of which are necessarily consistent. For instance, a victim of sexual harassment could sue under Title VII of the Civil Rights Act of 1964 or for intentional infliction of emotional distress. In the former action, relief is limited to the "make whole" remedy of reinstatement and back pay, while tort remedies in the latter action could include pain and suffering and punitive damages. To the extent that the trend toward increased recognition of individual rights continues, there will be more and more cases where statutory and common law rights and remedies overlap—and sometimes conflict.

Should an aggrieved employee be permitted to pursue several possible remedies simultaneously, should she have to make an election among them, or should the existence of one preclude access to the others? Prior developments in other employment cases establish two quite distinct—indeed, contradictory—lines of precedent, one arising under the National Labor Relations Act and the other under Title VII.

In San Diego Building Trades Council v. Garmon, 359 U.S. 236 (1959), the Supreme Court held that the primary jurisdiction of the National Labor Relations Board preempted state regulation of behavior which was either "arguably protected" or "arguably prohibited" under §§ 7 and 8 of the NLRA, unless the challenged activity was of only peripheral concern to the Act or the regulated conduct "touched interests so deeply rooted in local feeling and responsibility that, in the absence of compelling congressional direction, we could not infer that Congress had deprived the states of the power to act." In later cases, the Court elucidated its holding in *Garmon:* the federal statute would preempt state jurisdiction only if the controversy presented in state court was identical to the one which was or could have been presented to the NLRB.

In sharp contrast, the Supreme Court held in Alexander v. Gardner-Denver Co., 415 U.S. 36 (1974), that arbitration of a discrimination claim under a collective bargaining agreement did not foreclose subsequent administrative and judicial proceedings under Title VII. The Court concluded that the legislative history of Title VII manifested a congressional intent to permit independent claims under Title VII and parallel federal or state laws, as well as private contracts (e.g., a collective bargaining agreement): "Title VII was designed to supplement, rather than supplant, existing laws and institutions relating to employment discrimination." Individuals may file independent claims under Title VII and the grievance-arbitration provisions of a collective bargaining agreement; filing in one forum has no preclusive effect, substantively or procedurally, on the other action. For example, filing a grievance does not toll the statute of limitations for a Title VII complaint. For a further discussion, see *Pryner*, supra p. 57. The Supreme Court has extended this parallel remedies approach beyond Title VII to the Fair Labor Standards Act, Barrentine v. Arkansas-Best Freight Systems, 450 U.S. 728 (1981), and actions under the Civil Rights Act of 1871, McDonald v. City of West Branch, 466 U.S. 284 (1984).

Matters were further complicated with the Supreme Court's holdings in Belknap, Inc. v. Hale, 463 U.S. 491 (1983), and Allis-Chalmers, Inc. v.

Lueck, 471 U.S. 202 (1985).  In *Belknap,* the Court held that state actions for misrepresentation and breach of contract filed by "permanent replacements" who had been terminated by the employer following settlement of a strike were not preempted by the NLRA.  According to the Court, the issues which would be litigated in the state action would not have "anything in common" with issues before the Board on unfair labor practice charges, so no preemption was necessary in order to protect federal labor policy.  In contrast, in *Allis-Chalmers,* an employee's state law tort claim for bad faith handling of an insurance claim under a disability plan included in a collective bargaining agreement was preempted by § 301 of the LMRA.

Not surprisingly, these different approaches to parallel remedies raise a number of problems which have resulted in confusion, conflicting judicial interpretations, and considerable debate over the appropriate accommodation between common law and statute in regulating the employment relationship.  The debate focuses on the extent to which permitting parallel remedies undermines the statutory policies established by legislative action and on how to determine and strike the appropriate balance between competing causes of action.

## Lingle v. Norge Division of Magic Chef, Inc.

486 U.S. 399 (1988).

■ JUSTICE STEVENS delivered the opinion of the Court.

In Illinois an employee who is discharged for filing a worker's compensation claim may recover compensatory and punitive damages from her employer.  The question presented in this case is whether an employee covered by a collective-bargaining agreement that provides her with a contractual remedy for discharge without just cause may enforce her state law remedy for retaliatory discharge.  The Court of Appeals held that the application of the state tort remedy was preempted by § 301 of the Labor Management Relations Act of 1947, 61 Stat. 156, 29 U.S.C. § 185.  We disagree.

### I.

Petitioner was employed in respondent's manufacturing plant in Herrin, Illinois.  On December 5, 1984, she notified respondent that she had been injured in the course of her employment and requested compensation for her medical expenses pursuant to the Illinois Workers' Compensation Act.  On December 11, 1984, respondent discharged her for filing a "false worker's compensation claim."

The union representing petitioner promptly filed a grievance pursuant to the collective-bargaining agreement that covered all production and maintenance employees in the Herrin plant.  The agreement protected those employees, including petitioner, from discharge except for "proper" or "just" cause, and established a procedure for the arbitration of grievances.  The term grievance was broadly defined to encompass "any dispute between * * * the Employer and any employee, concerning the effect, interpretation, application, claim of breach or violation of this Agreement." Ultimately, an arbitrator ruled in petitioner's favor and ordered respondent to reinstate her with full back pay.

Meanwhile, on July 9, 1985, petitioner commenced this action against respondent by filing a complaint in the Illinois Circuit Court for Williamson County, alleging that she had been discharged for exercising her rights under the Illinois worker's compensation laws.  Respondent removed the case to the Federal District Court on the basis of diversity of citizenship, and then filed a motion praying that the Court either dismiss the case on pre-emption grounds or stay further proceedings pending the completion of the arbitration.  Relying on our decision in Allis–Chalmers Corp. v. Lueck, 471 U.S. 202 (1985), the District Court dismissed the complaint.  It concluded that the "claim for retaliatory discharge is 'inextricably inter-twined' with the collective bargaining provision prohibiting wrongful discharge or discharge without just cause" and that allowing the state-law action to proceed would undermine the arbitration procedures set forth in the parties' contract.

The Court of Appeals agreed that the state-law claim was preempted by § 301.  In an en banc opinion, over the dissent of two judges, it rejected petitioner's argument that the tort action was not "inextricably inter-twined" with the collective-bargaining agreement because the disposition of a retaliatory discharge claim in Illinois does not depend upon an interpretation of the agreement;  on the contrary, the Court concluded that "the same analysis of the facts" was implicated under both procedures.

## II.

Section 301(a) of the Labor Management Relations Act of 1947, 61 Stat. 156, 29 U.S.C. § 185(a), provides:

"Suits for violation of contracts between an employer and a labor organization representing employees in an industry affecting commerce as defined in this Act, or between any such labor organizations, may be brought in any district court of the United States having jurisdiction of the parties, without respect to the amount in controversy or without regard to the citizenship of the parties."

In Textile Workers v. Lincoln Mills, 353 U.S. 448 (1957), we held that § 301 not only provides federal-court jurisdiction over controversies involving collective-bargaining agreements, but also "authorizes federal courts to fashion a body of federal law for the enforcement of these collective bargaining agreements."  Id., at 451.

In Teamsters v. Lucas Flour Co., 369 U.S. 95 (1962), we were confronted with a straightforward question of contract interpretation:  whether a collective-bargaining agreement implicitly prohibited a strike that had been called by the union.  The Washington Supreme Court had answered that question by applying state-law rules of contract interpretation. We rejected that approach, and held that § 301 mandated resort to federal rules of law in order to ensure uniform interpretation of collective-bargaining agreements, and thus to promote the peaceable, consistent resolution of labor-management disputes.[3]

In Allis–Chalmers Corp. v. Lueck, 471 U.S. 202 (1985), we considered whether the Wisconsin tort remedy for bad-faith handling of an insurance claim could be applied to the handling of a claim for disability benefits that were authorized by a collective-bargaining agreement. We began by examining the collective-bargaining agreement, and determined that it provided the basis not only for the benefits, but also for the right to have payments made in a timely manner. We then analyzed the Wisconsin tort remedy, explaining that it "exists for breach of a 'duty devolv[ed] upon the insurer by reasonable implication from the express terms of the contract,' the scope of which, crucially, is 'ascertained from a consideration of the contract itself.'" Since the "parties' agreement as to the manner in which a benefit claim would be handled [would] necessarily [have been] relevant to any allegation that the claim was handled in a dilatory manner," we concluded that § 301 pre-empted the application of the Wisconsin tort remedy in this setting.

**3.** Our discussion of the pre-emptive scope of § 301 bears repeating:

* * * The dimensions of § 301 require the conclusion that substantive principles of federal labor law must be paramount in the area covered by the statute. Comprehensiveness is inherent in the process by which the law is to be formulated under the mandate of *Lincoln Mills,* requiring issues raised in suits of a kind covered by § 301 to be decided according to the precepts of federal labor policy.

"More important, the subject matter of § 301(a) 'is peculiarly one that calls for uniform law.' * * * The possibility that individual contract terms might have different meanings under state and federal law would inevitably exert a disruptive influence upon both the negotiation and administration of collective agreements. Because neither party could be certain of the rights which it had obtained or conceded, the process of negotiating an agreement would be made immeasurably more difficult by the necessity of trying to formulate contract provisions in such a way as to contain the same meaning under two or more systems of law which might someday be invoked in enforcing the contract. Once the collective bargain was made, the possibility of conflicting substantive interpretation under competing legal systems would tend to stimulate and prolong disputes as to its interpretation. Indeed, the existence of possibly conflicting legal concepts might substantially impede the parties' willingness to agree to contract terms providing for final arbitral or judicial resolution of disputes.

"The importance of the area which would be affected by separate systems of substantive law makes the need for a single body of federal law particularly compelling. The ordering and adjusting of competing interests through a process of free and voluntary collective bargaining is the keystone of the federal scheme to promote industrial peace. State law which frustrates the effort of Congress to stimulate the smooth functioning of that process thus strikes at the very core of federal labor policy. With due regard to the many factors which bear upon competing state and federal interests in this area, * * * we cannot but conclude that in enacting § 301 Congress intended doctrines of federal labor law uniformly to prevail over inconsistent local rules." 369 U.S., at 103–104 (citations omitted, footnote omitted).

Thus, *Lueck* faithfully applied the principle of § 301 pre-emption developed in *Lucas Flour:* if the resolution of a state-law claim depends upon the meaning of a collective-bargaining agreement, the application of state law (which might lead to inconsistent results since there could be as many state-law principles as there are States) is pre-empted and federal labor-law principles—necessarily uniform throughout the nation—must be employed to resolve the dispute.

### III.

Illinois courts have recognized the tort of retaliatory discharge for filing a worker's compensation claim, Kelsay v. Motorola, Inc., 74 Ill.2d 172, 384 N.E.2d 353 (1978), and have held that it is applicable to employees covered by union contracts, Midgett v. Sackett–Chicago, Inc., 105 Ill.2d 143, 473 N.E.2d 1280 (1984), cert. denied, 474 U.S. 909 (1985). "[T]o show retaliatory discharge, the plaintiff must set forth sufficient facts from which it can be inferred that (1) he was discharged or threatened with discharge and (2) the employer's motive in discharging or threatening to discharge him was to deter him from exercising his rights under the Act or to interfere with his exercise of those rights." Horton v. Miller Chemical Co., 776 F.2d 1351, 1356 (CA7 1985), cert. denied, 475 U.S. 1122 (1986). Each of these purely factual questions pertains to the conduct of the employee and the conduct and motivation of the employer. Neither of the elements requires a court to interpret any term of a collective-bargaining agreement. To defend against a retaliatory discharge claim, an employer must show that it had a nonretaliatory reason for the discharge; this purely factual inquiry likewise does not turn on the meaning of any provision of a collective-bargaining agreement. Thus, the state-law remedy in this case is "independent" of the collective-bargaining agreement in the sense of "independent" that matters for § 301 pre-emption purposes: resolution of the state-law claim does not require construing the collective-bargaining agreement.

The Court of Appeals seems to have relied upon a different way in which a state-law claim may be considered "independent" of a collective-bargaining agreement. The court wrote that "the just cause provision in the collective-bargaining agreement may well prohibit such retaliatory discharge," and went on to say that if the state law cause of action could go forward, "a state court would be deciding precisely the *same issue* as would an arbitrator: whether there was 'just cause' to discharge the worker." The Court concluded, "the state tort of retaliatory discharge is inextricably intertwined with the collective-bargaining agreements here, because it implicates the *same analysis of the facts* as would an inquiry under the just cause provisions of the agreements." We agree with the Court's explanation that the state-law analysis might well involve attention to the same factual considerations as the contractual determination of whether Lingle was fired for just cause. But we disagree with the Court's conclusion that such parallelism renders the state-law analysis dependent upon the contractual analysis. For while there may be instances in which the National Labor Relations Act pre-empts state law on the basis of the subject matter of the law in question, § 301 pre-emption merely ensures that federal law will be the basis for interpreting collective-bargaining agreements, and says nothing about the substantive rights a State may provide to workers when adjudication of those rights does not depend upon the interpretation of such agreements.[9]  In other words, even if dispute resolution pursuant to a collective-bargaining agreement, on the one hand, and state law, on the other, would require addressing precisely the same set of facts, as long as the state-law claim can be resolved without interpreting the agreement itself, the claim is "independent" of the agreement for § 301 pre-emption purposes.[10]

## IV.

The result we reach today is consistent both with the policy of fostering uniform, certain adjudication of disputes over the meaning of collective-bargaining agreements and with cases that have permitted separate fonts of substantive rights to remain unpre-empted by other federal labor-law statutes.

First, as we explained in *Lueck*, "[t]he need to preserve the effectiveness of arbitration was one of the central reasons that underlay the Court's holding in *Lucas Flour*. * * * A rule that permitted an individual to sidestep available grievance procedures would cause arbitration to lose

---

**9.** Whether a union may *waive* its members' individual, nonpre-empted state-law rights, is, likewise, a question distinct from that of whether a claim is pre-empted under § 301, and is another issue we need not resolve today.  We note that under Illinois law, the parties to a collective-bargaining agreement may not waive the prohibition against retaliatory discharge nor may they alter a worker's rights under the state worker's compensation scheme.  Before deciding whether such a state law bar to waiver could be pre-empted under federal law by the parties to a collective-bargaining agreement, we would require "clear and unmistakable" evidence in order to conclude that such a waiver had been intended.  No such evidence is available in this case.

**10.** Thus, what we said in Caterpillar Inc. v. Williams, 482 U.S. 119, ___ (1987) (emphasis in original), is relevant here:

"Caterpillar asserts that respondents' state-law contract claims are in reality completely pre-empted § 301 claims, which therefore arise under federal law. We disagree. Section 301 governs claims founded directly on rights created by collective-bargaining agreements, and also claims 'substantially dependent on analysis of a collective-bar-

gaining agreement.'  Electrical Workers v. Hechler, 481 U.S. ___, ___, n. 3 (1987); see also Allis–Chalmers Corp. v. Lueck, 471 U.S., at 220.  Respondents allege that Caterpillar has entered into and breached *individual* employment contracts with them.  Section 301 says nothing about the content or validity of individual employment contracts.  It is true that respondents, bargaining unit members at the time of the plant closing, possessed substantial rights under the collective agreement, and could have brought suit under § 301.  As masters of the complaint, however, they chose not to do so.

"Moreover, contrary to Caterpillar's assertion, * * * respondents' complaint is not substantially dependent upon interpretation of the collective-bargaining agreement.  It does not rely upon the collective agreement indirectly, nor does it address the relationship between the individual contracts and the collective agreement.  As the Court has stated, 'it would be inconsistent with congressional intent under [§ 301] to pre-empt state rules that proscribe conduct, or establish rights and obligations, independent of a labor contract.'  Allis–Chalmers Corp., supra, at 212."

most of its effectiveness, * * * as well as eviscerate a central tenet of federal labor contract law under § 301 that it is the arbitrator, not the court, who has the responsibility to interpret the labor contract in the first instance." Today's decision should make clear that interpretation of collective-bargaining agreements remains firmly in the arbitral realm; judges can determine questions of state law involving labor-management relations only if such questions do not require construing collective-bargaining agreements.

Second, there is nothing novel about recognizing that substantive rights in the labor relations context can exist without interpreting collective-bargaining agreements.

> This Court has, on numerous occasions, declined to hold that individual employees are, because of the availability of arbitration, barred from bringing claims under federal statutes. See, e.g., McDonald v. West Branch, 466 U.S. 284 (1984); Barrentine v. Arkansas–Best Freight System, Inc., 450 U.S. 728 (1981); Alexander v. Gardner–Denver Co., 415 U.S. 36 (1974). Although the analysis of the question under each statute is quite distinct, the theory running through these cases is that notwithstanding the strong policies encouraging arbitration, "different considerations apply *where the employee's claim is based on rights arising out of a statute designed to provide minimum substantive guarantees to individual workers.*" Barrentine, supra, 450 U.S., at 737.

Atchison, T. & S.F.R. Co. v. Buell, 480 U.S. 557, 564–565 (1987) (emphasis added).

Although our comments in *Buell*, construing the scope of Railway Labor Act pre-emption, referred to independent *federal* statutory rights, we subsequently rejected a claim that federal labor law pre-empted a *state* statute providing a one-time severance benefit to employees in the event of a plant closing. In Fort Halifax Packing Co. v. Coyne, 482 U.S. 1, 21 (1987), we emphasized that "pre-emption should not be lightly inferred in this area, since the establishment of labor standards falls within the traditional police power of the State." We specifically held that the Maine law in question was not pre-empted by the NLRA, "since its establishment of a minimum labor standard does not impermissibly intrude upon the collective-bargaining process." Id., at 23.

The Court of Appeals "recognize[d] that § 301 does not pre-empt state anti-discrimination laws, even though a suit under these laws, like a suit alleging retaliatory discharge, requires a state court to determine whether just cause existed to justify the discharge." The court distinguished those laws because Congress has affirmatively endorsed state anti-discrimination remedies in Title VII of the Civil Rights Act of 1964, 78 Stat. 241, see 42 U.S.C. §§ 2000e–5(c) and 2000e–7, whereas there is no such explicit endorsement of state worker's compensation laws. As should be plain from our discussion in Part III, this distinction is unnecessary for determining whether § 301 pre-empts the state law in question. The operation of the anti-discrimination laws does, however, illustrate the relevant point for

§ 301 pre-emption analysis that the mere fact that a broad contractual protection against discriminatory—or retaliatory—discharge may provide a remedy for conduct that coincidentally violates state law does not make the existence or the contours of the state law violation dependent upon the terms of the private contract. For even if an arbitrator should conclude that the contract does not prohibit a particular discriminatory or retaliatory discharge, that conclusion might or might not be consistent with a proper interpretation of state law. In the typical case a state tribunal could resolve either a discriminatory or retaliatory discharge claim without interpreting the "just cause" language of a collective-bargaining agreement.

### V.

In sum, we hold that an application of state law is pre-empted by § 301 of the Labor Management Relations Act of 1947 only if such application requires the interpretation of a collective-bargaining agreement.[12]

The judgment of the Court of Appeals is reversed.

## NOTES AND QUESTIONS

**1.** There have been a number of post-*Lingle* decisions interpreting § 301's preemptive reach. See, e.g., Smolarek v. Chrysler Corp., 879 F.2d 1326 (6th Cir.1989), cert. denied, 493 U.S. 992 (1989); Bettis v. Oscar Meyer Foods Corp., 878 F.2d 192 (7th Cir.1989); Nelson v. Central Illinois Light Co., 878 F.2d 198 (7th Cir.1989); Dougherty v. Parsec, Inc., 872 F.2d 766 (6th Cir.1989); Merchant v. American Steamship Co., 860 F.2d 204 (6th Cir.1988).

**2.** In *Lingle,* the Supreme Court held that Lingle's tort claim was not preempted, even though her employment was covered by a collective bargaining agreement. A few years earlier, the Court had preempted a state law tort claim in Allis–Chalmers v. Lueck, mentioned in the majority opinion. In upholding the employee's right to file a separate state law claim in *Allis–Chalmers,* the Wisconsin Supreme Court had held:

> [T]he tort of bad faith is not a tortious breach of contract. It is a separate intentional wrong, which results from a breach of duty imposed as a consequence of the relationship established by contract. * * * Lueck's claim is not for a breach of contract; rather,

---

**12.** A collective-bargaining agreement may, of course, contain information such as rate of pay and other economic benefits that might be helpful in determining the damages to which a worker prevailing in a state law suit is entitled. Although federal law would govern the interpretation of the agreement to determine the proper damages, the underlying state law claim, not otherwise pre-empted, would stand. Thus, as a general proposition, a state law claim may depend for its resolution upon both the interpretation of a collective-bargaining agreement and a separate state law analysis that does not turn on the agreement. In such a case, federal law would govern the interpretation of the agreement, but the separate state law analysis would not be thereby pre-empted. As we said in Allis–Chalmers Corp. v. Lueck, 471 U.S., at 211, "not every dispute * * * tangentially involving a provision of a collective-bargaining agreement is pre-empted by § 301 * * *."

it is a separate and independent claim arising out of the manner in which his disability claim was handled. For purposes of pursuing this claim, Lueck need only first establish that the defendants owed him a duty by virtue of the insurance contract. Even though that duty arose initially because of the insurance provided through the labor agreement, that fact alone does not persuade us that Lueck's claim is in essence a contractual claim.

Lueck v. Aetna Life Insurance & Casualty Co., 342 N.W.2d 699, 702 (Wis.1984), reversed, 471 U.S. 202 (1985).

Why is Lueck's claim preempted but not Lingle's? Why was the Supreme Court not persuaded by the Wisconsin Supreme Court's interpretation of the nature of the rights involved in *Allis–Chalmers?* Did the Supreme Court broaden or narrow the standard for § 301 preemption in *Lingle?* What is the new standard? To what extent should the characterization of a claim as tort or contract determine the preemptive effect of federal law in wrongful discharge actions?

**3.** Preemption problems arise in several different ways: there is the § 301 preemption addressed in *Lingle,* in which rights under a collective bargaining agreement and under state common law may overlap. Preemption may also be an issue when other federal statutes overlap state common law remedies, or when state statutory and common law causes of action overlap. One reason why Lingle's wrongful discharge claim was not preempted was because of the importance the Supreme Court attached to the process of collective bargaining and its concern that if Lingle's claim were preempted, unionized employees would have fewer rights than unorganized employees and collective bargaining under the National Labor Relations Act would be undermined. What the Court left open in *Lingle* is the extent to which that same, or analogous, reasoning would apply to other preemption problems.

In Screen Extras Guild, Inc. v. Superior Court, 800 P.2d 873 (Cal. 1990), the Supreme Court of California held that the Labor–Management Reporting and Disclosure Act (LMRDA) preempted state causes of action for wrongful discharge and related torts when brought against a union-employer by a former management or policymaking employee. The court cited to the strong federal policy favoring union democracy, which would be furthered by not interfering with the ability of elected union leaders to carry out the will of the members they represent.

**4.** An arbitration clause in a collective bargaining agreement bars a federal court lawsuit alleging unlawful discrimination on the basis of disability. Wright v. Universal Maritime Service Corp., 121 F 3d 702 (4th Cir. 1997), cert. granted, 118 S. Ct. 1162 (1998). The court of appeals relied on Gilmer v. Interstate/Johnson Lane Corp., 500 U.S. 20 (1991).

**5.** In Barnes v. Stone Container Corp., 942 F.2d 689 (9th Cir.1991), the Ninth Circuit held that an action brought under the Montana Wrongful Discharge From Employment Act was preempted by the NLRA.

**6.** If § 301 prevents unionized employees from using statutory and common law remedies to redress wrongful discharge, leaving them to their collective bargaining remedies, are they worse off than at-will employees? All at-will employees?

**7.** The NLRA is not the only federal statute which limits employees' access to state courts in cases of wrongful discharge. Another important bar is ERISA, § 514 of which provides that "any and all state laws insofar as they may now or hereafter relate to any employer benefit plan" are superseded. See the discussions of ERISA preemption in Chapters 6 and 13.

**8.** Title VII of the Civil Rights Act of 1964 applies to unionized and nonunionized individuals. It expressly provides, in § 708, "Nothing in this subchapter shall be deemed to exempt or relieve any person from any liability, duty, penalty or punishment provided by any present or future law of any State or political subdivision of a State * * *." What does this section mean with respect to preemption of state tort actions arising out of violations of federal law (regardless of the existence of a collective bargaining agreement)? For example, is emotional distress arising out of unlawful sexual harassment actionable under Title VII? See Blum v. Witco Chemical Corp., 829 F.2d 367 (3d Cir.1987), reversed in part on other grounds, 888 F.2d 975 (3d Cir.1989); Lapinad v. Pacific Oldsmobile–GMC, Inc., 679 F.Supp. 991 (D.Hawaii 1988); Ford v. Revlon, Inc., 734 P.2d 580 (Ariz. 1987).

**9.** In comparison to § 708 of Title VII, most workers' compensation statutes provide that workers' compensation will be the employee's exclusive remedy for injuries arising in the course of employment. How should the existence and availability of a workers' compensation statute affect an individual's ability to sue in state court for wrongful discharge? Compare Byrd v. Richardson–Greenshields Securities, Inc., 552 So.2d 1099 (Fla.1989) (state workers' compensation law does not provide exclusive remedy for female employees complaining about alleged sexual harassment by male co-workers) with Harrison v. Edison Brothers Apparel Stores, Inc., 724 F.Supp. 1185 (M.D.N.C.1989) (wrongful discharge suit for sexual harassment dismissed because of availability of other statutory remedies), affirmed in part and reversed in part, 924 F.2d 530 (4th Cir.1991). See also Johnson v. Delchamps, Inc., 715 F.Supp. 1345 (M.D.La.1989), affirmed, 897 F.2d 808 (5th Cir.1990) (Louisiana workers' compensation statute barred separate claim for negligent infliction of emotional distress by employee who was discharged after failing a polygraph examination). But an employee's suit against a co-worker may not be barred by a workers' compensation statute, see Meerbrey v. Marshall Field & Co., 545 N.E.2d 952 (Ill.App.1989).

**10.** Christine McKennon worked for the Nashville Banner for 30 years and was discharged in a work force reduction. McKennon, 62, alleged that she had been a victim of unlawful age discrimination. When the Banner took her deposition in the lawsuit, McKennon testified that she had copied confidential documents about the company's financial condition, taken them home, and showed them to her husband. The company then terminated her again, this time for violating its rule against unauthorized copying. The Banner said that had the company known of the copying earlier, it would have terminated her for that reason.

The court of appeals affirmed a district court decision that the employee's subsequently discovered misconduct precluded recovery on her age discrimination claim. The Supreme Court reversed, holding that the after-acquired evidence might limit appropriate damages and will generally render reinstatement and front pay inappropriate but that the new grounds for dismissal cannot bar all relief under the Age Discrimination in Employment Act. McKennon v. Nashville Banner Publishing Co., 513 U.S. 352 (1995).

**11.** Federal law is not the only limit on common law causes of action. In a number of cases, state statutes also have been held to preempt common law remedies, on the theory that the enactment of a comprehensive legislative scheme formally establishing the state's policy provides the exclusive remedy and preempts common law actions. But parallel common law claims such as breach of contract or intentional infliction of emotional distress may not be preempted. See Wolk v. Saks Fifth Avenue, Inc., 728 F.2d 221 (3d Cir.1984) (state employment discrimination statute precludes tort claim for sexual harassment); Strauss v. A.L. Randall Co., 194 Cal. Rptr. 520 (Cal.App.1983) (state age discrimination legislation preempts common law wrongful discharge action). But see Cancellier v. Federated Department Stores, 672 F.2d 1312 (9th Cir.), cert. denied, 459 U.S. 859 (1982) (recovery under ADEA did not preclude wrongful discharge action); Holien v. Sears, Roebuck & Co., 689 P.2d 1292 (Or.1984) (no preemption of common law wrongful discharge action based on sex discrimination; when legislature enacted statutory remedy, it had no idea common law remedy existed). See also Childers v. Chesapeake & Potomac Telephone Co., 881 F.2d 1259 (4th Cir.1989); Napoleon v. Xerox Corp., 656 F.Supp. 1120 (D.Conn 1987). Cf. Bernstein v. Aetna Life & Casualty Co., 843 F.2d 359 (9th Cir.1988); Helmick v. Cincinnati Word Processing, Inc., 543 N.E.2d 1212 (Ohio 1989).

**12.** At least one court has distinguished discharge claims "arising under" federal law for jurisdictional purposes from cases where the employee's state law alleges that he was discharged for refusing to violate state law. A former in-house counsel for a corporation alleged in a state wrongful discharge claim that he was fired for insisting that the corporation comply with state and federal environmental and securities laws and because he would not violate those laws. The employer removed to federal court, claiming that the federal issues pleaded as a part of the state law claim made it a federal case. The Seventh Circuit held that the state law case raised no "substantial issues" of federal law, and removal was improper. See Willy v. Coastal Corp., 855 F.2d 1160 (5th Cir.1988).

**13.** Lingle was a member of a union which had negotiated a collective bargaining agreement with the employer. Should § 301 preemption apply where the employees are not unionized? Consider the following case:

Virginia Chubb, an administrative clerk at a large insurance company, was fired, allegedly for poor work performance. Chubb claims that she was fired because of her efforts to obtain "a reasonably smoke-free environment in which to work." All of the administrative clerks work in a large open area with moveable barriers about five feet high separating individual groups of four work stations. Cigarette smoke can circulate freely throughout the area. Chubb, who is allergic to cigarette smoke, started her campaign after a coffee break conversation in which several other employees indicated their annoyance with the problem of having smokers and nonsmokers working in the same area, but she did not ask anyone else to join her in her crusade and no one else stepped forward. See Hentzel v. Singer Co., 188 Cal.Rptr. 159 (Cal.App.1982). See also Local 926, IUOE v. Jones, 460 U.S. 669 (1983); Sitek v. Forest City Enterprises, Inc., 587 F.Supp. 1381 (E.D.Mich.1984).

**14.** Hawaiian Airlines, Inc. v. Norris, 512 U.S. 246 (1994), held that the Railway Labor Act did not preempt state tort actions for wrongful discharge based on the policies of the Federal Aviation Act and the Hawaii Whistleblower Protection Act. Norris had refused to sign a maintenance record for a plane he considered unsafe.

**15.** An employee who brings a claim under New Jersey's whistleblower statute, the Conscientious Employee Protection Act, is not precluded by CEPA's waiver provision from asserting independent common law claims as well. Young had objected to his employer's testing of a veterinary drug without reporting it to several government agencies and was terminated. The court held that the retaliatory discharge claim did not preclude independent claims for owed but unpaid severance and defamation. Young v. Schering Corp., 660 A.2d 1153 (N.J.1995).

## PROBLEMS

Should the following claims be preempted? On what basis?

a. Plaintiff, covered by a collective bargaining agreement, sued her former employer for breach of the implied covenant of good faith and fair dealing and intentional infliction of emotional distress, alleging that she suffered humiliation and mental anguish arising out of her employer's decision to terminate her for alleged misappropriation of racetrack funds, without just cause or direct evidence of guilt. See Newberry v. Pacific Racing Association, 854 F.2d 1142 (9th Cir.1988).

b. Plaintiff, subject to a collective bargaining agreement, was fired for reporting health and safety violations. He sues his former employer for wrongful discharge. The employer argues that the lawsuit is preempted by both § 301 and the Occupational Safety and Health Act (OSHA). Preempted? See Paige v. Henry J. Kaiser Co., 826 F.2d 857 (9th Cir.1987), cert. denied, 486 U.S. 1054 (1988); LePore v. National Tool & Manufacturing Co., 557 A.2d 1371 (N.J.1989), affirming, 540 A.2d 1296 (N.J.Super.App.Div.1988), cert. denied, 493 U.S. 954 (1989).

c.  Female office workers, subject to a collective bargaining agreement, sued for sex discrimination under state law rather than federal; they alleged that they lost their jobs as a result of a merger between their original employer and another enterprise, in which male employees were offered transfers and female employees were not.  Jones v. Truck Drivers Local 299, 873 F.2d 108 (6th Cir.1989), cert. denied, 493 U.S. 964 (1989).

d.  After the employer announced proposed layoffs pursuant to a collective bargaining agreement, it offered a one-time lump sum payment to employees who voluntarily opted to cease working.  By accepting the severance payment, employees would forfeit their seniority and any rehire rights; a company spokesman allegedly told employees that they could be rehired if new jobs were created, but they would have to apply like anyone else.  A number of employees accepted the company's offer.  Two years later, new positions opened up, and when former employees applied, they were informed by management that they were ineligible for consideration.  The employees sued in state court for fraud and misrepresentation.  The employer moved for removal to federal court under § 301.  How should the court rule?  See Wells v. General Motors Corp., 881 F.2d 166 (5th Cir. 1989), cert. denied, 495 U.S. 923 (1990).

e.  An employee was induced by a rival company to leave his prior employment and move to a different city.  According to the employee, the new employer stated that he would be guaranteed employment for the reasonably foreseeable future and that any job offered would be permanent.  Five months after he started the new job, the employee was laid off as part of a company-wide reduction in force, pursuant to the terms of a collective bargaining agreement applicable to him.  He sued in state court for breach of contract, and the employer sought removal.  What result?  Berda v. CBS, Inc., 881 F.2d 20 (3d Cir.1989), cert. denied, 493 U.S. 1062 (1990). Cf. Terwilliger v. Greyhound Lines, Inc., 882 F.2d 1033 (6th Cir.1989), cert. denied, 495 U.S. 946 (1990).

f.  Two airline employees were discharged for union organizing activities, and they filed suit in state court for wrongful discharge.  Should their suit be preempted under the Railway Labor Act (which applies to airline employees)?  See Price v. PSA, Inc., 829 F.2d 871 (9th Cir.1987), cert. denied, 486 U.S. 1006 (1988).

g.  A customer requested that an employer fire one of its employees for filing an OSHA complaint relating to conditions at the customer's workplace, and the employer complied.  The employee was covered by the terms of a collective bargaining agreement.  He sued the customer for tortious interference with contractual relations; the customer sought removal to federal court.  Should the employee's action be preempted by § 301?  See Dougherty v. Parsec, Inc., 872 F.2d 766 (6th Cir.1989).

h.  An at-will employee was fired for refusing to drive vehicles that did not conform to state mandatory safety equipment requirements.  He filed a complaint with the Secretary of Labor alleging that his discharge violated the federal Surface Transportation Assistance Act and also sued in state court for wrongful discharge (breach of public policy).  The employer moved to dismiss the state claim on the basis of lack of subject matter jurisdiction. How should the court rule? See Todd v. Frank's Tong Service, Inc., 784 P.2d 47 (Okl.1989).

---

## D.   RECONSIDERING EMPLOYMENT SECURITY

### 1.   INTRODUCTION

Has the employment at will doctrine outlived its usefulness? Judicial recognition of wrongful discharge as an actionable wrong has naturally resulted in a dramatic increase in litigation of these cases. Virtually all of the states have permitted former employees to sue for wrongful discharge, although there is no uniformity in the legal basis on which such suits are allowed. Some states recognize only a narrow exception to the public policy rule; others permit plaintiffs to sue only in contract. In other jurisdictions, plaintiffs may sue under either theory. The proliferation of different legal standards on a case-by-case basis and wide variations in the amount of recovery in jury cases have caused many advocates on both sides to argue that the time has come to consider modification of the common law by legislative action rather than judicial fiat. Others maintain that the flexibility of judicial decisionmaking is desirable in this transitional area of the law in order to promote full, balanced, and nonpoliticized consideration of the nature of an employee's right to continued employment. Yet a third group argues that the employment at will rule has survived as long as it has because it serves the purposes of the parties in the majority of cases and that modification—judicial or legislative—would be ill-advised, if not actually counterproductive.

Ultimately, the question in actions for wrongful discharge is: should the presumption in favor of employment at will be modified or eliminated? If so, what theoretical structure should apply to the changed contours of the law? Compare the contract and tort approaches adopted in the cases above. Which form of action would do a better job of eliminating abusive discharges while at the same time permitting employers' productive activity to proceed in an efficient fashion? Should wronged employees be permitted to sue in both tort and contract? Or should these common law actions be replaced by a statutory scheme which imposes uniformity of treatment on all wrongful discharge cases?

## Richard Epstein, *In Defense of the Contract at Will*

51 U.Chi.L.Rev. 947 (1984).

There is today a widely held view that the contract at will has outlived its usefulness. But this view is mistaken. The contract at will is not ideal for every employment relation. No court or legislature should ever command its use. Nonetheless, there are two ways in which the contract at will should be respected: one deals with entitlements against regulation and the other with presumptions in the event of contractual silence.

First, the parties should be permitted as of right to adopt this form of contract if they so desire. The principle behind this conclusion is that freedom of contract tends both to advance individual autonomy and to promote the efficient operation of labor markets.

Second, the contract at will should be respected as a rule of construction in response to the perennial question of gaps in contract language: what term should be implied in the absence of explicit agreement on the question of duration or grounds for termination? The applicable standard asks two familiar questions: what rule tends to lend predictability to litigation and to advance the joint interests of the parties? On both these points I hope to show that the contract at will represents in most contexts the efficient solution to the employment relation.

\* \* \*

The recent efforts to undermine or abolish the contract at will should be evaluated not in terms of what they *hope* to achieve, whether stated in terms of worker participation, industrial harmony, fundamental fairness, or enlightened employment relations. Instead they should be evaluated for the generally harsh results that they actually produce. They introduce an enormous amount of undesirable complexity into the law of employment relations; they increase the frequency of civil litigation; and over the broad run of cases they work to the disadvantage of both the employers and the employees whose conduct they govern.

\* \* \*

The strong fairness argument in favor of freedom of contract makes short work of the various for-cause and good-faith restrictions upon private contracts. Yet the argument is incomplete in several respects. In particular, it does not explain why the presumption in the case of silence should be in favor of the contract at will. Nor does it give a descriptive account of *why* the contract at will is so commonly found in all trades and professions. Nor does the argument meet on their own terms the concerns voiced most frequently by the critics of the contract at will. Thus, the commonplace belief today (at least outside the actual world of business) is that the contract at will is so unfair and one-sided that it cannot be the outcome of a rational set of bargaining processes any more than, to take the extreme case, a contract for total slavery. \* \* \*

In order to rebut this charge, it is necessary to do more than insist that individuals as a general matter know how to govern their own lives. It is also necessary to display the structural strengths of the contract at will that explain why rational people would enter into such a contract, if not all the time, then at least most of it. The implicit assumption in this argument is that contracts are typically for the mutual benefit of both parties. Yet it is hard to see what other assumption makes any sense in analyzing institutional arrangements (arguably in contradistinction to idiosyncratic, nonrepetitive transactions). To be sure, there are occasional cases of regret after the fact, especially after an infrequent, but costly, contingency comes to pass. There will be cases in which parties are naive, befuddled, or worse.  Yet in framing either a rule of policy or a rule of construction, the focus cannot be on that biased set of cases in which the contract aborts and litigation ensues.  Instead, attention must be directed to standard repetitive transactions, where the centralizing tendency powerfully promotes expected mutual gain.  It is simply incredible to postulate that either employers or employees, motivated as they are by self-interest, would enter routinely into a transaction that leaves them worse off than they were before, or even worse off than their next best alternative.

From this perspective, then, the task is to explain how and why the at-will contracting arrangement (in sharp contrast to slavery) typically works to the mutual advantage of the parties.

* * *

The reason why these contracts at will are effective is precisely that the employer must always pay an implicit price when he exercises his right to fire.  He no longer has the right to compel the employee's service, as the employee can enter the market to find another job.  The costs of the employer's decision therefore are borne in large measure by the employer himself, creating an implicit system of coinsurance between employer and employee against employer abuse.  Nor, it must be stressed, are the costs to the employer light.  It is true that employees who work within a firm acquire specific knowledge about its operation and upon dismissal can transfer only a portion of that knowledge to the new job.  Nonetheless, the problem is roughly symmetrical, as the employer must find, select, and train a replacement worker who may not turn out to be better than the first employee.  Workers are not fungible, and sorting them out may be difficult:  resumes can be misleading, if not fraudulent;  references may be only too eager to unload an unsuitable employee;  training is expensive;  and the new worker may not like the job or may be forced to move out of town.  In any case, firms must bear the costs of voluntary turnover by workers who quit, which gives them a frequent reminder of the need to avoid self-inflicted losses.  The institutional stability of employment contracts at will can now be explained in part by their legal fragility.  The right to fire is exercised only infrequently because the threat of firing is effective.

* * *

The proposed reforms in the at-will doctrine cannot hope to transfer wealth systematically from rich to poor on the model of comprehensive systems of taxation or welfare benefits.  Indeed it is very difficult to identify in advance any deserving group of recipients that stands to gain unambiguously from the universal abrogation of the at-will contract.  The proposed rules cover the whole range from senior executives to manual labor.  At every wage level, there is presumably some differential in workers' output.  Those who tend to slack off seem on balance to be most vulnerable to dismissal under the at-will rule;  yet it is very hard to imagine why some special concession should be made in their favor at the expense of their more diligent fellow workers.

NOTES AND QUESTIONS

**1.**   Are you convinced by Professor Epstein's defense of the employment at will doctrine?   His argument is premised on a number of assumptions about the nature of the labor market.   What are they?   Do you agree with them?

**2.**   Epstein admits that the doctrine of employment at will is not appropriate for all types of employment relationships.   What types would he except from the rule's general application?

**3.**   Elsewhere in the article, Epstein specifically addresses long term relationships similar to those which existed in many of the previous cases in this chapter.   He asserts that both the employer and the employee have incentives to preserve such relationships because of the "capital" which they have built up over time:   the employee is entitled to greater vacation, sick leave, pension and other benefits because of job tenure, and the long-term employee is more valuable to the employer because of his or her intimate knowledge of the business.   Furthermore, it is costly for the employer to seek and train replacements.   What forces operate to counteract these incentives?

**4.**   In one response to Epstein, the author wrote:

> When we come down to cases, an employment contract is a very curious creature, since the nature of the exchange is not made very explicit in most instances.   On one hand, employment is an authoritarian relationship in which the employee undertakes an obligation to follow certain orders and commands of the employer.   On the other hand, it contains important elements of delegation in which the employee is given latitude within broad limits to behave in the interests of the firm.   Some elements of the contract are express or clearly implied and are actionable for breach (e.g., nonpayment for work done or misappropriation of firm property).   But most terms of the contract (not merely its duration), are left unspecified, precisely because it is too costly to write them down and to verify that they have been performed.   These therefore represent an *implicit understanding* about which there may be significant scope for disagreements through asymmetrical information.

> At-will contracts protect both parties against actions by the other that are beyond the terms of this mutual implicit understanding.   * * * But some of the cases discussed by Epstein left me uneasy.   I kept asking myself what the mutual understanding might have been and whether the actions taken were conformable with it.   If some monitoring is necessary to achieve efficiency in contracting, precisely why is it that these implicit terms should not be actionable, as they are, for example, in commercial law?   (Emphasis in original.)

Sherwin Rosen, Commentary:   In Defense of the Contract at Will, 51 U.Chi.L.Rev. 983 (1984).

**5.** Epstein questions whether employees as a class benefit from the erosion of the employment at will rule. When one employee is dismissed, another is typically hired to take his or her place, so that the net employment (or unemployment) effect is zero. In fact, Epstein argues, eliminating the rule is harmful to employees, in that under the at will rule, the employer is more willing to give marginal or risky employees a chance, since they can easily be terminated if their performance is unsatisfactory. What benefits, if any, do employees as a class gain from modifications of the at will doctrine?

**6.** Resistance to efforts to reform the at will doctrine come from pro-employee advocates as well as from the management community. See Catler, The Case Against Proposals to Eliminate the Employment at Will Rule, 5 Indus.Rel.L.J. 471 (1983), arguing that modification of the at will rule should be limited to breaches of public policy. The author contends that employee rights in the workplace are best secured through collective bargaining with the employer; in the long run, any legislated just cause provision will significantly undermine employees' incentive to unionize. The solution, according to Catler, is not for the government to provide job security for those who are not now protected by a just cause clause, but to eliminate barriers to their obtaining such security themselves, through such actions as extending coverage of the National Labor Relations Act to permit unionization by more employees, consolidating all legal actions relating to employment in one forum, and adopting broader protection against discrimination in employment than the narrow bases protected in Title VII and other statutes.

**7.** Although organized labor now supports efforts to reform the at-will rule, this was not always the case. Many union leaders were concerned that limiting an employer's ability to terminate employees at will would eliminate the most attractive feature that unions have to offer. See Nancy R. Hauserman & Cheryl L. Maranto, The Union Substitution Hypothesis Revisited: Do Judicially Created Exceptions to the Termination–At–Will Doctrine Hurt Unions?, 72 Marquette L.Rev. 317 (1989).

## 2.   ECONOMIC EFFECTS OF WRONGFUL DISCHARGE LAW

### James N. Dertouzos & Lynn A. Karoly, Labor–Market Responses to Employer Liability

35–40 (Rand Inst. for Civil Justice 1992).

#### THE ECONOMIC CONSEQUENCES OF
#### WRONGFUL TERMINATION

\* \* \*

#### THE DIRECT LEGAL COSTS OF LITIGATION

The evolution of court doctrines granting expanded protection to employees has led to a rapid escalation of legal activity. Even though virtually nonexistent before the 1980s, there are currently 20,000 wrongful-termination cases on court dockets. These suits have been highly concentrated in states that have adopted the most liberal standards. Although general information on case disposition is not readily available, a survey of cases filed in California indicates that the potential cost of these suits is quite high. For cases going to jury trial, plaintiffs were victorious almost 70 percent of the time. On average, jury awards were nearly $700,000. In addition, defense fees were escalating over the entire period. By late 1986, defense lawyer costs could exceed $250,000 in the course of a lengthy wrongful-termination trial.

Of course, these average jury awards overstate the expenses associated with the "typical" case outcome. To begin with, averages are inflated because of the existence of a few huge awards, generally involving particularly egregious (and avoidable) behavior on the part of employers. In actuality, half of all awards in California are less than $177,000. In addition, initial awards are typically reduced by post-trial adjustments. Because of subsequent settlements and rulings during the appeal process, final payments are generally less than half of the original jury awards. From a plaintiff perspective, the value of expected payments is further reduced by the cost of waiting (final payments are typically made about 6 years after the initial filing), the 40–percent contingency fee paid to their lawyers, and the uncertainty associated with a trial (about 30 percent of them receive nothing). Indeed, the majority of employees can expect a payment that, in present value dollars, is the equivalent of a half year of work.

Given the high transaction costs associated with conducting a trial, it is not surprising that the vast majority of wrongful-termination cases settle before reaching a jury. About 95 percent of all cases settle for an average of about $25,000. With legal fees of $15,000 per case, the total average cost of a settlement is $40,000. Since settlements occur more frequently, their aggregate costs are about 2.7 times the total cost of jury trials in wrongful-termination cases.[2]

On an annual basis, these aggregate costs summed to over $50 million for California in 1987. However, it is important to recognize that these direct legal costs are trivial on a per-worker basis. A rough computation suggests that California has about 6 million employment-at-will employees.[3] Thus, the average cost per employee is less than $10. Even if one considers the legal expenses on a per-termination basis, the costs appear to be insignificant. Involuntary terminations typically range between 6 and 12 percent of the labor force. So, the "expected" legal cost is, at the very most, $100 per termination.

## THE HIDDEN ECONOMIC COSTS OF UNJUST DISMISSAL

Even using the most liberal assumptions, it does not appear that direct legal costs are important in the aggregate. In fact, these average liabilities

**2.** Since 95 percent of all cases settle, there are 20 times as many settlements as there are jury trials. Even following post-trial reductions in jury awards, final payments and defense fees cost employers an average of $292,000 per jury trial. Thus, an average trial is nearly five times as costly.

**3.** This excludes unionized workers, civil servants, the self-employed, and other employees protected by explicit contracts.

and litigation costs are dwarfed in comparison with standard expenses incurred as a result of labor turnover. Such costs include recruiting expenses because of the search, advertising, and interview process. In addition, training costs for firm, industry, or occupation-specific human capital can be substantial. So, what accounts for the prevailing wisdom concerning the impact of unjust dismissal doctrines?

One simple hypothesis is that the public and the business community are misinformed about the true costs of wrongful termination. Certainly, the popular perception is fueled by media accounts of the largest jury awards. At the same time, the fear of potential litigation is probably encouraged internally by those likely to benefit from an increased emphasis on avoiding the legal risks. Defense counsel, personnel-management consultants and human-resource executives all have a personal stake in promoting the deployment of preventative measures.

Even if managers had access to accurate information about the true distribution of potential litigation costs, business behavior could be dramatically affected in risk-averse firms. The potential for huge negative outcomes, even if improbable, may be very important even if per-worker liabilities are trivial. Such risk aversion is likely to be more relevant for small businesses that are unable to distribute these potential risks across numerous employees. On the other hand, some insurance companies do offer protection against wrongful-termination liabilities and defense costs. If insurance is available, premiums will reflect the advantages of risk spreading and be based on expected costs that, as we have seen, are not very high.[4]

In assessing the likely consequences of the new doctrines, it is important to recognize that all the costs of unjust dismissal are not incurred by the "firm" or its stockholders. Instead, the individual decisionmakers or personnel managers bear a disproportionate share of the costs. This could be important for several reasons. First, the computations of direct expenses ignore what could be a major cost element associated with litigation, the manager's own time. At the same time, the benefits of a "correct" decision to terminate may not accrue to the decisionmaker. In addition, even if the risks of a dismissal are prudent from a firm, senior management, or stockholder perspective, a middle manager, having fewer opportunities to diversify via a "portfolio" of decisions, may be less willing to take personnel chances. Finally, the threat of litigation implies increased oversight and second-guessing of managers. Such controversies invariably include challenges to the supervisor's previous decisions and overall competence. It may well be in the interest of personnel managers to avoid legal confrontations even if, from the firm's perspective, the dismissal is justified.

---

**4.** In California jury trials, nearly 40 percent of all defendants had some form of insurance against wrongful-termination liabilities. See Dertouzos, Holland, and Ebener (1988). Presumably, risk-averse firms would have strong incentives to acquire such protection.

The aggregate direct costs of wrongful-termination litigation may not reflect potential risks if firms are avoiding litigation by engaging in preventative activities. These activities can be very expensive and need to be considered in any comprehensive accounting of the costs of the evolving employer liabilities. Most directly, firms can avoid the legal threat by not firing workers even when justified by economic conditions or poor job performance. Business might be reluctant to expand employment in response to changing product demand or other exogenous factors which increase the short-run need for labor input. The firm might adjust the employee mix, trading off production efficiency for diminished exposure to liability. Younger workers with short employment histories and unreliable references could be more risky. Older workers, despite their experience, might also be risky because of the higher sums they are awarded by juries. Changes in the utilization of overtime hours, part-time employees, or temporary workers are also possible. Managers might be reluctant to engage in risky ventures such as new product development or market expansion, out of fear of being left with a surplus of workers that can be terminated only at great expense. Firms would be prone not to adopt new technologies that displace labor in favor of capital equipment.

In addition to decisions that affect the utilization of labor, firms can avoid liability by changing the process of decisionmaking. Carefully screening potential employees, conducting extensive interviews, tracking down references, and maintaining rigorous qualifying standards diminish the risks of hiring the wrong person. Of course, this process is costly and could arbitrarily screen out higher risk persons with lots of potential. In addition to changes in hiring practices, firms will formalize the performance review, evaluation, promotion, and compensation process. Human-resource decisionmaking will become centralized, hierarchical, and systematic. Individuals will have less autonomy in personnel matters as internal mechanisms emerge for the purpose of exerting organizational oversight and risk management.

The decision to terminate an employee will no longer come at the discretion of immediate supervisors. Instead, grounds for termination will need to be well-documented and reviewed by senior executives, corporate counsel, and human resource specialists. Some firms will adopt an internal adjudication process for resolving workplace disputes without relying on the legal system. Decisions will be rendered by individuals perceived as having few vested interests in the disposition of the dispute.

The fact that many firms voluntarily provide implicit job guarantees and organize internal mechanisms to protect workers from unjust treatment, even in the absence of legal pressures, suggests that the marginal effects of employee protection might be less significant. For example, many businesses organized institutionalized procedures for ensuring fair treatment of personnel long before the erosion of employment at will. In many corporations, even nonunion employees can air grievances and appeal the decisions of supervisors. Although the 1988 Worker Adjustment and Retraining Notification Act mandates that some employers must provide workers 60 days advance notice of layoffs, recent studies of this legislation's effect suggest that workers are typically aware of impending employment reductions, even without formal notification requirements.

When workforce reductions are inevitable because of changing economic conditions or technological changes, firms frequently attempt to smooth the transition of displaced workers. Although lifetime employment is not feasible when long-run economic survival is at stake, the neoclassical caricature of the ruthless, profit-maximizing firm making instantaneous adjustments to the workforce does not represent reality. Firms are reluctant to lay off workers, preferring to rely on natural attrition, retraining, buyouts, and early retirement to achieve the desired level of employment.

Of course, such seemingly altruistic behavior does not imply that firms are not concerned with their long-run profitability. To begin with, there can be little doubt that a firm's treatment of a subset of its employees will affect the morale, loyalty, and productivity of remaining workers. Surely, a history of unfair labor practices will affect the ability to recruit high-quality employees in the future. Also, the reputation that a firm has a voluntary commitment to "fair" employment practices, though not providing an absolute lifetime guarantee, certainly reduces the expected probability that any given employee will lose his or her job. Since workers value such job security, firms will be able to pay lower wage rates in return for less flexibility in reducing the workforce. This has the potential for making both firms and workers better off. Finally, the higher probability of a long job tenure will induce workers to invest in training human capital that is firm-specific in nature.

NOTE

A study of 1,700 verdicts from 1988–1995 by Jury Verdict Research revealed that executives who sue after being fired win bigger awards than other workers. Executive managers win 64% of the time, compared with 42% for general laborers, 48% for professionals, and 58% for middle managers and salespeople. Only paraprofessionals matched the success rate of executives. The study found that plaintiffs won the largest awards, at an average of $219,000, in age discrimination suits, followed by $147,799 in race discrimination suits, $106,728 for sex discrimination, $100,345 for disability discrimination, $87,500 for pregnancy discrimination, and only $38,500 for sexual harassment. Men who brought lawsuits after being fired won more than twice as often as women. Margaret A. Jacobs, Wall St.J., April 15, 1996, at B5.

## 3. GOLDEN SHACKLES: THE TIES THAT BIND

### Mary Ann Glendon & Edward R. Lev, *Changes in the Bonding of The Employment Relationship: An Essay on the New Property*
20 B.C.L.Rev. 457 (1979).

Our thesis is that recent changes in the laws governing the termination of employment are part of a broader change in the bonding of the employment relationship, through which the web of relations that bind an individual's job to him and, more subtly, bind him to his job, is becoming tighter and more highly structured.

* * *

[After discussing developments in wrongful discharge law, the authors continue:]

We have considered above some recent additions to the legal, economic, and practical restraints upon an employer's ability unilaterally to terminate the employment relationship. Other current developments reinforce the ties that always have made it difficult for an employee to change occupations or employers. Together, these developments cut across legal, economic, and political lines. As job ties have tightened, simultaneously constraining and liberating the individual, the employment relationship has assumed a greatly enhanced importance for most persons.

An individual's decision to change or leave a job is more complex than her decision to take a job. Nevertheless, there is nothing particularly new about many of the factors that constrain an employee from shifting from one employer to another, or from one type of work to another. Inertia and the fear of unknown ills have always weighed against any prospective advantages of a job change. Job satisfaction, while extremely significant, usually yields to the employee's perception of his economic condition. This is an overriding consideration unless the employee's income is already well above a level which he deems appropriate to his needs, desires, and expectations. What is new, and what merits discussion here, is the increasing significance in recent years of pensions, and the benefits accruing from an accumulation of seniority, among the ties that bind an employee to his present job.

Pensions, in the private sector at least, are largely a post-World War II phenomenon. However, by 1973, according to one estimate, over half of the labor force was covered by pension plans, and enrollment was growing at a faster rate than the labor force. Significantly, until vesting occurs in private, nonambulatory pension plans, an employee can accumulate credits toward vesting only by staying with his present employer. Thus, at some point in the early years of employment, an employee begins to sense that he has made an investment which will be lost if he leaves before vesting occurs. By this time (ten years under ERISA) he may also be reluctant to forfeit the seniority, experience, and the other benefits of extended employment he has gained with his employer. The point at which an employee senses that he has accumulated sufficient pension or seniority credits to warrant staying where he is in order to avoid the forfeiture to be suffered by leaving varies with the particular employee, his family situation, his age, his health, and the perceptions he has of himself and his current job. In short, once it becomes distasteful for an employee to give up an accumulation of service credits toward vesting, he will tend to remain where he is. Just as the employee nearing the year in which his pension will vest is apt to remain with his employer, the vested employee feels the tug of the increase in retirement amount anticipated with each year's employment service. In both cases, each year is a strand which strengthens the cable binding the employee to his particular employer. The anticipated benefits of an increased pension, added to the difficulties older employees experience in securing new employment, are formidable deterrents to a change in jobs.

Seniority also significantly deters employees from changing jobs by reason of the monetary and other advantages, such as protection against layoff, priority in recall, promotion opportunities, and vacation entitlements, which accrue from length of service with a particular employer. * * *

Thus, the new ties that bind an employee to his job—seniority, pension rights, and related benefits—together with traditional constraining factors—fear of the unknown and economic pressure—simultaneously provide an employee with security and limit his freedom to change jobs as service with a particular employer accumulates.

* * *

[A]s perception of the importance of "new property" for economic security has widened, its legal protection has been increased. Sniadach v. Family Finance Corp. accorded heightened protection to wages. The Employee and Retirement Income Security Act of 1974 (ERISA) was a landmark in the protection of the form of new property represented by pensions. We already have described the legal protection crystallizing around the job itself, both in the public and in the private sector. With respect to government benefits, the Supreme Court, in Goldberg v. Kelly, accorded the most important of them the status of "property" for purposes of due process. Justice Brennan, in the majority opinion, held that welfare "benefits are a matter of statutory entitlement for persons qualified to receive them," and that New York could not terminate them without prior notice and hearing. * * *

Later cases have made clear that the Supreme Court is not prepared to redefine as "property" for due process purposes the whole spectrum of Reich's "entitlements." The Court has, however, reinforced the pervasive legislative and administrative schemes through which government increasingly becomes the insurer of health, employment, and retirement, as well as the provider of a minimum level of subsistence for those in need. Recent Supreme Court cases provide heightened protection to education (which in turn provides access to work-related new property), and also promote the right of an individual to follow his chosen profession. Protection of the individual's interest in a *particular* job, however, is coming primarily not through the Supreme Court, but through the developments traced above in the ties that bind the job to the employee.

The changing law has been a sensitive indicator of the fact that the most important relationship in the lives of most Americans, so far as economic security is concerned, is their own actual or potential employment relationship, with government and the family serving as back-up systems.

This is true even of spouses and children who may be dependent for periods of time on the employment of a family provider. We speak here of economic security not in the sense of the day-to-day pooling of contributions by members of a functioning family, but in the sense of an economic hedge against old age, illness, disability, unemployment, death of a family provider, and family disruption—the ills which all fear and to which all are susceptible. The importance of the employment relationship in assuring the economic security of the family is illustrated by the estimate made in 1977 by the Carnegie Council on Children that fully half of all American families cannot save. To the extent a middle-income family has savings apart from home equity, they are less likely to consist of bank accounts or tangible assets than employment-related pension plans, stock purchase plans, insurance and other benefits.

PROBLEM

Review the *Wagenseller* case in Chapter 1. Given what you now know about wrongful discharge, what rights do you think Wagenseller has in her employment? What rights *should* she have? What legal actions could she pursue?

# CHAPTER 11

# LEAVING A JOB

Just as the at-will doctrine allows an employer to fire an employee for any reason or for no reason, so long as the reason is not illegal, theoretically the at-will doctrine also allows an employee to quit for any reason or for no reason. In practice, this freedom to end the employment relationship tends to be less useful to employees than to employers. It is usually more difficult and disruptive for an employee to find a new job than it is for an employer to find a new employee, so quitting to resolve employment disputes is often a recourse of last resort for employees, particularly those who are unskilled or who possess skills that are widely held. Furthermore, like the employer's right to fire at-will, the employee's right to quit is also limited in various ways. Because these limitations tend to increase with the employee's skills and responsibilities, they effectively constrain the post-employment choices of those employees in better bargaining positions who would be better able to exercise the option to quit and to find suitable alternative employment. This chapter will cover limitations on an employee's right to quit that allow an employer to safeguard its investment in its employees.

## A. BREACH OF CONTRACT BY AN EMPLOYEE

### 1. BREACH OF EXPRESS TERMS

## Handicapped Children's Education Board v. Lukaszewski

332 N.W.2d 774 (Wis.1983).

■ CALLOW, JUSTICE.

This review arises out of an unpublished decision of the court of appeals which affirmed in part and reversed in part a judgment of the Ozaukee county circuit court, Judge Warren A. Grady.

In January of 1978 the Handicapped Children's Education Board (the Board) hired Elaine Lukaszewski to serve as a speech and language therapist for the spring term. Lukaszewski was assigned to the Lightfoot School in Sheboygan Falls which was approximately 45 miles from her home in Mequon. Rather than move, she commuted to work each day. During the 1978 spring term, the Board offered Lukaszewski a contract to continue in her present position at Lightfoot School for the 1978–79 school year.  The contract called for an annual salary of $10,760.  Lukaszewski accepted.

In August of 1978, prior to the beginning of the school year, Lukaszewski was offered a position by the Wee Care Day Care Center which was located not far from her home in Mequon.  The job paid an annual salary of $13,000.  After deciding to accept this offer, Lukaszewski notified Thomas Morrelle, the Board's director of special education, that she intended to resign from her position at the Lightfoot School.  Morrelle told her to submit a letter of resignation for consideration by the Board.  She did so, and the matter was discussed at a meeting of the Board on August 21, 1978.  The Board refused to release Lukaszewski from her contract.  On August 24, 1978, the Board's attorney sent a letter to Lukaszewski directing her to return to work.  The attorney sent a second letter to the Wee Care Day Care Center stating that the Board would take legal action if the Center interfered with Lukaszewski's performance of her contractual obligations at the Lightfoot School.  A copy of this letter was sent to the Department of Public Instruction.

Lukaszewski left the Wee Care Day Care Center and returned to Lightfoot School for the 1978 fall term.  She resented the actions of the Board, however, and retained misgivings about her job.  On September 8, 1978, she discussed her feelings with Morrelle.  After this meeting Lukaszewski felt quite upset about the situation.  She called her doctor to make an appointment for that afternoon and subsequently left the school.

Dr. Ashok Chatterjee examined Lukaszewski and found her blood pressure to be high.  Lukaszewski asked Dr. Chatterjee to write a letter explaining his medical findings and the advice he had given her.  In a letter dated September 11, 1978, Dr. Chatterjee indicated that Lukaszewski had a hypertension problem dating back to 1976.  He reported that on the day he examined Lukaszewski she appeared agitated, nervous, and had blood pressure readings up to 180/100.  It was his opinion that, although she took hypotensive drugs, her medical condition would not improve unless the situation which caused the problem was removed.  He further opined that it would be dangerous for her to drive long distances in her agitated state.

Lukaszewski did not return to work after leaving on September 8, 1978.  She submitted a letter of resignation dated September 13, 1978, in which she wrote:

> "I enclose a copy of the doctor's statement concerning my health.  On the basis of it, I must resign.  I am unwilling to jeopardize my health and I am also unwilling to become involved in an accident.  For these reasons, I tender my resignation."

A short time later Lukaszewski reapplied for and obtained employment at the Wee Care Day Care Center.

After Lukaszewski left, the Board immediately began looking for a replacement.  Only one qualified person applied for the position.  Although this applicant had less of an educational background than Lukaszewski, she had more teaching experience. Under the salary schedule agreed upon by the Board and the teachers' union, this applicant would have to be paid $1,026.64 more per year than Lukaszewski. Having no alternative, the Board hired the applicant at the higher salary.

In December of 1978 the Board initiated an action against Lukaszewski for breach of contract. The Board alleged that, as a result of the breach, it suffered damage in the amount of the additional compensation it was required to pay Lukaszewski's replacement for the 1978–79 school year ($1,026.64). A trial was held before the court. The trial court ruled that Lukaszewski had breached her contract and awarded the Board $1,249.14 in damages ($1,026.64 for breach of contract and $222.50 for costs).

\* \* \*

There are two issues presented on this review: (1) whether Lukaszewski breached her employment contract with the Board; and (2) if she did breach her contract, whether the Board suffered recoverable damages therefrom.

It is undisputed that Lukaszewski resigned before her contract with the Board expired. The only question is whether her resignation was somehow justified. Lukaszewski argues that, because she resigned for health reasons, the trial court erred in finding a breach of contract. According to Lukaszewski, the uncontroverted evidence at trial established that her employment with the Board endangered her health. Therefore, her failure to fulfill her obligation under the employment contract was excused.

We recognize that under certain conditions illness or health dangers may excuse nonperformance of a contract. This court held long ago that "where the act to be performed is one which the promisor alone is competent to do, the obligation is discharged if he is prevented by sickness or death from performing it." Jennings v. Lyons, 39 Wis. 553, 557 (1876). Even assuming this rule applies to Lukaszewski's failure to perform, we are not convinced that the trial court erred in finding a breach of contract.

A health danger will not excuse nonperformance of a contractual obligation when the danger is caused by the nonperforming party. Nor will a health condition or danger which was foreseeable when the contract was entered into justify its breach. It would be fundamentally unfair to allow a breaching party to escape liability because of a health danger which by his or her own fault has precluded performance.

In the instant case the trial court expressly found that the danger to Lukaszewski's health was self-induced. Lukaszewski testified that it was stressful for her to return to the Lightfoot School in the fall of 1978 because she did not want to work there and because she resented the Board's actions to compel her to do so. Citing this testimony, the court concluded: "The Court finds that the defendant's medical excuse was a result of the stress condition she had created by an attempted repudiation of her contract, and was not the product of any unsubstantiated, so-called, harrassment [sic] by the plaintiff's board." Lukaszewski further complained about the hazard of driving 45 miles to and from Sheboygan Falls each day. She alone, however, caused this commute by choosing to live in Mequon. The trial court pointed out in its decision from the bench that she could have eliminated this problem by simply moving to Sheboygan Falls. Thus the court clearly found that any health danger associated with performance of the employment contract was the fault of Lukaszewski, not the Board. This factual finding alone is enough to invalidate the medical excuse for Lukaszewski's breach.

The medical excuse is defective for a second reason. In order to excuse Lukaszewski's nonperformance, the trial court would have to have made a factual finding that she resigned for health reasons. The oral decision and supplemental written decision of the trial court indicate that it found otherwise. In its written decision the court stated:

> "[Lukaszewski's] reasons for resignation were succinctly stated in her testimony, upon cross-examination * * * as follows: ' * * * I had found a job that was closer in proximity to my home and it offered a different type of challenge, * * * also that the pay was, was more, and I asked them if I could be released from my contract.' "

The trial court did not include the health danger. Indeed, the court appeared to doubt that Lukaszewski resigned for health reasons. The trial judge observed that Lukaszewski had a history of hypertension dating back at least five or six years. Her blood pressure would fluctuate at the slightest provocation. He further noted that she was able to commute between Sheboygan Falls and Mequon from January, 1978, through the middle of the following summer. In short, the decisions indicate that the court believed Lukaszewski resigned for reasons other than her health.

These factual findings by the trial court invalidate Lukaszewski's medical excuse and thereby establish a breach.

* * *

We conclude that the trial court's findings of fact are not against the great weight and clear preponderance of the evidence and, therefore, must be upheld. Accordingly, we affirm that portion of the court of appeals' decision which affirmed the circuit court's determination that Lukaszewski breached her employment contract.

This court has long held that an employer may recover damages from an employee who has failed to perform an employment contract. Damages in breach of contract cases are ordinarily measured by the expectations of the parties. The nonbreaching party is entitled to full compensation for the loss of his or her bargain—that is, losses necessarily flowing from the breach which are proven to a reasonable certainty and were within contemplation of the parties when the contract was made. Thus damages for breach of an employment contract include the cost of obtaining other services equivalent to that promised but not performed, plus any foreseeable consequential damages.

In the instant case it is undisputed that, as a result of the breach, the Board hired a replacement at a salary exceeding what it had agreed to pay Lukaszewski. There is no question that this additional cost ($1,026.64) necessarily flowed from the breach and was within the contemplation of the parties when the contract was made. Lukaszewski argues and the court of appeals held, however, that the Board was not damaged by this expense. The amount a teacher is paid is determined by a salary schedule agreed upon by the teachers' union and the Board. The more education and experience a teacher has the greater her salary will be. Presumably, then, the amount of compensation a teacher receives reflects her value to the Board. Lukaszewski argues that the Board suffered no net loss because, while it had to pay more for the replacement, it received the services of a proportionately more valuable teacher. Accordingly, she maintains that the Board is not entitled to damages because an award would place it in a better position than if the contract had been performed.

We disagree. Lukaszewski and the court of appeals improperly focus on the objective value of the services the Board received rather than that for which it had bargained. Damages for breach of contract are measured by the expectations of the parties. The Board expected to receive the services of a speech therapist with Lukaszewski's education and experience at the salary agreed upon. It neither expected nor wanted a more experienced therapist who had to be paid an additional $1,026.64 per year. Lukaszewski's breach forced the Board to hire the replacement and, in turn, to pay a higher salary. Therefore, the Board lost the benefit of its bargain. Any additional value the Board may have received from the replacement's greater experience was imposed upon it and thus cannot be characterized as a benefit. We conclude that the Board suffered damages for the loss of its bargain in the amount of additional compensation it was required to pay Lukaszewski's replacement.

This is not to say that an employer who is injured by an employee's breach of contract is free to hire the most qualified and expensive replacement and then recover the difference between the salary paid and the contract salary. An injured party must take all reasonable steps to mitigate damages. Therefore, the employer must attempt to obtain equivalent services at the lowest possible cost. In the instant case the Board acted reasonably in hiring Lukaszewski's replacement even though she commanded a higher salary. Upon Lukaszewski's breach, the Board immediately took steps to locate a replacement. Only one qualified person applied for the position. Having no alternative, the Board hired this applicant. Thus the Board properly mitigated its damages by hiring the least expensive, qualified replacement available.

We hold that the Board is entitled to have the benefit of its bargain restored. Therefore, we reverse that portion of the court of appeals' decision which reversed the trial court's damage award.

The decision of the court of appeals is affirmed in part and reversed in part.

■ DAY, JUSTICE (dissenting).

I dissent. The majority opinion correctly states, "The only question is whether her resignation is somehow justified." I would hold that it was.

Elaine Lukaszewski left her employment with the school board. She suffered from high blood pressure and had been treated for several years by her physician for the condition. She claimed her hypertension increased due to stress caused when the Board refused to cancel her teaching contract. Stress can cause a precipitous rise in blood pressure. High blood pressure can bring on damage to other organs of the body.

She was upset over what she perceived was the unreasonable attitude of her employer in refusing to cancel her contract. Following an unpleasant exchange with the Board's Director of Special Education, Mr. Morrelle, she went to her physician. He found her blood pressure to be 180 over 100 which he testified was very high. He advised her to rest and to get out of the situation that was causing her symptoms which she properly interpreted to mean "quit the job." He also told her that her elevated blood pressure made it dangerous for her to drive the ninety miles round-trip each day, that commuting from her home in Mequon to Sheboygan Falls entailed.

The trial court and the majority of this court conclude she could have obviated the danger of driving by moving to Sheboygan Falls. But the fact is that would not have eliminated her illness nor the hazards to her health that her condition posed. There is not a shred of medical evidence that her blood pressure problems would be cured or appreciably alleviated if she moved from her home to Sheboygan Falls.

Once the dangerous hypertension is established, and here the only medical testimony did just that, it should follow that one should be relieved of a contractual obligation for services unless malingering is shown. In this case no one denies she has the condition. But, the trial court says, the condition was one "she had created," which the majority on this court refer to as "self induced." The majority here seized on the rationale that illness that is "self induced" is somehow less worthy of judicial consideration than illness caused by others, or by outside forces over which the patient has no control.

It seems clear from the trial judge's comments that if he had found her physical condition had been caused by the Board's "harassment," he would have let her out of the contract. This is the only logical conclusion from the statement by the trial judge that, "The Court finds that the defendant's medical excuse was a result of the stress condition she had created by an attempted repudiation of her contract, and was not the product of any unsubstantiated, so-called, harrassment [sic] by the plaintiff's board."

In either instance, whether "caused" by the Board or "self induced" because of her gnawing feeling of being unfairly treated, the objective symptoms would be the same.

Either, in my opinion, should justify termination of the contract where the physical symptoms are medically certifiable as they admittedly are here.

The majority makes the following assertion, "It would be fundamentally unfair to allow a breaching party to escape liability because of a health danger which by his or her own fault has precluded performance."

Happily no authority is cited for this sweeping statement which means that it will be easier to ignore it, gloss over it, "distinguish" it or overrule it in the future. Under this new found axiom, could a concert violinist under contract be sued to cover any added costs of his replacement if he lost an arm in an accident where he was found 100 percent negligent? Or could another party to a personal service contract be held liable if he was unable to perform because of a debilitating illness clearly caused by negligent health habits?

*Jennings* is cited by the majority to bolster its position. The case is not really in point. * * *

This court said that since the husband must have known his wife was four months pregnant when they took the job and that she would be unable to complete the year of work, therefore no recovery was allowed. This court said "For when performance becomes impossible by reason of contingencies which should have been foreseen and provided against in the contract, the promisor is held answerable." * * *

The precedential value of *Jennings* is doubtful but to the extent the rules stated may still be valid it provides no support for the majority. Here there is an illness, "an act of God," there is nothing in the record to show that the severe increase in Elaine Lukaszewski's hypertension was foreseeable when she signed the contract. Thus, even under *Jennings*, the teacher should be excused from performance.

Hypertension is a health problem that when caused by stress, however induced, may require a job change. That is what occurred here.

* * *

What the trial court said was that the desire to take the better job brought on the physical symptoms when release from her contract by the Board was refused.

If the trial court had found that she quit merely for the better job and *not* because of her health problems brought on by the high blood pressure, this would be an entirely different case. However, that is *not* what the trial court found in my opinion. The trial court found her medical problems were self induced and concluded they were therefore unworthy of consideration.

I would reverse the court of appeals decision that held she breached her contract.

Because I would hold that on this record there was no breach, I would not reach the damage question.

NOTES AND QUESTIONS

**1.** The majority and dissenting opinions construe somewhat differently the trial court's ambiguous statements about whether Lukaszewski's hypertension was the real reason for her resignation. Should the court have remanded the case to the trial court for a clearer finding on this issue?

**2.** The majority opinion in *Lukaszewski* recognizes that ill health on the part of the employee would excuse nonperformance, but that health problems brought on by the employee herself would not be a valid excuse. Is this a meaningful distinction? Suppose the health problems were self-induced through cigarette smoking, overeating, or skiing? Perhaps what the court means to hold as inexcusable were health problems resulting from the attempt to repudiate the contract. Is this distinction better? See pp. 870–873 supra on the distinctions between voluntary and involuntary disabilities in the Social Security program.

**3.** Other legal grounds for avoiding employment contracts include incapacity, undue influence, duress, fraud, act of God, illegality, intoxication, and misrepresentation. Can you think of examples of how these defenses could arise? When and how might these defenses be utilized by an employee seeking to avoid contractual obligations?

**4.** Employers often spend substantial sums of money in training new employees. Are these sums recoverable in the event the employee breaches the employment contract? A truck driver signed a three year contract which included a provision stating that if the employee terminated the agreement the employee would have to pay $1500 to reimburse the employer for training expenses. Colorado law allows employers to recoup training expenses for any employee who works less than two years with the employer. Such an arrangement, however, must be specified in the employment agreement. Dresser Industries v. Sandvick, 732 F.2d 783 (10th Cir.1984). New York State United Teachers v. Thompson, 459 F.Supp. 677 (N.D.N.Y.1978), upheld a cause of action in a lawsuit alleging that an employee should reimburse his employer for tuition paid by the employer when the employee refused to meet his contractual obligation to return to the job after an educational leave of absence.

**5.** With regard to damages, the court follows the general rule that damages for breach of an employment contract include the cost of obtaining equivalent services plus foreseeable consequential damages. Should the plaintiff or defendant have the burden of proving the reasonableness of the damages? Lukaszewski argued that even though the board hired a replacement at a higher salary, it obtained a more experienced teacher, and was therefore not damaged. The court rejected this line of reasoning. It awarded the board "the benefit of its bargain," which amounted primarily to the difference between the replacement's salary and Lukaszewski's salary. Is this an adequate measure of the damages suffered by the school board? In thinking about this, consider whether a higher salaried employee always confers a greater benefit on the employer. How would the calculus change if the only available replacement had a Ph.D. and 20 years experience and was paid twice as much as Lukaszewski?

## 2. BREACH OF IMPLIED TERMS

Depending on his or her position, an employee may be held to various standards of performance that are not mentioned in a contract but are implied under the law of agency.  Some employees owe their employers fiduciary duties, duties of care, and duties of loyalty which insure that the employee is acting in the best interests of the employer.

# Mercer Management Consulting, Inc., v. Wilde

920 F.Supp. 219 (D.D.C.1996).

■ JOYCE HENS GREEN, DISTRICT JUDGE.

After defendants Dean L. Wilde, II and Dean R. Silverman established a competing business, Dean & Co. Strategy Consultants, Inc., and, along with defendant Moray P. Dewhurst, left the employ of plaintiff Mercer Management Consulting, Inc., Mercer brought a ten-count complaint alleging, inter alia, breach of fiduciary duty, breach of contract, and tortious interference with contractual relationships.  Defendants Wilde and Silverman counterclaimed for breach of contract, stemming from Mercer's alleged failure to honor an agreement to make certain payments to Wilde and Silverman.

Following denial of defendants' second motion for summary judgment (except as to one claim relating to defendant Dewhurst), this case was tried to the Court.  After the trial, counsel submitted extensive proposed findings of fact and conclusions of law.  Upon consideration of the record and evidence introduced at trial, including the testimony of witnesses whose credibility, demeanor, and behavior the Court has had an opportunity to observe and fully evaluate, for the reasons set forth below judgment shall be entered in favor of plaintiff on its claims relating to breach of the 1982 Agreement by defendants Dean Wilde and Dean Silverman, and in favor of defendants on all of Mercer's other claims.  Judgment shall be entered in Mercer's favor on Wilde's and Silverman's counterclaim.

Mercer is a management consulting and strategic planning company incorporated under the laws of Delaware.  Mercer is an indirect subsidiary of Marsh & McLennan Companies, Inc.  In 1987, MMC acquired, through a subsidiary, a management consulting and strategic planning company known as Temple Barker Sloane, Inc.  On February 14, 1990, MMC acquired Strategic Planning Associates, Inc., by merging it with TBS.  The resulting company became known as Mercer Management Consulting, Inc., the plaintiff company in this case.

Defendants Wilde, Silverman, and Dewhurst were employed by SPA, and subsequently by Mercer, as management consultants.  Each defendant quickly rose through the ranks.  Wilde joined SPA in 1980 after his graduation from the Massachusetts Institute of Technology's Sloane School of Management.  He became a vice president of SPA in 1984 and an executive vice-president and member of SPA's Policy Committee in 1988.  Moreover, he served on Mercer's Board of Directors and Mercer's "inside board" from approximately October 1991 until his resignation on April 2, 1993.

Silverman, a graduate of Columbia Law School, joined SPA in 1979 after three years in a law firm and another management consulting business. Like Wilde, Silverman became a vice president in approximately 1984, and became an executive vice president and Policy Committee member in 1988. He too served on Mercer's Board of Directors and the "inside board" from approximately October 1991 until his resignation on April 2, 1993.

Dewhurst joined SPA in 1980 after his graduation from MIT's Sloane School of Management. He became a vice president of SPA in 1984 and served in that position until his resignation on March 15, 1993. In 1982, Wilde, Silverman, and Dewhurst each executed an employment agreement with SPA. The 1982 Agreement provides, inter alia, that each defendant will refrain from "render[ing] competitive services" to any client or active prospect of SPA, or from hiring or assisting in hiring any SPA employee, for a period of one year following the termination of employment with SPA. Such agreements are typical in the management consulting industry. Thomas Waylett, Chairman of Mercer Management, testified that the agreements served as Mercer's "protection that people wouldn't just walk out the door, set up in business, and take clients and employees." As part of its "due diligence" investigation prior to the TBS/SPA merger, Mercer sought to ascertain whether SPA's employees had previously signed non-solicitation agreements, and it learned of the 1982 Agreements in the course of that investigation.

In 1989, as a condition of the merger between TBS and SPA, Mercer required five senior employee-stockholders of SPA, including Wilde and Silverman, to enter into employment agreements. Wilde and Silverman each executed the 1990 Agreement in December 1989. The agreements became effective as of the merger date—February 14, 1990.

Among its key provisions, the 1990 Agreement assured continued employment at a guaranteed level of compensation for a period of three years from the date of the merger. The agreement obligated Wilde and Silverman to "perform and discharge well and faithfully the[ir] duties". For a three-year period commencing on the date of the merger, the agreement prohibited Wilde and Silverman from offering competitive services within a 50–mile radius, soliciting or accepting business from any Mercer client or active prospect, or soliciting any management consulting professional to terminate employment with Mercer.

Pivotal to the instant dispute is paragraph 14 of the 1990 Agreement, which concerns the relationship between the 1990 Agreement and prior employment agreements. Paragraph 14 states, in pertinent part:

14. Entire Agreement. This instrument contains the entire agreement of the parties with respect to employment following the Merger Date and supersedes all prior oral or written agreements and understandings between and among the Employee [and] the Company ... with respect to employment following the Merger Date, except for any agreements or understandings restricting or prohibiting the competition or solicitation activities of the Employ-

ee or the use of confidential information of the Company or its clients which shall remain in full force and effect, provided that in the event of a conflict between the provisions of this Agreement and those of any other agreement which survive hereunder, the provisions of this Agreement shall control.

The meaning of paragraph 14 and its effect on the survival of the 1982 Agreements is paramount to Mercer's breach of contract claims.

\* \* \*

The Court previously denied defendants' motion for summary judgment on Mercer's claims relating to breach of fiduciary duty, stating that "resolution of the question of whether defendants' actions constituted a breach of fiduciary duty ... requires 'a thoroughgoing examination of the facts and circumstances' presented in this case." Having heard and evaluated the testimony elicited at trial, the Court has concluded that defendants' actions, while perhaps questionable on moral or ethical grounds, do not rise to the level of a breach of fiduciary duty. The claims of breach of the "well and faithfully" clause in the 1990 Agreements, the facts and analysis of which parallel the fiduciary duty claim, similarly fail.

Corporate officers and directors owe "an undivided and unselfish loyalty to the corporation" such that "there shall be no conflict between duty and self-interest." Similarly, "an agent is subject to a duty not to compete with the principal concerning the subject matter of his agency." At the same time, however, the law is clear that "an agent can make arrangements or plans to go into competition with his principal before terminating his agency, provided no unfair acts are committed or injury done his principal."

Still, as the Court stated in Science Accessories, "[t]he right to make arrangements to compete is by no means absolute and the exercise of the privilege may, in appropriate circumstances, rise to the level of a breach of an employee's fiduciary duty of loyalty." The limitations of an officer's preparatory activities have been described as follows:

Prior to termination of employment, an officer may not solicit for himself or herself business which the position requires the employee to obtain for the employer. The officer must refrain from actively and directly competing with the employer for customers and employees, and must continue to exert his or her best efforts on behalf of the employer.

In preparing to compete, an employee may not commit fraudulent, unfair, or wrongful acts, such as misuse of confidential information, solicitation of the firm's customers, or solicitation leading to a mass resignation of the firm's employees. At the same time, failure to disclose plans to enter into competition is not itself necessarily a breach of fiduciary duty. Thus, "the ultimate determination of whether an employee has breached his fiduciary duties to his employer by preparing to engage in a competing enterprise must be grounded upon a thoroughgoing examination of the facts and circumstances of the particular case." The evidence at trial established that while still employed by Mercer, Wilde and Silverman in particular, and to a lesser extent Dewhurst, took numerous actions to establish what was to become Dean & Co., a competing business. Not only did they incorporate Dean & Co., but they made arrangements for office space, inquired about benefit packages, investigated computer systems, and met with an accountant.

It is evident to the Court that by at least late February 1993, Wilde and Silverman were intent upon forming their own company. The precise contours of the business might not have been fully developed, but Wilde and Silverman were plainly moving quickly down the road toward starting their own competing consulting business. Indeed, Dean & Co. was incorporated on February 25, 1993.

At no time prior to their departure did Wilde, Silverman, or Dewhurst disclose their actions or intentions to their colleagues at Mercer. They continued to perform work for Mercer, including meetings with clients they would later solicit on behalf of Dean & Co. Wilde and Silverman continued to attend with clients they would later solicit on behalf of Dean & Co. Wilde and Silverman continued to attend meetings of the Board of Directors and inside board, at which information of the most confidential sort was discussed.

At the same time, the record is clear that at no time prior to their departure from Mercer did Wilde, Silverman, or Dewhurst solicit Mercer's clients on behalf of what was to become Dean & Co., or perform any competing consulting work under the auspices of Dean & Co. Mercer urges the Court to find that defendants breached their fiduciary duty by performing work for Mercer until their departures, because, in Mercer's view, these efforts were plainly aimed at solidifying relationships to inure to the benefit of Dean & Co. While the Court does not doubt the sincerity of plaintiff's view, the Court is not persuaded that an employee breaches his fiduciary duty by performing work for his employer at a time when he is planning to leave his employment. The Court recognizes that personal relationships with clients are paramount in the management consulting business, and that defendants' contacts with Mercer's clients, if positive, could potentially work to the benefit of defendants' competing business. However, the Court finds unreasonable and unrealistic the proposition that any client contact prior to leaving one's employment and starting a competing business constitutes a breach of one's fiduciary duty. In the absence of evidence that any overt solicitation was made or other improper actions taken in the course of defendants' client contacts, the Court does not find the Bell Canada meeting or other client contacts to constitute a breach of fiduciary duty.

In the final analysis, upon full consideration and evaluation of all of the facts and circumstances presented in this case, the Court has determined that while defendants' covert actions in establishing Dean & Co. were not particularly admirable, they did not constitute a breach of their legal fiduciary duties of loyalty to Mercer. As previously noted, the Court finds that Wilde and Silverman did not solicit Dewhurst to leave Mercer and join Dean & Co. Moreover, while the record is clear that Wilde and

Silverman extended invitations to a dinner to solicit Mercer employees while they were still employed by Mercer, it is equally clear that the dinner did not take place until after the conclusion of Wilde's and Silverman's last day of employment at Mercer, albeit later that same day. Moreover, it appears that none of the individuals solicited by Wilde and Silverman at the dinner ultimately joined Dean & Co. Consequently, Mercer's damages resulting from the dinner are not evident.

Similarly, during the time they were establishing Dean & Co. and preparing to compete, all three defendants continued to perform fully their duties for Mercer. Indeed, Mercer's Chairman testified at trial that time was not the issue with respect to defendants' alleged disloyalty; rather, the issue was defendants' preparations to compete with Mercer while still on Mercer's payroll.

Apart from the stealth with which defendants established their competing business, the most troublesome aspect of Wilde's and Silverman's actions concerned their compilation and mailing to two major clients (AT & T and Sara Lee) tape diskettes containing the history of Mercer's work for those clients. The timing and unprecedented nature of these actions leaves no doubt that Wilde and Silverman intended for the diskettes to increase AT & T and Sara Lee's comfort level with switching their business from Mercer to Dean & Co. Arguably this action constituted misuse of confidential information in violation of Wilde's and Silverman's fiduciary duties. However, in view of the uncontroverted testimony of Wilde and Silverman that they have not had access to the information on the tape at any time, and the utter lack of testimony from relevant officials at AT & T or Sara Lee concerning the effect, if any, of the tapes on their decision to switch their business to Dean & Co., the Court finds that the compilation and mailing of the tapes, while certainly inappropriate, did not rise to the level of a breach of defendants' fiduciary duty.

For the foregoing reasons, judgment shall be entered for Wilde, Silverman, and Dewhurst on Mercer's claims relating to breach of fiduciary duty. Because Mercer's allegations concerning breach of the "well and faithfully" clause of the 1990 Agreements are based on the same facts and circumstances as the fiduciary duty claim, judgment shall similarly be entered in defendants' favor on this breach of contract claim.

A threshold question to be resolved in connection with Mercer's breach of contract claims relating to Wilde's and Silverman's 1982 Agreements concerns whether the Agreements survived the 1990 Agreement. As previously discussed, paragraph 14 of the 1990 Agreements states that the 1990 Agreement contains the full agreement of the parties, except for non-compete or non-solicit agreements or agreements relating to confidential information, which shall remain in full force and effect, unless a conflict existed between those provisions and the 1990 Agreement, in which case the 1990 Agreement controls.

"The basic rule of contract construction gives priority to the intentions of the parties." In ascertaining the meaning and intent of contract language, the starting point is obviously the language itself. A contract is construed as a whole, giving effect to all of the contract's provisions and avoiding a construction which would render one of those provisions meaningless. While extrinsic evidence may be considered when a contract is subject to a number of different interpretations, the greatest weight should be given to the express language of the contract itself. Finally, in determining intent, the overt acts and statements of the parties are examined through the eyes of an objective observer.

Because the Court previously determined that the language in paragraph 14 was subject to a number of different interpretations, the Court allowed extrinsic evidence on paragraph 14's meaning and intent. That evidence failed to elucidate a definitive explanation of the parties' expressed intentions at the time of contract formation. Thus, the Court must ascertain the reasonable meaning and effect of paragraph 14 primarily from the language itself, with the extrinsic evidence of the parties' negotiations as a backdrop.

Upon careful evaluation of the language of the contract and the evidence presented at trial, the Court is persuaded that paragraph 14's proviso clause did not eviscerate the exceptions clause. Moreover, the Court is persuaded that no conflict existed between the 1982 Agreement and the 1990 Agreement. Accordingly, the restrictions contained in the 1982 Agreements survived the 1990 Agreement.

* * *

No inherent conflict existed between the two contracts. Each provided Mercer a certain type of protection against competition and solicitation of its clients and employees. The 1990 Agreement assured Mercer that Wilde and Silverman would not compete with Mercer or solicit its clients or employees. However, those protections expired three years from the date of the merger. The 1982 Agreement provided Mercer protection against interference with its clients and employees for one year from the termination of Wilde's and Silverman's employment, whenever that termination occurred. If the termination happened to occur within two years of the merger, then the 1982 Agreement's restrictions would yield to the 1990 Agreement's restrictions, due to the stricter restrictions contained in the 1990 Agreement. In any other instance, the 1982 Agreement's one-year restriction would be triggered.

In any case, because the 1990 Agreement expired in February 1993, no conflict existed between its provisions and the restrictions contained in the 1982 Agreements. Even though the 1990 Agreement was no longer in effect at the time Wilde and Silverman left Mercer's employ, the 1982 Agreement was still viable.

Defendants contend that the 1982 Agreements are void as violative of the public policy against restrictive covenants. In order to be valid, covenants not to compete must protect some legitimate interest of the employer and must be reasonable in their scope. Restrictions are unreasonable if "the restraint is greater than is needed to protect the promisee's legitimate interest, or ... the promisee's need is outweighed by the

hardship to the promisor and the likely injury to the public." Significantly, a "restraint is easier to justify ... if the restraint is limited to the
taking of his former employer's customers as contrasted with competition
in general."

Here, the Court finds that Mercer has demonstrated a legitimate
purpose in requiring its employees to sign the 1982 Agreement—namely
that Mercer wished to protect the investment it made in its employees,
preserve the confidentiality of information gleaned in the course of employment at Mercer, and protect itself from its employees leaving and capitalizing on Mercer's client base.  The Court finds unpersuasive defendants'
argument that because Mercer's post-merger policy concerning restrictive
covenants was inconsistent, Mercer necessarily cannot demonstrate a legitimate interest in the agreements.  In the years prior to the merger, SPA
required all consultants to sign such agreements.  TBS required similar
agreements of its senior employees.  Mercer presently requires all senior
officials to sign such agreements.  The fact that for a period of time
following the merger not all employees of the former TBS were required to
sign such agreements does not eradicate Mercer's legitimate interests,
particularly in view of the disarray and multitude of issues facing the
merged company immediately following the merger.

Significantly, the 1982 Agreements do not broadly prohibit competition
with Mercer generally, but rather are limited to restricting the rendering of
services to Mercer's clients or hiring Mercer's employees.  The restrictions
are limited to a one-year period of time.  In view of the substantial
investment Mercer made in its employees, the vital importance of its client
base to its business, and the close contacts established between its consultants and its client base, the Court finds that the modest restrictions
contained in the 1982 Agreements are reasonable and enforceable.

The evidence at trial failed to establish that Dewhurst breached the
1982 Agreement.  Dewhurst attended two meetings with AT & T–DCS
immediately after joining Dean & Co., and he assisted in the preparation of
a proposal for AT & T–DCS, but both Dewhurst and Wilde presented
uncontroverted testimony that the proposal was rejected and Dean & Co.
obtained no work and no pay as a result of the proposal.  Thus, the Court
finds that Dewhurst did not "render competitive services" to a Mercer
client within one year of the termination of his employment.

Similarly, while Dewhurst was knowledgeable of Wilde's and Silverman's plan to solicit and hire Mercer employees, there is no evidence that
Dewhurst assisted in hiring either Adams or Lowell, who are the only
Mercer employees identified by Mercer as being hired by Dean & Co. within
one year of defendant's departure.  Accordingly, judgment in Dewhurst's
favor on the breach of contract claim is appropriate.

The situation differs with respect to Wilde and Silverman.  The
evidence at trial established that Wilde and Silverman both "render[ed]
competitive services" and hired Mercer employees, namely Lowell and
Adams, within one year of their termination of employment with Mercer.

These actions constituted material breaches of the 1982 Agreements for which Wilde and Silverman are liable.

\* \* \*

As previously noted, the 1982 Agreement does not expressly prohibit solicitation of SPA's (now Mercer's) clients, but states that the consultant shall not "render competitive services . . . to any person or firm" to which SPA (now Mercer) had rendered services or solicited business.  The agreement is clear that the prohibition on rendering services applies to the "firm," not a "client" or "division" or "department" within the firm.  This language is understandable in light of the intense efforts consulting companies make to develop business relationships with their clients, and is reasonable in light of the one-year limit on the restrictions.  Thus, Wilde and Silverman breached their agreements by rendering services not only to AT & T–DCS, but also to AT & T–FTS2000 and AT & T Trans Tech.

At the same time, the 1982 Agreement is clear that only "render[ing] competitive services," and not mere solicitation, is prohibited.  Mercer argues that it should be permitted to recover damages for work performed by Wilde and Silverman in the year following the expiration of the 1982 Agreement, insofar as the work was solicited or begun prior to the expiration of the agreement.  In detailing Dean & Co.'s revenues, Mercer did not differentiate between work begun prior to the expiration of the 1982 Agreement and work solicited but not begun prior to that time.  Because the 1982 Agreement does not prohibit solicitation, Wilde and Silverman cannot be held liable for those activities.  And because Mercer did not isolate those revenues resulting from work begun prior to the expiration of the 1982 Agreements, the Court has no reasonable basis upon which to award damages for that work.

With respect to "services rendered" in the year following Wilde's and Silverman's departure from Mercer, the Court has determined that the appropriate measure of damages is the profits Mercer would have received had the work been performed by Mercer instead of Dean & Co.  It is evident that Wilde and Silverman would not have been in the position to solicit and perform the work for AT & T and Sara Lee had they not developed close ties and vast experience with these companies during their tenure at Mercer.  Moreover, in estimating damages in the context of the management consulting business, the Court must be mindful of the paramount importance of a firm's client-consultant relationships.  It is reasonable to presume, given Mercer's close relationship and long experience with those companies, that Mercer would have been in a position to acquire and perform the work had Wilde and Silverman not left Mercer's employ and solicited the work on behalf of their new company.

According to the unrebutted testimony of Mercer's witnesses, Mercer's return on revenues from communications consulting was 20 percent in 1993, and 13.5 percent in other practice areas.  Thus, Mercer is entitled to 20 percent of the $1,664,597 in revenues received by Dean & Co. for its work for AT & T prior to April 2, 1994, or $332,919.40.  Mercer is also entitled to 13.5 percent of the $2,500 Dean & Co. received from Sara Lee, or $337.50, for total damages of $333,256.90.

In addition, Wilde and Silverman breached the 1982 Agreements by hiring Ware Adams and Gregory Lowell within one year of Wilde's and Silverman's departures from Mercer. According to Michael Muldowney, Mercer's replacement cost for hiring new consultant is $22,338 per consultant, and Mercer shall be awarded these costs as damages. In the absence of testimony demonstrating that work did not get performed due to Adams' and Lowell's departures, Mercer shall not be allowed to recover lost profits.

Counts VIII and IX allege that Wilde, Silverman, Dewhurst, and Dean & Co. interfered with Mercer's client and business relationships by soliciting business from Mercer clients. To sustain a claim of intentional interference with business relationships, Mercer must establish 1) the existence of a business relationship; 2) defendants' knowledge of the business relationship; 3) intentional interference with the relationship by defendants; and 4) resulting damages. Moreover, the defendants' interference must be improper. "Competitive activity does not by itself constitute intentional interference with prospective business advantage" unless accomplished by wrongful or improper means, such as fraud, violence, or civil suits.

Essentially, the facts underlying this claim are the same as Mercer's claims relating to defendants' breaches of their 1982 Agreements. The Court has determined that Dewhurst did not render competitive services to Mercer's clients; accordingly, Dewhurst's actions do not constitute intentional interference with Mercer's business relationships. Even if they did, Mercer has shown no damages stemming from Dewhurst's activities.

With respect to defendants Wilde and Silverman, unquestionably their actions in soliciting and rendering services to former Mercer clients interfered with Mercer's business relationships with these clients. Moreover, their actions were improper in the sense of being violative of the 1982 Agreements. However, during the time of their interference with Mercer's clients, Wilde and Silverman apparently did not believe they were under any restrictions against competitive activities. As such, the Court cannot find that they acted with the level of wrongful intent to constitute tortious interference. Nor has Mercer demonstrated that defendants wrongfully utilized confidential information in soliciting the work at issue. Accordingly, judgment shall be entered for defendants on this count. For the same reasons, judgment shall be entered for defendant Dean & Co. on the intentional interference count against it.

NOTE

An employee with sufficient authority must exercise a duty of care that a reasonable person in similar circumstances would use. In determining whether the duty of care was breached, courts generally use a business judgment rule. They do not question the wisdom of the judgment so long as the director or officer (1) had no conflict of interest when he or she made the decision, (2) gathered a reasonable amount of information before deciding, and (3) did not act wholly irrationally. There is more scrutiny of the procedure than of the content of the decision. A director in violation of the duty of care is personally liable for money damages to the corporation, whether or not the director derived personal benefit from the transaction.

---

## B.  POST-EMPLOYMENT RESTRICTIONS

Employers often spend a great deal of time and money training their employees, and often provide access to protected trade secrets developed at great expense. To safeguard these investments when employees leave their jobs, employers may try to place restrictions on future employment. Such post-employment restrictions impose another important practical limitation on the employee's freedom to quit.

## 1.  FUTURE EMPLOYMENT

### Arias v. Solis

754 F.Supp. 290 (E.D.N.Y.1991).

■ SPATT, DISTRICT JUDGE.

Pursuant to an order to show cause signed by Judge Edward R. Korman on December 26, 1990, plaintiff, a boxing manager, moves for a preliminary injunction to enjoin the defendant, Julian Solis, a professional boxer, from engaging in any boxing exhibitions, in particular a boxing match presently scheduled for Tuesday evening, January 8, 1991 with one Calvin Grove, without first obtaining the express prior approval and consent of the plaintiff pursuant to the contract between the parties.

Plaintiff Ciriaco Arias ("Arias"), is a boxing manager licensed by the New York State Athletic Commission. Defendant Julian Solis ("Solis"), is a professional boxer who was at one time the bantamweight champion of the world in the early 1980's.

Arias and Solis entered into a two-year contract on April 2, 1990 for Arias to act as a boxing manager for Solis ("Management Contract"). The contract is a standard one-page "Boxer–Manager Contract", filed with and approved by the New York State Athletic Commission ("NYAC"). The contract provides, in relevant part, as follows:

> "THIRD: The Boxer hereby agrees to render boxing services, including training, sparring, and boxing in exhibitions and contests at such times and places as designated by the Manager.
>
> FOURTH: The Manager hereby agrees to use his best efforts to provide adequate training for the Boxer, and to secure for the Boxer, reasonably remunerative boxing contests and exhibitions against fighters of similar qualifications or skill.

FIFTH: The Boxer hereby agrees not to actively participate in any sparring or boxing exhibitions, contests, or training exercises, except as specifically approved or required by the Manager.

\* \* \*

EIGHTH: It is understood and agreed by both parties that the services of the Boxer as provided herein are extraordinary and unique."

In accordance with the NYAC regulations, the contract further provides that Arias is to receive one-third of any monies earned by Solis.

Arias contends that he arranged for Solis to partake in several fights throughout 1990, but Solis thereafter refused or failed to participate in the fights. Arias also contends that despite the existence of the above contract, Solis entered into a separate agreement with a boxing promoter, defendant Peltz Boxing Promotions, Inc. and J. Russell Peltz (collectively "Peltz"), for Arias to fight Calvin Grove in Philadelphia on January 8, 1991 ("the Grove Bout").

It is undisputed that Solis entered into the Grove Bout agreement with the defendants in contravention of the express terms of the Management Contract, since he did not first obtain the approval of Arias. However, Solis has agreed to pay Arias his share of the purse due under the Management Contract from the Grove Bout.

Arias commenced this action seeking damages for breach of contract and a permanent injunction to enjoin Solis from participating in any exhibitions without the prior consent of Arias. In addition, Arias is suing Peltz for intentionally inducing Solis to breach his contract with Arias, and for interference by Peltz with his contractual relationship with Solis. Arias alleges that he has sustained damages by reason of the breach of contract by Solis since Arias has expended money to train Solis and in scheduling the various fights which Solis never fought. Arias also contends that Solis is not qualified to fight Calvin Grove; it would be detrimental to his career if he did so; and this fight would endanger the career of Solis thereby depriving Arias of income under the Management Contract.

\* \* \*

(c) *Availability of Injunctive Relief.*

In order to determine whether the plaintiff is entitled to the extraordinary relief of a preliminary injunction, the Court must first determine the availability of an injunction with respect to a personal services contract and, second, if so, whether Arias is entitled to preliminary injunctive relief in this case. Finally, the requirement of posting security is considered.

Under New York law, it is well settled that as a general rule a court of equity will not specifically enforce a contract for personal services. However, "where an employee refuses to render services to an employer in violation of an existing contract, and the services are unique or extraordinary, an injunction may issue to prevent the employee from furnishing those services to another person for the duration of the contract.''

Even though a contract may expressly state that the employee's services are unique or extraordinary, as in this case, the Court is not bound by that statement, and it does not preclude the Court from making a finding to the contrary.

Finally, as to the specific performance of personal services contracts involving athletes, before granting an injunction, it must be shown ''that the player [is] an athlete of exceptional talent.''

Here, the Court finds that Solis' services are ''unique and extraordinary'', and therefore the Court has the *power* to enforce the negative covenant in the Management Contract by enjoining Solis from engaging in any exhibitions or bouts without the prior approval of Arias.  * * *

First, the Court notes that in this regard, the defendants do not take issue in their papers in opposition with the characterization of Solis as ''unique and extraordinary''.  In fact, the issue first arose when the Court raised it *sua sponte*.  At oral argument, counsel for the defendants alleged that Solis is not even ranked at this point since he has not fought for an extended period of time.  However, the plaintiff offered into evidence two ranking lists as of November 1990, which indicate that in the Featherweight Division (126 pounds), Solis is ranked number ten by the International Boxing Federation and number seven by the United States Boxing Association.  This evidence is uncontroverted.

Accordingly, the Court finds the services of Solis to be ''unique and extraordinary.''

The Court also finds that the plaintiff Arias will suffer irreparable harm in the absence of an injunction.

Arias alleges that Solis is not fit to fight Grove for the scheduled bout. Specifically, Arias contends that the weight limit for the Grove Bout is 130 pounds, which is above the usual limit for Solis; that the purse is too small for a fighter of Solis' stature; and, in any event, that Solis suffered an arm injury from a recent automobile accident.

Significantly, however, Arias himself signed a contract on October 15, 1990 to have Solis fight the same Calvin Grove on November 13, 1990 in Baltimore, Maryland.  That fight was cancelled, not by Arias, but by the Maryland State Athletic Commission (''MSAC'') on the eve of the scheduled bout since Solis failed a state-required neurological examination.  The MSAC specifically found that Solis has shown ''progressive and ongoing neurological damage (brain damage).''

Arias alleges that even though he signed Solis to fight Grove in November 1990, he is now not fit to take part in the bout.  According to Arias, if he partakes in the match and loses, he will have no chance to fight Esparragoza or other higher ranked fighters.  Again according to Arias, in that event Solis will be ''washed up''.

The Court finds that Solis is a unique and extraordinary boxer and also that Arias will suffer irreparable harm if the fight with Calvin Grove goes forward on Tuesday, January 8, 1991. As Solis' manager, Arias has determined, in his judgment that the fight ought not take place and that it would not be in the best interests of Solis' career. Solis expressly agreed to this arrangement in the Management Contract which was approved and filed with the State Athletic Commission.

The Court also finds that the plaintiff is likely to ultimately succeed on the merits of the breach of contract claim against Solis. The contract specifically states that Solis shall not engage in any matches or contests without first obtaining the approval of Arias. It is undisputed that during the course of this agreement, Solis signed a contract with the Peltz defendants as promoters for the Grove Bout scheduled for January 8, 1991 in direct violation of this clause.

## NOTES AND QUESTIONS

**1.** Arias trained Solis to box, and Solis agreed not to participate in boxing matches unless they were approved by Arias. Other employers train employees to perform the same functions as the employers themselves. Reed, Roberts Associates trained John Strauman to advise clients on state unemployment laws. Despite an agreement by Strauman not to compete with Reed, Roberts after his employment ended, the court allowed Strauman to compete against Reed, Roberts and solicit their clients. Reed, Roberts Associates, Inc. v. Strauman, 353 N.E.2d 590 (N.Y. 1976).

Strauman had a well-paying executive position. He had promised not to compete. Is there any reason why the legal system should not enforce his promise? The ancient law was that promises not to compete would never be enforced. Apparently the earliest statement was in the Dyer's Case, Y.B.Mich. 2 Hen. 5, f. 5, pl. 26 (1414). See also Colgate v. Bacheler, 78 Eng.Rep. 1097 (Q.B. 1602). Beginning with Mitchel v. Reynolds, 24 Eng.Rep. 347 (Ch. 1711), this rule was replaced by a so-called "rule of reason," requiring courts to decide whether the limitations in the contract are reasonable in length and geographic extent, and whether the nature of the employer's business and the employee's work make such a restriction appropriate. Courts must therefore evaluate in detail the circumstances of each such contractual provision.

**2.** Most states test restraints by a rule of reason. That is the view of the Restatement of Contracts 2d § 188 (1981):

> (1) A promise to refrain from competition that imposes a restraint that is ancillary to an otherwise valid transaction or relationship is unreasonably in restraint of trade if
>
> > (a) the restraint is greater than is needed to protect the promisee's legitimate interest, or
>
> > (b) the promisee's need is outweighed by the hardship to the promisor and the likely injury to the public.

(2) Promises imposing restraints that are ancillary * * * include * * *:

\* \* \*

(b) a promise by an employee or other agent not to compete with his employer or other principal; * * *

**3.** A few states reject enforcement of such agreements altogether. See, e.g., Cal. Bus. & Prof. Code § 16600: "[E]very contract by which anyone is restrained from engaging in a lawful profession, trade, or business of any kind is to that extent void." California enacted this law in 1941.

Professor Kitch finds an irony: "Another bit of evidence that the real world does not operate as logic suggests is that California, a state that seems to harbor a disproportionate number of technologically progressive companies, does not permit any restrictive covenants to be enforced, even in the trade secrecy area. One would think that if legal protection of trade secrecy were of any significance, there would either be pressure from the firms to change the rule or this would be a significant factor in the location of such activities." Edmund W. Kitch, The Law and Economics of Rights in Valuable Information, 9 J.Legal Stud. 683, 710 (1980).

**4.** One remedy that is not available in employment or personal service contracts is specific performance. There are two reasons for this. First, it is considered undesirable to compel the continuance of a personal association after disputes have arisen and confidence and loyalty are gone. Second, ordering the performance of work can be considered involuntary servitude in violation of the Thirteenth Amendment. Restatement (Second) of Contracts § 367 (1981); Beverly Glen Music, Inc. v. Warner Communications, Inc., 224 Cal.Rptr. 260 (Cal.App.1986) (Thirteenth Amendment forbids injunction against performance by singer in violation of her contract).

**5.** In Pollock v. Williams, 322 U.S. 4 (1944), the Supreme Court struck down a Florida criminal statute making failure to perform services after receiving an advance payment prima facie evidence of misdemeanor fraud. Justice Jackson wrote for the Court: "The undoubted aim of the Thirteenth Amendment as implemented by the Antipeonage Act was not merely to end slavery but to maintain a system of completely free and voluntary labor throughout the United States. * * * When the master can compel and the laborer cannot escape the obligation to go on, there is no power below to redress [oppressive working conditions] and no incentive above to relieve a harsh overlordship or unwholesome conditions of work." See also Lorch, Inc. v. Bessemer Mall Shopping Center, Inc., 310 So.2d 872 (Ala. 1975).

*Pollock* was decided in the context of a post-emancipation practice, especially in the South, of retaining effective control over the employment mobility of blacks through onerous contracts. Is the case against recognizing a common law right of an employer to prevent an employee from leaving as strong today? Consider the argument made in Note, The

Implied Covenant of Good Faith and Fair Dealing:  Examining Employees'
Good Faith Duties, 39 Hastings L.J. 483 (1988):

> * * * Extension of tortious breach of the covenant of good faith
> and fair dealing liability to employees in special positions of trust
> and confidence would maintain a consistency between traditional
> common-law duties and the rapidly growing case law surrounding
> the implied covenant.  The public interest in protecting the "en-
> trustor" and deterring abuse by the "entrusted" is firmly estab-
> lished in the context of insurance contracts, and to a lesser degree
> employment contract terminations, loan agreements, and other
> contexts.  Certain employee's duties have been implied in law, or
> required by statute, with the purpose of balancing against the
> employee's interest in advancing his career.  In the context of
> employment termination disputes, the court balances the employ-
> er's interest in maintaining management control of its business
> against the employee's interests in job security and non-discrimi-
> natory application of company policy.  In all of these cases, the
> party entrusted with protecting the other party's interests (i.e.,
> "fiduciary") is subject to tort liability.  Consequently, in certain
> situations, tort liability for employee breach of the covenant is
> both logical and appropriate.

Do you agree with the author of the note that even if logic supports
such an employer's right, strong countervailing policy considerations ought
to prevent its recognition?  If not, why not?  If so, do consistency and
fairness demand that if the right is denied the employer it ought to be
denied the employee in an action to invalidate a dismissal?  Does your
answer turn on who is the stronger party?  See Hudson v. Moore Business
Forms, Inc., 836 F.2d 1156 (9th Cir.1987).

What effect do possible civil remedies for breach of contract have on an
employee's willingness to sever an employment relationship?  Injunctions
compelling work for a specific employer are not granted for breach of an
employment contract.  However, is it likely that an employee will sever an
employment relationship when confronted with a lawsuit and the concomi-
tant costs and monetary remedies?

**6.**  The rule of Lumley v. Wagner came to the American Courts from the
English Court of Equity.  *Lumley* held that although opera singer Johanna
Wagner could not be ordered to perform her contract, she would be
enjoined from singing at any competing music hall for the duration of the
remaining time on her contract.  After initial rejection in the United
States, the *Lumley* doctrine of enjoining other employment became accepted.  Lea VanderVelde, The Gendered Origins of the Lumley Doctrine:
Binding Men's Consciences and Women's Fidelity, 101 Yale L.J. 775 (1992),
asks why *Lumley,* rather than other rulings by eminent American judges,
became the canon:

> The answer appears to be related to the gendered context in which
> the rule was examined at the time that American courts construct-
> ed the canon.  Suits involving the services of women constituted

the core of cases and provided the central contextual focus in which the rule was examined. Many more actresses than actors were sued under this cause of action. Indeed, in the nineteenth century, all of the prominent cases in this line involved the services of women, and only women performers were subjected to permanent injunctions against performing elsewhere for the duration of the contract. In the corpus of reported cases, no male performer was ever permanently enjoined from quitting and performing elsewhere during the entire nineteenth century * * *.

[U]nlike male actors, nineteenth-century women performers were less likely to be viewed as free and independent employees. Nineteenth-century women were generally perceived as relationally bound to men. In this line of cases, that perception of women manifested itself in the need to bind actresses to their male theater managers. Moreover, in the view of the dominant culture, women performers were more likely to be perceived as subordinate than were their male counterparts. The decision in this line of cases reflect larger 'belief system out of which knowledge is constructed, [belief systems that] place constraints on thought [and] that have real consequences for the behavior of individuals who live within them.' This conceptualization of women in the nineteenth century paved the way for the adoption of the Lumley rule in America.

The *Lumley* rule is now applied to many kinds of performers and other employees with unique talents. Can you think of a better way to balance the rights of employer and employee than the *Lumley* rule? If not, do you nevertheless reject the *Lumley* rule because of its gendered origins?

## KGB, Inc. v. Giannoulas

164 Cal.Rptr. 571 (Cal.App.1980).

■ GERALD BROWN, Presiding Justice.

Viewed in its most obvious aspect, this controversy about a chicken suit poses the simple issue whether a local radio station may prevent its ex-employee/mascot from wearing a chicken suit. Silly though the issues appear at first glance, the underlying principles are serious. We deal with a conflict between an employer's asserted contract rights and the fundamental rights of an employee to earn a living, even in possible violation of the employer's bargain with him. We are also concerned with interpreting the application of California's restraint of trade statute (Bus. & Prof. Code, § 16600) to an entertainment contract which ostensibly restricts the entertainer from continuing to perform after a breach.

Appellant Ted Giannoulas seeks a writ of supersedeas to stay a preliminary injunction which he has appealed.

While employed by respondent radio station, KGB, Inc., Giannoulas made public appearances as a character known as the "KGB Chicken," a costumed chicken performing comic routines.  Giannoulas stopped working for KGB.  The station brought this lawsuit alleging breach of employment contract, unfair competition, servicemark infringement, and other causes. KGB sought both damages and an injunction preventing Giannoulas from appearing in a chicken suit.  Although at present all counts of the complaint except that for breach of contract have been dismissed on demurrer with leave to amend, the trial court granted KGB a preliminary injunction. Paragraph (1) [2] of the injunction prevents Giannoulas from appearing anywhere wearing the "KGB Chicken Ensemble," a described costume which includes a vest bearing the KGB initials.  Subsection (c) of paragraph (1) forbids appearing in a chicken costume "substantially similar" to the KGB chicken costume registered as a servicemark.  Paragraph (2) restrains Giannoulas from appearing in "any chicken ensemble or suit whatsoever" in San Diego County or any adjacent county.  Paragraph (3) similarly forbids appearances in any chicken suit at any sports or public event where a team from San Diego County appears.  The trial court found "likelihood of confusion" in the public mind if Giannoulas appears in the manner forbidden.  The meaning of that finding is when Giannoulas appears locally in a chicken suit the public probably thinks about KGB and may believe Giannoulas still works there.

We have decided to issue a writ of supersedeas to stay subsection (c) of paragraph (1) and all of paragraphs (2) and (3) of the injunction pending appeal.  Those provisions, preventing appearances in any chicken suit whatsoever, invalidly restrict Giannoulas' rights to earn a living and to express himself as an artist.  The burden is on KGB to justify an injunction restricting such vital rights.  When the injunction issued, KGB had not so much as pleaded a good cause of action for unfair competition or infringement.  Its factual showing to date is inadequate to sustain a prohibitory injunction, for reasons we will state.

Public policy disfavors injunctions restraining the right to pursue a calling.  On the national scene, the weight of authority shows great reluctance to issue such restraints unless the former employer can show irreparable injury.  California goes beyond judicial reluctance to possible illegality of such injunctions, under Business and Professions Code section 16600, which provides in relevant part:

> *"Invalidity of contracts.*  Except as provided in this chapter, every contract by which anyone is restrained from engaging in a lawful profession, trade, or business or any kind is to that extent void."

**2.**  Paragraph (1) prohibits Giannoulas from:

"Appearing anywhere wearing the KGB Chicken ensemble or suit.  The KGB Chicken is defined to be: (a) a design of a chicken red in color, with brown face, yellow beak, yellow webbed feet, blue eyelids, blue vest with the letters 'KGB,' and a red comb on the top of his head, or (b) a design of a chicken as depicted in Plaintiff's Certificate of Registration of Service Mark No. 5049 from the State of California attached as Exhibit 'C' to the complaint herein, or (c) any design substantially similar to (a) or (b) above."

Exhibit "C" is a picture of a chicken costume with KGB letters on it.

This statute presents an absolute bar to post-employment restraints and represents a strong public policy of this state. Although there are a few statutory exceptions to the ban against restraints of trade, none of them apply to this situation, where the employer seeks to restrain a performer from continuing to perform after the term of employment expires. Here it expired in September 1979.

The classic exposition of the topic of enforcement of employee covenants not to compete is Arthur Murray Dance Studios of Cleveland v. Witter, 105 N.E.2d 685 (Ohio C.P.1952), decided in a state (Ohio) which did not have a statute like California's Business and Professions Code section 16600. That case, with wit but also much scholarly erudition, documented the "sea" of authority evidencing judicial reluctance to enforce such covenants. According to the court, this hostility first judicially appears in the reign of Henry V in 1415, when a guild sought to restrain a dyer from working in a town for half a year, enraging the judge, who "in bad French * * * cursed the deal void: 'By God, if the plaintiff were here he should go to prison until he paid a fine to the king.' " Since then the courts have become more temperate, and will sometimes enforce such covenants at least in states not having statutes like Business and Professions Code section 16600, if such enforcement is reasonable; but even in those states, reasonableness is not lightly decreed, and always, the burden rests on the person seeking such a restraint to justify it. Further, of the many circumstances relevant to reasonableness, the most important is irreparable harm to the employer. Nothing less justifies preventing an employee from continuing to work. The court in that case compared the so-called sale covenant with the employee covenant and explained the stronger aversion to enforcing the latter:

> "In contrasting the employee covenant with the sale covenant, some of the typical pronouncements are—the employee covenant is more critically examined, more strictly construed—it is construed favorably to the employee—it is viewed with askance and more jealousy—it is not viewed as liberally or with the same indulgence—it is looked upon with less favor, more disfavor—courts are more loathe, less disposed and more reluctant to sustain or enforce it—not identical tests but different considerations apply—there is more freedom of contract between seller and buyer than between employer and employee,—the latitude of permissible restraint is more limited between employer and employee, greater between seller and buyer. The following are some of the reasons given for making the above distinction. The average, individual employee has little but his labor to sell or to use to make a living. He is often in urgent need of selling it and in no position to object to boiler plate restrictive covenants placed before him to sign. To him, the right to work and support his family is the most important right he possesses. His individual bargaining power is seldom equal to that of his employer. Moreover, an employee ordinarily is not on the same plane with the seller of an established business. He is more apt than the seller to be coerced into an oppressive

agreement.  Under pressure of need and with little opportunity for choice, he is more likely than the seller to make a rash, improvident promise that, for the sake of present gain, may tend to impair his power to earn a living, impoverish him, render him a public charge or deprive the community of his skill and training.  The seller has the proceeds of sale on which to live during his period of readjustment.  A seller is usually paid an increased price for agreeing to a period of abstention.  The abstention is a part of the thing sold and is often absolutely necessary in order to secure to the buyer the things he has bought.  Usually the employee gets no increased compensation for agreeing to the abstention; it is usually based on no other consideration than the employment itself."

\* \* \*

Further, even if the injunction were permissible despite section 16600, such an injunction must rest on a finding of injury to KGB.  As the court said in *Arthur Murray,* supra, we must consider whether an "ex-employee is a threatening menace."  There is no evidence of menace to KGB from the free publicity complained of, aside from a conclusionary allegation of irreparable harm.  The court noted in *Arthur Murray,* supra: "Remembering that the burden is on Arthur Murray to prove irreparable injury, where is the proof?  Certainly there is not one microscopic bit of evidence of actual injury.  It is not shown that Arthur Murray lost one pupil or one penny."  To paraphrase, where are the lost listeners?  Likelihood of confusion is insufficient; the confusion must be hurtful to the employer before an injunction is justified.

In this state, as elsewhere, under the general umbrella of the tort of unfair competition, a number of employee practices may be enjoined, such as purloining of trade secrets or misleading copying of products or services.  KGB seeks to justify this injunction on that basis, resting on the finding of likelihood of confusion, which is the jargon of unfair competition law.  We think, however, Giannoulas' performances in a chicken costume are neither competitive nor unfair because he does not sport the KGB logos or otherwise imply he represents KGB.  The essence of the tort of unfair competition is the inequitable pirating of the fruits of another's labor and then either "palming off" those fruits as one's own (deception) or simply gaining from them an unearned commercial benefit.

First, and probably most essential, the remedies sought in the above cases were not injunctions restraining pursuit of one's livelihood.  Thus, even if we had a case of unfair competition here, the injunctive remedy would probably be inappropriate for the reasons already stated.  Next, probably there is no case of unfair competition here, for the evidence so far shown to us does not establish misappropriation by Giannoulas of KGB's labor.  We are not in a position to determine the relative inputs of KGB and Giannoulas to the KGB chicken concept, but we note the inevitable significance of the performer's contribution to a fluid, changing, clownish role of the type here considered.  It is created spontaneously through gestures, movements and responses to changing situations. KGB cannot be said to own such a routine. * * *

We deal not with a stereotyped character such as The Lone Ranger or Yogi Bear, but with a clown in a chicken suit. His performances follow no set script. Only the costume itself has a fixed design, and we, by permitting subsections (a) and (b) of paragraph (1) of the injunction to stand, recognize KGB's probable rights in that particular design. KGB has not cited us a case, however, nor have we unearthed one, where it was regarded as unfair competition for a clown to change his employer.[3] Only in a breach of contract situation may such conduct be enjoinable, and then, probably only in a state where there is no statutory ban on restraints of trade as we have here.

The employment contract between KGB and Giannoulas does not expressly give KGB the right to prevent Giannoulas from performing. The most pertinent part of the agreement provides:

> "For a period of five years after termination of this agreement, employee agrees not to act as a mascot of any radio station other than KGB, Inc., in the San Diego market."

This language does not give KGB a perpetual monopoly of all chicken ensembles and routines; it refers only to employment by another radio station, i.e., competition.

KGB relies specifically on two other contractual provisions. The 1978 contract provides:

> " 'Employee agrees and acknowledges that the costume, concept, and the KGB Chicken are the exclusive property of employer, and the KGB Chicken is a registered tradename and a valid copyright of employer. Employee agrees not to take any action inconsistent with said rights of employer in and to the concept of the KGB Chicken.' "

KGB claims this language establishes its contractual monopoly of all rights in the KGB Chicken and of the "costume" or the "concept" of a chicken. The 1974 contract provides:

> " '(a) I hereby acknowledge that the * * * characters and all other subject matters broadcast over the station as well as any name assigned to me by the station for broadcast purposes, are and shall remain, both while this contract shall be in effect and at all times

---

**3.** The cases KGB relies on do not support its position. Lone Ranger, Inc. v. Cox (4th Cir.1942) 124 F.2d 650, involved a defendant who untruthfully billed himself as the "original Lone Ranger," which misled the public and constituted unfair competition. That case is different from this because the Lone Ranger is a specific well-defined character, with a name, specific garb, and appearance, unlike the case of an antic chicken dependent on individual performances for its life. Similarly inapposite are Boston Pro Hockey Ass'n. v. Dallas Cap. & E. Mfg. Inc. (5th Cir.1975) 510 F.2d 1004 [copying servicemark emblems of hockey teams], and Walt Disney Productions v. Air Pirates (N.D.Cal.1972) 345 F.Supp. 108, 116 [copyright infringement of character Mickey Mouse].

thereafter, the station's exclusive property in any and all fields, and that I shall not at any time obtain any right, title or interest whatsoever in or to such property or a part thereof.

" '(b) Any ideas, including, but not limited to, programs, themes, titles, characters, which are developed by me during the term of my employment, shall be the property of this station.' "

KGB claims these provisions indicate the parties' intent to vest exclusive ownership of the KGB Chicken character in KGB.

These arguments tend to buttress KGB's claim to an exclusive right to the specific character, the KGB Chicken, an antic chicken bearing the KGB insignia, colored in a definite manner, and appearing on behalf of the station. These contractual provisions do not, however, create a contractual monopoly of all appearances by Giannoulas in any chicken costume. In general, contractual language contained in employees' negative covenants not to compete is strictly construed against the employer because of the policy against such bargains which we have described. Here the specific chicken referred to is the KGB Chicken, and we have permitted the restriction on appearances as that character to stand. Further restriction is not warranted by the parties' express bargain.

* * *

However, because of the policies we have discussed, the employer has a weak case against his employee when he seeks to prevent future performances, unless he can point to a specific contract conferring such rights. His naked claim of having assisted the development of the role is not enough; presumably he has been compensated for that assistance by the revenues from performances while the employee still worked for him. Should he desire more, in the nature of continuing royalties or control of the character, then he must bargain for that control. Further, in California section 16600 limits his available remedies.

Both sides here have sought comfort in passages from Lugosi v. Universal Pictures, 25 Cal.3d 813, 160 Cal.Rptr. 323, 603 P.2d 425. That case discusses the inheritability of the rights to the "uniquely individual likeness and appearance of Bela Lugosi in the role of Count Dracula." The issues there determined do not decide this matter. The contest was not between employer and employee but between past employer and the employee's legal heirs. In his concurring opinion, Justice Mosk pointed out actors have protected rights in roles which they play and develop. That language gives some philosophic support to Giannoulas' propriety claim to his chicken routine, but does not advance the claim of KGB, inasmuch as Universal's rights to the Lugosi role were not in issue except insofar as they were abridged by exclusive exploitation rights in the heirs. Similarly, the dissent of Chief Justice Bird, with its emphasis on the individual's rights to decide how and when to exploit his identity and to enjoy the fruits of his labor, lends some support to Giannoulas, none to KGB.

Similarly inapposite, except in a philosophical sense, is Guglielmi v. Spelling–Goldberg Productions, 25 Cal.3d 860, 160 Cal.Rptr. 352, 603 P.2d

454. There, however, Chief Justice Bird discusses the vital role of the First Amendment in protecting entertainment. She regards performing as an integral part of self-expression: the development of ideas, exploration of the mind, realization of the self. The cases she cites all imply the right of expression through a fantastical role is fundamental: not only the commercial right to earn a living, but also personal freedom of artistic expression. These cases and others grant damages for exploitation of an artist's performance, based on the premise the developed character belongs to the performer and is his to exploit or leave alone.

Misappropriation of rights in a stage character can of course occur, but it takes a strong showing to restrict the allegedly infringing performer. For example, in West v. Lind, 186 Cal.App.2d 563, 9 Cal.Rptr. 288, Mae West lost her suit to enjoin defendant's appearance in the role of "Diamond Lil," which West claimed to have developed. The trial court found the role was not exclusively associated with West nor impressed with her identity in the public mind, hence she had no exclusive claim to it, despite her undisputed contributions to the role. It does not appear KGB has staked a valid claim to another's comic routine, at the preliminary injunction stage, when West could not monopolize the role she herself had played, for which she claimed sole credit. West's claim was also stronger than KGB's because the Diamond Lil character is well defined and specific, whereas here we deal with the ever changing performance of an antic routine.

KGB asserts because Lugosi played the Dracula role without a mask, the concept of the "unique individual likeness of the actor" as property, developed in the *Lugosi* opinion, does not apply to Giannoulas' performances in a chicken suit which hides his features. Facial expressions are hardly a necessary attribute of a fantastic character. Masked or not, both Lugosi and Giannoulas have made certain roles their own, by a combination of mannerisms, gestures, body language, and other behavior adding up in each case to a unique character. We see no reason why the concept of unique individual likeness should not apply to the role of antic chicken whose turns, kicks, tumbles and gyrations have become uniquely those of Giannoulas. What is more, we view with skepticism KGB's assertion it makes no difference who wears the costume. If that were so, why did KGB pay Giannoulas some $50,000 a year to wear it? The identity of the performer clearly has some relevance here.

KGB seeks to rely on Labor Code section 2860, asserting everything an employee "acquires by virtue of his employment" other than his wages, belongs to his employer. KGB has misinterpreted those authorities. The language in the statute has been applied to protect employee misappropriation of trade secrets and confidential information gained during employment; it has not been used to protect an actor's or artist's creations during employment in the absence of a contract providing express protection.

* * *

KGB also claims the service here involved is not entertainment, but is radio station broadcasting. The assertion is false. The service enjoined is entertainment in a chicken suit; Giannoulas is not in the radio broadcast business.  His performances are too fluid and changing to be a servicemark of some other service, such as broadcasting, and they cannot be owned by anyone, other than pursuant to a valid contract.

Finally, KGB claims we have no jurisdiction to make factual findings contrary to those of the trial court.  Specifically, it claims we have not honored the finding of secondary meaning, essentially a finding any costumed chicken at a sports or public event in the designated area is associated with KGB in the public mind.  We accept that finding.  It is insufficient to show irreparable harm, or indeed any harm, and it does not warrant a preliminary prohibitory injunction restricting constitutionally protected freedoms, and possibly violating a statute as well.  On the subject of irreparable injury, the record shows Giannoulas has become a nationally known figure.[4]  KGB is a station which can transmit, on a clear day, as far

---

**4.**  Giannoulas has also become an internationally known figure.  The Encyclopedia Britannica Book of the Year 1980 under Biographies, page 78, recognizes him in the following article in which KGB, no doubt to its delight, receives publicity.

© 1979 EILEEN MILLER—BLACK STAR

**Giannoulas, Ted**

When baseball's "chicken man" emerged from a giant egg in the San Diego Padres' infield on June 29, 1979, it was just a re-hatch.  He had first arrived fully fledged in Dayglow fluff five years earlier to hand out Easter eggs at the local zoo as part of radio station KGB's "promotional experiment."  But the bird's inner being, 5–ft 4–in Ted Giannoulas, had bigger ideas.  A communications student at San Diego State University,

he suggested that KGB send him to Padres games in the fine-feathered costume.  He became a fixture on and around the diamond, and the station rose from fifth to first place in local media standings.

Cavorting through the stands, lifting a web-footed leg at the umpires, smothering an occasional pretty fan's head in his yellow beak, the chicken man was soon responsible for attracting more than one out of ten spec-

as Oceanside. This station claims a perpetual monopoly on chicken routines in local counties; if that claim were not preposterous enough, it further contends injury because its former employee has made it nationally famous. The claim of irreparable injury in this context is ridiculous.

\* \* \*

KGB argues the preliminary injunction best preserves the status quo. It cannot be preserved. Giannoulas no longer works for KGB. The status quo has never been a situation where Giannoulas was not entitled to wear any chicken suit or ensemble.

Subsection (c) of paragraph (1) of the injunction preventing appearances in "any design substantially similar" to the KGB Chicken costume, is presumptively void because it is too uncertain to be a valid conduct regulation, whose violation may produce criminal sanctions. Such a broad restraint invites continual litigation and casts the constant shadow of possible criminal prosecution over Giannoulas' entertainment routines, impermissibly abridging his First Amendment freedoms which we have already discussed.

The injunction goes beyond authorizing law and is against public policy because it restricts Giannoulas' right to earn his living and to express his talents. Although subsections (a) and (b) of paragraph (1) of the injunction, referring to appearances in the defined KGB Chicken costume may stand, the remainder of the injunction is stayed pending the appeal of this matter.

\* \* \*

## NOTES AND QUESTIONS

**1.** Is it relevant whether an employee subject to a non-compete agreement quits or is fired? If the employee is dismissed, does it matter whether the employer had good cause? Robert S. Weiss & Assoc. v. Wiederlight, 546

tators to the stadium. Ted Turner, the Atlanta Braves' flamboyant owner, offered Giannoulas $100,000 to turkey trot down to Georgia. But the cackling celebrity decided to keep San Diego as his home base and turn free-lance—a decision that got his suit sued off.

The trouble started when he took off the vest showing KGB's call letters for an away-from-home game. The station fired him, shooed him into court claiming $250,000 in damages, and hired a substitute. But the fans threatened such mayhem that the substitute was fitted with a bulletproof vest, though nothing worse came his way than game-delaying boos. Enjoined from wearing KGB's outfit or calling himself a chicken, Giannoulas bought a new fowl suit to prance

the foul lines and went to work as an attraction without a name. Offered a percentage of the gate receipts by the Padres, he was escorted by motorcycle policemen onto the field inside the styrofoam egg atop an armoured truck and emerged to the tune of Thus Spake Zarathustra. KGB kept the legal heat on for a while but lost listeners and ended up eating crow.

Giannoulas was not alone in the world of professional sports clowns, nor was he the first "bleacher creature." But he was the most celebrated. Now earning more than $100,000 a year, he belly flopped around the bases on national television during one All-Star Game and received the legislature's official commendation for "comedy contributions to the State of California."

A.2d 216 (Conn. 1988), held that "the reasonableness of a restrictive covenant of employment does not turn on whether the employee subject to the covenant left his position voluntarily or was dismissed by the employer." In contrast, Iowa's highest court implied that termination can invalidate the covenant, and is certainly a factor opposing the grant of an injunction against the employee. Ma & Pa, Inc. v. Kelly, 342 N.W.2d 500 (Iowa 1984).

**2.** How should a court balance the policy considerations that support an employer's right to contract to protect its investments against an employee's right to earn a living? In the famous case of Kadis v. Britt, 29 S.E.2d 543 (N.C. 1944), E.G. Britt worked as a deliveryman and bill collector for Isaac Kadis, a retail clothing dealer in Goldsboro, N.C. Britt never made more than $27.50 per week. He signed a contract, promising "that he will not work for * * * any firm * * * engaged in any business * * * such as is conducted by [Kadis] in Wayne County, North Carolina, for a period of two years from the date of such cessation of employment, * * * nor will [Britt] * * * allow or permit his wife or any member of his family to engage in any business that is herein restricted * * * "

**3.** Who should bear the burden of proof when the reasonableness of a promise not to compete is at issue? In some states, presumably due to the general policy against restraints of trade, the party seeking enforcement has the burden of demonstrating the reasonableness of the non-competition clause. See, e.g., Curtis 1000, Inc. v. Youngblade, 878 F.Supp. 1224 (N.D. Iowa 1995). Is it fair that in these states the employer has the burden of proof in all cases, including those where an employee freely and knowingly consents to such a clause and later seeks to avoid it? Florida law does not place a burden on an employer to show that its non-competition agreement was reasonably necessary. See DeDantis v. Wackenhut Corp., 732 S.W.2d 29 (Tex. App. 1987), modified, 793 S.W. 2d 670 (Tex. 1990) (construing Florida law). What are the problems with this rule?

**4.** Subsequent to the commencement of an at-will employment relationship, should an employer's promise of continued employment constitute sufficient consideration for the employee's promise not to compete? This remains an unsettled issue. See 51 A.L.R.3d 825. Many courts have held that a promise of continued employment is illusory because the employer maintains the right to discharge at will. See George W. Kistler, Inc. v. O'Brien, 347 A.2d 311 (Pa.1975). Some jurisdictions, however, have upheld continued employment as adequate consideration. Many of these courts recognize that the employer would merely discharge the employee and reestablish the employment relationship in order to circumvent a decision to the contrary. Other courts have held that continued employment for a substantial period of time serves as sufficient consideration. See, e.g., Mattison v. Johnston, 730 P.2d 286 (Ariz.App.1986).

**5.** What interests should an employer be able to protect under a reasonable noncompetition agreement? Certainly, existing customer relationships can be protected; however, it is harder to justify restricting markets where the employer has little or no established presence. "The fact that an employer seeks to protect his interest in potential new customers in a reasonably limited market area as well as his existing customers at the time the employee leaves does not render the covenant unreasonable." Robert S. Weiss & Assoc. v. Wiederlight, supra note 1.

**6.** When is injunctive relief an appropriate remedy for an employee's breach of a promise not to compete? The New York Court of Appeals in *Reed Roberts,* supra, stated that the services of the employee must be "unique or extraordinary." Contrast this with the Supreme Court of Pennsylvania's decision to grant an injunction in John G. Bryant Co. v. Sling Testing & Repair Co., 369 A.2d 1164 (Pa. 1977):

> It is not the initial breach of a covenant which necessarily established the existence of irreparable harm but rather the threat of the unbridled continuation of the violation and the resultant incalculable damage to the former employer's business that constitutes the justification for equitable intervention. * * * The covenant seeks to prevent more than just the sales that might result by the prohibited contract but also the covenant is designed to prevent a disturbance in the relationship that has been established between appellees and their accounts through prior dealings. It is the possible consequences of this unwarranted interference with customer relationships that is unascertainable and not capable of being fully compensated by money damages. It is for this reason we noted * * * that where a covenant of this type meets the test of reasonableness, it is prima facie enforceable in equity.

**7.** Two disc jockeys quit WSHE, having promised not to be "connected in any manner" with a competitor for four months. However, during the four-month period WGTR used their names for promotion and to attract advertisers. A Florida court held that the disc jockeys had intentionally and materially breached the non-competition agreement. The court said WSHE had no adequate remedy at law, and ordered an injunction for a longer period of complete non-competition. T.K. Communications, Inc. v. Herman, 505 So.2d 484 (Fla.App.1987).

**8.** A law firm sought to enforce a promise that a withdrawing partner would forfeit earned but uncollected partnership revenues. The New York Court of Appeals said the agreement was unenforceable as against public policy. Cohen v. Lord, Day & Lord, 550 N.E.2d 410 (N.Y. 1989). An Illinois court refused to allow a law firm to enforce a promise not to solicit clients of the firm. Williams & Montgomery, Ltd. v. Stellato, 552 N.E.2d 1100 (Ill.App.1990).

**9.** Does the discharge of an employee for refusing to sign an allegedly unenforceable noncompetition agreement violate public policy? See Madden v. Omega Optical, Inc., 683 A.2d 386 (Vt.1996) (held: no).

**10.** An insurance firm's vice president, whose wife was employed by the same company, had a provision in his contract prohibiting him from competing "directly or indirectly." If his wife opens a competing business, has her husband violated his contract? See Rash v. Hilb, Rogal & Hamilton Co., 467 S.E.2d 791 (Va.1996) (held: yes).

## 2. TRADE SECRETS

### SI Handling Systems, Inc. v. Heisley

753 F.2d 1244 (3d Cir.1985).

■ A. LEON HIGGINBOTHAM, JR., CIRCUIT JUDGE:

\* \* \*

Appellee SI Handling Systems, Inc. ("SI"), founded in 1958 by its current Chairman and Chief Executive Officer L. Jack Bradt, is a Pennsylvania corporation with headquarters and principal manufacturing facilities located in Easton, Pennsylvania. SI employs approximately 300 persons and had sales of 20 million dollars in the fiscal year ended February 27, 1983. Through a number of subsidiaries and licensees SI's products are sold in much of the industrialized world.

SI is in the business of designing, manufacturing, and installing "materials handling systems". "Materials handling" is a generic term describing the transportation of materials, by any mechanized means, between locations in a factory or warehouse. Forklift trucks and conveyor belts are familiar examples of materials handling devices. A materials handling "system" connotes a combination of devices or components designed to integrate a number of warehouse or factory operations, in order to achieve greater automation and efficiency. SI, which at the outset made only manually-operated steel pushcarts, is today an industry leader with four sophisticated, highly automated product lines, each of which possesses the flexibility to be custom-designed for diverse systems applications.

This litigation involves only one of SI's product lines, known by the trade name "CARTRAC". CARTRAC was initially developed by a Swedish company which had limited success in marketing the product for light manufacturing applications during the 1960's. In 1971 SI purchased the worldwide rights to CARTRAC for 1.2 million dollars. SI's strategy with regard to acquisitions such as this is to identify products that can be further developed to meet market demands in a manner that secures SI a "unique proprietary advantage". Central to this strategy is the availability of patent or trade secret protection for SI's developments.

A somewhat detailed description of CARTRAC is helpful to understanding the issues raised in this appeal. CARTRAC is generically described as a "car-on-track" materials handling system. The track is a simple pair of steel rails, resembling railroad tracks. Materials are placed upon a carrier—the "car"—which transports them along the track. Propulsion for the car is provided by a cylindrical drive tube that is mounted in between the two rails and parallel to them. The car engages the tube via a urethane drive wheel mounted on the underside of the car in a pivoting, spring-loaded housing. When the tube is caused to spin by a drive belt connected to an electric motor, it imparts a force (or "thrust") to the drive wheel and causes it to turn. If the drive wheel's motion is perpendicular to the track the car cannot move and the energy expended is simply dissipated in spinning the drive wheel. If, however, the drive wheel is turned at an angle, a component of the thrust will be imparted in the direction parallel to the rails, thus enabling the car to move along the track. The car will accelerate as the angle of the drive wheel is increased, reaching a maximum velocity at 45 degrees. SI does not claim that these basic principles of CARTRAC propulsion are trade secrets.

SI's method of propelling the car along the track gives CARTRAC a number of capabilities not shared by other car-on-track systems. Among the advantages of the spinning tube approach are the capacity to operate different cars at different speeds at different points in the system ("asynchronous" operation), and to accelerate, decelerate, or stop an individual car at various points in the system with great precision and reliability.

\* \* \*

Beginning in 1978, "SI mounted a campaign to convince General Motors that CARTRAC could provide the automated system necessary for it to retool and meet the Japanese automotive challenge." This campaign included intensive engineering and sales efforts. In January 1981, after several small purchases by GM, the companies consummated what has been referred to as "the big buy"—an order for eight CARTRAC systems at a price of more than 17 million dollars. Since then SI has continued to sell CARTRAC systems to GM, and continues to view the GM market as its outstanding business opportunity.

\* \* \*

SI does not place any restrictions on how purchasers of CARTRAC use it, and it has publicized the basic principles and capabilities of the product extensively in trade shows, articles, and advertisements. With regard to SI's confidentiality policies, the district court found:

> SI has taken the usual and reasonable precautions at its Easton facility to preserve and protect the confidential nature of its development of the CARTRAC product. Entry into the building is limited and visitors are restricted. All visitors must have passes and be escorted throughout the operation when they are inside the building. Alarm systems are utilized when the business is closed. Certain documents of a highly proprietary nature are marked accordingly. Files containing sensitive documents are locked. Drawings are prestamped with a proprietary legend. In addition, the majority of employees at SI are required to sign an Employee Agreement which purports to limit disclosure by employees of confidential information. Licensees of SI are duly proscribed from disclosure of the licensed designs and processes received via their respective license agreements.

All Sales proposals for, and maintenance manuals provided with, CARTRAC systems contain restrictive use language. SI's purchase orders to suppliers also contain a restrictive provision.

The district court also found that "[i]n supplying product to General Motors SI took precautions not to give GM any more technical detail than is necessary for successful operation and maintenance of the systems."

* * *

Appellant Michael E. Heisley was an officer of SI from 1973 to mid-1978, serving as president for nearly all of that period. In that capacity he was involved in early discussions concerning SI's entry into the automotive manufacturing market, and he traveled to Japan to study IHI's technology. Heisley left SI at about the time of the early automotive CARTRAC sales to Chrysler. After leaving SI in 1978 Heisley formed appellant Heico, Inc. ("Heico"), an Illinois corporation. Appellant Philip L. Bitely, then SI's vice-president for finance, left the company and joined Heico shortly thereafter. Bitely had been with SI since 1971, and had also been involved in the early development of automotive CARTRAC. The record indicates that Heico is a diversified company employing over 300 persons with annual sales of approximately 25 million dollars. Heisley is the chairman of Heico and Bitely is its president. There is no evidence that, prior to 1982, Heico made any effort to develop a car-on-track system.

Appellant Thomas H. Hughes joined SI in 1976 as manager of field sales. In March 1977 he was promoted to vice-president of marketing, and in January of 1979 he became vice-president in charge of the computer controls division. It appears that in the latter two positions he had significant responsibility for the development of automotive CARTRAC. In July of 1981 Hughes left SI, with a number of other controls division employees, to form appellant Sy-Con Technology, Inc. ("Sy-Con"), a subsidiary of Heico. Sy-Con is located in Easton, Pennsylvania and is in the business of providing controls software for materials handling systems.

The watershed event leading to this litigation took place on April 17, 1982. On that date chief executive officer Bradt fired SI's vice-president of operations, appellant Richard O. Dentner. Dentner, it is fair to say, was the "father" of SI's automotive CARTRAC, with responsibility for coordinating both the engineering and marketing of this product. According to Bradt, he fired Dentner reluctantly, only after efforts to resolve tensions between Dentner and other SI officers had failed.

Dentner remained as vice-president of operations until May 9, 1982, and continued to receive severance pay until September 30, 1982. During that period he also did some consulting for SI on a per diem basis. Despite this continuing relationship with SI, Dentner was already making plans, in association with Heico, to market a competing spinning tube car-on-track system, ROBOTRAC.

* * *

On June 26, 1982 Dentner authored a letter to Midwest Conveyor—a Kansas City materials handling company—captioned "Proposed Plan of

Action for Midwest Conveyors Robotrac Product". Dentner proposed that Midwest establish a temporary office in Easton with the following "charter":

1.) Basic Concepts & Designs of Robotrac Components.

a.) Basic design of some critical long lead items such as drive wheel assemblies, drive tube components, & stop station components. These items require castings and will be needed for prototypes.

b.) Basic design of most recent GM body shop system components. * * * I feel it is important to get the basic designs completed while they are still fresh in our minds.

c.) Basic design of a car to car accumulation method that does not infringe upon the existing SI (Jacoby) patent.

* * *

e.) Basic concept & design of a Tugger system for use in GM Trim Line automation projects.

f.) Basic concept & design of Buffer Systems for use between various operating lines of automotive assembly plants.

* * *

3.) Sales Contact with GM and a few other customers that we have been working with while employees of SI Handling.

* * *

In an opinion handed down on March 1, 1984, the district court found that SI had made the requisite showings for preliminary injunctive relief, and in particular had demonstrated a reasonable probability of success on the merits of its trade secrets claim.

* * *

To be entitled to an injunction against use or disclosure of information, under Pennsylvania law, a plaintiff must show: (1) that the information constitutes a trade secret; (2) that it was of value to the employer and important in the conduct of his business; (3) that by reason of discovery or ownership the employer had the right to the use and enjoyment of the secret; and (4) that the secret was communicated to the defendant while employed in a position of trust and confidence under such circumstances as to make it inequitable and unjust for him to disclose it to others, or to make use of it himself, to the prejudice of his employer. In this case there is no serious dispute that the latter three elements were made out with respect to the trade secrets the district court found. Thus, our discussion will focus on the first element—the existence of trade secrets.

The Pennsylvania courts have adopted the definition of a trade secret given in the Restatement of Torts § 757 comment b. (1939):

A trade secret may consist of any formula, pattern, device or compilation of information which is used in one's business, and which gives him an opportunity to obtain an advantage over competitors who do not know or use it. It may be a formula for a chemical compound, a process of manufacturing, treating or preserving materials, a pattern for a machine or other device, or a list of customers.

"Novelty is only required of a trade secret to the extent necessary to show that the alleged secret is not a matter of public knowledge. * * * A trade secret may be no more than a slight mechanical advance over common knowledge and practice in the art." Matters which are fully disclosed by a marketed product and are susceptible to "reverse engineering"—i.e., "starting with the known product and working backward to divine the process which aided in its manufacture," cannot be protected as trade secrets.

Moreover, the concept of a trade secret does not include "[a] man's aptitude, his skill, his dexterity, his manual and mental ability, and such other subjective knowledge as he obtains while in the course of his employment, * * * the right to use and expand these powers remains his property. * * *"

* * *

In summary, we affirm the district court's factual and legal findings that SI has shown a reasonable probability of success on the merits as to the following claimed trade secrets:

(1) SI's method of examining drive tubes for concentricity;

(2) the dimensions, tolerances, and method of fit between drive tubes and drive plugs;

(3) use of a nonstandard maximum angular misalignment in conjunction with certain grease pack specifications in bearings;

(4) efficiency factors gained from component experience;

(5) the nonstandard coefficient of friction used by SI in making calculations for system design;

(6) the contents of three pending SI patent applications;

(7) SI's CARTRAC costing and pricing information; and

(8) nonstandard formulae for systems design developed by an IHI engineer (the "Tokunago formula book").

We reverse the district court's findings that the following were SI's trade secrets: knowledge of the existence of alternate suppliers of parts at lower prices; knowledge of long lead times in component supply; knowledge of key decisionmakers within General Motors, SI's identification of GM needs for "two-way accumulation", "tugger", and "buffer" systems; the two-way accumulation system developed by appellants for ROBOTRAC while they were still in SI's employ; methods developed by appellants, while they were still in SI's employ, for achieving car-to-car accumulation without infringing on the Jacoby patent; and SI's "know-how" in systems engineering.  * * *

Finally, appellants ask us to hold that the district court failed to properly weigh the public interest when it stated that "the preservation of commercial morality far outweighs any negative impact on free competition which might result from any order emanating from this litigation."  581 F.Supp. at 1562.  Appellants point to the numerous statutes and cases embodying the strong public policies favoring competition and economic mobility, apparently implying that these are overriding interests.  Appellants do not, however, explain why this case is different from numerous other trade secret cases, all implicating similar "commercial morality" issues and thus these same public policy concerns, where injunctions have issued.  Appellants here are not concerned about raising the morality of capitalism; rather their sole concern is raising the profitability of their ventures predicated on utilizing a competitor's trade secrets.  A classic statement of the competing policies appears in Wexler v. Greenberg, 399 Pa. 569, 160 A.2d 430 (1960) where the court found that trade secrets cases bring

> to the fore a problem of accommodating competing policies in our law: the right of a businessman to be protected against unfair competition stemming from the usurpation of his trade secrets and the right of an individual to the unhampered pursuit of the occupations and livelihoods for which he is best suited.  There are cogent socio-economic arguments in favor of either position.  Society as a whole greatly benefits from technological improvements.  Without some means of post-employment protection to assure that valuable developments or improvements are exclusively those of the employer, the businessman could not afford to subsidize research or improve current methods.  In addition, it must be recognized that modern economic growth and development has pushed the business venture beyond the size of the one-man firm, forcing the businessman to a much greater degree to entrust confidential business information relating to technological development to appropriate employees.  While recognizing the utility in the dispersion of responsibilities in larger firms, the optimum amount of "entrusting" will not occur unless the risk of loss to the businessman through a breach of trust can be held to a minimum.
>
> On the other hand, any form of post-employment restraint reduces the economic mobility of employees and limits their personal freedom to pursue a preferred course of livelihood.  The employee's bargaining position is weakened because he is potentially shackled by the acquisition of alleged trade secrets; and thus, paradoxically, he is restrained, because of his increased expertise, from advancing further in the industry in which he is most productive.  Moreover, as previously mentioned, society suf-

fers because competition is diminished by slackening the dissemination of ideas, processes and methods.

\* \* \*

■ ADAMS, CIRCUIT JUDGE, concurring.

\* \* \*

When deciding the equitable issues surrounding the request for a trade secret injunction, it would seem that a court cannot act as a pure engineer or scientist, assessing the technical import of the information in question. Rather, the court must also consider economic factors, since the very definition of "trade secret" requires an assessment of the competitive advantage a particular item of information affords to a business. Similarly, among the elements to be weighed in determining trade secret status are the value of the information to its owner and to competitors, and the ease or difficulty with which the information may be properly acquired or duplicated.

While the majority may be correct in suggesting that the trial court need not always "engage in extended analysis of the public interest," the court on occasion must apply the elements of sociology. This is so since trade secret cases frequently implicate the important countervailing policies served on one hand by protecting a business person from unfair competition stemming from the usurpation of trade secrets, and on the other by permitting an individual to pursue unhampered the occupation for which he or she is best suited.

"Trade secrets are not \* \* \* so important to society that the interests of employees, competitors and competition should automatically be relegated to a lower position whenever trade secrets are proved to exist."

These observations take on more force, I believe, when a case such as the present one involves the concept of "know-how." Under Pennsylvania law an employee's general knowledge, skill, and experience are not trade secrets. Thus in theory an employer generally may not inhibit the manner in which an employee uses his or her knowledge, skill, and experience— even if these were acquired during employment. When these attributes of the employee are inextricably related to the information or process that constitutes an employer's competitive advantage—as increasingly seems to be the case in newer, high-technology industries—the legal questions confronting the court necessarily become bound up with competing public policies.

It is noteworthy that in such cases the balance struck by the Pennsylvania courts apparently has favored greater freedom for employees to pursue a chosen profession. The courts have recognized that someone who has worked in a particular field cannot be expected to forego the accumulated skills, knowledge, and experience gained before the employee changes jobs. Such qualifications are obviously very valuable to an employee seeking to sell his services in the marketplace. A person leaving one employer and going into the marketplace will seek to compete in the area of his or her greatest aptitude. In light of the highly mobile nature of our society, and as the economy becomes increasingly comprised of highly skilled or high-tech jobs, the individual's economic interests will more and more be buffeted by employers' perceived needs to maintain their competitive advantage. Courts must be cautious not to strike a balance that unduly disadvantages the individual worker.

In achieving a proper balance, courts should be guarded in their use of older precedents. Perhaps the most "influential Pennsylvania holdings in the field of trade secrets" were decided in the early 1960's. Yet, quite significantly, those cases pre-date the rapid growth of several high-tech industries and the innovations which those industries have spawned.[1]

Furthermore, society has a fundamental interest in allowing an individual reasonable freedom to change his or her job and to make full use of acquired skills and experience for new employment. Reasonable movement promotes competition and the dissemination of ideas, which in turn benefit the consumer. Important values are served when the resources of skill and information are allocated in such a manner that they are utilized most efficiently to produce goods and services.

* * *

In my view a proper injunction necessarily would impose the minimum restraint upon the free utilization of employee skill consistent with denying unfaithful employees an advantage from misappropriation of information. Thus, as I see it, the district court, on remand, should fashion an injunction that extends only so long as is essential to negate any unfair advantage that may have been gained by the appellants.

## NOTES AND QUESTIONS

**1.** For the principal case on remand, see SI Handling Systems, Inc. v. Heisley, 658 F.Supp. 362 (E.D.Pa.1986).

**2.** Quoting from the Restatement of Torts, the court distinguished between a "compilation of information * * * which gives * * * an advantage over competitors," on the one hand, and on the other "aptitude, * * * skill, * * * dexterity, * * * and such other subjective knowledge as he obtains while in the course of his employment." Can judges or juries make this distinction? The defendants came away from SI Handling as experts on both the materials handling business and the detailed relationship between SI Handling and General Motors. Their new venture sought to capitalize

---

**1.** For example, before 1969 computer manufacturers apparently gave away "software" programs as part of their packaged product. Since then the estimated value of computer programs in use has surpassed $100 billion, and there is now an acute shortage of personnel capable of creating and improving computer programs. The status of a particular program in trade secret law is often extremely difficult to assess, partly be-cause the programs do not blend easily into a framework that utilizes such concepts as know-how and reverse engineering. In Pennsylvania, the idea of putting together computer programs to achieve a specific result and the expertise necessary to develop the programs are not subject to trade secret protection, but the specific programs developed to accomplish the purpose may be protected.

on all their knowledge. Can a court successfully tell them what information and ability they can use in a new undertaking and what they must refrain from using?

**3.** About half the states have enacted the Uniform Trade Secrets Act of 1979. The Commissioner's prefatory note states:

> Notwithstanding the commercial importance of state trade secret law to interstate business, this law has not developed satisfactorily. In the first place, its development is uneven. Although there typically are a substantial number of reported decisions in states that are commercial centers, this is not the case in less populous and more agricultural jurisdictions. Secondly, even in states in which there has been significant litigation, there is undue uncertainty concerning the parameters of trade secret protection and the appropriate remedies for misappropriation of a trade secret. One commentator observed:
>
>> Under technological and economic pressures, industry continues to rely on trade secret protection despite the doubtful and confused states of both common law and statutory remedies. Clear, uniform trade secret protection is urgently needed * * *

Comment, Theft of Trade Secrets: The Need for a Statutory Solution, 120 U.Pa.L.Rev. 378, 380–81 (1971).

The Act specifies:

## § 1.  Definitions.

As used in this [Act], unless the context requires otherwise:

(1) "Improper means" includes theft, bribery, misrepresentation, breach or inducement of a breach of a duty to maintain secrecy, or espionage through electronic or other means;

(2) "Misappropriation" means:

(i) acquisition of a trade secret of another by a person who knows or has reason to know that the trade secret was acquired by improper means; or

(ii) disclosure or use of a trade secret of another without express or implied consent by a person who

(A) used improper means to acquire knowledge of the trade secret; or

(B) at the time of disclosure or use, knew or had reason to know that his knowledge of the trade secret was

(I) derived from or through a person who had utilized improper means to acquire it;

(II) acquired under circumstances giving rise to a duty to maintain its secrecy or limit its use; or

(III) derived from or through a person who owed a duty to the person seeking relief to maintain its secrecy or limit its use; or

(C) before a material change of his [or her] position, knew or had reason to know that it was a trade secret and that knowledge of it had been acquired by accident or mistake.

\* \* \*

(4) "Trade secret" means information, including a formula, pattern, compilation, program, device, method, technique, or process, that:

(i) derives independent economic value, actual or potential, from not being generally known to, and not being readily ascertainable by proper means by, other persons who can obtain economic value from its disclosure or use, and

(ii) is the subject of efforts that are reasonable under the circumstances to maintain its secrecy.

## § 2.  Injunctive Relief.

(a) Actual or threatened misappropriation may be enjoined. Upon application to the court, an injunction shall be terminated when the trade secret has ceased to exist, but the injunction may be continued for an additional reasonable period of time in order to eliminate commercial advantage that otherwise would be derived from the misappropriation.

(b) In exceptional circumstances, an injunction may condition future use upon payment of a reasonable royalty for no longer than the period of time for which use could have been prohibited. Exceptional circumstances include, but are not limited to, a material and prejudicial change of position prior to acquiring knowledge or reason to know of misappropriation that renders a prohibitive injunction inequitable.

(c) In appropriate circumstances, affirmative acts to protect a trade secret may be compelled by court order.

## § 3.  Damages.

(a) In addition to or in lieu of injunctive relief, a complainant may recover damages for the actual loss caused by misappropriation.  A complainant also may recover for the unjust enrichment caused by misappropriation that is not taken into account in computing damages for actual loss.

(b) If willful and malicious misappropriation exists, the court may award exemplary damages in an amount not exceeding twice any award made under subsection (a).

A Minnesota court has held that under the Uniform Act an employee may have appropriated trade secrets by improper means when she utilized a former employer's policy and procedure manual in forming a rival business. Rehabilitation Specialists, Inc. v. Koering, 404 N.W.2d 301 (Minn.App. 1987).

**4.** What type and how much damage must an employer show before invoking trade secret protection against former employees?  Teradyne, Inc. v. Clear Communications Corp., 707 F.Supp. 353 (N.D.Ill.1989), held that a complaint invoking Illinois trade secret protection must do more than allege "a high degree of probability of inevitable and immediate * * * use * * * of trade secrets."  The complaint was dismissed:

> Here there is no allegation that defendants have in fact threatened to use Teradyne's secrets or that they will inevitably do so.  An allegation that the defendants said they would use secrets or disavowed their confidentiality agreements would serve this purpose.  An allegation that Clear could not operate without Teradyne's secrets because Teradyne's secret technology is the only one that will work would suffice though more technical facts may be necessarily included in such a pleading.  The defendants' claimed acts, working for Teradyne, leaving its business, hiring employees from Teradyne and entering the same field (though in a market not yet serviced by Teradyne) do not state a claim of threatened misappropriation.

The Seventh Circuit upheld the inevitable disclosure theory when it returned to the Illinois Trade Secret Act in PepsiCo, Inc. v. Redmond, 54 F.3d 1262 (7th Cir.1995).  There, an executive was prohibited from assuming new duties with a competing maker of sports beverages on the grounds that he would inevitably be led to rely on the former employer's trade secrets and confidential information.

**5.** A central holding of the principal case is that the employees would not have breached SI Handling's rights if they had made use of their knowledge of General Motors' "needs" and its "key decisionmakers."  Why should former employees of SI Handling be able to take away and use such valuable information, which they only obtained as employees on the former job?  In a case similar to *SI Handling,* a court said that the result should be heavily influenced by how much information the employee brought to the prior job when he was hired there.  The court distinguished the facts before it, in which the employee had worked for ten years for the Air Force and four years for the Draper Laboratory at MIT before joining plaintiff, a military contractor, from situations where an employee obtains all his knowledge on a job and then tries to use it elsewhere.  How well does this distinction capture the reality that individuals are constantly learning and developing, that they bring ability and knowledge even to their first job, and that later attempts to tell them what they can and cannot use will be difficult to enforce?  Dynamics Research Corp. v. Analytic Sciences Corp., 400 N.E.2d 1274 (Mass.App.Ct.1980).

**6.** What is the appropriate relief when a former employee has violated a valid restriction against using trade secrets?  In Lamb–Weston, Inc. v. McCain Foods, Ltd., 941 F.2d 970 (9th Cir.1991), the Ninth Circuit upheld the district court's eight-month injunction against McCain Foods for stealing Lamb–Weston's processing system that made curlicue french fries. The order banned McCain Foods from selling any curlicue french fries world-wide for the enjoined period. "An injunction in a trade secret case seeks to protect the secrecy of misappropriated information and to eliminate any unfair head start the defendant may have gained. Winston Research Corp. v. Minnesota Mining & Mfg., 350 F.2d 134, 141 (9th Cir.1965). A worldwide injunction here is consistent with those goals because it 'place[s the defendant] in the position it would have occupied if the breach of confidence had not occurred prior to the public disclosure, …' Id. at 142." The court also ruled that eight-months was not over-broad in time. "[T]he appropriate duration for the injunction should be the period of time it would have taken [the defendant], either by reverse engineering or by independent development, to develop [the product] legitimately without use of [plaintiff's] trade secrets." (citing K2 Ski Co. v. Head Ski Co., 506 F.2d 471, 474 (9th Cir.1974)). Was that a fair basis for deciding how long defendant should be barred?

**7.** As edited, the opinion in *SI Handling* does not contain a lengthy discussion of the technology of materials handling. Trade secret cases, like patent cases, are fact-specific, and a reader is sometimes uncertain whether a busy judge has in fact mastered the scientific or engineering issues.

**8.** Sometimes, disclosure of information obtained as an employee is a crime. See, e.g., Mass.Gen.Laws ch. 266 § 30(4): "Whoever steals, or * * * copies with intent to convert any trade secret of another, regardless of value, * * * shall be guilty of larceny * * *."

See Edmund W. Kitch, The Law and Economics of Rights in Valuable Information, 9 J.Legal Stud. 683 (1980):

> The difficulties of detection and enforcement make this a logical area for the use of strong criminal penalties. Since the number of detectable thefts is small, the activity can only be effectively deterred if heavy penalties are imposed on thieves who are caught. Trade secrecy skillfully executed is not a crime under the traditional criminal statutes. Entry only to copy is not entry with felonious intent and hence not burglary. Information is not the kind of property that falls within the scope of traditional theft statutes. Bribery of an employee to provide information, but not property of the employer, is not a crime. When property is taken, a crime has been committed. In the late 1960s and early 1970s, twenty-six states passed statutes to make trade-secrecy theft a crime. There have, however, been very few prosecutions under these statutes. The statutes came about as the result of a ring organized to steal systematically process secrets and materials from an American drug company and sell them to Italian manufacturers who at that time operated under an umbrella created by the lack of drug patents under Italian law. The ring proved very difficult for the company to break, and the problem highlighted a gap in the criminal laws that many legislatures were willing to fill.

The new statutes require the theft of a trade secret.  There-fore, in the criminal prosecution determining whether what was taken was a trade secret is a central issue.  The defense must prove that what was taken was not kept secret by the company nor known to other concerns in the industry.  To defend on that issue, the defense must ask for large amounts of material relevant to the technology in issue.  Procedures for protecting the confidentiality of this material exist, but its assembly and dissemination during the litigation process obviously increase the risk of further loss. In a California case, a convicted thief of trade secrets from IBM argued that his conviction should be set aside because he was the only one who had ever been prosecuted under the statute.

**9.**  (a) In some jurisdictions customer lists have been held to be trade secrets.  Under California trade secret law as long as a customer list is not generally known or readily accessible to others and is protected by efforts that are "reasonable under the circumstances" it is entitled to protection. Surgidev Corp. v. Eye Technology, Inc., 828 F.2d 452 (8th Cir.1987), employed this standard, holding that a list of physicians who were "high volume implanters" of intraocular lenses was a trade secret and was protected under California law.  The court upheld the enjoining of a former employee who attempted to utilize the information in setting up a compet-ing medical supply business.

Contrast the California standard with that recently utilized by a federal district court in applying New York law:

> As a general rule "where the customers are readily ascertainable outside the employer's business as prospective users or consumers of the employer's services or products, trade secret protection will not attach and courts will not enjoin an employee from soliciting his employer's customers."  Where customers are discoverable only through extraordinary efforts and the employer's clientele has been secured by many years expenditure of time and money then a court may confer trade secret status upon a customer list.

Consolidated Brands, Inc. v. Mondi, 638 F.Supp. 152 (E.D.N.Y.1986), quot-ing Leo Silfen, Inc. v. Cream, 278 N.E.2d 636 (N.Y.1972).

(b) What about the names and addresses of an accounting firm's clients?  Is this list not one of the most valuable assets of the firm? Nonetheless, a California court said the names and addresses were not trade secrets, and that the accounting firm's former professional employees did not engage in solicitation or unfair competition when they used the firm's address list in mailing announcements of their formation of a new accounting partnership.  Was the court holding that professional employees will often change jobs, and that customers have a right to know where their former accountant (or lawyer or dentist) now works, in case they want to move their business?  Moss, Adams, & Co. v. Shilling, 224 Cal.Rptr. 456 (Cal.App.1986).

(c) Should a former employee be able to assist plaintiffs in lawsuits against the employer?  Chrysler dismissed Rahn Huffstutler, a metallurgical engineer and manager at its Jeep Corp. subsidiary.  (Huffstutler also had a law degree.)  Huffstutler went into business as an expert witness for plaintiffs in product-liability suits in cases where Jeeps had rolled over.  Chrysler sued, saying Huffstutler's earlier participation in meetings discussing defenses to such lawsuits barred him from working for plaintiffs because of the attorney-client privilege.  Wall Street Journal, May 25, 1988.

**10.**  Businesses seek to protect commercially valuable information under both federal patent law and state trade secret law.  Even if patent law is relied upon, organizations often seek to ensure protection under state law because patents are often invalidated by the courts.  See Prefatory Note to Uniform Trade Secrets Act, 14 U.L.A. (Supp.) 369.  State trade secret law is not preempted by federal patent law.  Kewanee Oil Co. v. Bicron Corp., 416 U.S. 470 (1974).

**11.**  According to the Copyright Act, "the employer * * * is considered the author" unless an agreement is made to the contrary.  17 U.S.C. § 201(b).  This is the "works for hire" doctrine first enunciated in Bleistein v. Donaldson Lithographing Co., 188 U.S. 239 (1903).  The employer is entitled to the copyright if the work was created by the employee within the scope of his or her employment.  For a dispute over ownership of Superman, see Siegel v. National Periodical Publications, Inc., 508 F.2d 909 (2d Cir.1974).  What are the arguments for and against the "for hire" doctrine?

**12.**  Patent law grants the property rights in an invention to an employee who invents, but gives the employer a nonexclusive "shop right" to use the invention.  The parties can modify the arrangement by contract.  See, e.g., Francklyn v. Guilford Packing Co., 695 F.2d 1158 (9th Cir.1983).  The source of the "shop right" doctrine is McClurg v. Kingsland, 42 U.S. (1 How.) 202 (1843).

California Labor Code § 2870 provides that an employee's agreement to assign invention rights to the employer is unenforceable if:  (1) the employee did not use the employer's equipment or information;  (2) the employee developed the invention on his or her own time;  and (3) the invention does not relate to the employer's business.  See, e.g., Cubic Corp. v. Marty, 229 Cal.Rptr. 828 (Cal.App.1986).

Consider the case of Ingersoll–Rand Co. v. Ciavatta, 542 A.2d 879 (N.Y.1988).  Engineer Arnold Ciavatta joined Ingersoll–Rand in 1972.  As a condition of his employment, Ciavatta signed a Proprietary Agreement which assigned to the company his "entire right, title and interest in and to all inventions, copyrights and/or designs" which were developed by him during the period of employment and were related "directly or indirectly" to the business of the company, or were developed using company facilities.  The agreement also included a "holdover" provision which assigned to Ingersoll–Rand the right to inventions developed within one year of termination "if conceived as a result of and * * * attributable to work done during * * * employment."

During his tenure at Ingersoll–Rand, Ciavatta participated in the development of mining tools. As a result of this involvement Ciavatta became interested in the field of underground mining and began to develop his own mining instruments. Ciavatta's mining proposals were rejected by the company, and in June 1979 he was terminated for unrelated reasons.

Following his departure from Ingersoll–Rand, Ciavatta continued to develop mining tools. In March 1980, nine months after he left, Ciavatta filed for a patent on a mining stabilizing device which performed functions similar to existing Ingersoll–Rand products. Ciavatta's stabilizer achieved rapid market acceptance and became a competitive threat to Ingersoll–Rand's products. Ingersoll–Rand sued Ciavatta, alleging that he violated his employment agreement and was obligated to assign the rights to his stabilizing device.

The Supreme Court of New Jersey decided that Ingersoll–Rand was not entitled to an assignment. The court noted that the case illustrated the tension between the policy goals of encouraging individual creativity and maintaining an atmosphere of support for corporate subsidization of the inventive process. The court drew an analogy to general noncompetition agreements, which raise related policy concerns. Based on this analogy, the court applied the same reasonableness standard used in considering the enforceability of agreements not to compete. Under New Jersey law an agreement not to compete is enforceable if it "protects the legitimate interests of the employer, imposes no undue hardship on the employee and is not injurious to the public." The court concluded that the "holdover" agreement was not enforceable since protection of the information utilized by Ciavatta in developing his stabilizing device was not a protectable interest of the company, and enforcement would have worked an undue hardship on the inventor.

**13.** Steven P. Jobs, with Steve Wozniak, founded Apple Computer. Apparently starting with a small electronics lab in a garage, they created a major national company. After some years, Jobs, now 30 years of age, quit as chairman of the board of Apple and said he would set up a new firm (to be called Next, Inc.) with five former Apple employees and create new computer products. Apple sued, saying Jobs was inevitably taking information that belonged to Apple. It alleged that Jobs was violating his fiduciary responsibilities to Apple and was likely to misappropriate confidential and proprietary information. Apple sought to prevent Jobs from using information that might overlap with Apple projects, and also to stop him from hiring Apple employees. What is the right result? (The parties negotiated a settlement which placed some technological restrictions on Next's computer and allowed Apple a chance to inspect the machine before it went to market. See New York Times, Nov. 8, 1987, § 3, p. 1, col. 2.)

**14.** See Pat K. Chew, Competing Interests in the Corporate Opportunity Doctrine, 67 N.C.L.Rev. 435 (1989). Professor Chew argues that courts should give more protection to the interests of fiduciary employees by using a reasonable expectation test to evaluate claims that a fiduciary has violated the fiduciary duty by pursuing a business opportunity that a former corporate employer claims belonged to the entity. Currently, she contends, courts give too much weight to the corporate interest to the detriment of rights of individual employees.

> [T]he practical consequences for corporate fiduciaries are drastic. In many instances fiduciaries who lose corporate opportunity lawsuits are effectively prohibited from competing with their former corporations. This results even though the fiduciaries have not signed noncompetition agreements. Such de facto restraints are contrary to individuals' rights to pursue freely their interests and talents and to society's long-standing goal of promoting competition.

Id. at 438. In Allied Supply Co. v. Brown, 585 So.2d 33 (Ala.1991), the Alabama Supreme Court held that at-will employees do not breach a fiduciary duty by failing to give their employer advance notice of resignation before forming a new business.

# CHAPTER 12

# UNEMPLOYMENT

As chapter 10 shows, judicial decisions interpreting the common law and (as to government employees) the fourteenth amendment have reduced the vulnerability of workers to arbitrary dismissal. To some unquantifiable extent, a job has become "property." To that extent, workers have obtained a set of legally protected expectations in the continuation of the employment relationship.

Nevertheless, the U.S. remains committed to an economy in which there is risk, adaptation, and flexibility, and so to a labor market in which there is extensive mobility. The legal structure of our employment relationships must therefore balance legitimate worker expectations and entitlements with employer authority to hire, contract out, revise production methods, transfer operations elsewhere in the U.S. or abroad, diminish the scale of operations, and ultimately shut down. As in so many areas of employment relations, law restrains employer discretion. Regarding layoffs, there has been extensive litigation about whether Title VII of the 1964 Civil Rights Act prevents dismissals on the basis of seniority if the consequence is retention of most white workers and layoff of many nonwhites. That topic was considered in Chapter 4. This chapter begins with discussion of the bankruptcy system which gives workers certain limited rights: to wages they earned before bankruptcy, to compensation for work done after bankruptcy, and to a degree of protection for contractual expectations. The chapter then considers federal and state plant-closing legislation; those laws require notice to workers of impending shut-downs in some situations. The chapter also assesses the role of government in helping workers cope with technological change. Next, the chapter examines in depth the major national program dealing with dismissed workers—the federally mandated unemployment insurance system. That program offers broad coverage for the first six months of employment (and in some states for short additional periods). Finally, the chapter discusses the work requirements that are imposed as a condition in most programs supplying minimum income support. One set of questions is relevant to all the material in this chapter: Should long-term unemployment (for example, unemployment extending beyond the six months or nine months that unemployment insurance benefits usually last) be the target of a systematic national program? If so, what shape should that effort take?

## A.   BANKRUPTCY

In recent years, large and small American companies have become bankrupt—either as a means of terminating business, or as a way of reorganizing and continuing to operate.  Workers with years of service in the past and the hope of additional years in the future have many expectations that can be rudely interrupted by bankruptcy.  They may be owed wages on the day bankruptcy occurs.  They may believe they have a contractual right to benefits:  health care, disability protection, life insurance, pension.  They may have a written contract assuring continued employment or, more likely, implied contract rights to the job, or against arbitrary dismissal.

In the important case of NLRB v. Bildisco & Bildisco, 465 U.S. 513 (1984), the Supreme Court held unanimously that a collective bargaining agreement is only an "executory contract," and thus can be rejected by the employer after bankruptcy if the agreement "burdens the estate, and * * * after careful scrutiny, the equities balance in favor of rejecting the labor contract."  The Court also held, by five to four vote, that an employer commits no unfair labor practice if it unilaterally alters the terms of an existing collective bargaining agreement after a bankruptcy petition has been filed but before review by a bankruptcy court of the arguments for altering the contract.

Congress reacted speedily to prescribe the procedures that should be followed by a bankrupt company seeking relief from its collectively bargained obligations.  11 U.S.C. § 1113.

What of the nonunion worker not covered by a collective bargaining agreement?  Chapter 11 showed that in many states workers may now have a degree of protection against arbitrary dismissal.  Is that right an executory contract?  If the company approaches hard times and seeks to lay off workers, should the workers have rights of the sort created by 11 U.S.C. § 1113 for workers covered by a collectively bargained agreement?

## 1.   PROCEDURAL PROTECTION FOR EXECUTORY CONTRACTS
**11 U.S.C. § 1113.**

\* \* \*

(b)(1) Subsequent to filing a petition and prior to filing an application seeking rejection of a collective bargaining agreement, the debtor in possession or trustee * * *, shall—

(A) make a proposal to the authorized representative of the employees covered by such agreement, based on the most complete and reliable information available at the time of such proposal, which provides for those necessary modifications in the employees' benefits and protections that are necessary to permit the reorganization of the debtor and assures that all creditors, the debtor and all of the affected parties are treated fairly and equitably; and

(B) provide, subject to subsection (d)(3), the representative of the employees with such relevant information as is necessary to evaluate the proposal.

(2) During the period beginning on the date of the making of a proposal provided for in paragraph (1) and ending on the date of the hearing provided for in subsection (d)(1), the trustee shall meet, at reasonable times, with the authorized representative to confer in good faith in attempting to reach mutually satisfactory modifications of such agreement.

(c) The court shall approve an application for rejection of a collective bargaining agreement only if the court finds that—

(1) the trustee has, prior to the hearing, made a proposal that fulfills the requirements of subsection (b)(1);

(2) the authorized representative of the employees has refused to accept such proposal without good cause; and

(3) the balance of the equities clearly favors rejection of such agreement.

\* \* \*

(e) If during a period when the collective bargaining agreement continues in effect, and if essential to the continuation of the debtor's business, or in order to avoid irreparable damage to the estate, the court, after notice and a hearing, may authorize the trustee to implement interim changes in the terms, conditions, wages, benefits, or work rules provided by a collective bargaining agreement.

NOTES

Nonunion employees in many states have rights against arbitrary dismissal. Those rights can be considered a form of contract, implied or otherwise. See Chapter 10. If the employer of such employees seeks bankruptcy protection, those workers are likely to lose much of the value of their contractual rights. Looking at 11 U.S.C. § 1113, what statutory provision would you support for nonunion workers who have rights in their job but get no benefits from 11 U.S.C. § 1113 because they have no collective bargaining agreement? Could a court reason from 11 U.S.C. § 1113 and create such rights without new congressional action?

## 2. PRIORITIES IN BANKRUPTCY

Two statutory "preferences" provide a degree of advantage for employees of a bankrupt firm. First, § 507(a)(3) of the federal bankruptcy law gives workers preference over general creditors as to wages earned but uncollected before bankruptcy. This preference is limited to $2,000 per employee.

Second, and far more important, once the bankruptcy filing occurs, those who supply goods and services to the bankrupt firm have a right to be paid. Under the statutory scheme, these are "administrative expenses" of the bankruptcy, and must be paid before prebankruptcy creditors receive money. Under § 503(b)(1)(a) of the Bankruptcy Code, these goods and services are considered administrative expenses, which include "the actual, necessary costs and expenses of preserving the estate, including wages, salaries, or commissions for services rendered after the commencement of the case," and which must be paid before prebankruptcy creditors receive money. The reason for this policy is that the law seeks to encourage continued operation of the enterprise, and such operation requires assurance that new obligations will have priority over those still unpaid from the past. Clearly, therefore, wage claims for post-bankruptcy work are administrative expenses. The law is less clear about, and is currently wrestling with, how to handle claims against employers such as severance pay and accrued pension obligations that are at the intersection between new obligations and leftover duties contracted before bankruptcy.

## Law v. Law Trucking Co.

488 A.2d 1225 (R.I.1985).

■ BEVILACQUA, CHIEF JUSTICE.

This is an appeal from a petition by the permanent receiver of Law Trucking Company seeking instructions whether or not to pay claims filed with the receiver by * * * five employees. * * * [F]ive former Law Trucking employees claim back wages and seek priority to the extent permitted by the United States Bankruptcy Code, 11 U.S.C.A. § 507(a)(3) and (4) (1979).

* * *

The company evidently had fallen upon hard times, and in hopes of surmounting the financial difficulty, Robert Law, president of Law Trucking, approached the drivers and asked for certain wage concessions that he would plow back into the company with the aim of keeping it afloat. In return, he promised that if the company made a profit at the end of the year, the employees would be entitled to reimbursement for their "loan."

At the time of this agreement, the drivers were working under a union contract that paid them $12.71 for straight time and $19.06 for overtime, based upon a forty-hour week. Law asked that they accept $10 an hour for straight time and $15 an hour for overtime. Only five of the twelve drivers agreed to accept the wage-cut proposal. The acceptors then signed an agreement to this effect.[5]

**5.** The text of the agreement signed by the employees:

"I will loan to Law Trucking Company without interest, my earnings over $10.00 per hour straight time, over $15.00 per hour of overtime, and the 5 personal holidays due in 1981.

The employees contend that the terms of a collective-bargaining agreement cannot be altered individually to conflict with the terms of the contract originally entered into by the employer and the union representatives. This issue, however, was not raised below and we will not entertain it now for the first time.

In addition, employees contend that because there was no mutuality of obligation in the alleged agreement, it should fail. The trial justice found that testimony elicited at the hearing provides ample evidence of mutual obligation. Such evidence consisted of the following: Law promised to keep the company open for a year in exchange for the loans; the bookkeeper testified that the company was in serious debt at that time; and because employees were aware of the financial difficulty that the company was facing, the trial justice could have easily inferred that the employees understood the risk involved. We find no error in the trial justice's conclusion that mutuality of obligation sufficient to support an enforceable contract was present.

Finally, we examine the employees' claim for priority status under the Bankruptcy Code * * * Priority status operates upon the premise that the moneys withheld constitutes wages. If the moneys withheld did not constitute wages, we need not proceed to the issues of statutory application and construction.

The trial justice found that the moneys withheld were loans and not wages. There is ample evidence in the record to support this finding, which is further buttressed by reference to the written agreement signed by the employees. The language in the agreement refers to a loan to the company. Moreover, the moneys withheld were not treated as wages by the bookkeeper; no taxes, and no social security or disability deductions were withheld from sums earned above the wage-rate ceiling set forth in the new agreement.

In our review of these findings we detect neither error nor misconstruction of evidence; therefore, we will not disturb the findings of the trial justice.

## NOTES AND QUESTIONS

**1.** Why should the bankruptcy preference for uncollected wages not include "loaned" wages?

The following expenses and claims have priority in the following order:

> Third, allowed unsecured claims for wages, salaries, or commissions, including vacation, severance and sick leave pay—

>> (A) earned by an individual within 90 days before the date of the filing of the petition or the date of the cessation of the debtor's business, whichever occurs first; but only

"This money is refundable to me at the end of the year in the event of a        company profit."

(B) to the extent of $2,000 for each such individual.

Fourth, allowed unsecured claims for contributions to an employee benefit—

(A) arising from services rendered within 180 days before the date of the filing of the petition or the date of the cessation of the debtor's business, whichever occurs first; but only

(B) for each such plan, to the extent of—

(i) the number of employees covered by each such plan multiplied by $2,000; less

(ii) the aggregate amount paid to such employees under paragraph (3) of this subsection, plus the aggregate amount paid by the estate on behalf of such employees benefit plan.

11 U.S.C. § 507.

**2.**   Having read this case, how would you have structured this transaction to protect the employees' right to their wages?

**3.**   In re Growers Seed Association, 49 B.R. 17 (Bkrtcy.Tex.1985), refused to allow a priority claim for moving expenses on the ground that the statute gives priority only to employee claims for wages, salaries, commissions, vacation pay, sick pay, and severance pay.

**4.**   An independent contractor selling mobile homes on commission for a bankrupt company received no § 507(a)(3) preference for his commissions. In re American Shelter Systems, Inc., 40 B.R. 793 (Bkrtcy.W.D.La.1984).

**5.**   By statute in most states, a discharged or laid off employee must be paid back wages immediately.  See, e.g., Cal.Lab.Code § 201.

a.  VACATION PAY

## In re Ionosphere Clubs, Inc.

22 F.3d 403 (2d Cir.1994).

MINER, CIRCUIT JUDGE:

On this appeal we once again concern ourselves with the bankruptcy of Eastern Air Lines. . . .   The Air Line Pilots Association, International, the International Association of Machinists and Aerospace Workers and the Transport Workers Union appeal from a May 24, 1993 order of the United States District Court for the Southern District of New York affirming a September 10, 1991 order of the United States Bankruptcy Court for the Southern District of New York classifying pre-petition vacation pay claims asserted by former Eastern employees in part as unsecured claims eligible for third-priority status under section 507(a)(3) of the Bankruptcy Code, 11 U.S.C. § 507(a)(3), and in part as general unsecured claims. . . .   On appeal, the Unions contend that section 1113(f) of the Code supersedes the priority scheme of section 507, giving the vacation pay claims a superpriority status.... For the reasons that follow, we affirm.

On March 9, 1989, Eastern filed a petition for relief under chapter 11 of the Code, 11 U.S.C. §§ 1101–1174.... On January 18, 1991, Eastern ceased operations, and all employees of Eastern were terminated by February 1, 1991.

ALPA represents the airline pilots formerly employed by Eastern, IAM represents ground services personnel and other employees formerly employed by Eastern and TWU represents all former Eastern flight attendants. The collective bargaining agreements at issue on this appeal were entered into between Eastern and the Unions pursuant to the Railway Labor Act, 45 U.S.C. §§ 151–188. The vacation pay provisions of the CBAs are essentially alike. Union employees "accrued" vacation on a day-to-day basis in one year and "earned" the right to take it on January 1 of the following year. Employees generally are entitled to full payment for earned, unused vacation upon their separation from Eastern ...

On July 26, 1991, Eastern moved the bankruptcy court for an order determining the priority of the pre-petition vacation pay claims. There was a dispute between Eastern and the Unions concerning the portion of the employees' unused pre-petition vacation pay eligible for treatment under section 507(a)(3) of the Code, which gives third-priority status to unsecured claims for wages, salaries or commissions, including vacation pay, "earned by an individual within 90 days before the date of the filing of the petition ...; but only to the extent of $2,000 for each such individual." The Unions asserted that all claims for payment of unused vacation accrued in 1988 were entitled to third-priority status, since the "earn" date fell on January 1, 1989, which was within ninety days of the petition date. The Unions also contended that section 1113(f), which prohibits a trustee from unilaterally terminating or modifying a CBA, superseded the priority scheme of section 507 and required that vacation pay be accorded the equivalent priority of an administrative expense pursuant to section 507(a)(1). Eastern urged the bankruptcy court to adopt the reasoning of In re Northwest Engineering Co., 863 F.2d 1313, 1319 (7th Cir.1988), that for purposes of section 507(a)(3) only claims for vacation pay attributable to work performed in the ninety days immediately prior to filing are entitled to third-priority status, subject to the statutory $2000 cap, regardless of when the "earn" date occurred.

In a September 10, 1991 order, the bankruptcy court granted Eastern's motion, holding that only claims for vacation pay attributable to work actually performed during the ninety-day period immediately preceding the petition date were eligible for third-priority status, regardless of the earn date. The bankruptcy court also concluded that the remainder of the pre-petition vacation pay claims would be general unsecured claims. Finally, it rejected the Unions' contention that section 1113 should be construed to supersede the priority scheme established by section 507.

The Unions appealed the bankruptcy court's order. In a May 24, 1993 order, the district court affirmed the bankruptcy court's disposition in all respects, phrasing the primary issue as "whether judicial application of the priority scheme of § 507 constitutes a unilateral termination or alteration of the provisions of the collective bargaining agreement by the trustee as contemplated by § 1113, and whether the granting of 'superpriority' status to all unrejected pay claims is an appropriate method of enforcing the protections of § 1113."

On appeal, the Unions . . . continue to maintain that all vacation pay claims are entitled to a superpriority status equivalent at least to an administrative expense. Thus, we must determine whether, as the Unions assert, section 1113(f) of the Code preempts the application of the priority scheme of section 507. We conclude that it does not.

Section 1113 of the Code provides the sole means by which a trustee may assume, reject or modify a CBA. We have described the purposes of this provision as follows:

> It ensures that the debtor attempt to negotiate with the union prior to seeking to terminate a collective bargaining agreement. § 1113(b). In the event such negotiations fail, it delineates the standard by which an application by the debtor to terminate the collective bargaining agreement is to be judged by the bankruptcy court and establishes a time frame in which this determination is to be made.

Section 1113(f) provides that "[n]o provision of [the Code] shall be construed to permit a trustee to unilaterally terminate or alter any provisions of a collective bargaining agreement prior to compliance with the provisions of this section." The Unions argue that section 1113(f) preempts the priority scheme of section 507 and mandates that the claims for prepetition vacation pay receive first priority as administrative expenses. Whether section 1113(f) trumps section 507 to create a superpriority for claims arising under CBAs is an issue that has divided the courts within this Circuit and elsewhere. We find the Third Circuit's holding in Roth—that sections 1113(f) and 507 can be reconciled—to be the better reasoned position and the one most consistent with our analysis of the preemptive scope of section 1113(f) in Ionosphere I.

In Ionosphere I. . . . (w)e recognized that section 1113(f) was intended to reverse that portion of the decision in NLRB v. Bildisco & Bildisco, in which the Supreme Court held that a CBA was an executory contract which the trustee could unilaterally reject pursuant to section 365(a) of the Code. Accordingly, we held that section 1113(f) "prohibit[ed] the application of any other provision of the Bankruptcy Code when such application would permit a debtor to achieve a unilateral termination or modification of a collective bargaining agreement without meeting the requirements of § 1113." As applied to a particular section of the Code, however, we cautioned that section 1113(f) was "circumstance specific rather than section specific."

Applying the analytical framework we established in Ionosphere I to the facts of this case, we hold that application of the priority scheme of section 507 will not allow Eastern unilaterally to modify or terminate its obligations under the CBAs. In holding as we do, we are not drawing a mere semantical distinction. Eastern's obligation to satisfy in full the vacation pay claims remains unchanged. Section 507 only establishes the priority of those claims, it does not affect the underlying obligation. As the district court recognized, "Judicial ordering of benefit claims pursuant to § 507 is not equivalent to employer avoidance of obligations under a collective bargaining agreement. The collective bargaining agreement is respected, but the financial obligations issuing from it are accorded priority consistent with the Bankruptcy Code." Moreover, application of the priority scheme does not conflict with the purpose of section 1113. As the Third Circuit recognized in Roth,

> The congressional goal embodied in section 1113 to give special consideration to a collective bargaining agreement and encourage the debtor and the union to reach a mutually acceptable agreement while the provisions of the current agreement remain in effect until the bankruptcy court authorizes unilateral rejection or modification of the agreement pursuant to section 1113 can be satisfied without interfering with the previously established statutory priorities.

In enacting section 1113, Congress was concerned with preventing employers from using bankruptcy as an offensive weapon to rid themselves of burdensome collective bargaining agreements, not with re-ordering the priority in which claims would be paid.

Implying a superpriority for claims arising under CBAs also would disrupt the careful balancing of competing policies embodied in section 507. "Section 507 is intended to be the exclusive list of priorities in bankruptcy.... Recognizing this restriction, we are loath to create a class of claims with superpriority status absent express statutory authority. Section 1113 does not address the priority to be accorded claims arising from a debtor's obligations under a CBA. We must therefore assume that Congress intended that the priorities set forth in section 507 should apply to these claims. When Congress has intended to alter the general priority scheme, it has done so explicitly. For example, section 1114(e)(2) expressly confers upon retiree benefits owed by the debtor the status of an allowed administrative expense. Finally, we note that the Unions' proposed priority scheme is inconsistent with the established rule in this Circuit that vacation pay claims are accorded first-priority status as administrative expenses only to the extent the vacation pay is attributable to post-petition work.

For the foregoing reasons, the order of the district court is AFFIRMED.

NOTES

**1.** As shown above, in a Chapter 11 bankruptcy, a trustee or debtor in possession may request the court to approve rejection of a collective bargaining agreement only after seeking modifications of the agreement "that are necessary to permit the reorganization of the debtor and assures that all creditors, the debtor, and all of the affected parties are treated fairly and equitably." 11 U.S.C. § 1113(b)(1)(A). The union must be provided with relevant materials to evaluate the agreement and the debtor in possession must meet with the union at reasonable times and in good faith. The requirements of section 1113 were transformed into a nine-part test in In re American Provision Co., 44 B.R. 907 (Bankr.D.Minn.1984), which has been restated in numerous later decisions. This test may be phrased simply as:

1. The debtor in possession must propose modification of the agreement;

2. The proposal must be based on the most complete and reliable information available;

3. The modification proposed must be necessary to reorganization;

4. The modification proposed must treat creditors and affected parties equitably;

5. The debtor in possession must provide the labor union with relevant information to review the proposal;

6. The debtor in possession must meet at reasonable times with the labor union;

7. The debtor in possession must negotiate in good faith with the labor union;

8. The labor union must have refused the proposed modification without good cause; and

9. The balance of the equities must clearly favor rejection of the agreement.

A split has developed among the circuits as to the interpretation of part three of the test, the requirement that the modification proposed must be necessary to reorganization. The Third Circuit has held that "necessary" must be strictly construed and that any modifications proposed must be the minimum necessary to allow the Chapter 11 trustee or debtor in possession to avoid short-term liquidation. Wheeling–Pittsburgh Steel Corp. v. United Steelworkers of America, 791 F.2d 1074 (3d Cir.1986). The Second Circuit has held that the debtor in possession or trustee satisfies the necessary requirement when the proposal contains necessary although not absolutely minimal changes which will enable it to reorganize successfully. Truck Drivers Local 807 v. Carey Transp., Inc., 816 F.2d 82 (2d Cir.1987). What arguments could be made to support the strict construction of the Third Circuit? What arguments support the Second Circuit's conclusion?

**2.** For a case involving severance pay in lieu of notice of dismissal, see In re Tucson Yellow Cab Co., 789 F.2d 701 (9th Cir.1986). On September 1, 1978, Mary Ingrum lost the lower part of one leg in a collision between a taxicab and a motorcycle on which she was a passenger. She sued the Tucson Yellow Cab Company for negligence and received a judgment of $437,016. However, because the company had the bare minimum of insurance, Ingrum received only $100,000 and the company filed for bankruptcy under Chapter 11 on January 27, 1981.

In March 1982, the company was sold.   In accordance with the wishes of the purchaser of the company, on April 5, 1982 the bankruptcy court approved rejection of the collective bargaining agreement which included a provision for two weeks notice of firing or two weeks severance pay in lieu of notice.   On April 16, 1982 the employees were fired.   Despite the obvious equitable considerations against allowing the employees to recover from the estate at the expense of Ingrum, the court held that this severance pay was a form of wages that has administrative expense priority.   The court reasoned that the fair value of the work under the collective bargaining agreement had been the take-home wages and the severance pay provision, and that there was no reason to value the work less in the eleven days between the rejection of the collective bargaining agreement and the firing of the employees.

Was this form of "severance pay" earned by post-bankruptcy work? Prebankruptcy, it was already an entitlement of the workers.   Why is it considered an "administrative expense" of the bankruptcy?   Why should it receive priority over Mary Ingrum's tort claim?   Certainly, her claim has far more significance to her than any of the severance pay claims could have had to any of the fired employees.

**3.**   The $2,000 limit established under 29 U.S.C. § 1113 has not been increased for many years.   This failure to raise the monetary limit for workers in a bankruptcy setting has diluted the value of this protection in real dollars.

### b.   UNFUNDED PENSION OBLIGATIONS

## In re Chateaugay Corp.

130 B.R. 690 (S.D.N.Y.1991), decision vacated and withdrawn.
1993 WL 388809 (S.D.N.Y.1993).

■ KEVIN THOMAS DUFFY, DISTRICT JUDGE.

Beginning in the early 1950's, major corporations began funding employee pensions plans.   Trustees no longer required that funds be invested in employer corporations and diversified investments assuring the safest and most efficient use of the funds in order to earn benefit monies ultimately paid to employees upon retirement.   These pension funds became major players in the financial marketplace, but even so, with an aging workforce, smart investment policy did not necessarily cover the benefits to be paid, particularly in those cases where funding by the employer is still incomplete.

Congress and the President, spreading a federal safety net in order to protect retiree benefits, enacted the Employee Retirement Income Security Act ("ERISA"), 29 U.S.C. §§ 1001 et seq.   Formation of the Pension Benefit Guarantee Corporation ("PBGC") was established thereunder, it was developed, among other reasons, to rescue underfunded pension plans of bankrupt corporations.   ERISA guarantees payment of pensions to retirees and employees of corporations which fail or become bankrupt leaving incompletely funded pension plans, causing them to be terminated. In order for such terminated funds to make good on shortfalls, money is generated by: "insurance premiums," exacted from all pension funds, "charge-backs" assessed against defunct or bankrupt employers and officers, and as a last resort, a "call" on the United States Treasury.

This case revolves around the bankruptcy of plaintiff Chateaugay Corporation, Reomar, Inc. and the LTV corporation (collectively "LTV"), a major nation wide conglomerate, the pension plans of which are not completely funded. The case is difficult and important because it involves fundamental questions of valuation, procedure, and methodology. Complicating matters further is the fact that such procedures have never before been decided in connection with a major bankruptcy where practically every possible type of interest is present. The resolution of these issues is of grave concern not only to the parties involved here but potentially to the national economy.[1]

On July 17, 1986, LTV and its sixty six subsidiary organizations, filed for reorganization in bankruptcy. On November 24, 1987, PBGC filed proofs of claim against LTV, after which LTV filed an adversarial proceeding in the bankruptcy court, objecting to PBGC's September 13, 1989 claims. I withdrew the reference from the Bankruptcy Court on October 17, 1989, but, in acknowledgement of Judge Lifland's familiarity with the issues and the parties, the matter was referred to him for findings pursuant to 28 U.S.C. § 157(c)(1), subject to my *de novo* review. Defendants PBGC and the Department of Labor (the "DOL") now seek review of Judge Lifland's Report and Recommendation.

Specifically, by Recommended Decision dated May 24, 1990, the Bankruptcy Court advised that: (1) federal bankruptcy law is determinative of the discount rate to be applied in calculating the present value of PBGC's claims; (2) post-petition termination of pension plans did not entitle PBGC's claims to administrative status; (3) post-petition termination of pension plans did not entitle PBGC's claims to tax or lien status; (4) PBGC must give effect to certain limits imposed by 29 U.S.C. § 1362(b) (1986); (5) PBGC is entitled to a single, non-duplicative recovery; (6) PBGC's priority claims must be set off by payments made by LTV; and (7) PBGC's trust claims, pursuant to 29 U.S.C. § 1349 (1986), must be expunged. Both PBGC and the DOL also move pursuant to Fed.R.Civ.P. 12(b)(6) for judgment on the pleadings, dismissing paragraphs 14, 15 and 17 of LTV's complaint. Additionally, LTV moves for a declaratory judgment which would include rulings that: (1) any DOL claims arising from the LTV pension plan obligations are pre-petition claims and are therefore not entitled to priority; (2) payment of such claims may only be made pursuant to a plan of reorganization; and (3) the DOL may not compel payment of LTV's pension plan obligations.

---

**1.** Although the legal arguments advanced here have been very helpful, I cannot help but recognize that part of the reason underlying the government's position is occasioned by the potential call upon the Treasury and memory of the recent and on-going Savings and Loan insurance debacle.

LTV and its affiliates are principally engaged in the steel, aerospace/defense and energy products industries. LTV Steel Company, Inc. is one the country's largest steelmakers as a result of its acquisition of the Republic Steel Corporation in June of 1984, and the subsequent merger of an LTV subsidiary corporation, J & L Steel, with the LTV Steel Company, Inc. PBGC is a corporation owned by the United States government which administers the pension plan termination insurance program.

LTV filed petitions for relief under Chapter 11 of the Bankruptcy Code on July 17, 1986, in part because of the difficulty in maintaining its pension plan obligations in an increasingly competitive steel industry. At the time that LTV filed for bankruptcy, it was the sponsor of at least the four pension plans in question here. The pension plans have a wide range of benefits including those for medical and dental care, contributions to savings plans, and profit sharing. Since the time that LTV filed for bankruptcy, it has continued to operate its businesses as debtor in possession pursuant to 11 U.S.C. §§ 1107 and 1108.

On September 30, 1986, and January 12, 1987, PBGC moved before this court to terminate the plans after LTV filed for reorganization in bankruptcy. LTV consented to each of the terminations. Pursuant to the Bankruptcy Court's orders, LTV has been paying approximately 92% of the benefits for current retirees. Subsequently, PBGC attempted to administratively restore three of the four pension plans.[6] This restoration was ultimately permitted. In re Chateaugay Corp., 87 B.R. 779 (S.D.N.Y.1988), aff'd sub nom., Pension Ben. Guaranty Corp. v. LTV Corp., 875 F.2d 1008 (2d Cir.1989), rev'd, ___ U.S. ___, 110 S.Ct. 2668, 110 L.Ed.2d 579 (1990), on remand, 122 B.R. 863 (S.D.N.Y.1990).

While the above restoration action was *sub judice* in the United States Supreme Court, PBGC took over the assets and liabilities of the pension plans, which were sponsored and administered by related debtors in the LTV bankruptcy proceeding. PBGC filed numerous claims of liability for pension plan obligations.

## DISCUSSION

The parties are in agreement that there are no issues of material fact which would prevent the court from disposing of the issues at bar.[7] See Quinn v. Syracuse Model Neighborhood Corp., 613 F.2d 438, 444 (2d Cir.1980) (summary judgment pursuant to Fed.R.Civ.P. 56 is appropriate where there is no genuine dispute as to issues of material fact and the court may decide the issues as a matter of law).

---

**6.** The PBGC did not seek to restore the Republic Retirement Plan.

**7.** On June 18, 1990, the Supreme Court held that PBGC could properly restore a terminated pension plan without reference to policies other than those embodied in ERISA. Pension Ben. Guaranty Corp. v. LTV Corp., ___ U.S. ___, 110 S.Ct. 2668, 110 L.Ed.2d 579 (1990). In so far as PBGC's claims were rendered moot by restoration, they were withdrawn. The following discussion therefore addresses only PBGC's claims against the Republic Plan and the DOL's claims against the restored plans.

The Employee Retirement Income Security Act of 1974, as amended ("ERISA"), 29 U.S.C. § 1302 (1982 & Supp.1986) [8], governs both ongoing and terminated pension plans. Under Titles I and IV of ERISA, the DOL enforces the funding requirements for ongoing pension plans. 29 U.S.C. §§ 1132(a)(5) and 1132(b)(1). Section 4002 of ERISA establishes the PBGC, a wholly-owned United States Government corporation, created to administer a pension plan termination insurance program. *See* 29 U.S.C. §§ 1301–1461.

Single employer pension plans may be involuntarily terminated by the PBGC for, among other reasons, inability by the participant to fund its employee benefits programs. 29 U.S.C. § 1342. Here, the pension plans were involuntarily terminated. When a pension plan covered by Title IV of ERISA terminates without sufficient funds, PBGC takes over the assets and liabilities of the plan and makes up any deficiency in plan assets from its own funds. PBGC funds are drawn from the annual insurance premiums paid by administrators of covered plans as well as employer liability payments collected when a plan terminates for insufficient funds. 29 U.S.C. §§ 1306, 1307, and 1362. As aforementioned, there is also a potential for a call on the Treasury if PBGC funds are insufficient to cover its liabilities.

## I. *Computation of PBGC's Claims*

An employer liability claim, as defined under ERISA, is a claim for the unfunded benefit liabilities to all participants and beneficiaries under the plan. 29 U.S.C. § 1362(b)(1). Computing proper amounts to allot claims is based upon the total amount of unfunded guaranteed benefits as of the termination date of the plan, plus interest. 29 U.S.C. § 1362(b). Unfunded guaranteed benefits constitute an amount by which the actuarial present value of guaranteed benefits exceeds the current value of plan assets allocable to payment of requisite employee benefits. 29 U.S.C. § 1301(a)(17).

PBGC is responsible for determining the amount of unfunded guaranteed payments under a plan when an underfunded plan terminates. In addition, PBGC is responsible for determining the present value of all future plan benefits, applying certain discount rates to determine termination liability, depending on when the plan must pay out benefits. PBGC contends here that the assignment of a present value is properly an administrative decision under ERISA even though the employer is in the process of reorganization under the Bankruptcy Code.

LTV does not contest that determination of the value of the aggregate future liabilities of the plan generally is properly done by PBGC. However, LTV argues that in the context of a bankruptcy proceeding, the right of

---

**8.** Congress amended Title IV of ERISA on December 22, 1987, by enacting the Pension Protection Act (the "PPA"). Subtitle D of Title IX of the Omnibus Budget Reconciliation Act of 1987, Pub.L. No. 100–203, 101 Stat. 1330. The PPA was enacted subsequent to the events which gave rise to this litigation. This decision does not reflect the amendments.

PBGC to determine its own claims for liability must be subordinated to other policies. Further, LTV argues that bankruptcy law requires interest rate assumptions, used to determine the gross value of the claims, be reflective of the market discount rate, and that this rate is properly set by the bankruptcy court, insuring equitable treatment of claims. While this case arose under ERISA, the concerns of the Bankruptcy Code must also be satisfied.

On the one hand, the Bankruptcy Code primarily looks to rehabilitate the business of the debtor/employer in a reorganization proceeding. NLRB v. Bildisco & Bildisco, 465 U.S. 513, 528 (1984). On the other hand, PBGC's primary purpose is to further the statutory goals of ERISA, encouraging the continuation and maintenance of voluntary private pension plans for the benefit of their participants. Pension Ben. Guaranty Corp. v. LTV Corp., 110 S.Ct. 2668, 2677 (1990).

ERISA provides that if a conflict should arise with other federal policies, that "nothing in this subchapter shall be construed to alter, amend, modify, invalidate, impair or supersede any law of the United States." The Bankruptcy Court properly credited PBGC's ability to determine the value of the future liabilities of the plan according to its administrative procedures. PBGC's calculation of future liabilities will then be used by the Bankruptcy Court in order to set the present value of PBGC's claims. There has been no compelling information adduced by PBGC supporting the subordination of the Bankruptcy Code to the terms of ERISA.

In order for a debtor-in-possession to continue in business, the Bankruptcy Code allows certain claims and expenses first priority as "actual, necessary costs and expenses of preserving the estate, including wages, salaries, or commissions for services rendered after the commencement of the case." Although PBGC asserts that a number of its claims are entitled to such administrative priority, the Bankruptcy Court suggested that, except to a very limited extent, PBGC's claims are not entitled to administrative priority. I agree.

There is a clear policy favoring ratable distribution among similar claimants. Consequently, priority status is rarely allowed. That which constitutes a claim, however, is broadly construed. Under the Bankruptcy Code, a claim is defined as any "right to payment, whether or not such right is reduced to judgment, liquidated, unliquidated, fixed, contingent, matured, unmatured, disputed, undisputed, legal equitable, secured, or unsecured." PBGC and the DOL have stated claims here. The burden of establishing entitlement to priority, however, rests with the claimant and should only be granted under extraordinary circumstances.

In order to allow the debtor to start anew, a claim is deemed to exist "when the acts giving rise to the alleged liability were performed." For priority status, the claimant must show that the claim arose post-petition.

In this case, PBGC argues that its statutory obligations under the plan at bar were triggered by post-petition termination, thus according its obligations post-petition priority status.  I disagree.  PBGC's claims are pre-petition contingent claims because the labor giving rise to the pension obligations was performed pre-petition.  The contingent right to payment arose only when the Republic Retirement Plan was terminated.  There being nothing adduced here compelling me to find that these claims are post-petition, neither the DOL nor PBGC are entitled priority status of their claims.

Neither are PBGC's pre-petition claims entitled to administrative status on the alternative theory of providing "actual and necessary" expenses of preserving the estate.  LTV did not induce retirees to provide post-petition services by promising pension benefits.  Only those employees who provided post-petition services to LTV could benefit the company post-petition.  Thus, only that portion of pension liabilities arising from post-petition labor of employees would be entitled to administrative priority as "actual and necessary" expenses of preserving the estate.

\* \* \*

The Bankruptcy Code allows as a priority an "unsecured claim for contributions to an employee benefit arising from services rendered within 180 days before the date of the filing of the petition \* \* \*."  The statute expressly does not apply to services rendered prior to the 180 day period before filing for bankruptcy.  Therefore any claims by PBGC for services rendered prior to that period must be treated as general unsecured claims.

The extent to which a claim may be accorded priority if it falls within the 180 day period is further limited.  Pursuant to § 507(a)(4) of the Bankruptcy Code, the maximum that PBGC may recover on behalf of a terminated plan is $2,000 multiplied by the number of employees covered by the plan.

At the direction of the Bankruptcy Court, LTV has made payments in the form of "fringe benefits" such as life, health, and disability insurance, as provided under §§ 507(a)(3) and (a)(4).  As PBGC concedes, the aggregate amount paid by LTV to the pension plan participants under § 507(a)(3) reduces the amount that PBGC may recover under § 507(a)(4).  Therefore, PBGC's claims entitled to § 507(a)(4) status must be reduced by the amount of the claims paid to the employees directly.  A determination of the amount of allowable priority is purely a question of fact which need not be determined or reviewed at this juncture.

\* \* \*

For the foregoing reasons the Report and Recommendation of the Bankruptcy Court is adopted except insofar as noted herein.

NOTES

1.  This opinion was "vacated and withdrawn" when the PBGC and LTV negotiated a settlement agreement, 1993 WL 388809 (S.D.N.Y. June 16, 1993).

**2.** The opposite case from the dismissed employee struggling for severance pay is the executive whose board of directors awards a "golden parachute," an extremely generous cash or stock payment usually triggered by the takeover of the firm by hostile interests. Critics say that golden parachutes waste stockholder assets by giving executives more compensation than they deserve. The allegation is that boards award such contracts in an effort to deter raids by outsiders seeking control of the company. For information about how widespread golden parachutes have become, and analysis of the legal questions they raise, see Note, Golden Parachutes: Executive Employment Contracts, 40 Wash. & Lee L.Rev. 1117 (1983).

---

## B. PLANT CLOSINGS

## Local 1330, United Steel Workers of America v. United States Steel Corp.

631 F.2d 1264 (6th Cir.1980).

■ EDWARDS, CHIEF JUDGE.

This appeal represents a cry for help from steelworkers and townspeople in the City of Youngstown, Ohio who are distressed by the prospective impact upon their lives and their city of the closing of two large steel mills. These two mills were built and have been operated by the United States Steel Corporation since the turn of the century. The Ohio Works began producing in 1901; the McDonald Works in 1918. The District Court which heard this cause of action found that as of the notice of closing, the two plants employed 3,500 employees.

The leading plaintiffs are two labor organizations, Locals 1330 and 1307 of the United Steel Workers of America. This union has had a collective bargaining contract with the United States Steel Corporation for many years. These local unions represent production and maintenance employees at the Ohio and McDonald Works, respectively.

In the background of this litigation is the obsolescence of the two plants concerned, occasioned both by the age of the facilities and machinery involved and by the changes in technology and marketing in steelmaking in the years intervening since the early nineteen hundreds.

For all of the years United States Steel has been operating in Youngstown, it has been a dominant factor in the lives of its thousands of employees and their families, and in the life of the city itself. The contemplated abrupt departure of United States Steel from Youngstown will, of course, have direct impact on 3,500 workers and their families. It will doubtless mean a devastating blow to them, to the business community and to the City of Youngstown itself. While we cannot read the future of Youngstown from this record, what the record does indicate clearly is that we deal with an economic tragedy of major proportion to Youngstown and

Ohio's Mahoning Valley.   As the District Judge who heard this case put the matter:

> Everything that has happened in the Mahoning Valley has been happening for many years because of steel.   Schools have been built, roads have been built.   Expansion that has taken place is because of steel.   And to accommodate that industry, lives and destinies of the inhabitants of that community were based and planned on the basis of that institution: Steel.

In the face of this tragedy, the steel worker local unions, the Congressman from this district, and the Attorney General of Ohio have sued United States Steel Corporation, asking the federal courts to order the United States Steel Corporation to keep the two plants at issue in operation. Alternatively, if they could not legally prevail on that issue, they have sought intervention of the courts by injunction to require the United States Steel Corporation to sell the two plants to the plaintiffs under an as yet tentative plan of purchase and operation by a community corporation and to restrain the piecemeal sale or dismantling of the plants until such a proposal could be brought to fruition.

Defendant United States Steel Corporation answered plaintiffs' complaints, claiming that the plants were unprofitable and could not be made otherwise due to obsolescence and change in technology, markets, and transportation.   The company also asserts an absolute right to make a business decision to discharge its former employees and abandon Youngstown.   It states that there is no law in either the State of Ohio or the United States of America which provides either legal or equitable remedy for plaintiffs.

The District Judge, after originally restraining the corporation from ceasing operations as it had announced it would, and after advancing the case for prompt hearing, entered a formal opinion holding that the plants had become unprofitable and denying all relief.   We believe the dispositive paragraphs of a lengthy opinion entered by the District Judge are the following:

> This Court has spent many hours searching for a way to cut to the heart of the economic reality—that obsolescence and market forces demand the close of the Mahoning Valley plants, and yet the lives of 3500 workers and their families and the supporting Youngstown community cannot be dismissed as inconsequential.   United States Steel should not be permitted to leave the Youngstown area devastated after drawing from the lifeblood of the community for so many years.
>
> Unfortunately, the mechanism to reach this ideal settlement, to recognize this new property right, is not now in existence in the code of laws of our nation.

\* \* \*

This Court is mindful of the efforts taken by the workers to increase productivity, and has applauded these efforts in the preceding paragraphs. In view of the fact, however, that this Court has found that no contract or enforceable promise was entered into by the company and that, additionally, there is clear evidence to support the company's decision that the plants were not profitable, the various acts of forebearance taken by the plaintiffs do not give them the basis for relief against defendant.

Plaintiffs-appellants claim that certain of the District Judge's findings of fact are clearly erroneous, that he has misconstrued federal and state contract law, and that he failed to grant a hearing on their antitrust claims.

With this introduction, we turn to the legal issues presented by this appeal.

Plaintiffs assert jurisdiction in the federal courts, pursuant to Section 301 of the National Labor Relations Act, as amended, 29 U.S.C. § 185 (1976). They also assert diversity jurisdiction, pursuant to 28 U.S.C. § 1332 (1976). By so doing they claim that this action is brought under the fundamental labor law of the country and under the laws of Ohio which federal courts follow when a cause of action between citizens of one state is brought against citizens of another state.

The primary issue in this case is a claim on the part of the steel worker plaintiffs that United States Steel made proposals to the plaintiffs and/or the membership of the plaintiffs to the general effect that if the workers at the two steel plants concerned put forth their best efforts in terms of productivity and thereby rendered the two plants "profitable," the plants would then not be closed. It is clear that this claimed contract does not rest upon any formal written document, either authorized or signed by the parties to this lawsuit.

Plaintiffs themselves recognize that they cannot rely upon any formal contract law. Nonetheless, in this section we shall discuss relationships between the parties which plaintiffs have not raised in order to place their issues in proper context.

As noted above, the steelworkers have a formal collective bargaining contract with the U.S. Steel Corporation. In this record there is no indication that there ever was any formal negotiation or amendment of that contract in relation to the issues of this case.

* * *

The collective bargaining agreement applicable in this period also contains three sections which management asserts bear directly upon its claim of unilateral right to close any plant. These provisions are two rather general paragraphs on page 15 of the contract entitled "Management" which recite as follows:

### SECTION 3—MANAGEMENT

The Company retains the exclusive rights to manage the business and plants and to direct the working forces. The Company, in the exercise of its rights, shall observe the provisions of this Agreement.

The rights to manage the business and plants and to direct the working forces include the right to hire, suspend or discharge for proper cause, or transfer and the right to relieve employees from duty because of lack of work or for other legitimate reasons.

More directly applicable to the present case is Section 16 entitled "Severance Allowance." This section provides in detail for severance allowances in terms of weeks of pay of employees with more than three years seniority, and concludes with the sentence which says, "Acceptance of severance allowance shall terminate employment and continuous service for all purposes under this Agreement."

\* \* \*

We are unable to construe any claims set forth in the instant litigation as being based upon any language contained in this collective bargaining agreement. Indeed, plaintiffs make no claim in this case that the United States Steel Corporation has violated the provisions of this section (or any section) of the collective bargaining agreement.

\* \* \*

Appellants' principal argument in this appeal is, however, that the District Court should have found a contract based upon the equitable doctrine of promissory estoppel, which contract is enforceable in the federal courts under § 301 of the National Labor Relations Act. The doctrine of promissory estoppel recognizes the possibility of the formation of a contract by action or forbearance on the part of a second party, based upon a promise made by the first party under circumstances where the actions or forbearance of the second party should reasonably have been expected to produce the detrimental results to the second party which they did produce.

\* \* \*

Thus, appellants' contract claim depends essentially upon oral statements and newspaper releases concerning the efforts of the company to secure increased productivity by enlisting the help of the workers of the plant and upon the employee responses thereto. The representations as set forth in the steelworkers' complaint include many oral statements made over the "hotline" employed by management in the plants to advise U.S. Steel employees of company policy.

\* \* \*

[The court quoted at length from statements by U.S. Steel executives. It then described examples of individual worker reliance on the company's statements.]

As we read this lengthy record, and as the District Judge read it, it does not contain any factual dispute over the allegations as to company statements or the responsive actions of steelworkers in relation thereto. It is beyond argument that the local management of U.S. Steel's Youngstown plants engaged in a major campaign to enlist employee participation in an all-out effort to make these two plants profitable in order to prevent their being closed. It is equally obvious that the employees responded wholeheartedly.

The District Judge, however, rejected the promissory estoppel contract theory on three grounds. The first ground was that none of the statements made by officers and employees of the company constituted a definite promise to continue operation of the plants if they did become profitable. The second ground was that the statements relied upon by plaintiffs were made by employees and public relations officers of the company and not by company officers. The third ground was a finding of fact that "The condition precedent of the alleged contract and promise—profitability of the Youngstown facilities—was never fulfilled, and the actions in contract and for detrimental reliance cannot be found for plaintiffs."

The District Judge's fundamental disposition of plaintiffs-appellants' contract claims is stated in this finding of fact:

> [T]here is clear evidence to support the company's decision that the plants were not profitable, the various acts of forebearance taken by the plaintiffs do not give them the basis for relief against defendant.

Our examination of this record offers no ground for our holding that this finding of fact is "clearly erroneous."

\* \* \*

We believe that this record demonstrates without significant dispute that the profitability issue in the case depends in large part upon definition. The plaintiffs wish to employ the direct costs of operating the two plants, compared to the total selling price of their products. The difference, they contend, is "profit." This formula would eliminate such charges as corporate purchasing and sales expense allocable to the Youngstown plants, and allocable corporate management expenses including, but not limited to marketing, engineering, auditing, accounting, advertising. Obviously, any multiplant corporation could quickly go bankrupt if such a definition of profit was employed generally and over any period of time.

Plaintiffs-appellants point out, however, that this version of Youngstown profitability was employed by the Youngstown management in setting a goal for its employees and in statements which described achieving that goal. The standard of Restatement (Second) of Contracts § 90, upon which plaintiffs-appellants rely, however, is one of reasonable expectability of the "promise" detrimentally relied upon. The District Judge did not find, nor can we, that reliance upon a promise to keep these plants open on the basis of coverage of plant fixed costs was within reasonable expectability. We cannot hold that the District Judge erred legally or was "clearly erroneous" in his fact finding when he held that the "promise" to keep the plants open had to be read in the context of normal corporate profit accounting and that profitability had not been achieved.

Complete analysis of plaintiffs-appellants' promissory estoppel claims against the background of the collective bargaining agreement and Section 301 of the National Labor Relations Act would be a formidable task. We decline to undertake it, however, since even if we decided those issues favorably to plaintiffs, we would nonetheless be forced to decide the contract claim adversely to them because of failure to prove profitability.

### THE COMMUNITY PROPERTY CLAIM

At a pretrial hearing of this case on February 28, 1980, the District Judge made a statement at some length about the relationship between the parties to this case and the public interest involved therein. He said:

> Everything that has happened in the Mahoning Valley has been happening for many years because of steel. Schools have been built, roads have been built. Expansion that has taken place is because of steel. And to accommodate that industry, lives and destinies of the inhabitants of that community were based and planned on the basis of that institution: Steel.
>
> * * *
>
> We are talking about an institution, a large corporate institution that is virtually the reason for the existence of that segment of this nation [Youngstown]. Without it, that segment of this nation perhaps suffers, instantly and severely. Whether it becomes a ghost town or not, I don't know. I am not aware of its capability for adapting.
>
> * * *
>
> But what has happened over the years between U.S. Steel, Youngstown and the inhabitants? Hasn't something come out of that relationship, something that out of which—not reaching for a case on property law or a series of cases but looking at the law as a whole, the Constitution, the whole body of law, not only contract law, but tort, corporations, agency, negotiable instruments—taking a look at the whole body of American law and then sitting back and reflecting on what it seeks to do, and that is to adjust human relationships in keeping with the whole spirit and foundation of the American system of law, to preserve property rights.
>
> * * *
>
> It would seem to me that when we take a look at the whole body of American law and the principles we attempt to come out with—and although a legislature has not pronounced any laws with respect to such a property right, that is not to suggest that there will not be a need for such a law in the future dealing with similar situations—*it seems to me that a property right has arisen from this lengthy, long-established relationship between United States Steel, the steel industry as an institution, the community in Youngstown, the people in Mahoning County and the Mahoning*

*Valley in having given and devoted their lives to this industry.*
Perhaps not a property right to the extent that can be remedied by
compelling U.S. Steel to remain in Youngstown. But *I think the
law can recognize the property right to the extent that U.S. Steel
cannot leave that Mahoning Valley and the Youngstown area in a
state of waste, that it cannot completely abandon its obligation to
that community, because certain vested rights have arisen out of
this long relationship and institution.*

Subsequently thereto, steelworkers' complaint was amended, realleging
the first cause of action, paragraphs 1–49, claiming pendent jurisdiction
over claims arising out of the laws of the State of Ohio and asserting as
follows:

52. A property right has arisen from the long-established
relation between the community of the 19th Congressional District
and Plaintiffs, on the one hand, and Defendant on the other hand,
which this Court can enforce.

53. This right, in the nature of an easement, requires that
Defendant:

a. Assist in the preservation of the institution of steel in
that community;

b. Figure into its cost of withdrawing and closing the
Ohio and McDonald Works the cost of rehabilitating the
community and the workers;

c. Be restrained from leaving the Mahoning Valley in a
state of waste and from abandoning its obligation to that
community.

This court has examined these allegations with care and with great
sympathy for the community interest reflected therein. Our problem in
dealing with plaintiffs' fourth cause of action is one of authority. Neither
in brief nor oral argument have plaintiffs pointed to any constitutional
provision contained in either the Constitution of the United States or the
Constitution of the State of Ohio, nor any law enacted by the United States
Congress or the Legislature of Ohio, nor any case decided by the courts of
either of these jurisdictions which would convey authority to this court to
require the United States Steel Corporation to continue operations in
Youngstown which its officers and Board of Directors had decided to
discontinue on the basis of unprofitability.

This court has in fact dealt with this specific issue in Charland v.
Norge Division, Borg-Warner Corp., 407 F.2d 1062 (6th Cir.), cert. denied,
395 U.S. 927.

\* \* \*

This court's response to Charland's claims bears repetition here:

\* \* \*

The claim presented by this appellant brings sharply into focus such problems as unemployment crises, the mobility of capital, technological change and the right of an industrial owner to go out of business.   Thus far federal law has sought to protect the human values to which appellant calls our attention by means of such legislation as unemployment compensation.   These statutes afford limited financial protection to the individual worker, but they assume his loss of employment.

Whatever the future may bring, neither by statute nor by court decision has appellant's claimed property right been recognized to date in this country.

\* \* \*

In the view of this court, formulation of public policy on the great issues involved in plant closings and removals is clearly the responsibility of the legislatures of the states or of the Congress of the United States.

NOTES

**1.**   The court found insufficient evidence that U.S. Steel's statements encouraged justifiable reliance by workers.   Do you know other cases, from Chapter 11 or from your Contracts course, that you could cite in opposition to this conclusion?   The tone of the court's opinion suggests a view that "something should be done" but Congress or the state legislature should do it.   What legislation would you support?   How much help would these workers have gotten if the Worker Adjustment and Retraining Notification Act, infra, had been law?   Would worker ownership be a desirable alternative to the plant closing?   On that, see pp. 1091–1095 infra.

**2.**   In Charter Township of Ypsilanti v. General Motors, 8 Indiv.Empl.Rts.Cases (BMA) 385 (Mich.Cir.Ct.1993), a Michigan Circuit Court judge enjoined General Motors from transferring production of cars from a plant in Ypsilanti to a plant in Arlington, Texas.   The judge distinguished Local 1330 and another federal case because of the specific representations made by General Motors when it sought a tax abatement, and because General Motors stipulated that economic necessity was not a defense.

The judge concluded:

[T]his Court, perhaps unlike the judges there, simply finds that the failure to act in this case would result in a terrible injustice and that the doctrine of promissory estoppel should be applied. Each judge who dons this robe assumes the awesome, and lonely responsibility to make decisions about justice, and injustice, which will dramatically affect the way people are forced to live their lives. Every such decision must be the judge's own and it must be made honestly and in good conscience \* \* \*.   Perhaps another judge in another court would not feel moved by that injustice and would labor to find a legal rationalization to allow such conduct.   But in

> this Court it is my responsibility to make that decision.  My
> conscience will not allow this injustice to happen.

The decision was later reversed because the trial court's finding of a
promise to maintain production in Ypsilanti was found to be clearly
erroneous.  Charter Township of Ypsilanti v. General Motors, 506 N.W.2d
556 (Mich.App.1993);  remanded, 509 N.W.2d 152 (Mich.1993).

**3.**  See Daniel A. Farber & John H. Matheson, Beyond Promissory Estoppel:  Contract Law and the "Invisible Handshake," 52 U.Chi.L.Rev. 903,
929 (1985):

> A revised rule of promissory obligation should accept the
> fundamental fact that commitments are often made to promote
> economic activity and obtain economic benefits without any specif-
> ic bargained-for exchange.  Promisors expect various benefits to
> flow from their promise-making.  A rule that gives force to this
> expectation simply reinforces the traditional free-will basis of
> promissory liability, albeit in an expanded context of relational and
> institutional interdependence.

> Our proposed rule is simply that commitments made in fur-
> therance of economic activity should be enforced.  * * *  The
> proposed rule is a major departure from traditional contract law in
> that it requires neither satisfaction of traditional notions of consid-
> eration nor the specific showing of detriment associated with
> promissory estoppel. * * *

> According to the approach set forth by our proposed rule,
> *Local 1330* was wrongly decided.  The employees and the company
> had, over the years, developed the kind of interdependent relation-
> ship that promotes action on the basis of an "invisible hand-
> shake."  U.S. Steel must be understood to have sought economic
> benefits by leading employees to increase their efforts.  A traumat-
> ic time such as that surrounding a possible plant closing creates
> both a need to cooperate to salvage the operations and an atmo-
> sphere of distrust.  In such a setting, the need to reinforce trust
> with legal sanctions is especially strong. * * *

> The representations of profitability were unequivocal and
> were calculated to invoke the workers' trust.  Nonetheless, both
> the district and appellate courts found that the employees should
> not have relied on these representations. * * *

> We find this result unconscionable.  Whatever the prevailing
> definition of "profit" in corporate accounting, a continuous and
> consistent pattern of declaring the plants profitable, commending
> the employees for their achievements, and urging them forward
> should have tipped the scales against defendant U.S. Steel on this
> issue.  There can be little doubt from the steady stream of
> communications about the achievement of profitability that em-
> ployees did as they were expected to do when they relied on the
> representations of profitability.

The fact that the *Local 1330* courts placed such emphasis on the meaning of one term, "profitability," may well underscore the need for a rule which * * * examines the full context in which promises are made with a view to their social effects.   * * * The company had a strong community base and a stable work force that was willing to engage in the kind of long-term planning and commitment which is economically beneficial and perhaps even essential to a major industry. * * *

In the long run, allowing breach of the employer's promise in this situation injures society as a whole.  Employees will be less likely to put forth the extra effort to save a plant if employers can violate their promises by semantic quibbles.  In breaching its understanding with its employees, U.S. Steel polluted the pool of trust from which it had drawn.  The pool is large and individual breaches of trust may be small, but the effect of pollution is cumulative.  Not only justice to the employees, but also society's interest in preserving the integrity of a vital social resource, require enforcement of the employer's promise in this situation.

Do you agree?  What are the problems with the proposed rule?  Does it act as an incentive for the company to say nothing to induce greater worker productivity?  Does this expansive notion of reliance devalue the importance of positive reinforcement?  Will the company say "If you don't work harder, we'll close," rather than "If you work harder we'll stay open"?  Is this an accurate statement of the company's options?

What about the proprietary interests of workers?  Do the authors imply that inviolable rights accrue with each promise made?  Are these rights contractual or proprietary?  Does it make a difference in terms of the courts' likely willingness to grant relief?

**4.**  Sidney Degan sued Ford Motor Company and the UAW, alleging breach of an oral agreement to pay special early-retirement benefits.  The court of appeals held that common-law contract claims concerning pensions are preempted by ERISA, and that under ERISA only the written plan documents have legal force.  "Oral agreements would undermine Congress's goal of fashioning a comprehensive system of federal law designed to strengthen and protect the interests of employers in their expected retirement benefits."  Thus, there is no legal forum for Degan's "sympathetic, estoppel-based argument."  Degan v. Ford Motor Co., 869 F.2d 889 (5th Cir.1989).

**5.**  Singer Company took millions in union "give-backs" and agreed in return to spend $2 million to restructure its Elizabeth, N.J., sewing machine factory.  Eight months later, Singer announced plans to shut the plant.  The court found no promise by Singer to "surrender * * * the prerogative of any company to go out of business when it so desires."  Therefore, it refused to enter an injunction preventing closure of the plant.  But it found that Singer breached "a clearcut obligation both to spend $2 million to restructure the plant and to use its best efforts to * * * maintain the facility * * *."  It said money damages would be the greater of the value of the "give-backs" or the promised $2 million. Singer had argued that it owed no damages because decreased demand for sewing machines would have forced closing of the plant even if the company had spent the $2 million, so the failure to spend it had no effect on the workers' welfare. The court did not reach (but expressed "serious doubts" about) claims made by residents of the Elizabeth community as "third-party beneficiaries of the collective bargaining agreement." Local 461, IUERM v. Singer Co., 540 F.Supp. 442 (D.N.J.1982).

## NOTE ON FEDERAL PLANT-CLOSING LAW

In 1988, Congress enacted the first federal statute restricting employer authority to shut factories. The Worker Adjustment and Retraining Notification Act (WARN), 29 U.S.C. §§ 2101–2109, applies to businesses that employ at least 100 workers. A "plant closing" is defined as a shutdown at a single site resulting in loss of work for at least 50 employees. Employers cannot engage in such a plant closing without giving 60 days notice to a union (if there is one), to each worker (if there is no union), and to state and local government officials. Workers laid off without appropriate notice are entitled to back pay and any fringe benefits they may have lost.

## Carpenters District Council of New Orleans v. Dillard Department Stores, Inc.

15 F.3d 1275 (5th Cir.1994), cert. denied, 513 U.S. 1126 (1995).

■ E. GRADY JOLLY, CIRCUIT JUDGE:

For the first time, this court is called upon to address the Worker Adjustment and Retraining Notification Act ("WARN Act"), 29 U.S.C. § 2101 et seq. (Supp.1993). It requires some employers—generally those who are curtailing or closing an operation—to provide sixty days notice to those employees who will be laid off or whose hours will be substantially reduced. In 1989, D.H. Holmes Co., Ltd. merged with Dillard Department Stores, Inc., resulting in the layoff of a large number of people—mostly former Holmes employees—whose job functions had become redundant. These former employees sued Dillard, alleging that in the course of the ongoing merger efforts, Holmes and Dillard had failed to provide adequate notice of the pending terminations.

* * * On March 3 and 6, 1988, the (merger) agreement was approved by the respective boards of directors of both Dillard and Holmes.... One of the conditions of the agreement was that no less than eighty percent of Holmes's stockholders must approve the merger.... Further yet, the Securities and Exchange Commission ("SEC") required that such registration statements must be preapproved by the SEC before issuance.... [Neither] Holmes nor Dillard could anticipate precisely when the SEC would approve the registration statement. Approximately one month after the statement was filed, the SEC approved the registration statement.

Having received SEC approval, Holmes then scheduled a stockholders' meeting for May 9, 1989.

On April 19, 1989, at the direction of Dillard's personnel, Holmes notified its employees assigned to the corporate planning division and the warehouse facilities that they would be terminated as of May 9 if Holmes's stockholders approved the proposed merger with Dillard. Certain "transitional" employees at the warehouse facilities and the corporate offices received notification between April 21 and 28, informing them that they would be laid off sometime between May 9 and July 1. Finally, on May 12, employees in the Canal Street retail store were notified that they would be laid off between June 10 and July 8.

Because it was clear that the WARN Act sixty-day notice requirement would not be met with respect to certain employees, Dillard made efforts to comply with WARN's damages provision. First, Dillard determined which employees were entitled to payments under the WARN Act, and as to those employees, the amount owed. Under Dillard's interpretation of the statute, part-time employees were not entitled to the notice, and, as such, they were not entitled to any damages in lieu of notice. Dillard further determined that the sixty-day penalty period in 29 U.S.C. § 2104(a)(1)(A) referred to the number of work days within that period rather than the number of actual calendar days. This interpretation meant that each full-time employee who had not received the full sixty-day notice would be entitled to payment for those days the employee would have worked had the full sixty-day notice been given. Relying on the provisions of § 2104(a)(2) of the Act, Dillard also concluded that it could deduct from this amount any severance pay or vacation pay that Dillard owed the employee.

After the two companies merged, and as a direct result of the merger, numerous employees were involuntarily terminated between May 8 and August 9, 1989. These former employees sued a number of defendants, arguing that Dillard violated the WARN Act when it failed to provide the "affected employees" the required sixty-day notice of termination. In addition, the employees argued that Dillard failed to pay them the proper amount of damages in lieu of notice.

* * * Ultimately, the court granted the employees' motion for partial summary judgment, stating that Dillard violated the WARN Act.

Dillard argues that the district court erred in holding that Dillard violated the WARN Act ... In cross-appeal, the former employees * * * contend that the district court mistakenly determined that certain employees—the Bienville employees—were not "affected employees" as defined by the statute, and, as a result, those employees were erroneously denied benefits under the Act * * *

Although Dillard and Holmes acknowledge that certain affected employees did not receive the full sixty days notice of termination, they argue that they were excused from the notice requirements because they fell within one of the two statutory exemptions. Under the facts of this case,

Dillard and Holmes can escape WARN Act liability only if either the "faltering company" exception or the "unforeseen business circumstances" exception applies * * *

To fall within the "faltering company" exemption, an employer must meet four requirements. The Act states that

> an employer may order the shutdown of single site of employment before the conclusion of the 60–day period if as of the time that notice would have been required the employer was actively seeking capital or business which, if obtained, would have enabled the employer to avoid or postpone the shutdown and the employer reasonably and in good faith believed that the giving the notice required would have precluded the employer from obtaining the needed capital or business.

29 U.S.C. § 2102(b)(1) (Supp.1993). This exception applies only when a layoff is caused by the employer's failure to obtain sufficient capital. In this case, however, there is no causal connection between Holmes's search for capital and the ultimate reduction in work force. Although it is true that at the time notice should have been provided Holmes was actively searching for a new line of credit, the actual cause of the mass layoff was not a failure to obtain an adequate line of credit; instead, the cause of the layoff was the merger between Holmes and Dillard. Because there was no causal relationship between Holmes's search for additional capital and the reduction in its work force, the "faltering company" exception does not apply to exempt it from liability for failing to give notice for the ultimate layoff, which was in fact caused by the merger.

Next, Dillard contends that its failure to provide the full sixty days notice was excused under the "unforeseen business circumstances" exemption. This exemption provides that "[a]n employer may order a plant closing or mass layoff before the conclusion of the 60–day period if the closing or mass layoff is caused by business circumstances that were not reasonably foreseeable as of the time that notice would have been required." According to the proposed rules, an unforeseeable circumstance is "caused by some sudden and unexpected action or condition outside the employer's control." [9] As with the "faltering company" exception, this exception to the general rule is to be narrowly construed.

Dillard argues that there was some uncertainty as to when, or even if, the SEC would approve the registration statement, and as to whether Holmes's stockholders would approve the merger. Therefore, it asserts, the resulting merger was an "unforeseen business circumstance." We cannot agree. For several months prior to March 9—the date notice should have been given for the May 9 layoff—Dillard and Holmes had been intensely negotiating an agreement that would allow the two companies to merge. On March 6, three days before notice should have been given, a

---

**9.** Examples provided by the regulations include "a principal client's sudden and unexpected termination of a major contract with the employer, a strike at a major supplier of the employer, and an unanticipated and dramatic major economic downturn."

tentative agreement was reached. Both companies then sought SEC approval, and both companies actively promoted the merger. It is difficult to see how two companies that were busy promoting their merger can now argue that the resulting merger was unforeseeable. The fact that there were some uncertainties in the merger process does not make the resulting merger unforeseeable. We conclude that the merger was in fact foreseeable. Consequently, we hold that neither the merger itself nor any of the individual steps taken to effect the merger constitute "unforeseen business circumstances." Because Dillard and Holmes are unable to satisfy the requirements of either exception under the WARN Act, sixty days notice of termination was required.

The next issue concerns whether the district court erred by calculating damages on the basis of calendar days instead of work days. Dillard contends that the district court improperly included in the damage award payment for non-work days i.e., Saturdays, Sundays, and holidays. The district court held that "the time period for which penalty payments would be due are 60 individual work days and not the number of work weeks contained within a 60 day period."

Section 2104 spells out in some detail the amount of damages an employer must pay if it does not provide its employees with adequate notice of a mass layoff or a plant closing. If an employer violates the notice provision, the employer must pay the aggrieved employee "back pay for each day of the violation [period]." On one hand, the term "back pay" connotes a remedy that would require the payment of a sum such that the employees would be put in the same position they would have been had the violation never occurred. On the other hand, "each day of the violation" appears to require payment of "back pay" damages for each calendar day within the violation period, which would put the employees in a significantly better position than they would have enjoyed had the employer provided the full sixty-day notice.

Interpreting WARN's damage provision as requiring payment for work days only is well supported by the language of the section. First, the term "back pay" commonly means pay, i.e., wages, benefits, etc., that an employee would have earned, or to which she would have otherwise been entitled, if the event that affected such job related compensation had not occurred. Indeed, the Supreme Court has said that "back pay" requires "payment ... of a sum equal to what [the employees] normally would have earned" had the violation never occurred.... Further, the Supreme Court has explained that "back pay" suggests a remedy such that the damaged employee is restored "as nearly as possible, to that which would have [been] obtained but for the [violation]." If aggrieved employees are paid only for days they ordinarily would have worked during the sixty-day notice period, then those employees are placed in the position they would have occupied had the violation never occurred.

Second, the legislative history makes it clear that Congress intended the "back pay" language in WARN to connote the traditional back pay remedy as discussed in Phelps Dodge Corp. v. NLRB (damages "of a sum equal to what [the employees] normally would have earned" had the violation never occurred) * * *

Damages calculated by measuring the wages the employee would have received had the employee continued working requires a calculation using the number of work days in the violation period rather than the number of calendar days. To use calendar days would provide an employee with damages in excess of what he or she would have received had the plant remained open, or had the layoff been deferred until the conclusion of the notice period.

Finally, unlike the "calendar-day" approach, * * * the "work-day" interpretation of WARN's damages provision does not lead to anomalous results. * * * In United Steelworkers, defendant North Star Steel Co. provided the court with a hypothetical situation which, they argued, demonstrated the inequities inherent in the "calendar-day" approach. The Third Circuit, however, dismissed North Star's argument, but we find North Star's hypothetical to be a good example of why the "calendar-day" approach cannot be the approach Congress intended. In this hypothetical situation, an employer violates the WARN Act by terminating employees without providing any advance notice. Thus, the violation period contains sixty days. Employee "A" is a full-time employee who works a regular eight-hour shift each weekday. However, employee "B" is a part-time employee who works just one ten-hour shift each Saturday. Under the Third Circuit's calendar-day approach, employee "A" would receive 480 hours pay in lieu of notice (eight hours per day times sixty days), while part-time employee "B" would receive 600 hours pay (ten hours per day times sixty days). As North Star Steel argued, it would be anomalous for the one-day-per-week part-time employee to receive 120 hours pay over and above that paid to the five-days-per-week full-time employee. Under this calendar-day system, not only is the employer severely penalized for choosing to pay damages in lieu of notice, but the full-time employee is treated inequitably, and the part-time employee gets a windfall.[16] Under the "workday" approach, however, such bizarre results do not occur. Employee "A" is paid for the number of work days Employee "A" would have worked within the sixty-day period, which would work out approximately to eight hours per day times five days per week times eight weeks. Employee "B", on the other hand, would receive payment in lieu of notice that would reflect the employee's part-time status, i.e., approximately ten hours per week times eight weeks. This is a plain-sense result in a day and time when it is common to find employees with work schedules that vary from the traditional eight-hour day, forty-hour work week. It is for the forego-

---

**16.** The number of examples demonstrating the inequitable effects of the "calendar-day" approach are seemingly never ending. For example, a similarly inequitable result is achieved if one full-time hourly-wage employee works eight hours per day, five days per week, while another full-time hourly-wage employee works ten hours per day but only four days per week. Under the calendar day approach, the first employee would be entitled to 480 hours worth of pay over a sixty-day violation period while the second employee would be entitled to 600 hours of pay, notwithstanding that each was paid the same wages, and worked the same number of hours per week.

ing reasons that we now hold that damages in lieu of the WARN Act notice are to be calculated using on the number of work days within the violation period.

Dillard argues that the district court abused its discretion by not reducing its liability because Dillard acted in good faith and reasonably believed that it had complied with the Act. Any assessment of an employer's good faith or grounds for its belief in the legal propriety of his conduct is necessarily a finding of fact, to be disturbed on appeal only if clearly erroneous.

The WARN Act states that

[i]f an employer which has violated this chapter proves to the satisfaction of the court that the act or omission that violated [the WARN Act] was in good faith and that the employer had reasonable grounds for believing that the act or omission was not a violation of this chapter the court may, in its discretion, reduce the amount of the liability or penalty provided for [in the Act].

In this case, after the damages issues were tried to the court, the district court held that no good faith reduction of damages was warranted. First, the court found that Dillard did not subjectively believe that it complied with the notice requirements of the Act. The court noted that there was evidence that at the time the WARN Act requirements were discussed with Dillard's legal advisors, Dillard knew that it was well within the sixty-day notice period based on the projected date of the layoffs, and Dillard conceded that it was not relying on the two exceptions to establish its qualification for a reduction in damages based on its good faith. Moreover, throughout the process of calculating the WARN Act damages, when faced with any arguable point of law, Dillard consistently resolved any questionable issue in its favor. Dillard concluded, for example, that it could deduct from damages any vacation pay it already owed its employees, a conclusion that Dillard's own legal advisors characterized as "aggressive" or "on tenuous grounds." The district court concluded that at some point, Dillard's conclusions concerning the calculation of damages become objectively unreasonable, and as such, Dillard was not entitled to a "good faith" reduction in damages. Although we are mindful that Dillard was caught in a difficult position with respect to the notification requirements, and although we recognize that Dillard made significant WARN payments to a significant number of employees, we cannot say that the district court's refusal to reduce damages is clearly erroneous.

### F.   The "Bienville" Employees

In its cross-appeal, the employees contend that the district court erred in determining that certain employees who were terminated on May 9 were not entitled to WARN notice. These employees made up part of Holmes's corporate division, although they were not based in the "regular" corporate office in the Canal Street site. Instead, because of space considerations, they were located some distance away from the Canal Street location in offices known as the "Bienville site." The district court held that the

Canal Street corporate division and the Bienville site did not comprise a "single site of employment" under the WARN Act. Further, the district court held that "there were insufficient numbers of employees assigned to [the Bienville site] to [bring the Bienville site itself] within the Act." As such, the district court held that those Bienville site employees were not entitled to notice of termination. The employees have appealed this decision, contending that the two offices constituted a "single site of employment" under the WARN Act.

\* \* \*

Under the WARN Act, notice of mass layoffs or plant closings is required if there is a sufficiently large "plant closing" or "mass layoff" at a single site of employment. Dillard argued, and the district court held, that Holmes's corporate division at the Canal Street location and the employees at the Bienville site were two separate and distinct sites of employment under WARN. Specifically, the court noted that the two sites were several miles apart, that the personnel assigned to the Bienville site—those employees who performed construction facilities management, energy management and store planning—performed functions different from the functions provided by the workers in the Canal Street corporate division. The court noted that although the Bienville site employees' payroll checks were issued from the Canal Street location, "this was an insufficient connection by itself to view the Bienville location and the Canal Street store as one site."

On appeal, the employees contend that the Bienville site and the Canal Street corporate division were a "single site of employment" because the job functions of the Bienville employees were closely integrated with the job functions of the Canal Street corporate division. A complete review of the underlying facts leads us to agree with the employees' contention.... In an effort to relieve overcrowding in th[e Canal Street] offices, certain divisions—including construction facilities management, energy management, and store planning—were relocated to the Bienville site. Once moved to the Bienville site, those employees continued to perform precisely the same company-wide functions they provided when housed in the Canal Street location. The Bienville site employees remained integrated with the Canal Street corporate division after the move. The Bienville site had no support staff, and the Bienville employees continued to rely upon the support staff at the corporate division office. In spite of the move to the Bienville site, the employees nevertheless considered themselves part of the corporate division, and Holmes continued to consider them corporate employees for payroll purposes. It is not irrelevant that the employees—precisely, like the Canal Street employees—were made redundant and lost their jobs directly because of the merger. These factors lead us to conclude that the Bienville site and the Canal Street corporate division were merely one site of employment that was separated because of space considerations. In our view, this situation may be classified as "an unusual organizational situation" under the DOL regulations. See 20 C.F.R. § 639.3(i)(4) (1988) (proposed regulations). These employees were entitled to the WARN Act notice of termination, and, consequently, Dillard is liable for any damages associated with providing inadequate notice.

NOTES AND QUESTIONS

**1.** In February 1993, the General Accounting Office released a report on the operation of WARN in eleven states during the first three years that it was in force. The report found that 70% of covered employers failed to given advance notice to employees before a mass layoff or plant closing and 54% failed to file advance notice with state officials as required by the Act.

The GAO Report found that the Act's numerous exceptions limited its effectiveness. In many cases, employers were able to avoid coverage by spreading layoffs across various work sites, by firing employees gradually over a period of months, or by firing 49 employees (one short of the statutory minimum).

The Report also found that enforcement under the Act was inadequate. In its current form, the Act is enforced through private actions by employees and public actions by local governments. However, available remedies are so limited that costly and time consuming federal cases are impractical for most employees. Moreover, local governments are reluctant to bring cases for fear of appearing anti-business. The GAO concluded that better enforcement would improve compliance with the Act and suggested that the Department of Labor should be given enforcement authority. See also Richard W. McHugh, Fair Warning or Foul? An Analysis of the Worker Adjustment Retraining and Notification (WARN) Act in Practice, 14 Berkeley J. Empl. & Lab. L. 1 (1993).

**2.** In Cruz v. Robert Abbey, Inc., 1990 WL 84349 (E.D.N.Y.1990), a lamp manufacturer employing mostly Hispanic immigrants, laid off more than 50 employees without notice and for an indefinite period of time. The employer then recalled several employees for weekly or bi-weekly periods before laying them off again. The employees filed an action for violation of the WARN Act's notice provisions. In court, the employer argued that "of the * * * employees enough were recalled to work at Abbey during the two 90 day periods so that 50 or more employees were not laid off for a full 90 days." The court apparently perceived the employer's actions as an attempt to evade the requirements of the WARN Act. Those actions were covered under section 2102(d), "an attempt by employer to evade numerical predicates to WARN notice requirement of section 2102[a][3] [mass layoff] negates separate and distinct layoff defense." The court found an issue of material fact whether the layoffs constituted a "mass layoff" or "plant closing" under the Act.

**3.** In Rifkin v. McDonnell Douglas Corp., 78 F.3d 1277 (8th Cir.1996), the defendant laid off 609 employees in a two-month period, none of whom received the WARN Act's required 60 days notice. The court ruled that in discounting for part-time employees, rehired employees, employees electing for early retirement, and the "single site" requirement, only 481 employees actually suffered employment loss. Thus, the WARN Act did not apply to this series of lay-offs.  How does this compare with the ruling in Cruz v. Robert Abbey, Inc., supra?

**4.**  Prior to enactment of the federal law, more than half the states had enacted "plant closing" laws.  In Fort Halifax Packing Co. v. Coyne, 482 U.S. 1 (1987), the Supreme Court decided by 5 to 4 vote that these laws were not preempted by ERISA.  Section 2105 of the new federal law explicitly permits state regulation of this subject.  .

**5.**  Massachusetts has enacted special protection for employees laid off after a "takeover" of the employer.  See Mass.Gen.Laws Ch. 149, § 183(b) (1989):  "Any employee * * * whose employment is terminated within twenty-four calendar months after the transfer of control of his employer is entitled to a one time lump sum payment * * * equal to the product of twice his weekly compensation multiplied by each completed year of service."

**6.**  A 1985 Connecticut law requires an employer relocating or closing a plant to continue group health insurance for 120 days.  Conn.Stat. § 31–51o(a).

**7.**  Atari, Inc. v. Carson, 212 Cal.Rptr. 773 (Cal.App.1985), discussed in Note, Advantages and Limitations of Current Employee Ownership Assistance Acts to Workers Facing a Plant Closure, 36 Hastings L.J. 93, 100 n. 53 (1984), was a class action brought by nonunion employees seeking damages for the harm caused to them when the employer did not notify them of a decision to relocate a plant.  The workers claimed breach of an implied contract and breach of an implied covenant of good faith and fair dealing.  There is a close connection between this cause of action and the right of the worker to protection against arbitrary dismissal considered in Chapter 11.  The case was eventually settled, with the employees receiving an amount equal to four weeks' wages.  Barbara Rhine, Business Closings and Their Effects on Employees—Adaptations of the Tort of Wrongful Discharge, 8 Indus.Rel.L.J. 362, 371–72 n. 50 (1986).

**8.**  Communities have recently been offering incentives in the form of tax concessions in order to keep existing and attract new businesses.  In a related development, cities have been bidding for new and existing professional sports teams by building stadium facilities to house them.  While these facilities are usually built at taxpayer expense, in theory the teams add jobs, wealth and prestige to the community in return.

---

## C.  EMPLOYEE OWNERSHIP

## Alan Hyde, In Defense of Employee Ownership
67 Chi.–Kent L.Rev. 159 (1991).

Our inquiry is into the economic success or failure of the business owned in the majority, and actually controlled, by the people who work there....

First, the vision of an economy of worker-owned businesses is an old and resilient one;  it is, in fact, one of the things meant by "communism" in political discourse until an analyst named Marx argued that such an economic vision was "utopian" unless joined with a program for capture of political power.  The worldwide disenchantment with all or part of Marx's alternative program—a disenchantment that long predates 1989—has assisted a fresh look at the "utopian" vision he rejected—a vision that always had particular resonance in the resolutely pro-capitalist, anti-socialist segments of the American working class.

Second, in the past decade, the prospect of mass employee ownership has passed decisively from utopian proposal to big business.  Several hurdles have been jumped here.  One common argument against the utopian cooperative vision was that such worker owned firms could never attain any size.  However, there are now very large and successful companies that are over seventy percent owned by employees, such as Weirton Steel, ranking 288 on the Fortune 500, and Avis Corporation, now privately held but (as everyone knows) America's Number 2 car rental company.  "Employees own a majority of the stock in three of the country's ten largest integrated steel manufacturers, two of the ten largest private hospital management companies, two of the three largest shipbuilders, two of the ten largest construction companies, and many others."

Third, the spread in popularity in the United States of Employee Stock Ownership Plans (ESOPs) has suddenly created the possibility of an economy of firms in which the employees are in most cases the dominant shareholders.  Already there are more Americans working for firms, more than 4 percent owned by their employees, than there are represented by labor unions.  If, as is often asserted, a 15 percent ownership stake permits dominance, "[b]y the year 2000, more than a quarter of the companies traded on the New York Stock Exchange, the American Stock Exchange and Over-the-Counter Market will be more than 15 percent owned by their employees."

Now a firm with an ESOP, even an ESOP that owns 15 or 25 or 75 percent of stock, is not necessarily a firm that workers control or manage.  The ESOP, as envisioned by attorney Louis Kelso and later sanctioned by statute, was carefully designed to permit companies to donate stock to employees without necessarily parting with any control.  Today, the typical ESOP is a stock savings plan in which shares are held in trust for employees and voted by a trustee appointed by corporate management.  The company continues to be managed traditionally, and on the whole is less likely than a conventionally investor-owned firm to experiment in worker involvement of various kinds.  Until quite recently, sincere believers in worker management wanted nothing to do with ESOPs, which were seen as inevitably associated with control by conventional managers.  Their preferred institutional model was the cooperative, highly democratic, perhaps organized without any supervisors or leaders, and with jobs rotating.

It is possible, perhaps likely, that most of today's ESOPs will never amount to more than savings plans....

There are good reasons however to think that a significant number of the ESOPs of the 1980's will evolve during the 1990's into a new and exciting form of partial worker control.  In the next few years the loans that established these leveraged ESOPS will be paid off, more stock will vest in employees, and the sheer quantity of employee-held stock creates interesting possibilities, for example, of alliance with pension funds and other institutional investors. Meanwhile, a corps of lawyers, bankers, and other professionals experimented with combining workplace democracy with ESOP organization, and discovered that the ESOP is not inevitably associated with hierarchical management; indeed, there are ESOPs as "democratic" as the wildest cooperative. It is likely in the 1990's that many firms with ESOPs will evolve somewhere in between, with workers exercising the kind of control that shareholders with 15 percent stakes do, though not the kind of control associated with worker cooperatives. This trend makes more pressing a fresh look at the economic desirability of worker management.

Fourth, as I said, the few existing examples of real employee ownership have generated a large academic literature.

. . .

It is not really an exaggeration to say that the existing economic, political science, and legal literature answers that question in one of two ways. The answer is either "always" or "never." Here are slightly caricatured—but really, only slightly—explanations of the "always" and "never" simplified models of employee ownership that dominate the conceptual literature by political theorists and some economists.

The model that suggests that employee ownership is just about always good for just about everybody does so because it sees employee ownership as the solution to more or less universal problems experienced by employees of modern industrial or service firms: loss of control of work, alienation, an experience of passively following orders.

. . .

Across the Library, perhaps, in the economics section, lies a competing body of theoretical literature that suggests that employee ownership cannot possibly ever work for anybody. In this version, employee owners would (like other neoclassical economic actors) maximize their current income, so that every dollar that comes in would be paid out in wages; the firm would never plan or invest; it would never expand, since each new employee would just divide this static income stream into a smaller rivulet; the firm could generate no internal funds for investment, while no sane outside investor would ever finance such a firm; which would go to a speedy grave unless imposed on the unwilling through force of law.

B.  Empirical Literature on Employee Ownership

The most important point to emerge from study of the empirical literature on employee ownership is that neither conceptual model—neither "always" nor "never"—could possibly be correct. Let me sum up six of the most significant findings, and the challenges they present to the competing conceptual models. These are the central facts about employee ownership, which a more convincing model will eventually have to explain.

First, there are in fact a great many successful, long-lived, employee-owned and managed firms in the United States and elsewhere. These firms have survived without government subsidy, often in hostile environments. This fact alone should give pause to one drawn to the "never" school.

Second, such genuine employee-owned businesses succeed in almost any imaginable industry, with all types of employees. Among those studied in the greatest depth include: plywood manufacturing cooperatives; refuse collection; the Weirton Steel Corporation, for a time the best-performing company in the American steel industry; professional partnerships, such as law and accounting firms; taxi cab collectives; construction companies; artisanal manufacturing; supermarkets; the complex of industrial enterprises at Mondragon, Spain.

In short, successful employee ownership and management is found in the production of goods and services; among educated and less-educated employees; performing tasks both simple and complex; in enterprises as large as several hundred workers and in some cases larger. Few of these firms are subsidized. In short, the "never" models have a tough time explaining the successes of employee ownership.

Third, however, we do not observe entire industries that are dominated by employee-owned firms, except where alternative arrangements are legally prohibited, such as law firms. This is a significant and embarrassing fact for the "always" school, which tends to explain the low spread of employee ownership in terms of the weight of tradition, cognitive awareness of options, cultural factors that limit employee ownership to extreme risk-takers, high start-up costs in training a democratic workforce, free-rider and coordination problems, and similar factors. Without denying these, it is harder to explain why, even after successful employee ownership, there are so few industries in which it is the dominant form. In countries and industries that have seen successful employee ownership, there would then be cognitive awareness of options, a break with tradition and other cultural factors, lower training costs. Yet even here one sees plenty of investor-owned plywood companies, steel mills, Italian artisanal factories, and (in medicine and accounting) professional partnerships.

Fourth, substantial anecdotal evidence links the adoption of employee ownership to substantial productivity gains in individual firms.

Fifth, however, large-scale comparisons of employee-owned firms with controlled groups of conventional firms reveal a more mixed, but basically positive, picture on productivity.... The sharpest productivity differences between employee-owned and conventional firms occur in some of the long-lived firms listed above, firms with real employee control—not, typically, through an ESOP—over a long period of time. Even this literature lacks the "smoking gun" that would be necessary to support the thesis of the "always" school, that all or just about all firms would benefit from employee ownership. Moreover, if employee ownership is limited to shares in an ESOP, and there is little direct employee participation, it is difficult to demonstrate much, or any, productivity gain for whole groups of firms as compared with other whole groups of firms.

Sixth, employee-owned firms often go through a distinctive life cycle described by several economists. Employee-owned firms often begin during economic recessions, when employees buy out failed or failing conventional firms. (Note how damaging is this simple fact to the "never" school; there are many examples of successful employee-owned firms where the identical firm, when conventionally owned, was failing or actually failed). Such recession births succeed because workers will make concessions to themselves—lower wages, reduced staffing levels, other productivity gains—that they would not make to a management that might use them opportunistically. When the general economic climate improves, the employees sell the firm to private investors. (Obviously damaging to the "always" school. Yet employee-owned firms do indeed frequently sell out to private investors.)

It seems to me that the empirical literature on employee ownership is difficult if not impossible to interpret within the frameworks of the existing conceptual literature. The answer to the riddle of employee ownership simply cannot be, in our economy, either "never" or "always." This points out the need for newer models of the employee owned firm, that will better explain its pattern of successes. The answer to Professor Hansmann's question, "When Does Worker Ownership Work?", will have to start with the word "sometimes."

NOTES

**1.** For examples of state legislation encouraging employee ownership and analysis of their content, see Virginia L. Duquet, Note, Advantages and Limitations of Current Employee Ownership Assistance Acts to Workers Facing a Plant Closing, 36 Hastings L.J. 93 (1984).

**2.** For a further discussion of worker participation in business management and ESOPs, see generally Jeffery N. Gordon, Employee Stock Ownership as a Transitional Device: The Case of the Airline Industry, in The Handbook of Airline Economics (1996); Henry Hansmann, When Does Worker Ownership Work? ESOPs, Law Firms, Codetermination and Economic Democracy, 99 Yale L.J. 1749 (1990); Joseph R. Blasi, Employee Ownership: Revolution or Ripoff (1988); Charles S. Mishkind & David E. Khorey, Employee Stock Ownership Plans: Fables and Facts, 11 Employee Rel. L.J. 89 (1985); Robert B. Moberly, New Directions in Worker Participation, 87 W.Va.L.Rev. 765 (1987); Corey Rosen & Alan Cohen, Employees to the Rescue: The Record of Worker Buyouts, 6 J. Law & Commerce 213 (1986).

---

## D. DISPLACED WORKERS

## Office of Technology Assessment, U.S. Congress, Technology and Structural Unemployment: Reemploying Displaced Adults

6–9, 29–30 (1986).

Worker displacement is a continuing problem in a growing, dynamic economy. In the industrialized world, conditions of production and competition are constantly changing: new production technologies are developed, new products are made, and old products and techniques fall by the wayside. New competitors enter the field, forcing existing enterprises to adjust or go out of business. Increasingly, this competition is international. The number of countries whose products can hold their own in industrialized countries is growing. There is also a growing conviction that the pace of such change is accelerating: That the adjustments must be made more often, that the pressure to change before the competition changes is intensifying. Most experts agree that this dynamism is good for the economy as a whole. The processes of competition and change allow people to choose from a wider variety of goods and services, at lower cost, than would be possible in a static economy.

However, technological change and world economic interdependence mean that millions of American workers are displaced, and some must make forced work transitions several times during their lives. Automation, changing conditions of trade, offshore production, and changing consumption patterns have displaced millions of workers, and made it necessary for others to learn new skills, relocate, or change jobs.

Between January 1979 and January 1984, 11.5 million workers lost jobs due to plant closings or relocation, abolition of a position or a shift, or slack work. Of those, 5.1 million had had the job for at least 3 years, and were considered displaced according to a special survey conducted by the Census Bureau in January 1984 and analyzed by BLS. This definition underestimates the number of displaced workers, primarily because workers (such as younger workers and people who have just changed jobs) who have not held their former jobs for 3 years are not counted as displaced. However, it is inappropriate to count all 11.5 million workers who lost their jobs during the period as displaced, because some of the loss of jobs—particularly that due to "slack work"—probably was cyclical.

By January 1984, 1.3 million of the 5.1 million displaced workers were still unemployed; some 500,000 had been unemployed for more than 27 weeks. About 730,000 people had left the labor force, some by choice but many out of discouragement or by retiring earlier than they might have wished. During the entire 5–year period, nearly one-fourth of the 5.1 million displaced workers were without work for more than a year. Many of the 3.1 million workers who were reemployed had experienced real difficulties finding new jobs. During the 5 years, nearly one-third of those who found jobs and who reported their earnings had taken pay cuts of 20 percent or more, and over one-tenth of former full-time workers had taken part-time work.

Displaced workers are typically white males of prime working age with a steady work history in a blue-collar job in the Midwest or Northeast. However, many other groups are represented. One-third of displaced workers are women; 12 percent are black; 18 percent are over 55. Forty percent of the full-time work force is female, 11 percent is black, and 12 percent is over 55. Even though women are actually underrepresented in the population of displaced workers, and black people are represented in proportion to their share of the work force, these groups fared significantly worse than white men in regaining employment after being displaced.

Less skilled and less educated workers are more likely to be displaced, and more likely to have trouble finding a new job. Among the 5.1 million workers displaced from 1979 to 1983, the most overrepresented occupational group by far was machine operators, assemblers, and repairers, who comprised 22 percent of the displaced workers but only about 7.5 percent of the work force. Less likely to be displaced and more likely to find replacement jobs were professionals; executive, administrative and managerial workers; technicians; salespeople; and service workers.

\* \* \*

Displaced workers are likely to experience prolonged unemployment. Of the 5.1 million workers displaced between January 1979 and January 1984, 43 percent were out of work for at least 27 weeks, and nearly one-fourth of them had periods of joblessness adding up to a year or more. Many of these people are out of work long enough to exhaust unemployment insurance and family savings. Of the nearly 2.5 million manufacturing workers displaced, less than 60 percent had found jobs as of January 1984; the rest had either dropped out of the labor force or were unemployed.

The costs of displacement do not usually end with reemployment. Many displaced workers take jobs at lower pay and status than they had in their old jobs. Of the workers who reported their earnings in the Census Bureau survey, 45 percent had taken a pay cut, and two-thirds of those were earning less than 80 percent of their former income. Even workers who find jobs that pay as well as their former jobs may still lose earnings over time, for they might have received raises and adjustments for inflation if they had been able to keep the old job. The Congressional Budget Office found that, on average, displaced workers experience long-term wage losses, and the greater the worker's seniority in the old job, the greater the loss. Moreover, displaced workers lose benefits: health benefits usually stop, and pension benefits suffer. The loss of health benefits is a matter of urgent concern to many displaced workers. A score of bills in the 98th Congress proposed funding mechanisms for health insurance for the unemployed, and three such bills have been introduced in the 99th Congress.

The economic stresses of displacement take a toll in mental and physical health. Prolonged unemployment, which most displaced workers suffer, typically brings with it increases in stress, anxiety, depression, physical ailments, alcoholism, and family strife. While these emotional costs are difficult to quantify, they are very real.

The number of jobs available is the result of a variety of strategic choices, including choices of technology. Often, the choice is to replace human labor with technology, a factor that has helped double output per labor hour in the United States since World War II. At the same time, a growing population and rising affluence—thanks in part to the rising productivity made possible by the capital-for-labor shift—brought increasing demands for goods and services. The increasing demand, together with new products made possible by new technologies, were major factors in the growth of U.S. employment.

Labor-saving technology can have a job-destroying effect, but the drive for greater labor productivity can help maintain or increase the ability of U.S. firms to compete with foreign producers. However, greater labor productivity, by definition, means that fewer workers can produce equivalent output; unless demand for output rises faster than productivity, jobs will be lost. At the same time, without productivity increases, declining competitiveness may cause even more jobs to be lost. Changing production technology often saves some jobs at the expense of others.

* * *

If the effect of current technological changes is to raise the proportion of more highly skilled jobs in the Nation's occupational mix, that effect will continue a long-standing trend. Throughout the 20th century, higher skilled occupations such as professional and technical workers, managers, and administrators have grown faster than some lower skilled occupations such as farmworkers, nonfarm laborers, and operatives. It would be misleading, however, to conclude that the economy is moving rapidly toward a future where highly skilled occupations predominate. Millions of lower skilled jobs have been created in fast-growing service industries, which accounted for nearly 95 percent of the growth in employment between 1970 and 1984. In general, service sectors have higher concentrations of both high- and low-skilled jobs than manufacturing.

NOTES AND QUESTIONS

**1.** Displaced workers are individuals who once had good jobs but are now occupational dinosaurs because of technological and economic change. What should society do for them? See generally Symposium, Workers' Rights and New Technology, 8 Nova L.J. 481 (1984).

**2.** The major U.S. programmatic effort is the Job Training Partnership Act of 1983, 29 U.S.C. § 1501 et seq., discussed in Chapter 2. Among proposed legislation is an effort to enact a United States Skills Corporation, which would be an independent agency committed to providing workers with skills that are in short supply. See S. 2811, 98th Cong. (1984). At least four states currently operate state skills corporations.

---

## E.   UNEMPLOYMENT INSURANCE

## 1.   HISTORY

## John A. Garraty, Unemployment in History:  Economic Thought and Public Policy *

6–7, 134–136, 213–214 (1978).

*Genesis* tells us that work is punishment for sin and the fate of humankind, that idleness is the normal condition of the blameless soul (it was the Lord, not Adam, who planted the Garden of Eden), and that even the Lord, despite his omnipotence, felt the need to take a day off.  Historically, the tension between the wish to work and the wish to be idle has been a source of confusion to statesmen, employers, social workers, and others concerned with the problem of unemployment.  Aside from persons physically unable to work, there appear to be in any society numbers of individuals who for emotional, cultural, or perhaps even philosophical reasons are simply unwilling to work.  Separating these "unemployables" from the rest of the jobless has always been difficult, in large measure because every person is in a sense "unwilling" to work.  Because of this human ambivalence toward labor, policy makers have for centuries debated the relative merits of the carrot and stick approaches to the unemployed.  To the extent that the work ethic predominates, it pays to encourage and sustain them;  if it does not, then leaving them to their own devices or even punishing the idle may appear reasonable.

\* \* \*

The [British] unemployment-insurance system was the world's first;  the much-admired German social-welfare legislation of the 1880s had not dealt with unemployment.  The person most responsible for the measure was Winston Churchill, president of the Board of Trade and then Home Secretary in the cabinet of Prime Minister Herbert Asquith.  Churchill knew relatively little about the technicalities of either insurance or the unemployment problem, but he recognized unemployment (the "Achilles heel" of British labor) as an important political and social issue.  He quickly availed himself of the most advanced thinking on the subject—his mentors were Sidney and Beatrice Webb, who recognized Churchill's "capacity for the quick appreciation and rapid execution of ideas," and William H. Beveridge, an authority on labor exchanges, whom he met through the Webbs.  Like many other English social reformers of the period, Churchill was also impressed by German welfare programs;  before entering the cabinet he wrote an important article proposing "a sort of Germanized network of state intervention and regulation'' for the protection of the jobless.

Churchill did not, however, merely assimilate the ideas of others. The Webbs in particular, being ardent preventionists, were wary of compulsory unemployment insurance, which might seem ''an easy alternative to complicated measures of prevention,'' but which they believed would encourage malingering and be extremely expensive. Under a compulsory system, Beatrice Webb wrote in 1909, ''the state gets nothing for its money in the way of conduct.'' The Webbs favored instead a voluntary insurance program of the Ghent type, which, they argued, would encourage workers to develop thrift, foresight, independence, and ''the willingness to subordinate the present to the future,'' and also free the government from the need to administer a complex system. Insurance was, in any case, only a palliative; the true task was to get rid of unemployment.

\* \* \*

For various reasons, Churchill did not follow the Webbs's advice. Preventing unemployment might, as they said, be possible, but it would take longer than the politician in Churchill could afford to wait. Moreover, he rejected the argument of the Webbs and so many other social workers and reformers that programs of relief ought to aim at improving the character and morals of recipients. Getting something from the unemployed ''in the way of conduct'' did not appeal to him. ''I do not like mixing up moralities and mathematics,'' he wrote in 1909. ''Our concern is with the evil, not with the causes. With the fact of unemployment, not with the character of the unemployed.'' Even a worker discharged because of drunkenness should be entitled to unemployment benefits if he had paid insurance premiums. Conversely, where the Webbs favored compulsory labor exchanges, seeing them as a way to organize the labor market and prevent the malingering they believed an inherent danger in any insurance system, Churchill considered such a restriction on individuals unjust. Compulsory insurance, on the other hand, did not restrict anyone's freedom. Furthermore—in this he was following Beveridge—it would create ''a motive for the voluntary support of Labour Exchanges,'' a point which the Webbs eventually conceded. Churchill and the Asquith government went ahead with compulsory insurance and, after linking it with a health-insurance measure devised by Lloyd George, pushed it through Parliament in December 1911. The scheme covered about two and a quarter million workers and provided modest benefits, roughly equivalent to a third of the wage of a low-paid worker, for up to fifteen weeks of joblessness.

\* \* \*

The most important result of the high unemployment of the depression in the United States was the passage in 1935 of a national unemployment-insurance law. The measure did not come earlier because of the same popular prejudice against expanding federal authority and also because of disagreements among the advocates of insurance. The idea that an unemployment-insurance system could *prevent* unemployment, which had been advanced before the Great War by John R. Commons and others, was put to the test in Commons's own state of Wisconsin in 1932. The Wisconsin law required each company employing ten or more workers to build up an unemployment reserve fund, financed by the employer but administered by the government, from which that employer's workers would draw benefits when unemployed. The law provided that once the fund had reached a sum equal to $75 for each worker, the employer would not have to add to it except to make up for what was paid out to workers that had been laid off—presumably, therefore, employers would use every means possible to spread out work to avoid having to discharge anyone.

Other supporters of insurance preferred some variant of the British system, with workers as well as employers contributing to a single national fund. The issue was complicated by the opposition, until 1932, of many important labor leaders to any compulsory insurance system and their resistance thereafter to employee contributions, and by fears that no system could remain actuarily sound in the face of political pressures. There were also genuine constitutional concerns—it seemed likely that the Supreme Court would throw out any law setting up a nationally administered system. To get around the constitutional problem, Senator Robert F. Wagner of New York introduced a bill calling for a national payroll tax against which employer payments into any state insurance fund could be offset—thus federal law would force all states to enact unemployment insurance laws, yet not interfere with the Wisconsin system or for that matter prevent other states from devising whatever forms of insurance they wished.

President Roosevelt's position on unemployment insurance was not unlike Winston Churchill's in 1910, although he played a much smaller role in planning and pushing through the necessary legislation. Like Churchill, he did not allow the lack of detailed knowledge to keep him from espousing the principle whole-heartedly. He actually told Secretary of Labor Frances Perkins that he favored "cradle to the grave" insurance for all Americans against illness, unemployment, and old age, "operated through the post offices," but aside from insisting that workers should contribute to the insurance fund so as to have an irrefutable claim to benefits, he did not commit himself to any particular system. He accepted the idea of separate state insurance embodied in Wagner's bill, and when experts who wanted a centralized system objected, he pointed out the political and constitutional problems and put them off with the bromide "We cannot eat the whole cake at one meal." The Social Security Act of 1935 insured against both old age and unemployment. By leaving the particulars to the individual states it created a confused and inequitable unemployment-insurance system. But, under the impetus of the tax offset provision, all the states swiftly established systems. Despite its limitations, the act was, as the historian Arthur M. Schlesinger, Jr. wrote, "a tremendous break with the inhibitions of the past" and in the American context a "prodigious achievement."

## 2.    THE UNEMPLOYMENT INSURANCE SYSTEM

### Daniel N. Price, *Unemployment Insurance, Then and Now 1935–85*

48 Social Security Bull. No. 10 at 22 (1985).

On August 14, 1935, the Social Security Act was signed. It included the mechanism for establishing an unemployment insurance system in all States. The unemployment insurance provisions of the new law were contained in titles III and IX. A payroll tax on covered employers was established. It was 1 percent of payroll in 1936, 2 percent in 1937, and 3 percent in 1938 and thereafter. However, up to 90 percent of this tax (or 2.7 percent beginning in 1938) could be reduced by contributions that employers paid under an approved State unemployment insurance law. In addition, employers could credit against the 2.7 percent Federal tax any reductions in the State tax made under an approved State experience rating plan. That is, if the State tax was less than 2.7 percent as a result of reductions allowed employers who laid off fewer workers than other employers, the difference between 2.7 percent and the actual tax rate was also creditable against the Federal tax.

Employers of eight persons or more in at least 20 weeks in a year were subject to the Federal payroll tax, which, in effect, made this size firm the minimum size to be covered. Railroad workers were covered, but in 1938 a separate, completely Federal system of railroad retirement and unemployment insurance was legislated, superseding the Social Security Act coverage. Farm workers, government employees, employees in nonprofit industry or in domestic service, family members of employers, and seamen were the main groups excluded from coverage.

In addition, the Federal law provided broad standards still in effect today for approval of State programs. For example, compensation cannot be denied to any otherwise eligible claimant who refuses to accept new work that violates labor standards (such as work at a subminimum wage). As another condition of approval of a State program, all State tax funds must be deposited in the Federal Unemployment Trust Fund created by the Federal law. These deposits are credited to the State's account and may be withdrawn only to pay unemployment insurance benefits.

Grants are authorized to each State to administer the State unemployment insurance program. To receive these grants, the States are required to meet certain standards of administration, including procedures to pay benefits when due, allowing unemployed workers an appeal procedure if they are denied benefits, and providing information about the operation of the program to the Federal Government. All compensation under the State plan has to be paid through public employment offices or other approved agencies. The State staff administering the program must be employed in accordance with personnel standards on a merit basis.

The unemployment insurance provisions of the Social Security Act established a different system than that enacted for the old-age insurance and later the survivor, disability, and health insurance parts of the law. A tax offset device was used to promote passage of the unemployment insurance laws in all the States. The Federal Government retains an overseer's role in assuring that the States' programs meet certain broad standards of administration and in channeling the collection and disbursal of funds for benefit payments. But the States operate their programs directly and they determine eligibility conditions, the waiting period to receive benefits, benefit amounts, minimum and maximum benefit levels, duration of benefits, disqualifications, and other administrative matters.

* * *

In 1938, when all the State laws were in place and benefit payments began in most of them, 20 million workers were covered by the program nationally. This number represented less than two-thirds of employed wage-and-salary workers in that year. From then until 1985, the labor force has grown and so has the extent of statutory protection—to 92.5 million workers covered (96 percent of wage-and-salary workers) in January 1985. Thus, aside from some workers in very small firms and in agricultural work, and some specialized occupational groups such as elected officials and persons who work for family members, almost all wage-and-salary workers are now covered by the unemployment insurance laws.

In 1940, the second year for which benefits were paid in all States, 5.2 million workers received an average of $10.56 per week for almost 10 weeks. Altogether, $519 million was paid under the State programs in that year. By 1982, the year with the highest unemployment insurance expenditures, $20.6 billion was paid by the States to 11.6 million workers (excluding amounts under extended benefits programs). In that year, an average beneficiary received $119.39 per week for almost 16 weeks. Most recently, as the economy has improved, the total amount of benefits has declined: The $1.0 billion in benefits paid for August 1984 represented a $12 billion annual rate in benefit expenditures.

In general, the basic structure of unemployment insurance continues today much the same as when it originally was enacted 50 years ago: Joint Federal-State administration, weekly benefits of about 50 percent of a worker's wage (up to a stated maximum) for workers with recent work experience, protection for temporary periods with a set maximum duration, program financing through a payroll tax on employers, and experience rated tax schedules. Nevertheless, unemployment insurance has also changed. As indicated, the proportion of workers with this type of income-maintenance protection has grown to a point where coverage is nearly complete. The scope of protection has been enhanced in a major way by the provision for automatic increases in weekly benefit maximums to account for rising wages in about two-thirds of the States and through the extension of the maximum potential duration of benefits under the regular program and the establishment of extended benefit provisions.

The Federal agency originally responsible for overseeing the operation of the State programs was the Social Security Board, which also administered the old-age insurance and income-support provisions of the law.   In August 1949, the Federal responsibility was transferred to the Department of Labor, where it remains.   A number of the financing provisions also have been changed from those in the original program—namely, a much wider range of payroll tax rates on employers, but with a corresponding cutback from taxing all covered payrolls to taxing up to a set maximum (currently $7,000 per worker under Federal requirements).   Further, when they first were enacted, 10 State laws called for employee contributions as well as employer contributions.   By 1940, only five States required employee contributions, and since 1955 only three have retained this provision.

* * *

All the States have raised benefit maximums greatly but by considerably different amounts over the years.   All but two States provided a maximum weekly benefit of $15 in 1938; all the States provided a range of maximums from $84 to $225 by 1985.   The States generally still adhere to the principle of paying a weekly benefit that replaces about half of the worker's wage.   However, the benefit formulas vary considerably in implementing this general goal.   Some States have a weighted formula to give lower paid workers a somewhat higher proportion of lost earnings; others provide an allowance for dependents.

* * *

The question of disqualification from benefits is another area in which the States have acted with great diversity—both in defining what types of circumstances should result in disqualification and in determining the appropriate manner of reducing (or eliminating) benefits because of specified disqualifying acts.   More important, in certain respects, the State laws have become more stringent with the passage of time.   In the first 25 years of the program, "The causes for which benefits are denied have multiplied and the periods of disqualification have been made more severe."

Since 1960, the same patterns have continued.   For refusal to accept suitable work, for instance, just 15 States imposed a disqualification for the duration of unemployment in January 1960 (as opposed to disqualification for a specified fixed or variable period), but 40 States imposed this disqualification in January 1985.   Similarly, for voluntarily leaving the job or for discharge for misconduct, the number of States disqualifying a claimant for the duration of his unemployment rose significantly:

| Date | Voluntarily leaving | Misconduct |
|---|---|---|
| January 1960 .................. | 17 | 10 |
| January 1985 .................. | 47 | 39 |

These changes and other similar changes represent an attempt to discourage inappropriate use of the unemployment insurance program and to conserve funds, especially during periods of high unemployment when large amounts of benefits are being paid.

Experience rating has become a basic part of the unemployment insurance financing structure to maximize employment stabilization efforts by employers. Under experience rating, employers who maintain a stable work force are assigned favorable tax rates compared with the rates of other employers. First, although many States have encountered difficulties in financing benefits, especially during recessions, some States continue to allow a tax rate as low as zero to employers under the most favorable schedule (11 States in 1985). The conservative approach used in financing benefits early in the history of the program is discernible from the fact that, even under the most favorable schedule, the majority of States imposed a rate of at least 0.9 percent in 1937, but the minimum rate in almost all States had declined to 0.5 percent or less in 1960 and remained at that level in 1985. The maximum tax rates rose sharply between 1960 and 1985 for employers with unfavorable experience. But this change is largely a result of the federally mandated increase in the Federal tax instituted in 1985 (raising the Federal tax from 3.5 percent to 6.2 percent). One result of the most recent changes is that the range of experience rates has been expanded, allowing the States to better match employers' experience with their tax rate.

\* \* \*

As the present system evolved, three legislative patterns developed concerning duration of benefits. First, the number of weeks of benefits allowed under regular State programs increased substantially and stabilized at 26 weeks as a typical maximum amount for workers with substantial work experience before a period of unemployment. Second, despite the program objective stated through the mid-1950's—that benefit duration should be at least 26 weeks for all claimants who qualify for benefits—the States have moved in a different direction since 1941. All but eight States now vary potential duration—from 4 weeks to 26 weeks (except for a 28-week maximum in Washington)—by the extent of previous work experience. Variable duration provides some limited degree of protection even to workers who have not had stable full-time employment. Third, some States, and, in 1970, all States (under Federal law), added a supplementary set of benefits to regular program duration. This extended benefit feature for periods of high unemployment continues to be reexamined. The Congress has modified the duration provisions to meet the needs of the unemployed in succeeding business cycles, which have been accompanied by different patterns of unemployment.

NOTES

**1.** For certain workers, whose unemployment results "importantly" from the competitive impact of increasing foreign imports, additional cash benefits are available under a program of Trade Adjustment Assistance, 19 U.S.C. §§ 2271–2322. After reductions in eligibility and benefit amounts made since 1981, the program now pays at the rate of unemployment insurance benefits, but can extend the benefit period to 52 weeks from termination, plus up to 26 additional weeks if the former worker is in an approved retraining program.

**2.** A 1986 amendment to ERISA provides that under certain circumstances employers must continue group health benefits for terminated employees. Former workers can stay in the group health plan for up to 18 months, but can be required to pay the full cost of their coverage. Title X, Consolidated Omnibus Budget Reconciliation Act of 1985, P.L. No. 99–272, April 7, 1986, amending § 162 of the Internal Revenue Code.

## Daniel S. Hamermesh, Jobless Pay and the Economy
4–6 (1979).

In order to understand the main general features of state UI systems let us consider a person who has just been separated from his firm. (The state could be one of the fifty states, the District of Columbia, or Puerto Rico.) Immediately after separation he (or she) files an *initial claim* for benefits at a local Employment Security office. Upon receipt of this claim the office must determine three things. First, is the former employee covered by the state UI system? Essentially all who are employed in manufacturing firms would be covered, but those working in agriculture, the self-employed, domestic household workers, and persons employed in certain state and local government activities or in certain small nonprofit operations probably would not be covered and thus would be ineligible for benefits. (Railroad workers, ex-servicemen, and federal employees are covered by small, special programs which we will ignore in this discussion, and there are minor interstate differences in coverage.)

Second, is the claimant *eligible* for benefits? Eligibility is defined in terms of prior work attachment and the reason for separation. The regulations on prior work attachment differ from state to state. Among the five states used as examples throughout this book Colorado requires the worker to have earned thirty times the *weekly benefit amount* and $750 in the *base period*. (In thirty-five states in 1975 the base period was the first four of the five calendar quarters preceding the filing of a claim; in most of the remaining states, including Massachusetts and New York, it was the fifty-two weeks preceding the claim or the receipt of benefits.) In Massachusetts a flat amount of annual earned income is required for eligibility; in New York and Oregon there are requirements for both weeks worked and earnings in the base period; and in South Carolina the claimant must have earned 1.5 times his *high-quarter earnings* and $300 during the base period. Other states use different criteria for eligibility, but these examples illustrate the main types of provisions. The purpose of all such provisions is to ensure that the individual has a strong attachment to the labor force and is really interested in finding work.

The other criterion for eligibility in most states is whether or not the worker quit or was laid off for cause. If he quit voluntarily or was fired, he will be declared ineligible, although this decision can be appealed. In a few states such workers will receive UI benefits after a long waiting period (usually six weeks or more).

Third, if the individual is eligible for benefits, the office must determine what his weekly benefit amount is and how long he may receive it (his *potential duration* of benefits).   Potential duration is uniform in eight states (including New York), but in others it varies depending on the claimant's base-period earnings and/or weeks of employment.   In most states the *maximum potential duration* is twenty-six weeks.   Weekly benefits may be some fraction of a worker's high-quarter earnings (Colorado, Massachusetts, and South Carolina), a variable fraction of his average weekly wage during the base period (New York), with the fraction equal to .5 in most cases, or a portion of his entire base-period earnings (Oregon); or some other method of determination may be used.   In eleven states, including Massachusetts, the claimant can also receive extra benefits (*dependents' allowances*) linked to his weekly benefits, his base-period earnings, and the number of dependents in his household.   In all states there is a *maximum weekly benefit*, which cannot be exceeded regardless of prior earnings or work history.   This maximum is defined either in dollar amounts or relative to the state average weekly wage in covered employment (in thirty-two states, including Colorado, Massachusetts, Oregon, and South Carolina).   This maximum is not higher than two thirds of the state average weekly wage except in those states where dependents' allowances are also paid.

When the claimant returns (after the one-week *waiting period* in all but eight states), assuming he has not been disqualified, he is told what his weekly benefit is;  when he must report to pick up his benefit check, or in some states, when it will be mailed to him;  and what his potential duration is.   In most cases both potential duration and amount of benefits depend on the individual's attachment to the labor force.   Every two weeks (in most states) the beneficiary returns at the appointed time to receive a check for his UI benefits.   If he moves elsewhere, his claim will be filed *interstate,* with the charges assessed against his former location and his check receivable at his new location.

So long as he can show he is looking for work and that he has not refused *suitable work* in a job found for him by the Employment Service, the worker may continue to receive his payment.   *Suitable work* is necessarily an ambiguous term, and its interpretation is subject partly to the discretion of local UI officials.   In general, it is work that uses the skills employed on a previous job.   In all states except Montana the beneficiary may take part-time work and receive partial benefits up to his potential duration.   If the beneficiary has not found suitable work by the end of the period equaling his potential duration, he is said to have *exhausted his regular benefits.*

## 3.   LEGAL ISSUES IN UNEMPLOYMENT INSURANCE

### a.   ONE STATE STATUTE

**Mass.Gen.Laws Ch. 151A**

§ 24.   Eligibility

An individual, in order to be eligible for benefits under this chapter, shall—

*(a)* Have been paid wages in the base period amounting to at least thirty times the weekly benefit rate; provided, however, that * * * the individual has been paid wages of at least two thousand dollars during said period * * *.

*(b)* Be capable of, available, and actually seeking work in his usual occupation or any other occupation for which he is reasonably fitted; and

*(c)* Have given notice of his unemployment, by registering * * *

## § 25.   Disqualification for benefits

No waiting period shall be allowed and no benefits shall be paid to an individual under this chapter for—

*(a)* Any week in which he fails without good cause to comply with the registration and filing requirements of the Commissioner.  * * *

*(b)* Any week with respect to which the Commissioner finds that his unemployment is due to a stoppage of work which exists because of a labor dispute at the factory, establishment or other premises at which he was last employed; * * *

*(c)* Any week in which an otherwise eligible individual fails, without good cause, to apply for suitable employment whenever notified so to do by the employment office, or to accept suitable employment whenever offered to him, and for the next seven consecutive weeks in addition to the waiting period provided in section twenty-three, and the duration of benefits for unemployment to which the individual would otherwise have been entitled may thereupon be reduced for as many weeks, not exceeding eight, as the director shall determine from the circumstances of each case.

"Suitable employment", as used in this subsection, shall be determined by the Commissioner, who shall take into consideration whether the employment is detrimental to the health, safety or morals of an employee, is one for which he is reasonably fitted by training and experience, including employment not subject to this chapter, is one which is located within reasonable distance of his residence or place of last employment, and is one which does not involve travel expenses substantially greater than that required in his former work.

No work shall be deemed suitable, and benefits shall not be denied under this chapter to any otherwise eligible individual for refusing to accept new work under any of the following conditions:—

(1) If the position offered is vacant due directly to a strike, lockout or other labor dispute;

(2) If the remuneration, hours or other conditions of the work offered are substantially less favorable to the individual than those prevailing for similar work in the locality;

(3) If acceptance of such work would require the individual to join a company union or would abridge or limit his right to join or retain membership in any bona fide labor organization or association of workmen.

* * *

*(d)* Any period with respect to which he is receiving or has received or is about to receive compensation for total disability under the worker's compensation law of any state or under any similar law of the United States,

\* \* \*

*(e)* For the period of unemployment next ensuing and until the individual has had at least eight weeks of work and in each of said weeks has earned an amount equivalent to or in excess of the individual's weekly benefit amount after he has left his work (1) voluntarily unless the employee establishes by substantial and credible evidence that he had good cause for leaving attributable to the employing unit or its agent (2) by discharge shown to the satisfaction of the commissioner by substantial and credible evidence to be attributable to deliberate misconduct in wilful disregard of the employing unit's interest, or to a knowing violation of a reasonable and uniformly enforced rule or policy of the employer, provided that such violation is not shown to be as a result of the employer's incompetence, or (3) because of conviction of a felony or misdemeanor.

No disqualification shall be imposed if such individual establishes to the satisfaction of the commissioner that he left his employment in good faith to accept new employment on a permanent full-time basis, and that he became separated from such new employment for good cause attributable to the new employing unit. An individual shall not be disqualified under the provisions of this subsection from receiving benefits by reason of leaving his work under the terms of a pension or retirement program requiring retirement from the employment notwithstanding his prior assent, direct or indirect, to the establishment of such program. An individual shall not be disqualified from receiving benefits under the provisions of this subsection, if such individual establishes to the satisfaction of the commissioner that his reasons for leaving were for such an urgent, compelling and necessitous nature as to make his separation involuntary. \* \* \*

*(f)* For the duration of any period, but in no case more than ten weeks, for which he has been suspended from his work by his employing unit as discipline for violation of established rules or regulations of the employing unit.

*(g)* Any week which commences during the period between two successive sports seasons or similar periods if such individual performed services substantially all of which consisted of participating in sports or athletic events or training or preparing to so participate if such individual performed such services in the first of such seasons or similar periods and there is a reasonable assurance that such individual will perform such service in the later of such seasons or similar periods.

*(h)* Any period, after December thirty-first, nineteen hundred and seventy-seven, on the basis of services performed by an alien, unless such alien was lawfully admitted for permanent residence at the time such services were performed, was lawfully present for purposes of performing

such services, or was permanently residing in the United States under color of law at the time such services were performed, * * *

NOTES AND QUESTIONS

**1.** Most state unemployment insurance laws are like the Massachusetts statute in stating reasons for *disqualification* as exceptions to a general declaration of *qualification.*

**2.** Is it right to refuse unemployment insurance benefits to persons out of work because of a labor dispute? Several states pay benefits to strikers. The Supreme Court interpreted the federal unemployment insurance statute as permitting state law to decide this issue. See Ohio Bureau of Employment Services v. Hodory, 431 U.S. 471 (1977) (Ohio does not violate federal law when it disqualifies those deprived of jobs by a strike); New York Telephone Co. v. New York State Department of Labor, 440 U.S. 519 (1979) (New York does not violate federal law when it pays unemployment insurance benefits to strikers). The latest Supreme Court attention to this complicated subject is Baker v. General Motors Corp., 478 U.S. 621 (1986), upholding Michigan's policy of denying unemployment insurance benefits to workers who do not strike but are laid off due to a strike if they provided financing for the strike. In *Baker,* auto workers did not get benefits because they had contributed to a UAW emergency strike fund.

**3.** Section 25(c) of the Massachusetts law defines "suitable work." Cases interpreting the "suitable work" requirement appear infra. For certain periods during the 1970s, federal law provided extended Unemployment Insurance benefits (they once reached 65 weeks). The extended benefits programs sometimes required claimants to take *any* work, not just work that was "suitable" in light of the person's former work. Is this the right approach: 26 weeks of benefits while waiting for the former employer to recall or for another similar job to arise, and then additional benefits only on the condition of willingness to accept a less desirable job? Can government supervise such individualized rules?

**4.** Look at § 25(g) applying to professional athletes. The economy includes many seasonal jobs. Why is this one job the subject of a specific Massachusetts provision? (It is also the subject of a provision in the federal statute. See 26 U.S.C. § 3304(a)(13).)

b. YEAR–ROUND JOBS

# Toledo Area Private Industry Council v. Steinbacher

534 N.E.2d 363 (Ohio App.1987).

■ STRAUSBAUGH, PRESIDING JUDGE.

Appellant filed an appeal with the court of common pleas claiming the decision rendered by appellee Board of Review, Ohio Bureau of Employment Services ("review board"), was not supported by reliable, probative or substantial evidence and was contrary to R.C. 4141.33(A). The trial court affirmed the decision of the review board and appellant appeals.

Appellant operates under a federally funded program, the Job Training Partnership Act ("JTPA"), which is administered in Ohio by appellee, Dr. Roberta Steinbacher, Administrator of the Ohio Bureau of Employment Services. Pursuant to guidelines established by the administrator, appellant administers a summer youth employment program ("SYEP") which can operate only between May 1 and September 30. In order to properly administer the SYEP, appellant has hired office and field support employees who have never worked more than thirty-four weeks per year.

Appellant filed an application in May 1985 with the administrator seeking classification as a seasonal employer for its SYEP employees. Appellant's application was denied by the administrator and her decision was upheld upon reconsideration. Appellant appealed this reconsideration to the review board, which upheld the decision.

Appellant then initiated the instant suit seeking review by the common pleas court. The court below found that the decision of the review board was supported by reliable, probative and substantial evidence and was in accordance with law.

Appellant asserts a single assignment of error:

"The trial court erred in determining that climatic conditions are controlling under the seasonal employment exemption of the Unemployment Compensation Act."

The review board, in upholding Dr. Steinbacher's reconsidered decision, found that:

" * * * It is clear that the seasonal employment classification is one which can only be assigned to employers who work during reoccurring periods of 40 weeks or less due to climatic conditions or because of the seasonal nature of the business. The work performed by the supervisors is clearly not controlled by climatic conditions. A seasonal industry is one which due to reoccurring nature patterns such as agriculture are unable to operate on a year round basis. The processing and canning of foodstuffs is one such industry which can only be operated during a harvest season when the products have grown to maturity.

"The only reason the individuals who are hired as summer youth supervisors do not work in excess of 40 weeks is because of a contractual obligation. This is clearly not an industry which is limited by its seasonal nature or by climatic conditions, but one which is limited due to a legal obligation." * * *

Both the court below and the review board concluded that because appellant's SYEP was contractually limited to the period of May through September, it failed to qualify as seasonal employment. This court finds the conclusions of the administrative body and the common pleas court to be erroneous.

R.C. 4141.33(A) defines "seasonal employment" as employment in an industry which, because of climatic or seasonal conditions, customarily operates on a regularly recurring basis of forty weeks or less per year.

This court has previously held that the determination of whether employ- ment is seasonal turns, not on the totality of the employer's industry, but on the nature of the specific industries in which an employer may engage. Thus, although appellant may "also be engaged in a non-seasonal industry, to the extent that * * * [appellant] is engaged in a seasonal industry, the employment of the individuals in such seasonal industry is seasonal em- ployment within the contemplation of R.C. 4141.33(A)." It is clear, then, that appellant's SYEP may be evaluated by the review board as a separate industry for purposes of R.C. 4141.33(A), despite the overall nonseasonal nature of appellant's industry. Appellees contend, however, that because the SYEP is contractually limited to a specific period a finding that the program is seasonal is improper.

The Supreme Court of Ohio and the courts of appeal have yet to address the specific issues raised by appellees. The majority of cases which have considered the seasonal employment statute have done so only in the context of horse racing. While those cases can be readily distinguished from this case, they nevertheless establish two factors which the adminis- trator should consider when deciding whether a particular employment is seasonal. First, absent evidence regarding the climatic or seasonal nature of the industry, the controlling factor is whether the industry operates in regularly recurring periods of less than forty weeks. The second, and overriding, factor to be considered is whether, due to the nature of the industry or the climate, it is customary to operate on a seasonal basis. This is true whether or not some employers operate more than forty weeks per year.

The court finds that had the review board considered these factors, the only conclusion it could properly have reached is that the SYEP is a seasonal industry. Clearly, the evidence supports a finding that the SYEP operates for less than forty weeks. The parties agree that no SYEP employee worked more than thirty-four weeks per year. Appellees main- tain, however, that despite this finding, the SYEP does not operate for less than forty weeks because of seasonal or climatic conditions. Rather, the reason the SYEP operates only for limited recurring periods is because of a contractual limitation placed upon it.

We hold that merely because an SYEP is contractually limited in its operation to less than forty weeks is an insufficient basis for the review board to find that employment under the program is nonseasonal. There is no reason why an industry cannot be both seasonal in nature and also be limited by contract to a specific period of operation. * * *

Moreover, the federal Act under which SYEPs are funded contemplates seasonal employment. Part B is titled "Summer Youth Employment and Training Programs." Section 1633(a), which was in effect at the time the review board affirmed the administrative decision, dictated that programs operated under Part B "be conducted during the summer months." The congressional purpose for Section 1633(a) was the recognized need for youth employment during the *summer months*. These factors all militate in favor of a finding that the SYEP is, despite the contractual limitation on its period of operation, a seasonal industry.

Accordingly, the common pleas court abused its discretion when it found that the decision of the review board was supported by reliable, probative or substantial evidence. Appellant's sole assignment of error is well-taken, and the judgment of the court below is reversed.

Judgment reversed.

NOTES AND QUESTIONS

**1.** For treatment of the same issue in a different context, see Denver Symphony Associates v. Industrial Commission, 526 P.2d 685 (Colo.App. 1974) (permitting musicians to collect unemployment insurance during weeks when the orchestra had no work for them).

**2.** In a few states school teachers collect unemployment insurance benefits in the summer. What are the arguments for and against such a policy?

**3.** The "year-round jobs" issue pinpoints a central feature of the U.S. unemployment insurance system. An employer pays a tax that bears a relationship to the claims made by that employer's former workers. But the relationship of tax to claims is imperfect. There is a maximum tax rate and a minimum. Also, small employers are in a "pool." Thus for some employers, arranging their work in a seasonal way transfers wage costs to the general unemployment insurance fund. Also, to the extent that unemployment insurance benefits are not subject to income tax, regular, employees paid in part through unemployment insurance have an effective pay increase. Since 1978, changes have gradually been made in the unemployment insurance system tightening the relationship between the employer's tax rate and that employer's claims, and also subjecting unemployment insurance benefits to income tax when received by the former worker (they were made fully subject to the federal income tax by the Tax Reform Act of 1986).

c. SEPARATIONS

An unemployed person seeking benefits files a claim in the appropriate state office. The state notifies the former employer and offers the employer an opportunity to contest the claimant's eligibility. The employer has an incentive to challenge claimants believed ineligible, because the employer's annual unemployment insurance tax is substantially based on claims paid to that employer's former workers. If there is a challenge, the dispute will be heard and decided by the state agency.

Most disputes about initial eligibility concern whether the claimant left the former job "voluntarily and with 'good cause'," or whether he or she was fired "for just cause." Because the law generally favors the continuation of an employment relationship, it punishes the party that is responsible for the termination of the relationship. Thus, when an employee quits for good cause or is fired without just cause, the employer is viewed as responsible for terminating the relationship; the employee receives unemployment insurance benefits and the employer pays a higher unemployment tax rate. On the other hand, an employee who is fired for just cause or who quits without good cause is viewed as responsible for the end of the employment and loses some or all entitlement to benefits.

## (i) Good Cause Quit

## Raytheon Co. v. Director of Division of Employment Security

307 N.E.2d 330 (Mass.1974).

■ TAURO, CHIEF JUSTICE.

On January 5, 1970, Etta L. Miller left her job as an assembler on the night shift at the Raytheon Company's plant in Dighton because she lacked means of transportation. A co-worker who had been providing her with passenger service to the plant had been laid off by Raytheon, and she was unable to find other means of transportation, public or private. She requested transfer to the day shift, which would have been accessible to her, but there were no openings. On January 12, 1970, she was granted unemployment benefits by the director of the division of employment security. Raytheon protested this immediate award of benefits, contending that Mrs. Miller was subject to temporary disqualification in accordance with the provisions of § 25(c) of G.L. c. 151A, as amended through St.1973, c. 899, § 2, which reads in pertinent part, "No waiting period shall be allowed and no benefits shall be paid to an individual under this chapter for * * * (e) A period of four to eight weeks, as the director shall determine, after the effective date of his claim if an individual has left his work (1) voluntarily without good cause attributable to the employing unit or its agent * * *."

\* \* \*

* * * On one level, this case presents a pure question of law: can a departure from work for *personal* reasons ever be considered involuntary within the meaning of c. 151A, § 25(e)(1), if the position given up by the employee was still available at the time of leaving? For reasons set out below, we answer that question in the affirmative. The next level of analysis—were the personal reasons which caused an employee in a particular instance to leave work so compelling as to make the departure an involuntary one—brings into play the "experience, technical competence, and specialized knowledge" of the Division of Employment Security, and its finding on that question is entitled to considerable weight, and should not be disturbed by a reviewing court unless it is unsupported by substantial evidence. Section 25(c)(1) establishes two distinct prerequisites to temporary disqualification from unemployment benefits. The departure from work must be both (1) voluntary *and* (2) without good cause attributable to the employing unit or its agent. We think that the element of voluntariness was included in § 25(e)(1) for the purpose of avoiding temporary disqualification for persons who for compelling personal reasons are forced

to give up an otherwise available position.  The purpose and history of the unemployment compensation statute in general, and of § 25(c)(1) in particular, allow for no other interpretation.  The grant of benefits to unemployed persons is not premised on the concept of employer fault: "Relief of the physical needs of the unemployed who are without resources of their own is manifestly a duty of government.  The Unemployment Compensation Law * * * puts that burden upon the employers and employees not exempted from its operation.  * * * The harm to the common weal arising from unemployment of large numbers of people is beyond question.  * * * This law affords some defence against that hazard."  * * * There is therefore little force to the argument that the benefits are intended only for those who have been fired or otherwise forced to leave by their employers.  The broader purpose of the law is to provide temporary relief for those who are realistically compelled to leave work through no "fault" of their own, whatever the source of the compulsion, personal or employer-initiated.  Intrinsically, the law discourages those who are not truly compelled to leave work by temporarily disqualifying those who leave their jobs voluntarily.

The history of § 25(c)(1) indicates that the Legislature has been well aware of the significance of the exclusion or inclusion of the word "voluntarily."  In its decision, the board of review noted the interaction between various formulations of § 25(e)(1) and its own decisions: "From 1951 to 1953, Section 25(e)(1) * * * provided that a person would be disqualified from receiving unemployment benefits if he 'left his employment voluntarily without good cause attributable to the employing unit or its agent.  * * * ' During this period * * * the Board took notice of the significance of the word 'voluntarily' * * * and found that persons who were obliged to leave their work for causes over which they had no control, that is, involuntarily, were not subject to disqualification * * *.  [In 1953] the Law was amended only to the extent that the word 'voluntarily' was deleted.  In decisions of the Board made subsequent to the elimination of the word 'voluntarily' from the * * * statute, no differentiation was made between a voluntary or involuntary leaving of work, the sole consideration being whether or not the claimant left with or without good cause attributable to the employing unit.  Again in 1958 * * * [the law] was altered to read as follows: '* * * if an individual has left his work (1) voluntarily without good cause.'  * * * [A 1969] revision * * * adds the words 'attributable to the employing unit or its * * * [agent].' "  On the basis of the legislative history and responsive variations in board decisions, it is fair to say that the Legislature, in reinserting the word "voluntarily" in its 1958 version of § 25(c)(1), fully intended that the board revert to its recognition of compelling personal reasons as sufficient grounds for avoiding disqualification.

* * *

Decision of the District Court affirmed.

## NOTES AND QUESTIONS

**1.**  Employers were unhappy with the *Raytheon* decision.  They saw unemployment insurance benefits, for which they pay, as proper where the employer no longer offers a job. Here Raytheon was happy to keep employing Etta Miller, but she stopped coming to work. Yet surely the court was right that her resignation was reasonable, involuntary, and not her fault. Should the country, and the economy, provide 26 weeks of benefits to someone in Miller's situation? If so, is the court justified in changing established law in this way, or should the matter await statutory change? Is the decision part of a general decline in the work ethic or, on the other hand, an appropriate improvement in the security of all workers?

**2.** Antoinette Reedy was a sales person, floor manager, bookkeeper, and sexual harassment officer at M.H. King Co. George Anne Renfrow, another employee and Reedy's sister-in-law, told Reedy of a sexually inappropriate comment made by Todd Taylor, a male employee, concerning John Salcido, the store manager. Renfrow had not been offended by the comment, but Reedy checked with the company's sexual harassment coordinator and was told to file a complaint regarding the incident. When Reedy returned from a ten day vacation, Salcido told her that he had issued a reprimand based on her filing the complaint and that Renfrow had not been harassed or offended. Some of Reedy's tasks were reassigned. Reedy felt that co-workers were giving her the "cold shoulder" and discussing her behind her back. Suffering from stress, she resigned.

The Idaho Supreme Court upheld the commissioner's grant of unemployment benefits and found that Reedy had good cause for her resignation. Reedy v. M.H. King Co., 920 P.2d 915 (Idaho 1996).

**3.** A Pennsylvania court granted unemployment benefits to a claimant who quit her job as a nurse's aide after realizing that her arthritis did not permit her to do the lifting that the job required. "Because Claimant had a necessitous and compelling reason to terminate her employment, and because Employer did not adequately and accurately inform Claimant of the requirements of the job, thereby necessitating Claimant's informing Employer of her back condition, we conclude that Claimant was unemployed through no fault of her own." Schnee v. Unemployment Compensation Board of Review, 701 A.2d 994 (Pa.Cmwlth.1997).

**4.** Paul Platt worked as a locker room attendant at a private golf and tennis club for 70 to 80 hours a week, including 64 consecutive days without a full day off. Both Platt and his fellow attendant quit when no additional help was hired. A claims adjudicator and appeals referee both ruled that Platt quit his work without good cause. The appeals court reversed, holding that the reasons for quitting are good cause when the "average, able-bodied, qualified worker" would quit and noted that Platt's fellow attendant also quit. Platt v. Unemployment Appeals Commission, 618 So.2d 340 (Fla.App.1993).

**5.** Petitioner, a Jehovah's Witness, quit his job because his religious beliefs forbade participation in production of weapons. Indiana denied unemployment insurance benefits. The Supreme Court reversed, finding a violation of the free exercise of religion. Thomas v. Review Board, 450 U.S. 707 (1981). In a similar case, a referee determined that a fired public school teacher was ineligible for unemployment benefits because her wearing of a religious head wrap was insubordination and thus misconduct. The teacher was a member of "the original African Hebrew Israelites out of Ethiopia." The Supreme Court of Mississippi held that wearing the religious head wrap was constitutionally protected religious and cultural expression, and so she should receive UI benefits. Mississippi Employment Security Commission v. McGlothin, 556 So.2d 324 (Miss.1990) (5–4), cert. denied, 498 U.S. 879 (1990).

**6.** Tenner Jones worked as a cook for three months from 9 a.m. to 3 p.m. Told that if she could not work to 6 p.m. someone else would be hired, she accepted a change to a 9–6 day. One day later she said she could not work those hours because she had four children at home. Because Ms. Jones accepted the change in hours, she did not have good cause for her quit and was disqualified from eligibility for UI. Jones v. Review Board, 399 N.E.2d 844 (Ind.App.1980).

**7.** Marilyn Davis, hired to set up pre-schooling for three to five year-olds, was told to work with emotionally disturbed children when funding for the other program ran out. Feeling unqualified for the new work, she developed headaches and became upset. When she resigned, an Illinois appellate court said she had not left the job "without good cause attributable to the employing unit" and therefore should be eligible for unemployment insurance benefits. "A substantial, unilateral change in the employment may render the job unsuitable and entitle the worker to benefits even if he leaves voluntarily." Davis v. Board of Review, 465 N.E.2d 576 (Ill.App. 1984).

Compare an Indiana decision that it is not "good cause in connection with the work" to quit because a shift change causes transportation and child care problems. Gray v. Dobbs House, Inc., 357 N.E.2d 900 (Ind.App. 1976).

**8.** Francisco Olmeda could not get to work because his driver's license was suspended for traffic violations. Eligibility for unemployment insurance was denied because "he brought his unemployment on himself." Olmeda v. Director of the Division of Employment Security, 475 N.E.2d 1216 (Mass.1985).

## Norman v. Unemployment Insurance Appeals Board
663 P.2d 904 (Cal.1983).

■ RICHARDSON, JUSTICE.

Does the voluntary termination of one's employment in order to follow a nonmarital "loved one" to another location constitute "good cause" for purposes of determining eligibility to receive unemployment compensation benefits? Concluding that it does not, we will reverse the trial court's judgment which sets aside a decision of the Unemployment Insurance Appeals Board (Board) denying unemployment compensation benefits.

Section 1256 provides in relevant part: "An individual is disqualified for unemployment compensation benefits if the director finds that he left his most recent work voluntarily without good cause * * *.'' We apply this standard to the record before us.

On January 4, 1979, plaintiff commenced her employment with Mohawk Data Sciences Corp. in California. In July 1979, plaintiff's boyfriend, with whom she had been living, found employment in the State of Washington. Plaintiff thereupon gave notice to her employer that she intended to quit her job as of September 7, 1979, in order to move to Washington to join him.

Plaintiff inquired about work in Washington before leaving California but was told that no positions were available. She nonetheless felt that she could obtain employment and moved as she had intended. After her further job search was unsuccessful she filed a claim for unemployment compensation benefits with the California Employment Development Department (Department). On October 4, 1979, she was informed by Department that she was ineligible to receive benefits because "There was no compelling reason for the move," and therefore there was no "good cause" for leaving her work with Mohawk.

During the hearing of her administrative appeal, plaintiff acknowledged that she had no definite job prospects in Washington and had left her position "Because my fiance was moving to Washington and I moved up here with my fiance." In her words, the "sole reason" she quit work was to join her fiance and "it kind of put me on the spot, either come up here and live with him up here in Washington or to break up." Plaintiff further testified that in January 1979 she and her fiance decided to marry in June 1980. She did not, however, represent that her marriage was imminent, that her presence in Washington was required to prepare for the wedding, or, indeed, that she had any definite or fixed marital plans.

\* \* \*

In section 100, the Legislature described its policy underlying the creation of an unemployment insurance system as "providing benefits for persons unemployed through no fault of their own, and to reduce involuntary unemployment and the suffering caused thereby to a minimum." It has been said that in determining whether an employee has "left work voluntarily" within the meaning of section 1256, "the cases have not given that phrase its literal meaning. An employee need not actually choose to be unemployed; it is enough that his unemployment is the result of his own fault—a willful act causing or instigating his unemployment." However, a voluntary departure does not disqualify an employee from benefits so long as "good cause" is shown which we have defined very generally as "an adequate cause, a cause that comports with the purposes of the California Unemployment Insurance Code and with other laws." * * * One court has suggested that "Good cause may exist for personal reasons but those reasons must be so imperative and compelling as to make the voluntary leaving 'involuntary.' "

Former section 1264, repealed in 1976, had provided that an employee who left "employment to be married or to accompany his or her spouse to join her or him at a place from which it [was] impractical to commute" was deemed *in*eligible for benefits unless the individual at the time of his or her voluntary departure and filing of the claim was "the sole or major support of his or her family."   The repeal of this section followed the decision of the Court of Appeal in Boren v. Department of Employment Dev. (1976) 59 Cal.App.3d 250, 130 Cal.Rptr. 683.   *Boren* held that the effect of section 1264 was to disqualify improperly a group of claimants from certain benefits without any demonstration by the state of a compelling governmental interest justifying the discriminatory statutory classification.

\* \* \*

In Marvin v. Marvin, 18 Cal.3d 660, 134 Cal.Rptr. 815, 557 P.2d 106 (1976), we emphasized the property rights of nonmarital partners when their relationship terminated, holding that "adults who voluntarily live together and engage in sexual relations are nonetheless *as competent as any other persons to contract* respecting their earnings and property rights \* \* \*.   So long as the agreement does not rest upon illicit meretricious consideration, the parties may order their economic affairs as they choose, and no policy precludes the courts from enforcing such agreements."   As to the marital relationship, however, we carefully emphasized that "the structure of society itself largely depends upon the institution of marriage, and nothing we have said in this opinion should be taken to derogate from that institution."   \* \* \* The essence of *Marvin* thus was that nonmarital partners were not *barred* by virtue of their relationship from asserting those contractual rights and remedies which are available to other persons.

\* \* \*

Recent appellate opinions have recognized the limitations of *Marvin* and have declined to equate a nonmarital relationship with marriage. Thus, in People v. Delph (1979) 94 Cal.App.3d 411, 156 Cal.Rptr. 422, the court was examining the term "spouse" within the "marital communications" privilege.   In declining to extend this privilege to nonmarital partners, the court accurately characterized *Marvin* as providing: "... a method for equitable resolution of property disputes in situations where the parties not only carried on a relationship that, except for the formal ceremony, was marriage-like, but where they also entered into an implied contract or agreement as to ownership of property, thus protecting the reasonable expectations of the parties.   This in no way signals a general elevation of meretricious relationships themselves to the level of marriages for any and all purposes.   It is for the Legislature to determine whether such relationships, because of their commonness in today's society or for other policy reasons, deserve the statutory protection afforded the sanctity of the marriage union."

\* \* \*

Nothing in plaintiff's unmarried state *precludes* her from receiving benefits to which she would otherwise be entitled.   The Legislature's decision to give weight to marital relationships in the determination of "good cause" supports public policy encouraging marriage and is a reasonable method of alleviating otherwise difficult problems of proof.

* * *

Plaintiff here did not demonstrate the "imminency of her marriage" or any need for termination of employment at the time that she left work because of marriage related obligations. Plaintiff's decision to move to Washington came 10 months before her marriage was anticipated. It may be of some interest that, indeed, at oral argument more than 2 years later, we were informed that no marriage had as yet occurred. More significantly, nothing in her notification of termination to her employer or in her request for unemployment compensation benefits indicated that her presence in Washington was necessary because of concrete marriage plans which required "on-the-spot" arrangements.

We reaffirm our recognition of a strong public policy favoring marriage. No similar policy favors the maintenance of nonmarital relationships. We therefore conclude that plaintiff did not, as a matter of law, establish "good cause" for her voluntary departure from her employment within the meaning of section 1256. In the absence of legislation which grants to members of a nonmarital relationship the same benefits as those granted to spouses, no basis exists in this context for extending to nonmarital relations the preferential status afforded to marital relations.

Plaintiff also asserts a constitutional claim, arguing that to deny her the benefits accorded to those who are married violates her right of privacy and freedom of association, * * * In essence, plaintiff's argument is that nonmarried persons must be afforded all the rights and benefits extended to married persons. We do not agree. Underlying the unemployment compensation scheme is the state's legitimate interest in promoting marriage.

* * *

Recognizing and favoring those with established marital and familial ties not only furthers the state's interest in promoting such relationships but assures a more readily verifiable method of proof. Plaintiff here has demonstrated no compelling obligations requiring termination of her employment; she was neither following a spouse nor moving because of imminent plans to marry. [N]umerous problems of standards and difficulties of proof would arise if we imposed upon an administrative agency the function of deciding which relationships merited treatment equivalent to the treatment afforded those with formal marriages. The inevitable questions such as the factors deemed relevant, the length of the relationship, the parties' eventual plans as to marriage, and the sincerity of their beliefs as to whether they should ever marry. The potential for administrative intrusions into rights of privacy and association would be severe if agencies bore the burden of ferreting out the "true depth" and intimacy of a relationship in order to determine whether the existence and nature of the relationship was the equivalent of marriage.

Nothing, of course, would prevent claimants in such situations from establishing "good cause" based on compelling circumstances which make the voluntary leaving akin to an involuntary departure. Thus, for example, where there are children of a nonformalized relationship, and an employee leaves his or her position to be with a nonmarital loved one and their children, good cause might be shown. However, neither the statutes nor our decisions beginning with *Marvin* require that we extend to partners in nonmarital relationships such as plaintiff, the evidentiary benefits extended to marital partners.

The judgment of the trial court is reversed and the cause is remanded to the trial court with directions to deny the writ.

■ BROUSSARD, JUSTICE, dissenting.

* * *

In my opinion, section 1256 envisions a case-by-case determination of "good cause." While the courts may reasonably create an evidentiary presumption that a married person, or one about to be married, acts with "good cause" when he leaves work to join his spouse, we have no authority to create a rule denying a nonmarital partner the right to prove that he too acted with "good cause" in leaving employment. We cannot deny the fact that a nonmarital relationship can acquire such significance and importance in the lives and hopes of the persons involved that one partner may reasonably and in good faith decide that preserving the relationship justifies terminating current employment. If the partner can thus prove "good cause" without resort to any evidentiary presumption, he is entitled to unemployment benefits.

* * *

I do not claim that the state must equate marriage and nonmarital relationships in determining rights to unemployment compensation. To the contrary, the board and the courts may properly invoke a presumption of good cause to benefit a claimant who moves to maintain a present or imminent marriage, without granting a like presumption for persons in nonmarital relationships. But the presumption in favor of marriage should not lead us to refuse to recognize that there exist close, enduring, and significant nonmarital relationships, that such relationships may give rise to moral and (under *Marvin* ) legal obligations, and that in a particular case the maintenance of such a relationship may constitute "good cause" for leaving employment. Finding that the plaintiff's reasons for terminating employment in the present case meet the test of "good cause" under section 1256, I would affirm the judgment of the trial court granting unemployment benefits.

NOTES

**1.** In Reep v. Commissioner of Dept. of Employment and Training, 593 N.E.2d 1297 (Mass.1992), a Massachusetts woman who quit her job to move with her male domestic partner of 13 years received unemployment insurance benefits. The court found that the "urgent, compelling, and necessitous nature" clause treating separations as involuntary should be read liberally and that a "legally cognizable relationship" was not necessary for statutory protection.

**2.**   See Austin v. Berryman, 878 F.2d 786 (4th Cir.1989), cert. denied, 493 U.S. 941 (1989), where the Fourth Circuit upheld the denial of benefits to a wife who moved to be with her husband as mandated by her religion.  The court found that the denial of benefits did not infringe unconstitutionally on the marital relationship, nor was the Virginia statute which dictated the denial of benefits an unconstitutional restriction of the free exercise of religion.  The decision was on en banc rehearing, by 6–4 vote.  Is Austin v. Berryman inconsistent with *Frazee,* infra p. 1144?  If the wife prevailed in *Austin,* would the state be preferring religion unconstitutionally?

**3.**   Patricia MacGregor quit her job as a waitress to move with her fiance and their child to live with and take care of the fiance's ailing father.  The Supreme Court of California granted benefits, recognizing that despite the lack of a formal marriage there was a family unit which needed to stay together.  The court reaffirmed California's view that "the importance of preserving the marital or familial relationship may provide good cause for the other spouse's decision to follow."  MacGregor v. Unemployment Insurance Appeals Board, 689 P.2d 453 (Cal.1984).  But cf. Davis v. Employment Security Department, 737 P.2d 1262 (Wash.1987) (must take "immediate family" literally—no fundamental right to live in a meretricious relationship, and not good cause for UI purposes to move for the purpose of continuing such a relationship).

## Garner v. Horkley Oil

853 P.2d 576 (Idaho 1993).

■ McDEVITT, CHIEF JUSTICE.

Claimants James A. Garner ("Garner") and Chris D. Hadley ("Hadley") applied for unemployment benefits after each had voluntarily quit his previous employment to accept offers of new employment which proved unsuccessful.  Garner quit his part-time work as a truck driver with Horkley Oil to accept a full-time position as a salesman for Anderson Lumber Company.  Garner became partially unemployed after three months with Anderson Lumber due to a slow down.  Hadley quit work as a house framing laborer for Roger Carney after he received an offer of employment from Y–J Foods for work as a butcher.  Hadley's offer was later rescinded.

Although both claimants were initially determined to be ineligible for benefits, the appeals examiner reversed that determination, finding that each claimant had satisfied the requirements of IDAPA 09.30.483 and 09.30.484, and thus were entitled to benefits.[1]

---

**1.  IDAPA § 09.30.483**—For purposes of Idaho Code § 72–1366(e), to be connected with employment, a claimant's reason(s) for leaving the employment must arise from the

Both Horkley Oil and Roger Carney protested the appeals examiner's decisions to the Commission, which reversed the decision of the appeals examiner in both cases. The Commission determined that IDAPA 09.30.484 was inconsistent with I.C. § 72–1366(e),[2] and therefore, the appeals examiner's conclusion that Garner and Hadley had met their burdens of proving they quit their jobs with good cause in connection with their employment, as required by I.C. § 72–1366(e), was incorrect.

In support of its decision, the Commission relied on Schafer v. Ada County Assessor, 111 Idaho 870, 728 P.2d 394 (1986), which held that a county employee, who resigned his job voluntarily because he thought he had a firm job offer from another employer, left his job with "good cause." At the time *Schafer* was decided, the words "connected with his employment" were not part of the definition of "good cause." However, a few months after *Schafer* was decided, I.C. § 72–1366(e) was amended to require that a claimant show that such individual "left his employment voluntarily [with] good cause *connected with his employment.*" Based on this history of the law the Commission concluded the following:

> The Commission concludes that the legislature intended, in amending the statute to again require that "good cause" be "connected with" an individual's "employment," to disallow benefits where an employee quit only because he or she intended to take another job. The fact that such a job would meet the requirements of [IDAPA 09.30.484] is irrelevant. The employee's decision to quit his or her employment in order to take a "better" job is subjective, personal and unique to the employee and is not "connected with" the individual's prior employment. Because [IDAPA 09.30.484] contravenes I.C. § 72–1366(e), it cannot stand.

Following the Commission's decisions, the Department filed a motion to reconsider both cases. The Commission issued a consolidated "Order on Reconsideration" which affirmed its previous decision that both Garner

working conditions, job tasks, or employment agreement. If the claimant's reason(s) for leaving the employment arise from personal/non job-related matters, the reasons are not connected with the claimant's employment.

**IDAPA § 09.30.484**—In addition to satisfying the requirements of Rule 30.483, a claimant who quits suitable work to accept other suitable work must prove both of the following in order to establish that the claimant quit with good cause in connection with employment:

(1) That the claimant had a good faith and reasonable belief that the claimant had a definite job offer, that the job was expected to begin immediately or in the shortest reasonable time, and the job would be a continuing one; and

(2) That after comparing the old job (and all reasonable alternatives available with that employer) to the offer of the new job, the new job would provide better compensation or other more favorable term(s) of employment, to such a degree that a reasonable and prudent person would feel compelled to leave the old job and accept the offer of the new job.

**2. I.C. § 72–1366—PERSONAL ELIGIBILITY CONDITIONS.** The personal eligibility conditions of a benefit claimant are that—

(e) His unemployment is not due to the fact that he left his employment voluntarily without good cause connected with his employment, or that he was discharged for misconduct in connection with his employment.

and Hadley left work for personal reasons unconnected with their employment. The Commission also reaffirmed its ruling that IDAPA 09.30.484 was invalid, finding the Department's interpretation of I.C. § 72–1366(e) to be unreasonable. This appeal followed.

\* \* \*

At the heart of the Commission's decision is the long standing rule that "good cause" for voluntarily terminating employment cannot be based on reasons which are subjective and personal to the employee. The Commission determined that an employee's decision to quit his or her employment in order to take a better job is subjective, personal and unique to the employee and is not "connected with" the individual's prior employment. Thus, the Commission determined that whether or not an employee could meet the requirements of IDAPA 09.30.484 is irrelevant.

However, *Schafer* did not hold that quitting employment for other employment is never a personal decision. Rather, *Schafer* merely held that I.C. § 72–1366(e) at that time did not require that good cause be "connected with" an individuals employment. Although the 1987 amendment to the statute would now require such a finding, the issue of whether or not it is always a personal decision to leave one job for another was not before the Court in *Schafer*. Therefore, any legislation subsequent to that decision cannot be interpreted as overruling such a holding.

\* \* \*

\* \* \* In light of IDAPA 09.30.483, the Commission's conclusion that IDAPA 09.30.484 effectively deletes the phrase "connected with his employment" is unfounded. IDAPA 09.30.484, when combined with IDAPA 09.30.483, is completely consistent with I.C. § 72–1366(e). Therefore we find that IDAPA 09.30.484 is a reasonable interpretation of I.C. § 72–1366(e). \* \* \*

Finally, we believe that judicial deference is justified in this case. IDAPA 09.30.484 provides a practical and reasonable guideline to determine "good cause in connection with employment" for situations when an employee leaves one job for another. Most importantly, as we determined above, IDAPA 09.30.484 is consistent with the long standing rules regarding good cause and the need to avoid subjective and personal reasons in establishing good cause. Accordingly, we hold that IDAPA 09.30.484 is valid and entitled to deference.

However, the primary policy in the act is still to prevent "involuntary" unemployment, not to encourage the voluntary upgrading of employment. In this respect, IDAPA 09.30.483 requires the claimant to prove that the leaving of his employment must arise from "working conditions, job tasks or employment agreement." The requirements of IDAPA 09.30.484 specifically state that they are "in addition to satisfying the requirements of regulation 483."

\* \* \*

* * * On remand the Commission should consider the claimants' compliance with both IDAPA 09.30.483 and 09.30.484, and set out specifically whether the claimants' unemployment arise from "working conditions, job tasks or [the] employment agreement" which were sufficiently unreasonable, or unbearable, to justify the claimants' voluntary termination.

The order of the Commission is reversed, and the matter is remanded for further findings consistent herewith.

NOTES AND QUESTIONS

**1.**   Eileen Dohoney had a full-time job in a bank. When she became pregnant, she switched to part-time work until she finally left her job without indicating a desire to return. When she was again available to work, she declined to accept her previous part-time position and proceeded to file for unemployment benefits. While the court would have allowed Dohoney unemployment benefits if her reason for leaving was involuntary because it was due to "an urgent, compelling and necessitous nature" according to General Laws c. 151A, § 25(e), the court found that Dohoney did not take reasonable measures to preserve her job and was therefore ineligible for unemployment benefits. Dohoney v. Director of the Division of Employment Security, 386 N.E.2d 10 (Mass.1979). Although Dohoney denied benefits to the claimant due to the specific facts of the case, the court generally would allow for a subjective determination by the employee that good cause existed. In contrast, Garner allows for subjective determinations only in the specific case of taking another job and Norman restricted statutory good cause to marital relationships. Is it more true to the purposes of the unemployment compensation system to use subjective or objective determinations of good cause for quitting?

**2.**   See George Dahm & William Fineshriber, Disqualifications for Quits to Meet Family Obligations, in 1 Unemployment Compensation: Studies and Research 9, 13–14 (National Commission on Unemployment Compensation 1980):

> Overall the States treat the causes grouped as marital obligations as follows: leaving to marry is a disqualifying reason in eight States; leaving to accompany or join spouse is disqualifying in six States; leaving because of marital, parental, filial, or domestic obligations or circumstances is disqualifying in nine States. In three States the marital-obligation disqualification is not applicable if the claimant is or becomes "main support" or "sole or major support" of self or family, and, in the case of Pennsylvania, if "such work is not within reasonable commuting distance." * * *

> Although the relationship of penalties for general and special disqualifications differs among the States, a marital-obligation disqualification is automatic in all 13; the specific cause and circumstances cannot be considered. By contrast, 11 of these States have an unrestricted good-cause disqualification, under which special circumstances can be considered. It is very hard for

the disqualified claimants to reestablish eligibility in the benefit year. They would have to be reemployed and work long enough to meet the additional earnings requirement, which can be as much as 8 times the weekly benefit amount, and then happen to become unemployed for a nondisqualifying reason. The only exception is in "main support" or "sole or major support" situations. This exception approaches, if it does not constitute, a needs test. It does have the effect of reducing the number of men penalized by the marital-obligation provisions. Although they are less likely to leave a job for family obligations, they are doing so more often than they used to.

In a few of the appeals cases reviewed for this report, the wife had the better job and initiated the move to another area; the husband left his work to take his chances on getting work in the new location. In these situations, the husband was disqualified or found unavailable, depending on the State law.

UI was never intended for the individual who was not available for work—ready, willing, and able to work—or not doing what a reasonable person would do to get another job. The determination of an individual's availability can only be made *week by week*. Special family disqualifications are unnecessary for the purpose of denying benefits to those who are not in the labor force. While the child or the husband is ill, or until child care arrangements can be made, benefits would not be payable. Thus, the normal voluntary quit and availability requirements provide an adequate basis for paying or denying benefits. The special provisions are undesirable because they preclude consideration of the facts and because they may continue to cause denial of benefits long after any unavailability has ended.

Do you agree?

**3.** Missouri denied benefits to a claimant who left work as a cashier and sales clerk at J.C. Penney because of pregnancy and was denied reinstatement even though she was available to return to her old job. The U.S. unemployment law, 26 U.S.C. § 3304(a)(12), says that "no person shall be denied compensation * * * solely on the basis of pregnancy or termination of pregnancy." The Missouri Supreme Court said the U.S. provision did not apply in this case because the state disqualifies everyone who leaves work voluntarily and without good cause attributable to the employer, and thus this disqualification was not "solely" due to pregnancy. Wimberly v. Labor & Industrial Relations Commission, 688 S.W.2d 344 (Mo.1985). The U.S. Supreme Court unanimously affirmed: "[I]f a State adopts a neutral rule that incidentally disqualifies pregnant or formerly pregnant claimants as part of a larger group, the neutral application of that rule cannot readily be characterized as a decision made 'solely on the basis of pregnancy.'" Wimberly v. Labor & Industrial Relations Commission, 479 U.S. 511, 517 (1987). Lawsuits have challenged state presumptions that mothers of newborns are not "available" for work and are therefore ineligible for unemployment insurance benefits. See, e.g., Connecticut National Organization for Women v. Peraro, 23 EPD (CCH) ¶ 31,169 (D.Conn.1980) (consent decree forbidding various state agencies from declaring women who are recovering from delivery, who are breast feeding, or who have young children not yet in child care, as unable to work and thus ineligible for unemployment compensation), cited in Lucinda Finley, Transcending Equality Theory: A Way Out of the Maternity and the Workplace Debate, 86 Colum.L.Rev. 1118, 1125 n. 24 (1986).

**4.** State courts disagree over whether a worker who quits because other employees smoke should receive unemployment insurance benefits. Among cases awarding benefits are Alexander v. Unemployment Insurance Appeals Board, 163 Cal.Rptr. 411 (Cal.App.1980) (benefits for X-ray technologist allergic to cigarette smoke; employer did not enforce its no-smoking policy), and McCrocklin v. Employment Development Department, 205 Cal.Rptr. 156 (Cal.App.1984) (even if medical evidence is ambiguous, worker reasonably feared effects of exposure to smoke so quit was not disqualifying for benefits). Contra: Rotenberg v. Industrial Commission, 590 P.2d 521 (Colo.App.1979) (benefits disqualification for computer programmer who quit when employer refused to create no-smoking work area). Is it relevant whether a state or local smoking ordinance is in effect?

**5.** A Louisiana appellate court found "good cause" when an employee volunteered to resign in the face of company lay-offs in lieu of allowing a less senior colleague to be dismissed. South Central Bell Telephone Co. v. Department of Labor, 527 So.2d 1113 (La.App.1988), cert. denied 532 So.2d 153 (La.1988).

*(ii) Discharge for Misconduct*

## Pesce v. Board of Review

515 N.E.2d 849 (Ill.App.1987).

■ Presiding JUSTICE SCARIANO delivered the opinion of the court:

Plaintiff, Barry Pesce, brought an administrative review action in the circuit court of Cook County, seeking review of a decision of the Illinois Department of Employment Security, Board of Review. The Board found, pursuant to section 602(A) of the Unemployment Insurance Act, that plaintiff was ineligible for unemployment insurance benefits because he was discharged from his job for misconduct. The circuit court reversed the Board's decision, and the Board has appealed, contending that its decision was supported by the manifest weight of the evidence and was in accordance with the law.

Plaintiff was employed as a driver of a medicar, used to transport patients to and from hospitals and nursing homes, for A.C.S. Medicar (employer) for approximately three and one-half months. During that time, he was involved in four accidents with the employer's vehicle. Each of these accidents occurred while plaintiff was backing up and resulted in plaintiff striking a stationary object with the vehicle. There were no patients in the medicar at the times of these accidents and none of the accidents caused severe damage. Plaintiff was suspended from work for three days after the first accident, paid the employer for the damage to the medicar after the second accident, and was again suspended after the third accident. After the fourth accident, the plaintiff was discharged because his involvement in the accidents violated a company rule.

Plaintiff's application for unemployment insurance benefits was denied by a claims adjudicator and plaintiff filed an appeal of that determination. An administrative hearing was conducted at which plaintiff appeared pro se. The employer was represented by Steve Rabin, vice president of operations. Rabin testified that the employer felt that there was no choice but to terminate the plaintiff because he had some type of problem when he was backing up the medicar. Rabin also stated that plaintiff was a member of a union while working for the employer and that a union rule provided for discharge after two accidents. When asked by the hearing referee whether the employee is allowed leeway for accidents that are not his fault, Rabin answered affirmatively and indicated that was why plaintiff was discharged after four accidents rather than after two. The hearing referee issued a decision denying benefits, finding plaintiff ineligible because his actions constituted misconduct within the meaning of the Act.

Plaintiff thereafter retained counsel and appealed the referee's decision to the Board. The Board affirmed the denial of benefits pursuant to section 602 A of the Act. Plaintiff subsequently filed a complaint in the circuit court for administrative review of the Board's determination. The circuit court reversed the Board's decision finding it to be incorrect as a matter of law. On appeal the Board contends that the circuit court erred.
* * *

Every justifiable discharge does not disqualify the discharged employee from receiving unemployment benefits. An employee's conduct may be such that the employer may properly discharge him. Such conduct may not, however, constitute "misconduct connected with the work" which disqualifies him from receiving unemployment benefits. Misconduct has been defined as conduct evincing such wilful or wanton disregard of an employer's interests as is found in deliberate violations or disregard of standards of behavior which the employer had the right to expect of his employee, or in carelessness or negligence of such degree or recurrence as to manifest equal culpability, wrongful intent or evil design, or to show an intentional and substantial disregard of the employer's interests or of the employee's duties and obligations to his employer.

Every violation of a company rule will not constitute misconduct. The rule must be a reasonable rule governing the conduct or performance of an employee. In addition to the existence of such a rule, it must be shown that the breach of the rule is deliberate or its equivalent, as indicated in the above definition.

In this case, the record shows that the plaintiff had four accidents with stationary objects while backing up in the employer's vehicle. There is no evidence of deliberate conduct or a wilful or wanton disregard of the employer's interests. Similarly, we do not find that the plaintiff's conduct can be characterized as carelessness or negligence of such a degree or recurrence as to manifest equal culpability, wrongful intent or evil design, or to show an intentional and substantial disregard of the employer's interests or of the plaintiff's duties and obligations to his employer. We hold that a finding of misconduct is improper where there was no showing of an unreasonable and improper course of conduct from which could be imputed a lack of proper regard for the employer's interests.

The Board states in its reply brief that plaintiff was discharged due to his inability to back up the employer's vehicle. The Board then goes on to equate the plaintiff's inability to back up the vehicle with gross indifference to the interests of his employer, thereby disqualifying him from receiving unemployment insurance benefits. We do not agree with this conclusion. The Board argues that a finding of misconduct is necessary to avoid the potential of his injuring or aggravating an existing injury of one of the patients who relied on him for transportation. This is, however, an erroneous construction of section 602 A of the Act. As previously stated, although the employer's discharge of the plaintiff may have been proper, there is insufficient evidence in the record to establish that plaintiff's conduct constituted misconduct under the statute.

For the foregoing reasons, we hold that the circuit court's reversal of the Board's decision finding it to be incorrect as a matter of law was proper. The judgment of the circuit court of Cook County is affirmed.

## NOTES AND QUESTIONS

**1.** The common cases about discharge for misconduct concern breach of employer rules. The unemployment insurance administrators evaluate the validity of the rule and the reasonableness of its application. The unemployment insurance system thus gives us a body of law on the subject of whether a discharge was "for misconduct." That body of law will now be relevant if discharges themselves become administratively or judicially reviewable. Wrongful discharge is the subject of Chapter 10.

An example of a "run-of-the-mill" discharge-for-misconduct case is Smith v. Director of Division of Employment Security, 382 N.E.2d 199 (Mass.1978). In that case, the state agency refused unemployment insurance benefits to a plaintiff whose employer had fired him for drinking alcohol in his car during a break. The Supreme Judicial Court remanded for a decision as to whether the employer had enforced the rule with dismissal in the past. On another appeal after remand, the Supreme Judicial Court found that the claimant had failed to establish discriminatory application of the rule to him, 429 N.E.2d 700 (Mass.1981). A later Massachusetts case shifted to employers the burden of persuading the factfinder that a dismissed employee's conduct evidenced "deliberate misconduct in willful disregard of the employing unit's interest." Cantres v. Director, 484 N.E.2d 1336 (Mass.1985).

A Pennsylvania court found no violation of the free exercise clause of the First Amendment when a parochial school teacher, dismissed for violating church doctrine, was denied unemployment benefits because of her misconduct in marrying a non-Catholic man previously divorced from a Catholic woman. Bishop Leonard Regional Catholic School v. Unemployment Compensation Board of Review, 593 A.2d 28 (Pa.Cmwlth.1991), appeal denied, 600 A.2d 540 (Pa. 1991), cert. denied, 503 U.S. 985 (1992).

**2.** Cases interpreting statutes using the "willful misconduct" standard sometimes yield different results from "just cause" cases. See, e.g., Wedgewood v. Director of Division of Employment Security, 514 N.E.2d 680 (Mass.App.Ct.1987) (repeatedly sleeping on the job is not "willful misconduct"). Which standard better serves the policy goals of unemployment insurance?

Under the willful misconduct standard, the Supreme Court of Montana held that an employee must show "intentional disregard of the employer's expectation." Negligence will not suffice to cut off unemployment benefits. LaVe v. Montana State Department of Labor & Industry, 780 P.2d 189 (Mont.1989).

**3.** In Southern Pacific Transport Co. v. Doyal, 289 So.2d 882 (La.App. 1974), a truckdriver was dismissed for refusing to cut his long hair. The court found the dismissal to be for cause, disqualifying the dismissed employee from unemployment insurance benefits. There had been no hair length rule when the employee was hired, but later the company and the union agreed that "the employer has the right to establish and maintain reasonable standards for wearing apparel and personal grooming." Compare *Doyal* to the hair-length and other grooming issues discussed in Chapter 7. Does the employer need the unilateral power to determine hair length? Is the right rule that the employee should have no right to prevent discharge for this reason but a right to collect unemployment insurance benefits?

**4.** Rudy Castaneda, employed as a social worker at a boys ranch, did his supervisor a favor by accompanying a resident juvenile to a hearing. While at the hearing, Castaneda received a call from his fiancee who believed she was miscarrying and who was without transportation. After informing the juvenile's attorney and his case worker of a personal emergency and determining that the juvenile's presence was not necessary at the hearing, Cataneda returned the juvenile to the ranch and went to his fiancee. When Castaneda appeared at the ranch the next morning he declined to discuss the details of the emergency with his supervisor, preferring to discuss it instead with his former supervisor or with the assistant director of the ranch. The assistant director fired him less than a week later. The state court of appeals found that Castaneda's absence was due to urgent domestic responsibility and rejected the argument that he did not have a "legally sufficient relationship" with his fiancee for the miscarriage to qualify as a "domestic" matter. Castaneda v. Arizona Department of Economic Security, 815 P.2d 418 (Ariz.App.1991).

**5.** A laboratory employee was discharged for refusing to perform assigned tasks on vials of bodily fluids with AIDS warnings attached. The Indiana Court of Appeals held that the worker was dismissed for just cause and so was not eligible for UI benefits. Stepp v. Review Board, 521 N.E.2d 350 (Ind.App.1988).

**6.** Claimant, a cashier, pleaded guilty to shoplifting and was discharged. The Washington Supreme Court said that since the off-the-job misconduct violated no rule of the employer, the discharge was not for "misconduct connected with his or her work," and therefore she could receive unemployment insurance benefits. Nelson v. Department of Employment Security, 655 P.2d 242 (Wash.1982).

**7.** After several warnings, an assistant professor of geography was dismissed because he had made insufficient efforts to complete his Ph.D. work. The college opposed award of unemployment insurance benefits, saying the termination was for misconduct. A Pennsylvania court agreed with the college. Millersville State College v. Commonwealth, 335 A.2d 857 (Pa.Cmwlth.1975). Do you agree? Is unsatisfactory performance the same thing as misconduct?

**8.** Opara v. Carnegie Textile Co., 498 N.E.2d 485 (Ohio App.1985), held that an employee fired for using anti-Semitic epithets against a co-worker who was Jewish had no claim to benefits under an unemployment insurance scheme denying benefits to those terminated for just cause:

> [S]ome language can be so disruptive and provocative that the employer's ability to maintain a productive environment is severely compromised. * * * [The employee's] extreme anti-Semitic remarks were presumably intended to provoke a bitter response. They successfully disrupted employment that day and were likely to impair his working relationship for an extended interval with the subjects of his attack. The employer was justified in discharging him to alleviate the problem he created.

*Opara* concerned a private company. Would the result have been different if the employer had been a government agency? Cf. Rankin v. McPherson, supra p. 613.

**9.** Employee, the director of physical education for a boy's club, was arrested for the possession of marijuana and admitted sufficient facts before trial for a finding of guilty. He was discharged by the club and subsequently applied for unemployment compensation under a statute denying benefits to employees fired solely for "deliberate misconduct in willful disregard of the employing unit's interests." His application was denied by the state administrative authority. The Massachusetts Supreme Judicial Court held: "An admission to sufficient facts [for a judicial finding of guilt] is not an act of 'misconduct.' [The boy's club] suggests that [such an] admission creates an 'appearance of impropriety.' However such an appearance does not constitute misconduct." Santos v. Director of Division of Employment Security, 498 N.E.2d 118 (Mass. 1986).

**10.** Is failing or refusing to take a drug test "misconduct"? Compare Glide Lumber Products Co. v. Employment Division, 741 P.2d 907 (Or. App. 1987) (no; minority rule) with Johnson v. Department of Employment Security, 782 P.2d 965 (Utah Ct.App.1989) (yes; majority rule).

Fred Weller was fired for violating the company drug testing policy after failing a drug test in which his urine sample was determined by two separate methods to be 60 nanograms of cannabinoids per milliliter of urine (ng/ml). The court held that notwithstanding the failure of the drug tests, the termination was not for work-related misconduct and should not disqualify Weller from unemployment benefits. The court found that the employer could not demonstrate that Weller was ever impaired while on the job, and that it "introduced no evidence whatever to show that its 50 ng/ml value for a positive test result was anything more than its own arbitrarily established figure" or that the 60 ng/ml level of Weller's sample was a result of direct intentional inhalation rather than passive inhalation of second-hand smoke. As a result, the court found that where the only evidence of misconduct was a "positive" urinalysis which did not indicate impairment of the employee's abilities at work, the employee was not terminated for misconduct which would disqualify him from unemployment benefits, although he was unlikely to have a wrongful discharge claim. Weller v. Arizona Department of Economic Security, 860 P.2d 487 (Ariz. App.1993).

## Amador v. Unemployment Insurance Appeals Board

677 P.2d 224 (Cal.1984).

■ BIRD, CHIEF JUSTICE.

Is a worker disqualified from collecting unemployment insurance benefits when she has been discharged for wilfully refusing to perform work which she reasonably and in good faith believed would jeopardize the health of others?

Nelly Amador appeals from a judgment of the superior court rejecting her petition for a writ of mandate. She sought to compel the Unemployment Insurance Appeals Board (board) to vacate its ruling that she was ineligible for unemployment insurance benefits because she had been discharged for "misconduct."

The San Mateo County (Chope) Community Hospital hired Nelly Amador as a histotechnician in May of 1976. Histotechnicians prepare tissue samples for microscopic analysis by pathologists, physicians who specialize in the interpretation and diagnosis of changes in tissues caused by disease. During Amador's tenure at Chope, she was one of two histotechnicians on the staff.

Amador completed her training in histology at Stanford University. She was licensed as a histotechnician by the American Society of Clinical Pathologists. Prior to her employment at Chope, she worked as a histotechnician for about four years at hospitals operated by Stanford University and by Oxford University.

Beginning about six months after Amador started work at Chope, two doctors asked her on several occasions to perform a procedure known as "grosscutting." Grosscutting consists of the selection and removal of small tissue samples of approximately one centimeter in breadth from organs or other large (gross) specimens removed by a doctor from a patient. On the basis of a microscopic examination of these samples, a pathologist diagnoses the patient's condition.

Amador declined to perform grosscutting on tissue removed from live patients. She explained that in her view grosscutting exceeded her capabilities as a histotechnician. She believed that the accuracy of a pathologist's diagnosis depends in large part on the selection and cutting of the small samples. And, in turn, a patient's life and health could hinge on the quality of the diagnosis. In her view, such life-and-death matters should be handled by physicians or by specially trained technicians. This view accorded with her experience at Stanford and Oxford, where histotechnicians had not been permitted to perform grosscutting.

Amador did not object to grosscutting on organs taken from cadavers. Nor did she decline to process small-size specimens selected and removed from live patients by doctors.

Until September of 1978, Chope respected Amador's objection. Her supervisors rated her performance "standard" in a May 1978 evaluation.

Eventually, however, the other histotechnician complained about having to do all of the grosscutting work. On September 29, Amador was again asked to perform the work. She refused. A Chope official warned her that she could be subject to discipline. She maintained her position and was suspended from work for two days in October. After a full adversary hearing, the county civil service commission (commission) upheld the suspension on February 2, 1979.

Sometime before the hearing, Amador contacted three outside pathologists. One, a professor of pathology at Stanford, had been a teacher of hers. Another had worked with her at the Stanford University Medical Center. The third was an official of the American Society of Clinical Pathologists, from which Amador held her license as a histotechnician. These three physicians supported her refusal to perform grosscutting.

In the week following the decision of the commission, Amador was repeatedly ordered to perform grosscutting or face discharge. Standing on her past experience and on the opinions of the outside pathologists, she continued to refuse. On February 26, Chope discharged her for incompetence and insubordination.

Shortly after her discharge, Amador applied for unemployment benefits. Chope objected, arguing that Amador was ineligible under section 1256 of the code, which provides that employees discharged for "misconduct" are disqualified for benefits. The claims interviewer rejected Chope's argument and awarded benefits.

Chope pursued an administrative appeal.  At the hearing, it relied primarily on the fact-finding report of the commission, which had found that Chope's orders were "reasonable" and that Amador had committed "insubordination" in disobeying them.  In addition, Amador's supervisor and another Chope official testified regarding her repeated refusals to perform the work in spite of warnings of possible disciplinary action.

Amador gave uncontroverted testimony as to the reasons for her refusal.  She presented signed statements by two of the outside pathologists, and testified that the third was available to testify by phone.  The statements set forth the doctors' opinions that histotechnicians should not perform grosscutting, and indicated that Amador had consulted with them regarding those opinions.

The administrative law judge (ALJ) ruled that Amador had committed misconduct by repeatedly and wilfully violating her employer's orders.  He gave collateral estoppel effect to the commission's findings on the reasonableness of Chope's orders and on Amador's "insubordination."  He concluded that her deliberate violation of a reasonable order constituted misconduct within the meaning of section 1256.

Amador appealed to the board, which held that the evidence was sufficient to support the ruling on misconduct.  She then petitioned the superior court for a writ of mandate.  After an independent review of the record, the court denied the petition.

"An individual is disqualified for unemployment compensation benefits if the director finds that he or she left his or her most recent work voluntarily without good cause or that he or she has been discharged for misconduct connected with his or her most recent work."   (§ 1256.)

The term "misconduct," as used in the code, is limited to "conduct evincing such wilful or wanton disregard of an employer's interests as is found in deliberate violations or disregard of standards of behavior which the employer has the right to expect of his employee, or in carelessness or negligence of such degree or recurrence as to manifest equal culpability, wrongful intent or evil design, or to show an intentional and substantial disregard of the employer's interests or of the employee's duties and obligations to his employer.  On the other hand mere inefficiency, unsatisfactory conduct, failure in good performance as the result of inability or incapacity, inadvertencies or ordinary negligence in isolated instances, or good faith errors in judgment or discretion are not to be deemed 'misconduct' within the meaning of the statute."

The policy of the code is to provide benefits to "persons unemployed through no fault of their own."  (§ 100.)  "Accordingly, fault is the basic element to be considered in interpreting and applying the code sections on unemployment compensation."  The determination of fault is not concluded by a finding that the discharge was justified.  The claimant's conduct must evince culpability or bad faith.  "The conduct may be harmful to the employer's interests and justify the employee's discharge; nevertheless, it evokes the disqualification for unemployment insurance benefits only if it is wilful, wanton or equally culpable."

\* \* \*

A claimant may not be denied benefits solely on the basis of a "good faith error in judgment."

Although this case involves a discharge for "misconduct," the law concerning voluntary terminations for "good cause" is also relevant. If a claimant's reasons for refusing work constitute "good cause" sufficient to justify resignation, it follows that they should also justify the less drastic step of refusing a work assignment.

In view of the statutory objective of "reducing the hardship of unemployment" "the concept of 'good cause' cannot be arbitrarily limited; the board must take account of ' "real circumstances, substantial reasons, objective conditions, palpable forces that operate to produce correlative results, adequate excuses that will bear the test of reason, just grounds for action, and always the element of good faith." ' "

\* \* \*

Applying the substantial evidence test, this court concludes that the record lacks sufficient evidence to support the denial of benefits.

\* \* \*

This court's duty "[t]o construe the code liberally to benefit the unemployed" precludes the adoption of a draconian rule that would require an employee who reasonably and in good faith fears harm to herself or others to sacrifice her right to unemployment benefits because she has acted on that concern. Accordingly, this court holds that a worker who has been discharged for wilfully refusing to perform work which she reasonably and in good faith believed would jeopardize the health of others has not committed "misconduct" within the meaning of section 1256. \* \* \*

The judgment is reversed. The trial court is directed to issue its writ of mandate ordering respondent to pay to appellant the unemployment insurance benefits withheld.

■ Mosk, Justice, dissenting.

I dissent. Apparently everyone in the administrative and judicial hierarchy is out of step but my colleagues.

\* \* \*

In view of the \* \* \* record, reviewed over and over by five successive layers of administrative and judicial authority, I cannot allow sympathy for one who is denied unemployment benefits to outweigh the well established principle that misconduct and insubordination should not be rewarded. This employee was ordered to perform tasks that, as the trial court found, were within her job description. She received numerous warnings, not the least of which was from the civil service commission, that in refusing to follow reasonable orders of her employer she was being insubordinate. Nevertheless she persisted in prescribing her own rules of conduct.

\* \* \*

There are occasions when stubbornness in devotion to even misguided principle is to be respected. That is euphemistically called "good faith error in judgment."

Under these circumstances, however, the law does not permit a recalcitrant employee to dictate employment conditions in conflict with the job description pursuant to which she was hired.

The judgment should be affirmed.

## NOTES AND QUESTIONS

**1.** Compare this case with *Whirlpool,* supra p. 772. Compare it also with the public policy discharge cases, supra pp. 912–929.

**2.** In Hobbie v. Unemployment Appeals Commission, 475 So.2d 711 (Fla.App.1985), a Florida court said a claimant was terminated for "misconduct connected with work" when she refused to work on Saturdays after converting to a religion observing Saturday as the sabbath. The Supreme Court reversed, holding that "the state may not force an employee 'to choose between following the precepts of her religion and forfeiting benefits.'" Hobbie v. Unemployment Appeals Commission, 480 U.S. 136 (1987), quoting Sherbert v. Verner, 374 U.S. 398, 404 (1963).

But see Cargal v. Review Board, 428 N.E.2d 85 (Ind.App.1981), refusing UI to a former claims deputy for the State Employment Security Division who refused for religious reasons to be Employment Service Interviewer for liquor, movie, and dancing establishments. The court was influenced by the fact that Mr. Cargal had known the requirements of the job when he obtained it (although he had worked successfully for five months interviewing for "sales, domestics, and laundry" before being given the new assignment).

In Employment Division v. Smith, 494 U.S. 872 (1990), the Supreme Court vacated an Oregon Supreme Court decision in favor of UI eligibility for drug and alcohol abuse rehabilitation counselors who were discharged after ingesting peyote during a religious ceremony of the Native American Church. The Supreme Court noted that possession of peyote is a felony in Oregon. *Smith* was legislatively overruled by the Religious Freedom Restoration Act of 1993, 42 U.S.C. §§ 2000bb et seq. The Act declares that *Smith* "virtually eliminated the requirement that the government justify burdens on religious exercise imposed by laws neutral toward religion." It "restores" the "compelling interest test" set forth in Sherbert v. Verner, 374 U.S. 398 (1963) and Wisconsin v. Yoder, 406 U.S. 205 (1972), and provides that it should apply to all cases where the free exercise of religion is substantially burdened. The Act was declared unconstitutional in City of Boerne v. Flores, 117 S.Ct. 2157 (1997).

**3.** After nine weeks on the job Victoria Genier was dismissed as a secretary-receptionist by Oral Surgery Associates. The employer contested her claim for unemployment insurance benefits on the ground that she misrepresented her qualifications when she obtained the job. At her interview (there was no written application form), she had named previous jobs but had not said she had held them only on a temporary basis. Also, she had not volunteered the information that she had recently been terminated by another employer. The Employment Security Board said Genier's "misrepresentations" had evidenced "substantial disregard for the employer's business interests." The Vermont Supreme Court reversed, saying a job applicant is "under no duty to disclose more than she was asked. The information she gave was accurate." Thus unemployment insurance benefits could not be denied. Genier v. Department of Employment Security, 438 A.2d 1116 (Vt.1981).

**4.** Judith Granel was hired by Euclid Manor Nursing Home as a supervisor of registered nurses. The nursing administrator who hired her knew that Granel had only one year's experience as a nurse and none as a supervisor. After four weeks, Granel was terminated. The employer's challenge to a determination of UI eligibility was rejected: "[W]hatever problems Miss Granel was having were attributable to her inexperience and lack of proper training by the appellant, neither of which was the fault of the claimant. * * * She was inexperienced and yearning to learn, but found herself in a position where she was at first criticized for asking too many questions, and then criticized for either not asking enough questions or for asking the wrong people." The dissenting judge said that "an employee who accepts a probationary position implicitly represents that he or she can perform to the minimum standards for that trade or profession. * * * If the employee fails to perform * * *, the employee is 'at fault.' In that situation, the employer has just cause to discharge the employee without suffering any adverse effect on unemployment compensation premiums." Euclid Manor Nursing Home v. Board of Review, 501 N.E.2d 635 (Ohio App.1985).

**5.** In Colorado, alcoholism is not "misconduct" as long as the condition has progressed to a point at which drinking has become non-volitional. See City & County of Denver v. Industrial Commission, 756 P.2d 373 (Colo. 1988).

**6.** Often, the determination of initial eligibility for unemployment benefits reaches an official conclusion about the circumstances of the former employee's departure from work: whether the employee committed the misconduct; whether the employer enforced its rules fairly; what the employer's motivation was. For the argument that that determination should carry significant weight in a later proceeding by the employee for reinstatement or back pay under a collective bargaining agreement, see Stephen A. Mazurak, Effects of Unemployment Compensation Proceedings on Related Labor Litigation, 64 Marquette L.Rev. 133 (1980). See also Note, Issue Preclusion: Unemployment Compensation Determinations and Section 301 Suits, 31 Case W.Res.L.Rev. 862 (1981). If state law actions for wrongful discharge proliferate, see Chapter 11, questions will arise about the relevance and admissibility of unemployment insurance eligibility decisions in those proceedings. Currently, many companies do not contest unemployment insurance claims. Also in some states it is relatively easy for former workers to establish eligibility, since the consequence is "only" 26 weeks of benefits. If UI eligibility becomes the first step toward proving wrongful discharge (with the possibility of large money damage awards or even reinstatement), will employers invest more resources in contesting UI claims? Will more workers then need legal representation to establish their claim?

## d.  CONTINUING ELIGIBILITY

As well as deciding who is initially eligible, the state must supervise "continuing eligibility." Statutes require benefit recipients to be "available" and not to refuse "suitable work." Usually claimants are required to report weekly to the state unemployment insurance office, but it is difficult to make sure that they are trying sufficiently hard to find work. Also, whereas the former employer is at least sometimes the adversary in the initial eligibility proceeding, no private adversary is available to contest continuing eligibility.

For a sense of the magnitude of the decision-making burden, in 1979, the year studied by the National Commission on Unemployment Compensation, there were 20 million initial claims for unemployment insurance benefits. Of these claimants, 1.3 million were disqualified for voluntary quit and 600,000 because they had been discharged for misconduct. Also, 1.3 million were disqualified because of unavailability for work, and 80,000 for refusing suitable work. National Commission on Unemployment Compensation, Unemployment Compensation: Final Report 46 (1980).

### (i) Availability

## Glick v. Unemployment Insurance Appeals Board

591 P.2d 24 (Cal.1979).

■ Tobriner, Acting Chief Justice.

This case presents the issue whether under section 1253, subdivision (c), of the Unemployment Insurance Code an applicant who is ready and willing to work, but whose status as a student necessarily curtails her availability for work, is eligible for unemployment benefits. Section 1253, subdivision (c), provides that an unemployed individual is eligible to receive unemployment compensation benefits with respect to any week only if he is "able to work and available for work" for that week.

In the instant case, the California Unemployment Insurance Appeals Board concluded that the claimant satisfied this statutory requirement for eligibility by demonstrating her availability for work in a potential employment field. The trial court affirmed. The Director of the California Employment Development Department now seeks review of the board's decision, contending that because the restrictions which the claimant "voluntarily" imposed upon herself materially reduced the labor market available to her, she is ineligible for unemployment benefits.  As we shall explain, however, we reject the director's contention.

Claimant Enid G. Ballantyne's testimony at an administrative hearing establishes the details of her extensive employment history.  From 1968 to 1970 Ballantyne worked full time as a service representative.  Thereafter, because she was caring for her three small children, Ballantyne restricted her employment to part-time and intermittent day and night work at a department store.

In 1973 Ballantyne began attending college full time after separating from her husband.  Needing "more stable employment," she went to work at a movie theater as assistant manager and night cashier.  Ballantyne worked an average of 30 hours per week, from 6 p.m. until 1 a.m., at the theater until it closed in April 1974.  Meanwhile, in March 1974 Ballantyne began work for the Pasadena Unified School District administering and evaluating tests; Ballantyne worked 20 hours per week there for four months.

In July 1974 Ballantyne ceased working for the school district and accepted a secretarial job with the Los Angeles Times.  She worked four days a week, approximately 25 to 30 hours per week, "from 6 in the morning until whenever I was let go."  In March 1975 Ballantyne, through no fault of her own, lost this employment and began receiving unemployment insurance benefits.

In September 1975 Ballantyne entered law school at the University of California at Los Angeles.  She attended classes Monday through Friday, at varying hours, and studied four hours each day.[2]  When her employment office asked her in a written questionnaire, "If offered work that conflicts with the hours you are attending school, what provisions could you make to take such work?", Ballantyne answered "none."  The department thereupon found her "not available for work" and ineligible for continued benefits.

Ballantyne pursued an administrative appeal from this determination, and at the hearing testified as to the above stated facts of her employment history.  At the time of the hearing itself Ballantyne was earning $5 an hour for two hours each week as a private tutor; moreover, she was preparing to begin weekend work as a credit checker.  Ballantyne explained that although she would not be willing to forego schooling for a full-time job, she had been searching for work "in no special field," and had not limited her search to weekend or night work.

Aside from Ballantyne's own testimony, the only other evidence received at the hearing concerned the size of the potential market for labor within Ballantyne's time restrictions.  A department representative testi-

---

**2.** During her first quarter of law school, Ballantyne attended classes from 9 a.m. to 2 p.m. on Monday and Tuesday, 10 a.m. to 4 p.m. on Wednesday, and 11 a.m. to 4 p.m. on Thursday and Friday.

fied that "The labor market is extremely small regardless of what she does for a living. There are just too many people out of work and there is very little night work now."

\* \* \*

We recently examined the concept of availability for work in Sanchez v. Unemployment Insurance Appeals Board (1977) 20 Cal.3d 55, 141 Cal.Rptr. 146, 569 P.2d 740. In that case claimant Sanchez applied for unemployment insurance benefits when her employment as a restaurant waitress was terminated. She informed the department that she could not accept work on either Saturdays or Sundays because on those days she was required to care for her four-year-old son. Nevertheless, she was ready to accept either restaurant or factory work during the week when her sister-in-law was available to tend the child, and she imposed no time restrictions on such weekday work. The board concluded, however, that Sanchez was not "able to work and available for work" within the meaning of section 1253 of the code, in that her self-imposed exclusion from weekend employment eliminated a "major portion of her labor market" as a waitress, and therefore denied her benefits.

In our decision reversing the board's ruling, we recognized that the requirement of section 1253 was intimately related to the code's penalties for rejection of offers of "suitable work" without "good cause." While the requirement that an applicant for unemployment benefits be 'able to work and available for work' establishes a prerequisite to eligibility for any benefits, the code also provides a temporary disqualification from eligibility for an individual who 'without good cause, refused to accept suitable employment when offered to him, or failed to apply for suitable employment when notified by a public employment office.' \* \* \* "

We concluded that "[t]he combined effect of those sections is to allow a claimant to refuse, without risk of disqualification, work which is either unsuitable or which the claimant has other 'good cause' to refuse."

Nevertheless, we did not find the availability requirement satisfied "merely by a willingness to accept all such 'non-refusable' work." Rather, because the policy underlying availability "normally entails accessibility to work for which there is some social demand," we held that "a second element of the inquiry into availability consists of the determination whether, after a claimant has restricted his market to 'suitable work which he has no good cause for refusing,' he remains available for work for which there is a substantial field of potential employers." Thus we concluded that " '[a]vailability for work' within the meaning of section 1253, subdivision (c), requires no more than (1) that an individual claimant be willing to accept suitable work which he has no good cause for refusing and (2) that the claimant thereby make himself available to a substantial field of employment."

Applying this availability standard to the facts before us we found in *Sanchez* that "a claimant who is a parent or guardian of a minor has 'good cause' for refusing employment which conflicts with parental activities reasonably necessary for the care or education of the minor if there exist no reasonable alternative means of discharging those responsibilities."

Furthermore, we explained that by requiring claimant Sanchez to make herself available to a substantial field of employment we did not mean "to foreclose the possibility that even if an employment field is not large in absolute terms, it may nevertheless satisfy the availability requirement if it presents a substantial employment opportunity" for the claimant. In light of the board's failure to apply these correct criteria of availability, we remanded the case to the board for further proceedings.

\* \* \*

In the present case claimant Ballantyne seeks unemployment benefits although she does not accept employment which would conflict with the requirements of a full-time law student. Given the "indispensable role which education plays in the modern industrial state" we cannot impose upon Ballantyne the Hobson's choice of the neglect of her professional education or the sacrifice of entitlement to benefits. Indeed, Ballantyne's full-time attendance at school comports ideally with the purposes of the Unemployment Insurance Code to provide benefits to persons unemployed through no fault of their own, and to reduce involuntary unemployment to a minimum Ballantyne's training in law school will enable her most effectively to alleviate the hardships of involuntary unemployment, which she has suffered in the past, as well as to avoid the recurrence of such hardships in the future. We therefore affirm the trial court's holding that Ballantyne's status as a student, and the necessary curtailment of availability which that status entails, did not render claimant unavailable for work within the meaning of section 1253.

Claimant's own testimony at the hearing justifies the conclusion that she is available to a substantial number of potential employers in Los Angeles. As she stated, "I have been a student since 1973, and I have worked—let's see—as a cashier in a movie theater. I have worked for the Pasadena Unified School District. I have worked for Pasadena City College and then I went to work for the Los Angeles Times. All of this time, I was taking care of three children and attending school full time." She also testified that between 1970 and 1975 she worked at Bullocks department store between 9 a.m. and 9 p.m., or on weekends, depending on the store's needs. She was assistant manager and cashier at a movie theater from 6 p.m. to 1 a.m.

This evidence shows that claimant could indeed balance full-time law school attendance—which allowed her to leave school as early as 2 p.m. two days a week and arrive as late as 11 a.m. two other days—with a *substantial* array of suitable employment. Her movie theater work is obviously completely compatible with the restrictions imposed by the law school, and her longest job—working at Bullocks—could easily be arranged around a law school program. In light of this concrete evidence indicating claimant's availability to a substantial number of potential employers, the trial court correctly held that Ballantyne was available for work within the meaning of section 1253.

We conclude that claimant has established that she is available for work for which there is a substantial field of potential employers. She has adduced substantial evidence to sustain that proposition. We recognize that availability for a negligible, insignificant labor market will not suffice; the claimant, however, has shown in this case, and future claimants must show, availability for work in a substantial field of potential employers.

\* \* \*

The judgment is affirmed.

■ Clark, Justice, dissenting.

I dissent.

Is a person who devotes 46 hours per week to law studies, keeps an irregular and inflexible schedule, maintains a home, and cares for three children "available for work" within the statutory definition? By answering yes, the majority reduce to a nullity the "availability for work" requirement of Unemployment Insurance Code section 1253, subdivision (c).

Although the majority set forth claimant's school requirements, they refuse to give full effect to them. During her first quarter of law school, she attended classes from 9 a.m. to 2 p.m. on Monday and Tuesday, 10 a.m. to 4 p.m. on Wednesday, and 11 a.m. to 4 p.m. on Thursday and Friday. She studied four hours a day. Her law school activities required more of her than the ordinary full time worker spends on the job. In addition to her schooling, claimant has time burdens of transportation, caring for herself, and maintaining her three children. While claimant had worked part-time during undergraduate school, there is nothing to indicate the school time burdens were nearly so great as her present law school burdens.

The claimant stated that if offered a full-time job she would not be willing to forego her schooling in order to accept unless paid at least $1,000 per month. Obviously, claimants should not be able to remain eligible while rejecting all jobs paying less than $1,000 per month.

Given the claimant's responsibilities and undertakings apart from employment, it is obvious that accepting substantial employment would be a herculean undertaking. In the circumstances, there is no basis for a finding that she was "available for work" within the meaning of Unemployment Insurance Code section 1253, subdivision (c). The instant case differs substantially from Sanchez v. Unemployment Insurance Appeals Board, where the claimant's family duties rendered her unable to work on Saturdays and Sundays. There is substantial difference in the limited unavailability in *Sanchez* compared to the unavailability in the instant case.

Awarding benefits in the instant case and others like it means employers must effectively subsidize education. This is not the function of the

Unemployment Compensation Act. The statute "is fundamentally designed to act as a buffer or hedge against the ravages of sudden and unexpected loss of one's livelihood." The program is not one funded out of general taxes but through compulsory contributions by employers.

In an attempt to minimize the employer subsidization of education, the majority assert that granting the present claim does not require equal treatment for the typical student worker whose summertime employment terminates each fall with the start of classes. Yet, if anything just the opposite should ordinarily be true. The typical student is much more "available for work" than the present claimant. Relatively few students must set aside as much as 46 hours per week for study commitments. Few have undertaken the additional child care and home responsibilities the present claimant has. As such students who wish to work are far more "available for work" during the school term than the present claimant, fairness would seem to require they be eligible for benefits if claimant is.

Moreover, today's decision can only make it more difficult for students to secure part-time employment. Because employers are required to provide the benefits, they will be reluctant to hire either students or potential students. Faced with the choice between hiring students or others, employers can be expected to avoid the disproportionate exposure to increased unemployment insurance contributions.

I would reverse the judgment.

NOTES AND QUESTIONS

**1.** But see Shreve v. Department of Economic Security, 283 N.W.2d 506 (Minn.1979), upholding a conclusive presumption that a fulltime law student was unavailable for work, and so ineligible for unemployment compensation benefits. Such a presumption was upheld against constitutional challenge in Idaho Department of Employment v. Smith, 434 U.S. 100 (1977). Is there a way to distinguish Turner v. Department of Employment Security, 423 U.S. 44 (1975), which overturned per curiam a Utah statute making pregnant women ineligible for unemployment insurance benefits for a period extending from 12 weeks before expected birth to six weeks after? (The rule was held to be an invalid conclusive presumption under Cleveland Board of Education v. LaFleur, 414 U.S. 632 (1974)). See also Rosenbaum v. Johnson, 377 N.E.2d 258 (Ill.App.1978), accepting the possibility that someone whose medical problems permit only part-time work should nonetheless be considered "available."

**2.** Stephen Spangler had been a sales manager. The California Department of Employment said he was ineligible for unemployment compensation benefits because he refused to shave his beard and otherwise adjust his appearance to increase his chance of finding work. The court accepted the agency's view: "We might take judicial notice from everyday life and business that sales managers in the $850 per month class are not ordinarily men wearing jeans, tennis shoes and tee-shirts, with long hair and a straggly beard, with a braided belt hanging down at their side." Spangler

v. California Unemployment Insurance Appeals Board, 92 Cal.Rptr. 266 (Cal.App.1971).

Should employers be able to deny work to men with beards? See Chapter 6. Even if some employers do so, should a person be able to keep his beard while searching for an employer who will hire him? Do we want to let the unemployment insurance system control individual appearance and dress? Should the same rule apply to initial terminations as to continuing eligibility?

**3.** A Mexican citizen who was no longer eligible to work in the United States sought benefits for work performed while she was legally qualified to work in California. However, a California appellate court found that she could not receive benefits because her lack of work authorization from the Immigration and Naturalization Service rendered her no longer available for work. Gutierrez v. Employment Development Department, 18 Cal. Rptr.2d 705 (Cal.App.1993). Should today's involuntary inability to work preclude an alien from the benefits earned through work legally performed in the past?

### (ii) Suitable Work

## Frazee v. Illinois Department of Employment Security

489 U.S. 829 (1989).

■ JUSTICE WHITE delivered the opinion of the Court.

The Illinois Unemployment Insurance Act provides that "An individual shall be ineligible for benefits if he has failed, without good cause, either to apply for available, suitable work when so directed * * * or to accept suitable work when offered him. * * *" In April 1984, William Frazee refused a temporary retail position offered him by Kelly Services because the job would have required him to work on Sunday. Frazee told Kelly that, as a Christian, he could not work on "the Lord's day." Frazee then applied to the Illinois Department of Employment Security for unemployment benefits claiming that there was good cause for his refusal to work on Sunday. His application was denied. Frazee appealed the denial of benefits to the Department of Employment Security's Board of Review, which also denied his claim. The Board of Review stated: "When a refusal of work is based on religious convictions, the refusal must be based upon some tenets or dogma accepted by the individual of some church, sect, or denomination, and such a refusal based solely on an individual's personal belief is personal and noncompelling and does not render the work unsuitable." The Board of Review concluded that Frazee had refused an offer of suitable work without good cause. The Circuit Court of the Tenth Judicial Circuit of Illinois, Peoria County, affirmed, finding that the agency's decision was "not contrary to law nor against the manifest weight of the evidence," thereby rejecting Frazee's claim based on the Free Exercise Clause of the First Amendment. * * *

We have had more than one occasion before today to consider denials of unemployment compensation benefits to those who have refused work on the basis of their religious beliefs. In Sherbert v. Verner, the Court held that a State could not "constitutionally apply the eligibility provisions [of its unemployment compensation program] so as to constrain a worker to abandon his religious convictions respecting the day of rest." Thomas v. Review Bd. of Indiana Employment Security Div., also held that the State's refusal to award unemployment compensation benefits to one who terminated his job because his religious beliefs forbade participation in the production of armaments violated the First Amendment right to free exercise. Just two years ago, in Hobbie v. Unemployment Appeals Comm'n of Florida, Florida's denial of unemployment compensation benefits to an employee discharged for her refusal to work on her Sabbath because of religious convictions adopted subsequent to employment was also declared to be a violation of the Free Exercise Clause. In each of these cases, the appellant was "forced to choose between fidelity to religious belief and * * * employment," and we found "the forfeiture of unemployment benefits for choosing the former over the latter brings unlawful coercion to bear on the employee's choice." In each of these cases, we concluded that the denial of unemployment compensation benefits violated the Free Exercise Clause of the First Amendment of the Constitution, as applied to the States through the Fourteenth Amendment.

It is true, as the Illinois court noted, that each of the claimants in those cases was a member of a particular religious sect, but none of those decisions turned on that consideration or on any tenet of the sect involved that forbade the work the claimant refused to perform. Our judgments in those cases rested on the fact that each of the claimants had a sincere belief that religion required him or her to refrain from the work in question. Never did we suggest that unless a claimant belongs to a sect that forbids what his job requires, his belief, however sincere, must be deemed a purely personal preference rather than a religious belief. Indeed, in *Thomas,* there was disagreement among sect members as to whether their religion made it sinful to work in an armaments factory; but we considered this to be an irrelevant issue and hence rejected the State's submission that unless the religion involved formally forbade work on armaments, Thomas' belief did not qualify as a religious belief. Because Thomas unquestionably had a sincere belief that his religion prevented him from doing such work, he was entitled to invoke the protection of the Free Exercise Clause. * * *

Frazee asserted that he was a Christian, but did not claim to be a member of a particular Christian sect. It is also true that there are assorted Christian denominations that do not profess to be compelled by their religion to refuse Sunday work, but this does not diminish Frazee's protection flowing from the Free Exercise Clause. *Thomas* settled that much. Undoubtedly, membership in an organized religious denomination, especially one with a specific tenet forbidding members to work on Sunday, would simplify the problem of identifying sincerely held religious beliefs, but we reject the notion that to claim the protection of the Free Exercise Clause, one must be responding to the commands of a particular religious organization.   Here, Frazee's refusal was based on a sincerely held religious belief.   Under our cases, he was entitled to invoke First Amendment protection.[2] * * *

The State offers no justification for the burden that the denial of benefits places on Frazee's right to exercise his religion.   The Illinois Appellate Court ascribed great significance to America's weekend way of life.   The Illinois court asked: "What would Sunday be today if professional football, baseball, basketball and tennis were barred.   Today Sunday is not only a day for religion, but for recreation and labor.   Today the supermarkets are open, service stations dispense fuel, utilities continue to serve the people and factories continue to belch smoke and tangible products," concluding that "[i]f all Americans were to abstain from working on Sunday, chaos would result."   We are unpersuaded, however, that there will be a mass movement away from Sunday employ if William Frazee succeeds in his claim.

As was the case in *Thomas* where there was "no evidence in the record to indicate that the number of people who find themselves in the predicament of choosing between benefits and religious beliefs is large enough to create 'widespread unemployment,' or even to seriously affect unemployment," there is nothing before us in this case to suggest that Sunday shopping, or Sunday sporting, for that matter, will grind to a halt as a result of our decision today.   And, as we have said in the past, there may exist state interests sufficiently compelling to override a legitimate claim to the free exercise of religion.   No such interest has been presented here.

The judgment of the Appellate Court of Illinois for the Third District is therefore reversed and the case is remanded for further proceedings not inconsistent with this opinion.

NOTES AND QUESTIONS

**1.**   James Graves worked for 19 years as a mattress tape edger at Eclipse Sleep Products of New England.   He was paid on a piecework basis, his earnings ranging from $100 to $300 per week.   After a layoff, Graves was recalled to work, but at a much lower rate of pay.   "An employer cannot defeat the payment of unemployment benefits by offering to reemploy claimants at sharply reduced wages."   Graves v. Director, 429 N.E.2d 705 (Mass.1981).

**2.**   Shirley Martin was offered work that the prior employer said was "under basically the same terms and conditions [at] which she had been previously employed."   But she said that transportation and babysitting problems prevented her from accepting the offered hours, 4 p.m. to midnight.   The court held that good cause for refusing a new job is "a less strict standard" than good cause for voluntarily leaving a job.   A claimant

---

**2.** We noted in Thomas v. Review Board, that an asserted belief might be "so bizarre, so clearly nonreligious in motivation, as not to be entitled to protection under the Free Exercise Clause." But that avails the State nothing in this case. As the discussion of the Illinois Appellate Court itself indicates, claims by Christians that their religion forbids Sunday work cannot be deemed bizarre or incredible.

may impose restrictions on her availability if they "do not effectively remove her from the labor market." Martin v. Review Board, 421 N.E.2d 653 (Ind.App.1981).

**3.** Martha Biggerstaff worked the 8 to midnight shift at a fast food restaurant until she was forced to leave work for four weeks due to injury. When she was able to return to work, her shift was no longer available, but the restaurant offered her a new shift from 11 a.m. to 2 p.m. on weekdays. The grandmother told the restaurant that she could not take that shift due to babysitting responsibilities. After determining that the issue was one of suitability rather than availability, the court found that Biggerstaff had rejected suitable work:

> Biggerstaff's child care responsibilities are not related to her own minor children for whom she is the primary care-giver. Rather, Biggerstaff has voluntarily taken on the responsibility of baby-sitting for her grandchildren. We also note that there is no evidence that other arrangements could not be made for the grandchildren. We therefore hold that the Board's decision that this does not constitute good cause was not unreasonable.

Biggerstaff v. Review Board, 611 N.E.2d 184 (Ind.App.1993).

## 4. THE POLICY DEBATE

## Daniel S. Hamermesh, Jobless Pay and the Economy
97–102 (1979).

### Conclusions: "What We Now Know"

1. It is probable that employers ultimately pay at most only a small fraction of the taxes that finance UI benefits, for they are able to shift part of the tax burden backward onto labor and most of the rest forward onto their customers. Nonetheless, this process does not begin immediately, and for at least the first year after an employer's UI tax rate is increased he bears most of the increase.

2. UI payments are distributed nearly proportionately among families ranked by their other income, except that the poorest families receive few UI benefits, while the very well-to-do also receive a relatively small share.

3. The combined effect of taxes and benefits on the distribution of income is small. Benefits are distributed more equally than are incomes, but because of the limitation on the tax base, the part of the tax burden supported by workers is probably borne most heavily by low-wage labor.

4. The amount of income, net of taxes, transportation costs, and so forth (including fringe payments) replaced by UI benefits is below two thirds for individuals who just qualify for the maximum benefit; for most individuals it is probably close to 50 percent.

5. The system has numerous effects on the measured unemployment rate. These include changes in the duration of unemployment of UI

recipients, in the number of people seeking work, and in the labor-force status of recipients during a recession.

\* \* \*

13.  A substantial fraction of the experienced unemployed work very few weeks during the year prior to their current spell of unemployment. Determining eligibility for UI benefits based on high-quarter or annual earnings enables these workers, whose attachment to the labor force often is apparently quite weak, to qualify for benefits.

\* \* \*

Our best estimates are that the civilian unemployment rate is .7 percentage points higher at low unemployment and .45 percentage points higher during a deep recession than it would be in the program's absence. Expressed differently, if low unemployment in the late 1970s is 4.7 percent, it could be as low as 4 percent if regular UI benefits are not paid.  The .7 figure implies that nearly one third of the insured unemployed during low-unemployment periods would be at work (.7 divided by 2.2, the hypothetical insured-unemployment rate based on the assumption that insured unemployment as a fraction of civilian unemployment would be .47, as in 1969). This estimate may appear high, but most of the induced unemployment is based on the well-documented effect of UI benefits on the duration of unemployment when labor markets are tight.

\* \* \*

The induced unemployment should be construed partly as an investment made by society to subsidize job search, which can result in a more efficient labor market.  In part, however, it is a needless diversion of human resources away from their best uses, produced by the combined effects of legislated accretions to the program and changes in the labor market and the tax system.  Whether the real and measured effects are too large or too small depends on one's beliefs about the importance of efficiency in the labor market.  Observers who believe that any inefficiency in the labor market must be removed, regardless of its other beneficial effects, will regard these effects as too large to justify the program;  those who feel that society should be willing to pay a high price to aid the unemployed or that UI offsets the effects of other inefficiency in the economy will consider these effects small.  The appropriate question for this second group is, can the same improvement in the stabilization of incomes of the experienced unemployed be achieved without the likely loss in efficiency?

NOTE

It is often said that the unemployment insurance system reduces the work effort of covered employees.  Hamermesh quantifies that effect, based on a review of the empirical evidence.  Is what he reports a serious phenomenon?  Do his conclusions suggest changes that ought to be made in the structure of the program?

# Martin Feldstein, *The Social Security Explosion*

The Public Interest No. 81, at 94 (Fall 1985).*

The unemployment compensation program was created in the 1930s at the depth of the Depression. The unemployment rate was 25 percent and many men had not seen steady work for a year or more. Individual resources were exhausted and the prospects for finding work were generally bleak.

The structure of the unemployment compensation program has remained essentially unchanged since the 1930s even though the nature of unemployment has changed radically. In recent years, most unemployment has been relatively short with more than half of the spells of unemployment ending in less than six weeks. Nearly half of the unemployed did not become unemployed by losing their previous job but are either young people who are looking for their first job, or people returning to the labor force after a period in which they were neither working nor looking for work, or people who quit their last job in order to look for something better. And more than one-quarter of those who are officially classified as "job losers" are actually on temporary layoff from firms where they have regular jobs and expect to be recalled.

Under current conditions, unemployment compensation raises the rate of unemployment. The most obvious effect of unemployment compensation is to increase the length of time that individuals remain unemployed. Some individuals use the period of compensated unemployment to have a little extra vacation and do odd jobs around the home. Others are induced by unemployment compensation to keep waiting in the hopes that a better job will come along while still others don't bother to take temporary work that would reduce their total unemployment.

The current unemployment compensation system also encourages employers to lay workers off for short periods of time instead of finding other ways to smooth production and employment by varying inventories or cutting prices. And the presence of unemployment compensation makes it easier and cheaper for employers to find people willing to take temporary or seasonal jobs that add to the unemployment rate.

Although the absolute level of unemployment benefits is not high, the benefits are large relative to the lost wages that they replace. In most states, unemployment benefits are set at 50 percent of the individual's past wage, with additional benefits for dependents paid to about one-third of the unemployed. Although there is a limit on the weekly benefit, most beneficiaries do receive benefits that equal or exceed half of their past wage.

Until the late 1970s, unemployment benefits were completely free of tax. The high marginal tax rates on wages meant that untaxed unemployment compensation frequently replaced 75 percent or more of lost net income. In a 1973 article in *The Public Interest* I gave the following example:

---

* Reprinted by permission of the author.

Consider a worker in Massachusetts in 1971 with a wife and two children. He earns $500 per month or $6000 per year if he experiences no unemployment. She earns $350 per month or $4200 per year if she experiences no unemployment. If he is unemployed for one month, he loses $500 in gross earnings but less than $100 in net income. How does this occur? A reduction of $500 in annual earnings reduces his federal income tax by $83, his Social Security payroll tax by $26, and his Massachusetts income tax by $25. The total reduction in taxes is $134. Unemployment compensation consists of 50 percent of his wage plus dependents' allowances of $6 per week for each child. Total unemployment compensation is therefore $302. This payment is not part of taxable income. His net income therefore falls from $366 for the month if he is employed (i.e., his $500 gross earnings less $134 in taxes) to the $302 paid in unemployment compensation. The combination of taxes and unemployment compensation imposes an effective marginal tax rate of 87 percent—i.e., the man's net earnings fall by only 13 percent of his gross pay ($64) when he is unemployed for a month.

The balance between protection and distortion was clearly wrong. The protection of the standard of living of the unemployed was so complete that there was little incentive to find work or to avoid unemployment. Substantial statistical evidence has accumulated during the past decade that indicates that individuals who are eligible for higher unemployment benefits relative to their net wage have longer durations of unemployment, are more likely to become unemployed, and require relatively higher wages as a condition of accepting new employment.

In 1978 the Carter administration proposed and Congress enacted a partial taxation of unemployment compensation for upper-income taxpayers. [The 1986 Tax Reform Act made benefits fully taxable.] Although benefits are still exempt from the Social Security payroll tax (with a combined employer-employee rate of more than 14 percent) and from many state income taxes, subjecting benefits to the federal income tax is a significant step toward reducing distortion and increasing the fairness of the unemployment compensation system. Recent studies have shown that the average duration of unemployment declined for individuals whose benefits became taxable while remaining unchanged among individuals whose incomes kept benefits exempt from taxation.

The Reagan administration, in the tax reform plan released by the Treasury in November 1984, proposed taxing all unemployment compensation. Unfortunately, this proposal was eventually dropped in an effort to make the final plan politically more attractive. It is noteworthy, however, that the leading Democratic alternative, the Bradley-Gephardt bill, would tax all unemployment compensation. It is probably only a matter of time before all benefits are taxable.

The effect of the unemployment compensation system depends not only on the relative level of benefits but also on the way that the program is financed.

The method of financing unemployment benefits can either reduce or exacerbate the distortion of incentives that leads to higher unemployment. Employers now pay more than $25 billion in special payroll taxes to finance the unemployment compensation benefits.  Each firm's tax is in principle related to the benefits collected by workers who were laid off by that firm. If this system of experience rating were fully effective, each firm would face the full cost of the unemployment benefits that result from its layoffs.  A combination of full taxation of benefits to employees and a complete experience rating of firms would eliminate the incentive for excess layoffs and for an excessive amount of temporary and seasonal jobs.

In practice, however, the experience rating system is far from complete.  Firms with high layoff rates pay a relatively low maximum rate of unemployment compensation tax that does not increase or decrease as they raise or lower their layoff rates.  To make up for the taxes not paid by firms with high layoff rates, firms with very good unemployment experience must pay a relatively high minimum rate of tax.  Because this minimum tax cannot be lowered by better unemployment performance, these firms also have no incentive to reduce their layoff rate.

An improvement in the method of experience rating could improve incentives for higher employment without reducing the protection to unemployed workers or to firms.  A good start would be to require firms to pay 100 percent of the first month's unemployment compensation.

Some progress has been made in correcting the balance between protection and distortion in the unemployment compensation system.  The legislation to tax unemployment compensation that has been enacted is clear evidence that policymakers at last understand that the current system causes unnecessary unemployment.  The next steps should take us toward full taxation of benefits and a more complete method of experience rating.

NOTE

While some unemployed workers do not draw benefits, by choice or otherwise, participation in the funding of the system is still mandatory for almost all workers.  In part due to the crowding-out by mandatory government insurance and the outlawing of private unemployment insurance during the 1930s by some states, there is no private unemployment insurance market in the United States.  For the argument that we should reconsider such a system see Michael B. Rappaport, The Private Provision of Unemployment Insurance, 1992 Wis.L.Rev. 61 (1992).

## Gary Burtless, *Is Unemployment Insurance Ready for The 1990s?*, Social Insurance Issues for the Nineties: Proceedings of the Third Conference of the National Academy of Social Insurance

164–174 (Paul N. Van De Water, ed. 1992).

*Effects of Unemployment Insurance*

What are the wider effects of the system?  Unemployment insurance offers vital income protection to experienced workers who become jobless because of involuntary layoff. In spite of the crucial economic role the program plays, it suffers from a shameful reputation among some economists, journalists, and policymakers. It has such a reputation because unemployment benefits can prolong spells of joblessness. Workers collecting a weekly unemployment check may not devote as much time or effort to finding a new job as workers who do not collect benefits. Even more important, insured workers may reject a job offer that an uninsured worker would accept because the income cushion UI provides permits the insured to be choosier. Economists like to say that these behavioral effects of unemployment insurance represent adverse incentives of the program.

Policymakers were aware of adverse incentives when they designed the current system. To reduce the influence of these incentives, federal and state legislatures imposed two important conditions on insurance. First, benefits are paid only to unemployed workers who can demonstrate that they are available for and actively seeking work. This requirement gives rise to the mountains of forms that jobless workers are now asked to fill out in order to receive benefits. Second, benefits are denied to workers who reject an offer of suitable employment (meaning a job roughly equivalent to the job that was lost). These two conditions are notoriously difficult to enforce in practice, so the American system of unemployment insurance possesses one other notable feature: Benefits are generally limited to twenty-six weeks. Unemployment beyond that is not ordinarily compensated in this country. By international standards, this period of protection is very brief. Virtually all other industrialized countries offer at least a year of benefits, and in several countries the duration is much longer.

In spite of these limitations on American benefits, many economists and policymakers suspect that unemployment insurance contributes to the high level of unemployment we now suffer. A variety of analysts have examined the size of the adverse impacts of unemployment insurance and have concluded that more generous benefits do indeed lengthen the average duration of unemployment among insured workers. A good guess is that a 10 percent increase in weekly benefits prolongs the average spell of unemployment by around one week. A one-week increase in the potential duration of benefits (from, say, twenty-six weeks to twenty-seven weeks) would increase the average length of an insured unemployment spell by about one-tenth of a week, or perhaps a bit more. An honest assessment of jobless benefits must therefore conclude that some of the adverse consequences that economists worry about do in fact occur.

These adverse consequences do not take us very far, however, in explaining the current level and trend in national unemployment. Only about four in ten unemployed workers collect unemployment benefits, and nearly all of the insured became jobless because of a layoff that was in no way caused by the existence of the program. Thus, if insurance were eliminated tomorrow, the level of joblessness would fall only slightly. Furthermore, if some of the insured unemployed experience longer spells of unemployment because of the existence of the program, it must also be the case that some uninsured unemployed workers experience shorter spells because they are more likely to land a job that has been turned down by an insured unemployed worker. In a labor market with a long queue of workers seeking jobs, a job that is rejected by a worker collecting benefits will be promptly snapped up by a desperate uninsured worker.

More fundamentally, it is the goal of unemployment insurance to permit insured workers to reject unsuitable job offers. We provide jobless benefits in this country (as do other advanced industrialized economies) precisely because our workers must acquire costly skills that can often be applied only in specialized occupations or jobs. When workers lose these jobs because of a downturn in demand, it is advantageous for them and for the wider economy if they carefully seek out the best opportunity to apply their specialized skills. In an economy with two unemployed workers and two job vacancies, it is efficient to subsidize the two workers to sort themselves into the job openings so that their skills are put to best use and their joint earnings are maximized. The two workers benefit and the wider economy gains if the best possible match is made between workers and vacancies. Furthermore, the insurance protection provided under UI encourages workers to undertake investments in specialized skills that otherwise might be regarded as excessively risky. On balance, I think that some economists (and most op-ed writers at the *Wall Street Journal*) tend to exaggerate the adverse effects of unemployment insurance and ignore the vital function it plays in protecting skilled and semi-skilled workers against the hazards of job loss. Sadly, they also ignore the way it promotes efficiency.

### Declining Unemployment Insurance Coverage

Whether the effects of unemployment insurance have been positive or negative, they have shrunk in recent years. In the 1980s, joblessness rose to new postwar highs, but the share of unemployed workers drawing unemployment benefits fell to new lows. The percentage of jobless workers collecting benefits has risen modestly in the past couple of years, but still remains well below the levels prevailing before the mid–1980s.

The proportion of the unemployed collecting benefits declined for several reasons. First and most important, fewer unemployed workers now apply for benefits when they lose their jobs. In part, the drop in applications is due to a change in eligibility requirements for unemployment insurance, which are established both at the state and the national levels. In addition, some unemployed workers may have decided against applying for benefits as the after-tax value of those benefits fell. Finally, the nature of unemployment has changed.

* * *

### Extended Unemployment Insurance Benefits

The extended benefit UI program offers insurance protection beyond twenty-six weeks of unemployment for workers who have exhausted regular benefits and who live in states with high unemployment. The drop in the percentage of unemployed job losers collecting regular benefits has directly affected the insured unemployment rate (IUR), which serves as the basis for triggering extended UI benefits. If I am correct in estimating that the number of regular UI claimants has fallen one-fifth, then the IUR is also about one-fifth too low relative to the civilian or total unemployment rate (TUR), which provides a more accurate gauge of current labor market conditions.

The relationship between the insured and the total unemployment rates is shown in the two panels of figure 3. Although the IUR and TUR tend to move in parallel fashion over the business cycle, they have drifted apart since 1960. Before 1980, this drift could be easily explained by changing regulations about the insurance coverage of employed workers and by the changing composition of the civilian unemployed—who were younger, less likely to be job losers, and drawn more from industries with low levels of insurance coverage than their earlier counterparts. After 1980, however, the sharp decline in the IUR relative to the TUR has been due almost entirely to the sharp drop in the fraction of new job losers collecting benefits.

As a result of the drop in the IUR, the extended benefit program has virtually ceased to function. Even with unemployment approaching 7 percent, only a handful of states offer extended benefits. When the employment situation in a state deteriorates, its total unemployment rate rises, but its insured unemployment rate often does not rise enough to trigger extended benefits. The result is that the extended benefit program either fails to be triggered or is triggered late in an economic downturn. Moreover, even when extended benefits become available, the IUR can be expected to fall below the critical threshold relatively early in an economic recovery. Many beneficiaries are thus dropped from the insurance rolls even though the local job market remains very weak.

The extended benefit program also contracted over the past decade because of significant changes in federal law passed in 1981. Before 1982, the extended benefit trigger rate was computed by including recipients of both regular and extended benefits in the count of insured unemployed. (Thus, the trigger rate used before 1982 was not identical to the IUR, which excludes recipients of extended benefits from the numerator.) Since extended benefit recipients are now excluded, the level of insured unemployment needed to keep the extended benefit program turned on has effectively been raised. Also, before 1981, the extended benefit program could be triggered in all states if the national trigger rate exceeded 4.5 percent. The national trigger rate was eliminated by the 1981 legislation. Beginning in October 1982, extended benefits have been available only in states in which the IUR exceeds 5 percent and is at least 120 percent of the rate over the previous two years. Some states also provide benefits when the IUR reaches 6 percent, regardless of the rate in previous years. These 09 trigger rates are one percentage point higher than the comparable rates in effect before 1982.

Figure 3
Insured Unemployment Rate
and Civilian Unemployment Rate, 1960–91

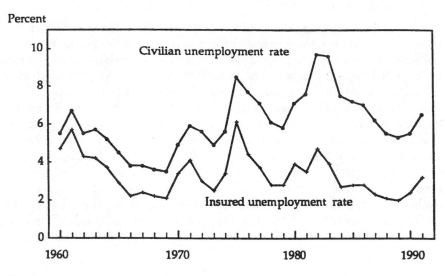

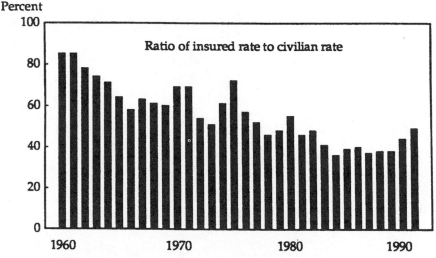

Source:  U.S. Department of Labor, Employment and Training Administration.          [G11024]

   The legislative reforms of 1981, along with the sharp drop in the
number of regular UI claimants, had a calamitous effect on the extended
benefit program.  At the end of 1982, when the civilian unemployment rate
reached 10.8 percent—a postwar record—only fourteen states with particularly high insured unemployment rates offered extended benefits.   By
October 1983, with unemployment still hovering above 9 percent, only two
states and Puerto Rico offered extended benefits.  In contrast, during the
1974–76 recession, when unemployment reached a high of 9.0 percent, all
fifty states offered extended benefits for prolonged periods.  As a practical
matter, the extended benefit program no longer operates as an effective

countercyclical stabilizer. Except in extraordinarily severe recessions, the program is unlikely to offer benefits to a sizable number of workers.

*Policy Implications*

An important implication of these developments is that the unemployment insurance system has become a much weaker source of countercyclical stimulus during economic downturns. The effectiveness of the extended benefit program has been cut at least in half as a result of the legislative changes passed in 1981 and the continued weakness of the IUR as a measure of the labor market situation. The stimulus provided by the regular twenty-six-week program has dropped one-fifth because of the decline in the number of claimants relative to the number of unemployed job losers. And the stimulus provided under both the regular and the extended benefit programs has dropped an additional 15 to 20 percent as a result of the taxation of benefits. In comparison with the level of countercyclical stimulus available during the 1960s and 1970s, the stimulus provided by the current system has dropped at least a third. The income protection available to jobless workers has dropped a similar proportion.

# CHAPTER 13

# RETIREMENT

America's population is aging. In 1995, 33.5 million people were 65 or older, of whom more than 15 million were 75 or older. (Sixty-five is the retirement age treated as "normal" in many pension systems, and the "normal" age under current Social Security rules. Most American workers cannot be retired on account of age; until enactment of a 1986 law, mandatory retirement had been permitted at age 70. The age for receiving full Social Security benefits is scheduled to rise gradually from 65 to 67, a change that will affect persons born in 1938 and later.)

As the population ages (a result of longer life expectancy and of demographic cycles), more of the nation's income must be devoted to retirees. Retirees consume their savings. In addition, they live on income transfers from government and on pension payments earned during their years at work. In 1995, Social Security paid about $298 billion in old age and survivors benefits to about 37.5 million retirees and dependents. In 1994, Supplemental Security Income (SSI), a federal program for the needy, paid $4.4 billion to 1.5 million elderly persons. Other programs, including food stamps, fuel assistance, and housing benefits, also transferred money to the elderly poor. In 1992, more than 15 million elderly persons received about $150 billion in income from private sector pension plans. About the same number of people receive public pensions under civil service, military, and railroad retirement systems. In 1995, the assets of these plans were greater than $5 trillion, more than two-thirds of that in private plans.

Social Security (technically, Old Age and Survivors) payments are thus the largest part of the income of America's elderly. Entitlement is earned by labor force participation and benefit levels are related to the wages on which the Social Security tax (FICA) was paid. Thus Social Security is very much a work-based and work-tied system of retirement income. Pensions are obviously earned through work. Pension law was largely a matter of state law (and most of that created by common law court adjudications) until 1974, when Congress preempted the field with the Employee Retirement Income Security Act. This complicated law, partly located within the Internal Revenue Code (because the law establishes conditions which pension plans must meet to be eligible for income tax treatment benefiting both the employing companies and the pension recipients), has become an important area of legal specialization. This chapter will not make you a specialist on either "government" Social Security law or "private" pension law, but it will introduce you to important issues and especially to some of the inter-connections between the two systems, which after all are performing the single task of providing retirement income to former workers.

## A.  BACKGROUND

## U.S. Senate Special Committee on Aging, Aging America:  Trends and Prospects

45 (1981).

### YOUNG AND ELDERLY SUPPORT RATIO

The combined effect of decreased fertility levels and increased numbers of elderly persons will result in growth in the ratio of persons of working age (18 to 64 years of age) to elderly persons (Chart 4 and Table 2).

The figure used to describe the number of persons of "working age" as compared to the number of "retirement age" is often referred to as a "support ratio," reflecting the economic fact that the working population supports the non-working age groups.  The ratio reflecting those who have retired, as opposed to children, is especially important since it is primarily publicly-funded programs which serve retirees.  The expected dramatic growth in the very old age group will require proportionately higher levels of "support" than is true today.

At the turn of the century, there were about 7 elderly persons for every 100 persons 18 to 64 years.  By 1982, that ratio was almost 19 elderly persons per 100 persons of working age.  By 2000, the ratio is expected to increase to 21 per 100 and then to surge to 38 per 100 by 2050.

Table 2

TOTAL SUPPORT RATIO, AGED SUPPORT RATIO, AND
YOUNG SUPPORT RATIO ACTUAL
AND PROJECTED 1900–2050

Number of Persons Per 100 Aged 18 to 64 Years)

|  | 1900 | 1920 | 1940 | 1960 | 1980 | 1982 [1] | 1990 | 2000 | 2025 | 2050 |
|---|---|---|---|---|---|---|---|---|---|---|
| Total support ratio (under 18 and 65 and over) . . . . . . . . | 83.65 | 75.69 | 62.84 | 81.95 | 64.39 | 62.86 | 62.57 | 61.86 | 71.00 | 74.46 |
| Aged support ratio (65 years and over) | 7.35 | 7.99 | 10.90 | 16.84 | 18.59 | 18.82 | 20.70 | 21.16 | 33.31 | 37.85 |
| Young support ratio (under 18) . . . . . . . . | 76.30 | 67.70 | 51.94 | 65.11 | 45.80 | 44.04 | 41.87 | 40.70 | 37.69 | 36.61 |

[1] Based on estimates

**Source:**  U.S. Bureau of the Census, Projections of the Population of the United States:  1982 to 2050 (Advance Report).  Series P–25, No. 922, October 1982, and Estimates of the Population of the United States, by Single Years of Age, Color, and Sex:  1900 to 1959, Series P–25, No. 311, July 2, 1965.  Projections are the middle series.

**Chart 4**
**YOUNG AND ELDERLY SUPPORT RATIO**
**ACTUAL AND PROJECTED**
**1900–2050**

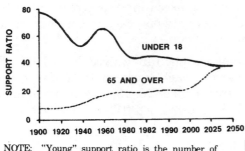

NOTE: "Young" support ratio is the number of
persons under 18 per 100 aged 18–64 years.
"Elderly" support ratio is the number 65+
per 100 18–64 years.

### Relative Contribution of Retirement Income Sources for the Elderly—1979 [1]

| Cash Income in 1979 | Employment Earnings | Social Security | Employer Pensions | Income from Assets | Government Assistance and Other | Total |
|---|---|---|---|---|---|---|
| Less than $5,000 | 3% | 76% | 3% | 6% | 12% | 100% |
| $5,000–9,999 | 10 | 59 | 12 | 15 | 4 | 100 |
| $10,000–14,999 | 18 | 43 | 17 | 19 | 3 | 100 |
| $15,000–24,999 | 34 | 26 | 16 | 22 | 2 | 100 |
| $25,000 and over | 48 | 11 | 13 | 27 | 1 | 100 |
| All Elderly | 27% | 37% | 13% | 20% | 3% | 100% |

**Source:** March 1980 Current Population Survey data.

[1] Percentages are based on the number of married couples headed by an individual age 65 and over and single persons age 65 and over.

## B. MANDATORY RETIREMENT

## Carr v. Armstrong Air Conditioning, Inc.

817 F.Supp. 54 (N.D.Ohio 1993).

■ JOHN W. POTTER, SENIOR DISTRICT JUDGE.

* * *

Plaintiff was employed with Armstrong Air Conditioning for approximately twenty-nine years. On December 19, 1990, plaintiff executed a severance agreement in which he received various benefits in exchange for being terminated. Plaintiff now alleges he was wrongfully discharged based upon age discrimination. Defendants deny plaintiff's allegations and filed a counterclaim based upon the severance agreement.

Plaintiff asserts that the counterclaim is based upon an invalid and unenforceable severance contract with defendant. According to plaintiff, the severance contract is in violation of the Age Discrimination in Employment Act (ADEA) and of the Older Workers Benefit Protection Act (OWBPA) in the following four ways: (1) it failed to specifically refer to rights or claims arising under the OWBPA; (2) plaintiff was never advised in writing to consult with an attorney prior to executing the agreement; (3) it failed to provide plaintiff with at least twenty-one days to consider it; and (4) it failed to allow seven days for revocation.

In order to ascertain whether plaintiff waived his ADEA claim, the court must determine whether any such waiver was "knowing and voluntary." OWBPA became effective October 16, 1990 as an amendment to the ADEA. Section 626(f), 29 U.S.C., captioned "Waiver" states in pertinent part:

(1) An individual may not waive any right or claim under this chapter unless the waiver is knowing and voluntary. Except as provided in paragraph (2), a waiver may not be considered knowing and voluntary unless at a minimum—

(A) the waiver is part of an agreement between the individual and the employer that is written in a manner calculated to be understood by such individual, or by the average individual eligible to participate;

(B) the waiver specifically refers to rights or claims arising under this chapter;

(C) the individual does not waive rights or claims that may arise after the date the waiver is executed;

(D) the individual waives rights or claims only in exchange for consideration in addition to anything of value to which the individual already is entitled;

(E) the individual is advised in writing to consult with an attorney prior to executing the agreement;

(F)(i) the individual is given a period of at least 21 days within which to consider the agreement; * * *

(G) the agreement provides that for a period of at least 7 days following the execution of such agreement, the individual may revoke the agreement, and the agreement shall not become effective or enforceable until the revocation period has expired;

* * *

(3) In any dispute that may arise over whether any of the requirements, conditions, and circumstances set forth in [the above subparagraphs] have been met, the party asserting the validity of a waiver shall have the burden of proving in a court of competent jurisdiction that a waiver was knowing and voluntary pursuant to (1) or (2).

The Court finds that plaintiff did not waive any rights he may have under ADEA since the severance agreement is in violation of OWBPA. In particular, this Court finds that as a matter of law the waiver was not "knowing and voluntary" as defined by the OWBPA for the following reasons: (1) the severance agreement fails to specifically refer to any rights or claims arising under the OWBPA in violation of § 626(f)(1)(B); (2) plaintiff was never advised in writing to consult with an attorney prior to signing the agreement, although plaintiff admits to consulting with an attorney regarding the severance agreement, in violation of § 626(f)(1)(E); (3) plaintiff was given only five days to consider the agreement instead of the required twenty-one days in violation of § 626(f)(1)(F)(i); and (4) plaintiff was not given seven days to revoke the agreement in violation of § 626(f)(1)(G).

Defendants next argue that if the waiver does not comply with OWBPA, Armstrong is still entitled to reimbursement of the consideration it paid for the waiver, under the tender-ratification theory.

* * *

This Court finds that a tender requirement is not consistent with ADEA since it would deter meritorious challenges to releases in ADEA claims. Therefore, plaintiff is not required to tender benefits back to defendants before he can proceed with a lawsuit under ADEA, and his retention of severance benefits during the pendency of this suit does not constitute ratification of the release. Nevertheless, any benefits paid by defendants shall be set off from any damage award received by plaintiff.

The Court now turns its attention to defendants' motion to dismiss plaintiff's state law claims pursuant to Fed.R.Civ.P. 12(b)(6) or 56. Again, the Court will construe the motion to dismiss as one for summary judgment pursuant to Rule 56 since defendants have attached an affidavit and other documents.

Defendants contend that plaintiff's state law claims must be dismissed because he signed a valid waiver. A valid release is an absolute bar to a later action on any claim encompassed within the release, unless the release was obtained by fraud.

Plaintiff now contends that he was induced to sign the severance agreement through fraud. In particular, plaintiff alleges that he signed the severance agreement under economic duress. The Supreme Court of Ohio has set forth a standard for determining economic duress:

> A person who claims to have been a victim of economic duress must show that he or she was subjected to ' * * * a wrongful or unlawful act or threat, * * * ' and that it ' * * * deprive[d] the victim of his unfettered will.' Further, ' * * * [m]erely taking advantage of another's financial difficulty is not duress. Rather, the person alleging financial difficulty must allege that it was contributed to or caused by the one accused of coercion.' The Restatement of Law 2d, Contracts * * * also requires that the one who coerces the victim be the other party to the agreement: 'If a

party's manifestation of assent is induced by an improper threat by the other party that leaves the victim no reasonable alternative, the contract is voidable by the victim.'

According to plaintiff's affidavit, plaintiff was unexpectedly informed that he was being terminated. Plaintiff was then shown a severance agreement and asked to sign it that day. Plaintiff also was informed that if he did not sign the agreement, he would be terminated with no severance pay. Plaintiff was in the process of building a house and was therefore concerned about his economic future. Lastly, plaintiff alleges that he felt "disturbed, confused, devastated and dumbfounded," due to the unexpected termination.

Whether particular facts are sufficient to constitute duress is a matter of law for the court to decide. However, the question of whether the facts alleged actually exist is a matter for the fact finder. The plaintiff in the case *sub judice* has stated a viable claim of economic duress if the trier of fact believes the facts as alleged by plaintiff. Since there are genuine issues of material fact, summary judgment is inappropriate.

It should be noted that if the trier of fact finds that economic duress exists, plaintiff, under Ohio law, would have to first tender back to defendant the consideration given in order to maintain his state law actions. Plaintiff has neither done nor alleged to have done this. Consequently, plaintiff is faced with two alternatives: he may tender back to defendant the consideration given and file an amended complaint alleging the fact of such tender or he may dismiss his state law claims.

## NOTES AND QUESTIONS

**1.** OWBPA allows employers to offer severance contracts on the basis of age so long as they meet the statutory waiver requirements in 29 U.S.C. § 626(f). OWBPA also allows employers to discriminate on the basis of age in employee benefits in certain circumstances. See note 11, infra.

For an example of a waiver that satisfies the Older Workers' Benefit Protection Act, see Seroka v. American Airlines, Inc., 834 F.Supp. 374 (S.D.Ala.1993).

**2.** The Age Discrimination in Employment Act, considered supra at pp. 328–337, makes it unlawful for an employer "to * * * [discriminate] against any individual * * * because of such individual's age." When the statute was first enacted in 1967, discrimination was prohibited until age 65. In 1978, the age of 65 was raised to 70. In 1986, the cap at age 70 was removed altogether. Thus for most jobs, no mandatory retirement age is permitted, and elder workers cannot be terminated or retired on the basis of age. At least 13 states had previously said that retirement on the basis of age could not be forced at any age. Although legal protection for older workers has increased, the age at which workers actually retire has been dropping steadily for the 50 years for which we have data. The average private sector worker retires at 62. Most other countries continue to permit mandatory retirement because of age, and in some countries—Japan is a conspicuous example—mandatory retirement from many jobs occurs at age 60 or earlier. Is the United States wrong to ban age-based retirement (1) because younger persons need and deserve the jobs, or (2) because retirement based on age is a humane alternative to telling people that their skills have declined and they are no longer adequate workers, or (3) because without mandatory retirement, a significant number of workers will work past the age at which their efforts become inefficient due to loss of skills?

**3.** By its own force (without a congressional statute), the equal protection clause does not bar mandatory retirement on account of age. Massachusetts Board of Retirement v. Murgia, 427 U.S. 307 (1976). Colonel Murgia was a state police official forced to retire at age 50 by a state law. (The law allowed officers to work beyond age 50 if necessary to complete 20 years of service.) A per curiam opinion said strict scrutiny was inappropriate because the aged have not suffered purposeful unequal treatment on the basis of stereotyped characteristics. Justice Marshall dissented arguing that discrimination based on age should be subject to intermediate scrutiny. Murgia was not helped by the federal ADEA, because that law was not amended to cover public sector workers until 1974. The extension to state and local government workers was upheld against a constitutional challenge (that the tenth amendment limits federal power to trespass on state sovereignty in this way) in EEOC v. Wyoming, 460 U.S. 226 (1983) (5–4). At issue was Wyoming's policy that game wardens must retire at age 55.

**4.** Discrimination by age is permitted by the ADEA "where age is a bona fide occupational qualification." An FAA rule prohibits commercial airline pilots from working beyond age 60, but allows flight engineers to work beyond that age. TWA's union contracts allowed displaced pilots to "bump" flight engineers if they became medically unfit to work as pilots before age 60, or if there was insufficient work for pilots. But a pilot forced to retire at age 60 could not switch to a flight engineer position. The Supreme Court held that "if TWA does grant some disqualified captains the 'privilege' of 'bumping' less senior flight engineers, it may not deny this opportunity to others because of their age." Trans World Airlines, Inc. v. Thurston, 469 U.S. 111 (1985). Does this mean that if a company lets workers stay until they choose to retire or are determined no longer capable, it must offer jobs to qualified applicants no matter how old?

**5.** Georgia's rule that state police officers retire at age 55 was held to be exempt from the ADEA's general ban on mandatory retirement rules. Knight v. Georgia, 992 F.2d 1541 (11th Cir.1993).

**6.** Western Air Lines v. Criswell, 472 U.S. 400 (1985), invalidated that airline's attempt to maintain an age–60 retirement age for flight engineers. The airline had attempted to justify the age rule as a bona fide occupational qualification "reasonably necessary" to safe operation of the airline. The Court emphasized the focus of the Age Discrimination in Employment Act on individualized determination of "the process of psychological and physiological degeneration caused by aging," rather than use of a bright-line retirement age applicable to all. It endorsed a two-part test first enunciated in Usery v. Tamiami Trail Tours, Inc., 531 F.2d 224 (5th Cir.1976): (1)

Can the employer show that substantially all persons above a prescribed age would be unable to perform the job safely and efficiently? (2) If not, can it show that it is impossible or highly impractical to deal with the older employees on an individualized basis? May an employer require more medical tests at a certain age to make necessary individualized determinations?

**7.** Who has the burden of proof when an employer seeks to establish a business justification for retiring an older worker? For one view, see Marshall v. Westinghouse Electric Corp., 576 F.2d 588, 591–92 (5th Cir. 1978), quoting Marshall v. Goodyear Tire & Rubber Co., 554 F.2d 730, 736 (5th Cir.1977):

> In race discrimination cases this circuit has recently held that an employer must prove by a preponderance of the evidence some legitimate, non-discriminatory reason for a race plaintiff's dismissal. * * * "Because the aging process causes employees constantly to exit the labor market while younger ones enter, simply the replacement of an older employee by a younger worker does not raise the same inference of improper motive that attends replacement of a black with a white person in Title VII cases." * * * To require a defendant to prove that his differentiating factors other than age criteria were evenly applied to all similarly situated employees * * * is inconsistent with prior case law under the ADEA. * * * [A] defendant in an ADEA case bears only the burden of going forward with the evidence to demonstrate reasonable factors other than age for the plaintiff's discharge.

The statutory language provides no basis for a different judicial attitude to age discrimination than to race or sex discrimination. What reasons might a court give for regarding age discrimination as a different (and lesser) social problem? For an example of a strong judicial attitude against age discrimination see Western Air Lines v. Criswill, note 6 supra, and EEOC v. Francis W. Parker School supra p. 328.

**8.** Can older workers be laid off because they cost more? "Both the legislative history and the Department of Labor regulations tend to support the proposition that higher labor costs associated with the employment of older employees constitute 'reasonable factors other than age' which an employer can consider when faced with possible termination of an older employee." Mastie v. Great Lakes Steel Corp., 424 F.Supp. 1299, 1318 (E.D.Mich.1976). Is cost a defense to race or sex discrimination under Title VII?

**9.** Lester E. Schlitz, circuit judge for the City of Portsmouth Virginia, sued the state claiming that the failure of the Virginia General Assembly to re-elect him constituted age discrimination in violation of the ADEA. Judge Schlitz had reached the age of seventy 25 days prior to the election, and claimed that the failure to renew his tenure was based on a normally unenforced—and possibly unenforceable—mandatory retirement law for judges. In response, the Commonwealth set forth alternative bases for the dismissal of Judge Schlitz including complaints regarding his capabilities and demeanor. The question presented to the court was whether the Assembly's motives for declining to re-elect the plaintiff were a pretext for age discrimination.

Summary judgment was ordered in favor of the Commonwealth. The court concluded:

> Plaintiff does not and cannot maintain that the failure to re-elect plaintiff was other than a legislative decision, but rather maintains that the ADEA proscribes the General Assembly from discriminating based on age. The flaw in this argument is that the Commonwealth would be unable to defend this action unless the legislators testify as to their motives for declining to re-elect the plaintiff. This the doctrine of legislative immunity will not allow.

Schlitz v. Commonwealth of Virginia, 854 F.2d 43 (4th Cir.1988). However, "municipalities are not entitled to such an immunity." Berkley v. Common Council of City of Charleston, 63 F.3d 295, 296 (4th Cir. 1995). Does this decision leave the Virginia General Assembly free to practice age discrimination?

EEOC v. Commonwealth of Massachusetts, 858 F.2d 52 (1st Cir.1988), upheld Massachusetts' mandatory retirement law for judges on the basis that state judges fall within the ADEA's exception for "appointee[s] on the policy making level."

**10.** Much current litigation concerning age discrimination in employment, concerns "voluntary" retirement "deals" offered to senior employees. Is it illegal age discrimination to offer these opportunities only to workers older than a specified age? Rock v. Massachusetts Commission Against Discrimination, 424 N.E.2d 244 (Mass.1981), held that it was not age discrimination in violation of the state statute, Mass.Gen.Laws c. 151B, § 4(1), for Westinghouse to offer early retirement benefits only to former employees over age 55 at the time of a plant shutdown. The court deferred to the agency's interpretation that the major legislative concern was for discrimination *against* older workers. See also Cipriano v. Board of Education, 785 F.2d 51 (2d Cir.1986), finding no violation of the ADEA in a policy of offering teachers financial incentives to retire early. Is it illegal (and if so for what reason) to offer them only to selected workers, whom the company would like to see depart?

**11.** United Air Lines v. McMann, 434 U.S. 192 (1977), held that Title VII was not violated when the airline forced retirement at age 60 pursuant to its retirement plan, which had been adopted in 1941. The Court relied on § 4(f)(2) of the ADEA which permits companies to "observe the terms of * * * any bona fide employee benefit plan * * * which is not a subterfuge to evade the purposes of this chapter." The Supreme Court decision was speedily overturned by P.L. 95–256 which added language to § 4(f)(2) forbidding seniority systems and employee benefit plans if they "require or permit the involuntary retirement of any individual ... because of the age of such individual."

A court of appeals considered the meaning and scope of § 4(f)(2) in EEOC v. Westinghouse Electric Corp., 869 F.2d 696 (3d Cir.1989). Defendant Westinghouse set up a benefit system under which employees who were laid off normally received Layoff and Income Benefits (LIB). Employees who were eligible for retirement, however, were denied the option of receiving LIB, and could only receive pension benefits in the event of a layoff. After concluding that this benefit scheme treated older employees less favorably than younger employees and that such treatment was based on age, the court rejected defendant's argument that even if its plan was otherwise in violation of the ADEA, it was exempt from coverage under § 4(f)(2):

> In order to qualify as exempt under § 4(f)(2), a plan must involve age related cost factors: i.e. the cost of providing benefits pursuant to the plan must increase with age. Westinghouse severance pay plans do not meet this requirement. The amount of severance pay an employee receives under the Westinghouse plans is based on the employee's length of service with the company, the employee's salary at the time of layoff, and the reason for the layoff. These factors are not directly related to age, and the costs of supplying severance pay to employees therefore does not increase with age.

The court concluded that the Westinghouse scheme was in violation of the ADEA. But after the Supreme Court's decision in *Betts,* infra, making the relevant issue whether the company's benefit decisions were a "subterfuge" for age discrimination, the Third Circuit found that EEOC had failed to prove age discrimination by Westinghouse. EEOC v. Westinghouse, 925 F.2d 619 (3d Cir.1991).

Public Employees Retirement System v. Betts, 492 U.S. 158 (1989), presented the following facts. The retirement system (PERS) offered disability retirement benefits to employees 60 or younger; older employees were only eligible for age and service benefits or unpaid medical leave, and were denied the option of disability retirement regardless of physical condition. June Betts, 61, suffered a disabling illness while a public employee but due to her age was denied disability benefits by PERS. She brought suit charging age discrimination under the ADEA. The district court and court of appeals agreed that because PERS did not demonstrate a cost-based justification for the differential treatment, it was not entitled to a § 4(f)(2) exemption.

The Supreme Court reversed, holding that under § 4(f)(2) defendant's benefit scheme was permitted by the Act. The Court flatly rejected any requirement that employers show a cost-based justification for age-related reductions in benefits. The Court reasoned that such a requirement is contrary to the plain language of the statute requiring intentional "subterfuge," not merely the absence of cost-based justifications, to make the ADEA applicable to valid benefit plans. Describing the purpose of § 4(f)(2) and the subterfuge requirement Justice Kennedy's opinion explained:

> § 4(f)(2) is not so much a defense to a charge of age discrimination as it is a description of the type of employer conduct that is

prohibited in the employee benefit context. By requiring a showing of actual intent to discriminate in those aspects of the employment relationship protected by the provisions of the ADEA, § 4(f)(2) redefines the element of the plaintiff's prima facie case instead of establishing a defense to what otherwise would be a violation of the Act. Thus, when an employee seeks to challenge a benefit plan provision as a subterfuge to evade the purposes of the Act, the employee bears the burden of proving that the discriminatory plan provision actually was intended to serve the purpose of discriminating in some nonfringe benefit aspect of the employment relation.

Justice Marshall, in a dissent joined by Justice Brennan, said the majority's decision "immunizes virtually all employee benefit programs from liability under the ADEA * * * even if an employer is unable to put forth any justification for denying older workers the benefit younger ones receive." But there is a business reason for the discrimination: a disabled employee (as in *Betts* ) or a laid off worker (as in *Westinghouse*) needs income if too young to retire but will receive a pension if older. Is that an adequate justification for the difference in treatment according to age?

Leaving unresolved the internal tension between § 4(f)(2)'s "subterfuge" and "involuntary retirement" clauses, the Court in *Betts* did not express an opinion as to whether Ms. Betts was unlawfully forced to retire due to the terms of the PERS benefit plan. On remand the court of appeals held that PERS forced Ms. Betts' retirement in violation of the "involuntary retirement" provision. Betts v. Hamilton County Board of Mental Retardation, 897 F.2d 1380 (6th Cir.1990). Relying on Trans World Airlines v. Thurston, 469 U.S. 111 (1985), supra p. 1163, the Court reasoned that forcing older workers into less desirable programs on the basis of age is "coercive conduct" constituting involuntary retirement.

Congress then acted, adopting the Older Workers' Benefit Protection Act of 1990 (OWBPA). (The other provision of the OWBPA, regulating early retirement "deals" is discussed in Carr v. Armstrong Air Conditioning, Inc., supra p. 1159. Specifically rejecting *Betts,* the OWBPA bans discrimination against older workers in employee benefits "except when age-based reductions in employee benefit plans are justified by significant cost considerations." The "actual amount of payment made or cost incurred on behalf of an older worker" must be no less than that made for a younger worker."

OBRA, enacted in 1986, barred refusing benefits because of age after January 1, 1988. The Supreme Court held that this provision does not require employers to credit pre-OBRA years of service in determining benefit levels for employees who worked in 1988 and thereafter. The Court also concluded that ERISA was not violated when the company offered certain enhanced benefit options only to employees who agreed to release the company from potential legal claims. Lockheed Corp. v. Spink, 517 U.S. 882 (1996).

**12.** Hazen Paper Co. hired Biggins as its technical director in 1977. They fired him in 1986, when he was 62. He said he was fired because of his age. Robert and Thomas Hazen, the owners of the company, said he was dismissed for doing business with competitors. The jury found that the company "willfully" interfered with Hazen's rights under the ADEA. It likely was influenced by the fact that the company's pension plan had a 10–year vesting period and Biggins would have reached that mark several weeks after he was fired.

The Supreme Court was unpersuaded that the jury had sufficient evidence to establish disparate treatment age discrimination. (Biggins had not alleged disparate impact, and the Court made clear that the applicability of disparate impact analysis under the ADEA remains undecided. See EEOC v. Francis W. Parker School, supra p. 328.) "[A]n employee's age is analytically distinct from his years of service * * * [T]hus, it is incorrect to say that a decision based on years of service is necessarily 'age-based.' " The Court recognized that firing Biggins to prevent his pension from vesting might well be a violation of § 510 of ERISA. See Phelps v. Field Real Estate Co., p. 490; see also EEOC v. Westinghouse Electric Corp., supra pp. 1166–1167.

Hazen Paper Co. v. Biggins, 507 U.S. 604 (1993).

**13.** The Texas Supreme Court created a public policy exception to at-will employment for an allegation that an individual was fired because the company sought to avoid contributing to his pension fund. The U.S. Supreme Court reversed, citing ERISA preemption. Ingersoll–Rand Co. v. McClendon, 498 U.S. 133 (1990).

**14.** Robert Gilmer, age 62, was fired after six years from his position as a manager of financial services. When registering with the New York Stock Exchange, and required as a term of his employment contract, Gilmer had "agree[d] to arbitrate any discharge . . . arising out of the employment or termination of employment." Gilmer alleged age discrimination. The Supreme Court upheld the agreement to arbitrate. The Court rejected three arguments: that an individual cannot waive the right to bring a statutory employment claim in a judicial forum; that the arbitral forum is inadequate; and that the purposes of the ADEA require availability of a judicial forum. Gilmer v. Interstate/Johnson Lane Corp., 500 U.S. 20 (1991). For a recent decision showing judicial skepticism of the move from judicial to arbitral proceedings in employment disputes, see Prudential Insurance Co. v. Lai, 42 F.3d 1299 (9th Cir.1994) cert. denied, 516 U.S. 812 (1995) (plaintiffs can take sexual harassment claims to court because they did not know they were agreeing to arbitrate). The issue of contractually agreed arbitration terms as conditions of employment has relevance for many of the substantive issues considered in this book.

**15.** An employer considering offering an early-retirement plan cannot actively mislead employees who ask about it. The employer need not disclose internal deliberations but must "speak truthfully" when questioned. Mullins v. Pfizer, Inc., 23 F.3d 663 (2d Cir.1994).

It is also a breach for a fiduciary to fail to investigate his suspicions that there were problems with a pension fund and to mislead participants with reassurances that funds will be available. Barker v. American Mobil Power Corp., 64 F.3d 1397 (9th Cir.1995).

**16.** Consider the case of Thomas Long, a long-time Sears employee, who signed a general release of all future ADEA claims in exchange for a reorganization package that included considerable severance benefits. Long was laid off while, he claimed, younger employees with less experience were retained and his department was not closed down, as he had been told when he signed the release. He filed discrimination charges with the EEOC, claiming a violation of ERISA by the termination of his employment to avoid paying future pension benefits. Sears' affirmative defense was the signed waiver, but the court of appeals found the release non-compliant with the OWBPA, and the employee therefore was not barred from pursuing claims under ADEA. The dissent argued that an employee may ratify a release invalid under OWBPA, and as such, Long's ERISA claim should be barred. Long v. Sears Roebuck & Co., 105 F.3d 1529 (3d Cir.1997).

**17.** The Supreme Court has held that an individual who accepted payment in exchange for a release that did not comply with OWBPA need not return or offer to return the money before filing a discrimination claim under the ADEA. Oubre v. Entergy Operations, Inc., 118 S.Ct. 838 (1998).

## C. PRIVATE PENSIONS

### 1. BACKGROUND

## Alicia Haydock Munnell, The Economics of Private Pensions

7–12 (1982).

The development of the social security program and private pension system, in the wake of the Great Depression, reflected a shift in the nation's preference away from individual saving for retirement and toward organized savings plans. The two systems developed simultaneously, since neither program provided adequate retirement income. Yet they clearly are alternative ways to accomplish the same goal—namely, providing an adequate retirement income. In fact, many private plans are explicitly integrated with social security and so reduce private pension benefits as social security benefits are increased. Because of the substitutability of the two programs, as the gap between desired and actual retirement assets narrows, an expansion in either social security or private pensions will lead to a decline in the relative role of the other.

The recent expansion of social security, therefore, has profound implications for the development of private plans. In the 1970s social security benefits grew particularly fast as a result of ad hoc increases and automatic cost-of-living adjustments. Despite this growth, a substantial gap still

exists—especially for workers with above-average earnings—between retirees' income needs and social security benefits.  Whether the gap is filled by
private pensions or a larger social security program will depend on the
relative ability of the two programs to provide good retirement protection.

THE GROWTH OF PRIVATE PLANS

Although private pension plans date officially from 1875, the early
plans were financially vulnerable and most were bankrupted by the Great
Depression.  Contemporary U.S. pension plans, both public and private, are
rooted in the desire for financial security that became part of the national
psychology after the onset of the Depression.  The expansion of private
plans was stimulated by the inflation, tax changes, and wage controls of
World War II.

The introduction of a few private plans by large industrial employers
during the last quarter of the nineteenth century reflected the United
States' transition from a rural agricultural society to an urban industrial
economy.

\* \* \*

While large industrial employers were establishing pension plans, a
small number of trade unions were instituting their own schemes for
retirement benefits.  Mutual benefit societies for survivors, sickness, and
disability were traditional among unions, but the first union old-age plan,
established by the Granite Cutters' International Association of America,
did not appear until 1905.

\* \* \*

The Great Depression had a disastrous effect on both the industrial
and trade union plans.  Many railroads had become unprofitable during the
late 1920s, and by the early 1930s they were operating in the red.  Despite
emergency measures to cut costs through reduction of wages and pension
benefits, the railroads' financial situation continued to deteriorate.  Approximately 25 percent of railway workers were approaching retirement,
but the railroads, with virtually no reserves, were incapable of fulfilling
benefit promises.  Because so many people were involved, strong pressure
developed for legislative action to bail out the railroads.  Thus the Railroad
Retirement Act of 1935 was enacted, which rescued the failing pension
plans by establishing a quasi-public retirement system for railway employees.

Employees covered by other industry plans were not so fortunate as
the railroad workers.  Beginning in 1929, as business activity declined,
many companies were unable to meet both operating expenses and rising
pension payments.  In response, they made substantial cutbacks in pension
benefits, ranging from tightening eligibility requirements and suspending
pension credit accumulation to abolishing pension plans and terminating
benefit payments even for retired employees.  The trade union plans also
floundered;  with high unemployment and competing demands on the
union treasuries, it was impossible to increase dues enough to support the

growing number of union retirees.  Within a few years after the Depression began, almost all union welfare plans had collapsed.

The Depression not only bankrupted most trade union and industrial pension plans but also undermined American confidence in the historic tradition of self-reliance and in the virtue of individual thrift as a way to provide for old age.  By 1933 nearly 13 million people were unemployed and the lifetime savings of many were erased.  The nation was therefore sympathetic to the need for the Social Security Act of 1935 and the subsequent development of negotiated funded private pension plans.

Although World War II initially consumed much of the nation's resources that might have been directed toward improved provisions for old age, two wartime factors—wage control policies and tax changes—greatly stimulated the expansion of private plans.  The wage stabilization program instituted during the war impeded employers' ability to attract and hold employees in the tight civilian labor market.  However, the War Labor Board attempted to relieve the pressure on management and labor from the legal limitations on cash wages by permitting employers to bid for workers by offering attractive fringe benefits.  The cost to the firms of establishing pension plans to attract workers was minimal in light of the tax deductibility of contributions and the wartime excess profits tax on corporate income.

The rate of growth of new pension plans fell off markedly during the immediate postwar period as employees focused on cash wage increases in an attempt to recover the ground lost during the period of wage stabilization.  By 1949, however, pension benefits again became a major issue of labor negotiation because of the increased resistance to further wage increases and a weak economy.  The importance of pensions was highlighted by a presidential fact-finding board, which concluded that while a cash wage increase in the steel industry was not justified, the industry did have a social obligation to provide workers with pensions.  This decision was based in part on the obvious inadequacy of social security benefits, which averaged $26 a month at the time.  Labor's drive for pension benefits was aided further when the Supreme Court confirmed a 1948 ruling of the National Labor Relations Board that employers had a legal obligation to negotiate the terms of pension plans.  Both the United Steelworkers of America and the United Automobile Workers then launched successful drives for pension benefits under the influence of the 1949 recession.

The main expansion of today's private pension system, then, actually began during the 1950s.  Private pension coverage grew rapidly during this period, not only in union plans but also among nonunionized industries. The economic impact of the Korean War further stimulated the pension movement as employers once again competed for workers in the face of wage and salary controls and excess profits taxes.  The mid-1950s marked the beginning of substantial collective bargaining gains in multiemployer pension plans.  These plans were established in industries containing many small companies and involving frequent job changes that prevented employees from remaining with a single employer long enough to qualify for pensions.  The multiemployer pension movement, encouraged by the success of the United Mine Workers of America, spread to such industries as construction, food, apparel, and transportation.

The growth of private pensions continued into the 1960s. But much of the increase in coverage during that decade was due to an expansion of employment in firms that already had pension plans, in contrast to the growth during the 1950s, which resulted primarily from the introduction of new plans. Coverage under multiemployer plans grew more than twice as fast as single-employer plans during the 1960s, owing in part to the merging of single-employer plans into multiemployer ones.

Table 2–1

Private Pension Plans: Coverage, Contributions, Benefits, and Assets, Selected Years, 1940–80

| Year | Workers covered (thousands) | Contributions (millions of dollars) | | | Number of beneficiaries (thousands) | Benefits Amount of payments (millions of dollars) | Assets end of year (billions of dollars) |
|---|---|---|---|---|---|---|---|
| | | Total | Employer | Employee | | | |
| 1940 | 4,100 | 310 | 180 | 130 | 160 | 140 | 2.4 |
| 1945 | 6,400 | 990 | 830 | 160 | 310 | 220 | 5.4 |
| 1950 | 9,800 | 2,080 | 1,750 | 330 | 450 | 370 | 12.1 |
| 1955 | 14,200 | 3,840 | 3,280 | 560 | 980 | 850 | 27.5 |
| 1960 | 18,700 | 5,490 | 4,710 | 780 | 1,780 | 1,720 | 52.0 |
| 1965 | 21,800 | 8,360 | 7,370 | 990 | 2,750 | 3,520 | 86.5 |
| 1970 | 26,300 | 14,000 | 12,580 | 1,420 | 4,750 | 7,360 | 137.1 |
| 1975 | 30,300 | 29,850 | 27,560 | 2,290 | 7,050 | 14,810 | 212.6 |
| 1980 | 35,800 | 68,970 | 64,840 | 4,130 | 9,100 | 35,177 | 407.9 |

The growth of private pension plans since 1940 is summarized in table 2–1. By 1980 approximately 36 million wage earners and salaried employees were covered by private retirement plans financed either by the employer alone or jointly by employers and employees. Coverage under private plans nearly doubled between 1950 and 1980, from 25 percent of the private nonfarm labor force to 48 percent. Annual contributions to private pension funds increased almost thirty-five times, from $2 billion in 1950 to $69 billion in 1980. On the benefit side, an estimated 9 million retirees and survivors were receiving periodic payments from private pension plans in 1980. These beneficiaries received a total of $35 billion, an average of almost $3,870 per recipient.

## 2.   Pre–ERISA Employee Rights Under Trust Law

Before enactment of ERISA in 1974, pensions were regulated (if at all) by state contract and trust law and by federal labor law. Frequently, employees learned as they approached retirement age that the pension they expected would not be provided. Sometimes employers relied on the small print of their brochures to deny entitlement. These disputes produced state contract cases such as Wilson v. Rudolph Wurlitzer Co., 194 N.E. 441 (Ohio App.1934). There, the employee worked for 24 years pursuant to a booklet promising a pension "to employees of good standing, who in the opinion of the officers of the company, have been loyal and faithful * * *." At age 65, he was discharged for refusing on one occasion to work overtime.

The company refused the pension. The court held that under Ohio contract law the employee had a right to a pension if he was faithful and loyal, "and that such an opinion was to be based upon substantial reasons, and not upon mere whim or caprice * * *." In other situations, employers promised pensions but were insolvent when the workers reached retirement age. The most important judicial intervention in the period leading up to ERISA was the United Mine Workers litigation, a proceeding brought by the Washington Research Project, one of the first public interest law firms, on behalf of miners in disagreement with the leadership of W.A. (Tony) Boyle, successor to John L. Lewis as president of the United Mine Workers.

## Blankenship v. Boyle

329 F.Supp. 1089 (D.D.C.1971).

■ GESELL, DISTRICT JUDGE.

This is a derivative class action brought on behalf of coal miners who have a present or future right to benefits as provided by the United Mine Workers of America Welfare and Retirement Fund of 1950.

\* \* \*

The Fund was created by the terms of the National Bituminous Coal Wage Agreement of 1950, executed at Washington, D.C., March 5, 1950, between the Union and numerous coal operators. It is an irrevocable trust established pursuant to Section 302(c) of the Labor-Management Relations Act of 1947, 29 U.S.C. § 186(c), and has been continuously in operation with only slight modifications since its creation.

The Fund is administered by three trustees: one designated by the Union, one designated by the coal operators, and the third a "neutral party designated by the other two." The Union representative is named Chairman of the Board of Trustees by the terms of the trust. Each trustee, once selected, serves for the term of the Agreement subject only to resignation, death, or an inability or unwillingness to serve. The original trustees named in the Agreement were Charles A. Owen for the Operators, now deceased; John L. Lewis for the Union, now deceased; and Miss Josephine Roche. The present trustees are W.A. (Tony) Boyle, representing the Union; C.W. Davis, representing the Operators; and Roche, who still serves.[2]

Each coal operator signatory to the Agreement (there are approximately fifty-five operator signatories) is required to pay a royalty (originally thirty cents, and now forty cents per ton of coal mined) into the Fund. These royalty payments represent in excess of ninety-seven percent of the total receipts of the Fund, the remainder being income from investments.

---

**2.** Lewis and Boyle have been the only Union trustees. There has been a succession of Operator trustees. Owen served until 1957, followed in sequence by Henry Schmidt, George Judy, Guy Farmer and C.W. Davis.

In the year ending June 30, 1968, royalty receipts totalled $163.1 million and investment income totalled $4.7 million. Total benefit expenditures amounted to $152 million.

In general, the purpose of the Fund is to pay various benefits, "from principal or income or both," to employees of coal operators, their families and dependents. These benefits cover medical and hospital care, pensions, compensation for work-related injuries or illness, death or disability, wage losses, etc. The trustees have considerable discretion to determine the types and levels of benefits that will be recognized. While prior or present membership in the Union is not a prerequisite to receiving welfare payments, more than ninety-five percent of the beneficiaries were or are Union members.

* * *

From its creation in 1950, the Fund has done all of its banking business with the National Bank of Washington. In fact, for more than twenty years it has been the Bank's largest customer. When this lawsuit was brought, the Fund had about $28 million in checking accounts and $50 million in time deposits in the Bank. The Bank was at all times owned and controlled by the Union which presently holds 74 percent of the voting stock. Several Union officials serve on the Board of Directors of the Bank, and the Union and many of its locals also carry substantial accounts there. Boyle, President of the Union, is also Chairman of the Board of Trustees of the Fund and until recently was a Director of the Bank.[3] Representatives of the Fund have also served as Directors of the Bank, including the Fund's house counsel and its Comptroller. The Fund occupies office space rented from the Union for a nominal amount, located in close proximity to the Union's offices.

The precise duties and obligations of the trustees are not specified in any of the operative documents creating the Fund and are only suggested by the designation of the Fund as an "irrevocable trust." There appears to have been an initial recognition by the trustees of the implications of this term. Lewis, who was by far the dominant factor in the development and administration of the Fund, stated at Board meetings that neither the Union's nor the Operators' representative was responsible to any special interest except that of the beneficiaries. He declared that each trustee should act solely in the best interests of the Fund, that the day-to-day affairs of the Fund were to be kept confidential by the trustees, that minutes were not to be circulated outside the Fund, and that the Fund should be soundly and conservatively managed with the long-term best interests of the beneficiaries as the exclusive objective. While he ignored these strictures on a number of occasions, as will appear, his view is still accepted by counsel for the Fund in this action, who took the position at oral argument that the duties of the trustees are equivalent to the duties of a trustee under a testamentary trust. Counsel stated, "You can't be just a

---

**3.** Boyle resigned from the Bank board after the record in this case was closed and following his indictment for other alleged misconduct.

little bit loyal. Once you are a trustee, you are a trustee, and you cannot consider what is good for the Union, what is good for the operators, what is good for the Bank, anybody but the trust."

This view, which corresponds with plaintiffs' position, is not accepted by all parties. While acknowledging that a trustee must be "punctilious," counsel for some of the parties urge that trustees as representatives of labor or management may properly operate the Fund so as to give their special interests collateral advantages (e.g., managing trust funds so as to increase tonnage of Union-mined coal), and that this is not inconsistent with fiduciary responsibility since such actions ultimately assist beneficiaries by raising royalty income. But there is nothing in the Labor-Management Relations Act or other federal statutes or in their legislative history which can be said to alleviate the otherwise strict common-law fiduciary responsibilities of trustees appointed for employee welfare or pension funds developed by collective bargaining.

* * *

It is true that trustees are allowed considerable discretion in administering a trust as large and complex as the Fund. In determining the nature and levels of benefits that will be paid by a welfare fund and the rules governing eligibility for benefits, the trustees must make decisions of major importance to the coal industry as well as to the beneficiaries, and their actions are valid unless arbitrary or capricious. On these matters, trustee representatives of the Union and the Operators may have honest differences in judgment as to what is best for the beneficiaries. Congress anticipated such differences in enacting § 302(c) of the Labor-Management Relations Act, and sought to temper them by the anticipated neutrality of the third trustee. The congressional scheme was thus designed not to alter, but to reinforce "the most fundamental duty owed by the trustee"; the duty of undivided loyalty to the beneficiaries. This is the duty to which defendant trustees in this case must be held.

* * *

The Fund's affairs were dominated by Lewis until his death in 1969. Roche never once disagreed with him. Over a period of years, primarily at Lewis' urging, the Fund became entangled with Union policies and practices in ways that undermined the independence of the trustees. This resulted in working arrangements between the Fund and the Union that served the Union to the disadvantage of the beneficiaries. Conflicts of interest were openly tolerated and their implications generally ignored. Not only was all the money of the Fund placed in the Union's Bank without any consideration of alternative banking services and facilities that might be available, but Lewis felt no scruple in recommending that the Fund invest in securities in which the Union and Lewis, as trustee for the Union's investments, had an interest. Personnel of the Fund went on the Bank's board without hindrance, thus affiliating themselves with a Union business venture. In short, the Fund proceeded without any clear understanding of the trustees' exclusive duty to the beneficiaries, and its affairs were so loosely controlled that abuses, mistakes and inattention to detail occurred.

The major breach of trust of which plaintiffs complain is the Fund's accumulation of excessive amounts of cash.

\* \* \*

It is contended that the trustees failed to invest cash that was available to generate income for the beneficiaries, and in total disregard of their duty allowed large sums to remain in checking accounts at the Bank without interest. It is further claimed that this breach of trust was carried out pursuant to a conspiracy among certain trustees, the Union, and the Bank through its President, and that all these parties are jointly liable for the Fund's loss of income resulting from the failure to invest.

That enormous cash balances were accumulated and held at the Bank over the twenty-year period is not disputed. The following figures are representative.

| Fiscal Year | Amount of cash in Demand Deposits at End of Year | Percentage of Cash to the Fund's Total Re- sources |
|---|---|---|
| 1951 | $29,000,000 | 29% |
| 1956 | 30,000,000 | 23 |
| 1961 | 14,000,000 | 14 |
| 1966 | 50,000,000 | 34 |
| 1967 | 75,000,000 | 44 |
| 1968 | 70,000,000 | 39 |
| 1969 | 32,000,000 | 18 |

\* \* \*

The beneficiaries were in no way assisted by these cash accumulations, while the Union and the Bank profited; and in view of the fiduciary obligation to maximize the trust income by prudent investment, the burden of justifying the conduct is clearly on the trustees.

Three explanations were seriously presented in justification of the cash accumulations: the trustees' general concern as to the future course of labor relations and other developments in the coal industry which might make it necessary to have money readily at hand on short notice; tax factors; and what was characterized as inadvertence or accident. None of these explanations will withstand analysis.

\* \* \*

The inference is also unavoidable that Lewis made more than a mistake of judgment as a trustee. He acted to benefit the Bank and to enhance its prestige and indirectly the prestige of the Union, not simply to keep money needed by the Fund in a safe place. The minutes show that he knew the large demand deposits were unnecessary for any legitimate purpose of the Fund. Moreover, he was not lacking in financial sophistication. He had been president of a bank himself and the record shows his many financial dealings and the manner in which, as President of the Union, he utilized the considerable financial resources of the Union for the Union's benefit. The conclusion is clear that Lewis, in concert with Roche, used the Fund's resources to benefit the Union's Bank and to enhance the Union's economic power in disregard of the paramount and exclusive needs of the beneficiaries which he was charged as Chairman of the Board of Trustees to protect.

* * *

This issue relates to the Fund's purchases of stock of certain electric utility companies, principally Cleveland Electric Illuminating Company and Kansas City Power & Light Company. While these stocks are on the list approved for trustees, the propriety of these investments is challenged on the ground that they were made primarily for the purpose of benefiting the Union and the operators, and assisting them in their efforts to force public utilities to burn Union-mined coal. The investments have declined in value and are said to have been in violation of the trustees' duty of undivided loyalty to the beneficiaries.

In the late 1950's and early 1960's, the Union was engaged in a vigorous campaign to force public utility companies to purchase Union-mined coal. Public relations and organizational campaigns to this end were pressed vigorously in several cities. Lewis, then a trustee, worked closely with Cyrus S. Eaton, a Cleveland businessman. It is undisputed that between February and April 1955 the Fund purchased 30,000 shares of Cleveland Electric, and in March of that year the Union loaned Eaton money to enable him to buy an additional 20,000 shares. Eaton then went on the Board of Directors of Cleveland Electric. Similarly, between January and March 1955 the Fund purchased 55,000 shares of Kansas City Power & Light, and in June of the same year the Union loaned Eaton money to buy an additional 27,000 shares. In each of the years from 1956 to 1965 the Fund gave a general proxy for all of its shares in Cleveland Electric and Kansas City Power & Light to Eaton. The Union and Eaton were pressing the managements of each company to force them to buy Union-mined coal. The Fund purchased both Cleveland Electric and Kansas City Power & Light stock on the recommendation of Lewis, who was then fully familiar with the Union's activities affecting these companies and proxies were given to the Union by the Fund at Lewis' request.

Schmidt, who became a trustee of the Fund in 1958, was president of the principal coal operator standing to benefit from Cleveland Electric's additional purchases of Union-mined coal. He was acquainted with the activities of the Fund and of the Union with respect to Cleveland Electric, and actively encouraged them. When the Union's campaign to push Union-mined coal focused on Cleveland Electric in 1962 and 1963, the Fund purchased an additional 90,000 shares, with the hearty approval of Schmidt.

Further indication that these particular challenged stock purchases were made primarily for the collateral benefits they gave the Union is found in a general course of conduct. Lewis and Widman, the Union man spearheading the efforts to force utilities to buy Union-mined coal, discussed some seventeen utility companies on the Fund's investment list, looking toward the possibility of obtaining proxies from fifteen. Proxies were in fact given the Union by the Fund not only on Cleveland Electric and Kansas City Power & Light, but on the shares the Fund held in Union Electric, Ohio Edison, West Penn Electric, Southern Company and Consolidated Edison. The intimate relationship between the Union's financial and organizing activities and the utility investment activities of the trustees demonstrates that the Fund was acting primarily for the collateral benefit of the Union and the signatory operators in making most of its utility stock acquisitions. These activities present a clear case of self-dealing on the part of trustees Lewis and Schmidt, and constituted a breach of trust. Roche knowingly consented to the investments, and must also be held liable. The Union is likewise liable for conspiring to effectuate and benefit by this breach of trust.

* * *

One of the principal subjects of inquiry at the trial involved the circumstances under which monthly pensions were raised from $115 to $150 on June 24, 1969. This $35 increase was not without consequences, since it involved an additional annual disbursement from the Fund of approximately $30 million. Plaintiffs do not seek a rollback of the pension increase, but assert that the motives for which it was made, and the manner in which it was made, are grounds for removal of Boyle as a trustee, and for monetary relief from Boyle, Judy, and the Union for any injuries the Fund may suffer as a result of the action. A full discussion of the incident is required.

* * *

When Lewis died and Boyle was named trustee, an election contest for presidency of the Union was looming. Boyle undoubtedly recognized that if he delivered on his pension promises to the rank and file, his position would be strengthened in the campaign. These election considerations account for the timing of his actions, but they were not the primary factor motivating Boyle. He genuinely believed that a pension increase should be made in the interests of the miner beneficiaries. Boyle knew that Roche was opposed to a pension increase, but with her hospitalized he was in a position to force the issue with Operator trustee Judy, and undoubtedly felt that the end—that is, the increase in pensions—justified the means. Even if Judy refused to go along, the Union's position in subsequent bargaining would be strengthened. Thus, Boyle decided to see if he could bully it through. As soon as he was designated trustee, Boyle called a meeting of the trustees for the next day at his offices at the Union.

Judy approved the increase in a private session with Boyle immediately before the formal meeting, * * * The increase was formally approved a few minutes later and an announcement was thereafter sent out over Boyle's name to all pensioners and potential beneficiaries.

This action was taken in unnecessary haste. The trustees did not adequately consider the implications of their action, and while the increase was not wholly irresponsible it was not approached with adequate regard for the trustees' fiduciary obligations. Roche was not consulted or even advised of the action in advance, and in fact continued vigorously to oppose the pension increase. No detailed projections of the Fund's long-term ability to pay were made, nor were possible alternative changes in benefit payments considered. The trustees took no contemporaneous steps partially to offset the added payout by eliminating unnecessary administrative expenses or by investing cash in income-producing securities. In short, the increase was handled as an arrangement between labor and management with little recognition of its fiscal and fiduciary aspects.

* * *

The most revealing document in this entire episode is the full text of the press release which the Fund's public relations man issued on the day of the pension increase. It reads as follows:

Washington, D.C.—W.A. "Tony" Boyle, President of the United Mine Workers of America, succeeded John L. Lewis today as the Chief Executive Officer and Trustee of the Union's Welfare and Retirement Fund, and immediately boosted the pension of retired soft coal miners from $115 to $150 monthly.

The new pension rate will be effective August 1. It was voted at the first session of the Trustees attended by the Union chief. He was chosen trustee at a meeting of the International Executive Board yesterday, and as chief executive officer of the Fund, as set forth under the UMWA contract with the bituminous coal industry, called a meeting of the trustees, and the pension boost was adopted. Other trustees are George Judy, for the coal operators, and Josephine Roche, also director of the Fund, as the neutral.

Pensions now are going to approximately 70,000 retired soft coal miners. Last year, the Fund paid out $96 million in this benefit alone. Other benefits are complete hospital care for miners and their families, and death benefits to widows and survivors.

Chairman Boyle also called for an immediate in-depth study of all benefits of the 23 year-old-Fund, with complete analysis of the entire program for miners, their widows and families. He has received scores of suggestions for possibly improving the benefits at a series of rallies in the coal fields of West Virginia, Pennsylvania and Illinois in recent months.

The new chief executive of the Fund, like his predecessor, will accept no pay for serving as Trustee.

Nothing could more blatantly expose the realities of what had occurred in this instance and had been occurring for some time. However correct or incorrect the pension increase decision may have been, it reflected the Union's influence over Fund policy and the loss of independence that the Fund's continuous deferences to the Union's self-interest had by this time achieved.

\* \* \*

Alongside these serious deficiencies must be placed the pioneer role of the Fund, which by constant effort has led in the development of a broad program of welfare benefits for a distressed segment of the working population.  The many beneficial and well-motivated actions cannot, however, excuse the serious lapses which have resulted in obvious detriments to many beneficiaries.  There is an urgent need for reformation of policies and practices which only changes in the composition of the Board of Trustees, an adjustment of its banking relationship, and other equitable relief can accomplish.

Further proceedings must be conducted on the measure of damages, but as the Court indicated before trial it is desirable at this stage to establish the nature of equitable relief which must be taken for the protection of the beneficiaries.  Equitable relief shall take the following form.

Neither Boyle nor Roche shall continue to serve as a trustee.  Each shall be replaced by June 30, 1971, under the following procedures.  A new trustee must first be named by the Union.  Consonant with the provisions of the Agreement, the new Union trustee and the existing trustee representing the Operators shall then select a new neutral trustee.  The neutral trustee shall be designated on or before June 15, 1971, and the designation will then be submitted for approval by this Court before the new trustee takes office on June 30.

The newly constituted Board of Trustees selected as required by the decree shall then immediately determine whether or not Roche shall continue as Administrator of the Fund.  No trustee shall serve as Administrator after June 30, 1971.

Upon the selection of a replacement for Boyle and the neutral trustee, the newly constituted Board of Trustees shall be required to obtain independent professional advice to assist them in developing an investment policy for creating maximum income consistent with the prudent investment of the Fund's assets, and such a program shall be promptly put into effect.

The Fund shall by June 30, 1971, cease maintaining banking accounts with or doing any further business of any kind with the National Bank of Washington.  Following termination of this relationship, the Fund shall not have any account in a bank in which either the Union, any coal operator or any trustee has controlling or substantial stock interest.  No employee, representative or trustee of the Fund shall have any official connection with the bank or banks used by the Fund after June 30, 1971. The Fund shall not maintain non-interest-bearing accounts in any bank or other depository which are in excess of the amount reasonably necessary to cover immediate administrative expenses and to pay required taxes and benefits on a current basis.

A general injunction shall be framed enjoining the trustees from the practices here found to be breaches of trust and generally prohibiting the trustees from operating the Fund in a manner designed in whole or in part to afford collateral advantages to the Union or the operators.

NOTES AND QUESTIONS

**1.** In the midst of the case, John L. Lewis died, Boyle replaced Lewis, Boyle defeated Yablonski in an election for UMW president, Yablonski was murdered, Boyle was convicted of ordering the murder, and reformer Arnold Miller was elected union president. The case was an important part of the scenario.

**2.** If the source of law is the common law of trust and fiduciaries, what should pension fund trustees be allowed to do:

(a) Should union leaders manage pension funds? Employer representatives?

(b) Should unions be able to invest in employer companies (e.g. Western Kentucky Coal Co.)?

(c) Should the pension fund be able to own a bank? If not, in what businesses should they be able to invest?

(d) Who should decide the size of benefits and the eligibility rules? Who should decide how much the employer should pay in compensation today and how much in future benefits?

**3.** See Nedd v. UMW, 556 F.2d 190 (3d Cir.1977), cert. denied, 434 U.S. 1013 (1978), permitting dissident UMW pensioners to sue the pension fund trustees. The complaint, asserting a conflict between the union's duties to beneficiaries and its obligations to working miners, was held to allege violations of the federal common law rights of the plaintiffs. The court thought it important to avoid letting these cases be decided "depending upon the vagaries of the state law of trusts."

See also NLRB v. AMAX Coal Co., 453 U.S. 322 (1981), holding that it was not an unfair labor practice for the United Mine Workers to "restrain or coerce" an employer in the selection of the employer's representative as trustee of the pension plan. The reason is that under the strict fiduciary duties of the law of trusts, codified in ERISA, the pension fund trustee is not the "representative" of the employer.

## 3. RETIREE HEALTH BENEFITS AND THE PROBLEM OF REPRESENTATION

Before ERISA, workers hoping for pensions depended on uncertain contract and trust rights and were always at risk of finding the cupboard empty when they reached retirement age. As discussed infra, ERISA vests pension rights, requires current funding, and supplies federal insurance through the Pension Benefit Guaranty Corporation. Today, workers expecting post-retirement health benefits are in the situation faced by pension plan participants before ERISA. That is, the law is unclear about when expectations of future health benefits are legally enforceable. The law does not require employers to provide retiree health benefits, and it does not force employers who do so to set aside the funds while the future retirees are working. When heavy industry reduces the size of the workforce, a company can end up with many more retirees than current workers, leading the firm to consider slashing health benefits for retirees as a way of avoiding bankruptcy. When that happens, the interests of current workers and of current retirees come into conflict. Who can speak for retirees?

## In re Century Brass Products, Inc.

795 F.2d 265 (2d Cir.1986), cert. denied, 479 U.S. 949 (1986).

■ CARDAMONE, CIRCUIT JUDGE:

Century Brass Products, Inc. came into existence in 1976 when it purchased the major assets of the Scovill Manufacturing Company located in Waterbury and New Milford, Connecticut. Included in the sale were a metals and a general products divisions; the former operated brass mills and the latter manufactured products for the automotive industry and the United States' military program. The purchase price was $30 million, $12 million of which was paid in cash. The remainder was accounted for by the Company's assumption of Scovill's $18 million vested pension and insurance obligations due its hourly and salaried employees.

Since 1976 Century has recognized the International Union, United Automobile, Aerospace & Agricultural Implement Workers of America (UAW) and its Local 1604 (collectively referred to as the Union) "for the purpose of collective bargaining in respect of wages, rates of pay, hours of employment, and other conditions of employment * * * as the sole and exclusive representative of all hourly and incentive paid production and maintenance employees employed in the metals division including the New Milford plant, the General Products division, and Waterbury services." Following the acquisition, Century and the Union entered into a series of collective bargaining agreements.

From the time of acquisition, Century experienced a downturn in business precipitated primarily by worldwide events that had a negative impact on the American brass industry. Operating losses were incurred for the fiscal years ending in April 1980–1983. The 1983 loss exceeded $9 million. In fiscal year 1984 Century realized a minimal profit of $523,704 on sales of $141 million, with this small profit due in large part to an insurance settlement. By February 1985 the availability of cash under its financing arrangement approached zero. To deal with its urgent need for operating funds, Century devised plans to reduce operating costs.

Those salaried employees not represented by the Union agreed to wage and benefit reductions totaling $2.3 million. Coupled with this, Century's president met with the UAW on February 25, 1985 to discuss wage and benefit concessions. The company emphasized that unless the UAW agreed to a $2.5 million reduction, the historically unprofitable metals division would be closed. Were this to occur, the inevitable transfer of overhead expenses to the general products division would then jeopardize its existence. On March 3, 1985 the UAW members voted to reject any modifications of the collective bargaining agreement. The following day Century closed the metals division and laid off 700 employees. Attempts by a local Congressman and the Mayor of Waterbury to resolve the conflict were unavailing.

Shortly thereafter, Connecticut Light & Power Company told Century that its electrical power would be turned off in 15 days unless an overdue payment of $2.5 million was made together with a one-month deposit. Connecticut Power also attached Century's bank accounts. On March 15, 1985 Century filed a bankruptcy petition under Chapter 11. Scheduled liabilities totaled over $103 million, while assets listed in the petition amounted to only $71 million. A loss of $7 million was projected for the fiscal year ending April 30, 1985 with anticipated net sales of $62 million and costs of approximately $69 million. The bankruptcy court found that Century faced $40 million of non-modifiable expenses, leaving $22 million for payment of wages and benefits to all of its non-union salaried and bargaining unit employees. Labor costs under the existing collective bargaining agreement amounted to $19,912,000. Thus, were Century unable to modify its labor agreement, it would be forced to reduce its non-union salaried employees' wages from over $9 million to about $2 million.

After filing its Chapter 11 petition Century initiated a series of meetings with the UAW to discuss the changes essential to the survival of the general products division and to answer questions regarding its Chapter 11 petition. During these informal negotiations held on April 3, 9 and 10, 1985, Century raised the possibility of terminating the pension plan, which cost it approximately $3 million annually. The UAW rejected this proposal. By letter dated April 16 Century's vice president for corporate services requested a formal negotiating session. Century and the UAW negotiating committees met again on April 23.

At this meeting, the company again proposed the following modifications of the collective bargaining agreement: termination of the existing pension plan and institution of a new plan, changes in the medical plan through the addition of a deductible and/or employee contributions, waiver of negotiated changes in wages for 1985 and 1986, and a new vacation plan. The UAW responded that the retiree insurance benefits for those already retired were vested and of lifetime duration. As a consequence, the Union maintained that it could not negotiate these benefits through collective bargaining. Rather, if Century wanted to reduce those benefits, direct negotiation with the retirees to obtain their consent was necessary. On April 26 the UAW and Century met with officials of the Pension Benefit Guaranty Corporation (PBGC) and were advised as to the benefits the

PBGC would guarantee to eligible persons should the existing plan be terminated.

The debtor provided the UAW with information on April 29 that detailed the status of the company, its financial data, and its proposed resolution of various operational problems. The parties met again on April 30, May 8, and May 13. The Union reiterated that it could not consider any proposal involving modification of retirees' benefits. At the May 8 meeting Century presented an economic proposal that was part of an overall plan to reduce its projected losses from $7 million in the ensuing year to a profit of $287,000 on sales of $62 million. The proposal called for contract modifications and the termination of vested retiree insurance benefits. The UAW wanted retiree insurance benefit reductions removed as a topic of negotiation. In response, Century presented a revised proposal at the final pre-hearing negotiating session. Because the proposal still called for the complete elimination of retiree insurance benefits for approximately 700 pre-acquisition hourly retirees and for a significant reduction in the insurance benefits of 500 post-acquisition retirees, the UAW refused to take Century's offer to its active employee membership for a vote.

On May 17 Century filed the present application in the bankruptcy court for an order pursuant to § 1113 terminating its collective bargaining agreement with the UAW. The Union appeared and objected. From May 31 through July 12 hearings were held on the application. On July 26 the bankruptcy court (Kreckevsky, B.J.) granted Century's application. On November 7 the United States District Court for the District of Connecticut (Cabranes, J.) affirmed the order rejecting the labor agreement and this appeal followed.

*Bildisco* [supra p. 1058,] resolved a disagreement among the circuits as to the proper standard for rejecting a collective bargaining agreement.

\* \* \*

[A]n equitable standard was devised which requires that the bankruptcy court make four findings before the debtor's petition for rejection may be granted. These are as follows: (1) the collective bargaining agreement burdens the estate; (2) the equities favor rejecting the labor contract; (3) reasonable efforts to negotiate a voluntary modification have been made and are not likely to produce a prompt and satisfactory solution; and (4) allowing rejection would further the policy of Chapter 11 to permit successful rehabilitation of debtors.

The first part of *Bildisco*—which established the proper standard for judicial determinations of when a collective bargaining agreement can be rejected—was decided unanimously. But in a controversial 5–4 vote, the Supreme Court further held that a debtor in bankruptcy, prior to obtaining judicial approval to reject the collective bargaining agreement, may unilaterally terminate or modify provisions of the agreement without committing an unfair labor practice under either § 8(a)(5) or § 8(d) of the NLRA.

\* \* \*

Section 1113 reversed the second part of *Bildisco*. It created an expedited form of collective bargaining with several safeguards designed to insure that employers did not use Chapter 11 as medicine to rid themselves of corporate indigestion. Employers may only propose modifications in an existing labor contract that are necessary to permit an effective reorganization of the debtor. Further, the debtor must propose these modifications to the union before seeking approval to reject its collective bargaining agreement. Only if the expedited bargaining fails does § 1113 permit a debtor to apply for rejection of the labor agreement. At that point, a modified version of the unanimously decided first part of *Bildisco* applies.

\* \* \*

Applying these standards to the instant case, we address the threshold question of whether Century made a proposal under § 1113(b)(1)(A) to the employees' authorized representative covered by the agreement. The answer to this question is central to the resolution of the case before us.

The UAW claims that it is not the authorized representative of retired union members who, although covered by the agreement, are no longer active workers. Retirees lack the essential rights of union members. For example, under the Union constitution retirees are members of the union, but they are not entitled to vote in ratification of collective bargaining agreements. In Allied Chemical & Alkali Workers v. Pittsburgh Plate Glass Co., 404 U.S. 157 (1971), the Court held that the union had no statutory duty to represent the interests of retirees—as nonbargaining unit members—when making economic decisions for those it does represent. The Supreme Court further observed that vested retirement rights may not, absent the retirees' consent, unilaterally be altered without giving rise to a § 301 Labor Management Relations Act suit for breach of contract.

The bankruptcy court rejected this argument on the ground that the "unavoidable conflict between federal labor law and bankruptcy law" was resolved by the Supreme Court in *Bildisco,* and thus "[t]he union, having voluntarily negotiated benefits for its retired members, has the accompanying responsibility, at least initially, to act in the bankruptcy context as the retirees' representative under § 1113." The district court reached the same result, reasoning that "[t]he Congress that enacted Section 1113 most likely assumed, consistently with *Pittsburgh Plate Glass,* that the rights of retired workers 'vitally affect' the rights of current workers whenever their common employer files for protection under Chapter 11."

We agree with the district court that the rights of retired workers "vitally affect" the rights of active workers within the meaning of *Pittsburgh Plate Glass* when their employer files a Chapter 11 petition. In a Chapter 11 context a refusal to negotiate a reduction in retiree benefits under § 1113 will "vitally affect" active employees in two possible ways: first, it could mean that, as is the case here, they will have to bear a much larger reduction in wages and benefits in order to permit reorganization because of the significant cost of the retiree benefits; second, and more importantly, if retiree benefits cannot be renegotiated, the debtor's reorganization may well fail, in which case the active employees would most likely lose their jobs and benefits.

The district court further correctly observed that the level of benefits provided to retirees affects "the ability of Century Brass to remain in business," an effect far more serious than any identified by the Supreme Court in *Pittsburgh Plate Glass*. Labor law jurisprudence therefore does provide a basis for finding that a change in retirees' benefits is properly a mandatory subject of bargaining between Century and the UAW.

The policies of bankruptcy law also compel this result. It is true that *Pittsburgh Plate Glass* held that retirees are not employees as defined in § 2(3). Yet, if retirees benefits are subjects of bargaining between the union and the employer, and no modification can occur absent the retirees' consent, those retirees must be represented in the negotiations. In order to promote "the policies of flexibility and equity built into Chapter 11 of the Bankruptcy Code," retirees should properly be characterized as "employees" for purposes of applying § 1113. Therefore, they are generally capable of being represented by the union as their "authorized representative."

Concededly, the most "workable" interpretation of § 1113 would logically then require that a union always represent both current and former employees of the debtor in any negotiation for collective bargaining modifications made under Chapter 11. To state such a requirement as an absolute may, as here, pose a serious question as to whether the Union has a conflict of interest. It may not always be appropriate for a union to represent both active and retired workers in modification negotiations. The Supreme Court acknowledged the conflict in *Pittsburgh Plate Glass,* and though it was in another context, this view is relevant when construing § 1113. Therefore, we decline to adopt a per se rule holding that a union is always the appropriate party to represent the interests of retirees whose former employer is in a Chapter 11 reorganization proceeding.

When the suitability of representation on account of a conflict of interest is raised the bankruptcy court should make a determination as to whether a conflict actually exists. If a conflict is found, a representative for the class of retirees should be appointed by the bankruptcy judge. Although this departs somewhat from a literal reading of § 1113, well-established precedent for an appointment of this sort is found in other areas of the law.

* * *

The UAW has steadfastly refused throughout the expedited collective bargaining negotiations and all judicial proceedings to represent the retirees. Further, the record amply demonstrates that a conflict of interest exists between active and retired employees. For example, after Century closed its metals division, its workforce was reduced to about 900 employees, 650 of whom the Union represented. The general products division was forced to absorb all of the overhead and many of the metals division's personnel costs. The collective bargaining agreement provided for payment of medical and pension benefits to more than 1,300 retired employees and their families. The workforce reduction at the metals division did not eliminate these costs. As a result, each of the 650 remaining active bargaining unit employees must now support medical and pension benefits for two retired employees and their families. The active workers are interested in decreasing this heavy financial burden. Conversely, dependent on their pension and health benefits and no longer drawing salaries, retirees want their benefits reduced as little as possible.

Doubtless, it would be more expedient if a union could always represent both active and retired workers. Yet to allow that here would cast doubt on the value of bargained-for rights and call into question the adequacy of pre-deprivation representation in the collective bargaining process. The same union cannot fairly represent two such divergent interests. Here, we conclude that a conflict exists as a matter of law. The UAW therefore may not represent the retired employees. Such must be the rule if, as Congress aimed, bankruptcy law is to be reconciled with labor law principles. Our sister circuit in Wheeling-Pittsburgh Steel Corp. v. United Steel Workers of America, 791 F.2d 1074 (3d Cir.1986) apparently thought that Congress swung the pendulum back in favor of labor as a reaction to *Bildisco*. The predicate of this opinion is rather that the Senate and House Conferees made the point clear that the road to resolution of the conflict between labor and bankruptcy principles lies in honest compromise.

The debtor as the moving-party seeking rejection of its collective bargaining agreement has the burden of persuasion on the procedural requirements and substantive standards of § 1113. Inasmuch as Century has failed to meet its threshold burden of negotiating with a representative of the company's retired employees covered by that agreement, it therefore has failed to comply with the procedural requirements of § 1113.

## NOTES AND QUESTIONS

**1.** Was it right for Scovill to transfer its vested pension and insurance obligations to Century Brass? Why should that transfer limit the contractual rights of retirees against Scovill? Or is the relevant standard of inquiry whether Scovill's transfer was a fraudulent conveyance—intended to defeat legitimate claims?

**2.** At issue here are health benefit claims of retirees. ERISA, discussed infra, required gradual funding of pension claims. As of 1986 big U.S. pension plans as a whole were overfunded. Meanwhile, there was virtually no ongoing funding of future obligations for retiree health benefits. A major reason is that the Internal Revenue Code does not permit companies to take a business expense deduction if they set aside such funds for current workers. Most private plans provide retiree health care until age 65, at which point they provide only coverage that supplements Medicare. With workers retiring earlier and living longer, and with medical expenses growing rapidly, especially for the elderly, these costs are a major unfunded liability of the U.S. economy. Especially when a business turns sour, so that—as with Century Brass—few current workers are being asked to support many retirees, this problem will recur. What should Congress do about it?

**3.** 11 U.S.C. § 1113 requires communication between a bankrupt company and worker representatives before an executory collective bargaining contract is modified or repudiated. See supra pp. 1058–1059. The same principle seems applicable as to benefits contractually owed to retirees. Why did the UAW refuse to speak for the Century Brass retirees? Why not permit (or require) the union to serve as a political organization involved with the tradeoff of worker and retiree rights? The union would indeed have conflicting concerns, but it has those anyway when it trades off competing claims of current workers—wage cuts versus job losses, for example. Will there be a satisfactory process if the debtor company talks separately with worker and retiree representatives?

For a discussion of collective bargaining, see pp. 46–62. It is interesting to note that the interests of future union members, like those of retirees, may not be represented by unions. For example, the collective bargaining agreement between the National Basketball Association and the National Basketball Players Association includes a rookie salary cap. The rookie salary scale used to determine the possible salaries of all first-round draft picks was proposed by the NBPA and accepted by the NBA.

**4.** If there is to be a separate spokesperson for retirees, are you happy with having the representative chosen by the bankruptcy judge? Why not elect a representative? Does the U.S. need a structure for selection of exclusive bargaining agents for retirees?

**5.** In re Unimet Corp., 842 F.2d 879 (6th Cir.1988), cert. denied sub nom. Unimet Corp. v. United Steelworkers of America, 488 U.S. 828 (1988), held that 11 U.S.C. § 1113 protects retirees covered by health insurance provisions of a collective bargaining agreement against unilateral reduction of benefits by a bankrupt employer.

The *Unimet* holding received statutory ratification in the Retiree Benefits Bankruptcy Protection Act of 1988, P.L. 100–334, codified at 11 U.S.C. § 1114. The provision allows bankruptcy courts to name committees of retired employees if a labor union chooses not to speak on behalf of retirees or if retirees were not covered by a collective bargaining agreement. The trustee in bankruptcy can alter retiree benefits only after meeting procedural requirements and making substantive showings similar to those required by 11 U.S.C. § 1113 for revision of collectively bargained wages due current workers. The provision does not protect retirees whose gross income exceeds $250,000 per year.

**6.** The district judge permitted the Pension Benefit Guaranty Corp. to terminate the Century Brass pension plan, in an effort "to prevent further deterioration of the plan's financial condition." In re Century Brass Products, Inc., 1986 Westlaw 20957 (D.Conn. Nov. 28, 1986).

**7.** For a further discussion of retiree health benefits, see Curtiss–Wright Corp., v. Schoonejongen, supra p. 534.

**8.** *Century Brass* indicates the importance of employment law to corporate attorneys. Attorneys involved in mergers and acquisitions need to be familiar with the legal responsibilities attendant to employee benefit plans and pension plans when acquiring a company.

# In re Speco Corp.

195 B.R. 674 (Bankr.S.D.Ohio 1996).

\* \* \*

SPECO Corporation, the debtor in possession, manufacturers helicopter rotor transmissions, air craft and marine gear drive assemblies, aircraft flight control systems, and accessory gearboxes for military and commercial aircraft.... Although the team was able to stabilize sales at approximately $15 million/year in 1994 and 1995, it has been unable to rid the company of operating losses (approximately $11 million in 1994 and an estimated $15 million in 1995).

During this period the debtor's cost of providing employee pension benefits and post retirement health benefits increased. Of importance to the motion before the court, the debtor's cost for retiree benefits in 1992 was approximately $500,000 per year, but has risen to almost one million. \* \* \* Currently, approximately 240 retirees (about 420 individuals when spouses are included) and 18 surviving spouses receive Retiree Benefits from Debtor; approximately 40 of this total (about 70 individuals when spouses are included) and 4 surviving spouses are on Medicare. \* \* \*

In March 1995, the current CBA was signed with the Union as part of an effort to return the Debtor to profitability and to reduce costs. \* \* \*

Despite Debtor's aggressive cost containment measure implemented under the CBA, Debtor's cost incurred in paying the applicable insurance premiums for the Retiree Benefits remains at almost $1 million annually, or more than $80,000 per month.... Debtor's expense is calculated based on the number of employees enrolled. Thus, this cost can be expected to continue to increase as a result of Debtor's aging work force and an unusually large number of retirements since Debtor filed its Chapter 11 bankruptcy proceeding. \* \* \*

Debtor filed its petition for relief on December 22, 1995, under chapter 11 of the Bankruptcy Code.

On December 29, 1995, the debtor made a written proposal to the retirees' union to provide retiree benefits as part of an employee K/ESOP plan. Under that plan the debtor was to be converted from a wholly-owned subsidiary of LBG, Inc., into a company owned by its employees and management in roughly the following manner: union employees (40%), salaried employees (30%) and management (30%). Under such plan, debtor's retirees were to receive lump sum distributions from their defined benefit plan and use these distributions (or a portion thereof) to purchase stock in the "new" SPECO. As part of the overall transaction, money would also be placed in a trust fund to pay for the retirees' future medical benefits.

After a series of meetings between the debtor's representatives and representatives for the Union, the Union rejected the debtor's proposal for financing retiree health benefits. . . .

It does not appear that the Union ever offered a concrete counter proposal to the debtor's original proposal, and on approximately February 13, 1996, the debtor submitted a second bargaining proposal to the Union in which it is stated that:

> The costs for continued retiree medical insurance for current retirees and future retirees is a severe financial drain on the company and one of the most significant liabilities impeding the possibility of a successful sale.  Therefore, the company proposes that its obligation to fund insurance premiums for retiree medical benefits be eliminated effective immediately and that the pertinent contract provisions be amended accordingly.  Unfortunately, absent the funding through the K/ESOP approach, the Company is unable to provide the financial resources for continued retiree medical benefits.

Prior to the enactment of § 1114 of the Bankruptcy Code, a debtor in possession was generally able, under § 365, to reject a contract to provide health benefits to its retirees.  As a result of the 1986 bankruptcy filing of LTV Corporation, Congress sought to afford more protection to retirees:

> In July of 1986, LTV filed a petition under Chapter 11 of the Bankruptcy Code in the United States Bankruptcy Court for the Southern District of New York.  Almost immediately thereafter, LTV announced that it would no longer pay health benefits to its approximately 78,000 retirees and their dependents.  LTV's affected retirees consisted of both former salaried employees who received benefits under programs terminable at will and former union employees whose benefits were governed by collective bargaining agreements.

> Congress acted immediately to address LTV's action.  On July 28, 1986, the Senate Judiciary Committee held a hearing addressing the cutoff of retiree benefits and two days later the Senate passed a bill ordering LTV to reinstate benefits.  The House of Representatives commenced hearings the following week, which resulted in the passage of a bill protecting union retiree benefits by explicitly including such benefits within the protection of section 1113 of the Bankruptcy Code.  At the same time as the Senate action, and in response to a steelworkers' strike at several of its profitable plants, LTV sought and obtained authorization from the bankruptcy court to continue paying retiree benefits.

> Neither the original Senate nor the original House bill was enacted.  Instead, Congress passed much broader stopgap legislation to give itself time to deal more thoroughly with the issue.  The provision was made applicable to pending Chapter 11 cases, such as that of LTV.  On June 16, 1988, after twice extending its stopgap legislation, Congress

passed [The Retiree Benefits Bankruptcy Protection Act of 1988], which has been codified as § 1114 of the Bankruptcy Code.

Although the precise congressional intent in enacting § 1114 may be difficult to glean, the language of the statute makes it quite clear that— absent the occurrence of two statutory conditions—the debtor in possession is required to continue the payment of retirement benefits at prepetition levels:

(e)(1) Notwithstanding any other provision of this title, the debtor in possession, or the trustee if one has been appointed under the provisions of this chapter (hereinafter in this section "trustee" shall include a debtor in possession), shall timely pay and shall not modify any retiree benefits, except that—

(A) the court, on motion of the trustee or authorized representative, and after notice and a hearing, may order modification of such payments, pursuant to the provisions of subsections (g) and (h) of this section; or

(B) the trustee and the authorized representative of the recipients of those benefits may agree to modification of such payments;

after which such benefits as modified shall continue to be paid by the trustee.

11 U.S.C. § 1114(e)(1).

The statute contains no other basis for debtors to modify or cease the payment of retiree benefits.

If a debtor in possession has decided to attempt the modification of benefit payments it is otherwise required to make to its retirees, there are several conditions a debtor in possession must fulfill before it may make an application to the court to modify those benefits:

(f)(1) Subsequent to filing a petition and prior to filing an application seeking modification of the retiree benefits, the trustee shall—

(A) make a proposal to the authorized representative of the retirees, based on the most complete and reliable information available at the time of such proposal, which provides for those necessary modifications in the retiree benefits that are necessary to permit the reorganization of the debtor and assures that all creditors, the debtor and all of the affected parties are treated fairly and equitably; and

(B) provide, subject to subsection (k)(3), the representative of the retirees with such relevant information as is necessary to evaluate the proposal * * *

11 U.S.C. § 1114(f).

Once a debtor in possession has met the conditions of § 1114(f)(1), it may then file an application for modification, and the court will hold a hearing to determine whether a modification should be ordered. 11 U.S.C.

§ 1114(g), (k).   Under § 1114(g),[3] however, the first question before the court in considering the question of modification is whether the debtor in possession has fulfilled the conditions of § 1114(f)(1) of the Bankruptcy Code.   It is this court's opinion that in the instant case the debtor in possession has not met its burden of proof to demonstrate that it has complied with § 1114(f)(1).   The court is satisfied that complete and reliable information has been supplied to the retirees' authorized representative.   The court is not convinced, however, that the debtor in possession's proposal to pay none of the retirees' health benefits constitutes modifications "that are necessary to permit the reorganization of the debtor."   The reason that the debtor in possession has been unable to demonstrate to the court that its proposed modification is necessary to permit its reorganization is that the debtor in possession has not yet determined whether it will be proceeding as a going concern or electing to liquidate its assets.   The debtor has argued that it is too early in the administration of this case for it to make such a determination, and it is not yet required to submit a plan of reorganization.   While this may be true, it is equally true that nothing in § 1114 appears to contemplate that a company's retiree's should give up their retiree benefits while the company decides whether to reorganize or liquidate.   In short, if the debtor in possession will not inform the court, at least in general terms, of its future plans, it is by definition impossible for the court to determine whether a proposed modification of retiree benefits is "necessary" to permit a debtor's reorganization.   Nor does the court believe it appropriate to require the retirees to pay for the debtor's privilege of remaining in a "holding pattern" with respect to its decision to liquidate its assets or to proceed with a reorganization.

For similar reasons, the court finds it impossible to gauge whether the debtor in possession's proposed modification "assures that all creditors, the debtor and all of the affected parties are treated fairly and equitably."   The court knows that the debtor wishes to pay nothing in the way of retiree health benefits but has been told little concerning what the debtor proposes to pay other creditors.   Without knowing how other creditors, besides the retirees, are to be treated by the debtor, the court simply cannot make a determination regarding fair and equitable treatment.   Again, the debtor has a right to withhold its decisions regarding the proposed treatment of creditors, but nothing in § 1114 suggests to the court that retirees should give up their benefits while the debtor makes its financial decisions.   To

---

**3.**   (g) The court shall enter an order providing for modification in the payment of retiree benefits if the court finds that—

(1) the trustee has, prior to the hearing, made a proposal that fulfills the requirements of subsection (f);

(2) the authorized representative of the retirees has refused to accept such proposal without good cause; and

(3) such modification is necessary to permit the reorganization of the debtor and assures that all creditors, the debtor, and all of the affected parties are treated fairly and equitably, and is clearly favored by the balance of the equities;

except that in no case shall the court enter an order providing for such modification which provides for a modification to a level lower than that proposed by the trustee in the proposal found by the court to have complied with the requirements of this subsection and subsection (f). . . .

11 U.S.C. § 1114(g).

hold otherwise would, in this court's opinion, severely diminish the protection Congress has afforded retirees.

At this point, then, having found that § 1114(g)(1) has not been satisfied, the court's inquiry must end. In the interest of judicial economy, the court will point out that even if § 1114(g)(1) had been satisfied by the debtor, § 1114(g)(2) has not. The debtor in possession did not demonstrate that "the authorized representatives of the retirees has refused to accept such proposal without good cause" as required by 11 U.S.C. § 1114(g)(2). The debtor in possession's latest proposed modification, and the one currently before the court, is for the debtor in possession's retirees to surrender their § 1114 statutory rights to health benefits in exchange for absolutely nothing. (The debtor in possession's contention that the retirees would be given an unsecured claim in exchange for their surrendering their rights is unpersuasive.) The court cannot conceive, at this time, of arriving at a decision that the retirees' refusal to accept nothing in exchange for their rights constitutes a lack of good cause. The latest proposal constitutes nothing more than an attempt to unilaterally terminate the retirees benefits and is precisely what § 1114 was intended to prevent.

NOTES

**1.** For a discussion of bankruptcy law, see pp. 1058–1073.

**2.** Recall Varity Corp. v. Howe from Chapter 6. Does giving individuals the right to recover for breach of the fiduciary duty solve the representation problem of retirees?

**3.** See also In re Unisys Corp. Retiree Medical Benefit "ERISA" Litigation, 58 F.3d 896, 906–07 (3d Cir.1995), cert. denied, 517 U.S. 1103 (1996):

> Although it is true that the [Plaintiffs] retired early, foregoing future salary and pension accruals in order to secure the retiree medical benefits under their existing plans, the plans pursuant to which the [Plaintiffs] received retiree medical benefits contained clear and unequivocal reservation of rights clauses that permitted the company to end the plans at any time. [T]he plan pursuant to which the retiree medical coverage was to be provided, contained an unambiguous reservation of rights clause. While the [Plaintiffs] point out that the offering materials for their incentive plans promised the incentive benefits without any reference to a reserved right by the company to amend or terminate the plans, we find that this is not dispositive of their claim because the benefits which the [Plaintiffs] were to receive were described in summary plan descriptions containing unambiguous RORs. Consequently, the district court did not err in rejecting the [Plaintiffs'] claim.

## 4.  ERISA

### a.  THE ERISA SCHEME

For many years there was an effort in Congress to offer statutory protection for private sector pensioners. Federal regulation was sought by some national companies, for whom varying state laws made decisions difficult. It was also supported by "Wall Street": big banks and insurance companies sought to manage the billions in pension fund assets. Major stimulus for the ERISA legislation came from Ralph Nader's exposure of defects in the existing largely unregulated system. In 1973 Nader and Kate Blackwell published *You and Your Pension,* a book sharply critical of the private pension system. To illustrate their criticisms, Nader and Blackwell documented numerous instances of workers who were denied their pension benefits even though they had held their jobs for twenty years or more.

In one example, a man worked 24 years for a Colorado manufacturing company before the company closed its factory. Believing he could soon collect his pension, he declined a job in one of the company's other facilities. When he reached age 65 and applied for his pension, however, he found he was ineligible because he had left the company before retirement.

In another case, a company laid off a coal miner with 23 years of service, forcing him to find a job outside the coal industry. When he applied for his pension 13 years later based on his 23 years of continuous service, he found he was ineligible because he had not had 20 years of service within the 30 years preceding his application for benefits.

In a third example, a woman who had been with a company for 17 years left for five years when paralysis of her arm and fingers, the result of an industrial accident, forced her to work at another job. After she recovered, she returned to her former employer and worked an additional nine years. Despite a total of 26 years with the same company, she was denied her pension because she had not spent 20 consecutive years at her job. In a similar case, a man with 32 years' service was forced by a stroke to quit work at age 48, only to find that he had no pension because he had stopped working before age 50.

When the Studebaker company closed its plants in 1964, it left more than 8500 employees with reduced or no pensions at all. Because the company's pension plan had been severely underfunded, only employees who were 60 or older with at least ten years of service received full benefits. Workers between 40 and 59 with ten years of service received only 15 percent of their promised benefits, and the remaining employees received nothing.

Congress responded to the calls of Nader and others with the Employee Retirement Income Security Act of 1974 (ERISA). ERISA does not require employers to provide pensions. Rather, it says that persons and firms conforming to its provisions receive income tax advantages—essentially the opportunity for employers to deduct pension costs when funds are set aside, while beneficiaries do not declare income until decades later when they receive both the employers' contribution and the interest and dividends compounded to those contributions. It makes no economic sense to operate a pension plan that forfeits these tax advantages. Thus plans have a major incentive to comply with ERISA's rules, and all the big ones do.

ERISA is administered by the Department of Labor and the Internal Revenue Service of the Department of the Treasury. An important aspect of the ERISA scheme, discussed infra pp. 1197–1234, is that it preempts state and local laws on participation and vesting, funding, fiduciary responsibilities, plan termination insurance, and disclosure and reporting procedures.

ERISA's participation and vesting standards enable workers to establish a legal claim to benefits. By requiring all employees who have reached age 21 and who have completed one year of service (at least 1000 hours of work) to be covered by their company's pension plan, the Act broadens the number of people eligible to participate in private pension plans. Once workers begin to participate, their benefits become vested after they have completed a minimum period of service. Employers can choose one of two alternative minimum vesting standards: (1) 100 percent vesting after five years of service (with no vesting prior to five years); (2) gradual vesting over seven years (20 percent vesting after three years followed by 20 percent vesting per year for the fourth, fifth, sixth, and seventh years). These vesting requirements do not apply to multi-employer benefit plans; participants in these plans need not be 100 percent vested until after ten years of service. Once they are fully vested, employees cannot lose their pension benefits even if they leave their jobs before retirement. Thus ERISA encourages job mobility by permitting a worker to accumulate pension rights while working at different jobs.

In addition to its participation and vesting provisions, ERISA imposes minimum funding standards. These include the requirement that employers fund the normal costs of plans each year and amortize their employees' liabilities from previous service over not more than 40 years and from formation of new plans or benefit liberalizations in old plans over 30 years.

To guard against abuses of pension plan assets, ERISA sets various fiduciary requirements. Individuals identified as fiduciaries by ERISA include persons who exercise discretionary control over pension plan assets or who, for a fee, offer investment advice relating to pension plan assets. Fiduciaries must, among other things, exercise the investment skill and care of a "prudent man," diversify the pension portfolio (without investing more than ten percent of the plan's assets in the employer's securities), and refrain from using their access to plan assets to benefit themselves or other "parties-in-interest."

In addition to imposing fiduciary requirements, ERISA created the Pension Benefit Guarantee Corporation (PBGC), a nonprofit corporation within the Department of Labor, to insure against loss of pension benefits when plans are terminated. The Act requires that employers providing defined benefit plans purchase termination insurance through annual premiums. The premium rates are based on the number of participants in the pension plan and the plan's status as a single-employer plan (covering the employees of one employer) or a multi-employer plan (maintained under a collective bargaining agreement to which more than one employer contributes). A 1986 statutory change raised the maximum annual premium from $2.60 per worker to $8.50. The PBGC fully insures benefits only after a plan has been in effect for five years. Whereas retired employees are insured in full, vested employees who are still working are insured only for the benefits they have accrued up to the time the pension plan terminates. For both groups, ERISA insures pension benefits only up to a dollar limit.

Under ERISA's reporting and disclosure provisions, plan administrators must provide employees summaries of their benefit plans, updates of major alterations, and synopses of annual reports on the financing and operation of the plans. Although employees may request a report on the status of their accrued pension benefits at any time, these reports must automatically be given to employees who leave their jobs temporarily or permanently. Plan administrators must also report certain detailed financial and actuarial data annually to the IRS.

ERISA allocates responsibility for the administration and enforcement of its provisions between the IRS and the Department of Labor. The IRS is responsible for enforcing ERISA's participation, vesting, and funding standards. It enforces the participation and vesting requirements by disqualifying offending plans from tax-exempt status. It achieves compliance with the minimum funding standards through an excise tax on accumulated funding deficiencies. The Labor Department has general responsibility for investigating possible violations of all of ERISA's provisions and specific responsibility for handling breaches of the Act's fiduciary standards and reporting and disclosure requirements. It enforces ERISA's fiduciary standards by relieving fiduciaries of their duties, suing fiduciaries to recover losses they cause, and assessing civil penalties against parties-in-interest who engage in prohibited transactions. It administers the Act's reporting and disclosure requirements by suing plan administrators to force compliance or by retaining accountants and actuaries to gather information plan administrators should have provided. ERISA supplements these means of enforcement by granting the right to sue to plan participants and beneficiaries who are harmed by violations of the Act's provisions.

ERISA does not apply to government employees—federal, state, or local. Many state and local government pension plans are severely underfunded, and will present a social problem when obligations come due that can only be met by tax increases.

NOTE ON DEFINED CONTRIBUTION PLANS

During the past decade, defined contribution pension plans have grown in importance. Defined benefit plans provide a formula, related to final years' salary, for computing benefits that extend from retirement to death. Thus the employer sets aside and invests funds and accepts the risks of investment performance. Defined contribution plans, on the other hand, do not specify the amount of benefits to be paid at retirement. Instead, the employer sets aside money during the employee's working years, the employee may add to that money, and the employee chooses investment vehicles from the options—various stock and bond funds—offered by the employer. Thus the retiree's retirement resources depend on the amount that was invested and the performance of the investments. These plans are often known as 401(k) plans and permit pretax contributions. ERISA compliance costs are substantially lower than in heavily regulated defined benefit plans.

Should the employer be at risk if it offers investment options to employees that perform badly? If it is not careful in selecting investment options? If it does not fully inform employees about risks? The leading case is In re Unisys, which refused the employer a directed verdict when substantial amounts of employee funds were invested in Guaranteed Investment Contracts (GICs) which performed badly because the insurance company that issued them invested heavily in junk bonds. The court of appeals said that the case should go to trial on the issues of whether the company investigated the GICs sufficiently, whether it shared with employees all of the information it had, and whether the employees should have been encouraged to diversify their retirement dollars. The court was influenced by the fact that the chairman of the board moved his retirement funds out of the GIC but other employees were not warned to do the same. In re Unisys, 74 F.3d 420 (3d Cir.1996), cert. denied, 117 S.Ct. 56 (1996).

b.   FIDUCIARY DUTIES UNDER ERISA

ERISA makes the pension plan trustee a fiduciary on behalf of future retirees. The statute tells them to make investment decisions "with the care, skill, prudence, and diligence under the circumstances then prevailing that a prudent man acting in a like capacity and familiar with such matters would use in the conduct of an enterprise of a like character and with like aims." This statutory standard leaves unclear such vital questions as the level of risk that the portfolio manager should assume.

In thinking about fiduciary duties under ERISA, it is important to distinguish between the two kinds of pension plans. In a defined contribution plan, a fixed amount of money is set aside annually. The money is invested, and the retiree will receive the funds eventually accumulated. Thus, the worker will receive the benefits from successful investments but will suffer if performance is bad. On the other hand, a defined benefit plan is a commitment to the worker of a future pension according to a defined formula (such as 2 percent per year of final salary times years of service up to 25). Then, the pension plan is at risk, and if performance is especially good, the employer will be better off (because it will have a smaller obligation to make contributions in succeeding years). For discussion of the implications of the two kinds of pension plans for the legal obligations of fiduciaries, see Note, Fiduciary Standards and the Prudent Man Rule Under the Employee Retirement Income Security Act of 1974, 88 Harv. L.Rev. 960 (1975).

## Donovan v. Bierwirth

680 F.2d 263 (2d Cir.1982), cert. denied, 459 U.S. 1069 (1982).

■ FRIENDLY, CIRCUIT JUDGE.

This action was brought on October 19, 1981, by the Secretary of Labor (the Secretary) under § 502(e)(1) of the Employee Retirement Income Security Act of 1974 (ERISA), in the District Court for the Eastern District of New York, against John C. Bierwirth, Robert G. Freese and Carl A. Paladino, Trustees of the Grumman Corporation Pension Plan (the Plan). The action stems from the unsuccessful tender offer by LTV Corporation (LTV) in the fall of 1981 for some 70% of the outstanding common stock and convertible securities of Grumman Corporation (Grumman) at $45 per share. At the time of the offer the Plan owned some 525,000 shares of Grumman common stock, which it had acquired in the mid–1970's. As hereafter recounted, the Plan not only declined to tender its stock but purchased an additional 1,158,000 shares at an average price of $38.27 per share, at a total cost of $44,312,380. These acts, the Secretary's complaint alleged, constituted a violation of §§ 404(a) and 406(b) of ERISA.

\* \* \*

[Trustees appeal from entry of a preliminary injunction stopping them from dealing in Grumman securities and appointing a receiver to serve as an "Investment Manager" for Grumman securities owned by the plan.]

The LTV tender offer followed a scenario that has become familiar. On September 21, 1981, in the absence of defendant Bierwirth, Chairman of the Board of Grumman, who was on vacation, Joseph O. Gavin, Jr., President of Grumman, received a telephone call from Paul Thayer, Chairman of the Board and Chief Executive Officer of LTV, inviting him to discuss a possible merger. Gavin rejected the invitation. Evidently unsurprised, LTV, prior to the opening of trading on the New York Stock Exchange on September 23, issued a press release announcing that it was planning to make a cash tender offer at $45 per share for up to 70% of Grumman's common stock and securities representing or convertible into common stock. According to the press release, the offer constituted "the first step in a plan to acquire 100% of the voting equity of the Grumman Corporation". On September 21 and 22 Grumman stock had sold on the New York Stock Exchange at prices ranging between 23⅞ and 27¼. Later in the morning of September 23 Grumman put out a release on the Dow Jones News Service in Bierwirth's name stating that the Grumman directors would promptly consider the proposed offer. The release noted that the board would "consider legal factors including antitrust implications," warned stockholders not to act hastily and said that Dillon, Read & Co. had been retained to provide advice regarding the LTV offer. On the same day LTV delivered to Bierwirth's office a letter expressing regret at the lack of a meeting in which LTV would have had an "opportunity to spell out in a personal way how \* \* \* combination would be beneficial to the shareholders, employees, and communities served by Grumman", and stating that "[t]he headquarters of a combined Grumman-Vought aerospace operation would be established in Bethpage, Long Island [Grumman's headquarters] under a top management team that would include you as CEO as well as Joe Gavin and George Skurla from Grumman and Bob Kirk from Vought."

Thayer continued to hope for "the opportunity to explain to you in more detail the advantages of the synergistic combination" he had proposed and enclosed a copy of the press release.

The LTV offer was made on September 24. It was conditioned upon the tender of a minimum of 50.01% of Grumman's common stock and securities representing or convertible into common stock. The withdrawal/proration date was 12:01 A.M. on October 16, 1981; the termination date was 12:01 A.M. on October 23. Bierwirth cut short his vacation and reached the Grumman office at midday on September 24.

Although SEC Rule 14e–2, 17 C.F.R. § 240.14e–2, gave the Grumman board 10 business days from the commencement of the offer to communicate its position, if any, the board lost no time in going into action. It met on September 25. By then the LTV offer had caused the price of Grumman stock to rise to a range of 32⅝ to 34¼. The board had before it a two page letter of Dillon, Read & Co., Inc., which had served Grumman as investment banker, stating in a conclusory fashion that it was "of the opinion that the offer is inadequate from a financial point of view to holders of the Grumman securities." The letter said this conclusion was based on

> certain information of a business and financial nature regarding Grumman which was either publicly available or furnished to us by Grumman and [on] discussions with the management of Grumman regarding its business and prospects.

The letter made no attempt at quantification of these factors, and no representative of Dillon, Read attended the meeting for questioning, although apparently there were some supporting financial materials available. Defendant Robert G. Freese had also prepared some projections which are not in the record. The board unanimously adopted a resolution to oppose the tender offer, and issued a press release to that effect, saying that the board had concluded that "the offer is inadequate, and not in the best interests of Grumman, its shareholders, employees or the United States."

On September 28 Grumman began the previously mentioned action which was to lead to the injunction of the tender offer. On the same day defendant Bierwirth, Chairman of the Board of Grumman, sent a letter to the company's shareholders seeking their help in defeating the offer. The letter stated:

> We're very optimistic about our chances of defeating the takeover bid. About a third of all shares are held by Grumman's employee investment and pension plans. These plans are managed by Grummanites who will look long and hard at how well their fellow members would be served by selling off Grumman stock. Much of the rest is owned by Grumman people who, I believe, understand their future is worth more than a quick return on a block of shares.

The reasons given for opposing LTV's offer were the inadequacy of the price and others, relating to the pension fund, set forth in the margin.[3] The letter concluded by announcing that "Grumman's management is totally committed to defeating this takeover attempt", and by pleading "If you own Grumman shares, don't sell out to LTV".

On September 30, at the invitation of George Petrilak, President of the Grumman Retirees Club, Bierwirth met with 300 retirees to discuss the LTV offer.  An affidavit of Petrilak avers that "there was great concern expressed by the members as to the possible impact of LTV succeeding in their tender offer upon their pensions," and said that "[t]he overwhelming attitude of the retirees was 'what is good for Grumman is good for retirees' ".  The Club purchased an advertisement appearing in Newsday, a Long Island newspaper, on October 13, headed

> Grumman retirees protect your pension.
> Do not tender your stock to LTV.

Expectably, Bierwirth spent about 90% of his time during the next fortnight in activity directed to opposing the LTV offer.

* * *

On September 28 Freese mentioned to Bierwirth that the trustees "are going to have to get together here at some point and decide what [to] do in regard to the holdings of Grumman stock."  Bierwirth agreed and said he would call Paladino.  During the next ten days, the three trustees had casual conversations as they happened to meet each other.  Nothing was said about the Plan's buying Grumman shares and no financial data were assembled for the meeting.  Bierwirth had been informed by Mullan that if LTV succeeded, it could "merge the pension Plan though it may take them some time" and also "could cancel the Plan to the extent that they eliminate the Fund although of course they would retain the corporate obligation to pay", and by unidentified other sources that changing the presumed earnings rate would permit the declaration of some of the fund as surplus and recapture for the corporation.

What occurred at the Plan trustees' meeting, which was held on October 7, was described in the depositions of the three trustees.  Freese's is the most detailed; we shall follow it, with supplementation from the others when required.  Mullan made a ten minute presentation dealing with ERISA, pointing out that the trustees' decisions "as far as the Grumman stock was concerned had to be predicated solely upon the best interests of the participants of the Plan".  There was then a general discussion of how the trustees felt about LTV, the Dillon, Read opinion letter, and Freese's five year financial projections for Grumman.  Elaborating on the discussion of LTV, Freese mentioned concern about the underfunding of "their pension plan", LTV's highly leveraged debt situation

---

**3.**  There's one other factor to keep in mind: your pension fund.  It's Grumman's policy to fully fund its employee pension fund.  In contrast, LTV's pension fund right now is underfunded by almost a quarter of a billion dollars.  Grumman people could lose if the two funds were to be merged.

which would be aggravated by the need for borrowing to finance the acquisition of Grumman, contingent liability with respect to environmental problems and a large number of pending lawsuits and alleged SEC violations, all of which was revealed in a recent LTV prospectus.[5] The same information was contained in LTV's annual report and in its other publicly available filings. Freese expressed concern that the assumed rate of return used by LTV's pension plan was higher than that used by other companies and that LTV would have trouble making contributions to their pension plan. Bierwirth testified that the trustees "were aware of" a report about Grumman by Lehman Brothers Kuhn Loeb Inc. (Lehman Brothers). This report, dated July 8, 1981, which recommended purchase of Grumman common stock, then selling at $28 per share, projected a 1981–84 earnings progression of $2.75, $5.00, $6.50 and $7.50, and contained financial analysis supporting the estimates. The report's projection of greater sales was stated to be based primarily on "[i]ndications * * * that [President] Reagan's request [for increased expenditures for military aircraft] will be approved by Congress" and Grumman's "promising diversification into aerospace subcontracting. * * *"

After a half hour's discussion the trustees voted not to tender the 525,000 Grumman shares held by the Plan. According to Bierwirth the trustees "then discussed whether we should take a second step. If we did not want to tender the stock at $45 a share, should we then consider buying additional shares, the market then being in the 30's?" A merit of such a purchase would be in making it more difficult for LTV to gain control of the pension fund. However, "it was also important that a further investment in Grumman shares be the right thing for us to do." "[A] number of fortuitous events had occurred during the summer and early in September which greatly enhanced the outlook for Grumman" and had made Bierwirth "feel earlier that a further investment in Grumman was desirable and should be recommended to the Trustees come this fall." While it had been "very difficult to accumulate substantial positions in Grumman stock", which ordinarily traded at volumes of 20,000 shares a day, the daily volume of half a million shares induced by the LTV offer made it "possible to accumulate a major position in Grumman stock without affecting the price all that much." Bierwirth was then of the view that "probably a majority of the stock would not be tendered" but could not feel confident about it. He recognized that if the LTV tender offer were abandoned, selling by arbitrageurs would push the price down. Following their discussion of these ideas, the trustees concluded that purchases of Grumman stock up to the maximum of 10% of the value of the Plan's assets permitted by § 407(a)(2) of ERISA, 29 U.S.C. § 1107(a)(2), would be prudent.

\* \* \*

5. The prospectus, dated May 28, 1981, was in connection with a public offering of 4,000,000 shares of LTV of $24.50 per share. The syndicate managers were Lehman Broth- ers Kuhn Loeb Incorporated and Merrill Lynch White Weld Capital Markets Group. On September 24, 1981, the closing price of these shares was $14.75.

The request to the SEC was granted on Friday, October 9. The trustees met briefly on Monday, October 12, and authorized the Plan's purchase of 1,275,000 additional Grumman shares—just short of ERISA's 10% limitation. A press release issued on October 13 stated that use of the authorization would increase the Plan's ownership of Grumman stock from 3.8% to approximately 8% of the outstanding fully diluted shares. The Plan, acting through Dillon, Read, purchased 958,000 shares at an average price of $38.61 per share on October 12 and an additional 200,000 shares on October 13 at an average price of $36.62, for a total cost of $44,312,380.

On the next day, October 14, as previously indicated, the district court temporarily enjoined the LTV offer, thereby drastically reducing its chances for success. The price of Grumman stock fell on October 15 to a range of 28¼–29½. After this court affirmed the temporary injunction, the price of Grumman shares was 28–28¾; the market value of the newly purchased shares was approximately $32,500,000. As this is written, the price is 26¼–26⅜.

We deal first with the contention, advanced by the Secretary in passing, that the result reached by the district judge was compelled on a ground rejected by him, namely, that the trustees, at least in their purchase of Grumman stock, violated the specific prohibitions of § 406(b) of ERISA.

We hold that the section does not apply.  * * *

Sections 404(a)(1)(A) and (B) impose three different although overlapping standards. A fiduciary must discharge his duties "solely in the interests of the participants and beneficiaries." He must do this "for the exclusive purpose" of providing benefits to them. And he must comply "with the care, skill, prudence, and diligence under the circumstances then prevailing" of the traditional "prudent man".

The trustees urge that the mandates of § 404(a)(1)(A) and (B) must be interpreted in the light of two other sections of ERISA. One is § 408(c)(3), 29 U.S.C. § 1108(c)(3), which permits the appointment of officers of the sponsoring corporation as trustees. The other is § 407(a)(3), 29 U.S.C. § 1107(a)(3), which, as here applicable, permitted the Plan to acquire Grumman stock having an aggregate fair market value not exceeding 10% of the fair market value of the assets of the Plan. This provision, the trustees point out, was the result of a lengthy debate in which the Department of Labor played an important role.  * * *

* * *

We accept the argument but not the conclusion which appellants seem to think follows from it. Although officers of a corporation who are trustees of its pension plan do not violate their duties as trustees by taking action which, after careful and impartial investigation, they reasonably conclude best to promote the interests of participants and beneficiaries simply because it incidentally benefits the corporation or, indeed, themselves, their decisions must be made with an eye single to the interests of the participants and beneficiaries. This, in turn, imposes a duty on the trustees to avoid placing themselves in a position where their acts as officers or directors of the corporation will prevent their functioning with the complete loyalty to participants demanded of them as trustees of a pension plan.

There is much to be said for the Secretary's argument that * * * the only proper course was for the trustees immediately to resign so that a neutral trustee or trustees could be swiftly appointed to serve for the duration of the tender offer.[8]

* * *

We are not, however, required to go so far in this case. The record contains specific instances of the trustees' failure to observe the high standard of duty placed upon them. Bierwirth and Freese should have been immediately aware of the difficult position which they occupied as a result of having decided as directors some of the same questions they would have to decide as trustees, and should have explored where their duty lay.[10]

* * *

An even more telling point against the trustees is their swift movement from a decision not to tender or sell [15] the shares already in the fund to a decision to invest more than $44,000,000 in the purchase of additional Grumman shares up to the 10% maximum permitted by § 407(a)(2) of ERISA. Their argument is that once they had reasonably decided not to tender the shares already in the fund since success of the offer would run counter to the interests of the beneficiaries, it followed that they should do everything else they lawfully could do to thwart the offer. This, however, should have involved a calculation of the risks and benefits involved. Bierwirth properly conceded that a further investment in Grumman shares had to be "the right thing for us to do." The trustees' consideration of this was woefully inadequate. Although Grumman shares may have seemed attractive when selling in the high 20's, with what appeared a good chance of appreciation, they were not necessarily attractive when, under the

**8.** It could be said against this that Bierwirth and Freese were fiduciaries for the Grumman stockholders and that if their actions before the trustees' meeting on October 7 met their duties as such, no harm was done by their prejudgment. However, as Justice Frankfurter observed in a famous passage, "to say that a man is a fiduciary only begins analysis; it gives direction to further inquiry. To whom is he a fiduciary? What obligations does he owe as a fiduciary?" The fiduciary obligations of the trustees to the participants and beneficiaries of the plan are those of trustees of an express trust—the highest known to the law. The trustees do not even contend that the quick judgment made at the directors' meeting of September 25 satisfied

their obligations under § 404(a)(1)(A) and (B). Whether it satisfied their obligations to Grumman shareholders is not before us.

**10.** Bierwirth was a law school graduate and had practiced for 3 years.

**15.** The record does not indicate that sale was even considered, although that course had some attractions. It would have eliminated the possibilities that if the Plan did not tender and the offer succeeded, the Plan might be left as a minority stockholder in an LTV controlled Grumman, and that, if the Plan did tender and the offer succeeded, the Plan might be left with some Grumman stock, because of the 70% maximum in the tender offer.

impetus of the tender offer, they had risen to the high 30's.  Moreover, and even more important, in purchasing additional shares when they did, the trustees were buying into what, from their own point of view, was almost certainly a "no-win" situation.  If the LTV offer succeeded, the Plan would be left as a minority stockholder in an LTV-controlled Grumman—a point that seems to have received no consideration.  If it failed, as the Plan's purchase of additional 8% of the outstanding Grumman stock made more likely, the stock was almost certain to sink to its pre-offer level, as the trustees fully appreciated.  Given the trustees' views as to the dim future of an LTV-controlled Grumman, it is thus exceedingly difficult to accept Bierwirth's testimony that the purchase of additional shares was justified from an investment standpoint—or even to conclude that the trustees really believed this.  Investment considerations dictated a policy of waiting.  If LTV's offer were accepted, the trustees would not want more Grumman shares; if it failed, the shares would be obtainable at prices far below what was paid.  Mid-October 1981 was thus the worst possible time for the Plan to buy Grumman stock as an investment.  It is almost impossible to believe that the trustees did not realize this and that their motive for purchasing the additional shares was for any purpose other than blocking the LTV offer.  Moreover, even if we were to make the dubious assumption that a purchase for this purpose would have been permissible despite all the investment risks that it entailed, the trustees should at least have taken all reasonable steps to make sure the purchase was necessary.

\* \* \*

We do not join in all of the district judge's pejorative adjectives concerning the trustees.  They were caught in a difficult and unusual situation—apparently, so far as shown in the briefs, one that had not arisen before.  We accept that they were honestly convinced that acquisition of Grumman by the debt-ridden LTV would mean a less bright future for Grumman and also that an LTV acquisition posed some special dangers to the participants of the Plan.  However, they should have realized that, since their judgment on this score could scarcely be unbiased, at the least they were bound to take every feasible precaution to see that they had carefully considered the other side, to free themselves, if indeed this was humanly possible, from any taint of the quick negative reaction characteristic of targets of hostile tender offers displayed at the September 24 board meeting, and particularly to consider the huge risks attendant on purchasing additional Grumman shares at a price substantially elevated by the tender offer.  We need not decide whether even this would have sufficed; perhaps, after the events of late September, resignation was the only proper course.  It is enough that, for the reasons we have indicated, as well as others, the district judge was warranted in concluding, on the materials before him, that the trustees had not measured up to the high standards imposed by § 404(a)(1)(A) and (B) of ERISA.  How the situation will appear after a trial is a different matter which we cannot now decide.

NOTES AND QUESTIONS

**1.** In *Bierwirth,* the court criticized Bierwirth, Freese, and Paladino for their financial judgment, but the court specifically declined to answer the question whether the Grumman directors were legally bound to resign from the trusteeship of the plan. Could the court have answered this question in view of the legislative history of ERISA; namely, the Senate testimony that recognizes that employers will often be administrators or trustees of a plan and that this "limited exception to the listed proscription against self-dealing * * * is made in recognition of the *symbiotic relationship* existing between the employer and the plan covering his employees"?

Given the "symbiotic relationship" between Grumman and its employee pension plan, can one argue that the court was wrong in criticizing even the directors' financial judgment? If Grumman's claim that it will best protect the employee's plan is true, what difference does it make if the plan loses money in the short term as long as the employees are protected for the future? Indeed, would the Grumman directors have breached their fiduciary duty if they had resigned in the face of a takeover battle?

Under a typical pension trust instrument, the outgoing trustees would have selected their successors. In a situation like *Bierworth,* however, is there any guarantee that the fiduciaries chosen by the outgoing trustees would be neutral?

**2.** ERISA does not specifically bar anyone from serving on the board of an employee pension plan merely by virtue of a position within the company or union. Instead, ERISA more generally bars a fiduciary from dealing with assets for "his own interest." See 29 U.S.C. § 1106. What are the problems posed by leaving ambiguous the matter of who can be a fiduciary? Does this wording insure that the judiciary will have an active role in the administration of employee pension plans?

Is the solution to have pension plan participants decide how risky the investments should be and what political goals should be pursued along with investment decisions? Or does that idea run counter to the paternalism that is one aspect of the ERISA scheme? Did not Congress want all workers to have their pension assets invested "prudently"? And does not *Century Brass* show the difficulty of finding an institutional method for letting workers and retirees choose investment strategies? How would decisions be made if plan participants disagreed (as they would be likely to do)? These questions are also relevant with regard to Social Security, infra pp. 1241–1278.

**3.** Professors Daniel Fischel and John Langbein contend that ERISA's Exclusive Benefit Rule engenders conflicts of interest between classes of plan beneficiaries and between beneficiaries and trustees. They note that this is evident upon careful consideration of cases such as Donovan v. Bierwirth:

> The court viewed *Bierwirth* as an easy case. ERISA required the trustees to act with an "eye single" to the interests of the plan's participants and beneficiaries. The trustees' conduct in

helping to defeat LTV's offer failed to meet this standard. Thus, the trustees breached their fiduciary duty to act solely in the interests of the plan's beneficiaries.

In reality, *Bierwirth* is a very hard case. Because the plan was a well funded defined benefit plan—the sort of plan in which almost all of the investment risk incides on the sponsor—Grumman's stockholders would bear the capital losses from adverse investment results. Pension plan participants, by contrast, would be relatively unaffected by investment losses. In their capacity as active employees, however, many of these same participants might have been harmed by the takeover if, for example, LTV would have closed Grumman plants or transferred or terminated Grumman employees. Thus, it was rational for workers to oppose the LTV offer and support plan purchases of Grumman stock to defeat the offer. This is precisely the position that most Grumman employees apparently took; recall that it was the Secretary of Labor, not the employees, who brought the *Bierwirth* lawsuit.

From the perspective of Grumman's stockholders, the situation was different. Not only did they bear the investment losses incurred by the plan,[126] but they would have received a substantial premium for their shares had LTV been able to complete its offer.

The irony of the *Bierwirth* case should now be clear. The Secretary of Labor sued to redress an injury allegedly suffered by the participants and beneficiaries of the plan. Most of them, however, thought that they benefited from the defeat of LTV's offer and supported the trustees' actions. And in any event, because the plan in question was a well funded defined benefit plan, the investment risk was borne by the employer, not by the employees or the government insurer, the PBGC. The shareholders of the firm, by contrast, on whom the risk did incide, suffered the true injury, yet they went unrepresented in the case.

*Bierwirth* illustrates the problems created by literal application of the exclusive benefit rule when a takeover defense works to the advantage of one of the groups beneficially interested in the plan (employees) but harms another (shareholders). Under a different plan, the same underlying facts would have produced a different sort of conflict. If the Grumman pension plan had been a defined contribution plan instead of a defined benefit plan, the

---

**126.** The Second Circuit held in a subsequent decision that the Plan did not incur any losses because the Grumman securities purchased by the Plan were eventually sold for a higher price than that paid by the Plan. Donovan v. Bierwirth, 754 F2d 1049 (2d Cir. 1985). We think that decision is quite wrong. The sale occurred almost two years after the initial purchases. Grumman stock, like other defense stocks, rose in value during the early 1980s as a result of the defense build up. This increase in the value of defense stocks should have been irrelevant in determining whether the plan incurred any losses at the time of the trustees' decision to oppose the offer. Instead, the Second Circuit allowed the trustees to appropriate by way of setoff the appreciation in trust assets.

takeover defense would not have affected shareholders, since they bear no investment risk; but conflicts of interest between different subclasses of employees would have become noticeable. In a defined contribution plan that holds employer securities in individual employees' accounts, the capital gain on the sale of shares in a successful takeover would accrue to the employees' accounts. This result is simply an application of the general principle that investment risk in a defined contribution plan incides on the participants rather than the sponsor. For younger employees, however, the concern over loss of employment may outweigh the benefit from receiving this capital gain. For older employees whose future income from prospective employment is smaller and whose prospective capital gain from the sale of shares is larger (since longer-service employees will have built up larger balances of plan shares), the capital gain may outweigh the risk of employment loss. And for retirees who cannot benefit from future employment with the firm, only the capital gain has value.

Daniel Fischel & John Langbein, ERISA's Fundamental Contradiction: The Exclusive Benefit Rule, 55 U.Chi.L.Rev. 1105, 1139–41 (1986).

**4.** Is it consistent with ERISA's Exclusive Benefit Rule to invest fund assets so that some plan participants receive additional financial benefits? What if such investments detract from overall plan performance? Brock v. Walton, 794 F.2d 586 (11th Cir.1986), held that mortgage loans made to fund participants below prevailing market rates are not in violation of ERISA. The court concluded:

> The Secretary has presented no evidence of imprudence except as to the differential in the rate of interest. There is little question that a rate could be so far below the market rate that it could not be justified as being in the best interest of the plan or within the realm of prudence. But such is not the case here. This case is quite unlike other cases involving self-dealing or preferential loans to plan officers where the trustees run afoul of the rule prohibiting transactions with parties in interest.

Is this a fair or correct result when the interests of participants not receiving the loans are considered? How does the decision fare when viewed in light of the arguments made by Lanoff, supra.

**5.** Consider the case of Evans v. Bexley, 750 F.2d 1498 (11th Cir.1985). Plaintiffs, disabled retirees of the International Brotherhood of Electrical Workers (IBEW), received benefits from IBEW Local 613 and the Contributing Employers Health and Welfare Fund (the H & W Fund). Certain trustees of the H & W Fund were also trustees of Local 613 and the Contributory Employers Pension Fund (the Pension Fund), another benefit plan serving members of the IBEW. In order to facilitate a collective bargaining agreement, the common trustees accepted a plan whereby payments by disabled retirees would be made to the H & W Fund so that employer contributions could be decreased. Pursuant to the same agreement, employer contributions to the Pension Fund were increased. Plaintiffs sued the trustees for breach of fiduciary duty, contending that the trustees sacrificed the interests of the H & W Fund beneficiaries for those of the Local and the Pension Fund.

The court found no violation of fiduciary duty:

> A fiduciary may * * * also serve as an officer, employee, agent, or other representative of a union or an employer. Logic demands that if a fiduciary may hold such positions, then he may fulfill the concomitant responsibilities. Thus, a trustee of an employee benefit plan does not violate ERISA merely by serving in a position with an employee organization or employer that requires him to represent such entity in the collective bargaining negotiations that determine the funding of the plan. In those negotiations, the bargaining representative represents either the employer or the employees. To require him to consider only the best interests of the plan at the negotiation table would be to require him to breach the trust of his constituents. We decline to do so.

Is this decision consistent with Donovan v. Bierwirth? What about "the trust of his constituents" who are beneficiaries of the H & W Fund? Why not simply require the appointment of a neutral trustee?

**6.** *Bierwirth* deals with trustees who wheel and deal with pension fund assets in takeover contests. What if union officials serving as trustees of a pension plan refuse to invest in stock of nonunion or antiunion companies? What if some workers urge the trustees to sell stock in companies doing business in South Africa (or Haiti or Iraq) but other workers favor seeking maximum return? Which investment policy is "solely in the interest" of plan beneficiaries, as ERISA requires? So far there have been no cases, but a Labor Department official addressed the central issue. Ian D. Lanoff, [Administrator, Office of Pension and Welfare Benefit Programs, U.S. Dept. of Labor], The Social Investment of Private Pension Plan Assets: May It Be Done Lawfully Under ERISA?,* 31 Labor L.J. 387 (1980):

> It is not consistent with the prudence standard for the fiduciary to make his or her investment decision based on other objectives, such as to promote the job security of a class of current or future participants. While it may sound harsh to say that the pension plan fiduciary cannot make his or her investment decision on such a basis, it is the fiduciary's duty of loyalty to plan beneficiaries which provides the participants' greatest protection.

> * * *

> In other words, what the pension plan fiduciary needs to determine about an investment is not, first, whether it is socially good or bad but how the proposed investment will serve the plan's participants and beneficiaries. The stability of a company's labor relations, the

* Reproduced from the July 1980 issue of the LABOR LAW JOURNAL, published and copyrighted 1980 by Commerce Clearing House, Inc., 4025 W. Peterson Avenue Chicago, Illinois 60646.

political situation in a country in which the investment is located or with which a company does business, and the effect that the public view of a company's social commitment may have on the profitability of a company are all factors which may properly enter into the evaluation of an investment.

If, after evaluating other factors, two investments appear to be equally desirable, then social judgments are permissible in determining which to select. The point is that social judgments may not properly be substituted for any factors which would otherwise be considered in a given case.

\* \* \*

On the other hand, ruling out certain investments completely, such as nonunion companies or competitors, runs the risk of violating ERISA. It is difficult to square an investment policy of exclusion on the basis of nonobjective economic investment criteria, whether the exclusion of union organized companies or nonorganized companies, with ERISA standards that plan assets be managed prudently, solely in the interest of the participants, and for the exclusive purpose of paying benefits.

Analysis of these ERISA standards, which encompass duties of care and loyalty, leads to the inescapable conclusion that any plan which for so-called social purposes excludes investment possibilities without consideration of their economic and financial merit is showing insufficient care for and disloyalty to individuals covered by the plans. Fiduciaries following such a course would, in my view, be acting at their peril.

\* \* \*

See also Note, Legal Standards Governing Investment of Pension Assets for Social and Political Goals, 128 U.Pa.L.Rev. 1340 (1980).

**7.** For consideration of damages due to plaintiffs in this case see Donovan v. Bierwirth, 754 F.2d 1049 (2d Cir.1985), and Ford v. Bierwirth, 636 F.Supp. 540 (E.D.N.Y.1986), ultimately concluding that the money would have earned $4.5 million less if invested legally than was earned through purchase of Grunman stock.

**8.** The fiduciary administering a company's benefit plan allegedly mishandled an employee's disability claim. The claim was ultimately paid, but the plaintiff said she suffered psychological damages from the unwarranted delay and that she should also receive punitive damages. Reversing a decision by the Ninth Circuit, the Supreme Court said § 409 of ERISA does not provide for extracontractual compensatory or punitive damages. Justices Brennan, White, Marshall, and Blackmun concurred, suggesting that the employee might have recovered had she sued under other sections of the ERISA statute. Massachusetts Mutual Life Insurance Co. v. Russell, 473 U.S. 134 (1985).

**9.** While extracontractual tort remedies may not be available to plan participants, the Ninth Circuit has ruled that courts have broad authority to fashion remedies for redressing a breach of fiduciary duty. See Donovan v. Mazzola, 716 F.2d 1226 (9th Cir.), cert. denied, 464 U.S. 1040 (1984), holding that the district court acted within its discretion when it found pension fund trustees liable for potential losses in connection with a questionable loan they had granted and required the trustees to post a $1 million cash or corporate surety bond to cover potential losses. The district court was also within its power in ordering the appointment of an investment manager to manage the pension fund's assets.

**10.** In Leigh v. Engle, 727 F.2d 113 (7th Cir.1984), cert. denied, 489 U.S. 1078 (1989), administrators of an employee pension plan used pension funds to participate in corporate-control contests in which they had an interest. The administrators won the takeover battles and the plan reaped enormous benefit. Nevertheless, the Seventh Circuit held the administrators liable for their breach of fiduciary duty:

> [The Trust's] investments * * * produced in the aggregate the extraordinary return on investment of 72%, exclusive of dividends. It is clear that the trust lost no money in the challenged transactions. The district court held that ERISA creates no cause of action where a breach of fiduciary duty does not cause financial harm to the benefit plan, but the district court erred in this statement of the law. ERISA clearly contemplates actions against fiduciaries who profit by using trust assets, even where the plan beneficiaries do not suffer direct financial loss. A fiduciary who breaches his duties "shall be personally liable * * * to restore to such plan any profits of such fiduciary which have been made through use of assets of the plan by the fiduciary." 29 U.S.C. § 1109(a).

> The nature of the breach of fiduciary duty alleged here is not the *loss* of plan assets but instead the *risking* of the trust's assets at least in part to aid the defendants in their acquisition program. ERISA expressly prohibits the use of assets for purposes other than the best interests of the beneficiaries, and the language of section 1109(a) providing for disgorgement of profits from improper use of trust assets is the appropriate remedy. On the record before us, we are unable to determine the extent of the defendants' total profits, and we certainly cannot measure the extent, if any, to which any profits resulted from the defendants' use of the trust assets. However, those questions are relevant only in measuring damages. At this point in the analysis, we need only say that plaintiffs are not required to show that the trust lost money as a result of the alleged breaches of fiduciary duties. If ERISA fiduciaries breach their duties by risking trust assets for their own purposes, beneficiaries may recover the fiduciaries' profits made by misuse of the plan's assets.

727 F.2d at 121–22.

**11.** Curtis Guidry served 17 years as the chief executive officer and business manager of Sheet Metal Workers Association Local No. 9, and 5 years as a trustee of the Sheet Metal Workers pension fund. In 1981, the year of his departure, an audit revealed that $1 million had been stolen from the union trust funds. Following investigation and indictment, Guidry pleaded guilty to embezzling $377,000 of union funds, and agreed to the entry of a $275,000 judgment against him on the union's civil claims.

Guidry later brought suit against the Sheet Metal Workers National Pension fund, claiming that his early retirement pension benefits were being unfairly withheld. The district court awarded Guidry the pension money over the union's argument that the funds were forfeited due to his misconduct. As a protective measure, however, the court placed the funds in a constructive trust so that if necessary they could be used in satisfaction of the stipulated civil judgment. Guidry appealed, contending that the constructive trust arrangement was in violation of ERISA's anti-alienation provision, 29 U.S.C. § 1056(d)(1), which states that "[e]ach pension plan shall provide that benefits provided under the plan may not be assigned or alienated." Guidry v. Sheet Metal Workers National Pension Fund, 856 F.2d 1457 (10th Cir.1988), held that the ERISA provision did not bar the district court from utilizing traditional equitable remedies such as the constructive trust. The court reasoned that "[g]iven the express purpose of ERISA to protect the financial security of employees * * * it [is] extremely unlikely that Congress intended to ignore equitable principles by protecting individuals such as the plaintiff from the consequences of their misconduct." The Supreme Court reversed, holding that because Guidry was convicted of stealing only from the union, and not from the pension plan, a judgment against him should not extend to his pension, given ERISA's strong anti-alienation provision. Guidry v. Sheet Metal Workers National Pension Fund, 493 U.S. 365 (1990). Is *Guidry* the ultimate declaration that pension funds and other union affairs are formally distinct? Reconsider Blankenship v. Boyle, supra p. 1173. Justice Blackmun wrote in *Guidry*: "[T]here may be a natural distaste for the result we reach here." Would you support a statutory change to overturn the decision?

## c. ARBITRARY AND CAPRICIOUS DECISIONS BY PENSION FUND TRUSTEES

Reacting to the post World War II growth of union-managed pension funds, Congress included § 302 in the Taft-Hartley Act, 29 U.S.C. § 186(c), permitting only bona fide fringe benefit trust funds. Enforcing § 302, the federal courts borrowed from state trust law and established a federal common law of fiduciary duties to plan beneficiaries. The Supreme Court then said that ERISA "essentially codified the strict fiduciary standards that a § 302 trustee must meet." NLRB v. AMAX Coal Co., 453 U.S. 322 (1981). Applying § 302 of the Taft-Hartley Act, the courts invented an ERISA standard. They banned "arbitrary and capricious" decisions by plan trustees. For example, courts held that similarly situated participants must be treated alike. See, e.g., Frary v. Shorr Paper Products, 494 F.Supp. 565 (N.D.Ill.1980). But sometimes courts played a more active role, intervening to "avoid an unjust result" or to "prevent a violation of fundamental fairness." See, e.g., Burroughs v. Board of Trustees, 542 F.2d 1128 (9th Cir.1976), cert. denied, 429 U.S. 1096 (1977). The Supreme Court's latest contribution to this debate is *Firestone,* infra.

## Firestone Tire & Rubber Co. v. Bruch

489 U.S. 101 (1989).

■ JUSTICE O'CONNOR delivered the opinion of the Court.

This case presents two questions concerning the Employee Retirement Income Security Act of 1974 (ERISA), 88 Stat. 829, as amended, 29 U.S.C. § 1001 et seq. First, we address the appropriate standard of judicial review of benefit determinations by fiduciaries or plan administrators under ERISA. Second, we determine which persons are "participants" entitled to obtain information about benefit plans covered by ERISA.

Late in 1980, petitioner Firestone Tire and Rubber Company (Firestone) sold, as going concerns, the five plants comprising its Plastics Division to Occidental Petroleum Company (Occidental). Most of the approximately 500 salaried employees at the five plants were rehired by Occidental and continued in their same positions without interruption and at the same rates of pay. At the time of the sale, Firestone maintained three pension and welfare benefit plans for its employees: a termination pay plan, a retirement plan, and a stock purchase plan. Firestone was the sole source of funding for the plans and had not established separate trust funds out of which to pay the benefits from the plans. All three of the plans were either "employee welfare benefit plans" or "employee pension benefit plans" governed (albeit in different ways) by ERISA. By operation of law, Firestone itself was the administrator, 29 U.S.C. § 1002(16)(A)(ii), and fiduciary, 29 U.S.C. § 1002(21)(A), of each of these "unfunded" plans. At the time of the sale of its Plastics Division, Firestone was not aware that the termination pay plan was governed by ERISA, and therefore had not set up a claims procedure, 29 U.S.C. § 1133, nor complied with ERISA's reporting and disclosure obligations, 29 U.S.C. §§ 1021–1031, with respect to that plan.

Respondents, six Firestone employees who were rehired by Occidental, sought severance benefits from Firestone under the termination pay plan. In relevant part, that plan provides as follows:

> "If your service is discontinued prior to the time you are eligible for pension benefits, you will be given termination pay if released because of a reduction in work force or if you become physically or mentally unable to perform your job.

> "The amount of termination pay you will receive will depend on your period of credited company service."

Several of the respondents also sought information from Firestone regarding their benefits under all three of the plans pursuant to certain ERISA disclosure provisions.  See 29 U.S.C. §§ 1024(b)(4), 1025(a).  Firestone denied respondents severance benefits on the ground that the sale of the Plastics Division to Occidental did not constitute a "reduction in work force" within the meaning of the termination pay plan.  In addition, Firestone denied the requests for information concerning benefits under the three plans.  Firestone concluded that respondents were not entitled to the information because they were no longer "participants" in the plans.

Respondents then filed a class action on behalf of "former, salaried, non-union employees who worked in the five plants that comprised the Plastic Division of Firestone."  * * *

Although it is a "comprehensive and reticulated statute," ERISA does not set out the appropriate standard of review for actions under § 1132(a)(1)(B) challenging benefit eligibility determinations.  To fill this gap, federal courts have adopted the arbitrary and capricious standard developed under 61 Stat. 157, 29 U.S.C. § 186(c), a provision of the Labor Management Relations Act (LMRA).  In light of Congress' general intent to incorporate much of LMRA fiduciary law into ERISA, and because ERISA, like the LMRA, imposes a duty of loyalty on fiduciaries and plan administrators, Firestone argues that the LMRA arbitrary and capricious stand and should apply to ERISA actions.  A comparison of the LMRA and ERISA, however, shows that the *wholesale* importation of the arbitrary and capricious standard into ERISA is unwarranted.

In relevant part, 29 U.S.C. § 186(c) authorizes unions and employers to set up pension plans jointly and provides that contributions to such plans be made "for the sole and exclusive benefit of the employees * * * and their families and dependents."  The LMRA does not provide for judicial review of the decisions of LMRA trustees.  Federal courts adopted the arbitrary and capricious standard both as a standard of review and, more importantly, as a means of asserting jurisdiction over suits under § 186(c) by beneficiaries of LMRA plans who were denied benefits by trustees.  Unlike the LMRA, ERISA explicitly authorizes suits against fiduciaries and plan administrators to remedy statutory violations, including breaches of fiduciary duty and lack of compliance with benefit plans.  Thus, the raison d'étre for the LMRA arbitrary and capricious standard— the need for a jurisdictional basis in suits against trustees—is not present in ERISA.  Without this jurisdictional analogy, LMRA principles offer no support for the adoption of the arbitrary and capricious standard insofar as § 1132(a)(1)(B) is concerned.

ERISA abounds with the language and terminology of trust law. ERISA's legislative history confirms that the Act's fiduciary responsibility provisions "codif[y] and make[ ] applicable to [ERISA] fiduciaries certain principles developed in the evolution of the law of trusts."  Given this language and history, we have held that courts are to develop a "federal common law of rights and obligations under ERISA-regulated plans."  In determining the appropriate standard of review for actions under § 1132(a)(1)(B), we are guided by principles of trust law.

Trust principles make a deferential standard of review appropriate when a trustee exercises discretionary powers. A trustee may be given power to construe disputed or doubtful terms, and in such circumstances the trustee's interpretation will not be disturbed if reasonable. Whether "the exercise of a power is permissive or mandatory depends upon the terms of the trust." Hence, over a century ago we remarked that "[w]hen trustees are in existence, and capable of acting, a court of equity will not interfere to control them in the exercise of a *discretion vested in them by the instrument* under which they act." Firestone can seek no shelter in these principles of trust law, however, for there is no evidence that under Firestone's termination pay plan the administrator has the power to construe uncertain terms or that eligibility determinations are to be given deference.

Finding no support in the language of its termination pay plan for the arbitrary and capricious standard, Firestone argues that as a matter of trust law the interpretation of the terms of a plan is an inherently discretionary function. But other settled principles of trust law, which point to de novo review of benefit eligibility determinations based on plan interpretations, belie this contention. As they do with contractual provisions, courts construe terms in trust agreements without deferring to either party's interpretation. * * * A trustee who is in doubt as to the interpretation of the instrument can protect himself by obtaining instructions from the court. The terms of trusts created by written instruments are "determined by the provisions of the instrument as interpreted in light of all the circumstances and such other evidence of the intention of the settlor with respect to the trust as is not inadmissible."

The trust law de novo standard of review is consistent with the judicial interpretation of employee benefit plans prior to the enactment of ERISA. Actions challenging an employer's denial of benefits before enactment of ERISA were governed by principles of contract law. If the plan did not give the employer or administrator discretionary or final authority to construe uncertain terms, the court reviewed the employee's claim as it would have any other contract claim—by looking to the terms of the plan and other manifestations of the parties' intent.

Despite these principles of trust law pointing to a de novo standard of review for claims like respondents', Firestone would have us read ERISA to require the application of the arbitrary and capricious standard to such claims. ERISA defines a fiduciary as one who "exercises any discretionary authority or discretionary control respecting management of [a] plan or exercises any authority or control respecting management or disposition of its assets." A fiduciary has "authority to control and manage the operation and administration of the plan," and must provide a "full and fair review" of claim denials. From these provisions, Firestone concludes that an ERISA plan administrator, fiduciary, or trustee is empowered to exercise *all* his authority in a discretionary manner subject only to review for arbitrariness and caprice. But the provisions relied upon so heavily by Firestone do not characterize a fiduciary as one who exercises *entirely* discretionary authority or control. Rather, one is a fiduciary to the extent he exercises *any* discretionary authority or control.

ERISA was enacted "to promote the interests of employees and their beneficiaries in employee benefit plans," and "to protect contractually defined benefits." Adopting Firestone's reading of ERISA would require us to impose a standard of review that would afford less protection to employees and their beneficiaries than they enjoyed before ERISA was enacted. * * *

As this case aptly demonstrates, the validity of a claim to benefits under an ERISA plan is likely to turn on the interpretation of terms in the plan at issue. Consistent with established principles of trust law, we hold that a denial of benefits challenged under § 1132(a)(1)(B) is to be reviewed under a de novo standard unless the benefit plan gives the administrator or fiduciary discretionary authority to determine eligibility for benefits or to construe the terms of the plan. Because we do not rest our decision on the concern for impartiality that guided the Court of Appeals, we need not distinguish between types of plans or focus on the motivations of plan administrators and fiduciaries. Thus, for purposes of actions under § 1132(a)(1)(B), the de novo standard of review applies regardless of whether the plan at issue is funded or unfunded and regardless of whether the administrator or fiduciary is operating under a possible or actual conflict of interest. Of course, if a benefit plan gives discretion to an administrator or fiduciary who is operating under a conflict of interest, that conflict must be weighed as a "factor in determining whether there is an abuse of discretion."

Respondents unsuccessfully sought plan information from Firestone pursuant to 29 U.S.C. § 1024(b)(4), one of ERISA's disclosure provisions. That provision reads as follows:

> "The administrator shall, upon written request of any participant or beneficiary, furnish a copy of the latest updated summary plan description, plan description, and the latest annual report, any terminal report, the bargaining agreement, trust agreement, contract, or other instruments under which the plan is established or operated. The administrator may make a reasonable charge to cover the cost of furnishing such complete copies. The Secretary [of Labor] may by regulation prescribe the maximum amount which will constitute a reasonable charge under the preceding sentence."

When Firestone did not comply with their request for information, respondents sought damages under 29 U.S.C.A. § 1132(c)(1)(B) (Supp.1988), which provides that "[a]ny administrator * * * who fails or refuses to comply with a request for any information which such administrator is required by this subchapter to furnish to a participant or beneficiary * * * may in the court's discretion be personally liable to such participant or beneficiary in the amount of up to $100 a day." * * *

In our view, the term "participant" is naturally read to mean either "employees in, or reasonably expected to be in, currently covered employment," or former employees who "have * * * a reasonable expectation of returning to covered employment" or who have "a colorable claim" to vested benefits. In order to establish that he or she "may become eligible" for benefits, a claimant must have a colorable claim that (1) he or she will prevail in a suit for benefits, or that (2) eligibility requirements will be fulfilled in the future.

So ordered.

## NOTES AND QUESTIONS

**1.** Professors Langbein and Wolk have cast a quizzical eye at the *Firestone* Court's borrowing from the law of trusts to support its "de novo" standard for judicial review of trustee decisions. The Court cites the Restatement of Trusts (Second) § 187 (1957). That section states: "Where discretion is conferred upon the trustee with respect to the exercise of a power, its exercise is not subject to control by the court except to prevent an abuse by the trustee of his discretion." However, this section of the Restatement seems to call for a standard of review very much like—if not identical to—the arbitrary and capricious standard rejected by the court in *Firestone*. The Court manages this judicial sleight of hand by quoting a passage from Nichols v. Eaton, 91 U.S. 716 (1875). *Nichols* called for a deferential standard when discretion is vested in trustees "by the instrument under which they act." From this premise, the *Firestone* Court draws the conclusion that a deferential standard is proper *only* when discretionary power is specifically delegated by a trust instrument.

This analysis raises two troubling issues. First, while *Nichols* holds that a deferential standard is proper when called for by the terms of the instrument, the case does not say that such a standard should be employed only when set forth by the instrument. Second, the Court's conclusion that the instrument must confer discretionary powers contradicts Restatement of Trusts § 187, the source from which its analysis originated. Comment (a) to that section states: "The exercise of a power is discretionary except to the extent to which its exercise is required by the terms of the trust or by the principles of law applicable to the duties of the trustees."

In any event, company pension plan documents are regularly revised by company lawyers. After *Firestone*, wouldn't most plans be revised to grant discretion to trustees? If so, what will be the significance of the *Firestone* decision? See John H. Langbein & Bruce A. Wolk, Pension and Employee Benefit Law 610–14 (1990).

**2.** Some pre-*Firestone* cases had held that the appropriate standard of review should vary depending on whether pension plan trustees have an interest adverse to that of beneficiaries. The clearest example is where the trustees are also officers of a company that will save money if the pension plan makes fewer or smaller payments. Look again at Donovan v. Bierwirth and Donovan v. Mazzola, supra, and consider whether it is usually feasible to distinguish the trustee conflict-of-interest cases.

**3.** The issue in *Firestone* was whether workers qualified for severance benefits when a factory was sold. What is the right answer? Since pension plans last for a long time and over time issues frequently arise that were not expected when the plan was written, who should—in effect— create the terms not decided at the onset? If this is a task for the courts, isn't it likely to be an onerous undertaking, prompting a large volume of disputes?

**4.** Consider Judge Posner's defense of the arbitrary and capricious standard in Van Boxel v. Journal Co. Employees' Pension Trust, 836 F.2d 1048 (7th Cir.1987).

> [In the] ERISA setting, the arbitrary and capricious standard may be inapt, a historical mistake, or a mechanical extrapolation from different settings, at once too lax and too stringent, but even if it is any or all of these things it is saved from doing serious harm by its vagueness and elasticity. There are more verbal distinctions among the standards of judicial review than there are real differences. It is easier to multiply standards than actually to differentiate among them—to keep them from overlapping—in the setting of a particular case. The fundamental difference in the depth or penetration or exactingness of judicial review is between deferential and nondeferential review, that is, between reversing a tribunal's decision because it is unreasonable and reversing it merely because it is wrong. Sometimes even this difference blurs. When the members of the tribunal—for example, the trustees of a pension plan—have a serious conflict of interest, the proper deference to give their decisions may be slight, even zero; the decision if wrong may be unreasonable. The less likely it is that the trustees' judgment was impaired by their having a stake, however indirect, in the outcome, the less inclined a reviewing court will be to override their judgment unless strongly convinced that they erred.

> As this example shows, flexibility in the scope of judicial review need not require a proliferation of different standards of review; the arbitrary and capricious standard may be a range, not a point. There may be in effect a sliding scale of judicial review of trustees' decisions—more penetrating the greater is the suspicion of partiality, less penetrating the smaller that suspicion is. * * *

> Flexibly interpreted, the arbitrary and capricious standard, though infelicitously—perhaps even misleadingly—worded, allows the reviewing court to make the necessary adjustments for possible bias in the trustees' decision. So there is no urgent need to throw it overboard and cast about for an alternative verbalization. Where the claimant does not argue or is unable to show that the trustees had a significant conflict of interest, we reverse the denial of benefits only if the denial is completely unreasonable. The greater the conflict of interest of a majority of the trustees, the less we defer to a denial of benefits that appears to be wrong.

*Van Boxel* was decided while Firestone's appeal to the Supreme Court was pending. Does Judge Posner's analysis adequately address the concerns expressed in *Firestone?*

**5.** A benefit plan made payments to employees and dependents who entered an extended care facility before age 70 but not to those who entered after. The age 70 rule was not included in the plan handbook. Suing under ERISA § 102(b), plaintiff survived a motion to dismiss with her plea that her costs should be paid because she would not have entered the Northside Convalescent Center had she known the rule. Zittrouer v. Uarco Inc. Group Benefit Plan, 582 F.Supp. 1471 (N.D.Ga.1984).

**6.** Marjana Vucic, daughter of an employee of Solo Cup Company, was hospitalized at Michael Reese Hospital's Psychosomatic and Psychiatric Institute for eight months for anorexia nervosa. Solo's Employee Health Benefit Plan paid for only seven weeks, saying its doctor said further inpatient care was not justified. The hospital sued the plan for $91,314.73 plus interest, costs, and attorney's fees. Applying *Bruch,* the court of appeals affirmed a decision that de novo review supported the plan's refusal to pay for more treatment. Michael Reese Hospital & Medical Center v. Solo Cup Employee Health Benefit Plan, 899 F.2d 639 (7th Cir.1990).

**7.** ERISA bars amendments which decrease "accrued benefits." Plaintiff worked for the Machinists Union. At the time he retired, the union's pension plan had a cost-of-living feature indexing benefits to salary increases in the position held before retirement. When the pension plan looked underfunded, delegates to the union convention voted to phase out this provision of the plan. Shaw v. International Association of Machinists & Aerospace Workers Pension Plan, 750 F.2d 1458 (9th Cir.), cert. denied, 471 U.S. 1137 (1985), said the formula for benefit increases was an "accrued benefit" and could not be reduced.

**8.** Even if a plan says benefits are limited to the amount in the fund, ERISA declares "nonforfeitable" the participant's right to the full set of promises made in the plan. Thus solvent employers are liable to the full extent of plan commitments. Nachman Corp. v. Pension Benefit Guaranty Corp., 446 U.S. 359 (1980). Four justices dissented because *Nachman* imposed this obligation on a company that sought to limit its obligations by terminating its plan before the ERISA statute took effect.

**9.** ERISA benefits are often important to survivors of deceased employees. A construction worker's pension fund brought an interpleader action, asking the court to decide whether a death benefit should be paid to the deceased worker's former spouse or to his mother. Laurine and James Brown were married in 1982. In 1986, he designated her as his beneficiary for the pension plan's death benefit. Later that year they were divorced, signing an agreement that said: "The parties each waive any interest * * * in and to any retirement, pension * * * ." Laurine and James continued to live with each other until his death in 1987. The court of appeals, en banc, affirmed a decision that Laurine waived her claim, and the money should go to Dessie Brown, James' mother, under a provision in the pension plan providing that the benefit of a decedent who did not designate a beneficiary goes first to a spouse, then to children, then to parents.  Judge Easterbrook, dissenting, said that honoring Laurine's waiver violates the spendthrift clause in ERISA, 29 U.S.C. § 1056(d)(1), which says "benefits * * * may not be assigned or alienated."  The majority said that provision applies only to plan participants.  Fox Valley & Vicinity Construction Workers Pension Fund v. Brown, 897 F.2d 275 (7th Cir.1990) (8–4).

## d.   FEDERAL PREEMPTION OF STATE LAW

## Alessi v. Raybestos–Manhattan, Inc.

451 U.S. 504 (1981).

■ JUSTICE MARSHALL delivered the opinion of the Court.

Some private pension plans reduce a retiree's pension benefits by the amount of workers' compensation awards received subsequent to retirement.  In these cases we consider whether two such offset provisions are lawful under the Employee Retirement Income Security Act of 1974 (ERISA), and whether they may be prohibited by state law.

Raybestos-Manhattan, Inc. and General Motors Corp. maintain employee pension plans that are subject to federal regulation under ERISA.  Both plans provide that an employee's retirement benefits shall be reduced, or offset, by an amount equal to workers' compensation awards for which the individual is eligible.  In 1977, the New Jersey Legislature amended its Workers' Compensation Act to expressly prohibit such offsets.  The amendment states that "[t]he right of compensation granted by this chapter may be set off against disability pension benefits or payments but shall not be set off against employees' retirement pension benefits or payments." N.J.Stat.Ann. § 34:15–29 (West 1979) (as amended by 1977 N.J.Laws, ch. 156).

Alleging violations of this provision of state law, two suits were initiated in New Jersey state court.  The plaintiffs in both suits were retired employees who had obtained workers' compensation awards subject to offsets against their retirement benefits under their pension plans.  The defendant companies independently removed the suits to the United States District Court for the District of New Jersey.

* * *

Retirees claim that the workers' compensation offset provisions of their pension plans contravene ERISA's nonforfeiture provisions and that the Treasury Regulation to the contrary is inconsistent with the Act.  Both claims require examination of the relevant sections of ERISA.

As we recently observed, ERISA is a "comprehensive and reticulated statute," which Congress adopted after careful study of private retirement pensions plans.  Congress through ERISA wanted to ensure that "if a worker has been promised a defined pension benefit upon retirement—and if he has fulfilled whatever conditions are required to obtain a vested benefit—[* * *] he actually receive[s] it."  For this reason, the concepts of vested rights and nonforfeitable rights are critical to the ERISA scheme. ERISA prescribes vesting and accrual schedules, assuring that employees obtain rights to at least portions of their normal pension benefits even if they leave their position prior to retirement. Most critically, ERISA establishes that "[e]ach pension plan shall provide that an employee's right to his normal retirement benefits is nonforfeitable upon the attainment of normal retirement age."

Retirees rely on this sweeping assurance that pension rights become nonforfeitable in claiming that offsetting those benefits with workers' compensation awards violates ERISA. Retirees argue first that no vested benefits may be forfeited except as expressly provided in § 1053. Second, retirees assert that offsets based on workers' compensation fall into none of those express exceptions. Both claims are correct; § 1053(a) prohibits forfeitures of vested rights except as expressly provided in § 1053(a)(3), and the challenged workers' compensation offsets are not among those permitted in that section.

Despite this facial accuracy, retirees' argument overlooks a threshold issue: what defines the content of the benefit that, once vested, cannot be forfeited? ERISA leaves this question largely to the private parties creating the plan. That the private parties, not the government, control the level of benefits is clear from the statutory language defining nonforfeitable rights as well as from other portions of ERISA. ERISA defines a "nonforfeitable" pension benefit or right as "as a claim obtained by a participant or his beneficiary to that part of an immediate or deferred benefit under a pension plan which arises from the participant's service, which is unconditional, and which is legally enforceable against the plan."

\* \* \*

It is particularly pertinent for our purposes that Congress did not prohibit "integration," a calculation practice under which benefit levels are determined by combining pension funds with other income streams available to the retired employees. Through integration, each income stream contributes for calculation purposes to the total benefit pool to be distributed to all the retired employees, even if the nonpension funds are available only to a subgroup of the employees. The pension funds are thus integrated with the funds from other income maintenance programs, such as Social Security, and the pension benefit level is determined on the basis of the entire pool of funds. Under this practice, an individual employee's eligibility for Social Security would advantage all participants in his private pension plan, for the addition of his anticipated Social Security payments to the total benefit pool would permit a higher average pension payout for each participant. The employees as a group profit from that higher pension level, although an individual employee may reach that level by a combination of payments from the pension fund and payments from the other income maintenance source. In addition, integration allows the employer to attain the selected pension level by drawing on the other resources, which, like Social Security, also depend on employer contributions.

Following its extensive study of private pension plans before the adoption of ERISA, Congress expressly preserved the option of pension fund integration with benefits available under both the Social Security Act and the Railroad Retirement Act. Congress was well aware that pooling of nonpension retirement benefits and pension funds would limit the total income maintenance payments received by individual employees and reduce the cost of pension plans to employers. Indeed, in considering this integration option, the House Ways and Means Committee expressly acknowledged the tension between the primary goal of benefiting employees and the subsidiary goal of containing pension costs.

\* \* \*

In setting this limitation on integration with Social Security and Railroad Retirement benefits, Congress acknowledged and accepted the practice, rather than prohibiting it. Moreover, in permitting integration at least with these federal benefits, Congress did not find it necessary to add an exemption for this purpose to its stringent nonforfeiture protections in 29 U.S.C. § 1053(a). Under these circumstances, we are unpersuaded by retirees' claim that the nonforfeiture provisions by their own force prohibit any offset of pension benefits by workers' compensation awards. Such offsets work much like the integration of pension benefits with Social Security or Railroad Retirement payments. The individual employee remains entitled to the established pension level, but the payments received from the pension fund are reduced by the amount received through workers' compensation. The nonforfeiture provision of § 1053(a) has no more applicability to this kind of integration than it does to the analogous reduction permitted for Social Security or Railroad Retirement payments. Indeed, the same congressional purpose—promoting a system of private pensions by giving employers avenues for cutting the cost of their pension obligations—underlies all such offset possibilities.

Nonetheless, ERISA does not mention integration with workers' compensation, and the legislative history is equally silent on this point. An argument could be advanced that Congress approved integration of pension funds only with the federal benefits expressly mentioned in the Act. A current regulation issued by the Internal Revenue Service, however, goes further, and permits integration with other benefits provided by federal or state law. We now must consider whether this regulation is itself consistent with ERISA.

Codified at 26 CFR §§ 1.411(a)–(4)(a), the Treasury Regulation provides that "nonforfeitable rights are not considered to be forfeitable by reason of the fact that they may be reduced to take into account benefits which are provided under the Social Security Act or under any other federal or state law and which are taken into account in determining plan benefits." The regulation interprets 26 U.S.C. § 411, the section of the Internal Revenue Code which replicates for IRS purposes ERISA's nonforfeiture provision, 29 U.S.C. § 1053(a). The regulation plainly encompasses awards under state workers' compensation laws. In addition, in revenue rulings issued prior to ERISA, the IRS expressly had approved reductions in pension benefits corresponding to workers' compensation awards.

\* \* \*

Without speaking directly of its own rationale, Congress embraced such IRS rulings. Congress thereby permitted integration along the lines already approved by the IRS which had specifically allowed pension benefit offsets based on workers' compensation. Our judicial function is not to second-guess the policy decisions of the legislature, no matter how appealing we may find contrary rationales.

As a final argument, retirees claim that we should defer to the policy decisions of the state legislature. To this claim we now turn.

The New Jersey Legislature attempted to outlaw the offset clauses by providing that "[t]he right of compensation granted by [the New Jersey Workers' Compensation Act] may be set off against disability pension benefits or payments but *shall not be set off against employees' retirement benefits or payments.*" To resolve retirees' claim that this state policy should govern, we must determine whether such state laws are pre-empted by ERISA.

\* \* \*

In this instance, we are assisted by an explicit congressional statement about the pre-emptive effect of its action. The same chapter of ERISA that defines the scope of federal protection of employee pension benefits provides that

> "the provisions of this Subchapter \* \* \* shall supersede any and all state laws insofar as they may now or hereafter relate to any employee benefit plan described in section 1003(a) of this title and not exempt under 1003(b) of this title." 29 U.S.C. § 1144(a).

We agree with the conclusion reached by the Court of Appeals but arrive there by a different route. Whatever the purpose or purposes of the New Jersey statute, we conclude that it "relate[s] to pension plans" governed by ERISA because it eliminates one method for calculating pension benefits—integration—that is permitted by federal law. ERISA permits integration of pension funds with other public income maintenance moneys for the purpose of calculating benefits, and the IRS interpretation approves integration with the exact funds addressed by the New Jersey workers' compensation law. New Jersey's effort to ban pension benefit offsets based on workers' compensation applies directly to this calculation technique. We need not determine the outer bounds of ERISA's pre-emptive language to find this New Jersey provision an impermissible intrusion on the federal regulatory scheme.

## NOTES AND QUESTIONS

1. The ERISA provision allowing "integration" of pensions with Social Security retirement benefits (actually, allowing Social Security benefits to offset in full entitlement to private pension payments) was changed in

1986. Now the retiree can only "lose" one-half of his or her pension—only half of Social Security payments can offset pension entitlements. Tax Reform Act of 1986, P.L. 99–514.

In 1981, Michigan enacted a law allowing coordination of workers' compensation benefits with employer-funded pension plan payments. Workers injured before the effective date of the statute were subjected to these provisions, prompting some concern about the legality of the changes. In 1987, the Michigan legislature passed a law which clearly indicated that the coordination of benefits provision of the 1981 law was not intended to reduce benefits for injuries occurring before the 1981 law's enactment. Michigan employers contended that the 1987 law violated their constitutional rights under the due process and contract clauses of the state and federal constitutions by retroactively altering the level of benefits due and payable prior to the amendment. The Michigan Supreme Court, and later the United States Supreme Court, upheld the 1987 law. Romein v. General Motors Corp., 462 N.W.2d 555 (Mich.1990), affirmed, 503 U.S. 181 (1992).

**2.** ERISA does not preempt California matrimonial law. Thus vested retirement benefits were community property, and upon divorce, the superior court ordered the Retirement Fund Trust to pay half the benefits directly to the former wife. Johns v. Retirement Fund Trust, 85 Cal. App.3d 511, 149 Cal.Rptr. 551 (1978), appeal dismissed and cert. denied, 444 U.S. 1028 (1980). Non-preemption of state law on marital property rights (i.e., how the spouses divide the pension on divorce) is now part of the statute: Retirement Equity Act of 1984, 29 U.S.C. § 1056(d).

The first wife of a deceased pension plan participant brought an action to declare the decedent's second wife disqualified from receiving benefits under the plan on the ground of her conviction for manslaughter of the decedent. The district court held that New York law prohibiting a killer from profiting from her crime is not preempted by ERISA. Mendez–Bellido v. Board of Trustees, 709 F.Supp. 329 (E.D.N.Y.1989).

**3.** The leading commentators on ERISA preemption believe that § 514(a) is fundamentally misguided:

> On the basis of the experience in the courts and Congress in the * * * years since ERISA's enactment, it is clear that the inclusion of section 514(a) in ERISA was a mistake. Given well-established judicial doctrines of preemption, section 514(a) was unnecessary. And, while judicial doctrines, have been molded by sensitivity to what is practicable and a reasonable balancing of competing interests, the categorical language and wider scope of 514(a) has unavoidably at times called for unreasonable and impracticable results. In short, the adoption of section 514(a) not only failed to fill any real need, but also created unnecessary problems for both the judiciary and those affected by private employee benefit plans. * * *

The clearly mandated but sweeping application of section 514(a) not only voids myriad state laws, it leaves grave uncertainties about how and whether to fill the gaps they created. Because there are enormous gaps to fill, the absence of guiding policy creates unfortunate difficulties and pressures for the courts. If the gaps are to be filled, the courts must derive a federal common law concerning trusts, fiduciary duties, contracts, remedies, and the like by reference to existing, largely state law sources. * * * The only safe prediction is that the process will continue to lurch forward and backward unpredictably, in large part because the rigidity and sweep of section 514(a) defy credibility and common sense in many cases, and because, when applied as written, it leaves courts without adequate guidance with respect to how and the extent to which to fashion a federal common law for employee benefit plans.

Leon Irish & Harison Cohen, ERISA Preemption: Judicial Flexibility and Statutory Rigidity, 19 U.Mich.J.L.Ref. 109 (1985).

Consider this opinion in light of the preemption rulings in the following notes.

**4.** Should ERISA preempt state laws regulating the testamentary transfer of assets? What if such preemption results in a disposition of assets contrary to a specific provision in a valid will?

Consider the case of MacLean v. Ford Motor Co., 831 F.2d 723 (7th Cir.1987). During his employment with Ford Motor Company David Pithie participated in Ford's Savings and Stock Investment Plan (SSIP). The Plan's 1983 prospectus provided that if the employee failed to file a written document with the administrators of the Plan designating a beneficiary, the member would be deemed to have designated as beneficiary the person who was entitled to receive the proceeds of the member's company life insurance policy. Pithie never filed the required documentation identifying a beneficiary for his SSIP but had designated his son, Allen Pithie, as the beneficiary of his company life policy. David Pithie's will, however, included the SSIP as part of his estate, only one quarter of which was to be distributed to his son, the balance going to his sister. Following Pithie's death, the executor of his estate sued Ford to collect the assets accumulated in Pithie's SSIP in order to distribute them pursuant to the terms of the will. Following the Supreme Court's analysis of the ERISA preemption problem in *Fort Halifax Packing,* supra, p. 469, the court of appeals held that the assets must be distributed in accordance with the terms of the SSIP:

[W]e must determine whether ERISA preempts state testamentary transfer law in determining the beneficiary of the decedent's SSIP assets. We agree with the district court that the state law "relates to" the terms of the SSIP and, therefore, the state law is preempted.

In this situation, the state testamentary law has "a connection with or reference to [the SSIP] because, if applied the state law would determine the distribution of assets under the Plan. The SSIP includes a specific method of identifying the designated beneficiary. Applying state testamentary transfer law to determine the beneficiary under the terms of the decedent's will would not only relate to the Plan, but would interfere with the administration of the Plan and violate its terms. When, as here, the terms of an employee pension plan under ERISA provide a valid method for determining the beneficiary, that mechanism cannot be displaced by the provisions of a will.

Such strong preemption rulings simplify administration. But is it necessary that preemption go so far as to enforce what may be a complicated and perhaps unread prospectus provision over the terms of a written will? If the answer is no, given the present statutory scheme is it proper for the courts to implement such a decision or must it be the result of legislative action?

**5.** When an underfunded pension plan cannot meet retirees' contractual claims, ERISA gives the retirees a degree of protection from the Pension Benefit Guaranty Corporation, which can then recover from the employer for up to 30 percent of the employer's net worth. Murphy v. Heppenstall Co., 635 F.2d 233 (3d Cir.1980), cert. denied, 454 U.S. 1142 (1982), said that this right of retirees does not preempt their separate right to bring a federal common law action against the employer for the full pension promised to them in the collective bargaining agreement. But cf. Lafferty v. Solar Turbines International, 666 F.2d 408 (9th Cir.1982).

**6.** ERISA preempts state law as to some fringe benefit programs considered in Chapter 6, see pp. 470–485, and as to some protections against layoffs considered in Chapter 12, see pp. 1073–1091. Fort Halifax Packing Co. v. Coyne, 482 U.S. 1 (1987), see p. 1091 supra, upheld Maine's plant-closing law against an ERISA preemption challenge. Justice Brennan's majority opinion in that case provided a cogent description of the problems the preemption requirement was intended to address:

> In the House, Representative Dent stated that "with the preemption of the field [of employee benefit plans], we round out the protection afforded participants by eliminating the threat of conflicting and inconsistent State and local regulation." Similarly, Senator Williams declared, "It should be stressed that with the narrow exceptions specified in the bill, the substantive and enforcement provisions of the conference substitute are intended to preempt the field for Federal regulations, thus eliminating the threat of conflicting or inconsistent State and local regulation of employee benefit plans."
>
> These statements reflect recognition of the administrative realities of employee benefit plans. An employer that makes a commitment systematically to pay certain benefits undertakes a host of obligations, such as determining the eligibility of claimants, calculating benefit levels, making disbursements, monitoring the availability of funds for benefit payments, and keeping appropriate

records in order to comply with applicable reporting requirements. The most efficient way to meet these responsibilities is to establish a uniform administrative scheme, which provides a set of standard procedures to guide processing of claims and disbursement of benefits. Such a system is difficult to achieve, however, if a benefit plan is subject to differing regulatory requirements in differing States. A plan would be required to keep certain records in some States but not in others; to make certain benefits available in some States but not in others; to process claims in a certain way in some States but not in others; and to comply with certain fiduciary standards in some States but not in others.

We have not hesitated to enforce ERISA's pre-emption provision where state law created the prospect that an employer's administrative scheme would be subject to conflicting requirements. * * *

It is clear that ERISA's pre-emption provision was prompted by recognition that employers establishing and maintaining employee benefit plans are faced with the task of coordinating complex administrative activities. A patchwork scheme of regulation would introduce considerable inefficiencies in benefit program operation, which might lead those employers with existing plans to reduce benefits, and those without such plans to refrain from adopting them. Pre-emption ensures that the administrative practices of a benefit plan will be governed by only a single set of regulations.

**7.** Before Congress required disability plans to include pregnancy-related disabilities, supra p. 263, no federal rule barred plans from refusing coverage for pregnancy. General Electric Co. v. Gilbert, 429 U.S. 125 (1976). In a case dealing with pregnancies that occurred prior to the Pregnancy Discrimination Act of 1978, the Supreme Court found that ERISA preempted the attempt by the New York Division of Human Rights to apply the state Human Rights Law to require coverage. In the same case, however, the Court found that ERISA did not preempt New York's Disability Benefits Law, which required employees to pay sick-leave benefits to employees unable to work because of pregnancy. Complicated provisions in ERISA explained the two holdings. Shaw v. Delta Air Lines, Inc., 463 U.S. 85 (1983).

**8.** The Georgia legislature's attempt to stop garnishment of federally regulated pensions is preempted by ERISA, and benefits are subject to garnishment under the general state garnishment law. Mackey v. Lanier Collection Agency & Service, Inc., 486 U.S. 825 (1988).

**9.** State law fraud and misrepresentation claims brought by early retirees who allegedly relied on their employer's misleading statements about planned future increases in an early retirement package when they retired are preempted by ERISA, even though the statute provides no remedy. Lee v. E.I. DuPont de Nemours & Co., 894 F.2d 755 (5th Cir.1990).

**10.** ERISA has been held to preempt Louisiana's community property laws. Isaac and Dorothy Boggs married and had three sons. When Dorothy died, she left her share of Isaac's ERISA plan to their sons. Isaac then remarried. When he died four years later, his second wife sued for the benefits that the three sons were due from Dorothy's will. The Court held that ERISA preempted Louisiana's community property laws, which would have permitted the first wife to transfer her interest in undistributed pension plan benefits to her sons. Boggs v. Boggs, 117 S.Ct. 1754 (1997).

**11.** Congress has several times created statutory exceptions to ERISA preemption. The Hawaii Prepaid Health Care Act was held to be preempted by ERISA in Standard Oil Co. v. Agsalud, 442 F.Supp. 695 (N.D.Cal. 1977), affirmed, 633 F.2d 760 (9th Cir.1980), affirmed mem., 454 U.S. 801 (1981). ERISA was amended to save the substantive portions of the Hawaii law from preemption. ERISA § 514(b)(5), added in 1983. In 1984, § 104 of the Retirement Equity Act amended both ERISA and the Internal Revenue Code to save from preemption certain state policies allowing spouses to reach pension assets. See ERISA §§ 206(d)(3) and 514(b)(7) and IRC § 414(p).

### e. PENSION PLAN TERMINATION

Pension plans can become overfunded for several reasons. One major cause of overfunded pensions has been the existence of a strong stock market. In the past, companies looked at their pension plan assets when stock prices were high and decided they had better uses for the money. They also feared that a surplus would make the company a takeover target. As a result, companies would terminate their pension plans and start new plans with the proper amount of cash reserves, keeping the excess funds.

Employees have argued that the pension plan is "their money," and the company should not be able to withdraw it. Employers have replied that they are responsible for increasing contributions if plans turn out to be underfunded, so if their estimates are conservative and excess funds accumulate, those funds belong to the company.

Where terminations did not comply with contractual provisions in the plan, courts have invalidated them. See, e.g., Delgrosso v. Spang & Co., 769 F.2d 928 (3d Cir.1985), cert. denied, 476 U.S. 1140 (1986). But any legal doubts about the basic legitimacy of excess fund recovery were put to rest by Title XI of the Consolidated Omnibus Budget Reconciliation Act of 1985, P.L. No. 99–272, which imposes procedural requirements on plan termination. The company must buy a fully-funded annuity for plan beneficiaries who are already retired, and must create an adequately funded new plan for current workers. See also ERISA § 4044(d)(1), permitting (in limited circumstances) excess earnings to be withdrawn without termination of the plan.

## Pension Benefit Guaranty Corp. v. LTV Corp.
496 U.S. 633 (1990).

■ JUSTICE BLACKMUN delivered the opinion of the Court.

In this case we must determine whether the decision of the Pension Benefit Guaranty Corporation (PBGC) to restore certain pension plans under § 4047 of the Employee Retirement Income Security Act of 1974 (ERISA) was, as the Court of Appeals concluded, arbitrary and capricious or contrary to law, within the meaning of § 706 of the Administrative Procedure Act.

Petitioner PBGC is a wholly owned United States Government corporation, * * *. The Board of Directors of the PBGC consists of the Secretaries of the Treasury, Labor, and Commerce. The PBGC administers and enforces Title IV of ERISA. Title IV includes a mandatory Government insurance program that protects the pension benefits of over 30 million private-sector American workers who participate in plans covered by the Title.[1] In enacting Title IV, Congress sought to ensure that employees and their beneficiaries would not be completely "deprived of anticipated retirement benefits by the termination of pension plans before sufficient funds have been accumulated in the plans."

When a plan covered under Title IV terminates with insufficient assets to satisfy its pension obligations to the employees, the PBGC becomes trustee of the plan, taking over the plan's assets and liabilities. The PBGC then uses the plan's assets to cover what it can of the benefit obligations. The PBGC then must add its own funds to ensure payment of most of the remaining "nonforfeitable" benefits, i.e., those benefits to which participants have earned entitlement under the plan terms as of the date of termination. * * *

The cost of the PBGC insurance is borne primarily by employers that maintain ongoing pension plans. Sections 4006 and 4007 of ERISA require these employers to pay annual premiums. The insurance program is also financed by statutory liability imposed on employers who terminate underfunded pension plans. Upon termination, the employer becomes liable to the PBGC for the benefits that the PBGC will pay out. Because the PBGC historically has recovered only a small portion of that liability, Congress repeatedly has been forced to increase the annual premiums. Even with these increases, the PBGC in its most recent Annual Report noted liabilities of $4 billion and assets of only $2.4 billion, leaving a deficit of over $1.5 billion.

As noted above, plan termination is the insurable event under Title IV. Plans may be terminated "voluntarily" by an employer or "involuntarily"

---

**1.** Title IV covers virtually all "defined benefit" pension plans sponsored by private employers. A defined benefit plan is one that promises to pay employees, upon retirement, a fixed benefit under a formula that takes into account factors such as final salary and years of service with the employer.

It is distinguished from a "defined contribution" plan (also known as an "individual account" plan), under which the employer typically contributes a percentage of an employee's compensation to an account, and the employee is entitled to the account upon retirement. ERISA insurance does not cover defined contribution plans because employees are not promised any particular level of benefits; instead, they are promised only that they will receive the balances in their individual accounts.

by the PBGC. An Employer may terminate a plan voluntarily in one of two ways. It may proceed with a "standard termination" only if it has sufficient assets to pay all benefit commitments. A standard termination thus does not implicate PBGC insurance responsibilities. If an employer wishes to terminate a plan whose assets are insufficient to pay all benefits, the employer must demonstrate that it is in financial "distress" as defined in 29 U.S.C. § 1341(c). Neither a standard nor a distress termination by the employer, however, is permitted if termination would violate the terms of an existing collective-bargaining agreement.

The PBGC, though, may terminate a plan "involuntarily," notwithstanding the existence of a collective-bargaining agreement. Section 4042 of ERISA provides that the PBGC may terminate a plan whenever it determines that:

"(1) the plan has not met the minimum funding standard * * *

"(2) the plan will be unable to pay benefits when due,

"(3) the reportable event described in section 1343(b)(7) of this title has occurred, or

"(4) the possible long-run loss of the [PBGC] with respect to the plan may reasonably be expected to increase unreasonably if the plan is not terminated."

Termination can be undone by PBGC. Section 4047 of ERISA provides:

"In the case of a plan which has been terminated under section 1341 or 1342 of this title the [PBGC] is authorized in any such case in which [it] determines such action to be appropriate and consistent with its duties under this subchapter, to take such action as may be necessary to restore the plan to its pretermination status, including, but not limited to, the transfer to the employer or a plan administrator of control of part or all of the remaining assets and liabilities of the plan."

When a plan is restored, full benefits are reinstated, and the employer, rather than the PBGC, again is responsible for the plan's unfunded liabilities.

This case arose after respondent The LTV Corporation and many of its subsidiaries, including LTV Steel Company Inc., in July 1986 filed petitions for reorganization under Chapter 11 of the Bankruptcy Code. At that time, LTV Steel was the sponsor of three defined benefit pension plans (the Plans) covered by Title IV of ERISA. Two of the Plans were the products of collective-bargaining negotiations with the United Steelworkers of America. The third was for non-union salaried employees. Chronically underfunded, the Plans, by late 1986, had unfunded liabilities for promised benefits of almost $2.3 billion. Approximately $2.1 billion of this amount was covered by PBGC insurance.

It is undisputed that one of LTV Corp.'s principal goals in filing the Chapter 11 petitions was the restructuring of LTV Steel's pension obligations, a goal which could be accomplished if the Plans were terminated and responsibility for the unfunded liabilities was placed on the PBGC. LTV Steel then could negotiate with its employees for new pension arrangements. LTV, however, could not voluntarily terminate the Plans because two of them had been negotiated in collective bargaining. LTV therefore sought to have the PBGC terminate the Plans.

To that end, LTV advised the PBGC in 1986 that it could not continue to provide complete funding for the Plans. PBGC estimated that, without continued funding, the Plans' $2.1 billion underfunding could increase by as much as $65 million by December 1987 and by another $63 million by December 1988, unless the Plans were terminated. Moreover, extensive plant shutdowns were anticipated. These shutdowns, if they occurred before the Plans were terminated, would have required the payment of significant "shutdown benefits." The PBGC estimated that such benefits could increase the Plans' liabilities by as much as $300 million to $700 million, of which up to $500 million was covered by PBGC insurance. Confronted with this information, the PBGC, invoking § 4042(a)(4) of ERISA, determined that the Plans should be terminated in order to protect the insurance program from the unreasonable risk of large losses, and commenced termination proceedings in the District Court. With LTV's consent, the Plans were terminated effective January 13, 1987.

Because the Plans' participants lost some benefits as a result of the termination, the Steelworkers filed an adversary action against LTV in the Bankruptcy Court, challenging the termination and seeking an order directing LTV to make up the lost benefits. This action was settled, with LTV and the Steelworkers negotiating an interim collective-bargaining agreement that included new pension arrangements intended to make up benefits that plan participants lost as a result of the termination. New payments to retirees were based explicitly upon "a percentage of the difference between the benefit that was being paid under the Prior Plans and the amount paid by the PBGC." Retired participants were thereby placed in substantially the same positions they would have occupied had the old Plans never been terminated. * * *

The PBGC objected to these new pension agreements, characterizing them as "follow-on" plans. It defines a follow-on plan as a new benefit arrangement designed to wrap around the insurance benefits provided by the PBGC in such a way as to provide both retirees and active participants substantially the same benefits as they would have received had no termination occurred. The PBGC's policy against follow-on plans stems from the agency's belief that such plans are "abusive" of the insurance program and result in the PBGC's subsidizing an employer's ongoing pension program in a way not contemplated by Title IV. The PBGC consistently has made clear its policy of using its restoration powers under § 4047 if an employer institutes an abusive follow-on plan. * * *

In early August 1987, the PBGC determined that the financial factors on which it had relied in terminating the Plans had changed significantly. Of particular significance to the PBGC was its belief that the steel industry, including LTV Steel, was experiencing a dramatic turnaround. As a result, the PBGC concluded it no longer faced the imminent risk, central to its original termination decision, of large unfunded liabilities stemming from plant shutdowns. * * *

The Director issued a Notice of Restoration on September 22, 1987, indicating the PBGC's intent to restore the terminated Plans. * * *

The Court of Appeals first held that the restoration decision was arbitrary and capricious under § 706(2)(A) because the PBGC did not take account of all the areas of law the court deemed relevant to the restoration decision. The court expressed the view that "[b]ecause ERISA, bankruptcy and labor law are all involved in the case at hand, there must be a showing on the administrative record that PBGC, before reaching its decision, considered all of these areas of law, and to the extent possible, honored the policies underlying them." * * *

The PBGC contends that the Court of Appeals misapplied the general rule that an agency must take into consideration all relevant factors by requiring the agency explicitly to consider and discuss labor and bankruptcy law. We agree.

First, and most important, we do not think that the requirement imposed by the Court of Appeals upon the PBGC can be reconciled with the plain language of § 4047, under which the PBGC is operating in this case. This section gives the PBGC the power to restore terminated plans in any case in which the PBGC determines such action to be "appropriate and consistent with its duties *under this title*." The statute does not direct the PBGC to make restoration decisions that further the "public interest" generally, but rather empowers the agency to restore when restoration would further the interests that Title IV of ERISA is designed to protect. Given this specific and unambiguous statutory mandate, we do not think that the PBGC did or could focus "inordinately" on ERISA in making its restoration decision.

Even if Congress' directive to the PBGC had not been so clear, we are not entirely sure that the Court of Appeals' holding makes good sense as a general principle of administrative law. The PBGC points up problems that would arise if federal courts routinely were to require each agency to take explicit account of public policies that derive from federal statutes other than the agency's enabling act. To begin with, there are numerous federal statutes that could be said to embody countless policies. If agency action may be disturbed whenever a reviewing court is able to point to an arguably relevant statutory policy that was not explicitly considered, then a very large number of agency decisions might be open to judicial invalidation.

The Court of Appeals' directive that the PBGC give effect to the "policies and goals" of other statutes, apart from what those statutes actually provide, is questionable for another reason as well. Because the PBGC can claim no expertise in the labor and bankruptcy areas, it may be ill-equipped to undertake the difficult task of discerning and applying the "policies and goals" of those fields. * * *

The Court of Appeals also rejected the grounds for restoration that the PBGC *did* assert and discuss. The court found that the first ground the PBGC proffered to support the restoration—its policy against follow-on plans—was contrary to law because there was no indication in the text of the restoration provision, § 4047, or its legislative history that Congress intended the PBGC to use successive benefit plans as a basis for restoration. The PBGC argues that in reaching this conclusion the Court of Appeals departed from traditional principles of statutory interpretation and judicial review of agency construction of statutes. Again, we must agree. * * *

Respondents argue that the PBGC's anti-follow-on plan policy is irrational because, as a practical matter, no purpose is served when the PBGC bases a restoration decision on something other than the improved financial health of the employer. According to respondents, "financial improvement [is] both a necessary and a sufficient condition for restoration. The agency's asserted abuse policy * * * is *logically irrelevant* to the restoration decision." We think not. The PBGC's anti-follow-on policy is premised on the belief, which we find eminently reasonable, that employees will object more strenuously to a company's original decision to terminate a plan (or to take financial steps that make termination likely) if the company cannot use a follow-on plan to put the employees in the same (or a similar) position after termination as they were in before. The availability of a follow-on plan thus would remove a significant check—employee resistance—against termination of a pension plan.

Consequently, follow-on plans may tend to frustrate one of the objectives of ERISA that the PBGC is supposed to accomplish—the "continuation and maintenance of voluntary private pension plans." In addition, follow-on plans have a tendency to increase the PBGC's deficit and increase the insurance premiums all employers must pay, thereby frustrating another related statutory objective—the maintenance of low premiums. In short, the PBGC's construction based upon its conclusion that the existence of follow-on plans will lead to more plan terminations and increased PBGC liabilities is "assuredly a permissible one." Indeed, the judgments about the way the real world works that have gone into the PBGC's anti-follow-on policy are precisely the kind that agencies are better equipped to make than are courts. * * *

We conclude that the PBGC's failure to consider all potentially relevant areas of law did not render its restoration decision arbitrary and capricious. We also conclude that the PBGC's anti-follow-on policy, an asserted basis for the restoration decision, is not contrary to clear congressional intent and is based on a permissible construction of § 4047. Finally, we find the procedures employed by the PBGC to be consistent with the APA. Accordingly, the judgment of the Court of Appeals is reversed and the case is remanded for further proceedings consistent with this opinion.

■ JUSTICE STEVENS, dissenting.

In my opinion, at least with respect to ERISA plans that the PBGC has terminated involuntarily, the use of its restoration power under § 4047 to prohibit "follow-on" plans is contrary to the agency's statutory mandate. Unless there was a sufficient improvement in LTV's financial condition to justify the restoration order, I believe it should be set aside. I, therefore, would remand the case for a determination of whether that ground for the agency decision is adequately supported by the record.

A company that is undergoing reorganization under Chapter 11 of the Bankruptcy Code continues to operate an ongoing business and must have a satisfactory relationship with its work force in order to complete the reorganization process successfully. If its previous pension plans have been involuntarily terminated with the consequence that the PBGC has assumed the responsibility for discharging a significant share of the company's pension obligations, that responsibility by PBGC is an important resource on which the company has a right to rely during the reorganization process. It may use the financial cushion to fund capital investments, to pay current salary, or to satisfy contractual obligations, including the obligation to pay pension benefits. As long as the company uses its best efforts to complete the reorganization (and, incidentally, to reimburse PBGC for payments made to its former employees to the extent required by ERISA), the PBGC does not have any reason to interfere with managerial decisions that the company makes and the bankruptcy court approves. Whether the company's resources are dedicated to current expenditures or capital investments and whether the package of employee benefits that is provided to the work force is composed entirely of wages, vacation pay, and health insurance, on the one hand, or includes additional pension benefits, on the other, should be matters of indifference to the PBGC. Indeed, if it was faithful to the statement of congressional purposes in ERISA, it should favor an alternative that increases the company's use and maintenance of pension plans and that provides for continued payment to existing plan beneficiaries. The follow-up plans, in my opinion, are wholly consistent with the purposes of ERISA.

\* \* \*

In the case of an involuntary termination, if a mistake in the financial analysis is made, or if there is a sufficient change in the financial condition of the company to justify a reinstatement of the company's obligation, the PBGC should use its restoration powers. Without such a financial justification, however, there is nothing in the statute to authorize the PBGC's use of that power to prevent a company from creating or maintaining the kind of employee benefit program that the statute was enacted to encourage.

Accordingly, I respectfully dissent.

NOTES AND QUESTIONS

**1.** Why does the PBGC object to "follow-on" plans? Is the situation worse for the government-guaranteed pension insurance program if companies *and* unions have an incentive to transfer pension obligations to the insurance fund? If workers must lose 20 percent of their benefits upon termination of the plan, will the company be deterred from following that course?

**2.** Is it appropriate to separate ERISA law from bankruptcy law as the PBGC did and the Supreme Court approved? If LTV is in fact in economic trouble and the bankruptcy process will find that the company cannot meet its pension obligations, what will be the practical significance of the *LTV* decision?

**3.** Under Mead Corporation's retirement plan the normal retirement age was 65 but participants of age 62 with 30 years of service could retire with full benefits. Mead terminated the plan, giving workers lump sum payments of between $50,000 and $87,000 depending on their years of service. The payments were based on an assumption that the recipient would work until age 65; thus they did not compensate workers for the early retirement feature of the plan. Compensation for the early retirement provision would have increased benefits to these employees by about $9,000 each. After making the lump-sum payments, the company "recouped" the $10 million left in the plan.

The Supreme Court held that the early retirement benefits had not yet "accrued," since these workers had not yet reached age 62. Thus it read the relevant statutory language—§ 4044(a) of ERISA—as permitting the company to terminate the plan without providing the cash value of this provision to affected workers. Justice Stevens dissented. Mead Corp. v. Tilley, 490 U.S. 714 (1989).

**4.** In Patterson v. Shumate, 504 U.S. 753 (1992), the Supreme Court held that ERISA-protected pensions are excluded from a bankruptcy estate and thus protected against the attempt by the bankruptcy trustee to seize them for the benefit of creditors.

**5.** The Retiree Benefits Act of 1988 was enacted as a result of the bankruptcy by LTV. The legislation codified the requirement that Chapter 11 debtors continue to pay retiree benefits. 11 U.S.C. § 1114(b)(2). The Act has had a profound impact on the way courts look at the priority that all benefits, including pension plans, must receive if a company goes bankrupt. Often, when the Retiree Committee of a corporation in Chapter 11 petitions the court for priority against other creditors, the trustees file cross motions claiming economic hardship. Frequently, the result is delays or decreases in retiree payments.

## 5. DISCRIMINATION IN PRIVATE PENSIONS

## City of Los Angeles v. Manhart
435 U.S. 702 (1978).

■ MR. JUSTICE STEVENS delivered the opinion of the Court.

As a class, women live longer than men. For this reason, the Los Angeles Department of Water and Power required its female employees to make larger contributions to its pension fund than its male employees. We granted certiorari to decide whether this practice discriminated against individual female employees because of their sex in violation of § 703(a)(1) of the Civil Rights Act of 1964, as amended.

For many years the Department has administered retirement, disability, and death-benefit programs for its employees. Upon retirement each employee is eligible for a monthly retirement benefit computed as a fraction of his or her salary multiplied by years of service.[3] The monthly benefits for men and women of the same age, seniority, and salary are equal. Benefits are funded entirely by contributions from the employees and the Department, augmented by the income earned on those contributions. No private insurance company is involved in the administration or payment of benefits.

Based on a study of mortality tables and its own experience, the Department determined that its 2,000 female employees, on the average, will live a few years longer than its 10,000 male employees. The cost of a pension for the average retired female is greater than for the average male retiree because more monthly payments must be made to the average woman. The Department therefore required female employees to make monthly contributions to the fund which were 14.84% higher than the contributions required of comparable male employees. Because employee contributions were withheld from paychecks a female employee took home less pay than a male employee earning the same salary.

Since the effective date of the Equal Employment Opportunity Act of 1972, the Department has been an employer within the meaning of Title VII of the Civil Rights Act of 1964. In 1973, respondents brought this suit in the United States District Court for the Central District of California on behalf of a class of women employed or formerly employed by the Department. They prayed for an injunction and restitution of excess contributions.

\* \* \*

There are both real and fictional differences between women and men. It is true that the average man is taller than the average woman; it is not true that the average woman driver is more accident prone than the average man. Before the Civil Rights Act of 1964 was enacted, an employer could fashion his personnel policies on the basis of assumptions about the differences between men and women, whether or not the assumptions were valid.

It is now well recognized that employment decisions cannot be predicated on mere "stereotyped" impressions about the characteristics of males or females. Myths and purely habitual assumptions about a woman's

---

**3.** The plan itself is not in the record. In its brief the Department states that the plan provides for several kinds of pension benefits at the employee's option, and that the most common is a formula pension equal to 2% of the average monthly salary paid during the last year of employment times the number of years of employment. The benefit is guaranteed for life.

inability to perform certain kinds of work are no longer acceptable reasons for refusing to employ qualified individuals, or for paying them less. This case does not, however, involve a fictional difference between men and women. It involves a generalization that the parties accept as unquestionably true: Women, as a class, do live longer than men. The Department treated its women employees differently from its men employees because the two classes are in fact different. It is equally true, however, that all individuals in the respective classes do not share the characteristic that differentiates the average class representatives. Many women do not live as long as the average man and many men outlive the average woman. The question, therefore, is whether the existence or nonexistence of "discrimination" is to be determined by comparison of class characteristics or individual characteristics. A "stereotyped" answer to that question may not be the same as the answer that the language and purpose of the statute command.

The statute makes it unlawful "to discriminate against any *individual* with respect to his compensation, terms, conditions, or privileges of employment, because of such *individual's* race, color, religion, sex, or national origin." The statute's focus on the individual is unambiguous. It precludes treatment of individuals as simply components of a racial, religious, sexual, or national class. If height is required for a job, a tall woman may not be refused employment merely because, on the average, women are too short. Even a true generalization about the class is an insufficient reason for disqualifying an individual to whom the generalization does not apply.

That proposition is of critical importance in this case because there is no assurance that any individual woman working for the Department will actually fit the generalization on which the Department's policy is based. Many of those individuals will not live as long as the average man. While they were working, those individuals received smaller paychecks because of their sex, but they will receive no compensating advantage when they retire.

It is true, of course, that while contributions are being collected from the employees, the Department cannot know which individuals will predecease the average woman. Therefore, unless women as a class are assessed an extra charge, they will be subsidized, to some extent, by the class of male employees.[14] It follows, according to the Department, that fairness to its class of male employees justifies the extra assessment against all of its female employees.

But the question of fairness to various classes affected by the statute is essentially a matter of policy for the legislature to address. Congress has decided that classifications based on sex, like those based on national origin or race, are unlawful. Actuarial studies could unquestionably identify

---

**14.** The size of the subsidy involved in this case is open to doubt, because the Department's plan provides for survivors' benefits. Since female spouses of male employees are likely to have greater life expectancies than the male spouses of female employees, whatever benefits men lose in "primary" coverage for themselves, they may regain in "secondary" coverage for their wives.

differences in life expectancy based on race or national origin, as well as sex.[15] But a statute that was designed to make race irrelevant in the employment market, see Griggs v. Duke Power Co., [supra p. 233], could not reasonably be construed to permit a take-home-pay differential based on a racial classification.

Even if the statutory language were less clear, the basic policy of the statute requires that we focus on fairness to individuals rather than fairness to classes. Practices that classify employees in terms of religion, race, or sex tend to preserve traditional assumptions about groups rather than thoughtful scrutiny of individuals. The generalization involved in this case illustrates the point. Separate mortality tables are easily interpreted as reflecting innate differences between the sexes, but a significant part of the longevity differential may be explained by the social fact that men are heavier smokers than women.

Finally, there is no reason to believe that Congress intended a special definition of discrimination in the context of employee group insurance coverage. It is true that insurance is concerned with events that are individually unpredictable, but that is characteristic of many employment decisions. Individual risks, like individual performance, may not be predicted by resort to classifications proscribed by Title VII. Indeed, the fact that this case involves a group insurance program highlights a basic flaw in the Department's fairness argument. For when insurance risks are grouped, the better risks always subsidize the poorer risks. Healthy persons subsidize medical benefits for the less healthy; unmarried workers subsidize the pensions of married workers;[18] persons who eat, drink, or smoke to excess may subsidize pension benefits for persons whose habits are more temperate. Treating different classes of risks as though they were the same for purposes of group insurance is a common practice that has never been considered inherently unfair. To insure the flabby and the fit as though they were equivalent risks may be more common than treating men and women alike;[19] but nothing more than habit makes one "subsidy" seem less fair than the other.[20]

**15.** For example, the life expectancy of a white baby in 1973 was 72.2 years; a nonwhite baby could expect to live 65.9 years, a difference of 6.3 years. See Public Health Service, IIA Vital Statistics of the United States, 1973, Table 5–3.

**18.** A study of life expectancy in the United States for 1949–1951 showed that 20-year-old men could expect to live to 60.6 years of age if they were divorced. If married, they could expect to reach 70.9 years of age, a difference of more than 10 years. Id., at 93.

**19.** The record indicates, however, that the Department has funded its death-benefit plan by equal contributions from male and female employees. A death benefit—unlike a pension benefit—has less value for persons with longer life expectancies. Under the Department's concept of fairness, then, this neutral funding of death benefits is unfair to women as a class.

**20.** A variation on the Department's fairness theme is the suggestion that a gender-neutral pension plan would itself violate Title VII because of its disproportionately heavy impact on male employees. This suggestion has no force in the sex discrimination context because each retiree's total pension benefits are ultimately determined by his *actual life span*; any differential in benefits paid to men and women in the aggregate is thus "based on [a] factor other than sex,"

An employment practice that requires 2,000 individuals to contribute more money into a fund than 10,000 other employees simply because each of them is a woman, rather than a man, is in direct conflict with both the language and the policy of the Act. Such a practice does not pass the simple test of whether the evidence shows "treatment of a person in a manner which but for that person's sex would be different." It constitutes discrimination and is unlawful unless exempted by the Equal Pay Act of 1963 or some other affirmative justification.

[The Court considered and rejected the argument that the Bennett Amendment authorized the Los Angeles practice.]

NOTES AND QUESTIONS

**1.** The Supreme Court opinion in *Manhart* held that the new policy should not apply retroactively. Justice Marshall dissented from that part of the holding. Chief Justice Burger and Justice Rehnquist agreed only with that part.

**2.** In Arizona Governing Committee for Tax Deferred Annuity & Deferred Compensation Plans v. Norris, 463 U.S. 1073 (1983), the Supreme Court held that Title VII prohibits an employer from offering its employees the option of receiving retirement benefits from one of several companies, all of which pay women lower monthly benefits than men because women as a group live longer than men. Citing *Manhart,* the Court majority said the "classification of employees on the basis of sex is no more permissible at the pay-out stage of a retirement plan than at the pay-in stage." The decision was by five to four vote. A different five to four decision (with Justice O'Connor as the "swing vote") said that the holding of *Norris* should apply only prospectively, as to pension plan benefits derived from contributions collected after the effective date of the judgment. The consequence of the nonretroactivity of *Manhart* and *Norris* is that workers will be receiving sex-determined pension benefits for several decades into the twenty-first century. For the argument that this wrongly "compromised Title VII's goal of full relief in favor of third-party contractual rights and employer solvency," see Wendy A. Wolf, Sex-Discrimination in Pension Plans: The Problem of Incomplete Relief, 9 Harv. Women's L.J. 83 (1986).

**3.** Formerly, many employers permitted women to retire at age 62 with full pension benefits, while men were not permitted to draw full benefits until age 65. Is this practice unlawful under *Manhart*?

**4.** As a class, blacks do not live as long as whites. The insurance industry has not used race-segregated actuarial tables similar to the sex-segregated tables at issue in *Manhart* because most states have had for many years

and consequently immune from challenge under the Equal Pay Act. Even under Title VII itself—assuming disparate-impact analysis applies to fringe benefits,—the male employees would not prevail. Even a completely neutral practice will inevitably have *some* disproportionate impact on one group or another. *Griggs* does not imply, and this Court has never held, that discrimination must always be inferred from such consequences.

statutes which prohibit discrimination in insurance on the basis of race. Should employers be permitted to charge gay men more for life or health insurance because of the risk of AIDS?

**5.** Where an employer's practice adversely affects a member of a group protected under Title VII, the employer is required to seek less discriminatory alternatives.   What factors other than race or sex could the insurance industry use to separate individuals into appropriate risk groups for insurance purposes?

**6.** The insurance industry contended in *Manhart* that forcing it to combine male and female mortality tables would result in male retirees subsidizing female retirees.   Many annuity plans offered to retirees include a survivors' benefits option for spouses of the annuitant;  as a result, males have been subsidizing females (the widows of other retirees who died earlier) for years.

**7.** Will the use of unisex mortality tables make it more expensive for an employer to hire a female, and so discourage female hiring?   How should the cost of female longevity be spread?   Would reducing retirement benefits for men in order to pay men and women the same benefits violate the Equal Pay Act, which states that no one's wages may be reduced in order to bring an employer into compliance with the law?

**8.** Life insurance presents the reverse side of the annuity problem: because women live longer than men, the use of unisex mortality tables for life insurance will result in women "subsidizing" men.   Does a switch to unisex mortality tables result in a net financial gain or loss for women, when one combines life and retirement insurance benefits?

**9.** The Retirement Equity Act of 1984, 29 U.S.C. § 1052(b)(5)(A), allows men and women to take parental leave for up to five years and not lose their pension rights.

## 6.   Government Pensions as Contract

ERISA does not apply to state and local government pension plans. Historically, those pensions were treated legally as gratuities. But "new property" thinking led to lawsuits in which some courts held that reductions in pension rights were unconstitutional.   In addition, many states, either by constitutional amendment or by judicial decision, have declared public pensions to be a contractual right rather than a gratuity.

NOTES AND QUESTIONS

**1.** The Supreme Judicial Court of Massachusetts held that "[l]egislation which would materially increase present [pension] members' contributions without any increase of the allowances finally payable to those members or any other adjustments carrying advantages to them appears to be presumptively invalid ... unless saved by the reserved police powers." Opinion of the Justices, 303 N.E.2d 320, 329 (Mass.1973).

**2.**  Connecticut required male state employees to work until age 60 (with 10 years' service; 55 with 25 years' service) to earn pension benefits, while females could collect the same benefits at 55 (with 10 years' service; 50 with 25 years'). This was held to be unlawful sex discrimination in *Fitzpatrick v. Bitzer*, 390 F.Supp. 278 (D.Conn.1974), affirmed and reversed on other grounds, 519 F.2d 559 (2d Cir.1975), affirmed in part, reversed in part, 427 U.S. 445 (1976) (eleventh amendment does not bar award against the state of back pay or attorneys' fees because Title VII is authorized by § 5 of the fourteenth amendment). The legislature changed the law to put females in the situation of males. Thus, in the name of equality, women were required to work until a later age before being entitled to their pensions. Some of these women sued, saying the change was an unconstitutional impairment of express and implied contract rights. Their argument was similar to the view that prevailed in *Opinion of the Justices*, supra note 1. The district court held that as to females who were working under the earlier rules, the change was unconstitutional. The court also granted relief to males, saying they remained in service after *Fitzpatrick* in reliance on the expectation of earlier retirement for males that they assumed would be the legislature's response to the initial decision. *Pineman v. Oechslin*, 494 F.Supp. 525 (D.Conn.1980). The judgment in Pineman v. Oechslin was vacated because the district court should have abstained and permitted an initial state court decision on the contract claim. 637 F.2d 601 (2d Cir.1981). The Connecticut Supreme Court said female employees had no contractual right to the lower retirement ages. *Pineman v. Oechslin*, 488 A.2d 803 (Conn.1985). The court said: "Although there is a seductive appeal in the contract-oriented approaches [to construing rights to government pensions] adopted by other jurisdictions, we decline to depart from the well established rules of statutory construction discussed earlier, namely, that a statute does not create vested contractual rights absent a clear statement of legislative intent to contract." 488 A.2d at 808.

Is the result ultimately reached in this dispute correct? If not, what would be a better result? If so, is there any way the legal system could have reached it without quite so many rounds of trial and appellate consideration?

In Pineman v. Fallon, 662 F.Supp. 1311 (D.Conn.1987), the court held that the change in retirement age did not violate contract clause, taking clause, or due process rights under the United States Constitution for those employees who under prior law would have been entitled to such benefits. This decision was affirmed by the Second Circuit in Pineman v. Fallon, 842 F.2d 598 (2d Cir.1988), cert. denied, 488 U.S. 824 (1988).

**3.**  See also the formulation by the Supreme Court of California: the public employer may make "reasonable" modifications in its pension program in order to meet "changing conditions" and to "maintain the integrity of the system," provided that "changes in a pension plan which result in disadvantage to employees [are] accompanied by comparable new advantages." Allen v. Long Beach, 287 P.2d 765 (Cal.1955).

---

## D. SOCIAL SECURITY RETIREMENT BENEFITS

## 1. BACKGROUND

## Social Security Administration, Social Security: Report to Our Customers

http://www.ssa.gov/pubs/10617.html (1996).

### A Message From the Commissioner of Social Security

The Social Security Administration (SSA) is committed to providing you service of the highest possible quality—not just good service, but world-class service. We take pride in making sure that benefits are delivered on time and in the right amount every month to about 47 million people entitled to Social Security and Supplemental Security Income (SSI). It's a job we do to the best of our ability. And it's a job we do well.

But we also believe we owe you so much more. * * *

We are committed to providing world-class service.

* * * When you contact a Social Security office, you have the right to be treated with courtesy, to have your requests handled by knowledgeable, helpful public servants, and to receive service quickly. We are working to make certain your needs and expectations are met.

And you've told us we're getting there.

You have told us that overall we are doing well. In a survey of people who were served by SSA in 1995, 79 percent said that our service was good or very good And I'm very proud of the fact that 94 percent said SSA's service was as good or better than the best service they had received from other government agencies.

And we will never stop working to improve our customer service, knowing that we can always find ways to do our work better, to serve you better, and to respond to your requests and needs in a manner that is unmatched by any public or private organization.

We have made promises to you. And we are committed to keeping them. * * * [P]lease let us know how we can do better.

Shirley S. Chater

Commissioner of Social Security

## Social Security Administration, Social Security: Basic Facts

http://www.ssa.gov/pubs/10080.html (1996).

### BASIC FACTS ABOUT SOCIAL SECURITY

Social Security is part of almost everyone's life. Social Security protects more than 142 million workers and pays benefits to 43 million people.

You and your family are probably protected by Social Security and you probably pay taxes that help make the system work. But you may also be unsure about what Social Security does, who it helps, and how much it costs.

This booklet gives you some basic facts about Social Security ... and tells you how to get more information if you want it.  * * *

### ALMOST EVERY RETIREE GETS SOCIAL SECURITY BENE-FITS

Social Security pays monthly retirement benefits to more than 30 million retired workers and their families. More than 9 out of 10 Americans who are age 65 or older get Social Security benefits.

Full retirement benefits are now payable at age 65, with reduced benefits available as early as age 62. The age for full benefits will gradually rise in the next century, until it reaches age 67 in 2027 for people born in 1960 or later. (Reduced benefits will still be available at age 62.)

### SOCIAL SECURITY IS A FOUNDATION FOR BUILDING A COMFORTABLE RETIREMENT

A recent national poll found that 3 in 4 workers "worry that they won't have enough money to live comfortably in retirement." Often the difference between retirees who enjoy retirement and those who struggle is financial planning.

Social Security has always been part of a "three-legged stool" that could solidly support a comfortable retirement. The other two legs of the stool are pension income and savings/investments.

Financial advisers often tell people that, when they quit work, they'll need about 70 percent of preretirement income to live comfortably. By itself, Social Security replaces about 42 percent of an average wage earner's salary.

### SOCIAL SECURITY—A FOUNDATION

Social Security benefit amounts, as of January 1996, are shown below for low, average, and high wage earners who retire at age 65:

## SOCIAL SECURITY RETIREMENT BENEFITS

| Monthly Retirement Benefits | Wage Earner | Wage Earner and Spouse |
|---|---|---|
| Low | $537 | $805 |
| Average | 886 | 1,329 |
| High | 1,248 | 1,872 |

The benefit amounts above are based on steady lifetime earnings from age 22 through the year before retirement (1995). For 1995, these earnings are approximately $11,100 for a low earner; $24,700 for an average earner; $61,200 or above for a high earner. Married workers can receive benefits based either on their own work record or their spouse's, whichever is higher. * * *

### YOUR SOCIAL SECURITY TAX DOLLARS

Employers match a worker's Social Security tax payment. Self-employed people pay Social Security taxes equal to the combined employee/employer tax, although half of their tax is deductible as a business cost.

Generally, out of every dollar paid in Social Security and Medicare taxes:

- 69 cents goes to a trust fund that pays retirement and survivors benefits;
- 19 cents goes to a trust fund that pays Medicare benefits;
- 12 cents goes to a trust fund that pays disability benefits.

Your Social Security taxes also pay for administering Social Security. The administrative costs are paid from Social Security trust funds and are less than 1 cent of every Social Security tax dollar collected.

The Social Security trust funds now take in more money than they pay out each month—about $5 billion more per month. These reserve funds are then invested in U.S. Treasury bonds, the safest of all possible investments. Those reserves will accumulate, earn interest and be used to help pay for the retirement of the baby boom generation beginning around 2010.

### WHY SOCIAL SECURITY?

Over the past six decades, Social Security has become the most successful domestic government program in history.

A basic understanding of why Social Security came about is important to understanding today's Social Security program ... and also to deciding what Social Security should be in the 21st century.

### ITS HISTORY

Before the industrial revolution, America was mostly a country of small farmers. But we soon became a country where more people worked for wages and fewer worked the land. This change helped make America strong, and it raised our standard of living. It also created new risks to family security and made it more difficult for families to take care of their own in hard times.

The Great Depression of the 1930s dramatized the fact that many American workers were financially dependent on factors beyond their own control. The Social Security Act, signed into law by President Franklin Delano Roosevelt in 1935, helped to alleviate this situation.

In the years that followed, Social Security was broadened to include survivors benefits, disability benefits and health care benefits.

ITS PHILOSOPHY

The Social Security system provides a minimum "floor of protection" for retired workers, and for workers and their families who face a loss of income due to disability or the death of a family wage earner.

Social Security payments are based on two underlying philosophies. First, the system is designed so that there is a clear link between how much a worker pays into the system and how much he or she will get in benefits. Basically, high wage earners get more, low wage earners get less.

At the same time, the Social Security benefit formula is weighted in favor of low wage earners, who have fewer resources to save or invest during their working years. Social Security retirement benefits replace approximately 60 percent of the pre-retirement earnings of a low wage earner, 42 percent of an average wage earner, and 26 percent of a high wage earner.

Basically, the Social Security program is a way of providing a base of economic security in today's society. It allows older Americans to live independently and with dignity and relieves their families of the financial burden for their retirement years. And Social Security provides a valuable package of disability and survivors insurance to workers over their working lifetimes.

ITS FUTURE

Our Social Security system has been a basic part of American life for 60 years. It has changed frequently over the years to meet new needs of workers and of beneficiaries. It will undoubtedly change in the future to meet the needs of 21st century workers and beneficiaries.

## Social Security Administration, Understanding the Benefits

http://www.ssa.gov/pubs/10024.html (1997).

\* \* \*

## You Become Eligible For Social Security By Earning "Credits"

You must work and pay taxes into Social Security in order to get benefits. (Of course, some people get benefits as a dependent or survivor on another person's Social Security record.)

As you work and pay taxes, you earn Social Security "credits." In 1997 you earn one credit for each $670 in earnings you have—up to a maximum of four credits per year. (The amount of money needed to earn one credit goes up every year.)

Most people need 40 credits (10 years of work) to qualify for benefits. Younger people need fewer credits to be eligible for disability benefits or for their family members to be eligible for survivors benefits if they die.

During your working lifetime, you probably will earn more credits than you need to be eligible for Social Security. These extra credits do not increase your eventual Social Security benefit. However, the income you earn will increase your benefit.

* * *

## Full Retirement

If you were born before 1938, you will be eligible for your full Social Security benefit at the age of 65.

However, beginning in the year 2003, the age at which full benefits are payable will increase in gradual steps from 65 to 67. This affects people born in 1938 and later.

## Reduced Benefits As Early As 62

No matter what your "full" retirement age is, you may start receiving benefits as early as 62. However, if you start your benefits early, they are reduced five-ninths of one percent for each month before your "full" retirement age. For example, if your full retirement age is 65 and you sign up for Social Security when you're 64, you will receive 93 percent of your full benefit. At 62, you would get 80 percent. (Note: The reduction will be greater in future years as the full retirement age increases.)

*Here's An Important Point:* There are disadvantages and advantages to taking your benefit before your full retirement age. The disadvantage is that your benefit is permanently reduced. The advantage is that you collect benefits for a longer period of time. Each person's situation is different, so make sure you contact Social Security before you decide to retire.

## What About Late Retirement?

Some people continue to work full time beyond their full retirement age—and they don't sign up for Social Security until later. This delay in retirement can increase your Social Security benefit in two ways:

- Your extra income usually will increase your "average" earnings, and the higher your average earnings, the higher your Social Security benefit will be.

- In addition, a special credit is given to people who delay retirement. This credit, which is a percentage added to your Social Security benefit, varies depending on your date of birth. For people turning 65 in 1997, the rate is 5 percent per year. That rate gradually increases in future years, until it reaches 8 percent per year for people turning 65 in 2008 or later.  * * *

### If You Disagree With A Decision We Make

Whenever we make a decision that affects your eligibility for Social Security or SSI benefits, we send you a letter explaining our decision. If you disagree with our decision, you have the right to appeal it. In other words, you can ask us to review your case. If our decision was wrong, we will change it.  * * *

### How Your Earnings Affect Your Benefits

The law limits the amount of money you can earn and still collect all your Social Security benefits. This provision affects people under the age of 70 who collect Social Security retirement, dependents, or survivors benefits. (Earnings in or after the month you reach age 70 won't affect your Social Security benefits.) People who work and collect disability or SSI benefits have different earnings requirements and should report all their income to Social Security.

If you are under age 65, you can earn up to $8,640 in 1997 and still collect all your Social Security benefits.

However, for every $2 you earn over $8,640, $1 will be withheld from your Social Security benefits.

If you are age 65 through 69, you can earn up to $13,500 in 1997 and still collect all your Social Security benefits.

However, for every $3 you earn over $13,500, $1 will be withheld from your Social Security benefits.

We count only the earnings you make from a job, or your net profit if you're self-employed. This includes compensation such as bonuses, commissions, and vacation pay. It doesn't include pensions, annuities, investment income, interest, Social Security, veterans, or other government benefits.  * * *

**OVERVIEW**

Social Security helps people help themselves!

Click on any animal & it will tell you a story.

People work and give a little money to Social Security.

When some people get so sick that they can't work, they get money from Social Security.

When people get older and don't work anymore, they can get money from Social Security.

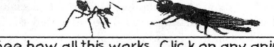

When people die, the family gets money from Social Security.

See how all this works...Click on any animal

## 2.   THE RETIREMENT TEST

### Taubenfeld v. Bowen

685 F.Supp. 237 (S.D.Fla.1988).

■ EDWARD B. DAVIS, DISTRICT JUDGE.

\* \* \*

The issue before this Court is whether the final decision of the Secretary, denying Plaintiff, WOLF TAUBENFELD ("TAUBENFELD"), Social Security retirement benefits, is supported by the evidence in the administrative record.  The Secretary's findings must be accepted as conclusive if supported by "substantial evidence."  \* \* \*

TAUBENFELD was born on November 12, 1917.  He was the president of Kontrol Men's Wear Corporation, Inc., a small, family-owned, closed corporation which operates a retail men's clothing store.  TAUBENFELD asserts that he retired in April, 1984.  At that time he resigned as president and operator of the business, and reduced his working hours from 200 hours per month to 72 hours per month, with a commensurate reduction in salary compensation.  TAUBENFELD claims that his wife, Luisa Taubenfeld, and two sons, Abraham and Isaac, have taken over the bulk of his duties, at substantially increased wages, and now run the business.

In August, 1984, TAUBENFELD filed a claim for retirement insurance benefits with the Social Security Administration ("SSA").  On November 23, 1984, the SSA informed the Claimant that he was not entitled to payments because he was "still in a position to control all the business activities and inasmuch, control [his] own earnings."  This decision was reaffirmed upon TAUBENFELD's request for reconsideration.  After a de novo hearing, an Administrative Law Judge also determined that TAUBENFELD was not "retired" within the meaning of the Social Security Act ("The Act"), 42 U.S.C. § 401 et seq.

TAUBENFELD requested review of this decision.  The SSA Appeals Council granted review and amended the ALJ's decision to reflect that undistributed corporate earnings could be allocated to TAUBENFELD as excess wages.  The Council found no eligibility for old-age benefits, reasoning that the Claimant had the ability to pay himself additional income based on his share of retained earnings in Kontrol Men's Wear Corp.  Furthermore, the Appeals Council found that TAUBENFELD was not retired because although his hours were reduced, the value of his services had not diminished.  Specifically, the Appeals Council held as follows:

> [T]he sole purpose for the claimant's presence at the business is to make important decisions and attract customers, both functions vital to the success of the business.  The Council believes he retains authority to set his salary despite the fact that he is a minority owner, and his services continue to be worth more than $580 per month.  \* \* \* The corporate returns for 1983 and 1984 \* \* \* show retained earnings which are sufficient to pay the claimant for his services.  Thus, the Council believes it was reasonable for the Administration and the Administrative Law Judge to determine that the claimant continues to earn at the same rate; i.e., at an amount sufficient to cause full suspension of old-age insurance benefits.  \* \* \*

Plaintiff appealed the Secretary's decision to this Court, asserting that he was legitimately "retired" and that the Secretary's allocation of retained corporate earnings as additional wages is an error of law.  The Magistrate considered two issues:  1) whether the Secretary erred in finding no retirement where the Secretary failed to make proper credibility findings;

and 2) whether substantial evidence supports the Secretary's conclusion that the Claimant was not entitled to retirement insurance benefits. With respect to the first point, the Magistrate found that the Secretary had stated in sufficient detail why it was rejecting the Claimant's testimony on credibility grounds. See Owens v. Heckler, 748 F.2d 1511 (11th Cir.1984); Appeals Council decision at 8 ("The foregoing evidence is inconsistent and therefore unreliable."). As to the second contention, the Magistrate found that because "the Administration has not acquiesced to any decision by a circuit court on the issue of allocation of undistributed corporate earnings," it was proper for the SSA to reallocate TAUBENFELD's income in the manner in which it did.

For the reasons stated below, the Court DISAFFIRMS the Magistrate and remands for further proceedings.

## DISCUSSION

The Court agrees that the Secretary "properly assessed the credibility of the plaintiff and witnesses, [and] considered the entire record." Nonetheless, the Secretary's determination that TAUBENFELD was not retired in the subject years is incorrect as a matter of law.

Under sections 203(b) and (f) of the Act, 42 U.S.C. § 402(b) and (f), a beneficiary aged 65 and over could earn $6,960 in the 1984 taxable year without suffering a loss of retirement insurance benefits. Deductions are taken from benefits for any month the beneficiary engaged in self-employment or rendered services for wages in excess of $580.

The "Retirement Test Exempt Amounts" for the 1985 taxable year are $610 per month for $7,320 per year. 42 U.S.C. § 403(f)(4)(B) provides that an individual will be presumed, with respect to any month, to have rendered services for wages of more than the applicable exempt amount until it is shown to the Secretary's satisfaction that excess wages were not so received. Wages are defined in 20 C.F.R. § 404.1041 to mean "remuneration *paid* to you as an employee for employment." The name given to the remuneration and the method of payment are immaterial.

Because TAUBENFELD is an employee, not a self-employed person, the inquiry is focused on whether he received payment of wages in excess of $6,960 for 1984 and $7,320 for 1985. The receipt of wages may be actual or constructive. "Wages are constructively paid when they are credited to the account of, or set aside for, an employee so that they may be drawn upon by the employee at any time although not then actually received." TAUBENFELD presented evidence that he substantially curtailed his work activity from a yearly salary of some $32,000 to an annual salary of $6,960 after March 31, 1984, and a $7,320.00 salary in 1985.

Clearly, TAUBENFELD deliberately arranged his affairs to be eligible for retirement. This he could do so long as he was "legitimately retired" and the arrangement was bona fide.

However, it appears that the Secretary found TAUBENFELD's arrangement to be a sham, for while he curtailed his work hours, reduced his salary, and resigned as president of the business, he "remained in control" and "had the ability to set his own salary".

"The Secretary has, without question, the authority and the duty to pierce any fictitious arrangements among family members, and others, to shift salary payments from one to the other when the arrangement is not in accord with reality."  Before the Secretary may treat a salary arrangement as a "sham" or "scheme of shifting wages", three factors must be considered:

> (1) whether the claimant continues to contribute substantial and valuable services to the corporation;  (2) whether the family member receiving the income increases his or her duties commensurate with the increase in salary;  and (3) whether the family member's income is used to support the claimant.

Here, the Secretary determined that TAUBENFELD continued to contribute substantial services despite the reduced work hours.  This is supported by substantial evidence.  However, there is no finding that Ms. Taubenfeld or the two sons received wages not commensurate with their allegedly increased duties.  Should the Secretary have made such a finding, the monies allocated by the Secretary to TAUBENFELD would necessarily have had to consist of the sham payments to these family members, not undistributed corporate earnings.

As to the third factor, the record is devoid of any facts that TAUBENFELD is supported by a family member's increased income or by money shifted elsewhere.  The record does not make this a case of income shifting to another family member constituting an indirect payment to the Claimant.

There is also no evidence that the corporate form of Kontrol Men's Wear is a sham or other than bona fide.  For example, there is no indication that TAUBENFELD intermingles his personal funds with corporate funds, or that he runs the business as a sole proprietorship.  * * *

Thus, one is left wondering under what authority the Secretary added to TAUBENFELD's reported wages the undistributed corporate profits. While this Court has been unable to locate an Eleventh Circuit decision addressing this issue, the published decisional law of other circuits is unanimous, and the result here inescapable.  There is no legitimate basis for allocating the funds in question to TAUBENFELD, for "where corporate profits remain undistributed and are not available 'at any time' for the personal use of the applicant, the Secretary has no authority to allocate any portion of the funds to the applicant."

In the present case, there is no evidence that TAUBENFELD or any other person received, directly or indirectly, any of the corporate profits in question.  The profits were not "credited to the account of, or set aside for" TAUBENFELD in such a manner that they could be drawn upon by him at any time.  Again, "[t]reating undistributed profits as constructively received wages by reasoning that the majority stockholder had unrestricted access to corporate funds ignores the corporate existence". Thus, the Secretary erred in attributing to TAUBENFELD those funds.

QUESTIONS

**1.** Why tell elderly persons they must stop working to receive full Social Security benefits? In particular, why would Mr. Taubenfeld not be penalized if he received dividends (even if he had very large unearned income), but lose some of his benefits if he received compensation for work? Is Social Security's "retirement test" inconsistent with the Age Discrimination in Employment Act, supra pp. 328–337, which bans involuntary retirement on the basis of age?

**2.** Under current law, persons can receive Old Age benefits after age 70 even if they work. Why is the law different depending on whether the person is older or younger than 70?

**3.** This case presents complicated facts "close to the line." Should we delegate this line drawing to the Social Security Administration? Is anything gained by allowing judicial review on a matter like this?

## 3. IS SOCIAL SECURITY PROPERTY?

### Flemming v. Nestor

363 U.S. 603 (1960).

■ MR. JUSTICE HARLAN delivered the opinion of the Court. From a decision of the District Court for the District of Columbia holding § 202(n) of the Social Security Act unconstitutional, the Secretary of Health, Education, and Welfare takes this direct appeal. The challenged section provides for the termination of old age, survivor, and disability insurance benefits payable to, or in certain cases in respect of, an alien individual who after September 1, 1954 is deported under the Immigration and Nationality Act on any one of certain grounds specified in § 202(n).

Appellee, an alien, immigrated to this country from Bulgaria in 1913, and became eligible for old-age benefits in November 1955. In July 1956 he was deported for having been a member of the Communist Party from 1933 to 1939. This being one of the benefit-termination deportation grounds specified in § 202(n), appellee's benefits were terminated soon thereafter, and notice of the termination was given to his wife, who had remained in this country. * * *

We think that the District Court erred in holding that § 202(n) deprived appellee of an "accrued property right." Appellee's right to Social Security benefits cannot properly be considered to have been of that order. * * *

The Social Security system may be accurately described as a form of social insurance, enacted pursuant to Congress' power to "spend money in aid of the 'general welfare,'" whereby persons gainfully employed, and those who employ them, are taxed to permit the payment of benefits to the retired and disabled, and their dependents. Plainly the expectation is that many members of the present productive work force will in turn become beneficiaries rather than supporters of the program. But each worker's benefits, though flowing from the contributions he made to the national economy while actively employed, are not dependent on the degree to which he was called upon to support the system by taxation. It is apparent that the noncontractual interest of an employee covered by the Act cannot be soundly analogized to that of the holder of an annuity, whose right to benefits is bottomed on his contractual premium payments. * * *

To engraft upon the Social Security system a concept of "accrued property rights" would deprive it of the flexibility and boldness in adjustment to ever-changing conditions which it demands. It was doubtless out of an awareness of the need for such flexibility that Congress included in the original Act, and has since retained, a clause expressly reserving to it "[t]he right to alter, amend, or repeal any provision" of the Act. 42 U.S.C. § 1304. * * *

We must conclude that a person covered by the Act has not such a right in benefit payments as would make every defeasance of "accrued" interests violative of the Due Process Clause of the Fifth Amendment.

This is not to say, however, that Congress may exercise its power to modify the statutory scheme free of all constitutional restraint. The interest of a covered employee under the Act is of sufficient substance to fall within the protection from arbitrary governmental action afforded by the Due Process Clause. In judging the permissibility of the cut-off provisions of § 202(n) from this standpoint, it is not within our authority to determine whether the congressional judgment expressed in that section is sound or equitable, or whether it comports well or ill with the purposes of the Act. * * * Particularly when we deal with a withholding of a noncontractual benefit under a social welfare program such as this, we must recognize that the Due Process Clause can be thought to interpose a bar only if the statute manifests a patently arbitrary classification, utterly lacking in rational justification.

Such is not the case here. The fact of a beneficiary's residence abroad—in the case of a deportee, a presumably permanent residence—can be of obvious relevance to the question of eligibility. One benefit which may be thought to accrue to the economy from the Social Security system is the increased over-all national purchasing power resulting from taxation of productive elements of the economy to provide payments to the retired and disabled, who might otherwise be destitute or nearly so, and who would generally spend a comparatively large percentage of their benefit payments. This advantage would be lost as to payments made to one residing abroad. For these purposes, it is, of course, constitutionally irrelevant whether this reasoning in fact underlay the legislative decision, as it is irrelevant that the section does not extend to all to whom the postulated rationale might in logic apply. * * *

We need go no further to find support for our conclusion that this provision of the Act cannot be condemned as so lacking in rational justification as to offend due process. * * * It is said that the termination of appellee's benefits amounts to punishing him without a judicial trial, that the termination of benefits constitutes the imposition of punishment by legislative act, rendering § 202(n) a bill of attainder; and that the punishment exacted is imposed for past conduct not unlawful when engaged in, thereby violating the constitutional prohibition on ex post facto laws. Essential to the success of each of these contentions is the validity of characterizing as "punishment" in the constitutional sense the termination of benefits under § 202(n). * * *

Turning, then, to the particular statutory provision before us, appellee cannot successfully contend that the language and structure of § 202(n), or the nature of the deprivation, requires us to recognize a punitive design. Here the sanction is the mere denial of a noncontractual governmental benefit. No affirmative disability or restraint is imposed, and certainly nothing approaching the "infamous punishment" of imprisonment, as in Wong Wing v. United States, 163 U.S. 228, on which great reliance is mistakenly placed. * * *

■ MR. JUSTICE BLACK, dissenting. * * * I agree with the District Court that the United States is depriving appellee, Ephram Nestor, of his statutory right to old-age benefits in violation of the United States Constitution.

Nestor came to this country from Bulgaria in 1913 and lived here continuously for 43 years, until July 1956. He was then deported from this country for having been a Communist from 1933 to 1939. At that time membership in the Communist Party as such was not illegal and was not even a statutory ground for deportation. From December 1936 to January 1955 Nestor and his employers made regular payments to the Government under the Federal Insurance Contributions Act, 26 U.S.C. §§ 3101–3125. These funds went to a special federal old-age and survivors insurance trust fund under 42 U.S.C. § 401, in return for which Nestor, like millions of others, expected to receive payments when he reached the statutory age. In 1954, 15 years after Nestor had last been a Communist, and 18 years after he began to make payments into the old-age security fund, Congress passed a law providing, among other things, that any person who had been deported from this country because of past communist membership under 66 Stat. 205, 8 U.S.C. § 1251(a)(6)(C) should be wholly cut off from any benefits of the fund to which he had contributed under the law. 68 Stat. 1083, 42 U.S.C. § 402(n). After the Government deported Nestor in 1956 it notified his wife, who had remained in this country, that he was cut off and no further payments would be made to him. This action, it seems to me, takes Nestor's insurance without just compensation and in violation of the Due Process Clause of the Fifth Amendment. Moreover, it imposes an ex post facto law and bill of attainder by stamping him, without a court trial, as unworthy to receive that for which he has paid and which the Government promised to pay him. The fact that the Court is sustaining this action indicates the extent to which people are willing to go these days to overlook violation of the Constitution perpetrated against anyone who has ever even innocently belonged to the Communist Party.

In Lynch v. United States, 292 U.S. 571, this court unanimously held that Congress was without power to repudiate and abrogate in whole or in part its promises to pay amounts claimed by soldiers under the War Risk Insurance Act of 1917, §§ 400–405, 40 Stat. 409.  This Court held that such a repudiation was inconsistent with the provision of the Fifth Amendment that "No person shall be * * * deprived of life, liberty, or property, without due process of law; nor shall private property be taken for public use, without just compensation."  The Court today puts the *Lynch* case aside on the ground that "It is hardly profitable to engage in conceptualizations regarding 'earned rights' and 'gratuities.'"  From this sound premise the Court goes on to say that while "The 'right' to Social Security benefits is in one sense 'earned,'" yet the Government's insurance scheme now before us rests not on the idea of the contributors to the fund earning something, but simply provides that they may "justly call" upon the Government "in their later years, for protection from 'the rigors of the poor house as well as from the haunting fear that such a lot awaits them when journey's end is near.'"  These are nice words but they cannot conceal the fact that they simply tell the contributors to this insurance fund that despite their own and their employers' payments the Government, in paying the beneficiaries out of the fund, is merely giving them something for nothing and can stop doing so when it pleases.  This, in my judgment, reveals a complete misunderstanding of the purpose Congress and the country had in passing that law.  It was then generally agreed, as it is today, that it is not desirable that aged people think of the Government as giving them something for nothing.  * * * The people covered by this Act are now able to rely with complete assurance on the fact that they will be compelled to contribute regularly to this fund whenever each contribution falls due.  I believe they are entitled to rely with the same assurance on getting the benefits they have paid for and have been promised, when their disability or age makes their insurance payable under the terms of the law.  The Court did not permit the Government to break its plighted faith with the soldiers in the *Lynch* case; it said the Constitution forbade such governmental conduct.  I would say precisely the same thing here.

The Court consoles those whose insurance is taken away today, and others who may suffer the same fate in the future, by saying that a decision requiring the Social Security system to keep faith "would deprive it of the flexibility and boldness in adjustment to ever-changing conditions which it demands."  People who pay premiums for insurance usually think they are paying for insurance, not for "flexibility and boldness."  I cannot believe that any private insurance company in America would be permitted to repudiate its matured contracts with its policyholders who have regularly paid all their premiums in reliance upon the good faith of the company.  It is true, as the Court says, that the original Act contained a clause, still in force, that expressly reserves to Congress "[t]he right to alter, amend, or repeal any provision" of the Act.  Congress, of course, properly retained that power.  It could repeal the Act so as to cease to operate its old-age insurance activities for the future.  This means that it could stop covering new people, and even stop increasing its obligations to its old contributors. But that is quite different from disappointing the just expectations of the contributors to the fund which the Government has compelled them and their employers to pay its Treasury. There is nothing "conceptualistic" about saying, as this court did in *Lynch,* that such a taking as this the Constitution forbids. \* \* \*

## Charles A. Reich, *The New Property* \*

73 Yale L.J. 733 (1964).

### THE NEW FEUDALISM

The characteristics of the public interest state are varied, but there is an underlying philosophy that unites them. This is the doctrine that the wealth that flows from government is held by its recipients conditionally, subject to confiscation in the interest of the paramount state. This philosophy is epitomized in the most important of all judicial decisions concerning government largess, the case of Flemming v. Nestor. \* \* \*

The implications of Flemming v. Nestor are profound. No form of government largess is more personal or individual than an old age pension. No form is more clearly earned by the recipient, who, together with his employer, contributes to the Social Security fund during the years of his employment. No form is more obviously a compulsory substitute for private property; the tax on wage earner and employer might readily have gone to higher pay and higher private savings instead. No form is more relied on, and more often thought of as property. No form is more vital to the independence and dignity of the individual. Yet under the philosophy of Congress and the Court, a man or woman, after a lifetime of work, has no rights which may not be taken away to serve some public policy. The Court makes no effort to balance the interests at stake. The public policy that justifies cutting off benefits need not even be an important one or a wise one—so long as it is not utterly irrational, the Court will not interfere. In any clash between individual rights and public policy, the latter is automatically held to be superior.

The philosophy of Flemming v. Nestor resembles the philosophy of feudal tenure. Wealth is not "owned," or "vested" in the holders. Instead, it is held conditionally, the conditions being ones which seek to ensure the fulfillment of obligations imposed by the state. Just as the feudal system linked lord and vassal through a system of mutual dependence, obligation, and loyalty, so government largess binds man to the state. And, it may be added, loyalty or fealty to the state is often one of the essential conditions of modern tenure. In the many decisions taking away government largess for refusal to sign loyalty oaths, belonging to

\* Reprinted by permission of The Yale Law Journal Company and Fred B. Rothman & Company from *The Yale Law Journal,* Vol. 73, pp. 768–74, 787.

"subversive" organizations, or other similar grounds, there is more than a suggestion of the condition of fealty demanded in older times.

\* \* \*

The public interest state is not with us yet.  But we are left with large questions.  If the day comes when most private ownership is supplanted by government largess, how then will governmental power over individuals be contained?  What will dependence do to the American character?  What will happen to the Constitution, and particularly the Bill of Rights, if their limits may be bypassed by purchase, and if people lack an independent base from which to assert their individuality and claim their rights?  Without the security of the person which individual wealth provides and which largess fails to provide, what, indeed, will we become?  \* \* \*

The public interest state, as visualized above, represents in one sense the triumph of society over private property.  This triumph is the end point of a great and necessary movement for reform.  But somehow the result is different from what the reformers wanted.  Somehow the idealistic concept of the public interest has summoned up a doctrine monstrous and oppressive.  It is time to take another look at private property, and at the "public interest" philosophy that dominates its modern substitute, the largess of government.

\* \* \*

During the industrial revolution, when property was liberated from feudal restraints, philosophers hailed property as the basis of liberty, and argued that it must be free from the demands of government or society.  But as private property grew, so did abuses resulting from its use.  In a crowded world, a man's use of his property increasingly affected his neighbor, and one man's exercise of a right might seriously impair the rights of others.  Property became power over others; the farm landowner, the city landlord, and the working man's boss were able to oppress their tenants or employees.  Great aggregations of property resulted in private control of entire industries and basic services capable of affecting a whole area or even a nation.  At the same time much private property lost its individuality and in effect became socialized.  Multiple ownership of corporations helped to separate personality from property, and property from power.  When the corporations began to stop competing, to merge, agree, and make mutual plans, they became private governments.  Finally, they sought the aid and partnership of the state, and thus by their own volition became part of public government.

These changes led to a movement for reform, which sought to limit arbitrary private power and protect the common man.  Property rights were considered more the enemy than the friend of liberty.  The reformers argued that property must be separated from personality.  \* \* \*

The struggle between abuse and reform made it easy to forget the basic importance of individual private property.  The defense of private property was almost entirely a defense of its abuses—an attempt to defend not individual property but arbitrary private power over other human beings. Since this defense was cloaked in a defense of private property, it was natural for the reformers to attack too broadly. Walter Lippmann saw this in 1934:

> But the issue between the giant corporation and the public should not be allowed to obscure the truth that the only dependable foundation of personal liberty is the economic security of private property. * * * For we must not expect to find in ordinary men the stuff of martyrs, and we must, therefore, secure their freedom by their normal motives. There is no surer way to give men the courage to be free than to insure them a competence upon which they can rely. [Lippmann, The Method of Freedom 101 (1934).]

The reform took away some of the power of the corporations and transferred it to government. In this transfer there was much good, for the power was made responsive to the majority rather than to the arbitrary and selfish few. But the reform did not restore the individual to his domain. What the corporation had taken from him, the reform simply handed on to government. And government carried further the powers formerly exercised by the corporation. Government as an employer, or as a dispenser of wealth, has used the theory that it was handing out gratuities to claim a managerial power as great as that which the capitalists claimed. Moreover, the corporations allied themselves with, or actually took over, part of government's system of power. Today it is the combined power of government and the corporations that presses against the individual.

From the individual's point of view, it is not any particular kind of power, but all kinds of power, that are to be feared.

\* \* \*

If the individual is to survive in a collective society, he must have protection against its ruthless pressures. There must be sanctuaries or enclaves where no majority can reach. To shelter the solitary human spirit does not merely make possible the fulfillment of individuals; it also gives society the power to change, to grow, and to regenerate, and hence to endure. These were the objects which property sought to achieve, and can no longer achieve. The challenge of the future will be to construct, for the society that is coming, institutions and laws to carry on this work. Just as the Homestead Act was a deliberate effort to foster individual values at an earlier time, so we must try to build an economic basis for liberty today—a Homestead Act for rootless twentieth century man. We must create a new property.

## United States Railroad Retirement Board v. Fritz
449 U.S. 166 (1980).

■ JUSTICE REHNQUIST delivered the opinion of the Court.

The United States District Court for the Southern District of Indiana held unconstitutional a section of the Railroad Retirement Act of 1974, and the United States Railroad Retirement Board has appealed to this Court pursuant to 28 U.S.C. § 1252.

The 1974 Act fundamentally restructured the railroad retirement system. The Act's predecessor statute, adopted in 1937, provided a system of retirement and disability benefits for persons who pursued careers in the railroad industry. Under that statute, a person who worked for both railroad and nonrailroad employers and who qualified for railroad retirement benefits and social security benefits, received retirement benefits under both systems and an accompanying "windfall" benefit.[1] The legislative history of the 1974 Act shows that the payment of windfall benefits threatened the railroad retirement system with bankruptcy by the year 1981.[2] Congress therefore determined to place the system on a "sound financial basis" by eliminating future accruals of those benefits.[3] Congress

1. Under the old Act, as under the new, an employee who worked 10 years in the railroad business qualified for railroad retirement benefits. If the employee also worked outside the railroad industry for a sufficient enough time to qualify for social security benefits, he qualified for dual benefits. Due to the formula under which those benefits were computed, however, persons who split their employment between railroad and nonrailroad employment received dual benefits in excess of the amount they would have received had they not split their employment. For example, if 10 years of either railroad or nonrailroad employment would produce a monthly benefit of $300, an additional 10 years of the same employment at the same level of creditable compensation would not double that benefit, but would increase it by some lesser amount to say $500. If that 20 years of service had been divided equally between railroad and nonrailroad employment, however, the social security benefit would be $300 and the railroad retirement benefit would also be $300, for a total benefit of $600. The $100 difference in the example constitutes the "windfall" benefit.

2. The relevant Committee Reports stated "Resolution of the so called 'dual benefit' problem is central both to insuring the fiscal soundness of the railroad retirement system and to establishing equitable retirement benefits for all railroad employees." The reason for the problem was that a financial interchange agreement entered into in 1951 between the social security and railroad systems caused the entire cost of the windfall benefits to be borne by the railroad system, not the social security system. The annual drain on the railroad system amounted to approximately $450 million per year, and if it were not for "the problem of dual beneficiaries, the railroad retirement system would be almost completely solvent."

3. Congress eliminated future accruals of windfall benefits by establishing a two-tier system for benefits. The first tier is measured by what the social security system would pay on the basis of combined railroad and nonrailroad service, while the second tier is based on railroad service alone. However, both tiers are part of the railroad retirement system, rather than the first tier being placed directly under social security, and the benefits actually paid by social security on the basis of nonrailroad employment are deducted so as to eliminate the windfall benefit.

The Railroad Retirement Act of 1974 had its origins in 1970 when Congress created the Commission of Railroad Retirement to study the actuarial soundness of the railroad retirement system. The Commission submitted its report in 1972 and identified "dual benefits and their attendant windfalls" as a principal cause of the system's financial difficulties. It also found that windfall benefits were inequitable, favoring those employees who split their employment over those employees who spent their entire career in the railroad industry. It therefore recommended that future accruals of windfall benefits be eliminated by the establishment of a two-tier system, somewhat similar to the type of system eventually adopted by Congress. It also recom-

also enacted various transitional provisions, including a grandfather provision, § 231b(h), which expressly preserved windfall benefits for some classes of employees.

In restructuring the Railroad Retirement Act in 1974, Congress divided employees into various groups. *First,* those employees who lacked the requisite 10 years of railroad employment to qualify for railroad retirement benefits as of January 1, 1975, the changeover date, would have their retirement benefits computed under the new system and would not receive any windfall benefit. *Second,* those individuals already retired and already receiving dual benefits as of the changeover date would have their benefits computed under the old system and would continue to receive a windfall benefit. *Third,* those employees who had qualified for both railroad and social security benefits as of the changeover date, but who had not yet retired as of that date (and thus were not yet receiving dual benefits), were entitled to windfall benefits if they had (1) performed some railroad service in 1974 or (2) had a "current connection" with the railroad industry as of December 31, 1974, or (3) completed 25 years of railroad service as of December 31, 1974. *Fourth,* those employees who had qualified for railroad benefits as of the changeover date, but lacked a current connection with the railroad industry in 1974 and lacked 25 years of railroad employment, could obtain a lesser amount of windfall benefit if they had qualified for social security benefits as of the year (prior to 1975) they left railroad employment.

Thus, an individual who, as of the changeover date, was unretired and had 11 years of railroad employment and sufficient nonrailroad employment to qualify for social security benefits is eligible for the full windfall amount if he worked for the railroad in 1974 or had a current connection with the railroad as of December 31, 1974, or his later retirement date. But an unretired individual with 24 years of railroad service and sufficient nonrailroad service to qualify for social security benefits is not eligible for a full windfall amount unless he worked for the railroad in 1974, or had a current connection with the railroad as of December 31, 1974 or his later retirement date. And an employee with 10 years of railroad employment who qualified for social security benefits only after leaving the railroad industry will not receive a reduced windfall benefit while an employee who

mended that "legally vested rights of railroad workers" be preserved. An employee who was fully insured under both the railroad and social security systems as of the changeover date (i.e., by having at least 10 years of railroad employment and the requisite length of social security employment) was deemed to have "legally vested rights."

Following receipt of the Commission's report, Congress requested members of management, labor, and retirees to form a Joint Labor Management Railroad Retirement Negotiating Committee (hereinafter known as the Joint Committee) and submit a report,

"taking into account" the recommendations of the Commission. The Joint Committee outlined its proposals in the form of a letter to Congress. Although it agreed with the Commission that future accruals of windfall benefits be eliminated, it differed as to the protection to be afforded those already statutorily entitled to benefits and recommended the transitional provisions that were eventually adopted by Congress. A bill embodying those principles was drafted and submitted to Congress, where the relevant committees held lengthy hearings and submitted detailed reports.

qualified for social security benefits prior to leaving the railroad industry would receive a reduced benefit. It was with these complicated comparisons that Congress wrestled in 1974.

Appellees filed this class action in the United States District Court for the Southern District of Indiana, seeking a declaratory judgment that 45 U.S.C. § 231b(h) is unconstitutional under the Due Process Clause of the Fifth Amendment because it irrationally distinguishes between classes of annuitants.

* * *

The initial issue presented by this case is the appropriate standard of judicial review to be applied when social and economic legislation enacted by Congress is challenged as being violative of the Fifth Amendment to the United States Constitution. There is no claim here that Congress has taken property in violation of the Fifth Amendment, since railroad benefits, like social security benefits, are not contractual and may be altered or even eliminated at any time. And because the distinctions drawn in § 231b(h) do not burden fundamental constitutional rights or create "suspect" classifications, such as race or national origin, we may put cases involving judicial review of such claims to one side.

* * *

[The Court reviewed prior "rational relationship" cases.]

In more recent years, however, the Court in cases involving social and economic benefits has consistently refused to invalidate on equal protection grounds legislation which it simply deemed unwise or unartfully drawn.

* * *

Applying those principles to this case, the plain language of § 231b(h) marks the beginning and end of our inquiry. There Congress determined that some of those who in the past received full windfall benefits would not continue to do so. Because Congress could have eliminated windfall benefits for all classes of employees, it is not constitutionally impermissible for Congress to have drawn lines between groups of employees for the purpose of phasing out those benefits.

The only remaining question is whether Congress achieved its purpose in a patently arbitrary or irrational way. The classification here is not arbitrary, says appellant, because it is an attempt to protect the relative equities of employees and to provide benefits to career railroad employees. Congress fully protected, for example, the expectations of those employees who had already retired and those unretired employees who had 25 years of railroad employment. Conversely, Congress denied all windfall benefits to those employees who lacked 10 years of railroad employment. Congress additionally provided windfall benefits, in lesser amount, to those employees with 10 years railroad employment who had qualified for social security benefits at the time they had left railroad employment, regardless of a current connection with the industry in 1974 or on their retirement date.

Thus, the only eligible former railroad employees denied full windfall benefits are those, like appellees, who had no statutory entitlement to dual benefits at the time they left the railroad industry, but thereafter became eligible for dual benefits when they subsequently qualified for social security benefits.   Congress could properly conclude that persons who had actually acquired statutory entitlement to windfall benefits while still employed in the railroad industry had a greater equitable claim to those benefits than the members of appellees' class who were no longer in railroad employment when they became eligible for dual benefits.   Furthermore, the "current connection" test is not a patently arbitrary means for determining which employees are "career railroaders," particularly since the test has been used by Congress elsewhere as an eligibility requirement for retirement benefits.   Congress could assume that those who had a current connection with the railroad industry when the Act was passed in 1974, or who returned to the industry before their retirement, were more likely than those who had left the industry prior to 1974 and who never returned, to be among the class of persons who pursue careers in the railroad industry, the class for whom the Railroad Retirement Act was designed.

Where, as here, there are plausible reasons for Congress' action, our inquiry is at an end.   It is, of course, "constitutionally irrelevant whether this reasoning in fact underlay the legislative decision," because this Court has never insisted that a legislative body articulate its reasons for enacting a statute.   This is particularly true where the legislature must necessarily engage in a process of line drawing.   The "task of classifying persons for * * * benefits * * * inevitably requires that some persons who have an almost equally strong claim to favored treatment be placed on different sides of the line," and the fact the line might have been drawn differently at some points is a matter for legislative, rather than judicial, consideration.

Finally, we disagree with the District Court's conclusion that Congress was unaware of what it accomplished or that it was misled by the groups that appeared before it.   If this test were applied literally to every member of any legislature that ever voted on a law, there would be very few laws which would survive it.   The language of the statute is clear, and we have historically assumed that Congress intended what it enacted.   To be sure, appellees lost a political battle in which they had a strong interest, but this is neither the first nor the last time that such a result will occur in the legislative forum.   What we have said is enough to dispose of the claims that Congress not only failed to accept appellee's argument as to restructuring in toto, but that such failure denied them equal protection of the laws guaranteed by the Fifth Amendment.

For the foregoing reasons, the judgment of the District Court is

*Reversed.*

■ JUSTICE STEVENS, concurring in the judgment.

* * *

As is often true, this legislation is the product of multiple and somewhat inconsistent purposes that led to certain compromises.  One purpose was to eliminate in the future the benefit that is described by the Court as a "windfall benefit" and by JUSTICE BRENNAN as an "earned dual benefit." That aim was incident to the broader objective of protecting the solvency of the entire railroad retirement program.  Two purposes that conflicted somewhat with this broad objective were the purposes of preserving those benefits that had already vested and of increasing the level of payments to beneficiaries whose rights were not otherwise to be changed.  As JUSTICE BRENNAN emphasizes, Congress originally intended to protect *all* vested benefits, but it ultimately sacrificed some benefits in the interest of achieving other objectives.

Given these conflicting purposes, I believe the decisive questions are (1) whether Congress can rationally reduce the vested benefits of some employees to improve the solvency of the entire program while simultaneously increasing the benefits of others;  and (2) whether, in deciding which vested benefits to reduce, Congress may favor annuitants whose railroad service was more recent than that of disfavored annuitants who had an equal or greater quantum of employment.

My answer to both questions is in the affirmative.  The congressional purpose to eliminate dual benefits is unquestionably legitimate;  that legitimacy is not undermined by the adjustment in the level of remaining benefits in response to inflation in the economy.  As for the second question, some hardship—in the form of frustrated long-term expectations—must inevitably result from any reduction in vested benefits.  Arguably, therefore, Congress had a duty—and surely it had the right to decide—to eliminate no more vested benefits than necessary to achieve its fiscal purpose.  Having made that decision, any distinction it chose within the class of vested beneficiaries would involve a difference of degree rather than a difference in entitlement.  I am satisfied that a distinction based upon currency of railroad employment represents an impartial method of identifying that sort of difference.  Because retirement plans frequently provide greater benefits for recent retirees than for those who retired years ago—and thus give a greater reward for recent service than for past service of equal duration—the basis for the statutory discrimination is supported by relevant precedent.  It follows, in my judgment, that the timing of the employees' railroad service is a "reasonable basis" for the classification as well as a "ground of difference having a fair and substantial relation to the object of the legislation."

Accordingly, I concur in the judgment.

■ JUSTICE BRENNAN, with whom JUSTICE MARSHALL joins, dissenting.

\* \* \*

The third way in which the Court has deviated from the principles of rational basis scrutiny is its failure to analyze whether the challenged classification is genuinely related to the purpose identified by the Court. Having suggested that "equitable considerations" underlay the challenged classification—in direct contradiction to Congress' evaluation of those considerations, and in the face of evidence that the classification was the product of private negotiation by interested parties, inadequately examined and understood by Congress—the Court proceeds to accept that suggestion without further analysis.

An unadorned claim of "equitable" considerations is, of course, difficult to assess. It seems to me that before a court may accept a litigant's assertion of "equity," it must inquire what principles of equity or fairness might genuinely support such a judgment. But apparently the Court does not demand such inquiry, for it has failed to address any equitable considerations that might be relevant to the challenged classification.

In my view, the following considerations are of greatest relevance to the equities of this case: (1) contribution to the system; (2) reasonable expectation and reliance; (3) need; and (4) character of service to the railroad industry. With respect to each of these considerations, I would conclude that appellees have as great an equitable claim to their earned dual benefits as do their more favored coworkers, who remain entitled to their earned dual benefits under § 231b(h).

\* \* \*

Even if I were able to accept the notation that Congress considered it equitable to deprive a class of railroad retirees of a portion of their vested earned benefits because they no longer worked for the railroad, I would still consider the means adopted in § 231b(h) irrational. Under this provision, a retiree is favored by retention of his full vested earned benefits if he had worked so much as one day for a railroad in 1974. This is a plainly capricious basis for distinguishing among retirees, every one of whom had worked in the industry for at least 10 years: the fortuity of one day of employment in a particular year should not govern entitlement to benefits earned over a lifetime.

I therefore conclude that the Government's proffered justification of "equitable considerations," accepted without question by the Court, cannot be defended. Rather, as the legislative history repeatedly states, equity and fairness demand that appellees, like their coworkers, retain the vested dual benefits they earned prior to 1974. A conscientious application of rational basis scrutiny demands, therefore, that § 231b(h) be invalidated.

Equal protection rationality analysis does not empower the courts to second-guess the wisdom of legislative classifications. On this we are agreed, and have been for over 40 years. On the other hand, we are not powerless to probe beneath claims by Government attorneys concerning the means and ends of Congress. Otherwise, we would defer not to the considered judgment of Congress, but to the arguments of litigators. The instant case serves as an example of the unfortunate consequence of such misplaced deference. Because the Court is willing to accept a tautological analysis of congressional purpose, an assertion of "equitable" considerations contrary to the expressed judgment of Congress, and a classification patently unrelated to achievement of the identified purpose, it succeeds in effectuating neither equity nor congressional intent.

I respectfully dissent.

## QUESTIONS

**1.**  Has Professor Reich's criticism of Flemming v. Nestor been answered in *Fritz?*  Who had what expectations?  Were they legitimate?  Is it wrong for Congress to reduce expected benefits?  What would be the gains and costs from giving such expectations constitutional protection?

**2.**  Would judicial review of legislative actions in this field be feasible?  Justice Brennan seems to want courts to find the "general purpose" of Congress.  Does a body like Congress have "*a*" purpose?  Can it be known?

**3.**  Do you prefer the judicial role described by the majority in *Fritz,* or that undertaken in Opinion of the Justices, supra p. 1239?

## 4.   Gender Discrimination in Social Security

## Califano v. Goldfarb

430 U.S. 199 (1977).

■ Mr. Justice Brennan announced the judgment of the Court and delivered an opinion in which Mr. Justice White, Mr. Justice Marshall, and Mr. Justice Powell joined.

Under the Federal Old-Age, Survivors, and Disability Insurance Benefits (OASDI) program, 42 U.S.C. §§ 401–431 (1970 ed. and Supp. V), survivors' benefits based on the earnings of a deceased husband covered by the Act are payable to his widow.  Such benefits on the basis of the earnings of a deceased wife covered by the Act are payable to the widower, however, only if he "was receiving at least one-half of his support" from his deceased wife.  The question in this case is whether this gender-based distinction violates the Due Process Clause of the Fifth Amendment.

\* \* \*

Mrs. Hannah Goldfarb worked as a secretary in the New York City public school system for almost 25 years until her death in 1968.  During that entire time she paid in full all social security taxes required by the Federal Insurance Contributions Act.  She was survived by her husband, Leon Goldfarb, now aged 72, a retired federal employee.  Leon duly applied for widower's benefits.  The application was denied with the explanation that

> "You do not qualify for a widower's benefit because you do not meet one of the requirements for such entitlement.  This requirement is that you must have been receiving at least one-half support from your wife when she died."

\* \* \*

Weinberger v. Wiesenfeld, 420 U.S. 636 (1975), like the instant case, presented the question in the context of the OASDI program. There the Court held unconstitutional a provision that denied father's insurance benefits to surviving widowers with children in their care, while authorizing similar mother's benefits to similarly situated widows. Paula Wiesenfeld, the principal source of her family's support, and covered by the Act, died in childbirth, survived by the baby and her husband Stephen. Stephen applied for survivors' benefits for himself and his infant son. Benefits were allowed the baby but denied the father on the ground that "mother's benefits" under § 402(g) were available only to women. The Court reversed, holding that the gender-based distinction made by § 402(g) was "indistinguishable from that invalidated in [Frontiero v. Richardson, 411 U.S. 677 (1973)]" and therefore:

> "[While] the notion that men are more likely than women to be the primary supporters of their spouses and children is not entirely without empirical support, * * * such a gender-based generalization cannot suffice to justify the denigration of the efforts of women who do work and whose earnings contribute significantly to their families' support.

> "Section 402(g) clearly operates, as did the statutes invalidated by our judgment in *Frontiero,* to deprive women of protection for their families which men receive as a result of their employment. Indeed, the classification here is in some ways more pernicious. * * * [I]n this case social security taxes were deducted from Paula's salary during the years in which she worked. Thus, she not only failed to receive for her family the same protection which a similarly situated male worker would have received, but she also was deprived of a portion of her own earnings in order to contribute to the fund out of which benefits would be paid to others."

Precisely the same reasoning condemns the gender-based distinction made by § 402(f)(1)(D) in this case. For that distinction, too, operates "to deprive women of protection for their families which men receive as a result of their employment": social security taxes were deducted from Hannah Goldfarb's salary during the quarter century she worked as a secretary, yet, in consequence of § 402(f)(1)(D), she also "not only failed to receive for her [spouse] the same protection which a similarly situated male worker would have received [for his spouse] but she also was deprived of a portion of her own earnings in order to contribute to the fund out of which benefits would be paid to others." *Wiesenfeld* thus inescapably compels the conclusion reached by the District Court that the gender-based differentiation created by § 402(f)(1)(D)—that results in the efforts of female workers required to pay social security taxes producing less protection for their spouses than is produced by the efforts of men—is forbidden by the Constitution, at least when supported by no more substantial justification than "archaic and overbroad" generalizations, or " 'old notions,' " such as "assumptions as to dependency," that are more consistent with "the role-typing society has long imposed," than with contemporary reality. Thus § 402(f)(1)(D) " '[b]y providing dissimilar treatment for men and women who are * * * similarly situated * * * violates the [Fifth Amendment].' * * *"

Appellant, however, would focus equal protection analysis, not upon the discrimination against the covered wage earning female, but rather upon whether her surviving widower was unconstitutionally discriminated against by burdening him but not a surviving widow with proof of dependency. The gist of the argument is that, analyzed from the perspective of the widower, "the denial of benefits reflected the congressional judgment that aged widowers as a class were sufficiently likely not to be dependent upon their wives that it was appropriate to deny them benefits unless they were in fact dependent."

* * *

From its inception, the social security system has been a program of social insurance. Covered employees and their employers pay taxes into a fund administered distinct from the general federal revenues to purchase protection against the economic consequences of old age, disability, and death. But under § 402(f)(1)(D) female insureds received less protection for their spouses solely because of their sex. Mrs. Goldfarb worked and paid social security taxes for 25 years at the same rate as her male colleagues, but because of § 402(f)(1)(D) the insurance protection received by the males was broader than hers. Plainly then § 402(f)(1)(D) disadvantages women contributors to the social security system as compared to similarly situated men. The section then "impermissibly discriminates against a female wage earner because it provides her family less protection than it provides that of a male wage earner, even though the family needs may be identical." In a sense, of course, both the female wage earner and her surviving spouse are disadvantaged by operation of the statute, but this is because "Social Security is designed * * * for the protection of the *family,*" and the section discriminates against one particular category of family—that in which the female spouse is a wage earner covered by social security. Therefore decision of the equal protection challenge in this case cannot focus solely on the distinction drawn between widowers and widows but, as *Wiesenfeld* held, upon the gender-based discrimination against covered female wage earners as well.

* * *

We conclude, therefore, that the differential treatment of nondependent widows and widowers results not, as appellant asserts, from a deliberate congressional intention to remedy the arguably greater needs of the former, but rather from an intention to aid the dependent spouses of deceased wage earners, coupled with a presumption that wives are usually dependent. This presents precisely the situation faced in *Wiesenfeld.* The only conceivable justification for writing the presumption of wives' dependency into the statute is the assumption * * * that it would save the Government time, money, and effort simply to pay benefits to all widows, rather than to require proof of dependency of both sexes. We held in *Wiesenfeld,* and therefore hold again here, that such assumptions do not suffice to justify a gender-based discrimination in the distribution of employment-related benefits.

*Affirmed.*

[Justice Stevens concurred, focusing on the husband's claim for benefits rather than on the wife's tax obligation, but concluding that "this discrimination against a group of males is merely the accidental byproduct of a traditional way of thinking about females."

[Justice Rehnquist, for four dissenters, would have upheld the provision's constitutionality.]

## NOTES AND QUESTIONS

**1.** Congress responded to Califano v. Goldfarb by repealing the dependency requirement for widowers and husbands but (to avoid an unacceptable fiscal problem for the Social Security trust fund) mandating that retired federal and state workers offset their government pensions against what they would receive as the spouse of a Social Security participant. Social Security Amendments of 1977, codified at 42 U.S.C. § 402(b)(4)(A), c(1), (c)(2)(A), (f)(1). But, to protect the reliance interests of those counting on benefits under the old rules, the new law exempted those eligible for special benefits for the five-year period 1977–82. The effect was to continue for five years the discrimination in favor of undependent widows and wives that had been held unconstitutional in *Goldfarb.* The Supreme Court unanimously upheld this phase-in of the end of gender-based discrimination. Heckler v. Mathews, 465 U.S. 728 (1984).

**2.** *Goldfarb* was followed with respect to Missouri's Workers' Compensation law in Wengler v. Druggists Mutual Insurance Co., 446 U.S. 142 (1980) (striking down provision that widower collects only if incapacitated or dependent, but widow collects without such showing).

**3.** The Social Security Act provided that illegitimate children ineligible to inherit under state law could receive benefits based on their father's disability only if he had acknowledged paternity by paying for their support prior to the onset of the disability. The Supreme Court held that the rule denied plaintiff "the equal protection of the law guaranteed by the due process provisions of the Fifth Amendment." The Court found the statutory distinctions both overinclusive (compensating some, for example some legitimate children, who had not been dependent on their disabled father) and under-inclusive (denying certain illegitimates the opportunity to show dependence). Justice Rehnquist, dissenting, called the Court's opinion "a rather impressionistic determination that Congress' efforts to cope with spurious claims of entitlement * * * are simply not satisfactory to the members of this Court." Jimenez v. Weinberger, 417 U.S. 628 (1974).

But in Califano v. Boles, 443 U.S. 282 (1979), the Court upheld denial of "mother's insurance benefits" (a misnomer: they are also paid to fathers) to the mother or father of the decedent's illegitimate children. The Court split five to four, the opinions differing over whether the benefit was mainly cash for the spouse or a way to permit the surviving parent to stay home and care for the children. If the latter, a categorization that refuses the advantage to illegitimate children is hard to distinguish from *Jimenez*.

**4.** The Social Security Act provides for widow's benefits only to women who were married to the deceased for at least nine months before his death. The purpose is to prevent marriages arranged solely to obtain the benefits. A three-judge district court found this an unacceptable irrebuttable presumption. The Supreme Court, per Justice Rehnquist, reversed. "The question is whether Congress, its concern having been reasonably aroused by the possibility of an abuse which it legitimately desired to avoid, could rationally have concluded both that a particular limitation or qualification would protect against its occurrence, and that the expense and other difficulties of individual determination justified the inherent imprecision of a prophylactic rule. We conclude that the duration-of-relationship test meets this constitutional standard." Among Justice Rehnquist's distinctions from earlier irrebuttable presumption decisions was the statement that "unlike the claims involved in *Stanley* [parental fitness] and *LaFleur* [job], a noncontractual claim to receive funds from the public treasury enjoys no constitutionally protected status * * * Unlike the statutory scheme in *Vlandis* [in-state tuition at state university], the Social Security Act does not purport to speak in terms of the bona fides of the parties to a marriage, but then make plainly relevant evidence of such bona fides inadmissible." Justices Douglas, Brennan, and Marshall found the result "flatly contrary to several recent decisions, specifically * * * Jimenez v. Weinberger." Weinberger v. Salfi, 422 U.S. 749 (1975).

**5.** See Davis v. Califano, 603 F.2d 618 (7th Cir.1979), where the Court upheld the Social Security Administration's denial of widow's benefits to decedent's second "wife," Mary, because decedent had only obtained from his first wife, Novella, a "divorce from bed and board," a form of legal separation, not a final divorce. Decedent and Mary were married in 1942, divorced in 1954, and remarried in 1955. He died in 1972. Under 42 U.S.C. § 416(h)(1)(B), there can be a "deemed spouse," but not if a legally entitled widow also claims. The district judge had ordered that the two women split the benefits. The idea of dividing the benefits apparently traces to Rosenberg v. Richardson, 538 F.2d 487 (2d Cir.1976).

**6.** Bowen v. Owens, 476 U.S. 340 (1986), upheld against a "rationality" challenge Social Security's policy of paying more to widowed spouses than to divorced spouses upon remarriage. Justices Brennan, Marshall, and Blackmun dissented, saying the discrimination is unconstitutional.

## Social Security Administration, What Every Woman Should Know

http://www.ssa.gov/pubs/10127.html (1997).

### Social Security And Today's Woman

Nearly every American—man, woman and child—has Social Security protection, either as a worker or as a dependent of a worker. When the program began in 1935, Social Security benefits were limited to retired or deceased workers and their families, and most workers were men. Most women did not work outside the home.

Today, the role of women is far different. Nearly 60 percent of all women are in the nation's workforce. Many women work throughout their adult life. Although Social Security has always provided benefits for women, it has taken on added significance. More women work, pay Social Security taxes and earn credit toward a monthly income for their retirement. Women with children earn Social Security protection for themselves and their families. This could mean monthly benefits to a woman and her family if she becomes disabled and can no longer work. If she dies, her survivors may be eligible for benefits.

Although some women choose a lifetime career outside the home, many women work for a few years, leave the labor force to raise their children, and then return to work. Some women choose not to work outside their home. They usually are covered by Social Security through their husband's work and can receive benefits when he retires, becomes disabled or dies.

Whether a woman works, has worked or has never worked, it is important that she know exactly what Social Security coverage means to her. She also should know about Social Security coverage for anyone she may hire as a household worker or provider of child care. She needs to know what to do if she changes her name. And she needs to know that if she receives a pension for work not covered by Social Security, her Social Security benefits could be affected.  * * *

## When You're Employed Or Self–Employed

* * *

If you are married and your husband is age 62 or older, he may qualify for payments if you become disabled. He may qualify at any age if he is caring for your child, who is under age 16 or disabled and entitled to benefits.

When you die, both your widower and your dependent children may receive monthly survivors benefits. A one-time payment of $255 also may be payable to your widower or dependent children.

If there are no dependent children, your widower must be either age 60 or older or between the ages of 50 and 60 and disabled to qualify for benefits on your work record. If you have dependent parents age 62 or older, they may be eligible for payments when you die.

* * *

## When You Retire

* * *

If you're married, you can receive retirement benefits on your own record or spouse's benefits on your husband's. Your husband can get retirement benefits at age 62 or older, either on his record, or as a spouse on your record. People who are eligible for benefits on more than one work record generally receive the larger benefit amount. (The same rule applies to children who are eligible for benefits on both parents' record.)

If you've had high earnings, it's likely that your own benefits will be higher than a spouse's benefit. On the other hand, if you stopped working for several years or had low earnings, the spouse's benefit may be higher. At age 65, a wife receives 50 percent of what her husband is entitled to at age 65. When you apply for retirement benefits, a Social Security representative can tell you whether you will get a higher benefit on your own record or on your husband's.

If you earned your own Social Security credits, you have certain options at retirement. For example, suppose your husband continues to work past age 65 and doesn't collect Social Security benefits. You can retire and get benefits based on your own record. Then when he retires, you can receive benefits on his record if they would be higher.

Or, you can take reduced benefits on your wage record before age 65. If you do, your benefit will always be reduced—even if you take reduced benefits on your own record and then take wife's benefits when your husband retires. The same benefit rules and options apply to a husband who's eligible for retirement benefits on both his own and his wife's work record.

Your husband may qualify for benefits on your work record at any age if he is caring for your child who is under age 16 or disabled and entitled to benefits. When you retire, your children can qualify for benefits on your record if they meet the same conditions as if you were disabled.

* * *

## If You've Never Been Employed

You may be eligible for spouse's benefits if you are married. If you make your home and family your career, you and your family have Social Security protection through your husband's work. You can receive benefits when he retires, becomes disabled or dies.

You can receive benefits if you are caring for a child who is under age 16 or disabled and entitled to benefits. If you don't have a child in your care, you must be age 62 or older to get benefits when your husband becomes disabled or retires.

If you choose to begin receiving retirement benefits before age 65, your benefit amount will be permanently reduced. If you wait until you're age 65, you'll get the full wife's benefits, which is 50 percent of the amount your husband is entitled to at age 65. (The age at which full benefits are payable will increase in the future.)

* * *

## When Your Marital Status Changes

If your husband dies, you can receive widow's benefits if you are age 60 or older. If you're disabled, you can get widow's benefits as early as age 50.

The amount of your monthly payment will depend on your age when you start getting benefits. It also will depend on the amount your deceased husband would have been entitled to, or was receiving, when he died.

Widow's benefits range from 71 percent of the deceased husband's benefit amount, if they begin at age 60, to 100 percent, if they begin at age 65. So, if you start receiving benefits at age 65, you'll get 100 percent of the amount your husband would be receiving if he were still alive. (Starting in 2005, the age at which the 100 percent widow's benefit is payable will be increased gradually until it reaches age 66 in 2011 and age 67 in 2029.)

If you are a disabled widow between the ages of 50 and 59, your monthly benefit would be 71 percent of your deceased husband's benefit amount.

The following are some points to remember:

- If you are entitled to retirement benefits on your own work record, you can take reduced retirement payments at age 62 and then receive the full widow's benefit at age 65.

- If you are eligible for benefits on your own work record, you may want to take reduced widow's benefits until you are age 65 and file a claim for retirement benefits on your own record.

- If you delay your retirement beyond age 65, your future benefits will increase each year by a certain percentage. For example, if you were born in 1935, your benefit will increase six percent each year you delay retirement between ages 65 and 70.

\* \* \*

If you remarry, you will continue to receive benefits on your deceased husband's Social Security record. However, if your current husband is a Social Security beneficiary, you may want to apply for a wife's benefit on his record if it would be larger than your widow's benefit. You cannot get both.

If you are a widow with children, you may be eligible for a widow's benefit at any age when you are caring for a child who is under age 16 or disabled and entitled to benefits. Unmarried children may receive survivors benefits on your husband's record until they are age 18, or until age 19 if they are attending elementary or secondary school full time.

Your benefits will stop when you no longer have a child under age 16 or disabled in your care. Usually, your benefits also will stop if you remarry, but there are some exceptions to this rule (see above). Benefits to your children will continue as long as they remain eligible for payments, even if you remarry.

* * *

### If You Are Divorced

You can receive benefits on your ex-husband's Social Security record if he is receiving Social Security benefits (or is deceased); and

- your marriage lasted 10 years or longer;
- you are presently unmarried; and
- you are age 62 or older (if he is deceased, you can collect benefits at age 60 and age 50 if you become disabled).

If your ex-husband has not applied for benefits, but can qualify for them and is age 62 or older, you can receive benefits on his record if you have been divorced from him for at least two years and meet the requirements listed above.

If your ex-husband is deceased, you can receive benefits on his record even though you were not married to him for 10 years—

- if you are caring for his child who also is your natural or legally adopted child and is under age 16 or disabled; and
- you are unmarried.

Your benefits will continue until the child reaches age 16 or the child's disability ceases.

The amount of benefits you receive as a divorced spouse does not affect the amount of benefits another spouse receives on your ex-husband's record.

Many women get a higher benefit based on their ex-husband's work record than they get on their own record, especially if he is deceased.
* * *

(Note: the same conditions apply to a divorced husband whose eligibility for benefits is based on his ex-wife's Social Security record.)

### You Also Need To Know

Make sure that your Social Security record shows your correct name. This is especially important if you are employed because your employer reports your earnings under the name you supply.

Whenever you change the name you use in employment—whether because of marriage, divorce or other reasons—be sure to report the change to Social Security. Otherwise, your earnings may not be properly recorded and you may not receive all the Social Security credit due you for your work.

Even if you don't work, you should report any name change so that your record will show the correct name when you apply for benefits. * * *

If you hire a household worker, you're responsible for seeing that wages you pay him or her are properly reported. You must deduct Social Security taxes from the wages if you pay the person $1,000 or more during the year. (The amount is indexed for inflation and could rise in future years.) You must pay an equal amount of tax because you are the employer and send the combined taxes to the Internal Revenue Service. You can report the earnings and pay the taxes when you file your federal income tax return. * * *

NOTE AND QUESTION

A 1979 publication of the Social Security Bulletin described the concerns about the treatment of women by the Social Security program.

"These concerns include:

- Married women workers get substantially lower benefits than men workers both because they frequently spend time out of the paid labor force (or work part time) to perform homemaker or childcare activities and because average wages for women are lower than for men.

- The divorced wife's benefit of 50 percent of the worker's benefit is often not adequate to support a divorced homemaker living alone. A divorced person has no social security protection based on the marriage if it lasted less than 10 years. * * *

- Widowed homemakers under age 60 cannot receive benefits unless they are either at least age 50 and disabled or are caring for children. Many widows have no social security protection during a period when they may face difficulty entering or reentering the labor force.

- Women working in the home have gaps in disability protection. Benefits are not provided for disabled homemakers or their children if the homemaker has no recent attachment to the paid work force. Widows who become disabled under age 50 do not have disability protection.

- Aged widows frequently remain on the benefit rolls for many years; they often do not have resources to supplement their social security benefits, may live in poverty, and may need additional protection.

A second area of concern centers on the equity of benefits between one- and two-earner couples and married and single workers. These concerns include:

- * * * Married women may find that the social security protection they earn as workers may duplicate, rather than add to, the protection they already have as spouses.

- Some two-earner couples are concerned that benefits are often higher for couples where one spouse earned all (or most) of the income than for couples where both spouses had earnings even though their total family earnings are the same.

- Since benefits are payable to dependents, married workers receive greater protection under social security than single workers, even though both pay social security taxes at the same rate; single workers may view this situation as inequitable.

See *Men and Women: Changing Roles and Social Security,* Hew Summary of Study by Social Security Administration Required by Social Security Amendments of 1977.

In light of the 1997 Social Security Administration publication, do any of these concerns appear to have been addressed?

## 5.   SOCIAL SECURITY POLICY

## Social Security Administration Advisory Council, Findings, Recommendations and Statements of the 1994–96 Advisory Council

http://www.ssa.gov/policy/adcouncil/findings.htm overview (1997).

In her charge to the Advisory Council, the Secretary of Health and Human Services, in consultation with the Commissioner of Social Security, asked the Council to look particularly at the long-term financing of Social Security.   This is the first Advisory group since 1979 to give its major emphasis to long-term financing questions in its review of the system. * * *

While the Council has not found any short-term financing problems with the Old–Age, Survivors, and Disability (OASDI) program, there are serious problems in the long run.   Because of the time required for workers to prepare for their retirement, and the greater fairness of gradual changes, even long-run problems require attention in the near term.   * * *

The Council identified four major areas of concern.

*Long–Term Balance*

Under their intermediate assumptions, the Trustees of the Social Security Funds estimated that income (the sum of the revenue sources plus interest on accumulated funds) will exceed expenses each year until 2020. The trust fund balances will then start to decline as investments are cashed in to meet the payments coming due.   The Trustees estimated that although 75 percent of costs would continue to be met from current payroll and income taxes, in the absence of any changes full benefits could not be paid on time beginning in 2030.

The deficit over the traditional 75–year projection period was 2.17 percent of taxable payroll.   This means that if payroll tax rates had been increased in 1995 by just over 1 percentage point each on employers and employees—from their present level of 12.4 percent combined rate to 14.57 percent combined rate (excluding Medicare)—the system would be in balance over this 75–year period.   In the early decades of the projection period there would be surpluses, followed by deficits later in the projection period, but because of earnings on the trust funds, the 2.17 percent payroll tax increase would eliminate the 75–year deficit.

Little support exists today for increasing payroll tax rates by 2.17 percentage points to provide long-term balance. But there are other ways to address the financing issue, including other ways of increasing income to the system and changes in benefits. The program can be brought into long-run balance without departing from its basic principles or undermining the economic well-being of future workers and program beneficiaries.

The Council's work, and the work of a task force of experts appointed by the Council to review the estimates of the Trustees, basically confirm the 1995 Trustees' estimates of the finances of the program. Consequently, one of the three major tasks the Council set for itself in the area of financing was to make recommendations that would eliminate the 2.17 percent of taxable payroll deficit. All members of the Council agree that this should be done, though there are differences of opinion on how the goal should be met.

## Long–Term Balance Beyond the 75–Year Horizon

The second major problem with Social Security financing is the deterioration in the program's long-range balance that occurs solely because of the passage of time. Because of the aging of the U.S. population, whenever the program is brought into 75–year balance under a stable tax rate, it can be reasonably forecast that, without any changes in assumptions or experience, the simple passage of time will put the system into deficit. The reason is that expensive years previously beyond the forecasting horizon, with more beneficiaries getting higher real benefits, are then brought into the forecast period. There is no simple answer to the question of how much higher the long-term actuarial deficit is above the 2.17 percent to bring Social Security into balance beyond the 75–year horizon, but there could be a significant increase. All members of the Council agree that it is an unsatisfactory situation to have the passage of time alone put the system into long-run actuarial deficit, though there are again differences on how the problem should be corrected.

## Contribution/Benefit Ratios

The third area of concern for the Council arises from the fact that from now on many young workers and workers of future generations under present law will be paying over their working lifetimes employee and employer taxes that add to considerably more than the present value of their anticipated benefits. This is the inevitable result of a pay-as-you-go system such as the United States has had, and an aging population. Although the money's worth that workers get from Social Security is only one of many criteria for judging the value of the Social Security system, the Council believes that the system should meet a test of providing a reasonable money's worth return on the contributions of younger workers and future generations, while taking account of the redistributive nature of the Social Security system.

The Council is breaking new ground by dealing so explicitly with money's worth issues. It does so because of concerns about equity from one generation to another. The Council feels that equity among generations is a serious issue and that it is important to improve the return on retirement saving for young people.

All members of the Council favor the objective of improving the money's worth given by Social Security to younger generations. There are again differences on how this objective should be achieved.

*Public Confidence*

The final issue involves public confidence in the system. Polling data suggest that younger people have unprecedentedly low levels of confidence that Social Security benefits "will be there" for them when they retire. Polling data also suggest some erosion in public confidence in Social Security over time. While some of this skepticism runs well beyond issues the Council was dealing with, the Council does want to reassure people about the future viability and fairness of Social Security.

\* \* \*

In the past, efforts to deal with Social Security's financial difficulties have generally featured cutting benefits and raising tax rates on a pay-as-you-go basis. All Council members agree that the pay-as-you-go approach should be changed. But despite its best efforts, the Council was not able to agree on one single plan for dealing with Social Security's financial difficulties. Rather, Council members expressed interest in three different approaches to restoring financial solvency and improving money's worth returns. One group of members favors an approach, labeled the Maintenance of Benefits (MB) plan, that involves an increase in income taxes on Social Security benefits, a redirection to the OASDI funds beginning in 2010 of the part of the revenue from taxes on OASDI benefits now going to the Hospital Insurance (HI) Trust Fund, coverage of newly hired State and local government workers not currently covered by Social Security, a payroll tax increase in 2045, and serious consideration of a plan allowing the Government to begin investing a portion of trust fund assets directly in common stocks indexed to the broad market. Historically, returns on equities have exceeded those on Government bonds (where all Social Security funds are now invested). If this equity premium persists, it would be possible to maintain Social Security benefits for all income groups of workers, greatly improving the money's worth for younger workers, without incurring the risks that could accompany individual investment.

Another group of members supports an approach, labeled the Individual Accounts (IA) plan, that creates individual accounts alongside the Social Security system. This plan involves an increase in the income taxation of benefits (though not the redirection of HI funds), State and local coverage, an acceleration of the already-scheduled increase in the age of eligibility for full benefits up to year 2011 and then an automatic increase in that age tied to longevity, a reduction in the growth of future Social Security benefits is structured to affect middle- and high-wage workers the most, and an increase in employees' mandatory contribution to Social Security of 1.6 percent of covered payroll, which would be allocated to individual defined contribution accounts. These individual accounts would be held by the Government but with constrained investment choices available to individuals. If individuals were to devote the same share of their IA funds to equities as they now do for their 401(k) private pension funds, the combination of the annuity income attributable to their individual accounts and their scaled-back Social Security benefits would on average yield essentially the same benefits as promised under the current system for all income groups.

A third group of members favors an approach, labeled the Personal Security Accounts (PSA) plan, that creates even larger, fully-funded individual accounts which would replace a portion of Social Security. Under this plan, workers would direct 5 percentage points of the current payroll tax into a PSA, which would be managed privately and could be invested in a range of financial instruments. The balance of the payroll tax would go to fund a modified retirement program and modified disability and survivor benefits. When fully phased in, the modified retirement program would offer all full-career workers a flat dollar benefit (the equivalent of $410 monthly in 1996, the amount being automatically increased to reflect increases in national average wages prior to retirement) plus the proceeds of their PSAs. This plan also would involve a change in benefit taxation, State and local coverage, an acceleration of the already-scheduled increase from 65 to 67 in the age of eligibility for full retirement benefits, with the age increased in future years to reflect increases in longevity, a gradual increase from 62 to 65 in the age of eligibility for early retirement benefits (although workers could begin withdrawing the proceeds of their PSAs at 62), a reduction in future benefits for disabled workers, a reduction in benefits for women who never worked outside the home, and an increase in benefits for many elderly widows.

If individuals allocated the assets in their PSAs in the same proportion as they do for their 401(k) private pension plans, the combination of the flat benefit payment and the income from their PSAs would, on average, exceed the benefits promised under the current system for all income groups. There would be a cost associated with the transition to this new system equivalent to 1.52 percent of payroll for 72 years. This transition cost would be met through a combination of increased tax revenues and additional borrowing from the public.

All of these approaches have in common that they seek to achieve more advance funding of Social Security's long-term obligations. They would also result in a higher level of national saving for retirement, although the impact on the nation's overall retirement saving would differ under the plans. The two individual account plans would raise overall retirement and national saving much more than the MB plan in the early years of the forecast horizon through the mandatory contributions of the IA plan or the transition tax of the PSA plan. These two plans are then likely to generate higher national income in the 21st century. While each of the proposals would increase investment in the stock market, one approach invests new Social Security funds directly into equities to realize a higher rate of return; another approach adds additional, mandatory saving on top of a scaled-back version of the existing benefit system; and the third approach moves from the current pay-as-you-go, largely unfunded system to one in which future benefits are more than 50 percent funded through PSAs. Each of these plans has different potential to create real wealth for retirement and provides for different ownership of that wealth. And each involves a very different vision for the future evolution of the U.S. retirement system.

* * *

## NOTES AND QUESTIONS

**1.** Section 706 of the Social Security Act requires an Advisory Council on Social Security to review the status of the Social Security Trust Funds and their relationship to their long-term commitments every four years. Advisory Council members are appointed every four years, two years after Presidential election years.

**2.** Which of the three approaches given by the Council is most appealing?

**3.** Who speaks for the future generations who will pay into Social Security "considerably more than the present value of their anticipated benefits"? Shouldn't young people have "low levels of confidence that Social Security benefits 'will be there' for them when they retire"?

**4.** Should there be concern about allowing the Social Security Trust Funds to invest in common stocks? Don't government bonds have a lower return than common stocks because government bonds are less risky investments?

**5.** If the Council wants to create funds like 401(k) private pension funds, why have Social Security at all? Isn't Social Security supposed to be part of a diversified "retirement portfolio?" If private 401(k) plans are governed by ERISA, should similar plans offered by Social Security also be required to comply with ERISA?

**6.** Could women who have never worked outside the home and who will lose benefits under the third proposal claim that they have been discriminated against on the basis of sex? Does this proposal discount the imputed economic value of unpaid work performed by homemakers?

# INDEX

References are to Pages